THE VOLUNTARY SECTOR

LEGAL HANDBOOK

2nd edition

The Directory of Social Change is an independent voice for positive social change,
set up in 1975 to help voluntary organisations become more effective.
We do this by providing practical, challenging and affordable information and training
to meet the current, emerging and future needs of the sector.

Further copies of this book, a copy of the current booklist and information about courses,
conferences and other events may be obtained by contacting:
Directory of Social Change
24 Stephenson Way, London NW1 2DP
08450 77 77 07; fax 020 7391 4804
e-mail info@dsc.org.uk
website www.dsc.org.uk

THE VOLUNTARY SECTOR LEGAL HANDBOOK

2nd edition

SANDY ADIRONDACK and JAMES SINCLAIR TAYLOR

THE CHARITY TEAM AT RUSSELL-COOKE, Consulting editors

DIRECTORY OF SOCIAL CHANGE

Published by the Directory of Social Change
24 Stephenson Way, London NW1 2DP
tel 08450 77 77 07, fax 020 7391 4804
e-mail info@dsc.org.uk
website www.dsc.org.uk

Registered charity no. 800517

First published 1996
Second edition 2001
Reprinted 2005

ISBN 1 900360 72 1
British Library Cataloguing in Publication Data
A catalogue record for this book is available from the British Library

Designed and typeset by Sandy Adirondack
Cover design by Gabriele Kern
Printed by Page Bros, Norwich

This book does not give a full statement of the law, nor does it fully reflect changes after 1 January 2001. It is intended for guidance only, and is not a substitute for professional advice. No responsibility for loss occasioned as a result of any person acting or refraining from acting can be accepted by the publisher or authors.

Double-underlined section headings indicate additions or significant changes since the first edition.

Updates can be found at www.russell-cooke.co.uk and www.sandy-a.co.uk. Updates on Sandy's website are cross-referenced to *The Voluntary Sector Legal Handbook*.

CONTENTS

Double-underlined section headings in the text indicate significant changes or additions since the first edition.

ACKNOWLEDGEMENTS

It would not be possible to produce a book of this size and complexity without the assistance of very many people.

Final responsibility for the contents rests with us, but we are very grateful to all those who checked our text and provided helpful advice:

Lindsay Driscoll, Martyn Fisher, Mark Harvey, James McCallum, Charles Robinson and **Shivaji Shiva** of Sinclair Taylor & Martin Solicitors;

Simon Chrystal, the Pensions Trust;

Karen Cobham, CHAT Project (Liverpool Occupational Health Partnership);

Jonathan Dawson, solicitor and consultant;

James Dutton and **Sue Smith**, Charity Commission;

Peter Gotham. Gotham Erskine (accountants);

Bill Hyde, Community Transport Association;

Kate Kirkland, independent consultant;

Keegan and Pennykid (insurance brokers);

Mark Lattimer;

John Littman, Littman & Robeson Planning Consultants;

Christine Rigby, Bates, Wells & Braithwaite (solicitors);

Ian Oakley Smith, PricewaterhouseCoopers;

Kate Sayer, Sayer Vincent (accountants);

Dr **Michael Stuart**, formerly of the National Centre for Volunteering;

Jo Szwarc;

Paul Ticher, independent consultant;

Andrew Watt, Institute of Charity Fundraising Managers.

We remain grateful to those who provided advice and assistance on the first edition: Phil Allen, Paul Bater, Charlie Cattell, John Claricoat, Sally Collett, Graham Goodchild, Roger Jenkinson, Stephen Lee, Stephen Lloyd, Christina Morton, Helen Mountfield, Hilary Phillips, Jonathan Pinkney-Baird, Richard Poynter, Gill Taylor, and Robert Venables.

Very special thanks are due to **Aidan Merritt**, sub-editor, indexer and proofreader extraordinaire, **Fran Sinclair Taylor** for her support, **Jessica Sinclair Taylor** for continuing to forgive an absent parent, and **Peter Firkin**, for ongoing support and trips to the cinema.

Alison Baxter at the Directory of Social Change has been patiently supportive. In addition to these people, many other friends and colleagues provided support in all sorts of ways: providing information, listening to us, and telling us at appropriate intervals that the first edition was so useful that we really did need to do a second one.

Finally, continuing thanks to each other. The only thing we can say is that working together remains a pleasure.

Sandy Adirondack
James Sinclair Taylor

London, July 2001

ABOUT THE AUTHORS

Sandy Adirondack has been a freelance management trainer and consultant in the voluntary sector since 1980, working primarily with community-based and user-based organisations and now specialising in governance and legal aspects of voluntary sector management. She is author of *Just About Managing? Effective management for voluntary organisations and community groups* (London Voluntary Service Council 1989, 4th edition 2005), often called 'the voluntary sector's management bible', and *The Good Governance Action Plan for Voluntary Organisations* (National Council for Voluntary Organisations, 2002). She has written, edited or contributed to many other publications on campaigning and voluntary sector management. She can be contacted at:

39 Gabriel House
10 Odessa Street
London SE16 7HQ
tel 020 7232 0726; fax 020 7237 8117
sandy@sandy-a.co.uk
www.sandy-a.co.uk

James Sinclair Taylor is a senior partner at Russell-Cooke Solicitors, where he heads the Charity Team of 12 solicitors specialising in work with voluntary organisations. He is involved with the charitable and voluntary sector both professionally and personally, and has advised charities ranging from small and community groups to national organisations. His work involves assisting social care charities, educational bodies, community and development trusts, regeneration and partnership bodies, as well as campaigning, environmental, grant-making, benevolent and learned health organisations, as well as their trading and other subsidiaries. Much of his work is in governance, restructuring and mergers of charities. He also provides training, and has contributed to a variety of publications. He can be contacted at:

The Charity Team
Russell-Cooke Solicitors
2 Putney Hill
London SW15 6AB
tel 020 8394 6480
taylorj@russell-cooke.co.uk
www.russell-cooke.co.uk

James and Sandy are co-authors of the *Sinclair Taylor & Martin Company Handbook and Registers for Voluntary Sector Companies Limited by Guarantee* (1999 updated 2003), which combines a guide to company law and the company secretarial function with the necessary company law registers. It costs £39.50 including p&p from Sandy Adirondack at her address above.

INTRODUCTION TO THE 2nd EDITION

Since the first edition of *The Voluntary Sector Legal Handbook* was published in late 1996, many legal changes have affected charities and voluntary organisations. To make it easier to find these changes, we have double-underlined section headings where there have been additions or significant changes since the first edition.

Working time rights, minimum wage and dozens of other changes in employment law, the extension of employment rights to a wider category of 'workers', new disability rights, data protection, the ongoing review of the register of charities—hardly a week went by without a new case or regulation which had a significant impact on the voluntary sector. The criminal and civil justice systems have been reviewed and significant procedural changes introduced. A whole new area of law, around the internet, electronic communication and electronic commerce, has emerged. Much of the European Convention on Human Rights has been incorporated into UK law, and cases relating to Convention rights can be brought in domestic courts, without having to go to Strasbourg.

But perhaps more significant than specific legal changes is the accessibility of legal information. The progress of draft legislation can be tracked on the internet, and all new Acts and statutory instruments are online within a few days of parliamentary approval. Government departments have websites with vast amounts of information, from the introductory to detailed technical guidance. The lay person now has much improved access to information about legal rights and obligations.

Equally important is the changing language of the law. While many statutes and much guidance are still incomprehensible, there is a noticeable trend towards plain English. So not only is information available, but people can understand it. Some of the time, at least.

But organisations still need a starting point, something to guide them to what they should know, and that's where this book comes in. We hope it will continue to be an essential source of basic information for staff and governing bodies, and a guide to when they really should find out more, or seek professional legal or financial advice. When professional advice is necessary, we hope the book will provide an understanding of the legal context in which the advice is given.

What it includes

The book is in nine parts:

1 **Setting up an organisation**: the various legal structures for voluntary organisations, how to set up an organisation and register as a charity, drawing up and amending a governing document (constitution), relationships with branches and subsidiaries, mergers

2 **Governance and membership**: the roles and responsibilities of the organisation's members, its governing body (management committee, board of trustees, board of directors etc) and its officers

3 **Running an organisation**: the organisation's registered office, paperwork requirements, meetings and decision making, entering into contracts and other legal arrangements, personal and organisational liabilities, insurance, winding up

4 **Employees, volunteers and other workers**: employment rights and obligations

5 **Services and activities**: health and safety, equal opportunities in service delivery, confidentiality, data protection, intellectual property, publicity, publications, campaigning and public activities

6 **Funding and fundraising**: fundraising, tax-effective giving, trading, contracts and service agreements

7 **Finance**: financial procedures, annual accounts and audit, tax, VAT, investment, reserves and borrowing

8 **Property**: forms of tenure, leases and licences, property management, the environment

9 **Background to the law**: the English legal system, dispute resolution and litigation.

This book covers the law only as it applies to England and Wales. Much law is the same or very similar in Scotland and Northern Ireland, but there are significant differences. Organisations based or operating in these countries should contact the Scottish Council for Voluntary Organisations (0131-556 3882, www.scvo.org.uk) or the Northern Ireland Council for Voluntary Action (028-9032 1224, www.nicva.org).

Our intentions

In writing this book we have tried to make it:

- **comprehensive**: covering as many aspects as we could of the law as it relates to voluntary organisations, although inevitably we have had to omit some topics and abridge complex areas of law;

- **relevant to all voluntary organisations**: covering not only charities but also non-charitable organisations, and where relevant clearly differentiating between trusts, associations, companies and industrial and provident societies;

- **detailed**: giving enough information so that readers can understand not only what the law says, but why it says it;

- **up to date**: updating it to reflect the law at 1 January 2001, and including significant information after that date where it was available before the book went to press;

- **easy to use**, with significant changes since the first edition clearly indicated by double-underlined section headings;

- **comprehensible**: avoiding jargon, and explaining technical terms whenever they are used;

- **useful**: explaining the implications of the law for real voluntary organisations operating in the real world;

- **technical**: providing the source of the law (statute, statutory instrument or case references), with detailed tables of cases and statutes at the end, to make it easy to find out more.

Readers must, of course, be aware that large areas of law are summarised and some are not covered at all, and the law will continue to change. Quite apart from those two factors, no book can replace good legal advice from suitably experienced legal advisors.

In order to make the book affordable we decided not to do it as a looseleaf with regular updates and not to put it, for the moment, on CD-ROM—although that is a potential future development, and the Directory of Social Change would welcome readers' views about this.

We are aware that with heavy usage, the book's spine may break. To avoid this, organisations may want to remove the cover, punch holes in the pages, and put the pages into ring binders or a lever arch file.

Keeping up to date

One major change since the first edition is that there is now easy access to bills as they go through Parliament (www.parliament.the-stationery-office.co.uk), Acts after they are passed and draft and final statutory instruments (all at www.opsi.gov.uk), and press releases and guidance issued by government departments and other agencies. We have included website addresses at the end of each chapter.

Russell-Cooke Solicitors and Sandy Adirondack both have websites which include legal updates for voluntary organisations, with links to other relevant sites. They are at www.russell-cooke.co.uk and www.sandy-a.co.uk. Items on Sandy's website are cross-referenced to this edition of the *Legal Handbook*.

TERMS USED IN THIS BOOK

LANGUAGE AND THE LAW

The law uses language in strange and often perverse ways, causing frustration for non-initiates trying to come to grips with legal issues. Words have specialist technical meanings—referred to by lawyers as **terms of art**—which are often far removed from their use in everyday language. Worse, the same word may have differing technical meanings depending on the context in which it is found.

A **licence**, for example, may be a right to use land rather similar to a lease. But it may also be a permission given by a court or statutory body to undertake a restricted activity such as the sale of alcohol, or a legal document by which an organisation grants a permission to someone, perhaps to use its logo or copyright material. Without knowing the context, a detailed definition of what a 'licence' is cannot be given.

Where we use such a term of art it initially appears in bold, and is defined. All terms of art used in this book are included in the index at the end.

Getting the labels right

Because so many everyday words have specific legal meanings, they must be used properly. A licence to occupy property generally confers fewer rights than a lease, so something intended to be a licence must not be called a lease, or vice versa. Employees have rights which self-employed people do not, so if people are being hired by an organisation on a self-employed basis, they must be given a **contract for services** rather than a **contract of service** (contract of employment).

But a four-pronged digging instrument is not a spade, whatever it says on the label. The courts, taking all the surrounding circumstances into account, will find that something which fulfils the legal criteria to be a lease is a lease even if it is called a licence [see **56.5.1**]; and a person who fulfils the legal criteria to be an employee will be an employee even if he or she is treated by the organisation as self-employed [see **22.1**].

So the law places great importance on how things are labelled, but is prepared to ignore those labels if they are inappropriately used.

The meaning of words

Constitutions, leases, contracts and other legal documents often contain words or phrases incomprehensible to a non-specialist. These documents do not have to be in complex legal language, and some solicitors now seek to ensure that legal documents are in straightforward English. But the 'translation' from legal terminology to everyday language needs to be carefully done, because even words which appear to have a clear meaning may have a technical and surprising legal meaning, evolved through years of legal interpretation.

In common usage, for example, 'person' refers only to a human person. But in legal terms a person can be either a human person or a **corporate body**. A corporate body is a registered company or other form of organisation recognised in law as having **corporate personality**. If a constitution says that an organisation is open to 'persons who support the organisation's objects and pay a subscription', it may not be clear whether this applies only to human persons or to corporate 'persons' as well. And while the plural 'persons' may mean both humans and corporate bodies, the plural 'people' means only humans.

Another example of words possibly not meaning what they appear to is a lease which contains an obligation for the tenants to 'keep in repair' the premises they are renting. Tenants can easily assume that this means they must not let the building get into any worse a state than it was in when they first rented it. It can come as quite a shock to learn that 'keep in repair' means putting a building into a fully repaired state—even if it was completely dilapidated when the tenants took the tenancy [see **58.2.4**].

DEFINING THE VOLUNTARY SECTOR

In addition to the language of the law, people in voluntary organisations must also understand the particular terminology of their own sector.

How can it be a **voluntary** sector if it is staffed by employees rather than volunteers, and is funded through public sector grants and fees rather than through 'voluntary' donations? But calling it the **charitable** sector can be misleading, because not all voluntary organisations are charitable. **Not-for-profit** sector is an alternative but it is a misnomer, because voluntary organisations *can* make a profit (although they do not have profit making as their primary objective, and usually must use any profits only for the purposes of the organisation). **Third sector**? Still an unfamiliar term, although it is coming into more widespread use to describe all organisations which are not clearly in the public sector or commercial sector. **Non-governmental organisations** or **NGO** sector? Usually used only for organisations operating at national or international level, to distinguish them from governmental agencies. What about the continental term *économie sociale*? Includes workers' cooperatives and similar organisations which in Britain are not generally considered part of the voluntary sector.

Whatever the sector is called, it encompasses a huge and diverse range of organisations with radically different origins, traditions and terminologies. Because of this there is no consistency in the terms used to describe the organisations in the sector, the rules which govern them and the people responsible for managing them.

Charity, for example, might refer only to an organisation registered with the Charity Commission, or to any organisation set up for purposes recognised in law as charitable, even if it is not registered with the Commission, or to any organisation set up for any good cause, even if the cause is not recognised as charitable in law. A **management committee** or **executive committee** might be the body which is ultimately responsible in law for managing the organisation, or it might be a subcommittee of the body which is ultimately responsible in law. **Secretary** might mean a company secretary with responsibilities under company law, an honorary or elected secretary with duties set out in the organisation's constitution, or an employee with duties set out in a job description. Even among similar organisations, it should never be assumed that terms are being used in the same way.

TERMS USED IN THIS BOOK

To avoid confusion, we have tried to use a consistent language throughout this book for terms relating to the voluntary sector. Some of the main terms are set out here.

The organisation

Organisation is used to refer to any group of people who come together for a common purpose and have some agreed rules for how they operate together. These rules are usually written into a governing document [see below], but for some organisations the rules might be unwritten, based on assumptions: 'this is why we exist and how we do things'.

This book is only about **voluntary organisations**, which are:

* set up for charitable, social, educational, philanthropic, religious, political or similar purposes;
* required to use any profit or surplus only for the organisation's purposes; *and*
* not part of any government department, local or health authority or other statutory body.

6

Some organisations, such as grant-maintained schools, colleges and public museums are on the border between the public sector and the voluntary sector. Others, such as independent schools, cooperatives and mutual societies, are on the border between the private (commercial) sector and the voluntary sector. Most of this book—for example on employment, health and safety and intellectual property rights—apply to these 'border' organisations in exactly the same way as to voluntary organisations. Other parts of the book apply only if the organisation is recognised as charitable and/or has a particular legal structure.

Legal structure

All voluntary organisations have a **legal structure** or **legal status**. The most common are **unincorporated association**, **trust** and **company limited by guarantee**. Less common structures for voluntary organisations are **industrial and provident society**, or a body created by **royal charter** or **statute**. Legal structures are described in chapters 1 and 2. When we refer in this book to associations, trusts, companies or IPSs, we mean only organisations with that particular structure.

We use the term **incorporated organisation** or **corporate body** for organisations incorporated as a company, as an industrial and provident society, or by statute or royal charter. We use **unincorporated organisation** for bodies which are not incorporated.

Charitable status

Charitable status is separate from legal structure. We use the term **charitable organisation** to refer to organisations set up for purposes recognised in law as charitable, and **registered charity** for charities registered with the Charity Commission. Charitable status is explained in chapter 3.

Non-charitable organisations are those set up for purposes which are not recognised in law as charitable, such as organisations set up to campaign politically or as closed self-help groups.

The governing document

Most voluntary organisations have some sort of document describing the purposes for which they are set up (their **objects**), and how they are to operate. In practice it is often called a constitution, but we use the term **governing document**.

Governing documents take a variety of legal forms:

- if the organisation is registered as a company, the governing document is its **memorandum and articles of association**;
- if it is registered as an industrial and provident society, the governing document is its **rules**;
- if it is set up as a trust, its governing document is generally a **trust deed** or **declaration of trust**;
- if it is an association, its governing document is usually called a **constitution** or **rules**.

We use these terms when we refer to governing documents of organisations with a particular legal structure.

Governing documents are explained in detail in **chapter 5**.

The governing body

The **governing body** is the group of people who are legally responsible for running the organisation. In practice it might be called the council, board, committee, council of management, management committee, executive committee, steering committee, board of directors, board of trustees, board of governors or any similar name.

We use the term **members of the governing body** for the people who have full (voting) rights on this body. If other people are entitled to attend governing body meetings but not to vote, we call them **non-voting members** of the governing body or **observers**.

Regardless of what the governing body is called, the members of the governing body may have a specific role in law:

- if the organisation is charitable, the voting members of the governing body are **charity trustees**, even if they are not called this;
- if the organisation is registered as a company, the voting members of the governing body are **company directors**;
- if the organisation is both a company and a charity, the voting members of the governing body are company directors as well as charity trustees.

We use these terms when we need to make clear that we are referring specifically to members of governing bodies of charitable organisations or companies.

Although most members of governing bodies are individuals, it is also possible under some governing documents for corporate bodies (companies and industrial and provident societies) to be members of a governing body.

There is more about governing bodies in **chapter 11**.

The organisation's members

Some voluntary organisations, especially those set up as trusts, are generally made up only of the members of the governing body. Associations generally have a wider membership, which elects some or all of the members of the governing body. Companies and industrial and provident societies might have either a narrow or wider membership.

Where there is a wider membership, the governing document generally sets out who is eligible to be a member and their rights. This varies tremendously, from the simple rights to attend general meetings and elect some of the members of the governing body to the right of National Trust members to visit NT properties.

In organisations with a wider membership the governing document may specify that only members of the organisation can be members of the governing body, or it may not make this restriction.

Membership is described in **chapter 10**.

Officers

In many voluntary organisations, special titles and responsibilities are allocated to some members of the governing body. These are typically the chairperson (chair, chairman etc), vice-chair, treasurer and secretary. Some organisations have one set of officers for the organisation as a whole, and another for the governing body. Matters relating to officers may be based on tradition, or detailed provisions may be included in the governing document.

These officers may be called **honorary officers** to indicate that they are unpaid.

In company law the term **officers** encompasses all the members of the company's governing body and the company secretary, and in some contexts senior staff and the company's auditor as well. In this book we always make clear when we are referring to officers in this sense.

The roles of officers are explained in **chapter 12**.

Beneficiaries

We use the term **beneficiaries** for the people or organisations which the voluntary organisation exists to serve—the persons who are intended to benefit from the organisation. The beneficiaries may be only the members of the organisation, or may consist of a very large group such as 'poor people anywhere in the world'. In practice, many organisations use terms such as clients, service users or residents rather than beneficiaries.

If the organisation has a membership, beneficiaries can be members unless the governing document specifies otherwise.

If the organisation is charitable, it may or may not be possible for beneficiaries to be members of the governing body. This is a complex area which depends on the provisions of the governing document, and may need clarification from the Charity Commission [see **14.5**].

One individual may have several roles within an organisation. In an organisation which is registered as a charity and a company, for example, the same person could be a member of the organisation, a beneficiary, a member of the governing body (and therefore a charity trustee and company director), the chairperson, a volunteer providing the organisation's services (such as working in a lunch club or on a helpline), a volunteer fundraiser, and a volunteer helping with administrative tasks or publicity. That person will have to be clear which 'hat' he or she is wearing in any particular situation.

LEGAL REFERENCES

Although this book covers a large area of the law, it can only summarise the main points. For readers who want more detail we refer throughout to the relevant statutes and statutory instruments (regulations or orders, abbreviated as SIs), and to key cases.

Statute law

To understand what the law really says, there is no substitute for reading the statutes and statutory instruments. These are available from various sources:

- statutes and SIs are on the internet at www.legislation.hmso.gov.uk;
- they can be purchased from the Stationery Office;
- *Halsbury's Statutes*, a multi-volume series, contains all statute law and is available in many public reference libraries.

Case law

Similarly, to understand how the law is interpreted there is no substitute for looking at relevant cases. The judgment sets out the factual background and the legal reasons for the judge's decision, and provides a real depth of understanding. Whenever we cite a case in this book., we say where it was reported [see **60.2.1.2** for an explanation of these citations, and **page 868** for a list of law reports cited in this book]. Unfortunately case law is reported in a wide variety of journals, and it may require some research to discover where a particular journal is available.

Anyone involved in an important or contested legal issue may find it worthwhile to ask their solicitor to obtain copies of key cases for them.

Throughout this book we seek to explain why a particular action is required. In many cases this is because a particular statute applies, but many duties and rights arise from the **common law** [see **60.2.1**]. The common law is based on earlier cases which set **precedents.** These precedents are recognised by the courts of England and Wales as the law, even though Parliament has not passed any detailed statute covering those matters.

10

PART I
SETTING UP AN ORGANISATION

The people involved in setting up a voluntary organisation must decide whether to become an incorporated body or remain unincorporated, and whether to be charitable or non-charitable. The first choice gives the organisation its **legal status** or **legal structure**, while the second gives its **charitable status** (or lack of it).

Part I explains how to set up a voluntary organisation, and looks at issues around setting up branches and other complex structures or undertaking mergers.

11

FOR FURTHER INFORMATION

Charitable status, charity law and charity registration. Charity Commission: 0870-333 0123; www.charity-commission.gov.uk

The Charities Acts Handbook by Fiona Middleton and Stephen Lloyd (Jordans, 0117-923 0600)

Butterworths Charity Law Handbook (Butterworths, 020-7400 4623)

Charity governing documents. Charity Law Association: 01904-625790

Charities and tax. Inland Revenue (Charities): 0151-472 6036; www.inlandrevenue.gov.uk

Unincorporated associations. *Unincorporated Associations: Law and practice* by Jean Warburton (Sweet & Maxwell, 020-7449 1111)

Company law and registration. Companies House: 0870-333 3636; www.companieshouse,gov.uk

Sinclair Taylor & Martin Company Handbook and Registers for Voluntary Sector Companies Limited by Guarantee by James Sinclair Taylor & Sandy Adirondack (Sinclair Taylor & Martin Solicitors). £35 from Sandy Adirondack: 020-7232 0726, bookorders@sandy-a.co.uk

Industrial and provident society law and registration. Mutual Societies Registration and Registrar of Friendly Societies: 020-7676 1000; www.fsa.org.uk

ICOM (industrial Common Ownership Movement): 0113-246 1737

Handbook of Industrial and Provident Society Law by Ian Snaith (Holyoake Books, 0161-832 4300)

New incorporated charitable structure. Charity Commission [see above]

Department of Trade and Industry: www.dti.gov.uk

General information about legal structures, charitable status and setting up. National Council for Voluntary Organisations: 0800-2 798 798; www.ncvo-vol.org.uk

Wales Council for Voluntary Action: 029-2043 1700; www.wcva.org.uk

Chapter 1
TRUSTS AND UNINCORPORATED ASSOCIATIONS

Topics covered in this chapter

The vast majority of voluntary organisations are unincorporated, which means they are not registered as a company or incorporated in another way. This chapter explains unincorporated associations and trusts, the two main forms of unincorporated structure. It covers:

For sources of further information see page 12.
Double-underlined section headings indicate additions or significant changes since the first edition.

1.1 UNINCORPORATED ORGANISATIONS

An unincorporated body is a group of persons bound by a common purpose and a set of rules or procedures, and not incorporated as a company or an industrial and provident society or by an Act of Parliament or royal charter.

Unlike incorporated organisations [see **chapter 2**], unincorporated organisations are not recognised for legal purposes as being legal entities. The law recognises only the individuals who make up the organisation. So Anyville Community Association is not a legal entity; rather, the law sees it as 'the members of Anyville Community Association acting together', or 'the members of the governing body of Anyville Community Association acting together on behalf of the members of the association'.

If the organisation cannot meet its financial obligations or gets into legal trouble, the members of the governing body have **unlimited personal liability**. In some situations this liability could extend to all the members of the organisation.

For voluntary organisations, the main forms of unincorporated organisation are the **unincorporated association** (typically a membership body) and the **trust** (typically used when a small group will manage money or property for a specific purpose or purposes).

If the purposes of an unincorporated body are wholly and exclusively charitable, it is then a **charitable association** or **charitable trust**.

For information about how to set up an unincorporated association or trust see **chapter 6**.

1.2 UNINCORPORATED ASSOCIATIONS

1.2.1 What unincorporated associations are

An association has been defined in law as 'two or more persons bound together for one or more common purposes, not being business purposes, by mutual undertakings each having mutual duties and obligations, in an organisation which has rules which identify in whom control of it and its funds rests and on what terms, and which can be joined or left at will'.

Conservative and Unionist Central Office v Burrell [1982] 1 WLR 522, 525

An **association** is formed when a group of people come together:

- for an agreed lawful purpose of benefit to themselves or others;
- for a purpose which is not to make a profit for themselves or others; *and*
- with the intention (even if it is not explicit) of creating a legal relationship among themselves.

When organisations, or organisations and individuals, come together in the same way they also form an association.

An association is **unincorporated** if it is not registered as a company or an industrial and provident society, and is not incorporated under statute or a royal charter [see **chapter 2**].

An association must have rules setting out, for example, who can be a member and how decisions are made about what the association does. If the rules are written they form the association's **governing document** [see **chapter 5**] and might be called a **constitution** or **rules**. The governing document generally sets out not only the procedural rules but also the purposes (objects) of the association, and the members' duties and their responsibilities to each other.

An association might be called a club, society, trust, organisation, campaign, project, federation, forum or anything similar. It might even be called a company (as in the case of an unincorporated theatre company). What it is called has no significance in terms of its legal structure. If it is not part of another organisation [see **9.2**], is not formally set up as a trust, company or industrial and provident society and is not incorporated under statute or royal charter, it is an unincorporated association.

Family and friendship groups are not associations because there is no intention to create this sort of legal relationship between the individuals. Unincorporated businesses involving two or more persons are **partnerships** rather than associations.

1.2.2 Associations without a governing document

Even if a group does not have a written constitution, it is nonetheless an association if it fulfils the criteria described above. An association which has a governing document is sometimes referred to as **constituted**, and one which does not have a governing document as **unconstituted**, but these terms have no meaning in law.

1.2.3 Regulation of unincorporated associations

There is no statute law relating to unincorporated associations as a whole, although there is some case law and there are some statutes regulating specific types of unincorporated association, most notably trade unions. If an association is charitable [see **3.1**], it must comply with charity law.

Associations established to promote science, literature or fine arts or to provide adult education are in some very limited situations regulated by the Department of Trade and Industry under the **Literary and Scientific Institutions Act 1854**.

The rules or constitution of an unincorporated association form a contract between the members and can be enforced in the courts.

1.2.4
Advantages of associations
1.2.4.1
Flexibility

The main advantage of the unincorporated association structure is that it is **uncomplicated** and **flexible**. Associations can be set up or wound up quickly, easily and cheaply.

An association can have a **simple governing document** which the members can, if they want, draw up themselves without involving lawyers or other advisors. They can create their own rules and procedures, and if the association's purposes are not charitable the rules and procedures will not have to comply with external requirements. If the people setting up the association want the benefits of charitable status it is advisable to obtain advice while drawing up the governing document, to ensure it meets the requirements of charity law [see **7.2.2**].

If the governing document includes procedures for **amendment**, an association's rules can usually be changed quickly and easily. If the association is charitable, prior Charity Commission approval is needed for some changes [see **5.5.1**] and all changes, even those for which prior approval is not required, must be notified to the Commission.

An association can be **wound up** quickly and simply. Usually all it needs to do is comply with the procedures set out in its governing document [see **21.7** and **21.8**], and notify the Charity Commission if it is a charity. Incorporated organisations are more difficult to dissolve.

1.2.4.2
Privacy

A non-charitable association has the advantages of **privacy** and **absence of external accountability**. No one outside the association needs to know who its members are, what they do, how they operate or how much money they have. However this does not apply to charitable associations, which are publicly accountable under charity law.

Even non-charitable associations may lose their privacy if they enter into agreements with third parties (such as funders) by which they become externally accountable.

1.2.5
Disadvantages of associations
1.2.5.1
Personal liability

The overwhelming disadvantage of being an unincorporated association is that the members of the governing body, and in some cases all the members of the association, can be held **personally liable** for the organisation's debts and for other claims [see **chapter 19**].

If **creditors**—the people to whom the organisation owes money—take legal action, it must be against the individuals who authorised or incurred the debt, rather than against the organisation. Similarly if a person suffers loss or damage and wants to bring legal action against the organisation, the lawsuit will be brought against some or all of the members of the governing body or other individuals who authorised or carried out the activities which caused the loss.

There are ways to reduce the risk to individuals [see **19.6**].

1.2.5.2
Entering into contracts and taking legal action

Another disadvantage of being unincorporated is that because an unincorporated association is not a legal entity, it **cannot enter into legal agreements** or take legal action in its own right. If it rents a telephone line, hires staff, opens a bank account or orders goods or services from a supplier, those contracts are entered into by individuals—the signatories and/or the members of the governing body who authorised the transaction—who could be held personally liable if there is **breach of contract**. If the individuals cease to be a member of the governing body or the association, this does not end their legal liability, unless the legal agreement is transferred to a new signatory [see **18.10.1**].

If an unincorporated association wants to take **legal action** [see **61.4**], the action must be brought in the name of an individual or individuals.

If the association is charitable this disadvantage can be overcome by incorporating the governing body [see **1.4**].

1.2.5.3
Holding property and investments

Because land, buildings, other property and investments must be held by individuals or by a body which is recognised as being a legal entity, they cannot be directly held by an unincorporated association. Unless it is a charitable association which has incorporated its governing body [see 1.4], the association appoints individuals or a corporate body to hold the assets on its behalf. These are called **nominees** (**holding trustees** or **custodian trustees**) or a **nominee company** [see 18.4].

The individuals appointed as holding trustees may or may not also be members of the association's governing body. If the association is charitable, the governing body members will be **charity trustee**s [see 11.1.7]; this role is separate from any holding trustee role.

The holding trustees are the legal owners of the property, but can use it or allow it to be used only for the purposes of the association, and only as directed by the association's members or governing body. If the association is charitable, the property is treated as being held on trust by the **charity trustees**—the governing body members—even though they may not be the 'legal' owners.   *Charities Act 1993 s.97*

When holding trustees resign or die they must be replaced, which can cause expense and other problems.

1.2.5.4
Gifts to non-charitable associations

A gift or grant given to an unincorporated association in effect creates a trust [see 1.3.1], with the association's members entrusted to use the money or property for the purposes of the association. But except in very exceptional circumstances, a trust can be created only for identifiable individuals or for charitable purposes [see 1.3.4], and trusts created for non-charitable purposes are invalid.

Re Astor's Settlement Trust [1952] Ch 534

If property or any other significant gift is being given to a non-charitable association, legal advice may be needed to ensure that the terms are worded in a way that makes clear:

- the purposes for which the gift is given are charitable in law; *or*
- if the purposes are non-charitable, that the gift is given 'for the benefit of the members of the association for the time being' or for other identifiable beneficiaries.

If the wording is not correct and the gift is challenged, it could be declared invalid.

1.2.6
Choosing to be an unincorporated association

An unincorporated association may be an appropriate structure if:
- the organisation does not expect to own significant property or to employ staff, will have a secure income, and will not undertake risky or financially burdensome activities; *and*
- it wants to be a membership organisation; *and/or*
- it wants more privacy than it could get as a company or industrial and provident society (but much of this privacy will not be available if it is charitable).

If it is financially secure and does not intend to have a membership, a trust may be more appropriate [see 1.3.1].

If the organisation will have larger scale financial dealings, for example hiring staff, or if it owns land or buildings, or if it is in situations of financial risk, for example being dependent on unpredictable grant funding, it should consider incorporation [see **chapter 2**].

1.3
TRUSTS

1.3.1
What trusts are

Early in the development of English law the courts, particularly the church courts, felt that moral obligations should be recognised even where they were not enshrined in statute law, a contract [see 18.6 for definition] or a deed [see 18.3]. These courts began to enforce promises under a type of law known as **equity** [see 60.2.2].

Within equity, promises are enforced as a **trust** where money or property of any sort (the **corpus**) is given by a **settlor** or **donor** to a person (the **trustee**) with the intention that they hold it not as their personal property, but on behalf of another person (the **beneficiary**).

For a trust to be enforced there must be a benefit for a third party. A trust is not created when the intention is merely to benefit the settlor and/or trustee. Nor is a trust generally created if either of them has the right to revoke the intention to benefit the third party, for example if the settlor is entitled to cancel the benefit by diverting it to him or herself. However this rule is subject to many exceptions.

As soon as the property has been given to the trustees it belongs to them, not to the settlor, even if the settlor is a trustee. The trustees own the property (the **legal interest**), but they are required to use it only for the defined beneficiaries or purposes. The beneficiaries have the **beneficial interest** in the property.

1.3.2
Trusts established by trust deed or will

A trust comes into being, without any formalities, as soon as money or property is given to a person to be used for an identifiable beneficiary or for a charitable purpose. The term **trust** defines the relationship between parties, rather than an organisational structure.

However some trusts are created under the terms of a will, or through a trust deed or declaration of trust [see **6.2.1**]. Where these are set up for charitable purposes they are referred to in this book as organisations with the legal structure of a trust. Organisations which are formally set up as trusts are sometimes called **strict trusts** or **simple trusts**. The trust deed or declaration needs to be stamped by the Inland Revenue stamping office [see **6.2.2**].

1.3.3
Private and public trusts

A **private trust** is intended to benefit one person or a specific group of private individuals (for example, a trust created by a will for the benefit of the deceased person's children). A trust intended to benefit the public or a section of the public, rather than identifiable beneficiaries, is a **public trust**. A public trust must in virtually all cases be **charitable**, which means:

- the objects for which it is set up must be wholly charitable [see **4.3**]; *and*

- it must benefit the public, or a substantial section of the public [see **4.3.8**]. There is an exception for charitable trusts set up for the relief of poverty, which can have a small group of beneficiaries.

1.3.4
Valid trusts

The requirements for setting up a valid private or public trust are:
- it must be clear that the donor(s) intended to set up a trust (**certainty of intention**);

- it must be clear what the trust's property is;

- a trust cannot be required to accumulate its income, without spending it, for more than the common law perpetuity period, which is 21 years after the death of the donor (**rule against excessive accumulations**).   *Perpetuities and Accumulations Act 1964 s.13*

A trust which does not meet these requirements is void (invalid).

Other rules apply in different ways to private and public trusts.

- If the gift to create a private trust, the selection of beneficiaries, or the use of the trust funds is conditional on something happening, the event must happen within the **perpetuity period** of 80 years or a lifetime plus 21 years. This **rule against perpetuities** (also known as the **rule of inalienability** or **rule against perpetual trusts**) does not apply if the gift is given for charitable purposes or is given to one charity on condition that it be given to another charity if a specific event occurs (a **gift over**).   *ss.1, 3*

- A private trust must have identifiable beneficiaries (**certainty of objects**). These might be defined by name, by reference to a named individual or employer or in any other way, but they must be capable of being identified. A public trust cannot be for named individuals.

- A private trust may have any number of beneficiaries, from one to a very large group. A public trust must in virtually all cases benefit the public or a section of the public, rather than only a small group.

- A public trust must have stated purposes or objects. These do not have to be precisely defined, so long as it is clear that they are completely charitable as defined by law [see **4.3**] or fall into the very small number of objects which are allowed for non-charitable public trusts [see next paragraph]. A private trust does not have to have stated objects.

A trust which does not define identifiable beneficiaries and is set up for a purpose which is not charitable is called a **trust of imperfect obligation** and is nearly always void (invalid). There are a few exceptions—trusts to maintain individual tombs or monuments, to support one or more specific animals ('my beloved dog Fifi'), and for the furtherance of fox hunting—but these are anomalous. Apart from these, it is not possible to set up a trust without identifiable beneficiaries for non-charitable purposes.

1.3.5
Common confusions about trusts and trustees

The terms **trust** and **trustee** are used in many different ways and cause great confusion within voluntary organisations.

Not all trusts are charities. Most trusts are private and have nothing to do with the voluntary sector or with charitable purposes.

All charities hold their assets **on trust**, in the sense that they have a special duty to apply those assets only for their charitable purposes, but only some charities are set up with the **legal structure** of a trust. However, even those which are not set up as trusts often have 'trust' in their name.

1.3.5.1
Trustees under charity law and trust law

For the purposes of **charity law**, members of the governing body of *all* charitable organisations are **charity trustees** and are subject to **charity law** even if they are actually called committee members, governors or something else.   *Charities Act 1993 s.97*

Trustees of charitable unincorporated associations, trusts, and bodies established by charter are all subject to relevant aspects of **trust law**, and in particular have statutory duties and powers under the **Trustee Act 2000** [see **13.5.2** and **54.1.2**]. Governing body members in companies and industrial and provident societies, even if charitable, do not have these powers except in situations where property is held on trust.

1.3.5.2
Holding and custodian trustees

If an unincorporated association wants to own land, buildings or other property, the individuals in whose names the property is held will hold it **on trust**. It is good practice to set out the terms of this trust in a **trust deed** [see **18.3**], but even if nothing is written the law will imply a trust and the associated duties. In this case the settlors are the members or committee of the unincorporated association, the new trustees are called **holding trustees** or **nominees**, and the objects are the purposes for which the property can be used (in a charitable association) or the benefit of the members of the association (in a non-charitable association). This kind of trust is simply a legal device for holding property and does not create a new organisation or charity.

1.3.6
Regulation of trusts

A *private* trust does not need to be registered with any regulatory or supervisory body, and so long as the trustees fulfil the terms of their trust, they are not externally accountable to anyone. If they do not fulfil the terms of their trust, the beneficiaries can take legal action against them.

A *charitable* trust must comply with the requirements for charity registration and accountability [see **7.1**]. The terms of the trust are enforceable not by the beneficiaries but by the Charity Commission or the High Court in proceedings involving the attorney general, although persons with an interest in the charity may be able to bring charity proceedings [see **61.8**] if they object to the way a charity is operating.

Rules providing for the appointment of new trustees and some matters relating to the powers of trustees are contained in the **Trustee Acts 1925 and 2000,** the **Trusts of Land and Appointment of Trustees Act 1996** and the **Trustee Delegation Act 1999** [see **11.4.1** and **11.5.5**]. Investments by trustees are controlled by the governing document and legislation [see **54.1.2**].

1.3.7 Advantages of the trust structure

Organisations set up as trusts share with unincorporated associations many of the advantages of simplicity, flexibility and ease of creation and winding up [see **1.2.4.1**].

The **number of trustees** can be small. For private trusts it is possible to have only one trustee although it is usual to have at least two if the trust property includes land. The Charity Commission usually presses for a minimum of three trustees for charitable trusts.

Trustees are generally appointed by the existing trustees or sometimes by an outside body, rather than being elected. This creates a **self-perpetuating governing body,** which may be perceived as an advantage.

1.3.8 Disadvantages of the trust structure

As in an unincorporated association [see **1.2.5.1**], the trustees of a trust are **personally liable** for the trust's debts if it cannot meet them.

Because trustees are usually appointed rather than elected, the trust structure is typically **undemocratic**. It is not well suited for a membership organisation, although it can be adapted to have members and give them the right to elect the governing body.

Trust governing documents can include a power of amendment [see **5.5.1**]. But if the power is limited or is not included, they cannot not be altered except by an order of the court or, in the case of a charitable trust, by the Charity Commissioners. Inflexibility can be avoided by including a power of amendment and a wide objects clause [see **4.6.1**].

Unlike unincorporated associations, the trustees **can hold land or investments** without having to appoint separate holding trustees, a custodian trustee or a nominee company [see **18.4**]. But it is the trustees, rather than the trust itself, who hold the trust's property. If a trustee changes, a new trustee must be appointed to hold the property. To overcome this, property can be held by a corporate body (a custodian trustee or nominee company) or the trustee body can be incorporated and can then hold property as a corporate body [see **1.4**].

1.3.9 Choosing the trust structure

A trust may be a suitable legal structure if:

- the organisation will have substantial assets (for example an endowed or grant-making trust); *or*

- the organisation will have very secure funding and/or it will not have long-term financial commitments, so it can with some certainty ensure it will be able to meet all its financial obligations;

- it will not employ staff; *and*

- it will not have a large membership.

1.4 INCORPORATING THE GOVERNING BODY

Trustee incorporation is a process by which the governing body (the charity trustees) of a charitable unincorporated association or charitable trust can incorporate, without incorporating the organisation as a whole as a company limited by guarantee or industrial and provident society.

Charities Act 1993 ss.50-62

This gives them legal personality and permanent succession [see **2.1.1**] and the right to own property, enter into legal agreements and take legal action in the name of the trustee body as a whole rather than in the name of individuals.

It does not, however, limit the liability of members of the governing body or the organisation. They still have the same responsibilities and liabilities as if the organisation was unincorporated [see **1.2.5.1**].

Trustee incorporation might be appropriate if the organisation:

- is a registered, exempt or excepted charity [see **7.1** for definitions];

- owns or expects to own property or investments and/or is involved or expects to be involved in leases or long-term contracts; *and*

- does not consider that it needs the additional protection it would get by incorporating the charity as a company or industrial and provident society.

Trustee incorporation involves making an application to the Charity Commission. The process is explained in Charity Commission booklet CC43 *Incorporation of Charity Trustees*.

1.5 CHARITY SCHEMES

Many older charitable associations or trusts are now regulated by a **scheme**, made by the court or more commonly by the Charity Commission [see **5.5.4**]. Under this procedure the charity is given a new governing document or the old one is varied. The governing body under a scheme has the powers and duties of the type of body it was before the scheme—generally an association or trust.

1.6 FRIENDLY SOCIETIES

Friendly societies were originally set up in the 18th century as mutual aid or self-help associations. Under the **Friendly Societies Act 1974**, registration was available to certain types of self-help and benevolent organisations, including some which were legally charitable. Until the Charities Act 1992 these charitable friendly societies were classed as **exempt charities** and did not have to register with the Charity Commission. Since the 1992 Act exempt charities have not been allowed to register, and registration has ceased to have effect for those which were registered.

The **Friendly Societies Act 1992** ended registration under the 1974 Act. Since 1 February 1993 only mutual assurance societies have been able to register, and the structure has been changed from unincorporated to incorporated. The structure is therefore no longer available for voluntary organisations, and information about it is not included in this book.

Chapter 2
COMPANIES AND OTHER
INCORPORATED STRUCTURES

2.1
INCORPORATION

Before deciding whether to incorporate, the main points to be aware of are:

- an incorporated organisation exists as a legal entity separate from its members, and can own property, enter into contracts and take other legal action in its own right rather than having to do it in the name of individuals as an unincorporated body must do;

- there are a variety of forms of incorporation, but some are not appropriate for voluntary organisations;

- most voluntary organisations which choose to incorporate become a **private company limited by guarantee**, with smaller numbers becoming an **industrial and provident society**;

- some bodies become incorporated by statute, such as schools, or by royal charter;

- in most incorporated organisations the members have **limited liability**, so they are protected from unlimited personal liability if the organisation cannot meet its financial obligations;

- a company or IPS is governed by **directors** (often called the management committee, trustees or something similar), who in most situations have **limited liability** if the organisation cannot meet its financial obligations but who may in some situations be made personally liable;

- company law requires a certain amount of paperwork, and the people responsible for managing a company may be fined if it does not comply with the requirements;

- at the time of writing (early 2001) there were plans for a new form of incorporated body, a **charitable incorporated institution** [see

21

2.2], which would provide limited liability for the members and governing body but without the onerous requirements of company law;

- a form of incorporation for charity trustees allows them to act as a legal entity, but without giving limited liability [see **1.4**].

For how to set up an company or IPS see **6.3** and **6.4**.

2.1.1
Advantages of incorporation

For most organisations, the overriding advantage of incorporation is the limited liability it offers to the members of the organisation and its governing body. But there are other advantages as well.

2.1.1.1
Legal personality

When an organisation incorporates, it takes on **legal personality** (legal person-hood) as a **corporate body** or **body corporate**. Unlike an unincorporated organisation it can, in its own right, enter into contracts, rent or own property, take legal action and be sued. It is considered to be a **legal person**, and within the bounds of common sense can do anything a human person can do. So when governing documents and other official documents refer to **persons**, they are generally referring to corporate bodies as well as human persons.

Because an incorporated organisation can enter into legal agreements in its own right, there is no need to appoint **holding trustees, custodian trustees** or a **nominee company** [see **18.4**] to hold its land, buildings or investments.

2.1.1.2
Limited liability

Apart from gaining a legal existence and therefore being able to enter into legal agreements in its own name, the main advantage of incorporation is that it nearly always gives **limited liability** to the organisation's members. In an unincorporated organisation the members are potentially liable for the organisation's debts if the organisation does not have enough money to pay them [see **1.2.5**]. But an incorporated organisation is liable for its own debts. If it does not or cannot pay its bills, the people to whom it owes money (its **creditors**) can take legal action against the organisation and very occasionally against the members of its governing body, but not against the organisation's members.

If the organisation ultimately cannot afford to pay its debts, it goes into **insolvent liquidation** [see **21.5**], and its assets are sold and distributed among its creditors. The organisation becomes insolvent, but the members of the organisation and in most cases the members of its governing body are protected from any personal liability for its debts.

2.1.1.3
Permanent succession

An incorporated organisation has **permanent succession**, which means there is no need to transfer contracts, leases or other legal agreements to new signatories whenever the persons who signed them cease to hold their position in the organisation.

2.1.1.4
Permanence

An incorporated organisation is **permanent**. Unlike an unincorporated association which can simply fade away if its members cease to meet, it continues to exist until it is formally dissolved [see **21.3** and **21.6**].

2.1.2
Disadvantages of incorporation

2.1.2.1
Cost

Incorporation involves some **costs**. In setting up a company limited by guarantee there will be legal costs unless a law centre, council for voluntary service or similar organisation is willing to do it free, and there is a registration fee (£20 as at 1/4/01) and an annual filing fee (£15 as at 1/4/01). An audit, if required, may be more expensive than for an unincorporated organisation.

There are similar set-up costs in becoming an industrial and provident society, and the registration fee is much higher (£90 as at 1/4/01 if approved model rules are used; £250 to £875 if model rules with amendments are used and £980 if the society does not use model rules). There are also fees for many transactions after the IPS is registered, for example up to £800 (as at 1/4/01) if it amends its rules, £180 if it changes its name and £40 if it changes its registered address.

2.1.2.2
External accountability

All organisations are accountable to their members, funders and (for charitable organisations) the Charity Commission. But incorporation also means **accountability** to the registrar of companies or, for industrial and provident societies, the registrar of friendly societies, and companies and IPSs must make certain information available to the public. Non-charities, in particular, may consider it a disadvantage to have to make publicly available details of their financial position and names of their governing body members. Charities have to do this anyway, regardless of whether they are incorporated.

2.1.2.3
Paperwork

Primarily because of this public accountability, incorporation involves **detailed paperwork** [see **chapter 16**] and compliance with the relevant **legislation**. Before an organisation incorporates, it must have the capacity to cope with increased paperwork and administration.

For a company this involves keeping various registers (lists), notifying Companies House every time certain changes are made to some of these registers, sending in annual accounts and returns, and operating according to company law. Failure to comply with company law could lead to the company being fined or struck off the register, and/or the company's directors, the company secretary and senior managers being fined.

Paperwork and rules for IPSs are less burdensome, but nonetheless must be dealt with.

2.1.2.4
<u>**Public access to records**</u>

Information about a company's directors and secretary, including directors' home addresses, is publicly available at Companies House. In addition a company's registers of company members, company directors and company secretaries must be open to members of the public every weekday, and information from the registers must be provided to any member of the public who asks for it [see **16.3.2** and **16.3.4**]. While this is generally not a problem, some voluntary organisations would not want this information to be available to the public. Access rules for industrial and provident societies are less intrusive [see **16.4.1** and **16.4.2**].

In exceptional circumstances consent may be given for company directors' home addresses not to be made available either at Companies House or through the register of directors [see **16.3.4**].

2.1.2.5
Limitations on limited liability

The ordinary members of an incorporated organisation are protected from personal liability for the debts or actions of the incorporated body. But the members of the governing body may be **personally liable** if they act outside their powers, act fraudulently or without due care, commit an offence, or allow the organisation to carry on operating when they know, or should reasonably have known, that it is inevitably going to become (or already is) insolvent.

Incorporation does not protect directors from liability for failure to comply with certain statutory duties [see **13.2**] nor, if the organisation is charitable, does it protect directors from liability arising from their duties as charity trustees [see **13.3**].

The protection of limited liability is extensive, but it is not absolute. For more about liability of governing body members, see **chapter 19**.

2.1.2.6
Permanent endowment

Permanent endowment [see **13.3.5**] is money given to a charitable organisation on condition that it not be spent, or property given on condition that it not be disposed of (or if it is disposed of, the proceeds cannot be spent). Trust law generally prevents permanent endowment held by a charitable unincorporated association or trust from being disposed of, but assets subject to these conditions and held by a charitable company or IPS are not protected in the same way. In the case of a company or IPS liquidation, the assets would be available for sale to meet the organisation's liabilities [see **22.4-22.6**].

For this reason a charitable trust or unincorporated association which holds permanent endowment and becomes incorporated will generally be required to agree, with the Charity Commission, special trust arrangements for holding the permanent endowment. In relation to such arrangements the company directors will be trustees for the purposes of the **Trustee Act 2000** [see **54.1**].

2.1.2.7
Winding up

Because an incorporated organisation is permanent, it must go through a formal process to bring it to an end [see **22.3-22.6**]. It cannot simply fade away or pass a resolution to dissolve itself, as unincorporated associations often do.

2.1.3
Choosing to incorporate

It is sensible to consider incorporation if an organisation:

- employs or expects to employ staff;
- owns, or expects to own, land, buildings, investments or other substantial property; *or*
- is, or expects to be, involved in activities, leases or contracts where there is financial risk.

Incorporation may not be suitable if an organisation:

- does not employ staff, own property or investments, or have long-term leases or contracts;
- does not expect to last a long time;
- does not have the administrative capacity (or desire) to comply with paperwork requirements and external rules about how it operates;
- does not want its registers of members and directors to be open to the public, and directors' details to be available at Companies House;
- is not a charity, and does not want to make its accounts available to the public; *or*
- does not want to put onto the members of its governing body the extra responsibilities and liabilities involved with incorporation (but without incorporation, they will have all the responsibilities and risks which arise from *not* being incorporated).

2.1.4
Incorporation without limited liability

Trustee incorporation [see **1.4**] enables the governing body of a charitable trust or charitable association to incorporate itself. This gives the trustee body legal personality and enables them to enter legal agreements, own property or take legal action as a corporate body, but does not give the trustees limited liability.

2.2
PROPOSED NEW STRUCTURE

The legal structures available for voluntary organisations are all less than perfect. In an unincorporated association or trust, members of the governing body may be at risk of potential personal liability. Registration as a company or IPS substantially reduces this risk, but company paperwork is overly cumbersome, especially for small organisations, and IPS registration is not always appropriate.

A second complicating factor is the need for registration with the Charity Commission if a company limited by guarantee has charitable objects [see **4.3** and **7.1**]. This creates a complex dual accountability, which becomes even more complex for organisations such as registered social landlords which have additional registration requirements [see **6.5.2**].

These factors have led various bodies to consider new structures for voluntary organisations.

Proposals for a **charitable incorporated institution** (CII), a new incorporated structure for charities, were published in mid-2000 as part of a wide review of company law. This would have the advantages of legal identity and limited liability but without overly burdensome paperwork and the confusion of dual charity/company accountability.

At the time of writing (early 2001) it remained unclear whether the structure would be available only for charities, or for non-charitable voluntary organisations as well, and who the registration body would be. It was also unclear whether existing charitable companies would have to convert to the new structure or could remain as charitable companies, and whether new organisations could register as charitable companies or charitable IPSs or would have to become a charitable incorporated institution.

Organisations wishing to incorporate should contact the Charity Commission, National Council for Voluntary Organisations or Wales Council for Voluntary Action, the Department of Trade and Industry website [see **page 12** for details] or a professional advisor to find out whether the new structure has become available. Note that it may end up being called something other than a charitable incorporated institution.

2.3 COMPANIES

A company is a membership organisation in which the **company members** generally elect **directors** as the governing body. The company legal structure is appropriate even for charities and other organisations which are not businesses.

2.3.1 Types of company

The members of a company may have limited liability or in some cases unlimited liability. A voluntary organisation which incorporates as a company will become a **limited liability company**.

A limited liability company can be **public** or **private**.

2.3.1.1 Public and private limited companies

A **public limited company** is one which has a share capital [see below] of at least £50,000, and states in its memorandum of association that it is a public limited company. It is identified by the words 'public limited company', the initials 'plc' or the Welsh equivalent in its name. A plc can raise money by selling shares publicly on the stock exchange, and the shareholders become company members.

If a company is not explicitly public, it is a **private limited company** (usually identified by 'limited', 'ltd' or the Welsh equivalent). A voluntary organisation which incorporates as a company becomes a **private limited company**. Most voluntary sector companies can choose not to use 'limited' or 'ltd' as part of their name [see **8.4.3**].

A private limited company may be **limited by shares** or **limited by guarantee**.

2.3.1.2 Companies limited by shares

A company limited by shares, whether public or private, has members (**shareholders**) who each purchase at least one share in the company. Private companies limited by shares can invite people to invest in them through buying shares, subject to rules set out in the **Financial Services Act 1986**. But unlike plc's they cannot raise money by selling their shares on the stock exchange.

Members may be individuals or corporate bodies. They provide money (**share capital**) for the company, and generally hope to make money for themselves through **dividends** (a proportion of profits paid to shareholders).

Often shareholders do not immediately pay to the company the full value of their shares, and pay by instalments instead. Their personal liability if the company becomes insolvent is limited to the amount they still owe on their shares. If the company becomes insolvent after they have paid in full they lose what they have paid for their shares, but they do not owe anything more towards the company's debts.

Shares may generally be sold or transferred. Normally each share carries one vote in the company, so members are entitled to multiple votes if they hold multiple shares.

2.3.1.3
Company limited by guarantee

A **company limited by guarantee** does not issue shares. Instead the members promise (guarantee) to contribute a sum, usually between £1 and £10, if the company becomes insolvent and is wound up. Their personal liability to the company is limited to this amount [see **10.4.1**].

The vast majority of voluntary organisations which incorporate become **private companies limited by guarantee and not having a share capital**.

Some companies set up before December 1980 are companies limited by guarantee *with* a share capital. These companies must comply with most company legislation but there are some differences. This book does not deal with them, or with public companies.

2.3.2
Regulation of companies

Companies limited by guarantee are regulated by a variety of Acts, of which the most important are the **Companies Acts 1985** and **1989**, the **Business Names Act 1985**, the **Company Directors Disqualification Act 1986**, and the **Insolvency Act 1986**. At the time of writing (early 2001) company law was under review, and significant changes were expected in 2002.

As well as statutes there are many statutory instruments (regulations containing the detailed rules for implementing the statutes) and a substantial body of case law. It is the responsibility of the company secretary [see **12.3**] and all members of the governing body to ensure the requirements of company law are met.

Questions about company law can sometimes be answered by Companies House [see **page 12**] but they will often advise the enquirer to consult a legal advisor. Many solicitors are reasonably well versed in company law, but may not be aware of differences in the treatment of companies limited by guarantee. It is generally sensible to consult a legal advisor who is a voluntary sector specialist [see **60.10.3** for how to find a specialist advisor].

If asked to do so by the company itself or by at least 20% of the company's members, the secretary of state for trade and industry can appoint inspectors to investigate a company's affairs. The secretary of state or the court can order an investigation of a company to be carried out. Even without an investigation, the secretary of state can require anyone involved in a company to provide and explain any documents.

Companies Act 1985 ss.431-437

2.3.3
Advantages of the company structure

For the main advantages and disadvantages of incorporation, see **2.1.1** and **2.1.2.1**. Specific advantages of the company structure are that it is **flexible** and can be adapted for any size and type of voluntary organisation, and that it is **widely understood** by solicitors and funders.

The structure is intrinsically **democratic**, giving company members the right to elect and remove directors. But there is nothing to stop an organisation from adapting it in an undemocratic way, for example having only three company members who keep electing themselves as directors, or having directors who serve for life or until they resign.

The company structure is suitable for any size of organisation. A private company only needs to have one member, and one director and a company secretary. A sole member and sole director can be the same person, but the director and secretary must be separate. For a charitable company the Charity Commission generally presses for a minimum of three directors, one of whom may be the company secretary. *ss.282, 283*

A company gets a **detailed constitution** (the memorandum and articles of association) covering many of the problematic situations which organisations get themselves into. Even where the procedures are not explicit, there may be a **default procedure** in company law. This can be helpful in difficult situations, for example if the company members want to remove a member of the governing body.

There is a **statutory right to amend** the articles and the objects clause by special resolution [see **5.5.2**], although any amendment altering a charity's objects or any other provision affecting the way its money or property is used requires written consent from the Charity Commission before it is passed.

Companies Act 1985 ss.4, 9, 17; Charities Act 1993 s.64(2)

2.3.4 Disadvantages of the company structure

As indicated in **2.1.2**, the main disadvantages of becoming a company are the cost, the paperwork, and the risk of fines for the company, being struck off the register of companies and/or potential personal liability for directors if the paperwork is not dealt with on time or for not complying with other aspects of company legislation. For some organisations, public access to the registers of members and directors may also be a disadvantage.

Another disadvantage is that members or supporters who do not understand that 'company' is simply a legal structure and can be used for not-for-profit as well as well as profit-making bodies may misunderstand the term and think that the organisation is becoming inappropriately commercial.

People who would happily 'just be a committee member' might not like the idea of being a company director, even though they are almost certainly more at risk on the committee of an unincorporated body.

Companies need to comply with detailed company regulations concerning their **annual accounts**. Charities now need to comply with similar requirements, so incorporation does not make a significant difference for them. But for non-charitable unincorporated associations, incorporation brings the obligation to prepare accounts according to company law. [For more about accounting see **chapter 50**.]

The administrative requirements imposed by company law are significant, and *the importance of complying with the legislation cannot be over-emphasised*. The company's officers (its directors, the company secretary and possibly senior employees) could, for example, be fined for:

- failure to hold an annual general meeting;
- failure to circulate a resolution properly submitted by members;
- failure to notify Companies House of resolutions which must be notified (a fine for each officer, plus a further fine for each day of default);
- failure to submit the annual accounts to Companies House within 10 months of the end of the company's financial year (automatic penalty of £100 for the company if the accounts are even one day late, rising to £1,000 if they are more than a year late, plus the possibility of fines or imprisonment for the officers);
- etc etc; altogether there are over 200 criminal offences within company law.

The penalty for failure to submit annual accounts on time is levied by the computer at Companies House, not by the courts, and is automatic. Apart from this, companies and their officers are generally prosecuted only if a default has been deliberate and persistent, so the risk of legal action and the resultant fines or imprisonment is very low.

A more likely outcome is that failure to comply will result in the company being removed from (**struck off**) the register of companies, thus ending the limited liability of the members and directors. A company which has been struck off can be reinstated, but this requires application to the court and is an expensive procedure.

2.3.5
Choosing the company structure

The company limited by guarantee structure is suitable if:

- the organisation has decided to incorporate [see **2.1.3**];

- it wants a flexible structure suitable for any size organisation;

- the people involved are prepared to ensure that the administrative responsibilities under company law are dealt with;

- they do not mind the public having access to the registers of members and directors; *and*

- the industrial and provident society structure [see **2.4**] is not suitable, or is suitable but has been rejected as an option.

2.3.6
Companies limited by shares

The structure of public or private company limited by shares is used for businesses which incorporate. It is generally not suitable for charities or other voluntary organisations, but **trading companies** or **trading subsidiaries** set up by charities and other organisations [see **47.3.2**] are usually incorporated as private companies limited by shares. The parent organisation or, in the case of an unincorporated body, a person or persons appointed by the parent body, generally own all the shares.

A charity or other voluntary organisation which wants to set up a company limited by shares must get specialist legal advice. In particular, the relationship between a charity and a company limited by shares must be very carefully worked out to ensure the affairs and accounts of the two bodies are kept completely separate, the charity's assets are not used for non-charitable purposes, and the tax and VAT arrangements are appropriate [see **chapter 47**].

Most company law which applies to companies limited by guarantee also applies to private companies limited by shares. But there are some significant differences, and share companies must comply with additional requirements which are not covered in this book.

2.4
INDUSTRIAL AND PROVIDENT SOCIETIES

A less common form of incorporated organisation is the industrial and provident society (IPS), in which members agree to purchase one or more shares. Members' liability is limited to the amount unpaid on the purchase of the shares.

Unlike the company structure, which is available to virtually any sort of organisation, the IPS structure is available only to *bona fide* cooperative societies, and to voluntary organisations carrying on an industry, trade or business for the benefit of the community.

Industrial and Provident Societies Act 1965 s.1(1),(2)

A consultation on the law relating to IPSs was undertaken in the late 1990s, and legislation may be forthcoming.

2.4.1
Cooperatives

A *bona fide* (genuine) cooperative:

- carries on a business or trade for the mutual benefit of its members;

- is democratically run by its members, with each member having one vote at general meetings; *and*

- has rules (the governing document) which reflect the principles agreed in 1966 by the International Cooperative Alliance Commission on Cooperative Principles.

Some co-ops allow for the profits of the business to be distributed to the members. Examples are a wholefood co-op or jewellery manufacturing business whose members are its workers, and whose profits are distributed among the workers.

Other co-ops are set up on a not-for-profit basis, which means that any profits cannot be distributed, but must be used solely for the objects of the co-op. An example is a housing co-op where any profit or surplus from the rents must be used to improve the housing or provide more housing for members in housing need. This type of co-op may be, on paper, virtually indistinguishable from a charitable housing association. But it does not have charitable status, because it provides housing only to its members. To be legally charitable an organisation must show that it operates 'for public benefit' [see **4.3.8**] and not solely for the benefit of a small, limited group of members.

A co-op is not obliged to register as an IPS. Depending on the sort of co-op it is, it may be unincorporated as a partnership or association, or may incorporate as a company limited by shares or by guarantee.

This book does not cover cooperatives. For more information contact the Mutual Societies Registration or ICOM [see **page 12**].

2.4.2
Community benefit societies

If an organisation is not a genuine cooperative, it can register as an industrial and provident society only if:

- it is carrying on some sort of industry, trade or business which is in the interests of the community;
- it will benefit people other than, or in addition to, its own members;
- it is democratically controlled by its members;
- all profits made from the business will be applied solely for the benefit of the community (with none distributed as profits or dividends to members or anyone else); *and*
- there are convincing reasons why it should be registered as an IPS rather than a company limited by guarantee.

Report of the Chief Registrar of Friendly Societies 1989-90, para.2.5

These organisations are called **community benefit societies**, or sometimes **bencoms**. If the organisation is being paid for its services or activities, it is likely to be considered to be carrying on a trade or business and will be eligible for registration as a community benefit IPS. Payments might come, for example, as rents, fees or admission charges, or as payments by customers or under a contract or service agreement.

The meaning of 'business' is not necessarily interpreted strictly when community benefit IPSs are registered, and it may be possible to register community organisations which are not trading in a conventional sense. Consult Mutual Societies Registration or ICOM [see **page 12**] or a specialist solicitor for advice.

Social and recreational clubs which provide services to their members can register as industrial and provident societies. One-third of registered IPSs fall into this category.

2.4.3
Community businesses

There is no agreed definition of what constitutes a **community business** or **community enterprise**. The terms are generally used to refer to businesses which are run in a commercial way, such as a café, launderette or bookshop, but which are run by an elected unpaid committee and whose profits must be reinvested in the business or in other community activities. A community business can register as a community benefit IPS, company limited by shares or company limited by guarantee.

2.4.4
Charitable IPSs

If a community benefit IPS is set up exclusively for charitable purposes [see **4.3**] and all profits will be used for those purposes, the IPS can apply to the Inland Revenue for recognition as a charity. If recognised it will be an **exempt charity** [see **7.1.2**].

Exempt charities cannot register with the Charity Commission and do not have a Charity Commission registration number, but are eligible for the tax benefits available to charities [see **3.2.1**]. Most of the provisions of the Charities Acts do not apply to exempt charities but some do; these are explained in the relevant sections of this book.

In the past charitable IPSs could register voluntarily with the Charity Commission, but since the Charities Act 1992 they have not been able to do this, and IPSs which were voluntarily registered have been deregistered. It is unlawful for an IPS, even if it is set up for charitable purposes, to say it is a registered charity or to use a registered charity number. It can, however, say 'a charity exempt from registration' or similar wording and/or use its Inland Revenue charity reference number.

2.4.5
Regulation of IPSs

All IPSs register with Mutual Societies Registration, part of the Financial Services Authority, under the **Industrial and Provident Societies Act 1965**. For the registration process, see **6.4**.

Mutual Societies Registration and the Registry of Friendly Societies take more of a direct interest in the administration of IPSs than Companies House does in the administration of companies. The registrar has a supervisory responsibility for IPSs, and can appoint an inspector to investigate a society's affairs.

2.4.6
Advantages of the IPS structure

IPSs have all the advantages of incorporation [see **2.1.1**]: limited liability of members, legal personality, permanent succession and the right to own property and take legal action in their own name.

The legislative requirements are less detailed, intrusive and cumbersome than for companies, and the risk of prosecution for non-compliance is low. Members of the IPS and persons with an interest in the funds of the IPS have a right to see its register of members, but the register is not open to the public in general as it is for a company.

For a larger membership organisation costs can be lower, as full accounts do not have to be sent to every member but can instead be advertised or displayed at the IPS's premises.

The use of **model rules** produced by **promoting bodies** [see **6.4.1**] eliminates the need to write a governing document and reduces the registration fee.

Charitable IPSs are eligible for the tax advantages of charitable status without having to register with the Charity Commission. They must seek recognition of their charitable status from the Inland Revenue, but this is generally quicker than registration with the Commission. Unlike charitable companies, charitable IPSs do not have to comply with most charity legislation and in general are not subject to scrutiny and intervention by the Charity Commission.

2.4.7
Disadvantages of the IPS structure

2.4.7.1
Unfamiliarity

The industrial and provident society structure is still unfamiliar and not well understood, and it is surprisingly difficult to get detailed information about the requirements. Non-specialist legal advisors are unlikely to know anything about IPSs, and even voluntary sector specialist legal advisors may be able to give only sketchy advice.

It can be difficult to explain to funders that the IPS has charitable status even though it is not registered with the Charity Commission and does not have a charity registration number.

2.4.7.2
Size and structure

An IPS must have at least three members, which could be a disadvantage for very small organisations. A private company needs only one member and a secretary.

IPSs must generally be democratic, and any constitutional provision which is not democratic—such as places on the governing body which are filled by outside bodies rather than being elected by the IPS's members—may be challenged during the registration process.

2.4.7.3
Slower registration

The registration process for IPSs is slower and more expensive than for companies, and the governing document will be scrutinised before registration. After registration, however, the requirements are less strict than for companies.

If model rules are used the process is quicker and cheaper (though still slower and more expensive than registration as a company), but the model rules must be used *exactly* as they are. Any deviation increases the registration fee and the time.

It can be difficult to convince the Inland Revenue that a charitable IPS is indeed charitable, and there can be problems in getting the tax benefits to which the IPS is entitled.

2.4.7.4
Cost

The cost of registration is substantially higher than for a company [see **2.1.2.1**]. There is no annual filing fee, but there are many substantial additional charges, for example when changing the registered office.

2.4.7.5
Winding up

Company winding up procedures are clear and well defined, but for IPSs which are being wound up—especially if they are insolvent—the process can be complex and confused [see **21.6**].

2.4.8
Choosing the IPS structure

An IPS may be a suitable structure if:

- the organisation is charging for all or some of the services it provides;
- suitable model rules already exist;
- it wants to avoid the detailed requirements of company law; *and*
- if it is charitable, it will not be affected by not having a charity registration number.

2.5
OTHER INCORPORATED BODIES

Some organisations are incorporated under **royal charter** or by **statute**. These companies must comply with most company legislation but there are some differences. This book does not deal with them, and organisations with these structures should contact a specialist advisor.

From April 2001 the structure of **limited liability partnership** is available but is unlikely to be appropriate for voluntary organisations.

Chapter 3
CHARITABLE STATUS, CHARITY LAW AND REGULATION

Topics covered in this chapter

As well as deciding the appropriate legal structure [see chapters 1 and 2] for an organisation, the people involved in setting it up must decide whether they want it to have charitable status—although in some cases they have no choice. This chapter covers:

For sources of further information see page 12.

Double-underlined section headings indicate additions or significant changes since the first edition.

**3.1
DEFINING
CHARITABLE
STATUS**

In England and Wales an organisation, regardless of its legal structure, is by definition a charity and has charitable status if:

- its objects or purposes are **wholly and exclusively charitable** [see **4.3**];
- it is of a **charitable nature** [see **4.3.9**]; *and*
- it provides a **public benefit** [see **4.3.8**].

An organisation does not become a charity by registering with the Charity Commission, the Inland Revenue or anyone else; by definition it is a charity and has charitable status if it meets the above criteria. However, most charities in England and Wales are required to register with the Commission and/or have their charitable status recognised by the Inland Revenue. This process is explained in **chapter 7**.

An organisation which does not want to register must word its objects in a way which makes it clear that they are not wholly and exclusively charitable, but the organisation will then not be eligible for most of the tax reliefs available to charities.

**3.1.1
Charitable status
and legal structure**

Charitable status is completely separate from the organisation's legal structure. Regardless of whether an organisation is an **unincorporated association** [see **1.2**], **trust** [see **1.3**], **company limited by guarantee** [see **2.4**] or **industrial and provident society** [see **2.3**], it is also a charity if its objects are charitable. It is not possible to be 'a charity' on its own, without also having another legal status.

3.1.2
Charities
as trusts

Under charity law, the members of the governing body of all charities, regardless of their legal structure, are **charity trustees**, and have duties under charity law [see **13.3**].   *Charities Act 1993 s.97*

The members of the governing body of a trust, charitable association or body established by charter hold money, property and other assets **in trust** [see **1.3.1**] for the charity's beneficiaries, and have a range of duties and powers as **trustees** under the **Trustee Act 2000** [see **54.1**]. In some situations governing body members of charitable companies may also have these duties and powers.

In a narrow sense, a person is a trustee if he or she is on the governing body of an organisation established as a trust [see **1.3**].

3.2
ADVANTAGES OF CHARITABLE STATUS
3.2.1
Tax benefits

The tax advantages of charitable status include:

- exemption from income tax or corporation tax on profits or surplus and capital gains tax on gains from the sale of assets [see **52.5** and **52.6**], provided the profits are used wholly for the charity's purposes;

- exemption from having to pay stamp duty on conveyancing [see **57.10.1**] and on most other transactions;

- mandatory 80% relief on non-domestic rates for property used wholly or mainly for charitable purposes, and the possibility of up to 20% further discretionary relief [see **59.2.4**];

- the right to reclaim tax on donations made under gift aid [see **46.2**];

- donors able to make donations free of tax through a payroll deduction scheme [see **46.3**], and the charity able to recover an additional 10% from the government from until 5 April 2003;

- donors do not generally pay inheritance tax on legacies to a charity or capital gains tax on assets donated to a charity [see **46.5.2** and **46.4.1**];

- eligibility for zero rate VAT instead of standard rate on some goods and services purchased by the charity [see **53.2**];

- for a charity which is registered for VAT, the right to charge zero rate VAT instead of standard rate for some goods and services provided by the charity [see **53.5.1**].

To qualify for these fiscal benefits, the organisation and its activities must fall within the definition of charity for tax purposes [see **52.5.1**].

3.2.2
Other advantages

Further advantages of having charitable status are:

- many funders are allowed (or choose) to fund only charities;

- charities have, for the most part, a good public image, and most people think of charity as 'a good thing', so it may be easier to raise money or obtain cooperation and help as a charity;

- the Charity Commission provides help and guidance to charities on some matters;

- charities are subject to scrutiny by the Charity Commission or other bodies, which can help prevent abuse.

3.3
RESTRICTIONS ON CHARITIES

All charities must comply with certain restrictions:

- the charity's assets can be used only for its objects and within its powers as set out in the governing document;

- any use of the charity's property outside its objects or powers may be a breach of trust for which the members of the governing body can be held personally liable;

- in general, members of the governing body cannot be paid for serving on the governing body or for any other work they do for the charity, unless this is authorised by the governing document or the Charity Commission [see **14.3**];

- members of the governing body cannot profit in any other way or benefit from the charity unless the governing document allows this or the Charity Commission has authorised it [see **chapter 14**];

- charities can charge for charitable activities or services which they provide for their beneficiaries, and for goods produced or services provided by their beneficiaries, but there are limits on other trading which they can undertake [see **47.1.2**];

- although charities can undertake non-party political activities which are directly related to their objects, there are limits on other political activities and campaigning which they can undertake [see **41.3**];

- there may be restrictions on how a charity's funds can be invested [see **54.4**];

- a charity must comply with certain requirements in dealing with its property [see **57.11** and **57.12**].

Other possible disadvantages of charitable status are:

- charities are public bodies, open to public scrutiny;

- all charities must prepare annual accounts, and most must prepare annual reports [see **50.2**];

- registered charities with income or expenditure over £10,000 must have their accounts examined or audited and submit them every year to the Charity Commission [see **50.2.12**] (but many charities have to have their accounts audited anyway, to comply with funders' or constitutional requirements);

- charity trustees are required to act 'with prudence' which may inhibit their activities, for example their ability to invest in ethical investments [see **54.6.2**];

- the Charity Commissioners have considerable powers to investigate complaints, and if there is serious mismanagement to step in and even bring legal action against the charity, the members of its governing body and its employees. This may be seen as a disadvantage by those involved in the mismanagement.

3.4 REGULATION OF CHARITIES

3.4.1 Charity legislation

3.4.1.1 Early legislation

Charity regulation is not new. The preface to the **Charitable Uses Act 1601** gave examples, four centuries ago, of the purposes for which charitable property could be used [see **4.3.1**]. The purpose of this Act was 'to redress the misemployment of lands, goods and stocks of money heretofore given to certain charitable uses'—making it very clear that misuse of charity funds and other property is not a new phenomenon.

The **Charitable Trusts Act 1853** set up a permanent Charity Commission under the Court of Chancery [see **60.2.2**] to oversee the running of charities, and a series of other Charitable Trusts Acts in the latter half of the 19th century sought to ensure charities were properly managed. Most of these were replaced by the **Charities Act 1960**, which consolidated and extended charity law, clarified the role of the Charity Commission, set up a register of charities, and made it easier for charities to update their objects. But it did not include any replacement for the 1601 definition of charitable purposes, which had been repealed in 1891. The **Recreational Charities Act 1958** [see **4.3.7**], which made the provision of recreational facilities charitable, is the only statute law defining charitable purposes.

The **Charities Act 1985** allowed small local charities to alter their objects more easily, and in some cases to spend capital assets.

3.4.1.2 Charities Act 1992 (originally)

The **Charities Act 1992** was in four main parts:

- part I, primarily increasing the powers of the Charity Commission, clarifying requirements for charity registration, accounting and reporting and bringing in some new requirements for this, and repealing and replacing the **War Charities Act 1940** and the **Charities Act 1985**;

- part II, on professional and commercial involvement in fundraising;
- part III, on public collections, which was intended to replace legislation on street collections (the **Police, Factories etc (Miscellaneous Provisions) Act 1916**) and house-to-house collections (the **House to House Collections Act 1939**);
- part IV, on the liability of trustees in charitable companies and on various administrative matters.

The Act strengthened the Charity Commission and made it, for the first time, a criminal offence for charity trustees not to comply with some of the administrative requirements.

3.4.1.3
Charities Act 1993

Before the ink was dry on the 1992 Act, the **Charities Act 1993** was enacted. This was a consolidating Act and did not include any new legislation. It brought together:

- the **Charitable Trustees Incorporation Act 1872**, which allowed the trustee body of unincorporated charities to incorporate [see **1.4**];
- the **Charities Act 1960**;
- part I of the **Charities Act 1992**;
- the sections in part IV of the 1992 Act which related to part I.

The 1993 Act then included, in one place, all the legislation relating to charity management and administration.

The **Recreational Charities Act 1958** was not consolidated in the 1993 Act, because it relates to charitable purposes rather than to charity administration.

The other piece of charity legislation which was not consolidated in the 1993 Act was the **Charitable Trusts (Validation) Act 1954**, which clarified the status of trusts set up before 16 December 1952 for objects which were both charitable and non-charitable.

Implementation of the 1993 Act was in stages, with the last major section, on annual accounts, audit and annual reports, coming into effect on 1 March 1996.

3.4.1.4
Charities Act 1992 (now)

The remaining **Charities Act 1992** now includes:

- **part II**, on professional and commercial involvement in fundraising [see **44.5**];
- **part III**, on public collections [see **45.2**];
- some miscellaneous sections in part IV.

The provisions in parts II and III apply not only to charities but also to **benevolent** and **philanthropic** organisations [see **44.5.1**], so it is reasonable for them to be separated from the legislation which applies only to charities.

At the time of writing (early 2001) there was no timetable for implementation of Part III. Until it comes into effect, the 1916 and 1939 legislation [see above] remains in force.

3.4.1.5
Since the 1993 Act

Some Charities Act procedures were simplified through provisions of the **Deregulation and Contracting Out Act 1994** and through detailed Charities Act regulations issued by the Home Office in the mid-1990s. The government announced in mid-2001 that charity law and the role of the Charity Commission would be reviewed.

3.4.2
Other legislation

As well as duties under charity law, charitable trusts [see **1.3**] and charitable unincorporated associations [see **1.2**] have a duties and powers under trust law, including the **Trustee Act 2000** [see **54.1**]. All charities are also subject to all relevant aspects of UK and European law. These statutory obligations are outlined throughout this book.

3.4.3
Case law

Governments have for hundreds of years recognised the need to ensure that charity management and administration are effective, to ensure that organisations which call themselves charities are eligible for the tax benefits available to them, and to reassure the public that funds or property given for charitable purposes are used as they should be.

But they have resisted the temptation to define too closely what is and is not a charitable purpose, preferring to rely on case law decisions about whether a new purpose is within the spirit and intention of the **Charitable Uses Act 1601** [see **4.3.1**]. Even the charitable categories defined in 1891 in the Pemsel case [see **4.3.2**] included the general 'other purposes beneficial to the community', rather than requiring all charities to fall within defined categories.

If a potential charity is dissatisfied with a decision about the charitable nature of its objects, or if the Inland Revenue believes that tax benefits are being given for purposes which it does not consider charitable, a case may be brought through the High Court. As a result there is a substantial body of case law on what charities can and cannot do. The Charity Commission refers to this when deciding whether a new purpose is or is not charitable.

In 1998 the Charity Commission launched a review of the register of charities, and is systematically looking at areas of charitable activity and criteria for charitable status. As a result of this review several new charitable purposes have been defined [see **4.3.7**].

3.4.4
Home Office

The charity law section in the Home Office's Active Community Unit is responsible for charity legislation, but the regulation of charities is the responsibility of the Charity Commission. The home secretary appoints the charity commissioners and reports annually to Parliament on the general work of the Commission.

3.4.5
Charity
Commission

The Charity Commission is a non-ministerial government department which acts on behalf of Parliament and the courts to help charities be more effective and to deal with abuse. Much of its work is as a gatekeeper, seeking to ensure that only appropriate organisations are registered. The work of the Charity Commission is described in **3.5**.

3.4.6
High Court

For the purposes of charity law, a charity is 'any institution, corporate or not, which is established for charitable purposes and is subject to the control of the High Court in the exercise of the court's jurisdiction with respect to charities'.   *Charities Act 1993 s.96(1)*

The court's jurisdiction is England and Wales, so the Commission cannot register a body if the promoters do not intend it to be regulated under the laws of England and Wales. Factors which may be taken into account in determining the intentions of the promoters include the residence of the original trustees and whether the organisation's property is based in England or Wales, but these factors are not conclusive. For charitable companies, the determining factor is where the company is registered.   *Gaudiya Mission v Brahmachary [1998] Ch 341*

The High Court retains final jurisdiction in charity matters, and if individuals or an organisation do not accept the Commission's view or ruling, they can apply to the court. However such applications are expensive, and are therefore rare.

Even though the home secretary appoints the charity commissioners, ministers cannot intervene in or overturn decisions of the commissioners in individual cases, because in those cases the Commission is acting on behalf of the courts.

3.4.7
The charity's governing document

Every charity must comply with the requirements in its governing document. If a charity acts outside its defined objects or powers [see **5.4.3**], the trustees can be personally liable for **breach of the charity's trust**, and can be required by the Charity Commission or court to repay to the charity any money used for that unlawful purpose.

Trustee liability insurance [see **20.10**] can provide protection for trustees if they make an honest mistake in good faith. But it does not cover breaches which the trustees knew were outside the charity's objects or powers, or which they undertook in 'reckless disregard' of whether they were outside the objects or powers. Nor does trustee liability insurance cover other liabilities such as redundancy payments, the organisation's debts if it becomes insolvent, or compensation for negligence. [For more about potential liability and insurances, see **chapters 19 and 20**.]

The administrative procedures set out in the governing document are also important. The improper appointment of a trustee or a meeting called with inadequate notice, for example, could be held to be invalid.

This is why it is essential to get good advice when drawing up the governing document and to give careful thought not only to what the charity wants to do and how it wants to operate now, but also to how it might want to change in future. **Chapter 5** looks at the process of drawing up a governing document.

3.5
WHAT THE CHARITY COMMISSION DOES

The Charity Commission covers only England and Wales, although it has some supervisory powers over Scottish charities which are controlled from England or Wales.   *Charities Act 1993 s.80*

Charities in Scotland and Northern Ireland must apply directly to the Inland Revenue if they want formal recognition of their charitable status (and the resultant tax benefits). At the time of writing (early 2001), Scottish charity law was being reviewed and is likely to be reformed.

The Commission consists of a chief charity commissioner and between two and four other commissioners. The Commission's staff are divided between offices in London, Liverpool and Taunton.

The role of the Charity Commission is described in its booklet CC2 *Charities and the Charity Commission*. It defines its overall role as:

- **support** for charities and the charity sector;
- **supervision** of charities, including monitoring, investigation of complaints, inquiries, and ultimately bringing legal proceedings against a charity or individuals involved with it.

On behalf of the courts, the Commission acts in a quasi-judicial capacity to:

- determine charitable status;
- make orders and schemes to improve the administration of individual charities and to allow trustees to take actions which would otherwise be outside their powers;
- authorise transactions by charities which need consent, such as some land disposals;
- investigate alleged or actual cases of mismanagement or fraud;
- safeguard charitable funds from misuse;
- take remedial action against those responsible for abuse.

On behalf of Parliament, it:

- maintains a register of charities and makes it available to the public;
- receives charity accounts and annual reports, and makes them available to the public;
- monitors charities' activities.

The Commission produces free booklets on many charity matters, available from the Commission or on its website [see **page 12**]. The Commission's detailed internal operational guidance is also on its website.

Some of the main aspects of the Commission's work are reported in its annual report, which is available on its website or from the Stationery Office. The reports explain the Commission's views and are often referred to when the Commission makes a ruling or gives guidance.

3.5.1
Register of charities

The Charity Commission maintains a register of all charities in England and Wales except those which are exempted or excepted from having to register [see **7.1.2** and **7.1.3**]. Inclusion in the register is conclusive proof for all purposes that an organisation is charitable.

Charities Act 1993 ss.3, 4(1)

The Commission is required to keep the register up to date and to remove any organisation which is no longer charitable, was registered in error, ceases to operate or no longer exists. Updating is done through a database update form [see **50.2.16**] which all registered charities are required to submit. Trustees of registered charities are required to notify the Commission of changes in the charity's name, objects or address, or the name or address of the contact person. *s.3(4),(7)(b)*

Information about the register is in Charity Commission booklet CC45 *Central Register of Charities*. The register itself is on the Commission's website [see **page 12**], and can be searched by registered number, name of charity, a key word in the name of the charity, location, or objects. Alternatively requests for information can be made in person at Commission offices, or by phone or letter.

3.5.2
Information and advice

The Charity Commission provides informal information and advice, either about charity law in general or about a specific situation, to charity trustees and managers. This may be done by telephone or in writing.

There is sometimes a lack of consistency between Commission offices, or even between staff within an office. A charity which feels it is getting wrong or inconsistent advice should consult the Commission's operational guidance (available on its website) and discuss the issues with relevant Commission staff. If it is still dissatisfied it should seek legal advice or use the Commission's review procedure [see **3.5.11**].

3.5.2.1
Section 29 advice

The charity trustees and other people connected with a charity will not be held liable for a breach of trust [see **19.3**] arising from any situation related to their duties as trustees if they:

- write to the Commissioners for an opinion;
- provide, to the best of their knowledge, the full facts; *and*
- act on the Commissioners' formal advice given under the **Charities Act 1993** s.29.

3.5.3
Official custodian for charities

The official custodian for charities is a person appointed by the Commission to serve as a **custodian trustee** [see **18.4.4**], holding charity land on behalf of unincorporated charities. Until the Charities Act 1992 the Official Custodian also held investments, but these were **divested** (returned to the charities).

If the Commissioners think that any of a charity's assets are at risk of being misused, they can vest the assets (not only land) in the Official Custodian [see **3.5.9**].

3.5.4
Orders

Sometimes a charity may want to do something which it does not have the power to do under its governing document. The Commissioners have the power to authorise some actions which are outside the trustees' powers but are considered to be in the best interests of the charity. It does this by **order** or by a **scheme** [see below]. Orders can be obtained reasonably quickly, but schemes can be very slow. *s.26*

An order might be made, for example, to allow a charity:

- to pay a trustee or former trustee for work done for the charity, or appoint a trustee or former trustee to a paid position;

- to provide, on a one-off basis, a charitable service or benefit to someone who is not within the charity's defined beneficiary group or lives outside the geographical area covered by the charity;

- to appoint trustees, if the governing document does not specify how this is to be done or if the trustees are unable to appoint;

- to discharge trustees, if they have ceased to be active but have not resigned and there is no power under the governing document to remove them;

- to spend its permanent endowment (money held by the charity on condition that it not be spent).

If the action requires changing the governing document or doing something which is expressly prohibited by the governing document, a scheme may be necessary [see below]. Even where a scheme is not necessary, the Commission sometimes makes a scheme rather than an order if it seems more suitable to the particular situation.

It is a breach of trust, for which the members of the governing body and others involved with the management of the charity may be held personally liable, to take action outside the charity's objects and powers without authorisation from the Charity Commission.

3.5.5
Schemes

Making a **scheme** is the procedure by which the Commission alters or extends the purposes of a charity, or authorises acts which are expressly prohibited under the charity's governing document or under other conditions. The procedure may also be used for other amendments to the governing document. A scheme is not always necessary for amendment [see **5.5**].   *Charities Act 1993 ss.16-18*

A scheme to alter or extend a charity's objects will not change the existing objects more than is necessary to ensure that those purposes remain socially useful, and capable in practice of being carried out [see **5.5.4**]. The term for this is **cy près**: that any change must be as near as possible to the original purposes. (*Cy près* is pronounced 'see pray'.)

Another form of scheme is when the governing document contains unworkable or cumbersome administrative procedures, and there is no procedure to amend it. The Commission can, in this situation, make a scheme to change the procedures [see **5.5.4**].

Schemes are generally made on the application of the charity, although the Commission can make one itself if it feels a scheme should be made but the trustees have unreasonably refused to apply for one. The process for requesting a scheme is set out in Charity Commission booklet CC36 *Making a Scheme*.   *s.16(6)*

3.5.6
Consents and other powers

The Commission has many other powers in relation to individual charities (but not exempt charities, see **7.1.2**). These include power to:

- require a charity to change its name [see **8.8.2**];   *s.6(9)*
- require information or documents;   *s.9(1)*
- authorise *ex gratia* payments [see **49.2.7**];   *s.27(1)*
- make directions about dormant bank accounts;   *s.28(2)*
- authorise charity proceedings [see **61.8**];   *s.33(2)*
- authorise mortgages or the disposal of property [see **8.11, 57.11** and **57.12**].   *ss.36-39*

3.5.7
Monitoring

The Commission's computerised monitoring system for annual returns, supported by examination of accounts and annual reports, is designed to identify charities at risk or in need of assistance and to enable the Commission to help charities avoid serious problems. The Commission monitors the largest charities regularly, along with a sample of smaller charities and those selected through the computerised system. It also carries out routine monitoring visits.

If the monitoring shows cause for concern, an approach is made to the trustees. The intention is to clarify the issues involved, and provide advice and assistance or take action as appropriate to resolve any difficulties and ensure that the charity functions effectively.

Circumstances which might lead to Commission enquiries include:

- lack of trustee meetings;
- lack of expenditure, or exceptional expenditure in certain areas;
- excessively high payments to staff;
- payments or other benefits to trustees;
- high fundraising expenses compared to funds raised;
- high legal or accountancy fees;
- loans to or from associated companies;
- inappropriate accumulation of income;
- potential insolvency.

3.5.8
Dealing with disputes

Charity Commission leaflet CC25 *Resolving Charity Disputes* explains when the Commission can help resolve disputes affecting charities. It can intervene only when significant assets or funds are at risk, the charity is not operating within its governing document or charity law, there is real danger of the name of the charity being brought into disrepute, or the charity is not working effectively due to poor management or administration.

It cannot intervene in contractual disputes with third parties, or in internal disagreements or disputes about how the charity should be run (provided it is operating within its governing document and charity law). The Commission can, however, be asked for advice in these situations [see **3.5.2**].

Any person connected with the charity or any member of the public may contact the Commission in writing if they believe there is cause for concern. The Commission does not normally respond to anonymous complaints, but will try to respect a complainant's wishes for confidentiality as much as possible.

3.5.9
Section 8 inquiries

Only if a situation cannot be informally resolved, or if there are indications of serious problems, will a **section 8 inquiry** be initiated. The procedure is explained in CC47 *Inquiries into Charities*. Such an inquiry might concern one charity or several. An inquiry cannot be undertaken in relation to exempt charities [see **7.1.2**].   *Charities Act 1993 s.8*

Trustees and others connected with the charity can be required to attend an inquiry or to provide accounts and any other relevant information. It is a criminal offence knowingly to conceal, destroy or falsify relevant documents or other information or to give false evidence to the Commission.   *s.11*

The purpose of an inquiry into an individual charity is not to punish the charity or its trustees, but to identify problems or potential problems and to help the charity strengthen its management and administration. But if the inquiry shows that mismanagement or maladministration has already occurred, or that the charity's property is at risk of not being used properly, the Commission has the power to:

- suspend any trustees, officers or employees for up to 12 months ('officers' include members of the governing body, the company secretary in a charitable company, and senior executives or managers);
- appoint additional trustees;
- freeze debts owed to the charity;

- freeze the charity's bank accounts and other property held by third parties;
- transfer any of the charity's property to the official custodian for charities [see **3.5.3**] for safekeeping;
- restrict any of the charity's activities and transactions; *and/or*
- appoint a receiver or manager (who must not be a Commission employee) to run the charity's affairs temporarily, with powers and duties specified by the Commissioners.   *Charities Act 1993 s.18(1)*

If the investigation shows that serious mismanagement or maladministration has already occurred, the Commission may also:

- remove the responsible trustees, officers, agents (persons authorised to act on behalf of the charity) or employees permanently;
- make a scheme [see **3.5.5**] to reorganise the charity, even if the trustees do not cooperate;   *s.18(2)*
- bring the results of its investigations to the attention of the police or other bodies.

The Commission maintains a list, available for public inspection, of everyone removed in this way or by the court. It is an offence for anyone on the list to serve as trustee of any charity.   *s.72*

The Commission publishes the findings of all inquiries on its website, and some in its annual report. These make instructive reading on how things can go wrong.

3.5.10
Legal proceedings

Some orders of the charity commissioners, for example those requiring documents or other information to be provided, property transferred or payments made, are enforceable as if they were High Court orders. Non-compliance is treated as contempt of court and is punishable by a fine or imprisonment. For some appeals against an order made by the commissioners there is a statutory time limit of three months. Appeals are brought in the High Court.

Non-compliance with some Charities Act requirements is a criminal offence punishable by a fine. In other cases the Commission can make an order requiring a default (for example a failure to apply for registration) to be made good. Such orders are also enforceable as if they were High Court orders.

Although the Commission has extensive powers and there are criminal penalties for some non-compliance, it reserves these for wilful breaches of the rules. An innocent mistake, even where it has serious consequences, rarely causes the Commission to take penal action.

In the past, only the attorney general could bring legal proceedings against a charity. Since 1993 the charity commissioners have also been able to, but only with the consent of the attorney general.

3.5.11
Complaints and appeals

A formal complaint against a Commission decision or action is made initially to a customer complaints manager, then to a regional operations manager and finally to an independent complaints reviewer. At the time of writing (early 2001) the reviewer does not have power to require the Commission to change its decision or action.

If the outcome of the complaints procedure is unsatisfactory a case may be brought against the Commission in the High Court [see **3.4.6**].

Chapter 4
THE OBJECTS CLAUSE

4.1 OBJECTS AND POWERS

Objects are the purposes for which an organisation is established, as set out in its governing document (constitution, trust deed, memorandum of association etc). The objects clause may also define:

- the people the organisation will provide services or activities for (**beneficiaries** in a charitable organisation, members in a membership organisation); *and/or*

- the geographical area covered by the organisation (the **area of benefit** or **beneficial area**).

Powers define activities which can be undertaken in order to achieve the objects. For example, the payment of rent or salaries does not *directly* achieve the object of providing support for elderly people, improving the quality of life for local people, or whatever else the organisation seeks to achieve. Acquiring premises and hiring staff are *means to an end*, rather than the end. For more on powers, see **5.4.3**.

Any action outside the objects or powers is ***ultra vires*** ('beyond the powers'). The person(s) who authorised or undertook an *ultra vires* action could be required to make good any losses to the organisation and in some cases, to third parties [see **4.7**].

If the objects or powers as set out in the governing document are very narrow, there is a risk that the governing body or the organisation's members could unintentionally find themselves acting *ultra vires*. This is why many organisations have relatively wide objects [see **4.6.1**] and why the powers clause in many governing documents gives power to do anything which is lawful and achieves, or helps to achieve, the objects [see **5.4.3**]. But even a catch-all powers clause such as this does not entitle the organisation to do anything it wishes. Everything the organisation does must be solely in furtherance of the objects.

Objects are described in detail in this chapter. Powers are covered throughout the book, and especially in **5.4.3-5.4.8** and **chapter 13**.

4.2 MYTHS ABOUT CHARITABLE OBJECTS

Certain misconceptions about charitable objects are very widespread. One is that charitable objects must always include some element of relieving poverty. Only some charities have such an element, and even they could be relieving the relative poverty of beneficiaries with significant incomes [see **4.3.3**]. Other charities—Eton College, the Royal Opera House—provide services clearly intended for people who are not poverty stricken.

A second misconception, arising from the label **not-for-profit** or **non-profit-making** [see **4.3.9**], is that charities must provide services free, below cost or at cost. Many do, but many others quite properly charge fees and seek to make a reasonable surplus or profit on the fee charged.

Another myth is that charities cannot be involved in political activities. Charities cannot be set up to promote the interests of a political party, nor can they be set up to seek or oppose changes in the law or in government policy in the UK or abroad. But they can have the object of educating the public on political issues or a range of other objects which could be seen as 'political' [see **4.3.8.4**], and can take part in a range of political activities [see **41.3**].

A further misconception is that the definition of what is charitable is immutable. While it is rooted in a 400-year-old law [see **4.3.1**] and based on categories drawn up more than 100 years ago [see **4.3.2**], new definitions are constantly evolving through Charity Commission rulings and court cases, and more recently through the Charity Commission's review of the register of charities.

A final myth is that definitions of what is and is not charitable represent a coherent body of law. In reality a wide range of political and social factors, as well as individual prejudices, have led to very disparate (and apparently unjustifiable) distinctions as to what is and is not charitable. For example, securing the release of prisoners of conscience is not charitable, but rescuing cruelly treated animals is.

McGovern and others v Attorney General (Amnesty International Trust) [1981]
3 All ER 493;

Re Green's Will Trusts: Fitzgerald-Hart v Attorney General [1985] 3 All ER 455

Small variations in the wording of the objects clause in the governing document can make all the difference as to whether an organisation is accepted as a charity. Organisations should seek advice from a solicitor with charity law experience if their objects do not clearly fit with one of the traditional heads of charity law, or are at the boundaries of what is regarded as legally charitable [see **4.3.2**].

4.3 WHAT IS CHARITABLE?

To be charitable, an organisation's objects must be **wholly and exclusively charitable**—although occasionally charities might have been registered with ancillary objects which are not charitable [see **4.3.10**].

What is legally charitable is a largely artificial concept that has grown organically as a result of many pressures over hundreds of years. In recent years there has been some pressure from the voluntary sector for a statutory definition of charity. But no attempt at a total legislative definition has ever been attempted in the UK, and eligibility for charitable status is still decided on the basis of case law.

4.3.1
The Statute of Elizabeth I

The preamble to the **Charitable Uses Act 1601** (often referred to as the **Statute of Elizabeth I**) contained a long list of activities then seen as charitable:

- relief of aged, impotent [weak or powerless] and poor people;
- maintenance of sick and maimed soldiers and mariners;
- maintenance of schools of learning, free schools, and scholars in universities;
- repair of bridges, ports, havens, causeways, churches, sea banks and highways;
- education and preferment [advancement] of orphans;
- relief, stock or maintenance for houses of correction;
- marriages of poor maids;
- supportation, aid and help of young tradesmen, handicraftsmen and persons decayed [fallen into misfortune];
- relief or redemption of prisoners or captives;
- aid or ease of any poor inhabitants concerning payment of fifteens [a tax on movable property], setting out soldiers [a tax to equip soldiers], and other taxes.

This list has come to be used as the starting point for making decisions on what is and is not charitable. An **analogy** or **stepping stones** approach is taken, to show that a proposed purpose is sufficiently close to one of the 1601 purposes, either directly or by analogy. For example 'the repair of churches' in the 1601 Act is analogous to the upkeep of churchyards, which is analogous to provision of burial grounds, which is analogous to provision of a crematorium; therefore provision of a crematorium is charitable. By this rather tortuous route, activities which could never have been foreseen in 1601 can be defined as charitable.

Scottish Burial Reform Cremation Society v Glasgow City Corporation [1968] AC 138; [1967] 3 All ER 215 HL

The Charity Commissioners seek to take a 'generous as opposed to a restrictive view' in finding an analogy.

Report of the Charity Commissioners 1985, pp.11-12

4.3.2
The Pemsel case: the four heads of charity

In a landmark case in 1891, known as the **Pemsel case**, Lord Macnaghten drew on the 1601 Act and an 1804 definition of charitable objects to divide charitable purposes into four heads or categories: the relief of poverty, the advancement of education, the advancement of religion, and other purposes beneficial to the community. Despite constant pressure to update, clarify and modernise them, these remain the headings into which charitable purposes must be squeezed.

Income Tax Special Purpose Commissioners v Pemsel [1891] AC 531

In most cases it does not matter which category the objects fit into, and many charities' objects fit into two or more.

4.3.3
Relief of poverty

The first category, relief of poverty, includes relief, support, help or services for people who are poor, either to help them directly or to help them to become self-supporting. 'Poor' applies not only to people who are destitute or who are in receipt of means-tested welfare benefits, but also to those who are suffering deprivation compared to their normal standard of living. *Re Coulthurst [1951] Ch 66*

Unlike charities registered under the other heads, those for the relief of poverty may have a very small class of beneficiaries, such as the residents of a particular street [see **4.3.8**].

Activities to remedy the **effects** of poverty and deprivation are charitable. Activities to deal with their **causes** may also be charitable if such activities are not inappropriately political [see **4.3.8.4**].

Charity Commission booklet CC4 *Charities for the Relief of the Poor* states that charity funds should not be used to replace assistance which people are receiving, or are entitled to receive, from the state. Replacing state benefits would, the Commission says, relieve the state rather than the beneficiary.

4.3.4
Relief of people who are aged, ill or disabled

As defined by Lord Macnaghten, the first head of charity referred only to relief of poverty. The first purpose listed in the Statute of Elizabeth was 'relief of people who are aged, impotent *and* poor', so Lord Macnaghten might have considered it redundant to include 'aged' and 'impotent' in his first head. Nearly 60 years later, the courts decided that the first head should be interpreted as encompassing people who are poor *or* aged *or* 'impotent' (meaning ill or disabled).

Re Glyn [1951] 2 WLR 1150n

This head may also include the relief of human suffering and distress in general.   *McGovern and others v Attorney General [1982] 1 Ch 321*

Purposes under this head include relief, support, help, advice and services for people who are not necessarily poor but who are elderly, physically or mentally ill or convalescing; people with a disability; people addicted to alcohol or drugs; victims of abuse, violence or crime; and families or carers of people who are elderly, ill, disabled etc.

There is no clear definition of when people become 'aged'. The cut-off was defined in an 1889 case as 50, but this would be unlikely to be accepted as a limit now.   *Re Wall [1889] 42 ChD 510*

Activities to deal with the causes of ill health or disability, such as medical research and health promotion, may also be charitable if such activities are not inappropriately political [see **4.3.8.4**]. For more information see Charity Commission booklet CC6 *Charities for the Relief of Sickness*.

Some authorities on charity law define the first head as covering only relief of poverty, and put relief of people who are elderly, ill or disabled under the fourth head.

4.3.5
Advancement of education

Educational charities include many bodies which are not usually considered to be charities, such as universities and colleges, city technology colleges, voluntary controlled and voluntary aided schools, schools which have opted out of local education authority control, private schools run on a not-for-profit basis [see **4.3.9**], museums, libraries, galleries, concert halls and theatres.

Other examples of educational charities are:
- nurseries;
- youth organisations;
- training organisations (which may also come under the first head);
- music, arts, dance and drama societies, arts centres and festivals;
- provision of sports equipment and facilities (but sport clubs and the promotion of sport are not, at the time of writing, charitable);
- organisations to educate and inform people about different cultures;
- city farms;
- conservation and environmental organisations (which may also come under the fourth head);
- organisations undertaking research 'of educational value';
- education about politics, citizenship or political principles (but propagandising is not charitable);
- fundraising trusts to provide financial support for schools or for people attending the schools;
- students' unions, if their purpose is educational rather than 'political'.

There are many anomalies. In one case education was seen as extending to students' physical development, so a trust to build sports facilities and provide sports prizes at a school was held to be charitable. In a later case, education was defined as 'training the mind' and therefore did not cover training in manual skills—although manual skills training would become 'educational' if it also included job-search skills or confidence-building.

Re Mariette [1915] 2 Ch 284;
Barry v Hughes [1973] 1 All ER 537

To be charitable, scholarship funds and research grants must not only benefit the individuals who receive them, but must have a clear public benefit. Scholarships must be shown to encourage high standards of learning, thus promoting the advancement of education in general. Charities which promote research may be required to publish their findings, so the public gets the benefit of the research.

4.3.6
Advancement of religion

Places of worship which are registered under the **Places of Worship Registration Act 1855** do not have to register as charities [see **7.1.3**]. Other religious groups generally do need to register, although some are excepted until 1 October 2002.

For a charity to be established under this head:

- the religion must be of a kind which is accepted by the courts as a religion;
- the activities of the organisation must promote or advance that religion; *and*
- the purposes of the organisation must benefit the public, not just the adherents of the religion or members of the organisation.

In refusing to register an organisation as a charity, the courts defined religion as involving 'faith in a God and worship of that God'.

Re South Place Ethical Society [1980] WLR 1565

Although this definition applies only to religions which worship one god, in practice it has been extended to established religions which have many gods, such as Hinduism, or those such as Buddhism which do not require belief in a god or gods.

For new religious groups or 'cults' the Commission may require evidence from independent sources about the nature of the public benefit. But in general the Commission acts on the assumption that religious groups benefit the public and that 'any religion is at least likely to be better than none'. *Neville Estates v Madden [1962] Ch 832*

The advancement of religion includes, for example, maintenance of places of worship, including the church grounds and furniture and other items within the church; carrying on religious services; provision of music in a place of worship; supporting clergy, former clergy, their families, lay workers, and people such as caretakers employed at a place of worship; translating and/or distributing religious literature; and missionary work.

Because there must be some element of public benefit, prayer and contemplation on their own have been held not to be charitable, so an enclosed order of nuns could not be granted charitable status.

4.3.6.1
Religious charities and human rights

The current limitations on the registration of charities for the advancement of religion may be attacked as contravening the right to freedom of thought and religion under article 9 of the **European Convention on Human Rights** and the **Human Rights Act 1998** s.13 [see **60.3.1**].

4.3.6.2
Other activities by religious charities

Many religious groups have a wide range of associated charities for social welfare or educational purposes. These charities do not fall under the 'advancement of religion' head and must be registered under the relevant other head.

4.3.7
Other purposes beneficial to the community

This is the broadest head, and many new charities are registered under it by analogy with the Statute of Elizabeth I [see **4.3.1**]. Among the many types of organisations under this head are those which:

- promote racial harmony;
- promote equality of women and men in political and economic opportunity;
- provide public amenities which are not provided by the local authority, such as park benches and village halls;
- protect the public or promote public safety;
- promote industry, commerce or the arts;
- protect the environment, the countryside, or buildings of historic or aesthetic interest;
- promote the prevention of cruelty to animals.

4.3.7.1
New charitable purposes

The Charity Commission's **review of the register of charities** is identifying further charitable purposes. By early 2001 promotion of **urban and rural regeneration**, the **relief of unemployment** and the promotion of **community capacity building** had been recognised as charitable, provided strict criteria relating to public benefit are met (see Charity Commission booklets RR2, RR3 and RR5). **Preservation** of buildings and **conservation** of the environment had been confirmed as charitable, provided certain criteria are met (see RR9). At the time of writing (early 2001) **museums and art galleries** and the promotion of **sport** were being considered, and there were plans to review other purposes. Consultation documents and review publications are available free from the Commission or on its website [see **page 12**].

Other purposes may be accepted as charitable because of social and political changes [see **4.3.8.4**].

4.3.7.2
Recreational charities

The **Recreational Charities Act 1958** covers village halls, community centres, women's institutes, and other facilities for recreation and leisure activities. Such provision is charitable only if it is for the benefit of the public [see below] and is 'in the interests of social welfare', which means the facilities must be:

- intended for people who need them because of their youth, age, infirmity, disability, poverty or social and economic circumstances;
- available to the public at large, or only to female members of the public; *and*
- intended to improve the conditions of life of the people for whom they are primarily intended.   *Recreational Charities Act 1958 s.1*

The criteria for recreational charities were clarified as part of the review of the register, and are explained in Charity Commission booklet RR4.

4.3.8
The requirement of public benefit

Charities must be for the benefit of the public or a section of the public. A public benefit is assumed to exist in charities to relieve poverty or to advance education or religion, but must be demonstrated for fourth head charities (other purposes beneficial to the community).

Even for poverty, education and religion charities, the presumption of public benefit can be challenged, for example if an educational charity is being set up to promote ideas which are clearly redundant or false.

At the time of writing (early 2001) a charity law reform advisory group had proposed that all charities—not only those falling under the fourth head—should be required to demonstrate public benefit in order to be recognised as charitable.

4.3.8.1
Section of the public

The definition of **section of the public** varies depending on the purpose for which the charity is established. A charity established for purposes under the 'relief of poverty' head may define its beneficiaries more narrowly than charities established under other heads. So, for example, a trust to help poor employees of a company was accepted as charitable but an educational programme limited to employees of a company probably would not be. *Dingle v Turner [1972] AC 601*

There are no clear definitions as to what constitutes 'a section of the public'. In Dingle v Turner Lord Cross said it is 'a matter of degree', which is not particularly helpful. So long as the beneficiaries are defined in a broad way, it may not matter that only a few people qualify. For example an organisation set up to help people with a rare illness would almost certainly be charitable, even though there were only a few people with the illness. *Neville Estates v Madden [1962] Ch 832*

A specialist legal advisor or the Charity Commission should be asked for advice before attempting to set up any charitable organisation which will be restricted to a relatively small group or to a group defined by reference to an individual or an employer.

4.3.8.2
Individual benefit

Individual or private benefit obviously occurs in charities. But it must arise directly from the achievement of the charity's objects, for example education provided to a child or services provided to a person with a disability, or it must be legitimately incidental to the achievement of charitable objects, for example a local business improving as a result of urban regeneration.

4.3.8.3
Clubs and self-help groups

An organisation set up solely as a members' club or for the self-improvement of narrowly defined members is not charitable. Even if its objects are charitable, a club or self-help group will be considered charitable only if can show that it also provides some benefit to others who are not members, and/or that it is open to all members of the public who meet the criteria for membership.

4.3.8.4
'Political' charities

A number of rulings by the courts have made it clear that seeking to achieve a political purpose cannot be charitable. This is because charities must exist for the public benefit, and the courts will not decide whether a particular political purpose is or is not for the public benefit.
Bowman v Secular Society Limited [1917] AC 406; National Anti-Vivisection Society v Inland Revenue Commissioners [1948] AC 31

However, once a 'political' purpose has become enshrined in law, its promotion or education in its principles may be accepted as charitable. Promotion of racial harmony, for example, was accepted as charitable after the Race Relations Act 1976 was passed, and the promotion of human rights may well be accepted as charitable in the wake of the Human Rights Act 1998.

Political purposes include:
- promoting the interests of a political party whether local, national or international;
- seeking to change or oppose changes to the law or government policy at home or abroad, or supporting existing law or policy;
- seeking to educate the public in accordance with one particular set of political views.

If the dominant purpose of an organisation is charitable, the fact that it has a power to seek to change legislation along with other powers does not prevent it being a charity. It is crucial to differentiate here between political **objects** (which are not acceptable for a charity) and a power to carry out political **activities** (which may be acceptable, if it is directly related to the achievement of the charity's objects).
National Anti-Vivisection Society [see above]

Education and research on political matters generally and on forms of government can be charitable, if the education or research are made available to the public. In these cases it will be necessary to show that educational programmes are objective and balanced, and do not consti-

tute propaganda. This can be difficult, for example with peace education charities.
Re The Trustees of the Arthur McDougall Fund
[1956] 3 All ER 867

4.3.8.5
Charities working abroad

Organisations set up for the relief of poverty, the advancement of education and the advancement of religion are presumed to be for the public benefit, and therefore eligible for registration as charities, even if they will operate abroad. For organisations with international activities seeking to register under the fourth head, the Commission considers whether they would be charitable if their activities were carried out in the UK. If so, they are presumed to be for the public benefit and will be registered, unless it would be 'contrary to public policy' to do so. A charity cannot be set up for objects which are unlawful in the country where it is working.
Decisions of the Charity Commissioners vol.1, August 1993, pp.16-17

To qualify for tax reliefs [see **3.2.1**], a charity must be established in the UK. But activities undertaken abroad by a UK charity are generally eligible for UK tax relief.
Camille and Henry Dreyfus Foundation Inc
v Inland Revenue Commissioners [1954] 1 Ch 672

4.3.8.6
Disaster appeals and appeals for individuals

The attorney general has drawn up special guidelines (reprinted in Charity Commission booklet CC40) for disaster appeals and appeals for individuals or groups of individuals. A legally enforceable **trust** will always be implied (assumed to be created) when funds are sought for a particular purpose [see **44.2.1**]. If there is no formal declaration of trust, the terms of the appeal form the basis for the trust.

The guidelines clarify the distinction between:

* the establishment of a **charitable trust**, which is eligible for all the tax benefits of charitable status [see **3.2.1**] but under which individuals cannot be named and can only receive funds or benefits appropriate to their needs, with any surplus being used for other appropriate charitable purposes;

* a **non-charitable** (private) **trust**, which is not entitled to tax reliefs but which can distribute funds or benefits in any way defined by the appeal or other document setting out the terms of the trust.

The Charity Commission will give advice as a matter of urgency on disaster appeals. An inappropriately worded appeal could result in the loss of tax benefits; an appeal which does not indicate what will happen to surplus funds could result in any surplus having to be returned to donors.

The Red Cross has a disaster appeal scheme, with a 24-hour helpline, to assist in setting up appeals (tel 0800-777100).

4.3.9
The requirement to be not-for-profit

Charities must be set up on a **not-for-profit** or **non-profit** basis. This does not mean that charities cannot charge for their goods or services, or cannot make a profit. It does mean that charities cannot be set up specifically for commercial or profit-making purposes, and that under the terms of their governing document they must be **non-profit-distributing**. Any profits or surplus made by the organisation:

* must be used solely for the purposes of the organisation; *and*

* generally must not be distributed as profits, dividends, bonuses etc to members of the organisation or members of the governing body, as they can be in a business.

So long as it meets these criteria, an organisation is charitable even if it charges a commercial rate for its charitable activities or services. 'Charitable' does not intrinsically mean providing services free or below cost.

Even if a charity charges a commercial rate (or more) for its charitable activities and services and makes a profit, it will not be charged income or corporation tax on the profits so long as they are used solely for the charity's purposes. But *there can be VAT implications* if a charity charges for its activities or services, even if it does not charge a commercial rate or does not make a profit [see **chapter 53**].

4.3.10
Ancillary objects

Despite the requirement that the charity's objects must be wholly and exclusively charitable, it used to be possible to be accepted as a charity even if some **ancillary objects** were not in themselves charitable. Ancillary means related to the main object, but incidental to it.

If such purposes are to be included now, they must be written into the governing document as **powers** [see **4.1**]. This enables the organisation to carry out that type of activity, but only in furtherance of its charitable objects.

4.4
NON-CHARITABLE
OBJECTS

Non-charitable associations and companies may be set up for any lawful purposes, without having to meet the specific requirements for charities. Non-charitable industrial and provident societies may be set up for any purposes which meet the requirements for IPS registration [see **2.4**].

4.5
EQUAL
OPPORTUNITIES
AND THE OBJECTS

In general it is unlawful for organisations to discriminate on racial grounds (race, colour, ethnic origin, national origin, nationality), sex or disability in providing access to services, facilities or goods [see **chapter 37**]. But charities and some other voluntary organisations may have constitutional objects which limit their membership or their beneficiary group on the basis of race, sex, or physical or mental capacity. Before drawing up an objects clause which seeks to limit membership or the beneficiary group in this way it is sensible to take legal advice to ensure the proposed objects do not contravene the relevant legislation.

In some situations, even organisations which do not have a membership or beneficiary group defined by racial group or sex can provide activities for a specified racial group or groups or for one sex [see **37.2.2** and **37.3.1**].

4.5.1
Racial groups

Charities are allowed to limit their beneficiary group to people of a particular racial group or groups, provided the beneficiary group is not defined by reference to colour. This is why the Charity Commission cannot register groups which define their beneficiary group simply as 'black'. *Race Relations Act 1976 s.34*

Unless the charity's objects fall under the 'relief of poverty' head [see **4.3.3**] the charity will need to demonstrate that it will serve a sufficient group to fulfil the public benefit requirement [see **4.3.8**].
Decisions of the Charity Commissioners vol.4, September 1995, pp.17-21

Non-charitable clubs and associations are allowed to define their main object as enabling the benefits of membership to be enjoyed by people of a particular racial group, not defined by reference to colour. An example is a cultural association open only to members of a particular ethnic group and providing its services only to its members.
Race Relations Act 1976 s.26

Even where an organisation's governing document limits its membership or beneficiaries to a particular racial group, it can provide ancillary (related) services to people of other racial groups.

4.5.2
Sex

Charities are allowed to limit their beneficiary group to members of one sex. Non-charitable membership organisations set up on a not-for-profit basis may restrict their membership, and the services they provide to members, to one sex. *Sex Discrimination Act 1975 ss.34, 43*

Single-sex organisations can provide ancillary services to people of the other sex.

4.5.3
Disability

A charity may define its beneficiaries by reference to any physical or mental capacity or capacities, and may carry out activities specifically for people defined in that way. This would cover, for example, an educational charity specifically for children with learning difficulty as well as one for gifted children.   *Disability Discrimination Act 1995 s.10(1)*

Non-charitable organisations may not define their beneficiaries by reference to physical or mental capacity and may not limit their activities on this basis.

4.6
THE OBJECTS CLAUSE

When setting up any organisation it is important to ensure the objects as set out in the governing document are clear and are suitable for the organisation's planned activities and for its development well into the future. This is especially important for charities, because:

- if their objects are not properly worded considerable time is likely be added to the charity registration process;
- they may need Charity Commission consent to change their objects in future, and the consent may not be forthcoming [see **5.5**].

For a non-charitable organisation it is somewhat less critical if the objects clause is not quite right. Provided the governing document contains an amendment clause which allows for the objects to be amended [see **5.4.26**], there is generally no need for external consent, although under some funding agreements the funder may have to give consent.

4.6.1
Breadth of the objects

If a charity's objects are narrowly defined the founders can ensure the charity will not get sidetracked into other activities or into working with other beneficiaries. But it is also very limiting. Unless the governing document contains power to change the objects or the Charity Commission allows a change—which it will do only if there is good reason—the charity will not be able to broaden its activities or client group.

Geographical limitations can cause particular problems, especially where only residents can be beneficiaries. Defining the **area of benefit** very narrowly may reflect the intentions of the charity's founders, but the governing body will always have to ensure that services and activities benefit only residents of that area. Flexibility can be achieved by adding 'and neighbouring districts' to the area, and by defining beneficiaries as 'persons who live or work' in the area, or even those who 'live or work or have a connection with' the area.

Widely defined objects allow the charity flexibility. Despite the wide objects, the charity does not have to be all things to all people; it is completely free to make its own policy decisions limiting its activities to specific types of work, beneficiary groups or geographic areas. But it can at any time alter its policies if it wants to take on new activities or start working with a new client group.

With widely defined objects, however, the charity may end up doing something completely different from what the founders intended, or it may be difficult to set priorities.

One solution is to define the objects relatively narrowly, but to add an additional wide object of 'any other charitable purpose'. This makes clear the intentions and priorities of the founders, without limiting the charity's future development. However the Charity Commission often insists on **certainty** (explicitness) **of objects**, and may refuse to allow a catch-all tacked onto a defined object.

There is no right level of specificity. The people involved in each potential charity must define the limits for themselves, in consultation with a charity advisor or solicitor.

During the process of applying for registration as a charity [see **7.2**], the Charity Commission may suggest narrowing wide objects to reflect more closely the founders' plans, or widening narrow objects to allow for future development. It is not always necessary to make these changes. Provided all the objects are clear and are charitable in law, the Charity Commission cannot insist that they be changed.

4.6.2
Problematic objects

The boundaries of what is and is not charitable are inconsistent and constantly changing. Specialist advice is needed for any organisation whose objects are not clearly within the recognised categories.

In many cases, the bar to registration disappears if a slightly different approach is adopted. For example, promotion of sport is not (at the time of writing) charitable, but sport in schools or associated with improving the effectiveness of the police or armed forces would be, as would sport for recreation. A sport centre open to all, offering all its activities without charge and promoting excellence in a *single* sport would not, at the time of writing, be registered as a charity, but the same centre offering a *range* of sports would be likely to be accepted on the basis that it is a recreational centre [see **4.3.7.2**].

Only a specialist solicitor or charity advisor is likely to be able to advise on the nuances that can make the difference between registration as a charity and non-registration.

4.6.3
Altering the objects clause

If the objects clause is too narrow or is inappropriate for other reasons, it may be possible to alter it [see **5.5**]. Such alteration must not be made unless the governing document allows it. Even where such governing document allows such change, it may say that the change requires the prior consent of the Charity Commission.

Alteration of the objects of a charitable company, or any clause in the memorandum or articles of association governing or controlling trustee benefits or the use of money or assets, always requires the prior consent of the Charity Commission [see **5.5.2**].

Alteration of the objects or powers of an industrial and provident society, whether charitable or non-charitable, always requires the prior consent of the registrar of friendly societies [see **5.5.3**].

The Charity Commission allows charitable objects to be altered only if there is good reason to do so. Any change must be *cy près* (as near as possible to the original objects) [see **5.5.4**].

4.7
ACTING OUTSIDE THE OBJECTS OR POWERS

The possible adverse consequences of acting *ultra vires*—outside the organisation's objects or powers as set out in the governing document—mean that it is absolutely essential for those running an organisation to be aware of *and understand* the organisation's objects and powers. This includes the members of the governing body, members of the governing body's sub-committees and senior staff.

4.7.1
Companies

Until the Companies Act 1985 was amended in 1989, all *ultra vires* acts by a company or its directors were void (invalid). Now the company members may by special resolution [see **17.4.7** for procedure] authorise a company to do anything, so long as the company is *not charitable* and the transaction is not with a director or person connected with a director [see **4.7.1.3**]. But the directors must abide by the objects and powers as set out in the memorandum, and unless an *ultra vires* action by the directors is ratified by the company members it is invalid and the directors are personally liable.   *Companies Act 1985 ss.35, 35A*

4.7.1.1
Transactions with third parties

The *ultra vires* rules could mean that a person entering into a contract with a company could find that the contract is invalid because the directors did not have the power to enter into it. This would then harm that person. To prevent this happening, any transaction with a third party which the directors, or anyone authorised by them, enters into on behalf of a *non-charitable* company is generally valid, even if it is *ultra vires* and even if the person who is dealing with the company knew it was *ultra vires*. The exceptions to this are transactions with directors or their associates, where special rules apply [see **4.7.1.3**].

Companies Act 1985 ss.35A, 35B

4.7.1.2
Charitable companies

Unlike the *ultra vires* actions of a non-charitable company, an action which is outside the objects or powers of a charitable company is valid only if:

- a third person enters into an *ultra vires* transaction without knowing that the company is a charity;

- a third party pays the charity full money or money's worth in relation to the transaction, and does not know that the transaction is *ultra vires*;

- the transaction involves the transfer of property to someone who has paid a full price for it and who was not informed that the transaction might be invalid;

- the Charity Commission makes an order or scheme [see **3.5.4** and **3.5.5**] to authorise the act; *or*

- the Charity Commission gives prior written consent to ratification of an *ultra vires* act and the company members then pass a special resolution ratifying the act.

Charities Act 1993 s.65; Companies Act 1985 s.35(3)

Any other *ultra vires* act is a breach of trust for which the members of the governing body could be held personally liable to the charity.

4.7.1.3
Transactions involving directors or connected persons

An *ultra vires* transaction by the directors of any company is voidable (can be invalidated) by the company members if it is with a person who is:

- a director of the company;

- a director of the company's holding (parent) company;

- connected with such a director as a family member or business associate [see **13.2.2** for definition of connected person]; *or*

- connected with any other company with which the director is associated. *Companies Act 1985 s.322A(1),(2)*

The company may require the director or connected person, and/or the directors who authorised the transaction, to repay any profit they have made from the transaction, or repay to the company any losses it has suffered as a result of the transaction. *s.322A(3)*

A person connected with a director does not have to repay any losses if he or she did not know, when entering into the transaction, that the directors were exceeding their powers. *s.322A(6)*

4.7.2
Industrial and provident societies

Unlike a company, every act outside an industrial and provident society's objects or powers is invalid, and an *ultra vires* contract is not binding on the IPS or the other party.

Ashbury Railways Carriage and Iron Company v Riche [1875] 7 HL 653;
Warburton v Huddersfield Industrial Co-operative Society Ltd [1892] 1 QB 178

The members of the governing body of an IPS must therefore take great care to act within the objects and powers, and third parties entering into contracts with an IPS should ensure the contract is within the IPS's objects and powers.

An *ultra vires* act by an IPS's governing body act cannot be approved by the members. All they can do is amend the rules [see **5.5.3**] to allow the action in future. Any such amendment must be approved by the registrar of friendly societies, and is not valid until it is approved.

IPSs generally have very detailed objects and powers but may also have a clause allowing any action to achieve the objects.

4.7.3
Trusts

In a charitable trust, any action outside the objects or powers must be authorised by an order or scheme of the Charity Commission [see **3.5.4** and **3.5.5**]. If this is not done, trustees could be held personally liable for any *ultra vires* act. This liability would be enforced by the courts or through the Charity Commission. In a private (as opposed to charitable) trust the liability may be enforced by the beneficiaries.

4.7.4
Unincorporated
associations

There is no statute law governing the objects or powers of non-charitable unincorporated associations. If all the members agree, an unincorporated association can do anything it wants, even if it is *ultra vires*. But if any member disagrees with the action:

- he or she can insist that the governing document or other rules are followed, and could get an injunction to stop the others from taking the action;
- members who approved or undertook the action could be held liable to repay to the organisation any money which had been used for that purpose; *and/or*
- members who enter into a contract outside the organisation's objects or powers could be held personally liable for the contract, without being able to claim the funds from the organisation.

If the governing document contains a power of amendment, the governing document may be amended to make further acts lawful. If there is no explicit power of amendment, such a change would require the unanimous consent of all the members. If the amendment clause prohibits amendment of the objects and/or powers clauses, such amendment cannot be made even if all the members agree.

A charitable association must always act within its objects or powers, unless it obtains a Charity Commission order or scheme [see **3.5.4** and **3.5.5**] authorising an *ultra vires* act. Even if all the members agree, it cannot decide to do something *ultra vires* without this authorisation.

Chapter 5
THE GOVERNING DOCUMENT

Topics covered in this chapter

This chapter explains the significance of the governing document (constitution), how to create it, what it usually includes and how to alter it. It covers:

For sources of further information see page 12.
Double-underlined section headings indicate additions or significant changes since the first edition.

5.1
THE IMPORTANCE OF THE GOVERNING DOCUMENT

Anyone can set up a voluntary organisation. If the group is very small, rules may be made up as they are needed, and perhaps changed whenever anyone feels like it. But as the group gets larger or seeks public recognition and funding, there will be pressure to produce a written description of what the organisation is and the rules by which it operates. This is its **governing document** or **governing instrument**.

The governing document is the organisation's central document, setting out its purposes, powers and rules. Because it is so important, all members of a governing body should receive a copy as soon as they are elected or appointed, and should understand that they have a legal obligation to ensure the organisation complies with it. If the governing document is very long or complex, they should also receive a summary of the main points. In a membership organisation it is good practice to give the members a copy of the full version or a summary. If this is not practical a copy should be posted in a prominent place where the members can see it, or copies should be available on request.

Companies and industrial and provident societies have a statutory obligation to provide a copy of their governing document to anyone who requests it [see **6.3.10** and **6.4.7**].

5.1.1
Form of the governing document

The form of the governing document depends on the legal structure of the organisation [see **chapters 1** and **2**]:

- for an unincorporated association, the governing document is generally called the **constitution** or **rules**;

- for a trust, the governing document is generally a **trust deed** or **declaration of trust**;

- for an industrial and provident society, the governing document is the **rules**;

- for a company limited by guarantee, the governing document is in two parts: the **memorandum of association**, setting out the company's objects, powers and the liability of its members, and the **articles of association**, setting out its administrative procedures.

The fact that an organisation is charitable affects the content of the governing document, in particular the objects clause [see **4.3**], but does not affect the form.

The term **constitution** is often used to refer to all governing documents, of whatever form.

5.1.2
Legal nature of the governing document

In unincorporated associations, companies, and industrial and provident societies the governing document is a type of contract, setting out:

- the mutual rights and obligations of members and the organisation;

- the rights and obligations of the members in relation to each other;

- the powers and obligations of the governing body in relation to the members and the organisation.

As contracts, the terms of these governing documents are enforceable in the courts.

In charitable organisations the governing document embodies the terms of the **trust** between the charity's donors or funders, the governing body (the charity's trustees), and the charity's beneficiaries [see **1.3.1** for more about this relationship]. Any action outside the charity's objects or powers may constitute a **breach of trust** for which the trustees could be held personally liable.

5.1.3
Getting it right

A governing document:

- for a new organisation, should reflect not only what the organisation is now but what it might become [see **4.6.1**];

- should be written in as straightforward a manner as possible;

- should be reasonably comprehensive, so rules and procedures do not need to be constantly re-discussed and agreed;

- should not be unduly restrictive, and should allow for amendment;

- should include provision for dissolving the organisation, unless there are statutory procedures for this [see **5.4.27**], and should indicate what happens to any remaining assets;

- after it is agreed, should be reviewed every three to five years to be sure it is still appropriate and the organisation is complying with it;

- if it is not still appropriate, should be amended if this is necessary and permissible [see **5.5** for how to alter a governing document];

- must include all amendments with every copy, either attached to the end or retyped with the amendments included.

5.2
GETTING ADVICE

There is no obligation to consult a legal advisor to set up any kind of voluntary organisation. However many organisations do so, in order to ensure the governing document is appropriate and meets any legal requirements [see **60.10.3** for how to find a specialist legal advisor]. Even if legal advice is not necessary when the organisation is first set up, it may be needed later when the organisation wants to change its legal structure or develop a more detailed governing document.

5.2.1
Using a legal advisor

Legal advice should always be sought when setting up a **trust**. There is no obligation to involve a solicitor or legal advisor in setting up a **company**, but most organisations do so, in order to ensure the memorandum and articles meet the legal requirements and all the necessary paperwork is completed.

Regardless of legal structure, it is sensible to consult an advisor if:

- charitable status is desired, or a decision needs to be made about whether the organisation should be charitable;
- the governing document is not being based on a well proven model;
- it is important that the process not be delayed; *or*
- the organisation is likely to need advice on other legal matters such as contracts of employment, property or service agreements.

Most solicitors can help in setting up a trust or company, but one who specialises in the voluntary sector is far more likely to be able to advise specifically on how to phrase the objects and powers so they are acceptable to the Charity Commission, what forms of membership and governing body are most appropriate, and similar issues. It may be tempting to use a solicitor who offers to deal with the governing document free or at reduced cost as a favour, but this could be a false economy if he or she does not have a clear understanding of relevant areas of the law and how to put it into practice, and broad experience of issues affecting voluntary organisations.

Industrial and provident societies are generally set up through a **promoting body**, using model rules [see **6.4.1**]. Anyone setting up an IPS without going through a promoting body should seek advice from an advisor with expertise in IPSs.

5.2.1.1
The cost

Solicitors and other advisors with voluntary sector experience should be able to give a good estimate of the likely cost of drawing up the governing document and, if required, registering the organisation as a company, industrial and provident society and/or charity. If they quote an hourly rate, they should be able to indicate of how long the process is likely to take. If they quote a flat fee, it is important to clarify what is included and whether there are likely to be any extras.

An additional cost which may be justified is the solicitor or advisor attending a meeting of the whole group. This might be at the start of the process, to deal with fundamental issues such as what the organisation is about now and is likely to be about in future, or might be at final draft stage, to allow all members of the group to ask questions.

5.2.1.2
The process

Unless only two or three people are involved in setting up the organisation, the process of meeting with the advisor and discussing the details of the governing document should be delegated to a small group. They should have a clear indication of what sorts of issues they can agree on their own and what needs to come back to the larger group for discussion and decision.

Before meeting a solicitor or other legal advisor, the people involved should:

- be familiar with the choice of legal structures [see **chapters 1** and **2**] and the pros and cons of charitable status [see **chapter 3**];

- send the solicitor background material, especially on the proposed objects of the organisation [see **chapter 4**], and any model or draft governing document they have;
- prepare for the meeting by writing a list of questions and issues and if possible, sending this to the advisor beforehand.

At the meeting it is important to:

- ensure the advisor is made aware of any values or political issues which are particularly important for the group;
- ask for clarification of anything which is not clear;
- make full notes;
- agree a timetable for progress, and highlight any critical dates.

If notes are written up or a report to a meeting of the group is minuted, a copy should be sent to the advisor.

5.2.2
Guidance

Some councils for voluntary service and other voluntary sector support bodies may not be able to provide detailed technical advice, but can offer general information and support. This may be very helpful in the early stages, but for a trust, company or industrial and provident society it may be necessary to consult a legal advisor at a later stage.

5.2.3
Do-it-yourself

It may be appropriate for the people involved with the organisation to draw up the governing document without consulting a legal advisor if:

- the organisation is a simple unincorporated association, or its governing document will follow an appropriate existing model with little or no variation;
- there is a national association or parent body prepared to help or advise;
- the people involved in drawing up the governing document have a high level of relevant skills, and have the time and inclination to become personally involved in the process; *and/or*
- the organisation places a high value on involvement and democracy, and therefore wants to involve people directly in the process.

The temptation simply to adopt another organisation's governing document should be resisted, as it may lead to the organisation ending up with something inappropriate to its needs. Other governing documents may be used as examples, but they should be gone through line by line to ensure they are appropriate for the new organisation.

Another temptation is to cobble together sections from a range of other organisations' governing documents. This can create a document which is internally inconsistent and is therefore unworkable.

A third temptation is to put in anything that sounds legal, on the assumption that if it sounds important, it probably is. Nothing should be included in the governing document unless people understand what it means and the implications of including it.

5.2.3.1
The process

To get it right, the people involved in drafting a governing document themselves will need to:

- find out whether key third parties, such as funders, have particular views about what sort of structure and governing document is appropriate for the organisation;
- be sure everyone involved understands the difference between unincorporated and incorporated structures;
- decide whether the organisation should be unincorporated or incorporated [see **chapters 1** and **2**];
- be sure everyone understands what charitable status means, and the implications of being or not being charitable [see **3.2** and **3.3**];

- decide whether they want the organisation to be charitable or non-charitable;
- if the organisation is to be charitable, clarify whether it has to register with the Charity Commission [see **7.1**];
- understand the relevant registration procedures [see **6.2-6.4** and **7.2**];
- agree the proposed objects for the organisation, ensuring they either are or are not charitable [see **chapter 4**];
- if the organisation is charitable and experienced solicitors are not being used, get model governing documents [see **7.2.2**] for the desired structure from similar organisations, the Charity Commission or Charity Law Association [see **page 12**];
- if there is a national or coordinating body for similar organisations, find out whether they have model governing documents;
- go through the models, think about each section and how it would need to be adapted to fit in with what *this* organisation will do and how *this* organisation is to be run;
- if the governing document is to be based on a model or one from another organisation, remember that every organisation is unique, and someone else's governing document should never be adopted without thinking through every clause in it very carefully;
- when drawing up the draft use familiar language, without trying to put it into legal language or pompous-sounding jargon.

When the draft is drawn up, it should be very carefully read by two or three people involved with the organisation or with relevant experience, and any confusions or anomalies should be sorted out at this stage. In particular they should look for any clauses whose meaning is not clear.

Key areas are the objects [see **chapter 3**], provisions for admission and removal of members [see **chapter 10**], the quorum for general meetings [see **17.2.8**], and how members of the governing body are selected, elected or co-opted [see **11.4**].

5.2.3.2
Getting it checked

Even organisations which for cost or ideological reasons want to draw up their own governing document, may decide to have the final version checked by a legal advisor.

If the motive for doing it themselves was cost, they may find that this approach saves very little. Even at final draft stage a good advisor will need to become thoroughly familiar with the aims and style of the organisation. Because the governing document will be unfamiliar, it may take the advisor almost as much time to consider it as to create one from **precedents** (previously used models) with which he or she is familiar. In addition, the advisor may at this late stage raise fundamental questions—such as whether to incorporate— which put the process back to square one.

5.3
THE LANGUAGE OF CONSTITUTIONS

Many governing documents, especially older ones, are written in legal terminology. With careful reading they should become comprehensible; if in doubt ask for an explanation from a solicitor or voluntary sector advisor. Most of the terms used in governing documents are explained in this chapter or in the relevant section of this book.

Governing documents, even for companies and trusts, do not need to be written in legal jargon. Models are now available from the Charity Law Association, Charity Commission and other sources [see **page 12**] which are reasonably clear and straightforward.

Some of the terms used in governing documents are likely to be unfamiliar. The problem is made worse because the same term may have a different meaning in different governing documents, or different terms may be used to describe the same thing.

5.3.1
Should and shall, may and must

For all governing documents, clarity is essential. For example, a common confusion arises from the use of the word 'should'. Anything which says it **shall** be done means it **must** be done. Anything which says it **may** be done means it is **optional**. Beware of anything which says it **should** be done. It is often unclear whether this is intended to mean 'must' (as in 'you should stop at red lights') or 'it is good practice' (as in 'you should brush your teeth after every meal'). If something *must* be done, use **must** or **shall**.

5.3.2
Terms relating to people
5.3.2.1
Governing body

The **governing body** is the body which, according to the governing document, is responsible in law for managing the organisation [see **11.1**]. It is unlikely to be called this in the governing document; instead, it will be called the management committee, executive committee, council of management, board of directors, board of trustees, board of governors or a similar name.

Regardless of what they may be called in the governing document or in practice, voting members of the governing body of a charitable organisation are **charity trustees**, and the voting members of the governing body of a company are **company directors**. It is not possible to be a voting member of the governing body of a charity without being a charity trustee, or to be a voting member of the governing body of a company without being a company director. If the organisation is a charitable company, governing body members are charity trustees as well as company directors.

5.3.2.2
Officers

The term **officers** is used in a number of ways. In company law it includes the company directors, and possibly shadow directors as well [see **11.1.3** for definition], the honorary officers (chairperson, vice chair, secretary, treasurer etc), the company secretary, and senior employees or executives.   *Companies Act 1985 s.744*

The term is used in a similar way for industrial and provident societies.

In unincorporated associations and trusts 'officers' typically refers only to honorary officers, and in many company and IPS governing documents the term is used in this way as well.

5.3.2.3
Secretary

Similarly the term **secretary** has a specific meaning as the person responsible for various administrative matters under company and IPS law. A company or IPS secretary may be a member of the governing body, but could be an employee or someone such as a solicitor or accountant who is not directly connected with the organisation.

In trusts, the term **trust secretary** is often used for a person who is not a member of the governing body but attends meetings to take minutes. It may also refer to the chief executive. In associations—and sometimes in trusts or companies as well—secretary refers to a member of the governing body who is elected by the governing body or at a general meeting to carry out certain administrative duties. This is often called an **honorary secretary**, to distinguish it from company secretary or a person employed as a secretary.

5.3.2.4
Agents

As well as being 'officers', members of the governing body of an incorporated organisation are **agents** of the organisation, and members of the governing body of an unincorporated organisation may be either agents or **principals** [see **18.5** for more about agents and principals]. An agent is anyone who has authority, in general or for specific purposes, to act on behalf of the organisation (or anyone else). The person or organisation on whose behalf an agent acts is the **principal**.

5.3.2.5
Servants

The term **servants** as used in governing documents refers to employees who carry out the work of the organisation as directed by an officer (as defined above).

5.3.3
Terms relating to property

The governing document might refer to:

- **demise**: to lease property, or the lease itself;
- **bequest**: personal property (money or goods) left to the organisation under a will;
- **devise**: real property (land or buildings) left to the organisation under a will;
- **endowment**: money or property which produces an income for the organisation, through interest on money, dividends on investments, or rent on property;
- **permanent endowment**: money or property given on condition that the capital or principal sum of money is not spent or that the investments or property are not sold or disposed of, or that if they are sold the proceeds from the sale are not spent.

5.3.4
Latin and French terms

Some governing documents contain Latin or other phrases which have a specific meaning in law. Some of the more common ones are:

- *ad hoc* (Latin, literally 'for this'): for a specific purpose, usually short term e.g. 'The management committee may set up standing [permanent] or *ad hoc* [temporary] sub-committees';
- *cy près* (Norman French, 'so near'): as near as possible, applied to changes in a charity's objects or purposes when the original objects can no longer be met [see **5.5.4.1**];
- *ex gratia* (Latin, 'out of gratitude' or 'as a favour'): a payment made where there is no legal obligation to do so but the organisation feels a moral obligation [see **49.2.7**];
- *ex officio* (Latin, 'by virtue of office'): holding a position by virtue of holding another position e.g. 'The chairperson is a member *ex officio* of all sub-committees';
- *inter alia* (Latin, 'among others'): among other things e.g. 'a governing document may contain, *inter alia*, rules for general meetings';
- *inter se* (Latin, 'among themselves'): between or among themselves, e.g. 'The members of the committee shall decide *inter se* or by drawing lots which one-third of their number shall retire';
- *intra vires* (Latin, 'within powers'): actions authorised by the organisation's governing document or in any other way;
- *mutatis mutandis* (Latin, 'changing the things that need to be changed'): the rules relating to one situation are adapted for another, e.g. 'The rules relating to meetings of the governing body shall be applied *mutatis mutandis* to meetings of its committees';
- *sine die* (Latin, 'without a date'): with no date set, e.g. 'If a date within seven days is set for an adjourned meeting no notice of the adjourned meeting need be given, but a minimum of seven days notice must be given for any meeting adjourned *sine die* or to be held more than seven days after the original meeting';
- *status quo* (Latin, 'the situation which is'): the current situation;
- *ultra vires* (Latin, 'beyond powers'): with no legal authority; actions which are not authorised by the organisation's governing document or in any other proper way [see **4.7**].

5.3.5
General terms

It is not only Latin or ancient French terms which cause difficulty; even English words can be unfamiliar.

These presents means this document; **heretofore** means before this; **hereinafter** means after this; **whereas** means 'here's why we are doing this'. **From time to time** means 'when they choose to do it', rather than once only or at a set time (as in 'Members must pay the subscription as determined from time to time by the executive committee'). **For the time being** means 'at the time the action takes place', as in 'Notice must be sent to all members for the time being'. **Save that** or **saving that** means except.

Determine and **determination** can mean the same as terminate and termination. It is necessary to look at the context of the sentence to determine whether determine means 'decide' or 'terminate'.

5.3.6
Interpretation

Within the governing document there may be an **interpretation** section which defines what is meant by some of the terms used in the governing document. Examples are:

* what the organisation will be called in the governing document, in order not to keep repeating its name (it might be 'the Company', 'the Charity', 'the Organisation' etc);

* what the governing body will be called ('the Committee', 'the Management Committee', 'the Board of Directors', 'the Board of Trustees' etc);

* what the members of the governing body will be called ('Committee Members', 'Directors', 'Trustees' etc).

Use of capital letters within the governing document usually signals that the word has been defined in the interpretation section. For example, a charity's governing document might state '"the Charity" means the company intended to be regulated by these articles', and '"the Objects" means the objects of the Charity'. The importance of the capital letters is seen in this dissolution clause: 'The Charity's assets shall be given to some other charity or charities having objects similar to the Objects.'

There may be a section stating 'the masculine imports [or includes] the feminine', meaning that wherever the governing document says 'he', it means 'he or she'. This statement does not have to be included, because 'he' in English is still (unfortunately) assumed to include 'she'. 'He or she' or 's/he', or other non-sexist language, can be used throughout the governing document. 'They' can also be used as a way of avoiding the cumbersome 'he or she', but can be confusing because 'they' is a plural implying more than one person.

Women's organisations whose members and members of the governing body must all be women may use 'she' throughout. There is nothing to stop mixed organisations from using 'she' throughout and saying that 'the feminine includes the masculine'.

There may be a section stating something like 'the singular imports [or includes] the plural'. This means that if the governing document refers to 'a member', 'a trustee', 'an auditor' etc, the provisions apply to all of them that there may be, not just one of them.

There may be a section which says that if words or expressions are not specifically defined in the interpretation section (if there is one), and if they do not obviously have a different meaning, they should be interpreted as they would be within the **Interpretation Act 1978** as it applies to an Act of Parliament. This Act sets out what words mean when they are used in statutes. The section is included in the governing document to indicate the Act should be referred to if there is a dispute about what the governing document means. The section does not have to be included, and certainly should not be included unless the people who draw up the governing document are clear that they *are* using words as they would be used within the Interpretation Act.

The articles of association of a company usually say that words or expressions in the articles have the same meaning as in the Companies Acts. Again, it is important to ensure that if this clause is included, words are used in this way.

5.4
WHAT A GOVERNING DOCUMENT INCLUDES

There are significant differences between a trust's trust deed or declaration of trust, a company's memorandum and articles of association, the rules of an industrial and provident society, and the constitution of an unincorporated association. Despite these differences, most governing documents cover the following matters.

5.4.1
Name and location

The governing document generally starts with the name of the organisation [see **8.1-8.4**], and if it is a company or industrial and provident society, where the registered office will be located [see **15.1** and **15.2**]. For companies, the country where the registered office must be located is called **domicile**.

5.4.2
Objects

The objects clause [see **chapter 4**] is the most important clause in the governing document, and must be carefully drafted to ensure it covers not only what the organisation is set up to do at present, but also what it might do in future. The clause includes:

- the **objects** or purposes for which the organisation is established;
- if appropriate, the **beneficiaries** (clients, users) whom the organisation is set up to serve or work with;
- if appropriate, the **area of benefit** (geographic area).

5.4.3
Powers

Strictly speaking, a voluntary organisation has the right to carry out only activities *directly* related to its objects as set out in its governing document. So an arts organisation whose purpose is the advancement of education of the public by promoting artistic activities can put on a concert or an art exhibition. But it may not be able to fundraise, hire staff, rent premises, set up a committee to organise the concert or exhibition, hire an organiser or charge admission to the event—because none of those activities *directly*, by itself, promotes artistic activities. They are the means to an end, rather than the end in itself.

An organisation's right to undertake these secondary activities is called its **powers**. A power may be:

- given by **statute**;
- **implied** (implicit) in case law or common law;
- **express** (explicit) within an organisation's governing document; *or*
- included in a general catch-all power.

If a power to do something does not exist, *the organisation may not be able to do it*. If it does it anyway, the action could be *ultra vires* (outside its powers) and the individuals who authorised or undertook the action could be personally liable to repay to the organisation all funds used for it [see **4.7**]. The powers clause may, especially in older governing documents, be written in legal terminology but it is important to understand it and to ensure the organisation operates within it.

Powers may rest with:

- the organisation, if it is a corporate body;
- the organisation's members, acting as a body;
- the governing body;
- committees (which may be called sub-committees);
- individuals such as the treasurer, chairperson or chief executive/senior staff member.

In a company or industrial and provident society the powers given in the powers clause rest with the organisation. In an unincorporated association they rest with the members of the organisation or, if specified in the governing document, with the governing body. In a trust the powers rest with the trustees. Further on in the governing document, other powers may be given to the governing body, committees or individuals.

5.4.3.1
Statutory powers

Powers given under statute automatically apply to organisations of that type or their governing body. A company, for example, has a power to amend its memorandum or articles of association, even if there is no amendment clause in the memorandum or articles [see **5.5.2**]. Similarly, trustees of trusts and charitable unincorporated associations have certain investment powers [see **54.1.2**] and powers to delegate and insure [see **13.5.2** and **20.2.1**] under the **Trustee Act 2000**.

Some statutory powers can be varied or excluded by clauses in the governing document. Trustees, for example, may have under the governing document investment powers narrower than those allowed by legislation [see **54.1**].

5.4.3.2
Implied powers

Some powers exist because a court would find that they were so directly and necessarily linked to the achievement of the organisation's objects or to other activities imposed on the organisation that they must be assumed—for example the power to open a bank account. Such powers can be exercised even if they are not explicit in statute or in the governing document. But implied powers are likely to be narrow, and should only be relied upon after taking legal advice.

5.4.3.3
General power

A well drafted governing document should contain a general power, such as 'power to do any other acts the committee thinks fit' or 'power to do any lawful act necessary for the achievement of the objects'. This gives the organisation the right to do acts which are not specifically mentioned, so long as the action:

- is lawful;
- is for the purpose of achieving the organisation's objects;
- is not one for which explicit power has to be given in the governing document;
- is not explicitly prohibited by the governing document; *and*
- falls within the wording of the general power.

A company memorandum of association nearly always includes a general power. Even if it does not, the members of a non-charitable company have a statutory power to ratify any lawful action taken by the company's directors which is outside the company's express powers. Members of a charitable company may be able do so, but should first get advice from the company's solicitor or the Charity Commission [see **4.7.1**].

It is vital to include a general power in the list of powers. Without it, the organisation may not in future be able to do things it wants to do without amending its governing document or going to the Charity Commission for a scheme [see **5.5.4**].

If in doubt about whether an action falls within implied or general powers, advice should be sought from the Charity Commission (for charities) or an experienced solicitor.

5.4.3.4
Express powers

If a power does not exist under statute and cannot properly be implied in case law or common law, and there is no general power in the governing document, the organisation is able to do something only if there is an **express** (expressed, explicit) power to do so within its governing document. This is the reason for the long lists of powers in most voluntary organisations' governing documents.

If, for example, a charity's governing document does not include an express power to set up committees and delegate some decision-making powers to them, and if there is no statutory power, the governing body will not be able to delegate any of its decision-making powers to committees [see **13.5**]. All decisions and actions will have to be undertaken by the governing body as a whole, although such decisions could be based on proposals or recommendations made by committees.

Even with a general power, it is good practice to list most powers in detail, in order to avoid future doubt about whether an action is allowed.

Some powers, such as the power to use a charity's funds to purchase trustee liability insurance [see **20.2.4**], must be explicit. These powers cannot be implied within a general power.

5.4.3.5
Powers requiring consent

Even with a statutory or express power, some powers require the consent of a third party. A charitable company, for example, has a statutory right, subject to certain limitations, to amend its memorandum and articles, but has a statutory duty to get prior consent from the Charity Commission before amending clauses relating to the organisation's objects and some powers [see **5.5.2**]. A charitable organisation may have a constitutional power to sell or mortgage property, but in certain situations requires, under the **Charities Act 1993** ss.36-39, Charity Commission consent before doing so [see **57.11** and **57.12**].

Even where there is no statutory obligation to obtain external consent, the governing document may impose a requirement. The governing document of an unincorporated organisation, for example, might include an amendment power, but require prior consent from the Charity Commission, the local authority or another external body.

5.4.3.6
Powers subject to special duties

The exercise of some powers, most notably in relation to investment and property, may be subject to specific statutory requirements or to requirements arising from fiduciary duty, duty of care and duty of prudence [see **13.1** and **54.1**].

5.4.4
Powers relating to money

5.4.4.1
Raising funds

The governing document generally includes the power to raise funds and to invite and receive contributions. Difficult issues of interpretation can arise as to whether various ways in which the funds might be raised—for example by charging fees or subscriptions, receiving donations, organising fundraising events—fall within the power.

If this power is not explicit, advice should be sought from the Charity Commission or a specialist solicitor before relying on a general or implied power.

The governing document may say that in raising funds the organisation must comply with all relevant legal requirements, but this applies even if it is not explicit.

A charity's governing document may say that the charity must not engage in substantial or permanent trading. A restriction worded in this way relates only to permanent or large-scale trading for fundraising purposes. It does not refer to charges made for goods or services provided directly in furtherance of the charity's objects [see **47.1.2**], and would not prevent fundraising events and activities which are exempt from tax [see **52.8.1** and **52.8.2**].

If the trading restriction is narrower, preventing all trading, it is still allowed to charge for goods or services provided directly in furtherance of the charity's objects [see **47.1.2**] but advice should be taken before making other charges for goods, services or activities.

5.4.4.2
Borrowing

Raising money through loans or other forms of borrowing may be *ultra vires* unless there is an explicit power to do so, or such power can be clearly implied under a general power. The power to borrow money or to charge the organisation's property (use it as security for a loan or mortgage) should be explicit if the organisation is ever likely to need to borrow [see **chapter 55** for more about borrowing].

5.4.4.3
Financial transactions

A governing document generally includes the power to operate bank accounts and undertake financial transactions to carry out the organisation's business, although this power would be likely to be implied even if it is not explicit.

5.4.4.4
Investment

Statutory investment powers were widened by the **Trustee Act 2000** for the governing body of trusts, charitable unincorporated associations and bodies established by charter [see **54.1**], and where a charitable company or other incorporated body holds assets in trust. The statutory powers may be restricted by an organisation's governing document.

The governing document of companies and industrial and provident normally include wide investment powers.

The wording of the investment clause is very important for any voluntary organisation, including a company, which might want to invest in or make loans to a trading subsidiary [see **47.4.4** and **47.4.5**].

It may also be important to include power to appoint investment managers with powers to make investment decisions. This would normally require such decisions to be made within a broad framework set by the governing body [see **54.3**], and provide for regular reporting and review.

5.4.4.5
Insurance

Where there is a statutory obligation to take out insurance (such as employer's liability insurance) or a statutory power to insure, for example under the **Trustee Act 1925** ss.19-20 (as amended by the **Trustee Act 2000** s.34), there is no need for a specific power in the governing document [see **20.2.1**]. Taking out other insurances requires either an express power to do so or a general power.

A charity may take out **trustee liability insurance** only if it has express power to do so or the Charity Commission has given written authorisation [see **20.2.4**]. Insurances are covered in more detail in **chapter 20**.

5.4.4.6
Set-up costs

For new organisations the governing document often includes the power to pay the costs of setting up the organisation and registering it as a charity, trust, company and/or industrial and provident society.

5.4.5
Powers relating to property

If the organisation is likely ever to own or use land, buildings or other property, such as vehicles or major equipment, the governing document should include a full range of powers to buy, let, take in exchange, mortgage, build, sell, etc [see **56.2**]. Where there are no explicit powers, the governing body of trusts and charitable unincorporated associations has statutory powers under the **Trustee Act 2000** ss.8-10 to acquire and manage land [see **56.2.3**], and there are powers to manage land under the **Trusts of Land and Appointment of Trustees Act 1996**.

For an unincorporated association, the governing document may usefully make provision as to whether the title to any property is to be held by **holding trustees**, the **official custodian for charities**, another **custodian trustee** or in some other way [see **18.4**].

Industrial and provident societies have a statutory power to acquire, maintain and alter land and buildings. This statutory power may be excluded in the governing document.

Industrial and Provident Societies Act 1965 s.30(1)

5.4.6
Power to employ staff and agents

Even if it is not explicit in their governing document, companies and industrial and provident societies have an implied power to employ staff. *Ferguson v Wilson [1866] 2 Ch App 77;*
Burnley Equitable and Co-operative Society v Casson [1891] 1 QB 75

The governing bodies of trusts and charitable unincorporated associations have statutory power to employ and pay agents, including staff [see **18.5**], nominees and custodians [see **18.4**] to transact any business or carry out any other act necessary for the organisation's work. This might be a solicitor, banker, stockbroker, or other person. The trustees must properly supervise the appointed person.

Trustee Act 2000 ss.11-23, 32

For other organisations, if the power to employ staff is not explicit in the governing document it may be covered by a general power.

For charities and many other organisations, there is generally a proviso that members of the governing body cannot be employed or remunerated by the organisation [see **14.3.7**].

If there is an express power to employ staff, there is usually also an express power to contribute to pensions for staff and their dependants. If this is not explicit it may covered by a general power.

5.4.7
Ancillary powers

Many governing documents include a range of powers enabling the organisation to undertake activities which do not directly further its objects, but are related or ancillary. These might include, for example, the power to undertake research, produce publications, hold conferences, set up advisory committees, set up branches etc. If they are not explicit, these powers may be covered under a general power.

5.4.8
Power to undertake joint activities

The governing document is likely to include powers to support, cooperate with, join or amalgamate with other charities, voluntary organisations and statutory or public authorities which carry out work related to the organisation's own objects.

Charities have a statutory right to undertake joint activities with other charities, local authorities and joint boards carrying out the functions of local authorities, provided the activities promote the charity's work or make it more effective.   *Charities Act 1993 s.78(2)*

5.4.9
Restrictions

The governing document may set out restrictions on activities or on how the organisation's property and income can be used.

5.4.9.1
Restrictions on charities

The governing document of a charitable organisation usually contains some or all of the following restrictions [see **chapter 14** for more information].

These following restrictions apply even if they are not express:

- All of the charity's income and property must be used only to promote its objects. Any other use constitutes **breach of trust**.
- None of the charity's money or property can be paid or given as a dividend, bonus or other form of profit to any member of the charity.
- If the charity is wound up, any assets remaining after all its debts have been paid must be given to another charitable organisation with the same or similar purposes, unless the governing document specifies disposition for different charitable purposes.

The members of a charity's governing body cannot receive any direct or indirect 'benefit in money or money's worth' from the charity [see **14.1.1**]. This means that unless the governing document authorises otherwise or the Charity Commission gives consent:

- the members of the governing body cannot generally be paid any salary or fees by the charity;
- spouses of governing body members, other very close relatives, business partners, and companies in which any of these people or the governing body member has an interest cannot generally be paid for work done for the charity.

If the intention is for the governing body to include beneficiaries or users of the charity, it is advisable to make clear in the governing document that this is allowed [see **14.5**].

The 'no benefit' rule is not absolute, and some exceptions may be allowed by the governing document or can be authorised by the Charity Commission, either on a one-off basis or by authorising amendment of the governing document. For example the governing document or Commission may:

- give power to pay members of the governing body who charge the charity professional fees as a solicitor, accountant or person engaged in a profession, provided the person being paid does not take part in the decision [see **14.3.5**];

- authorise payments to members of the governing body, for serving as a trustee and/or for providing other services to the charity [see **14.1.1**];

- allow for an employee or employees to be governing body members [see **14.3.7**];

- allow a member of the governing body to be a beneficiary (client, user etc) of the charity, or charitable benefits to be given to governing body members [see **14.5**];

- make explicit the statutory and implied rights for members of the governing body to be reimbursed for reasonable travel and similar genuine out-of-pocket expenses [see **14.2**];

- allow payment of interest on money lent to the charity by a member of the charity or its governing body, although there is likely to be a limitation on the rate of interest which can be paid [see **14.4.3**];

- allow the payment of reasonable rent to a member of the charity or its governing body [see **14.4.2**];

- authorise the purchase of goods or services from a company in which a member of the governing body owns shares, although this generally applies only if the member's shareholding is less than 1% of the company's issued share capital [see **14.4.1**];

- authorise the use of charity funds to pay for liability insurance for members of the governing body [see **20.2.4**].

A charity's governing document cannot be amended to include any of the above powers unless the Charity Commission gives prior consent.

Re French Protestant Hospital [1951] 1 All ER 938; Charities Act 1993 s.64

The memorandum of association of a charitable company may in addition include a range of restrictions which apply even if they are not explicit:

- any property given to the charity for a specific purpose must be used for that purpose only, and must be separately accounted for;

- if the company has any property requiring the Charity Commission's approval before it can be disposed of or dealt with in any way, it must obtain such consent [see **57.12**];

- it must not become involved in the regulation of relationships between employers and employees (cannot become a trade union);

- in relation to charity law, the members of the governing body are personally accountable in the same way as if the charity were not incorporated. Despite having limited liability in general, they may still be held personally liable for misuse of the charity's funds or property, breach of charity law, or other breaches of trust.

**5.4.9.2
Non-charities**

A non-charitable voluntary organisation's governing document might have restrictions (and exceptions) virtually the same as a charity's, and might include a prohibition on amending certain clauses.

Non-charitable **trading subsidiaries** or **trading companies** set up by charities may have particular restrictions in their memorandum of association [see **47.5.1**]. For example, a charity's trading company might have a restriction requiring it to pay all profits to the parent charity. This could have the unforeseen effect of preventing the company from being able to retain profits in order to finance expansion. Such restrictions should not be necessary if the trading company is wholly owned by the charity, and should in general be avoided.

5.4.10
Conflict of interest

A member of a governing body must be careful to avoid conflicts of interest [see **13.2.2** and **13.3.4**]. This general duty may be buttressed by particular restrictions, for example a clause in the governing document saying that no member of the governing body can own or hold any interest in land belonging to the organisation, unless he or she is doing so as a trustee, and/or may not have a financial interest in any contract entered into by the organisation.

The governing document may include a clause relaxing the rules which are normally implied in situations where a conflict of interest might arise. For example the governing document might say that a member of the governing body may continue supplying goods or services to the organisation if, prior to election or appointment to the governing body, he or she was supplying the goods or services to the organisation at or below the fair market price and on normal trade terms. If this clause is not in the governing document, a member of a charity's governing body may continue being paid for goods or services only if the services are professional and the governing document authorises payment to professionals, or if the Charity Commission authorises the payment.

5.4.11
Membership

If the organisation has a membership the governing document should set out the requirements for membership, including eligibility, rights and benefits of membership, any right of members to resign, and any right of the organisation to terminate membership. If there are different classes of membership, these may be specified.

Instead of specifying classes of membership, eligibility, rights or benefits and application procedures, the governing document may say that these are to be determined by the members at a general meeting, or by the governing body. These rules may then be set out in **standing orders** [see **5.4.25**].

The governing document might set out a process for applying for membership and for the application to be approved. If this is not included, it can be set out in standing orders or rules.

Membership is covered in **chapter 10**.

5.4.12
General meetings

If the organisation has a membership, the governing document should set out the requirements for meetings of all the members. These might include:

- the requirement to have an **annual general meeting**, including the amount of notice which must be given for the AGM and the business which must be transacted at an AGM;
- any requirements relating to other meetings of the members, which might be called **general**, **special** or **extraordinary meetings**;
- procedures by which members can request (**requisition**) a general meeting to be held;
- procedures for general meetings, for example chairing, quorum, proxies and voting;
- the majority required to approve resolutions at meetings;
- whether decisions may be made by telephone or electronic means [see **17.2.6**] or by all members signing a written resolution [see **17.2.16**], so that a meeting does not need to be held.

Chapter 17 covers meetings and decision making in detail.

5.4.13
Governing body

The governing document should set out:

- who the first members of the governing body are or how they are to be selected;
- who is eligible to serve on the governing body;

- the maximum and minimum number of people on the governing body;

- how the members of the governing body are elected or appointed, how long they serve, whether they can be re-elected or re-appointed, and how they can be removed;

- how vacancies are filled;

- whether and how others can be appointed or co-opted as non-voting members of the governing body or observers;

- powers of the governing body.

Governing documents often do not make it clear that the voting members of the governing body are charity trustees if the organisation is a charity, and/or company directors if the organisation is a limited company. This should be made clear to everyone on a governing body.

Chapter 11 covers the governing body in detail.

5.4.14
Governing body
meetings

The governing document might specify how often the governing body must meet and the quorum and procedures for its meetings, or may specify that the governing body decides how it will operate. It may also specify that decisions may be made by telephone or electronic means, or by a written resolution signed by all or a specified number of the members [see **17.6.6**].

5.4.15
Committees
and delegated
powers

Members of the governing body have the right to delegate decision making to individuals, committees, employees or others only if this is authorised by statute, by the governing document, or (for charities) by the Charity Commission. Even where they have power of delegation, the members of the governing body remain ultimately responsible for ensuring the organisation is properly managed and decisions are properly made.

The governing document should state that the governing body may delegate some or all or its powers to committees [see **13.5**]. If the governing body is called a board these are likely to be called **committees**, but if the governing body is itself called a management committee, executive committee or something similar, the delegated bodies are generally called **sub-committees**.

The governing document may state that any such committee must include a minimum number of members of the governing body, and should make clear whether people who are not members of the governing body can serve as members of committees.

Sometimes the governing document states that any committee must:

- act only within the authority delegated to it by the governing body;

- keep proper minutes and make them available to the governing body, and/or report back as soon as reasonably practical.

These rules apply even if they are not explicit.

The governing document may also specify that some powers can be delegated to individual officers or members of the governing body.

If the power to delegate decision making does not exist, the governing body may delegate only the right to make proposals or recommendations. It is then up to the governing body to make the decision.

For more about delegation see **13.5**.

5.4.16
Officers

The governing document may specify that certain officers (sometimes called **honorary officers**) must be elected or appointed, and should indicate whether this is to be done by the organisation's members or by the governing body. The officers usually include a chairperson, vicechair and treasurer, and may also include a secretary [see **12.1** and

12.2]. The governing document may set requirements, for example that they be members of the organisation or live in the area of benefit.

References in a company's articles of association to a secretary mean the **company secretary**, a post required under company law [see **12.3**].

The governing document may list other officers which must or may be elected or appointed. It may also say how long officers serve, whether they can be re-elected or re-appointed, and how they can be removed.

5.4.17
Minutes

There is often a clause in the governing document requiring minutes to be kept of all general meetings, meetings of the governing body, and meetings of committees. Even if this clause is not there, minutes should, and in most cases must, be kept. [See **17.2.15** and **17.4.11** for more about minutes.]

5.4.18
The seal

The seal is a stamping device used when an incorporated body enters into a legally binding agreement. Companies no longer need to have a seal, but many continue to use one. The company's articles of association may have a clause setting out how the seal is used. Industrial and provident societies must have a seal. An incorporated trustee body [see **1.4**] does not have to have a seal but may do so if it wishes.

5.4.19
Bank accounts

The governing document should specify how money is to be held, and how cheques and other transactions are to be authorised. If these matters are not clear in the governing document, charities have a statutory power to delegate authorisation of financial transactions to two or more governing body members.   *Charities Act 1993 s.82*

5.4.20
Accounts and audit

The governing document may specify in detail the types of financial records which must be kept, the type of annual accounts to be prepared and how the accounts are to be checked or audited.

If the organisation is a charitable trust or charitable association the governing document may simply say that accounts are to be prepared in accordance with the relevant provisions of the Charities Acts; if the organisation is a company (whether charitable or non-charitable) the governing document may say that the accounts must be prepared in accordance with the Companies Acts. These requirements apply even if they are not explicit in the governing document.

Accounting and audit procedures are covered in **chapter 50**. If the Charities Act or Companies Act does not require a full audit, but the governing document does, the organisation must comply with the governing document. However, it may be possible to amend it [see **5.5**] so the organisation only has to comply with the relevant legislation. Funders may require a full audit even if this is not required under legislation or the organisation's governing document.

If the governing document does not require an audit but legislation does, the organisation must comply with the legislation.

5.4.21
Property and
insurance

The governing document may make provision for aspects of property acquisition, management, insurance and disposal, for example that any land not required may be sold or leased.

5.4.22
Indemnification

The governing document should say that members of the organisation, members of the governing body, officers [see **5.3.2.2** for definition] and staff have a right to be indemnified (repaid) out of the organisation's assets:

- in trusts and unincorporated associations, for any liability incurred in connection with their position, unless they have acted negligently or fraudulently; *or*

- in charitable companies, for costs incurred in defending legal proceedings brought against them in that capacity—but only if judgment is given in their favour, or if the court grants relief from liability for negligence, default, breach of duty or breach of trust [see **19.2.5**].

For more about the right to be indemnified see **19.6.7**.

5.4.23
Notices

The governing document usually sets out how **notices** (official communications required by statute or the governing document, such as notice of meetings) are given, and who is entitled to receive them [see **17.2.3**, **17.4.4** and **17.6.2**].

5.4.24
Branches

If the organisation is to have branches or affiliates [see **9.2** and **9.4**], the governing document might set out how these are to be set up and rules for the relationship between the main organisation and its branches or affiliates. It should be clear whether branches are autonomous or are part of and controlled by the parent organisation.

5.4.25
Standing orders

The governing document may say that the members in general meeting or the governing body may make **standing orders, by-laws, regulations, rules** or **secondary rules** about specified matters, or about any matters relevant to how the organisation operates. These rules might cover matters such as eligibility for membership and application procedures, subscriptions, procedures for governing body nomination and election, procedures for general and governing body meetings, or terms of reference for committees. Standing orders, rules etc cannot contradict anything in the governing document, or exempt the organisation from a statutory duty. The National Council for Voluntary Organisations [see **page 12**] can provide examples of standing orders.

In general a governing document should not be too specific about matters which are likely to change. It is better to provide a broad framework, and to authorise the members in general meeting or the governing body to make rules of standing orders to deal with the detail.

Unincorporated associations and trusts generally have no power to make standing orders unless this is explicit in the governing document. An exception is literary or scientific institutions [see **1.2.3**], in which the governing body has a statutory power to make by-laws.

Literary and Scientific Institutions Act 1854 s.24

In a company, even if there is no express power to make standing orders, the members may pass an ordinary resolution [see **17.4.7**] setting out how the provisions of the memorandum and articles of association are to be implemented or covering any other matter, or they may authorise the governing body to make such rules. The members of an industrial and provident society have a statutory right to make such rules. *Industrial and Provident Societies Act 1965 s.13(4)*

Any rules and procedures relating to company or IPS directors' meetings can either be formally adopted by ordinary resolution, or informally by agreement of the directors.

Standing orders and other rules relating to the governing document or to the organisation's procedures should be kept with the governing document. Unlike amendments [see **5.5**], they do not need to be circulated with all copies of the governing document.

Standing orders can be changed in the same way they are made.

5.4.26
Amendment

Company law includes a procedure for amending the memorandum and articles of association [see **5.5.2**]. It may be sensible to spell it out in the memorandum or articles, but this is not necessary unless it is desired to make amendment more difficult than the statutory procedure.

For non-companies the governing document should include a procedure for amendment. If it does not, the governing document of a non-charitable association can be altered only by unanimous agreement of every member, and the governing document of a charitable association or trust can generally be altered only by a scheme made by the Charity Commission. Amendment procedures are covered in **5.5**.

5.4.27
Dissolution

Company law and industrial and provident society law provide procedures for dissolution (winding up the organisation). For other organisations the governing document should specify how dissolution is authorised, and what happens if the organisation has assets left after meeting all its financial obligations. Dissolution arrangements are covered in **chapter 21**.

5.5
ALTERING THE
GOVERNING
DOCUMENT

Alteration of a governing document is a particularly complex area, and in many cases legal advice may be necessary.

The procedures for altering a governing document depend on:

- whether the organisation is an unincorporated association, trust, company or industrial and provident society [see **chapters 1** and **2** for definitions];

- whether the organisation is charitable;

- whether the governing document contains specific provisions for amendment and/or there are statutory provisions; *and*

- whether the alteration is being made to a **fundamental** or **charitable provision** (the objects clause, and anything relating to how the organisation's money or property is or is not to be used), or to an **administrative provision**.

Complex issues may also arise as to whether money or property received before a change in the objects or powers can properly be used for different or wider purposes. Any use for the new objects or under the new powers could be a breach of trust. To prevent this, that money or property may need to be ringfenced and used only for its original purpose.

A general rule relating to amendments is that they should be within the spirit of the original objects or intentions. Dissatisfied members who feel that an amendment is contrary to those intentions may be able to ask the courts to decide whether the amendment is lawful.

Hole v Garnsey [1930] AC 472, 496, 500

Once an amendment has been properly approved, it should be attached to all copies of the governing document, or the governing document should be reprinted including the new provisions. It is sensible to put 'as amended [date]' on the amended version.

5.5.1
Trusts and
unincorporated
associations

Amending the governing document of an association or trust depends on whether it contains a power of amendment, and whether the organisation is charitable or non-charitable. Failure to follow the proper procedure could result in a claim for breach of trust against governing body members, or court action by members of an association.

If an unincorporated association has only one object, it may not be possible to change it. In this case the association would have to be wound up if the original object was no longer appropriate.

Thellusson v Viscount Valentia [1907] 2 Ch 7; Doyle v White City
Stadium Ltd and British Boxing Board of Control [1935] KB 110, 121

5.5.1.1
With power of
amendment

If the governing document of an unincorporated association or trust allows for amendment, the procedures must be strictly followed. In particular, the amendment power may not apply to alteration of the objects clause or certain other fundamental clauses.

A non-charitable association may make any amendment, provided it is not prohibited by the governing document and is not in itself unlawful. If it has a general power to amend but this does not apply to certain clauses, alteration of those clauses must be treated in the same way as for an organisation without power of amendment [see below].

Charity Commission consent must be obtained for any use of a charitable association's or trust's amendment power to authorise personal gain for members of the governing body, for example allowing them to be paid by the charity [see **5.4.9.1**]. It is advisable to seek Commission authorisation before making any change to the objects clause or any clause affecting how the charity's money or property is to be used. Without such authorisation there is a risk that the organisation's charitable status could be jeopardised or the members of the governing body could find themselves in breach of trust.

Amendment to a trust deed or declaration of trust is generally made by each trustee executing a supplemental deed [see **18.3**].

Charitable associations registered with the Charity Commission must send a copy of the amended governing document to the Commission, and charitable trusts must send a copy of the supplemental deed and the amended trust deed or declaration of trust.   *Charities Act 1993 s.3(7)*

5.5.1.2
Without power of amendment

If the governing document does not allow for amendment, the objects or powers clauses can be changed only:

- if an association is non-charitable, by agreement of *all* the members;
                                        Abbatt v Treasury Solicitor [1969] 1 WLR 1575, 1583

- if an association or trust is charitable, by having the Charity Commission make a scheme to alter the constitution [see **5.5.4**];

- if an association is legally defined as a literary or scientific institution, by following a statutory procedure; *or*
                                        Literary and Scientific Institutions Act 1854 s.27

- under special procedures for some charities with annual income of £5,000 or less [see **5.5.5**].

5.5.2
Companies

All companies have the right to alter their objects, their articles and anything in the memorandum which could have been in the articles, by special resolution at any general meeting [see **17.4.7** for procedure].
                                        Companies Act 1985 ss.4, 9, 17

However, some amendments require consent or special procedures. Charitable companies, for example, must obtain Charity Commission consent for some changes [see below]. Companies which are **registered social landlords** must obtain the Housing Corporation's consent under seal for any amendment of their memorandum or articles. Without such consent, the alteration is invalid.
                                        Housing Act 1996 sch.1 para.11.2

Because of the statutory right to amend the memorandum and articles, company governing documents often do not contain an amendment clause. If such a clause is included in the memorandum or articles, it must be carefully followed.

Any amendment must be for the benefit of the company as a whole.

Within 15 days of passing any special resolution, the company must send a copy of the resolution to Companies House, along with a copy of the Charity Commission's consent if this was required [see below] and an amended copy of the full memorandum and/or articles. If the company is charitable, a copy of the amendment and the amended memorandum and/or articles must also be sent to the Charity Commission.
                                        Companies Act 1985 ss.380, 18(2); Charities Act 1993 ss.3(7), 64(3)

5.5.2.1
Amendment of fundamental clauses

If amendment of the memorandum is expressly prohibited within the memorandum, any change must be agreed by the High Court.

The liability of members (for example, the amount of the members' guarantee) cannot be increased without the written consent of all the affected members.   *Companies Act 1985 s.16*

A charitable company must have written authorisation from the Charity Commission before it can propose a special resolution [see **17.4.7**]. amending the objects clause or any clause relating to how the charity's income or property is used, or which gives any benefit to trustees.

Charities Act 1993 s.64(2)

If 15% or more of a company's members object to an alteration of the objects or a related clause in the memorandum, they can apply to the High Court within 21 days of the resolution being passed.

Companies Act 1985 ss.5, 6

After the memorandum has been amended, every copy which is distributed must include the amendment.

s.20

**5.5.2.2
Amendment of administrative provisions**

Unless the memorandum or articles specify otherwise, the ordinary clauses in the articles—relating for example to membership, the governing body, meetings and the company's internal procedures—may be amended at a general meeting by a special resolution [see **17.4.7** for procedure]. For charitable companies Charity Commission consent is not required, but a copy of the amended articles must be sent to them.

**5.5.3
Industrial and provident societies**

An IPS's rules must include provision for amendment. The legislation does not specify what the procedure should be, but typically amendment requires a two-thirds majority of members present and voting at a general meeting.   *Industrial and Provident Societies Act 1965 sch.1 para.5*

If a charitable IPS's objects or powers are being amended, the Inland Revenue should be consulted to ensure the organisation's charitable status is not jeopardised.

Two signed copies of the approved amendment must be sent to the registrar of friendly societies, with the appropriate forms (available from the registrar) and a fee which depends on the nature and extent of the amendment (generally £220-£800, as at 1/4/01). The amendment does not come into force until the IPS receives formal notification from the registrar that it has been registered.

**5.5.4
Charity Commission schemes**

If a charitable association's or trust's governing document does not contain an amendment procedure, or if the governing document of a charitable association, trust or company expressly prohibits amendment of certain parts of the governing document, the Commission must authorise the alteration, and if necessary make a **scheme** for it. A scheme is an agreed and approved way to alter the provisions under which the charity was originally set up.

Schemes are explained in Charity Commission booklet CC36 *Making a Scheme*. The Commission has a standard form for a resolution applying for a scheme. Except for very small charities [see **5.5.4.3**], the resolution must be passed at a meeting of the charity or its trustees. Except in relation to exempt charities, application may also be made by the attorney general.   *Charities Act 1993 s.16(4)(a),(b)*

Trustees are under an obligation to request a scheme if one is necessary in order to ensure that the charity's assets are effectively used. *s.13(5)*

If the Charity Commission believes that a scheme is necessary but the trustees refuse to apply for one the Commissioners have power to make a scheme anyway, but only if the charity has been in existence for at least 40 years.   *s.16(6)*

**5.5.4.1
Cy près schemes**

Cy près is a Norman French expression meaning 'as near as possible'. It means that if a charity's objects or purposes have to be changed, the new ones must be as close as possible to the original ones.

The general presumption is that a charity's objects cannot be changed, because money and other property has been given to the charity in trust [see **3.1.2**] to be used only for the purposes for which the charity was established. However, a *cy près* alteration is possible if:

- the original purposes of the charity have been fulfilled as much as they can be;
- the original purposes cannot be carried out, or cannot be carried out according to the instructions given or within the spirit of the original objects;
- the original objects only cover part of the property given to the charity (for example, if a charity raises more money than can be used for the objects as specified);
- the charity can operate more effectively if it amalgamates with other charities;
- the area of benefit (geographical area) defined in the objects has changed, for example because of local government reorganisation;
- the area of benefit is no longer appropriate;
- the definition of the beneficiaries is no longer appropriate;
- all or some of the original objects are being adequately provided for by other means;
- all or some of the objects for which the charity was established have ceased to be charitable in law; *or*
- all or some of the original objects are no longer suitable or effective.

Charities Act 1993 s.13(1)

A *cy près* scheme is frequently slow and expensive to undertake.

If a scheme is very complex or contentious, the Charity Commission may advise trustees to apply to the High Court for a scheme.

The secretary of state for education has powers to make schemes for charities which are schools or provide educational services, without referring to the Charity Commission. *Education Act 1996*

5.5.4.2
Administrative schemes

If a charitable association's or trust's governing document does not contain amendment procedures, it must apply to the Charity Commission if it wants to amend the administrative provisions. Such a scheme is straightforward and involves convincing the Commission that the change is in the best interests of the charity and its beneficiaries, is in keeping with the spirit of the original trusts, and is workable.

The Commission's emphasis now is not on making schemes to deal with specific alterations, but on making schemes which give trustees the power to amend the governing document. Such powers of amendment will generally exclude the power to amend the charity's objects, to dissolve the charity or to spend its permanent endowment, and will require the charity to get authorisation before making any amendments relating to remuneration of trustees or powers of investment.

Decisions of the Charity Commissioners vol. 3, January 1995, pp.29-31

5.5.4.3
Very small charities

If a charity's annual income is less than £500 and it is not an exempt charity [see **7.1.2** for definition], application for a Charity Commission scheme does not have to be made by a resolution of the charity's members or its governing body. It may be made by one trustee of the charity, by any person 'interested in the charity', or, if it is a local charity, by any two or more inhabitants in the area of benefit.

Charities Act 1993 s.16(5)

5.5.5
Amendment without a scheme

There is no need for a charitable association or trust to apply for a scheme if:

- its gross income in the last financial year was £5,000 or less; *and*
- it does not hold any land subject to trusts which allow it to be used only for one or more purposes of the charity. *s.74*

In these charities the trustees may amend the administrative provisions by passing a resolution with a two-thirds majority of those voting.

If the trustees are satisfied that the existing objects no longer provide for suitable and effective use of the charity's resources, they may pass a resolution, also requiring a two-thirds majority, to replace all or some of their objects with other charitable purposes. The new purposes must be as similar as is reasonably practicable to the existing objects.

The charity must publicise its resolution, and must send a copy to the Charity Commission with a statement of the reasons for the alteration. The Commission will notify the charity within three months if it accepts the resolution, and if it does, the governing document is considered to be altered from the date specified in the notification.

These provisions are explained in Charity Commission booklet CC44 *Small Charities*. They cannot be used by exempt charities. [see **7.1.2**].

5.6 ALTERNATIVES TO AMENDING THE GOVERNING DOCUMENT

Alteration of the governing document may be slow, expensive or impossible, especially where a change to the objects is desired. In this situation it may be appropriate:

- to set up a new organisation with additional or broader objects, and transfer the organisation's activities to the new body; *or*
- for a charitable, trading or campaigning organisation to be set up with the new objects, to undertake the new work.

Before doing this, careful consideration must be given to:

- whether the original organisation has power to create the new organisation;
- whether the new organisation is intended to be short-term and therefore perhaps needs only a simple unincorporated structure [see **chapter 1**], or whether it is likely to be complex, risky or long-term and should therefore be incorporated [see **chapter 2**];
- the possible need to obtain Charity Commission consent if the original organisation is charitable;
- possible restrictions on the use of the original organisation's funds for any purposes which are not within its objects, which may mean that funds cannot be transferred to the new organisation if its objects are completely different, or that transferred funds need to be ring-fenced within the new organisation;
- the additional administrative burden in running a separate organisation; *and*
- the relationship between the original and new organisations [see for example **47.5**].

Chapter 6
SETTING UP AN ORGANISATION

Topics covered in this chapter

This chapter explains how to set up an organisation as an unincorporated association, trust, company or industrial and provident society. Chapter 7 covers how to register any of them as a charity. This chapter covers:

6.1 Setting up an unincorporated association
6.1.1 Coming into existence
6.1.2 Deciding whether to be charitable
6.1.3 Drawing up a draft constitution
6.1.4 Adopting the constitution
6.1.5 Charity registration
6.1.6 Circulating the constitution
6.1.7 Other registrations
6.1.8 First meeting of the committee

6.2 Setting up a trust
6.2.1 The trust deed
6.2.2 Executing and stamping
6.2.3 Charity registration
6.2.4 Circulating the trust deed
6.2.5 Other registrations
6.2.6 First meeting of the trustees

6.3 Setting up a limited company
6.3.1 Buying an off-the-shelf company
6.3.2 The promoters
6.3.3 Memorandum and articles
6.3.4 The subscribers
6.3.5 The first directors
6.3.6 Applying for registration
6.3.7 Same day registration
6.3.8 Certificate of incorporation
6.3.9 Charity registration
6.3.10 Circulating the memorandum and articles
6.3.11 Other registrations
6.3.12 First meeting of the directors

6.4 Setting up an industrial and provident society
6.4.1 Model rules
6.4.2 Applying without model rules
6.4.3 Consulting Inland Revenue
6.4.4 Adopting the rules
6.4.5 Applying for registration
6.4.6 Certificate of registration
6.4.7 Circulating the rules
6.4.8 Other registrations
6.4.9 First meeting of the directors

6.5 Other registration requirements
6.5.1 Organisations with employees
6.5.2 Registered social landlords
6.5.3 Provision of care and accommodation
6.5.4 Work with children
6.5.5 Other registrations

6.6 Changing from unincorporated to incorporated
6.6.1 Transfer of assets, liabilities and responsibilities
6.6.2 Notification of incorporation
6.6.3 The process

6.7 IPS/company conversion
6.7.1 Changing from IPS to company
6.7.2 Changing from company to IPS

6.8 Changing from incorporated to unincorporated

For sources of further information see page 12.

Double-underlined section headings indicate additions or significant changes since the first edition.

6.1 SETTING UP AN UNINCORPORATED ASSOCIATION

6.1.1 Coming into existence

Unincorporated associations and their advantages and disadvantages are explained in **1.2**.

Unlike other legal structures which generally require legal recognition before they come into being, an unincorporated association is generally assumed to exist as soon as:

- two or more people start doing something together for a common purpose which is not primarily for business and is not purely a family or friendship relationship;

- they call themselves a 'group' or anything else which signifies that they intend to be bound together in some sort of membership;

- they develop rules, even informal and non-written ones, for who can be a member, what the group is doing and how they are doing it.

An unincorporated association can exist even if the members do not identify themselves as an association. It is not necessary to have a name, a constitution or a bank account, or even any money.

In a case in 1996, the Court of Appeal ruled that an unincorporated association did not formally come into existence until its first annual general meeting—even though the organisation had already been operating and had a bank account and a constitution. This was a surprising decision, and legal advice may be necessary in situations where the legal existence (or not) of an unincorporated association is significant.

Hanuman v The Guyanese Association for Racial Unity and Democracy,
13/6/1996 CA unreported

6.1.1.1
The governing document

At some point, either early on or after a group has been in existence for a while, there may be pressure to adopt a constitution (a **governing document**). This often arises when the group wants to open a bank account, seek funding, or clarify who is eligible for membership.

The governing document is a legally enforceable agreement between the association's members. Even if nothing is written, the verbally agreed rules by which the association operates form the agreement. And even if nothing has been agreed verbally, any rules which have been consistently used over a long period form the agreement.

Re Buckinghamshire Constabulary Widows' and Orphans' Fund Friendly
Society No.2 [1979] 1 WLR 936, 952; John v Rees [1970] Ch 345, 388

6.1.2
Deciding whether to be charitable

If the association is to be set up for purposes which are wholly and exclusively charitable [see **4.3**] it is likely to have to register with the Charity Commission [see **7.1**]. The association must register if it meets all the requirements for registration; it does not have a choice.

The people involved in setting up the organisation should consider the advantages and disadvantages of charitable status [see **3.2** and **3.3**]. If they do not want to be charitable, they should ensure the governing document includes provisions which make the organisation non-charitable. If they want to be charitable they should read **chapter 4** on charitable objects and **chapter 7** on the charity registration process, and obtain a registration pack from the Charity Commission [see **page 12**].

6.1.3
Drawing up a draft constitution

An unincorporated association does not need to comply with any requirements in drawing up its governing document unless it wants to be charitable. **Chapter 5** explains what should be in an unincorporated association's governing document and additional clauses which might be included.

The Charity Commission provides a list of approved standard constitutions for charitable associations, and the Charity Commission and Charity Law Association [see **page 12**] have model constitutions for unincorporated charitable associations if none of the standard ones is appropriate. A model constitution for a non-charitable unincorporated association is included in *Unincorporated Associations* by Jean Warburton (published by Sweet & Maxwell). A solicitor with voluntary sector experience can create a tailor-made constitution.

The constitution of an unincorporated association can be in any language. If it is registering as a charity, it will have to supply a certified English translation to the Charity Commission. Even if it is not registering as a charity it may want to have a certified translation available for funders, bank managers and others outside the organisation.

6.1.4
Adopting the constitution

The **draft constitution** should be formally adopted by the members at a general meeting called in accordance with the rules in the constitution.

When the governing document is adopted it should be signed and dated. This is generally done by the association's chairperson and secretary. This signed copy should be kept in a safe place.

6.1.5
Charity registration

If the association is charitable and is required to register with the Charity Commission, the constitution and supporting documents must be submitted [see **chapter 7**]. Some charities may need to apply to the Inland Revenue for recognition of their charitable status [see **7.1.2**].

6.1.6
Circulating the constitution

A copy of the agreed constitution should be given to the chairperson, secretary, treasurer, other honorary officers, other members of the governing body (committee) and senior staff. If possible a copy should be given to all members but if this is impractical they should be given a summary, or a copy of the full constitution or a summary should be posted on a noticeboard or kept in a place where the members have access.

Procedures should be put in place to ensure:

- all new members of the association get a full or summarised copy of the constitution or know where they can see it; *and*

- all new members of the governing body get a copy of the full constitution as soon as they join the governing body.

6.1.7
Other registrations

When setting up, consideration should be given as to whether it is necessary to register with the Inland Revenue or other bodies [see **6.5**].

6.1.8
First meeting of the committee

At its first meeting after adoption of the governing document the governing body (or the members of the organisation) should:

- arrange for minutes to be taken;

- consider any further appointment of governing body members, if the constitution allows;

- elect or appoint a chairperson, treasurer and possibly other officers [see **12.1.2**], unless the governing document says it must be done at a general meeting or through another process;

- decide on frequency and procedure for calling meetings of the governing body [see **17.6**];

- declare and record any conflicts of interest of governing body members—this is obligatory for charitable associations [see **13.3.4**], and good practice for non-charitable associations;

- if the organisation is taking over from a previous body, ensure legal advice has been or will be taken and proper steps are being taken to transfer any assets, liabilities, contracts of employment, leases or agreements [see **6.6.1**];

- appoint auditors, if required [see **51.1**, and **60.10.3** for how to find an auditor];

- decide on the organisation's financial year [see **50.2.1**];

- select bankers and account signatories, pass a resolution in the bank's required wording, and complete the bank mandate and other forms to open accounts;

- agree any contracts the organisation will enter into, for example with landlord or employees, and for telephone, gas, electricity, photocopier etc;

- agree insurances [see **chapter 20**];

- appoint solicitors, if necessary [see **60.10.3** for how to find a suitably experienced solicitor];

- admit any members who have applied for membership of the organisation (if the governing document requires this);
- consider and if appropriate agree dates for the annual general meeting and other general meetings (meetings of all the members);
- ensure that stationery and financial and fundraising documents carry correct details [see **16.1**];
- carry out any other business required by the governing document for the first meeting;
- consider arrangements for correspondence and other communications;
- consider what the organisation is actually going to do.

Proper minutes must be kept and should be signed at the next meeting as an accurate record [see **17.2.15**].

6.2 SETTING UP A TRUST

6.2.1 The trust deed

Trusts and their advantages and disadvantages are covered in **1.3**.

The Charity Commission provides a list of sources of standard **trust deeds** (also called **declaration of trust**), and the Charity Commission and Charity Law Association [see **page 12**] have models if none of the standard deeds is appropriate. **Chapter 5** explains what must be in a trust deed for a charitable trust, and optional clauses. A trust should not be set up without legal advice.

A trust deed must be carefully worded, because the trust may fail (be declared void or invalid) if there is any uncertainty about the intentions of the persons who set up the trust, or about whether they intended the money or property to be used solely for charitable purposes [see **1.3.4**].

Individuals often set up personal or family charitable trusts as a tax-effective way of donating to charities [see **46.6**]. A charitable trust can also be set up under the terms of a **will**. Setting up these types of trust is not covered in this book but a solicitor can advise.

6.2.2 Executing and stamping

The persons setting up the trust and those who will be the trustees execute the trust deed by signing and dating it in the presence of a witness. The deed must then be sent to the Inland Revenue stamping office within 30 days, with the stamping fee (£5 as at 1/4/01). The process of executing and stamping is explained in **18.3**.

6.2.3 Charity registration

When the deed is returned from the stamping office the charity registration process must be carried out if the trust is charitable and is required to register with the Charity Commission [see **chapter 7**].

6.2.4 Circulating the trust deed

A copy of the declaration should be given to every trustee (member of the governing body). A procedure should be put in place to ensure a copy is given to all new trustees as soon as they are appointed.

6.2.5 Other registrations

The people involved in setting up the trust must consider whether they must register with the Inland Revenue or other bodies [see **6.5**].

6.2.6 First meeting of the trustees

At their first meeting the trustees should consider the same matters as at the first meeting of an association's committee [see **6.1.8**].

6.3 SETTING UP A LIMITED COMPANY

Companies limited by guarantee and the advantages and disadvantages of this structure are explained in **2.3**. Information about registration and the necessary forms are available from Companies House or its website [see **page 12**].

6.3.1 Buying an off-the-shelf company

A ready-formed **off-the-shelf company** can be bought from a company formation agent (listed under 'company registration agents' in the Yellow Pages) or through an accountant or solicitor. Off-the-shelf companies are nearly always limited by shares rather than by guarantee, so great care must be taken to get the right structure if this method of setting up is used.

Registration agents keep their fees low by providing a basic service. They give little or no advice, and the purchaser of the company is expected to specify exactly what they want and to understand the duties and responsibilities of companies and company directors.

An off-the-shelf company can be useful if a company is needed in a very great hurry, for example to sign a lease. The company name can later be changed [see **8.7.1** for procedure] and the memorandum and articles can be amended [see **5.5.2** for procedure]. But in the meantime the organisation is likely to be operating an inappropriate company, so this step should be taken only in exceptional circumstances.

6.3.2
The promoters

The persons involved in setting up the company are called the **promoters**. The promoters might or might not be involved in the company when it is finally set up. A solicitor or other person who assists the formation by acting in a professional capacity is not a promoter.

6.3.3
Memorandum and articles

A company's governing document is in two parts: the **memorandum of association**, which sets out the company's objects and powers and the limit on members' liability, and the **articles of association**, which set out its internal rules and procedures. A section in the memorandum is a **clause**; a section in the articles is an **article**.

Model formats for company memoranda and articles are set out in the **Companies (Tables A-F) Regulations 1985**. Table C provides the format for a company limited by guarantee. The Act says that this should be followed as closely as is practical, but in reality the promoters have almost complete freedom in the way they word the memorandum and articles, so long as what is included is not contrary to company law.

Companies Act 1985 s.8(4)

A company limited by shares can choose not to draw up articles, and table A is used by default. A company limited by guarantee must draw up and submit articles. *s.7(1)*

The Charity Commission registration pack includes a list of organisations which provide standard memoranda and articles of association for charitable companies. If none of these is appropriate, the Charity Commission and Charity Law Association have model memoranda and articles which can be adapted. It is especially important to ensure the membership structure and criteria [see **10.2**] and provisions for general meetings, election or appointment of the governing body, governing body meetings and other matters are suitable for the new company.

Particular issues apply to the choice of company name [see **8.4**], and where the company is being set up as a trading company [see **47.5.1**].

A company whose registered office [see **15.1.1**] must be in Wales may, if it wishes, submit its memorandum and articles in Welsh with a certified translation into English. All other memoranda and articles must be in English. *s.21(1)*

Chapter 5 explains some of the obligatory and optional clauses for the memorandum and articles for all companies limited by guarantee, whether charitable or non-charitable.

6.3.4
The subscribers

The memorandum of association ends with the **association clause**, in which at least one person (but generally more) signs the memorandum, to state that they want to form the company. The same **subscribers** also sign the articles. Their signatures on the memorandum and the articles must be witnessed. Anyone can witness the signatures so long as they can understand what they are witnessing, but it is sensible to ensure the witness is at least 18 years old.

These **subscribers** are the company's founder members, but have no special rights unless these are stated in the articles. Typically the subscribers are the people who want to start the company, but in the case of an off-the-shelf company [see **6.3.1**] they may be two companies, or employees of the agents who form the company. In this case they will resign their membership as soon as the company is sold to the organisation which purchases it.

6.3.5
The first directors

The articles might say the subscribers are the first directors of the company or that they appoint the first directors, or that the first directors are named in the articles or are the persons named in companies form 10 [see **6.3.6.1**]. If the articles do not say anything, the first directors are the persons named as directors in form 10.

Unless the articles specify otherwise, the first directors constitute the governing body only until new directors are elected (at the first annual general meeting, or at a general meeting held before this) or until new directors are appointed under the procedures set out in the articles.

6.3.6
Applying for registration

The final version of the memorandum and articles must be typed in numbered paragraphs on white A4 paper with margins of at least 1cm (2cm on the edge which is to be bound).

The memorandum and articles are signed by the subscribers and the signatures witnessed, and are sent to Companies House with the forms listed below and the registration fee (£20 as at 1/4/01). The original of the memorandum and articles is kept at Companies House, so the organisation should keep its own copies and should also keep photocopies of all documents and forms sent to Companies House.

Copies of all company forms are available free from the stationery section at Companies House, and most can be printed from the Companies House website [see **page 12**].

Most forms are available in a bilingual Welsh version. Companies whose registered office [see **15.1.1**] must be in Wales may submit forms in Welsh with a certified translation into English.

Companies Act 1985 s.21(3)

6.3.6.1
Form 10

Companies form 10 names the company secretary and the first directors, and gives the address of the registered office.   *s.10; sch.1*

It includes:

- full name, previous name, usual home address and signature of the person who will be company secretary [see **12.3**];
- name, previous name, usual home address, date of birth, nationality, occupation (if any), other directorships and signature of each person who will be a director (member of the first governing body);
- the signatures of the subscribers to the memorandum and articles, or the signature of a solicitor or other person acting on behalf of the subscribers;
- the address of the intended registered office.

The form has space only for two directors. For more directors a blank form may be photocopied, or continuation sheets are available from Companies House or its website.

For the question on previous name a married woman does not have to give the name by which she was known before marriage. No one has to give a name they have not used since age 18, or for the past 20 years.

All directorships of bodies incorporated in Great Britain must be listed on form 10. This includes voluntary sector as well as commercial companies and industrial and provident societies. All current directorships, and any directorships held in the past five years must be listed, unless the company is dormant [see **50.3.7**], or was dormant at all times when the person was director during the past five years, or is the parent company of the company which is being set up, or is another subsidiary of the same parent company.

If the same person will be both company secretary and a director he or she must fill in and sign both sections of the form.

If there are very pressing reasons, the company can apply not to have its directors' home addresses made public at Companies House [see **16.3.4**].

6.3.6.2
Form 12

Companies form 12 is a declaration of compliance with the requirements for registering a company.   *Companies Act 1985 s.12(3)*

The company secretary or a director named in form 10, or the solicitor or other person who has advised the new company about its formation, certifies on this form that all the legal requirements for setting up the company have been met. The person who signs it is certifying that:

- the memorandum and articles of association have been properly drawn up;

- the objects as set out in the memorandum accurately reflect what the company is being set up to do;

- the directors and company secretary named on form 10 can legally hold these posts. [For details about who is not eligible to be a company director or secretary, see **11.3.3** and **12.3.1**].

Form 12 must be sworn in the presence of a commissioner for oaths, notary public, justice of the peace or solicitor (fee £5 as at 1/4/01). The date on which this is sworn must be on or after the dates on which the other paperwork is dated.

6.3.6.3
Form 30(5)(a)

If the company is exempt from having to use the word 'limited' in its name [see **8.4.3**], as most voluntary organisations will be, and does not want to use the word as part of its name, **form 30(5)(a)** must be sworn in the same way as form 12.   *s.30(5)(a)*

6.3.6.4
Form 225

The final form, signed by a company director or the secretary, may be submitted at any time. **Form 225**, 'notice of **accounting reference date**' (ARD) sets out the date when the company's **accounting reference period** (financial year) will end [see **50.3.1**].   *s.224(2)*

The company can choose any date it wants, and may wish to choose a date which corresponds with its funding cycle. If form 225 is not sent in, the default ARD is the last day of the month in which the anniversary of incorporation falls.   *s.224(3)*

6.3.7
Same day
registration

For those who need a company in a hurry, while-you-wait registration is possible by attending at or delivering documents to Companies House in London, Birmingham, Cardiff, Leeds, Manchester or Edinburgh, and paying an increased fee (£80 as at 1/4/01).

6.3.8
Certificate of
incorporation

When Companies House is satisfied that the company's name is acceptable [see **8.4**] and that all the paperwork is in order, a registration number is allocated and a certificate of incorporation is issued. This generally takes about two weeks from the time the forms are sent in. The most common cause of delay is a small error in the paperwork, such as the subscribers signing the memorandum but not the articles, or directors not filling in their occupation on form 10.

The company comes into existence as a body corporate, under the name specified in the memorandum, from the date on the certificate.

A private company can start operating as soon it is incorporated. A public company (plc) needs a second certificate, called a trading certificate, before it can start operating, but voluntary organisations are not plc's so this does not apply to them.

6.3.9
Charity registration

If the company is charitable it must submit its memorandum and articles and the other required documents to the Charity Commission for registration as a charity [see **chapter 7**], or may have to apply to the Inland Revenue for recognition as a charity [see **7.1.2**]. It may start its activities immediately, without waiting for registration.

6.3.10
Circulating the
memorandum and
articles

At least one copy of the memorandum and articles should be kept in a safe place. A copy, perhaps with a summary of the main points, should be given to all company directors (voting members of the governing body), and procedures should be put in place to ensure it is given to all new directors in future.

It is good practice to give the memorandum and articles, or a summary of the main points, to all company members and to have procedures in place to ensure it is given to all new members when they join. If members do not automatically receive the memorandum and articles they have a statutory right to a copy, and cannot be charged more than 5p for it. Any copy given to members must include all amendments.

Companies Act 1985 ss.19, 20

It is also good practice to give all directors (members of the governing body) a copy of Companies House leaflet GBA1 *Directors and Secretaries Guide* which summarises their responsibilities under company law. It is available free from Companies House or its website [see **page 12**].

6.3.11
Other registrations

The company is likely to have to register with the Inland Revenue and other bodies [see **6.5**].

6.3.12
First meeting
of the directors

At their first meeting after incorporation the directors should deal with the matters set out at **6.1.8**, and also:

- receive the certificate of incorporation, memorandum and articles, and form 10 appointing the first directors;

- consider any further appointment of directors, if the articles allow, and ensure they complete company form 288a [see **16.3.4**];

- if the company was off-the-shelf [see **6.3.1**] or for any other reason the directors named in form 10 are not to remain directors, ensure form 288c is completed and submitted for them;

- appoint auditors if required under the articles or company law [see **50.2.12** and **50.5**, and **60.10.3** for how to find an auditor];

- ensure steps are taken to notify any party with whom contracts may be made that the organisation is incorporated [see **6.6.2**];

- confirm the location of the registered office and ensure a plaque is put up [see **15.1**], approve the location for the register of members if it is to be kept elsewhere [see **16.3.2**], and instruct the company secretary to file the relevant forms;

- decide when the company's financial year will end (accounting reference date) and instruct the company secretary to file company form 225, unless the ARD is to be the last day of the month in which the anniversary of incorporation falls [see **6.3.6.4**].

6.4
SETTING UP AN
INDUSTRIAL AND
PROVIDENT
SOCIETY

Industrial and provident societies and the advantages and disadvantages of this structure are explained in **2.4**.

The rules of an industrial and provident society must follow a prescribed format (form A), available from Mutual Societies Registration [see **page 12**]. Unlike company legislation, IPS legislation does not provide detailed models. It simply provides a list of what must be included in the rules. *Industrial and Provident Societies Act 1965 sch.1*

The rules may also include other matters which are not prescribed, and may specify the documentation to be used for any procedure set out in the rules, for example a membership application form or committee nomination form.   *s.13(1),(4)*

6.4.1
Model rules

Registration as an IPS is quicker and less expensive if model rules from a **promoting body** are used. Model rules are available for a range of voluntary organisations, including transport schemes, housing associations, credit unions, allotment societies and licensed bars in village halls or community centres. Mutual Societies Registration [see **page 12**] can provide a list of promoting bodies.

To qualify for the lower registration fee (£90 as at 1/4/01) the rules must be exactly as they are in the model. If model rules are used with minor amendments the fee can be as high as £875 (as at 1/4/01), depending on the number of amendments.

In addition to the registration fee, the promoting body will add its own fee.

6.4.2
Applying without model rules

If there is no relevant promoting body, or if the organisation does not want to register through a promoting body, it is sensible to contact an experienced solicitor or other advisor or Mutual Societies Registration to obtain confirmation that the organisation is appropriate for registration as an IPS. The fee for registration without model rules is much higher (£980 as at 1/4/01).

Before registering, draft rules must be drawn up and submitted to Mutual Societies Registration. If the draft is based on model rules, this should be stated. Mutual Societies Registration will give advice on draft rules, but will not draw them up.

Unlike Companies House, Mutual Societies Registration scrutinises rules in detail and the registration process can take several weeks.

6.4.3
Consulting Inland Revenue

IPSs whose objects are wholly charitable [see **4.3**] are **exempt charities** and do not register with the Charity Commission [see **7.1.2**]. Unless the organisation is using model rules which have been accepted as charitable, it is sensible to send a copy of the draft rules to Inland Revenue (Charities) [see **page 12** for details] at the same time as they are submitted to Mutual Societies Registration, to ensure the proposed purposes will be considered charitable for tax purposes.

If the society's purposes are unusual, or if it is not clear that all its trading will be carried on for the benefit of the community, the Inland Revenue may consult the Charity Commission for its opinion as to whether the organisation is indeed charitable.

To avoid any future problems about eligibility for tax reliefs, copies of all correspondence with the Inland Revenue about the society's charitable status should be kept safely.

6.4.4
Adopting the rules

When the rules have been agreed in principle by Mutual Societies Registration and, for a charitable IPS, are acceptable to the Inland Revenue, or if model rules are being used, the members must formally adopt the rules at a general meeting. The final rules must be typed on paper no larger than A4 with at least 2cm margins, and should be presented in book form (bound or stapled).

6.4.5
Applying for registration

An application (**form A**) is submitted to Mutual Societies Registration along with two bound printed copies of the rules and the registration fee. Form A lists all the clauses which must be included in the rules.

6.4.5.1
Ordinary IPSs

For cooperatives and community benefit societies, form A and both copies of the rules must be signed by at least three members of the society, the secretary, who can be one of the members and, if model rules are being used, the promoting body.

**6.4.5.2
Secondary IPSs**

A **secondary IPS** is one which is made up of other IPSs. It only needs two member societies and a secretary. Form A and both copies of the rules must be signed by the secretary of the secondary IPS, the secretary of at least two member societies and, if model rules are being used, the promoting body.

**6.4.5.3
Credit unions**

For a credit union, form A must be signed by 21 members; the secretary, who may be one of the members; and the promoting body.

Credit Unions Act 1979 s.6(1)(a)

**6.4.6
Certificate of
registration**

Mutual Societies Registration sends a certificate of registration (**form B**) to the society, with its registration number and date of registration. Form B is conclusive evidence that the organisation is registered as an IPS.   *Industrial and Provident Societies Act 1965 s.2(3)*

Form B is also conclusive evidence that the society's rules are registered, except for companies which have converted to the IPS structure [see **6.7.2**], which need a separate certificate to show that their rules are registered.   *ss.9, 53(3)*

If Mutual Societies Registration does not register the society on the basis that it is not a genuine cooperative or business operating for the benefit of the community, the decision cannot be appealed. But if a refusal to register is based on any other grounds, the members of the organisation may appeal against the decision.   *s.18(1)(a),(2)*

**6.4.7
Circulating the rules**

All directors should have a copy of the rules, and members should have either a full copy or summary. Procedures should be in place to ensure new members get a copy of the rules as soon as they join.

A copy of the rules must be given to any person who requests it, at a charge not exceeding 10p.   *s.15(1)*

**6.4.8
Other registrations**

The IPS will have to register with the Inland Revenue and possibly with other bodies [see **6.5**].

**6.4.9
First meeting
of the directors**

The first meeting of the directors of the IPS should consider the same business as the first meeting of company directors [see **6.3.12**].

**6.5
OTHER
REGISTRATION
REQUIREMENTS**

Many organisations must be registered with other bodies. These registrations are additional to the obligatory registration with the Charity Commission for most organisations with wholly charitable objects [see **7.1.1**] and to the optional registration as a company or industrial and provident society.

The Department of Trade and Industry produces a useful leaflet *Setting Up in Business: A guide to the regulatory requirements* which is also relevant for voluntary organisations [see **page 12**]. Some of these registrations are listed here and at the relevant points in this book. There are many registrations and new organisations, or organisations undertaking a new type of work, should take advice from an experienced solicitor and/or the relevant professional body.

**6.5.1
Organisations with
employees**

If an organisation employs anyone for whom it must operate PAYE [see **27.3**] it must register with the Inland Revenue for PAYE (new employer's helpline tel 0845-60 70 143).

Every place where people are employed must be registered with the local authority's environmental health department or, in some cases, the Health and Safety Executive [see **36.1.3**].

Premises at which more than 10, or in some cases 20, people are employed must be registered with the fire authority [see **36.5.2**].

6.5.2
Registered social landlords

Housing associations and other **registered social landlords** which receive funding from the Housing Corporation or other public sources must be registered with the Corporation. *Housing Act 1996 ss.1-6*

Housing associations and RSLs are subject to particularly complex regulatory requirements, which are beyond the scope of this book. Information is available from the National Housing Federation (020-7278 6571, www.housing.org.uk).

6.5.3
Provision of care and accommodation

New procedures for the registration and inspection of care services are in effect from 1 April 2002, under the control of the National Care Standards Commission in England and an arm of the Welsh Assembly in Wales. The new procedures cover residential care homes, nursing homes, children's homes, domiciliary care agencies, fostering and adoption agencies, healthcare services, hospices, and welfare arrangements in boarding schools and further education colleges which accommodate children. Information is available on the National Care Standards Commission website (www.doh.gov.uk/ncsc) or from the local social services department. *Care Standards Act 2000*

6.5.4
Work with children

Most organisations which work with children under eight years old, including playgroups, nurseries, clubs, and organisations providing out-of-school activities, must be registered with the local authority. The social services department can advise on specific requirements.

Residential accommodation for children under 16 must be registered with the social services department, or with the National Care Standards Agency [see above] when it is established.

Organisations offering adventure activities (caving, climbing, water sports etc) to under-18s may need to be registered with Tourism Quality Services Ltd (029-2075 5715; www.aala.org), the adventure activities licensing authority. *Activity Centres (Young Persons' Safety) Act 1995*

6.5.5
Other registrations

An organisation may need to register:

- with the Inland Revenue, if the organisation is not a charity and will therefore be liable to income tax or corporation tax on its profits or surplus [see **52.4**], or if it is a charity and has taxable income [see **52.4**], or if it is a charity and will want to recover tax [see **52.5.1**];

- with Customs and Excise, if the organisation is required to register for VAT or chooses to register voluntarily [see **53.6**];

- with the information commissioner, for data protection [see **38.3.9**];

- with the Community Legal Service if it provides legal information, advice or specialist legal services to the public, even if this is only part of its work (020-7813 8691; www.legalservices.gov.uk);

- with the Office of the Immigration Service Commissioner if it provides any immigration advice to members of the public—not actually registration for non-profit organisations, but an application for exemption (020-7211 1500; www.oisc.org.uk);

- with the Office of Fair Trading, if the organisation gives advice about debts or makes loans and this work is covered under the **Consumer Credit Act 1974** (08457-224499; www.oft.gov.uk);

- with the local authority's environmental health department, for premises where food will be prepared, sold or provided [see **43.2.1**];

- with the licensing justices at the magistrates' court, for the sale of alcoholic beverages [see **43.3**];

- with the local authority, for premises where public music, dancing or sports events will take place, plays will be performed or films or videos will be shown [see **42.2**];

- with the Performing Right Society, Phonographic Performance Limited, Video Performance Limited and/or the Mechanical Copyright Protection Society, for the performance of live or recorded music [see **42.3**];

- with the local authority, for premises where there are amusement machines or where other forms of gaming take place [see **45.12.3**].

Even where the organisation does not have to register when the organisation is set up, it may need to register or get a licence or permission later if it undertakes a new activity or service, or for a one-off activity such as a public event [see **chapter 42**], a public collection [see **45.2**] or a lottery [see **45.6**].

6.6 CHANGING FROM UNINCORPORATED TO INCORPORATED

If an unincorporated association or trust wants to change from unincorporated to incorporated it cannot simply go through a company or IPS registration procedure. Legally the new incorporated body has to be set up, the assets and legal obligations of the existing organisation are transferred to it, and usually the existing organisation is dissolved. The new organisation will have its own company or IPS number, and if it is a charitable company it will have a new charity number because legally it is a new charity.

Most recent constitutions for unincorporated associations and trust deeds include a power to make payments to another organisation with the same or similar objects, and/or a procedure for dissolving the organisation and transferring its assets to another organisation with the same or similar objects. In this case the unincorporated organisation must follow the relevant constitutional procedures.

If a non-charitable association does not have a transfer or dissolution procedure, any transfer of assets must be agreed by *all* of the association's members. If a charitable association or trust does not have a transfer or dissolution procedure, it must apply to the Charity Commission before it can dissolve the original organisation or transfer its assets.

Charities Act 1993 s.74

6.6.1 Transfer of assets, liabilities and responsibilities

Even if the new organisation has exactly the same objects as the original body, will carry on exactly the same activities and involve exactly the same people, it is a new organisation and everything must be legally transferred from the old to the new. If this is not done, there could be problems later about the ownership of assets or who is responsible for outstanding liabilities.

Before winding up, the original organisation must ensure that all its assets, liabilities and obligations will be transferred or discharged. This may take some time, and the original organisation and the new one may have to run in parallel for a period [see **6.6.3.3**].

In all but the simplest situations, a formal deed will need to be drawn up setting out the relationship between the old and new bodies [see **18.3** for an explanation of deed and the process]. The deed generally transfers the original organisation's assets and liabilities to the new one. Legal advice should be sought before drawing this up.

The deed may:

- include information and assurances about the extent of assets and liabilities transferred (**warranties**);

- give promises by the new organisation, for example to protect members of the old body against later claims (**indemnities**);

- authorise the new organisation to enforce obligations or collect monies due to the old organisation, generally by power of attorney;

- oblige each party to preserve and make available for inspection key records or documents;

- provide for any steps that need to be taken after the transfer date, such as notification to various parties [see **6.6.2**].

Branches of national bodies and some other organisations may have governing documents requiring all assets to be transferred, on dissolution, to the national body or some other named body. To ensure that assets are not lost as a result of such transfer, the recipient body should give prior consent to any such transfer.

6.6.1.1
Property and investments

If the original body owns or occupies land or buildings, they must be transferred by a legal agreement. The transfer of a lease or tenancy agreement [see **58.2.7**] may require consent of the landlord or superior landlord (one above the landlord with whom the organisation has the lease or licence). These transactions should be done by a solicitor.

Investments must also be formally transferred.

Movable property such as equipment, furniture and vehicles can be transferred **by delivery**, simply by handing it over. Some guarantees on equipment are invalidated if ownership is transferred, so legal advice should be taken before transferring any item subject to such conditions.

6.6.1.2
Contracts of employment

If the original organisation employs staff, they must be consulted before any transfer to the new organisation [see **26.4.7**]. Their transfer is covered by the **Transfer of Undertakings (Protection of Employment) Regulations 1981** (TUPE) [see **26.4**], and their contracts, statutory rights and virtually all contractual rights are transferred automatically to the new body [see **26.4.5**].

New contracts do not need to be issued, but employees must be notified in writing of the identity of the new employer. There is no break in employment, so employment rights related to length of service are not affected [see **23.4.6**].

6.6.1.3
Other contracts

If the unincorporated body has equipment leases, hire purchase agreements, service contracts with other people (for example for office cleaning), maintenance contracts (for example to look after computers), or contracts to provide goods or services (for example with clients or a local authority), it must seek the consent of the parties to the contracts in order to transfer the contracts to the new organisation. This is called a **novation agreement**, and ideally contains clauses releasing the original signatories from their obligation for the contract.

However, a supplier or purchaser cannot be forced to agree to such a transfer. If the supplier or purchaser of goods or services will not agree to novation, the new organisation faces some difficult decisions, particularly if the contract cannot be terminated or can be terminated only on disadvantageous terms.

Many organisations simply ignore the issue, on the assumption that problems will not arise so long as the supplier is paid or the purchaser gets whatever it has paid for. But problems can arise if the organisation does not meet its obligations. The contract cannot be enforced against the new organisation because it is not legally a party to it and has not taken on any obligation for it, so the original signatories could find themselves liable.

One solution is to create a deed by which the new organisation promises to indemnify the original signatories against any claim and which appoints the new organisation as an agent with power to enforce the original signatories' rights. Whether this is entirely effective will depend on the wording of the original agreement.

6.6.1.4
Funding arrangements

Grant-aid agreements, service agreements, contracts and other funding arrangements under which the original organisation provides services must be transferred to the new organisation. This must be discussed with funders/purchasers prior to making any final decision to incorporate, because in most cases, consent of the funder or purchaser will be needed. This is, in effect, a form of novation [see **6.6.1.3**].

6.6.1.5
Gift aid and covenants

Provided the new organisation is essentially the same as the old, donors with deeds of covenant and current gift aid declarations should be notified of the change. The deeds and declarations can simply be transferred provided the donors are notified and do not object.

If the organisation has changed its name or objects, donors with gift aid declarations should be asked to make new declarations. Donors with deeds of covenant should assign (transfer) the deed to the new organisation by deed, or replace it with a gift aid declaration and standing order. Where the organisation's objects have changed, income from assigned covenants should be ringfenced and used only for the original objects.

Advice is available from Inland Revenue (Charities) [see end of **chapter 46**].

6.6.1.6
Legacies

Legacies to an unincorporated charity will generally take effect as a gift to a successor incorporated charity, provided both charities' objects are the same. However if the successor body has different objects, or if the legacy is worded in a way that precludes it being given to any body other than the original one, the gift may fail. Organisations should seek to ensure that known legators make new wills or codicils, and should take legal advice about safeguarding legacies from unknown donors or those who do not change their wills.

6.6.1.7
Bank accounts

All bank, building society and other types of accounts must be in the full registered name of the new organisation, exactly as it is on the certificate of incorporation (if a company) or certificate of registration (if an IPS). Even where the new organisation has exactly the same name as the old, accounts will generally be closed and new ones opened.

If the new body is a charitable company with annual income over £10,000 and does not have 'charity' or 'charitable' as part of its name, its cheques must say 'registered charity' [see **16.1**].

6.6.1.8
Insurances

Insurances must be transferred to the new organisation, or the old policies cancelled and new ones taken out. It may be necessary to continue some of the old policies, if there is any risk of potential liability relating to that insurance. It is essential to take advice from the insurers and a legal advisor on these matters.

6.6.1.9
Debts and indemnities

There is always the possibility of liabilities or claims against the old organisation. But having transferred all its assets to the new company or IPS, there will be no funds to meet these. To avoid the risk of personal liability, the old organisation should obtain an indemnity for current and former members of the organisation and its governing body.

In drawing up the terms of this indemnity, especially any limitation of liability, there is a conflict of interest between the new and old organisations. Careful drafting will be necessary, and in some situations the members or governing body members of the old organisation may want to take independent legal advice.

Occasionally an organisation in financial difficulties wishes to transfer its assets and liabilities to a new company or IPS. It cannot do this if the transferred liabilities will exceed the transferred assets and the new organisation does not have adequate assets of its own to cover the difference. In this situation the new organisation would be insolvent, and it is not permissible to set up an insolvent company or IPS.

6.6.1.10
Membership

There is no way that membership can be automatically transferred, so members of the original organisation must apply for membership of the new body and be entered in a new register of members [see **16.3.2** and **16.4.1**]. Considerable publicity may be needed to reassure members that the organisation is still essentially the same even though it will have a new legal structure.

6.6.1.11
Policies and procedures

The new organisation must formally adopt (or change) all of the original organisation's policies, procedures, activities etc. This can be done through a minuted decision at the first meeting of the directors of the new organisation [see **6.3.12**].

6.6.1.12
Written materials

New stationery, cheques, leaflets, posters and other written materials must be produced with the required information [see **16.1**]. Printed stickers with the new information can be used, so long as they completely cover all reference to the old name and/or charity number. It is unlawful to continue to use stationery with the old charity number, or without the new company/IPS number, charity status (if appropriate) and other required information.

6.6.2
Notification of incorporation

Accounts for gas, electricity, telephone, non-domestic rates and credit cards, as well as accounts with contractors, advisors, suppliers etc have to be transferred to the new company's name. Inland Revenue (for corporation tax registration, PAYE and national insurance, and tax recovery) must be notified. If the organisation is registered for VAT, Customs and Excise must be notified. All other relevant registration bodies must also be notified.

Even if the new company or IPS is going to have exactly the same name as the existing organisation all these notifications must be made, because everyone who does business with the new organisation or who may have any claim against it must know that they are now dealing with an incorporated body rather than an unincorporated organisation.

A protective measure is to advertise the change in the *London Gazette*, which effectively gives notice of the change to everyone. A solicitor can advise on this.

Failure to take the above steps or to provide notification of the change may mean that a personal liability remains for individuals. A supplier whose bill was not paid, for example, could say they thought they were still supplying the unincorporated organisation, and could claim against the person(s) who authorised an order or contract rather than claiming against the new company.

6.6.3
The process

The initial discussions for all these steps can be undertaken well in advance and the paperwork can be drawn up, but no date should be set for any of the transfers until:

- it is clear that there are no adverse consequences;
- if required, the Charity Commission has authorised the transfer of assets to the new body [see **57.12**];
- the new organisation has been registered by Companies House or Mutual Societies Registration;
- the new organisation has passed at a directors' meeting or a general meeting of its members an ordinary resolution [see **17.4.7** for procedure] to accept the transfer on the agreed terms.

The first meeting of the governing body of the new organisation should formally deal with all the matters normally considered at an ordinary first meeting [see **6.3.12**].

It is important to remember that even where the new organisation seamlessly carries on the previous body's function, it is legally a completely new and separate body. So not only do the tangible assets and liabilities need to be transferred, but the new body must also re-adopt policies, procedures and delegation of responsibilities.

6.6.3.1
Transferring the assets

The original organisation must pass, in accordance with its governing document, a resolution to transfer its assets to the new company or IPS, or must carry out such other procedures as are required by its governing document to make this decision. It may be convenient to do this earlier, perhaps when the decision to become incorporated is first taken. That meeting may resolve not only to form the new incorporated body but also to make the transfer of assets and liabilities and to dissolve the existing body [see below], at a date or dates to be decided by the governing body. Such a resolution may be conditional, for example on consent being given by funders and/or the Charity Commission.

Regardless of when the incorporated body is actually registered, many organisations choose to delay the transfer until the end of the financial year. This makes it easier to prepare accounts.

6.6.3.2
Dissolving the original organisation

To dissolve the original organisation, a resolution must be passed in accordance with its governing document. The accounts of the existing association or trust will have to be prepared up to the date of winding up. If required by funders and/or charity law [see **50.2.12**], those accounts will have to be audited.

When its final accounts have been prepared and if necessary audited, the old organisation holds a final general meeting or takes whatever other steps are necessary under its governing document to accept the accounts and to dissolve itself. If the resolution to dissolve was already passed and the governing body authorised to set the date [see **6.6.3.1**], it may not be necessary to hold this final meeting.

If the original organisation was a charity the Charity Commission must be notified and final accounts filed, so it can be deregistered.

6.6.3.3
Retaining the original organisation as a shell

If the original body is being retained, for example to ensure legacies are not lost, its governing document is likely to need amendment to enable the organisation to function in its new role. The new company, for example, may become the sole member of the original body, so procedures for meetings, quorums etc are likely to need to be changed.

6.7
IPS/COMPANY CONVERSION

Changing from an industrial and provident society to a company, or a company to an IPS, does not give any advantage in terms of limited liability and permanent succession [see **2.1.1**], since both are incorporated. There are, however, other reasons to consider such a change.

Specialist legal advice should be sought before undertaking a transfer or conversion between a company and IPS or *vice versa*.

6.7.1
Changing from IPS to company

An IPS might wish to become a company because:

- a private company only needs one member plus a company secretary, while an IPS needs a minimum of three individual members;

- an IPS which is a genuine cooperative [see **2.4.1**] might want to stop being a co-op;

- a charitable community benefit IPS [see **2.4.2**] might want to register with the Charity Commission and get a charity registration number, which it cannot do as an IPS.

The ways of doing this, as set out in the IPS legislation, are:

- by setting up a company and then **amalgamating** the IPS with it;

- by setting up a company and then transferring all the IPS's assets and liabilities to it (this is called **transferring engagements**); *or*

- by **converting** the IPS to a company.

Industrial and Provident Societies Act 1965 s.52

In amalgamation and transfer the IPS and new company exist side by side; in conversion the IPS becomes the company.

The IPS must pass a special resolution [see **17.5.2** for procedure]. If the IPS is amalgamating or transferring engagements, all property owned by the IPS must be legally transferred to the company. If it is converting, this is not necessary. The wording of the resolution is crucial, and should be approved in advance by the registrar of friendly societies to ensure it will be acceptable.

Housing associations and credit unions which are registered as IPSs cannot amalgamate with, transfer engagements to, or convert to a company. *Housing Associations Act 1985 s.21(2);*

Credit Unions Act 1979 s.22

6.7.2
Changing from company to IPS

Reasons for changing from a company to an IPS might include:

* the regulatory requirements are less burdensome [see **2.4.6**];

* a charitable IPS is not registered with the Charity Commission and is not for most purposes under the scrutiny of the Commission;

* the statutory status of 'democratic society for the benefit of the community' may sound more ideologically acceptable than 'private company limited by guarantee without a share capital';

* an IPS's register of members does not have to be open to the general public, as a company's does [see **16.3.2**];

* an IPS's register of directors does not have to be open to the general public, as a company's does, and is not open to public scrutiny the way a company's is at Companies House [see **16.3.4**];

* for large membership organisations the costs of a company can be considerable, because accounts and notices of all general meetings must be sent by post to all company members (unless members have agreed that they can be posted on a website or sent by email; see **17.4.4** and **50.3.5**), while an IPS can simply advertise in the press or at its place of business that accounts are available or that a general meeting is to be held, and paperwork only has to be sent to members who ask for it. This could be a significant factor for mass movements or other very large organisations.

A company which becomes an IPS cannot use the word 'company' in its new name. *Industrial and Provident Societies Act 1965 s.53(6)*

To convert, the procedures set out in the **Industrial and Provident Societies Act** s.53 must be followed. If unamended model rules are not being used, the rules are agreed by Mutual Societies Registration, as with a new registration [see **6.4.1** and **6.4.2**]. The company passes a special resolution [see **17.4.7** for procedure] agreeing to convert into an IPS and appointing three company members to sign the new IPS rules with the secretary. The resolution and rules are sent to Mutual Societies Registration When the new IPS is registered, a copy of the resolution and the IPS registration are sent to Companies House. As soon as Companies House registers the special resolution, the conversion takes effect.

6.8
CHANGING FROM INCORPORATED TO UNINCORPORATED

A decision to deregister as a company or industrial and provident society and continue operating as an unincorporated association is extremely unusual and should never be taken lightly, because the members of the organisation and its governing body will be giving up the protection of limited liability [see **2.1.1**].

The organisation will have to wind up as required under company or IPS law [see **21.4** or **21.6**], all assets and liabilities will need to be transferred to the members of the new governing body or holding trustees [see **6.6.1**], and if the organisation is charitable, it will have to apply for charitable status as a new body. Particular care may need to be given to the appointment of holding trustees to take on any property or investments [see **18.4**].

Chapter 7
REGISTERING AS A CHARITY

For sources of further information see page 12.
Double-underlined section headings indicate additions or significant changes since the first edition.

7.1 WHO HAS TO REGISTER

7.1.1 Compulsory registration

Every organisation in England and Wales which meets the legal definition of a charity [see **3.1**] must register with the Charity Commission unless it is explicitly exempt or excepted from registration [see **7.1.2** and **7.1.3**].
Charities Act 1993 s.3(7)(a)

An organisation is likely to be charitable and have to register if:

- all of its main purposes are charitable as defined by the Charity Commission and the courts [see **4.3**];

- it is set up with the intention of benefiting the community or the public, rather than simply benefiting private individuals;

- all money raised by the organisation will be used only for the organisation's purposes; *and*

- its income is more than £1,000 per year, or it occupies rateable premises or has permanent endowment [see **7.1.3.1**].

An organisation which is charitable but is not registered, and is not exempt or excepted from registration, is unlikely to receive the tax benefits to which it is entitled. If the Commission becomes aware of the charity's existence it may direct the members of the governing body to register; failure to do so can lead to contempt of court proceedings.

Being 'a charity' is only one aspect of an organisation. The organisation is also defined by whether it is an unincorporated association [see **1.2**], a trust [see **1.3**], a company limited by guarantee [see **2.3**] or an industrial and provident society [see **2.4**].

In registering as a charity, there are three separate processes:

- drawing up the governing document (constitution) [see **chapter 5**];

- formally establishing the organisation as an association, trust, company or industrial and provident society [see **chapter 6**]; *and*

- registering the organisation as a charity.

7.1.2
Exempt charities

Exempt charities are subject to the jurisdiction of other supervisory bodies. They include charitable industrial and provident societies [see **2.4.4**], the statutory governing body of foundation and voluntary schools, and some universities, medical schools and national museums.

Charities Act 1993 s.3(5)(a), sch.2

Exempt charities:

- do not register with the Charity Commission;
- must keep proper accounting records [see **49.3**], but generally prepare accounts under legislation other than the Charities Act;

ss.45, 46(1)

- do not need to comply with most Charities Act requirements on the sale, leasing, mortgage or disposal of land [see **57.11** and **57.12**]; *and*

ss.36(10), 37, 38(7), 39(1)

- are not subject to inquiry by the Commission under s.8 of the Act [see **3.5.9**], nor does the Commission have the power to take steps to protect the charity's property. *ss.8(1), 18(16)*

The Charity Commission can, if asked to do so by the charity or by order of the court, make orders and schemes [see **3.5.4** and **3.5.5**] in relation to exempt charities. *s.16(4)*

Exempt charities gain formal recognition of their charitable status by applying to Inland Revenue (Charities) [see end of **chapter 46**].

7.1.3
Excepted charities

The Home Secretary can issue regulations and the Charity Commission can issue orders **excepting** some charities from the need to register.

s.3(5)(b),(13)

Some excepted charities do not have to register because they are registered elsewhere. These include some small funds of the Scout and Guide Associations, some armed forces charities, and places of worship registered under the **Places of Worship Registration Act 1855**. Charities which hold only property (no other assets) for foundation schools and voluntary schools which are now in the state sector are excepted. Some religious charities are excepted until 1 October 2002. *Charities Act 1993 s.3(5),(14); Schools Standards and Framework Act 1998 s.23*

At the time of writing (early 2001) the Home Office and Charity Commission were considering widening the types of excepted charity.

An excepted charity:

- does not have to register with the Commission but may, if the Commission agrees, register voluntarily and thereby get a charity number; *s.3(2)*
- if voluntarily registered, may at any time ask to be removed from the register; *s.3(2)*
- must keep proper accounting records and produce annual accounts [see **49.3** and **50.2**]; *ss.41-42*
- if not registered, may not have to comply with the Charities Act requirements on examination and audit of accounts, unless this is required by the governing document or funders [see **50.2.12**];

ss.43-44, 46(3)

- does not have to submit annual accounts to the Commission, unless specifically required to do so by the Commission or unless voluntarily registered with the Commission and having an income over £10,000;

s.46(4)

- is subject to Charities Act requirements on sale, leasing, mortgage or disposal of land [see **57.11** and **57.12**]; *and*
- is subject to the Commission's supervisory powers [see **3.5.4-3.5.10**].

7.1.3.1
Very small charities

Excepted charities also include some **very small charities**. A charity is very small if:

- its income from all sources is £1,000 or less per year;
- it has no permanent endowment (money which under the terms of the governing document or terms of a trust cannot be spent as income, or land or buildings which cannot be sold or whose proceeds of sale may not be used as income); *and*
- it does not use or occupy rateable land or buildings.   *s.3(5)(c)*

A very small charity which does not want to register voluntarily with the Commission should simply follow the steps for setting up an unincorporated association [see **6.1**] or trust [see **6.2**]. Care should be taken to monitor its income and to register when it exceeds £1,000 per year, or when it occupies premises or receives any permanent endowment.

7.2
THE REGISTRATION PROCESS

Organisations should obtain a registration pack from the Charity Commission at an early stage in setting up, but do not apply for registration as a charity until they have adopted their governing document [see **chapter 5**] and, if necessary, have had the trust deed executed and stamped or have registered as a company [see **chapter 6**].

Assistance from an experienced solicitor or voluntary sector support body can make registration much smoother, especially if the organisation is not using a standard or model governing document [see **7.2.2**] or its objects are unusual or on the fringes of what might be considered charitable in law [see **4.6.2**]. In such situations it may be advisable to discuss the proposed objects or activities with the Commission prior to adopting the governing document, so there is less likelihood of it having to be amended during the registration process.

7.2.1
Promoters

The person or persons setting up the charity are sometimes called the **promoters**. It is their responsibility to:

- make the initial contact with the Charity Commission [see **page 12**] to get the necessary information (especially Charity Commission booklet CC21 *Registering as a Charity*) and registration pack;
- choose a legal structure [see **chapters 1** and **2**];
- if appropriate, obtain model governing documents [see **7.2.2**] from the Charity Law Association [see **page 12**] or the Charity Commission, an approved standard governing document [see **7.2.2**], or sample governing documents from other organisations with the same legal structure (association, trust or company), similar objects and a similar organisational and membership structure;
- get legal and professional advice, if necessary [see **60.10.3** for how to find an appropriate legal advisor];
- draw up the governing document.

Anyone may be a promoter. But if they are to be the first trustees (governing body members) they must generally be at least 18 years old and must not be disqualified from acting as a charity trustee [see **11.3.2**].

7.2.2
Standard and model governing documents

The registration pack includes guidance on the minimum requirements for a governing document, and suggests that if a standard or model governing document is adopted the registration process will be easier.

The Commission has approved standard governing documents as **precedents** for various types of organisation. These are available from umbrella or parent bodies such as national Mind, Age Concern, Community Matters (for community associations), ACRE (for village halls), the National Housing Federation, and a wide range of other organisations. The registration pack contains a list.

If a standard governing document is not available or is not suitable, model governing documents for charitable unincorporated associations, trusts and companies are available from the Commission and from the Charity Law Association [see **page 12**].

There is no obligation to use a standard or model governing document. However, organisations which try to draw up their own without legal advice are likely to find their registration is a lengthy process, and they may have to amend their newly adopted governing document before the Charity Commission will accept it for registration.

**7.2.3
Establishing the
organisation**

To establish the organisation:

- an **association** must formally adopt its governing document at a meeting of the members [see **6.1.4**];
- a **trust** must execute and stamp its trust deed [see **6.2.2**]; *or*
- a **company** must register with Companies House [see **6.3.6-6.3.8**].

**7.2.4
Application form
and supporting
information**

After the organisation has been established, the trustees must fill in the Charity Commission's application (**APP1**). The form is intended to:

- enable the Commissioners to decide whether the organisation's purposes and intended activities are wholly and exclusively charitable [see **4.3**];
- clarify whether the organisation needs to register, or whether it is exempt or excepted from registration [see **7.1.2**];
- ensure the organisation will not duplicate the work of another charity;
- ensure the governing document adequately covers everything it needs to;
- identify any problems which should be sorted out;
- obtain information to be held on the register of charities [see **3.5.1**].

The application form and two copies of the governing document are sent to the Commission along with details of the organisation's bank account(s) and any other information which might help the Commission in the registration process, including:

- minutes of the meetings held to set up the organisation;
- leaflets, newspaper articles or other publicity about the organisation and its activities;
- a list of planned activities for the next 12 months;
- longer-term plans, if available;
- for new organisations, evidence of its actual or anticipated income;
- for organisations already in existence, annual accounts for the last three years;
- accounts of any other organisations which are, or will be, controlled by the organisation which is registering;
- contracts with any fundraisers or others who are not directly employed by the organisation but are paid to raise money for it;
- copy of the certificate of incorporation, if the organisation is registered as a company limited by guarantee.

Charities engaging in various specified activities should supply additional information. For example:

- research charities must give full details of how the research is to be conducted, supervised and evaluated;
- fundraising charities should give details of the fundraising methods to be used;
- charities engaging in counselling must give details of the proposed counsellors' qualifications or training.

The organisation will often be asked to supply a business plan setting out its proposed activities, expenditure budget and anticipated income.

All the charity trustees must complete a **declaration** (form **DEC1**) in which they certify that they are willing to act as charity trustees, are not disqualified from acting as a charity trustee [see **11.3.2**], and have read specified booklets supplied with the registration pack.

If the trustees do not understand any question or are not certain how to reply or what information to submit, they should seek legal advice or contact the Charity Commission's registration department. It is an offence knowingly or recklessly to supply false information on the questionnaire or in any other way. *Charities Act 1993 s.11(1)*

The Commission may ask for additional information, and may ask to meet with the trustees. This is because the Commission does not have enough information to be certain that the organisation is indeed charitable in law, or to explore any other concerns or ambiguities.

**7.2.5
Consultation with
the Inland Revenue**

Because a charity is entitled to tax benefits [see **3.2.1**], the Inland Revenue has the right to object to its registration. If the Commission thinks this might happen it consults the Inland Revenue at this stage, before registration.

The Inland Revenue stands to lose money if an organisation is registered as a charity, so it is sometimes more strict than the Charity Commission in defining whether a proposed purpose is or is not charitable. It is also particularly concerned about a charity's powers to trade. Although the decision about whether an organisation is charitable is the Commission's or ultimately the High Court's, the Commission takes into account the Revenue's views.

**7.2.6
Consideration of the
application**

The registration process can be lengthy and difficult. If the Commission is not satisfied that the organisation is being established for exclusively charitable purposes, it may propose changes to the objects. These suggestions are open to negotiation, but this is most effectively done by an experienced solicitor. If the organisation agrees to make these changes, either before or after negotiation, it will have to amend its governing document [see **5.5** for the procedure]. Otherwise it will have to resign itself to not being allowed to register as a charity, or seek a review or appeal against the Commission's decision [see **7.2.9**].

Changes to internal procedures may also be suggested. These changes reflect the Commission's views on good governance, but may not reflect the charity's values and priorities, and may not be in its best interests in the longer term. Failure to comply with these suggestions should not affect registration, unless the Commission considers that the changes are necessary to ensure the organisation is exclusively charitable.

**7.2.6.1
Children's charities**

Since implementation of the **Protection of Children Act 1999** [see **26.3.3**], the Commission checks proposed trustees of children's charities, to ensure they are not on the Department of Health or Department for Education and Skills lists of people considered unsuitable to work with children, and checks that they have not been banned by the courts from working with children.

**7.2.7
Decision of the
Commission**

After its consideration and, if necessary, discussions with the trustees the Charity Commission will inform the trustees that:

- the organisation has been registered as a charity;
- the organisation is not set up for exclusively charitable purposes and therefore cannot be registered; *or*
- the application is complex and will require further consideration.

**7.2.8
Entry on the
register**

When the charity is registered it receives its registration number and a certificate (**form RE5**) setting out the details as entered in the index to the register. This certificate should be kept in a safe place.

Entry on the register is conclusive proof for all purposes that the organisation is legally a charity. *Charities Act 1993 s.4(1)*

7.2.9
Reviews and appeals against decisions

If registration is refused, there is an internal review procedure [see **3.5.12**]. If that fails, the organisation can further appeal internally to the Board of the Charity Commissioners. To make an appeal against a refusal to register on the grounds of charitable status, the organisation must have enough assets to make it eligible for compulsory registration, so must have permanent endowment or an annual income of at least £1,000. For organisations below this level, an appeal can be made against a decision not to consider the organisation for registration.

Charities Act 1993 s.4(4) s.4(2)

If the organisation remains dissatisfied after appealing to the Board of the Charity Commissioners, an appeal may be brought in the High Court. However few recent appeals have been successful.   *s.4(3)*

Reviews or appeals on questions of charitable status are complex and legal advice is essential

Any person affected by the registration of an organisation may appeal *against* a registration. Objections usually come only from the Inland Revenue or the rating authority.

7.3
AFTER REGISTRATION

7.3.1
Registered status on documents

As soon as it is registered, a charity whose annual income is over £10,000 must include a statement saying that it is a registered charity on all its cheques, most documents for other financial transactions, fundraising materials, and many other documents [see **16.1.4**]. It is an offence to issue cheques and certain documents without the statement, or allow them to be issued. Until new paper and cheques are printed the statement can be handwritten or typed, or put on with a rubber stamp or sticker.

7.3.2
Trustees' duties

All governing body members have a very wide range of common law and statutory duties [see **chapter 13**], but charity trustees have special responsibilities [see **13.3**]. It is each trustee's responsibility to know, understand and comply with these duties, and to take all reasonable steps to ensure the trustee body as a whole complies with them as well.

7.4
LOCAL AUTHORITY REGISTERS, REVIEWS AND REGISTRATION

The Charity Commission is required to provide information about any or all charities in their area to any local borough, district or county council which asks for it. The council may then keep an index of local charities.   *s.76*

Borough, district and county councils have the right to undertake reviews of charities in their area involved in similar types of work, and to make recommendations about the charities to the Commission. This might include, for example, recommendations that small charities be merged. Such reviews cannot be undertaken without the consent of the charities' trustees, and cannot include ecclesiastical charities.   *s.77*

Chapter 8
THE ORGANISATION'S NAME

8.1 CHOOSING A NAME

When choosing a name for an organisation:

- non-charitable associations must not use any name whose use is prohibited [see **8.3**];

- charitable associations, trusts and companies must comply with the rules on charity names [see **8.2**];

- companies and industrial and provident societies, whether charitable or non-charitable, must comply with the rules on company names [see **8.4**].

A charity, company or IPS which does not comply with the relevant rules could be required to change its name.

Any organisation which uses a name which is the same as, or very similar to, another organisation's name could have a claim brought against it for passing off [see **39.5**] or infringement of trade mark rights [see **39.4**].

It is important to choose a name which reflects not only what the organisation is now, but what it might become. There is no point calling it 'Anyville Dance Centre' if in a few years it will be serving a wider geographic area, and will have drama and music activities as well as dance. However the mere fact that the name is Anyville Dance Centre does not stop it from operating outside Anyville or carrying on activities other than dance. It is limited to Anyville and dance only if its objects and area of benefit, as defined in its governing document, are limited in this way [see **4.6**].

8.2
CHARITY NAMES

A registered charity's name must not be the same as, or in the Charity Commission's opinion too like, the name of any other registered or un-registered charity. Names can be checked with the central register of charities on the Charity Commission website or at its offices [see **page 12**].
Charities Act 1993 ss.6(2)(a),(7)

Charities may enter on the register their abbreviated name, informal name or any other **operating name** they use. This helps prevent other charities from using those names as well as the registered name.

A charity's name must not be offensive, give a misleading impression of the charity's purposes or activities, or give a misleading impression that the charity is connected with the government, a local authority, an individual or a group.
s.6(2)(b),(d),(e)

A charity's name needs explicit Charity Commission approval if it includes certain words or expressions:

* *British, England, English, Europe, European, Great Britain, Great British, International, Ireland, Irish, National, Nationwide, North-ern Ireland, Northern Irish, Scotland, Scottish, United Kingdom, Wales* and *Welsh*, which can be used only if they correctly describe the charity's area of benefit;

* *assurance, authority, benevolent, church, official, registered*;

* words suggesting a royal connection;

* *bank, building society, cooperative, friendly society, grant main-tained, industrial and provident society, polytechnic, school, trade union* and *university*, which can be used only if they are legally accurate.   *Charities (Misleading Names) Regulations 1992 [SI 1992/1901]*

A charity must also comply with the requirements for its legal structure [see below and **8.4**].

8.3
TRUSTS AND UNINCORPORATED ASSOCIATIONS

Apart from a few words which are prohibited by specific legislation, a non-charitable trust or unincorporated association can use virtually any name it chooses. A charitable trust or association must comply with charity law requirements [see above].

Organisations should be very careful about using a name already used by another body if there is any risk of an action for **passing off** [see **39.5**] being brought.

It is an offence for an unincorporated body to trade or to carry on a business using a name with *limited, public limited company*, their abbreviations or the Welsh equivalents as the last word. Voluntary organisations should avoid using 'limited' as the last word in their name.
Companies Act 1985 s.34

8.4
COMPANY AND IPS NAMES

Strict rules apply to the names of companies and industrial and provident societies. Detailed information is available from the business names section at Companies House [see **page 12**].

8.4.1
Similarity to other names

The registered (corporate) name of a company or industrial and provi-dent society cannot be **the same as** any other name on the register of company names kept by Companies House.
ss.26, 714(1)(g)

In deciding whether a name is the same, the following are ignored:

* punctuation, accent marks and spaces;

* *the* as the first word of a name;

* *company, and company, co, limited, ltd, unlimited, public limited company* etc as the last word of a name;

* *and* and *&*.

As part of the company or IPS registration process, Companies House consults the register and advises if a name has to be changed. However it is sensible to check the register before reaching the registration stage. This can be done on the Companies House website, in person at Companies House or at main reference libraries, or by ringing Companies House.

If a company is a registered charity, its name must not be too similar to that of any other charity [see **8.2**].

8.4.1.1
Using symbols in names

Symbols such as @, which are not ordinary punctuation, are treated as being different from their word equivalent. So *Care@Home* is not 'the same as' *Care at Home*, and one can be registered even if the other is already on the register.

8.4.1.2
'Too like' names

A company or IPS name is rejected only if it is 'the same as' one on the register. Sometimes, therefore, a name is registered which is very similar to another name—such as *Care@Home* and *Care at Home*. If the new organisation's name is **too like** one which is already on the register, the original company or IPS can object to the registration within 12 months. If the similarity could cause confusion, the new company or IPS could be required to change its name [see **8.7.1**.] It is sensible to check beforehand for similar names as well as names which are 'the same'.

Companies Act 1985 s.28(2)

8.4.2
Misleading and sensitive names

A company or industrial and provident society cannot use a name which:

- in the opinion of the secretary of state for trade and industry is offensive or constitutes a criminal offence;

- includes certain **sensitive words and expressions**, as set out in the **Company and Business Names Regulations 1981** *[SI 1981/1685]*, without authorisation from the secretary of state for trade and industry or other authorities; *or*

- contains words or expressions whose use is governed by other legislation. *ss.26(1)(d),(e), 26(2), 29*

An IPS's name cannot include the word *company* in a way which implies that it is registered under the Companies Acts.

8.4.2.1
Approval from the secretary of state

Some of the 'sensitive' words which need approval from the secretary of state are:

- anything which might give the erroneous impression that the organisation is connected with the government or a local authority;

- *British, English* and similar national and international words, as on the list for charities [see **8.2**];

- *board, council* and *authority*, because they imply government patronage or sponsorship;

- *association, federation, society, institute, institution*, because they imply pre-eminence or representative status;

- words which imply specific objects or functions, such as *benevolent, charter, cooperative, foundation, friendly society, fund, group, register, registered, trade union, trust*.

The complete list is available on the Companies House website or in GBF2 *Company Names*, available free from Companies House or its website [see **page 12**]. An organisation intending to use one of the words requiring authorisation may need supporting evidence, for example a letter from a government department or large organisation confirming that the new organisation is genuinely national or pre-eminent, or documentation showing that it has already used the word in its name for a long time and should therefore be allowed to continue using it. The supporting evidence and a letter of application should be sent to the secretary of state for trade and industry c/o Companies House.

8.4.2.2
Approval from the relevant body

Some words need approval from the defined **relevant body** before applying to the secretary of state [see GBF2 for details]:

- *charity* or *charitable* need authorisation, before the memorandum and articles are sent to Companies House, from the Charity Commission in London if the organisation is planning to register as a charity, and from the Charity Commission in Liverpool if the organisation is not intending to register as a charity;

- most words with a medical connection, including *abortion, health centre, health service, nursing home, pregnancy, termination;*

- words implying a royal connection (so the *Prince of Wales* Road Community Centre or *Windsor* Association of Disabled People would need consent, even though they are located in those places);

- words implying a specific function such as *police, polytechnic, special school, university.*

8.4.2.3
Included in other legislation

Some words are covered by other legislation, and cannot be authorised by the secretary of state. Any organisation wanting to use one of these words should consult a solicitor prior to contacting the relevant body [see GBF2 for details]. A name which includes one of these words will not be approved as a company name without the relevant authorisation:

- *Red Cross;*

- *credit union, building society, patent agent* and *patent office;*

- *architect,* words relating to *bank* and *banking,* words relating to *insurance* and *assurance;*

- words implying medical qualifications such as *dentist, optician, pharmacist, radiographer.*

The names of a few associations (British Legion, Girl Guides Association, National Society for the Prevention of Cruelty to Children, Royal Life Saving Society, Scout Association, Venerable Order of Saint John of Jerusalem) are protected under the **Chartered Associations (Protection of Names and Uniforms) Act 1926.**

8.4.2.4
Misleading names

As well as the use of sensitive words and expressions, a company or IPS needs to be careful not to use a seriously misleading name. If it does, it could be required to change the name [see **8.7.1**].

8.4.3
Use of 'limited' and 'unlimited'

The name of a company or industrial and provident society cannot include the word *limited, unlimited* or *public limited company,* or their abbreviations or Welsh equivalents, anywhere except at the end of the name. *Companies Act 1985 s.26(1),(2)*

8.4.3.1
Companies

Public limited companies must end their name with *public limited company* (or *plc*). Most private limited companies must end their name with *limited, ltd* (with no full stop) or *ltd.* (with a full stop), or with *cyfyngedig* if they are Welsh. *s.25*

8.4.3.2
Companies exempt from having to use 'limited'

A private company limited by guarantee does not have to use *limited* or *cyfyngedig* at the end of its name if:

- its objects are the promotion of commerce, art, science, education, religion, charity or any profession;

- its memorandum of association requires the company's profits or other income to be used to promote its objects [see **5.4.9**];

- its memorandum or articles prohibit payments of dividends to its members [see **5.4.9**]; *and*

- its memorandum or articles require all the company's assets to be transferred, if the company is wound up, to another body with similar objects or to one whose objects are the promotion of charity. *s.30(3)*

The requirements are explained in more detail in GBF2 *Company Names*, available from Companies House [see **page 12**].

If a company does not want to use the word *limited* in its name on registration, the solicitor or other person helping to set up the company, or a director or the company secretary named in form 10 [see **6.3.5**], must fill in **form 30(5)(a)**, declaring that the company meets these criteria, and swear and sign it before a commissioner for oaths, notary public, justice of the peace or solicitor with powers conferred on a commissioner for oaths (fee £5 as at 1/4/01).

A company which does not use *limited, ltd* or the Welsh equivalent at the end of its name must disclose that it has limited liability on its stationery and many other documents [see **16.1.1**].

A company which does not use *limited* cannot change its memorandum or articles in any way which would mean that s.30(3) no longer applies. If it acts in ways which mean that s.30(3) no longer applies, it can be required to change its name to include *limited*.

A qualifying company which is registered with *limited* and subsequently decides it does not want to use it must pass a special resolution [see **17.4.7** for procedure]. A director or secretary swears **form 30(5)(c)** in the same way as 30(5)(a) and submits it with the change of name fee (£10 as at 1/4/01). *Companies Act 1985 s.31(1),(2)*

8.4.3.3
Industrial and provident societies

An industrial and provident society must end its name with *limited*. It cannot use the abbreviation *ltd* or *cyfyngedig* when registering its name.
Industrial and Provident Societies Act 1965 s.5(2)

Voluntary sector IPSs may apply to the registrar of friendly societies [see **page 12**] for exemption from having to use *limited* as part of their name. This will be allowed only if the society is financially viable, so the society may need to be registered with *limited* and apply later for it to be dropped. *s.5(5)*

8.5
USING OTHER NAMES

8.5.1
Company and IPS business names

Companies are legal entities which must legally be identified by their full name (called **registered name** or **corporate name**). This name must be used exactly as it is on the certificate of registration. It is not permitted to abbreviate words which are written out in the corporate name, or write out words which are abbreviated. Nor is it allowed to put in or take out commas or full stops, or to use & instead of *and* or *vice versa*. An exception is that from September 2000 all names are shown on the certificate in uppercase (capital) letters, and the capitalisation can be ignored when using the registered name.

The rule is slightly less strict for industrial and provident societies, which are allowed to abbreviate *limited* to *ltd* when using their registered name. *s.5(2)*

Many companies and IPSs operate under abbreviations or names other than their registered name, or allow projects or parts of the organisation to operate under other names. Any name other than the full registered name—even if the difference is only very slight—is a **business name** (often called **trading name** or **operating name**). It is called a business or trading name even if the organisation is not actually carrying on a business or trade.

For example if the registered name is 'The West Anyville Neighbourhood Team Limited', the following would be business names:

- The West Anyville Neighbourhood Team (without 'Limited');
- West Anyville Neighbourhood Team;
- WANT;
- Anyville Under Fives or any other name used for all or some of its work instead of, or in addition to, its registered name.

Members of the governing body and staff or volunteers who enter into agreements on behalf of the organisation must be aware of the difference between the registered name and business names. The consequences of getting this wrong can be serious:

- a contract signed under a business or abbreviated name is not legally a contract with the company or IPS, but is a contract with the signatories for which they are personally liable;

- a cheque which does not have the registered name on it is, in effect, personally guaranteed by the person who signs the cheque.

**8.5.1.1
Permitted business names**

A business name cannot end in *limited* or *ltd*, so 'WANT Limited' cannot be used. In other words, a company or IPS can use *limited* or any variation as the last word *only* in its registered name.

A word needing approval from the secretary of state or other body for use in a registered name [see **8.4.2**] also needs approval for use in a business name. *Business Names Act 1985 ss.2, 3*

The rules about 'same as' and 'too like' names do not apply, so the Business Names Act does not prevent a company or IPS from using a business name which is the same as, or very similar to, a registered name or someone else's trading name. But this opens the organisation to the risk of legal action for passing off [see **39.5**]. When choosing a trading name, it is sensible to check the register of company names to be sure the name is not too similar to a registered name.

The registered name must be on certain documents [see **16.1.1**] and outside the organisation's registered office and any premises where it carries on its work [see **15.1.2**]. If the business name is also included on these documents or outside the premises, it must be clear which is the registered name.

**8.5.2
Voluntary registration of business names**

A business name does not have to be registered in any way. It is, however, possible to register it with a commercial **business names registration agency**. The agency will:

- check that the business name is not the same as any other registered company name;

- on payment of an additional fee, check that the business name does not infringe any UK trade mark rights [see **39.4**];

- undertake legal proceedings if anyone else uses the business name in a way which constitutes passing off.

Such registration is optional and is not linked in any way with any official registration.

**8.5.3
Trusts and unincorporated associations**

The **Business Names Act 1985** does not apply to trusts or unincorporated associations.

The names of non-charitable trusts and unincorporated associations are not registered with any registration authority. It is however possible to register the name voluntarily with a commercial business names registration agency [see above]. This might reassure the organisation that it is not using someone else's corporate or business name, and can provide it with a way to take action if someone else is passing off as the organisation. However the organisation can check the company names register itself [see **8.4.1**], and can take appropriate legal advice when and if it needs to take action against someone passing off.

**8.5.4
Charity operating names**

A charity which uses any names other than its full registered name should register these **operating names** or **working names** with the Charity Commission. This includes acronyms and names used for fundraising purposes, and could include project names.

8.6
PROTECTING A NAME

Logos, names, designs etc are part of the organisation's **intellectual property** and as such are valuable assets which should be protected against exploitation and unauthorised use [see **39.9**].

Organisations' names, logos, designs, brand names, symbols, slogans, abbreviations etc can generally be registered as **trade marks** (for goods) or **service marks** (for services) [see **39.4**].

A logo, design, symbol or other visual representation of the organisation's name is automatically **copyright** if it has any artistic merit, however small [see **39.2**]. But a name cannot, in itself, be copyright.

8.7
CHANGING A NAME

Changing an organisation's name does not change its legal status, so it is not necessary to undertake novation agreements [see **18.10.1**] or other formal procedures to transfer the assets, liabilities and contracts to the organisation with the new name. Nor does a name change alter any legal proceedings the organisation is involved in.

It is, however, important to notify everyone with whom the organisation has any dealings, and to notify the name to the Land Registry if the organisation owns any registered land [see **56.6.4**].

8.7.1
Companies

A company may change its registered name by a special resolution at any general meeting [see **17.4.7** for procedure] so long as the name meets all the usual requirements for a company name [see **8.4**].

Companies Act 1985 s.28(1)

A charitable company should check with the Charity Commission to ensure the new name meets charity requirements [see **8.2**]. A company which is a registered social landlord will require consent from the Housing Corporation.

A fee (£10 as at 1/4/01) is payable when a special resolution to change the company's name is submitted to Companies House. This must be submitted within 15 days after the resolution has been passed. The name change takes effect from the date Companies House issues a revised certificate of incorporation, which is usually within five working days of receiving the documents. For an additional fee (£80 as at 1/4/01) the certificate can be issued on the same day the documents are received at any Companies House office [see **page 12**].

The old name can continue to be used as a business name [see **8.5.1**] but it must not be used with *limited* or *ltd* at the end. Any new documents, including cheques, which are required to include the registered name must be changed to the new name.

8.7.2
Industrial and provident societies

An IPS must have consent from the registrar of friendly societies [see **page 12**] before it can change its name. Approval is usually granted only if there is a good reason for the name change.

Industrial and Provident Societies Act 1965 s.5(3)(b)

If there is a procedure in the society's rules for passing a resolution to change its name, this procedure must be followed. If there is no such provision in the rules, the usual procedures for amending the rules must be followed. *s.5(3)(a)*

The new name is registered on **form C** (fee £180 as at 1/4/01) and is acknowledged on **form K**.

8.7.3
Trusts

If a trust deed includes a procedure for alteration, the name can be changed in this way. This will involve passing a resolution of the trustees and preparing a **supplemental deed** [see **18.3**]. If there is no procedure for amending the trust deed, a charitable trust can approach the Charity Commission for a scheme [see **5.5.4**].

**8.7.4
Unincorporated
associations**

If the constitution of an unincorporated association includes a procedure for amendment, the name can be changed in this way. If there is no such procedure, the name of a non-charitable association can be changed only by agreement of all the members, and a charitable association requires a Charity Commission scheme [see **5.5.4**].

Abbatt v Treasury Solicitor [1969] 1 WLR 1575,1583

**8.7.5
Charities**

Change of a charity's name does not require the Charity Commission's prior consent. But it is sensible to check with it beforehand, since the change must be notified to the Commission anyway and it can then require a change in the new name. *Charities Act 1993 s.3(7)(b)*

The notification is made by sending the Commission:

* for a charitable association, a copy of the resolution and the minutes of the meeting at which it was passed, signed by the chairperson or secretary to certify that it is an accurate copy;

* for a charitable trust, a certified copy of the supplemental deed;

* for a charitable company, a copy of the new certificate issued by Companies House.

If a charitable trust or association does not have the power to amend its governing document, the Commission has to make a scheme [see **5.5.4**].

So long as its objects are not changed, a charity which changes its name can still retain all property given to it under its previous name.

**8.8
COMPULSORY
CHANGE OF NAME**

Any organisation can be required by the court to change its registered name or any other name it uses if it is found guilty of passing off or infringement of trade mark rights [see **39.4** and **39.5**].

**8.8.1
Companies**

The secretary of state for trade and industry can require a company to change its registered name:

* within 12 months of registration, if the name is the same as or too like the name of another registered company;

* within five years of registration, if the company gave misleading information at the time of registration;

* at any time, if the name is so misleading that it could cause harm to the public. *Companies Act 1985 ss.28(2),(3), 32(1)*

**8.8.2
Charities**

The Charity Commission can require a registered charity to change its name within 12 months of registration, if its name is the same as or too like the name of another charity, whether registered or not.

Charities Act 1993 s.6(2)(a),(3)

It can require any charity other than an exempt charity [see **7.1.2**] to change its name at any time if the name:

* gives a misleading impression of the charity's purposes or activities;

* misleadingly includes one of the words in the **Charities (Misleading Names) Regulations 1992** [see **8.2**];

* gives a misleading impression of its connections with the government, a local authority, an individual or a group; *or*

* is offensive. *s.6(2)(b)-(e)*

If the charity is required to change its name, the trustees can choose the new name but it must be approved by the Commission. *s.6(1)*

If a charitable company is required by the Commission to change its name this can be done by a resolution of the directors. The name change must be notified to Companies House in the usual way [see **8.7.1**].

s.6(7)

Chapter 9
BRANCHES, SUBSIDIARIES, PARTNERSHIPS AND MERGERS

Topics covered in this chapter

This chapter looks at relationships which may exist between organisations and their branches or subsidiaries, between private or public sector bodies and voluntary organisations, and in networks and partnerships. It also looks at mergers. It covers:

For sources of further information see page 12.
Double-underlined section headings indicate additions or significant changes since the first edition.

9.1 THE RANGE OF RELATIONSHIPS

Voluntary organisations may be involved in many complex organisational relationships, for example:

- a parent body with non-autonomous projects or branches, with the parent ultimately responsible for what happens in the projects or branches;

- a parent body with a network of autonomous 'branches', more properly called affiliates, where each affiliated body is independent and responsible for itself, but is accountable in some way to the parent;

- a group structure where a central organisation controls, generally as subsidiaries, a range of organisations, often providing diverse services but sharing central administrative functions;

- an international organisation with branches, either autonomous or non-autonomous, operating in different countries under different laws and legal requirements;

- a voluntary organisation which franchises its name and way of operating;
- a federation made up of independent organisations which join a coordinating or umbrella organisation;
- a partnership where a number of organisations and agencies, perhaps including local authorities, health authorities and businesses as well as voluntary organisations, work together on a project;
- a charity which sets up a non-charitable campaigning organisation;
- a campaigning organisation which sets up a charity;
- a charity which sets up a non-charitable trading body;
- a business which sets up a charity;
- a charity which sets up and controls another charity;
- a funding body which sets up a charity or other voluntary organisation to carry out activities or provide services it wants to fund;
- a purchasing body such as a health authority which sets up a charity to provide services it wants to purchase;
- two 'sister' organisations with different objects but the same people on their governing bodies;

... and that's just for starters.

Faced with the need or desire to grow, to replicate activities in other locations, to develop new activities or to undertake new forms of campaigning or fundraising, voluntary organisations can choose from this rich variety of organisational solutions.

Unfortunately, in many cases a choice is not actively made and the 'solution' is allowed to develop piecemeal. The relationship which seems straightforward in the early stages can very quickly become a legal, financial and managerial nightmare, with serious implications:

- potentially dangerous confusion about the responsibilities and obligations of the various bodies;
- use of charitable assets for purposes for which they were not intended, and possibly even for non-charitable purposes;
- tax and/or VAT implications;
- potential liability of the parent body if a branch or project fails to meet its financial or legal obligations;
- similar liability for organisations involved in a partnership if a partner fails to meet its financial or legal obligations.

It is beyond the scope of this book to consider these types of relationship in detail; however, this chapter outlines the main legal issues.

Another type of relationship is created when an independent organisation uses another organisation's charity number for its fundraising [see **44.4**].

9.2 PROJECTS AND BRANCHES

A successful organisation may give rise to a range of projects and a network of local branches. These may be deliberately and systematically developed by the parent organisation, or may emerge spontaneously as a result of supporters' interest. There are no legal problems so long as everyone is clear that the governing body of the parent organisation is ultimately responsible for the activities of the branch or project, and that therefore those responsible for the branch or project must be accountable to the parent.

But problems can arise if the branch or project is operating at a distance from the main organisation with very little contact or accountability, or if the branch or project has its own committee, provides services, raises its own funds, has bank accounts and employs its own staff. Everyone may be unclear whether the branch or project is part of the main organisation or is independent and autonomous.

Another type of problem arises if the project's or branch's objectives or activities do not fall within the objectives of the parent organisation and are therefore in breach of trust or *ultra vires* [see **4.7**].

9.2.1
Clarifying the situation

It is essential to clarify whether for legal purposes branches or projects are part of the parent, or are separate entities. To complicate matters:

- they may be separate for legal purposes but for accounting purposes may have to have their accounts consolidated with those of the main organisation;
- they may be part of the parent, but may be treated as separate for VAT purposes; *and/or*
- some branches may be separate, and others not.

The questions below can help clarify whether the branch or project is independent [see **9.2.2**], is an integral part of the main organisation [see **9.2.3**], or is in the highly undesirable situation of being semi-autonomous [see **9.2.5**]. In many cases advice from a solicitor, the organisation's accountant or the Charity Commission may be necessary.

- Does the branch or project use the name of the main organisation for its activities and fundraising? Or does it use its own name?
- If the main organisation is a registered charity, does the branch or project use its charity number? Or does the branch or project have its own charity number?
- Does the branch or project have its own committee, and if so, do its members accept that they are accountable to the main organisation and are, in effect, a sub-committee of the main organisation? Or do they feel that they are an independent committee?
- Does the branch or project say it is raising funds for the main organisation? Or for itself?
- Does the branch or project need authorisation from the main organisation for anything new? Or can it choose how to spend its money and what activities to run?
- Does the branch or project account for its income and expenditure to the main organisation?
- If the branch or project has employees, who is the employer? (This is not necessarily the same as who operates PAYE.)

9.2.2
Separate entities

If the branch or project is **separately registered** with its own company or charity number, it is a separate organisation.

It may choose to affiliate to the main organisation, or may agree to comply with conditions set by the main organisation in exchange for being able to use its name and logo and to get support from it [see **9.3**]. For accounting, tax or VAT purposes it may form a group with the parent body [see **9.6**]. It may even be a subsidiary of the main organisation, if it is controlled by the main organisation [see **9.6**]. But regardless of these relationships, the 'branch' or 'project' is independent and:

- is fully responsible for its finance, funding, employees and other legal and financial obligations;
- can use the main organisation's name only by agreement;
- cannot use the charity or company number of the main organisation.

Even where the 'branches' or 'projects' are separately registered and are therefore legally independent, the main organisation could be held liable for their actions if the separation is not absolutely clear or if, for example, contracts originally held by the main organisation were not transferred to the new one when it became independent.

If there is any possibility of the main organisation being seen as responsible for the independent bodies, it is sensible for both parties to seek legal advice to ensure the position is clear.

111

9.2.3
Integrated branches or projects

A branch or project which is not legally separate is part of the parent organisation, even if it is given considerable freedom of action. The parent organisation will need to:

- recognise that it is fully responsible and potentially liable for the activities of the branch or project, and take appropriate steps to monitor and control it;

- if the branch or project has its own branch committee or project committee, set clear terms of reference for that committee and its relationship to the main governing body;

- ensure clarity about decisions delegated to the branch or project, and what needs to be referred to the parent for decision;

- ensure clarity about how much scope the branch or project has for determining its own activities, fundraising approaches etc, and what can be done only within a framework determined by the parent;

- ensure the funds of the branch or project are properly safeguarded;

- if the parent is a charity, company and/or industrial and provident society, ensure that the full accounts of the branch or project are consolidated with those of the parent organisation;

- ensure all the policies and safeguards implemented in the main organisation are properly implemented and monitored in the branches or projects;

- ensure proper contracts of employment are issued, naming the parent organisation as employer;

- ensure the activities and risks of the branch or project are appropriately insured;

- clarify membership arrangements, in particular whether voting members can join the parent organisation through membership of branches or only by direct application to the parent;

- establish rules and effective communication with the branch or project to ensure it complies with all legal and organisational requirements;

- ensure the branch or project accepts that final control of the branch legally rests with the parent organisation, including, where necessary, power to wind up branches and transfer assets.

For charitable associations and trusts, and for all companies whether charitable or non-charitable, the obligation to include the branch's or project's income and expenditure with the parent's may take the parent to the level where it has to prepare more detailed accounts and/or have a full audit [see **50.2.3** and **50.3.2**].

Because the branch or project is legally part of the parent organisation, its assets legally belong to the parent. If the branch or project stops operating, any money or property passes to the parent unless there is a formal agreement specifying otherwise.

9.2.4
Fundraising and supporters' groups

Fundraising or 'friends' groups which raise money solely for a specific named charity generally do not have to register as a separate charity, because they do not have discretion as to how the funds they raise will be used. If such groups have a formal long-term existence they should generally be treated legally and administratively in the same way as a branch or project of the parent charity [see **9.2.3**].

A friends or supporters' group which can choose how to use or donate its funds will probably have to register as a charity if it receives more than £1,000 per year from all sources [see **7.1**].

9.2.4.1
Informal fundraising groups

A more informal group which occasionally fundraises for one charity is not treated as part of the charity for which it is fundraising. But even an informal fundraising group may need to register as a charity if it receives more than £1,000 per year from all sources and:

- raises funds for a charitable purpose or purposes, rather than for a specific named charity;

- raises funds for a number of charities, rather than always for one named charity; *or*

- has discretion about how it uses the funds it raises.

Where a group raises funds for a named organisation which is not itself registered as a charity, such as a school or hospital, it is not always clear whether registration is necessary. Advice should be sought from the Charity Commission or an experienced solicitor.

**9.2.4.2
Responsibilities of the
fundraising group**

Anyone who raises funds for any organisation(s) or purpose(s) holds the funds as a **constructive trustee** [see **44.2.1**], must comply with all relevant legislation on fundraising [see **chapters 44** and **45**], and must use the funds only for the purpose(s) for which they were collected. If the funds are collected for charitable, benevolent or philanthropic purposes those involved in raising the funds are subject to the control of the Charity Commission, even if they have not registered their fundraising group as a charity.

The individuals involved in the fundraising group are responsible for ensuring the group complies with all its legal obligations, and could be held personally liable if the group does not. It is especially important for them to be aware of their responsibilities if they occupy premises, employ staff, are required to pay tax on their income or are required to register for VAT.

**9.2.5
Semi-autonomous
branches or projects**

Some organisations have allowed their branches or projects to achieve a semi-autonomous status, where the branches or projects use the parent body's name and charity number, particularly for fundraising purposes, but in all other ways act independently with their own committee, bank accounts, premises, employees etc. The branches may be in regular contact with the main organisation and cooperate with it, but do not see themselves as accountable to it.

This semi-autonomous status is fraught with potential legal difficulties. For example:

- if the 'branch' gives the impression when raising funds that the money will be used only within the objects of the main organisation, it is a breach of trust to use the funds for any other purpose;

- the members of the main organisation's governing body could be found to be negligent in failing to ensure the proper application of funds raised in their name and for which they are legally trustees;

- the members of the main organisation's governing body could find themselves liable for the debts of the branch or project.

The governing body of the main organisation must clarify the situation either by ensuring the branch is clearly within its control (albeit with considerable delegated powers) or by allowing the branch to become truly independent [see below], perhaps with a franchising type relationship to the main organisation [see **9.4.4**].

**9.3
PROJECT OR
BRANCH BECOMING
INDEPENDENT**

Because of the difficulties in maintaining adequate control over a network of branches or over self-sustaining projects, parent organisations may be happy for these offshoots to move to independent status. Or the move to independence may be part of a planned process, through which projects are set up and supported within an organisation and are then, when viable, established as independent entities.

Decisions about independence are arrived at through negotiation between the parent organisation and the affected branches or projects, but the final decision must always be made by the governing body of the parent organisation. When it is agreed that a branch or project should become independent, it will have to draw up a governing document [see

chapter 5], register as a company if this is desired, and register as a charity and obtain its own charity number if it has charitable objects and its annual income from all sources exceeds £1,000 [see **7.1.1**].

The process of becoming independent is complex and raises most of the same issues that occur when an unincorporated organisation incorporates as a company limited by guarantee [see **6.6**]. Issues likely to need particular attention include:

- ensuring the new organisation is registered with all the relevant authorities [see **6.5**];

- ensuring all restricted funds received for the branch or project, including tax recovered on gift aid donations and interest, are used only for the branch or project or are transferred to the new body;

- ensuring assets purchased from the branch's or project's restricted funds are transferred to the new body (but beware that some equipment warranties may be invalidated by transfer of the equipment);

- the transfer of staff under TUPE rules [see **26.4**];

- data protection issues around the transfer of information to the new organisation about clients, donors and other individuals [see **38.2**];

- agreeing any use by the new organisation of the parent organisation's name, logo, policies, procedures, research and other intellectual property [see **chapter 39**];

- agreeing whether the parent body will continue to provide premises, facilities, training or other support, and/or will continue to require key principles or standards to be observed, and if necessary putting these arrangements into a contract, licence or the new organisation's governing document.

Specialist legal advice will ensure the separation, handover and new registration are done properly, and will reduce the risk of later problems.

9.3.1
Use of parent organisation's name or logo

If a branch or project which becomes independent is to continue to use the parent organisation's name or logo in any form, the parent should consider whether ongoing monitoring or control is appropriate.

One form of control is requiring a branch, on becoming independent, to affiliate to the national organisation [see **9.4.1**] and adopt a standard form of governing document which includes restraints and other clauses which provide the parent with safeguards. Typically these would include one or more of the following provisions:

- the objects and other key clauses cannot be changed without the consent of the parent organisation;

- if the new organisation is wound up, any surplus funds must be transferred to the parent organisation or be used in a specified way;

- the parent organisation must be provided with annual returns or reports and given access on request to other information about the new organisation;

- the parent organisation has the right to be represented on the governing body of the new organisation either as a fully voting member or as an observer;

- the parent organisation has powers of veto to remove officers or members of the governing body if this is considered necessary (for example, if an officer of the new organisation brings the parent organisation into disrepute);

- the new organisation must cease using any name associating it with the parent organisation if it breaches any of the requirements.

The relationship might be further buttressed by a formal legal agreement licensing the branch to use the logo or other copyright material [see **39.11** for details of such arrangements].

Although organisations with this arrangement are separately registered, their accounts might in some cases need to be consolidated with those of the parent organisation [see **9.6**].

9.3.2
Ongoing support

If the parent organisation does not want to retain such control over its former branches, it may set up a franchise arrangement [see **9.4.4**] or federation [see **9.4.2**].

If this is not appropriate, the parent organisation may maintain a link by providing advice and encouragement, perhaps developing training and consultancy services which can be purchased by the former branches and other similar bodies. Within this framework the original organisation has no legal link with its former branches other than a contractual arrangement to provide advice, training or consultancy. This is the weakest sort of structure, and may lead to a final break-up of any links.

9.4
NETWORKS OF INDEPENDENT ORGANISATIONS

Independent organisations may become involved in a range of networks and joint activities, some of which have legal implications. These include affiliated structures, federations, franchises, partnerships and joint local authority committees.

Where one organisation pays a membership or similar fee to another or enters into a contractual relationship there may be VAT implications [see **53.5.3**].

9.4.1
Affiliated structures

The term **affiliated structure** is used here to refer to a structure where a number of independent organisations agree to be bound by rules set by another organisation. The organisations are independent but choose to accept certain obligations as a condition of affiliation, for example adopting a common model of governing document [see **9.3.1**] or operating within a framework set by the main organisation.

An affiliation agreement should make clear what the affiliate is obliged to do, what the main organisation will provide, and under what circumstances affiliation may be terminated by either party. It is especially important to be clear about situations in which the affiliate could be required to give up use of the main organisation's name and logo.

Depending on the nature of the affiliation relationship, the organisations may constitute a **group** for company and charity accounting purposes [see **9.6**].

The term 'affiliation' is often used to refer not to this type of close relationship, but to a looser federal relationship [see below].

9.4.2
Federal structures

A federal structure is one where completely independent organisations come together for coordination, mutual support, information and/or training. The federation is a membership association, with the organisations as its members.

A federation might be set up by one or more organisations, or by a parent body which wants to create a structure within which it can support its newly independent former branches or projects, but without the monitoring and control needed for an effective affiliated structure.

9.4.3
Licensing

The main body may allow independent bodies to use its name or logo under licence [see **39.9**]. This may not involve the same level of control as in an affiliation [see above] or franchise [see below]. But as with those approaches, there should be absolute clarity about how the name or logo can and cannot be used, and what happens in case of misuse.

9.4.4
Franchising

The concept of franchising developed in the business world and has been successfully transferred to the voluntary sector by organisations such as Crossroads Care and Home-start. The **franchisor** develops a blueprint which:

- provides the local organisation (the **franchisee**) with the information needed to set up a project;
- contains detailed guidance about the steps involved;
- provides complete details about what is required to run the project.

The blueprint is normally backed by training, regular information, access to commonly needed supplies or services at preferential rates, opportunities for networking and cooperation with other franchise operators, advice on problems, and an agreement not to compete or cover the same geographic area.

For the franchisee, the main advantages are the franchisor's name and reputation, which may well make it easier to build credibility and attract funding; not needing to reinvent the wheel in developing services and management procedures; and access to resources such as tailor-made insurance packages. For the franchisor, the process enables replication of good practice—and can also bring in funds.

The franchise contract is likely to be detailed and needs very careful development, so it is essential to take legal advice.

The franchisor normally retains the right to terminate the franchise arrangement if the franchisee's behaviour becomes unsatisfactory or the quality of service is inadequate. Normally the franchisee will have to cease using the name and any copyright material or other intellectual property, return all documents and manuals, inform all parties it deals with that it has lost the franchise, and possibly even cease to deliver similar services even under another name.

9.5 PARTNERSHIP ARRANGEMENTS

The term 'partnership' is used in many ways. In the business world, the most common is where two or more individuals carry on a business in common with a view to making a profit, and do not register their enterprise as a company. This type of partnership is the commercial equivalent of an unincorporated association [see **1.2.1**], and is governed by the agreement between the parties or, if there is no agreement, by the **Partnership Act 1890**. Business partnerships may also obtain limited liability under the **Limited Liability Partnerships Act 2000**.

In voluntary sector usage the term **partnership** covers a wide range of joint ventures between voluntary organisations, or between voluntary organisations and commercial businesses, local authorities, central government or other statutory bodies. Such partnerships take many forms: contractual relationships, informal associations, the creation of separate bodies or, in some cases, local authority joint committees.

It is important to be clear about the nature of any 'partnership' arrangement and to exclude the possibility of a legal partnership being implied. If such a legal partnership is considered to exist, the partners each have unlimited liability for the partnership's debts.

9.5.1 Partnerships without creating a new organisation

Most simply, a 'partnership' might operate as an informal group of representatives from various organisations who come together for a common purpose. Such a group might be called an action group, steering committee, coordinating group, consultative group, forum, network or a range of other names.

There are few legal implications so long as the members of the group merely share information or discuss ideas. But if the group starts to take any action with legal or financial implications, the members should clarify whether:

- one of them will undertake the activity or activities and will therefore take legal and financial responsibility (although the other partners may agree to contribute financially); *or*
- they will undertake the activities jointly, and therefore share legal and financial responsibility.

9.5.1.1
<u>Lead body arrangement</u>

A typical example of the first scenario is where one organisation provides the premises and employs the staff, but policy and direction for the work is set by the group. Unless the legal situation is clear problems can arise if, for example, an employee's work is unsatisfactory, or there are differences between the host organisation and the group about how the work should develop. To reduce the risk of this, the relationships between the participating organisations may be set out in either a contract [see **9.5.3**] or a non-legally binding **memorandum of understanding**. Such a memorandum should make clear that it is not intended to be legally binding, but to be binding in honour only.

9.5.1.2
Joint responsibility arrangement

If the group chooses the option of undertaking activities jointly, they will probably be operating as an unincorporated association [see **1.2.1**]. The members of the group—corporate bodies, or individuals representing unincorporated bodies—could be held responsible for the actions of the group in the same way that the members of the governing body of any unincorporated association can be held liable for the association's acts. However if both the paperwork and practice make clear that they are acting jointly only on the basis of a non-legally binding cooperation, a court may in some situations say that separate members of the group are not liable for the group's activities.

9.5.2
Partnership organisations

Partnership arrangements are sometimes implemented by creating a new organisation, in which the 'partners' become members of the new organisation with the right to elect or nominate the governing body. Development trusts, Sure Start programmes and similar bodies which bring together charities, local authorities and businesses are typical examples. The relationship between the partners is set out in the governing document of the new body. The new organisation is formally independent of the bodies which set it up, although it generally retains close links with them.

If the new organisation is set up as a company or industrial and provident society and one or more local authorities is involved, it could be a local authority controlled or influenced company [see **9.7.3**]. The implications of this should be considered before drawing up the governing document or appointing members of the governing body.

An alternative is to have a lead agency, which has contractual relationships with the partners and accepts direction from a steering group made up of partners [see **9.5.1.1**].

9.5.3
Contractual arrangements

If two or more organisations choose to work together without setting up a new organisation, they may enter into a contractual relationship with each other. For example, a housing association might build residential care accommodation and retain responsibility for maintenance and repairs, while passing to a specialist charity the responsibility for day-to-day care of residents, day care and support services. In this situation, the mutual responsibilities and liabilities need to be incorporated in a carefully drafted agreement. This might be called a contract, service agreement, management agreement, memorandum of agreement or any such term. In addition, there might be a supporting tenancy or licence agreement.

Such arrangements often start informally, and may continue satisfactorily without any detailed written agreement. But serious problems can arise if one party does not do what the other thinks it should, or if someone is injured or suffers loss because of the actions of one party. To avoid these problems it is wise to seek legal advice and draw up a proper agreement between the parties right from the beginning.

9.5.4
Joint ventures

A more commercial type of partnership arrangement is a **joint venture**, for example when several organisations jointly set up a trading company. This might happen where a number of small organisations wish to run a joint trading venture such as a charity shop, or if an organisation wishes to share the risks and capital expenditure of a large venture.

The trading body is set up as an separate organisation, and the rights and responsibilities of the parties are set out in a **shareholders' agreement** or **joint venture agreement**. A joint venture agreement typically sets out:

- objects of the venture, and limitations on other activities;
- shares of ownership and of profit;
- right to positions on the governing body;
- special rules controlling governance, for example that the quorum for meetings must include a representative from all parties, or that key decisions such as budget setting are subject to special controls;
- provision for resolving deadlocks;
- provision for withdrawal of a partner;
- valuation provisions for buy-out of partners or bringing in new partners;
- restrictions on competitive behaviour.

The initial glow of goodwill and the pressure of time and work often mean that the parties do not think about such agreements until a dispute arises—which is too late.

9.6 GROUP STRUCTURES

In legal terms, a **group** exists when an organisation sets up **subsidiaries** which it controls, or when one organisation can, by agreement, control another. The control is usually exercised by the main organisation being able to appoint all or a majority of the members of the governing body of the subsidiary or other organisation. A group might be formed:

- when a charity sets up a non-charitable company to carry out non-charitable fundraising or trading activities;
- when a non-charitable campaigning organisation sets up a charity;
- when a commercial business sets up a charity;
- where a group of organisations are controlled by the largest or holding organisation, for example a housing association which merges [see **9.9.1**] with a number of charities which remain separate legal entities, but are under the control of the housing association.

A branch structure [see **9.2.3**] is not a group because the branches are all legally part of one organisation. A federation [see **9.4.2**] is not a group because the organisations which make up the federation are independent of each other. An affiliation structure [see **9.4.1**] may or may not be a group, depending on the level of control exercised by the main organisation on the governing bodies of the affiliated organisations.

The creation of a group can have important implications for tax, VAT and accounting. It is therefore essential to be clear about what constitutes a group for these purposes and when one exists.

9.6.1 Company law and groups

For company law purposes, a group exists if one corporate body (the **parent undertaking**) is legally able to control one or more undertakings (the **subsidiary undertakings**).

The parent undertaking does not necessarily have to be a registered company; it can be any corporate body, including an industrial and provident society. If the parent body is a company it may be called a **parent company** or **holding company**.

Companies Act 1985 s.736(1),(3)

Nor does the subsidiary undertaking need to be a company. The term includes all corporate bodies, including IPSs, as well as partnerships (unincorporated businesses involving two or more individuals); and unincorporated associations which carry on a trade or business, whether on a for-profit or not-for-profit basis.　　*Companies Act 1985 s.259(1)*

A **parent undertaking** is a corporate body which:

- holds a majority of the voting rights of another undertaking;
- is a member of another undertaking, and has the right to appoint or remove a majority of its governing body;
- is a member of another undertaking, and has an agreement with the other members of the second undertaking which gives it control of a majority of the voting rights; *or*
- has the right to exercise a dominant control over another undertaking because of provisions contained in the governing document of the second undertaking, or because the two undertakings have a control contract.　　*s.258(2)*

A **subsidiary undertaking** is a body subject to one of the above types of control.

A parent undertaking may also exist if the parent has a **participating interest** in another undertaking, defined as owning 20% or more of the shares or holding 20% or more of the voting rights in an undertaking, and either:

- the parent actually exercises a dominant influence over the other undertaking; *or*
- the parent and the other undertaking are managed on a unified basis.　　*ss.258(4), 259, 260*

An undertaking is a **wholly owned subsidiary** if its only members are its parent undertaking, the parent undertaking's other wholly owned subsidiaries, and/or persons who are acting on behalf of the parent undertaking or its wholly owned subsidiaries.　　*s.736(2)*

Special accounting regulations apply to groups [see **50.3.2**].

9.6.2
Charity groups and accounting

The Statement of Recommended Practice for charity accounts (Charities SORP) requires accounts to contain information about **connected charities**, and requires the accounts of a charity's subsidiaries to be **consolidated** with those of the primary charity [see **50.2.7**].

9.6.2.1
Connected charities

Two charities are **connected** if:

- they have common, parallel or related objects and activities; *and*
- they have either common control or unity of administration.
　　Charities SORP 2000 app.1 para.5

Common control exists if:

- the same person or persons (or persons connected with each other through family or business relationships) have the right to appoint a majority of the charity trustees of both or all the charities; *or*
- the same person or persons, or persons connected with each other through family or business relationships, hold a majority of the voting rights in the administration of both or all the charities.

A person may be either an individual person or a corporate body.

Unity of administration is not defined in SORP.

9.6.2.2
Subsidiary undertakings

A parent charity's **subsidiary undertakings** are defined in the same way as in the Companies Act [see **9.6.1**].

The type of accounts which must be prepared depends on whether the subsidiary undertakings are themselves charities or non-charitable, and whether the parent and/or subsidiary is incorporated.

9.6.2.3
Subsidiary charities

The Charity Commission uses the phrase **subsidiary charity** to mean a subsidiary with the same objects as, or narrower objects than, the parent controlling charity. In these circumstances it allows both to share the same charity number, so they are not a group for charity law purposes—but if the parent charity is a company, the parent and subsidiary *will* be a group for company law purposes. For charity law purposes the parent and subsidiaries submit one set of reports and accounts, with subsidiary charities being shown as restricted funds within the accounts.

9.6.2.4
Affiliates treated as branches

Where one charity is able to exert a substantial degree of influence over another, the influenced charities may have to be treated in the same way as non-independent branches and their accounts may have to be consolidated with those of the main charity [see **50.2.7**]. This would apply, for example, in the sort of affiliation arrangement where the main charity prescribes the governing document for the affiliated charities [see **9.4.1**] and exercises substantial control over the work of affiliates, even if the affiliated charities are themselves separately registered. An organisation to which this requirement might apply should take advice from its auditor or the Charity Commission.

9.6.3
Unincorporated non-charitable parent bodies

A 'group' exists if the parent body is incorporated, or if the parent body is a charity whether incorporated or unincorporated. If the parent body is neither an incorporated body nor an unincorporated charity, it is not obliged to consolidate its accounts with those of its subsidiaries unless failure to do so would give a misleading picture.

9.7
SETTING UP A SUBSIDIARY

There are many reasons for setting up subsidiaries, for example:

- a non-charitable voluntary organisation might set up a charitable subsidiary, thus getting the tax and funding advantages of charitable status [see **3.2**] for that part of its work;

- a business might set up a charitable subsidiary to channel its support for charitable activities;

- a charity unable or unwilling to change its objects might set up another charity to undertake different charitable activities;

- a charity might set up a non-charitable but not-for-profit subsidiary to undertake activities which are not charitable in law;

- a charity might set up a non-charitable trading subsidiary to undertake substantial trading and fundraising activities [see **47.2**];

- an organisation of any type might wish to separate the risks and liabilities of an activity from the parent so that if these risks cause insolvency, the parent's assets are not at risk.

In these situations there is good reason for creating the subsidiary, because without it the first organisation would not be able to achieve all of its objectives, or would not be able to achieve them in the most efficient way. But the complexity of a group structure increases cost and administration, so subsidiaries should be set up only if necessary and only if the advantages warrant the extra work.

9.7.1
Formal control

A parent may exercise control of a subsidiary by a variety of means, most commonly through:

- absolute control of votes at general meetings of members, where the parent owns 100% of the shares of a company limited by shares or is the only member of a company limited by guarantee;

- majority control of votes at general meetings of members, for example where the parent owns a majority of the shares of a company limited by shares;

- the subsidiary's governing document giving the parent the right to nominate all or most of the members of the subsidiary's governing body or the right to remove them; *or*

- a contractual agreement between the parent and subsidiary.

9.7.2
Typical group structures

A huge range of structures is possible, with combinations of charities, non-charities or both. Vital underlying principles are that a charity cannot generally use its funds to create or subsidise a non-charitable body, and a charity's finance and financial records must be kept completely separate from those of any non-charity [see **47.5.2**].

9.7.2.1
Charity with for-profit subsidiary

A common voluntary sector group structure consists of a charitable organisation which sets up a trading subsidiary to undertake commercial activities as a way of raising funds for the charity. The trading subsidiary is likely to take the form of a company limited by shares, with the charity holding all the shares [see **47.3.2** for more about how trading subsidiaries are set up]. Such a subsidiary may also be set up to obtain VAT benefits in the delivery of charitable services [see **53.4.1**].

The profits of the trading subsidiary are subject to tax, but if all or most of the pre-tax profits are passed to the charity through gift aid, the tax is avoided or reduced [see **47.7**].

9.7.2.2
Charity with non-charitable not-for-profit subsidiary

If a charity wants to take on activities which are not themselves charitable, for example some types of political campaigning, it can set up a non-charitable not-for-profit organisation. This might take the form of an unincorporated association or, if limited liability is important, a company limited by guarantee. In either case the charity generally retains the right to appoint all or most of the members of the subsidiary organisation's governing body, but cannot use its assets or resources to create or subsidise the non-charitable organisation.

9.7.2.3
Non-charity with charitable subsidiary

The reverse scenario is when a non-charitable organisation wants to set up a charity in order to take advantage of tax benefits for the properly charitable aspects of its work.

If the charity is likely to be fairly inactive—existing primarily to channel funds to the primary organisation for its charitable activities—and will not be exposed to significant financial risks, the legal form is likely to be a charitable trust. If the charity will itself undertake activities, the structure will probably be a charitable trust or charitable company limited by guarantee. Whatever the legal form, the primary organisation will generally retain the right to appoint all or most of the charity's trustees.

9.7.2.4
Charity with charitable subsidiary

A charity may set up a charitable subsidiary because its own objects are too narrow to allow it to undertake an activity. Or even where there is no legal need to do so, a charity might choose to set up a separate charity with the same or similar objects. An example is a charity which creates a subsidiary to undertake a major project funded under a contract [see **48.1.2**]. The advantages for the parent charity include:

- risks and liabilities associated with the contract are isolated within the subsidiary, thus protecting the assets of the parent charity;

- the pressure to use the parent charity's own funds to subsidise the contracted services may be minimised by the clear accounting separation;

- the contract project may need to develop a separate public image or internal culture which may be facilitated by the legal separation;

- fundraising for the parent charity may be less likely to be threatened by the contract;

- if purchasers of the contracted services or others want to be represented on the organisation's committee or require full disclosure of information, this can be done within the subsidiary, leaving the parent charity's internal arrangements untouched;

- if the parent charity has limitations within its objects which would be breached if it delivers the service, it can create a subsidiary with wider objects—provided it does not use any of its resources to subsidise any activities by the subsidiary that are outside its own objects.

Where a charity is setting up a charitable subsidiary, a decision will need to be made about whether the new charity has its own number and the two charities thus form a group [see **9.6.2**], or whether the new charity should be a 'subsidiary charity' using the parent's charity number [see **9.6.2.3**].

In the type of situation outlined above—where separation of activities and/or separation of risk is desirable—the same structure can be used for a non-charity setting up another non-charity. It can also be used for a non-charity setting up a charity or a charity setting up a non-charity, so long as the charity does not subsidise non-charitable activities.

9.7.2.5
Non-charity with charitable and trading subsidiaries

Various structures may be combined in more complex configurations. An example is a non-charitable voluntary organisation—perhaps an organisation set up primarily for political objects, or a professional association providing services primarily for its members—which sets up a charitable subsidiary to support and raise funds for those of its activities which are properly charitable.

Even though the primary organisation is not charitable, its governing document may prohibit it from undertaking substantial trading activities, or it may feel it is inappropriate to be involved in these. To overcome this, it also sets up a trading subsidiary.

The trading subsidiary would then raise funds for the non-charitable organisation, but these would be subject to tax. So any funds which were to be used solely for charitable purposes could be passed to the charity through gift aid, thus taking advantage of tax relief on gift aid donations. The charity could then make a grant to the non-charitable organisation for those parts of its activities which are charitable, or the charity itself could undertake these functions.

9.7.2.6
Charity with trading and non-charitable subsidiaries

A variant on this structure has a charity setting up a trading subsidiary to raise funds and also setting up a non-charitable organisation to undertake its non-charitable campaigning or similar activities. The trading subsidiary can take advantage of tax reliefs by donating its profits to the charity under gift aid, or donate them to the non-charity and forgo the tax relief.

Because a charity must take advantage of all possible tax reliefs [see **13.3.5**], the charity would have to be able to demonstrate that the non-charitable campaigning organisation was receiving no more than its proper share of the profits of the trading subsidiary.

This structure might be simplified by dispensing with the non-charitable voluntary organisation and having all non-charitable activities—whether trading or campaigning—undertaken by the trading subsidiary. However, it might not be appropriate for a trading subsidiary whose name is associated primarily with the sale of Christmas cards and other fundraising activities to appear on, for example, petitions to MPs. More importantly, if the campaigning or non-charitable activities involve any significant expenditure, the charity could be criticised for allowing its wholly owned subsidiary to expend funds in that way rather than passing its profits to the charity.

9.7.3
Issues in group arrangements

As well as the VAT [see **53.6.6** and **53.6.7**] and accounting [see **50.2.7** and **50.3.2**] implications of group structures, there are also issues internal to the group.

**9.7.3.1
Control**

It is not unusual for the parent/subsidiary relationship to break down. One common scenario is when a community association or community centre wishes to obtain, through the club registration procedure, a licence to sell alcohol on its premises [see **43.3.2**]. To meet the requirements of the licensing legislation, it must create a genuinely independent members' club. There is no problem with this—unless the members of the bar association become so powerful a voting bloc that they come to control the community association. This has happened in some community centres which have become little more than drinking clubs which happen to have a community association attached to them.

Even when a parent organisation appears to have complete control of a subsidiary through being the only member, that control may be undermined in a variety of ways. If a trading subsidiary, for example, is highly dependent on key staff who develop specialist expertise, the staff may come to exercise *de facto* control of the subsidiary because only they have the contacts and expertise to ensure its continued success. The risk of this can be reduced by ensuring adequate staff accountability, and by creating restrictive covenants by which the staff promise not to set up competing operations [see **24.44**].

If a charitable trust structure is used for a charitable subsidiary there is a particular risk of loss of control. Trust deeds tend, unless specially drafted, to provide for a self-selecting group of trustees, and may include no provision for removal or retirement. If trustees become entrenched they may fail to change and develop with the parent, and may fail to respond to the directions of the parent organisation. The parent may then be powerless to remove them. This situation can be prevented by including appropriate provisions in the trust deed. Here, as in virtually every arrangement involving creation of a group structure, it is important not just to seek legal advice but to seek it from advisors with real experience of these types of situation.

**9.7.3.2
Duality and conflict
of interest**

Some **duality of interest** is inherent in the legal rules governing the separate parts of a group structure. Each director of a company must, when sitting on the board of that company, make decisions in the best interests of that company [see **13.2.1**], and those decisions might conflict with directions given by a parent organisation. Similarly, every person while sitting on the governing body of a charity must ensure that their duties as a charity trustee are observed and must act always in the best interests of the charity and its beneficiaries, even if this involves disregarding the directions of the parent body [see **13.3.3**].

For example if a charity's trustees are also directors of its trading subsidiary they might be tempted, in their role as trustees, to continue to vote loans to prop up an unsuccessful subsidiary, even though this would be in breach of their duties of prudence to the charity. The Charity Commission report on the Royal British Legion highlights the disastrous consequences of such confusion of roles.

Decisions of the Charity Commissioners vol. 1, August 1993, pp.24-25

There is no easy way around this duality of interest where individuals have more than one role. It can be prevented by not having anyone sitting on two governing bodies, but this may be impractical and undesirable if a truly integrated group is to be maintained. It may be more appropriate to have some overlap to ensure integration, but to have some members of the subsidiary governing body who are not on the governing body of the main organisation, and *vice versa*.

It is essential to ensure that meetings clearly separate business for one part of the group from that of business for other parts. Confusion can also be reduced by having clear role descriptions for each role, and by ensuring each part of the group has its own clear mission statement and business plan highlighting its objectives.

9.7.3.3
Liability for subsidiaries

The isolation of risk within a part of the group is a great advantage, but this advantage can only be retained if care is taken. Even something as minor as using the wrong notepaper may result in a contractual liability being inadvertently taken on by the parent body.

A parent organisation—especially one which is charitable—should think very carefully before guaranteeing loans, bank overdrafts, leases and other liabilities of subsidiaries. The parent organisation may well not have power to take on such liabilities [see **55.5.3**]. Even if it does, it may not want to jeopardise its own future. If it does take on such potential liabilities it should first take legal advice and should make every effort to limit the risks.

9.7.3.4
Closure or liquidation

When setting up any group, thought needs to be given as to what will happen if any part of the group ceases to exist or goes into liquidation [see **chapter 21**]. This problem is likely to be particularly important where significant assets are being accumulated within a charity which is a subsidiary of a non-charity. When a charity is dissolved or liquidated, its assets may generally only be passed to another charity or applied for charitable purposes. This might prevent the subsidiary's assets being passed to a non-charitable parent.

When a subsidiary fails, the governing body of the parent organisation may feel morally bound to meet the subsidiary's debts. Such debts should be paid only after legal advice, because in most cases there will be no legal obligation to pay, and such non-obligatory payments may well be in breach of the governing body's duties [see **49.2.7**].

9.8
STRUCTURES INVOLVING PUBLIC SECTOR BODIES

Many local authorities, health authorities and other public sector bodies have very close links with voluntary organisations. Where these links simply involve sharing information and consulting, there are no structural implications for the organisations. However, other relationships may have legal implications.

9.8.1
Local authority joint committees

Local authorities have powers to create **joint committees** with one or more other local authorities. Such joint committees may also have members other than local authorities, provided such members make up no more than one-third of the total membership.

Local Authorities Act 1972

These committees may be appropriate for initiatives in which local authorities want to involve voluntary sector or commercial bodies. As with all such arrangements, responsibility needs to be clarified if the group undertakes any action with legal or financial implications.

9.8.2
Organisations created by public sector bodies

Local authorities, health authorities and other public sector bodies have a long history of setting up voluntary organisations. Among the reasons for this are:

- the authority wants to undertake activities which government rulings or legislation do not allow it to undertake directly;

- it has to take on a purchaser role and wants to set up a separate agency to become a provider of services; *or*

- there needs to be a separate body in order to release matching funds from outside sources.

The organisation might be charitable or non-charitable, depending on its purposes. It might be a completely new organisation set up by the authority, or—increasingly—might involve floating off into the voluntary (or private) sector a project or service that previously formed part of the parent authority.

The parent authority would typically maintain a close working relationship with the independent organisation, perhaps by providing a long-term contract under which the organisation provides services directly to the public sector body or to members of the public whom the public sector body has a duty to assist [see **chapter 48** for more about such contracts].

These relationships can cause difficulties. Anyone serving on the governing body of the new organisation is under an obligation to act always in the best interests of that organisation and its beneficiaries [see **13.2** and **13.3**]. If the person is an employee, officer or member of a local or health authority or other public body this can create a conflict of interest [see **9.7.3.2**].

Another potential difficulty is that if the organisation is incorporated as a company or industrial and provident society, it may be a **local authority regulated company** [see below]. Even if it does not fall into this category, any organisation which has close structural links with a public sector body needs to be aware of the potential legal implications.

9.8.3
Local authority interests in companies

Specific restrictions apply to companies limited by guarantee, companies limited by shares and industrial and provident societies which are influenced or controlled by, and are effectively an operating unit of, one or more local authorities. Such bodies are called **regulated companies**. The rules are set out in the **Local Government and Housing Act 1989** pt.V, the **Local Authorities (Companies) Order 1995** *[SI 1995/849]* and the **Local Authorities (Companies) (Amendment) Order 1996** *[SI 1996/621]*. The restrictions do not apply to unincorporated associations and trusts.

At the time of writing (early 2001) these restrictions were being reviewed. Up-to-date information is available from the local government section in the Department for Transport, Local Government and the Regions (020-7944 3000, www.dtlr.gov.uk).

9.8.3.1
Local authority controlled companies

A company or IPS is a **local authority controlled company** if:

- it is defined under the Companies Act as a subsidiary of the local authority [see **9.6.1**];
- the company or IPS is not a subsidiary for Companies Act purposes but the local authority has the power to control a majority of the votes at a general meeting of the organisation;
- the company or IPS is not a company for Companies Act purposes but the local authority has the power to appoint or remove a majority of the organisation's board of directors; *or*
- the company or IPS is under the control of another local authority controlled company.   *Local Government and Housing Act 1989 s.68*

Typically a company or IPS is a local authority controlled company if the local authority holds more than 50% of the membership rights.

If two or more local authorities act jointly in relation to an organisation, and together are able to control the organisation, the organisation is held to be under the control of each authority.   *s.73*

9.8.3.2
Local authority influenced companies

A company or IPS is a **local authority influenced company** if:

- people **associated** with the local authority [see below] hold 20% or more of the total membership voting rights, *or* make up 20% or more of the directors, *or* hold 20% or more of the total voting rights at a meeting of the directors; *and*
- the company or IPS has a **business relationship** with the local authority.   *s.69*

A person is **associated** with a local authority if he or she:

- is a member of the local authority, or has been at any time in the previous four years;
- is an officer of the local authority; *or*

- is employed by a local authority controlled company and is also a director, manager, secretary or similar officer of the company.

Local Government and Housing Act 1989 s.69(5)

It does not matter whether the person associated with the local authority is a member of the organisation or its governing body in a personal capacity, or as a representative of the local authority.

If the local authority has the right to 20% or more of the places, but does not take up these places, the organisation is not a local authority influenced company.

Business relationship is defined in a variety of ways. The ones most likely to apply to voluntary organisations are where:

- in any 12 month period, payments from the local authority or a local authority controlled company account for more than half of the organisation's income;

- local authority capital grants or shares or stock owned by the local authority exceed more than half the net assets of the organisation;

- more than half the organisation's turnover is derived from assets in which the local authority has an interest; *or*

- the organisation occupies local authority land or buildings at less than the market rent, or intends to enter into such an arrangement.

s.69(3)

Payments from the local authority include grants of all types, fees for services provided under a service agreement or contract, or any other payment made by the local authority to the organisation.

An example of a local authority influenced company is a voluntary sector company or IPS which receives more than half its income from a local authority and/or occupies local authority premises at below market rent, and where 20% or more of its members or the members of its governing body are associated with the local authority.

9.8.3.3
Regulated companies

The restrictions apply only to **regulated companies**. A body is a regulated company if it is:

- a local authority controlled company [see **9.8.3.1**];

- a local authority influenced company [see **9.8.3.2**], and also registered as an industrial and provident society;

- a local authority influenced company, and the local authority, if it were a company, would have the right to exercise a **dominant influence** over the company, or has exercised such an influence; *or*

- a local authority influenced company, and the local authority, if it were a company, would have to prepare group accounts in respect of the influenced company.

Local Authorities (Companies) (Amendment) Order 1996 [SI 1996/621]

The effect of the rules on regulated companies is to exempt many influenced companies from the restrictions.

9.8.3.4
Implications of
being regulated

The rules on local authority regulated companies deal primarily with how such bodies are financed by local authorities. They:

- require the company to state on business letters, notices and other documents that is influenced or controlled by a local authority or authorities, and name the authorities;

- limit payments to directors of the company;

- prevent the organisation from publishing material which the local authority would be prevented from publishing [see **40.2.5**];

- require certain information to be provided to local authority members, the local authority's auditors and the Audit Commission;

- require controlled companies to obtain Audit Commission consent to the appointment of auditors;

- specify that the local authority's capital spending powers are reduced if a controlled or influenced company borrows money or receives certain grants. *Local Authorities (Companies) Order 1995 [SI 1995/849]*

9.8.3.5
Exemption

It is possible to apply for a **direction** to exempt the company and local authority (or authorities) from the relevant provisions of the Act. Information is available from the Department for Transport, Local Government and the Regions.

Local Government and Housing Act 1989 ss.68(1), 69(1)

Some organisations are exempt under directions made in 1995. These include Groundwork Trusts, area museum councils, regional or area arts boards, building preservation trusts, citizens advice bureaux, registered housing associations, and companies which received less than £2,000 from the local authority in the previous year.

9.8.3.6
Avoiding the restrictions

An organisation which thinks it might be caught by these restrictions should take specialist legal advice to clarify its position, the position of the local authority and the possible implications, and if appropriate to decide whether to apply for exemption.

Alternatively it may be able to alter its membership or governing document [see **5.5** for the procedure] so the local authority no longer has the right to control or influence it.

9.9
MERGERS
9.9.1
Forms of merger

Merger is the process of formally bringing together two or more organisations. Many different approaches are colloquially referred to as 'merger', including arrangements where:

- both organisations wind up and transfer their assets and liabilities to a new organisation;
- one existing organisation takes over the assets and liabilities of the other, either directly or into a subsidiary [see **9.6**];
- the organisations create a group structure or extend an existing group structure, with the merging organisation becoming a subsidiary [see **9.6**];
- an incorporated organisation becomes the sole corporate trustee of an unincorporated organisation.

Whatever mechanism is adopted, the bodies concerned must ensure that the action is within their powers [see **5.4.3**]. Merger or takeover always involves complex legal, financial, managerial and organisational issues. Specialist advice and support are vital.

Sinclair Taylor & Martin Solicitors [see **page 2**] maintain a register of voluntary organisations seeking merger partners.

9.9.1.1
Merging into an existing organisation

Rather than creating a new organisation, it may be easier simply to amend the governing document of one organisation—even, perhaps, changing its name—then wind up the other and transfer its assets and liabilities. With this approach, only one set of staff transfer under TUPE [see **26.4**] and have their terms and conditions protected.

9.9.1.2
Creating a new organisation

For some mergers it may be appropriate to create a new organisation, with both existing organisations transferring their assets and liabilities and then winding up. This may reduce the sense that one organisation is being taken over by the other, make it easier to work towards a new organisational culture, and reduce the risk of a transfer of liabilities attached to the old organisations.

9.9.1.3
Group structures

For some mergers it may be appropriate for both organisations to continue existing, but within a new or existing group structure [see **9.6**]. One organisation may become the subsidiary of the other, or both may become subsidiaries of a parent body. Legal advice will be needed about the company and/or charity law implications of this arrangement, as well as the tax and VAT implications.

9.9.1.4
Industrial and provident societies

An industrial and provident society which wishes to merge, either with another IPS or a company, can take advantage of special provisions. These allow two or more IPSs to pass special resolutions to become **amalgamated** as one IPS. All assets and liabilities transfer automatically to the new IPS. *Industrial and Provident Societies Act 1965 s.50*

Alternatively one IPS can by special resolution **transfer its engagements** to another IPS, or can by special resolution agree to convert itself into, or amalgamate with or transfer its engagements to, a company registered under the Companies Acts. *ss.51-52*

9.9.2
Transferring assets and liabilities

Where the merger involves a transfer of assets and liabilities, either to an existing organisation or to a new one, the process is similar to the transfer from an unincorporated body to an incorporated body [see **6.6**]. But a merger situation is more complex, because:

- the organisations may have different objects, so the assets of each may need to be ringfenced for its own objects within the new body;

- different membership and governance structures will need to be brought together in a way acceptable to both;

- the organisations are likely to have different funding sources, and different financial systems and procedures;

- bringing the organisations together may take them into higher brackets for the purposes of company accounts and audit [see **50.3.2**], charity accounts and audit [see **50.2.3**], and/or VAT registration [see **53.6.1**];

- the organisations are likely to have different contracts of employment, and the fact that each set of employees retains its existing terms and conditions [see **26.4**] can lead to problematic differentials;

- the fact that transferred staff may bring with them employment claims relating to their previous employer can lead to problems;

- even where on paper the organisations look quite similar, they may in reality have very different organisational cultures and ways of doing things. Even if objects, priorities, systems and procedures can be sorted out on paper, it may be difficult to change the way things are actually done on the ground.

It is crucial to gain the support of key stakeholders, such as funders, staff, clients and any regulators through the process.

9.9.2.1
Transfer without winding up

Normally, after a transfer of assets and liabilities, the transferring body is wound up. But if a company or industrial and provident society is wound up any charitable legacies or gifts to it may be lost, because the body is no longer in existence to receive them. It may therefore be sensible to keep such a party to a merger in existence, simply to ensure that such gifts are not lost. Winding up a charitable trust or association may pose less risk of loss of future legacies, but legal advice should be taken if this is likely to be an issue.

9.9.3
Due diligence

Whatever the form of merger, the merging bodies have separate histories, which may have involved acquisition of actual and contingent (potential) liabilities, obligations and risks. Each partner must ensure it is not involving itself with a partner with an unacceptable level of exposure to such risks. This is common good sense, but it is also a duty, arising from the obligations of the governing body [see **13.2-13.4**] if the organisation is a trust, company or industrial and provident society, or is a charity. The process of finding out about potential risks is called **due diligence**, and is normally carried out with the assistance of experienced solicitors and accountants.

PART II
GOVERNANCE AND MEMBERSHIP

Once the organisation is set up, its members—if it is a membership organisation—and its governing body must ensure it operates effectively and legally. The governing body might be called a management committee, executive committee, council of management, board of directors, board of trustees, board of governors or any similar name. Regardless of what it is called, the governing body as a whole and its individual members have a range of legal duties, which are explained in this part.

Part II also looks at the requirements for being a member of an organisation and for being on a governing body, the duties of officers, and restrictions on payments or benefits to members of the governing body and members of the organisation.

Chapter 10
MEMBERS OF THE ORGANISATION

10.1
DEFINING
MEMBERSHIP

An organisation's **members** are individuals or organisations, who are defined as members by the governing document or who meet criteria for membership defined in other ways, and who have agreed to abide by the organisation's rules. Companies, industrial and provident societies and unincorporated associations all have members; trusts generally do not.

The legal basis of members' rights and obligations is contractual. In incorporated bodies the contract is between the member and the organisation; in unincorporated associations it is between all the members.

Where there are members they have a constitutionally defined role in the organisation, usually as the governing body itself [see **11.1**] or as the people who elect all or most of the members of the governing body.

Members as defined here must be distinguished from others, such as **supporters**, **service users** or **participants**, who may be called members but do not have any constitutional role in the organisation. These 'members' have only such rights as the members of the organisation or its governing body agree to give them.

Members as defined here must also be distinguished from the **members of the governing body**. The organisation's members and the members of the governing body may in some organisations be one and the same, but usually the governing body is smaller than the overall membership, and may include people who are not members of the organisation. **Chapter 11** covers governing body membership in detail.

10.1.1 Membership records

An accurate list or database of members (often called a **register**) is vital and in some cases is a statutory requirement [see **16.3.2**, **16.4.1** and **16.6**]. Failure to keep up-to-date membership records frequently causes serious problems, because members generally have the final say on key issues such as electing the governing body, amending the governing document and winding up the organisation.

10.1.2 Constitutional provision

Voluntary organisations have hugely varied membership provisions. When drawing up the membership clauses in the governing document it is important to think through what is appropriate for each organisation, rather than simply adopting the clauses from a model governing document or another organisation's constitution.

Many organisations have only one class or type of member, while others have several classes. The governing document might set out the different classes of membership, the eligibility criteria, the procedure for becoming a member, how they stop being members and the rights of each class, or might give a general meeting or the governing body power to make regulations or standing orders [see **5.4.26**] about these and related matters. If such power is not given to the general meeting or governing body, classes or rights of members can be changed only by amending the governing document [see **5.5** for procedure].

10.1.3 Eligibility

Membership eligibility criteria range from the very specific to the very broad ('anyone who supports our objects'). The governing document or membership regulations may set any criteria for membership so long as they do not discriminate unlawfully on the basis of racial group, sex or disability [see **10.3**]. Typical membership criteria include living within a defined geographical area; having a particular illness or disability; being in a defined situation, for example being a parent of a child at a particular school, or being a carer; supporting the objects of the organisation; agreeing to abide by the organisation's governing document; and/or paying an annual subscription.

10.1.4 Rights, benefits and obligations

In considering membership classes a distinction must be made between:

- **membership rights**: rights which exist in law or are granted by the governing document;
- **membership benefits**: additional benefits conferred on some or all classes of membership;
- **membership obligations**: obligations in law or in the governing document, for example an obligation to pay a subscription or to attend a certain number of meetings each year. Members who do not meet their obligations may become ineligible for membership.

Members of an organisation may in some cases be held personally liable for the organisation's actions or debts [see **19.1**].

10.1.5 Rights akin to membership

A governing document may provide for some non-members to have rights similar to those of members, for example the right to appoint some officers or members of the governing body, to attend meetings or to approve constitutional changes. Non-members with such rights might include honorary members [see **10.2.7**], patrons [see **10.2.7**], a president, or a funder or other outside body. The governing document may need to be carefully considered to discover whether true membership is intended, or only some membership rights.

10.2
CLASSES OF MEMBERS

Where there is more than one class or type of member, the governing document or standing orders [see **5.4.26**] should clearly set out the differing rights and obligations of each class. There is no consistency within voluntary organisations about what members are called or their rights and obligations, so the examples here are purely illustrative.

10.2.1
Full membership

Full members (sometimes called **individual** or **ordinary** members, or simply **members**) have full voting rights and are usually eligible to become members of the governing body. Payment of a subscription might be a requirement for membership, but does not have to be.

10.2.2
'Open' membership

Some organisations have governing documents which state that everyone, or everyone who lives in a certain area or meets some other criterion, is entitled to membership. People who are entitled to membership in this way may have membership rights, but have no obligations as members unless they have formally joined the organisation or have taken action in a way which implies they have consented to be a member (for example, voting in the organisation's election).

10.2.3
Junior or youth membership

Junior or **youth membership** is typically a separate category for **minors** (people who are under 18 years of age). If the governing document does not set a minimum age limit, minors can be full members of a company or association. For industrial and provident societies, there is a statutory minimum age limit of 16.

Industrial and Provident Societies Act 1965 s.20

Even if minors can be members of the organisation, there may be restrictions on their serving on the governing body [see **11.3**].

10.2.4
Family membership

Where an organisation offers **family membership**, the governing document or membership regulations must be clear what is meant by 'family' and whether it includes, for example, couples without children, single parent families, same-sex couples, grandparents or other carers. It is also essential to be clear whether every member of the family has a vote or whether there is only one vote per family. If there is only one vote per family, there should be a clear rule about whether family members can join instead as individual or junior members, and in that way get several votes.

10.2.5
Organisational, corporate and group membership

Many organisations make provision for other organisations to be members. The term **corporate member** generally refers to corporate bodies (companies, industrial and provident societies, local authorities and other public bodies). The term **group member** generally refers to unincorporated bodies, and **organisational member** might refer to either or both. In practice the terms are used interchangeably, but membership affects incorporated and unincorporated bodies differently.

Some organisational members, for example larger ones, may be entitled under the governing document to more than one vote.

10.2.5.1
Corporate bodies

An incorporated body can become a member of any other body if its objects or powers allow this. The incorporated body then appoints an individual or individuals to be its **representative(s)** at meetings of the organisation of which it is a member. A representative acts on behalf of the corporate member because it is the corporate body, not the individual, which is the member. The governing document might state that corporate members can appoint an alternate as well as their representative.

If a company is a corporate member of another organisation, any documents which must be signed by 'the member' must be signed by a director, the company secretary, or any person authorised by that company to sign [see **12.1.1**]. *Companies Act 1985 s.41*

If an industrial and provident society is a corporate member of an organisation, any documents must be signed by two members of the IPS's governing body and its secretary.

Industrial and Provident Societies Act 1965 s.19(2)

Unless the governing document specifies otherwise, corporate bodies, acting through their representatives, have all the rights of members. Provided the representative is acting within the powers authorised by the corporate body, the obligations and liabilities of members rest with the corporate body and not with the representative.

10.2.5.2
Unincorporated bodies

Because unincorporated associations and trusts are not legal 'persons' [see **1.1**], technically they cannot be members of another organisation. If they want the right to participate in the incorporated body, they must generally appoint a **nominee** to join on their behalf [see below].

In practice many organisations ignore this and allow unincorporated organisations to join in the same way as corporate bodies, and to appoint a representative to act on behalf of the organisation. In the unlikely event of such membership being challenged it seems likely that the individual who signed the membership application would be held to be the organisation's nominee.

10.2.6
Nominees

The governing document may contain provisions for organisations to nominate members who join on their behalf. This **nominee**, not the appointing organisation, is the member. The nominee and the appointing body should have a clear agreement about whether the nominee is expected to represent the organisation's views, or her or his own.

In this situation the individual has the same rights and liabilities as any other individual member.

10.2.7
Other types of
membership

Voluntary sector governing documents use a wide variety of labels to describe types of members, and the same labels may be used in quite different ways by different organisations. The key issue is always what rights and obligations, if any, are given by the governing document or standing orders to a particular type of membership.

Some typical classes of membership are:

- **branch members**: could refer either to groups set up as branches of the organisation [see **9.2**], or members of those branches;

- **affiliates**: may refer to organisational members [see **9.4.1** and **9.4.2**], or to individuals or organisations who do not meet the criteria for full membership;

- **associate members**: may refer to individuals or organisations who do not meet the criteria for full membership, or those who are in a trial period prior to full membership;

- **honorary members**: may refer to individuals invited to become members even though they do not meet the criteria for membership, or people who fulfil the role of patrons;

- **patrons**: generally refers to well known or illustrious individuals who lend their name and support to the organisation, who may or may not have membership rights;

- **co-opted members**: individuals invited to become members, who might be treated in the same way as full members, associate members or honorary members;

- *ex officio* **members**: people who under the governing document are automatically members by virtue of the position they hold, for example local clergy, the head teacher, the MP or local councillors;

- **life members**: typically defined as those who remain members of the organisation until they die or resign, without needing to renew their membership in the same way as other members.

10.2.8
Subscribers

The term **subscribers** generally refers to individuals or organisations who pay a subscription in order to receive the organisation's publications and/or have access to its activities and services, without becoming members or having any of the rights or obligations of membership.

'subscriber' has a specific meaning when a company is being set up [see **6.3.4**]. In this situation, the subscribers are the persons who sign or 'subscribe to' the memorandum and articles of association and become the first members of the company.

10.2.9
Supporters or 'friends'

Supporters or **friends** are typically individuals or organisations who want to support the organisation, but who do not have any of the rights or obligations of members. They may be required to pay a subscription, and may receive mailings or other benefits in return.

10.2.10
Observers

In addition to the various classes of members and supporters, some people might be invited to attend the organisation's meetings as observers. Observers generally have no right to participate unless invited to do so, and have no right to vote.

10.3
EQUAL OPPORTUNITIES AND MEMBERSHIP

In general the law prohibits discrimination on the basis of racial group (race, colour, ethnic origin, nationality or national origin), sex or disability when selecting members of an organisation, providing benefits or services to them, or terminating membership.

There are some exceptions. A club or association can use racial group as a factor in membership if:

- it has fewer than 25 members, and is not an organisation of workers or employers or a trade or professional organisation; *or*
- the main object of the club or association is to enable people of a particular racial group, which must not be defined by reference to colour, to enjoy the benefits of membership.

Race Relations Act 1976 ss.11(2),(3), 25, 26

A not-for-profit organisation can be set up to provide services to one sex, and can limit its membership to that sex.

Sex Discrimination Act 1975 s.34

Charities (but not most other voluntary organisations) can be set up to provide services to one or more groups of people defined by reference to any physical or mental capacity, and can limit their membership to those people. *Disability Discrimination Act 1995 s.10(1)*

For more about equal opportunities see **chapter 37**.

10.4
LEGAL STRUCTURE AND MEMBERSHIP

Although an organisation might have full, junior, corporate and any of the other types of membership outlined above, there are some differences depending on the organisation's legal structure.

10.4.1
Companies

In a company the members are:

- the subscribers to the memorandum of association [see **6.3.4**]; *and*
- individuals and corporate bodies who agree to become members, and whose names are entered in the register of members [see **16.3.2**].

Companies Act 1985 s.22

In a company limited by shares, the shareholders are the company members. Typically each share gives a right to vote, so a shareholder has as many votes as he or she has shares.

In a company limited by guarantee, the members agree to contribute a guaranteed amount to the company's winding up costs if necessary [see **2.3.1**]. Typically in a modern company limited by guarantee the guarantee is for a nominal £1, and each member has only one vote.

The minimum number of members for a private company, whether limited by shares or guarantee, is one. Voluntary sector companies virtually always have more than one member, but a trading company [see **47.3.2**] might have its parent charity as its sole member.

Companies Act 1985 s.3A

The standard company structure assumes that there will be two tiers: the **company members**, and the **directors** who are elected by the company members. But where there is no intention to have a separate body of members, the company can be set up with the directors as the only company members.

It is important to differentiate between a company's legal members, who have been entered in the register and who have rights under the governing document and company law, and people who might be called members but are simply users of services, supporters etc.

10.4.2 Industrial and provident societies

In an industrial and provident society, the members are shareholders. Shares can be used to raise capital for a society, but in a community benefit IPS [see **2.4.2**] the shares are usually simply used as a token of membership and have a nominal value of £1. The rules must state the maximum shareholding, which in a community benefit society might be only £1 but can be anything up to the statutory maximum of £10,000 per member. The statutory maximum does not apply if the member is another IPS, a company, or a local authority which acquired its holding under the **Housing Associations Act 1985**.

Industrial and Provident Societies Act 1965 sch.1 para.7, s.6(1)

An IPS must have at least three members at all times unless it is a credit union (21 members) or an IPS made up solely of other IPSs (in which case it must have at least two IPSs as members).

IPSA s.16(1)(a); Credit Unions Act 1979

Unless the rules indicate otherwise, membership is open to individuals who are at least 16 years old. Members under 18 years old have the same rights as other members, but cannot be the treasurer or a member of the governing body.

IPSA s.20

The rules might say that corporate bodies cannot be members of the society. If they do not say this, any corporate body can hold shares in the society.

ss.2(2), 19(1)

Unlike the members of a company limited by shares, each member of an IPS has only one vote, regardless of the size of shareholding.

Joint membership is possible unless the rules prohibit this. Joint members have only one vote; clear provision should be made as to who exercises this.

The rules may give the society power to impose reasonable fines on its members if they contravene the rules.

s.13(2)

10.4.3 Trusts

Generally trusts do not have members in the conventional sense, and the only 'members' are the trustees. However it is possible to create a trust similar to an unincorporated association where, for example, the power to appoint or replace trustees is vested in a group of individuals who would have some of the rights of members.

10.4.4 Unincorporated associations

Unincorporated associations often have many classes of membership [see **10.2**]. If these are not carefully defined considerable confusion can arise.

10.4.5 Charities

Membership of a charity depends on whether it is a company, industrial and provident society, trust or association.

Although employees, others paid by a charity and persons under 18 cannot in general be members of the governing body of a charity [see **14.3.7** and **11.3.2**], they can be members of the charity itself unless this

135

is prohibited by the governing document or the organisation's internal rules.

10.5 ADMISSION PROCEDURES

The governing document often outlines the procedure for agreeing new members. Arrangements vary widely. Membership may be **automatic** on application provided the applicant meets the membership criteria, or it may be **subject to approval** by a general meeting of the members, the governing body, a membership committee or an individual.

The application and admission procedures as set out in the governing document or the membership regulations must be strictly followed.

Some governing documents require members to be proposed and seconded by an existing member. This may constitute unlawful racial discrimination, if all the existing members are of one racial group.
Re Handsworth Horticultural Institute, The Guardian 29/1/1993,
Birmingham County Court

Where it appears that an applicant's motives may be destructive, a membership charity may consider these motives and the impact on the organisation. *Royal Society for the Prevention of Cruelty to Animals*
v Attorney General & others [2001] 98(11) LSG 43; TLR 13/2/2001

Where membership affects a right protected under the **Human Rights Act 1998** [see **60.3**], refusal of or removal from membership may be subject to that right. An example might be where membership of a professional body is a precondition to practising a profession, and a person is denied or removed from membership without a fair hearing.

10.5.1 Companies

The first members of a company are the subscribers (signers) of the memorandum and articles of association. Thereafter, to join a company limited by guarantee, an individual or corporate body should sign the register of members [see **16.3.2**] or an application or consent to join, agreeing to pay the guarantee amount [see **2.3.1**] if the company is wound up. By signing, the members agree contractually to join together and to be bound by the memorandum and articles of association.

The name, address and date of joining must be entered in the register of members [see **16.3.2**], but only after the applicant has satisfied all the conditions for membership of the company. These might include, for example, approval by the governing body or a membership committee, and/or payment of a subscription. The date of joining is the date the membership details are entered in the register. Entry in the register is the key evidence of membership of the company.

10.5.2 Industrial and provident societies

The rules of an industrial and provident society must set out the membership criteria for individuals and organisational members and the procedure for admission to membership. The rules usually authorise membership decisions to be delegated to the governing body, a committee or officer. The governing document may include the possibility of an appeal to a general meeting.
Industrial and Provident Societies Act 1965 sch.1 para.4

To join a community benefit IPS a member purchases at least one share and receives a share certificate, and the member's name and details are added to the register of members [see **16.4.1**].

10.5.3 Unincorporated associations

If an unincorporated association does not have a procedure in its governing document or rules about how members are admitted, any membership decision must be made by all the members.

In general no one has a right to membership even if they are eligible, and no reason for refusing membership needs to be given.
Nagle v Feilden [1966] 2 QB 633, 644, 653;
McInnes v Onslow-Fane [1978] 1 WLR 1520, 1529, 1531

However, if the governing document or membership rules state that membership is open to anyone who agrees with the objects, then anyone who says they agree and who pays any necessary subscription cannot generally be refused admission.   *Woodford v Smith [1970] 1 WLR 806*

If membership of an association is necessary in order to carry on a particular trade or profession, any decision not to admit a member must be reached honestly and without bias, but no reason for rejection needs to be given. This provision could in some situations be open to challenge under the Human Rights Act [see **10.5**].   *Nagle v Feilden*
[see above] 645, 653; McInnes v Onslow-Fane [see above] 1533

Unless its governing document requires it, there is no obligation for an unincorporated association to keep a register of members. But it is good practice to do so, and to keep it up to date.

10.6 SUBSCRIPTIONS

Many governing documents contain provision for membership to be conditional on payment of a monthly, annual or one-off subscription. If there is to be a subscription, the governing document normally provides for it to be fixed by a general meeting or the governing body. If the amount is specified in the governing document, it can be changed only by amendment [see **5.5** for procedure].

Non-payment may result in suspension of certain rights or termination of membership, and could lead to the person being sued for the amount by the organisation (if it is incorporated) or by the other members (in an unincorporated association).

Even if the governing document does not authorise a subscription to receive membership *rights* (granted by company law, industrial and provident society law or the governing document), the organisation may charge a subscription to receive membership *benefits* (additional rights given as a result of a decision by the membership or governing body). If members receive benefits in return for payment of a subscription, the subscription may be subject to VAT [see **chapter 53**].

10.7 ASSIGNMENT OR TRANSFER OF MEMBERSHIP

The governing document of most voluntary organisations prohibits the transfer of membership to another person. This is in contrast to companies limited by shares, where the right to transfer shares and therefore membership is virtually universal.

Membership of some organisations, for example a sports association, may bring valuable rights, and provision may be made in the governing document for the assignment or transfer of these. Provision for assignment of membership rights is more common where it is a requirement of membership that an investment or loan is made to the organisation, for example to fund construction of facilities. Difficult issues can arise, such as how much control the organisation has over the assignment, and whether membership can be assigned at a premium or profit. Matters may be simplified by drawing up a loan agreement for any capital input, and separating the loan from membership rights. This should not be done without appropriate legal advice.

10.8 RESIGNATION AND TERMINATION

The membership clause in the governing document should set out procedures for resignation or removal of members, or should give the governing body or a membership committee power to make such regulations. It may also provide procedures for appeal against expulsion. Any procedure for resignation or termination of membership must be followed, and any human rights issues [see **10.5**] should be considered.

Companies and industrial and provident societies must keep their registers of members [see **16.3.2** and **16.4.1**] up to date by entering the date of resignation or termination of membership. If an association has a register of members (and it is good practice to do so) the date of resigning or termination of membership should be entered in it.

10.8.1 Resignation

There is sometimes a clause in the governing document saying that a member cannot resign if by doing so, it brings the number of members below a specified number.

The rules of an IPS must include procedures for deciding whether and if so how members can withdraw. The 'whether' implies that members do not automatically have a right to withdraw, unless this is explicit in the rules. *Industrial and Provident Societies Act 1965 sch.1 para.9*

Unless the governing document specifies otherwise, a member of an unincorporated association has a right to resign at any time by following the procedure in the governing document or membership rules, or by notifying the secretary. Resignation is then automatic, from the date the letter or other communication is received, and cannot be revoked unless the rules allow this. *Finch v Oake [1896] 1 Ch 409, 415*

10.8.2 Lapsing

The governing document might provide that once a person becomes a member, membership lasts until resignation, automatic termination or expulsion. Or it may say that in order to remain a member, certain criteria must be fulfilled, for example paying a membership subscription within a defined period, or attending a general meeting at least once every three years. If members do not take the action necessary to meet these criteria, their membership lapses.

10.8.3 Automatic termination

The governing document or membership rules may specify that membership terminates automatically in certain circumstances, for example if the member moves away from the area, or if membership depends on another contractual relationship—such as being a tenant of a housing association—and the contractual relationship ends.

10.8.4 Death

When a member of a share company dies, his or her shares normally pass to the executor or administrator of the estate (called a personal representative). This is unlikely to be the case in a company limited by guarantee, where the death of a member generally brings the company membership to an end.

As in a share company, shares in an industrial and provident society pass to a personal representative when a member dies. The rules must include procedures for dealing with this. Members have a right, during their lifetime, to nominate a person to succeed to their interest in the society when they die, and the society must keep a record of this.
 Industrial and Provident Societies Act 1965 sch.1 para.11; s.23(1),(5)

Death terminates membership of an unincorporated association unless the governing document allows membership to pass to another person.

10.8.5 Suspension and expulsion

A member may be suspended or expelled from an organisation only if:

- there is a power to do so in the governing document or membership rules;

- the rules are strictly followed;

- the organisation acts in good faith;

- where Human Rights Act issues arise, the provisions of the Act are not breached [see **60.3**]; *and*

- the rules of **natural justice** are followed. This means that the person to be suspended or expelled has the right to know the reasons for the action, to put his or her case in response to the accusation, and to have any decision made by an unbiased body.
 John v Rees [1970] Ch 345, 397; Dawkins v Antrobus [1881] ChD 615, 620

If a suspension or expulsion is not properly carried out the member can bring a case in court to have it declared invalid, and may be awarded damages. An exception is a short-term suspension needed in order to investigate possible wrongdoing, for example suspending the treasurer while the accounts are checked after an allegation of fraud. In situations such as this the organisation's rules must be followed and those initiating the suspension must act in good faith, but the person being suspended does not have to be given an opportunity to present his or her case before being suspended. *Lewis v Heffer [1978] 1 WLR 1069, 1073*

10.9 MEMBERS AND THE GOVERNING BODY

In a membership organisation, the governing body is accountable to the membership. The boundaries between the organisation's members and the governing body can be complex and sometimes problematic. The governing document should clearly specify which rights and powers are reserved for the members, and which are granted to the governing body. Generally the organisation's members have the right to elect or appoint the governing body, and the governing body is given full control over the management of the organisation.

The organisation's members can pass resolutions which the governing body has to implement, provided they do not require the governing body to do anything which is unlawful or conflicts with their duties as charity trustees, and provided they do not take action on anything which the governing document delegates exclusively to the governing body.

In companies and industrial and provident societies a majority of the members can remove the directors [see **11.5.6**], and the governing document of many unincorporated associations contains similar provision. Members may also be able to amend the governing document to limit the powers of the governing body.

10.10 RIGHTS OF INDIVIDUALS AND MINORITIES

Individuals or minorities of members who do not like the way the majority or the governing body is operating have very little recourse, because the courts generally will not intervene in an organisation's internal business unless the members or the governing body are acting outside the organisation's objects or powers [see **4.7**], are acting unlawfully, or are infringing the rights of individuals. In other cases the only action open to dissatisfied members may be to leave the organisation.

In a company, the individual company members cannot in general bring an action against any person, including members of the governing body, even if they have harmed the company or its members.

Foss v Harbottle (1843) 2 Hare 461

There are several exceptions to this rule, and individual company members may bring legal action if:

- the company's affairs are being or have been conducted in a manner which is **unfairly prejudicial** to the interests of some or all members, or an actual or proposed act or omission by the company is or would be prejudicial; *Companies Act 1985 ss.459-461*
- an action taken by the organisation is *ultra vires* or illegal [see **4.7**];
- a decision made by the members requires a special or extraordinary resolution [see **17.4.7**] but was passed by an ordinary resolution;
- a majority of members are committing fraud on a minority;
- the members of the governing body are using their powers fraudulently or negligently, and in a way which benefits themselves at the expense of the company; *Daniels v Daniels [1978] Ch 406*
- an individual's personal rights as a member of the company have been infringed; *or* *Edwards v Halliwell [1950] 2 All ER 1064*
- a company meeting cannot be called in time to be of practical effect in stopping an action. *Hodgson v National and Local Government Officers Association [1972] 1 WLR 130*

Chapter 11
MEMBERS OF THE GOVERNING BODY

11.1 MAKE-UP OF THE GOVERNING BODY

The governing body are the persons who are responsible in law for managing the organisation. A governing body may have many names, such as board of directors, board of trustees, board of governors, management committee, council of management, executive committee, steering committee or steering group. Regardless of what it is called:

- in a company, the members of the governing body are the **company directors**;
- in a trust or charitable association they are **trustees** for the purposes of the **Trustee Act 2000** and most other trust law;
- if a trust, association, company or industrial and provident society is charitable [see **3.1**], the members of the governing body are **charity trustees** for the purposes of charity law.

What matters is not what the governing body is called, but the powers and duties it has under the organisation's governing document and under charity, company, IPS, trust and general law.

If a group is not formally constituted, for example if it is a steering committee or 'just a group of members', the governing body are the persons who control the group's activities.

Just as there is no standardisation in what the governing body is called, so is there no standardisation in how large it is, who is on it and how they get appointed or elected.

Typically the governing body of an organisation with members (companies, industrial and provident societies and unincorporated associations) is a smaller group elected by those members. But there is no reason why the whole membership should not itself be the governing body. This is especially appropriate for small organisations, or where a high premium is put on members' direct involvement in managing the organisation.

Especially where there is a complex web of committees and sub-committees, it may not be straightforward to work out which is the governing body. But it is important to be clear about this, because it has implications for decision making, legal responsibility and potential liability.

11.1.1
Voting members

To be a full member of the governing body, a person must have a vote. So the members of the governing body are those persons who the governing document defines as voting members of the governing body, regardless of what they are called.

Confusion sometimes arises about the rights of co-opted members [see **11.4.1.6**], representatives of other organisations [see **11.4.1.3** and **11.4.1.4**], people who serve *ex officio* [see **11.4.1.2**], and others who are not appointed or elected in the usual way. If the governing document refers to such persons as members of the governing body and does not say anything about whether they have the right to vote, they will generally be full voting members of the governing body unless the governing document makes clear in some way that they are not.

Some governing documents specify that only members of the organisation (in a membership organisation) can be full members of the governing body; other governing documents allow anyone to be a full member.

11.1.2
Non-voting members

The governing document sometimes specifies that co-opted members, representatives of other organisations and/or people who serve *ex officio* do not have voting rights or are observers or advisors on the governing body. This might apply, for example, to funders' representatives or the organisation's employees.

Non-voting members generally have a right to participate in discussions, but are not entitled to vote or make decisions in other ways. **Observers** generally have no right to participate in discussions or decisions but they may, with the consent of the person chairing the meeting, participate in discussions. **Advisors** are there to give advice, either generally or on specific matters. They cannot take part in decisions.

Anyone who does not have a vote will not count towards the quorum [see **17.6.4**] unless the governing document states that they do.

In general, persons who do not have a vote are not legally considered to be members of the governing body and are not liable for the organisation's actions. However a person who in fact takes part in decisions could be held liable in the same way as other governing body members, or in a company could be considered to be a **shadow director** [see **11.1.3.2**].

11.1.3
Companies

11.1.3.1
Company directors

Not very helpfully, a **company director** is defined in company law as 'any person occupying the position of director, by whatever name called'. The first directors are the persons named in company form 10 (and sometimes in the articles of association as well) as the first directors [see **6.3.5**]. Subsequent directors are persons elected or appointed under the provisions in the articles.   *Companies Act 1985 s.741(1)*

All voting members of the governing body of an organisation registered as a company are company directors. Under company law they must formally consent to be a director by signing company **form 288a** and their details must be entered in the register of directors [see **16.3.4**].

All company directors are **officers** of the company, and are also agents of the company [see **5.3.2**, **12.1.1** and **18.5**]. In most voluntary organisation companies the directors are not paid by the company, but if they are paid solely for their services *as directors* they are not generally classed as employees. Directors who are paid in another capacity—for example as a chief executive, a finance officer or a care worker—are generally classed as employees in that capacity.   *Companies Act 1985 s.744*

If the company is charitable, its directors are also **charity trustees** [see **11.1.7**].

11.1.3.2
Shadow directors

A **shadow director** is a person who does not have voting rights on the board but 'in accordance with whose directions or instructions the directors of the company are accustomed to act'.   *s.714(2)*

A chief executive, representative of a funding body, consultant, advisor or other person who dominates or controls the board could be considered to be a shadow director. However if a person gives professional advice, for example as a solicitor or accountant, and it is only on that advice that the directors act, the person is not a shadow director.

For many company law purposes, shadow directors are treated in the same way as ordinary directors. For example they must sign form 288a, their names must be entered in the register of directors and they are liable in the same way as company directors if the organisation becomes insolvent and is involved in fraudulent or wrongful trading [see **21.2.4**].
s.288(6)

The concept of shadow director has caused considerable concern within voluntary organisations. If, for example, a chief executive of a charitable company is a shadow director, he or she would also be a charity trustee and might not be able to be paid by the charity. While an awareness of the risks is important, the tests for shadow directorship require the person virtually to control the other directors. This is different from providing information and recommendations, and is a rare situation.

11.1.4
Industrial and provident societies

The rules of an industrial and provident society must specify how members of the board or committee, managers and other officers are elected. Their names must be entered in the register of officers [see **16.4.2**].
Industrial and Provident Societies Act 1965 sch.1 para.6

Governing body members of charitable IPSs have some duties as **charity trustees** [see **11.1.7**].

11.1.5
Unincorporated associations

In a small unincorporated association with a single-tier organisational structure, where there is only one identifiable group of people ('the members', 'the committee' etc), those people will be the governing body.

However, the governing document often explicitly states that the members of the association are to elect or appoint a committee of some sort. If this committee is empowered to take decisions on behalf of the members or to manage the organisation, it is clearly the governing body. In situations where it is less clear that management responsibility is being delegated, the committee will usually be considered to be the governing body on the assumption that by electing such a committee, the members are authorising them to manage the organisation on their behalf. But it could perhaps be argued that the full membership is the governing body, and the elected or appointed committee is only a sub-committee. If there is a dispute about the powers held by the committee it will be necessary to get specialist legal advice.

11.1.6
Trusts

In a trust the original trustees are generally named in the trust deed [see **6.2.1**]. The deed may have provision for the appointment of subsequent trustees. If it does not, the remaining trustees may appoint new trustees [see **11.4.1.5**].

11.1.7
Charities

The voting members of the governing body of a charitable organisation are **charity trustees**, regardless of whether the charity is set up as a trust, unincorporated association, company or industrial and provident society. Charity trustees are 'the persons having the general control and management of the administration of a charity'. *Charities Act 1993 s.97*

Charity trustees are not the same as **holding trustees** [see **18.4.4**], who hold property and investments on behalf of unincorporated bodies. But the same people may hold both roles.

Some, but not all, charity trustees are also trustees for the purposes of the **Trustee Act 2000**, and have specific duties and powers under the Act [see **54.1**].

11.2 NUMBER ON THE GOVERNING BODY

The **minimum** number of people who must be on the governing body is set down in law and/or in the organisation's governing document. If different numbers are specified, the higher number prevails.

A governing body which does not have the minimum number or does not have enough members to make a quorum [see **17.6.4**] cannot take any action, other than to elect or appoint new governing body members (if it has that power) or to call a general meeting where the members of the organisation can elect new governing body members.

There is no **maximum** number of governing body members set out in law, but the governing document may set a maximum. It is generally advisable not to have too large a governing body, because of the difficulty in calling meetings and making decisions efficiently.

11.2.1 Trust law

A trust may have only one trustee, if that trustee is a corporate body such as a local authority or other **trust corporation**. Otherwise it must have at least two trustees. *Trustee Act 1925 s.14(2)*

A trust is unlikely to be registered by the Charity Commission if it has fewer than three individuals as trustees.

11.2.2 Company law

A private company—which virtually all voluntary sector companies are—must have at least one individual or corporate director as well as a company secretary. If there is more than one director, one of the directors can also be the secretary. *Companies Act 1985 ss.282, 283*

The Charity Commission generally requires a charitable company to have at least three directors unless a corporate body is a sole director.

11.2.3 Industrial and provident societies

An industrial and provident society must consist of at least three individuals or two IPSs. The governing body cannot be any smaller than this. *Industrial and Provident Societies Act 1965 s.2*

11.2.4 Unincorporated associations

An unincorporated association must have at least two members [see **1.2.1**] but apart from this the only rules about minimum or maximum numbers are those in the governing document.

11.3 ELIGIBILITY AND DISQUALIFICATION

A person may be prohibited from serving on a governing body because he or she:

- does not meet criteria set down in the organisation's governing document or rules and is thus **ineligible** to serve on its governing body;
- does not fulfil the statutory criteria for charity trustees and is therefore **disqualified** from serving on a charity governing body; *or*
- does not fulfil the statutory criteria for serving as a company director or has been **disqualified** by the court from being a company director.

11.3.1 The governing document

A governing document may set out eligibility requirements, for example that a member of the governing body must live in a particular area or be a member of the organisation at the time of nomination or election.

The governing document may also specify that a governing body member must stand down in certain situations [see **11.5**].

11.3.2
Charity law

To serve as a charity trustee or as a holding trustee [see **18.4.4**] for a charity, a person must:

- meet any requirements set out in the governing document;

- be properly elected or appointed as set out in the governing document; *and*

- not be disqualified from serving as a charity trustee [see **11.3.2.4**].

In charities set up as trusts, trustees must be at least 18 years of age. Although this does not strictly apply to charities set up as associations or companies, the Charity Commission generally requires members of the governing body to be 18 or over.   *Law of Property Act 1925 s.20*

Two principles of equity [see **60.2.2**], on which charity law is based, are that trustees must not profit or benefit from their trust [see **13.3.6**], and that they must not be in a position where they may have a conflict of interest [see **13.3.4**]. These principles have important implications for charities which want to have employees or users/beneficiaries, or persons closely connected to them, as trustees, or which want to pay trustees for work they do for the charity. These rules are explained in **chapter 14**.

11.3.2.1
Payments to trustees and persons close to them

Trustees have a right to be reimbursed for genuine out-of-pocket expenses [see **14.2**]. Most governing documents prohibit or restrict other payments to trustees, but in some situations it is acceptable for trustees to be paid for their services as trustees, or for trustees or persons close to them to be paid for work for the charity [see **14.3** and **14.4**].

11.3.2.2
Employees as charity trustees

An employee cannot be a charity trustee—and a charity trustee cannot be employed by the charity—unless this is authorised by the governing document or the Charity Commission [see **14.3.7**]. There is nothing to stop employees from attending and participating in trustees' meetings.

11.3.2.3
Beneficiaries as charity trustees

A charity's beneficiaries or users of its services benefit from the charity and could easily be in a position where, if they were trustees, they would have a conflict of interest. A strict interpretation of charity and trust law could therefore be that beneficiaries or users of a charity's services should not be trustees. In practice the interpretation is usually not this strict, and the Charity Commission has issued guidance on this [see **14.5** for more about beneficiaries as trustees and *vice versa*].

Beneficiaries/users who are not trustees may be invited to attend governing body meetings and may, with the consent of the meeting, participate in discussions.

11.3.2.4
Disqualification

The grounds for disqualification apply to trustees and holding trustees of all charities, including exempt and excepted charities [see **7.1.2** and **7.1.3**]. They are:

- having been convicted for any offence involving dishonesty or deception, unless the conviction is spent under the terms of the **Rehabilitation of Offenders Act 1974** [see **25.10**];

- having been declared bankrupt or (in Scotland) having assets sequestered, unless the bankruptcy or sequestration has been discharged or permission has been granted under the **Company Directors Disqualification Act 1986** s.11 for the person to act as director of a charitable company;

- having made a composition or arrangement with creditors under the **Insolvency Act 1986** which has not been discharged;

- having been removed by the Charity Commission or the High Court from being a trustee of or for any charity;

- having been removed by the Court of Session in Scotland from being involved in the management of any charitable body;

- being subject to a disqualification order under the **Company Directors Disqualification Act 1986**, unless permission has been given to act as a director of a charitable company;

- being subject to an order made under the **Insolvency Act 1986** s.429(2)(b) for failure to make payments under a county court administration order, unless permission to act as a charity trustee has been granted by the court which made the order. *Charities Act 1993 s.72*

The Charity Commission keeps a register, open to the public, of people removed from charity trusteeship by the Commission or High Court.

**11.3.2.5
Charity Commission
waiver**

Any person disqualified on any of these grounds may apply to the Charity Commission for a waiver either in relation to a particular charity or type of charity, or in general. However, a Commission waiver cannot override a disqualification provision in a charity's governing document.
Charities Act 1993 s.72(4)

A waiver is not possible in relation to a charitable company if the person is prohibited from being a charity trustee by a disqualification order under the **Company Directors Disqualification Act 1986**, and permission has not been granted for him or her to act as director of any other company.

**11.3.2.6
Serving while
disqualified**

It is an offence, punishable by a fine and up to two years imprisonment, to serve as a trustee of or for a charity while disqualified.
Charities Act 1993 s.73(1)

The charity law penalties do not apply if the charity is a charitable company and the person is disqualified only because of bankruptcy, sequestration of assets, disqualification under the Company Directors Disqualification Act 1986 or an order under the Insolvency Act. But the same penalties apply to these under company law [see **11.3.3.2**]. *s.73(2)*

Any person who serves as a trustee while disqualified may be required by the Charity Commission to repay to the charity any payments received as remuneration or for expenses while disqualified, or the monetary value of any benefits received while disqualified. The Commission does not have this power in relation to exempt charities. *s.73(4)*

A charity's governing document may specify that the trustee automatically ceases to be a member of the governing body as soon as he or she becomes disqualified. If it does not specify this, the person should resign or, if necessary, be removed from the governing body under the procedure in the governing document or under the provisions of the **Trustee Act 1925** [see **11.5.5**]. While waiting for this procedure the person remains a trustee but must not attend meetings or take part in any way in managing the charity.

People who are not trustees and are disqualified can attend trustee meetings in a non-voting capacity, but need to be careful not to act in ways which could be seen as influencing or taking part in decisions.

**11.3.2.7
Protecting trustees**

To ensure an individual does not inadvertently serve while disqualified, it is good practice to devise an information sheet or consent form listing the grounds for disqualification, and to ensure trustees receive this before accepting the position. The sheet can make clear that the person can apply to the Charity Commission for a waiver if he or she is disqualified [see **11.3.2.5**].

**11.3.3
Company law**

To serve as a company director an individual must:

- meet any requirements set out in the articles of association;

- be properly elected or appointed as set out in the articles; *and*

- not be disqualified from being a company director and, in a charitable company, not be disqualified from serving as a charity trustee [see **11.3.2.4**].

There is no minimum age limit for being a company director in England and Wales, although it would generally be considered unwise to have directors under the age of 18 and the Charity Commission generally does not allow it for charitable companies. There is an upper age limit of 70 for directors of public companies, but this does not apply to directors of private companies, which virtually all voluntary sector companies are.

Companies Act 1985 s.293

11.3.3.1 Disqualification

The **Company Directors Disqualification Act 1986** sets out the reasons for which a court must or may disqualify a person from serving as a company director for a specified period. Disqualification also extends to taking any part in promoting, forming or managing a company.

A person cannot be involved in setting up or managing a company or serve as director without permission from the court if he or she is an undischarged bankrupt or, in Scotland, has had an estate sequestered, or fails to make payments under a county court administration order.

Company Directors Disqualification Act 1986 ss.11, 12(2)

A person may be disqualified by the court because of **general misconduct** in connection with companies if:

• the person is, or has been judged to be, persistently in default in sending annual returns, accounts or other required documents [see **50.3.5**] to the Registrar of Companies;

• the person is convicted of an indictable offence in relation to the promotion, formation, management or liquidation of a company, or with the receivership or management of a company's property; *or*

• it appears, in the course of winding up a company, that the person has been guilty of fraudulent trading [see **21.2.4**]. *ss.2-5*

A person may be also disqualified after being found liable for wrongful trading [see **21.2.4**] while a company was being wound up. *s.10*

A person must be disqualified for **unfitness** if:

• he or she is or has been director or shadow director [see **11.1.3.2**] of a company which has become insolvent, either while he or she was a director or afterwards, *and*

• the court believes that the person's conduct as a director makes him or her unfit to be involved in managing a company. *ss.6-9*

Companies House maintains a public register of persons disqualified from serving as company directors. Information is provided by telephone, or the register can be searched at Companies House or on its website [see **page 12**].

11.3.3.2 Serving while disqualified

It is a an offence, punishable by a fine and up to two years imprisonment, to be involved in promoting, forming or managing a company while disqualified. *s.13*

In addition, a person who acts while disqualified becomes personally liable for all the debts of the company incurred while he or she was involved in managing the company. A person who knowingly acts or is willing to act on instructions given by a person who is subject to a disqualification order or is an undischarged bankrupt becomes personally liable for all the debts of the company incurred while he or she acted or was willing to act on such instructions. *s.15*

To protect individuals from these risks, it is good practice to devise an information sheet or consent form [see **11.3.2.7**].

A company's governing document usually specifies that the director ceases to be a member of the governing body as soon as he or she becomes disqualified. If it does not specify this, the person should resign or be removed from the governing body [see **11.5.6.1** for procedure]. While waiting for this procedure the person remains a director but must not attend meetings or take part in any way in managing the company.

After resignation or removal there is no prohibition on the disqualified person attending board meetings in a non-voting capacity, but he or she must not take a dominant or significant role because of the risk of being seen as a shadow director [see **11.1.3.2**] while disqualified.

11.3.4
Industrial and
provident societies

A person under the age of 18 may not serve on the governing body of an industrial and provident society, or as its manager or treasurer.

Industrial and Provident Societies Act 1965 s.20

IPSs are not covered by the **Company Directors Disqualification Act 1986**, nor is there anything about disqualification in IPS law. However, many IPSs have provisions in their governing document disqualifying anyone subject to company disqualification. Charitable IPSs must comply with charity rules regarding eligibility for and disqualification from trusteeship [see **11.3.2**].

11.3.5
Trusts and
unincorporated
associations

Charitable trusts and charitable associations must comply with charity rules in relation to their trustees and any holding trustees [see **11.3.2**].

Non-charitable associations do not have to comply with any requirements other than those set out in their governing document.

11.3.6
Children's charities

It is an offence to serve on the governing body of a children's charity or an educational institution while banned or disqualified from work with children [see **26.3.4**]. It is also an offence for anyone knowingly to offer such a position to a person who is banned or disqualified from work with children.

Criminal Justice and Court Services Act 2000 ss.35-36

11.4
JOINING THE
GOVERNING BODY

The process by which the governing body members are appointed or elected, and the length of time they serve, depend on the organisation's governing document and, to a lesser extent, its legal structure.

For companies, all changes relating to directors must be entered in the register of directors [see **16.3.4**] and must be notified to Companies House within 14 days on **form 288a** (new directors), **288b** (resignation or removal) or **288c** (change of name, address or other details).

When new governing body members are appointed or elected in a trust, the trust's assets should be vested in the new trustees [see **18.4.5**]. In an association, if the governing body members are holding trustees for the association's property or investments, it may be necessary to vest the property in new trustees when the governing body members change. Without this vesting, the original trustees continue to hold the assets.

11.4.1
Appointment
11.4.1.1
By founders

An organisation's founders may name some or all members of the governing body in the governing document.

In a **trust** the trustees named in the trust deed serve until they resign, are removed or die, unless the trust deed indicates otherwise.

In a **company**, the first directors are named in company **form 10** when the company is registered [see **6.3.5**]. If it is known beforehand who all the directors will be, form 10 will list all of them, and their names may appear in the articles of association. If it is not known beforehand who the directors will be, interim directors will be listed on form 10 and will serve until new directors are appointed or elected.

Where the articles of association refer to first directors as 'directors' but then refer to 'management committee members' or something similar, it is a common mistake to think that the directors named in form 10 remain company directors forever, and that the management committee is separate from the directors. This is not the case. Unless the articles of association explicitly name someone as a **permanent director**, the directors named in form 10 serve only as the first governing body and only until they are replaced by the election or appointment of new directors at a general meeting.

11.4.1.2
Ex officio

Some people are entitled to a place on the governing body *ex officio*, by virtue of a position they hold (for example as the mayor or chief executive of the organisation). They generally retain their place on the governing body for as long as they hold the relevant position, and are then replaced by the new post holder.

11.4.1.3
Nomination

The governing document may give other organisations, the local authority or other bodies the right to appoint one or more members of the governing body. These appointees are called **representative**, **nominated** or **nominative members** of the governing body. The individual person, not the nominating body, is the member of the governing body.

11.4.1.4
Corporate body representatives

A corporate body (but not an unincorporated body) may under the terms of the governing document be a member of a governing body. Local authorities, for example, are often trustees for charitable trusts.

In this case the corporate body, rather than any individual who acts on its behalf, is the member of the governing body and has the duties and liabilities of governing body membership. Despite this, the individual who represents the corporate body could be held liable on the basis that he or she had the powers and duties of a trustee.

When public sector bodies are reorganised it may be necessary to take advice to determine which successor authority has the right to serve as trustee or appoint members of the governing body.

11.4.1.5
Appointment by existing members of governing body

The governing document may give the members of the governing body the power to appoint further members. A maximum may be set.

If a charity is set up as a trust [see **1.3**] and the charity's governing document gives the members of the governing body, the members of the charity or other persons the right to appoint and discharge trustees, the transfer may be done by producing a memorandum stating that the trustee has been appointed or discharged.   *Charities Act 1993 s.83*

The memorandum gives the name of the charity and says,

> At a meeting of the trustees held on [date], it was resolved, in exercise of the power in clause ___ of the charity's trust deed/ constitution, that the following should be appointed as trustees: [names and addresses] in place of [name and address] who wished to retire [or has died].

The memorandum must be signed and delivered [see **18.3.2**] by the person who chaired the meeting at which the appointment or discharge was made, or by another person authorised by the meeting to sign. The memorandum must be witnessed by two people who were at the meeting. Additional procedures are needed to transfer investments and land [see **18.4.5**].

If the governing document of a charitable trust does not contain provision for appointment of further trustees, the trustees have the power to replace trustees when they retire, but not to appoint additional trustees.   *Trustee Act 1925 s.36*

11.4.1.6
Co-option

The governing document may give the members of the governing body and/or the members of an association, company or IPS power to **co-opt** additional people onto the governing body, either to fill vacancies which arise between elections (**casual vacancies**) or to bring additional members onto the governing body.

The governing document should set out how long they serve (usually until the next annual general meeting), and whether they can be re-co-opted. Unless the governing document indicates otherwise, co-opted members of the governing body have the same voting rights, other rights and obligations as other governing body members.

People cannot be co-opted if the governing document does not allow this, but the governing document may be amended in the usual way [see **5.5**], or people may be invited to attend meetings as observers.

11.4.1.7
By the Charity
Commission

The Charity Commission may appoint or discharge (remove) charity trustees if requested by trustees to do so, or if it considers such action necessary for the proper management of the charity, or if a defunct charity is being revived.   *Charities Act 1993 s.16(1)(b)*

11.4.2
Election

In membership organisations, some or all of the members of the governing body are generally elected by those members who have the right to take part in elections [see **10.2**]. Procedures set out in the governing document must be carefully followed.

In small membership organisations, all the members may be the governing body. If the governing document requires an AGM to be held and requires the organisation's members to elect the governing body, these procedures must be followed—even though the members of the organisation simply elect themselves as members of the governing body.

11.4.2.1
Nomination

Some governing documents specify that anyone standing for election to the governing body must be **nominated** by another member or members; others allow individuals to nominate themselves. Some require nominations to be made a specified period before the AGM; others allow nominations from the floor on the day of the election; others require nomination only if the candidate is not a current member of the governing body or approved by the governing body.

Standing orders [see **5.4.25**] may be put in place to clarify nomination arrangements, provided they do not contradict anything in the governing document. In designing nomination arrangements, a balance often needs to be drawn between ensuring that nominees are well supported and good notice is given of who they are, and the realities of the last-minute struggle to find people willing to stand. Where an organisation fears sudden change or takeover, it may try to prevent this by imposing elaborate nomination requirements.

11.4.2.2
Uncontested elections

In many organisations, candidates for an uncontested post are automatically elected. However some organisations have a procedure for uncontested elections which allows members to vote against the candidate, or requires a minimum number of votes in favour of him or her. This prevents a person genuinely considered unsuitable from being elected simply because no one else was nominated.

If an election in a private company (which virtually all voluntary sector companies are) is uncontested, with the number of available places equal to or more than the number of candidates, all the directors may be elected as one block rather than individually.   *Companies Act 1985 s.292*

11.4.2.3
Voting methods

The governing document may require members to vote in person, or may allow voting by postal ballot or proxy [see **chapter 17**].

For contested elections (more candidates than places), many voting systems exist. Members may vote by ticking the candidates they want on a **first past the post** system (the ones with the most votes win), or voting in order of preference on a **single transferable vote** system. The Electoral Reform Society [see end of **chapter 17**] can provide advice on STV, and Electoral Reform Services can manage elections for any organisation.

11.4.2.4
Open voting

While many organisations allow only members to vote in elections, some allow wider participation. Community associations, for example, may allow voting by 'anyone who lives or works in the parish of X', or a residents' association may allow any resident of the estate to vote.

11.4.2.5
Electoral colleges

The governing document may specify that groupings within the organisation—for example members who live in the Midlands, a black section or a users' group—elect one or more members of the governing body. These groupings are sometimes called **electoral colleges**. Especially in large organisations this procedure can make it easier for people to vote for people they know, and can make it more likely that minority interests will be represented on the governing body.

11.4.3
Alternates

If the governing document allows, a governing body member may temporarily delegate his or her authority to an **alternate**. This could happen, for example, if a member of the governing body is hospitalised or is going to be away. The alternate is a substitute for the original member and serves only until the original member returns.

An alternate should not be confused with:

- a permanent change of representative [see **11.4.1.3**], where a body has the right to appoint a member of the governing body;
- where a corporate body is itself a member of the governing body [see **11.4.1.4**], and changes the person acting on its behalf.

11.4.3.1
Companies

The articles of association of both charitable and non-charitable companies may allow appointment of alternate directors.

Virtually all the statutory requirements applying to company directors apply to alternates as well. An alternate must not be disqualified from serving as a director [see **11.3.3.2**], her or his name must be entered in the register of directors [see **16.3.4**] and the appointment and revocation must be notified to Companies House in the usual way [see **11.4**].

Alternate directors are not agents [see **18.5**] of the directors who appointed them, and are liable for their own acts.

11.4.3.2
Trusts and charitable associations

Trustees are required to act personally [see **13.3.8**], so the Charity Commission is generally unwilling to approve a governing document for a charitable trust or association which allows appointment of alternate trustees. However a trustee may delegate any or all powers and duties for a period of up to one year [see **11.5.5**]. The original trustee is liable for the acts of the appointed person.

11.4.3.3
Non-charitable associations

A governing document for a non-charitable association which allows alternates should make clear that the alternate is acting in his or her own right and not as an agent [see **18.5**]. If this is not made clear the original member could be held liable for the acts of the alternate.

11.5
LEAVING THE GOVERNING BODY

A person may leave a governing body by:

- **retiring**, when the term of office set under the governing document comes to an end;
- **resigning**, before the end of the term;
- being **replaced** by the body which appointed him or her;
- becoming **disqualified** from serving as a company director and/or charity trustee [see **11.3.2.4** and **11.3.3.2**], and resigning or being removed from the governing body;
- being removed for a reason set out in the **governing document**, for example missing meetings or no longer living in the area;
- in a trust, being replaced by the other trustee(s);
- being removed by a vote of the members of a company, industrial and provident society or association;
- being removed by the Charity Commission or the High Court;
- dying;
- in the case of a corporate body, being **dissolved** [see **21.3-21.6**].

**11.5.1
Restrictions on
retirement and
resignation**

Governing documents sometimes contain restrictions relating to retirement or resignation, for example:

- a member of the governing body cannot resign if the resignation would bring the number of members below the quorum for governing body meetings;

- retiring members of the governing body are automatically re-elected or re-appointed at the end of their term if there is no one to replace them.

A trustee of a charitable or non-charitable trust cannot resign if the resignation would leave less than two individual trustees or a trust corporation. *Trustee Act 1925 s.39(1)*

The Charity Commission is likely to take the view that members of the governing body who resign leaving a charity without an effective governing body remain liable to discharge their duties as charity trustees.

**11.5.2
Incapacity**

The governing document may state that a person automatically ceases to be a member of the governing body if he or she 'suffers from mental disorder', or 'becomes incapable by reason of mental disorder, illness or injury of managing and administering his or her own affairs'. It is then up to the organisation to determine whether the person is incapable of serving on the governing body.

The standard Companies Act article in the articles of association provides for the office of director to be vacated if the director is, or may be, suffering from mental disorder *and* he or she either is admitted to hospital under the **Mental Health Act 1983** or **Mental Health (Scotland) Act 1960,** or is subject to a court order in matters concerning mental disorder. This has the advantage of defining mental disorder, but means that the governing body has no choice about whether to remove the director. *Companies Act 1985 table A para.81(c)*

Unless the governing document specifies otherwise, an incapacitated person remains a member of the governing body until he or she resigns or his or her term of office comes to an end. In extreme cases it may be possible to obtain a court order excluding the person from attending meetings until they recover.

**11.5.3
Non-attendance**

The governing document may state that a member is automatically removed from the governing body, or may be removed if the other members agree, if he or she is absent from meetings for a specified time or from a certain number of meetings without consent of the governing body. If the governing document does not contain this provision it can be amended in the usual way [see **5.5** for procedure].

Unless the governing document specifies otherwise, membership continues even if the member never attends meetings. However for charity trustees and company directors, persistent non-attendance could constitute a breach of their duties, and could even lead to disqualification as a company director [see **13.3.8** and **13.2.3**].

**11.5.4
Misconduct**

Unless the governing document allows, the members of the governing body generally have no power to remove another member, even one who engages in misconduct. In limited circumstances, the trustees of a trust or charitable association may be able to remove a trustee [see below]. If the misconduct threatens a charity's assets, the Charity Commission may be asked to investigate, and has power to remove trustees [see **3.5.8-3.5.10**].

**11.5.5
Replacement by
trustees**

Unless the governing document specifies otherwise, trustees of non-charitable and charitable trusts may replace a trustee who:

- is out of the UK for a continuous period of more than 12 months;

- wishes to be discharged from responsibilities as a trustee;

- refuses to act as a trustee;
- is unfit to act as a trustee;
- is incapable of acting as a trustee; *or*
- is under the age of 18. *Trustee Act 1925 s.36*

'Unfit' is not defined but generally applies to matters covered by the charity trustee disqualification rules [see **11.3.2.4**]. Incapacity to act includes senility, mental disorder etc [see **11.5.2**].

For the process of removal and replacement, see **13.5.2**. This procedure is not available for companies and industrial and provident societies, whether charitable or non-charitable, or for non-charitable unincorporated associations. Legal advice should be sought before using it in a charitable association.

11.5.6
Removal by members

11.5.6.1
Companies

Members of a company always have a right to remove a director and to appoint a replacement by ordinary resolution with special notice [see **17.4.7** for procedure]. The right to remove a director cannot be taken away or amended by anything in the articles or by any agreement with directors, and applies even to 'permanent' directors.

Companies Act 1985 s.303

Notice of intention to put a resolution to remove a director and/or appoint a replacement must be delivered to the company's office at least 28 days before the meeting. As soon as the company receives this notice of intention, it must send a copy to the director whose removal is proposed. *s.304*

This director has the right to be heard on the resolution at the meeting, and also has the right to make written representations of a reasonable length to the company and request that these be notified to members. The company must then, in the notice of the resolution given to members, state that representations have been made, and send a copy of them to every member to whom notice of the meeting has been sent. If the representations are received too late to send them out or if the company does not send them out, the director can require them to be read out at the meeting.

If the representations are considered to be defamatory, either the company or any aggrieved person may apply to the High Court, which may rule that the representations involve 'needless publicity for defamatory matter' and do not need to be circulated or read out.

11.5.6.2
Other membership organisations

Provision for removal of governing body members must be included in the rules of an industrial and provident society. IPSs and associations often have removal provisions similar to those for companies.

11.5.7
Vote of no confidence

Unincorporated associations do not have a statutory procedure for removing members of the governing body, and the governing document may not include a provision. In this situation members of the organisation or governing body may call for a **vote of no confidence**, in the hope of putting the relevant person(s) in a position where they will resign. But vote of no confidence has no meaning legally, and there is no obligation on the person to resign, even if 100% of those voting say they have no confidence. In some situations they may even be prevented from resigning, because generally the governing document will say that governing body members cannot resign if the number would then fall below the quorum, or below three.

Anyone proposing a vote of no confidence should consider the potential impact of such action on funders, beneficiaries and other key stakeholders.

Chapter 12
OFFICERS, COMMITTEES AND SUB-COMMITTEES

12.1
WHO'S WHO

As with so many other aspects of organisational description, the terms used to describe voluntary organisations' officers and committees are inconsistent, overlapping and confusing, and it is important to be clear about how they are used in *this* organisation. For example:

- the governing body might be called a **management committee** or **executive committee**;

- the governing body might be called something else, such as a **board of directors**, **board of trustees**, **board of governors** or **council of management**, and a body called a management committee or executive committee might be a committee of that board or council;

- if the governing body is called a **board**, the sub-groups it sets up are likely to be called **committees**—but if the governing body is called a **committee**, the sub-groups it sets up are likely to be called **sub-committees**;

- people called **committee members** might be company directors and/or charity trustees, or might not;

- a person called a **director** might be a member of the governing body, or might be the chief executive or the head of a department or team;

- a **president** might have all the responsibilities of a chairperson, or might be a figurehead with no responsibilities;

- a **secretary** might be elected at the AGM to deal with the organisation's paperwork, or be a company secretary with a range of duties under company law, or be an employee.

This chapter looks at these roles and relationships—whatever they are called.

12.1.1
Officers of a company

In most voluntary organisations the term **officers** is used narrowly, to refer only to honorary officers [see below]. In company law, however, the term refers to a much wider group, including:

- the **company directors**: the voting members of the governing body;
- the **honorary officers**;
- **shadow directors** [see **11.1.3**];
- the **company secretary**;
- the **chief executive**, general secretary, director or other senior employee(s). *Companies Act 1985 s.744*

A company's officers have certain rights and duties under company law, which are referred to throughout this book.

12.1.2
Honorary officers

In general usage, the term **officer** or **honorary officer** refers to the elected or appointed chairperson, vice-chair, treasurer, honorary secretary and others who have special responsibilities which distinguish them from the other members of the organisation or its governing body.

When the term 'officers' is used in a governing document, standing orders or other contexts, it is important to be absolutely clear whether it refers only to honorary officers or to a broader group, or even to staff.

There is no statutory obligation to have honorary officers, although governing documents often specify that the organisation must have certain officers. Even if it is not required by the governing document it is generally sensible to have at least a **chairperson** and **treasurer**, and possibly a **vice-chair**. If a company wants to have a **secretary** to deal with minutes and/or correspondence this post should be called **honorary secretary** to distinguish it from the **company secretary** [see **12.3**].

If there are to be honorary officers the governing document may specify that they should be elected by the members in a membership organisation, elected by the governing body, or appointed by the governing body. For new organisations, the procedure for electing or appointing officers should be clarified before drawing up the governing document.

Some governing documents provide that even when the chairperson and vice-chair are elected, the company secretary (in a company) and treasurer are appointed by the governing body members. This helps ensure that the people chosen for these posts are considered by the members of the governing body to be suitable to oversee the organisation's finances and company law responsibilities, and are not in the post simply because they happen to be the only people nominated or are the most popular.

Some governing documents provide for other posts such as **president** or **patron**. These might be members of the governing body, or purely honorary posts with very limited or no rights [see **10.2.7** and **12.2.3**].

12.1.3
Vacancies

A **casual vacancy** occurs if a post is not filled by the usual election or appointment process or if the post falls vacant between elections, usually because the post holder resigns or dies.

If the governing document contains a procedure for filling casual vacancies, this must be followed. If there is no such procedure, the body which would ordinarily have elected or appointed the officer may appoint someone to serve in an **acting** capacity until the next scheduled election. 'Acting' indicates that they were not elected in the usual way.

12.2
DUTIES AND POWERS OF HONORARY OFFICERS

The duties of honorary officers and their powers (if any) are not, in general, set out in law. They arise primarily from the organisation's governing document, its internal standing orders [see **5.4.25**], and resolutions of the governing body. It is therefore important for anyone elected or appointed as an officer to clarify what is required and expected in that particular organisation.

12.2.1
Chairperson

The role of chairperson carries no legal rights or responsibilities except in relation to chairing meetings [see **17.2.7** and **17.4.5**]. Additional responsibilities may be set out in the governing document or standing orders, or may have developed through custom and practice. Typical responsibilities of the chairperson include guiding the strategic development of the organisation, overseeing the work of the chief executive, and representing the organisation publicly.

12.2.1.1
Chair's action

Chair's action is where a decision must of necessity be made before the next meeting, and the chairperson has the authority to make it. There is no implicit right to take chair's action. A chairperson may do so if, and only if:

- the governing document or standing orders allow such action; *or*
- the chairperson has been explicitly authorised to take such action, generally through a minuted decision of the governing body.

The organisation's custom and practice may be for the chairperson to make essential decisions between meetings when they genuinely cannot wait until the next meeting. While common, this will leave legal doubts as to the legitimacy of such action, so explicit authorisation is preferable.

All decisions taken under chair's action must be reported to the next meeting, and if they have financial or legal implications or are outside the organisation's agreed policy must be ratified (confirmed).

12.2.2
Convenor

The term **convenor** is used in a variety of ways. Examples include:

- especially in Scotland, it may be synonymous with chairperson;
- the convenor may be a person who arranges meetings but does not chair them; *or*
- it may be a person who chairs meetings, but does not take on the typical chairperson's roles of representing the organisation and overseeing its work.

12.2.3
President

The term **president** is also used in a variety of ways. A president may:

- be the same as a chairperson;
- represent the organisation publicly, but not chair meetings; *or*
- have a figurehead role with no responsibilities.

12.2.4
Vice-chair

A **vice-chair** typically stands in when the chairperson is not available to chair meetings. Depending on the organisation, the vice-chair may take on other roles, to ease the burden on the chairperson. If there is a vice-chair it is good practice to keep him or her as fully briefed as the chairperson. It may also be good practice to use the vice-chair position as a way of training people to take on the position of chairperson.

12.2.5
Honorary secretary

The term **honorary secretary** typically refers to the person responsible for dealing with correspondence and/or organising and minuting meetings, but the post may involve other duties. There is no obligation to have an honorary secretary unless this is required by the governing document or standing orders.

12.2.6
Treasurer

Even if the governing document does not require the organisation to have a **treasurer** it is good practice to appoint one, so a named person has particular responsibility for monitoring the organisation's finances and keeping the members of the governing body informed. The appointment of a treasurer does not relieve the other members of the governing body of their responsibility for overseeing the finances.

No matter how trustworthy and reliable the treasurer it is not good practice to allow her or him sole control of the finances, because it does not provide opportunity for mistakes or fraud to be detected [see **49.2.8**].

**12.3
COMPANY
SECRETARY**

Every company must have a company secretary, who cannot be the same person as a sole director. *Companies Act 1985 s.283(1)*

The company secretary is responsible for ensuring that the administrative responsibilities set out in company law and the articles of association are properly carried out. The post has no executive or management responsibilities unless these are explicitly delegated by the governing body. So a company secretary cannot, for example, authorise expenditure, borrow money, alter the registers or appoint auditors without the authority of the directors or the company members.

A company secretary who attends general meetings of the company's members has no vote unless he or she is a member of the company, and a company secretary who attends meetings of the governing body has no vote unless he or she is also a company director.

Although the company secretary may have no say in the company's decisions, he or she is an officer for the purposes of company law [see **12.1.1**] and can be held liable in the same way as a company director for breach of company law duties [see **19.2**].

**12.3.1
Who can be
company secretary**

The company secretary is normally appointed by the members of the governing body (the company directors), but the articles of association may specify that the appointment must be made in another way, for example by the company members in a general meeting. Unless the articles specify otherwise the secretary may be a member of the governing body, an employee, the company's accountant or solicitor, a company, or anyone else. Two persons can be appointed as joint secretary. The secretary may be paid, but if the company is charitable and the secretary is a member of the governing body, there may be restrictions on this [see **14.3.1**].

In public companies (plc's), the company secretary must be properly qualified and/or have relevant knowledge and experience. There is no such requirement for private companies, which is what virtually all voluntary sector companies are. But the directors would be failing in their duty of care to the company [see **13.2**] if they appoint someone who does not have the ability to carry out the administrative tasks for which the secretary is responsible, or who does not have access to relevant advice to enable her or him to carry out the tasks. *s.286*

Appointing the organisation's accountant or solicitor as company secretary may seem like a good idea, but someone within the organisation must provide all necessary information to them. The company forms and paperwork are not difficult, so it may make more sense and be less expensive to appoint a member of the governing body, senior employee or reliable volunteer as company secretary.

Where under company law or the articles of association something must be done or signed by a director and the company secretary, it must be done by two persons. A director who is also company secretary cannot in this situation serve in both roles simultaneously.

**12.3.2
Duties**

The company secretary's duties as set out in company law must be carried out by the company secretary or, if the articles of association allow delegation, by a person to whom the duties are delegated. The company directors are responsible for ensuring the company secretary carries out the duties.

Training specifically for voluntary sector company secretaries is provided by the Directory of Social Change (020-7209 4949; www.dsc.org.uk) and the Institute of Chartered Secretaries and Administrators (020-7580 4741; www.icsa.org.uk), and may be available from local councils for voluntary service and other voluntary sector training providers.

The duties of company secretaries and directors, and all necessary forms, are included in the *Sinclair Taylor & Martin Company Handbook and Registers for Voluntary Sector Companies Limited by Guarantee* [see **page 2** for details].

12.3.2.1
When a company
is set up

As soon as a company is registered [see **6.3.8**] the secretary must:

- open a register of members [see **16.3.2**], and if it is not to be kept at the company's registered office, send form 353 to Companies House;

- open a register of directors and secretaries [see **16.3.4** and **16.3.5**] and file company form 288a for any directors who were not named in form 10 when the company was formed, and form 288b for any initial directors who are resigning immediately;

- open the relevant register of charges if there are any mortgages or debentures, and notify the charges to Companies House [see **16.3.9-16.3.11**];

- display the company's full registered name outside the company's registered office [see **15.1.2**];

- arrange for printed materials such as stationery and chequebooks to be produced with the necessary details [see **16.1.1**], or get a rubber stamp or stickers with the details;

- add the same details to the organisation's website and the 'signatures' used on its outgoing emails;

- arrange for safekeeping of the seal (if there is one), registers, minute books and the certificate of incorporation.

There are additional responsibilities in companies limited by shares, which are not covered in this book.

12.3.2.2
Taking over as a
company secretary

A company secretary appointed for an existing company should obtain from the outgoing secretary, or from whoever has them:

- the original of the certificate of incorporation and any certificate changing the company's name;

- a copy of the memorandum and articles of association and any amendments;

- the company's statutory books [see **16.3**];

- copies of company forms 288a, 288b and 288c (details of directors and secretary) which have been submitted to Companies House;

- copies of other forms which have been submitted;

- contact addresses and phone numbers of directors and key staff;

- copies of the company notepaper, cheques, and forms used for invoices, receipts, orders and other financial documents;

- print-outs from the company's website and outgoing emails, showing company and (if applicable) charity registration details;

- correspondence files of the previous company secretary;

- copies of the previous year's company annual accounts, reports and return [see **50.3**] and, for a charitable company, the previous year's charity return [see **50.2.16**];

- an up-to-date company search [see **12.3.2.3**], unless the company secretary is absolutely certain the company's documentation at Companies House is completely up to date;

- blank copies of company forms 288a, 288b and 288c;

- the company seal, if there is one [see **5.4.18**].

If any of these items is missing the company secretary should alert the governing body and take action to find or replace the missing items.

The secretary should also:

- complete and sign form 288a and sent it to Companies House within 14 days of being appointed;

- find out when the end of the accounting year (**accounting reference date**) is, and ensure that company form 225 has been filed if necessary [see **50.3.1**];

- check the correspondence file and if necessary notify key people of any change of address for correspondence;

- if one does not already exist, create a diary with all the key dates (end of financial year, deadline for submitting annual accounts, dates for general and governing body meetings, deadlines for giving notice of general and governing body meetings, etc);

- locate the originals of the certificate of incorporation and any certificates recording a change of name, if these are not to hand;

- find out who the company's accountant (if there is one), auditor and solicitor are, and introduce herself or himself to them;

- if there is no company solicitor, ask the board how they expect the secretary to obtain advice on company matters.

12.3.2.3
Company search

A **company search** provides a **company record** showing what information has been registered at Companies House. Searches can be done on the Companies House website, in person at Companies House offices [see **page 12**], or by post or by a company registration agent (listed in the Yellow Pages). The fees for the company record (as at 1/4/01) are £9.50 by post, £6.50 if collected from a Companies House information centre, or £5 if downloaded from the Companies House website. Other documents such as annual accounts are also available.

The company record should be compared with the company's registers and documents to ensure that Companies House has:

- an accurate record of all the company's directors, including co-optees, representatives and others who have a vote on the governing body [see **11.1.3**];

- current name and address for all company directors;

- current registered address for the company;

- up-to-date version of the memorandum and articles of association, with all amendments included;

- details of all charges or mortgages on the company's property;

- up-to-date accounts and returns.

If there are discrepancies, the appropriate information and forms must be filed (form 287 to notify change of registered office, 288a for notification of new directors, 288b for directors who are no longer serving, 288c to update details of directors and company secretary).

It is particularly important for a new secretary to check that **annual returns** and **annual accounts** have been filed, as there are penalties for late submission [see **50.3.5** and **50.3.8**]. For a charitable company, the secretary should also check that the charity accounts and return have been sent to the Charity Commission [see **50.2.14** and **50.2.16**].

12.3.2.4
Maintaining the registers

The secretary must ensure the **register of directors** [see **16.3.4**] is up to date, all voting members of the governing body appear on it, and their details are complete. These can be obtained from the copies of the form 288a which they signed when they became directors, or which they would have just signed if new forms have had to be submitted, and the forms 288c which have been submitted to Companies House to update their details. The new secretary's name and details must be entered in the **register of secretaries**. The registers of directors and secretaries must be held at the registered office.

The company secretary must ensure the **register of members** [see **16.3.2**] is kept up to date. This involves ensuring that:

- Companies House knows where it is kept if it is not at the company's registered office (form 353);

- the proper procedures have been followed to admit members (for example if membership applications must be approved by the governing body, ensuring that they have been approved and minuted);

- if there are more than 50 company members, the register is alphabetical or there is an alphabetical index [see **16.3.3**];

- the register contains not only the names of members, but also up-to-date addresses;

- the register cannot be altered without proper authority.

The secretary must ensure that the registers of members, directors and secretaries are available for inspection by members and the public for at least two hours every working day [see **16.3.2-16.3.5**]. The register of members can be unavailable for up to 30 days per year, but the closure must be advertised in a local newspaper.

If any members have lapsed, for example by failing to pay subscriptions or no longer qualifying for membership, the company secretary should inform the governing body and take steps to remove them from membership. But the company secretary must not enter the date they ceased to be a member without the governing body's authority.

Even if members resign, die or move away their names may not be removed from the register until at least 20 years after they ceased to be a member [see **16.3.2**].

12.3.2.5
Disclosure of status

The company secretary should know the location of the original **certificate of incorporation** and any certificates altering the company's name. If the original is lost, a duplicate should be obtained from Companies House.

The company secretary should carefully check that the full name of the company, exactly as it appears on the certificate of incorporation or on any subsequent certificate of name change, appears on all stationery, financial documents, cheques, outgoing emails, websites etc, along with the other required information [see **16.1.1**]. (Capitalisation on the certificate can be ignored.) If the company uses a name other than the registered name, this must also appear on some documents.

The secretary must ensure that the full name of the company is displayed outside the registered office [see **15.1.2**]. If the registered office is not the company's usual address or the company secretary's address, the secretary must ensure there are clear and workable arrangements for post to be forwarded as soon as it is received at the registered office.

12.3.2.6
Memorandum and articles of association

The company secretary should become familiar with the **memorandum and articles of association**. The objects clause is particularly important, and the secretary should alert the governing body immediately if he or she thinks any of the company's activities might be outside the objects or powers (*ultra vires*).

If the memorandum and articles have been amended, the secretary should ensure that all amendments were properly passed [see **17.4.7**]; that where necessary the Charity Commission's consent was obtained [see **5.5.2**]; and that proper notice of the amendments, with Charity Commission consent if necessary, was sent to Companies House and a copy of the amended version was sent to the Charity Commission.

If amendments have simply been attached to the memorandum and articles, the secretary should consider having the whole thing retyped. If this is done, a copy of the new version must be sent to Companies House and, for charitable companies, the Charity Commission. It is useful to include a summary of amendments made during the history of the company.

12.3.2.7
Meetings

The company secretary may be involved in organising meetings of the governing body (board of directors) and general meetings of the company members [see **17.4.3** for the tasks involved in this]. The secretary must ensure:

- proper notice is given as required under company law and/or the articles of association [see **17.4.4** and **17.6.2**];
- decisions are made with the appropriate type of resolution [see **17.4.7**] and with proper voting procedures [see **17.4.8**];
- proper minutes are kept and entered in the minutes book [see **17.2.15** and **17.6.7**];
- all necessary changes are made to the registers after the meeting (for example members' names and the date they were admitted to membership entered in the register of members, and changes of director entered in the register of directors);
- all necessary information and forms are sent to Companies House within the required period.

12.3.2.8
Legal information

The company secretary can perform a valuable role in helping to ensure that directors are aware of all their statutory obligations. To carry out this duty effectively, the company secretary should seek to ensure the company has access to a legal advisor with experience not only in company law, but also in charity law if the company is charitable, employment law, and perhaps also with experience in any specialist field within which the company operates, such as housing.

A company secretary might want to suggest to the company directors that the company asks a suitably experienced solicitor to undertake a regular review or annual 'legal audit' of the company's affairs, to ensure the company is keeping up with the changing requirements of the law.

12.3.3
Vacancy

A company must have a company secretary at all times. A vacancy must be immediately filled and details of the retirement and replacement must be entered in the register of secretaries and notified to Companies House on forms 288b and 288a.

A company secretary may be removed at any time by the body which elected or appointed him or her.

12.3.4
Liability

The company secretary has personal liability if he or she fails to perform duties required under the Companies Acts. Usually such liability arises only if the default was knowing or deliberate. The company can generally insure against such liability, but if the company is charitable and the secretary is also a member of the governing body, the rules on liability insurance for trustees apply [see **20.2.4**].

12.4
IPS SECRETARY

Industrial and provident societies must also have a secretary. Their duties are less onerous than those of a company secretary, but are similar in nature.

12.5
COMMITTEES AND SUB-COMMITTEES

The term **committee** as used here means a group set up by the members (in a membership organisation) or the governing body to undertake specific tasks. If the governing body is itself called a committee, the group is a **sub-committee**. A governing body may delegate to a committee only if this is allowed by law or the governing document [see **13.5**].

Committees are accountable to the body which set them up. In a membership organisation the governing body and any committees set up by the members are accountable to the members; committees set up by a governing body are accountable to the governing body. Lines of accountability should always be clear.

A **standing committee** is one which is permanent, usually set up by the governing document or under standing orders [see **5.4.25**]. A committee set up for a specific short-term purpose is sometimes called a

working group or an ***ad hoc*** ('for this purpose') **committee**. A group which sets up a committee may disband it at any time, but a committee set up under the provisions of the governing document can be disbanded only if the governing document allows.

12.5.1
Terms of reference

Committees may act only within the **terms of reference** set by the governing document, standing orders or the body which set up the committee. The terms of reference generally cover:

- the purpose(s) of the committee;
- the topics, issues or areas of work it is authorised to cover;
- its tasks;
- whether it can make decisions about those matters, or can only make proposals or recommendations to the body to which it is accountable;
- how its members are elected or appointed, how long they serve and how they are removed;
- how often it must meet, its procedures and similar administrative matters;
- how its work is funded, whether it controls a budget for its work, and if not how expenditure is authorised;
- how, and how often, it must report to the body to which it is accountable.

Committees must always act within agreed policies and budgets and must properly minute their decisions [see **17.2.15** and **17.4.11**].

12.5.2
Delegated powers

Decision-making powers can be delegated to a committee or individuals only if there is statutory power to do so, or the power is explicit within the governing document [see **13.5**]. The body which appointed the committee or sub-committee remains liable for its acts and must supervise its work [see **13.5.2**].

12.5.3
Management or executive committee

The term **management committee** or **executive committee** sometimes refers to the governing body as a whole. But a governing body, especially if it is very large, may appoint a committee called a management committee or executive committee which has delegated powers to act on behalf of the governing body between meetings. This sort of committee usually includes the honorary officers [see **12.1.2**] and perhaps a small number of other key individuals.

A variation is when the governing body is very small—perhaps a trust with only three or four trustees—and they appoint a larger and more representative executive or management committee with some decision-making powers.

12.5.4
Advisory committee

A committee which can only make proposals or recommendations to the main body and has no decision-making powers may be called an **advisory board** or **advisory committee**.

12.5.5
Steering committee

A steering committee is usually a type of working party or *ad hoc* group set up specifically to start a new project or organisation. If the project is completely within an organisation, the steering committee is simply an internal committee. If it is a group working together to set up a new organisation, it is in effect an unincorporated association [see **9.5** for more about this situation, and the implications for liability].

Typically a steering committee hands over to the first governing body when the organisation is set up. If members of the steering committee have entered into legal agreements in their own names or in the name of their organisations, it may be necessary to transfer these to the new governing body [see **18.4.5** and **18.10.1**].

Chapter 13
DUTIES AND POWERS OF THE GOVERNING BODY

For sources of further information see page 12.

Double-underlined section headings indicate additions or significant changes since the first edition.

13.1 THE RANGE OF DUTIES

A duty is a legal obligation. The flip side of virtually all duties is **liability** if the duties are not fulfilled. Members of the governing body may in many situations be held personally liable, either jointly or separately, if they or their organisation do not comply with its legal duties [see **chapter 19**].

Statutory and other legal duties may arise:
- through particular activities carried out by the organisation such as being an employer, occupying premises, providing services, organising public activities or engaging in fundraising;
- by being registered as a charity and/or a company or industrial and provident society;
- by having charitable objects, even if not registered as a charity;
- by being a trust [see **1.3**], whether charitable or non-charitable.

Contractual duties arise:
- from the organisation's governing document, which in a membership organisation forms a contract between the organisation and its members and/or among the members;
- from legally binding agreements such as contracts of employment, leases, and contracts to purchase or provide goods or services.

General information about obligations arising from contracts and other legal agreements is included in **chapter 18**.

Duties as trustees [see **13.3**] arise from charity law and trust law. **Trustee** is defined differently for different aspects of law, so a person may be a trustee in some contexts but not others.

Good practice goes beyond legal duties. There are as many views of what constitutes good practice as there are commentators, and to a large extent it depends on the nature of the organisation and its values. But a good starting point is the Charity Commission's CC60 *Hallmarks of a Well Run Charity*, available free from the Commission or on its website [see **page 12**]. These 'hallmarks' also apply to non-charities.

Moral obligations may arise because of promises made or a belief that the organisation 'should' do something, even when there is no legal obligation to do so. *Ex gratia* payments [see **49.2.7**] are an example of an organisation fulfilling what it sees as a moral duty.

13.2
DUTIES OF COMPANY AND IPS DIRECTORS

As well as their specific duties under company or industrial and provident society law and the general law, the courts have imposed on company and IPS directors two broad duties to their organisation: **fiduciary duty** and **duty of care**. Directors of charitable companies and IPSs have additional duties as charity trustees [see **13.3**].

A director in breach of fiduciary duty or duty of care may be sued by the company or IPS, or by one or more members of the organisation.

13.2.1
Fiduciary duty

Fiduciary means 'in good faith', from the Latin *fides* (trust, faith, trustworthiness). **Fiduciary duty** means that everything done by a director must be done in good faith *(bona fide)*, for the benefit of the organisation as a whole, and for a proper purpose.

In making decisions the directors must:

- act in the best interests of the organisation as a whole and all its members (in a non-charitable company or IPS) or all its beneficiaries (in a charitable company or IPS);

- in a company, have regard to the interests of the company's employees;
  Companies Act 1985 s.309

- not misuse the organisation's property;

- not misuse information for personal gain even after they have left the governing body; *and*

- not allow their personal interests or the interests of any other body, even one which appointed them as a director, to override the interests of the company or IPS.

This duty is to the organisation *as a whole*. Directors must not place the interests of any individual members, employees or beneficiaries, or any group of them, above the interests of the whole company or IPS.

This duty changes dramatically when a company or IPS is, or is becoming, insolvent. The primary duty immediately becomes to act in the best interests of its creditors (the persons to whom it owes money) and to minimise the potential loss to them [see **21.2.3**].

Most directors of a company or IPS are also ordinary members of the organisation. Their fiduciary duty does not extend to their role *as a member*. When voting as company or IPS members at a general meeting, directors may vote however they wish.
North-west Transportation Co Ltd v Beatty [1887] 12 AC 589

13.2.2
Conflict of interest

A **conflict of interest** exists when a member of a governing body has a financial interest in or stands to gain (or lose) financially from any contract, transaction or other agreement entered into by the organisation or its governing body. 'Financial interest' and 'financial gain' apply not only to money, but to anything with a monetary value.

A potential gain may arise directly (for example goods or services purchased from the governing body member) or indirectly (for example if purchased from a partnership in which the director is a partner, or from a company in which the member of the governing body owns shares and therefore stands to gain from the company's profits).

One aspect of fiduciary duty is that a governing body member must not make a **secret profit** from their organisation. This means that any potential conflict of interest must be disclosed. In the case of trustees the duty is even higher, as they have a duty not to make *any* profit from their organisation, whether secret or otherwise [see **13.3.6**].

13.2.2.1
Connected persons

Under company law a conflict of interest also exists if someone **connected** with a director stands to gain. This applies to:

- the director's spouse;
- the director's child or stepchild under the age of 18, including an illegitimate child; *and*
- the director's business partner(s), or the business partner of the director's spouse or child.   *Companies Act 1985 s.346*

It also applies if:

- the director is trustee of a trust whose beneficiaries include the director and/or the director's spouse or children (but not if the trust is an employees' share scheme or pension scheme); *or*
- the director is **associated** with a corporate body. This means that the director and the persons connected with him or her have an interest in 20% or more of the equity share capital of a company, or are entitled to more than 20% of the voting rights at any general meeting of a company.   *s.346*

13.2.2.2
Disclosure of conflict of interest

A company director's conflict of interest must be declared at the meeting of the governing body at which the contract or other arrangement is first considered. The disclosure may be verbal or in writing. If a director does not initially have an interest but subsequently does, the conflict of interest must be declared at the first governing body meeting thereafter. If a director becomes interested in a contract or other arrangement after it has been agreed, this must also be declared at the next meeting of the governing body.   *s.317(1),(2)*

The disclosure must be to the full governing body, not to a committee or sub-committee of it.   *Guinness plc v Saunders [1988] BCLC 43*

The disclosure may be specific to a particular transaction, or may be a general notice stating that he or she is to be regarded as having an interest in any future transactions or potential transactions with named companies where the director is a member or the firms where he or she is a partner, and/or named connected persons [see above].

    Companies Act 1985 s.317(3)

Once this general notice has been given and minuted, it does not have to be given every time a relevant transaction is discussed.

A director who does not disclose an interest may be fined, and the contract may be voided (invalidated) by the company.   *s.317(7)*

Special rules apply to loans made by the company to directors and persons connected with them, and to substantial property transactions involving directors.   *ss.320-322B, 333-343*

Unless the articles of association explicitly allow, a director may not take part in a decision on any matter in which he or she has a conflict of interest, and does not count towards the quorum for that part of the meeting [see **17.2.8**].   *Re North Eastern Insurance Co [1919] 1 Ch 198;*
Yuill v Greymouth Point Elizabeth Railway and Coal Company Ltd
[1904] 1 Ch 32

There is also a common law duty for a director to disclose any conflict of interest at a general meeting, although the articles may say this is unnecessary so long as the interest has been declared at a governing

body meeting. If a director who is required to disclose to a general meeting does not do so and the company subsequently enters the contract, the director may be required to repay to the company all profits from the transaction.
Hely-Hutchinson v Brayhead Ltd [1968] 1 QB 549

If all the directors have an interest in a transaction, it must be referred to a general meeting of the company's members.
Re Express Engineering Works [1920] 1 Ch 466

A shadow director [see **11.1.3**] with a conflict of interest must declare it in writing to the governing body.
Companies Act 1985 s.317(8)

13.2.2.3
Duality of interest

Conflict of interest is not the same as **duality of interest**, where a governing body member is associated with another body and may have divided loyalties, but does not stand to gain financially. Where there is duality of interest the person should declare it and ensure it is minuted, and must always act in the best interests of the organisation on whose governing body he or she is then sitting.

13.2.2.4
Industrial and provident societies

Governing body members in industrial and provident societies have the same duties as company directors to avoid conflicts of interest. There is no obligation to disclose such interests unless this is required by the governing document, but if it is not disclosed the IPS can void (invalidate) the contract or recover from the director the amount paid on the contract.

13.2.2.5
Registered social landlords

Housing associations and other registered social landlords are prohibited from making payments, apart from reimbursement of genuine out-of-pocket expenses, to governing body members and also to former members and relatives of governing body members [see **14.1.3**].

13.2.3
Duty of care

As well as their duty to act in good faith, company and IPS directors have a **duty of care**. This means they must act carefully and responsibly. If they do not they may be considered **negligent**, and may face civil claims or be prosecuted under criminal law.

In general a director 'need not exhibit in the performance of his duties a greater degree of skill than may reasonably be expected from a person of his knowledge and experience'. There is no obligation actually to *have* any relevant knowledge and experience, so long as the director acts honestly and in good faith.
Re City Equitable Fire Insurance Co Ltd [1925] Ch 407

13.2.3.1
Duties in insolvency

The duty is greater in relation to financial matters when a company or IPS is, or is becoming, insolvent [see **21.2** for explanation of insolvency]. In this situation a director or shadow director [see **11.1.3**] is expected to act on the basis of:

- the general knowledge, skills and experience which might reasonably be expected of a person carrying out that particular director's functions or the functions entrusted to her or him; *and*

- the general knowledge, skills and experience which that director actually possesses.
Insolvency Act 1986 s.214(4),(5)

In the context of actual or imminent insolvency ignorance is not a defence, and a director must be able to show reasonable competence *as a director*. At the very least, this means that all directors have a duty to ensure they receive proper financial information and have the skill to identify problems which could lead to insolvency.

Directors concerned that they lack appropriate skill or knowledge, especially on financial matters, should seek training or obtain advice from specialists such as the organisation's solicitor or accountant.

13.2.3.2
Duty to attend meetings

Company and IPS directors are not obliged to attend all meetings of the governing body, although they have a duty to attend when they are 'reasonably able to do so', and the governing document may say that `they are removed from office if they do not attend for a specified period [see **11.5.3**].   *Re City Equitable Fire Insurance Co Ltd [1925] Ch 407*

A director who does not take part in the company or IPS over an extended period could be held to be in breach of duty of care. If a company or IPS becomes insolvent, a director who has consistently failed to attend governing body meetings could be disqualified from being a company director.   *Dorchester Finance v Stebbings [1989] BCLC 498*

13.2.3.3
Duty to third parties and statutory duties

The duties of care outlined above relate to the director's relationship to the company. Other duties of care also exist in relation to the general law, and to third parties such as employees, users of the organisation's services and people on its premises. A director who directs or authorises a breach of statutory duty, a criminal act or a tort (a civil wrong such as negligence or libel) could be held liable for the act [see **19.2** and **19.5**].

13.3
DUTIES OF TRUSTEES

Duties as **trustees** arise under both charity law and trust law. In considering these duties a distinction must be made between:

- trust law duties and powers that apply only to trustees of bodies set up as trusts [see **1.3**], whether charitable or non-charitable (referred to in this chapter as **trustees**);

- trust law duties and powers, such as those under the **Trustee Act 2000** [see **54.1**], that apply to trustees of all trusts, whether charitable or non-charitable, and to governing body members of charitable associations [see **1.2**] and bodies established by royal charter (all referred to in this chapter as **trustees under the Trustee Act 2000**);

- charity law duties that apply to governing body members of all charities, regardless of their legal structure and regardless of whether they are registered with the Charity Commission (**charity trustees**);

- charity law duties that apply only to governing body members of charities registered with the Charity Commission (**trustees of registered charities**);

- trust and/or charity law duties that apply to holding or custodian trustees [see **18.4**] who hold property on behalf of trusts or charities;

- trust and/or charity law duties that may arise in many other situations where one or more individuals or a corporate body holds property, money or other assets on behalf of another person or persons, even if there is nothing in writing saying that a trust has been created [see, for example, **44.2.1**].

Because all trustees have been entrusted with managing property or money for beneficiaries or for a charitable purpose, they have a **duty of trust** which is analogous to, but wider than, the fiduciary duties of company and IPS directors. Failure to comply with the relevant trustee duties constitutes a **breach of trust** for which a trustee can be held personally liable.

Trustees have an obligation to meet often enough to exercise their duties properly. The Charity Commission recommends, in CC48 *Charities and Meetings*, an absolute minimum of two meetings per year.

13.3.1
Initial duties

Before agreeing to become any type of trustee, the person must disclose any circumstances which might lead to a conflict between personal interest and duties as a trustee.   *Peyton v Robinson [1823] 25 RR 278*

After being appointed or elected, a trustee has a duty to:

- ensure he or she has been properly appointed or elected;

- understand the organisation's objects and the trustees' powers;

- become familiar with the governing document and other relevant documents;

- ascertain what assets the organisation has and that they are appropriately safeguarded;
- ensure that if necessary, property is properly vested in her or him [see **18.4.5**];
- take reasonable steps to find out whether the organisation has been properly managed, and if necessary take steps to put it right. A trustee who does not do this could be held liable for the actions of previous trustees.

13.3.2
Duty to comply with governing document

All trustees, of any type, must act at all times strictly within the objects, powers, rules and administrative provisions set out in the governing document. Action outside the governing document must be authorised by the Charity Commission (if the body is charitable) or the court.

If a charity's property cannot be used for the original purposes a charity's trustees have a duty to apply to the Charity Commission for a *cy près* scheme [see **5.5.4**]. *Charities Act 1993 s.13(5)*

13.3.3
Duty to act in the best interests of beneficiaries

All trustees, of any type, must act at all times in the best interests of the trust or charity and all its beneficiaries, both current and future. **Duality of interest** [see **13.2.2.3**], where the trustee is torn between two (or more) different roles, should be declared and minuted. Decisions must be made without regard for the trustee's own interests and views, and without regard for the views of any individual or body which appointed the trustee. A trustee who does not feel able to comply with this requirement should not take part in the decision.
Report of the Charity Commissioners 1991, para.41-43

A local authority or other corporate body which serves as a charity trustee must act in the best interests of the charity, not in accordance with its own policy. *paras.44-45*

13.3.4
Duty to avoid conflict of interest

All trustees have an obligation to avoid conflict of interest [see **13.2.2** for definition]. If a trustee's personal interest is likely to conflict with that of the trust or charity this must be disclosed to the other trustees, and the trustee must not take part in any discussion or decision in which he or she has such a conflict. Particular issues around beneficiaries as trustees as considered in the Charity Commission's CC24 *Users on Board*, available free from the Commission or on its website [see **page 12**]. *Peyton v Robinson [1823] 25 RR 278*

13.3.5
Duty to safeguard assets

Under their duty to safeguard the organisation's assets, all trustees, of any type, must:
- receive all sums due to the trust or charity, for example grants, dividends, rate relief and recovered tax;
- invest prudently [see **54.3**];
- take reasonable precautions to safeguard against fraud and dishonesty [see **49.2**];
- in general, not refuse money, property or other assets offered to a charity unless the governing document gives them the power to **disclaim assets** [see **44.3.2**].

Trustees under the **Trustee Act 2000** should make good use of the investment powers granted under that Act [see **54.1.2**].

A governing body which does not insure its buildings and valuable assets [see **20.6**] could be in breach of its duty to safeguard its property.

13.3.5.1
Duty to safeguard permanent endowment

One aspect of the duty to safeguard assets is the obligation to safeguard a charity's permanent endowment. Permanent endowment may include:
- money given to the charity on condition that only the income from the fund, not the fund itself, can be spent (often called an **endowment fund** or **capital fund**);

- land or other assets given on condition that they not be sold or otherwise disposed of;

- land or other assets given on condition that if they are sold or disposed of, the money received is retained as a capital fund.

Charity trustees must ensure that money or property held as permanent endowment is not treated as expendable, is separately shown in the annual accounts as a capital fund [see **50.2.8**], and is not used, sold or disposed of without the consent of the Charity Commission unless such consent is not required [see **21.8.1**]. The Commission can give consent for income earned on permanent endowment to be spent, rather than having to be added to the capital fund [see **54.7.1**].

13.3.6
Duty not to profit

Unless the governing document specifies otherwise, a trustee has a duty to serve gratuitously (without payment) and not to make any profit or receive any benefit from the trust unless this is authorised by statute, the governing document, the Charity Commission or the court [see **chapter 14** for more about payment of expenses, remuneration and provision of benefits to trustees].

Trustees of *non-charitable* trusts have a statutory right to be remunerated in some circumstances, and the secretary of state has power to make regulations authorising payment of charity trustees. At the time of writing (early 2001) no such regulations had been made.

Trustee Act 2000 ss.29-30

Any unauthorised payment, profit or benefit having a monetary value must be returned to the trust or charity or, if it cannot be returned, the trustee must repay the value.

Special rules apply when a charity sells land to or buys land from a trustee or person connected with a trustee [see **57.12.1**], and to registered social landlords [see **14.1.3**].

13.3.7
Duty of care

In most situations a company director only has to act at a level commensurate with her or his knowledge and experience [see **13.2.3**]. A trustee must meet a higher standard of care: the standard a prudent businessperson would have in managing her or his own affairs.

Re Luckings Will Trust [1968] 1 WLR 866

This does not mean that trustees must have detailed technical knowledge, but they must have a general awareness of financial and legal issues and must take proper professional advice when appropriate.

In appointing advisors, nominees and custodians, making investments, acquiring land, delegating to agents or others, or exercising other powers under the **Trustee Act 2000**, the standard required for trustees under the Act is higher [see **54.1.2**]. They must exercise such care and skill as is reasonable in the circumstances, having particular regard to any special knowledge or experience the trustee has or holds himself or herself out as having.

Trustee Act 2000 s.1

Where a trustee has special knowledge or skill, a higher level of care is required. Trustees acting in the course of their business or profession must exercise a duty of care in keeping with any special knowledge or experience that it is reasonable to expect of a person acting in the course of that kind of business or profession.

s.1

These duties of care relate only to the trustees' duty to the trust or charity and its beneficiaries. Trustees have other duties of care to employees, people who use its premises etc.

13.3.8
Duty to act personally

Trustees of any type must act personally unless delegation is allowed by statute or explicitly authorised in the governing document [see **13.5.2** for more about delegation]. Failure to attend meetings or to participate in decisions about the trust could constitute a breach of the duty of care.

13.3.9
Duty to act collectively

Charity trustees may make decisions by majority unless the governing document specifies that they must be unanimous. Provided the governing document allows delegation to committees [see **13.5**] these may be set up. They must report to the trustees who are not on the committee at the earliest opportunity.

In making decisions the trustees must act as a group. An individual trustee or a minority group of trustees may not make decisions or take action unless they are authorised to do so by the trustees as a body.

13.3.10
Duty to keep accounts

All trustees have an obligation to keep proper financial records [see **49.3**]. All charities must prepare annual accounts, have them examined or audited if this is required under the Charities Act 1993 or other legislation or by the governing document, and make them available to the public [see **chapter 50**].

13.3.11
<u>Duties when investing</u>

When investing, all trustees must comply with the charity's governing document and any statutory requirements [see **chapter 54** for more on investment and these requirements].

Trustees under the **Trustee Act 2000** must comply with the Act when exercising powers under it, including powers of investment [see **54.1**]. They must exercise their statutory duty of care [see **54.1.2**], and ensure investments are suitable. Proper advice must be sought before investing unless the trustees conclude that it is unnecessary or inappropriate to obtain such advice.   *Trustee Act 2000 ss.3-5*

The Trustee Act significantly widened the investment powers of many trustees. Trustees who obtained wider powers under the Act must review their investments and consider whether they need varying.

13.3.12
Statutory duties

Charity trustees must ensure that the charity is registered if it is required to be [see **7.1**], and that they and their charity comply with the Charities Acts and all legislation relevant to its work and activities.

13.4
DUTIES OF COMMITTEE MEMBERS OF AN ASSOCIATION

If an unincorporated association is set up exclusively for charitable purposes it is a charity. The members of its governing body are charity trustees and have all the duties of charity trustees, and are also trustees for the purposes of the **Trustee Act 2000** [see **13.3**].

If it is set up for non-charitable purposes, the members of its governing body have fiduciary duties, a duty not to misuse powers and a duty of care comparable to the common law and case law duties of company directors [see **13.2**]. Apart from this their duties are determined by the governing document.

13.5
DELEGATION

13.5.1
'A delegate may not delegate'

Governing body members act not on their own behalf, but:

- in a trust or any form of charity, on behalf of the people who have given property or money for the trust's beneficiaries or purposes;
- in a company or industrial and provident society, on behalf of the company or IPS as a corporate body and its members;
- in a membership association, on behalf of the members.

Thus all governing body members, as persons to whom duties and powers have been delegated, are already delegates. As such they are subject to the basic principle *'delegatus non potest delegare'*—a person to whom any responsibility has been delegated may not delegate it further, unless such delegation is explicitly authorised by statute or by whoever did the initial delegating.

It follows that a governing body may delegate duties, powers and functions to committees, individual members of the governing body, employees or others only if they are allowed to do so by the governing document or statute, by the members in a membership organisation, or by the Charity Commission in a charity. It may be possible to alter the governing document to allow delegation [see **5.5** for procedure].

13.5.2
Delegation by trustees

Specific rules apply to trustees in charitable and non-charitable trusts and charitable associations. Like other governing body members, these trustees 'have no right to shift their duty on other persons' and may delegate only if they have explicit authorisation to do so. Such authorisation may come from powers of delegation in the governing document [see **5.4.15**], statute [see below], or a Charity Commission scheme or order [see **3.5.4** and **3.5.5**].   *Turner v Corney [1841] 5 Beav 515;*
Pilkington v Inland Revenue Commissioners [1964] AC 612

13.5.2.1
Statutory powers

Unless specifically excluded under the governing document, trustees under the **Trustee Act 2000** [see **13.3**] have statutory power:

• to appoint nominees and custodians to hold property [see **18.4**], unless the governing document already provides for property to be held only by a custodian trustee or the official custodian for charities; *and*

• to appoint one or more **agents** to exercise any delegatable function.
Trustee Act 2000 ss.11, 16-27

A **nominee** in this context holds land, investments or money on behalf of the trustees in his, her or its own name, but has no powers of management. In this book nominees are generally referred to as **holding trustees** or **custodian trustees** [see **18.4.4**].

A **custodian** looks after records, documents of title etc on behalf of the trustees. A custodian has no powers in relation to the assets.

An **agent** is someone to whom functions are delegated. The Trustee Act 2000 allows delegation only of specific functions, and only to certain persons [see below].

Nominees and custodians are generally appointed to eliminate the need to transfer the title to trust property when trustees change, to facilitate the sale and purchase of shares and similar assets, and to reduce the risk of loss of documents. Agents may be appointed to undertake a wide range of activities, such as discretionary investment of the trustees' funds.

In appointing nominees or custodians or delegating to agents, trustees must exercise a duty of care as defined by statute [see **54.1.2**].

Charities also have a statutory power to appoint custodian trustees (a form of nominee), and to have land held by the official custodian for charities [see **3.5.3**]

13.5.2.2
Who can be a nominee or custodian

The only persons who can be nominees or custodians in relation to duties under the **Trustee Act 2000** are:

• two or more trustees of the trust, to act as joint nominees or joint custodians, or one of the trustees if it is a trust corporation;

• individuals or corporate bodies which carry on a business which consists of or includes acting as a nominee or custodian;

• a corporate body controlled by the trustees; *or*

• a solicitor's nominee company recognised under the **Administration of Justice Act 1985** s.9.   *Trustee Act 2000 s.19*

In appointing nominees or custodians, trustees or charitable trusts or associations must act in accordance with Charity Commission guidance, available from the Commission or on its website [see **page 12**].

13.5.2.3
Who can be an agent

The only persons who can be appointed as agents to exercise powers under the **Trustee Act 2000** are:

• a person or body properly appointed as a nominee or custodian; *or*

• one or more trustees.   *s.12*

If two or more persons are appointed as agents for a particular function, they must act jointly. *s.12(2)*

The Trustee Act 2000 says that beneficiaries cannot be appointed as agents, even if they are trustees. The Charity Commission's view is that this provision applies only to non-charitable trusts. The reasoning is that in this context charities technically do not have beneficiaries, because they are established for charitable *purposes* rather than for the beneficiaries. *Trustee Act 2000 s.12(3)*

Agents with asset management functions (property and investments) must be appointed in writing, and must operate within a written policy statement. *s.15*

13.5.2.4
What can be delegated

In exercising their **Trustee Act 2000** powers, trustees of *charitable* bodies may delegate only:

* carrying out decisions taken by the trustees;
* functions relating to investment and land management;
* functions relating to fundraising, other than carrying on a trade which is integral to the charity's primary purpose [see **52.6**];
* other functions which may be set out in orders made by the home secretary. *s.11(3)*

In relation to any functions not covered by the Trustee Act, trustees of charitable trusts and associations may also:

* delegate responsibilities to one trustee or to committees made up of trustees, provided all decisions are made by a majority of the trustee body; *Re Whiteley [1910] 1 Ch 600*
* authorise two or more trustees to sign deeds, contracts or other documents on behalf of all the trustees. *Charities Act 1993 s.82*

13.5.2.5
Liability for acts of agents, nominees and custodians

Trustees are not liable for any losses arising from the work of an agent, nominee or custodian appointed under Trustee Act 2000 powers provided the trustees exercise all aspects of their statutory **duty of care** [see **13.3.7** and **54.1**]. *Trustee Act 2000 ss.1, 22*

For other issues around liability for acts of agents see **18.5**.

13.5.2.6
Delegation by an individual trustee

Unless it is prevented or restricted by the governing document, individual trustees in a charitable or non-charitable trust or charitable association have a statutory right to delegate virtually all of their powers, including their decision-making power, by power of attorney. They can do this for up to 12 months.
Trustee Act 1925 s.25 amended by Trustee Delegation Act 1999 s.5

The rules for this procedure are:

* the power of attorney must be worded as specified in the **Trustee Delegation Act 1999** s.5;
* it must be executed as a deed [see **18.3**];
* before or within seven days after giving power of attorney, the trustee must give notification in writing to every other trustee and to anyone having the power to appoint trustees, setting out the date the power comes into effect, its duration, who it is being delegated to, the reason for the delegation, and what is being delegated;
* the trustee remains personally liable for anything done, or not done, by the person to whom he or she has delegated.

Such delegation may be by an **enduring power of attorney**. Unlike an ordinary power of attorney, this continues to be effective even if the trustee who gave the power becomes mentally incapable.

13.5.3
Effective delegation

When duties, powers or tasks are delegated to individual members of the governing body, committees whether permanent or short-term, outside professionals or employees, the governing body generally remains primarily responsible for decisions and actions taken by the delegatees. To protect themselves, the members of the governing body should:

- where applicable, ensure they comply with their statutory duty of care under the Trustee Act 2000 [see **13.3.7** and **54.1.2**];

- ensure all decisions about delegation are properly made and minuted;

- be clear whether what is being delegated is the right to *make decisions*, the right to *make recommendations* to the governing body, or the right to *take action* within the scope of decisions made by the governing body;

- ensure that the limits to the delegation are clear;

- exercise reasonable supervision over any individuals or groups acting on their behalf;

- ensure that committees have clear terms of reference and employees have up-to-date job descriptions;

- ensure that all decisions and actions are within policies and budgets approved by the governing body;

- require all decisions and actions to be fully and promptly reported to the governing body;

- retain the right to revoke the delegation.   *Report of the Charity Commissioners 1981 para.108; 1984 para.45; 1986 para.28; 1993 para.83*

Governing body members must also supervise any outsiders who are appointed to undertake specific functions on behalf of the governing body. Governing body members remain liable for any losses to the organisation arising from the acts of those persons unless the governing document provides otherwise or they have been appointed under the provisions of the **Trustee Act 2000** [see **13.5.2.5**].

Any governing body, even one which does not have powers of delegation, can appoint individuals to collect information and make a recommendation to the governing body, provided the final decision clearly rests with the governing body.

While the primary liability remains with the governing body, case law makes it clear that where a properly selected employee causes loss to the trust, the members of the governing body are unlikely to be required to make good the loss.

13.6 POWERS OF THE GOVERNING BODY

Powers give the organisation, its members or its governing body the right to take certain actions in order to achieve the organisation's objects [see **4.1** and **5.4.3-5.4.8**]. Powers must generally be explicit in statute or the governing document, although some powers may be implied (assumed to exist). The first requirement for governing body members is therefore to read the governing document and understand the powers outlined there and who has the right to exercise them.

Most governing documents in membership organisations give the governing body power to manage the organisation on behalf of the members. But some governing documents limit this power, for example by saying that certain actions must be done by the organisation's members in a general meeting. Where it is not clear whether a specific power rests with the membership as a whole or with the governing body, legal advice may be needed to clarify the situation.

The governing body operates *as a body*. Individual governing body members—including the chairperson—can act on its behalf only if they have been explicitly authorised to do so by the governing document or by a decision of the governing body or the organisation's members. An unauthorised action taken by an individual is *ultra vires* unless it is subsequently properly ratified.

Chapter 14
RESTRICTIONS ON EXPENSES, REMUNERATION AND BENEFITS

14.1 RESTRICTIONS ON PAYMENTS AND BENEFITS

Charities and many non-charitable voluntary organisations are characterised by restrictions on the payments which may be made to members of the governing body, and sometimes restrictions on payments to members of the organisation who are not on the governing body.

In looking at this, a clear distinction must be made between:

- **reimbursement** for genuine expenses which is allowed under trust law or the governing document [see **14.2**];

- reimbursement for expenses which is not allowed under trust law or the governing document and has not been authorised by the Charity Commission, and is therefore unlawful;

- **remuneration** for services provided to the organisation [see **14.3**];

- **payment** for goods provided to an organisation, rent on property or interest on a loan to the charity [see **14.4**];

- being a user of the organisation's **services** or activities or receiving a **benefit**, such as a scholarship or accommodation, as a beneficiary of the charity [see **14.5**];

- getting **preferential treatment** from the organisation, or benefiting in other ways;

- benefiting **indirectly** through a closely linked person or company being remunerated by or benefiting from the organisation [see **14.7**].

Anyone who is remunerated by an organisation, receives reimbursement which is not allowed free of tax by the Inland Revenue, or receives other taxable income may be liable to income tax through PAYE [see **27.3**] or self-assessment [see **34.1.4**], and may be entitled to minimum wage [see **27.2.1**]. If the person receives state benefits, these may be affected by remuneration or other taxable income [see **35.10**]. Even if the person receives only allowed reimbursement of genuine expenses the organisation may have to declare these to the Inland Revenue on form P9D or P11D and the recipient may have to declare them on income tax self-assessment [see **27.4.8**].

14.1.1
Governing body members

One of the basic principles of trust law which applies to all charities is that trustees must not profit or benefit from their trust unless this is explicitly allowed under the terms of the governing document or authorised in some other valid way [see **13.3.6**]. These rules are explained in this chapter and in more detail in Charity Commission booklet CC11 *Payment of Charity Trustees*. Even in non-charities, the governing document often contains the same restrictions.

It is important to read the governing document carefully to determine which payments and benefits are explicitly allowed or prohibited, and to be clear about which payments are prohibited even if this is not explicit in the governing document. A governing body member who receives an improper payment or benefit may have to repay to the organisation all the money received or any element of profit in the money received, or all or some of the value of non-financial benefits.

Where the governing document allows payment to a member of the governing body, the other governing body members must consider whether that person is truly the best person to provide those goods or services. Their decision should be clearly minuted, along with the fact that the person concerned was (in a charity) not present for the discussion or decision or (in a non-charitable company) had declared their interest in the decision and not taken part in it [see **13.2.2**].

A charitable or non-charitable company, charitable trust or charitable association which makes any payment, including reimbursement of expenses, or provides any material benefit to its governing body members must include certain information in the notes to the accounts if its annual accounts are prepared on an accruals basis [see **50.2.10** and **50.2.11**]. Even where the accounts are prepared on a receipts and payments basis [see **50.2.9**] it is good practice to include the disclosures.

14.1.2
Members of the organisation

14.1.2.1
Charities

Where a membership organisation—whether a company, industrial and provident society or unincorporated association—is charitable, profits or surplus cannot be distributed or paid to the members.

This restriction does not prevent members receiving charitable benefits where the costs of the benefit are covered by the profit or surplus. For example a charitable school or nursery which has parents as members can use its surplus funds to reduce fees, thus providing a benefit for the members, but could not simply pay out the cash to its members. There is more information about provision of benefits to members in Charity Commission booklet CC24 *Users on Board: Beneficiaries who become trustees*.

14.1.2.2
Non-charities

The governing document of many non-charitable organisations contains similar restrictions. An organisation with such restrictions is often referred to as **not for profit**. Where there are no such restrictions, a non-charitable organisation may distribute its assets among its members or in any other way agreed by the members or the governing body.

14.1.3
Registered social landlords

For **registered social landlords**, additional rules govern the circumstances under which employment, a tenancy, a grant, or purchase of goods or services can be entered into with a current or former member of the governing body, an employee, or a person connected with a governing body member or employee. Information about these rules is available from the Housing Corporation.   *Housing Act 1996 pt.1 sch.1*

14.2 REIMBURSEMENT OF EXPENSES

14.2.1 Allowed expenses

Members of a governing body can be reimbursed for expenses only if this is allowed by trust law [see **14.2.3**] or the governing document. Ordinary members of an organisation (not on the governing body) can be reimbursed unless this is prohibited by the governing document.

Even where reimbursement is allowed under trust law or the governing document, it is subject to tax unless it is allowed free of tax by the Inland Revenue. Where the person receives no payment other than allowed reimbursement, the tax rules are the same as for volunteers [see **35.2.1**]. Where the person receives further payment, the tax rules are the same as for paid employees [see **27.4.3** and **27.4.8**].

Allowed expenses for volunteers (but not necessarily for people who receive additional payment) include, for example, reimbursement for postage, stationery, telephone calls etc, as well as childminding, travel and, if necessary, accommodation and meal costs to attend meetings and other essential events. For reimbursement for meals, hotels, childminding etc, it is good practice for the organisation to have guidelines on maximum reimbursable amounts. The National Council for Voluntary Organisations [see **page 12**] can provide a factsheet *Expenses for Trustees* giving examples of NCVO's rates, but each organisation should set rates which are reasonable in its circumstances.

Reimbursement for genuine expenses allowed by the Inland Revenue is not subject to income tax, does not create an entitlement to minimum wage [see **27.2.1**] and does not affect eligibility for state benefits. It may, however, have to be declared by the organisation on tax form P9D or P11D and by the recipient as part of self-assessment [see **27.4.8**].

14.2.2 'Expenses' as remuneration

Some payments which are traditionally called 'expenses' are actually taxable income rather than reimbursement and must be treated as such [see **14.3**]. These include:

- lump sum payments for expenses (for example, being paid £10 regardless of how much was actually spent);
- payment for expenditure which the person would have incurred anyway, such as rent or telephone line costs;
- mileage payments above the Inland Revenue rates [see **35.2.1**];
- an **attendance allowance** or payment for **loss of earnings** when the person attends meetings or takes part in other activities;
- sessional fees or one-off payments for work.

These are taxable [see **35.2.2**], may create an entitlement to minimum wage [see **27.2.1**] and may affect state benefits [see **35.10**].

14.2.3 Governing body members

Trustees of all trusts and charitable associations, as well as holding or custodian trustees [see **18.4**], have a statutory right to be reimbursed for expenses genuinely incurred in serving as a trustee and for other costs properly incurred in administering the trust. Expenditure which has not been authorised by the trustees cannot be reimbursed unless it is subsequently ratified (approved) by them.   *Trustee Act 2000 s.31*

Governing body members in companies (whether charitable or non-charitable) and non-charitable associations do not have a right to reimbursement unless it is explicit in the governing document or has been approved by the members of the organisation. In industrial and provident societies, the rules must provide for the right of governing body members to be reimbursed for expenses.

Industrial and Provident Societies Act 1965 sch.1

**14.2.4
Members of the
organisation**

Ordinary members of a membership organisation—those who are not members of the governing body—do not have a statutory right to be reimbursed for expenses incurred on behalf of the organisation, but neither is there any prohibition on it. If the governing document prohibits payments to members, any reimbursement must be limited to genuine out-of-pocket expenditure.

**14.2.5
Documentation for
expenses**

Receipts, mileage records or other documentation (**vouchers**) should always be provided by anyone claiming expenses unless it is genuinely impossible to do so. If the expenses ever have to be proved to the Charity Commission, Inland Revenue and/or Benefits Agency, the vouchers should be adequate to satisfy them that the expenditure was genuinely incurred, necessary and properly authorised. Minutes should be kept of all decisions authorising reimbursement, especially for unusual expenses.

**14.3
REMUNERATION
FOR SERVICES**

Remuneration for services involves being paid for work done for the organisation, whether as an employee or on a freelance or self-employed basis. Many payments which are called 'payment for expenses' are in fact remuneration and must be treated as such [see **14.2.2**].

**14.3.1
Ordinary members**

Ordinary members of an organisation—those who are not members of the governing body—may be paid by the organisation unless this is prohibited by the governing document. This applies regardless of whether the organisation is charitable or non-charitable.

**14.3.2
Governing body
members**

In all organisations, whether charitable or non-charitable, there may be restrictions on payment to members of the governing body for services provided to the organisation. Failure to comply with these restrictions could lead to the governing body member having to return the payment.

**14.3.2.1
Charities**

For payments to governing body members in all charities and in non-charitable trusts, the main principles which apply are:

- a trustee cannot profit from her or his trust [see **13.3.6**], so charity and other trustees cannot receive any remuneration or other payment unless this is specifically authorised by the governing document, statute, the Charity Commission or the court;

- trustees may not alter their governing document to authorise payment to themselves, so any such amendment requires the consent of the Charity Commission or court.

    Re French Protestant Hospital [1951] 1 All ER 938; Charities Act 1993 s.64

For charities, guidance on remuneration is set out in Charity Commission booklet CC11 *Payment of Charity Trustees*.

**14.3.2.2
Non-charities**

If a properly authorised decision is taken, members of the governing body of non-charitable associations, companies and industrial and provident societies may be paid unless this is prohibited by the governing document. If such payment is prohibited, the organisation may be able to amend its governing document to allow it [see **5.5** for procedure].

**14.3.2.3
Payments to company
directors**

In a company, whether charitable or non-charitable, there is a statutory obligation for directors to disclose any interest in any contract or in any piece of work from which they might profit [see **13.2.2**].

If company directors are paid for their work as directors or are employed by their company, a copy of their service contract or a memorandum setting out the terms of their remuneration must be kept and must be open to company members [see **16.3.6**].

A resolution by a general meeting is required if a company wants to give a director a contract of employment or a contract to provide services on a self-employed basis which is for five years or more and cannot be terminated by the company by giving notice, or can be terminated only in specific circumstances. *Companies Act 1985 s.319*

14.3.3 Serving on the governing body

Most voluntary sector governing documents do not allow members of the governing body to be paid for their services as members of the governing body, but some do allow it. Some organisations argue that only by paying can they recruit governing body members with suitable experience and skills; others argue that such payments violate the fundamental principles of the voluntary sector.

14.3.3.1 Charities

New charities may be registered with the power to pay trustees for serving as trustees, provided the governing document limits the remuneration to a reasonable amount.

Existing charities which do not have an explicit power in the governing document to remunerate trustees cannot do so. If they want to pay trustees, they must get Charity Commission authorisation. Factors taken into account when deciding whether to allow a charity to remunerate its trustees include:

- the size and complexity of the charity;
- whether it has sufficient income to be able to remunerate trustees without affecting its charitable work;
- whether the charity's activities need constant oversight by trustees;
- whether the charity relies on trustees to do its day-to-day work, or has employees to do it;
- whether the trustees need specialist skills not available through staff or external advisors;
- the relative cost of paying trustees to provide those skills compared to paying others; *and*
- whether people are excluded from trusteeship because of their economic circumstances.

14.3.3.2 Non-charities

Non-charitable associations, companies and industrial and provident societies often have similar restrictions in their governing document. Such constitutional provisions can be amended in the usual way [see **5.5**], unless such amendment is explicitly prohibited.

14.3.4 Serving on an associated governing body

Charity trustees who are also members of the governing body of a subsidiary non-charitable company [see **47.5.1**] and are paid a fee as directors of that company may keep the fee if the governing document *of the charity* explicitly allows them to. If it does not, they may apply to the Charity Commission for authorisation to keep the fees, or must pay over the fee to the charity. Charity Commission consent to keep the fee is likely to be given only if evidence is given that from the charity's point of view it is necessary that:

- the trustees should be directors of the subsidiary;
- they should receive remuneration for their services in that capacity;
- the level of remuneration is reasonable for the services which they actually render; *and*
- the work cannot be done by someone who is not a trustee.

14.3.5 Professional services

Depending on the nature of the organisation and its governing document, it may be possible to pay governing body members for professional services provided to the organisation.

14.3.5.1 Charities

Governing documents of charities often contain provisions allowing payments to governing body members who are members of specified professions, such as accountants and solicitors, for professional services provided to the charity. Payments to governing body members for professional services which are not authorised by the governing document need the consent of the Charity Commission.

Some charity governing documents contain a similar provision but without naming specific professions. Such provision should be used only for services which an 'ordinary reasonable person in the street' would consider 'professional' (accountants, solicitors, architects, surveyors etc).

These provisions apply only to 'professional' work, not work related to the general running of the organisation. If in doubt about whether a particular payment is authorised under the governing document or whether a service such as computer consultancy or graphic design is 'professional', the Charity Commission should be consulted.

The restriction on being paid for services applies not only to payments to individual governing body members, but also to businesses owned by a governing body member or in which he or she is a partner. It may also extend to a business where a governing body member is managing director or has a significant interest as an employee or shareholder. However the governing document, particularly in a charitable company, may state that the charity may enter into a contract with a business in which a member of the governing body holds shares, provided the person's holding is less than 1% of the voting rights.

Report of the Charity Commissioners 1981 para.105; 1990 para.66

Trustees in charitable and non-charitable trusts and in charitable associations, including holding or custodian trustees [see **18.4**], who are solicitors may hire their business partner(s) to undertake professional work for the trust, and the partner may then be paid. It must be clear that the partner, not the firm, is being hired, and any payment from the charity must be to the partner and not to the firm.

Clack v Carlon [1861] 30 LJ Ch 639; Re Gates [1933] Ch 913

If the governing document does not authorise payments for services or if the payment is outside what is allowed by the governing document or the provisions on solicitor-trustees, the Charity Commission may make an order [see **3.5.4**] authorising the payment. They will need to be convinced that:

- the work is exceptional, and not part of the trustee's normal duties;
- the work is necessary;
- the trustee is not being paid more than would ordinarily be paid for such work; *and*
- the payment is reasonable for the work done.

14.3.5.2
Non-charities

Non-charities often have similar provision in their governing document. They must comply with the governing document, although they may be able to amend it to allow such payment [see **5.5** for procedure].

14.3.6
'Non-professional'
services

Governing body members may be involved in providing 'non-professional' services to their organisation, for example printing, building works or typing. There is no problem if these are provided free or with only genuine expenses reimbursed [see **14.2**], but if the governing body member is actually paid anything for the work the rules on remuneration of governing body members apply.

14.3.7
Services as an
employee

Where employees are allowed to be governing body members, the duties on avoidance and disclosure of conflict of interest [see **13.2.2** and **13.3.4**] apply.

A governing body member who is likely to become employed by the organisation, is applying or might apply for a job should not take part in discussions or decisions about the job or terms of employment.

Some governing documents explicitly prohibit persons closely connected with an employee (spouse, co-habitee, business partner) from serving as a member of the governing body. If in doubt about a particular situation, advice should be sought from the Charity Commission or a solicitor who specialises in voluntary organisations.

14.3.7.1
Charities

In all charities, employees are prohibited from being members of the governing body (and governing body members from being employees) unless the governing document provides otherwise or the Charity Commission authorises it. Where the prohibition applies, a member of the governing body who becomes employed by a charity, even for a short time, must resign. But charity trustees cannot resign in order to receive a benefit from their charity, so even though the trustee has resigned or will resign the charity must get an order [see **3.5.4**] from the Charity Commission authorising the employment.

The Charity Commission is willing to register new charities which allow employees to be trustees, provided the governing document prohibits the employee trustees from taking part in any discussions or decisions relating to their terms of employment. Before registering the charity, the Commission will want to know why employees should be trustees. They will be especially concerned if employees make up more than a small minority of the governing body.

For existing charities whose governing documents do not allow employees to serve as trustees, the Commission will not allow the governing document to be altered unless there is a very strong reason to do so.

Employee trustees, like all trustees, are under a duty to act in the best interests of the charity as a whole and its beneficiaries, even if this is in conflict with their best interest as an individual or employee.

14.3.7.2
Non-charities

In non-charitable organisations, the governing document often prohibits employees from serving on the governing body. It may be possible to amend the governing document [see **5.5** for procedure].

14.4
OTHER PAYMENTS

In general, the rules on governing body members or their businesses receiving other types of payment from the organisation follow the same basic principles as payments for non-professional services [see **14.3.6**].

14.4.1
Payment for goods

Goods must not be purchased from a charity trustee, a holding or custodian trustee for the charity, a business closely associated with a trustee or a business in which a trustee owns shares unless the governing document or the Charity Commission authorises such transactions. Non-charities are not subject to this restriction unless it is included in the governing document.

14.4.2
Rent

A charity trustee or a holding or custodian trustee may be paid rent by the charity only if the governing document or Charity Commission authorises this. The rent must be 'reasonable'. If there is any doubt, the governing body should take and record independent valuation advice. Non-charities are not subject to this restriction unless it is in the governing document.

14.4.3
Loans

14.4.3.1
Loans to the organisation

Any governing body member may make an interest-free loan to their organisation. But interest may be paid on a loan only if this is explicitly authorised by the governing document or, for a charity, by the Charity Commission. Governing documents which allow payment of interest to governing body members usually specify the maximum level of the interest. If the amount is specified by reference to a rate at a bank which is now defunct, the comparable business rate at its successor bank should be used. The Bank of England (020-7601 4444) can advise.

All the details of the loan arrangement should be put in writing at the time the loan is made.

14.4.3.2
Loans from the organisation

A charitable organisation, of any legal status, may not make a loan to a member of its governing body unless it is authorised by the governing document or the Charity Commission.

Non-charitable companies cannot generally make loans to directors of the company or its holding company. Exceptions apply to loans under £5,000, and to companies making a loan enabling a director to meet costs properly incurred for the purposes of the company or for performing her or his duties as a director. A loan for this purpose:

- must have prior agreement at a general meeting of the members, with full disclosure of the reason for the loan and the conditions;

- must be approved at or before the next AGM, with full disclosure; *or*

- if it is not so approved, must be properly used for the company's purposes or be repaid to the company within six months from the end of that AGM. *Companies Act 1985 ss.330, 334, 337*

14.4.4
Land and assets

Special provisions apply when a company director or any person connected with a director [see **13.2.2**] acquires land or substantial non-cash assets from a company, or when a company acquires them from a director or connected person. *ss.320-322*

Special provisions also apply when a charity is selling land or giving a tenancy or lease to a trustee of the charity or to a person connected with a trustee [see **57.12.1**] *Charities Act 1993 s.36*

A charity which wishes to purchase land or other assets from a trustee or former trustee must take advice from the Charity Commission.

14.5
BENEFITS AS A USER OR BENEFICIARY

Strictly speaking, anyone who benefits from a charity should not be a trustee [see **13.3.6**]. But this is inconsistent with the reality of many charities, whose governing document states that some or all governing body members must or may be users of the charity's services. It is also inconsistent with charities such as community associations where all members, including its governing body members, are eligible to use the association's facilities. These anomalies have arisen because of the misfit between traditional trust law, and user or local control of charities.

Guidance on how to encourage user involvement in charities—including involvement as governing body members—while staying within trust and charity law is set out in Charity Commission booklet CC24 *Users on Board: Beneficiaries who become trustees.*

14.5.1
The legal position

In any organisation, whether charitable or non-charitable:

- if the governing document states that members of the governing body may (or must) be users of the organisation's services, or that they may (or must) be members of an organisation whose members are entitled to use services, then beneficiaries/users may be members of the governing body;

- if the governing document excludes beneficiaries/users from the governing body, they cannot be members of the governing body.

If the governing document of a *non-charitable* organisation does not say anything one way or the other, beneficiaries/users may be members of the governing body.

If the governing document of a *charitable* organisation does not say anything one way or the other or if it is unclear, advice should be sought from the Charity Commission before electing or appointing a beneficiary/user as a member of the governing body or providing a charitable benefit to an existing governing body member.

It may be possible to alter the governing document [see **5.5** for procedure] but Charity Commission advice should be sought before making any alteration allowing beneficiaries or service users to serve as governing body members in a charity.

Any material benefits provided to governing body members in a charity may have to be disclosed in the notes to the annual accounts [see **50.2.11**].

180

14.5.2
Avoiding conflict of interest

Where beneficiaries/users are permitted to be on a charity's governing body, the rules on disclosing conflict of interest, not taking part in discussion or decisions where there is a conflict of interest, and acting always in the best interest of the charity and all its beneficiaries apply [see **13.3.3** and **13.3.4**]. They must not use their position to gain an advantage for themselves or their relatives. In practice, this means:

- because of the duty to avoid conflict of interest, a governing body member should not take part in any discussion or decision relating to benefits *specific* to her or him, such as a research grant or scholarship, allocation of a flat, or selection for a holiday;

- there is probably no significant conflict of interest in taking part in discussions or decisions about services or activities which are equally available to all, or very large numbers, of the organisation's users (for example an advice line or a school);

- everything between is a grey area in which governing body members need to exercise common sense, remembering their overriding duties to avoid conflict of interest and to act not in their personal interest but in the best interests of the organisation as a whole and all its present and future beneficiaries (in a charity) or all its members (in a non-charitable membership organisation);

- all decisions about which beneficiaries or users should be chosen for a grant, service or activity must be scrupulously fair and must not give any unfair advantage to a member of the governing body;

- decisions must be properly minuted, and if they involve a benefit to a specific member of the governing body should make clear that he or she was not involved in the discussion or decision.

If in doubt—especially where a benefit of substantial value, such as a research grant, is to be given to a member of the governing body—the Charity Commission should be consulted or legal advice taken.

14.5.2.1
When everyone has a conflict of interest

Sometimes all or a majority of governing body members would stand to gain or lose from a decision, for example in a community nursery where the parents who make up the governing body have to decide whether to raise fees. They could not all withdraw, because there would then be no one to make the decision. They should all declare their conflict of interest, and then make the decision mindful of their duty to act in the best interests of all the beneficiaries rather than in their personal interest or in the interest of a particular group. If the situation is unworkable, advice should be sought from the Charity Commission.

14.6
OTHER BENEFITS

Charity trustees are not permitted to benefit from their charity in any other way, for example living in charity property, unless it is authorised by the governing document or the Charity Commission.

14.6.1
<u>Small gifts</u>

In principle the same rules apply to small thank you, get well and similar gifts for governing body members or former members—a charity's funds should not be used to purchase them. In practice the Charity Commission does not object to a modest token of appreciation. If in doubt about whether something is 'modest', the charity's funds should not be used or Charity Commission advice should be sought.

14.7
PROFITS/BENEFITS TO CONNECTED PERSONS

The governing document may prohibit some or all payments or benefits not only to members of the governing body, but also to persons (individuals or corporate bodies) connected to or associated with them. For companies, the same rules apply to connected persons as to company directors [see **13.2.2**]. For transactions involving charity land, the definition of connected person is very wide [see **57.12.1**].

PART III
RUNNING AN ORGANISATION

Part III starts by looking at the administrative aspects of running a voluntary organisation: the registered office, various paperwork requirements, and procedures for meetings and decision making. It moves on to look at the types of legal agreement organisations are likely to enter into, liability for those agreements and for other aspects of the organisation's work, insurance, and winding up the organisation.

Chapter 15
THE REGISTERED OFFICE
AND OTHER PREMISES

Topics covered in this chapter

This chapter looks at the legal requirements regarding the location of the office and the information which must be displayed at the registered office and other premises. It covers:

For sources of further information see page 12.

15.1
COMPANIES

Every company and industrial and provident society must have a registered office. Certain information must be displayed there, and at other premises where a company or IPS carries out its activities.

15.1.1
Domicile and registered office

A company's **domicile** is the country (England and Wales, Wales on its own or Scotland) where its registered office must be. Domicile must be included in the memorandum of association. A company whose domicile is England and Wales, and whose registered office is in Wales, can alter its memorandum by special resolution to change its domicile to Wales [see **17.4.7** for procedure]. Apart from this, domicile cannot be changed.

Companies Act 1985 s.2(1),(2)

A company must have a **registered office** at all times. This is the official address, where official company correspondence and legal documents are sent.　　　　　*s.287*

The registered office might be:

- the company's office;
- a box number at the company's premises;
- any place where the company carries out its activities;
- the address of the company secretary, treasurer, or any other person;
- the office of the company's accountant or solicitor;
- any other reasonable address.

The registered office cannot be a box number at the post office or at other premises which are not occupied by the company.

If the registered office is not the company's usual office, there must be very good arrangements to ensure any papers delivered to the registered office quickly reach the people who need to see them. If a writ or other notice is served at the registered office, time runs from the date it is served, not the date the company directors become aware of it. In most cases judgment can be entered against the organisation if it fails to respond to a writ within 14 days.

The address of the first registered office is notified to Companies House on **form 10** when the company is registered. As soon as the company is registered its registered name must be displayed on the outside of the registered office [see below], and stationery and order forms, including outgoing email and websites, must show the company's domicile and the address of the registered office [see **16.1.1**].

Many of the company's statutory books must be kept at the registered office [see **16.3**]. The register of members and the register of debenture holders (if there is one) do not need to be kept at the registered office, but if they are not, **form 353** and/or **form 190** must be submitted to Companies House.

15.1.2
Name on premises

A company's full registered name, exactly as it appears on the certificate of incorporation (apart from capitalisation), must be painted or affixed on the outside of its registered office and every office or place where it carries on its work. The plaque or other notice does not actually need to be out of doors; it can be indoors, provided it is visible during normal working hours from the outside (for example, through large glass doors). The name must be kept conspicuous and legible. The registered office does not have to be identified as such.   *Companies Act 1985 s.348*

A Welsh company whose name ends with *cyfyngedig* or *cyf* must state the fact that it is a limited company in a notice in English conspicuously displayed in every place where it carries on its work.   *s.351(4)(b)*

If a company uses a business name (a day-to-day name different from its registered name, see **8.5.1**) it must prominently display the registered name and registered address in all premises where the organisation operates and where its clients, customers, users or suppliers have access. If a business name is also displayed, it must be clear which is the registered name.   *Business Names Act 1985 ss.4(1)(b), 1(a)(iii)*

15.1.3
Changing the office

A company's registered office can be changed at any time by a resolution of the directors. **Form 287** must be sent to Companies House within 14 days of the decision. The change of address takes effect as soon as it is registered, but for 14 days after registration, legal documents may be delivered to the previous registered address as well as the new one.
Companies Act 1985 s.287

The plaque or nameplate needs to be removed from the old office and be displayed at the new office [see above] and stationery, other documents, outgoing emails and websites must be changed [see **16.1.1**]. Most of the statutory books must be moved to the new office and **forms 353** and **190** must be submitted if the register of members (and register of debenture holders, if there is one) are not to be kept at the new office.

15.1.3.1
Registered social landlords

Registered social landlords must inform the Housing Corporation of any change of registered office.   *Housing Act 1996 sch.1 para.11.2*

15.2
INDUSTRIAL AND PROVIDENT SOCIETIES

An industrial and provident society must have a registered office in its area of registration. The address of the registered office must be included in the society's rules.
Industrial and Provident Societies Act 1965 s.1(1)(c), sch.1 para.3

15.2.1
Registered office

There are two areas of registration: one for Scotland, and one for England, Wales and the Channel Islands. An IPS registered in one area cannot operate in the other until a copy of its rules has been **recorded** by being sent, with **form D**, to the registration body for the other area. If the rules are subsequently amended, the amendments must be sent to the other area.   *s.8*

If the registered office is not the society's usual place of business, there must be good arrangements to get all official communications delivered at the registered office to the relevant people immediately.

The registers of members and officers [see **16.4**] must be kept at the registered office, and a copy of the most recent balance sheet and auditors' report must be on public display there. Unless the society is a credit union, it must not display any unaudited accounts [see **50.4.1**].

Industrial and Provident Societies Act 1965 ss.44(1), 40

15.2.2
Name on premises

The IPS's full registered name must be painted or affixed on the outside of the registered office and at each place where the society operates, in the same way as for companies [see **15.1.2**]. *s.5(6)*

The provisions of the **Business Names Act 1985** relating to businesses which use a different name for their day-to-day work apply to IPSs in the same way as companies [see **15.1.2**].

15.2.3
Changing the office

An IPS can change its registered address by using the amendment procedure in its rules. The change must be notified to Mutual Societies Registration on **form I** (fee £40 as at 1/4/01). IPSs which are registered social landlords must notify the Housing Corporation [see **15.1.3.1**].

s.10(2)

15.3
TRUSTS AND UNINCORPORATED ASSOCIATIONS

Trusts and unincorporated associations do not need a registered office. Sometimes the governing document says the organisation's office or other premises must be in a specific area. This must be complied with, or the governing document may be amended to allow the premises to be located elsewhere [see **5.5** for procedure].

Trusts and unincorporated associations are not required to put their name on any premises they use.

15.4
CHARITIES

15.4.1
Address

Before a charity is registered, the Charity Commission must be satisfied that the trustees intend it to be governed by the laws of England and Wales [see **3.4.6**]. Apart from this, there are no location requirements specific to charities. *Charities Act 1993 s.96*

Charitable companies and IPSs must have a registered office, but there is no requirement for charitable trusts and associations to have one. All they need is a correspondent's address which is given in the Charity Commission's annual return and entered into the register of charities.

15.4.2
Status at premises

Charitable status does not, in itself, involve any requirements to display a name or other information on premises. But if a charity with total annual income over £10,000 displays a notice at a charity shop or any other premises encouraging people to donate money or goods to the charity, or encouraging them to purchase goods from the charity, the notice must state that the organisation is a registered charity [see **16.1.4**]. *s.5(1),(2)*

15.4.3
Changing address

Any change in the charity's address as shown in the register of charities, or in the address of the correspondent named in the annual return, must be notified to the Charity Commission. *s.3(7)(b)*

Chapter 16
PAPERWORK REQUIREMENTS

**16.1
PUBLICATION OF
NAME AND STATUS**

For companies, industrial and provident societies and charities it may be an offence to issuedocuments which do not include the required statements of name and/or status, or to authorise documents to be issued without them. The safest course is to include the required information on every publication, document, letter, outgoing email and website.

**16.1.1
Companies**

As soon as the **certificate of incorporation** [see **6.3.8**] is received, a company must immediately include certain information on some documents. The company's name on these must be exactly as shown on the certificate of incorporation, with no abbreviations or other changes (but capitalisation on the certificate or incorporation can be ignored).

**16.1.1.1
Name, status, number, registered office and charitable status**

All **business letters** and **forms used to order goods, services or money**, whether on paper or sent electronically, must contain:

- the company's **full registered name**, as on the certificate of incorporation;

- for a company which does not use *limited* as part of its name [see **8.4.3**], the fact that it is a limited company;

- the company's **domicile**, which is the country specified in the memorandum of association where the registered office must be located (for example 'Registered in England and Wales', if the registered office may be in either England or Wales, or 'Registered in Wales', if the office must be in Wales);

- the company's registration number;
- the address of its registered office [see **15.1.1**].

Companies Act 1985 ss.349(1), 351(1)

A Welsh company whose name ends with *cyfyngedig* or *cyf* must state in English that it is a limited company on all headed paper, notices and other official publications, and bill-heads. *s.351(4)(a)*

Strictly speaking the registered name does not have to be on business letters and forms if the company is not a charity and its registered name does not end in *limited, ltd* or the Welsh equivalents. But it is sensible even for these companies to include the registered name. *s.30(7)*

If another address is included as well as the registered office, it must be clear which is the registered office.

A charitable company must include a statement of charitable status [see **16.1.4.4**] if its name does not contain the words *charity* or *charitable*.

Charities Act 1993 s.68

There are no rules governing what must be on compliments slips or outgoing email, but they could become business letters and have to include full company details, so it is best always to include them.

16.1.1.2
Registered name and charitable status

The company's full registered name must be shown on:

- all its notices (for example, notice of meetings) and other official publications;
- cheques;
- endorsements (cheques signed over to a third party);
- invoices and receipts issued by the company;
- promissory notes (unconditional promises to pay);
- bills of exchange (authorisation for someone who owes money to the company to pay it to a third party);
- letters of credit (agreements to provide credit);
- conveyances (deeds transferring property). *s.349(1)*

The requirement to show the registered name does not apply to non-charitable companies whose registered names do not end in *limited, ltd* or the Welsh equivalents, but it is sensible to include it. *s.30(7)*

A charitable company whose name does not include *charity* or *charitable* must include a statement of charitable status on its notices and financial documents [see **16.1.4.4**]. *Charities Act 1993 ss.67, 68*

16.1.1.3
Business names

If a company uses a day-to-day **business name** (sometimes called its **trading name** or **operating name**) which is different from the registered name [see **8.5.1**], it must include its registered name on all the documents listed above and also on written demands for payment of debts to the company. *Business Names Act 1985 s.4(1)(a)*

On all documents where the trading and registered names are used it must be clear which is the registered name.

A company which uses a trading name must include its **registered address** on invoices and receipts issued by the company and written demands for payment of debts. *s.4(1)(a)*

16.1.1.4
Names of directors

There is no requirement to publish the **names of directors** on the company's stationery. But if the names of some directors are to be included on the company's stationery (except within the text of the letter or as a signatory) the names of *all* directors and shadow directors [see **11.1.3**] must be listed. *Companies Act 1985 s.305*

If the honorary officers (president, chairperson, treasurer etc), company secretary or senior staff are not directors, their names can be on the stationery. But if they are directors—as at least some of them are likely to be—their names cannot be on, even if they are identified as chairperson etc rather than as director, unless all the other directors are included as well.

The usual practice is not to include directors' names, so the paper does not have to be reprinted every time there is a change of directors.

16.1.1.5
VAT number

A company registered for VAT must include its name, address, VAT registration number and certain other information on invoices and receipts which it issues [see **53.6.2**].

16.1.2
Industrial and provident societies

An industrial and provident society must put its full name on all:

- business letters;
- notices, advertisements and other official publications;
- bills of exchange, promissory notes, endorsements, cheques, orders for money or goods, bills, invoices, receipts and letters of credit [see **16.1.1.2** for definitions].

Industrial and Provident Societies Act 1965 s.5(6)

Limited may be abbreviated to *ltd*. Other words must be exactly as on the certificate of registration.   *s.5(2)*

All business letters, orders and invoices should also include:

- address of the registered office;
- registration number;
- 'Registered in England and Wales' or 'Registered in Scotland'.

If a day-to-day business name [see **8.5.1**] is included it must be clear which is the registered name. If an address other than the registered address is included it must be clear which is the registered address.

A society registered for VAT must include its name, address, VAT registration number and certain other information on its invoices and receipts [see **53.6.2**].

16.1.3
Trusts and unincorporated associations

There are no legal requirements for publishing the name or address of non-charitable trusts or unincorporated associations, but clearly it is sensible for the name to be on all its business and official documents. Charitable trusts and associations must comply with charity requirements [see below].

A trust or association registered for VAT must include its name, address and VAT registration number and other required information on its invoices and receipts [see **53.6.2**].

16.1.4
Charities

16.1.4.1
Statement on business documents

All trusts and associations registered as charities with annual income of more than £10,000 in their last financial year, including excepted charities which are voluntarily registered, must include a **statement of charitable status** in the specified form [see **16.1.4.4**] on the following documents:

- cheques;
- the charity's invoices, receipts, bills and orders for money or goods;
- bills of exchange, promissory notes, endorsements and letters of credit [see **16.1.1.2** for definitions].   *Charities Act 1993 s.5*

Although charitable trusts and associations do not have to put the statement on all their correspondence, it is good practice to put it on headed paper, compliments slips and outgoing emails as these may be used for orders, receipts etc.

A charitable company with income of any amount whose name does not include *charity* or *charitable* must include the statement on all its letters and the documents listed above.   *s.68(1)*

16.1.4.2
Statement on
fundraising documents

The statement must also be included on written or printed documents, notices or advertisements which are intended to persuade the reader to give or pay money, goods or property to the charity.

Charities Act 1993 s.5(1),(2)

Examples of the types of written or printed materials on which the statement must appear include:

- a leaflet asking people to donate goods for a jumble sale;
- a recycling container outside a local supermarket, for aluminium cans which the charity is collecting to raise money;
- a poster or newspaper advertisement for a concert where admission will be charged or a collection will be taken;
- an article in the charity's newsletter about a fundraising event;
- a letter, email message or webpage asking for donations;
- an order form, on paper or the internet, for publications or other goods sold by the charity;
- a list of services provided by the charity, if a charge is made for them.

If in doubt ... include the statement.

16.1.4.3
Statement not required

An unincorporated association or trust which is registered as a charity but had income of £10,000 or less in its last financial year does not have to include the statement on any documents, but may do if it chooses.

Excepted charities which are not voluntarily registered [see **7.1.3**] must not use the statement. Exempt charities [see **7.1.2**] must not use the statement but may say 'Exempt charity' or indicate that they are recognised as charitable by the Inland Revenue [see **6.4.3**].

16.1.4.4
Form of the statement

The statement should be in one of the following forms:

- A registered charity
- Registered as a charity
- Registered charity number [*or* no.] 1234567
- Registered with the Charity Commission
- *Elusen cofrestredig* (acceptable only where the document on which it appears is wholly in Welsh).

The statement may be in any language but must be in English as well, unless the document and statement are wholly in Welsh.

The statement may be printed, rubber stamped, handwritten or put on in any other way so long as it is clear and readable.

16.1.4.5
Other information

A charitable association or trust may, if it wishes, put some or all of the names of its committee members/trustees on its headed paper. A charitable company can include directors' names only if it includes all of them [see **16.1.1.4**].

16.2
RECORD KEEPING
AND ACCESS TO
INFORMATION

All organisations should keep adequate minutes, membership lists and financial records for their own purposes. But for many organisations there are also legal requirements about what must be kept, its format, where and how long it must be kept, and who has access to the records. The following sections outline these requirements.

Funders or donors might request or require access to, or copies of, records not available to the public. Unless the law requires or prevents public access to the information, it is a matter for each organisation to decide and negotiate with the funder or donor. Funders and donors do have a proper interest in having full information about what is done with money they provide, but an organisation might feel that a funder or donor does not have a right to detailed information, or to information about other aspects of the organisation's work. This is especially important in relation to sensitive information about staff, beneficiaries, clients etc, and each organisation should develop appropriate confidentiality procedures [see **38.1**] and ensure that all rules on access to information comply with the **Data Protection Act 1998** [see **38.3**] and the **Human Rights Act 1998** [see **60.3**].

For companies, industrial and provident societies and charities, it is an offence not to provide information to which the public has a statutory right under company, IPS or charity law.

16.3
COMPANY RECORDS
16.3.1
The statutory books

Because companies are publicly accountable, company law places great emphasis on requiring them to keep certain information up to date and accessible. These records are called the **statutory books**.

At the time of writing (early 2001) company law was being reviewed, and some reporting requirements may change. Information is available from Companies House or on its website [see **page 12**].

As with other aspects of company law, there are penalties for not maintaining the statutory books, not keeping them up to date or persistently not notifying Companies House of changes where this is required. For example, if a company does not keep a register of company directors or does not allow members of the public to see it, the company can be fined up to £5,000, each officer (director, company secretary and salaried manager) can be fined up to £5,000, and the company and each officer can be fined £500 for each day there is no register or it is not open to the public. In practice such fines are rarely levied, but it gives an indication of the potential consequences of not treating seriously the detailed requirements of company law.

16.3.1.1
Format

Pre-printed **combined registers** are available from legal stationers, with sections for each set of books. But these registers are generally designed for companies with shareholders, so some sections are not relevant for companies limited by guarantee.

There is no need to buy a pre-printed register. Ordinary paper or a bound book with blank pages can be used. Pro formas specific to voluntary sector companies, which can be photocopied to make up registers, are included in the *Sinclair Taylor & Martin Company Handbook and Registers for Voluntary Sector Companies Limited by Guarantee* [see **page 2** for details].

A written version of the statutory records is called a **legible form**. Records kept on computer are **non-legible**. Non-legible records must be able to be printed out. *Companies Act 1985 s.723*

Data in the registers must comply with the **Data Protection Act 1998** [see **38.3**].

16.3.1.2
What must be kept

A company limited by guarantee must keep the following records:

- register of members [see **16.3.2**];
- if there are more than 50 members and the register is not alphabetical, an alphabetical index of members [see **16.3.3**];
- a register of directors (members of the governing body) [see **16.3.4**];
- a register of company secretaries [see **16.3.5**];
- if directors are employees or are paid for their services as directors, their contracts with the company [see **16.3.6**];
- minute books for general meetings, meetings of the directors and meetings of managers [see **16.3.7**];
- accounting records [see **16.3.8**];
- a register of charges (mortgages etc) and a copy of every charge [see **16.3.9**];

- a register of directors' interests in the company's shares and debentures, if any [see **16.3.10**];
- a register of holders of debentures, if any [see **16.3.11**].

Company law defines the information which must be kept, the form, how it is updated, whether Companies House needs to be notified of changes, where the information must be kept, how long it must be kept, who has access to it and who has the right to a copy of it.

**16.3.1.3
Access**

Documents which must be open to inspection by company members and/or the public must be available for at least two hours between 9 a.m. and 5 p.m. every day except Saturdays, Sundays and bank holidays.
Companies (Inspection and Copying of Registers, Indices and Documents) Regulations 1991 [SI 1991/1998] regs.2, 3(2)(a)

Where the company has a right to charge a fee to people inspecting its records, the maximum which may be charged is £2.50 per hour or part thereof (as at 1/4/01). People who have the right to inspect the documents also have the right to take notes. *sch.2 para.1; reg.3(2)(b)*

**16.3.1.4
Copies**

Where the company has an obligation to provide a copy of information from the registers and has a right to charge for this, the maximum fee (as at 1/4/01) is £2.50 for the first hundred entries, £20 for the next 1,000 entries or part thereof and £15 for each subsequent 1,000 entries or part thereof. A lower fee may be charged, or none. *sch.2 para.2*

**16.3.1.5
How long the records must be kept**

Apart from accounting records [see **49.3.2**], all statutory books must be kept throughout the life of the company.

If the company is dissolved [see **21.1.3**] the books should be kept for at least two years afterwards, as a court may declare the dissolution void (invalid). If the company is struck off the register [see **21.4**] the books should be kept for 20 years, because the company can be reinstated to the register during that period. *Companies Act 1985 ss.651, 653(2)*

**16.3.2
Register of members**

Membership gives the right to vote and therefore to control the company, so the records of who is and is not a member must be kept accurate and up to date. This vital task is very widely neglected.

What must be kept. For a company limited by guarantee the register of members must contain the name and address of every company member, the date of becoming a member (the date the name is entered in the register), the date of ceasing to be a member, and the class of membership if the company has different types of membership.
s.352(2),(4)

There is no obligation to assign membership numbers, but a numbering system can help to ensure that the register is complete and can make it easier to cross-reference to the index [see **16.3.3**].

If the company has only one member (for example, a trading company wholly owned by a charity), the register must state this and give the date on which the company became a single member company.

Form. In a bound or unbound book, or on computer so long as it can be printed out. The register must be kept in a form which cannot be altered without proper authority, and which makes it as easy as possible to discover falsification. If kept in an unbound book, each page should be numbered and initialled, and any alteration should be initialled. Errors should be crossed out and initialled, not covered with correction tape or fluid. *ss.722(1),(2), 723(1)*

Updates. Must be kept up to date with all changes to members' details, details of new members and the date of resignation.

The names of former company members cannot be removed from the register until 20 years after they ceased to be a member. *s.352(6)*

Where it must be kept. At the registered office or wherever the work of keeping it up to date is done, so long as it is in the country where the company is required to have its registered office [see **15.1.1**]. If the register of members is not kept at the registered office, Companies House must be notified where it is kept on **form 353**.

Companies Act 1985 s.353(1)

Access. Must be open to company members free of charge, and to the public for which a fee can be charged [see **16.3.1.3**]. *s.356(1)*

The company may pass an ordinary resolution [see **17.4.7**] to close the register for up to 30 days in each year. A notice saying it is closed must be placed in a local newspaper. *s.358*

Copies. Any person is entitled to a copy of the register of members or any part of it, within 10 days of their request being received. A fee may be charged [see **16.3.1.4**].

16.3.3
Index to register of members

What must be kept. If there are more than 50 members and the register is not alphabetical, an alphabetical index must be kept indicating where to find each member's name in the register. *s.354*

Form. As for the register of members [see above].

Updates. Must be updated within 14 days of a name being added to the register or any details being changed.

Where it must be kept. In the same place as the register of members.

Access. As for the register of members.

Copies. No statutory obligation for the company to provide a copy of any information in the index, but anyone can copy it themselves.

16.3.4
Register of directors

What must be kept. The register of directors [see **11.1.3** for who is a director] must contain for each director:

- full name, with forenames in full;
- any former name or names [but see below for exceptions];
- usual home address [but see **16.3.4.1**];
- nationality;
- date of birth;
- occupation (if any);
- details of directorships of all corporate bodies currently held or held in the previous five years [see below for exceptions];
- if the director is a corporate body, its corporate name and registered address;
- the date elected or appointed as a director;
- the date of ceasing to be a director. *s.289*

It can be helpful to have spaces on the register, next to 'date appointed' and 'date left post', for 'date form 288 sent' [see below].

A previous name does not need to be included if it was used by a woman before she was married, used only before the director was 18 years old or used before taking a title by a peer or other person usually known by a British title, or if the name has not been used for the past 20 years.

Date of birth is included because special provisions apply to directors of public companies when they reach age 70. The upper age limit does not apply to directors of private companies, unless the private company is a subsidiary of a public company. *s.293*

All current directorships in bodies incorporated in Great Britain must be listed, and all directorships held in the past five years unless:

- the company is now dormant [see **50.3.7** for explanation];
- the company was dormant at all times during the past five years when the person was a director of it;

- the company is this company's parent; *or*
- the company is another subsidiary of the same parent company.

Companies Act 1985 s.289(3),(4)

Directorships must be listed even if they are in voluntary sector companies or industrial and provident societies rather than 'traditional' companies.

Form. As for the register of members [see **16.3.2**].

Updates. Must be kept up to date.

Notification. Companies House must be notified within 14 days of:
- the appointment or election of a director (**form 288a**, signed by the director to show consent to serve);
- the resignation, death or removal of a director (**form 288b**);
- any change in a director's name, address, or other particulars entered in the register (**form 288c**). *s.288*

The forms can be downloaded from the Companies House website [see **page 12**].

Details of directors must also be updated, if necessary, in the company annual return [see **50.3.8**].

Where the register must be kept. At the registered office.

Access. Must be open to members free of charge, and to the public for which a fee may be charged [see **16.3.1.3**]. Unlike the register of members, the register of directors cannot be closed for 30 days.

Copies. No statutory obligation on the company to provide a copy of information from the register of directors, but anyone may copy information directly from the register.

16.3.4.1
Restricted access to home addresses

Where the director(s) or company secretary could be at serious personal risk, application can be made to the secretary of state for trade and industry for a **confidentiality order**. This enables the director or secretary to give an alternative (non-residential) address for the register of directors and for records open to the public at Companies House. A home address must also be given to Companies House, but is kept on a secure register. *Criminal Justice and Police Act 2001 s.45*

16.3.5
Register of secretaries

What must be kept. The register of secretaries must include:
- the name of each company secretary [see **12.3**] or, in the case of joint secretaries, all the names;
- former name or names [see register of directors, above, for exceptions];
- usual home address [but see **16.3.4.1**];
- date appointed;
- date of ceasing to be secretary. *Companies Act 1985 s.290*

Form; updates; notification; where it must be kept; access; copies. As for the register of directors [see above].

16.3.6
Directors' service contracts

What must be kept. Service contracts or contracts of employment for all company directors who are employed by the company or paid for their services as directors. *s.318*

Updates. If a contract is changed the new one must be kept.

Where they must be kept. At the registered office, the company's principal place of business, or where the register of members is kept. All service contracts must be kept together. If they are not kept at the registered office, Companies House must be notified on **form 318**.

Access. Open to company members free of charge [see **16.3.1.3**].

Copies. No statutory obligation on the company to provide a copy of directors' service contracts, but any company member may copy information directly from the contracts.

16.3.7
Minute books

What must be kept. Minute books containing the official (signed) copy of the minutes of all general meetings [see **17.4.11**] and meetings of the directors (governing body). *Companies Act 1985 s.382*

The articles of association generally require minutes of committees to be kept as well.

Form. Must be kept in a way which makes it as difficult as possible for anyone to alter them, and which makes it possible to detect falsification. *s.722(2)*

If minutes are in a ring binder or unbound book, each page should be numbered and initialled by the chairperson or secretary. Errors should be crossed out and initialled, not covered with correction tape or fluid.

Updates. Any alteration to the minutes (for example, to make a correction agreed at the next meeting) should be dated and initialled by the chairperson or secretary.

Where they must be kept. Minute books of general meetings must be kept at the registered office. Minute books of directors' meetings and managers' meetings may be kept anywhere convenient.

Access. Minutes of general meetings must be open to inspection by company members free of charge [see **16.3.1.3**]. Minutes of directors' meetings and managers' meetings do not have to be open to anyone.

Copies. Any company member is entitled to a copy of all or part of the minutes of any general meeting, within seven days of asking for it. The maximum fee which may be charged is 10p per 100 words or part thereof (as at 1/4/01).

There is no obligation to provide anyone with a copy of minutes of directors' or managers' meetings.

16.3.8
Accounting records

What must be kept. The financial records must include details of income, expenditure, assets and liabilities [see **49.3.1** for details]. If the company deals in goods, the records must also include an annual stock check. *1985 s.221*

Unlike the other statutory books the financial records do not have to be kept for the life of the company and at least two years after. They must, however, be kept for three years and should generally be kept for at least 13 years [see **49.3.2**].

Updates. Must be detailed and up to date enough to give, at any time, a reasonably accurate indication of the company's financial position, and must include day-to-day entries of all income and expenditure.

Where they may be kept Anywhere agreed by the directors.

Access. Open at all times to the company's officers (directors, company secretary, senior employees) and its auditors. *ss.222(1), 389(1)*

Copies. The company's officers must provide the auditors with any information and explanations considered by the auditors to be necessary for the performance of their duties [see **51.2.1**]. Apart from this there is no statutory obligation on the company to provide copies of the accounting records to anyone, including the company's officers, but the officers may copy information from the records.

16.3.9
Register of charges
and copy of charges

What must be kept. A charge is a mortgage or other loan secured on the company's assets [see **57.11** and **55.5**]. The register must include:

- date of the charge;
- names of the parties;

- details of the property secured by the charge;
- amount of the charge. *Companies Act 1985 s.401*

When the charge is vacated (paid off) the entry should be crossed through or there should be space for the date vacated. It is sensible to have columns for the dates Companies House was notified of the creation and vacation of the charge [see below].

In addition to the register, the company must also keep a copy of every charge. *s.406*

Information about registration of charges and mortgages is in Companies House booklet GBA8 *Company Charges and Mortgages*.

Form. As for register of members [see **16.3.2**].

Updates. Must be kept up to date.

Notification. Notice of a charge or mortgage being created must be given to Companies House, with a £10 fee, within 21 days on **form 395**. If this is not done the charge will be largely ineffective.

If debentures [see **55.5.2**] are issued this must be notified on **form 397**, but failure to do so does not invalidate the debentures. *s.397*

Any repayment, in full or in part, or any other change must be notified on **form 403a**.

The forms are available on the Companies House website [see **page 12**].

Where they must be kept. At the company's registered office.

Access. Open to company members and to creditors (people to whom the company owes money) free of charge, and to the public for which a fee may be charged [see **16.3.1.3**].

Copies. Any person is entitled, within 10 days of their request being received, to a copy of any entry in the register of charges and/or a copy of any charge. A fee may be charged [see **16.3.1.4**].

16.3.10
Register of directors' interests in shares and debentures

What must be kept. A director must notify the company in writing if he or she has any interest in the shares or debentures [see **55.5.2**] of the company, its parent company, its subsidiary company, or another subsidiary of the same parent company. Any change in the interest must be notified to the company within five days. *s.324; sch.13 para.14*

A debenture is a form of secured loan. The director's interest includes any shares or debentures held by the director's spouse, or by his or her children or step-children under the age of 18. *ss.328, 325*

Companies limited by guarantee do not have shares, and debentures are not usually issued by charities, so very few voluntary sector companies will have any entries in this register. It would be used if a non-charitable company issues debentures, or the directors of a charitable company have an interest in the shares or debentures of a non-charitable company which is the charity's parent or subsidiary.

Form. As for register of members [see **16.3.2**]. If the register is not alphabetical, there must be an index.

Updates. Must be entered in the register within three working days.

Where it must be kept. At the registered office or at the same place as the register of members. If it is not kept at the registered office, Companies House must be notified where it is kept on **form 325**.

Access. Open to company members free of charge, and to the public for which a fee may be charged [see **16.3.1.3**].

Copies. Any person is entitled to a copy of the register of directors' interests or any part of it, within 10 days of their request being received. A fee may be charged [see **16.3.1.4**].

16.3.11
Register of holders of debentures

What must be kept. Register of holders of the company's debentures [see **55.5.2**]. As indicated above, few voluntary organisations have debentures, so the register is unlikely to be used.

Companies Act 1985 ss.190, 191

Form. As for register of members [see **16.3.2**].

Where it must be kept. At the registered office, or wherever the work of keeping it up to date is done. If it is not kept at the registered office, Companies House must be notified on **form 190**.

Access. Open to company members and holders of debentures free of charge, and to members of the public for which a fee may be charged [see **16.3.1.3**]. The register may be closed for up to 30 days each year if this is authorised in the company's articles of association or in the debentures.

Copies. As for register of directors' interests [see above]. Holders of debentures also have a right to a copy of the trust deed for the issue of debentures, for a fee of not more than 10p per 100 words.

16.3.12
Register of sealings

What may be kept. A register of sealings is a list of documents the company has signed under seal [see **18.3**]. Companies no longer need to have a seal, and even if they have one there is no obligation to keep a record of when it is used. If a register is not kept it is good practice to keep a record in minutes of the directors' meetings of when the seal's use is authorised and when it has been used.

16.4
INDUSTRIAL AND PROVIDENT SOCIETY RECORDS

One of the advantages of an industrial and provident society is that the record keeping requirements are less onerous than for companies. There are fewer statutory requirements, and the registration authority does not need to be notified as frequently.

Registers must be kept permanently.

Industrial and Provident Societies Act 1965 s.44

16.4.1
Register of members

The register of members of an industrial and provident society must be up to date and must include:

- name;
- address;
- date when registered as a member;
- date when ceased to be a member;
- the number of shares held by the member and the amount paid or agreed to be considered as paid on them;
- other property such as loans or deposits held by each member.

The register must be kept at the registered office. If it is not in a bound book, there must be precautions against falsification.

Members and people with an interest in the funds of the society have the right to see basic information for all members (name, address, date of joining or ceasing to be a member) but they have no right to see any financial entries (relating to shares and other property) except their own. So a duplicate register with only the 'public' information must be compiled, or the original register must be produced in such a way that it can be shown with only the 'public' information revealed.

ss.44(3), 46(1)

The society's rules may specify that officers have the right to inspect financial entries, or that the members can pass a resolution authorising any person(s) to inspect the entries. A person who is not an officer or authorised by a resolution may inspect financial entries only with the written consent of the person whose entry it is. *s.46(2)*

The society's auditors and registration authorities have the right to inspect the whole register at any reasonable time, and to see all documents relating to the IPS's affairs.

Industrial and Provident Societies Act 1965 s.44(4);
Friendly and Industrial and Provident Societies Act 1968 s.9(5)

If asked to do so by at least 10 members who have been members for at least one year, the registration authority can appoint an auditor to inspect the records and report on the IPS's affairs.   *IPSA s.47*

16.4.2
Register of officers

The register of officers covers committee members/directors, secretaries and treasurers and must include name, address, date of becoming an officer and date of ceasing to be an officer. It must be kept at the registered office, and if not in a bound book must be in a format which minimises the risk of falsification.   *s.44*

The registrar of friendly societies must be notified in the annual return [see **50.4.2**] of changes in committee members, but does not need to be notified of changes at the time they occur.

The register of officers must be open in the same way as the register of members to society members, people with an interest in the society's funds, the society's auditor, the registration authority, and any auditor appointed by the registration authority.

16.4.3
Accounting records

The society must keep proper financial records showing its transactions, assets and liabilities [see **49.3.1** for details, and **49.3.2** for how long they should be kept]. Members have no statutory right to see the financial records, but they do have a right to see their own financial details.

ss.45, 46

In addition to these statutory rights, the rules may make provision for members to see the financial records and/or for officers to see individual members' financial details, or the members may pass a resolution allowing someone to see individual details [see **16.4.1**].

The most recent audited balance sheet must be conspicuously displayed at the IPS's registered office.   *s.40*

16.4.4
Charges on assets

All charges on the IPS's assets must be notified to the registrar of friendly societies on **form AI** within 21 days along with a certified copy of the document creating the charge and a fee (£60 as at 1/4/01). The charge may be inspected by the public, but a register of charges does not have to be kept.   *Industrial and Provident Societies Act 1967 s.1*

If the charge is not notified within 21 days, or if there is an error in the registration of the charge, an application must be made to allow late registration or to amend the error.

16.5
TRUSTS

Trustees must ensure the following are kept safely:

- the deed, declaration of trust or will which set up the trust;
- deeds of appointment of new trustees, if under the terms of the governing document they are appointed by deed rather than by election;
- deeds for vesting assets in the trustees [see **18.4.5**];
- details of retirement or death of trustees;
- financial records as required for tax, VAT and charity purposes;
- minutes of meetings of the trustees and their committees.

Charity requirements [see **16.7**] apply to charitable trusts.

Members of the public do not have a statutory right to know anything about a private trust but do have a right to some information about charitable trusts [see **16.7.2**].

16.6 UNINCORPORATED ASSOCIATIONS

There is no statutory requirement for a non-charitable unincorporated association to keep any registers of members or committee members, or even to keep minute books. But such records may be required by the association's governing document or funders, and it is good practice to keep them anyway. If the association is a charity, the requirements of charity law apply [see **16.7**].

It is implicitly the treasurer's duty to keep financial records and the secretary's duty to keep records of members and committee members and minutes of meetings, but the association's governing document, members or committee may assign these duties to anyone.

It is sensible to keep records for at least 13 years [see **49.3.2**].

Unless the governing document specifies otherwise, the records may be kept anywhere reasonable and the association may decide for itself who may see the records. Generally the lists of members, officers and committee members and minutes of general meetings should be open to members of the association. Minutes of meetings of the governing body should be open to members of the governing body. The governing document might say that they must also be open to all members of the association, or a general meeting or meeting of the governing body might agree that they should be open to all members.

Members of the public do not have a statutory right to know anything about the association unless it is charitable [see below].

16.7 CHARITIES

All charities must keep accurate and up-to-date records of income, expenditure, assets and liabilities and the records required for their particular legal structure [see **49.3**].   *Charities Act 1993 s.41*

16.7.1 Notification to Charity Commission

In order to keep the register of charities up to date, the Charity Commission must be notified in writing of the following changes in registered charities:

- change in the name of the charity;

- change to the charity's objects, powers, or any other provision in the governing document affecting the charity's use of its income or property;

- change in type of governing document;

- change of correspondent (the Commission's contact person in the charity), address or other information held in the register.

The register is updated annually through the Charity Commission's **data update form** [see **50.2.16**].

16.7.2 Access to Information

Members of the public may consult the register of charities, or request from the Charity Commission details of charities, their objects, gross annual income, and correspondent's name and address. The public may also see charity annual reports held by the Commission.   *ss.3(8), 47(1)*

At the time of writing (early 2001) the Commission was consulting on whether the names of all trustees, rather than only the correspondent, should be available to the public.

All charities, even those which are not registered with the Commission, must provide a copy of their most recent annual accounts and report within two months if asked to do so by a member of the public [see **50.2.14**]. The public does not have a statutory right to any other information about charities.

Chapter 17
MEETINGS AND DECISION MAKING

17.1 MEETINGS AND THE LAW

General meetings of an organisation's members and meetings of its governing body and committees are governed by:

- the organisation's governing document and its standing orders or other rules relating to its meetings;
- for companies, company law [see **17.4**];
- common law relating to private meetings, if the governing document (and company law, if relevant) are silent about a matter.

Industrial and provident society law [see **17.5**] and charity law [see **17.3**] say very little about meetings.

Decisions made at a meeting which is not properly convened or conducted could, if challenged, be held to be invalid.

General, governing body and committee meetings are **private meetings**. Different rules apply to **public meetings** [see **42.2**].

Basics of good practice on meetings are set out in Charity Commission booklet CC48 *Charities and Meetings*.

17.1.1
Decision making without meetings

If the governing document allows, decisions may be made without a meeting by postal voting [see **17.2.12**] or written resolution [**17.2.16**], or by holding meetings via telephone or the internet [**17.2.6**]. Companies have a statutory right to make general meeting decisions by written resolution [**17.4.12**]. Provided all participants can see and hear each other [see **17.2.5.3**], meetings can be held by video conference unless the governing document prohibits this.

If the governing document allows, a member may appoint a **proxy** to vote on their behalf at a meeting [see **17.2.11** and **17.4.9**].

17.1.2
<u>Conflicts of interest</u>

It is good practice for participants in any meeting to declare any conflict of interest. However the legal position distinguishes between meetings of the members of an organisation, and meetings of the governing body.

Governing body members normally have a legal duty to act in the best interest of the organisation, and in many cases must declare conflicts of interest [see **13.2.2** and **13.3.4**]. But ordinary members of an organisation—including governing body members, when they are taking part in a general meeting—are entitled, unless the governing document provides otherwise, to act and vote in their own interest.

17.2
COMMON LAW AND THE GOVERNING DOCUMENT

Company law includes detailed provisions for most aspects of meetings [see **17.4**], but the meetings of other organisations are governed primarily by common law and their governing document.

17.2.1
Annual general meeting

Under common law there is no requirement for a membership organisation to hold an annual general meeting, but the requirement is explicit in company law [see **17.4.1**] and is generally included in the governing document of other membership organisations. All requirements in the governing document must be met. The guidance on preparing for company general meetings [see **17.4.3**] is useful for non-companies as well.

17.2.2
Other general meetings

General meetings other than the AGM are called **general**, **ordinary**, **extraordinary** or **special meetings**. There is usually no significance in what they are called. The governing document usually sets out:

- any requirement for how often general meetings must be held;
- the procedure for calling a general meeting;
- the procedure, if any, for a minimum number or percentage of members to require (**requisition**) the secretary or governing body to call a general meeting;
- who is entitled to attend and vote at general meetings;
- others entitled to receive notice of general meetings.

17.2.3
Notice

17.2.3.1
Entitlement to notice

Notice must be given to everyone entitled to attend the meeting and to others entitled, under statute or the governing document, to receive notice.
John v Rees [1970] Ch 345, 402

Unless statute or the governing document says otherwise, the organisation is not obliged to give notice:

- to a member who is too ill to attend;
Young v Ladies' Imperial Club [1920] 2 KB 523
- to a member who is too far away to attend; *or*
Smyth v Darley [1849] 2 HL Cas 789
- if all members entitled to attend are present and agree to a meeting being held. *Re Express Engineering Works [1920] 1 Ch 466*

Unless they are too ill or too far away to attend, notice must be given to members who have said they are unable to attend.
Re Portuguese Consolidated Copper Mines [1889] 42 ChD 160

It is the member's responsibility to ensure the organisation has a correct address if notices are sent, or might be sent, by post.

17.2.3.2
Non-receipt of notice

Under common law, a meeting is invalid unless notice is given to every person entitled to receive it [see above]. Governing documents therefore nearly always provide that accidental failure to give notice or non-receipt of notice does not invalidate the meeting. Deliberately 'forgetting' or neglecting to give notice makes the meeting invalid.

17.2.3.3
How notice is given

If the governing document does not specify how notice is to be given, the governing body decides. Failure to give reasonable notice may invalidate decisions made at the meeting.   *Labouchere v Earl of Wharncliffe*
[1879] 13 ChD 346, 352; Young v Ladies' Imperial Club [1920] 2 KB 523

What is 'reasonable' depends on the circumstances. The notice might be, for example, given verbally, displayed at the organisation's premises, advertised in the organisation's newsletter or a relevant publication or on its website, advertised on posters, given by hand to each member, or ent by post, fax, email or other electronic means.

If important decisions about the organisation or the rights of individual members will be considered at the meeting, notice should be given individually to each member instead of being given publicly.
Re GKN Sports and Social Club [1982] 1 WLR 774, 2 All ER 855

17.2.3.4
Period of notice

If statute or the governing document does not specify a period of notice, the period must be 'reasonable' for an organisation of that type. The governing body decides the period. There is no default position in common law, but the company law requirements of 21 days for AGMs and 14 days for other general meetings could be used as a guide.

17.2.3.5
Clear days

Unless otherwise defined in the governing document, any period of notice referred to in the governing document means **clear days**.
Re Railway Sleepers Supply Company [1885] 29 ChD 204

Clear days do not include:

- the day on which the meeting is to be held; *and*
- the day on which the notice is handed to someone or left at their address, or the days on which it is posted, is in the post and is assumed to be delivered.

17.2.3.6
Contents of notice

Under common law a notice must contain:

- date, time and place of the meeting;
- type of meeting (annual general, special general etc);
- a clear indication of the business to be transacted, especially special business [see below], with any decisions to be made set out clearly enough to enable members to know what is being considered;
- date of the notice; *and*
- signature of the person calling, or authorised to call, the meeting.

If one meeting is to be held immediately after another, the time may be given as 'at the conclusion of the XXX meeting'.

Routine matters are **ordinary business**. **Special business** may be defined in the governing document, or if not defined, includes matters such as amending the governing document or expelling a member.

There is no obligation under common law to include in the notice the exact details of business or to give the full text of resolutions, but it is good practice to do so.   *Betts and Co Ltd v MacNaughton [1910] Ch 430*

The notice usually includes the **agenda**, showing the order in which the items of business will be taken. Unless a majority at the meeting agrees otherwise, the items must be considered in the order they are listed on the agenda.   *John v Rees [1970] Ch 345, 378*

Matters which are not included in the notice cannot be considered at the meeting unless they are minor and unimportant and are included under an 'any other business' item on the agenda.

Young v Ladies' Imperial Club [1920] 2 KB 523

17.2.4
Postponement or
cancellation

Postponement is delaying a meeting after notice has been given, but before the meeting has begun. It is different from **adjournment** [see **17.2.14**], which is stopping a meeting after it has started with the intention of continuing it at another time.

Unless the governing document specifies otherwise, a meeting for which notice has been properly given may not be postponed or cancelled. The meeting must technically be opened and then be properly adjourned.

Smith v Paringa Mines [1906] 2 Ch 193

17.2.5
Validity of meetings

A meeting is valid only if it is **properly convened, legally constituted** and **properly held**. These requirements have been defined in common law. Decisions made at an invalid meeting may be subsequently ratified at a valid meeting.

Re Sick and Funeral Society of St John's Sunday School, Golcare [1973] Ch 51

17.2.5.1
Properly convened

To be properly convened:

- the meeting must be called by a body or individuals having the right to do so under the governing document or under statute;

- a general meeting must be convened in the interests of the organisation as a whole, not in the interests of a particular individual or group of members;

- a general meeting must not be convened at an unreasonable time or place;

- in choosing the time and place for the meeting there must not be any deliberate intention of excluding certain members by making it impossible or very difficult for them to attend (but clearly no meeting can be at a time when everyone can attend);

- notice must be sent to everyone entitled to receive it [see **17.2.3.1**]; *and*

- the notice must give all legally required information [see **17.2.3.6**].

17.2.5.2
Legally constituted

To be legally constituted:

- there must be a properly appointed chairperson for the meeting [see **17.2.7**];

- a quorum must be present when the meeting starts and, if required, throughout the meeting [see **17.2.8**];

- for companies, the provisions of the Companies Acts relating to meetings must be complied with [see **17.4**]; *and*

- the provisions of the governing document must be complied with.

17.2.5.3
Properly held

For a meeting to be properly held:

- if those attending are not all in the same room, they must all be able to see and hear each other through audio-visual links;

Byng v London Life Assurance Ltd [1989] 2 WLR 738, 1 All ER 560

- for companies, decision making and voting must follow the procedures set out in the Companies Acts [see **17.4.8**];

- decision making and voting must follow the procedures set out in the organisation's governing document;

- the chairperson must ensure 'the sense of the meeting is ascertained' on all matters under discussion;

National Dwellings Society v Sykes [1894] 3 Ch 159, 162

- the chairperson must not refuse to allow relevant amendments to resolutions; *Henderson v Bank of Australasia [1890] 45 ChD 330*

- the meeting must be held fairly, people must have a right to be heard on matters which affect them individually, and other principles of natural justice [see, for example, **10.8.5**] must be followed.

17.2.6
Meetings by telephone or electronic means

Because one of the requirements for a valid meeting is that the participants must be able to see each other [see above], a decision made by conference telephone call, internet conferencing or email is not valid unless the governing document allows decisions to be made in this way. If the governing document does not allow telephone or internet meetings, an in principle decision made by telephone or via the internet may be ratified at a subsequent valid meeting, or it may be possible to ratify it by a unanimous written resolution [see **17.2.16**].

Re Associated Color Laboratories Ltd [1970] 12 DLR (3d) 338; 73 WWR 566

Community Network [see end of chapter] can provide advice on telephone meetings and suitable governing document amendments.

Provided all members participating can see and hear each other, a meeting held by video conferencing is valid.

The rules relating to notice, quorum, etc for meetings held by video conference or (where allowed) by telephone or internet conference are the same as for meetings in person.

17.2.7
Chairing meetings

17.2.7.1
Appointment of chairperson

Unless the governing document specifies how the chairperson is to be chosen, the members present at a meeting may elect any member present to chair the meeting.

Under common law if the chairperson is not present, or is unable or unwilling to chair, the deputy or vice-chair chairs, if one has been chosen under the requirements of the governing document. If there is no deputy or vice-chair in post, the meeting must elect someone to chair the meeting. The governing document may specify how this is done.

17.2.7.2
Chairperson's duties

The person chairing the meeting has a legal duty to:

- ensure that he or she has been properly appointed as chair;
- act in the interests of the organisation as a whole;
- ensure in a company that the requirements and procedures set out in the Companies Acts are followed;
- ensure that the requirements and procedures in the governing document and standing orders are followed;
- ensure that the meeting has been properly convened and proper notice [see **17.2.3**] has been given;
- ensure that the rules relating to quorum [see **17.2.8**] are followed;
- take the business in the order set out in the notice of the meeting or the agenda, unless a majority of members present agree that the order can be changed;
- ensure that no business is transacted unless it is within the scope of the notice which has been given [see **17.2.3.6**];
- ensure that when discussing any matter, the members keep their remarks to that piece of business;
- clearly state resolutions, ensure that voting or other decision making is properly carried out and only people authorised to vote take part in decisions, and declare the results of decisions [see **17.2.10**];
- organise a poll (counted vote) if one is demanded [see **17.2.10.2**];
- keep order;
- adjourn the meeting properly, if adjournment is necessary [see **17.2.14**];
- ensure that the meeting is minuted and any decisions recorded [see **17.2.15**];
- ensure that there is a clear end to the meeting.

The person chairing the meeting has the right to insist that a disorderly or abusive person leaves the meeting [see **42.4.1**], and to call the police if necessary.

**17.2.8
Quorum**

A quorum is the minimum number of members with voting rights who have to be present at a meeting. The governing document may provide that people present as proxies [see **17.2.11**] count towards the quorum.

Unless the governing document specifies otherwise, the quorum for a general meeting is a majority of the members. The quorum may not, except in a very few situations in company law [see **17.4.6**], be less than two.

*Ellis v Hooper [1859] 28 LJ Ex 1; Sharp v Dawes
[1876] 2 QBD 26; Re Sanitary Carbon Co [1877] WN 223*

If the governing document or legislation prohibits some members from taking part in some decisions—for example, if they have a conflict of interest [see **13.2.2** and **13.3.4**]—they do not count towards the quorum for that part of the meeting.

*Yuill v Greymouth
Point Elizabeth Railway and Coal Company Ltd [1904] 1 Ch 32*

**17.2.8.1
Members leaving during meeting**

A meeting may not transact business (vote or make a decision in any other way) unless it is **quorate**. If the meeting starts with a quorum but some members subsequently leave and the number falls below the quorum, generally no further decisions can be made and the meeting must be adjourned.

Re Romford Canal Co [1883] 24 ChD 85

If, however, the governing document specifies that a quorum needs to be present 'when the meeting proceeds to business' (or words to that effect), the quorum needs to be present only at the start of the meeting. Even if the numbers subsequently fall below the quorum, the meeting remains valid.

If the meeting must be quorate throughout and a person deliberately leaves in order to make it inquorate, that member would be unlikely to be able to claim successfully that decisions made after his or her departure were invalid.

Ball v Pearsall [1987] 10 NSWLR 700

**17.2.9
Motions and
resolutions**

A **motion** is any matter of business requiring a decision. A motion is **moved** or **proposed**, is **seconded** if this is required, is **put to the vote**, and if it is agreed becomes a **resolution**. But the terms proposal, motion and resolution are often used interchangeably.

A motion must be proposed as required by the governing document or by standing orders or other rules governing the meeting [see **5.4.26**]. Unless required by the governing document or rules, there is no need for any motion to be seconded.

Once a motion has been proposed, it can be withdrawn only if the meeting agrees.

**17.2.9.1
Amendments**

An amendment is a proposal to change a motion. Prior notice of an amendment must be given if required by the governing document or other rules; otherwise an amendment may be proposed at any time before a vote is taken on the motion.

If prior notice of the motion has been given, the amendment cannot create a situation where a substantively different matter is being voted on.

If the rules do not specify the procedure for amendments, the chairperson decides:

- whether to accept an amendment;
- whether to allow amendments to an amendment;
- whether to call a vote on each amendment separately, and then put the revised motion to the meeting;

- whether to wait and vote on all the amendments (and amendments to amendments) together. In this case they are voted on in the order in which they affect the motion, not the order in which they were proposed. The agreed amendments are then incorporated into the original motion, and the new version is put to the vote.

Amendments are always voted on before the original motion. The motion which is put to the meeting after all the agreed amendments have been incorporated into it is called a **substantive motion**.

17.2.9.2
Dropped motions

A motion is **dropped**, is **withdrawn** or **fails** if a seconder is required by the governing document or other rules and no one seconds it, or if the person who proposed the motion withdraws it and the meeting agrees to this withdrawal. A proposed amendment may be withdrawn only if the meeting agrees.

A motion is **shelved**, **deferred** or **not put** if the meeting decides through a procedural motion [see below] not to vote on it.

17.2.9.3
Procedural motions

Formal or **procedural motions** regulate how the business of a meeting is carried out, but are not directly concerned with the content of the business. If a procedural motion is misused, for example to call a vote before adequate time has been given to discussion, it is called a **dilatory motion**. A chairperson has the right to reject a procedural motion if it appears to have been proposed for a dilatory purpose.

The main procedural motions are:

- *That the question now be put*, proposed after adequate discussion, or sometimes as a way of curtailing discussion prematurely. In the latter case the chairperson has to decide whether to allow it to be voted on. This motion is called a **closure**. If approved, the original motion is voted on; if not approved, discussion continues.

- *That the meeting proceed to next business*, to move on without voting on the motion. If approved, the motion is shelved and the meeting moves to its next business; if not approved, discussion continues.

- *That the question not now be put*, called a **previous question**. If this is approved, the original motion is shelved and the meeting moves to its next business. If not approved, the original motion is immediately voted on, without further discussion.

- *That the meeting postpone consideration of the matter* until later in the meeting or until a subsequent meeting, usually because of inadequate information at present. If approved, discussion is postponed; if not approved, discussion continues.

- *That the debate be adjourned*, which has the same effect as postponement. Usually postponement is used before discussion starts on a motion, and adjournment after discussion has started.

- *That the recommendation be referred back to committee*, to require further work to be done or information to be provided by the committee which proposed the motion. If approved, discussion is curtailed; if not approved, discussion continues.

- *That the meeting be adjourned*, to close the meeting and re-open it at another time [see **17.2.14**].

17.2.10
Voting procedures

In many voluntary organisations formal voting is relatively uncommon, and the emphasis is on reaching a **consensus** decision with which everyone agrees (or which everyone agrees to accept, even if they do not fully agree with it). However, where a decision with legal or financial implications is being made there should be a vote, even if the vote comes at the end of a discussion in which consensus has been reached. Without a vote and an announcement of the result, it could subsequently be claimed that the decision had not been properly made.

Methods of voting are:

- by **show of hands** [see **17.2.10.1**];
- by **voice**, saying 'aye' and 'nay' or 'yes' and 'no', but this is imprecise and should be used only if there is a very clear majority;
- a **poll**, which is a counted vote [see **17.2.10.2**];
- a **ballot**, where secrecy is important (usually when voting for governing body members or officers, or on other matters involving individuals) or where voting is being done by post [see **17.2.12**];
- by **division**, as in Parliament, where members physically move into an area to show how they are voting.

The people who count votes are **scrutineers** or **tellers**.

Elections can be organised and overseen by Electoral Reform Services [see end of chapter].

17.2.10.1
Show of hands

The common law method of voting is by **show of hands**. This should generally be used unless the governing document specifies otherwise.

Where a corporate member [see **10.2.5**] is allowed more than one representative, each is allowed one vote on a show of hands. In other situations where members may be entitled to more than one vote, the governing document needs to be read carefully to determine whether they have these multiple votes on a show of hands, or only one vote.

If voting by proxy is allowed [see **17.2.11**], the governing document should be clear whether only members present may vote on a show of hands, or whether proxies may participate as well. If proxies are able to participate, it should be clear whether they have only one vote on a show of hands, regardless of how many proxies they hold, or have multiple votes if they hold multiple proxies.

For a show of hands, members are sometimes given a **voting card** to ensure that every hand raised actually represents a person entitled to vote. This may be particularly important if people present are entitled to multiple votes on a show of hands, or if a number of people who do not have voting rights are present.

Unless the governing document specifies otherwise, the person chairing the meeting has a right to vote. He or she may be entitled to a casting vote in case of a tie [see **17.2.13.3**].

Nell v Longbottom [1894] 1 QB 767, 771

17.2.10.2
Poll

A poll is a counted vote. It is sometimes a simple head-count, but usually each person's vote is recorded on a voting slip or by signing a voting list. There is a common law right for any member to demand a poll, but the governing document may remove or restrict this right.

R v Wimbledon Local Board [1882] 8 QBD 459

Proxies [see **17.2.11**] may vote in a poll.

A poll may be ordered by the chair or demanded by any member if:

- the vote on a show of hands is too close to be accurate without a better count or a written record of the vote;
- people present as proxies are not permitted to vote on a show of hands but could vote on a poll;
- people entitled to multiple votes can have only one vote on a show of hands, but want an opportunity to cast all their votes; *or*
- people want an adjourned poll so others can vote on the matter.

Unless the governing document specifies otherwise:

- the chairperson may decide to take the vote by poll without first having a vote by show of hands;
- if a vote by show of hands is taken, any demand for a poll must be immediately made, otherwise the vote stands;

- a poll, once demanded, must be taken;
- the original vote (by show of hands) ceases to have effect as soon as the poll is demanded;
- the poll should be taken immediately if possible;
- if it is not practicable to take the poll immediately, the chair may adjourn the meeting to allow the poll to take place at another time;
- if the poll is not taken immediately, members who were not present for the original show of hands have a right to vote in the poll;
- the demand for a poll does not stop a meeting from carrying on with its other business.

17.2.11
Voting by proxy

A proxy is a person appointed to represent a member who cannot attend a meeting. The term 'proxy' also refers to the form or document used for the purpose of making the appointment [see **17.4.9** for a sample form].

In common law there is no right to appoint a proxy, so proxies may be appointed only if the governing document or statute gives the right to do so, and their voting rights depend on the wording of the governing document or statute.   *Harben v Phillips [1883] 23 ChD 14*

17.2.12
Postal and
electronic voting

With a postal vote, the member fills in a ballot and returns it to the organisation by post or hand, or by fax if this is allowed. A postal voting procedure may be used alongside, or instead of, voting in person and proxy voting, but only if the governing document explicitly allows it.

Where postal voting is allowed, it can include voting by electronic means if secure encryption of electronic signatures is available.
Electronic Communications Act 2000 s.7

17.2.13
Counting the votes

In counting votes on a show of hands, only the votes of members present and entitled to vote are counted unless the governing document specifically states that postal votes are included and/or that proxies [see **17.2.10.1**] can vote on a show of hands.

17.2.13.1
Basis for counting

The governing document should specify whether voting is based on:
- the number of **members present and voting**;
- the number of **members present and entitled to vote**;
- the **total number of members**; *or*
- the number of **votes cast**.

It should also be clear whether voting by proxy is allowed.

As an example, an organisation has 100 members and the quorum for a general meeting is 20% of the membership. Twenty members attend the meeting, so it is just quorate. On a resolution requiring a simple majority, 14 vote and six abstain. One of the members holds a proxy for another member. In addition, two people who are not members attend as proxies, each holding proxies for two members.

- If majority is based on more than half of **members present and voting**, the motion needs eight votes to be carried (more than half of 14). The votes of proxies are not included because only the votes of members present and voting are counted.

- If majority is based on **members present and entitled to vote**, it needs 11 votes to be carried (more than half of 20), and proxies are not included.

- If majority is based on **total number of members**, it needs 51 votes to be carried (more than half of 100), and votes cast by proxies would be included.

- If majority is based on **number of votes cast**, it needs 10 votes to be carried (more than half of the 19 votes cast: 14 by members, and five by proxies).

In companies, majority is worked out on the basis of **votes cast**. In organisations which are not companies the majority is worked out, unless the governing document specifies otherwise, on the basis of **members present and entitled to vote**.

Knowles v Zoological Society of London [1959] WLR 823

The number of **abstentions** does not need to be counted or announced, but it may be appropriate to do so where there is a significant number of abstainers, or where the outcome of the vote requires a majority of members present and entitled to vote.

17.2.13.2
Majorities and percentages

Careful attention needs to be given to the governing document and, for companies, company law when counting votes.

A **simple majority** means more than half the votes. It is not necessarily the same as having the **highest number** of votes (**first past the post**). If, for example, 20 members vote and Ali gets seven votes, Ben gets five and Carol gets eight, Carol is elected on a highest number of votes basis, but not if the governing document requires a majority.

Some organisations use a transferable vote process, but this can be done only if the governing document specifically allows. Information about **single transferable vote** processes is available from the Electoral Reform Society [see end of chapter].

A resolution requiring 'at least 75% of the votes' or 'a three-quarters majority' would need 15 votes out of 20; a resolution requiring 'more than three-quarters of the votes' or 'more than 75%' would need 16.

17.2.13.3
Equality of votes

The governing document should set out what happens in case of an equality of votes (a **tie vote**). Usually the procedure is for the person chairing the meeting to have a **casting vote**, but this must be explicit in the governing document. *Nell v Longbottom [1894] 1 QB 767, 771*

If the chair is entitled to vote in his or her own right, the casting vote is a second vote. There is no obligation to use a casting vote.

If there is no provision for the chair to have a casting vote or if the chair does not use it, a poll may be called [see **17.2.10.2**] which might result in the tie being broken, or the motion is not passed because it does not have the necessary majority.

17.2.13.4
Announcing the result

The number of votes cast for and/or against does not have to be announced, but for anything requiring more than a simple majority it is good practice to say it has been passed by the required majority. This avoids any doubt in future.

A motion agreed by everyone who is entitled to vote is carried **unanimously**. A motion agreed by everyone who votes on it—but with some people abstaining—is carried *nem con* (*nemine contradicente*, 'with no votes cast against').

17.2.14
Adjournment

Adjournment means extending a meeting to another time in order to deal with unfinished business. A meeting may be adjourned by agreement of a majority of the members present and voting. Alternatively it may be adjourned by the person chairing the meeting:

- in situations where the governing document explicitly gives the chairperson power to adjourn;

- if the meeting has to be adjourned in order to take a poll [see **17.2.10.2**]; *R v D'Oyly [1840] 12 A&E 159*

- if the chairperson is unable to keep order at the meeting after making genuine attempts to do so, and the members will not pass a resolution for adjournment; *John v Rees [1970] Ch 345*

- if a quorum is not present [see **17.2.8**]; *or*

- if practical circumstances make it impossible for the members present to consider a resolution to adjourn, for example a breakdown of electricity in a large meeting dependent on microphones.

Byng v London Life Assurance Ltd [1989] 2 WLR 738, 1 All ER 560

If the governing document says that the chairperson *may* adjourn a meeting if asked to do so by a majority of the members present he or she is not obliged to do so. If it says that the chairperson *shall* adjourn the meeting there is an obligation to do so.

Salisbury Gold Mining Co v Hathorn and Others [1897] AC 298

An adjourned meeting is a continuation of the original meeting and under common law, resolutions passed at the adjourned meeting take effect as from the date of the original meeting. This does not apply to companies [see **17.4.10**], or to other organisations whose governing documents specify otherwise.

Jackson v Hamlyn and others [1953] 1 Ch 577, 1 All ER 887

Notice of an adjourned meeting needs to be given only if:

- required by the governing document;
- the original meeting was adjourned **sine die** (without fixing a date and time for the new meeting); *or*
- new business is to be considered at the adjourned meeting.

R v Grimshaw [1847] 10 QB 747

17.2.15
Minutes

Minutes are a written record of the business carried out at meetings. Their purpose is to provide a record, both for current use and for historical purposes, of decisions and actions.

17.2.15.1
Content

The minutes should include:

- name of the organisation;
- description of the meeting (annual general meeting, meeting of the management committee, meeting of the finance sub-committee etc);
- date, including the year, of the meeting;
- place of the meeting;
- list of members present, but for large general meetings it is sufficient to indicate the number of members present;
- list of others 'in attendance' (optional for large meetings);
- who chaired and took the minutes (optional);
- apologies for absence (optional);
- corrections, if any, to the minutes of the previous meeting;
- acceptance and signing of the (corrected, if necessary) minutes of the previous meeting;
- matters arising from the previous minutes;
- a separate minute for each item covered at this meeting (see below);
- date, time and place of the next meeting (optional).

The minute for each item must include any decision reached by the meeting, including a decision not to make one. It may also include:

- important points arising in the discussion;
- details of any document, report or advice relied on in reaching a decision;
- action required to implement the decision, who will take the action and any deadlines for the action.

For a general meeting or if legal business is being transacted, each minute should also include:

- full text of every motion [see **17.2.9**];
- names of proposer and seconder, if any;
- full text of any amendments;

- result of the vote on each amendment and the motion, as announced by the person chairing the meeting.

Errors in the minutes should be crossed through and visibly corrected, with all corrections initialled.

17.2.15.2
Minute books

Minutes should be written or permanently glued into a bound book, or kept in a ring binder with each page serially numbered and signed or initialled by the person who signs the minutes. Minute books must be kept for as long as the organisation exists, and for companies even after it ceases to exist [see **16.3.1**].

17.2.15.3
Approval and signature

If the minutes are written directly into a minute book, they may be read out at the end of the meeting and signed by the person chairing the meeting. More frequently the minutes are distributed before the next meeting, and at that meeting are approved and signed.

The minutes do not have to be read out unless required by the governing document or standing orders. Even if reading out is required, the minutes may be 'taken as read' at the meeting if they have been distributed beforehand.

Approval indicates that the minutes are an accurate record of the meeting. If they are not accurate, a motion to alter them is put to the meeting. Only the people who were at the original meeting should approve the minutes or vote on whether to alter them. The full text of the alteration should be included in the minutes of this meeting, and should also be written by hand into the minutes of the previous meeting and be initialled before they are signed.

Once the minutes are signed they are *prima facie* evidence of the proceedings at that meeting (accepted as accurate but can be rebutted). Some governing documents contain a clause saying that signed minutes are conclusive proof of the proceedings. This means they cannot be rebutted unless they were signed fraudulently or in bad faith.

Kerr v Mottram [1940] Ch 657

17.2.16
Written resolutions

Members of a company have a statutory right to pass virtually any resolution as a written resolution, without having to have a meeting [see **17.4.12**]. Members of an association or IPS may do so if the governing document allows.

There is a common law right for members of the governing body of an association, company or industrial and provident society to pass a resolution in writing [see **17.6.6**].

A written resolution must be agreed by 100% of the members entitled to vote on the matter. Each sheet containing one or more signatures must contain a full copy of the resolution. The signed sheets must be kept in the minute book.

Unless the governing document or the resolution itself specifies otherwise, a written resolution comes into effect when the final signature is received.

17.3
CHARITABLE TRUSTS AND ASSOCIATIONS

Notice of meetings of a charitable trust or association may be sent by post and is deemed to be given 'by the time at which the letter containing it would be delivered in the ordinary course of post'. It is not necessary to give notice to a member of a charitable trust or association if the charity does not have a UK address for him or her.

Charities Act 1993 s.81

Apart from this, meetings of charitable trusts and associations must comply with their governing document and the common law.

17.4 COMPANY MEETINGS

Company law contains many provisions relating to meetings, and a company's articles of association may also be very detailed. Where the articles say nothing about a particular point, company law prevails. If the articles are different from the company law requirements the articles take priority, except in a few situations where company law must prevail. Where they apply these exceptions are explained below.

Where neither company law nor the articles say anything, the common law [see **17.2.1**] applies.

Detailed guidance about company meetings is included in the *Sinclair Taylor & Martin Company Handbook and Registers for Voluntary Sector Companies Limited by Guarantee* [see **page 2**].

17.4.1 Annual general meeting

Unless it has elected not to hold AGMs [see below], a company must hold its first AGM within 18 months of incorporation. Thereafter no more than 15 months can elapse between AGMs, and at least one must be held in every calendar year. *Companies Act 1985 s.366*

A private company (which virtually all voluntary sector companies are) may pass an elective resolution [see **17.4.7.6**] to dispense with holding AGMs. It is unusual to do this unless the company is dormant [see **50.3.7**]. *s.366A(1)*

If an elective resolution is in place, any company member may require an AGM to be held by giving notice to this effect to the company at least three months before the end of the calendar year. *s.366A(3)*

17.4.1.1 Ordinary business

The articles may list the business which must be transacted at an AGM. If it is listed, it generally includes the **ordinary business** of:

- presentation and consideration of the accounts, balance sheet, directors' report and auditor's report (if one is required) for the previous year [see **50.3.5**];
- election of directors [see **11.4.2**];
- if required, appointment of auditor(s) for the period until the next AGM [see **51.3.2**];
- setting the remuneration of the auditor [see **51.3.3**] or authorising the directors to set it.

If the articles do not say that this ordinary business must be transacted at the AGM, it may be done at any general meeting within 10 months from the end of the financial year. *s.241*

It is possible to pass elective resolutions [see **17.4.7.6**] dispensing with the need to present annual accounts and reports to a general meeting and the need to appoint auditors every year.

17.4.1.2 Special business

Other business may be transacted at a company AGM, or the AGM may be closed and an extraordinary general meeting (EGM) convened for the other business. Anything which is not ordinary business is **special business** and depending on what is being proposed, requires a special, extraordinary, ordinary or elective resolution [see **17.4.7**]

17.4.2 Extraordinary general meetings

Any meeting of the company members which is not defined in the notice of the meeting as an AGM is an **extraordinary general meeting** (EGM). The directors may call an EGM at any time, provided they give proper notice [see **17.4.4.1**], and must call any EGMs required by the articles of association.

17.4.2.1 Members' rights to call EGMs

Company members holding at least 10% of the voting rights have a right to require (**requisition**) the directors to call an EGM. If the organisation only has individual members and/or organisational members with one vote each this will be 10% of the members, but this will not be the case if some members have more than one vote. The provision for requisitioned meetings is a key right of company members. It exists even if it is not included in the articles, and cannot be altered or amended.

Companies Act 1985 s.368

The requisition must state why the meeting is being requested, must be signed by the **requisitionists** (either with all signatures on one copy of the requisition, or with signatures on separate identical copies), and must be sent or delivered to the registered office. Within 21 days of delivery, the directors must send out notice of an EGM. Depending on the resolution the period of notice is the same as for a general meeting or for a special resolution at a general meeting [see **17.4.4.1**]. The EGM date cannot be more than 28 days after the notice date.

If the directors do not send out notice of an EGM within the 21 day period, the requisitionists (or those representing more than half their total voting rights) may call an EGM. The company must reimburse them for any reasonable expenses incurred in calling the meeting.

In addition to the right to requisition a meeting, there is a right in company law for 5% or more of the company's members to call a meeting. But the articles may alter or remove this right. *s.370*

17.4.3
Preparing for a general meeting

General meetings are normally called by the governing body, who direct the company secretary and/or others to undertake the necessary preparation. This involves ensuring:

- all time limits in connection with notice for the meeting are complied with [see **17.4.4.1**];
- the annual accounts, report of the auditor (if any) and report of the directors are completed, approved, signed as required, printed and circulated for any general meeting at which they will be presented [see **50.3**];
- a suitable location is booked for the meeting, and all necessary special provision (disability access, signers, creche etc) is arranged;
- notice and all necessary documentation is sent out as required, including the text of special, extraordinary and elective resolutions;
- the necessary forms are produced and sent out if proxy and/or postal voting is allowed [see **17.4.9** and **17.2.12**];
- people who might not be on the lists of those who must get notice are invited, if desired (funders, patrons etc);
- arrangements are made for attendance sheets and for proof of authority for representatives of corporate members;
- arrangements are made for voting, for example voting cards, ballots for elections and/or voting slips if a poll [see **17.4.8.1**] is expected;
- postal votes [see **17.2.12**] are totalled before the meeting, and proxy votes [see **17.4.9**] if the proxy has been given to the chairperson rather than to an individual who will attend the meeting;
- the governing document and any standing orders relating to general meetings are available at the meeting;
- if the accounts are being laid before the meeting, the originals of the signed accounts and report are available at the meeting;
- the meeting is run according to the articles, standing orders and company law;
- the meeting is properly minuted [see **17.2.15**];
- all necessary changes are made to the registers after the meeting [see **16.3**];
- all necessary information and forms are sent to Companies House within the required period, which is usually 14 or 15 days after the general meeting: signed copies of all resolutions which must be notified [see **17.4.7.1**], forms 288a and 288b [see **16.3.4**], etc.

17.4.4
Notice

17.4.4.1
Entitlement to notice

Notice of a company's general meetings must be given or sent to:

- all company members, unless the articles provide otherwise or they do not have a registered address in the UK and have not given the company a UK address for notices;
- all directors [see **11.1.3** for who is a director];
- the company's auditors, if any;
- debenture holders [see **55.5.2**] if the objects are to be changed.
  Companies Act 1985 ss.370(1),(2), 390(1), 5(8)

Notice must be given even if members are too ill to attend or too far away or have said they cannot attend, unless they are outside the UK and the company has no UK address for them.

17.4.4.2
How notice is given

Unless the articles specify otherwise, notice of company general meetings must be in writing and must be given:

- by posting to the member's registered address or to any UK address which they have given to the company for the purpose of notices;
- by leaving it at that address; *or*
- in person. *s.370(1),(2); table A para.111, 112*

All companies have a statutory right to give notice by sending it electronically to an email or other electronic address which the member has given to the company for the purpose of notices. They also have the right to place the notice on a website, and give electronic notice of how to access it to members who have agreed to being notified in this way. This avoids the difficulties of having to send annual reports, accounts and other substantial documents by email. Guidance on electronic communications with company members is available from Companies House and the Institute of Chartered Secretaries and Administrators [see end of chapter]. *Companies Act 1985 (Electronic Communications) Order 2000 [SI 2000/3373] art.18(2)*

17.4.4.3
Statutory period of notice

The period of notice for company meetings depends on whether it is for an annual or an extraordinary general meeting, and the nature of the business to be considered at the meeting. Except in very limited situations [see below], the **statutory period of notice** is **21 clear days** [see **17.2.3.5**] for:

- an annual general meeting;
- an extraordinary general meeting at which a special resolution [see **17.4.7.2**] is being proposed. *Companies Act 1985 ss.369(2), 378(2)*

All other meetings and types of resolution require at least **14 clear days notice**, although shorter notice may be permissible [see below].

If the articles require more than the above 21 or 14 days, the longer period must be given. If the articles require less than 21 days for an AGM or for an EGM at which a special resolution is proposed, that article does not apply and 21 days notice must be given. *s.369(1)*

17.4.4.4
Shorter notice

An annual general meeting may be called with less than 21 days notice if this is agreed by 100% of the members who are entitled to attend and vote. *s.369(3)(a)*

Members holding not less than 95% of the total voting rights of the company may agree that notice less than the required period is acceptable for:

- a general meeting at which a special resolution or other resolution requiring 21 days notice is being proposed;
- any other general meeting. *ss.378(3)(b), 369(3)(b),(4)(b)*

The consent to a shorter period of notice does not have to be in writing, but it would be sensible to get written consent. The consent may be given either before or at the meeting. But if consent is not sought until

213

the meeting and the required number of members do not agree, the meeting cannot be held.

A private company, which virtually all voluntary sector companies are, may reduce the 95% to 90% by elective resolution [see **17.4.7.6**].

Companies Act 1985 ss.369(4), 372(3)

**17.4.4.5
Contents of notice**

The notice of a company general meeting must contain:

- date (including year), time and place of the meeting;
- a statement that it is the annual general meeting, if it is;
- the exact wording of any special or extraordinary resolution [see **17.4.7.2** and **17.4.7.3**], and a statement that the resolution is special or extraordinary;
- the general nature of other business, including the exact wording or a general explanation of ordinary resolutions [see **17.4.7.4**];
- for companies limited by guarantee whose articles allow for proxies [see **17.4.9**], a statement that any member may appoint a proxy, who does not have to be a member of the company, to attend and vote instead of the member;
- if proxies are allowed, the deadline for returning proxy forms, which must not be more than 48 hours before the meeting;
- any members' resolutions [see below] which have been properly requisitioned;
- statements properly provided by requisitionists [see below] about any matter to be dealt with at the meeting. *ss.372, 376, 378*

The notice may also contain details of how to obtain a proxy form, if they are allowed but are not sent out with the notice.

A resolution which is not covered by the 'general nature of other business' as given in the notice may not be passed at the meeting. However company members may, after the formal business has been completed, discuss matters which are not specified in the notice. They may not take decisions, but the discussions and any informal resolutions may be taken into account by directors when they later make decisions.

**17.4.4.6
Members' resolutions
and statements**

Members representing 5% of the voting rights may requisition (request) the company:

- to circulate a **members' resolution** to be put to the next AGM;
- to circulate a statement of not more than 1,000 words about any resolution or other business to be dealt with at any general meeting. *s.376(1),(2)*

The signed resolution must be delivered to the company's registered address at least six weeks before the AGM at which it is to be proposed. The resolution or statement must then be circulated, insofar as possible, in the same way and at the same time as the notice of the meeting. If a statement does not arrive in time to be sent out, there is no obligation on the company to distribute it. *ss.377(1), 376(3)*

Circulation of members' resolutions and statements is at the requisitionists' expense unless the company members agree otherwise. If the members have not agreed to pay for the distribution, the requisitionists must provide to the company, when they make the requisition, a reasonable sum to cover mailing costs. If this is not provided, the company does not have to circulate the statement. *ss.376(1), 377(1)(b)*

**17.4.4.7
Circulation of accounts**

The annual accounts, auditor's report (if any) and the directors' report must be sent not less than 21 days before the AGM or other general meeting at which they are to be considered, to everyone who is entitled to receive notice of general meetings [see **17.4.4.1**]. Copies may be sent less than 21 days before the meeting if this is agreed by all the members entitled to attend and vote at the meeting. *s.238*

A private company may pass an elective resolution to dispense with laying accounts and reports before a general meeting [see **17.4.7.6**].

**17.4.5
Chairing general
meetings**

If the articles do not specify who chairs general meetings, any member at the meeting may be elected to chair. *s.370(5)*

The chairperson's duties arise from common law [see **17.2.7.2**].

**17.4.6
Quorum for general
meetings**

Unless the articles of association require otherwise, the quorum [see **17.2.8**] for a general meeting of a company is two members personally present (i.e. not represented by proxies). *s.370(4)*

A quorum of one is valid for a company's general meeting if it is a private company with only one member [see **10.4.1**]. *s.367(2)*

**17.4.7
Types of resolution**

The various types of company resolution need different notice periods or different majorities, and some must be notified to Companies House. Booklet GBA7 *Resolutions* is available free from Companies House or its website [see end of chapter]. A resolution which is not passed properly is invalid.

**17.4.7.1
Notification to
Companies House**

Special, extraordinary and elective resolutions and an ordinary resolution to revoke an elective resolution must be notified to Companies House within 15 days of being passed. The notification should be headed with the company name and number and should start:

> At a general meeting of the above-named company, duly convened and held at [town] on the [...] day of [month] [year], the following special/extraordinary/elective resolution(s) was/were duly passed.

If the resolution has been passed in writing rather than at a meeting [see **17.4.12**], the notification should start:

> The following special/extraordinary/elective resolution(s) was/were duly agreed by being signed by all of the members under the provisions of the Companies Act 1985 s.381A.

The resolution(s) should then be set out in full, and the notification should be signed and dated by the company secretary or a director.

**17.4.7.2
Special resolutions**

A **special resolution** requires at least 21 clear days notice [see **17.4.4.1**] and must have at least 75% of the votes cast. *s.378(2)*

In companies limited by guarantee a special resolution is required:

- to amend the articles of association, the objects clause of the memorandum of association or any clause in the memorandum which could have been in the articles [see **5.5.2**]; *ss.4, 9, 17(1)*
- to change the name of the company [see **8.7.1**]; *s.28(1)*
- to ratify an *ultra vires* act done by the directors [see **4.7.1**]; *s.35(3)*
- to agree not to have an audit for a dormant company [see **50.3.7**]; *s.250*
- in some situations, to wind up the company [see **21.4.3** and **21.5.4**];
- for any other decisions where the articles of association specifically require a special resolution.

Charitable companies must obtain prior written consent from the Charity Commission for a change of objects, and may need its consent to ratify certain *ultra vires* acts. *Charities Act 1993 ss.64, 66*

After notice of a special or extraordinary resolution has been given, the only changes allowed at the meeting are very minor ones which do not in any way alter the substance of the resolution.

A special resolution to change the name of the company [see **8.7.1**] takes effect only after it has been notified to Companies House and a revised certificate of incorporation has been issued.

**17.4.7.3
Extraordinary
resolutions**

An **extraordinary resolution** is sometimes required to wind up the company [see **21.4.3** and **21.5.3**], and may be required by the articles of association for other types of business. It requires a minimum of 14 days notice if it is proposed for an extraordinary general meeting and 21 days notice if proposed for an annual general meeting. It must be passed with at least 75% of the votes cast, and must be notified to Companies House [see **17.4.7.1**].   *Companies Act 1985 s.378(1)*

**17.4.7.4
Ordinary resolutions**

Unless company law or the articles of association specify that something must be a special or extraordinary resolution, an **ordinary resolution** will suffice. This requires 14 days notice for an extraordinary general meeting and 21 days notice for an annual general meeting, and needs a simple majority (more than half the votes).

Some ordinary resolutions require **special notice** [see **17.4.7.5**].

A company member may propose an amendment to an ordinary resolution without advance notice, but only if it does not substantively alter its nature and create a situation where a different matter is being voted on. The amendment must also not impose any new or different obligations on the company. Amendment procedures are dealt with in the articles or under common law [see **17.2.9.1**].

Ordinary resolutions do not need to be notified to Companies House unless they revoke an elective resolution [see **17.4.7.6**].

**17.4.7.5
Ordinary resolutions
with special notice**

Some ordinary resolutions require **special notice**. These are not the same as **special resolutions** [see **17.4.7.2**]. Resolutions requiring special notice are:

- to remove a director [see **11.5.6**];
- to appoint a director at the same meeting to replace one who has been removed;
- to fill a vacancy in the post of auditor [see **51.3.2**];
- to reappoint an auditor who was appointed by the directors to fill a vacancy;
- to appoint as auditor anyone other than the current auditor; *or*
- to remove an auditor before the end of their term of office [see **51.3.5**].   *ss.303, 388, 391A*

Special notice is intended to give the director or auditor being removed an opportunity to know what is happening and present their case.

When special notice is required:

- notice of intention to propose the resolution must be given to the company at least 28 days before the meeting;
- if possible, notice of the resolution must be given to the members at the same time and in the same way as the usual notice is given;
- if it is not possible to give notice in the same way, notice must be given at least 21 days before the meeting by advertising in an appropriate newspaper or, if the articles allow, in any other appropriate way.   *s.379*

When the company receives special notice, there is no obligation on the directors to call a meeting specifically to consider the resolution, and the resolution may be held over until the next annual or extraordinary general meeting. But if the directors do call a general meeting after the special notice has been given to the company, the resolution must be considered at that general meeting, even if the date of the meeting is less than 28 days after the special notice was given.   *s.379(3)*

**17.4.7.6
Elective resolutions**

Private companies (which virtually all voluntary sector companies are) may choose to dispense with certain requirements of the Companies Acts. Such an **elective resolution** requires 21 days notice stating the terms of the resolution, and must be agreed at the meeting by 100% of the members entitled to attend and vote at the meeting. The agreement can be given in person or, if allowed, by proxy [see **17.4.9**].

Companies Act 1985 s.379A(2)

By elective resolution a private company may elect:

- to reduce from 95% to 90% the majority required to call an extraordinary general meeting with less than 14 days notice and an AGM with less than 21 days notice [see **17.4.4.4**]; *s.369(4)*
- to reduce from 95% to 90% the majority required to agree to propose a special resolution at a meeting at which less than 21 days notice has been given [see **17.4.4.4**]; *s.378(3)*
- to dispense with holding an AGM [see **17.4.1**]; *s.366A*
- to dispense with having to present annual accounts and annual reports to a general meeting [see **50.3.5**]; *s.252*
- to dispense with having to appoint the auditor(s) every year [see **51.3.2**]. *s.386*

An elective resolution may be revoked by passing an ordinary resolution. Companies House must be notified of all elective resolutions and resolutions revoking them [see **17.4.7.1**]. *ss.379A(3), 380(4)*

17.4.8
Voting procedures

Unless the articles of association provide otherwise or a poll is demanded, decisions at company meetings are made by **voting on a show of hands** [see **17.2.10.1**].

A **proxy** [see **17.4.9**] cannot vote on a show of hands unless the articles of association allow this. *s.372(2)(c)*

17.4.8.1
Poll

Company members have a statutory right to demand a poll (a counted vote, see **17.2.10.2**) on any matter except the election of a person to chair a meeting and the adjournment of a meeting. *s.373(1)(a)*

A poll may be demanded:

- by five or more members who have the right to vote;
- by members with at least 10% of the total voting rights of all members who have the right to vote at the meeting. *s.373(1)(b)*

If the articles of association require more members to demand a poll, the statutory provision applies. If the articles allow for a poll to be demanded by fewer members, the articles apply.

A member entitled to more than one vote does not need to cast all the votes the same way. *s.374*

17.4.8.2
Resolutions without a meeting

If all company (or industrial and provident society) members entitled to vote are in favour of a resolution, it may be passed without any formalities and without a meeting. *Cane v Jones [1980] 1 WLR 1451*

This applies even to special and extraordinary resolutions. It is unlikely to be appropriate for voluntary sector companies unless they are very small, and even then it would be more sensible to pass a written resolution [see **17.4.12**]. The need to notify Companies House remains.

17.4.9
Voting by proxy

For companies, rules regarding proxies [see **17.2.11**] depend on the type of company. A member of a private company limited by guarantee, which is what most voluntary sector companies are, does not have the right to appoint a proxy unless the articles of association allow, and the proxy cannot speak at the meeting or vote on a show of hands unless the articles allow. *Companies Act 1985 s.372*

On a poll [see **17.4.8.1**], a proxy may exercise all the votes to which he or she is entitled. So a person who is proxy for several members may vote on behalf of all of them, and a person who is a member in her or his own right and is also proxy for another member has two votes.

A proxy has the right to take part in a demand for a poll.

Companies Act 1985 s.373(2)

If proxy voting is allowed, the articles of association usually prescribe the format and the deadline for delivering the proxy form. This cannot be more than 48 hours before the meeting. *s.372(5)*

If legally valid encryption facilities are available, proxy forms signed with an electronic signature and sent via electronic means are valid.

Electronic Communications Act 2000 s.7

A proxy may be revoked at any time up to the beginning of the meeting, and is automatically revoked if the member attends and votes in person.

A sample proxy form is given below. If the section in italics on the sample form is not included, it is an **ordinary form** which simply gives the proxy the right to vote on behalf of the member. If the section in italics is included, it is a **two-way form** which instructs the proxy to vote either for or against a resolution or resolutions. If a two-way form is filled in but the member does not instruct the proxy one way or the other, the proxy can decide how to vote. This is called a **special proxy**.

17.4.9.1
Example of a proxy form

[NAME OF COMPANY]

I/We_____ of [address]_____

being a member of [name of company] appoint the chairperson of the meeting (see note 1)

or _____ of _____

as my/our proxy to attend and vote for me/us and on my/our behalf at the [Annual/Extraordinary] General Meeting of the company to be held at [place] on [date] and at any adjournment thereof.

(Please indicate with an X in the spaces provided how you wish your votes to be cast on the resolutions specified.)

RESOLUTION	*FOR*	*AGAINST*
That	___	___
That	___	___

Subject to any voting instructions so given, the proxy will vote, or may abstain from voting, on any resolution as he or she may think fit.

Signature _____

Dated this _____day of _____ 20____

NOTES
1. If you desire you may delete the words 'the chairperson of the meeting' and insert the name and address of your own choice of proxy. Please initial such alteration.
2. This proxy form must reach the company's registered office not less than 48 hours before the time fixed for the meeting. In default the proxy cannot be treated as valid.
3. A corporation must execute this document under its seal or under the hand of an officer or attorney duly authorised.
4. If this proxy form is executed under a power of attorney or other authority such power of attorney or other authority must be lodged with the company along with the proxy form.

17.4.10
Adjournment

A company's articles of association generally contain rules on adjournment. If they do not, common law applies [see **17.2.14**].

A company resolution passed at an adjourned meeting is valid from the date on which it was actually passed, not the date of the original meeting. This is different from the common law position.

Companies Act 1985 s.381

17.4.11
Minutes

Company law requires minutes to be kept [see **16.3.7**], but does not say what needs to be included or in what form [see **17.2.15** for guidance].

Minutes signed by the chairperson of the meeting or of the next meeting are evidence of the proceedings.   *Companies Act 1985 s.382(2)*

17.4.12
Written resolutions

Private companies (which virtually all voluntary sector companies are) may pass most resolutions in writing, without a general meeting. This right exists even if the memorandum or articles of association specify otherwise.   *ss.381A, 381C*

The main exception is a resolution to remove a director or auditor before the end of his or her term of office. A resolution of this nature must always be dealt with at a meeting.   *s.381A(7)*

17.4.12.1
Notification to auditor

Unless the company's accounts do not have to be audited [see **50.3.4**], a copy of every written resolution must be sent to the company's auditors. If the resolution concerns them in any way as auditors, they may notify the company within seven days that they want the matter dealt with at a meeting rather than in writing.   *s.381B*

For a **written resolution** to be valid:

- the auditors must notify the company within seven days that the resolution does not concern them as auditors;
- the auditors must notify the company that the resolution concerns them as auditors, but does not need to be dealt with at a meeting; *or*
- the seven days must expire without any notice from the auditor.

17.4.12.2
Approving the resolution

A written resolution must be signed by 100% of the members entitled to attend and vote at meetings at the date of the resolution, which is the date on which the last member signs. Every signature must be on a document which states the full resolution, and every copy of the resolution must be exactly the same. Each copy may have any number of signatures, provided they all fit on the page.   *s.381A*

If encryption safeguards complying with the legal requirements are available, documents with an electronic signature are valid.
          Electronic Communications Act 2000 s.7

A written resolution which would require notification to Companies House if it had been passed at a meeting [see **17.4.7.1**] must be notified to Companies House in the usual way. Instead of giving the date and place of a meeting the notification should state that the resolution was passed under the provisions of Companies Act 1985 s.381A.

The resolution and signatures must be included in the company's minute book [see **16.3.7**] and must be signed by the company secretary or a director.   *Companies Act 1985 s.382A*

17.5
INDUSTRIAL AND PROVIDENT SOCIETY MEETINGS

Industrial and provident society legislation contains few requirements for meetings, apart from saying that an IPS's rules must specify which meetings must be held and who has voting rights. So IPS meetings are governed primarily by their governing document and common law [see **17.2.1** and **17.4.8.2**].

17.5.1
Notice

Notice of general meetings and all information sent to members about general meetings must also be sent to the society's auditor or auditors.
          Friendly and Industrial and Provident Societies Act 1968 s.9(7)

In general IPS legislation does not set out a period of notice, but it is included in each IPS's rules. The exception is when an auditor is being removed or is not being reappointed [see **51.5**]. The society must be given notice at least 28 days before the meeting and must then give notice to members and the retiring auditor with the notice of the meeting, or 14 days before the meeting, or by a notice in an appropriate newspaper or in some other way. *FIPSA ss.5(1)(a), 6*

17.5.2
Resolutions

In general, IPS law does not say anything about the form of resolutions or the majority required to pass them, leaving it to each IPS's rules. The main exceptions are when an IPS amalgamates with another IPS or a company, transfers its business to another IPS or a company, or converts into a company [see **6.7.1**]. These procedures require a **special resolution** with:

- two-thirds of votes cast in person or by proxy at a general meeting for a resolution to amalgamate with or transfer engagements to another IPS, and three-quarters of the votes cast to amalgamate with, transfer engagements to or convert into a company; *and*

- confirmation by a majority of votes cast at a second general meeting held between two weeks and one month after the first.
Industrial and Provident Societies Act 1965 ss.50-52

A copy of the special resolution, signed by the chairperson of the second meeting and by the secretary, must be sent to the registrar of friendly societies within 14 days of the second meeting, with the appropriate fee. The resolution does not take effect until it is registered.

Dissolution of an IPS [see **21.6**] requires the written consent of at least three-quarters of the members. *s.55(b)*

17.6
MEETINGS OF THE GOVERNING BODY

Common law principles [see **17.2.1**] apply to meetings of governing bodies. In addition, the governing document generally includes some rules for meetings of the governing body. If it does not, or if additional rules need to be agreed:

- in an unincorporated association, the committee members agree rules for their meetings; *Cassell v Inglis [1916] 2 Ch 211, 222*

- in a trust, the trustees agree the rules for their meetings;

- in a company, the articles of association may provide that rules for meetings of the directors are agreed by the directors;

- in an industrial and provident society, the governing document sets out how rules for governing body meetings are decided.

The rules may be agreed on a one-off basis, but usually they are fixed as standing orders [see **5.4.26**]. They generally cover frequency of meetings, notice, quorum, chairing, voting and minutes.

17.6.1
Frequency

Unless the governing document or standing orders specify otherwise, the members of a governing body may meet as frequently or infrequently as they like. They must, however, meet often enough in a company to fulfil their duties under the Companies Acts, and in a charity to fulfil their duties as charity trustees [see **chapter 13**]. The Charity Commission recommends an absolute minimum of two meetings per year.

17.6.2
Notice

Unless the governing document or standing orders specify otherwise, governing body meetings are generally called by the chairperson. In a company any director may call a governing body meeting (unless prevented from doing so by the articles of association), and the company secretary must call one if asked to do so by a director.

Unless the governing document specifies otherwise:

- reasonable notice needs to be given for governing body meetings, indicating when and where the meeting is to be held;

- notice does not have to be in writing;

- notice must be given to all members of the governing body, even if they have said they cannot attend;
Re Portuguese Consolidated Copper Mines [1889] 42 ChD 160

- notice does not have to be given if the governing body meets regularly at the same time and place.

Compagnie de Mayville v Whitley [1896] 1 Ch 788

A company's articles of association generally state that notice of governing body meetings does not have to be given to any director who is away from the UK. In charitable trusts and associations, notice of meetings of the governing body does not have to be given if the charity does not have a UK address for the governing body member.

Charities Act 1993 s.81(3)

17.6.2.1
Agenda

Unless required by the governing document, there is no legal requirement to notify governing body members beforehand of the agenda or purpose of any governing body meeting, but it is good practice to do so.

17.6.2.2
Meetings without notice

If all the members of a governing body are together and they all agree, they can hold a meeting there and then, without any notice, and can agree any resolution provided they are unanimous. The resolution should be recorded in the minute book or be included in the minutes of the next meeting. *Re Bonelli's Telegraph Co [1871] 12 Eq 246*

17.6.3
Chairing

If the governing document does not specify how the governing body chairperson is appointed, the members may elect one of their number to take that role. The duties arise from common law [see **17.2.7.2**].

17.6.4
Quorum

Unless the governing document specifies otherwise, the quorum for a meeting of the governing body is:

- in an unincorporated association, all the members of the governing body; *Brown v Andrew [1849] 18 LJQB 153*

- in a charitable trust, a majority of the trustees; *Re Whitely [1910] 1 Ch 600*

- in a company, a majority of the directors. *York Tramways v Willows [1882] 8 QBD 685*

If a company's articles empower the directors to set a quorum but do not say what the quorum is if it is not set, the default is 'the number of directors who usually act at meetings'.

Re Regents Canal Iron Co [1867] WN 79

If a governing body member cannot attend a meeting it may be possible in some situations to appoint an alternate [see **11.4.3**] who counts towards the quorum.

If the total number of governing body members falls below the quorum, those remaining may meet only to fill vacancies or, in a membership organisation, to call a general meeting of the members.

17.6.4.1
Disinterested quorum

For company and charity governing body meetings the quorum must be **disinterested**, and in general cannot include a member who has an interest in a contract under discussion [see **13.2.2** and **13.3.4**]. The governing document of other organisations may include a similar rule.

17.6.5
Decision making

Unless the governing document specifies otherwise, decisions at governing body meetings are made by a majority of votes, and the chairperson does not have a casting vote in case of a tie [see **17.2.13.3**].

17.6.6
Decisions without a meeting

A governing body may pass its resolutions in writing provided the resolutions are agreed by all the governing body members entitled to vote on the matter [see **17.2.16** for the procedure].

Re Bonelli's Telegraph Co [1871] 12 Eq 246

A company's articles often specify that a written resolution must be signed by all the directors entitled to receive notice of a board meeting. If the articles specify that notice does not need to be given to directors outside the UK, they do not need to sign a written resolution.

The rules on email, internet, telephone or video conference meetings are the same as for general meetings. Unless everyone can see and hear each other, decisions made by such means are not valid unless the governing document allows [see **17.2.6**]. Decisions made by such means should be ratified by a written resolution or at a valid meeting.

17.6.7
Minutes

Proper minutes [see **17.2.15**] must be kept for:

- all meetings of a company's governing body; *and*
  Companies Act 1985 s.382(1)

- all meetings where minutes are required by the governing document or standing orders.

Even where there is no statutory or constitutional obligation to keep minutes, it would be poor practice not to. Minutes should be approved and signed in the same way as meetings of general meetings.

Minutes of governing body meetings do not have to be kept in a specified location or be open to anyone other than members of the governing body, unless this is specified in the governing document.

17.7
COMMITTEES AND
SUB-COMMITTEES

Decisions may be delegated to committees if the governing document allows [see **13.5**]. (In general if the main body is called a general meeting, council, board etc the delegated body will be called a committee, but if the main body is called a management committee, executive committee etc, the delegated body is called a sub-committee.)

In general, committees set up by the membership or by the governing body [see **12.5**] must comply with the same requirements for meetings as the body which set them up—so a committee set up by the governing body has to follow the same procedures as the governing body. Unless specified otherwise in the governing document, standing orders, the terms of reference for the committee [see **12.5.1**] or the minute of the meeting which established the committee, the following rules apply:

- the common law relating to meetings [see **17.2.1**] applies to committee meetings;

- the members of the committee may decide how often to meet;

- the provisions applying to notice for governing body meetings [see **17.6.2**] apply to committee meetings;

- the quorum is all the members of the committee;
  Re Liverpool Household Stores Association [1890] 59 LJ Ch 616

- the chairperson does not have a casting vote [see **17.2.13.3**].

Minutes must be kept if required by the governing document, standing orders, the committee's terms of reference, or the resolution under which the committee or sub-committee was set up. Even if they are not required, it is poor practice not to keep minutes.

FOR FURTHER INFORMATION

Carrying out elections and ballots. Electoral Reform Services: 020-8365 8909; www.electoralreform.co.uk

Company meetings. Companies House: 0870-333 3636; www.companieshouse.gov.uk

Electronic communication. Institute of Chartered Secretaries and Administrators: 020-7580 4741; www.icsa.org.uk

Industrial and provident society meetings. Registrar of friendly societies: 020-7676 1000; www.fsa.gov.uk

Telephone meetings. Community Network: 020-7359 4594; www.community-network.org

Voting systems. Electoral Reform Society: 020-7928 1622; www.electoral-reform.org.uk

Chapter 18
LEGAL AGREEMENTS

For sources of further information see end of chapter.
Double-underlined section headings indicate additions or significant changes since the first edition.

18.1
LEGAL OBLIGATIONS

Legally enforceable obligations are those which the courts will enforce. They include legally binding **agreements**, and legal obligations which are imposed by the **common law** or **statute**. People responsible for the organisation and its activities must be aware of the organisation's legal obligations and the potential liabilities if the obligations are not met.

18.1.1
Agreements

The main types of enforceable agreement are:

- **contract**: a binding agreement between two or more parties, involving **consideration** [see **18.6**];

- **deed**: a binding agreement, not necessarily involving an exchange of consideration, which takes its validity from formalities [see **18.3**];

- **trust**: a binding arrangement where assets given by one party are held on trust for beneficiaries or charitable purposes [see **18.2**].

Even a signed agreement is generally not legally enforceable if no contract, deed or trust is created. For example if a funder agrees in writing to make a grant but does not do so, the agreement would be enforceable through the courts only if it was in the form of a contract, which grants generally are not [see **48.1**] or a deed [see **18.3**], or if the funder was under a statutory or other legal obligation to make the payment.

18.1.2
Common law and statutory obligations

Many statutes contain obligations which can be enforced through the civil courts [see **60.1**]. An employer, for example, has a **statutory duty** to provide a safe workplace for its employees [see **36.2.1**]. If it fails to do so, the Health and Safety Executive may bring an action against the employer, and/or any employee may sue the employer for breach of statutory duty. For more about statutory duties, see **19.2**.

Numerous other obligations are imposed by the common law, most notably in **tort** [see **19.5**]. An example is the duty of care, under which everyone has to take reasonable care where it is reasonably foreseeable that a lack of care could cause personal injury or damage.

18.2
TRUSTS

Obligations under **trust law** arise:

- where a trust, whether private, public or charitable [see **1.3.3** for the distinction] is created by deed or under the terms of a will; *or*

- where a trust would be assumed by the courts to exist, even if one has not been formally created. This is referred to as a **constructive** or **implied trust** [see **44.2.1**].

When a trust exists:

- those holding or controlling the assets are **trustees**, and have certain duties and powers [see **13.3** and **54.1**];

- any use of the assets for purposes or beneficiaries other than those intended is a **breach of trust** [see **44.2**], as is any action which contravenes trust law or, in a charity, charity law;

- the beneficiaries are entitled to the benefit of the trust (have a **beneficial interest**) even though they are not a party to the formal arrangement between the donor (settlor) and trustees;

- in a private trust, any beneficiary may sue to enforce its rights;

- in a public or charitable trust the individual beneficiaries generally cannot sue to enforce their rights, but the attorney general or Charity Commission may bring a claim on their behalf;

- a donor may sue if its donated assets are not used as intended.

18.3
DEEDS

A document which has been properly drawn up and signed (**executed**) as a **deed** is enforceable even though there may be no trust or contract. Deeds are used for a variety of reasons, including:

- where the law requires, as for leases of more than three years;

- where no contract is created but there is a need for the agreement to be legally enforceable;
- where there is a contract but greater formality is required;
- to create or record the terms of a trust;
- to record certain other important events such as a change of name, appointment of a trustee or the grant of a property right;
- to create a long-lasting obligation.

A **supplemental deed** adds to or amends an existing deed. It is executed in the same way as an ordinary deed.

18.3.1
Wording of the deed

A deed must make clear that it is intended as a deed, and that it has been executed and delivered [see below].

It often starts '*This deed* is made the ___ day of [month and year]', thus making clear that it is intended to be a deed. This may be followed by **recitals**, a short statement of why the deed is being created. These often start with 'whereas'. The detailed **operative provisions** follow.

The deed includes wording such as 'Executed and delivered on the date inserted above' or 'Executed and delivered by the parties on the date inserted above', if there are two or more parties. It ends with signatures or an organisation's seal.

18.3.2
Execution

A deed formerly had to be **under seal**, which originally meant sealing wax with a seal impressed in it had to be placed on the deed. More recently, a red wafer (sticker) could be stuck on the deed, or there had to be some other indication of the intention to seal.

Now to be validly executed by an individual, the deed merely needs to be signed by the individual making it, with the signature witnessed by one person. For organisations, the nature of the execution depends on the organisation's legal structure.

18.3.2.1
Companies

A company deed can be executed by being signed by two directors or by the company secretary and a director.   *Companies Act 1985 s.36*

Alternatively if the company has a seal [see **5.4.18**] it is impressed on the deed or on a red wafer stuck to the deed. The deed is signed by two directors or the secretary and a director to show the use of the seal is authorised.

18.3.2.2
Industrial and provident societies

Deeds executed by an industrial and provident society must be sealed with the IPS seal and signed by the secretary and two other committee members.   *Industrial and Provident Societies Act 1965 s. 29*

18.3.2.3
Charitable trusts and associations

Deeds executed by a charitable trust or association must be signed by at least two trustees properly authorised by the governing body. Each signature must be witnessed by a non-signatory, with the witness's name and address beside the signature. The witness's occupation should be included but is often omitted.   *Charities Act 1993 s.82*

18.3.2.4
Non-charitable trusts and associations

For private trusts and non-charitable associations, deeds are signed by at least one person properly authorised by the governing body, with the signature witnessed [see above].

18.3.3
Delivery

A deed is not valid until it is **delivered**. It does not physically have to be given to the person to whom the promise in the deed is made, but there must be some indication that the person now intends to be bound by it. The term 'executed and delivered' or 'signed and delivered' and a signature are adequate to show this.

A deed which is intended to take effect only on the occurrence of some event is delivered as an **escrow**, and comes into effect as a deed only if the event on which it is conditional occurs. For example, a deed promising a grant in a future year might be conditional on confirmation of matching funding being supplied by a third party.

If these formalities are observed the promise made in the deed is legally enforceable, but if the wording or execution is not right the deed may not be enforceable.

18.4
OWNERSHIP OF ASSETS

Assets—money, equipment, investments, land etc—can be owned only by **legal persons** [see **2.1.1**]. These are natural (human) persons, and corporate bodies (which are **corporate persons**). Companies, industrial and provident societies, and charitable trusts or associations which have incorporated their trustee body [see **1.4**] can own assets in their own right, but for unincorporated associations and trusts the situation is more complex.

18.4.1
How unincorporated bodies hold assets

An unincorporated association or trust is not a legal person [see **1.1**]. It may 'own' assets in the sense of having the **beneficial right** to them or a **beneficial interest** in them, the right to use and benefit from them. But the **legal title** must be held on its behalf by one or more legal persons (individuals or corporate bodies).

18.4.1.1
Investments, land and buildings

If an unincorporated trust or association purchases or is given assets, particularly investments, land or buildings, it should either:

- incorporate its governing body so the governing body can hold the property as a corporate body, even though the organisation itself remains unincorporated [see **1.4**];

- **vest** ownership in all of the members of the governing body; *or*

- vest ownership in one or more **nominees**—a legal person or persons, often referred to as **holding trustees** [see **18.4.4**] or a **custodian trustee** [see **18.4.2**], who hold assets on behalf of the members of the governing body.

For a non-charitable association, an alternative is for the investments, land or buildings to be held by all the members under terms set out in the governing document (a form of contract) or under another contractual agreement among the members.

Any rules in the governing document specifying how assets are held must be followed. In most cases, legal advice is advisable.

18.4.1.2
Other assets

Physical assets other than land and investments may be held by the members of the governing body of an unincorporated organisation without needing to be formally vested in them. They can be transferred by **delivery**, which simply involves handing them over, rather than having to be formally transferred.

18.4.2
Custodian trustees

A **custodian trustee** is a corporate body authorised under the **Public Trustee Act 1906** to hold investments or land on behalf of other organisations. They generally make a charge for holding assets.

18.4.2.1
Trust corporations

Trust corporations may hold land and/or investments. They include:

- corporate bodies appointed by the Charity Commission as charity trustees or custodian trustees;   *Charities Act 1993 s.35*

- banks, local authorities or other corporate bodies defined as trust corporations and authorised to act as custodian trustees by the **Public Trustee Act 1906** and the **Trustee (Custodian Trustee) Rules 1975** *[SI 1975/1189]*;

- corporate bodies prescribed as trust corporations by the lord chancellor.

18.4.2.2
Official custodian for charities

The **official custodian for charities** [see **3.5.3**] is a Charity Commission official who holds land, but generally not investments, on behalf of unincorporated charities. If a charity has investments as well as land, these will have to be held in another way. *Charities Act 1993 ss.21-23*

More details are in Charity Commission booklet CC13 *The Official Custodian for Charities' Land Holding Service*. There is no charge for having land held by the official custodian.

18.4.2.3
Public trustee

The **public trustee** is a government official who holds investments and land on behalf of individuals, private trusts and non-charitable bodies, but not charities.

18.4.3
Custodians

A **custodian** does not 'own' assets in the same way as a custodian trustee [see above] or a holding trustee [see below], but undertakes the safe custody of assets or of documents or records concerning the assets. For trusts, charitable associations and other bodies covered by the **Trustee Act 2000**, the rules on use of custodians are the same as for nominees [see **54.1**]. *Trustee Act 2000 ss.17-23*

A custodian cannot be appointed by an organisation which has a custodian trustee, or in relation to any assets vested in (held by) the official custodian for charities.

18.4.4
Holding trustees
or nominees

Holding trustees, increasingly called **nominees**, can hold legal title to land, investments or other assets for the benefit of the beneficiaries (in a charity) or for the members of the association (in a non-charity). Legal advice should be sought before appointing holding trustees or nominees to hold land.

Although the same person may have both roles, being a holding trustee is not the same as being a trustee of a trust [see **11.1.6**] or a charity trustee in a charitable organisation [see **11.1.7**]. Charity trustees are responsible for managing the charity (often called, in this context, **managing trustees**). Nominees—holding trustees or custodian trustees—hold assets on behalf of the managing trustees, but have no say in the management of the charity or the assets they hold.

18.4.4.1
Nominees for trusts and
charitable associations

Unless the governing document specifies otherwise, a nominee or custodian for a trust, charitable unincorporated association or other body subject to the provisions of the **Trustee Act 2000** must be:

- two or more of the trustees, who must act jointly;
- one of the trustees, if that trustee is a trust corporation [see **18.4.2.1**];
- a corporate body controlled by the trustees; *or*
- an individual or corporate body whose business consists of or includes acting as a nominee or custodian. *Trustee Act 2000 s.19*

For more about nominee companies, see **18.4.4.3**.

In appointing a nominee or custodian under the Trustee Act provisions, trustees must exercise their statutory duty of care [see **13.3.7** and **54.1.2**]. Appointments must be in writing, and must be kept under regular review If the organisation is charitable but is not an exempt charity [see **7.1.2**], the trustees must comply with Charity Commission guidance, available free from the Commission or on its website [see **page 12**]. *ss.16-22*

If the governing document allows, an individual or corporate body which does not meet the Trustee Act requirements may be appointed as a holding trustee. Where individuals are allowed to be appointed, a minimum of three is usually required. There is no maximum.

18.4.4.2
Nominees for
non-charitable
associations

Provided the governing document allows, any individual or corporate body may be a holding trustee or nominee for a non-charitable association. The maximum number of holding trustees for land is four.

Trustee Act 1925 s.34

18.4.4.3
Nominee companies

Nominee companies are set up for the purpose of holding property, and are most frequently used by investment managers to hold stocks and shares they are managing. As a nominee the company holds the title to the property, but the organisation is beneficial owner [see **18.4.1**].

Nominee companies typically hold shares owned by many owners, although it is possible to create a nominee company to hold the investments or land of only one organisation.

18.4.5
Vesting in trustees, nominees and custodians

The process of passing the legal ownership of investments or land to a new trustee, a nominee or a custodian is called **vesting**. Vesting must take place whenever a new trustee, nominee or custodian is appointed.

Where nominees (holding trustees or a custodian trustee) are to be appointed, the organisation's governing document may specify who they are to be. If it does not, the governing body can choose, provided that they comply with the requirements of the **Trustee Act 2000** [see above] and exercise their statutory duty of care [see **54.1.2**]. All appointments of nominees and custodians must be in writing.

18.4.5.1
Deed of appointment

If detailed provisions for appointing nominees (holding trustees and/or a custodian trustee) and the terms on which they hold property are not set out in the organisation's governing document, a **trust deed** should be drawn up. Even if this is not done the nominees have the responsibilities of trustees, but these will not be as clear or as easily managed.

If the organisation's governing document does not set out the procedure for removing and replacing nominees, this should be set out in the trust deed. A supplemental deed [see **18.3**] will need to be drawn up to appoint new nominees.

18.4.5.2
Model deed of appointment

This Deed of Trust is made on the ___ day of *[month]* *[year]* between:
[Name of organisation] ('the Organisation'),
acting by its Management Committee *[or insert what the governing body is called]* ('the Governing Body');
and *[Names and addresses of holding trustees]* ('the Trustees').

BACKGROUND

The Organisation is an unincorporated association // an unincorporated association registered as a charity // a charitable trust.

The Organisation wishes property that it owns which includes items in the attached schedule and other property acquired from time to time ('the Property') to be vested in the Trustees.

At a duly convened meeting of the Governing Body // a general meeting of the Organisation held on *[date]* at *[place]* it was resolved that the Trustees named above should be appointed to hold the title to the Property for the purposes of the Organisation.

> *Note that if the organisation is a charitable association or charitable trust, the property should be held 'for the purposes of the Organisation'. If the organisation is not charitable, the property should be held 'for the benefit of the members for the time being of the Organisation'. [See **18.4.5.3** for an explanation of this.]*

At the same meeting it was resolved that *[names of two persons authorised to sign]* were authorised to sign this Deed on behalf of the Governing Body // the members of the Organisation.

AGREEMENT

It is agreed that:

1. The Organisation hereby appoints the Trustees to act as trustees of the Organisation for the purpose of holding the Property.

2.   The Trustees agree jointly and severally to hold the Property for the Purposes of the Organisation // for the benefit of the members for the time being of the Organisation.

3.   The Trustees undertake that they will promptly follow all lawful and reasonable directions given by the Organisation, and that they will act only in accordance with such directions.

4.   The Organisation agrees that it will indemnify the Trustees against all costs, claims and liabilities properly incurred or arising out of their trusteeship of the Property.

5.   The Trustees have the following rights during the period of their trusteeship and during any further period in which they may be liable to any claim arising out of their trusteeship:

(a)   the right to receive notice of all meetings of the Governing Body and all general meetings of the Organisation;

(b)   the right to attend and speak at any meeting of the Governing Body or general meeting on any matter relevant to the Property;

(c)   the right of access to information reasonably required to discharge their duties as trustees;

(d)   the right to immediate payment of any outstanding liability arising from trusteeship of the Property.

6.   The Trustees agree to provide the Organisation with copies of all correspondence and to notify them of all communications in respect of the Property.

7.   The Trustees agree to notify the Organisation of any change of their name or address.

8.   New trustees may be appointed only by a resolution of the Governing Body or general meeting of the Organisation.

9.   Trustees may be removed only by a resolution of the Governing Body or a general meeting of the Organisation.

Unless it is made explicit that the power to appoint and remove trustees rests solely with the governing body of the organisation, trust law will place the power to appoint and remove in the hands of the holding trustees.

10. If a Trustee wishes to resign from his or her trusteeship the Organisation will use its best endeavours to obtain the Trustee's release from any obligation connected with the Property.

Signed and delivered as a Deed
by *[signature of authorised person]*
on behalf of the Governing Body of *[name of organisation]*
acting under their authority by resolution on *[date]*
in the presence of *[witness's signature, name, address and occupation]*

Signed as a Deed
by *[signature of Trustee no. 1]*
in the presence of *[witness's signature, name, address and occupation]*

[and the same for the remaining trustees]

18.4.5.3
Holding property for non-charitable associations

Apart from a few exceptions, trusts can be created only for charitable purposes or for the benefit of identifiable persons [see **1.3.4**]. Because assets cannot be held in trust for the purposes of a non-charitable association, they must be held for the benefit of identifiable members.

If the property is held 'for the members of the association', that would apply only to the members at the time the trust is established, and not future members. But the property cannot be held for 'the present and future members', because no one can know at this point who the future members will be, so they are not identifiable. The wording which should be used is 'for the members for the time being of the association'. 'For the time being' means at any given point in time. At any point, the members are identifiable from the organisation's membership records.

18.4.6
Powers, duties and liabilities

As nominees, holding and custodian trustees hold assets on behalf of the organisation, must carry out the wishes of the organisation unless doing so would be unlawful or in breach of trust, and do not have any management powers in relation to the organisation or to the property they hold. But if they are members of the organisation's governing body as well as being holding trustees, they have management responsibilities in that capacity.

A nominee or custodian may enter into an agreement to act as an **agent** [see **18.5**] of the organisation, buying and selling investments or signing leases as directed by the organisation and subject to the control of the organisation. But they cannot do this without such agreement.

18.4.6.1
Liability of nominees

If a *custodian* trustee undertakes an act which is unlawful or in breach of trust, full legal liability rests with the members of the governing body which authorised the act.

If *holding* trustees undertake such an act they, rather than the governing body which authorised the act, are liable—even if the holding trustees have acted at the bidding of the governing body. It is therefore especially important for holding trustees to be fully aware of the purposes for which the property is held, and any conditions attached to the property. If instructed to carry out an act which is in breach of those trusts, the holding trustees should refuse to do so.

18.4.6.2
Appointments under the Trustee Act 2000

Governing body members are not liable for the defaults of nominees or custodians appointed under the provisions of the Trustee Act 2000, provided the trustees exercised their statutory duty of care [see **13.3.7** and **54.1.2**] in entering into arrangements with the nominee or custodian, keeping the arrangements under review, and intervening if necessary.

Trustee Act 2000 s.23

18.5
AGENCY

Agency exists when one person or group (the **principal**) authorises another (the **agent**) to act on their behalf. Unlike the relationship with a holding or custodian trustee, which is based on a trust, the agency/principal relationship is based on contract [see **18.6**]. An agent may enter into contracts and do other acts which bind the principal.

18.5.1
The creation of agency

No particular formalities are required to appoint an agent, except:
- if the agent is to execute deeds [see **18.3**], he or she must be appointed by deed (a **power of attorney**);
- if the agent is appointed under the provisions of the **Trustee Act 2000** [see **13.5.2**], the appointment must be in writing.

18.5.1.1
Express appointment

The appointment of an agent may be express (explicit), where the parties agree that one party will become the other's agent. The agent's authority may be general ('to do anything'), or may be limited to a specific transaction or specific types of transactions. The person appointing the agent must be certain that all limitations are carefully set out. If the instructions are not clear, the principal may be bound by acts of the agent which are outside what the principal intended.

18.5.1.2
Implied authority

In certain situations, including some which might not be immediately recognised as contractual, the law implies that one party is authorised to act as another's agent. For example company directors are agents for the company, and the governing body members of an unincorporated association are agents for the members of the association.

18.5.1.3
Apparent and usual
authority

Once the principal has indicated that someone is their agent—for example, an employer authorising an employee to enter into contracts or undertake other binding actions—the principal will be bound by such contracts. This applies even if a contract exceeds the authority of the agent, unless the party with whom the contract was made was aware that the agent was acting outside his or her authority.

18.5.1.4
Agencies of necessity

In certain very limited circumstances, for example where a person is looking after the goods of another and it is necessary to protect them from damage, the person taking the protective steps may under the law of agency be able to recover the costs from the owner or principal.

18.5.2
Commission
payments

Whether the agent is entitled to a commission or other payment depends entirely on what has been agreed between the principal and agent. There is no presumption that an agent is entitled to be paid.

18.5.3
What can be
delegated

A governing body can delegate decision-making powers only if this is allowed in its governing document, by statute, or (for charities without such powers) by the Charity Commission. Governing body members of trusts, charitable associations and some other bodies have statutory power to delegate certain functions, providing they act in accordance with a statutory duty of care and other requirements imposed by the **Trustee Act 2000** [see **13.3.7**, **13.5.2** and **54.1.2**].

18.5.4
Duties of an agent

An agent must:

- act with care and skill;
- avoid conflicts of interest and duty;
- not take bribes or make secret profits;
- indemnify the principal for any losses incurred by the principal because of the agent's negligence or acting outside its authority.

Agents appointed by trusts and charitable associations have specific duties [see **13.5.2**].

18.5.5
Liability for
contracts made by
an agent

If when making a contract on behalf of the principal the agent names the principal, the agent has no rights under the contract. Only the principal can benefit from the contract or sue if it is not fulfilled.

Generally a principal is liable only for the acts of a properly authorised agent. If an unauthorised person enters into a contract, or if an agent enters into an unauthorised contract:

- the agent may be held liable to the person they contracted with; *or*
- if the principal is held liable under the contract, the agent will be liable to the principal.

Even when a contract is unauthorised, the principal may take on the liability by ratifying the contract.

If the agent did not have authority and knew it, the agent may be liable to be sued for the tort of **deceit**.

18.5.5.1
Liability for contracts
made by employees

A third party dealing with an employee is entitled to assume that the employee is authorised to act on behalf of the employer. A contract, even a very onerous one, entered into by an employee nearly always binds the employer. The only situation where it might not is where the employee did not have authority to enter into it and the third party actually knew, or ought reasonably to have known, that the employee had no such authority.

18.5.6
Ending an agency
arrangement

An agency arrangement is a contract and can be ended by anything that will bring a contract to an end [see **18.11**]. The end of a commercial agency arrangement may give the agent a right to substantial compensation. *Commercial Agents Regulations 1993 [SI 1993/3173]*

An agency arrangement may also end if either the principal or agent becomes unable to manage his or her own affairs. This terminates any informal agency or agency under a normal power of attorney, but individuals may make an **enduring power of attorney** which will continue despite their mental illness or other incapacity.

Enduring Powers of Attorney Act 1985

The death or bankruptcy of the principal terminates an agency arrangement. Inconsistent conduct, such as disposal by the principal of goods the agent has been asked to sell, may terminate the agency.

The principal should ensure that any third party likely to deal with the agent knows the agency arrangement has ended.

18.6
CONTRACTS

An agreement which meets the criteria to be a contract is enforceable in the courts. There is no need for a document to be signed and delivered or even, in most cases, for a document to exist.

18.6.1
Elements of a contract

For a valid contract:

- there must be at least two parties, who must have the **capacity** to enter into a contract [see **18.6.2**];
- an **offer** must be made, and must be **accepted**;
- there must be sufficient **certainty** about what has been agreed;
- there must be **consideration**;
- the parties must **intend** to create a legally binding relationship.

These terms are described below.

18.6.1.1
Offer

For a contract to be made an agreement must be reached. The law treats this in two parts: **offer** and **acceptance**. An offer may be quite straightforward—'I offer you £10 in exchange for that book'—or it may be inferred from behaviour, as the person stands silently at the till with the book in her hand and offers £10 to the sales assistant.

An offer may be withdrawn at any time before it is accepted.

Some situations in which there may appear to be an offer are actually an **invitation to treat**, which is a step prior to an offer. Some examples of this are:

- goods displayed on a bookshop's shelves, where the offer itself is not made until the purchaser takes a book to the till and seeks to buy it, and acceptance comes when the cashier agrees the sale;
- property put up for sale at an auction, where the offer is made by a potential purchaser calling out a price or simply raising a hand, and acceptance comes on the fall of the auctioneer's hammer;
- a house put up for sale, where the final offer and acceptance do not come until there have been detailed negotiations;
- an invitation to bid (tender) for work, where offers are made by the persons who bid for the work, and the purchaser might accept one of the offers.

18.6.1.2
Acceptance

Acceptance must be clear and unqualified. If it is ambiguous ('it sounds OK, but I'll have to check with the board') there is no acceptance.

Acceptance must be distinguished from **counter-offer**. In acceptance, the **offeror** makes the offer, and the **offeree** accepts the offer unconditionally. With a counter-offer, the offeree accepts the offer but seeks to change it, perhaps by changing the price, the specification of the goods or services to be provided, or other terms. The offeree thus becomes the offeror, and the original offeror becomes the offeree and has to decide whether to accept this counter-offer.

A common difficulty arises where one party offers goods or services on its **standard terms of supply**, and the other party then orders them but on its **standard terms of purchase**. In this situation it may be very difficult to determine whether agreement has been reached and if so on which set of terms.

Complex rules govern when acceptance takes place, particularly if it is undertaken by post.

18.6.1.3
Certainty

An offer and acceptance give rise to a contract only if there is sufficient **certainty** as to what has been agreed. If key terms are not agreed—who the parties are, what is to be provided, when it is to be provided, what is to be paid or given in return—there is generally no contract, although in some cases uncertainty may be resolved by looking at normal usage or custom in that trade or occupation.

18.6.1.4
Conditional contracts

Although the acceptance must be unconditional, the offer may make clear that the contract comes into being only if certain conditions are met. The contract may be conditional on an objective event occurring, for example a charity agreeing to provide services *when it is able to purchase a property in the area*, or may be dependent on more subjective conditions, for example an offer of employment *subject to receipt of references satisfactory to the employer*.

Even where the words are clear, it may be unclear whether the condition being met is simply the formal confirmation of a contract already in existence, or whether no contract is in existence until the condition is met. In the examples above, for example:

- the contract to provide services is in place, but does not come into effect until the charity purchases a suitable property;
- the contract of employment is not created until satisfactory references are received—but if the employer allows the person to start work before this, the courts are likely to consider that a contract of employment is in place [see **26.3.1**].

18.6.1.5
Consideration

A contract is created only if **consideration**—goods, services, money or something else of material value—is given in exchange for what is offered. Consideration may be something of value to the recipient, but can also be something which causes the giver to suffer a detriment.

Some key points relevant to consideration are:

- it need not be given immediately, so a promise to do or provide something in future is valid consideration;
- something given in the past, even five minutes ago, cannot be used as consideration for a contract which is being entered into now;
- the amount of the consideration does not make any difference, so a contract may be created by agreeing to pay a nominal amount such as a peppercorn or £1 in return for some very substantial benefit, or by paying 'pocket money' to a volunteer [see **35.3**];
- the consideration must come from the other party or parties to the contract, so consideration from a third party cannot support a contract between the other two parties. But contracts may involve more than two parties if each provides something to the others, and in some situations a third party can sue on a contract he or she is not party to [see **18.6.5**].

18.6.1.6
Contractual intention

Even where an agreement is made and there is consideration, the courts will not enforce it as a contract unless it is clear, or can be implied (assumed) from the circumstances, that the parties intended the agreement to be a binding contract.

The courts virtually always imply that arrangements of a business nature, where one party is paid to provide goods or services to another, are intended to be legally binding.

Agreements which might not be enforced by the courts include:

* where there is a clearly expressed intention for the agreement not to be enforceable, for example where the parties have agreed that it is **binding in honour only**;

* family or social agreements, because the parties do not generally intend to create a legal relationship (but if they make clear that they do intend this, the agreement will be enforceable);

* **subject to contract** agreements, because the parties have made clear that they do not consider that the agreement they have so far reached is yet a contract;

* **letters of intent**, where one party or both has said they intend to enter into a contract, but have not yet agreed the contract;

* where the maker of the agreement merely states its current policy or intentions, effectively reserving the right to change its intention.

If goods, services or money have already been provided by one party and accepted by the other, a court might well enforce subject to contract agreements, letters of intent and similar pre-agreements as a contract.

Other agreements which might not be enforced by the courts include:

* where the agreement gives one party complete freedom to vary the terms, because this would be an **unfair contract** [see **18.7.5**];

* **collective agreements** [see **32.3.5**] between employers and employees or between employers and trade unions, which are presumed not to be legally binding unless expressly stated to the contrary.

18.6.2
Capacity to contract

For a contract to arise the parties must have **contractual capacity**, which means they must be legally capable of entering into a contract.

18.6.2.1
Minors

Generally contracts by a person under the age of 18 are valid. But if the contract is to purchase goods or services, the contract is enforceable in the courts only if it is for **necessaries**. This includes contracts for obvious necessities—shelter, food, clothing—as well as for services such as education, medical care and legal advice, and for any goods or services 'which are appropriate for that person'.

From the other side, a minor who enters into a contract of employment or to *provide* goods or services is bound by the contract if it is as a whole for his or her benefit (a **beneficial contract of employment**), but is not bound by a contract which is as a whole oppressive or unfair.

A contract with a minor which is not valid under the above provisions may be **voidable**. It binds both parties, but the minor can **repudiate** (disclaim) it before or within a reasonable time after reaching age 18.

If a contract is neither valid nor voidable the adult or other party will be bound, but the minor will not. However, the minor becomes bound if he or she ratifies (confirms) the contract after becoming 18.

To avoid the risk of an invalid or voidable contract, an organisation should not allow a minor to enter into a contract on its behalf.

18.6.2.2
Mental illness

A contract with a mentally ill person is voidable by that person if the other party knew of the person's condition when the contract was entered into. To void the contract, the mentally ill person would have to show that he or she did not understand the transaction.

The property of some mentally ill people is under the control of the court. In this case the person is not able to dispose of it.

Mental Health Act 1983 pt. VII

18.6.2.3
Drunkenness

If a person entering into a contract is so incapacitated by alcohol or other substances as to be incapable of understanding the transaction and the other party knows this, the contract is voidable by the person who was incapable. He or she can ratify it to make it binding.

18.6.3
Contracts by an organisation

Just as individuals must have capacity to contract, so must organisations. A voluntary organisation should contract only if:

* the contract is within its constitutional objects [see **5.4.2**];

* the organisation (as a company or industrial and provident society) or the governing body (in a trust or unincorporated association) has the power to enter into such a contract [see **5.4.3**]; *and*

* the individuals who negotiate, agree and/or sign the contract on behalf of the organisation are authorised to do so, either by the governing document, other agreed rules, their job description or a decision of the governing body or other appropriate body.

A person who enters into a contract which does not meet these criteria could be held liable to the organisation for the contract. The other party to the contract will generally be able to enforce the contract, either against the organisation or against the individual(s) who authorised or entered into it.

18.6.4
Joint and several liability

If two or more individuals or organisations together promise to do or pay something under a contract, their liability may be joint, or joint and several.

Normally if two parties make a promise that they will together deliver money, goods or a service to someone else, the liability is **joint**. Joint contracted parties make only one promise binding all of them, and each is liable only for its share of the total.

If the liability is to be **joint and several** this must be explicit within the contract. The multiple parties make one promise binding all of them, and each also makes a separate promise binding her or him alone. This does not entitle the person receiving the promise to obtain more than was originally promised by all together, but that person may seek to obtain it from any one (or more) of the parties.

Where two or more individuals or organisations agree to provide goods or services on a joint and several basis, each is potentially liable to provide the full amount—even if they have an agreement between themselves that one will, for example, provide 75% and the other 25%.

In unincorporated organisations, the members of the governing body have joint and several liability for the organisation's debts and other contractual obligations [see **19.1.3**].

18.6.5
Privity of contract and third party rights

Until recently, only the parties to the contract gained rights under the contract. If, for example, a contract between two parties specified that goods or services were to be provided to a third party and this was not done, the contract had to be enforced by the contracting party rather than by the third party. This rule was known as **privity of contract**.

For contracts entered into since 11 May 2000, the rules on privity of contract have changed. Where a contract clearly intends a benefit for a third party, or where the contract explicitly gives a third party the right to enforce the contract, that person has the right to enforce the contract—unless the contract explicitly excludes this right.

Contracts (Rights of Third Parties) Act 1999

An example is where a care organisation enters into a contract with the local authority to provide services to named individuals, or to a class (group) of individuals. If those services are not provided the local authority can sue the organisation under the contract, and the individual could sue the organisation for failure to provide services to which he or she was contractually entitled. Other examples would be a contract between a charity's trading company and a commercial participator, under which the parties agree to raise funds for the charity, or a lease between an organisation and a landlord, under which the organisation agrees not to cause a nuisance to other tenants.

Other exceptions to the basic rule on privity of contract include:

- if two organisations enter into a contract with one another as a result of a representation made by a third party, that third party may become liable even though they are not a party to the contract (this is referred to as a **collateral contract**);

- third parties can very occasionally use trust law to obtain a benefit intended for them under a contract.

**18.6.6
Contract
documentation**

The vast majority of contracts do not have to be in writing. Statute law creates a limited number of exceptions:

- some consumer credit agreements are not enforceable unless certain formalities are complied with;   *Consumer Credit Act 1974*

- contracts for the sale of an interest in land must generally be in writing;

- guarantees, marine insurance and certain other agreements are not enforced by the courts unless there is written evidence of a contract.

Employers are obliged to provide a written **statement of employment particulars** to virtually all employees [see **23.5**], but a contract of employment may exist even if nothing is put into writing [see **23.2**].

**18.7
CONTRACT TERMS**

A vast body of contract law exists in relation to the terms of contracts. Where the terms are unusual or problematic or there is a dispute between the parties, it is important to take legal advice.

**18.7.1
Terms agreed
verbally**

In a dispute about a **verbal contract**, the court will look at what the expressed words meant. If the agreement has been put in writing the court will generally look at **verbal evidence** only if the written terms do not cover everything that was agreed verbally. If they cover everything but are (or are alleged to be) at variance with what was agreed verbally, the courts will not generally look at any verbal agreements. Organisations which receive assurances prior to signing a written contract should therefore ensure those promises are explicit in the contract.

**18.7.2
Terms implied by
the court**

Detailed rules govern how the courts ascertain terms of a disputed contract. In limited circumstances, terms omitted from a contract may be **implied** into it. One way this is done is by applying the **officious bystander test**. The court imagines an officious bystander overhearing the contract being made. If such a bystander were asked 'Would X be a term of this contract?' and would reply 'Yes, of course', the court will imply the term into the contract.

**18.7.2.1
Officious bystander test**

**18.7.2.2
Conduct**

Terms may also be implied into a contract because of the conduct of the parties in similar contracts or arising from custom and practice.

**18.7.2.3
Duty to cooperate**

In cases involving standard computer systems, the purchaser and supplier have an implied **duty to cooperate** The means that the purchaser should clearly state its needs, the supplier should be clear if these needs cannot or might not be able to be met and should inform the purchaser of suitable alternatives, and the purchaser should be willing to adapt working practices to the new system.

Anglo Group plc v Winther Brown & Co Ltd [2001] SJ 89

**18.7.3
Terms implied by
statute**

The original stance of the law on contracts was *caveat emptor*—'let the buyer beware'. It was up to buyers to inspect the goods or to specify in detail what they required. The seller had no duty to disclose any fault.

Purchasers now have some protection under statute, particularly where they are **consumers** (individuals who are acting for purposes outside of business). Consumer contracts for goods, for example, impliedly include the following terms, unless they are explicitly and lawfully excluded [see **18.7.5**]:

- the vendor owns the goods;
- goods sold by description or sample will correspond with the description or sample; *and*
- where the goods are sold in the course of business, they are of a satisfactory quality. *Sale of Goods Act 1979 ss.12-15*

Similar terms are implied in hire purchase agreements and in contracts for the supply of services. *Supply of Goods and Services Act 1982; Supply of Goods (Supplied Terms) Act 1973 ss.8-11*

18.7.3.1 Distance contracts

Where a contract for goods or services is agreed without face-to-face contact (by telephone, internet, post, catalogues, email, fax or media advertising) the customer must be made fully aware of key contractual issues, including the supplier's name, description of the goods or services, price inclusive of VAT, any delivery costs, the costs (if any) of using the distance communication, arrangements for payment, the period for which the offer or price is valid, and the minimum length of any contract. The information must be given verbally, or must be included in catalogues, websites, advertisements or similar material.

If not given in writing these details must be confirmed 'in good time' in writing or other 'durable medium'. At the time of writing (early 2001) it appeared likely that email would be accepted as a durable medium. *Consumer Protection (Distance Selling) Regulations 2000 [SI 2000/2334]*

Unless agreed otherwise, the goods or services must be delivered within 30 days. The consumer in most cases has the right to cancel the distance contract within seven days, and any advance payment must be returned within 30 days.

18.7.3.2 Interest on late payments

Small businesses (including voluntary organisations) with 50 or fewer employees have a right to charge interest on amounts due on contracts made with large businesses (over 50 full-time employees) and public sector bodies since 1 November 1998, and contracts made with small businesses since 1 November 2000. This is a statutory right, and does not need to be explicitly included in the contract. The maximum that can be charged under these provisions is the Bank of England base rate plus 8%. *Late Payment of Commercial Debts (Interest) Act 1998*

Interest can be charged from the payment date specified in the contract or, if no date is specified, from 30 days after invoice date or delivery of the goods or services, whichever is later.

At the time of writing (early 2001) the government had announced its intention to allow large businesses and the public sector to charge interest on contracts entered into after 1 November 2002.

18.7.4 Standard contracts

A **standard contract** is one whose terms apply to all of the provider's dealings of that nature, rather than being individually negotiated with the purchaser of the goods or services [see **18.8.1**].

The basic rule is that if a party agrees to a contract they are bound by all the terms even if they did not fully understand them, or if they read them and thought they meant something else. These terms may have been set out in a document they signed, may have been displayed on the wall of premises where they bought the goods or may simply have been referred to as being available for inspection elsewhere. They may also be implied on the basis that all the prior contracts were subject to them, and while they were not specifically referred to in this case it is to be implied that they applied here.

18.7.5 Unfair terms and exclusions

Providers of goods or services often seek to protect themselves by drawing up detailed standard terms which exclude certain liabilities. But both the courts and statute law are increasingly hostile to unfair terms and exclusions in standard contracts, particularly where the purchaser is a consumer [see **18.7.3** for definition]. For example:

- the court strictly interprets clauses in the agreement against the person who drew up the agreement and will give the narrowest application, so any doubt will be resolved in favour of the other party;

- liability for negligently causing death or injury cannot be excluded [see **19.6.6**];   *Unfair Contract Terms Act 1977 s.2(1)*

- liability cannot be excluded for loss or damage to a consumer arising from goods used by a consumer and due to negligence in manufacture or distribution;   *s.5(1)*

- guarantees cannot be used to restrict consumers' rights;   *ss.5-7*

- terms implied by statute [see **18.7.3**] cannot be excluded for consumers, and may only be excluded in other contracts if it is reasonable;
  ss.6(3), 7

- other clauses in written standard terms or where the purchaser is a consumer are allowed only if they are reasonable;   *s.3*

- liability for breach of the contract cannot be excluded;   *s.3(2)(a)*

- entitlement to perform the contract in a substantially different way from that originally agreed is not binding even if it is included in written standard terms.   *s.3(2)(b)*

The implications for voluntary organisations are:

- if the organisation provides goods or services to consumers in the course of a business and its standard terms are unfair, the consumer is not bound by the unfair terms;

- the rules apply, but to a considerably lesser extent, where the organisation is not acting in the course of a business when it makes the contract;

- in certain circumstances the members of the governing body of a trust or unincorporated association might be consumers and be protected if they enter into a contract which includes unfair terms.

Unfair Terms in Consumer Contracts Regulations 1999 [SI 1999/2083]

18.7.6
Misrepresentation

If an individual or organisation enters into a contract because of a **representation** (statement about the goods, services or terms of the contract) which has been made to them, whether verbally or in writing, and that representation turns out to be wrong, the purchaser has considerable common law rights.

The court may relieve the purchaser from the obligation to complete the contract or may award damages to the purchaser, but only if the representation was unambiguous and material to the contract, and the purchaser relied on it. Certain representations, such as non-specific sales talk designed to encourage purchase, or statements of law or opinion, do not generally give rise to a right to relief from the contract.

If a misrepresentation was made the purchaser may claim damages or rescind the contract [see **18.12.2** and **18.11.5**]. Misrepresentation may also give rise to rights outside the contractual relationship through the law of tort [see **19.5**].

Where a contract exists, the person who made a misrepresentation is always assumed to be liable. This applies even if the misrepresentation is not made fraudulently, unless they can prove they had reasonable grounds to believe and did believe that the facts represented were true.

Misrepresentation Act 1967 s.2(1)

18.7.7
Disclosure of information

Purchasers are expected to be aware of what they are purchasing, so there is generally no duty to tell them that there is a defect in the goods or a problem with the services. However, a supplier must disclose:

- where goods have a hidden or latent defect which later causes injury;

- where a representation is technically true, but misleading;

- generally, where a representation has been made but then circumstances change and it is rendered untrue;

- where there is a special relationship between the parties, for example where one relies on the other's expertise such as an organisation relying on their bank manager's financial advice;

  Hedley Burn and Co Ltd v Heller Partners Limited [1964] AC 465

- where there is a fiduciary relationship, for example where one party may have a position of undue influence over another [see **18.7.8.4**].

For certain contracts, such as contracts of insurance, there is a positive duty on both or all parties to disclose all information that might be of importance [see **20.3.4**].

18.7.8
Unenforceable contracts

Some agreements may meet all the criteria for being contracts, but will not be enforced by the courts. These include contracts tainted by illegality or where improper pressure has been applied.

18.7.8.1
Illegality

The courts will generally not enforce contracts:

- to commit a crime or deliberately to commit a civil wrong such as trespass or assault;

- where goods sold are to be used for an illegal purpose; *or*

- to indemnify others against liability for unlawful acts, for example a contract to pay an employee's fine if the employee is caught speeding while delivering for the organisation.

Contracts to commit a civil wrong where neither party realised that the wrong was being done are enforceable.

18.7.8.2
Contracts contrary to public policy

Contracts considered to be contrary to public policy will not be enforced by the courts, for example contracts which promote sexual immorality, interfere with the course of justice or seek to deprive the courts of jurisdiction which they would otherwise have, or are in **restraint of trade**. A contract in restraint of trade includes covenants (promises) by employees that they will not compete with their employer after they leave a job. A covenant such as this is enforceable only insofar as it is reasonable [see **24.41**].

18.7.8.3
Contracts that damage competition

Agreements that might distort competition—for example two organisations agreeing not to compete for local authority contracts—may be unlawful and therefore unenforceable. This area of law is extremely complex and advice must be sought before entering into any non-competition arrangement. Basic information is available from the Office of Fair Trading [see end of chapter].   *Competition Act 1998*

18.7.8.4
Duress and undue influence

Applying pressure to a person to enter into a contract may render the contract invalid. This may be threats of physical violence or any other threat which is legally wrong. Difficult issues arise as to the boundary between **duress** and normal commercial pressure.

Undue influence short of duress may also invalidate a contract, particularly where a special relationship exists between the parties. Such relationships will be implied in situations such as parent/child, doctor/patient, solicitor/client, and trustee/beneficiary. It may be implied in other situations, such as husband/wife fellow committee members.

18.8
CONTRACTS TO PURCHASE GOODS OR SERVICES

Voluntary organisations should seek to ensure that all contracts for goods and services they purchase are on terms which are advantageous to them. Many suppliers, if pressed, are prepared to offer a discount, especially to regular customers or charities. For the clauses which might be included in a contract to purchase services, see **34.3.1**.

18.8.1
Creating standard terms of purchase

An organisation which regularly purchases goods or services in commercial quantities should consider whether to develop its own terms of purchase. Such terms are incorporated into its standard contract and become part of the agreement with each supplier.

If the supplier has its own terms considerable confusion may arise as to whose terms apply, so these matters should be clarified at an early stage. If possible the organisation should get the supplier to sign and return a copy of the organisation's conditions to indicate their agreement to them. If there is a regular relationship it may not be necessary to do this on each occasion a supply is purchased.

18.8.2
Finance and hire purchase agreements

Hire purchase or finance agreements are often particularly complex and onerous. Faced with a complex agreement an organisation may:

- sign it without reading it (potentially disastrous);

- obtain professional advice (appropriate where substantial sums are involved, for example when commissioning software, acquiring substantial amounts of equipment or undertaking building works);

- carefully consider the terms and seek to negotiate improvements where necessary (possibly not easy, if the terms are written in technical language and/or the supplier is unwilling to negotiate); or

- consider going to another supplier who provides terms written in straightforward language and/or less onerous terms.

The legislative protection available in these cases is largely designed to assist individual consumers [see **18.7.5**], and may not cover voluntary organisations.

18.8.2.1
Advice on contracts

Organisations frequently seek advice on contract terms from the salesperson they are dealing with, which may be unwise. Standard terms often exclude any representations which are not actually written into the contract, and some go even further and provide that the salesperson making the representation should be treated as the agent of the purchaser and not the agent of the seller. If advice is needed, it should be sought from the local authority's consumer rights unit, an independent consumer rights organisation, or a solicitor.

18.8.2.2
Equipment contracts

Voluntary organisations may suffer very considerably from failure to take complex agreements seriously, particularly finance agreements for equipment such as photocopiers. Key problem include:

- allowing junior staff to sign agreements without appropriate advice;

- failing to ensure all the blanks are correctly filled in;

- entering into agreements for an unduly long period compared with the likely life of the equipment;

- failing to understand the implications and true costs of complex charging arrangements;

- signing a 'receipt' for replacement equipment without realising it is actually a new finance agreement;

- failing to understand that the contract cannot be terminated without incurring large costs;

- failing to understand that arrangements allowing purchase of equipment at a later date generally do not reduce total liability;

- failing to realise that termination may require positive steps on their part, and that inaction may trigger further periods of liability.

The Finance and Leasing Association [see end of chapter] can provide guidance.

18.8.3
Large-scale purchases

An order with a value of more than £134,800 (as at 1/4/01) for certain services, or more than £3,370,000 for building or other works, may be a **public procurement** and have to be openly advertised throughout the EU [see **48.5.2**]. The rules apply where:

- the organisation receives more than 50% of its funding from a purchasing authority (central government, a local authority or a government agency) or from the national lottery; and

- more than 50% of the organisation's governing body is appointed by the government, a government agency, local authorities etc.

The Office of Government Commerce [see end of chapter] can advise.

18.9 CONTRACTS TO SUPPLY GOODS OR SERVICES

A voluntary organisation may be involved in contracts for the supply of goods or services to a wide variety of parties, including individuals, other voluntary organisations, businesses and major institutional purchasers such as local authorities [see **chapter 48** for more about contracts for the provision of charitable and similar services].

A contract is not created if the organisation is supplying goods or services to a department, branch, project or other unit which is actually part of itself, rather than being autonomous [see **9.2** for information on when branches etc are and are not autonomous]. This is because both parts of the organisation are under the control of the same governing body, which could not enforce a contract against itself. Internal arrangements for one unit to purchase from another are often called **service agreements**, to distinguish them from contracts. But the term 'service agreement' is used in many other ways, and often refers to contracts [see, for example, **48.1.3**].

A contract is unlikely to exist if goods or services are being provided entirely free, because in order for a contract to exist there must be payment or some other consideration [see **18.6.1.5**] given in return for the goods or services. So an organisation might have a contract with a local authority to provide services to clients, but if the client does not pay or provide other consideration there is no contract with the client. The client may, however, be able to enforce the contract [see **18.6.5**].

Where the organisation is involved in substantial or routine provision of goods or services, thought should be given to whether standard terms should be developed. Legal advice should be sought before seeking to draw up standard terms.

18.10 TRANSFERRING OR CHANGING A CONTRACT

18.10.1 Transferring a contract

Assignment means transferring the benefit of a contract to someone who was not a party to the original contract, for example when an organisation converts to a company [see **6.6.1**] or merges [see **9.9**], and passes the benefit of a contract to the successor organisation. Assignment may take place under a contract or by deed. It does not normally require the consent of the other party, who has the burden of the contract.

A transfer of the burden of the contract is called **novation**. This requires the person who is owed the obligation or the money to enter into a new three-party contract, accepting that the obligation will be discharged by the new third party. The person who has the benefit of the contract is not obliged to accept this new arrangement, in which case the original contract remains in place.

Certain contractual rights are not assignable. These include:

- contracts of employment, unless they are transferred as part of a transfer of an undertaking [see **26.4**] or specifically allow transfer to another employer;
- where assignment is prohibited by provisions within the contract;
- assignment prevented by statute, such as pension rights.

18.10.2 Varying a contract

A contract may be varied (changed):

- where there is accord and satisfaction [see below];
- by deed [see **18.3**], in which case no consideration is needed;
- where estoppel applies [see **18.10.2.2**]. In this situation no consideration is needed but the variation must be negative only (an agreement *not* to enforce an existing obligation).

18.10.2.1
Accord and satisfaction

A variation other than by deed or estoppel must involve **accord** (agreement) and **satisfaction** (consideration). Some new consideration [see **18.6.1.5**], however nominal, will be needed.

If neither party has yet started its part of the contract, consideration is provided by mutual release. But if one or both parties have started performing their part of the contract, additional consideration must be provided. If an existing staff member, for example, agrees to accept a restrictive covenant [see **24.41**] in her or his contract of employment, the agreement is not binding unless the employer provides a payment or other consideration when the staff member agrees the change.

18.10.2.2
Estoppel

Estoppel occurs when one party to a contract (A) agrees not to enforce a contract condition in a way that benefits party B and disadvantages party A, but without A receiving any consideration from B. If party A then tries to enforce the original contract, they will be **estopped** (prevented) from enforcing it.

An example is a landlord (party A) with a right to evict a tenant (B) for failure to repair. Instead of evicting, the landlord tries to get the tenant to surrender (give up) the lease. The delay benefits the tenant (who is saved from eviction during the negotiations) and disadvantages the landlord (who doesn't get back the property). If these negotiations break down, the landlord is estopped from immediately forfeiting (ending) the lease [see **58.4.2**], because the tenant has been led to believe this action would not be taken. The landlord must give the tenant a reasonable time thereafter to repair, before the landlord is again able to forfeit. In some cases A may never be able to enforce its original rights.

18.11
ENDING
CONTRACTUAL
OBLIGATIONS

The obligations which are created when a contract comes into existence continue to bind the parties until:

- the contract is ended by performance, or discharged by agreement, breach, frustration or rescission [see below];
- it is repudiated by an individual who did not have capacity to contract [see **18.6.2**]
- it ceases to be enforceable because too much time has passed [see **18.12.9**]; *or*
- the obligation does not have to be carried out, as it has been estopped [see **18.10.2.2**].

18.11.1
Performance

The vast majority of contracts end by **performance**: fulfilling the terms of the contract by one party providing the required goods or services and the other paying for them.

18.11.2
Discharge by
agreement

If the contract is not fulfilled the parties may agree that it is **discharged** (completed by something less than that was originally agreed). This may involve an agreement:

- to end the contract completely;
- to end it and replace it with a new contract; *or*
- to vary (change) the existing contract [see **18.10.2**].

The discharge must involve accord and satisfaction [see **18.10.2.1**] unless it is done under a deed or estoppel [see **18.10.2.2**].

18.11.2.1
Forbearance

If the change in the arrangements is not formalised by a deed or by accord and satisfaction, the party to whom a right is owed may simply choose not to enforce the right. Generally such **forbearance** does not legally discharge the contract, and the party is able to change its mind and enforce its right unless it is estopped.

18.11.3
Frustration

The parties may be released from their obligations under a contract if an unforeseeable event makes its fulfilment illegal or impossible. Examples include:

- destruction of the subject matter of the contract, for example a work of art which was to have been exhibited being destroyed in a fire;
- the death or incapacity of an individual due to provide services;
- the means of performing the contract can no longer be undertaken, for example because of war or a disaster;
- performance becomes illegal because of a change in the law.

Sums due but not paid cease to become due, and sums already paid are recoverable. But the court may allow a party who has incurred costs or expenses to recover these or obtain sums in respect of them.

Law Reform (Frustration of Contracts) Act 1943 s.1

18.11.4
Force majeure

The court may or may not find that an event such as a strike, riot, explosion or hurricane frustrates a contract. Many contracts therefore include a *force majeure* clause which allows the contract not to be fulfilled if a specified event occurs.

18.11.5
Rescission

A contract based on a misrepresentation [see **18.7.6**] may be **rescinded** (set aside) by the party who was misled or by the court. **Rescission** is also possible for certain unfair contracts, or where a fundamental term has been breached [see below].

18.11.6
Discharge by breach

In certain circumstances where there has been a breach of contract [see **18.12**], the wronged party may choose to treat the contract as **discharged** (ended) by the breach. Unless otherwise agreed, the wronged party is entitled to damages [see **18.12.2**].

18.11.6.1
Repudiation

Repudiation occurs when one party shows an intention no longer to be bound by the contract, for example where an employer treats an employee so badly that the employee is entitled to believe that the employer has repudiated the contract [see **30.4.8**]. It is generally very difficult to ascertain whether one breach is enough to constitute repudiation, and there is considerable case law on the subject.

18.11.6.2
Condition precedent

In some contracts, one party must do something before the other party has any liability. Thus if one party agrees to pay for a service monthly in arrears, the liability to pay does not arise until that service has been received for a month. If less than a month of service is provided the **condition precedent** has not been met and no liability will arise.

18.11.6.3
Breach of
fundamental term

The law recognises two types of contractual terms: **conditions**, which are key terms, and **warranties**, which are minor terms. The breach of a warranty generally only gives the injured party a right to monetary compensation (**damages**). Breach of a condition gives the right to **rescind** (terminate) the contract as well as the right to damages.

Distinguishing between conditions and warranties can be difficult and depends on each particular contract.

18.11.6.4
Late delivery

The legal phrase **time is not of the essence** means that generally the timing of performance under a contract is not critical and is not treated as fundamental. Therefore late delivery of a service or goods will not generally in itself constitute a failure to perform a contract.

Where the contract makes clear that time is to be **of the essence**, failure to perform on time may constitute a breach of the contract, thus giving the injured party rights either for breach of a condition or for breach of a warranty.

Where there is no clear indication and there is a delay, the injured party may be able to make time of the essence by warning the defaulting party that if performance is not achieved within a reasonable time, they will take action.

18.12 REMEDIES FOR BREACH OF CONTRACT

Non-performance means not doing what is required under a contract. **Defective performance** means providing what is required, but not to the required timing, quantity, quality or standard. Non-performance or defective performance generally constitutes a **breach of contract**.

All breaches of contract, unless otherwise agreed, entitle the wronged party to damages [see **18.12.2**]. In addition, some breaches entitle the wronged party to treat the contract as discharged by the breach [see **18.11.6**].

A breach of contract is a civil wrong, entitling action to be taken in the civil courts. In limited circumstances it may also be a criminal offence, for example harassing a residential tenant who has a contractual right to quiet enjoyment.

Complex rules govern rights in breach of contract cases. Legal advice will be required if there is any likelihood that a contractual dispute will end up before the courts.

18.12.1 Alternatives to court action

Methods other than court proceedings should always be considered when there is a contractual problem. Depending on the circumstances, these may include:

- the wronged party agreeing to **discharge** the contract by accepting the defective performance [see **18.11.2**];
- forfeiting any deposit;
- appealing to a higher level in the other party's organisation or firm;
- using mediation or arbitration to resolve the dispute [see **61.2**];
- involving the other party's key customers or clients;
- involving the professional or trade association of the supplier or other contracting party;
- involving the local authority's consumer protection department;
- involving the media or local or national politicians;
- where one exists, involving the ombudsman for that type of work.

Practical solutions are usually the best. A workable solution at an early stage in a dispute may well be better than a slightly better solution after many weeks or months of discussions, letters, meetings and disagreements. A careful analysis of whether a contract dispute is worth pursuing may prevent much wasted time and energy.

18.12.2 Damages

A breach of a legally enforceable contract always gives rise to a right to **damages**, unless the agreement specifically excludes this right. To recover damages the wronged party must show that some sort of loss occurred, and the loss arose directly from the breach of the contract.

The purpose of damages is to put the wronged party, insofar as possible, in the position it would have been in if the contract had been performed. In most contract cases damages are **compensation**, rather than a penalty. **Punitive damages** or **exemplary damages** may be awarded in some court cases [see **61.4.7**], but generally not in contract.

Complex rules govern the level of damages. If the wronged party has suffered real financial loss, damages may be substantial. If the breach involves no financial loss they may be nominal, typically £1.

18.12.2.1 General damages

General damages are those which both parties could reasonably have anticipated would occur if either party had failed to honour their part of the contract.

In the classic case, a miller gave a carrier a broken mill shaft to be delivered for repair. The carrier was slow, and because the miller did not have a spare shaft he was unable to work during the period of delay. The carrier did not know that the miller did not have a spare, and so could not have anticipated that the miller would not be able to work. The carrier was therefore held to be liable only for damages for being slow, not for the additional loss of profit suffered by the miller.

Hadley v Baxendale [1854] 9 Ex 341

If the carrier had been told of the full situation, the miller's loss of earnings would have been reasonably foreseeable, and the carrier would have been liable for general damages in respect of them.

18.12.2.2
Loss partly caused by third party

If a loss results partly from a breach and partly from the acts of a third party, the party to the contract may still be liable if the act of that third party was reasonably foreseeable.

18.12.2.3
Special damages

Special damages are items of direct loss incurred by the wronged party. If, for example, a badly installed tank bursts, the purchaser will be entitled to general damages as assessed by the court to compensate for the inconvenience. If the purchaser had to hire a dehumidifier and replace all the carpets, those costs would be the special damages.

18.12.2.4
Mitigation

Where there is a breach of contract the wronged party cannot sit still and allow damages to build up. They must take steps to try to **mitigate** (minimise) the loss, and avoid any steps which might increase the loss.

An employee who is alleging wrongful dismissal, for example, has an obligation to look for a new job while waiting for the tribunal to determine whether the dismissal was indeed in breach of contract and therefore wrongful [see **33.4.2**]. If the employee does not take these steps, any eventual damages will be reduced. Similarly a community centre which is suing a manufacturer for installing a faulty boiler must take steps to minimise the loss caused by the malfunctioning boiler, even if this involves having it repaired or replaced.

18.12.2.5
Damages for injured feelings or reputation

The courts have for a long time resisted awarding damages for hurt feelings or damaged reputations arising from breach of contract. However in certain limited circumstances such awards may be made.

18.12.3
Liquidated damages and penalties

A contract may contain a clause providing that late delivery will require the defaulting party to make a fixed payment. A fixed payment which is based on a genuine estimate of the amount of loss is referred to as **liquidated damages**, and is enforceable.

Although such a clause is often colloquially called a **penalty clause**, the courts will not enforce a pre-quantified payment if it is a penalty whose object is to force performance by making the party in default pay an extravagantly large sum.

18.12.4
Deposits and part payments

A **deposit** is a sum paid by a purchaser as a guarantee that he or she will fulfil the contract by paying the remaining amount. A purchaser who defaults by not paying the remaining amount is generally unable to recover the deposit, unless the forfeited deposit is so large as to amount to a penalty [see above].

Where the contract is with a consumer [see **18.7.3**] rather than a business the consumer has even stronger protection against unfair penalties or forfeiture of deposit.

Unfair Terms in Consumer Contracts Regulations 1999 [SI 1999/2083]

Part payment is not made as a guarantee, but is simply a partial payment of the purchase price. A purchaser who defaults may recover the amount paid, minus any damages awarded to the person to whom the part payment was made.

18.12.5
Restitution

Where one party pays money for goods or a service and there is a total failure to provide what has been purchased, the court will order the payment to be returned. This is called **restitution**.

Where there is only a partial failure, for example a builder who only half finishes a job, there is no right to restitution. The wronged party will, however, have a right to claim damages.

18.12.6
Specific
performance

Specific performance is an order from the court that the party in breach must fulfil its obligations under the contract. The court will generally make this award only if damages are an insufficient remedy. Specific performance is unlikely to be awarded where:

- the goods or service are readily available elsewhere, so there is no particular need for them to be provided under this contract;

- specific performance would give rise to unfairness, for example where the purchaser paid only a nominal price;

- the wronged party has acted in an unfair way, but perhaps short of giving rise to any counterclaim by the party in breach;

- specific performance is impossible, for example where the vendor does not own the goods which they failed to deliver;

- the contract requires a service to be provided personally [see **22.1**], for example under a contract of employment;

- specific performance would require constant supervision by the court.

Building contracts are not generally specifically enforced.

18.12.7
Injunctions and
stop now orders

An **injunction** is a negative or **restraining** order. Where an injunction is to prevent future breaches, the court is generally willing to grant it. If it relates to a past act, for example to undo something already done by the defaulting party, the court will look at the balance of convenience. The injunction is unlikely to be granted if the disadvantage suffered by the party in breach, in having to undo the act, heavily outweighs the advantage to be gained by the wronged party.

From 1 June 2001, consumers and consumer protection bodies can apply to the court for a **stop now order**, a new form of injunction covering the sale of goods, consumer contracts, distance selling, guarantees, misleading advertising, unfair contract terms and similar matters.

Stop Now Orders (EC Directive) Regulations 2001 [SI 2001/1422]

18.12.8
Declaration

The parties to a contract may seek a **declaration** from the court, for example to clarify a disputed contractual term.

18.12.9
Extinction of
remedies

The wronged party may delay so long in bringing action for breach that its right to do so is extinguished. The rights contained within the contract itself are not lost, merely the right to bring a case in the courts to enforce those rights. The limitation period is three years for personal injury claims, six years for damages and other remedies arising from breach of contract, and 12 years if the contract was made under seal (as a deed) [see **18.3**]. Complex rules govern the date from which the start of the period runs. *Limitation Act 1980*

FOR FURTHER INFORMATION

Fair contracts, competition. Office of Fair Trading: 08457-22 44 99; www.oft.gov.uk

Equipment contracts. Finance & Leasing Association: 020-7836 6511; www.fla.org.uk

Public procurement contracts. Office of Government Commerce: 020-7211 1300; www.ogc.gov.uk

Chapter 19
ORGANISATIONAL AND
PERSONAL LIABILITY

19.1 NATURE OF LIABILITY

Liability means being held legally responsible for actions taken and for **defaults** (actions not taken). A corporate body, the members of a membership organisation, members of the governing body, employees, volunteers, agents (persons acting on behalf of an organisation) and persons saying they are acting on behalf of an organisation when they are not authorised to do so may all be held liable in various ways.

Most liabilities are not problematic. The people involved with an organisation ensure compliance with the law through training, information, supervision and access to appropriate advice. They know the organisation has financial obligations, and guard against problems by ensuring it has adequate funds to meet these as they fall due. They also know that a liability could arise if the organisation causes injury or loss, and guard against this by ensuring staff are properly trained and by taking out appropriate insurance.

Liability generally becomes an issue only if the organisation breaks the law, cannot pay what it owes, or faces a loss for which it is not insured. Few organisations ever get into such difficulty, and the likelihood of an individual facing personal liability is very small indeed. The prospect of liability is frightening, but needs to be kept in perspective.

19.1.1
Sources of liability

Liabilities might arise because a corporate body, a governing body, employees, volunteers or persons acting on behalf of the organisation or its governing body act:

- in breach of criminal law [see **19.2**];

- in breach of statutory duty [see **19.2**];

- in breach of covenants or other property rights or duties [see **56.7**];

- in breach of trust [see **19.3**], creating a liability to the organisation, its members, or third parties to whom a duty of trust or fiduciary duty is owed;

- in breach of contract [see **19.4.1**], creating a liability to the other party or parties or to third parties who benefit from the contract;

- in breach of duties in an insolvency [see **21.2.4**]; *or*

- in a way which causes a tort (a civil wrong against a person, such as negligence, libel or trespass) to be committed [see **19.5.1**].

Who is liable in any situation will depend on:

- whether the organisation is incorporated or unincorporated;

- who authorised an action or contract, and whether they were authorised to do so;

- who carried out the action or entered into the contract, and whether they were authorised to do so;

- who did not do something which they had a duty to do.

The question of liability is often very difficult to disentangle and will generally require legal advice.

19.1.2
Personal liability

The term **personal liability** is used here to mean situations where a member of the governing body, an employee or other individual associated with the organisation:

- has to use personal funds to meet the organisation's obligations;

- has to make good losses caused to the organisation because of his or her actions;

- has to repay to the organisation any personal profit from an unauthorised contract or transaction; *or*

- is held responsible in law for offences caused by or on behalf of the organisation.

Individuals held financially liable for the organisation's obligations may be entitled to be indemnified (repaid) by the organisation, the members of the governing body or the members of the organisation [see **19.6.7**]. In some situations a governing body member may apply to the court for relief from personal liability [see **19.2.5** and **19.3.5**].

19.1.2.1
Liability in companies and IPSs

Members of companies and industrial and provident societies have **limited liability**. The liability of the members of a company limited by guarantee is limited to the amount—usually £1—which they promise to contribute if the company is wound up with outstanding debts [see **21.5.3**]. In a company limited by shares or an IPS the liability of members is limited to the amount unpaid on the shares they hold.

All other liabilities rest with the company or IPS itself, or in some situations with the directors, the company secretary or senior employees. They have limited liability in most, but not all, situations [see **19.6.1.1**].

19.1.2.2
Liability in unincorporated associations and trusts

In unincorporated organisations liability in most situations rests with the members of the governing body, although in some situations members of the organisation who are not on the governing body (if there are any) could be liable. Where a charitable association or trust has incorporated its governing body [see **1.4**] the members of the governing body still have personal liability, rather than limited liability.

19.1.3
Joint and several liability

Where the members of an organisation or its governing body are held liable for the organisation's financial obligations, the liability is **joint and several** [see **18.6.4**]. This means that each could be held liable for all or any part of the obligation.

If two or more persons are held liable for the same loss or damage arising from tort [see **19.5.1**] or breach of contract [see **19.4.1**], but only some of them are sued, those who are sued are entitled to recover a contribution from the other liable persons. The court decides what each person's contribution should be, based on their responsibility for the loss or damage. *Civil Liability (Contribution) Act 1978 ss.1, 2*

19.1.4
Liability for the acts of others

The general rule of liability is that persons are liable for their own acts. But there are many situations where a person might be held liable instead of, or in addition to, the person who committed the act:

- if a person (an **agent**) who is authorised to act on behalf of someone else (the **principal**) enters into a contract on behalf of the principal, the principal is liable for the contract [see **18.5.5**];

- if an employee is negligent or commits another tort the employee is liable, but the employer has **vicarious liability** and may also be held liable for the acts of the employee [see **19.5.3**];

- trustees may be held liable for losses caused by persons acting on their behalf but not properly supervised by them [see **13.5.2**].

Statute law frequently makes one party liable for the acts of another. Employers, for example, are liable for unlawful race, sex or disability discrimination by their employees, even if they did not know about it, unless they can show that they took reasonable steps to prevent such discrimination [see **25.2.3**]. This is a civil matter. Statute law may also impose criminal liability on a person who authorised or allowed a criminal act, even if someone else actually committed the act.

19.1.4.1
Liability for acts of 'rogue trustees'

In general governing body members are not liable for unauthorised acts by other members of the governing body. However an employment tribunal found that a local authority, as an employer, was liable for the unauthorised acts of a councillor which led to an employee resigning and claiming constructive dismissal [see **30.4.8**]. The case illustrates the importance of being absolutely clear about who is authorised to speak for, make decisions or take action on behalf of the organisation and its governing body, and ensuring they do not overstep their authority.

19.1.5
Risk assessment and management

The trustees of charities with income over £100,000, or with lower income which prepare accrual accounts [see **50.2.10**], must confirm in the notes to the accounts that they have considered major risks to the charity and have taken steps to mitigate (reduce) those risks [see **49.1**]. The risk assessment must look not only at financial risks, but at the full range of risks outlined in this chapter.

19.2
CRIMINAL OFFENCES AND BREACH OF STATUTORY DUTY

Liability for criminal offences arises from offences against persons, property or the public interest. Action is generally brought by the state, rather than by individuals, and the person responsible may be fined or imprisoned.

19.2.1
What they are

The state also imposes many **statutory duties**, for example in relation to duties to employees [see **23.4**], health and safety [**chapter 36**], in connection with the supply of food and drink [**43.2**], and use of land [**59.5**]. Many statutory duties—such as the duty to send in company accounts and reports on time, or to put a charity's status on all its financial documents—are offences where failure to act (**default**) may be punishable by fines or in some cases imprisonment. Most people do not think of such acts as 'criminal' but the fact that they are punishable by the state means they are criminal offences.

Many other statutory duties can be enforced by the courts, but default is not in itself punishable. Examples include the duty to register a charity or to provide itemised pay statements to employees. A person ordered by the court to put right the default who does not do so may be found to be in contempt of court. Contempt is a civil wrong but may be punished by a fine or imprisonment.

19.2.2
Reducing the risk of liability

To reduce the risk of statutory duties not being fulfilled or offences taking place, members of the governing body should:

- ensure there are people (governing body members, employees, volunteers, professional advisors) who are aware of the full range of the organisation's legal obligations;

- put proper procedures in place and ensure adequate monitoring of staff and others, especially those who have access to money, children, vulnerable adults or dangerous equipment or are in other situations where unlawful or dangerous acts are most likely to occur;

- ensure they receive proper financial reports clearly setting out the organisation's financial position so that they are not at risk, in a company or industrial and provident society, of continuing to operate while the organisation is, or is becoming, insolvent.

19.2.3
Who is liable

A person who commits a criminal act or breach of statutory duty is liable. The person may be a corporate body or a human person.

An employer has vicarious liability [see **19.5.3**] for a breach of statutory duty by an employee, and in some cases may have vicarious liability for criminal offences by employees committed in the course of work. A funding body could possibly be held liable for breach of health and safety law by an organisation it funds, if the funder has some form of control over the funded project or activity [see **36.2.2**].

19.2.3.1
Corporate body

Under common law, corporate bodies were not generally held liable for criminal acts, on the basis that they could not be hanged or imprisoned. Now it is increasingly common for corporate bodies to be fined for criminal acts, as well as for breaches of statutory duty by the organisation itself or by its governing body or its employees.

For example a corporate body can be convicted of corporate manslaughter, but only if it can be shown that one or more directors was directly implicated. If this can be shown, the company can be fined and the responsible director(s) can be imprisoned. In a case in 1999, two directors of a transport company were convicted of corporate manslaughter after one of their drivers caused a fatal crash. It was held that they knew, or should have known, that the driver often worked 60 hours or more without a proper break.

In 2000 the Home Office proposed a new offence, **corporate killing**, where death is caused by a serious management failure on the part of the corporate body—even if the directors are not directly implicated. Unincorporated bodies could also be charged with corporate killing.

19.2.3.2
Governing body

Members of a governing body are personally liable for their own criminal acts as individuals or as a body. They may also be held vicariously liable for acts committed by employees in the course of their work [see **19.5.3**], and may be held liable for acts by other members of the governing body if it can be shown that they authorised the action and/or that they were negligent in allowing it to take place.

Authorising or assisting a criminal act or a breach of statutory duty, or allowing premises to be used for a crime, may also be an offence. Particular care must be taken to ensure premises are not used for drug-related offences [see **59.5.3**].

In trusts and unincorporated associations, the members of the governing body are responsible for ensuring that statutory obligations are met.

In incorporated organisations it is the organisation itself which is responsible and is generally liable if obligations are not met, but governing body members may be held personally liable for some defaults of the organisation, such as:

- failure to operate PAYE [see **27.3.3**];
- failure to comply with health and safety legislation [see **chapter 36**] and other statutory duties;
- failure to comply with most Companies Acts or Industrial and Provident Societies Acts requirements;
- in charitable companies, failure to comply with some Charities Act requirements;
- allowing the organisation to continue operating when it is, or is inevitably going to become, insolvent, or deceiving creditors or others when a company is or is becoming insolvent [see **21.2.4**].

19.2.3.3
IPS directors

In industrial and provident societies, every offence committed under the Industrial and Provident Societies Act 1965 or the Friendly and Industrial and Provident Societies Act 1968 is considered to have been committed by any officer who under the governing document is responsible for fulfilling that duty. If no such officer is named in the governing document, every member of the governing body is considered liable unless it can be proved that he or she did not know the offence was being committed, or attempted to prevent it.

Industrial and Provident Societies Act 1965 s.62

19.2.3.4
Ordinary members

Ordinary members of a company or IPS (those who are not officers or governing body members) are not liable for criminal acts or breaches of statutory duty committed by the organisation, its governing body or other members unless they authorised the acts or took part in them.

In unincorporated membership organisations, where the members *are* the organisation, the ordinary members could be held liable for criminal acts and breaches of statutory duty committed by the organisation, its governing body or other members. This is unlikely unless they authorised the acts or took part in them.

19.2.3.5
Individuals

Individuals are always liable for their own criminal actions, regardless of whether they do it as an individual or as an employee, volunteer, governing body member or in any other capacity.

19.2.4
What happens

A breach of statutory duty or a criminal offence may lead to a penalty, fine or imprisonment. It may also give rise to a civil claim [see tort, **19.5.1**].

Insurance cannot cover penalties or fines, but it is possible to take out insurance to cover some legal costs arising from a successful defence in criminal cases and breach of statutory duty [see **20.9.3** and **20.10.1**]. Insurance is available to cover civil claims [see **chapter 20**].

19.2.4.1
Civil enforcement

If an act which should have been done (for example, submitting charity accounts or providing a statement of employment particulars to an employee) has not been done, a court may order it to be done. Failure to comply with the ruling can lead to penalties for contempt of court.

19.2.4.2
Criminal penalties

On conviction for a criminal offence a corporate body may be fined, members of a governing body may be fined or imprisoned, and/or other individuals who carried out the act, authorised it or allowed it to happen may be fined or imprisoned.

For some statutory breaches a penalty is automatic without any need for a court case. An example is failure to submit company annual accounts on time, where a penalty is levied automatically against the company as soon as the accounts become overdue [see **50.3.5**].

19.2.5
Relief from liability

A company director, company secretary or senior employee who is or may be liable because of negligence, default or any breach of duty may apply to the court for relief from personal liability. An application may be made to the court even if the claim has not been brought.

Companies Act 1985 s.727

19.3
BREACH OF TRUST/ FIDUCIARY DUTY

19.3.1
What it is

Breach of trust or **breach of fiduciary duty** (duty to act in good faith) occurs when a person in a position of trust breaks that trust. In voluntary organisations, the members of the governing body have a duty of trust and fiduciary duty to the organisation, its members and its beneficiaries. [See **13.2** and **13.3** for more about these duties.]

A breach of trust or breach of fiduciary duty may arise where some or all governing body members:

- allow money or property to be used for purposes for which it was not intended or are not allowed under the governing document;
- allow a charity's money or property to be used for improper political activities or trading;
- fail to obtain the consent of the court or Charity Commission for an act requiring such consent;
- cause a loss to the organisation through mismanagement, failure to show a proper duty of care [see **13.2.3** and **13.3.7**] or failure to take professional advice;
- steal money or property from the organisation (which is a criminal offence as well as a breach of trust);
- make a personal profit or gain a benefit from the organisation when not allowed to do so;
- misuse information obtained through their position as a trustee or governing body member.

19.3.2
Reducing the risk of liability

Breaches of trust or fiduciary duty are unlikely if the members of the governing body:

- act honestly and reasonably;
- always act within the terms of the governing document and the authority delegated to them;
- obtain proper information and advice when making any decision with financial or legal implications;
- declare any conflict of interest and act accordingly [see **13.2.2** and **13.3.4**];
- understand clearly the rules on remuneration, profit or gain for members of the governing body [see **chapter 14**], and comply strictly with them;
- in charities, take advice from the Charity Commission if there is any doubt about whether an act could be in breach of trust.

19.3.3
Who is liable

Potential liability for breach of trust rests with:

19.3.3.1
Trustees

- all charity trustees, including directors of charitable companies and industrial and provident societies, trustees of charitable trusts and committee members of charitable associations;
- trustees in non-charitable trusts;
- nominees (holding trustees and custodian trustees) and custodians [see **18.4**], if they act outside the terms of their agreement with the body for whom they are holding assets;
- holding trustees [see **18.4.4**], if they do anything in breach of trust, even if it is authorised by the body for which they are holding assets;
- anyone who holds money or property on trust for someone else or for charitable purposes (for example someone who says they are raising

money for a named charity or a charitable purpose, but then uses it for other purposes).

Trustees may be held liable for losses to the trust arising from the acts of agents (persons authorised to act on their behalf) unless they can show that they have exercised their proper duty of care in appointing and supervising the agents [see **13.5.2**].

If more than one trustee is liable the liability is joint and several [see **19.1.3**]. Each trustee is liable for up to the full amount of the loss even if some of them were more involved in the breach than the others.

Attorney General v Wilson [1840] 47 RR 173

A trustee is not liable for breach by a former trustee, but if he or she becomes aware of the breach there is an obligation to take action as quickly as possible to recover the loss to the organisation.

Harvey v Olliver [1887] 57 LT 239

A trustee who retires remains liable for breaches which he or she committed, as does the estate of a trustee who dies. A trustee who retires or resigns knowing that a breach of trust is likely to take place could be liable along with those who actually commit the breach. A trustee who leaves the organisation in these circumstances should put his or her concerns in writing to the other trustees, and could apply to be relieved of liability [see **19.3.5**]. *Head v Gould [1898] 2 Ch 250*

19.3.3.2
Company and IPS directors

Limited liability does not protect against liability for breach of fiduciary duty. Potential liability rests with directors of all companies and industrial and provident societies, whether charitable or non-charitable.

The principles of fiduciary duty are broadly the same as for duty of trust, but the required standard of care is lower in a non-charitable company or IPS than in a charitable one [see **13.2.3** and **13.3.7**].

19.3.3.3
Non-charitable associations

There appears to be no English case law relating specifically to the fiduciary duties of governing body members in non-charitable associations, but it is reasonable to assume the duties are similar to those for company directors.

19.3.4
What happens

19.3.4.1
Reinstatement of losses

If the organisation suffers a loss as a result of breach of trust or breach of fiduciary duty, the liable persons could be required by the organisation, the other members of the governing body, the Charity Commission or the court to repay to the organisation, with interest:

- any losses arising to the organisation because the person did not show a proper standard of care [see **13.2.3** and **13.3.7**], for example where the governing body did not take proper advice before investing or did not put proper procedures in place to prevent fraud;

- any losses arising to the organisation because the person acted outside his or her powers or outside the organisation's objects or powers, or in ways which were not properly authorised;

- in trusts and charitable associations, any losses arising from the actions of agents acting on their behalf, but not if those people were properly appointed and supervised by the trustees [see **13.5.2**].

Trustee Act 2000 s.23

It may be possible to take out insurance to indemnify governing body members for personal liability in some situations [see **20.10**]. For charities, such insurance cannot cover any action which the trustees knew was wrong or did in 'reckless disregard' [see **20.10.1**] of whether it was wrong, so it is not likely to cover any of the above situations.

19.3.4.2
Reinstatement of profit or gain

Even if the organisation has not suffered any loss, the person could be required to repay to the organisation any profit or gain, or the value of any non-monetary benefits, which were not allowed or properly authorised [see **chapter 14**] or in which a conflict of interest was not properly disclosed and acted upon [see **13.2.2** and **13.3.4**].

19.3.5
Relief from liability

If the court finds that a member of the governing body of a trust or a charitable association is or may be liable for breach of trust, it may relieve the person of some or all personal liability for that breach if the person acted honestly and reasonably and 'ought fairly to be excused'.
Trustee Act 1925 s.61

Company directors may also apply to the court to be relieved from liability for breach of trust [see **19.2.5**].

19.4
BREACH OF CONTRACT

19.4.1
What it is

An organisation's liability under **contract** typically arises if:

• the organisation cannot or does not pay sums due under a contract;

• it cannot or does not provide goods or services it has committed itself to provide;

• the goods or services provided do not meet the standards specified in the contract, or required or implied by statute [see **18.7.3**]; *or*

• it breaches the conditions of the contract, for example by failing to insure hired equipment or to repair leased premises.

19.4.2
Reducing the risk of liability

To reduce the risk of liability arising from contracts:

• no contract should be authorised unless it is reasonably certain the organisation will be able to meet its contractual obligations;

• no one should enter into a contract or other agreement on behalf of any organisation unless they have explicit authorisation to do so;

• anyone entering into a contract should make clear they are doing so on behalf of the organisation (in an incorporated body) or its governing body (in an unincorporated body);

• legal advice should be taken about the possibility of limiting or excluding liability under the contract [see **19.6.5**];

• members of an unincorporated organisation should not enter into any arrangement to pay later for goods or services unless they have adequate resources in hand, or credit arrangements are authorised by the governing document;

• everyone involved with the contract should understand what the contract requires and the effects of not meeting the requirements.

19.4.3
Who is liable

In breach of contract situations, the distinctions between incorporated and unincorporated bodies, and between those whose members do or do not have limited liability, become significant.

19.4.3.1
Incorporated organisations

In an incorporated organisation (a company or industrial and provident society) the organisation as a corporate body enters into contracts. Those who agree the contract—the governing body, or persons with delegated authority such as committees, individual officers or employees—act as **agents** of the company or IPS and as such are not a party to the contract [see **18.5**].

Provided the contract is within the organisation's objects and powers and the individuals who agreed it had authority to do so, neither they nor the members of the governing body will be held liable for any obligations arising under the contract. The situation is different and they could be held personally liable if the contract is *ultra vires* (outside the organisation's objects or powers) [see **4.7.1** and **4.7.2**] or outside the authority of the persons who agreed it [see **18.5.5**].

There is also a risk of personal liability if a member of the governing body makes a negligent mis-statement in a way which indicates that he or she is accepting personal responsibility for the statement.
Williams v Natural Life Health Foods Ltd [1997] 1 BCLC 131

19.4.3.2
Disqualified company directors

A person who serves as a company director while disqualified [see **11.3.3**] may be held liable for all of the company's debts incurred while he or she was a director.   *Company Directors Disqualification Act 1986 s.15*

19.4.3.3
Governing body members during insolvency

A director, secretary or senior employer who allows a company or industrial and provident society to continue operating or to operate fraudulently while it is, or is becoming, insolvent may be held liable for all debts incurred during this period [see **21.2.4**].

19.4.3.4
Principals in unincorporated associations

An unincorporated association, not having a legal identity of its own [see **1.1**] cannot enter into contracts as an organisation. Only individuals or incorporated bodies can enter into the association's contracts, only those parties to the contract can be held liable and their liability is **unlimited**. The situation is slightly different where the association is charitable and the governing body has incorporated [see **19.4.3.6**].

The determination of who is liable may be complex and illustrates the importance of making clear decisions and keeping clear minutes or records of decisions and delegation of authority. This is especially important when entering into any long-term financial commitments, or when entering into agreements which commit the association to providing goods or services. The key issues are:

- who made the decision to enter into the contract; *and*
- who actually entered into the contract, by making a verbal agreement or signing a written agreement.

Primary liability rests with the **principals** (the individuals who authorise an action), but they may have a right to be indemnified by the association or its members [see **19.6.7**].

Depending on the situation the principals might be:

- all the members, if the decision is taken in a general meeting;
- all the members of the governing body, if they make the decision or explicitly delegate decision-making authority to one or more governing body members, officers, employees or others;
- one or more members of the organisation, governing body members, officers or employees, if they rather than the members as a whole or the governing body as a whole make the decision to enter into the contract;
- individuals, if they enter into a contract without authority from the members or the governing body, or enter into a contract which goes beyond what they are authorised to do.

The law in this area is not clear, but the general view is that members of an association's governing body are normally the principals.

A principal entering into a contract on behalf of other principals (for example, the treasurer acting on behalf of all the governing body members) must make clear that he or she is entering into it 'for and on behalf of the association'. If this is not made clear, the person entering into the contract could be held solely liable.

A person who is not a principal and who enters into a contract with proper authority to do so is an **agent**, and is generally not liable for the contract [see **18.5.5**]. For example if the governing body makes a decision to enter into a contract and an officer or employee then signs it, that person is the agent of the governing body.

If an agent enters into an unauthorised contract he or she is generally personally liable, and the contract does not bind the principal(s). But the principals could be held liable if they subsequently ratify the contract, or they ratify it by implication by using goods which have been ordered without authorisation.   *Delauney v Strickland [1818] 2 Stark 416*

No one in an unincorporated association has the right to commit the association to spending more money than it has, so the association cannot borrow money or purchase goods or services on credit unless authorisation to do so is explicitly given in the governing document or by the members. *Cockrell v Aucompte [1857] 2 CBNS 440*

If such authorisation is given by the members, only those who authorise it can be held liable if the association subsequently cannot repay the borrowing or meet its financial obligations. However such authorisation may be implied if the members have previously known about contracts on credit and allowed them to go ahead.

Todd v Emly [1841] 7 M&W 427; Harper v Granville-Smith [1891] 7 TLR 284

Contracts involving ongoing obligations, such as leases and contracts of employment, may be entered into even if the association may not have sufficient funds to pay them into the distant future, provided the governing document authorises such transactions. It is wise to ensure the contract contains a termination clause which allows the organisation to end the agreement if they do not have adequate assets in future.

Principals who leave an association remain liable for their contracts, and after death liability passes to their estate. A **novation agreement** [see **18.10.1**] enables a principal to be released from his or her contractual obligations and transfer them to a new member, but this is only possible if the new member and other party to the contract agree.

Where the principal has the benefit (rather than the liability) of a contract, for example where money is owed to the association under a contract entered into by the principal, the contract can be **assigned** to a new principal [see **18.10.1**]. This does not require the consent of the other party to the contract.

19.4.3.5
Trustees

A body established as a trust is unincorporated and therefore cannot enter into contracts in its own right. All contracts are entered into by one or more trustees or others authorised to act on their behalf, and those considered to be principals [see above] will be held liable for claims arising from the contract.

Unless a contract is transferred to new trustees by novation or assignment [see **18.10.1**], a trustee retains the right to enforce the contract and remains liable for it even after retiring. When a trustee dies, liability passes to her or his personal representatives.

19.4.3.6
Members of incorporated trustee bodies

To make it easier for charitable trusts and associations to enter into contracts, it is possible to incorporate the trustee body [see **1.4**]. This gives the trustees corporate personality and enables them to enter into contracts as a corporate body, rather than as individual trustees. It does not, however, limit the liability of the trustees in any way, so they remain fully liable as individuals in the same way as in any unincorporated association or trust.

19.4.3.7
Guarantors

Any person who gives a **personal guarantee** [see **55.5.3**] for any transaction—bank overdraft, loan, credit account with a supplier etc—is personally liable if the organisation defaults. The guarantor will be entitled to indemnification from the organisation, but that is not much use if the organisation has no assets.

19.4.4
What happens

If the organisation does not meet its contractual obligations, the organisation (if it is a corporate body) or the individuals liable for the contract (in an unincorporated body) may be sued. Where the organisation is unincorporated the suit may be brought against one or more members of the governing body, or where the other party wishes to claim against a larger group a **representative action** may be started. A representative action is a special procedure where a number of individuals are sued as representatives of a larger group.

A number of remedies are available through the courts, including damages (money compensation) and specific performance (ordering the organisation to provide the goods or services) [see **18.12** for more about breach of contract, and **chapter 61** for dispute resolution procedures].

It is possible to take out insurance to cover damages awarded by the court [see **20.5.8**]. If damages are not covered by insurance and are more than the organisation can pay, the organisation becomes insolvent (if it is a corporate body) or the individuals who have been sued are personally liable (in an unincorporated body). The individuals might be entitled to be indemnified by the organisation [see **19.6.7**] and/or a contribution from other principals [see **19.1.3**]. The right to be indemnified by the organisation is meaningless if the organisation has no assets.

If individuals who are held liable do not pay damages awarded by the court, the judgment may be enforced by seizure of possessions or a **garnishee** order, where the court orders sums to be deducted from wages and paid to the court. Individuals with insufficient assets to meet the financial obligations could be personally bankrupted.

19.5
TORT

19.5.1
What it is

Tort comes from the French *tort*, 'wrong', and refers to an injury, loss or damage caused to a person through acts such as negligence, nuisance, defamation or trespass. A tort is a civil wrong [see **60.1.2**], where action is brought by persons rather than the state. An act which causes a tort is **tortious** or **wrongful**. In some cases such as assault the act which gives rise to the tort may also be a criminal offence.

For most torts there must be either intention to commit the act (as in trespass or defamation) or negligence. But there are some acts for which there is **strict liability**, where the person is liable simply by committing the act, even without intention or negligence. Some of the more common torts are set out below.

19.5.1.1
Negligence

Negligence occurs when a person who has a **duty of care** towards another person does not take reasonable care, and the other person suffers injury, loss or damage as a result. For example:

- employers have a duty of care towards employees, to provide competent staff, safe equipment, and a safe workplace and work systems;
  Wilsons & Clyde Coal Co Ltd v English [1938] AC 57

- occupiers of land have a duty to take reasonable care to ensure that premises are safe for visitors, and even have a duty of care to trespassers [see **59.5.2**].

Negligence may occur in various aspects of a voluntary organisation's work, for example an injury caused by sports which are not properly supervised or where proper equipment is not provided, loss suffered as a result of inaccurate benefits advice, or theft of a client's property because the organisation did not have proper security systems. In general, the higher the risk, the greater the level of care required.

19.5.1.2
Harassment

Harassment is a tort and criminal offence. The term is not defined in the **Protection from Harassment Act 1997**, but includes causing alarm or distress, by verbal or other means, on at least two occasions.

19.5.1.3
Trespass

Trespass involves assaulting a person (which is also a criminal offence); entering or remaining on land without authorisation, which is also a criminal offence in some circumstances [see **59.5.2**]; or interfering with another person's goods.

19.5.1.4
Passing off

Passing off [see **39.5**] occurs where a supplier of goods or services makes a misrepresentation to actual or potential customers or clients, which is calculated to injure another supplier. An example is an organisation seeking care contracts and using a name which causes it to be confused with another organisation offering similar services.

19.5.1.5
Defamation

Defamation [see **40.3**] involves publishing material which lowers the public's view of a person. **Libel** is published in a permanent form; **slander** is transient, usually oral. A claim of slander requires the person to have been damaged in some way, but libel does not require this and can be a crime as well as a tort.

19.5.1.6
Nuisance

Public nuisance is a crime and may be a tort if it causes special damage to a person. Noise nuisance, for example, is both a tort and a criminal offence [see **59.10.3**]. **Private nuisance**, which is only a tort, is usually something which interferes with a person's enjoyment of their land, such as blocking light.

19.5.2
Reducing the risk of liability

The risk of tortious acts occurring can be reduced if:

- members of the governing body and everyone involved in the organisation's activities understand relevant aspects of the law and their duty of care to everyone who uses the organisation's premises, uses its services or takes part in its activities;

- employees, volunteers and others who carry out the organisation's activities are properly recruited, inducted, trained and supervised;

- there are clear rules for situations when an employee or volunteer must get authority from a superior before carrying out an act or dealing with a situation;

- the governing body is clear about what can and cannot be delegated to agents who will act on their behalf, and are aware of the obligation to exercise proper supervision;

- a person making a statement or representation makes clear that they are making it on behalf of the organisation, and is not taking personal responsibility for the statement;

- proper records are kept of all incidents involving personal injury, violence, trespass, damage to people's property etc;

- the organisation has a clear procedure for dealing with complaints and keeping records of action taken.

19.5.3
Vicarious liability

In general, persons are liable only for their own tortious acts and those they authorise. But employers have **vicarious liability** for the torts of their employees, even if the employer did not authorise or order the employee's act and even if the employer did not know about it.

Vicarious liability does not depend upon any fault on the part of the employer. All that must be proved is:

- the person committing the act is an employee of the employer;

- the act occurred during the course of the employee's employment; *and*

- the act committed by the employee is one which entitles the person who has been injured to bring court proceedings.

Considerable legal argument has gone into defining whether an act occurs 'in the course of employment', and it is difficult to say how the courts might interpret a particular set of facts. For example in one case an employer was found liable for damage caused when the employee had broken company rules by smoking while delivering petrol, and had started a fire. But in another case an employee had broken the rules by picking up a hitch-hiker, and the employer was found not liable for injuries sustained by the hitch-hiker in an accident.

Century Insurance Co Ltd v Northern Ireland Road Transport Board [1942] AC 509; Twine v Bean's Express Limited [1946] 62 TLR 458

An employer may be liable for an employee's act either directly, or through the employer's negligence. For example an employer who hired a porter who had custody of keys to flats, without checking to discover that the porter had a long criminal record, was found liable for the subsequent thefts.

Nahhas v Pier House (Cheyne Walk) Management [1984] 270 EG 328

There is no obligation for the employer to insure against most claims from third parties but it is wise to do so [see **20.5**].

A tortious act may also be a criminal act. In this case the person who authorises and/or carries out the act is criminally liable, and the employer could be held criminally liable as well.

**19.5.3.1
Injury to other
employees**

Vicarious liability covers not only injuries or losses caused to third parties, but also those caused to fellow parties (other employees of the same employer). An employer must take out **employer's liability insurance** [see **20.4.1**] to insure against claims by fellow employees. This covers situations where one employee injures another, and the injured employee successfully sues the employer.

**19.5.3.2
Torts by volunteers**

In general employers have vicarious liability only for the acts of employees. But there could be vicarious liability for the acts of volunteers if the 'volunteer' is in fact an employee [see **35.3**], or if the court felt that the relationship between the organisation and the volunteer was sufficient to justify a liability being imposed.

Even if the organisation is not vicariously liable it might be possible for a claim to be brought against the organisation for its own liability in, for example, not properly training or supervising the volunteer.

**19.5.3.3
Torts by secondees**

Unlike volunteers, secondees are employees [see **22.5.3**]. Vicarious liability generally rests with the organisation which controlled the secondee at the time of the negligent act, but it might not be clear whether this was the organisation from which the person was seconded, or the one to which he or she was seconded.

**19.5.3.4
Torts by contractors**

Employers or other principals are not generally liable for torts by independent contractors, including self-employed people carrying out work for an employer. But they could be held liable in some situations [see **34.2.3**], for example if they were negligent in hiring that contractor.

**19.5.4
Who is liable in other
situations**

Liability may arise not only for the acts of employees, but also for acts of volunteers, governing body members, ordinary members, service users and others involved with the organisation. It is important to be clear about who could be held liable in these situations.

**19.5.4.1
Corporate bodies**

Corporate bodies can commit torts and be sued in the same way as individuals. A director is not personally liable for a tort committed by a company unless the director directed or authorised the tort, or it occurred because of the director's negligence. *Performing Right Society Limited v Ciryl Theatrical Syndicate Ltd [1924] 1 KB 1*

**19.5.4.2
Governing body**

Members of a governing body are liable for their own torts, those of the governing body, those of the organisation or others which they authorise or allow to happen, and those of their employees even if they did not authorise them [see **19.5.3**].

A member of a governing body will not generally be held liable for wrongful or negligent actions of the governing body or organisation if:

- he or she did not know of their decision or action at the time it was taken; *or*
- he or she knew about it, but did not participate in it.

Liability in tort is similar to liability in contract [see **19.4.3**]. In incorporated organisations with limited liability, any claim for damages is generally against the organisation. If the organisation is not insured and its assets are insufficient to meet the claim, the organisation becomes insolvent. Even in a limited liability organisation, members of the governing body could be held personally liable if they authorise a tort.

**19.5.4.3
Governing body in
an unincorporated
association**

In unincorporated associations or trusts any legal action for tort would be brought against one or more named individuals. If they have to pay damages to the other party and the organisation does not have insurance to indemnify them they may be entitled to be indemnified by the organisation, its members and/or the other persons who authorised or committed the tort [see **19.6.7**].

The members of an unincorporated association are generally unable to bring a claim for personal injury against the governing body, on the basis that governing body members do not have a duty of care to the organisation's members [see **19.5.4.5**]. However in a case in 1998 it was held that a club committee did have a duty of care to its members, and had to compensate a member who was injured as a result of breach of that duty.

**19.5.4.4
Holding trustees**

If an unincorporated association's property is held by holding trustees [see **18.4.4**] they could possibly be held liable, for example for claims arising under the **Occupier's Liability Acts** if they, rather than the members of the governing body or all the members of the association, are considered to be the occupiers of the land.

**19.5.4.5
Ordinary members**

Ordinary members of an unincorporated association may all be liable in tort if:

- they all authorised or are all carrying on the activity which causes the injury, loss, damage, nuisance or defamation;

- only some of the members are carrying on the activity, but all the members are in overall control of it;

- all the members, rather than the governing body or holding trustees, are considered to be the occupiers of premises; *or*

- all the members, rather than the governing body, are considered to be the employer.

An individual member or a group of members could be found liable in tort if they are specifically responsible for an activity or for the safety of premises and are in breach of their duty of care.

Prole v Allen [1950] 1 All ER 476

The members of an unincorporated association do not have a general duty of care towards each other, beyond that owed between strangers. So in general a member of an unincorporated association cannot claim against the other members unless it can be shown that an individual had a specific responsibility, for example for keeping the premises in a fit state, or that an individual knew of a danger and failed to warn the other members. *Prole v Allen [see above]*

**19.5.5
What happens**

The award in tort is **damages** for the loss, injury, damage or nuisance caused. The person against whom the claim is brought has to pay. In some situations an **injunction** may be brought to stop the person from carrying out the tortious act.

Judgments against a corporate body or individual are enforced in the same way as for contracts [see **19.4.4**].

**19.5.5.1
Claims against
employers**

Both the employee and the employer are liable for a tortious act by an employee [see **19.5.3**]. Both may be sued, but because the employer normally has greater resources and is more likely to be covered by insurance, the injured party is more likely to sue the employer. If the claim is successful and is not covered by the employer's insurance, the employer may then seek to recover from the employee the losses which have been caused to the employer.

19.5.5.2
Contributory negligence

Where there is a successful claim, the person at fault may be able to show that the injured person's own negligence or actions contributed to his or her injury. In rare cases it might be shown that the claimant consented to the risk of injury, for example by deliberately breaching well known and properly enforced safety procedures. Damages awarded to a claimant may be reduced to such extent as the court thinks just and equitable, having regard to the claimant's share in the responsibility for the injury.   *Law Reform (Contributory Negligence) Act 1945*

19.6
PROTECTING
AGAINST LIABILITY

The best way to protect against a liability is not to incur it in the first place. But where liability might arise, there are a number of ways to protect individuals and the organisation.

19.6.1
Incorporation

Where an unincorporated organisation's potential liabilities are substantial, the possibility of becoming a company or industrial and provident society should be considered [see **6.6**]. Incorporation as a company or IPS limits the liability of the members in many situations, but not all.

If the organisation does not itself wish to incorporate it may in some situations be able to limit liability by setting up a separate company. The company could, for example, take on a potentially risky contract to provide services. It could then sub-contract provision of the services to the original unincorporated organisation, on contractual terms which specifically exclude the unincorporated organisation having any liability. Legal advice should be taken before including such terms in a contract.

19.6.1.1
Liabilities of governing body members

Incorporation does not protect the governing body members of a company or IPS from:

* fines or penalties for their own, or in some cases the organisation's, criminal acts or breach of statutory duty [see **19.2**];
* liability where they direct or authorise a tort (a civil wrong, see **19.5.1**) or breach of statute;
* liability to the organisation for their own breach of trust or fiduciary duty [see **19.3**], or breach which they knowingly allow to happen;
* liability if they enter into *ultra vires* or unauthorised contracts (unless the contract is, in a non-charitable company, subsequently ratified by the company members) [see **4.7.1**];
* liability for a company's debts while serving as a company director while disqualified [see **19.4.3.2**];
* liability for a company's or IPS's debts if the organisation operates while insolvent or while becoming insolvent, or seeks to defraud creditors while it is becoming insolvent [see **19.4.3.3**].

Trustee liability (or indemnity) insurance or directors and officers insurance can cover some of these, but not all [see **20.10**].

19.6.2
Insurance

Insurance protects the organisation and individuals from liabilities to third parties and, in some cases, to the organisation. Insurances are covered in detail in **chapter 20**.

19.6.3
Charity Commission advice

A charity trustee uncertain about whether an action could be a breach of trust may seek advice from the Charity Commission. Trustees who reveal all material facts and then act in accordance with advice given by the Commission under the provisions of the **Charities Act 1993** s.29 will not be held liable for any breach of trust arising from such action.

19.6.4
Limitation of liability under the governing document

The governing document of an unincorporated association may contain a clause saying that ordinary members (those who are not members of the governing body) are not liable for the organisation's debts or actions. This does not protect them if they are a member of the association's governing body, are a principal to a contract, enter into an unauthorised contract or are liable for criminal or tortious acts.

Overton v Hewett [1886] 3 TLR 246

Similarly the governing document of a trust may limit the liability of trustees for losses caused to the charity by, for example, poor investment performance, provided the trustees have taken proper advice and acted in good faith. *Armitage v Nurse [1997] TLR 31/3/1997*

19.6.5
Contractual limitation of liability

It is possible—and indeed highly desirable—for unincorporated associations and trusts to include in contracts a clause limiting the liability of its members or the members of its governing body to the extent of the assets of the organisation. *DeVries v Corner [1865] 13 LT 636*

Such a clause might say, for example,

> The personal liability of the person signing this contract on behalf of ABC, any member of the governing body of ABC and any other person held liable under this contract shall be limited to the amount of the net assets of ABC at the date of any claim.

This means that if the organisation does not have enough assets to meet its obligations under the contract, the person to whom money is due cannot bring a claim for more than the organisation actually has. Many parties to contracts are unwilling to include this, but a friendly landlord might, or a local authority purchasing services from a voluntary body.

19.6.6
Exclusion of liability

Liability may in some circumstances be limited by an **exclusion of liability** or **disclaimer** notice or clause. This might be on display, printed on documents such as admission or cloakroom tickets, or included in a contract [see above], licence or lease. Legal advice should be sought before attempting to exclude liability in this way, as the law restricts the effectiveness of exclusion clauses. Simply saying that the organisation is not liable, for example for incorrect advice, will not necessarily provide protection, and does not absolve the organisation of its obligation to take reasonable steps to ensure information and advice is accurate and up to date.

Liability for death or personal injury cannot be excluded.

Unfair Contract Terms Act 1977 s.2

19.6.7
Indemnity

To **indemnify** means to compensate someone for a loss suffered. Persons involved with voluntary organisations may have a statutory and/or common law right to be indemnified, or may be entitled to indemnity under the governing document.

The right to be indemnified by an organisation is not worth anything if the organisation does not have sufficient assets or insurance cover to do so. It should therefore not be relied on as protection for individuals.

If it is not possible to be indemnified from the organisation's funds and a governing body member—or anyone else connected with the organisation—has contributed a disproportionate amount in a situation where there is joint and several liability, he or she is entitled to a contribution from the others [see **19.1.3**].

There is no right to be indemnified for fines or penalties, or to be indemnified by an organisation in situations where the person is liable to the organisation itself, for example for breach of trust [see **19.3**].

19.6.7.1
Statutory rights: trustees

A trustee of a trust or charitable association is entitled to be reimbursed out of trust funds for expenses properly incurred on behalf of the trust, if he or she acted with proper authority and with due care.

Trustee Act 2000 s.31

Trustees cannot be indemnified by the trust or association for other liabilities, but some may be covered by trustee indemnity insurance [see **20.10**].

**19.6.7.2
Statutory rights:
companies**

A company cannot indemnify a director, company secretary, senior employee or auditor for liability arising from any offence in relation to the company for which the person is found guilty. A company may, however, cover legal costs of a successful defence, if the memorandum or articles allow, or may purchase insurance to indemnify the person [see **20.10.1**].

**19.6.7.3
Common law rights**

If a member of the governing body of a non-charitable association, or an ordinary member of any association, is successfully sued by a third party he or she is entitled to be indemnified by the association for damages and costs only if:

- he or she was sued as representative of all the members; *or*
- he or she was carrying out activities for, and with the approval of, the association and its members.

Egger v Viscount Chelmsford [1964] 3 All ER 406, 413

This right to be indemnified extends only to the assets of the association. If the association does not have adequate funds, there is no right to be indemnified by the ordinary members of the association unless this is explicit in the governing document [see below].

If some or all of the members of the governing body are liable for a contract, any member who pays more than a proper share is entitled to a contribution from the other liable governing body members.

Earl Mountcashell v Barber [1853] 14 CB 53

Similarly if some or all of the members of an unincorporated association are liable for a contract, any member who pays more than a proper share is entitled to a contribution from the other liable members.

Boulter v Peplow [1850] 9 CB 493

**19.6.7.4
Governing document**

The statutory and common law rights to indemnity may be extended if the governing document includes a clause indemnifying governing body members, or ordinary members of an association, from the organisation's funds for liabilities properly incurred in managing the organisation. Such a clause would not generally allow the person to be indemnified if he or she had acted outside the objects or powers as set out in the governing document, without proper authority, without proper duty of care to the organisation, or criminally.

The right to indemnity in an unincorporated association may be further extended if the governing document includes a clause entitling members of the governing body, or ordinary members of the association, to be indemnified by the organisation's *members* if they are successfully sued for an act properly undertaken on behalf of the members, and if the association does not have sufficient assets to indemnify them.

This reduces the liability of the member who can claim from the other members—but it increases the liability of all the other members, making them liable even where they are not a principal to a contract or have not authorised or taken part in a tort. Legal advice should be taken before putting into a governing document any clause giving members of an association the right to be indemnified by other members.

Without such a clause, individual members who are sued have no right to be indemnified by the other members of the association.

If an unincorporated association has property which is held by holding trustees [see **18.4.4**], the association's governing document or the deed of trust setting out the relationship between the association's members and the holding trustees should include provision for indemnifying the holding trustees from the association's funds for any losses they incur.

Chapter 20
INSURANCE

20.1
THINKING ABOUT INSURANCE

For many organisations, liabilities and insurance to provide protection against them are hidden issues which come onto the agenda only when something goes wrong. But they are so important that they should be considered automatically in relation to every activity or transaction of the organisation. The governing body should have procedures in place to ensure this is done.

Insurance is only one way to deal with potential liabilities. Other ways are covered in **19.6**.

20.1.1
Finding an insurer

It is sensible to obtain quotes from at least three insurers before making any decision about insurance, and important to ensure that like is being compared with like. Insurance contracts are not standardised and the names of insurance products are not used consistently, so two identically titled policies may offer very different cover.

Because insurance is such a vital and complex topic, organisations should consider taking advice from their solicitor or a qualified insurance broker. Geographical lists of registered brokers are available from the British Insurance Brokers Association [see end of chapter]. Details of brokers who specialise in insurance for voluntary organisations may be available from organisations such as the National Council for Voluntary Organisations and Wales Council for Voluntary Action [see end of chapter], voluntary sector umbrella bodies and local councils for voluntary service.

A good broker will provide advice on risks the organisation is exposed to, explain the types of insurance and cover available, ensure the organisation is fully covered without overlaps, advise on which insurances are the best value for the organisation, obtain competitive quotes from a range of insurers, remind the organisation in good time prior to renewal and provide assistance when claims have to be made.

Insurance and financial services are also available through other intermediaries, particularly solicitors, accountants and banks. Virtually all intermediaries receive a commission from the insurer for their services. This may be negotiable. In the case of solicitors the full amount of the commission will be disclosed and an agreement reached as to who receives it; other intermediaries must disclose the commission if asked.

20.1.2
Allocating responsibility

A named post holder—typically the treasurer, chief executive or senior employee, or head of finance—should have responsibility for:

- identifying the insurance requirements of the organisation;
- ensuring decisions about insurance are properly made by the governing body or by a committee or employee with delegated authority to make such decisions;
- taking out the insurance;
- notifying insurers of all relevant changes, including new activities, services and equipment;
- ensuring policies are renewed and premiums are paid on time;
- keeping the governing body informed about insurance matters.

The organisation's procedures for dealing with insurance should allow decisions to be made quickly when necessary.

20.1.2.1
Annual review

Insurance should be reviewed regularly by the governing body. At least once a year it should be an agenda item, and governing body members should receive a full report which includes:

- name of insurer for each policy held by the organisation;
- details of risks covered under each policy, and level of cover;
- exceptions (risks not covered);
- excess (the amount the organisation has to pay on each claim);
- cost of each policy;
- copies of the insurer's confirmation of payment of the most recent premium for each policy;
- current or potential developments in the organisation's activities, premises, equipment etc which might indicate the need for increased levels of cover or extended areas of cover.

The discussion provides a good opportunity for governing body members to confirm that full disclosure [see **20.3.4**] has been made to the insurer.

20.1.2.2
Related matters

The governing body should also:

- ensure the organisation is doing everything possible to reduce the risk of liability arising [see **chapter 19** and **49.1**];

- ensure the organisation complies with all legal requirements which could affect insurance, for example in relation to health and safety;

- allocate clear responsibility for dealing with emergencies (fire, theft, violence etc), and ensure procedures are in place to minimise risks to people and property;

- ensure copies of insurance policies and other key documents, such as the inventory of assets [see **20.6.2**], are kept off the premises.

20.2
POWER TO INSURE
20.2.1
Statutory power

Where there is a statutory duty to insure, all organisations have power to do so. Every employer has a statutory duty to take out employer's liability insurance [see **20.4.1**], and vehicles used on the road must be covered by third party insurance [see **20.8.1**]. Insurance may also be required for some registrations and licences, for example public liability insurance is likely to be a requirement for obtaining a public entertainment licence [see **42.2**].

Trustees of trusts and charitable associations have statutory power to insure any property against loss or damage, but not trustees' personal liability.   *Trustee Act 2000 s.34*

A company has statutory power to insure its officers (directors, company secretary and senior staff) and their auditors against personal liability arising from their actions, or inaction, as officers or auditors [see **20.10**]. A charitable company may do so only if its memorandum of association explicitly allows this, and may amend the memorandum to allow this only with the prior consent of the Charity Commission [see **20.2.4**].
                                                        Companies Act 1985 s.310(3)(a)

20.2.2
Implied power

The Charity Commission's view is that trustees of charities should insure charity property for its full value. Because trustees have a duty to safeguard a charity's assets [see **13.3.5**], they could in some circumstances be held to be in breach of trust if they do not insure property and it subsequently goes up in smoke or is stolen.

The Charity Commission allows charity funds to be used for insurance to cover:

- buildings, either as a freeholder or tenant [see **20.6.1**];
- contents [see **20.6.2**];
- public liability [see **20.5.1**];
- the organisation's vehicles [see **20.8**];
- additional premiums payable by an employee or volunteer for using their own vehicle for the organisation's work [see **20.8.1.1**].

Unless the power to take out other insurances is explicitly included in the governing document, charities need specific advice or consent to do so [see below]. Non-charities have power to take out insurances for which there is no statutory power only if there is an explicit or general power in the governing document [see **20.2.5**].

20.2.3
Advice

Charity Commission booklet CC49 *Charities and Insurance* states that charities may take out insurances for which there is no statutory or implied power or an explicit power in the governing document only if:

- the charity's circumstances make it necessary or prudent;

- paying the premiums will not affect the charity's charitable work; *and*

- the trustees are advised by their legal or other independent financial advisors to have such insurance.

20.2.4
Consent

A charitable organisation may take out trustee indemnity insurance (also called trustee liability insurance) or directors' and officers' insurance only if:

- for a charitable company, the memorandum of association contains explicit power to take out this insurance or the Charity Commission has allowed the memorandum to be amended to include such power;
- for a charitable industrial and provident society, the rules contain explicit power to take out this insurance or the Registry of Friendly Societies has allowed the rules to be amended to include such power;
- for a charitable trust or association, the Charity Commission has given written consent or has made a scheme to amend the governing document to allow such insurance [see **5.5.4**].

Before allowing a charitable trust or association to take out trustee indemnity insurance, the Commission needs to be satisfied that this use of the charity's funds is justified in relation to the charity's activities, the potential risk of personal liability for trustees, the number of trustees, the amount of protection required, and the cost.

See **20.10** for more about these insurances.

20.2.5
Governing document

The governing document may contain power 'to effect such insurances as the governing body thinks fit' or a similar wording [see **5.4.4** and **5.4.21**], or a catch-all power 'to do all such other lawful things as are necessary for the achievement of the objects' [see **5.4.3**]. These general wordings give non-charities the power to take out any insurances, but do not give charities power to take out insurances requiring advice or Charity Commission consent [see above].

A non-charity whose governing document does not contain an insurance power or general power should seek legal advice before taking out any insurance except those where there is a statutory duty or power to insure [see **20.2.1**].

20.3
TAKING OUT
INSURANCE

A company, industrial and provident society or incorporated governing body [see **1.4**] takes out insurance in its own name. Technically an unincorporated association or trust cannot take out insurance in its own name, and some insurers may require any insurance to be held in the names of one or more individual members of the governing body acting as representatives of the other governing body members. If the members in whose name the insurance is held cease to be on the governing body, new people should be appointed to hold the insurance and the insurer should be notified. The policy must clearly cover (indemnify) all potentially liable parties, not just those in whose name the insurance is held.

20.3.1
Basis of insurance

The organisation must be clear whether it is obtaining cover on:

- an **indemnity** basis, where the insurance company pays out only what the organisation has actually lost (so, for example, if an organisation loses a computer which cost £1,000 five years ago it could get only £75, the current open market second-hand value);
- **replacement**, **reinstatement** or **new for old**, where the insurer pays the actual cost of a replacement (so, for example, £800 to put in place a computer comparable to the one which was stolen);
- **fixed sum**, where a fixed amount is paid out if an event occurs, regardless of the actual loss. An example is pluvius insurance [see **20.9.2**], where the organisation receives a fixed sum if a fundraising event has to be cancelled because of rain.

Some replacement or reinstatement policies make a reduction if replacement means the organisation gets more than it lost. For example if the new £800 computer has more features than the old one, the insurance might not cover the value of the additional features.

20.3.2
Subrogation

If an organisation suffers loss, it may have a right to recover that loss from the person who caused it. But if the organisation receives payment from an insurer for its loss, the insurer then has the right to recover the amount it has paid out from the person who caused the loss. The insurer's right of recovery is **subrogated** to (substituted for) the organisation's right of recovery.

20.3.3
Average clauses

Most commercial insurance policies contain **average clauses**. The effect of these is to reduce the insurer's liability to pay the full amount of a partial loss. For example if a building having a reinstatement cost of £1 million is only insured for £600,000 (60% of the reinstatement cost) and is completely destroyed, the insurer's maximum liability is clearly only £600,000. But if the building suffers a loss of £200,000, the insurer would still pay only 60% of the loss, i.e., £120,000.

Regular revaluation of the assets or risk insured is vital. Some policies contain inflation clauses, but this should not mean that revaluation is neglected. Where a property is subject to a preservation or conservation order or is listed, the need for accurate valuation is even greater.

Where values have gone down, revaluation may mean that the level of coverage can be reduced.

20.3.4
Duties of good faith and disclosure

Insurance policies are **policies of the utmost good faith**. This means that any factor likely to affect the insurer's decision to insure or the level of premium charged must be disclosed to the insurer. Failure to do so can invalidate the policy. Because of this, some leases include obligations on tenants to disclose any such factors to the landlord.

The obligation to disclose covers a very wide range of factors likely to affect the risk of whatever is insured against. For example, various insurances might be invalidated by failure to disclose:

- appointment of a new employee who has a criminal conviction;
- previous refusal or imposition of specific conditions on insurance;
- earlier claims;
- non-standard construction of a building;
- sharing premises with another organisation or use by the public.

The organisation is obliged to disclose not only what it is actually aware of, but also what reasonable enquiry would have revealed. This means that procedures should be put in place to discover whether new employees, volunteers or members of the governing body are aware of any matters about themselves which should be disclosed. [For more about how to find out about these matters see disqualification of governing body members, **11.3**, Rehabilitation of Offenders Act, **25.10**, and criminal record checks, **26.3.3**.]

The fact that the proposal form does not ask about a particular matter does not relieve the organisation of the need to disclose.

The duty exists at the date of the start of the policy, so if further facts become known between completing the proposal form and acceptance by the insurer, these must be disclosed. A further duty of disclosure arises on each renewal.

Disclosure of matters seen by insurers as positive, such as installing a burglar alarm, may result in a lower premium.

20.3.5
Policy terms

The full policy should be obtained and checked. It can be useful to highlight key clauses. Particular concerns are likely to be:

- **conditions** to be complied with, such as reporting loss to insurers and police within a defined period;
- **warranties** (factual conditions which the organisation promises are true, as a condition of cover);

- **exclusion** of particular risks or circumstances, such as more than £50 cash kept on the premises, cash not in a locked safe overnight, lack of proper door or window locks;
- whether there is an **excess** (the organisation's obligation to meet the first part of the claim);
- **limitation**, such as no more than three claims in any period;
- **endorsements** (additions to or exceptions from cover).

20.3.6 Age exclusions

Some insurances which cover employees and/or volunteers in case of sickness, injury or death or for negligence in carrying out certain duties may be valid only up to age 60 or 65, or may not cover them under age 18. It is essential to check all policies for any age exclusions, and to extend the policy to cover staff in higher or lower age groups. The National Centre for Volunteering [see end of chapter] has details of insurers who provide cover for older volunteers.

20.3.7 Claims

The duty of good faith applies to all aspects of insurance, including claims. Any attempt to inflate the claim artificially or withhold information might invalidate the claim.

Conditions on the policy must be strictly adhered to. Brokers may assist, but for very large or potentially contested claims legal advice or the assistance of a professional claims adjuster may be needed. Where the claim involves potential liability to employees or third parties, the organisation must not admit any liability and must generally leave all negotiation to the insurer.

It is generally necessary to report to the insurer all incidents relevant to the policy, even if a claim is not made.

20.3.8 Complaints

The Association of British Insurers, Insurance Brokers' Registration Council and General Insurance Standards Council [see end of chapter] deal with complaints which cannot be resolved with the insurer.

20.4 INSURANCES RELATING TO EMPLOYEES AND OTHER WORKERS

Every employer has a legal obligation to insure all staff, and may be fined £2,500 for each day it does not have this insurance.

Employers' Liability (Compulsory Insurance) Act 1969;
Employers' Liability (Compulsory Insurance) Regulations 1998 [SI 1998/2573]

20.4.1 Employer's liability

The insurance must cover the organisation (or, in unincorporated organisations, the members of the governing body or others considered for legal purposes to be the employer) for claims of up to £5 million for each incident leading to illness, injury or death arising out of and in the course of the employee's work, if:

- the employer was in breach of a statutory duty to the employee, *or*
- the employer can be shown to have been negligent.

In practice most employer's liability policies have an upper limit of £10 million. Higher cover may be appropriate in some situations.

The employer must prominently display, within 30 days of the policy being renewed, a copy of the current certificate of insurance at all of its premises where employees work. Failure to do this can lead to a fine of up to £1,000 for day it is not displayed. For policies which expire on or after 1 January 1999, expired certificates must be kept for 40 years.

20.4.1.1 Who must be covered

Employer's liability insurance is required for all employees, including temporary, part-time and casual employees and apprentices. Some trainees, especially on government schemes, are considered to be employees for this purpose, and the employer must ensure they are covered by the employer's liability insurance. Organisations which provide work for people serving community service orders may be obliged to cover them under the policy as well.

There is no obligation to take out employer's liability insurance for other trainees or volunteers, but it is good practice to extend an employer's liability policy to include them, because a court could in some circumstances deem them to be 'employees' for these purposes. In certain circumstances this may also apply to self-employed people.

Where trainees, volunteers, members of the governing body and self-employed people are not covered under employer's liability, it may be appropriate to cover them under a public liability policy [see **20.5.1.2**].

20.4.1.2
What is not covered

Employer's liability insurance covers only illness, injury or death caused by the employer's negligence or breach of duty. It does not cover situations where the employer has shown the required standard of care. It covers only injury to the person, not to the person's clothing, property or other objects. If the employer wants to cover these risks, separate insurance is needed [see **20.4.3** and **20.6.2**].

20.4.2
Employer's
legal costs

Employer's **legal costs** or **legal expenses** insurance [see **20.9.3**] is sometimes called **employer's protection** or **employer's indemnity insurance**. This is not the same as employer's liability insurance, and is not legally required. Typically it covers the employer 's legal costs for claims of unfair dismissal, wrongful dismissal, breach of the contract of employment, or unlawful discrimination. It generally also covers employment tribunal awards .

20.4.3
Health care,
sickness, accident
and death

An organisation may choose to provide life insurance, sickness and/or accident cover, health care or permanent health cover as a benefit for employees or volunteers. They may cover illness, injury or death only if it is caused in the course of work, or regardless of how it is caused and whether it is linked to work.

There is no legal obligation for an employer to provide any of these unless they are promised in an employee's contract of employment. Most of these insurances are treated by Inland Revenue as a benefit in kind and are taxable [see **27.4.7**]. If the insurance pays an income to the employee, the organisation should make clear whether this is intended to cover all or some of its sick pay obligations [see **27.6** and **24.22**].

Some insurances provide a long-term income to an employee who becomes too ill or injured to work [see below]. Legal advice should be obtained before taking out any such insurance, because it may have the unforeseen consequence of making it very difficult to dismiss an employee who is receiving payments under the policy [see **30.8.3**].

Because these insurances provide a benefit to the individual covered (or his or her estate), they should not be provided for anyone who is a member of a charity's governing body unless the governing document explicitly allows governing body members to receive such benefit or consent has been obtained from the Charity Commission.

20.4.3.1
Types of insurance

Health care insurance provides for private health care in addition to, or instead of, NHS care, and may also cover employees' families. It does not pay any additional income to the insured person.

Permanent health or **income protection insurance** pays an ongoing income, generally monthly, to an employee who is unable to work for an extended period due to illness or disability. Sometimes the policy is narrowly defined to cover only permanent incapacity for any sort of work. 'Permanent' means that unlike the other insurances, it cannot be cancelled or changed by the insurer if the insured person's health changes, although the premium may be increased.

Critical illness insurance pays a fixed sum and/or an ongoing income if the employee is diagnosed as having a defined disease such as cancer or heart disease. **Sickness insurance** is similar but does not have to involve a critical illness.

Personal accident insurance covers injuries or death arising from an accident. The insurance generally provides a lump sum at the time of injury, and/or a weekly income for a fixed period.

Life insurance or **death-in-service insurance** pays a fixed sum and/or an ongoing income to the employee's spouse, or sometimes other partner or dependant, if the employee dies while employed.

**20.4.4
Key workers**

Key worker insurance provides payment to the organisation to help cover the cost of replacement staff while a key worker is unable to work.

**20.4.5
Travel**

If employees or volunteers travel outside the UK on behalf of the organisation, it is good practice for the organisation to take out **travel insurance** to cover their medical expenses, emergency travel costs, repatriation, and compensation in case of death or serious injury. The organisation may also want to insure their baggage, personal effects and money.

Travel insurance should also be considered for people who travel on behalf of the organisation within the UK. Such insurance usually applies only where the travel involves a minimum number of nights accommodation and/or pre-booked flights.

Advice should be sought from the Charity Commission before taking out travel insurance for governing body members.

**20.5
INSURANCE FOR CLAIMS BY THIRD PARTIES**

Most situations in which a third party or member of the public suffers injury or loss can be insured against. Organisations need to consider potential risks, and decide which are worth insuring against.

**20.5.1
Public liability**

Public liability, **personal injury (PI)** or **third party insurance** protects the organisation (or, in an unincorporated body, the members of the governing body) from claims by members of the public for death, illness, injury, or loss of or damage to property caused through the negligence of the organisation or someone working for it. It is generally linked to premises, or to specific activities such a lunch club, sports activities, a festival or open day. It does not cover liabilities arising from professional services [see **20.5.3**], products manufactured or supplied by the organisation [see **20.5.4**], and some other specific liabilities.

'Public' generally includes users/beneficiaries, visitors to the organisation's premises (and sometimes even trespassers), passers-by, and anyone other than employees with whom the organisation comes into contact. Volunteers and trainees need special attention [see **20.5.1.2**].

Many funders and registration bodies require organisations to have public liability insurance. Even where it is not required, every organisation which occupies premises or organises activities should have it.

Public liability insurance is often combined with employer's liability insurance, buildings insurance and/or contents insurance. Minimum cover is typically £2 million for any one incident, but may be much higher if the organisation's activities could cause serious injury or damage. The premium depends on the nature and scale of risk. Public liability insurance is generally renewed annually but it is possible to it take out for a specific event or activity of a few weeks, days or even hours.

To have a valid claim, the injured person must be able to show that the organisation or its worker(s) acted negligently, did not take reasonable care, or breached another duty.

**20.5.1.1
Limitation of liability**

Liability for damage to or loss of property, for example in car parks and cloakrooms, may be excluded or limited by putting up a disclaimer notice [see **19.6.6**]. But these should be considered a first line of defence only. To be effective they must satisfy certain conditions, and legal advice should be obtained as to their wording. Liability for personal injury or death can never be limited or excluded.

20.5.1.2
Volunteers, trainees etc

If volunteers, trainees and members of the governing body are not explicitly included under the employer's liability insurance [see **20.4.1**], they should be explicitly included in its public liability insurance.

As well as themselves becoming ill or injured as a result of the organisation's negligence, a volunteer or trainee might cause injury or property damage to a user of the organisation or to someone else. The organisation's public liability or professional indemnity [see **20.5.3**] insurance should clearly include liability for injury or damage caused by volunteers and others who are not employees but who carry out work on behalf of the organisation.

In some situations a volunteer or other person could be sued as an individual for damage or injury caused to a third party. The organisation's public or professional liability insurance should indemnify (repay) volunteers or trainees who have such claims brought against them.

20.5.1.3
Members

In some situations one or more members of an unincorporated association could be held liable for damage to another member [see **19.5.4**]. A membership association should therefore ensure that its public liability policy includes **member-to-member insurance** to cover this.

20.5.1.4
Contractors

The organisation should ensure that contractors and self-employed people it hires have, if appropriate, their own public liability insurance to cover them for injury or damage to the organisation's staff or property or members of the public, and/or professional liability insurance [see **20.5.3**]. If the contractor does not have appropriate insurance it raises potentially serious questions about their standing. In some cases the contract may require the organisation to arrange its own cover.

20.5.2
Special activities

Special events or **special activities insurance** should be arranged for activities or events which are not covered by the organisation's usual public liability policy, or for organisations which do not have public liability insurance.

Insurance for equipment, materials and valuable items at the event or in transit to or from it [see **20.6.2**], and pluvius, non-appearance or cancellation insurance [see **20.9.2**] should also be considered.

20.5.3
Professional liability

Professional liability, **professional indemnity**, **errors and omissions** or **malpractice insurance** covers the organisation (or, in an unincorporated organisation, the members of the governing body) for claims arising from loss or injury caused by services provided negligently or without reasonable care. Such loss might arise, for example, from:

- medical treatment which causes further illness, injury or death;
- incorrect welfare benefits advice which leads to a claimant not getting benefits to which he or she is entitled;
- misleading information about tenants' rights which leads to a tenant being evicted.

Even if information or advice is given free or on a telephone or internet helpline, the organisation may be sued if it is incorrect and leads to loss. The organisation may also be sued if the person to whom the advice or information was given repeats it, with the advice giver's knowledge, to a third party (for example, if it is published in a newsletter).

Professional liability insurance often covers defamation [see **20.5.5**], inadvertent breach of copyright [see **20.5.6**], inadvertent breach of confidentiality [see **20.5.7**] and/or loss of documents [see **20.6.5**].

Organisations may find that policies appropriate to their activities and services are available through a national umbrella or support organisation at better rates than are available on the commercial market. They may also find that professional liability cover is included as part of trustee indemnity insurance [see **20.10**].

272

In some situations liability may be excluded by drawing a disclaimer notice to the client's attention [see **19.6.6**]. Liability for personal injury or death cannot be excluded.

20.5.4
Product liability

Product liability arises from illness, injury, death or damage to property caused by a defect in a product, even if there is no negligence. **Product liability insurance** covers organisations which manufacture, sell or supply goods against claims arising from product defects. In some situations an organisation which allows its trademarked logo to be used on a product could be held liable for losses arising from defects in the product, so product liability insurance may be advisable.

20.5.5
Defamation

If the organisation publishes in any media (including the internet), if staff or others representing it send email outside the organisation, or if people representing it speak in public situations, it is advisable to have insurance to cover claims for defamation [see **40.3**]. This may be included as part of professional or trustee indemnity or other insurances.

20.5.6
Breach of copyright

If the organisation produces publications, advertisements, videos or other materials, including on the internet, it may want to insure against claims for inadvertent breach of copyright or other intellectual property rights [see **chapter 39**]. This may be included with other insurances.

20.5.7
Breach of confidentiality

If a worker, user/beneficiary or other person can show that he or she has been damaged because the organisation or someone working for it disclosed information which should have been kept confidential, he or she could bring a claim against the organisation (or, in an unincorporated organisation, the members of its governing body). Insurance is available to cover inadvertent breach of confidentiality and/or breach of Data Protection Act duties [see **chapter 38**].

20.5.8
Breach of contract

If an organisation is obliged to provide goods or services under contract and is unable to do so, the organisation may be liable to the other party for any loss it suffers as a result [see **19.4.4**]. For example, a local authority might place children in a community nursery which then fails to provide services as required under the contract. If the local authority has to move the children to another nursery, it can sue the first nursery for the costs of the transfer. Third parties who do not receive a benefit to which they are entitled—in this case, the children or their parents—may also have a right to sue for breach of contract [see **18.6.5**].

An organisation cannot insure against its own deliberate default on a contract. However it can take out **consequential loss insurance** [see **20.9.1**] to cover situations where a contract cannot be performed because of some act beyond its control, such as flood or fire. An alternative is to include a *force majeure* clause in the contract saying the organisation will not be liable if it cannot provide the service because of specified circumstances beyond its control [see **18.11.4**].

20.5.9
Debts to third parties

An organisation cannot insure against its inability to pay money it owes, because the insurer would in effect be guaranteeing its debts.

20.6
PROTECTING THE ORGANISATION'S ASSETS

Many insurances are available to protect the organisation from loss or damage to its premises and possessions.

If property belongs to the organisation itself, there is no statutory obligation to insure it. However all charity trustees have a duty to safeguard the charity's assets [see **13.3.5**], and the Charity Commission considers that failure to insure buildings and valuable contents could constitute a breach of trust [see **20.2.2**].

If property used by the organisation belongs to someone else—for example premises rented from a landlord, a photocopier leased from a photocopier company, paintings lent by the local art gallery or a local artist, a laptop computer belonging to an employee or volunteer—it is essential to be clear who is responsible for insuring it against loss, damage and theft. If an asset is being used as security for a loan, the lender will almost certainly require it to be insured.

Insuring property for less than the true value could invalidate the insurance or lead to only partial recovery on a claim. The amount insured should be regularly reviewed, even if the policy contains provision for regular inflation increases.

All policies should be carefully checked for exclusions. Many do not cover, for example, damage caused by riots, terrorism, explosion or impact of vehicles.

20.6.1
Buildings

Usually the freeholder [see **56.3**] takes out **buildings insurance** but in some cases, particularly with long leases, the responsibility may be shifted to the tenant. The insurance covers damage to the structure, and may also cover damage to its grounds and items such as fences.

Buildings insurance may include damage arising from:

- **fire only** (which may include lightning and some explosions);
- fire and **special perils**, which includes named perils such as storms, flood, earthquakes, aircraft, riots and malicious damage; *or*
- **all risks**, which covers all causes except those which are explicitly excluded. Exclusions might include subsidence, defective design etc.

Buildings cover does not always include the land, roads, pavements, bridges, culverts etc which could be damaged, by flood for example. Consideration should be given to their inclusion.

As well as insuring the premises, the organisation should consider other costs it might incur if its building is unusable, and possibly take out consequential loss insurance [see **20.9.1**].

20.6.1.1
Basis of insurance

Buildings insurance should normally be on a full **reinstatement** basis, including cover for site clearance, professional services and any special additional costs because, for example, the building is on a difficult site for rebuilding or has important historical detail. For an old or obsolete building the freeholder or other owner may insure for a lesser **first loss** value, in order to reduce outgoings. This is generally not advisable and in some situations, such as buildings subject to listing or a conservation order, it is inappropriate.

If a building is held on mortgage the building society or other mortgagor generally requires it to be insured for its full rebuilding cost.

If the organisation is unable to reclaim VAT [see **chapter 53**], the sum insured should include all VAT which the organisation would have to pay as part of the costs of rebuilding.

20.6.1.2
Insurance by a landlord

If the organisation rents and the landlord is responsible for insuring the premises, the organisation must:

- check that its fittings and fixtures [see **56.7.8**] are covered (or the organisation should insure them under its own policy);
- ensure the policy covers the value of any improvements made by the organisation (or the organisation can insure this itself);
- check that the policy covers rental losses, so the organisation is not responsible for paying rent while the building is unusable, and that the period is sufficient to allow rebuilding (and/or take out its own insurance to cover the rent it would have to pay while the premises are being repaired or rebuilt);
- ensure a full range of risks are covered, and either arrange or get the landlord to arrange cover for omitted risks;
- monitor the extent of cover and any excess (first part of any claim which will not be paid by the insurer) during the period of the lease;

- consider what additional costs the organisation might have to bear if the building was damaged, and take out additional insurance as appropriate [see **20.9.1**].

If the organisation as tenant is paying the landlord's building insurance premium, it should request a waiver of subrogation rights [see **20.3.2**].

The links between lease provisions and insurance arrangements should be carefully considered. For example if the building is damaged the lease may allow the landlord to terminate the lease and to keep all the insurance money, thus depriving the organisation of the value of improvements it has made. The easiest way to protect the organisation's improvements to leased property is to include them in the organisation's own policy. Even if covered by the landlord's policy, the organisation's interest should be noted in the landlord's policy.

The lease should also provide that if the landlord fails to reinstate the premises, the liability to pay rent ceases.

Organisations which are themselves landlords should consider the same issues. In particular they should generally ensure they are covered for two or three years loss of rent (or more, if necessary) while the building is being reinstated after damage.

20.6.1.3
Building works

Where building works or renovations are being undertaken, the organisation should ensure that the contractor is insured for public liability [see **20.5.1.4**], and for non-completion of the work if, for example, the contractor goes out of business. This is called a **performance bond**. The organisation should also ensure that the actual works are covered against loss or damage, through **contractor's all risks cover**. Some contracts may require this insurance to be arranged by the organisation or jointly by the organisation and contractor.

20.6.1.4
Terrorism

For non-domestic premises, insurance against damage or loss caused by terrorist attacks is generally limited to £100,000 each for buildings, contents and consequential loss [see **20.9.1**] at each insured location. Organisations which need higher cover must take out insurance through Pool Re (a government-backed insurance pool) or an alternative scheme. This can be arranged through the usual insurer or broker.

20.6.1.5
Glass

Plate glass windows are frequently excluded from the landlord's obligation to insure. If this is the case, the tenant will need to take out separate cover. This may also cover sanitary ware, sinks and similar items.

20.6.1.6
Engineering

Boilers, lifts, air conditioning and similar electrical or mechanical equipment can be insured against breakdown and some damage. The insurer will require the equipment to satisfy requirements for regular statutory inspections [see **36.4.12** and **36.4.15**].

20.6.2
Contents

Contents insurance generally covers loss of and damage to movable items in the building, and usually in the grounds: equipment, machinery, furnishings and stock or supplies. Some **fixtures and fittings** such as wall lamps, built-in display cases or fitted carpets might not fit easily into a buildings policy or a contents policy, and advice should be taken from the insurer or broker to be sure such items are covered.

Specific items such as bicycles, computers, anything with a value of more than a defined amount, cash, food in freezers, other food, documents [see **20.6.5**] and data stored on computer or disk may need separate extensions within the policy.

Some contents policies cover accidental damage; others do not. If it is an all risks policy or has an extension for theft, it generally covers theft of contents by persons other than staff, governing body members and others in a position of trust in relation to the organisation. Cover for theft by them needs separate fidelity insurance [see **20.6.3.1**].

275

The risks covered by the policy need to be carefully examined along with any exclusions and limitations. Cover against theft, especially, is increasingly qualified by requirements for alarms, specified types of lock and other safeguards. These limitations apply especially to cover for cash or vulnerable equipment such as computers and sound systems.

It is normally sensible for contents insurance to be on a **new for old** or **reinstatement basis** [see **20.3.1**]. If the organisation is prepared to replace its lost or damaged equipment with second-hand replacements or is willing to cover the additional cost of new items, the insurance may be on an **indemnity basis**, with the value adjusted to allow for wear and tear and depreciation. If the organisation cannot reclaim VAT it should include the cost of VAT when working out the value of contents.

To ensure that all items are covered and to make it easier to claim in case of theft or damage, an up-to-date inventory should be kept off the premises, listing all furniture, equipment and other items. It should show when items were obtained, the purchase price (or value, if received as a gift), and serial number or other identifying data.

20.6.2.1
Computers

Rather than including computers as part of the standard contents policy, it may be appropriate to take out a separate policy to cover:

- repair or replacement of the computer, regardless of how the damage or loss was caused;

- the cost of replacing software, reinstating data etc if information is erased or corrupted;

- consequential loss [see **20.9.1**] if the organisation could suffer financial loss as a result of having to operate without the computer.

Computer cover is generally only fully operative while the equipment is under warranty and/or a maintenance agreement, and only covers costs not covered by the warranty or maintenance agreement. Cover for systems and data is usually dependent on backups being kept at another location or in a fireproof cabinet.

20.6.2.2
Property of workers, users and members

Contents insurance covers equipment, goods etc belonging to the organisation. Additional cover will normally need to be arranged if the insurance is to cover personal property belonging to employees, volunteers, members, users of services or facilities, or visitors to the premises. It is especially important to be clear about this if people bring valuable equipment, such as computers or sound systems, onto the premises.

20.6.2.3
Items off the premises

Many contents policies cover items in transit or when away from the premises for limited periods, but some do not. Even if items are covered in transit, they may not be covered if the vehicle they are in is unattended. The organisation should consider the need for more extensive cover, for example if staff take equipment home or off site.

20.6.3
Money

The organisation should arrange insurance against loss or theft of money if it receives substantial amounts of cash or cheques; it keeps substantial cash, cheques or unused postage stamps on its premises or elsewhere; or individuals carry large amount of money to or from the bank or anywhere else.

A money policy is subject to strict limitations and may cover only theft by third parties, not by staff or governing body members. Some policies provide cover for theft of money by employees, where the loss is discovered within a specified period (generally three to seven days). Such cover can be extended to volunteers.

20.6.3.1
Fidelity

Fidelity or **fidelity guarantee insurance** covers the organisation for theft by, or dishonesty of, employees, volunteers, governing body members and/or others who handle money or valuable equipment for the organisation. The Charity Commission recommends that charities take out this cover if its financial advisors or insurance brokers advise it.

It is important to check the policy details carefully, since cover may be dependent upon safeguards such as the organisation obtaining a certain number of references, asking whether the person has any unspent convictions [see **25.10**] for offences involving deception, theft, fraud or dishonesty, or undertaking a criminal records check [see **26.3.3**]. Before arranging such insurance the insurer may investigate the individuals covered and the organisation's financial procedures.

As new individuals take on financial or similar responsibilities, they must be added to the policy unless the policy is explicitly 'all employees' or 'all employees, volunteers and trustees' (or whatever).

20.6.4
Money owed to the organisation

Where the organisation sells goods or provides services on credit, **credit insurance** may be available to cover purchasers' failure to pay in certain circumstances.

20.6.5
Documents and data

It is possible to take out insurance to cover costs arising from loss of documents or information. This is often included as part of another cover. Insurance to cover loss of computer data may be included as part of a separate computer insurance policy, and will require safe storage of backups [see **20.6.2.1**].

20.7
HIRING PREMISES

An organisation which hires out its premises should make absolutely clear, in writing, who is responsible for insuring against damage to the building, damage to or theft of contents, and public liability while all or part of the premises are in use. It may be possible to arrange extensions as required with the organisation's insurer, and to include the cost of these as part of the booking fee.

If the party hiring the premises is required to arrange its own cover, the organisation should have procedures to confirm that this has been done and to have its name included as joint insured. Such arrangements impose considerable administrative burden on the organisation.

Similarly an organisation which hires premises from someone else should be clear about its potential liability in case of damage, theft or injury to the public while it is using the premises.

20.8
VEHICLES

An organisation which operates its own vehicles or vehicles owned by other persons, or whose employees or volunteers use their own or other people's vehicles for work purposes, must ensure that they are properly insured. The Community Transport Association [see end of chapter] can provide information on insurances for vehicles and drivers.

Exclusions should be carefully examined. In particular, many policies do not cover use for business purposes [see **20.8.1.1**], or use by drivers under 25 unless they are individually named in the policy.

All relevant information, including medical conditions and driving convictions of anyone who might drive the organisation's vehicles, must be disclosed to the insurer, and the information must be kept up to date. The organisation should photocopy volunteer and employee drivers' driving licenses each year, and keep the copies on file.

20.8.1
Third party

No vehicle can be used on a road unless it is insured for injury to or death of passengers and third parties, and damage to the property of passengers and third parties. It is an offence for the owner or keeper of a vehicle to use it, or allow it to be used, without this insurance. There is no obligation for the insurance to cover injury or death of the vehicle owner or driver, or damage to their property.

Road Traffic Act 1988 s.143

Third party insurance also covers vehicle accidents on private property, and some legal expenses arising from vehicle accidents. It may also cover injury or damage caused by passengers or by trailers or caravans being towed by the vehicle.

20.8.1.1
Employees and
volunteers using
their own cars

Most insurance for private vehicles covers **social, domestic and pleasure use**, but not **business use**. 'Business use' means using the vehicle for the purposes of any paid employment, for example driving to work-related meetings, delivering the organisation's goods, or transporting clients. Journeys between home and the employee's usual place of work are generally 'domestic' rather than business use, but some insurers may charge an extra premium for regular commuting.

Some insurers consider that work as an unpaid volunteer falls within social, domestic and pleasure use, but others define it as business use. 'Unpaid volunteer' means receiving no more than reimbursement of genuine out-of-pocket expenses, with mileage reimbursed at no more than the Inland Revenue approved rate [see **35.2.1**].

Employees, volunteers, trainees and others who use their cars for business use must:

- inform their insurer that they are using the car for work; *and*

- ensure the insurer amends the policy to cover this use, or provides written confirmation that such amendment is not required.

Depending on the level of additional risk, the insurer might or might not charge an additional premium. (Using a car to attend occasional meetings does not create substantial additional risk; using it to carry children from the local playscheme to the park, library or swimming pool every day does.) The National Centre for Volunteering [see end of chapter] maintains a list of insurers who do not charge an extra premium for car use as a volunteer.

If there is an additional premium, the organisation should be clear about whether it will cover the cost. The Inland Revenue considers that its approved mileage rates for employees and volunteers [see **27.4.5**] include the cost of insurance, so anything additional paid to an employee or volunteer could be subject to tax, and could affect the amount of state benefits if a volunteer is receiving them [see **35.10**].

Although it is the responsibility of the individual to notify his or her insurer, it is good practice for the organisation to:

- inform all employees and volunteers who use or might use their car for work purposes that they must inform their insurer in writing (the organisation might provide a form letter for this purpose);

- ask to see proof of insurance which covers the vehicle *for this purpose* before the person is allowed to use their car for the organisation, and keep a copy of this with the worker's personnel records;

- ask to see proof of insurance once a year (this may be easier if it is the same date for all car users, rather than each car user's anniversary), and keep a copy of this; *and*

- on the mileage claim form, include a statement by which the worker confirms that his or her vehicle remains insured for the purpose for which it is being used (and is also taxed and if required has a valid MoT certificate), and that the driver has not been charged with or convicted of any motoring offence since the last mileage claim.

An organisation which fails to carry out these procedures could be found to be negligent if an uninsured vehicle is involved in an accident while being used for the organisation's business.

Even with these procedures, an organisation might want to ask its insurer to arrange **motor contingency insurance**. If this can be arranged, it provides third party cover for the organisation in case employees' or volunteers' own insurance has lapsed or is invalid.

If employees or volunteers use their cars only occasionally for the organisation, for example for one-off events, the organisation may be able to arrange **occasional business use cover**. The insurer should be approached in good time, in case insurance cannot be arranged and the employees and volunteers each have to contact their own insurer.

**20.8.2
Excess and
no claims discount**

The organisation can take out insurance providing **protection for a no claims discount** and/or **cover for an excess**. This has nothing to do with the legally required third party insurance [see above]. It indemnifies employees and volunteers who have to pay an excess or who lose their no-claims discount or have it reduced as a result of an accident while driving for the organisation. Where such insurance is being effected for members of the governing body of a charity the prior written consent of the Charity Commission must be obtained, because such insurance is considered to provide a benefit to the trustees.

**20.8.3
Insuring the vehicle**

Third party insurance does not cover damage to the user's own vehicle. **Third party, fire and theft insurance** adds to the basic third party policy additional protection if the vehicle is stolen or damaged by fire. Theft insurance may cover not only the vehicle but also items which form part of the vehicle and its equipment, such as the radio or toolbox. It may cover theft of other items left in the car, but generally only if they are locked in the boot or are otherwise out of sight.

Comprehensive insurance covers third party, fire, theft and a range of other risks such as collision (damage to the car caused by the driver), windscreen breakage, and theft of items left in the car.

**20.8.4
Charging for
journeys**

Vehicle insurance policies generally exclude any use of the vehicle 'for hire or reward'. But this exclusion does not generally apply to users of cars holding up to eight passengers who charge passengers only enough to cover the cost of each journey.

The Inland Revenue guidelines on allowable reimbursement for vehicle use by employees and volunteers [see **27.4.5**] are used to determine the allowable mileage rate for journeys. If the organisation charges more than this for use of its vehicles, or if employees or volunteers use their own cars to carry passengers and charge them more than this, the vehicles will need to have additional insurance for 'hire or reward' use.

Even where hire or reward insurance is not required, the organisation, employee or volunteer is still obliged to notify the insurer that passengers are being charged.

Organisations operating minibuses (seating nine to 16 passengers) and larger buses should contact the Community Transport Association [see end of chapter] for advice about insurance and driver licensing.

**20.8.5
Driving abroad**

UK insurance provides the minimum legally required third party insurance throughout the EU, but additional insurance must be specially arranged through the insurer. The **green card**, issued by insurance companies to show that the vehicle has EU third party insurance, is not legally required so long as the policy is available.

Detailed information about driving abroad or taking a car abroad is available from insurers and motoring organisations. Organisations which provide transport services (minibuses, dial-a-ride etc) should contact the Community Transport Association [see end of chapter].

**20.9
LOSS TO THE
ORGANISATION**

An organisation may suffer loss because it is liable to an employee or other person, but may also suffer direct losses not involving any loss to a third party. Theft of its property is an example, but many other types of direct loss can also be insured against.

20.9.1
Consequential loss

If flood, fire or other disaster prevents an income-generating body from operating for a period, it may suffer significant loss of income. Even small localised damage such as a fire near a desk or a flooded basement may have a significant impact if it destroys vital records or equipment.

Such losses can be covered under **business interruption, loss of business** or **consequential loss insurance**. These provide a guaranteed income until the organisation is able to restart the income generating activity. The insurance might cover loss of profit, the additional costs of carrying on work at different premises, or amounts due if work required under a contract cannot be performed as required.

Organisations which do not carry out trading or income generation should insure on an **additional expenses** basis, to take account of rent for alternative accommodation, one-off costs to make the premises suitable, reprinting stationery and similar costs.

In all cases it is crucial to allow for an adequate indemnity period. For some premises the standard period of 12 months may not be adequate for repairs or rebuilding, or may not allow enough time for the organisation's trading or operating position to be restored. If the indemnity period is set at two or three years, the sum insured should reflect the revenue or additional expenses for that period.

To prevent the organisation becoming completely immobilised by a fire, theft or other loss it is very good practice to keep duplicates or backups of crucial records off site and to have a disaster plan.

20.9.2
Failure of events

An organisation may suffer financial loss if a public event is cancelled or unsuccessful, by having financial obligations which it has to meet anyway and/or because it does not receive the income it anticipated. Some of these losses can be insured against, but a careful decision has to be made about whether the risk justifies the cost.

Cancellation insurance covers the organisation's financial obligations or loss of income if an event is cancelled for reasons beyond its control. Cancellation due to lack of support is not covered.

Non-appearance insurance covers loss of money or reputation as a result of a speaker or other key person not appearing.

Pluvius insurance (Latin, 'rain'), covers losses suffered because an event is wholly or partly stopped by rain. It is important to be clear about how much rain has to fall and where it will be measured. Cover is less expensive if the insurance is taken out well before the event.

20.9.3
Legal costs

Legal costs or **legal expenses insurance** covers the solicitor's and other costs incurred in specified court proceedings or employment tribunal claims. Some policies also cover any damages which the organisation is ordered to pay in a civil case (a case brought by a person rather than by the state), for example damages awarded to employees. Insurance cannot cover penalties or fines arising from criminal acts or breach of a statutory duty.

It is essential to be clear about whether the insurance covers only legal expenses (solicitor etc costs), or covers damages as well.

Policies may be linked to an advice line which provides initial advice on issues which may give rise to a claim. The insurance may require such advice not only to be taken but also to be followed, which will limit the organisation's freedom to resolve matters in the way it wishes.

20.9.4
Charity protection

Charity protection or **trust indemnity insurance** protects a charity from losses to the charity caused by one or more members of the governing body and not recoverable from the individuals involved. It is generally included in trustee indemnity insurance [see below].

20.10 TRUSTEE INDEMNITY AND DIRECTORS' AND OFFICERS' INSURANCE

The potential liabilities faced by members of the governing body and ordinary members of organisations are covered in detail in **chapter 19**. These liabilities might be to third parties (for example through the organisation's or their own breach of contract, negligence or breach of duty) or to the organisation itself (for example for using its funds for purposes for which they should not have been used).

Trustee indemnity insurance (also called **trustee liability insurance**) or **directors' and officers' insurance** (D&O) covers some of the losses caused by governing body members *to their organisation*. It does not generally cover losses caused to third parties.

Charitable organisations may pay for such insurance only if their governing document explicitly allows this or the Charity Commission has given consent [see **20.2.4**].

Details of the insurance must be disclosed in a company and/or charity annual report [see **50.2.11** and **50.3.3**].

In most situations ordinary members of an organisation (those who are not on its governing body) are unlikely to be liable to the organisation.

20.10.1 What is covered

When a governing body member causes a loss to the organisation because of breach of trust or breach of duty as a trustee or company director [see **19.3**], the governing body member normally has to make good the loss to the organisation. Trustee indemnity or D&O insurance covers some of these liabilities.

20.10.1.1 For charities

The Charity Commission does not allow indemnity insurance for charity trustees to cover any act which the trustee knew was a breach of trust or breach of duty, or committed 'in reckless disregard of whether it was a breach of trust or breach of duty'. **Reckless disregard** means it would have been reasonable for the trustee to realise that such an act might be in breach of trust or duty, but that he or she went ahead with the act without getting advice or finding out if it was a breach.

Examples of situations which might be covered are where one or more trustees are required by a charity or the Charity Commission to repay to the charity:

- funds used for activities outside the charity's objects or powers, provided the trustees genuinely believed and had reason to believe that the activity was within the charity's objects or powers;

- funds used for a political activity which the Commission considers to be outside what is allowed [see **41.3**], provided the trustees genuinely thought it was acceptable and, if appropriate, had taken and acted on proper advice about whether it was acceptable;

- losses caused by poor investments, provided the trustees had taken and acted on proper investment advice and had invested prudently [see **54.1.1**].

20.10.1.2 For companies and IPSs

For directors in *non-charitable* companies and industrial and provident societies the cover is wider and can include situations where the directors did not take proper advice. It may cover liability of directors arising from wrongful trading (operating while they knew, or reasonably should have known, that the organisation was insolvent or was becoming insolvent; see **21.2.4**).

In *charitable* companies and IPSs the insurance cannot cover such liability if the director knew that the company was insolvent or allowed the organisation to continue operating in reckless disregard of whether it was solvent or not. This seems to preclude most situations in which a director of a charitable company or IPS could be held liable for wrongful trading, so insurance should not be relied on to provide cover in this situation.

20.10.1.3
Legal costs

Trustee indemnity or directors' and officers' insurance may cover the cost of defending legal proceedings brought against a governing body member for beach of trust or breach of duty—but only if the defendant is found to be not guilty.

The insurance may also cover legal costs for cases such as Charity Commission investigations where the charity's funds cannot be used to pay the costs.

20.10.1.4
Additional cover

Trustee indemnity or D&O insurance generally includes a range of other cover, such as legal expenses [see **20.9.3**], professional indemnity [see **20.5.3**], fidelity [see **20.6.3.1**], loss of documents [see **20.6.5**], breach of copyright [see **20.5.6**] and/or breach of confidentiality [see **20.5.7**]. All policies are different, so it is important to check what is and is not covered and to be sure that the organisation is not paying twice for the same cover under two different policies.

20.10.2
What is not covered

Trustee indemnity or directors' and officers' insurance does not cover:

- liabilities to third parties, such as for breach of contract, redundancy payments or negligence, unless such cover is provided as an addition to the basic cover [see **20.10.1.4**];

- penalties for breach of statutory duty, or fines;

- liability arising from any act which the person knew was fraudulent or dishonest;

- losses arising from the trustees' or directors' failure to insure the organisation's assets, where such failure is a breach of trust [see **20.2.2**];

- in a company or industrial and provident society, liability arising from **fraudulent trading**, where the director deceived creditors or others while the organisation was, or was becoming insolvent [see **21.2.4**];

- in a charitable organisation, any act which the a trustee knew was in breach of trust, or committed in reckless disregard of whether it was in breach of trust.

If the act which gives rise to the liability is not covered under the insurance, the governing body member will be obliged to indemnify the organisation for its losses and will not be entitled to be indemnified under the insurance.

FOR FURTHER INFORMATION

Brokers. British Insurance Brokers Association: 020-7623 9043; www.biba.org.uk

Names of insurers for voluntary organisations. National Council for Voluntary Organisations: 0800-2 798 798; www.ncvo-vol.org.uk

Wales Council for Voluntary Action: 029-2043 1700; www.wcva.org.uk

Umbrella organisations, councils for voluntary service etc

Sports activities. Central Council of Physical Recreation: 020-7828 3163; www.ccpr.org.uk

Vehicles and drivers. Community Transport Association: 0161-367 8780, www.communitytransport.com

Volunteers. National Centre for Volunteering: 020-7520 8900, www.volunteering.org.uk

Complaints. Association of British Insurers: 020-7600 3333; www.abi.org.uk

Insurance Brokers' Registration Council: 01933-359083

General Insurance Standards Council: 020-7648 7800; www.gisc.co.uk

Chapter 21
FINANCIAL DIFFICULTIES AND WINDING UP

21.1 ENDING AN ORGANISATION

How an organisation ends depends on whether it is incorporated or unincorporated, and whether it is solvent or insolvent. The terms **winding up**, **liquidation** and **dissolution** describe different parts of the process, although in practice the terms are used interchangeably.

21.1.1 Winding up

Winding up is the process of ceasing to operate: making the decision, stopping activities and services, dismissing staff, closing premises, paying the bills, terminating contracts, dealing with liabilities etc.

21.1.2 Liquidation

Liquidation is a formal process governed by the **Insolvency Act 1986**. It involves selling or disposing of the assets of a company or industrial and provident society and dealing with the liabilities. **Insolvent liquidation** occurs when the organisation is insolvent.

Most corporate bodies (companies and industrial and provident societies) which wind up go through a formal liquidation, even if they are solvent. Confusingly all liquidations, even if the company or IPS is solvent, are covered by the Insolvency Act.

Unincorporated bodies (associations and trusts) do not have to go through a formal process comparable to liquidation. If they have enough funds to meet their financial obligations the bills are simply paid off, all

283

contracts are terminated and any remaining assets are distributed as specified in the governing document. But if an unincorporated association or trust will not be able to meet all its financial obligations, the members of the governing body should get urgent professional help to ensure that the organisation's assets are properly disposed of and to reduce the risk of personal liability for individuals.

21.1.2.1
Insolvency practitioners

Insolvency practitioners are individuals, usually accountants or solicitors, licensed under the **Insolvency Act 1986** ss.390-393 to carry out liquidations of solvent and insolvent companies and industrial and provident societies. Only a minority of accountants and a very small minority of solicitors are insolvency practitioners, and of those only a very small number have experience of voluntary sector insolvency.

The **official receiver** is a court official appointed by the court to deal with liquidations and bankruptcies.

Any accountant or solicitor may advise on liquidation or insolvency, but only an insolvency practitioner or the official receiver can carry out the role of liquidator or similar roles such as administrator. Costs for liquidation vary widely, and quotes should if possible be obtained from more than one potential liquidator before selecting one.

21.1.2.2
Distribution of assets

If any assets remain after all the organisation's liabilities and the costs of dissolution have been met, they may be distributed only as set out in the dissolution clause of the governing document [see **5.4.27**]. The most usual requirement is that they are given to one or more organisations which have similar objects and prohibit their profits from being distributed to at least the same extent as the dissolved organisation.

The decision as to how the assets should be distributed may be left to the members of a company, IPS or association in general meeting, or to the governing body. In some cases third parties must be consulted. Alternatively, the governing document may name a specific organisation or organisations to which the assets must be given.

Clubs and some other non-charitable organisations may be allowed by their governing document to distribute surplus assets to their members [see **21.7.1**].

21.1.3
Dissolution

Dissolution is the final stage in ending the organisation, when it ceases to exist. Companies and industrial and provident societies come into being by registration, and cease to exist only when they are removed from the relevant register. Unincorporated trusts and associations may dissolve themselves using the procedure in their governing document [see **21.7.1** and **21.8.4** for what happens if there is no procedure]. If the organisation is a registered charity, the Charity Commission must be notified that it has been dissolved.

21.1.3.1
Dissolution without winding up

An organisation may be dissolved without being liquidated or wound up, for example if its assets, liabilities and work are all transferred to another organisation, or if two organisations are dissolved and merge to form a new organisation [for more about merger, see **9.9**].

21.1.3.2
Between liquidation and dissolution

A company which is being liquidated, but has not yet been dissolved, is still in existence and can still receive legacies. This has implications where the company is insolvent, and the legacy therefore becomes available to meet the company's debts [see **46.4.1**].

ARMS (Multiple Sclerosis Research) Ltd: Alleyne v Attorney General & another
[1997] 2 All ER 679

21.2
SOLVENCY AND INSOLVENCY

An organisation does not become insolvent when it runs out of money. It is likely to have become insolvent much earlier, at the point when it became clear that there was no realistic hope of financial survival.

21.2.1
Tests for insolvency

Two 'tests' are used to determine if an organisation is, or is likely to become, insolvent. If an organisation fails on either, it needs to take urgent advice from an accountant or solicitor.

21.2.1.1
Cashflow test

An organisation fails the **going concern** or **cashflow test** if it cannot pay the money it owes when payment is due, or if this is likely to occur within the foreseeable future. 'Foreseeable' depends on the organisation and the situation, but is generally the next 12 months.

Companies and industrial and provident societies are considered unable to pay their debts if:

- a creditor (a person to whom money is owed) for more than £750 has demanded the amount due, and the organisation has not paid within three weeks or made satisfactory arrangements to pay;

- the organisation has not paid a creditor after being ordered by a court to do so; *or*

- the High Court is satisfied that the organisation is unable to pay its debts as they fall due.   *Insolvency Act 1986 s.123(1)*

21.2.1.2
Balance sheet test

An organisation fails the **balance sheet test** if the value of its total assets is less than its total liabilities, taking into account current and contingent liabilities and sometimes also prospective liabilities.

s.123(2)

Current liabilities are due now (generally defined as within the next 12 months). **Contingent** liabilities are those which will arise only if a specific event does or does not happen, such as redundancy payments. **Prospective** liabilities are those which the organisation knows it will have, such as a loan due for repayment in two years' time.

The liabilities included in the balance sheet test depend on assumptions about the organisation. If the governing body can reasonably assume that the organisation will be able to continue operating into the foreseeable future, it can do its balance sheet test on a **going concern** basis, and does not need to include liabilities contingent on winding up (redundancy payments, penalty clauses in contracts and leases, winding up costs, etc). But if this assumption cannot reasonably be made, the balance sheet test must be on a **break-up** basis, including all the liabilities contingent on winding up.

An organisation which passes the balance sheet test (has assets worth more than liabilities) but cannot pay its debts when they are due will not generally be considered insolvent if it can borrow against the value of its assets, sell the assets and use the money to pay the debts, or convince creditors to wait for later payment.

21.2.1.3
Technical insolvency

If an organisation is able to pay its debts as they fall due but fails the balance sheet test, it is sometimes said to be **technically insolvent**. An organisation in this situation should seek advice.

21.2.2
Insecure funding

Many voluntary organisations have virtually no assets and are wholly dependent on external bodies for their funding. There is often a period towards the end of the financial year when the organisation has no guarantee of funding for the next year, and has no reserves to cover its commitments beyond the end of the financial year.

If there is any risk that a company or industrial and provident society could find itself at the beginning of the financial year (or at any other time) without sufficient funds to cover its liabilities, it should strictly speaking take advice from an insolvency practitioner [see **21.1.2.1**], who might well advise winding up. Similarly, if there is any risk that an unincorporated organisation could find itself unable to pay its bills, it really should start winding up in order to avoid any increased personal liability for the governing body members.

But if these steps were taken every time an organisation with inadequate reserves faced uncertainty about funding, many viable organisations would close each year. Unfortunately, not taking them puts the members of the governing body at risk of personal liability [see **21.2.4**] in unincorporated organisations, and could also put them at risk even in incorporated bodies if the prospects for survival are not good. There is no easy solution here.

The risks inherent in this situation emphasise the importance of:

- building up enough reserves to cover a winding up period;
- not becoming over-dependent on a small number of funding sources;
- educating funders to make decisions in good time.

21.2.2.1
Precautionary
redundancy notices

An organisation facing closure if funding is not forthcoming should take steps to reduce its liabilities. This may include giving **precautionary notice of redundancy** [see **31.3.1**] to employees. Again a balance has to be struck between prudence and realism. Issuing redundancy notices is disruptive and demoralising, but not doing so may put the members of the governing body at risk of personal liability.

21.2.3
Action when facing
insolvency

Once it has become clear that the organisation is going to become or is already insolvent, certain steps are obligatory or advisable. These depend on whether the organisation is incorporated or unincorporated.

Charity Commission booklet CC12 *Managing Financial Difficulties and Insolvency*, free from the Charity Commission or its website, outlines some of the issues. But in any situation where insolvency is a realistic possibility, professional advice is likely to be necessary.

21.2.3.1
Companies and IPSs

When a company or industrial and provident society is in this situation its highest priority in law is to safeguard the interests of its creditors—the people to whom it already owes money. It must take advice as a matter of utmost urgency from its accountant or solicitor, and is likely to have to call in an insolvency practitioner [see **21.1.2.1**].

The organisation should do everything possible to collect all sums owing to it, and should not pay into any account which is overdrawn.

If a company or IPS knows, or should have known, that it cannot avoid liquidation it should not make or authorise any expenditure without taking appropriate advice. Continuing to operate could constitute **wrongful trading** [see **21.2.4.2**] or **preference** [see **21.9.3**].

21.2.3.2
Trusts and associations

Trusts and associations do not have the same legal duty to safeguard the interests of creditors, because the creditors may sue individuals involved in the organisation [see **21.2.4.1**]. Because of this risk to individuals the organisation would be very foolish indeed to continue incurring debt, and should take advice as a matter of utmost urgency from an accountant, solicitor or insolvency practitioner.

21.2.4
Personal liability

It is a very serious matter to continue operating while the organisation could become or is already insolvent. Doing so exposes members of the governing body and in some cases other individuals to risk of personal liability for the organisation's debts.

21.2.4.1
Insolvency in
unincorporated
associations and trusts

Anyone to whom money is owed by an unincorporated association or trust may be able to bring a claim against:

- any member or members of the current governing body;
- anyone who has been on the governing body at any time since the contract, lease or other arrangement on which the money is due was put in place [see **19.4.3**];
- in some situations, any ordinary member of the organisation (not a member of the governing body); *and/or*

- any individual who signed a contract, ordered goods or entered into any other agreement without being properly authorised by the governing body to do so [see **18.5.5**].

A person who has to pay more than a fair share of the organisation's debts is entitled to a contribution from other members of the governing body, but this involves taking further legal action.

Civil Liability (Contribution) Act 1978

Many governing documents provide for members of the governing body to be indemnified (compensated) by the organisation if they suffer any loss as a result of their position. This does not help if the organisation has insufficient assets to indemnify them.

The governing document may say that governing body members have a right to be indemnified by the organisation's members (rather than by the organisation itself) if they suffer any loss. In this situation the governing body members could bring a claim against any or all of the organisation's members.

Even without this clause in the governing document, the organisation's members could be liable for the association's debts if the decisions which led to the insolvency were taken by the members in a general meeting rather than by the governing body.

A person against whom legal action is taken could be personally bankrupted, and should take his or her own legal advice.

**21.2.4.2
Insolvency of
corporate bodies**

In a company or industrial and provident society the ordinary members have **limited liability** in the event of the organisation becoming insolvent. In a company limited by guarantee their maximum liability is the amount of the guarantee under the memorandum of association [see **10.4.1**]. In a company limited by shares or IPS the maximum is the amount unpaid on their shares.

In general the officers of a company or industrial and provident society (members of the governing body, the company/IPS secretary, and senior employees) are protected from personal liability if the organisation becomes insolvent. But they may, individually or as a group, lose the protection of limited liability if the organisation goes into insolvent liquidation and they have allowed it to continue operating while they knew or reasonably should have known that it was, or was inevitably going to become, insolvent. This is known as **wrongful trading**.

Insolvency Act 1986 s.214

Fraudulent trading occurs when an officer or employee of a company or IPS deliberately seeks to defraud any creditor while the organisation is or is becoming insolvent. This is a criminal offence.   *s.213*

Company or IPS officers may also be held personally liable if they:

- have entered a contract or taken other legal action without being authorised to do so [see **18.5.5**];
- have acted in breach of trust or in breach of fiduciary duty [see **19.3** and **21.2.4.3**];
- have acted dishonestly or fraudulently.

The company or IPS may be able to insure against some of these liabilities [see **20.10**], or in a company the directors may be able to apply to the court for relief from liability [see **19.2.5** and **19.3.5**].

A director of a company which becomes insolvent may be disqualified from serving as a director of any company or being involved with setting up or managing any company [see **11.3.3**].

**21.2.4.3
Insolvency of a charity**

In all charitable organisations, even those with limited liability, the members of the governing body may be found in **breach of trust** if they have not acted prudently, for example if they did not receive proper financial information, meet regularly, take and act on proper financial advice, or make decisions properly. In these situations the Charity Commission could require the trustees to repay to the charity any losses incurred by the charity.

Trustee indemnity insurance [see **20.10**] provides some protection against this but does not cover situations where the trustees knowingly acted in breach of trust, or acted in reckless disregard as to whether something was in breach of trust.

A trustee of a trust or charitable association may apply to the court for relief from some or all liability for breach of trust [see **19.3.5**].

21.3 ENDING A COMPANY

A company can cease to exist only in the following ways:

- it applies to the registrar of companies for a **voluntary striking off** from the register of companies [see **21.4.1**];

- it becomes defunct or consistently fails to comply with company legislation, and is **struck off** by the registrar [see **21.4.2**];

- there is a **members' voluntary winding up** [see **21.4.3**] and liquidation (if the company is solvent);

- there is a **creditors' voluntary winding up** [see **21.5.3**] and liquidation (if it winds up voluntarily when it is, or is about to become, insolvent);

- there is winding up by the High Court and **compulsory liquidation** [see **21.5.4**] (if the company is insolvent and action is brought against it by its creditors); *or*

- the attorney general takes proceedings to cancel the registration of a company which has been registered with illegal objects.

The procedures are explained in Companies House leaflets GBW2 *Strike-off, Dissolution and Restoration* and GBW1 *Liquidation and Insolvency*, available from Companies House, and in leaflets from the Insolvency Service [see end of chapter].

As soon as a decision to wind up is made, however informally, the organisation should notify its accountant, auditor and solicitor. Advice may be needed on the most appropriate type of winding up, and on the procedures. Failure to follow the procedures is in many cases an offence.

A company may be merged or amalgamated with or taken over by another company, without having to be wound up, if the High Court agrees. Legal advice is needed for this.

21.3.1 Alternatives to winding up

Winding up a company is a complex procedure involving an liquidator [see **21.1.2.1**] and costing several thousand pounds. If the company is solvent, alternatives are voluntary striking off [see **21.4.1**] or making the company dormant [see **50.3.7**]. If the company is insolvent, a company voluntary arrangement [see **21.5.1**] or administration order [see **21.5.2**] may be possible.

21.4 SOLVENT COMPANIES

21.4.1 Voluntary striking off

The **voluntary striking off** procedure enables a company which is not insolvent and has not operated in the previous three months to apply to be struck off the register and dissolved. The procedure contains detailed safeguards to protect members, creditors, employees and others involved with the company.   *Companies Act 1985 s.652A*

This is a useful and inexpensive way to close a company which is solvent and is no longer required. If it may be required in future, it may be more sensible to put it into dormancy [see **50.3.7**]. The procedure is:

- the company does not carry on its business for at least three months (though it can, during this period, carry out certain transactions necessary to close it down);

- send **form 652a**, signed by a majority of the directors, to the registrar of companies with the fee (£10 as at 1/4/01);

- send copies of the completed form 652a to all company members, creditors (people to whom money is owed), bodies such as the Inland Revenue to whom the organisation owes or will owe money, employees, managers or trustees of any employee pension fund, and any directors (governing body members) who did not sign form 652a;

- the registrar advertises the proposed striking-off;

- if no one objects, the registrar strikes off the company three months after the advertisement.

A company which has been struck off can be restored to the register within 20 years of dissolution, for example if a creditor says the former company owes it money and should not have been struck off.

Companies Act 1985 s.653

21.4.2
Striking off by registrar

A company may be struck off by the registrar and dissolved if it appears that the company is defunct. This could happen if the company persistently does not send in annual returns, accounts and forms which must be filed with Companies House, or if post sent to the company's registered address is returned undelivered. *s.652*

Assets of a company struck off are *bona vacantia*, which means they belong to the Crown. They can be recovered by making an application to the court for the company to be reinstated, but legal advice will be needed and the process is costly. *ss.654-657*

21.4.3
Members' voluntary winding up

If the company is solvent and the members want to end it, but the voluntary striking off procedure [see **21.4.1**] is not appropriate, the members must pass a special resolution [see **17.4.7** for procedure] to be wound up voluntarily. *Insolvency Act 1986 s.84*

Alternatively the articles of association may say that the company is to be dissolved at a particular time, or after a particular event occurs. In this case, if the company is solvent, the members must pass an ordinary resolution [see **17.4.7**] to be wound up voluntarily. *s.84(1)(a)*

These resolutions lead to a **member's voluntary winding up**. The winding up formally starts as soon as the resolution is passed. The company ceases to operate, except as far as is required to wind up, although it continues to exist as a company until it is dissolved.

The advantages of a members' winding up over a voluntary striking off are that the company cannot generally be revived, and the process is managed by a professional. In addition if an unexpected liability arises that makes the company insolvent, a members' voluntary winding up can relatively easily be converted into insolvent liquidation.

The procedure is:

- at any time in the five weeks before the resolution is made, a majority of the directors make a **declaration of solvency** at a board meeting, confirming that they believe the company will be able to pay its debts in full within a specified period, which cannot be more than 12 months from the start of the winding up;

- a **liquidator**, who must be an **insolvency practitioner** [see **21.1.2.1**], is appointed at a general meeting, usually the meeting at which the resolution to wind up is passed;

- the powers of the directors cease as soon as the liquidator is appointed, but a general meeting or the liquidator may agree to allow the directors to continue to operate;

- the liquidator and company members decide on the disposition of the company's assets;

- when the winding up is completed, the liquidator produces a detailed report and accounts and presents them to a general meeting;

- after the meeting, the liquidator sends the accounts and report to the registrar of companies;

- the company is deemed to be dissolved three months from the date the registrar receives the accounts and report.

If at any time during the winding up the liquidator believes the company will not be able to pay its debts in full within the period specified in the declaration of solvency, the winding up is converted into a **creditors' voluntary winding up** [see **21.5.3**].

21.5 INSOLVENT COMPANIES

If a company already is, or is about to become, insolvent a company voluntary arrangement or administration order may be an alternative to winding up. *Specialist advice should be taken at the earliest opportunity.*

21.5.1 Company voluntary arrangements

In a **company voluntary arrangement** the company directors make a proposal to the company members and to its creditors for a **composition** in satisfaction of its debts or a **scheme of arrangement** of its affairs. *Insolvency Act 1986 s.1*

Small companies [see **50.3.2** for definition] may apply for a 28-day **moratorium** to give directors time to put together proposals for the arrangement. During this period the company's creditors (persons to whom money is owed) cannot bring action against the company. *Insolvency Act 2000 ss.1-2*

The directors appoint an insolvency practitioner [see **21.1.2.1**] as **nominee**, and provide information about the company's financial position and their proposed arrangements for paying their creditors. The nominee obtains court approval to call meetings of the company members and its creditors, at which the proposed arrangements are considered and can be modified. When the company members and creditors agree a final arrangement, it takes effect and the nominee becomes the **supervisor**, with responsibility for ensuring the arrangement is implemented. *Insolvency Act 1986 ss.2-7*

21.5.2 Administration orders

An **administration order** is a procedure to try to rescue a failing company, either to bring it to solvency or, if that is not possible, to obtain more for its assets when it is liquidated. The High Court appoints an **administrator** who becomes responsible for managing all the affairs, business and property of the company. This procedure requires the approval of the company's creditors. *ss.8-27*

21.5.3 Creditors' voluntary winding up

A **creditors' voluntary winding up** does not start with the creditors, but with the company members passing an extraordinary resolution [see **17.4.7** for procedure] saying it cannot continue operating because of its liabilities and that it is advisable to wind up. *s.84(1)(c)*

If the company has passed the resolution to liquidate but a liquidator has not yet been appointed, the directors may not spend any money, even on salaries or rent, unless the expenditure is directed solely to winding up the organisation (for example, to collect money owing to it) or is to prevent loss (for example, maintaining insurance policies). Any other action by the directors needs High Court approval.

All powers of the directors cease when the liquidator is appointed. But the liquidation committee or, if there is no committee, the creditors may allow the directors to continue.

The procedure for a creditors' voluntary winding up is:

- the company calls a general meeting at which the resolution calling for the voluntary winding up will be proposed;

- it also calls a meeting of its creditors, to be held not more than 14 days after the general meeting;

- the directors produce a statement of the company's affairs in a prescribed format;
- the company may nominate a **liquidator** [see **21.1.2.1**] at its general meeting, and the creditors may nominate a liquidator at their meeting (there are statutory rules for the procedure if the company and the creditors nominate different people);
- in addition the creditors may appoint a **liquidation committee** made up of not more than five persons plus up to five more appointed by the company;
- as soon as the liquidator is appointed, all expenditure must be authorised by him or her;
- the liquidator, creditors and company members decide on the distribution of the company's assets, following a strict order for the payment of debts [see **21.9**];
- in an insolvent company limited by guarantee, all company members and anyone who has been a member in the year before winding up may be asked to contribute the amount they guaranteed when they became a member [see **10.4.1**];
- when the winding up is completed the liquidator presents a detailed report and accounts to a general meeting and creditors' meeting;
- the liquidator sends the accounts to the registrar of companies;
- the company is deemed to be dissolved three months from the date the registrar receives the accounts and reports.

21.5.4 Compulsory liquidation

The High Court and in some cases county courts may wind up a company in a variety of situations, including where:

- the company is unable to pay its debts [see **21.2.1.1**];
- the company members pass a special resolution [see **17.4.7** for procedure] asking to be wound up by the court; *or*
- the company does not operate in the year after incorporation, or suspends operation for a year. *Insolvency Act 1986 s.122(1)*

A petition for winding up may be presented to the court by the company, all the company directors, a creditor, the secretary of state, or the official receiver. Issuing or threatening to issue a petition is a classic way for a creditor to seek to enforce a debt. *s.124*

If the petition is accepted the court appoints the **official receiver** [see **21.1.2.1**] or other person as liquidator. The process is then broadly similar to the process in a creditors' voluntary winding up but is completely under the jurisdiction of the court. *s.135*

21.6 INDUSTRIAL AND PROVIDENT SOCIETIES

A solvent industrial and provident society may be wound up by an **instrument of dissolution** signed by at least 75% of the IPS's members. *Industrial and Provident Societies Act 1965 ss.55(b), 58*

Alternatively most IPSs may amalgamate with another IPS or company or may undertake a **transfer of engagements** to another IPS or company. An amalgamation creates a new organisation. With a transfer of engagements the organisation transferred to continues, but the one transferred from is generally wound up. *ss.50-52*

An insolvent IPS is wound up in the same way as a company under the **Insolvency Act 1986**. But the procedures for administration orders [see **21.5.2**] and voluntary arrangements [see **21.5.1**] are available only to companies and cannot be used for IPSs. *s.55(a)*

As with companies, there is a strict order for the payment of debts by an insolvent IPS [see **21.9**]. The **Company Directors Disqualification Act 1986** [see **11.3.3**] does not apply to IPSs.

21.7
NON-CHARITABLE ASSOCIATIONS

A non-charitable association must comply with any provisions for dissolution in the governing document. If there are none:

- the organisation may be dissolved if all the members agree (**acquiescence**);

- there may be **spontaneous dissolution** if the organisation has become inactive and it no longer has any assets, contracts or anything else that would indicate a continuing existence; *or*

- the **High Court** may wind up the organisation if application is made to the Chancery Division.

Notification should be given to members, employees, creditors (persons to whom money is owed), and bodies such as the Inland Revenue.

If the association is insolvent, the members of the governing body or in some cases the ordinary members of the organisation could be held liable for its debts [see **21.2.4.1**].

21.7.1
Distribution of assets

If the organisation is solvent and has remaining property after paying its debts, the distribution of the property must comply with any provisions in the governing document.

Donations or legacies received for charitable purposes or the very few types of non-charitable purposes for which a trust can exist [see **1.3.4**] are held on a **constructive trust** [see **44.2.1**]. They must be used only for the purposes for which they were given, or be transferred to an organisation with relevant objects [see **21.8.2** for issues to consider].

Other assets of non-charitable associations are held **on contract** for the members. In the absence of any provision in the governing document for their distribution, the assets are assumed to belong to the members at the time of dissolution, but not to former members. Members are entitled to equal shares unless some classes of members have different constitutional rights. The distribution is subject to income tax. Members dissatisfied with the distribution may apply to the High Court.

If an association has no members or only one member its property is *bona vacantia* (belongs to the Crown).

Re Brighton Cycling and Angling Club Trusts [1956] The Times 7/3/1956

21.8
CHARITABLE TRUSTS AND ASSOCIATIONS

The process for dissolving a charitable trust or association depends on whether it is solvent and whether its governing document contains a procedure for dissolution. It will also be affected by whether the charity has any permanent endowment (money which is held on condition that it not be spent, or property held on condition that it not be sold or that any proceeds from the sale not be spent).

When any charity is dissolved or ceases to operate, the Charity Commission must be notified and will remove the charity from the register. The charity's financial records must be kept for at least six years unless the Commission says they can be destroyed.

Charities Act 1993 ss.3(7)(b), 41(4)

21.8.1
Permanently endowed

A charitable trust or association which has permanent endowment [see above] generally cannot distribute that endowment. The Charity Commission must be consulted, and may suggest that the charity be amalgamated with another charity with the same or similar objects.

21.8.1.1
Very small charities with permanent endowment

There is an exception for very small charitable trusts and associations, which may spend their permanent endowment and wind up if:

- their permanent endowment does not include land;

- the charity's income from all sources in the last financial year was less than £1,000; *and*

- the trustees believe that the charity's assets are too small to achieve any useful purpose from the income alone, and that a transfer of the assets to another charity is not practical.   *Charities Act 1993 s.75*

The resolution to spend the permanent endowment must be passed by a two-thirds vote of the governing body, must be publicised in a reasonable way, and must be notified to the Charity Commission. Exempt charities [see **7.1.2** for definition] cannot use this procedure.

21.8.2
Transfer of assets

Before dissolving the charity, careful thought should be given to whether there are any potential claims against it. If its assets are completely used or are transferred to another organisation and a claim later emerges, the members of the governing body of the transferring organisation will have no funds to meet the claim. If assets are transferred, it is sensible for the transferring organisation to require an indemnity for any future claim. This is done by deed [see **18.3**].

21.8.3
Dissolution procedure

If a charitable association or trust does not have permanent endowment and its governing document contains a dissolution procedure, the charity must follow this and any assets must be distributed as specified.

21.8.4
No dissolution procedure

If the governing document does not include provision for dissolution, small charities may be able to use the procedure below. Other charities which want to wind up must contact the Charity Commission.

21.8.4.1
Small charities

In small charities the trustees may pass a resolution by a two-thirds majority to transfer the assets to one or more charities with similar objects, publicise the decision and notify the Commission. To do this:

- the charity's income from all sources must be less than £5,000 in its last financial year;
- it must not hold any land which must, under the terms on which it is held, be used only for the purposes of the charity; *and*
- the trustees of the recipient charity or charities must have indicated their willingness to accept the assets.   *s.74*

21.8.5
Insolvent charities

An insolvent charity must wind itself up in the manner appropriate to its legal structure, as a company, association, trust or industrial and provident society.

If the assets of a charitable association, trust or company (but not an exempt charity) are at risk because of mismanagement or misconduct, the Charity Commission may appoint a **receiver and manager** to take on the powers and duties of the charity's trustees and manage the charity [see **3.5.9**]. Part of the receiver's brief might be to put the charity on a more secure financial footing, but this type of receiver has nothing directly to do with solvency or insolvency.   *ss.18-19*

21.9
PAYMENT OF DEBTS

Strict rules govern the use of a company's or industrial and provident society's funds after a decision has been made to wind up the organisation, or after it has become clear that such a decision will have to be made. These rules are designed to protect creditors, and apply even if the company or IPS is solvent.

The rules do not apply to unincorporated organisations, but if the organisation is insolvent the members of the governing body will generally be advised to follow similar rules.

21.9.1
Solvent companies and IPSs

A company or IPS is not allowed to operate or make any expenditure after the liquidation meeting [see **21.4.3**], even if it is solvent, unless this is authorised by the liquidator. The liquidator will oversee the disposition of the organisation's assets and the fulfilment of its financial obligations, and must approve all expenditure.

21.9.2
Solvent trusts and associations

If an unincorporated association or trust is solvent, the governing body may decide how and when to pay off its bills and fulfil its other financial obligations during the winding up. If any money or property remains after all the organisation's liabilities have been met, it may be used or distributed only as specified by the organisation's governing document [see **21.7.1** and **21.8.2**].

21.9.3
Order of preference in insolvent companies and IPSs

When an insolvent company or industrial and provident society is wound up, its financial affairs must be settled in a defined **order of preference**. The process is supervised by the liquidator, and no payment can be made to anyone without his or her approval.

If the company or IPS does anything with the intention of putting one or more creditors in a better position at insolvency, this **preference** can be set aside by the court if it took place while the organisation was unable to pay its debts, or in the six months before insolvency, or in the two years before insolvency if the preference was to a connected person [see **13.2.2** for definition]. *Insolvency Act 1986 ss.239, 240*

Giving **preference** in this way could constitute **fraudulent trading** [see **21.2.4.2**].

21.9.3.1
Secured creditors with fixed charge

A company's or IPS's obligations must first be met to **secured creditors with a fixed charge**, such as a debenture or mortgage, on specific property [see **55.5**].

21.9.3.2
Winding up costs

Next priority is given to the costs of the **winding up**, including remuneration of the liquidator. Winding up costs are sometimes called **pre-preferential debts**. *s.115*

21.9.3.3
Preferential debts

The categories of **preferential debts** rank equally and must all be paid in full before any other debts can be paid. If they cannot all be paid in full, they are paid in equal proportions. *s.175*

Preferential debts are:

- remuneration of employees for the preceding four months, to a maximum of £800 (as at 1/4/01);
- full holiday pay due to employees;
- tax due to Inland Revenue under PAYE for the 12 months before the organisation became insolvent;
- debts due to Customs and Excise, including VAT due for the past six months before it became insolvent, and car tax and other duties due for the 12 months before;
- national insurance contributions due for the 12 months before;
- payments due as contributions to occupational pension schemes and state scheme premiums;
- money owed that has been lent to the company to enable it to pay its employees during the preceding four months. *sch.6*

In mid-2001 the government announced proposals to make the Inland Revenue and Customs and Excise unsecured rather than preferential creditors.

21.9.3.4
Secured creditors with floating charge

Next on the list are **secured creditors with a floating charge** over some or all of the organisation's assets. A floating charge is not linked to a specific asset [see **55.5.2**]. *s.175*

21.9.3.5
Unsecured creditors and shareholders

Next come **unsecured creditors**, including:

- salary and other pay due to employees above the amount classed as a preferential debt, and redundancy pay;
- tax, rates, VAT etc not included with the preferential debts;

- payments due under leases and contracts and due to the organisation's suppliers;
- everything else the organisation owes.

The liquidator allocates the assets among these creditors. If anything is left, it is distributed according to the dissolution clause in the governing document. In a share company or commercial industrial and provident society, if there is no provision in a dissolution clause any assets are distributed to the members (shareholders).

21.9.4
Insolvent trusts and associations

Unincorporated organisations are not covered by the order of preference rules [see **21.9.3**], because the members of the governing body are liable for the full amount of the organisation's debts. However unincorporated organisations are likely to be advised to pay their debts in this order, and if claims are brought against individual members of the governing body or others held liable for the organisation's debts, the claims should be paid in this order.

21.9.5
Payments to employees

In looking at the rights of employees in an insolvency, a distinction must be drawn between:

- what the employee is **entitled to**, under statute or his or her contract of employment;
- how much of this can be claimed from the **National Insurance Fund**, which the employee can therefore rely on getting;
- if the employer is a company or industrial and provident society, how much of the employee's entitlement becomes a **preferential debt** [see **21.9.3.3**] and therefore ranks above most other debts when the organisation's assets are being liquidated, and how much is an unsecured debt [see **21.9.3.5**].

Entitlements from the employer, the NI Fund and as a preferential debt are set out below.

If the employer is a company or industrial and provident society, the employee will receive the full amount of preferential debt only if the organisation has sufficient assets, and is very unlikely to receive the full amount of unsecured debt.

If the employer is any unincorporated association or trust, the employee will receive anything beyond what can be claimed from the NI Fund only if the organisation has sufficient assets, or if the employee sues one or more members of the governing body.

21.9.5.1
Claiming from the National Insurance Fund

The **National Insurance Fund** is run by the Redundancy Payments Service (part of the Department of Trade and Industry) and is intended to ensure that employees get at least some of what they are entitled to if their employer is insolvent. The liquidator or employee claims from the Fund. The Fund then recovers as much as it can of the amount it has paid from the assets of the organisation (or, if liable, the members of its governing body) in the same way as the employee would have done. *Employment Rights Act 1996 ss.166-170, 182-190*

In a company or industrial and provident society insolvency the liquidator will deal with these matters. For unincorporated associations and trusts it is essential to get proper advice. Governing body members in unincorporated organisations need to be aware that:

- if the NI Fund cannot recover what it has paid from the assets of the organisation, it could claim against any or all members of the governing body or others held to be the employer; *and*
- an employee could claim any entitlement not paid by the employer or the NI Fund from any or all members of the governing body.

21.9.5.2
Pay

Entitlement: full pay until notice of redundancy is given or up to the date the employer became insolvent.

From NI Fund: pay for maximum eight weeks, to a maximum of £240 per week (as at 1/4/01).

Order of preference: pay for the four months until the date of insolvency, to a maximum of £800 (as at 1/4/01), is a preferential debt. The remainder is an unsecured debt.

21.9.5.3
Holiday pay

Entitlement: contractual holiday pay entitlement accrued to the date of insolvency, with the daily rate worked out as 1/7th of weekly pay or 1/365th of annual pay.

From NI Fund: holiday pay accrued in the 12 months to the date of insolvency, to a maximum of six weeks at maximum £240 p.w. (as at 1/4/01).

Order of preference: the full entitlement is a preferential debt.

21.9.5.4
Pension contributions

Entitlement: contractual pension contribution entitlement accrued to the date of insolvency.

From NI Fund: occupational pension scheme entitlement.

Order of preference: unsecured debt.

21.9.5.5
Pay during notice

Entitlement: pay during statutory or contractual period of notice [see **24.33**], whichever is longer, or pay in lieu of notice.

From NI Fund: pay for statutory notice period [see **24.33**]; maximum £240 p.w. (as at 1/4/01).

Order of preference: unsecured debt.

21.9.5.6
Statutory redundancy pay

Entitlement: either one half, one or one and a half week's pay (maximum £240 p.w. as at 1/4/01) for each year of employment to a maximum of 20 years, if employed for at least two years [see **30.6**].

From NI Fund: full entitlement.

Order of preference: unsecured debt.

21.9.5.7
Contractual redundancy pay

Entitlement: as entitled by contract.

From NI Fund: none.

Order of preference: unsecured debt.

21.9.5.8
Other

Entitlement: as due to employee.

From NI Fund: any basic award made for unfair dismissal [see **32.4.2**]; all or part of the fee paid by an apprentice or articled clerk.

Order of preference: unsecured debt.

FOR FURTHER INFORMATION

Your organisation's accountant, auditor and/or solicitor

Charities. Charity Commission: 0870-333 0123; www.charity-commission.gov.uk

Companies. Companies House: 0870-333 3636; www.companieshouse.gov.uk

Industrial & provident societies. Registrar of Friendly Societies: 020-7676 1000; www.fsa.gov.uk

Insolvency. Insolvency Service: 020-7291 6895; www.insolvency.gov.uk

Redundancy. Redundancy helpline: 0500-848489; www.dti.gov.uk/er/redundancy.htm

Unincorporated associations. *Unincorporated Associations* by Jean Warburton (Sweet & Maxwell).

PART IV
EMPLOYEES, WORKERS, VOLUNTEERS AND OTHER STAFF

Any organisation depends on people to carry out its work. Part IV is about how the law governs an organisation's relationships with those people: its employees, volunteers, other staff and independent contractors.

Chapter 22
EMPLOYEES AND OTHER WORKERS

Topics covered in this chapter

This chapter explains the distinction between employees and other workers, and the significance of the distinction. It covers:

For sources of further information see end of chapter.

Double-underlined section headings indicate additions or significant changes since the first edition.

22.1 EMPLOYEES AND OTHERS

Whenever a person carries out work for an organisation, it is essential to clarify the nature of the relationship between them. The starting point is whether there is:

- a **contract of employment** (also called a **contract of service**), creating a relationship of employment [see **22.1.1**];

- a **contract for services**, creating a relationship of self-employment [see **22.1.3**];

- another type of contract, perhaps creating a **worker** relationship [see **22.1.2**]; *or*

- no contract, for example most (but not all) volunteers [see **35.3**].

'Contract' in this context does not depend on whether there is a document called a contract, or even whether there is anything in writing. The existence of a contract depends not on documentation but on the nature of the relationship between the individual and the organisation, and in particular whether the individual is receiving money or something else of value in return for doing the work [see **23.2**].

Organisations need to be absolutely clear which category each relationship falls into. Where the individual receives or is going to receive *any* payment (other than a volunteer receiving only reimbursement of genuine out-of-pocket expenditure), there should be an appropriate written contract setting out the details of the relationship. This applies not only to long-term staff, but also to temporary or casual workers. **Chapter 24** contains a model contract for employees, and **34.3.1** outlines points to be included in a contract with a self-employed person.

In many cases a written contract should also be provided where a person does not receive pay, but receives something else of value in return for work such as accommodation.

The nature of the relationship determines how employment and employment-related legislation affect the parties. This includes:

- employment legislation which sets the statutory rights available only to **employees**, such as rights to redundancy pay, maternity pay, a minimum period of notice and not to be unfairly dismissed;

- other employment legislation, which sets out rights such as minimum wage and working time rights which are available not only to employees but also to a wider category of **workers**;

- employment-related legislation such as health and safety [see **36.2.1**] and equal opportunities [see **chapter 25**], which in each case sets out who is covered by the legislation;

- tax and national insurance rules, which define the 'employees' for whom the employer must operate PAYE [see **27.3**]. The definition of employee for tax purposes is much wider than the definition of employee for the purposes of employment rights.

22.1.1 Employees

Employment legislation defines an **employee** as an individual who has entered into or works under a **contract of employment**, and defines a contract of employment as a **contract of service** or apprenticeship.

Employment Rights Act 1996 s.230

Individuals working under a contract of employment have employment and employment-related rights. Contracts of employment are explained in **chapter 23**, and **chapter 24** contains an annotated model contract.

The employer must operate PAYE if the employee's earnings are above the thresholds for tax and national insurance [see **27.4.1** and **27.5.1**].

22.1.2 Workers

Worker as a legal concept is defined in the **Employment Rights Act 1996** s.230(3) and subsequent employment legislation. It extends employment rights to casual workers [see **22.3.4**], **freelance** workers who do not run their own business as a self-employed person, and in some cases volunteers who are paid or receive something else of value [see **35.3**]. Such individuals previously did not have such rights because they fell outside the definition of an employee.

At the time of writing (early 2001) workers were entitled only to some statutory rights [see **chapter 23** for details]. However the government has wide powers to extend the range of rights available to workers, and had announced its intention to do so. It is possible that in due course all workers, other than those who are genuinely self-employed [see **34.1.3**], will have access to all employment rights.

Employment Relations Act 1999 s.23(2)

For most purposes a 'worker' is defined is anyone who:

- works under a contract of employment [see **23.1**]; *or*

- works under any other contract where they have to perform work or services personally for the other party to the contract—but the individual is not a worker if he or she is carrying out a business or profession, and the party for whom the work is performed is a customer or client of that business. *Employment Rights Act 1996 s.230(3)*

The contract may be written, verbal, or implied from the circumstances.

The definition of 'worker' includes most people who are paid or receive something else of value for their work or services. However under this definition a person is generally *not* a worker if:

- he or she can sub-contract the work or employ someone else to do it (and thus does not have to perform it personally); *and/or*

- the person is genuinely self-employed [see **34.1.1**] and the work is being done for a customer or client.

22.1.2.1
<u>Minimum wage</u>

For the purposes of national minimum wage [see **27.2**], the definition of worker is broadened to include:

- **home workers**, even though they may not be obliged to perform the work personally;

- **agency workers**, even though the contract is between the worker and the agency, rather than between the worker and the body for whom the work is done.   *National Minimum Wage Act 1998 ss.34, 35*

22.1.3
Contractors

A **contractor** is taken on to complete a piece of work and produce a result, and has a **contract for services**. A contractor may be:

- an individual undertaking work through their own business on a **self-employed** basis [see **chapter 34**];

- two or more persons undertaking work jointly as a formal or informal **partnership** [see **19.4**] or an unincorporated association; *or*

- a corporate body (company or industrial and provident society).

Statute law has attached many obligations, rules, rights and controls to employer-employee and employer-worker relationships which do not apply to contractors. Examples of these differences are:

- an employee or worker must provide his or her services personally to the employer, but a contractor—unless the contract specifies otherwise—does not have to provide the service personally and can **subcontract** it to someone else or employ someone to do the work;

- contractors do not have employment rights or the rights of workers;

- an employer must insure against claims if its employees become ill or injured as a result of the employer's negligence or breach of a statutory duty [see **20.4.1**], but does not generally have to insure against claims by its contractors (but note that the workers and contractors who are not employees for the purposes of employment law, may be classed as employees for the purposes of having to be covered by employer's liability insurance);

- an employer has **vicarious liability** in most circumstances for its employees' acts within employment [see **19.5.3**], but is not generally liable for the acts of contractors (but note that a court may say that an employer is also liable, in some situations, for the acts of workers or contractors);

- an employer owes a higher duty of care to its employees than to its contractors [see **36.1.2**] (but your organisation does not want to be the test case to decide the level of duty that applies to workers or contractors);

- an employer must provide safe materials, safe conditions and a safe system of work for employees [see **36.2.1**], but this is a contractor's own responsibility [see **34.3.2**];

- an employer must operate PAYE and pay employer's national insurance for employees and workers [see **27.3**], but contractors are generally responsible for dealing with their own tax and NI, provided they are registered as self-employed with the Inland Revenue.

22.1.3.1
Employment and
self-employment

The laws which apply to employees and self-employed individuals are inconsistently worded, and there is often no agreement as to where an individual falls. A person may, for example, be an employee for tax purposes but not for the purposes of employment rights, or *vice versa*.

Serious difficulties can arise for both the individual and employer if a person is treated as self-employed when he or she is legally an employee. Before taking on anyone on a self-employed, freelance or consultancy basis, the organisation should be satisfied that he or she meets the criteria for being genuinely self-employed—for the purposes of both tax and employment law—in relation to the particular piece of work. These criteria are explained in **chapter 34**.

22.1.4
Personal contracts

The term **personal** or **individualised contract** is used to refer to contracts of employment which have been re-issued to exclude incorporated terms [see **23.2.5**] based on collective agreements negotiated with trade unions. Workers on personal contracts are not self-employed. They have all the rights of employees, including protection if they refuse to enter into a personal contract.   *Employment Relations Act 1999 s.17*

22.2
PART-TIMERS
22.2.1
Part-time staff

Part-time employees or workers are those who are defined *by the employer* (not by statute) as working less than full time. Unless they are genuinely self-employed [see **34.1.3**] they are employees or workers for the purposes of employment-related legislation, and have the same statutory rights, *pro rata*, as full-time staff. They are also generally entitled to the same contractual rights, *pro rata*, as comparable full-time staff working for the same employer [see **23.4.2**].

The earnings of part-time employees and workers are subject to national insurance under PAYE if they are more than the NI employee's earnings threshold [see **27.5.1**], and to tax if earnings from all employments are more than the tax threshold [see **27.4.1**].

22.2.2
Job sharers

In legal terms job sharers who divide the work between them are the same as part-time employees [see above].

22.2.3
Sessional workers

A sessional worker may:

- be genuinely a casual worker [see **22.3.4**];
- be supplied by an employment agency [see **22.5.1**];
- be seconded by another employer [see **22.5.3**]; *or*
- meet the tests for genuine self-employment [see **34.1.3**].

If the sessional worker does not fit any of these categories he or she is almost certainly a part-time employee.

22.2.4
Zero-hours
contracts

With a **zero-hours contract** the employer agrees to offer work to the person and the person has to do it if it is offered, but there are no fixed hours. Even if no work is given to the person, there is a continuing employment relationship. This is different from casual workers [see **22.3.4**], where the employer has made no commitment to offer work to a particular person even if it is available, and there is no continuing obligation between the individual and employer.

Depending on the situation, a person on a zero-hours contract may be:

- self-employed, liable for his or her own tax and national insurance and not required to accept the work even if it is offered; *or*
- more commonly, an employee with the same employment rights as any other employee—because a contract of employment exists, even if during some weeks there is no work available for the worker.

Legal advice should be taken before offering a contract of this type.

22.3
NON-PERMANENT
WORKERS

Unless it is made explicit that a contract of employment is temporary, fixed-term, or for completion of a specific task, it is assumed to be open-ended or **continuing**.

22.3.1
Temporary workers

Temporary workers are employed on a basis which is not intended to be permanent, but do not have a fixed ending date. Unless they are genuinely self-employed [see **34.1.3**] or are supplied by an employment agency [see **22.5.1**], temporary workers are employees for all employment-related purposes. The employer has a duty to notify them that their employment is temporary, and if the work is going to last or has lasted at least one month the employer must indicate in a statement of employment particulars how long it is expected to continue [see **24.7**].

Temporary employees are generally treated in the same way as permanent employees. Exceptions are:

- a written statement of employment particulars does not have to be given to a temporary employee whose employment is expected to last less than one month [see **23.5.1**];

- statutory sick pay is not available to temporary employees on contracts of less than three months [see **27.6**];

- at the time of writing a person there was a 13 week qualifying period for paid annual leave, but this was due to be changed [see **28.4**].

Temporary employees who have worked for the statutory qualifying period have the right to claim unfair dismissal [see **30.9**] or redundancy pay [see **31.6.1**] if their contract is not renewed.

22.3.2
Workers on
fixed-term contracts

Unlike a temporary contract, a fixed-term contract has a defined ending date. Employees on fixed-term contracts are generally treated the same way as temporary employees [see above]. But unlike permanent or temporary employees, employees on fixed-term contracts of two years or more can be asked or required to waive the right to redundancy pay if their contract is not renewed when it ends [see **24.5**]. Prior to October 1999 employees on fixed-term contracts of one year or more could waive the right to claim unfair dismissal, but this is no longer possible.

If an employee continues working after the fixed-term period this may create, by implication, an open-ended contract. If the employee is to carry on, the fixed-term contract should be extended by written agreement or be changed to a continuing contract.

At the time of writing (early 2001), legislation had been proposed that would make it unlawful to treat a fixed-term worker less favourably than a non-fixed-term worker, and would automatically make fixed-term contracts open-ended after a specified period.

22.3.3
Contracts to
complete a task

Some contracts are not for a defined time period, but until a task is completed. Employees on these contracts have the same rights as other temporary employees [see above] but are not entitled to claim unfair dismissal or redundancy pay if the contract is not renewed [see **24.6**].

22.3.4
Casual workers

A casual worker is employed occasionally, with no continuing contract. There is no agreement as to whether or when any work is to be offered. If work is offered and accepted the contract is only to provide work for that day, session or period. There is no obligation on the employer to offer work or the worker to accept it on any other occasion, or for the employer to provide any minimum amount of work or pay. There is no **mutuality of obligation**, and without this there can be no contract of employment [see **23.2.3**].

Nethermere (St Neots) Ltd v Gardiner [1984] ICR 612; IRLR 240

If there is an ongoing contract extending beyond one week (with a week running from Sunday to Saturday), the person is an employee, rather than a casual worker, even if the work is very part-time. In one case, a person who was contracted to work 5½ hours on alternate Fridays was held to be an employee. *Colley v Corkindale [1996] 542 IRLB 8, EAT*

Even where the employer treats a series of contracts as separate casual contracts, the worker may be defined by the tribunal as an employee if in fact the person is regularly offered work—at least once in every week—and does not have the right to turn it down when it is offered. In one clear-cut case, a woman who had worked for a housing association for nine months on a series of one-day contracts was held to be an employee. *Brown v Chief Adjudication Officer, The Times 16/10/1996*

Legal advice may be necessary to clarify whether a worker is in fact:

- an employee who works fluctuating hours, perhaps under a zero-hours contract [see **22.2.4**];

- a very part-time employee, but one with an ongoing obligation to work for the organisation, as in the Colley case above;

- a person who started out as a casual but whose relationship with the organisation has become an employment relationship, as in the Brown case above;

- a self-employed worker undertaking occasional work for the organisation [see **34.1.3**];

- a genuine casual worker who is outside the scope of a contract of employment because there is no mutuality of obligation.

Even if casual workers are not legally employees for the purpose of employment rights:

- they are workers [see **22.1.2**] (unless they are genuinely self-employed) and are entitled to the rights that workers have [see **23.4**]; *and*

- PAYE must be operated unless the person earns less than the tax and national insurance thresholds [see **27.4.1** and **27.5.1**] *and* has no other taxable earnings, or is genuinely self-employed.

22.3.4.1
Keeping casual workers casual

Organisations which do not want casual workers to be legally employees should make very clear, in writing, that work will be offered on an 'as required' basis and there is no obligation on the part of the organisation to offer any work, and the worker is free to refuse any offer of work.

Carmichael v National Power plc [2000] IRLR 43

22.3.4.2
Contracts for casual workers

An organisation which uses casuals should draw up a contract which explicitly states that it applies each time the worker is offered and accepts work. Legal advice should be sought to ensure that the contract as written does not inadvertently create a contract of employment.

22.3.5
Bank or pool staff

Bank staff who are on an organisation's books and are offered work when it is available may be employees on a zero-hours contract [see **22.2.4**], or casual workers who are not employees [see above]. The key issue will be whether there is **mutuality of obligation**, with the organisation obliged to offer work and the worker obliged to accept it.

22.4
EMPLOYEES ON JOINT CONTRACTS

Joint employment by two organisations—for example a charity and its trading company—can avoid the restrictions on employment businesses and the VAT charge which might arise where one organisation provides an employee to another and charges for his or her work [see **53.5.3**]. However, difficult issues can arise concerning:

- which employer controls allocation of time;

- what happens if one employer is dissatisfied with the person's work;

- how liability for salary, sick pay, maternity pay etc is calculated;

- whether dismissal by one employer results in dismissal by the other (and the implications for a potential unfair dismissal claim, if there is no fair reason for dismissal by the second employer);

- what happens if one employer becomes insolvent, and in particular whether the other employer is liable for the failed employer's obligations to the employee.

Careful drafting of the contract is needed to avoid these problems.

22.5
WORKERS FROM SOMEWHERE ELSE

It is not uncommon for a voluntary organisation to use workers provided by agencies or other organisations. The workers may be supplied by:

- an **employment agency** [see below] which provides a recruitment service, being paid a fee to match employers and potential employees, with the worker becoming employed by the employer;

- an employment agency supplies staff on a temporary basis and pays the workers;

- an **employment business** [see **22.5.2**] which itself is an employer, employing people and supplying them to another person to be used in their business or organisation; *Employment Agencies Act 1973 s.13; Employment Relations Act 1999 sch.7*

- an employer which continues to pay the worker's salary but 'lends' the worker to another organisation, as a **secondee** [see **22.5.3**].

Basic information about employment agencies and businesses is available from the Department of Trade and Industry [see end of chapter]. At the time of writing (early 2001) new rules on employment agencies and businesses were expected to be introduced in 2001. The situation of workers supplied by employment agencies, employment businesses or other bodies can be complex, and legal advice may be necessary.

22.5.1 Employment agencies

When an organisation uses a worker from an employment agency it has a contract with the agency, but not with the worker. The worker also has a contract with the agency. In some circumstances this could be a contract of employment, but generally is not because the agency does not normally have the control necessary in an employment relationship.

Montgomery v Johnson Underwood [9/3/2001], CA

Similarly an agency worker generally does not have a contract directly with the body for which it is working (the agency's client). But where that body has sufficient control over the worker, a tribunal might find that the worker has a contract of employment with that body.

Motorola Ltd v (1) Davidson and (2) Melville Craig Group Ltd [2001] IRLR 4

Agency workers who are not employees of either the agency or its client have some statutory employment and workers' rights, including minimum wage [see **27.2**], working time rights [see **28.1**], and rights arising from equal opportunities and health and safety legislation. Additional employment and workers' rights may be extended to agency workers, and if legislation is introduced requiring all agency workers to be employed by the agency under a contract of employment, they are likely to have the full range of employment rights.

22.5.2 Employment businesses

Where a body which is not an employment agency provides a worker, it is an **employment business** if the receiving organisation pays the providing organisation, and the providing organisation then pays the worker. The worker has a contract of employment with the providing organisation, but as with employment agency arrangements, there could be a contract of employment with the receiving organisation if it exercises control over the worker.

An employment business is different from secondment [see below], where the receiving organisation does not pay the providing organisation. It is also different from an arrangement where an organisation simply arranges for another body to operate PAYE on its behalf.

Employment businesses must comply with relevant provisions of the **Employment Agencies Act 1973** and related regulations, but charities and certain other bodies which supply workers in this way are exempt. *Employment Agencies Act 1973 (Exemption) Regulations 1976 [SI 1976/710]*

Where staff are supplied the providing organisation is carrying out a service which is subject to VAT, and may have to register for VAT and charge VAT to the receiving organisation [see **53.5.3**].

22.5.3 Secondees

A secondee is an employee who is lent to another organisation while the first employer continues to pay his or her salary. The providing organisation is generally—but not always—considered to be the employer. Legal advice should be taken to ensure that the rights and obligations of all parties are clear, especially in relation to VAT, insurance, supervision and control, discipline, and terminating the arrangement. These arrangements should be set out in a written agreement.

If a secondee causes loss or injury, the organisation or employer which has control over the actions of the secondee is generally held to be vicariously liable [see **19.5.3**].

22.6 GENERALLY NOT EMPLOYEES

Trainees, volunteers and some other types of worker are neither employees, 'workers' nor self-employed. They are not generally covered under employment protection legislation, although some aspects of the legislation may apply. Nor are they covered by equal opportunities and health and safety legislation in the same way as employees, but it is good practice to apply the same basic principles to them. This is particularly important because of the difficulty in being completely sure of the individual's status [see, for example **22.1.3** and **22.6.2**].

Employer's liability insurance is unlikely to cover non-employees, so the organisation should ensure it is protected for claims by non-employees arising from its negligence [see **20.4.1**].

A person who is not an employee for the purposes of employment and employment-related legislation may still be considered an employee for the purposes of tax and national insurance, and the employer will have to operate PAYE [see **27.3**]. Conversely, a person could be an employee for the purposes of employment law, but not for PAYE.

22.6.1 Apprentices and trainees

Under employment law **apprentices** are employees, but others who are working as a way of being trained for work generally are not. It is a question of fact as to whether the training element is so predominant that the person is considered to be a trainee rather than an employee. A trainee who takes on additional tasks for the employer, perhaps for additional payment, may be both a trainee and employee.

Apprentices have the same rights as employees. Trainees do not have rights under employment legislation, but have the same rights as employees under health and safety legislation [see **36.2.1**], and may be covered by the employment provisions of equal opportunities legislation if the traineeship can be seen as a route to employment.

Work experience for school pupils is part of their education and is neither training nor employment. The status of work experience for college and university students depends on the particular circumstances. Advice should be sought, especially if the student is being paid by the organisation, perhaps for additional work 'on the side'.

22.6.2 Volunteers

For tax and national insurance purposes, volunteers who are paid anything more than reimbursement of genuine expenses are treated as employees or casual workers [see **35.2**]. This applies even if the payment is called an honorarium, sessional fee, pocket money or even 'expenses' (if it is not genuine reimbursement).

For employment law purposes, volunteers are normally not employees or 'workers' because there is generally no consideration (pay or something else of value), and even where there is consideration the parties may have explicitly stated that they do not intend to create legally binding obligations between them [see **35.3**]. However, a so-called volunteer may be entitled to workers' rights if:

- he or she is paid more than reimbursement of genuine out-of-pocket expenses, or receives something else of value (such as discounts or in some situations training) from the organisation; *and*

- the individual and the organisation have not explicitly stated that they do not intend their relationship to be legally binding.

If, in addition, the organisation says it will provide work and the individual makes a commitment to do it, the individual may be working under a contract of employment and be entitled to the full range of employment rights

The employment status and rights of volunteers are considered in more detail in **chapter 35**.

22.6.3
Others

Some people who carry out work are neither employees nor self-employed, and may or may not be 'workers' [see **22.1.2**]. Depending on the situation and the specific provisions of the relevant legislation they may or may not be entitled to workers' or employment rights, they may or may not be covered by employment-related legislation such as health and safety and equal opportunities, and they may be within PAYE or may be responsible for their own tax and national insurance.

22.6.3.1
Office holders

Office holders are distinguished from employees because their rights and duties are defined by the office they hold, rather than by a contract of employment. Some examples of office holders are:

- company directors and company secretaries [see **11.1.3** and **12.3**], whose duties are defined by company law and the memorandum and articles of association;

- trade union officials;

- police constables, judges and justices of the peace.

A person may be both an office holder and an employee. A company director, for example, may be paid under a **contract of service** with the company [see **16.3.6**]. In this situation one role can be terminated without losing the other.

22.6.3.2
Clergy

Members of the clergy are neither employees nor office holders. The exception is Salvation Army officers, who are office holders.

Davies v Presbyterian Church of Wales [1986] 1 WLR 323, 1 All ER 313

22.7
OVERSEAS
EMPLOYEES

22.7.1
UK workers abroad

Employees of a UK-based employer who work abroad are no longer automatically excluded from employment protection. Provided there is a sufficient connection with the UK, they have many of the same statutory rights as if they were employed in the UK. The rules about which rights do and do not apply are complex, and legal advice should be sought.

Employment Relations Act 1999 s.32(3)

One difference is that the statement of employment particulars may need to include information specifically about the overseas posting [see **23.4.3**], and a worker who is going abroad within the first two months of employment must be given the statement before they go [see **23.4.1**].

A UK employee working temporarily in the European Economic Area (EU member states plus Iceland, Liechtenstein and Norway) has, in relation to the work done there, at least the minimum employment rights available in that state as well as rights available in the UK, and can take advantage of whichever are more favourable.

Contracts (Applicable Law) Act 1990;
EU Posting of Workers Directive 96/71/EC

22.7.2
Workers from
abroad in the UK

Workers from abroad who are working in the UK, even temporarily, generally have most of the same rights as UK workers. For rules on entitlement to work in the UK, see **26.2.9**.

FOR FURTHER INFORMATION

Employment law. www.acas.org.uk; see telephone directory for local office

Department of Trade and Industry: www.dti.gov.uk; separate telephone helplines for various topics—see end of relevant chapters in this book

Employment agencies and businesses. DTI: 0845-955 5105; www.dti.gov.uk/er/agency.htm

---

Chapter 23
RIGHTS, DUTIES AND THE
CONTRACT OF EMPLOYMENT

Topics covered in this chapter

This chapter explains when a contract of employment comes into existence, the distinction between the contract and the statement of employment particulars, what the statement must contain, and the rights and duties of employers and employees. It covers:

For sources of further information see end of chapter 22.
Double-underlined section headings indicate additions or significant changes since the first edition.

23.1
THE CONTRACT OF EMPLOYMENT

Creating contracts of employment by employing staff brings the organisation into one of the most complex and litigated areas of law. It also creates clear conflicts of interest. The governing body members or others who agree contracts or are responsible for managing staff must ensure they obtain independent advice. It is not appropriate to act solely on the basis of information and advice provided by staff or trade unions.

The environment within which contracts of employment operate is not static, and contracts should be reviewed at least every 18-24 months to ensure they reflect not only current law, but also current best practice.

Confusion is often created because the term 'contract of employment' is used in four ways:

• the contractual relationship between the employer and employee, which exists as soon as an offer of employment is made and accepted, even if this is only verbal;

• all the terms and conditions which govern that relationship, regardless of whether they are explicit;

- the **written statement of employment particulars**, which by law must be given to virtually all employees; *and*

- a written contract which generally includes everything required in the statement of employment particulars and replaces the statement, and also includes additional terms and conditions.

Although the written statement or written contract is often called the contract, the contract of employment is much wider than any document and encompasses many rights and duties which are not written but are **implied** (assumed) by law. An example is the implied duty on both employer and employee to maintain trust and confidence [see **23.3.4**].

23.1.1
Other types of contract

Other types of agreement have different legal consequences from contracts of employment These include:

- contracts with people legally defined as **workers** who are not employees but have some employment rights, such as casual and freelance workers [see **22.1.2** and **22.1.3**];

- contracts with people who are **self-employed** [see **34.1**];

- arrangements with volunteers, which may or may not be contractual [see **35.3**].

23.2
CREATING THE CONTRACT OF EMPLOYMENT

The relationship between the employer and employee exhibits the key elements necessary in law to make a contract [see **18.6.1**]: clear agreement between the employer and employee, with pay or other **consideration** in return for service, and made with the intention of being legally bound. It is a contract **of employment** rather than any other type of contract because it gives the employer 'control' of the employee's work and because there is mutuality of obligation [see **23.2.2**].

23.2.1
Agreement

In all contracts, agreement is reached through a process of offer and acceptance. This may be done formally in writing or by an informal verbal exchange, or may even be inferred from conduct. The contract comes into being as soon as there is an agreement, even if it is verbal, apart from contracts of apprenticeship which must be in writing.

23.2.1.1
Offer and acceptance

When a potential employee applies for a job this is generally not the offer, more an enquiry about the possibility of an offer.

Following the selection process [see **26.2**], the employer makes the offer. If the employer offers the job unconditionally, the contract exists as soon as the future employee accepts it unconditionally.

The offer may be **conditional** on acceptance within a time limit, or upon one or more events such as passing a medical examination or receiving satisfactory references [see **26.3**]. If the employer makes the conditions clear, no contract is created until the conditions are met. If the employer does not make clear that the offer is conditional, a contract is created as soon as the employee accepts. The employee may then be able to claim for damages if the employer seeks to renege on the contract, for example because of an unsatisfactory reference.

Even if employment is made conditional on completion of a satisfactory probationary period, the contract of employment exists from the point when the offer of work is first made and accepted. The implications of a probationary period will depend on what, if anything, the contract says [see **24.31** and **30.5.2**].

The employee can accept the offer verbally, in writing, or simply by turning up and commencing work. If sent through the post, the employee's acceptance is treated as being made as soon as it is posted.

23.2.1.2
Withdrawal of offer

The employer may withdraw the offer if it is not accepted within a specified time limit or if the employer has a change of heart before the offer is accepted. A withdrawal becomes effective when it reaches the potential employee (*not* when it is posted). Once the offer has been accepted, withdrawal by the employer constitutes breach of contract.

23.2.1.3
Counter-offer

The employee may only accept the offer exactly as it is made. If the employee seeks to accept the offer but on a condition, for example that the paid holiday is longer than was specified by the employer, this is not an acceptance but a **counter-offer** by the employee. It is then open to the employer to accept or refuse this counter-offer.

It is important for the employer to respond if an employee attaches an unacceptable condition to the acceptance. If employment commences without clarification and there is later a dispute, the courts might rule that the employee's condition had been incorporated into the contract.

23.2.1.4
Redeployment

There is an important exception to the need for acceptance to be unconditional in order to create an agreement. If an existing employee is being made redundant but is offered the chance to try a different job within the organisation, the employee can in effect conditionally accept by taking the new job for a trial period before deciding whether to accept that job or opt for redundancy [see **31.5**].

23.2.2
Intention to create a legal relationship of employment

For a contract to exist, both parties must intend the agreement between them to be legally binding [see **18.6.1**]. There is a presumption that the relationship is intended to be legally binding and that a contract of employment exists if:

- the worker is paid or remunerated in other ways for doing work, and thus receives **consideration** [see below];
- there is **mutuality of obligation**, with the employer obliged to provide work and the worker obliged to do it; *and*
- the employee's work is controlled by the employer.

Although the relationship as a whole is a binding contract, either side may specify matters which they do not intend to form part of the contract. For example, an employer may say that when pressure of work allows, it is their practice to give sabbaticals to staff. It may need very careful analysis to ascertain whether an obligation binding on the employer has been created or whether the decision to grant a sabbatical is within the employer's discretion.

23.2.3
Consideration

Consideration is anything of material value. In a contract of employment both sides provide consideration—the employer generally in the form of a salary or wage, the employee by providing a service. If consideration is not provided by both parties, there is no contract.

Consideration does not need to be monetary. It may consist of meals, luncheon vouchers, accommodation, a car, training, membership of the organisation, preferential rates for the organisation's goods or services, or anything else of value.

23.2.4
Certainty

In order to create a contract, the agreed terms must be clear and certain [see **18.6.1**]. If they are too vague there is no contract. However the court seeks to prevent contracts failing because of an uncertainty about the terms, by **implying** terms or otherwise filling the gap [see **23.3.4**].

Many contracts contain terms which specify that a particular point is to be 'as agreed' between the employer and an employee. Such an agreement to agree creates no certainty and cannot itself be enforced. It should therefore be avoided.

23.2.5
Capacity to contract

A contract with a person under the age of 18 or person who is mentally ill may in some situations be voidable (able to be invalidated) by that person [see **18.6.2**].

23.3
CONTRACT TERMS

When a contract of employment comes into existence its terms may be express, imposed by statute, implied, or incorporated by reference to another document or source.

23.3.1
Express terms

Express terms are explicitly expressed, verbally or in writing. They include the **written statement of employment particulars** [see **23.5**] and, if provided, a more comprehensive written contract, as well as terms agreed verbally or in correspondence.

Where the contract seeks to exclude employees' rights to benefits and procedures to which they would otherwise be entitled (for example, by requiring the person to have worked a certain period before becoming entitled to a perk), or where a contractual terms is unreasonable, it is possible that a court would say that the term is unfair. At the time of writing (early 2001) this area was unclear, and legal advice should be sought if it is an issue. *Unfair Contract Terms Act 1977;*

Bridgen v American Express Bank Limited [1999] 10 PLC 69n

23.3.2
Imposed terms

Many contract terms are imposed by statute, for example the right to minimum wage and minimum period of notice [see **23.4**]. Imposed terms can be excluded from the contract only in the rare situations where the legislation specifically allows this.

Employment Rights Act 1996 s.203

23.3.3
Mutual duties

Within every employer-employee relationship there are core duties on both parties which are implied into the contract [see **23.3.4**]. Some of these duties arise from statute, and others from common law. Breach of these duties may, if sufficiently serious, justify immediate termination of the contract [see **30.4.7** and **30.4.8**].

23.3.3.1
Employers' duties

Employers have a duty:

* to pay wages, although in some cases the contract only gives the employee the *opportunity* to earn wages [see **22.2.4**];
* to provide work, or perhaps more accurately, not to withhold work unreasonably when there is work available to be done;
* to comply with rules on maximum working hours and rest breaks [see **28.1**]
* to repay costs or expenses incurred by an employee in carrying out the employer's requirements [see **27.4.3**];
* to provide a safe system of work, selecting proper staff and providing safe and adequate materials and equipment [see **36.2.1**];
* not to order the employee to do something illegal or dangerous or carry on a dishonest activity; *Malik v BCCI [1997] ICR 600*
* to maintain a relationship of trust and confidence with the employee, which generally can be characterised by behaving in a reasonable and fair way towards the employee.

23.3.3.2
Employees' duties

Employees' duties include:

* to maintain the trust and confidence of the employer;
* to provide services personally to the employer [see **22.1.1**];
* to cooperate with the employer;
* to accept the 'control' of the employer and carry out reasonable instructions;
* to take reasonable care in carrying out the job;
* to display proper competence in carrying out the job;
* to adapt, after training if necessary, to new ways of work;
* to be loyal and give honest and faithful service;

- to pass on to the employer the copyright or other rights for work produced in the course of employment [see **39.2.3**];

- not to obtain secret profits or compete with the employer;

- to tell the employer of any information relevant to the employment which comes into his or her possession;

- to treat the confidential information or trade secrets of the employer as secret, although if the employer is acting unlawfully there is a duty to bring this to the attention of the employer, and if the employer is acting unlawfully or against the public interest there may also be a 'just cause' defence in making this public and protection under the whistleblowing legislation [see **29.8**].

23.3.4
Implied terms

A contract normally has implied in it all the mutual duties which characterise the employee-employer relationship [see above]. If the mutual duties, the express terms or those imposed by statute do not deal with all the issues, a tribunal or court will, in case of dispute, seek to establish what has been impliedly agreed between the parties. A number of methods are used for this.

23.3.4.1
Implied by custom

Where there are well known, reasonable, and clear customs and practice which generally apply to this particular type of contract, it is assumed in the absence of evidence of a contrary intent that these apply to the contract of employment in question.

23.3.4.2
The officious bystander test

A term will be implied if it is obvious that the parties would have intended it. 'Obvious' is defined by imagining an officious bystander asking the parties, when the contract was made, what they intended. 'Do you intend for bank holidays to be paid holidays?' the nosey bystander would have asked. If the employer and employee would both have said 'Of course', the court will imply that term into the contract.

23.3.4.3
Implied by conduct

If both parties operate the contract in a way which shows that they agreed upon a particular issue, for example the office opens at 9.00 and closes at 5.00 and the employee attends during that period, the court will imply a term that the hours of work are 9.00 to 5.00.

23.3.4.4
Characteristic terms

A court may imply a term simply because such a term is typical or characteristic, reasonable and necessary. For example when a written contract provided that the employee was entitled to sick pay but did not specify for how long, the court implied a term that sick pay would not continue forever but only for a 'reasonable' period.

Howman & Son v Blyth [1983] IRLR 139, ICR 446 EAT

23.3.5
Incorporated terms

Incorporated terms exist when the parties have agreed that they will accept an outside source for contractual terms. Examples include:

- a staff handbook [see **23.6**], but depending on how the contract is worded this may simply be regarded as guidance as to how the contract is to be carried out rather than part of the contract itself;

- staff salaries linked to scales determined externally;

- agreeing to be bound by a collective agreement [see **32.3.4**].

Some contract terms must be included in detail in the written statement of employment particulars [see **23.5.3**], but for others the statement may refer to other documents.

If the terms of a national collective agreement between an employer and trade union are incorporated within a contract of employment, those terms continue to apply to the contract even if the employer withdraws and is no longer a party to the agreement, or if the employment is transferred to another employer.

Gibbons v Associated British Ports [1985] IRLR 376; Transfer of Undertakings (Protection of Employment) Regulations 1981 [SI 1981/1794] reg.6

23.4
STATUTORY RIGHTS AND DUTIES

All employees have a wide range of statutory rights, some of which are also available to workers who are not classed as employees. Employment rights are covered in detail in the relevant sections in **chapters 24-33**, but the most important are listed here.

Every employment right imposes a corresponding duty on the employer.

23.4.1
Rights of employees and other workers

Many rights apply from the first day of employment, and in some cases even before a contract comes into being (for example, the right not to be discriminated against in selection for employment).

23.4.1.1
Right not to be discriminated against

Anyone working under a contract of employment or a contract to provide services personally has the right:

- not to be discriminated against in recruitment or any other aspect of employment on the basis of **racial group** (race, colour, ethnic origin, national origin or nationality) unless this is a genuine occupational qualification for the work [see **25.2** and **25.3**];

- not to be discriminated against in recruitment or any aspect of employment on the basis of sex, gender reassignment or being married, unless being of a particular sex is a genuine occupational qualification for the work [see **25.2** and **25.3**];

- not to be unjustifiably discriminated against in recruitment or any aspect of employment on the basis of disability if the employer has 15 or more employees or others working under a contract [see **25.5**];

- when the **EU Employment Framework Directive** [see **25.1**] is implemented in the UK, not to be discriminated against on the basis of religious or other belief, sexual orientation or age, unless such discrimination is explicitly allowed;

- for men and women to receive **equal pay** for work of equal value [see **25.4**];

- not to be dismissed for any reason connected with the worker's racial group, sex, pregnancy, childbirth or being married, and if the employer has 15 or more employees the right not to be dismissed because of disability unless the dismissal is justified.

Unlike most other workers' rights, discrimination legislation extends not only to 'workers' [see **22.1.2**] but also to self-employed people.

These rights may in some situations also apply to volunteers. Even if they do not, a good employer will act as if they do.

All ex-offenders have the right not to disclose **spent convictions** and not to have them taken into account, except in specific situations where they must be disclosed [see **25.10**] or taken into account [see **26.3.4**].

23.4.1.2
Rights related to pay

All employees and workers [see **22.1.2**] including casual, freelance and agency workers, have a statutory right:

- if they are at least 18 years old, to be paid no less than the **national minimum wage** [see **27.2**];

- to receive an **itemised pay statement** [see **27.1.3**];

- not to have **unauthorised deductions** made from pay [see **27.1.4**].

Employees—but not, at the time of writing, other workers—have the right:

- in general, to receive **statutory sick pay** [see **27.6**];

- to be a preferential creditor for at least some of the money they are owed if the employer becomes **insolvent** [see **21.9.3**].

23.4.1.3
Trade union rights

All employees have a statutory right:

- to belong, or not to belong, to a **trade union**, to take part in trade union activities, and not to suffer a detriment or be unfairly dismissed because of trade union membership or activities [see **32.4**];

- to seek recognition for a trade union [see **32.3.3**];
- to have reasonable time off, with or without pay, to take part in **activities of a union** recognised by the employer [see **32.5**];
- to take reasonable time off, with pay, to carry out duties as an **official of a trade union** recognised by the employer [see **32.5.2**];
- not to be dismissed or suffer a detriment for taking part in **protected industrial action** [see **32.8.1**].

23.4.1.4
Health and safety rights

Employees, apprentices and trainees have a statutory right:

- to work in a **healthy, safe environment** [see **36.2.1**];
- not to be victimised or unfairly dismissed because of action taken to prevent or put right **health and safety risks** [see **36.3.3**].

Virtually all employees and other workers [see **22.1.2**], including casual, freelance and agency workers, have the right:

- not to be required to work more than 48 hours per week on average [see **28.2**];
- to four weeks paid annual leave [but see **23.4.5.2**];
- not to be required to work more than a maximum number of hours without daily and weekly rest periods [see **28.3**].

23.4.1.5
Other rights

All employees have a statutory right:

- to take reasonable time off, with or without pay, for **public duties** [see **28.10**];
- to take reasonable time off, with or without pay, to deal with emergencies relating to dependants [see **28.9**];
- to take reasonable time off, with pay, to serve as a trustee of the employer's occupational pension scheme [see **27.9.3**];
- to be paid **damages** if they are injured or become ill as a result of their employer's negligence or breach of duty [see **20.4.1**];
- not to be penalised for disclosing information about alleged wrongdoing by the employer [see **29.8**];
- not to be subject to **detriment**, dismissed or selected for redundancy because they have claimed a statutory **employment right**.

Employees and other workers [see **22.1.2**], including casual, freelance and agency workers, have a statutory right to be accompanied in hearings under a disciplinary or grievance procedure [see **29.3.4**].

Shop workers have a right not to work on Sundays [see **28.2.5**].

23.4.2
Rights of part-time workers

Part-time employees and other part-time workers [see **22.1.2**], including casual, freelance and agency workers, have the right not to be treated less favourably than a comparable full-time worker working under the same type of contract (permanent, temporary, fixed-term) [see **25.12**].

23.4.3
Rights of female employees

All female employees have the right:

- to paid time off for **ante-natal care** [see **28.7.1**];
- to 18 weeks ordinary **maternity leave**, with maintenance of all terms and conditions of employment apart from the right to remuneration [see **28.7.4**];
- if suspended on medical grounds while pregnant or breastfeeding [see **28.7.7**], to be offered alternative employment or to be paid during suspension;
- to **return to the same job** on the same pay and conditions after ordinary maternity leave [see **28.7.4**];
- **not to be dismissed or made redundant** for reasons connected with pregnancy, and the right to a written statement of reasons for dismissal or redundancy while pregnant or during ordinary or additional maternity leave [see **28.7.8**].

23.4.4
Rights of young workers

Young employees (under age 18) and in some cases other young workers [see **22.1.2**] have specific rights:

- some young employees have the right to paid time off for study [see **28.5.4**];

- young employees and other young workers, including casuals and agency workers, have the right to more frequent and/or longer rest breaks and rest periods [see **28.5.2**], and to at least one two-week break from employment during school holidays [see **28.5.3**];

- young employees, trainees and apprentices have the right to increased protection under health and safety legislation [see **36.3.1**].

23.4.5
Rights requiring continuous service

Some statutory rights are available only to employees who have completed a minimum period of **continuous service** or **continuous employment** with the same or an associated employer.

There is no longer any requirement to work a minimum number of hours per week. These rights therefore become available after the qualifying period even to employees who work a very low number of hours per week, and to employees on zero-hours contracts [see **22.2.4**] even if the employer provides no work. *Employment Rights Act 1996 s.210(4)*

23.4.5.1
One month

A qualifying period of one calendar month applies to employees' right to:

- a **written statement** of employment particulars [see **23.5.1**];

- pay during **medical suspension** [see **27.1.10**];

- if on wages, a **guarantee payment** for days when contracted to work but no work is available [see **27.1.9**];

- the statutory **notice** of termination of employment [see **30.6.1**].

23.4.5.2
13 weeks

At the time of writing employees and other workers [see **22.1.2**] had the right after 13 weeks employment to four weeks paid annual leave [see **28.4**]. The government announced in June 2001 that the 13-week requirement would be removed.

Employees on fixed-term contracts [see **22.3.2**] do not have a right to statutory sick pay until they have completed 13 weeks continuous service.

23.4.5.3
26 weeks

Women have the right to 18 weeks **statutory maternity pay** (SMP) if they have worked for at least 26 weeks up to and including the 15th week before the expected week of childbirth [see **27.8**].

23.4.5.4
One year

Employees have the right, after a qualifying period of one year:

- to **parental leave**, which may be paid or unpaid [see **28.8**];

- **not to be dismissed** without good reason [see **30.8**];

- to claim unfair dismissal if dismissed without good reason [see **30.9**] or without a fair procedure [see **30.8.2**];

- to receive a written statement of **reasons for dismissal** within 14 days of asking for it, if dismissed or if a fixed-term or temporary contract expires without being renewed [see **30.2**].

An employee may have specific rights if an employer, in trying to avoid the employee reaching the one-year mark, dismisses without going through a proper dismissal procedure or without giving the required notice [see **30.6** and **30.8**].

Women employees who have worked for at least one year up to the 11th week before the expected week of childbirth have the right to:

- **additional maternity leave** extending the maternity leave period to 29 weeks after the birth, with some (but not all) contractual rights continuing during this longer period [see **28.7.5**].

23.4.5.5
Two years

Employees have the right, after two years continuous service, to:

- the right to a statutory **redundancy payment**, and to take time off to look for work if being made redundant [see **31.4** and **31.6**].

23.4.6
Determining
continuous service

The determination of continuity is subject to complex regulations. Continuity might arise:

- from one continuous contract;

- from a series of continuous contracts with the same or an associated employer without any break of more than one week between contracts; *or*

- under provisions governing transfer of undertakings [see **26.4**].

The period of continuity starts on the first day of the contract, which may in fact be prior to the first day on which the employee arrives for work [see **23.2.1**]. *Employment Rights Act 1996 s.211*

23.4.6.1
Breaks in employment

Normally, if an employee ceases to be employed for a week or more and is then rehired by the same employer, this breaks the continuous employment and there is no continuity with the previous employment. But there are a number of exceptions, including:

- when an employee whose contract was terminated while he or she was away due to sickness, injury, pregnancy or childbirth is re-engaged within 26 weeks of the contract being terminated;

- when work ceases temporarily;

- absence from work which by arrangement or custom does not break continuity, such as a sabbatical. *s.212*

During some breaks in a contract continuity is not broken, but the date of commencement of continuous employment is brought forward by the number of days involved in the absence:

- if the reason for the work ceasing temporarily is a strike or lockout (but if the employee is dismissed during a strike and then rehired, this does break the continuity of employment);

- absence on military service.

Continuity is not broken if the employee is dismissed but subsequently re-employed as a result of an internal appeal, intervention by ACAS [see **33.3.3**] or a successful unfair dismissal claim.

23.4.6.2
Continuity for
redundancy purposes

Two groups of employees may have a separate date of commencement of employment for redundancy purposes only. These are:

- employees who started work with the employer before their 18th birthday, who for redundancy purposes are deemed to have commenced work on their 18th birthday;

- employees who have been employed overseas, whose date of commencement may be postponed by that period.

23.4.6.3
Change in employer

Employment with a new employer is continuous if:

- all or part of the previous employer's work is transferred to or taken over by the new employer [see **26.4**];

- the new employer is associated with the previous employer, for example is a company in the same group [see **26.4.8**]; *or*

- in an unincorporated organisation, there is a change in the governing body members or other persons who are technically the employer.

23.4.7
Rights and duties
dependent on
number of workers

Certain employment rights (and employer duties) apply only if the employer has a minimum number of employees or, in some cases, a minimum number of employees and workers together. As an organisation grows, the governing body must be aware of its additional duties.

As soon as there are **five** employees, the employer must:

- have a written health and safety policy and a written health and safety risk assessment [see **36.2.6** and **36.3.1**] (all other health and safety requirements apply even if there is only one employee);

- offer access to stakeholder pensions, unless other appropriate pension provision is offered [see **27.9.6**].

A woman returning from additional maternity leave *must* be given her old job or a comparable job if there are **six** or more employees at the time of her return from leave [see **28.7.5**]. If there are fewer than six employees, failure to allow return to work may not be unfair dismissal.

The employment provisions of the Disability Discrimination Act apply if the employer has **15** or more employees or other workers such as casual, freelance, agency or self-employed workers [see **25.5**].

An employer with **20** or more employees must have written disciplinary and grievance procedures [see **29.2.1**].

An employer with **21** or more employees must in some situations formally recognise a trade union [see **32.3.3**].

At the time of writing (early 2001) legislation had been proposed requiring employers with more than **50** employees in total or **20** on one site to consult workforce representatives on some issues [see **32.1.1**].

23.5 STATEMENT OF PARTICULARS

23.5.1 Section 1 statement

Employers must provide a written **statement of employment particulars** covering the major terms of employment to virtually all new employees. The statement is sometimes called the **section 1 statement** because it is required under the **Employment Rights Act 1996** s.1.

If a full contract of employment [see **23.5.5**] is provided containing all the required information, a separate statement is not necessary.

The statement must be given within two months of starting work to every employee who will work for more than one month, or sooner if he or she is to work abroad. If a person works for more than one month but leaves before two months, a statement must still be given. There is no minimum number of hours, so even if the employee works only for an hour a week or a fortnight, the statement must be given.

Employment Rights Act 1996 ss.1(1), 2(5),(6)

It is good practice to give two copies of the statement to the employee when the offer of employment is made and accepted, or before the employee starts work, or as soon as he or she starts. The employee should sign and return one copy and keep one. However, the statement is valid even if it is not signed by either the employer or employee.

23.5.2 Statement not provided

At any time during employment or within three months after the date of termination of employment, an employee can ask an employment tribunal to make a **declaration** if the employer has not given a written statement or has given only an incomplete statement, or there is a dispute about the accuracy of the terms in the statement provided. The tribunal's job is merely to ensure that terms are accurately set down. It cannot interpret what the terms actually mean

The tribunal has no power to make any monetary award or to change any of the terms, even if it feels they are unfair. It can, however, in limited circumstances change the statement or fill in omissions. For example, where the employer and employee have verbally agreed a particular term but this was wrongly stated in the written statement, the tribunal has power to alter the incorrect particulars.

The tribunal can also fill in gaps if required particulars have been left out. In doing this, it looks first at what was actually agreed. If this cannot be ascertained, the tribunal will see whether it can be implied from the other terms or from how the contract was operated in practice.

23.5.3
Required particulars

Unless the legislation specifically states otherwise, the details required in the statement must be given in full in one document, known as the **principal statement**. If there is nothing to be entered for a particular, this must be stated. The statement or a full contract containing the required particulars may be issued in instalments so long as all the instalments are issued within the two month period.

Employment Rights Act 1996 ss.1(2), 2(1),(4)

An outline contract, including all required particulars with details of each, is in **chapter 24**.

23.5.3.1
Principal statement

The principal statement must contain the following information:

- full name of employer;
- full name of employee;
- date when employment began, and date when continuous employment [see **23.4.6**] began;
- amount of salary, pay scale or method of calculating pay, any other benefits (payments in kind etc), and the intervals at which the employee is paid [see **24.13-24.16**];
- hours of work, with terms and conditions relating to normal working hours [see **24.9** and **24.10**];
- holiday entitlement [see **24.19** and **24.20**];
- job title or a brief description of the work of the employee;
- place of work or, if the employee is going to be working in several places, details of that and the address of the employer [see **24.11**].

23.5.3.2
Other written form

The following information must be included in the principal statement or in another written document given to the employee:

- for temporary employment, the period for which it is expected to continue; for fixed-term employment, the date on which it is to end; for a contract for a task, a brief description of the task whose completion will end the contract [see **24.5-24.7**];
- if an employee is going to be required to work outside the UK for more than one month, details of the period, the currency in which pay will be made outside the UK, any additional pay or benefits, and terms and conditions relating to return to the UK [see **24.8**];
- details of any collective agreements [see **24.61**].

23.5.3.3
Reference to other documents

The following particulars must be included either in the principal statement or in other documents. If included in other documents, this must be stated in the principal statement and the employee must have reasonable access to the documents. The particulars are:

- sick pay or the lack of it, any rules about notification or certification, and other rules about sick pay [see **24.22**];
- pension details or the lack of pensions [see **24.17**];
- details of disciplinary and grievance procedures, but if, at the time the employee starts work, the employer and associated employers have fewer than 20 employees, the only disciplinary and grievance matters which must be given are the name or position of the person with whom any grievances should be raised [see **24.37** and **24.38**].

If the following is not included in the statement of particulars the statement must refer the employee to the law, or to a collective agreement to which the employee has reasonable access:

- period of notice to terminate employment [see **24.33** and **24.34**].

23.5.4
Changes in the particulars

Any change in the particulars must be notified in writing to every employee affected by the change within one month after the change, or sooner if the employee is to go abroad.

s.4

If the change is one for which reference could be made in the statement of particulars to another document, the notification of change can also make reference to another document. *Employment Rights Act 1996 s.4(4)*

Notification must be given within one month but it is not necessary to issue new particulars if:

- the only change is that the employer has changed its name, but is still the same employer; *or*
- the only change is that there is a new employer, with no effect on the employee's continuity of employment [see **26.4** and **26.5**]. In this case, the notice must state when the employee's period of continuous service began.   *s.4(6),(8)*

23.5.5 Additional particulars

The statement of particulars sets out only part of the overall contract of employment [see **23.1**]. Only the statement legally has to be given to employees, but it is much the better for an employer to provide a longer **written contract of employment** or **statement of terms and conditions of employment** which includes all the statement particulars plus others which do not have to be in the statement.

The statement particulars must be given to each employee, but there is no legal requirement for any additional terms to be given to each employee. The additional terms could, instead, be made reasonably available to the employee in the course of work, or be agreed verbally or in some other way with the employee.

Where there is no dispute about additional terms, they are binding even if they are not in writing or not signed by the employer or employee. But to avoid subsequent disputes and court cases, it is good practice for the full terms to be set out in a contract.

23.6 STAFF HANDBOOK AND POLICIES

Staff handbooks are a very good way of bringing together guidance for employees on a variety of issues. A handbook might include detailed policies, operating procedures, guidance on how to deal with problems within the job, any documents referred to in the statement of particulars, and details relating to the contract of employment.

Unintended consequences can arise if it is not clear whether some or all of the handbook forms part of the contract of employment. So the handbook should clearly state whether it contains contractual terms, and if so which terms are contractual and which are not. If the contract or statement of particulars refers to the handbook, it should state whether the entire handbook, or only part of it, is incorporated into the contract.

If something in the handbook forms part of the contract, any changes are subject to the rules governing varying a contract [see **23.7**].

Even where the handbook is not explicitly part of the contract, it may have contractual consequences. If, for example, the handbook sets out safety procedures and makes clear that breach of these will be gross misconduct, and all employees were made aware of this, this will be taken into account in any subsequent tribunal hearing.

All but the smallest employers should aim to provide all employees with the following policies and procedures, either as part of the staff handbook or as separate documents:

- health and safety policy and any guidelines or procedures;
- equal opportunities policy and procedures;
- disciplinary and grievance procedures;
- whistleblowing policy;
- key operational guidance, such as data protection, confidentiality, and acceptable use of email and web access.

23.7
CHANGING THE CONTRACT

If a requirement is not part of the overall contract of employment the employer can reasonably **vary** (change) it at any time, although before doing so it would generally be good practice to consult the employees who will be affected. If the requirement forms part of the contract the usual rules on varying contracts apply [see **18.10.2**].

If a requirement is contractual it can be varied only if the change does not require consent (see below), or if the employee consents. Variation should be undertaken only after taking legal advice, and bearing in mind that all contracts of employment are governed by implied duties to maintain relationships of trust and confidence [see **23.3.3.1**].

If a change affects an item in the statement of particulars [see **23.5**] it must be notified to all affected employees within one month. Special rules govern changes to contracts following a TUPE transfer of staff [see **26.4.5**].

23.7.1
Changes not requiring consent

Some changes can occur without needing the employee's consent:

- contract terms which are imposed by statute are automatically changed when the legislation changes [see **23.3.2**];
- contract terms which are dependent on an external agreement or other source incorporated in the contract change when that agreement changes [see **23.3.5**];
- some contracts include express (explicit) clauses which allow the employer to make changes without the employee's consent, for example a **mobility clause** requiring the employee to work at any location, a **flexibility clause** requiring the employee to do 'any work reasonably requested by the employer', or a **variation clause** allowing the employer 'to make reasonable changes in the contract'.

23.7.2
Changes with consent

Any contractual provision, except those which are imposed by statute and cannot be altered unless the statute is changed, can be changed with the agreement of the employee and employer. Such change requires additional consideration [see **18.10.2**]. Where the change brings mutual benefit—such as longer hours provided to the employer and more pay provided to the employee—there is clear consideration for the new contract. Where the change is one-sided and there is no consideration it is not enforceable. An example is where a restrictive covenant preventing the employee from taking other work is added to the contract, without the employee receiving any consideration.

The agreement to vary a contract does not have to be in writing. However the change must be put in writing if it affects the statement of particulars, and it is good practice to put all changes in writing.

The nature of any work inevitably changes. It is good practice to review contracts at least every 18-24 months to ensure they reflect legal and organisational changes and best practice, and to update them by mutual consent if they do not. But even if the contracts are not formally updated, an employee and employer may be considered to have agreed tacitly to a change in the contract if they have gone along with a change in work practices.

23.7.3
Changes imposed by employers

Although any change to a contract by one or both parties must either be allowed for within the contract or must be agreed by both parties [see above], employers may feel they need to impose changes without the consent of the employee.

One way to do this is simply to operate as if the new terms were agreed and in place. If the employee accepts the change explicitly or by conduct, the change may be seen by the courts as part of the contract. However this course of action can be risky. In one case the court held that an employee who continued to work without protest following the employer's variation of the contract could not necessarily be held to have consented to the variation. The case involved a mobility clause which did not come into effect as soon as the variation was made, and indicates that particular caution is necessary where a condition that is not going to come into effect immediately is varied. From the employer's point of view, the only satisfactory practice is to ensure the new contract with the varied terms is actually signed by the employee(s) involved.

Aparau v Iceland Frozen Foods plc [1996] IRLR 119

Where a unilateral variation involves a cut in pay, the employee may be able to argue that this is an unauthorised deduction from pay [see **27.1.4**]. An employee who is dismissed or threatened with dismissal for refusing to accept the cut may be able to claim unfair dismissal for asserting the statutory right not to have deductions from pay made without consent [see **30.9.1**]. Such dismissal would automatically be unfair, regardless of length of service. *Mennell v Newell*

and Wright (Transport Contractors) Ltd, The Times 2/5/1996, EAT

If the employee explicitly rejects the new terms but continues to work, he or she reserves the right to claim damages at any time in the next six years. For example if the imposed change is a reduction in paid leave, the employee may wait until leaving the job, then sue for damages for **breach of contract** [see **33.6.2**] for the unpaid amounts.

If the change is serious enough, the employee may treat it as a **repudiation** of the contract by the employer and **constructive dismissal** [see **30.4.8**], and may be able to bring action against the employer for wrongful and/or unfair dismissal.

23.7.4
Terminating the contract and offering a new one

Some employers seek to change the contract by terminating the old contract, and offering a contract on new terms. This is a very complex area and should not be done without specialist legal advice.

Provided the required notice is given [see **30.6.1**], the employee will have no claim for **wrongful dismissal** [see **30.10**]. In some cases an employee who refuses to accept the new contract, leaves and has worked for the one-year qualifying period [see **23.4.5.4**] may be able to claim **unfair dismissal** [see **30.9**]. However in a number of cases the employment tribunal has found that a dismissal where the employee refused to accept the new contract was not unfair, on the basis that the dismissal was necessary for 'some other substantial reason' [see **30.8.7**].

In considering whether such a dismissal is fair or unfair, the tribunal will look particularly at:

- how substantial the change was (the more substantial the change, the more likely that the dismissal is fair);

- whether the change was really required by the business needs of the organisation (the greater the necessity, the more likely that the dismissal is fair);

- whether the employer behaved reasonably, for example in consulting on the change (the more reasonable the behaviour, the more likely that the dismissal is fair).

23.8
ENFORCING THE CONTRACT

Most disputes involving contracts of employment are resolved through negotiation. If a dispute cannot be resolved in this way, an employee can take legal action through an employment tribunal, the county court or High Court. An employer can take disciplinary action and, if the matter is serious, ultimately dismiss the employee. A court will not order an employee to perform the terms of the contract, but may restrain a breach of contract (prevent the employee from continuing the breach).

Procedures for dealing with contractual and other employment-related disputes are covered in **chapter 33**.

Chapter 24
MODEL CONTRACT OF EMPLOYMENT

Topics covered in this chapter

This chapter provides an outline contract of employment and commentary indicating what must be included in the principal statement of employment particulars [see **23.5**], what must be included but can refer to other documents, and optional matters. It gives details of the law and points to watch out for when agreeing a contract.

Parties to the contract
24.1   Name and address of employer
24.2   Name of employee
24.3   Job title

Duration, time and place of work
24.4   Period of continuous employment
24.5   Fixed-term contract
24.6   Contract for a task
24.7   Temporary employment
24.8   Work outside the UK
24.9   Normal hours of work
24.10   Overtime arrangements
24.11   Place of work
24.12   Accommodation

Remuneration and pensions
24.13   Starting salary
24.14   Pay period
24.15   Annual review
24.16   Increments
24.17   Pension
24.18   Deductions

Holiday entitlement
24.19   Public holidays
24.20   Annual leave

Sickness and maternity
24.21   Sick leave
24.22   Sick pay
24.23   Maternity leave
24.24   Maternity pay

Other leave and time off
24.25   Parental leave
24.26   Dependants leave
24.27   Special leave
24.28   Study leave
24.29   Sabbatical leave
24.30   Time off for public duties

Termination of employment
24.31   Probationary period
24.32   Retirement

24.33   Period of notice (employer)
34.34   Period of notice (employee)
24.35   Work during notice period
24.36   Redundancy

Disciplinary and grievance
24.37   Disciplinary procedure
24.38   Grievance
24.39   Suspension

Other work by the employee
24.40   Other paid work
24.41   Competition

Disclosure
24.42   Conflict of interest
24.43   Disclosure

Intellectual property rights
24.44   Copyright/patent

Internal policies
24.45   Confidentiality
24.46   Monitoring of communications
24.47   Personal data
24.48   Health and safety
24.49   Smoking
24.50   Equal opportunities
24.51   Media

Financial and other benefits
24.52   Removal expenses
24.53   Expenses
24.54   Car use
24.55   Childcare
24.56   Use of facilities
24.57   Outside remuneration
24.58   Gratuities

The contract
24.59   Transfer and secondment
24.60   Variation
24.61   Collective agreements
24.62   Signatures

For sources of further information see end of chapters 27-32.

Double-underlined section headings indicate additions or significant changes since the first edition.

MODEL CONTRACT

This contract sets out the main terms and conditions under which you are employed by [Organisation] and includes all particulars required by the Employment Rights Act 1996.

COMMENTS

Unless indicated otherwise, all statute references in this chapter are to the **Employment Rights Act 1996**.

Like any model, this model contract should be used with care and generally only after legal advice. For existing employees, changes can normally be made only with consent [see **23.7**].

This model can be adapted for part-time, sessional, fixed-term or temporary employees. Part-time workers must receive the same rights *pro rata* as comparable full-timers [see **25.12**].

This model must not be used for people who are hired on a self-employed basis [see **34.1**] or for volunteers [but see **35.3** and **35.4**].

Much of the information in this contract must be given to virtually all employees as part of the **statement of employment particulars** [see **23.5**]. If all the information required in the statement is included in the contract, a separate statement does not have to be given.

Employment law changes constantly, and the organisation's employment practices may also change over time. To ensure that contracts reflect these changes, it is vital to have an experienced solicitor review them regularly.

24.1 **Name and address of employer**:
[Organisation's full name and address]

The full name of the employer [see **26.1**] must be included in the principal statement. The employer's address must be given if it is not shown later as the place where the employee will work.

ERA 96 ss.1(3)(a), 2(4)

Consideration should be given to how to refer to the employer in the contract. If the contract says that notice (for annual leave etc) must be given 'to the employer', it may not be clear who it is to be given to. If the contract says notice is to be given to the manager, chairperson etc this is clearer, but may become inappropriate if the organisation's management structure changes. It is generally easiest to refer to 'the employer' throughout, and attach a memorandum indicating who the appropriate person is.

You may also be required to work for subsidiaries or other organisations associated with the employer.

This sentence should be included if the organisation has, or may create, subsidiary companies or associated organisations.

24.2 **Name of employee**: [Full name]

The name of the employee must be included in the principal statement. *ss.1(3)(a), 2(4)*

24.3 **Job title**: [Job title]

The job title, with a brief description of the job if this is not apparent from the job title, must be included in the principal statement. It is not advisable to include a detailed job description as part of the contract, as any variation would then require the consent of the employee [see **23.7**].

ss.1(4)(f), 2(4)

The following clauses cover the duration, time and place of work.

24.4 **Period of continuous employment:** This employment begins on [date] and is not continuous with any previous employment.

or

This employment begins on [date] and is continuous with your previous employment, which began on [date].

or

This employment begins on [date] and is continuous with your previous employment with [name of previous employer, if employment was with an associated employer or has been transferred from another employer], which began on [date].

The starting date for the employee's period of continuous employment [see **23.4.6**] must be included in the principal statement. This is extremely important, because significant employment rights depend on the length of the period.
Employment Rights Act 1996 ss.1(3)(c), 2(4)

Employment begins (or began) when the contract starts, which is not necessarily the first day of work. For example if the offer letter says the contract starts on 1 June but it is a Saturday and the person does not start work until Monday, the date of commencement is 1 June.

For new employees this clause should say that the contract is not continuous with any previous employment. For current employees who are starting a new post within the organisation or with a subsidiary or associated organisation, the start date for continuous employment will be the date they started working for this organisation.

For employees transferred from another employer [see **26.4**], continuous employment will have started when they commenced work with their previous employer.

If an employee's contract is terminated for a week or more and the employee is then rehired by the same employer, there is normally no continuity with the previous employment. But there are a number of exceptions [see **23.4.6**].

24.5 **Fixed-term contract:**

24.5.1 This is a fixed-term contract. Unless previously terminated, your employment will end on [date].

This clause should be included only if the contract is to end on a specified date. The ending date must be specified in the principal statement or in a letter or another document given to the employee. *s.1(4)(g)*

Fixed-term contracts need to be worded very carefully, as they can expose the employer to large claims for wrongful dismissal [see **30.7**]. The phrase 'Unless previously terminated' allows termination of the contract before the ending date by giving notice [see **24.32**].

At the time of writing (early 2001) legislation had been proposed to implement the **EU Fixed Term Workers Directive** *[1999/70/EC]* in the UK. Up-to-date information should be obtained before issuing or renewing fixed-term contracts or contracts for a task [see **24.6**].

24.5.2 In accordance with Section 197 of the Employment Rights Act 1996, as amended, you agree to waive your right to seek a redundancy payment on expiry of this contract on [date] without its being renewed.

An employee on a fixed-term contract for a specified period of two years or more can be asked or required to give up the right to redundancy pay if the contract is not renewed. The waiver can be in a written agreement separate from the written contract. It is no longer possible to include a waiver of the right to claim unfair dismissal.
Employment Rights Act 1996 s.197;
Employment Relations Act 1999 s.18

An employee can be *required* to accept a waiver only before the contract is in place. Once the contract is in place a waiver may be added at any time before the contract expires, but only if the employee agrees in writing.

Without the waiver, an employee who has worked for the necessary qualifying period is entitled to redundancy pay if the contract is not renewed when it ends.

If a contract with a waiver is renewed—either formally, or simply by the person continuing to work—a new waiver may be needed. Without a new waiver, the worker is likely to be entitled to redundancy pay when the contract ends.

24.6 **Contract for a task**: This contract will end on completion of [task].

This clause should be included only if the person is being taken on to do a specific time-limited piece of work, for example a piece of research.

Unlike employees on fixed-term contracts for a specified time period, an employee on a contract for a task cannot claim redundancy pay if the contract is not renewed when it ends. Therefore the waiver [see above] should not be used, because the employee cannot waive something there is no right to.

24.7 **Temporary employment**: This post is not permanent, and your employment is expected to last for _____ weeks/months.

This clause should be included if the employment is not intended to be permanent and does not have a fixed ending date. The period for which it is expected to continue must be included in the principal statement or in a letter or other document.   *ERA 96 s.1(4)(g)*

Employees on temporary contracts have the same rights as employees on open-ended contracts to claim unfair dismissal or redundancy pay when the contract comes to an end.

24.8 **Work outside the UK**: [Details as required]

This clause should be included only if the employee is to work outside the UK for more than one month. The principal statement or another document given to the employee must include the period of work outside the UK, the currency in which payment will be made, any additional payment or benefits arising from the work outside the UK, and any terms or conditions relating to returning to the UK. The information must be given before the employee leaves the UK.   *s.1(4)(k)*

24.9 <u>**Normal hours of work**</u>: Your normal hours are ___ a.m. - ___ p.m. Monday to Friday.

or

You are normally required to work ___ hours per week excluding meal breaks.

or

You are normally required to work ____ hours per week excluding meal breaks. The employer operates a flexi-time system with core hours from

The hours of work and the terms and conditions relating to normal working hours must be included in the principal statement. Employees cannot be required to work more than 48 hours per week, averaged over 17 weeks, unless they have opted out of the 48-hour limit [see **28.2.3**].   *ss.1(4)(c), 2(4)*

The employer may want to include something like 'The employer may vary the normal hours by giving you at least two weeks notice in writing, provided there is no increase in the hours of work per week.'

___ a.m. to ___ p.m. on Monday to Friday. You are expected to work ___ hours per day (excluding meals) during core hours, and to agree the remaining hours with the employer.

If flexitime operates, the core hours (if any) and the procedure for arranging hours of work should be stated.

If hours vary from week to week, this must be stated, for example 'The number of hours per week will vary between 10 and 25.' If hours vary, the contract should state how and when the employee will be notified.

Some contracts now operate on the basis of monthly or annual hours, rather than weekly.

The contract should state whether the hours of work include meal breaks. The employer might want to include something like 'You will have a lunch break of one hour each day, to be arranged with your manager to ensure there is adequate staffing throughout the day.'

24.10 **Overtime arrangements**: *For example:* There is no payment for overtime and you are not expected to work more than 35 hours per week. When more than 35 hours are worked, the additional hours should be taken as time off in lieu (TOIL) within one month. TOIL not taken within one month can be carried forward only with the written agreement of the employer. TOIL should be arranged in consultation with other staff. If regular overtime working seems necessary, this should be discussed as a matter of urgency with your manager.

or

You are expected to work a minimum of 35 hours per week plus such additional hours as are needed to meet the organisation's objectives [or the client's needs, or whatever]. There is no payment for overtime and time off in lieu is not normally given.

or

Overtime is paid at the rate of £____ per hour. No overtime will be paid unless the overtime work has been authorised in writing by your manager.

If overtime is or might be required, the arrangements for the overtime and for overtime pay (if any) must be included in the principal statement. *Employment Rights Act 1996 s.1(4)(c)*

This should include whether overtime working is essential, whether it must be authorised beforehand and if so by whom, and whether there is any limit on the amount of overtime which can be required, for example 'You may be required to work overtime not exceeding 10 hours in any week and not exceeding in total 20 hours in any calendar month'.

Unless the contract specifies it, there is no implied duty on an employee to work overtime, even when it is really necessary.

Most employees cannot be required to work more than an average 48 hours per week in total, unless they have signed an opt-out agreement [see **28.2.3**]. Employers have a duty to make reasonable enquiries about whether an employee has other work which could take them over the 48 hours [see **24.40**].

The principal statement should state whether overtime is paid, and if so at what rate. The law makes no presumption as to the level of overtime pay, or whether there are special payments for evenings, weekends or holidays. Where overtime attracts a special rate of pay, part-time workers do not have a statutory entitlement to this until they have worked as many hours as their full-time 'comparator' [see **25.12**].

If overtime is not paid, the contract should state whether time off in lieu is given, and if so how much overtime can be accumulated, whether TOIL has to be taken within a fixed period, and whether arrangements have to be made with a manager before taking TOIL.

Overtime where the person works 'voluntarily', with no pay and no right to TOIL, could bring pay below minimum wage level [see **27.2**] and/or take the worker over the 48-hour working time limit [see **28.2**].

If overtime pay or TOIL is to be given, the employer should consider how overtime working is to be recorded and verified. The employer should also be aware of its duty of care to ensure that employees do not suffer risks to their health as a result of overwork [see **36.4.6**].

24.11 **Place of work**: _____ or such other place as the employer may require

> *or*

> ...such other place within ____ miles of this location ...

> *or*

> ...such other place within [specified geographic area] ...

Place of work must be included in the principal statement, or an indication that the employee is required or allowed to work in more than one place. *Employment Rights Act 1996 ss.1(4)(h), 2(4)*

Legal advice should be sought before requiring employees to move house or work at any distance from where they were originally hired to work, because it could constitute unlawful sex discrimination [see **25.2.4**].

Even where the contract provides for a move, the employer must behave reasonably in asking the employee to work at a different place, and must give reasonable notice of the move.

If the contract does not include a mobility clause, the courts will imply mobility based on what is reasonable for that type of work.

If the employee is required to work from home this must be specified. The employer may want to indicate whether it will pay to insure equipment and other work items used at home, and whether it will pay public liability insurance if clients or others will visit the employee's home. [See **59.8** for issues on working at home.]

24.12 **Accommodation**: [Details]

If the employee is or could be required to live in accommodation provided by the employer, this should be indicated in the contract of employment. There should be a separate agreement for occupation of the accommodation. Legal advice should be sought for drawing this up, and on the tax implications of providing accommodation.

The following clauses cover remuneration and pensions.

24.13 <u>**Starting salary**</u>: £____ per ____.

> *or*

> You will start at point ___ on the _____ scale, for which the salary is currently £____ per _____.

The amount of salary, pay scale or method of calculating pay, and any other benefits such as payments in kind must be included in the principal statement [see **27.1** for more on salary]. If the worker is over 17 years old, pay cannot be less than the national minimum wage [see **27.2**].
ss.1(4)(a), 2(4)

If the salary is linked to an externally negotiated scale this must be stated. Unless an organisation has adequate reserves, it should think carefully before committing itself to an external pay scale over which it has no control.

24.14 **Pay period**: You will be paid monthly on the ____th of the month or, if it falls on a weekend or public holiday, on the working day before *[or as applicable]*.

The intervals at which the employee is paid must be included in the principal statement.
ss.1(4)(b), 2(4)

Examples are 'weekly on Fridays', 'monthly on the last Thursday in each month', 'monthly on the 15th of each month or on the working day before if the 15th is not a working day, half in advance'.

If payment is made direct into the employee's bank account, this should be stated.

24.15 Annual review: *For example:* Your salary will be reviewed annually, with any increase payable from 1 April.

There is no requirement to include arrangements for increases. The employer should not commit itself to automatic increases unless it is confident it will have adequate funds.

24.16 Increments: *For example:* Provided you have been in post for at least six months, you will go up one point on the salary scale on 1 April each year until you reach the ceiling for your post, which is at point ____.

or

You will go up one point on the salary scale each year on the anniversary of your starting the post, until you reach the ceiling for the post which is at point ____.

or

Provided you have satisfactorily completed the annual appraisal carried out by the employer, you will go up one point on the salary scale each year on the anniversary of your starting the post, until you reach the ceiling for the post which is at point ____.

If there are agreed provisions for annual increments, these should be included. Organisations with insecure funding and inadequate reserves should be very wary of making a commitment to automatic annual increments.

24.17 Pension:

[If the employer is exempt from having to provide a stakeholder pension] The employer does not provide a pension scheme and there is no contracting-out certificate under the Social Security and Pensions Act 1993.

or

[as the paragraph above, plus:] If you request it, the employer will make a contribution equivalent to ____% of your salary to a personal pension scheme of your choice [after you have been employed for ____ months].

or

[If the employer has a stakeholder pension scheme] The employer has created stakeholder pension arrangements with [name of company and contact details]. The employer makes a contribution of ____% of your salary to such pension [after you have been employed for ___ months]. [*or* The employer does not make a contribution to such pension.]

or

The pension arrangements or the lack of pensions must be included in the principal statement, or the statement must refer to another document. If the employer operates a pension scheme the statement or other document must indicate whether it is contracted out of the state scheme [see **27.9.2**].

Employment Rights Act 1996 ss.1(4)(d)(iii), 2, 6

Unless the employer is exempt from the obligation to provide access to a stakeholder pension [see **27.9.6**], employees must be given details of the stakeholder pension provider. There is no obligation for the employer to make a contribution to a stakeholder pension.

See **27.9** for more on pensions.

[If the employer has an occupational pension scheme or group personal pension scheme]
The employer provides a pension scheme with [name of institution] and will make a contribution to the scheme of _____% of your salary [after you have been employed for _____ months]. The scheme is/is not a contracted out scheme. Full details of the scheme are available from/in ____ .

or

[as the paragraph above, plus:] You are not obliged to join this scheme, and if you request it the employer will contribute an equivalent amount to a personal pension scheme of your choice.

24.18 **Deductions**: The employer may deduct from your salary or other sums due to you an amount to cover losses sustained in relation to property or money of the employer or of any client, customer, visitor or other employee during the course of your employment caused through your carelessness, negligence or recklessness or through breach of the employer's rules or any dishonesty on your part. [*Contracts for employees in charity shops and other retail outlets must add:* Except for any final payment of salary, this will be no more than 10% of salary for retail staff.]

The employer may also deduct from salary or other sums due to you a day or part day's pay for each day or part day of unauthorised absence. Unauthorised absence is failing to appear for work at the appropriate time unless absence is due to genuine sickness or injury which has been notified to the employer in accordance with this contract, or leave for which prior permission has been granted, or genuine reasons outside your control which are acceptable to the employer.

The employer may also deduct the amount of any accidental overpayment to you, and/or the amount of any loan made to you for any purpose, and/or any other amount due to the employer from you.

The employer will notify you in writing of the details of any such deduction, and will provide you with copies of any supporting documents reasonably requested in connection with the deduction.

There is no obligation to include a deductions clause in the principal statement. However an employer is prevented from making deductions except in limited circumstances [see **27.1.4**], unless the contract allows. A deduction which is not authorised by statute or the contract may be made only if the employee has given written consent to the deduction *before* the act to which the deduction applies took place.

Employment Rights Act 1996 ss.13-14

If an employer makes a deduction which is not authorised by statute, the contract or prior consent of the employee—for example, to recover a loan or to recover losses caused by the employee—it is then precluded from attempting to recover that money by going to court or in any other way.

The following clauses cover holiday entitlement.

24.19 **Public holidays**: Full-time employees are entitled to a paid holiday on all public holidays.

or

You may be required to work on public holidays. If so you will be entitled to take equivalent paid time off. [Such time off must be taken in the week in which the public holiday occurs or in the week immediately before or after.]

Part-time employees are entitled to paid time off for each public holiday, calculated as one-fifth of their normal weekly working hours. [Such time off must be taken in the week in which the public holiday occurs or in the week immediately before or after.]

There is no statutory requirement for an employer to give time off, either paid or unpaid, for public holidays [see **28.4.3**]. But if leave is given for public holidays, the principal statement must include details of how they are treated.

Employment Rights Act 1996 ss.1(4)(d)(i), 2(4)

If there is a comparable full-time worker on the same type of contract (open-ended, temporary or fixed-term), a part-time worker must be given the same leave entitlement *pro rata* [see **25.12**].

24.20 **Annual leave**:

24.20.1 *For example:* In addition to public holidays, full-time employees are entitled to ____ days holiday on full pay for each completed leave year, and *pro rata* for each partial leave year. [After ____ years, leave entitlement increases to ____ days and thereafter by one additional day for each year of service to a maximum of ____ days.]

Part-time employees are entitled to ____ weeks holiday on full pay for each completed leave year, and *pro rata* for each partial leave year. For these purposes a 'week' is the number of hours worked in a normal working week, or if this is not regular, the average number of hours worked in the 12-week period before the leave year starts. [After ____ years leave entitlement increases by one-fifth of your normal working week for each year of service, to a maximum of ____ days total.]

24.20.2 No annual leave can normally be taken during the first three months of employment.

24.20.3 The employer reserves the right to make any working day falling between Christmas and New Year's Day a compulsory holiday, to be taken from your annual leave entitlement.

24.20.4 All leave dates must be agreed by the employer.

24.20.5 The leave year is from 1 January to 31 December *[or 1 April to 31 March, or whatever]*.

All workers, including part-timers, are entitled to four weeks paid annual leave per year [see **28.4**]. At the time of writing there was a 13-week qualifying period, but the government had announced this would be dropped.

The principal statement must include details of annual leave entitlement, plus sufficiently detailed particulars to enable any accrued holiday pay due on termination of employment to be calculated. If additional holiday leave is available but without pay or with reduced pay, this must be stated in the principal statement.

ss.1(4)(d)(i), 2(4)

The statement must make clear whether public holidays [see **24.19**] are included as part of the holiday entitlement, or are additional to it.

Entitlement to leave continues to accrue during absence on sick leave or maternity leave.

A sample clause is given here, but each organisation should carefully think through what is appropriate in its circumstances.

The **Working Time Regulations 1998** *[SI 1998/1933]* allow the employer to specify that leave must or must not be taken at specified times. It is important to state whether holiday leave has to be agreed by anyone, and whether a minimum notice of intention to take it has to be given. The regulations set out procedures under which the employee may be required to give a minimum notice period, and the employer can then issue a counter-notice. If no counter-notice is issued, the employee may take leave at his or her desired time [see **28.4**].

24.20.6 Entitlement to leave cannot be carried forward into the new leave year without the written consent of the employer. If such consent is not obtained, leave not taken by the end of the leave year is lost. Consent generally will not be given if you have not taken at least four weeks annual leave, including paid public holidays, during the leave year.

or

Provided you have taken at least four weeks annual leave, including paid public holidays, during the leave year, a maximum of ___ days can be carried forward to the next leave year.

The right to annual leave is a health and safety right. If it is allowed to be carried forward, allowed, the contract should make clear that the employee is required to take at least their statutory entitlement of four weeks leave (including any paid public holidays) during the leave year.

24.20.7 At the end of your employment, you are entitled to be paid for any accrued leave not taken.

or

At the end of your employment you will at the discretion of the employer either be paid for accrued leave not taken or be obliged by the employer to take the remaining leave.

A deduction will be made from your final pay for leave taken in excess of your accrued entitlement.

Employees must be paid for holiday accrued but not taken at the date employment terminates [see **28.4.1**].

After a worker gives notice of leaving, the employer may want to be able to require the employee to continue working, in order to complete vital tasks. Conversely, it may be better to be able to require the employee to take any unused leave during this period.

The **Working Time Regulations** allow a deduction to be made for excess statutory leave taken. The contract should allow deduction for excess contractual leave (leave taken above the statutory four weeks).

24.20.8 Accrued holiday pay or a deduction will be calculated on the basis of:
- number of days from the beginning of the leave year up to and including the date of termination;
- divide by 365;
- multiply by the number of days annual leave entitlement;
- then subtract the number of days leave already taken.

The following clauses cover sickness and maternity arrangements.

24.21 **Sick leave:**

24.21.1 You must report sickness or injury to the employer as soon as possible on the first day of absence, with an indication of the likely period of absence.

Details about entitlement to sick leave, sick pay, notification procedures and certification must be included in the principal statement, or there must be reference to another document where the employee can get this information.
Employment Rights Act 1996 ss.1(4)(d)(ii), 2(2), 6

24.21.2 By the end of the fourth day's absence you must provide a self-certification note, available from the employer or your GP. For any period of one week or more a doctor's certificate must be provided. The employer

The self-certification form is SC2, employee's statement of sickness, which the employee or employer can obtain from GPs or the Contributions Office.

There is no obligation to require SC2 or a doctor's certificate, but without it an organisation which can recover SSP from the Contributions may require a doctor's certificate for a shorter period.

24.21.3 If you are ill or injured during a holiday and provide a medical certificate, the period covered by the certificate will be classed as sick leave rather than holiday leave.

24.21.4 The employer may require you to have a medical examination by a doctor appointed by the organisation and/or may require you to arrange for your own doctor to provide a full report. The employer will meet any costs incurred in this.

24.22 **Sick pay:**

24.22.1 *[Statutory sick pay only:]* During absence due to sickness or injury you will receive statutory sick pay to which you are entitled. Your qualifying days in respect of statutory sick pay are Monday to Friday *[or days the employee usually works]* or such other days as are agreed in writing by the employer.

   or

[SSP plus contractual sick pay:] During absence due to sickness or injury you are entitled to statutory sick pay plus additional sick pay to bring your total pay to the following amount:
- during your first [two] years of employment: a total of [two] weeks full pay during any 12-month period;
- during your [third] to [fifth] years of employment: a total of [three] weeks full pay and [two] weeks half pay during any 12-month period;
- in each subsequent year of employment: a total of [five] weeks full pay and [five] weeks half pay during any 12-month period.

Office may not have adequate evidence that the employee was entitled to it.

This clause is optional.

This clause is optional, but an employee cannot be required to undergo a medical examination (or other tests, such as drug or alcohol checks) unless the contract allows the employer to require this.

An employee who is unfit for work may be suspended by the employer until fit for work.

Employers with 15 or more employees or others working under a contract must take reasonable steps to adapt jobs or find alternative work for employees who are unable to work because of disability, which could include long-term sickness [see **25.5**]. Employers who unjustifiably fail to take such steps could be guilty of unlawful disability discrimination. The exemption for employers with fewer than 15 workers is expected to be removed by October 2004.

Employers are required to pay statutory sick pay to employees who are entitled to it. If only SSP is to be paid there is no need to state this, but doing so makes clear that there is no further entitlement. Most voluntary sector employers offer more than SSP, and the statement should include details of this.

Statutory sick pay is payable only in respect of qualifying days [see **27.6**], but these do not have to be included in the contract. The employer may be able to recover some SSP from the Contributions Office [see **27.6.1**].

There is no statutory requirement to pay employees more than SSP, so this clause is optional. However, most employers pay at least some additional (contractual) sick pay. The amounts suggested here are only examples. Before making any commitment to contractual sick pay, the employer should ensure it can afford to pay the sick pay as well as meet the cost of any locum staff to replace the person who is ill.

If a contract says nothing about sick pay entitlement, a court would try to infer from other sources what had been agreed. In the complete absence of any such evidence, the court may assume that salary was payable 'for a reasonable period' during sickness or injury.

If you are ill for longer than these periods you are entitled only to statutory benefits.

[If the employer wants to pay only SSP during the early days of employment, it might want to include at the start of this clause:] If you are absent due to illness or injury during your first ____ months of employment you will receive statutory sick pay to which you are entitled. Thereafter you will receive payments to give you the equivalent of: ...

24.22.2 For calculating sick pay a 12-month period commences 12 months before the date when the period of absence due to sickness began.

or

For sick pay purposes a year runs from 1 January to 31 December *[or whatever]*. Sick leave entitlement will be worked out *pro rata* from the beginning of this contract until next 31 December.

It may be administratively easier to have everyone on the same sick leave year, which would generally be the same as the annual leave year [see **24.20**]. However it is fairer to use a rolling year, based always on the previous 12 months.

24.22.3 <u>Termination of sick pay</u>: Contractual sick pay may be terminated, suspended or reduced if you fail to follow the notification procedure, or if your absence or continued absence is due to your:

a) taking a clearly unwarranted risk, even in your own time;

b) abusing alcohol or drugs, or other substance abuse;

c) breach of health and safety law or health and safety rules in the course of your work; or

d) being involved in conduct prejudicial to your recovery.

You will be given the opportunity to comment on any such proposal prior to it being implemented.

This clause is optional.

24.22.4 <u>Recovery of sick pay</u>: Where you receive sick pay for any period because of any injury caused to you by a third party which gives you a right to recover damages or compensation from that third party, the amount of such sick pay shall be a loan by the employer to the employee, repayable from damages or compensation you receive.

This clause enables the employee to include the sick pay in any damages claim, for example after a car accident. If the employee is awarded damages, the employer can then seek reimbursement from the employee.

24.23 **<u>Maternity leave</u>:**

24.23.1 *[statutory only:]* Female employees are entitled to ordinary and additional

There is no need to include this in the contract, because the employee has a statutory right to ordinary and additional maternity leave [see **28.6**].

maternity leave in accordance with statutes in force at the time.

or

[contractual:] Female employees are entitled to a total of ____ weeks maternity leave. The periods of notice and other requirements are the same as for statutory additional maternity leave.

Contractual maternity leave entitlement may be more than the statutory minimum, but may not be less [see **28.6.4** and **28.6.5** for details].

24.24 **Maternity pay**: *[statutory only:]* During ordinary maternity leave you may be entitled to statutory maternity pay. If you are not entitled to SMP you may be entitled to maternity allowance from the Benefits Agency.

As this is a statutory right, it does not need to be included in the contract. The organisation can recover from the Contributions Office most (or in some cases all) of the SMP payments it makes [see **27.8.4**].

[SMP plus contractual maternity pay:] [Where you have been continuously employed for at least ___ months/ years before the beginning of the expected week of childbirth,] you are entitled to maternity pay from the employer to bring your total pay to the equivalent of your usual full pay for ____ weeks [and one-half of your usual full pay for an additional ____ weeks].

If the organisation wants to pay more than the SMP entitlement and/or wants to pay for a longer period, this should be clearly set out. The organisation will not be able to recover this additional contractual entitlement from the Contributions Office.

See **27.8** for more about SMP and other payments for pregnant women and after childbirth.

The following clauses cover other entitlements to leave and time off.

24.25 <u>Parental leave</u>: If you are the mother, father, adoptive mother or adoptive father of a child, or have parental responsibility for a child under the Children Act, you are entitled to statutory parental leave. [If you are living with the mother as her partner but are not entitled to statutory parental leave, you will be entitled to equivalent contractual entitlement. The employer may require evidence of your relationship with the mother.]

In each case you will receive a total of ____ days paid leave, as part of your statutory or contractual entitlement. Further days of parental leave will be unpaid.

Notification procedures and rules with regard to leave periods are as set out in statutes in force at the time.

If circumstances require, additional leave may be requested as special leave (see below).

Parents and others with parental responsibility under the Children Act have a statutory entitlement to 13 weeks unpaid parental leave, generally to be taken before the child's fifth birthday or within five years of the child being placed with the family for adoption [see **28.8**]. At the time of writing (early 2001) parental leave was available only for children born on or after 15 December 1999, but this was due to be changed. It is available for each child, so parents with three eligible children are each entitled to 39 weeks leave. As these are statutory rights, they do not have to be included in the contract.

However the organisation might want to include provision in the contract for part or all of the leave to be paid, and/or for it to be available in relation to children born before 15 December 1999, and/or for the leave to be taken over a longer period. If paid leave is to be offered, the employer may wish to require it to be taken within a specified period, for example in the year after the child's birth or adoption.

The employer may also want to extend some parental leave entitlement to anyone, male or female, whose partner is having a baby. However difficult issues can arise, for example where a lesbian partner or male partner who is not the father does not live with the mother. An alternative is to define entitlement narrowly, for example by saying that such a partner must be living with the mother, and deal with exceptional cases as special leave [see **24.27**].

The **Maternity and Parental Leave etc Regulations 1999** *[SI 1999/3312]* include default provisions relating to notification, minimum leave periods etc [see **28.8.2**]. The employer may, if it wishes, set other rules.

At the time of writing the government had announced plans for two weeks paid paternity leave, and for adoptive parents to be entitled to maternity and paternity leave (with adoptive parents entitled to choose who takes each leave).

24.26 **Dependants leave**: You are entitled to reasonable time off to deal with unexpected or sudden emergencies relating to a child or other person dependent on you. A maximum of ____ days of such leave will be paid in any leave year.

Parents and others with responsibility for dependants are entitled to reasonable time off, which need not be paid, to deal with emergencies [see **28.9**]. For these purposes 'dependant' is very widely defined. This is a statutory right so does not need to be specified. The employer may wish to consider payment for a limited number of days, which should be specified.

24.27 **Special leave**: *For example:* Leave on a paid or unpaid basis may be granted in urgent or special personal circumstances. Leave of up to ____ working days may be granted by your line manager, the director or the chairperson. Special leave of more than ____ days, whether paid or unpaid, must be confirmed by _____.

There is no statutory requirement to include anything about special leave (sometimes called compassionate leave). But some contracts set out an entitlement and approval procedure for this, and may include a safeguard that any leave of more than a certain amount needs to be confirmed by someone else. It is important to be clear how special leave fits in with leave to deal with dependant emergencies [see above].

24.28 **Study leave**: *For example:* Requests for study leave on a paid or unpaid basis will be dealt with in the same way as special leave.

There is no statutory obligation to allow study leave except for some 16 and 17-year-olds [see **28.5.4**], but some employers consider it good practice to offer it more widely. The employer should have clear guidelines about this, for example whether the studies must be work-related, whether leave is paid or unpaid, maximum leave, any contribution by the employer towards the cost of the course or books, and whether the employer will require repayment of some or all contributions towards the costs and/or salary for paid leave if the employee leaves within a specified period.

24.29 **Sabbatical leave**: *For example:* After ____ years continuous employment you may apply for up to ____ months unpaid sabbatical leave. The application must be made at least six months before the intended start date. In deciding whether to grant leave, the employer's primary consideration will be whether your work can be covered in your absence.

If sabbatical leave is granted you will have the right to return to the same or a substantially similar post on the same terms and conditions as if the employment had been continuous, with no loss of rights.

A small number of employers allow all staff, or senior staff, to take time off after an extended period of service (such as five or seven years). Before offering even an unpaid sabbatical, the employer should consider the potential costs of recruiting, training and supporting a replacement worker during the sabbatical. Unless the organisation has and expects to maintain substantial reserves, it should be wary of making contractual commitments for significant periods into the future. Most organisations will not find it wise to include such a provision.

24.30 **Time off for public duties**: You have a statutory right to time off work for certain public duties.

You are entitled to be paid during such time off [for a maximum of ____ days in any 12-month period]. You are required to claim all available attendance allowances or loss of earnings payments and to remit them to the employer to offset the salary paid to you during time off.

or

Such time off is on an unpaid basis.

There is no statutory requirement to include in the contract of employment a statement about this, since it is a statutory right [see **28.10**].

Although there is a right to the time off, there is no right to be paid by the employer. If the employer is willing to make a contractual commitment to pay for this time, this should be stated in the contract, and it should be clear what happens to payments received by the employee from the outside body. The employer may wish to limit the number of paid days, or to make payment discretionary rather than contractual.

The following clauses cover termination of employment.

24.31 <u>**Probationary period**</u>:

24.31.1 This post is subject to a probationary period of ____ weeks/months, which may be extended by the employer. During the probationary period employment may be terminated by either side with one week's notice.

There is no obligation to have a probationary period. Some employers specify a period when either side may end the contract with shorter notice than will later apply [see **24.33**]. Even with a probationary period, the employee must be given a statement of employment particulars within two months of starting work.

It is not a good idea to set out supervision or appraisal procedures in the contract, because failure to comply with them could lead to a claim for breach of contract or wrongful dismissal [see **30.7**].

24.31.2 The disciplinary procedure does not apply to dismissal during the probationary period, unless you have been continuously employed for one year or more at the date of dismissal.

If there is a probationary period, the employer may wish to specify that during this period—provided the employee has worked for less than one year—the disciplinary procedure does not apply, or a simplified procedure applies. This reduces the burden on the organisation. However even with this provision the employer must be able to show that the dismissal was not discriminatory, and was not for another reason that is automatically unfair dismissal [see **30.9**].

24.32 **Retirement**: Retirement is at age 62 *[or whatever]*. Unless your employment has terminated at an earlier date, it will terminate without any further notice at the end of the month in which your 62nd birthday falls. By agreement employment may be continued after the normal retirement date.

There is no obligation to include anything about retirement in the principal statement, or to set a compulsory retirement age. If a retirement age is set it can be any age, but must be the same for men and women.

An employee cannot bring a claim for unfair dismissal if he or she is dismissed after the state retirement age or the employer's compulsory retirement age, so there are advantages for the employer in not setting too high an age.

See **30.4.5** for more about retirement.

24.33 **Period of notice (employer)**:

24.33.1 Except for dismissal for gross misconduct, the minimum notice of termination of employment to which you are entitled is:

The notice required to be given by the employer and employee to terminate the contract must be given in the principal statement, or the statement may refer the employee to the law or to a collective agreement provided the employee has reasonable access to it.

Employment Rights Act 1996 ss.1(4)(e), 2(3), 6

- in your first month of employment: no notice;
- then in the first two years of continuous employment: one week's notice;
- after two years of continuous employment, two weeks' notice,
- then one additional week for each completed year of employment, to a maximum of 12 weeks' notice after 12 years of continuous employment.

Notice will be in writing.

This clause sets out the statutory minimum notice to which employees are entitled [see **30.6.1**]. An employer can agree in the contract to give longer notice, but not less.

Employment Rights Act 1996 s.86(1)

Note that there is a contradiction between this notice clause, which sets out the statutory minimum, and the probationary period clause above, which commits the employer to giving (and requires from the employee) more than the statutory minimum in the first month. If a probationary period clause is included, the notice required should be consistent with the notice clause.

24.33.2 <u>Pay in lieu of notice</u>. The employer reserves the right to make a payment in lieu of notice should it so wish.

There is no obligation to include provision for pay in lieu of notice (PILON). In some situations where there is a PILON clause the employer may be entitled to pay a reduced amount if the employee obtains other employment during the notice period; in other situations the employer must pay the full amount even if the employee gets other work [see **30.6.6**]. The amount paid by the employer is subject to tax and national insurance in the usual way.

Technically PILON cannot be given unless the contract allows, but in practice it is often done [see **30.6.6**]. If a PILON clause is not included but the employer makes a payment in lieu of notice, this is technically **damages** for breach of contract [see **18.12.2**]. Damages are not generally taxable, so can be paid gross.

24.33.3 In the case of gross misconduct you may be dismissed without notice and without pay in lieu of notice.

This clause allows the employer to dismiss without notice (summary dismissal) in very serious cases [see **30.4.7**].

24.34 **Period of notice (employee)**: The notice you are required to give is:

- in your first month of employment: none;
- thereafter, one week's notice.

Notice must be in writing.

This clause sets out the legal minimum notice which employees are required to give [see **30.6.1**]. *s.86(2)*

Virtually all employers require longer notice. Many employees are required to give the same notice as they are entitled to receive.

Although the statutory minimum notice periods cannot be reduced in the contract, there is nothing to stop either party from waiving its right to notice on any occasion. *s.86(3)*

24.35 **Work during notice period**: During your notice period the employer reserves the right to require you to remain away from work, regardless of whether you or the employer gave notice. You will be required to comply with any conditions relating to your work laid down by the employer. While on full pay during such time you may not undertake any employment or work on a self-employed basis without the employer's prior written permission.

This clause should be included if there could be situations where the employer would prefer that the employee not come in to work during the notice period.

24.36 **Redundancy**: Before any redundancy is agreed, there will if possible be consultation with staff who might be affected.

In the event of your being made redundant, you will be entitled to such payment as the relevant statute in force at the time requires. You will also be entitled to reasonable time off for training or to look for work.

The period of notice for redundancy is the same as for dismissal.

There is no need to include anything about redundancy in the contract, if only the minimum statutory provisions apply. If the employer wishes to give redundancy pay more generous than the statutory provision, or wants to give it to employees who are not covered by the statutory provision, this should be included.

Many voluntary organisations have very generous contractual redundancy pay. This is good for the employees, but could create serious difficulties for the organisation if it cannot meet its contractual obligations.

See **chapter 31** for more about redundancy.

The following clauses cover disciplinary and grievance matters.

24.37 **Disciplinary procedure**: The disciplinary procedure is attached to this contract but does not form part of it.

If the employer and any associated employers [see **26.4.8**] have fewer than 20 employees at the time this employee's employment begins, the employer does not need to have a written disciplinary procedure. However it is good practice to do so. *Employment Rights Act 1996 s.3(3)*

If there are 20 or more employees, the principal statement must include a procedure or must refer to another document which is reasonably accessible to employees. *ss.3(1), 6*

If the disciplinary and grievance procedures form part of the contract, the rules governing variation of contract apply [see **23.7**]. It is better to have it as a separate document which is not part of the contract [see **29.2.2**].

See **chapter 29** for more about disciplinary matters and a model procedure.

24.38 **Grievance**: The procedure for dealing with any grievance you have in relation to your employment is attached but does not form part of this contract.

If there is a disciplinary procedure, it must include (or there must be separately) a procedure for dealing with employees' grievances. *ss.3(1), 6*

If the employer has fewer than 20 employees there is no statutory requirement for a grievance procedure, but the principal statement or another document must state who the employee should go to if she or he has a grievance.

See **24.37** for comment about including the grievance procedure as part of the contract, and **chapter 29** for more about grievance matters and a model procedure.

24.39 **Suspension**: You may be suspended from work during disciplinary proceedings. Suspension will be on full pay unless the allegation is of gross misconduct, when you may be suspended on reduced pay or without pay.

There is no obligation to include this in the contract. But unless the contract contains a provision allowing suspension, such action is in breach of contract. Hence even if the disciplinary procedure is excluded from the contract for the reasons stated above, the right to suspend should be included in the contract.

The following clauses deal with other work by the employee. Some are 'restrictive covenants', which can be used only in limited circumstances.

An employer normally has virtually no control of employees' activities outside working hours, so some seek to put into the contract **restrictive covenants** limiting what an employee can do outside work. The courts are reluctant to uphold provisions which they regard as being in **restraint of trade**, so will generally enforce a restrictive covenant only if:

• it protects a legitimate interest of the employer; *and*

• it is reasonable in relation to the employer and employee, and in the interests of the public.

Legal advice should always be sought before including any restrictive covenant.

24.40 **Other paid work**: If at the time you start this employment or at any time during the employment you are being paid for any other work, whether as an employee or on a self-employed or other basis, you are required to give details to the employer. If your total working hours exceed or may exceed an average of 48 hours per week, the employer will ask you to opt out of the 48-hour limit imposed by the Working Time Regulations.

or

While you are employed by the employer you may not undertake any other paid work as an employee, on a self-employed basis or on any other basis, without the prior written consent of the employer. If such consent is given and your total working hours exceed or may exceed an average of 48 hours per week, the employer will ask you to opt out of the 48-hour limit imposed by the Working Time Regulations.

The **Working Time Regulations 1998** *[SI 1998/1833]* put a duty on employers to ensure an employee does not work more than an average of 48 hours per week in *all* employments [see **28.2**]. Employers should therefore ask employees for details of other paid work.

The first clause asks only for information and does not give the employer any right to limit what the employee does—except to comply with the Working Time Regulations—so it is not a restrictive covenant. The second clause is restrictive and should not be included without taking legal advice.

Some voluntary organisations employing night staff who work long hours have found it sensible to include a clause limiting the outside work they can take, since those who also worked days were too tired to undertake the duties they were hired for. Such a clause is enforceable only if the employer can clearly show damage to its interests without the restriction.

24.41 **Competition**: During your employment and for the six months afterwards you must not, directly or indirectly, engage in or undertake any work which is or is intended to be in competition with the employer. This includes work undertaken on your own account, or as a partner, or as an agent, employee, officer, director, consultant or shareholder of any company or other entity, as a member of any firm, or in any other way.

The use of covenants restricting competitive behaviour is growing as organisations move increasingly into the contract culture. Employees have an implied duty not to make secret profits or compete with the employer during employment [see **23.3.3**], but attempts to protect the organisation from competition afterwards must fit the 'public interest' requirement [see above]. This could be difficult, but it is important to consider whether there are some areas of work which need the protection of such a covenant.

Where a restrictive covenant might be held to be unreasonable but the employer wants to restrict the employee's right to take other work after leaving this employment, the contract might allow for a period of **garden leave** where the person remains on the payroll but remains at home and is not allowed to work for anyone else [see **24.35**].

The following are disclosure clauses.

24.42 **Conflict of interest**: You must disclose to the employer any direct or indirect relationship that you or any close relative have with any customer, client or beneficiary of the employer.

If you or a close relative has any direct or indirect interest in any company or firm which may enter into a contract with the employer, this interest must be disclosed to the employer as soon as you become aware of it.

Although there is a duty to give honest and faithful service and to pass on information relevant to the employment [see **23.3.3**], there is generally no statutory obligation for an employee to declare conflicts of interest to the employer. If the organisation does work in which conflicts of interest might be significant, a clause such as this might be appropriate.

If the organisation is a company and/or charity and the employee is a company director and/or charity trustee, there is an obligation to disclose conflicts of interest [see **13.2.2** and **13.3.4**].

24.43 **Disclosure**: If at any time you are offered any gift or consideration as an inducement to influence a contract or obtain preferential treatment for any customer, client or beneficiary of the employer, or if any suggestion of this type is made to you, you must report it immediately to the employer.

There is no obligation to include this but in some situations it may be appropriate.

The following clause covers intellectual property rights.

24.44 **Copyright/patent**: Every work created, developed, invented, carried out or produced during your employment or arising out of or in consequence of this employment, shall be deemed to have been made by or on behalf of the employer. The work, together with the benefit of any such work, belongs exclusively to the employer.

You must give the employer full details of all and any such work. You must, at the employer's request and cost during the employment and thereafter, if required, take all steps as may be necessary or desirable to substantiate the employer's rights in respect of any such work.

There is no need to include this in a contract, because copyright material and inventions created during employment belong to the employer [see **39.2.3**]. But a clause like this provides additional clarity and protection for the employer.

The following clauses relate to the organisation's internal policies.

There is no obligation to include anything about the organisation's internal policies in the contract, but doing so makes clear that breach of the policy is also a breach of contract. The information could be included instead in a staff handbook, which might or might not have contractual force [see **23.6**].

24.45 **Confidentiality**: You must not at any time disclose any confidential information arising out of your employment, unless such disclosure is authorised under the employer's policy on data protection and confidential information, or is protected under the Public Interest Disclosure Act.

If the organisation does not have a confidentiality policy, replace the words from 'under' to 'protection' with 'by the employer'. For more about confidentiality see **38.1**, and for more about whistleblowing see **29.8**.

24.46 **Monitoring of communications**. Telephone, email and internet use are monitored by the employer, and your signature on this contract indicates your consent.

For more about employees' right to privacy and the employer's right to monitor communications see **38.1.5**. If the employer does not actually monitor but wishes to reserve the right to do so, replace 'are' with 'may be'.

24.47 **Personal data**: From time to time it may be necessary to process sensitive personal data, for example about your health. By signing this contract you agree that the employer may retain and process sensitive personal data about you as the needs of the organisation require.

The **Data Protection Act 1998** requires explicit consent to store or process in any way sensitive personal data, which includes information about racial or ethnic background, health, disability, religious belief, trade union membership etc [see **38.3**].

24.48 **Health and safety**: Every employee must comply with the employer's health and safety policy and procedures.

This is a statutory obligation for all employees, but it does not hurt to remind them.

24.49 **Smoking**: The employer operates a no smoking policy and smoking is not allowed anywhere in its buildings or grounds [is allowed only in designated areas in its buildings and grounds].

There is no obligation to include anything about smoking but the organisation may wish to do so. Once it is in the contract it can be changed only by agreement of the employer and employee, so if it is ever likely to change it should be included in a separate policy rather than in the contract. See **36.4.3** for more about smoking at work.

24.50 **Equal opportunities**: Every employee must act at all times in accordance with equal opportunities legislation and the employer's equal opportunities codes of practice.

As with health and safety, some employees may need reminding.

24.51 **Media**: Communication with the press, television or radio must be authorised by the employer if it is in any way connected with your employment or is likely to contain reference to the employer.

The organisation may wish to include a clause such as this, or may wish to include it in a non-contractual policy.

The following clauses relate to financial matters other than salary and pension, and to 'perks'. Note that some of these benefits may be subject to tax and national insurance.

24.52 **Removal expenses**: The employer will contribute £_____ towards your removal expenses to take up this post.

There is no obligation to pay relocation expenses. If payment for removal expenses meets certain requirements and is less than £8,000 (as at 1/4/01), it is not subject to tax or national insurance [see **27.4.4**].

24.53 **Expenses**: Out-of-pocket expenses and agreed travel and subsistence costs will be reimbursed in accordance with the employer's financial procedures.

There is no need to include anything about reimbursement of expenses, since employees have a right to be reimbursed for essential or authorised expenditure. Some reimbursements may be subject to tax [see **27.4.3**].

24.54 **Car use**: Use of your car for authorised work purposes will be reimbursed at a mileage rate set out in the employer's financial procedures. Mileage records must be kept and must be submitted in accordance with the procedures.

There is no obligation to include this, but if the employee might use a privately owned vehicle it is good practice to set out the rules in a handbook, or possibly in the contract. In particular, staff should be aware of the need to inform their insurer that the car is being used for work purposes. If a car comes with the job, this should be reflected in a clause in the contract.

24.55 **Childcare**: The employer cannot assist practically or financially with the provision of childcare.

or

The employer will contribute towards childcare costs for each week in which you have a child or children under school age normally living with you and being looked after by a registered childminder or in a registered childcare facility. The contribution will not be more than one-half of the fees paid by you for the childcare and will not exceed £___ per child [in total] per week. During weeks when you are on leave the contribution is reduced on a per day *pro rata* basis.

There is no obligation to provide childcare or contribute towards its cost, but if there are such arrangements, they must be made equally available to women and men.

Very careful thought must be given before making any contractual commitment to childcare (or anything with long-term financial implications). If the organisation wants to provide an allowance towards childcare it may be more sensible to do so as a policy, which can be changed by the governing body, rather than as a contractual commitment which can be changed only if the employee agrees.

The organisation will need to decide whether it will contribute only towards the cost of childcare with registered childminders or in registered facilities, or whether it will also contribute to the cost of nannies or informal childcare arrangements.

24.56 **Use of facilities** Use of the employer's facilities or equipment for personal use is not permitted without prior written consent from the employer.

There is no need to include this but the organisation may want to. It is generally preferable to include matters like this in the staff handbook, where they can be easily revised, rather than in the contract.

24.57 **Outside remuneration**: If you receive any outside remuneration for work undertaken on behalf of the employer or arising directly from your employment by the employer (for example, fees for a speaking engagement or an article), you are required to pay these to the employer.

There is no obligation to include anything about outside remuneration, but doing so avoids doubt if the employee receives outside fees.

24.58 **Gratuities**: You are not allowed to accept gratuities, money or non-monetary gifts from clients or users of the employer's services. If such gratuities are given to you without your prior knowledge, they must be given to the employer.

or

You are not allowed to accept money from clients, customers or

There is no need to include this in the contract. Rules such as these are generally better in a staff handbook, where they can be more easily changed.

users of the employer's services, nor may you accept a non-monetary gift with a value of more than £___ . If money or such a gift is given to you without your prior knowledge, it must be given to the employer. You may keep a non-monetary gift with a value under £___ provided you report it in writing to the employer.

The following clauses relate to the contract itself.

24.59 **Transfer and secondment**: The employer is entitled to assign its rights under this agreement to any subsidiary or associated employer, or any body with which it may be merged or which may succeed it, on giving you written notice of its intention to this effect. It may also require you to work for another organisation, while remaining employed by the employer.

This clause gives the employer the right to transfer the employee's contract to an associated organisation such as a trading subsidiary, a new organisation set up to undertake a specific project etc. It also allows the employer to require the employee to work for any organisation on a seconded basis. Both transfer and secondment raise significant issues [see **26.4** and **22.5.3**].

24.60 **Variation**: The employer reserves the right to make reasonable changes to any of your terms and conditions of employment. You will be notified in writing of minor changes of detail, and any such change takes effect from the date of the notice or such other date as specified in the notice. Other changes will be made only after consultation, and with at least one month's written notice.

A clause such as this can be very useful in enabling the employer to make minor or relatively minor changes to the contract. Even with this provision, the employer should be cautious about making changes without the employee's consent [see **23.7**].

24.61 **Collective agreements**: This contract is affected by the terms of a collective agreement between [trade union or unions] and [employer or other party to the agreement].

or

This contract is not covered by any collective agreement.

If any collective agreement directly affects the terms of employment it must be referred to in the principal statement. If the employer is not a party, the names of the parties to the agreement must be included.

Employment Rights Act 1996 s.1(4)(j)

This clause is optional.

24.62 **Signatures**
Signed: [Name]
For and on behalf of [Employer]
[Date]

I have read, understood and accept the above terms and conditions of employment.
Signed: [Employee]
[Date]

A written statement of employment particulars [see **23.5**] or broader written contract does not need to be signed by either the employer or employee. However signatures are proof that the employee has received the statement of particulars, and for a broader contract signatures show that each side has accepted the terms as set out.

Chapter 25
EQUAL OPPORTUNITIES IN EMPLOYMENT

Topics covered in this chapter

This chapter explains when it is and is not lawful to use race or sex as a factor in employing people, and the legal requirements for aspects of equal opportunities. It covers:

For sources of further information see end of chapter.

Double-underlined section headings indicate additions or significant changes since the first edition.

25.1 UNLAWFUL DISCRIMINATION

Discrimination involves treating people less favourably because they are members of a particular group or have a particular characteristic. At the time of writing (early 2001), it is unlawful to discriminate in any aspect of employment on the basis of racial group, sex, being married, pregnancy, gender reassignment, disability or working part-time, unless such discrimination is allowed under exceptions to the legislation.

Until new legislation required by EU directives is implemented [see below] there are many situations where discrimination is not specifically unlawful, for example in relation to age, sexual orientation, and in most cases religion. However discrimination on those grounds may constitute **indirect discrimination** [see **25.2.4**] on the grounds of race or sex. In particular discrimination against a particular religious group may be unlawful where religion is linked to ethnic origin [see **25.8**], and unjustified age discrimination may indirectly discriminate against one sex and thus be unlawful [see **25.9**].

25.1.1
European Union directives

New legislation will have to be implemented by 2 December 2003 outlawing discrimination in employment on the basis of religion or other belief and sexual orientation, and on the basis of age by 2 December 2006. Some provisions of the **Disability Discrimination Act 1995** must also be extended by 2 December 2006.

EU Equal Treatment in Employment Framework Directive [2000/78/EC]

In addition the UK must ensure that provisions are in place by 19 July 2003 to outlaw all discrimination (not only in employment) on the basis of racial and ethnic origin. Most of these provisions are already in place in the **Race Relations Act 1976** and **Race Relations (Amendment) Act 2000**, but new legislation or regulations may redefine indirect discrimination [see **25.2.4**], explicitly include racial harassment [see **25.2.5**], and/or further extend protection for ex-employees. In addition the **burden of proof** will fall to the employer or other person accused of discrimination to disprove discrimination, once the person bringing the claim has shown that he or she was treated less favourably.

EU Directive on Equal Treatment between Persons irrespective of Racial or Ethnic Origin [2000/43/EC]

In the same way the burden of proof will shift in sex discrimination cases when the **EU Burden of Proof Directive** is implemented in the UK in mid-2001.

EU Directive on the Burden of Proof in Cases of Discrimination Based on Sex [97/80/EC]

25.1.2
Who is covered

Discrimination legislation protects not only employees, but also applicants for jobs, workers supplied by an agency or by another person, and self-employed or freelance workers who are contracted to provide work personally to the employer. In some situations the legislation might also apply to volunteers [see **35.6.1**].

Protection may in some cases apply to discriminatory acts by the employer even after employment has ended. For example, if an employer refuses to give a reference to a person who has brought a sex discrimination claim against the employer, this may constitute victimisation under the sex discrimination legislation [see **25.2.3.1**]. At the time of writing (early 2001) it appeared that a claim cannot be brought for race or disability discrimination which occurs after employment ends, but this may change either through case law or legislation.

Coote v Granada Hospitality Ltd [1998] IRLR 656, 82 EOR 39 ECJ

Staff whose work is wholly outside Great Britain are not protected by the discrimination legislation. Those whose work is partly outside Great Britain are protected.

Equal Opportunities (Employment Legislation) (Territorial Limits) Regulations 1999 [SI 1999/3163]

25.1.3
Acts by employees and other workers

It is unlawful for an employer to require or pressure an employee to take part in any discriminatory act or practice, and unlawful for any worker, whether employed, self-employed or from an agency to do any discriminatory act in the field of employment.

An employee who is dismissed because of complaining about discrimination by other workers might be able to bring a claim of unfair dismissal [see **30.9.1**]. If an employee resigns because the employer has refused or neglected to investigate and take action about discrimination, this could constitute constructive dismissal [see **30.4.8**].

25.1.3.1
Vicarious liability of employer

An employer has vicarious liability [see **19.5.3**] for discriminatory acts by its employees carried out in the course of employment, unless the employer can show that it took all reasonably practicable steps to prevent the acts. In these cases much depends on the tribunal's view of whether the act occurred 'in the course of employment', and whether the employer could have prevented the action. Reasonable steps include:

- providing race, sex and disability awareness training;

- ensuring equal opportunities policies reflect changes in the law;

- making clear that racist, sexist, anti-gay, anti-disability and similar comments, behaviour, 'jokes' and harassment are unacceptable and will be treated as disciplinary matters;

- encouraging a positive approach to adapting premises, work and services to make them more accessible to people with disabilities and people from other cultures;

- monitoring the organisation's recruitment, selection, promotion and similar procedures, and taking appropriate action if it appears that unlawful discrimination is occurring.

An employer cannot have vicarious liability for harassment or discriminatory acts by customers, service users or other third parties. But allowing such behaviour to take place or to continue, in a situation where the employer could have prevented it, may constitute direct discrimination by the employer.   *Burton and Rhule v DeVere Hotels [1996] IRLR 596*

25.1.4
Equal opportunities policies

Many voluntary organisations have equal opportunities policies which go beyond the legislation and:

- say that the organisation will not discriminate on the basis of certain factors, even though such discrimination is not covered by legislation and would therefore not be unlawful;

- commit the organisation to going beyond the minimum required by the law, in order to ensure the organisation is genuinely open and welcoming to all employees, members, service users and others.

Where such policies form part of the contract of employment or other contract, they may give an enforceable right not to be discriminated against in relation to matters referred to in the policy—even where, as with age, there is (at the time of writing) no statutory protection.

25.1.5
Human rights and discrimination

Article 14 of the **European Convention on Human Rights** [see **60.3**] provides that the rights guaranteed by the Convention must be enjoyed without discrimination on any grounds. This is not a freestanding right not to be discriminated against, because the discrimination must be in relation to a Convention right.

The protections under article 14 are very broad, covering political or other opinion, language, religion, social origin, association with a national minority, property, birth or other status, as well as sex, race, colour and national origin. 'Other status' is likely to include disability, sexual orientation, age, marital status and illegitimacy.

Only public authorities and other bodies carrying out public functions are bound by the Human Rights Act. Some charities and voluntary organisations may fall into this category and thus have to comply with article 14 [see **60.3.2**]. Even where this is not the case, article 14 will have an impact on employment-related matters, primarily because all UK legislation must be interpreted compatibly with Convention rights.

At the time of writing (early 2001) the Council of Europe had proposed a protocol (additional provision) to the Convention creating a freestanding right to freedom from discrimination. This would apply only to acts by public authorities and other bodies carrying out public functions, but would not require the discrimination to be linked to a Convention right.

25.2
RACE AND SEX DISCRIMINATION

The **Sex Discrimination Act 1975** and **Race Relations Act 1976** are very similar, using the same concepts and language. They are therefore considered together here. Under these Acts, it is unlawful for an employer to discriminate on the basis of sex, being married, gender reassignment, or racial group in relation to the work provided (or not provided) to these workers, or in relation to their conditions of work.

Sex Discrimination Act 1975 s.9; Race Relations Act 1976 s.7

25.2.1
Racial groups

The Race Relations Act outlaws discrimination between racial groups or on racial grounds. **Racial grounds** means colour, race, ethnic origin, national origin or nationality, and a **racial group** is any group defined by reference to their colour, race, ethnic origin, national origin or nationality.   *Race Relations Act 1976 s.3(1)*

The Act does not define these terms, but case law has defined an ethnic group as 'a segment of the population distinguished from others by a combination of shared customs, beliefs, traditions and characteristics derived from a common or presumed common past, even if not drawn from what in biological terms is a common racial stock'.

Mandla v Dowell Lee [1983] 2 AC 548, 1 All ER 1062

Some religious groups have been defined as coming within this definition of ethnic group [see **25.8**].

25.2.2
<u>Sex</u>

The Sex Discrimination Act makes it unlawful to discriminate on the basis of sex or being married. It applies to discrimination not only on the basis of being a woman or a man, but also, in relation to employment and vocational training, on the basis of intending to undergo, undergoing or having undergone gender reassignment (transsexualism).

Sex Discrimination (Gender Reassignment) Regulations 1999 [SI 1999/1102]

25.2.3
Unlawful discrimination

Apart from very few situations [see **25.3**], an employer must not take racial group, sex (including gender reassignment) or the fact that someone is married into account when recruiting and selecting staff, determining conditions of employment, offering training or other benefits, transferring or promoting staff, or dismissing staff.

Sex Discrimination Act 1975 s.6; Race Relations Act 1976 s.4(1),(2)

The codes of practice of the Commission for Racial Equality and Equal Opportunities Commission [see end of chapter] set out good practice. Failure to comply with the codes is not unlawful, but is taken into account if a discrimination claim is brought against an employer.

25.2.3.1
Types of discrimination

Unlawful race or sex discrimination is defined as:

- treating someone less favourably on the basis of racial group, sex or marital status than a person from another group is or would be treated in the same or a similar situation (**direct discrimination**);

- applying a requirement or condition, even if it is applies to everyone equally, if the condition is not justifiable and has a detrimental effect on people of a particular racial group or sex, because they disproportionately cannot comply with the requirement or condition (**indirect discrimination**);

- treating someone less favourably because he or she has claimed that an employer has discriminated unlawfully, or because he or she has brought or been involved in proceedings against a discriminator (**victimisation**).   *SDA ss.1-4; RRA ss.1, 2*

25.2.3.2
Advertising

It is unlawful to publish advertisements which indicate, or could reasonably be interpreted as indicating, an intention to discriminate unlawfully. Use of terms such as 'waitress', 'postman' or 'stewardess' are assumed to indicate an intention to discriminate, unless the advertisement states otherwise.   *SDA s.38; RRA s.29*

25.2.4
Indirect discrimination

Indirect discrimination occurs when an employer uses a factor in selecting for a job, training, promotion etc which:

- is not justified by the objective demands of the job;

- has the effect of discriminating because a disproportionate percentage of one sex or one or more racial groups cannot comply with the requirement; *and*

- puts people of that sex or racial group at a disadvantage.

Examples of indirect discrimination include:

- a refusal to accept applicants from a particular postal district of a city where it could be shown that the district had a significantly higher proportion of potential applications from racial minorities;

  Hussein v Saints Complete House Furnishers [1979] IRLR 337 IT

- imposing longer periods of training on non-British graduates;

  IOM Mitchell v Common Professional Examining Board [1978] IRLR 525 IT

- setting age limits of 17-28 for a job without having a justifiable reason for doing so, because more women than men are off work looking after children at that age;

  Price v Civil Service Commission [1978] 1 All ER 1228

- requiring all employees to work full time when in fact the work could be done by part-time employees, or making part-time employees redundant before full-time employees, because more women than men work part-time. *Home Office v Holmes*

  [1984] IRLR 299; Clarke v Eley (IMI) Kynoch Ltd [1982] IRLR 131

A requirement which has a disproportionate impact on one group but is justified may not be unlawful discrimination. For example:

- a rule prohibiting employees from having a beard on hygiene grounds was found to be not unlawful, even though it meant that Sikhs were less likely to be able to be employed;

  Panesar v Nestle & Co Ltd [1980] IRLR 60 EAT

- a university careers office argued successfully that it needed to advertise for young workers, even though this might discriminate against women, because it was necessary to have someone young enough to identify with the majority of the students.

  Jones v University of Manchester [1993] IRLR 218

25.2.5
Harassment

Harassment is unacceptable behaviour which is unreasonable, unwelcome and/or offensive. It might be physical, verbal or non-verbal, and might be directed against an individual or arise in a gathering such as a meeting, public gathering or party. Racial and sexual harassment are not defined in the legislation, but have been held to be unlawful direct discrimination, on the basis that the person who is being harassed is being treated less favourably than a person of the other sex or another racial group would be. *for example,*

Porcelli v Strathclyde Regional Council [1986] ICR 564; IRLR 134

Employers are liable for harassment carried out by employees in the course of their employment, and allowing harassment by customers, service users or other third parties could constitute direct discrimination [see **25.1.3.1**].

Harassment on any basis—not only race or sex—may fall within the criminal offence of **intentional harassment** if it involves alarm or distress caused by threatening, abusive or insulting words or behaviour; disorderly behaviour; or writing, signs or other visible representations which are threatening, abusive or insulting. Where harassment puts a person in fear of violence a civil and criminal offence is committed.

Criminal Justice and Public Order Act 1994 s.4A;
Protection from Harassment Act 1997

Advice on harassment is included in the Commission for Racial Equality's code of practice and the Employment Service's *Sexual Harassment in the Workplace*, based on the EU Code on the Dignity of Women and Men at Work. These codes and decisions in harassment cases emphasise the importance of having proper procedures to deal with complaints of harassment.

Wiseman v Wadman Carpenter Partnership [1993] IRLR 374

25.2.6
Maternity

It is unlawful to refuse to hire a woman simply because she is pregnant at the time of interview. However, it may not be unlawful to reject a woman because of her pregnancy if the post is for a short fixed term [see

22.3.2], and maternity leave would mean she would not be available for the entire period of the fixed term.

Dekker v Stichting Formingscentrum voor Jongen Volwassenen-Plus [1991] IRLR 26; Webb v EMO Air Cargo (UK) Ltd [1995] ICR 1021, IRLR 645 HL

It is unlawful sex discrimination to subject a woman to detriment [see **25.1**] on maternity-related grounds. It is automatically unfair dismissal to dismiss a woman or make her redundant on maternity-related grounds, although there is an exception for small employers where the woman has taken additional maternity leave [see **28.7.5**].

Employment Rights Act 1996 s.104

Failure to carry out health and safety assessments required for new or expectant mothers [see **36.3.1**] may be sex discrimination.

Day v T. Pickles Farms Ltd [1999] IRLR 217 EAT

25.2.7
Workers from outside the EU

Most workers from outside the European Economic Area (the European Union member states plus Iceland, Liechtenstein and Norway) require permission to work in the UK [see **26.2.9**]. It is not unlawful race discrimination to refuse to hire a person who is not entitled to work in the UK. It *is* unlawful to refuse to hire a person on the basis of nationality if he or she is not required to have a work permit, or has a permit covering the type of employment.

To avoid the risk of prosecution under the **Asylum and Immigration Act 1996** s.8 [see **26.2.9**] the employer should ask to see proof of entitlement to work in the UK. But to avoid a claim of racial discrimination all potential employees, not only those who are or might be foreign nationals, should be asked for this.

25.3
RACE AND SEX DISCRIMINATION EXCEPTIONS

In some situations it may be lawful to:

*   recruit a person specifically because he or she is of a particular racial group or sex;
*   provide preferential access to training for people of a particular racial group or sex; *or*
*   encourage people of a particular racial group or sex to apply for some types of work.

Unless such discrimination is explicitly permitted, it is unlawful.

25.3.1
Genuine occupational qualification

Under the **genuine occupational qualification** (GOQ) provisions it is lawful to advertise for a person or a particular racial group or sex, and choose someone on the basis of their racial group or sex, if there is a genuine reason for needing a person of that particular group in the post. Training or other benefits to enable the person to do the job can also be provided. The GOQ provisions apply regardless of whether all of the job duties fall within the requirements, or only some of them.

Sex Discrimination Act 1975 s.7(3); Race Relations Act 1976 s.5(3)

An employer cannot define a job as a GOQ post if there are already employees of that sex or racial group who are capable of carrying out the relevant duties, whom it would be reasonable to employ on those duties, and who could be given those duties without causing undue inconvenience.

SDA s.7(4); RRA s.5(4)

Before advertising a post as a GOQ job, it is sensible to contact the Commission for Racial Equality if a person of a particular racial group is being recruited, and/or the Equal Opportunities Commission if a person of a specified sex is being recruited. They cannot give 'exemption', but can advise on whether a job is likely to fall within the GOQ exemptions. The fact that such advice has been requested (and acted or not acted on) is taken into account if a claim is subsequently brought that the employer acted unlawfully by defining the post as a GOQ job.

25.3.1.1
Sex

Being of a particular sex can be a GOQ if:

- the job requires a man or woman to undertake it for physiological reasons (other than strength), for example for authenticity for a part in a dramatic performance;   *Sex Discrimination Act 1975 s.7(2)(a)*

- there are considerations of decency or privacy, for example in situations involving physical contact, people in a state of undress or people using sanitary facilities;   *s.7(2)(b)*

- the job involves living or working in a private home and it would be inappropriate for a man to be in close physical or social contact with a woman, or *vice versa*;   *s.7(2)(ba)*

- the employee must live on premises provided by the employer, and it is unreasonable to expect the employer to provide separate facilities for the sexes (for example, on an oil rig);   *s.7(2)(c)*

- the job is within a institution such as a hospital and it is reasonable that it should not be held by a person of a particular sex;   *s.7(2)(d)*

- it is likely that the job will have to be undertaken outside the UK in a country whose customs or laws would make it difficult for it to be properly undertaken by person of a particular sex;   *s.7(2)(g)*

- the job is one of two to be held by a married couple; *or*   *s.7(2)(h)*

- statutory restrictions apply.

The provision which is most used by voluntary organisations allows an employer to recruit a person of a particular sex because:

- the worker provides individuals with personal services promoting their welfare or education or similar services, and those services can most effectively be provided by a person of that sex.   *s.7(2)(e)*

To fall within the s.7(2)(e) exemption, the post must involve the provision of **personal services** and must be **most effectively** filled by a person of that sex. Treating a post which does not meet these criteria as a s.7(2)(e) post constitutes unlawful sex discrimination.

25.3.1.2
Racial grounds

Racial grounds can be used as a factor in recruiting or selecting a person for a job, or promoting or transferring a person to a job, or providing training for the job, only:

- for reasons of authenticity in drama or entertainment (for example, portraying a black person);   *Race Relations Act 1976 s.5(2)(a)*

- for work as an artist's or photographic model, in order to achieve authenticity;   *s.5(2)(b)*

- in the public section of a restaurant for reasons of authenticity (for example, in a Chinese restaurant); *or*   *s.5(2)(c)*

- where the job holder will provide persons of a racial group with personal services promoting their welfare, and these services can most effectively be provided by a person of that racial group (for example, a Pakistani advice worker for that community).   *s.5(2)(d)*

A post can be filled under s.5(2)(d) only if the employee is going to be primarily involved in face-to-face or other direct contact with the members of the defined racial group. Posts which are largely managerial or administrative do not generally fall within the provision.

London Borough of Lambeth v Commission for Racial Equality [1990] IRLR 231

Where it is important that the employee understands the cultural and religious background of the people with whom he or she is working, it is accepted that those services may be most effectively provided by a person of the relevant racial group.

Tottenham Green Under Fives Centre v Marshall [1989] IRLR 147

As with sex GOQ posts, it is the employer's responsibility to be able to show the post involves personal welfare services which are most effectively provided by a person of a particular racial group.

The race relations legislation does not apply to employment in a private household, so it is not unlawful to specify that a person hired to work in a private household must be of a particular racial group. This is the only employment situation where race can be used purely as a matter of choice or preference. *Race Relations Act 1976 s.4(3)*

25.3.2
Positive action

The Race Relations and Sex Discrimination Acts do not encourage or require employers to take positive steps to recruit, appoint or promote people from particular groups. They do, however, contain very limited provision for some **positive action** by employers and by training providers.

In addition public authorities as defined under the Human Rights Act, which could include some voluntary organisations [see **60.3.2**], have a duty to eliminate racial discrimination and promote equality of opportunity. This could include setting targets for ethnic minority recruitment, retention and promotion. *Race Relations (Amendment) Act 2000*

25.3.2.1
Positive action by employers

Positive action can be undertaken by employers if at any time in the previous 12 months:

- there were no persons of a particular racial group or sex doing particular work at a particular establishment;

- the proportion of persons of that racial group or sex doing that work at that establishment was small in comparison to everyone employed there; *or*

- the proportion of persons of that racial group or sex doing that work at that establishment was small in comparison to the population of the area from which the employer normally recruits for there.
Sex Discrimination Act 1975 s.48; Race Relations Act 1976 s.38

An employer *cannot* in these situations specifically recruit, promote or transfer a person from the under-represented group to 'make up the numbers'. But the employer *can*:

- encourage people of the under-represented group to apply for the job or take advantage of opportunities to do the job, for example by encouraging applications from that group, placing advertisements in publications read by that group, or using agencies with particular skills in attracting staff of that group; *and/or*

- provide access to training for the work only for people from that group, to help them gain skills or knowledge needed for that work.

Even where positive action advertising or preferential training is allowed, racial group or sex cannot be used as a criterion for selection.

It is not unlawful to provide training specifically for people of a particular racial group if they are overseas residents whom the employer is training in skills which they will exercise outside the UK. This also applies to contract workers ordinarily resident overseas, and to overseas students provided they are not intending to remain in the UK after they have completed their education. *RRA ss.6, 7(4), 36*

In addition to training which can be provided by employers, training (but not employment) can in some situations be provided by others for one sex or racial group [see **37.2.2** and **37.3.1**].

25.3.3
Maternity

Special treatment is permitted for women in relation to pregnancy and childbirth, and such treatment does not constitute unlawful sex discrimination against men. *SDA s.2(2)*

25.4
EQUAL PAY AND CONDITIONS

The **Equal Pay Act 1970** applies not just to pay, but to all contractual terms of employment (for example entitlement to holidays, bonuses, travel concessions or redundancy pay). Its intention was to bring women's pay and other conditions up to the levels of men's, but it applies to men as well as women. It applies not only to employees but also to apprentices, others working under a contract, and people undertaking work on a self-employed basis.   *Equal Pay Act 1970 s.6(a)*

Every employee's contract of employment is considered to include an **equality clause** giving contractual equality:

- for like work to that of an employee of the other sex, when the work is of the same or a broadly similar nature;   *s.1(2)(a),(4)*

- for work rated in a job evaluation study as being equivalent to the work of an employee of the other sex; *and*   *s.1(2)(b),(5)*

- for work of equal value to that of an employee of the other sex, which makes comparable demands in terms of effort, skill and decision making.   *s.1(2)(c)*

Equal pay cannot be claimed with another person of the same sex, and men do not have the right to claim contractual benefits relating to special treatment of women in relation to childbirth.

For sex discrimination, it is enough to show that a hypothetical person of the other sex *would have been* treated differently. To claim equal pay, however, there must be an *actual* **comparator**. This person:

- must be of the other sex;

- must generally be employed by the same employer or an associated employer (two companies where one is controlled by the other, or two companies controlled by the same third person or company);

- must generally be employed at the same establishment (or must be employed at another establishment owned by the same or an associated employer, with common terms and conditions applied at the two establishments); *and*

- must be doing work which is like (the same or broadly similar), or rated as equivalent, or of equal value.   *s.6*

In some cases it may be possible to compare with a person employed by another employer in the same type of service and subject to the same standard terms and conditions, such as one education authority employee comparing with an employee from another education authority.

South Ayrshire Council v Morton [2001] IRLR 28

Unequal pay and conditions between a man and a woman doing comparable work are lawful only if the employer can show that the difference is due to a material factor other than sex. Lawful justifications for unequal treatment include:

- the different conditions (but not pay) relate to pregnancy or childbirth;

- the different entitlements relate to death benefits or retirement (but cannot relate to age of retirement); *or*

- the different conditions (but not pay) are legally required.   *s.6*

25.5 DISABILITY AND LONG-TERM SICKNESS

The employment provisions of the **Disability Discrimination Act 1995** prohibit **direct discrimination** on the basis of disability unless such discrimination is justified, prohibit victimisation [see **25.2.3.1**], and require employers to make **reasonable adjustments** to enable a disabled person to apply for a job, take up a job or continue working [see **25.5.4**].

Much of the detail is included in regulations, which have the force of law, and in a code of practice and guidance, which do not have the force of law but are taken into account in discrimination claims. The code and guidance are available from the Disability Rights Commission [see end of chapter].

The employment provisions of the Act apply only to employers with 15 or more employees or others working under a contract. However, smaller employers are encouraged to follow good practice. At the time of writing (early 2001) the government had announced its intention to remove the 15-workers limit by October 2004.

In calculating the number of employees, people employed by an associated employer, for example a charity's trading company, are not counted. Volunteers are not included unless they are being paid or receiving something else of value in a way that means they are working under a contract [see **35.3**].

Like the race and sex legislation, the DDA has anti-discrimination provisions. But unlike the earlier legislation, it imposes a positive duty on employers to make reasonable adaptations to enable a disabled person to apply for a job and do the work if hired, and to enable a person to be able to continue working if he or she becomes disabled. Failure to make reasonable adaptations is as serious as unjustifiably dismissing or refusing to hire a person because of their disability.

Under company law, an employer which is registered as a company and has more than 250 employees must include specified information about employees with disabilities in its annual report [see **50.3.3**].

25.5.1
Definition of disability

Disability is defined as a physical (including sensory) or mental impairment which has a substantial and long-term adverse effect on a person's ability to carry out at least one normal day-to-day activity: mobility; manual dexterity; continence; ability to lift, carry or move everyday objects; speech, hearing or eyesight; memory; ability to concentrate, learn or understand; or perception of the risk of physical dangers.

An effect is long-term if:

- it has lasted for at least one year;
- it is likely to last for at least one year; *and/or*
- it is likely to last for the rest of the person's life.

The definitions of disability and substantial adverse effect have been elaborated in regulations and many tribunal cases. The cases, in particular, set a fairly high threshold for disability. *Disability Discrimination (Meaning of Disability) Regulations 1996 [SI 1996/1455]*

If an impairment ceases to have a substantial adverse effect, it is treated as continuing to have the effect if the effect is likely to recur.
Disability Discrimination Act 1995 s.1; sch.1 para.2

Mental impairment can arise only from a clinically recognised mental condition, including learning disability. *sch.1 paras.1(1)*

An impairment which would have a substantial effect but does not because it is being treated or corrected (for example medically controlled epilepsy, or limb loss corrected with a prosthesis) is classed as a disability. This does not apply to sight impairments corrected with spectacles or contact lenses. *sch.1 para 6*

A progressive condition such as cancer, multiple sclerosis or HIV infection whose effects are likely to become substantial was, at the time of writing, classed as a disability as soon as there is any adverse effect on normal day-to-day activities. In early 2001 the government announced that such conditions would be defined as a disability as soon as they are diagnosed. *sch.1 para.8*

A serious disfigurement, such as a birthmark or burns injury, is classed as a disability even if it does not have a serious adverse effect on normal day-to-day activities. *sch.1 para.3*

25.5.1.1
Good practice in relation to long-term illness

It is good practice to have procedures:

- to ensure the organisation asks enough to ascertain whether job applicants or employees may have a disability and may need the employer to make adaptations to enable the person to apply for the job, do the work or carry on working [see below];

- to ensure that if information about an individual's health is made available to the organisation, it is known only to those people who have a need to know, and that no one is told without the individual being informed that this will happen [see **38.1.2**];

- to ensure procedures are in place and known to all staff, and equipment is available, for dealing with potential health risks posed by persons who are or may be ill;

- to offer suitable alternative work, if available, to employees who are unable to carry on with their usual work [see **25.5.4**].

Employers have a duty to be aware that workers who have frequent or long-term sickness absences may be, or become, legally classed as disabled and therefore have rights under the DDA. Employers are expected to take reasonable steps to determine the nature of the illness, and if appropriate to consider adaptations.

If an employee is genuinely incapable of carrying out the required work because of illness it may be possible to dismiss him or her, but legal advice should be taken before doing this [see **30.8.3**].

An employee cannot be required to have an HIV test or other medical examination unless this is specified in the contract of employment [see **26.3.2**]. Dismissal for refusing to have a test or medical examination could constitute constructive dismissal [see **30.4.8**].

25.5.2
Direct discrimination

The provisions relating to unlawful disability discrimination in employment are similar to those for race and sex [see **25.2**], and apply to employees, apprentices, agency workers, and self-employed and other workers with a contract to do the work personally. It is unlawful to treat a person who has, or has had, a disability less favourably than a person without that disability in relation to recruitment, appointment, dismissal, or terms and conditions of employment. This includes promotion, training and other employment-related benefits.

Disability Discrimination Act 1995 s.4

Case law has made clear that unlawful direct discrimination can take place even if the employer and employee are unaware at the time of the discriminatory act that the person has a disability. Where there are grounds for suspecting a disability—such as persistent absences—the employer has a duty to investigate the reasons for the absence and act accordingly. *H J Heinz v Kenrick [2000] IRLR 144*

It is unlawful discrimination to victimise any person who has brought, or is threatening to bring, proceedings under the Act, or who has given or may give evidence or information in relation to such proceedings. This is the one part of the Act which applies to people who are not disabled, so it is as unlawful to victimise a non-disabled person as one who is disabled. *DDA ss.55, 4(5)*

If an employer advertises in a way which suggests an intention to discriminate against people with disabilities or with a particular type of disability, an employment tribunal will assume unlawful discrimination if a person with a disability, or with the particular disability, is rejected for the job. It is the employer's obligation to show that disability was not the reason for the rejection. *s.11*

25.5.3
Exceptions

Discrimination on the basis of disability is poor practice, but at the time of writing was not unlawful if the employer has fewer than 15 employees or others working under a contract. (The 15-worker limit is expected to be removed by October 2004.) Even where the employer has 15 or more workers, discrimination on the basis of disability is not unlawful if the employer can show that it is justified. *s.5(1)(b)*

The legislation prohibits unjustifiable discrimination on the basis of disability, but does not say anything about discrimination against able-bodied people. So it is not unlawful for an employer to give preference to a disabled person, or to disabled people in general, in recruitment and selection or in other aspects of employment. However the organisation's funders or its own equal opportunities policy may require posts to be openly advertised and appointment to be made solely on the basis of merit, and this would prevent this type of positive discrimination.

It is discriminatory to favour people with a specific type or types of disability, for example to give preference to people with a visual impairment, because this then disadvantages people with other disabilities.

It is not unlawful for a charitable organisation whose objects are to help people with a specific type or types of disability to offer supported employment to that group, even though this has the effect of discriminating against people with other types of disability. This provision applies only to supported employment.

Disability Discrimination Act 1995 s.10(2)

25.5.4
Reasonable adjustments and redeployment

Employers with 15 or more employees or others working under a contract have a duty to take reasonable steps to adapt premises or equipment, make adjustments to the work or provide special assistance to enable a person with a disability:

* to be appointed (if the employer knows that a disabled person is or may be an applicant for a job);
* to take advantage of promotion, training or other benefits;
* to remain employed. *s.6*

At the time of writing (early 2001) the government had announced that the 15-worker limit would be removed by October 2004.

Employers do not have this duty if they 'do not know or could not reasonably be expected to know that the employee has a disability and would be affected by an arrangement or physical feature of the workplace'. However the code of practice on disability discrimination and case law make clear that employers should do all they can to find out whether a person has a disability. *s.6(6)*

In determining what is reasonable, factors taken into account are cost, disruption, the employer's resources, availability of financial assistance for the employer, and how effective the steps would be. *s.6(4)*

Adjustments include offering suitable alternative work if a person becomes disabled while employed. Giving priority for such work to other employees, even those threatened with redundancy [see **31.5**], could be discriminatory.

25.5.5
Employment Service schemes

The Employment Service runs schemes to encourage employers to hire people with disabilities and to help people with disabilities develop their job skills. These include the access to work scheme, which provides practical help to disabled workers, and the supported employment programme, which provides subsidies to employers. Information is available from the disability service team at the local job centre.

25.6
REDRESS

25.6.1
Race, sex and disability discrimination

Employers should have clear procedures for employees to raise concerns about discrimination. This may be done through the normal grievance procedure [see **29.7**], but given the sensitive nature of the issues it may be sensible to create a more private initial procedure.

The Advisory, Conciliation and Arbitration Service has a conciliation procedure for individual cases. Either the employee or employer may call in ACAS at any time [see **33.2.2** for conciliation procedures].

If the case is unresolved or the individual who is complaining of discrimination does not want to go to ACAS, the Commission for Racial Equality, Equal Opportunities Commission and Disability Rights Commission have powers to investigate complaints, issue non-discrimination notices, and institute legal proceedings.

Alternatively, an individual may take the case to an employment tribunal [see **chapter 33**]. A complaint must generally be made within three months of the date of the act being complained about. Although the tribunal can hear a complaint made later than this if it considers it just and equitable to do so, it may be advisable for a worker to bring a claim within the three months even if the employer's grievance and appeal procedures have not been exhausted.

Sex Discrimination Act 1975 s.63; Race Relations Act 1976 s.68(1),(6); Disability Discrimination Act 1995 sch.3

The tribunal procedure usually starts with a questions procedure which enables the complainant to obtain information from the employer. If the employer does not reply or gives evasive answers, this could be seen as evidence that the employer has discriminated unlawfully.

If unlawful discrimination is proved, the tribunal may award compensatory sums, including compensation for injury to feelings. There is no ceiling to the awards in discrimination cases, and in some cases the amounts awarded are very high. The tribunal may also make an order declaring the rights of the parties and make a recommendation of action to be taken to reduce the adverse effects of the discrimination.

25.6.2
Equal pay and conditions

Equal pay complaints also go to employment tribunals, although the procedure is different from the procedure for other ET cases, and cases are often very lengthy. Under the Equal Pay Act a complaint may be made at any time while the person is still doing the job to which the claim applies, or within six months of when she or he was last employed in that job. *Equal Pay Act 1970 s.2(4)*

The tribunal may award arrears of pay and damages for non-cash benefits for up to two years before the date on which application was made to the tribunal. At the time of writing (early 2001) the government had announced plans to extend the two year period.

Levez v T H Jenning (Harlow Pools) Ltd [1999] IRLR 36 ECJ

25.7
SEXUAL ORIENTATION

The **Sex Discrimination Act 1975** does not explicitly cover discrimination on the grounds of being gay or lesbian, and a series of cases in the late 1990s confirmed that sexual orientation was not covered by the SDA. In 2000 an employment appeal tribunal stated that the legislation was ambiguous and the word 'sex' could be interpreted to include sexual orientation, but this decision was overturned in June 2001.

The UK must implement, by 2 December 2003, legislation prohibiting discrimination in employment on the basis of sexual orientation. The legislation may include provision allowing discrimination where sexual orientation is 'a genuine and determining occupational requirement'.

EU Equal Treatment Framework Directive [2000/78/EC] art.4(1)

Advice on good practice is available from LAGER [see end of chapter].

25.8
RELIGION

At the time of writing (early 2001) discrimination on the basis of religion is unlawful in Northern Ireland, but in England, Wales and Scotland there is no legislation which specifically covers religion. Sikhs and Jews have been defined as coming within the definition of 'ethnic group' under the **Race Relations Act 1976** [see **25.2.1**], so discrimination against them on the basis of their religion/ethnic group is unlawful. Catholics, Muslims and Rastafarians have been held not to constitute ethnic groups.

Before specifying that an employee must be of a particular religious group it is important to consider whether the requirement has the indirect effect of discriminating against particular racial or ethnic groups, because they are disproportionately less likely to be of that religion [see **25.2.4** for explanation of indirect discrimination]. A requirement to be

Christian, for example, could constitute indirect racial discrimination against Asians. Such a requirement is unlawful unless the employer can show that it is a genuine occupational requirement [see **25.3.1**] for the post. If in doubt, advice should be sought from an experienced solicitor and/or the Commission for Racial Equality.

The UK must implement, by 2 December 2003, legislation outlawing discrimination in employment on the basis of religion or other belief. UK legislation is likely to allow churches, religious associations or communities, and philosophical organisations to require employees to respect the tenets of the organisation's religion or beliefs. The legislation may include further provision allowing such employers to specify that an employee must be of that religion or belief where it is a genuine, legitimate and justified requirement for the job.

EU Equal Treatment Framework Directive [2000/78/EC] art.4(2)

25.9
AGE

At the time of writing (early 2001) discrimination on the basis of age is not in itself generally unlawful, but in some cases may be unlawful as a form of sex discrimination.

The government issued in 1999 a voluntary code of practice on age discrimination. While this is not legally binding, a tribunal could consider it in the context of other employment claims, for example unfair dismissal where age was a factor.

The UK must implement, by 2 December 2006, legislation outlawing discrimination in employment on the basis of age. Such legislation may include provision for discrimination where age is a genuine and determining occupational requirement, or if it is objectively and reasonably justified, for example in relation to labour market or vocational training objectives. In particular, the legislation may say that a compulsory retirement age is not unlawful discrimination.

EU Equal Treatment Framework Directive [2000/78/EC] art 4(1), 6

25.9.1
Age limits

Setting an unjustified age limit for a job could constitute indirect sex discrimination if more women than men cannot apply because, for example, they are looking after children at that age [see **25.2.4**].

If an age limit is given for a job or type of work or for retirement, it must be the same for men and women. Setting different age limits is direct sex discrimination.

In one case, the employment tribunal found that the age limit of 65 on the rights to claim unfair dismissal and redundancy pay [see **30.10.3** and **31.6.1**] constitutes indirect sex discrimination, because more men than women work past age 65. Tribunal decisions do not set a precedent, and the claimant died before his employer's appeal could be heard in the employment appeal tribunal. At the time of writing (early 2001) the status of the 65 cut-off remained unclear. Organisations should take advice if dismissing an employee aged 65 or over for an unfair reason or through an unfair procedure, or making a person aged 65 or over redundant. *Nash v Mash/Roe Group Ltd [1998] 589 IRLB 13*

25.9.2
Young workers

Children cannot be employed before their 13th birthday. From 13 to school leaving age, limits on working hours [see **28.5.1**] and types of work [see **36.4.2**] are enforced by the local authority education department, and workers under 18 have specific protection under the working time regulations [see **28.5**] and health and safety law [see **36.4.2**].

These rules apply to paid work (including work for their family), but do not apply to unpaid voluntary work. However, good practice would generally be to stick to the limits even when the young person is volunteering.

Before a person under school-leaving age can be employed, the local education authority must grant a permit to the employer.

Employer's liability insurance [see **20.4.1**] should be checked to ensure it covers young employees and volunteers.

A person under 18 is bound by a contract of employment only if it is on the whole for her or his benefit [see **18.6.2**].

25.10
PEOPLE WITH
CRIMINAL RECORDS

The **Rehabilitation of Offenders Act 1974**:

* in most situations, gives ex-offenders the right not to reveal convictions when these have become 'spent' after a rehabilitation period without a further offence;   *s.4(1),(2)*

* for most jobs, makes it unlawful for an employer to dismiss an employee or refuse to employ a person because he or she has a spent conviction;   *s.4(3)*

* defines some jobs and occupations which are excepted from the Act and where, if asked, the person must declare the conviction even if it is spent, and where the employer can refuse to employ the person or can dismiss him or her because of the conviction.

The Act applies not only to convictions in the UK, but also to convictions abroad if the offence would be an offence in the UK.

Where convictions must be disclosed, this applies only if the person is asked. There is no obligation to reveal any information if not asked, either directly or by being asked to provide or give consent for the employer to obtain a criminal record check [see **26.3.3**].

Where convictions are disclosed or the employer becomes aware of them they are likely to have to be disclosed to the organisation's insurers [see **20.3.4**]. Failure to do so could invalidate some policies.

At the time of writing (early 2001) the Rehabilitation of Offenders Act was being reviewed. Advice about the regulations and good practice in employing people with criminal records is available from the Home Office, Apex Trust and NACRO [see end of chapter].

25.10.1
Rehabilitation
periods

The heavier the sentence, the longer it takes for a conviction to be spent. Starting from the date of conviction, rehabilitation periods are:

* 10 years if the sentence is imprisonment or detention in a young offender institution for six to 30 months;

* seven years if such a sentence is for six months or less;

* five years if the sentence is a probation, order, fine or other sentence, such as a compensation or community service order for which a rehabilitation period is not specified in the Act;

* one year if the sentence is a conditional discharge, bind-over, care order or supervision order (or until the order expires, if it is for more than one year);

* six months if the sentence is an absolute discharge.   *s.5*

The rehabilitation periods are halved if the offender was under 18 when convicted. A sentence of more than 30 months imprisonment or detention in a young offender institution can never become spent.

25.10.2
Exceptions

There are a number of exceptions to a person's right not to reveal a spent conviction. These include:

* anyone employed by a local authority or any other body for social services involving access in the course of normal duties to people over 65, people with mental disorders, people with serious disabilities or who are chronically ill, people who are blind or deaf, people who are drunk, or people who are addicted to alcohol or drugs;

* all workers, whether paid or voluntary, who have substantial access to people under 18 in the course of their duties, including the provision of accommodation, care, leisure and recreational facilities, schooling, training, supervision, or social services;

- posts involving access to persons receiving health services;
- all workers in any establishment which has to be registered under the **Registered Homes Act 1984** or, from 2001 and 2002, the **Care Standards Act 2000** [see **6.5.3**];
- teachers;
- barristers, solicitors, and chartered or certified accountants;
- medical practitioners and others in medical professions.

Rehabilitation of Offenders Act 1974 (Exceptions) Order 1975 [SI 1975/1023]
and (Exceptions) (Amendment) Order 2001 [SI 2001/1192]

Applicants for, or employees or volunteers already in, posts covered by the exceptions must if asked reveal all convictions, even those which are spent. The application form for jobs covered by the exceptions should ask whether the applicant has any convictions, and should include the statement, 'This post is exempt under the Rehabilitation of Offenders Act 1974 and you are required to reveal all convictions, even those which are spent.'

Unless the person is banned or disqualified from working with children or vulnerable adults [see **26.3.4**] it is not unlawful to take on a person with a conviction for an exempt job, but it would be up to the employer to take reasonable steps to supervise the person's work.

An employer could be found to be negligent if the worker is involved in an offence at work and the employer had not asked about convictions or done a criminal records check [see **26.3.3**], or knew about a relevant conviction but not taken reasonable steps to supervise the worker.

25.10.3
Other jobs

For some jobs, such as those involving unsupervised access to money or expensive equipment or going into people's homes, it may be appropriate to ask whether the applicant has any convictions, or any relevant convictions. The question should be followed by a statement that 'you are not required to reveal any convictions which are spent under the Rehabilitation of Offenders Act 1974'. The organisation may want to indicate that a conviction does not necessarily disbar an applicant from consideration for the post.

As with exempt posts, an employer could be considered negligent if the job involves risk to people or property, and information about relevant unspent convictions was not sought from the employee and/or through a criminal records check, or was not taken into account when offering paid or unpaid work.

25.10.4
Undisclosed convictions

Unless the applicant has been banned or disqualified from working with children or vulnerable adults or is specifically asked about convictions, he or she is under no obligation to disclose them. If an employer subsequently finds out about an unspent conviction (or a spent conviction, for an exempt post) disciplinary action or dismissal may—or may not—be justified. Legal advice should be sought before dismissing an employee, to ensure the dismissal is not unfair.

If the employee was asked during the application process about convictions but failed to disclose an unspent conviction (or a spent conviction, for an exempt post), this could constitute breach of contract. The employer could be justified in dismissing the employee, but there is no obligation on the employer to do so unless the work involves access to children or vulnerable adults and the person has been banned or disqualified from working with them. In other situations, if the employee has built up a good employment record with the employer, dismissal may not be necessary. The same basic principles apply to volunteers, except that volunteers are generally not working under a contract [see **35.3**] so breach of contract is not an issue.

Unless the post is exempt, information about spent convictions is irrelevant and should not be taken into account.

**25.10.5
Criminal record
checks**

Some employers must, and other employers may, obtain information about criminal records through the **Criminal Records Bureau** [see **26.3.3**]. All employers may require job applicants, employees or volunteers to obtain a criminal record check covering spent convictions. Where work is exempt under the Rehabilitation of Offenders Act [see **25.10.2**], employers registered with the CRB have access to details of unspent convictions, banning or disqualification from working with children or vulnerable adults, and other information.

**25.11
TRADE UNION
MEMBERSHIP
AND ACTIVITIES**

It is unlawful to refuse employment, dismiss, or subject an employee to a detriment because the person is or is not a member of a trade union, or has taken part in trade union activities. The detriment is unlawful regardless of whether it is because of an action taken by the employer, or failure by the employer to take an action. So-called 'blacklists', under which employers keep records of people who have taken part in trade union activities with a view to discriminating against them, are also unlawful.   *Trade Union and Labour Relations (Consolidation) Act 1992*
ss.137, 146; Employment Relations Act 1999 s.3, sch.2

Advertisements are unlawful if they indicate or imply that employment is only available to union members or non-members, or that any membership-related requirement will apply. Procedures where trade unions recommend people for employment are unlawful if they have the effect of discriminating against people who are not union members.
TULR(C)A s.137(3),(4)

Employment outside Great Britain is not covered.

**25.12
PART-TIME
WORKERS**

Part-time workers are entitled to the same statutory rights as full-time workers. They are also entitled to the same contractual rights *pro rata*, provided that:

• there is a **comparator**: a full-time worker doing the same or broadly similar work for the same employer on the same type of contract (permanent, temporary or fixed term); *and*

• there is no objective reason for the employer to treat the part-timer less favourably than the comparable full-timer.
Part-time Workers (Prevention of Less Favourable Treatment)
Regulations 2000 [SI 2000/1551]

Part-time rights apply not only to employees, but to virtually anyone who is working under a contract [see **22.1**]. This includes casuals and people who work on a freelance basis but are not genuinely self-employed. People who are genuinely self-employed (see **34.1.3**) are not protected by part-time workers' rights.

Full-time workers are defined as those who are paid wholly or in part by reference to the time they work, and are considered by the employer to work full-time. **Part-time workers** are defined as those who are paid wholly or in part by reference to the time they work, and are not identified by the employer as a full-time worker.   *reg.2*

In identifying a comparator, employees of associated employers (for example, a charity's trading company) or other employers cannot be considered.

There is no need to identify a comparator where a full-time worker:

• continues to work but for fewer hours, even if the new or varied contract is of a different type or for a different type of work; *or*

• after an absence of less than 12 months, returns to the same job or a job at the same level but at a lower number of hours, even if the new or varied contract is of a different type.   *regs.3, 4*

Where full-time workers who work overtime receive an enhanced rate of pay, part-timers do not become eligible for this higher rate until they have worked at least as many hours as the comparable full-timer.

A part-time worker may ask the employer, in writing, for an explanation for being treated less favourably, and the employer must provide this in writing within 21 days of the request.

Part-time Workers Regulations 2000 reg.6

Dismissal is automatically unfair if it is for a reason connected with asking or requiring the employer to comply with the regulations, alleging that the employer has infringed the regulations, asking for a written statement of reasons for less favourable treatment, or bringing a claim against the employer.

To ensure they do not discriminate against part-time workers, employers should ensure that part-timers:

- receive the same rate of pay as comparable full-timers;
- receive the same hourly rate of overtime pay as comparable full-timers, at least once they have worked more than the normal full-time hours;
- are not treated less favourably than comparable full-timers in terms of calculating the rate of sick pay or maternity pay, the length of service required to qualify for payment, and the length of time the payment is received;
- have the same access to pension schemes as comparable full-timers, unless different treatment is justified on objective grounds;
- are not excluded from training simply because they work part-time;
- are entitled to the same contractual holiday pay as comparable full-timers, on a *pro rata* basis;
- are entitled to the same contractual maternity and parental leave as comparable full-timers;
- are entitled to career breaks and other leave in the same way as for comparable full-timers, unless their exclusion is objectively justified on grounds other than their part-time status;
- must not be treated less favourably than comparable full-timers in selection for redundancy.

Less favourable treatment can only be objectively justified if the employer can show it to be necessary and appropriate in order to achieve a legitimate objective.

FOR FURTHER INFORMATION

Disability. Disability Rights Commission: 08457-622 633; www.drc-gb.org

Employment Service: via local jobcentre; www.employmentservice.gov.uk

Equal opportunities in employment. Equality Direct helpline: 0845-600 3344; www.equalitydirect.org.uk

Equal opportunities claims. ACAS: 020-7396 5100 or check local telephone directory; www.acas.org.uk

Ex-offenders. Apex CharitableTrust: 020-7638 5931; www.apextrust,com

NACRO: 020-7582 6500; www.nacro.org.uk

Race equality. Commission for Racial Equality: 020-7828 7022; www.cre.gov.uk

School-age workers. Children's Legal Advice Centre: 01206-873820

Sex equality. Equal Opportunities Commission: 0161-838 8312; www.eoc.org.uk

Sexual orientation: LAGER (Lesbian and Gay Employment Rights): 020-7704 2205; www.lager.dircon.co.uk

Chapter 26
TAKING ON NEW EMPLOYEES

26.1
DEFINING THE EMPLOYER

Before hiring a new employee, it is essential to clarify who the employer is. If the organisation is incorporated as a company or an industrial and provident society [see **chapter 2**], or if it is a charitable trust or association which has incorporated its trustee body [see **1.4**], it is able to enter into contracts, including contracts of employment, in its own right. The employer is the company, IPS or trustee body itself.

If the organisation is an unincorporated association or a charitable trust which has not incorporated its trustee body, the members of the governing body (the trustees of a trust or the management committee of an association) are legally the employer—even though the organisation itself is generally named as the employer in the statement of employment particulars [see **23.5.3**] or written contract.

Affleck & others v Newcastle Mind [1999] IRLR 405 EAT

If an employee is employed by one body and then lent or seconded to another [see **22.5.3**], it must be made clear—ideally in a formal secondment agreement—who is legally the employer and who is responsible for managing the employee.

Sometimes an employee is shared between two associated organisations, perhaps a charity and trading subsidiary, or a charity and its linked campaigning organisation. A decision needs to be made as to whether:

- one organisation employs the worker and charges the other for a share of salary and other costs (in which case VAT may need to be charged on payments between the organisations; see **53.5.3**);
- the employee is the joint employee of both [see **22.4**]; *or*
- the employee is separately employed on a part-time basis by each organisation.

Regardless of how the person is employed, salary and other costs must be apportioned in a way that ensures that a charity's funds and other resources are not used for non-charitable work [see **47.6**].

If a person is to be hired on a self-employed basis, the organisation must be very careful to ensure that the person genuinely meets the criteria for self-employment [see **34.1.3**].

26.2 THE RECRUITMENT PROCESS

To prevent discrimination and comply with the legislation [see **chapter 25**], good recruitment procedures should ensure that an employer does not deny anyone a job for reasons which are not connected with their competence or ability to do the job as specified.

An employer should always be able to show, if challenged, that neither direct nor indirect discrimination [see **25.2.3** and **25.2.4** for definitions] took place during the recruitment of staff. To do this, the whole process should be organised consistently, with proper records kept at each step.

If the organisation already has staff, it must consider whether any employees are currently being made redundant, or if there is a likelihood of this. If those at risk of redundancy could be suitable for the new post, or could with training be suitable, they should be offered the new job on a permanent or trial basis [see **31.5**]. If more than one suitable person is being made redundant, they are all entitled to apply for the post before it is openly advertised.

26.2.1 Job description

There is no statutory obligation to draw up a **job description**. However it is difficult to recruit successfully if the employer is not clear about the work to be done, and it can be difficult to monitor work and deal with unsatisfactory performance where there has been no agreement about what was supposed to be done and to what standards.

Even for new posts where it is unclear what the work will eventually involve, a job description should be drawn up for the initial months, with an indication of when and how it will be reviewed and revised.

A job description should reflect the need for flexibility.

The statement of employment particulars [see **23.5**] which must be given to virtually all employees (or written contract containing the required particulars) must contain a clear job title or a brief job description. It is not advisable to include a detailed job description in the statement of particulars or contract. Doing so means that it becomes part of the contract of employment and could be difficult to change.

26.2.2 Person specification

A **person specification** is a list of the key criteria needed for the job. The criteria may be classed as essential or desirable. It should be clear whether applicants must meet each criterion now, or whether that skill, knowledge or qualification can be gained on the job.

All criteria should be justifiable in terms of the duties set out in the job description. Great care should be taken to ensure that no person specification requirement has the effect of discriminating unjustifiably against one sex or against particular racial, ethnic or nationality groups—even if any such discrimination is unintentional. Unless such a requirement is justifiable in terms of the job, it could constitute unlawful indirect discrimination [see **25.2.4**]. Criteria which exclude persons with a particular disability or disabilities should be used only if they are objectively justified. By 2 December 2003 it will be unlawful to discriminate on the basis of religious or political belief or sexual orientation, and by 2 December 2006 it will be unlawful to discriminate on the basis of age [see **25.1.1**].

There is no statutory requirement for a person specification. But if there is no record of the key criteria and how individual candidates matched these, it could be difficult to demonstrate that shortlisting and selection were conducted in a non-discriminatory way.

26.2.3
Advertising

There is no statutory obligation to advertise jobs, but recruiting only through informal networks is particularly likely to give rise to discriminatory practices. It has, for example, been found to be discriminatory to publicise vacancies only through word of mouth.

Unless the advertisement clearly specifies otherwise, terms such as 'foreman' or 'Girl Friday' which imply that the job is open only to one sex are considered to be discriminatory [see **25.2.3**].

To avoid allegations of indirect discrimination, advertisements should be placed in publications which are read by all sectors of the community, and notices of vacancies should be circulated, if appropriate, to community organisations and job centres. Provided vacancies are widely advertised in this way, they can also be advertised in specialist publications such as the minority ethnic press.

26.2.3.1
GOQ jobs

If it is a genuine occupational qualification to be of a particular racial group or sex [see **25.3.1**] this must be specified in the advertisement and notices of the vacancy, with a statement that the post is exempt and the section of the Race Relations Act 1976 or Sex Discrimination Act 1975 which applies. Similar rules are likely to apply when discrimination on the basis of religious or political belief, sexual orientation and age become unlawful [see **25.1**].

It is lawful to place advertisements for GOQ posts only in publications targeted specifically at the group(s) for whom the post is intended. Advertisements for an Asian women's refuge worker, for example, could be placed only in publications likely to be read by Asian women.

26.2.3.2
Giving preference to people with disabilities

It is not unlawful to give preference to disabled applicants, for example to say that all disabled applicants who meet the person specification will be shortlisted, provided that all disabilities are treated equally. It is also not unlawful to say that only disabled applicants will be considered for a post [see **25.5.3**]. If the organisation is going to do this it should be stated in the advertisement and person specification.

26.2.4
Responding to enquiries

It is important to have guidelines for dealing with enquiries, to ensure that unlawful discrimination does not occur at this stage. There is no statutory obligation to provide an application form, but if there is one it should ask only for information relevant to the post.

26.2.5
Monitoring

There is no statutory obligation to monitor racial group, sex, disability or other information relating to job applicants, but such monitoring helps employers assess whether they have been effective in attracting applications from a broad cross-section of the community, and whether reasonable numbers from various groups were shortlisted. Information from the form about racial group, sex, married status or disability must not be used in shortlisting or selection decisions.

Because there is no statutory obligation to undertake monitoring, applicants cannot be required to fill in monitoring data and should not be rejected on the basis that they did not fill it in.

Much of the information on monitoring forms is classed as **sensitive data** under the **Data Protection Act 1998** [see **38.3.4**], and should be kept in an anonymised form which cannot be linked to any individual. If the information is used in relation to individuals or can be linked to identifiable individuals, it must comply with data protection requirements.

26.2.6 Adaptations for people with disabilities

Employers with 15 or more employees or others working under a contract [see **25.5.4**] must make reasonable adaptations to the recruitment or selection process, in order to remove or reduce any substantial disadvantage faced by a disabled person who has applied or wishes to apply. At the time of writing (early 2001) the government had announced that the 15-worker limit would be removed by October 2004. There is no duty to make such adaptations if the employer did not know or could not reasonably have known that the person had a disability, but the employer does have a duty to take reasonable steps to find out. The easiest way to do this is usually to ask on the application form whether the applicant has a disability, and would need any adjustments to enable them to apply, take part in the selection process, or do the job as advertised. *Disability Discrimination Act 1995 s.6*

26.2.7 Shortlisting and interview

An employer should be able to show that shortlisting, interviews and any tests were based on relevant criteria which did not discriminate unjustifiably on the basis of racial group, sex or disability. There is no statutory requirement to record the criteria used for shortlisting and interview and how candidates were assessed, but it is sensible to do so. The person specification provides a useful checklist for this purpose.

Interviewers must not create an impression of discrimination by asking inappropriate questions, for example asking whether candidates have children and what provision they would make for their care during school holidays. Such a question could be held to be discriminatory if it is irrelevant to the job or is asked only of women.

There is no statutory obligation to ask all candidates the same questions, or to ask them all in the same way. The intention should be to elicit comparable information, so candidates can be fairly compared.

26.2.8 Tests

Tests and exercises can be effective in assessing candidates' knowledge and skills, but great care should be taken to ensure they actually assess what they are supposed to, and to ensure the people evaluating them have clear criteria and know how to do it. If a person with a disability has applied, consideration should be given to adaptations to assist her or him to take the test, and to ensure the criteria for 'passing' the test do not unjustifiably put the disabled person at a disadvantage.

Tests must not involve unjustifiable questions or tasks which have the effect of discriminating on the basis of sex, racial group or disability. Questions which assume knowledge of British history, for example, discriminate against people from abroad—but such questions are permissible if the job requires knowledge of British history.

26.2.9 Workers from abroad

26.2.9.1 Work permits

A worker from abroad does not require a work permit if he or she:

- is a citizen of a European Economic Area state (European Union member states plus Iceland, Liechtenstein and Norway);
- is a Commonwealth citizen with at least one grandparent born in the UK;
- is a Commonwealth citizen aged 17-27 in the UK for a working holiday of up to two years (but see **26.2.9.3** for restrictions);
- is a student working part-time [see **26.2.9.4**];
- has been given the right to settlement in the UK;
- has been granted refugee status or exceptional leave to remain, or is an asylum seeker with permission to work;
- is a journalist, minister of religion or other person whose work requires entry clearance, but not a permit;
- is in the UK to obtain professional qualifications or specialist expertise under the Training and Work Experience Scheme.

Before hiring any other person from abroad, the employer must apply to Work Permits (UK) (formerly the Overseas Labour Service) for a work permit [see end of chapter for details]. The necessary forms are available from job centres. The employer usually has to show that it advertised the job for at least four weeks in a national newspaper or trade publication and no suitable UK or EEA citizen was available, and that the person has qualifications or skills not held by EEA applicants.

A permit is specific to the individual and the job, and is for a maximum of five years. It can be renewed on application to the Home Office and Work Permits (UK).

26.2.9.2
Asylum and Immigration Act 1996

An employer who hires a person who is not entitled to work in the UK is liable for a fine of up to £5,000. It is a defence for the employer to show that it has seen the original and kept a copy of a **specified document**:

- the worker's national insurance number (NINO) card, or the NI number on a P45 or P60 from the previous employer or on a document from the Inland Revenue, Benefits Agency, Contributions Office or Employment Service;

- an original (not photocopy) of a passport, birth certificate or certificate of naturalisation from an EU member state or Iceland, Liechtenstein or Norway;

- an original of a passport, other travel document or letter from the Home Office showing that the person has the right to work in the UK or that there are no restrictions on his or her right to work here.

Asylum and Immigration Act 1996 s.8

Information about acceptable documentation is available from the Immigration and Nationality Department (IND) helpline [see end of chapter]. It is acceptable to ask on an application form or at interview whether the applicant has the right to work in the UK, and to ask for the relevant documentation at any stage in the selection process. To avoid an allegation of racial discrimination, the employer should ask all potential employees, not only those known or assumed to be foreign, for documentation [see **25.2.7**]. Procedures should comply with the code of practice available from the IND, which came into effect on 2 May 2001.

The employer should be satisfied that the document appears to be one of the specified documents, appears to be an original, and appears to relate to the person in question. The employer does not need to investigate the validity or authenticity of the document. The IND helpline can give advice about the acceptability of documents.

Unless the document is a P45 part 2, the employer should photocopy it and immediately return the original to the individual. The copy should be kept for at least six months after the person ceases to be employed by the employer. A P45 part 2 must be kept for at least three years.

26.2.9.3
Working holidaymakers

Working holidaymakers are Commonwealth citizens aged 17-27, who can come to the UK for up to two years and can take employment incidental to their holiday. The fact that a potential employee is a working holidaymaker will be shown in his or her passport.

It is the employer's responsibility to ensure the work is incidental to the holiday. This means the work should be for less than 25 hours per week, or if for more than this should not last for more than half the person's stay in the UK. Working holidaymakers should not engage in business, work as a professional sportsperson or entertainer, or pursue a career.

26.2.9.4
Foreign students

Students from outside the European Economic Area can work unlimited hours during vacations, and a maximum of 20 hours per week during term. They must fill in form OSS1, available from the job centre. A student can be hired for a full-time job only by leaving the UK and having the employer apply for a work permit in the usual way.

26.2.10
Selection

Written records of the reasons for selection decisions do not have to be kept, but without such records it would be difficult for an employer to show that it had not discriminated unlawfully in reaching its decision.

Candidates do not have to be told why they were not selected. If such information is provided great care should be taken, because if a candidate subsequently makes a complaint of discrimination anything said about the reason for non-selection could be significant.

A complaint of discrimination must generally be made within three months of the date of the act being complained about, but an employment tribunal can hear a complaint made later than this if it considers it just and equitable to do so. An employer should keep shortlist and interview records and all other documentation relating to the recruitment process for at least six months, and preferably for one year.

Sex Discrimination Act 1975 s.63; Race Relations
Act 1976 s.68(1),(6); Disability Discrimination Act 1995 sch.3 para.3

26.2.11
Offer of
employment

An offer of employment and its acceptance may be verbal or in writing. Putting it in writing reduces the risk of misunderstanding.

If the offer is conditional upon satisfactory references, a criminal record check, a medical test [see **26.3**], provision of documentation showing the right to work in the UK, the granting of a work permit or any other condition, this must be clear and explicit. If this is not made clear and the offer of employment is subsequently withdrawn, this could constitute breach of contract and the employer could become liable for damages for wrongful dismissal (see below).

An offer subject to satisfactory completion of a probationary period generally creates a contract from day one [see **30.5.2**], but the contract will be subject to any special conditions, such as shorter notice, specified as applying during the probationary period.

Unless the offer of employment sets out all the key conditions of employment, there is a risk that an issue will be omitted by the employer and will later be contested by an employee. It is therefore advisable to send with the offer a written contract or statement of employment particulars [see **23.5**], even though this does not generally have to be provided until two months after the person starts work.

26.2.11.1
Pre-employment
dismissal

If an unconditional offer of employment is made and accepted and is subsequently withdrawn, the individual will be able to bring a claim for wrongful dismissal [see **30.7**]—even if he or she has not yet started work. The person may also be able to claim unfair dismissal if the reason is for a reason connected with pregnancy or childbirth or another automatically unfair reason [see **30.9.1**].

Sarker v South Tees Acute Hospitals NHS Trust [1997] IRLR 328

26.2.12
Misrepresentation

Misrepresentations made prior to the creation of the contract by either party may give rise to a right to claim damages. If a misrepresentation is sufficiently serious and has been incorporated into the terms of the contract, the wronged party might be entitled to terminate the contract without notice [see **30.4.7** and **30.4.8**].

The employer should guard against the possibility of misrepresenting its position by putting all its relevant information in writing. It should also reduce the risk of a potential employee's misrepresentation by, for example, requiring documentary proof from candidates of key qualifications and making enquiries of previous employers.

26.3
PRE-EMPLOYMENT
CHECKS

While some employers are satisfied with information provided by candidates, most require additional information in the form of references, medical checks and/or criminal record checks.

26.3.1
References

26.3.1.1
Duty of former
employer to employee

There is normally no obligation on a former employer to provide a reference. But if one is provided, the employer giving it has a duty of care to the employee, and must:

- exercise reasonable skill and care, and ensure the reference is true and accurate (although it does not have to be comprehensive);
  Spring v Guardian Assurance plc and others [1994] 3 All ER 129, IRLR 460 HL

- be fair, and ensure it does not give a misleading impression; *and*
  Bartholomew v Hackney LBC [1999] IRLR 246 CA

- ensure it does not include complaints against a worker unless the worker is aware of them. *TSB Bank plc v Harris [2000] IRLR 157 EAT*

An employee who is not hired or suffers other loss because a reference does not meet the above criteria may claim damages from the employer.

Failure to provide a reference to an employee who has brought, or threatened to bring, a discrimination claim may constitute victimisation [see **25.1**].

26.3.1.2
Duty of former
employer to prospective
employer

The employer providing the reference also owes a duty of care to the prospective employer. If, as a result of an inaccurate or negligent reference, the new employer hires an unsuitable worker and suffers loss, the employer who provided the reference could be held liable. A disclaimer of liability in the reference will only operate if it is reasonable.
Unfair Contract Terms Act 1977 s.2(2)

26.3.1.3
Duties of new employer

If the offer of employment is conditional on satisfactory references, it is up to the employer to decide whether a reference is or is not acceptable.
Wishart v NACAB [1990] ICR 794, IRLR 393

Some employers ask for written references; others prefer the telephone. For practical and equal opportunities reasons it is practical to make a list of questions to ask and to keep a written record of points raised in telephone references, especially if the reference is unsatisfactory.

It is not sensible to accept, without further investigation, written references produced by a potential employee or a very anodyne reference provided by a former employer, since the provision of such references is frequently a term of settlement for a contested dismissal.

Employees or potential employees generally have the right to see references received about them (including notes of telephone conversations) if, as is likely, the references are kept in a manner which makes them personal data under the **Data Protection Act** [see **38.3.2**]. However they do not have the right to see a reference if:

- the new employer has made clear to the referee and employee that the reference will be kept confidential;

- the previous employer has given the reference in confidence;

- reasonable efforts have been made to seek consent but the referee has withheld it, and such withholding of consent is reasonable; *or*

- the reference contains information about another person who has not consented to it being disclosed, and the information cannot be removed or made anonymous.

26.3.2
Medical checks

An employer does not have to undertake a medical check on prospective employees unless it is required by specific regulations, such as the obligation to do a health check for night workers [see **36.3.1**]. However, guidance note MS20 *Pre-Employment Health Screening* from the Health and Safety Executive [see end of **chapter 36**] advises that medical screening should be carried out if the work involves health or safety hazards which make it desirable to screen people before they are hired or when they are transferred to a new employer.

A medical test cannot be carried out if the employee refuses it. An employer generally can dismiss or refuse to employ a person who refuses to have a medical check only if there is a statutory requirement for a medical test or if a medical test is explicitly a condition of employment.

Failure to hire a person for medical reasons could in some situations constitute unlawful disability discrimination [see **25.5.1**].

26.3.2.1
Medical records

An employer can ask for a report from an employee's doctor only if the employee gives consent. The employee has the right to see a copy of the doctor's report before it is sent to the employer, query items in the report, and have her or his objection appended to the report if the doctor does not change the report.   *Access to Medical Records Act 1988*

The organisation should have proper procedures for keeping medical and other personal information strictly confidential [see **38.1.2**].

26.3.3
Criminal record checks and other safeguards

Until recently most voluntary sector employers had neither an obligation nor a right to undertake checks to discover whether potential or current staff had previous convictions. But from autumn 2001 individuals—and in some cases employers—will have access to their criminal records through the **Criminal Records Bureau** (CRB), and some organisations which work with children and vulnerable adults will be obliged to carry out checks [see **26.3.4.7**]. Detailed information about checks is available from the CRB [see end of chapter].

Police Act 1997 pt.V

A check will cost £12, but the fee will be waived for standard and enhanced disclosures [see below] provided to volunteers.

It is an offence to offer certain types of work with children, paid or unpaid, to a person who has been disqualified or banned from working with children [see **26.3.4.8**], and from April 2002 there are similar rules for work with vulnerable adults [see **26.3.4.9**]. Provided they have not been disqualified or banned from such work, people with criminal convictions can be hired, even for work involving children or vulnerable adults. The employer should ensure appropriate supervision is in place [see **25.10.2**].

Where an organisation discovers, through a criminal record check or in any other way that an employee or volunteer has a criminal conviction, this is likely to have to be disclosed to the organisation's insurers [see **20.3.4**]. Failure to do so may invalidate some insurances.

26.3.3.1
CRB registration

For work with children or vulnerable adults, work in registered homes and in certain professions such as accountancy and medical professions, the employer can from May 2001 become a **registered person** with the CRB. The registration costs £300, plus £5 for each additional registered signatory. Small organisations may, if they wish, group together and seek registration through an umbrella organisation.

Because registered persons have access to particularly sensitive information, they must adhere to a CRB code of practice. This requires them to:

• have written policies on the recruitment of ex-offenders;

• store criminal record disclosures securely and dispose of them once used;

• consider carefully the relevance of any convictions in assessing a person's suitability, so that those with convictions are not unfairly excluded from employment or volunteering opportunities.

26.3.3.2
Enhanced disclosure

For work that regularly involves caring for, training, supervising or being in sole charge of those aged under 18 or vulnerable adults, an **enhanced disclosure** (previously referred to as **enhanced criminal record certificate**) is available from autumn 2001, on joint application by the registered person and the worker. This is the highest level of disclosure and lists spent and unspent convictions, non-conviction information such as cautions, reprimands and warnings, and other information considered relevant to the work to be carried out by the individual.

Where the work involves close contact with children or vulnerable adults, details from the Protection of Children Act (PoCA) list and List 99 [see **26.3.4.1**] and/or the Protection of Vulnerable Adults (PoVA) list [see **26.3.4.2**], and details of any disqualification from working with children or vulnerable adults [see **26.3.4.6**], are also included.

26.3.3.3
Standard disclosure

From autumn 2001 other registered employers can apply jointly with the individual for an intermediate-level **standard disclosure** (previously called **criminal record certificate**). This is available for work involving regular contact with under-18s or vulnerable adults, but where an enhanced certificate is not justified. It is also available for some other occupations, such as accountancy.

It lists spent and unspent convictions and cautions, but does not include other information from criminal records. Where appropriate, it includes details from the PoCA and PoVA lists and List 99, and disqualification from working with children or vulnerable adults [see **26.3.4.6**].

26.3.3.4
Criminal conviction
certificate

From mid-2002, any employer can ask or require any employee or volunteer to provide a **basic disclosure** (previously called **criminal conviction certificate**). This shows only unspent convictions [see **25.10**]. The person obtains the certificate, then provides it to the employer. This certificate is not job-specific, and may be used more than once.

26.3.3.5
Pre-CRB access
to police records

Prior to gaining direct access to criminal record checks, some organisations may have access to police checks via the Voluntary Organisations Consultancy Scheme, the statutory sector or local police. Organisations working with children can access the Protection of Children Act (PoCA) list and List 99 through the Department of Health.

26.3.3.6
Procedures for police
and criminal record
checks

If police or criminal record checks are to be carried out, the organisation should have good procedures to ensure the information is properly used.

Applicants should be told that their permission is required for a police check or that they will be required to apply for a criminal record check, and that refusal could mean that their application is not considered further or that they will be rejected for the work. A check should not be undertaken until all the other recruitment procedures have been carried out. If work is offered to the person, it should be clear that the offer is subject to satisfactory police or criminal record checks.

A previous conviction does not necessarily mean that the person is unsuitable. A recent sexual offence where the person was dealing with vulnerable people is one thing, but what about taking and driving away 15 years ago when the person was 19 years old? Home Office circulars emphasise that 'a person's suitability should be looked at as a whole in the light of all the information available'.

If an employer finds out about spent convictions these may be taken into account only if the job is exempt under the **Rehabilitation of Offenders Act 1974** [see **25.10**]. It is not unlawful to take unspent convictions into account for any work. Any discrepancy between what the applicant says and what the criminal record reveals should be discussed with the applicant.

26.3.3.7
Other procedures

A very large proportion of people involved in abuse or fraud never come to the attention of the police. So police or criminal record checks, even when available, should never be used as a substitute for proper procedures. It is more important to develop the best possible procedures for recruiting, selecting, inducting and supervising employees and volunteers, and to ensure there are clear and well known procedures for complaining if any worker is acting in unsuitable ways. These procedures should apply not only to those working with under-18s, but to anyone working with vulnerable adults, in sensitive situations with other adults, or with access to money or valuable property.

Good procedures will not provide a guarantee against being found negligent if harm ever does come to a child or vulnerable adult or if money or property is misappropriated, but the use of detailed procedures would be evidence of good practice and management.

The following guidelines are adapted from Home Office guidance.

- The organisation should have policy statements on safeguarding the welfare of clients, access to money and property, and other matters where abuse, fraud or breach of trust might occur.

- The work of the organisation should be planned in ways which minimise the risk of abuse, fraud or breach of trust.

- All clients/users should be clear about how to complain to an independent person if they are unhappy about a worker. If clients are unable, because of age or disability, to make their own complaints, additional safeguards may be needed. All allegations should be properly investigated, with immediate action taken if required.

- The agreed procedures for protecting people or property should be applied to all staff, whether paid or unpaid, and to agency workers and temporary or locum workers.

- Staff should understand what their work involves, and the limits.

- Applicants for all relevant posts—whether paid or unpaid, permanent or temporary, part-time or full-time—should be asked at application or interview stage about previous convictions [see **25.10**]. If the post if exempt under the **Rehabilitation of Offenders Act 1974** it should be made clear that all previous convictions, even those which are spent, must be disclosed.

- Where police or criminal record checks are undertaken, they should be seen as only one part of the appointment process. As the Home Office itself acknowledges, 'criminal records may not be complete and will not give a full picture of a person's fitness for the job'.

- At least one reference should be taken up from a person who has experience of the applicant's paid or unpaid work in a comparable situation. This is especially important for work with children and vulnerable adults, or involving access to money.

- All applicants for sensitive posts should be interviewed, with the interview used to explore their relevant experience.

- All employees should have an induction programme during which they are clearly told what is expected of them, what records must be kept and how their work will be supervised.

- Supervision procedures and communication channels should encourage open discussion.

- The organisation should have, and all workers should be aware of, guidelines on how to deal with the disclosure or discovery of abuse, fraud or other serious matters. These procedures should conform with the requirements of the whistleblowing legislation [see **29.8**].

- Ongoing training should be provided on prevention of child and adult abuse, financial controls, security and similar matters.

26.3.4 Additional requirements for work with children and vulnerable adults

26.3.4.1 The PoCA list and List 99

Organisations working with children must comply with a number of statutory duties when recruiting staff or moving staff from non-childcare work into work with children. At the time of writing (early 2001), new legislation was being developed relating to work with vulnerable adults. Information is available from the Department of Health, Home Office and Criminal Records Bureau [see end of chapter], as well as from local social services and education departments.

Childcare organisations regulated by statute [see **26.3.4.3**] are required, and **other organisations** working with children are allowed, to notify the Department of Health (or National Assembly for Wales) in specified circumstances where a person who is or has been engaged in work with children is considered unsuitable for such work [see **36.8.2**].

After investigation the person may be included in the **Protection of Children Act (PoCA)** list of people banned from work with children in social or health care. This list was formerly the DoH Consultancy Service Index.   *Protection of Children Act 1999 ss.1-4*

Similar rules apply to the Department for Education and Skills' **List 99**, which lists people banned from working in schools and further education institutions or restricted from certain types of work.   *ss.5-6*

26.3.4.2
The PoVA list

From April 2002 the Department of Health will maintain the **Protection of Vulnerable Adults (PoVA)** list, similar to the PoCA list, of individuals banned from work with vulnerable adults. Some people on the PoCA list will automatically be included on the PoVA list.
Care Standards Act 2000 ss.80-104

26.3.4.3
Childcare organisations

A **childcare organisation** is one:

- which is concerned with the provision of accommodation, social services or health care services to children under 18 or the supervision of children; *and*

- whose activities are regulated by statute (for example social services, adoption, NHS and community care legislation, the Children Act or Registered Homes Act).   *Protection of Children Act 1999 s.12;*
Protection of Children (Child Care Organisations) Regulations 2000
[SI 2000/2432]

Organisations which work with children but do not fall into this definition are referred to as **other organisations**.

26.3.4.4
Regulated positions

The **Protection of Children Act 1999** referred to **childcare positions**, but this was replaced by the concept of **regulated positions** under the **Criminal Justice and Court Services Act 2000** s.36. Any work in a regulated position is classified as 'working with children'. Unless indicated otherwise, a child is a person under 18.

Regulated positions are:

- positions where normal duties involve carrying out any work in **establishments which are exclusively or mainly for children**, such as schools, children's homes or children's hospitals, even if the work does not involve direct access to children;   *CJCSA s.36(1)(a),(2)*

- positions where normal duties include work on **day care premises**, unless the duties are carried out in a completely separate part of the premises where children are not looked after, or at times when children are not being looked after;   *s.36(1)(b),(3)*

- positions where normal duties include **caring for, training, supervising or being in sole charge of children** in any type of organisation (even if it is not primarily for children), but not including persons who care for, train, supervise or are in sole charge of children in employment;   *s.36(1)(c),(4)*

- positions where normal duties involve **unsupervised contact** with children under arrangements made by a responsible person (for example a parent, guardian or primary carer, but not including persons who have unsupervised contact with children in employment;
s.36(1)(d),(4),(5),(13)

- positions where normal duties include caring for children who are under 16 (not 18) in the course of the **children's employment**;
s.36(1)(e)

- positions where a substantial part of the duties involve supervising or training children under 16 (not 18) as part of the children's employment;   *s.36(1)(f)*

- trustees of children's charities [see below], members of the governing body of educational institutions, and persons in certain local authority and other positions;   *s.36(1)(g),(6)-(9)*

- persons whose normal duties may not directly involve work with children but who supervise the day-to-day work of, directly line manage and/or have authority to dismiss, persons in regulated positions.
  Criminal Justice and Court Services Act 2000 s.36(1)(h),(10)

26.3.4.5
Trustees of children's charities

It is very important to note that being a trustee of a **children's charity** is a regulated position. A children's charity is one whose workers normally work in regulated positions. *s.36(11),(12)*

26.3.4.6
Disqualification

From 11 January 2001 a judge, as part of sentencing or disposing of a case against a person who has committed a serious offence against a child, can issue a disqualification order banning the person from all work with children in both a paid and unpaid capacity. It is an offence for a person disqualified in this way, included in the Protection of Children Act list [see **26.3.4.1**] or banned under List 99 [see **26.3.4.1**] to work in a regulated position, or for work in a regulated position to be offered to a person known to be disqualified or banned. *ss.26-38*

26.3.4.7
Pre-employment checks

Childcare organisations regulated by statute [see **26.3.4.3**] have a duty to check the Protection of Children Act and List 99 [see **26.3.4.1** and **26.3.4.1**] before offering work, paid or unpaid, in a **regulated position** [see **26.3.4.4**]. When criminal record checks become available they will have a duty to undertake these checks, which will include details from the PoCA list and List 99. Checks must also be carried out on current workers changing to a regulated position within the organisation. *Protection of Children Act 1999 ss.7, 9*

Where a childcare organisation recruits via an employment agency or nursing supply agency, the organisation must receive written confirmation that the agency carried out a check within the previous 12 months, and details of the check. *s.8*

Before criminal record checks become available, other organisations working with children may, if they wish, carry out PoCA and List 99 checks via the Department of Health, and may also have access to police checks [see **26.3.3.5**]. They do not generally have a statutory duty to carry out these checks but are strongly advised to do so. Even where there is no statutory duty to carry out checks, funders may require organisations to do them.

26.3.4.8
Work in regulated positions

It is an offence:
- for a disqualified or banned person to apply or offer to work, or to accept or carry on working, in a regulated position;
  Criminal Justice and Court Services Act 2000 s.35(1)
- for an individual in any organisation, not only those legally defined as childcare organisations, to offer work, paid or unpaid, in a regulated position to a person whom they know to be disqualified or banned from working with children, or to offer work to a person supplied by an agency who was disqualified or banned at the time the agency undertook its check; *s.35(2)(a)*
- for an individual in any organisation to allow a person whom they know to be banned or disqualified to continue working in a regulated position. *s.35(2)(b)*

Further information is available from local social services departments, the Department of Health and the Home Office [see end of chapter].

26.3.4.9
Work with vulnerable adults

At the time of writing (early 2001) provision was being developed for similar controls in relation to work with vulnerable adults. This will cover care homes for elderly people and people with a disability, domiciliary care agencies, private and voluntary healthcare services, and residential family centres, and is expected to come into effect from April 2002. *Care Standards Act 2000 ss.80-104*

26.4
TRANSFER OF
UNDERTAKINGS

Any organisation which is taking on work previously done by another employer, or which is transferring any of its work to another employer, is likely to be affected by the **Transfer of Undertakings (Protection of Employment) Regulations 1981** (TUPE). This area is particularly complex and is constantly changing, and it is vital to seek legal advice.

26.4.1
Effect of the
regulations

TUPE applies when an **undertaking** [see below for definition] is transferred from one employer (the **transferor**) to another (the **transferee**). Employees and apprentices employed by the transferor immediately before the transfer are automatically transferred to the transferee, on all the same terms (apart from, at the time of writing, occupational pension rights) and with continuity of employment preserved.

Transfer of Undertakings (Protection of Employment)
Regulations 1981 [SI 1981/1794] reg.5(1)

The regulations transfer not only the contracts of employment, but also all the rights, powers and duties in connection with the contract. This might include, for example, a liability for negligence or breach of statutory duty by the transferor (in this case the right to claim against the transferor's insurance also passes to the transferee), unpaid wages due to the employee while employed by the transferor, or a liability for compensation for unfair dismissal where a former employee was dismissed by the transferor.

Bernadone v Pall Mall Services Group and others [2000] 644 IRLB 15

Criminal liability, for example arising from non-compliance with health and safety regulations, does not transfer and remains with the transferor.

TUPE reg.5(2),(4)

The **Employment Rights Act 1996** also contains relevant provisions. TUPE's complexity, and the confusing overlap of Employment Rights Act and TUPE rules, reinforce the necessity of getting specialist legal advice in transfer situations.

Employment Rights Act 1996 ss.138, 218

26.4.2
Undertakings

26.4.2.1
Defining an
undertaking

An **undertaking** is a distinct **economic entity** which carries on the same sort of **economic activity** (work) after the transfer. An economic entity may be a whole organisation or a recognisable and identifiable part such as a branch, department or group of workers. Even a single person can be an economic entity. When a bank gave its cleaning contract to an outside contractor, the single cleaner who had been employed at the bank was entitled to be transferred to the new contractor.

Schmidt v Spar- und Leihkasse der füheren
Amter Bordesholm, Kiel und Cronshager, C-392/92 [1994] IRLR 302 ECJ

A contract to provide goods or services may be an undertaking, if it constitutes an economic entity. This is a complex area and legal advice should be sought.

Suzen v Zehnacker Gerbäudevereinigung GmbH Krankenhausservice [1997] IRLR 255 ECJ; Stirling v Dietsman [1991] IRLR 368

26.4.2.2
Changes in grant
funding

In a case with implications for voluntary organisations, a transfer was found to occur when a local authority switched a subsidy (grant) for work with drug dependants from one charity, the Redmond Foundation, to the Sigma Foundation and Sigma took on some of the Redmond employees.

Dr Sophie Redmond Stichting v Bartol [1992] IRLR 366

Although the transfer occurred because of a change in grant funding, it was held that a transfer of undertaking had occurred and that the employees' contractual rights and continuity were transferred.

In a similar case the Home Office stopped funding a local authority to provide education at a young offenders institution, and awarded the funding to a further education college. The court ruled that a transfer of an undertaking had occurred and the college was obliged to take on the local authority staff who had been providing the service.

Kenny v South Manchester College [1993] IRLR 265, ICR 934

**26.4.2.3
Voluntary sector
transfers**

Situations where a voluntary organisation could be obliged to take on transferred staff include:

- if it receives a grant or contract to run a service previously provided by the employees of another voluntary organisation, public or private sector body or any other body;
- if the organisation takes on a project or other piece of work previously run by another organisation;
- if a new (independent) organisation is set up to take on a project or piece of work previously run by a local authority, health authority, voluntary organisation or anyone else;
- if two organisations merge, or one takes over the other;
- if an organisation purchases, receives or rents property used for an undertaking and continues or restarts the undertaking.

Situations where voluntary sector staff could find themselves transferred include:

- if their organisation merges with or is taken over by another;
- if a contract, service agreement or grant for work they are currently doing is awarded to another body;
- if their work is contracted out to another body;
- if their work involves looking after or working from a building or other property which is transferred to another body;
- if their organisation sets up a subsidiary or another organisation and they are transferred to it.

In these and similar situations it is essential to take specialist advice to ensure it is clear whether TUPE does or does not apply.

**26.4.3
Transfers not
covered**

A change in control (for example through change of trustees in an unincorporated association or trust) or a change in ownership (for example through a sale of a majority shareholding) is not a transfer, because there is in fact no change in the employer—merely a change in the control or ownership of the employer.

Taking on an activity under a new contract, where the new contractor would use its existing staff to deliver the service in a different manner, would probably not be a transfer. However, legal advice should be sought.

The sale of assets only, without any of the connected activity or business, is generally not a transfer.

Transfers of undertakings outside the United Kingdom are not covered by the UK regulations, nor is the transfer of employees who ordinarily work outside the UK.   *Transfer of Undertakings*

(Protection of Employment) Regulations 1981 [SI 1981/1794] reg.13

**26.4.4
Employees' rights
before transfer**

Dismissing an employee for any reason connected with a transfer at any time prior to or at the time of the transfer is automatically unfair, and an employee will be entitled to bring a claim for unfair dismissal. The original employer's liability to the dismissed employee transfers with the undertaking, so if the claim cannot be brought against the old employer it will be brought against the new one.

Litster v Forth Dry Dock and Engineering Co Ltd [1990] 1 AC 546

An employee has the right to object to being transferred. This prevents the transfer of that employee, and terminates the contract of employment. The employee must give proper notice [see **30.6.1**], and will not have the right to claim unfair dismissal or redundancy.

TUPE reg.5(4A),(4B)

**26.4.5
Employees' rights
after transfer**

Once the transfer has been completed, the contract of employment made by the employee with the previous employer is deemed to have been made with the transferee employer, with automatic continuity of all rights and contractual terms except those relating to occupational pension schemes. The new employer does not have to provide new written particulars of employment [see **23.5**], but does have to notify the employee of the identity of the new employer. *TUPE reg.5(1)*

The employer and employee cannot subsequently agree to vary the contract, even by a clear and fair agreement.

Credit Suisse First Boston (Europe) Ltd v Lister [1998] IRLR 700 CA

**26.4.5.1
Variation without agreement**

If there is a detrimental change in an employee's working conditions to which the employee has not agreed, this may constitute constructive dismissal [see **30.4.8**] and the employee may be entitled to claim wrongful and/or unfair dismissal. *TUPE reg.5(5)*

**26.4.5.2
Dismissal and rehiring**

If the employer wants to vary the contract and the employee agrees, the employer can dismiss the employee under the terms of a settlement agreement [see **33.2.2**], then re-hire the employee on a new contract. If this is done prior to or at the time of the transfer, the settlement should be three-way, involving the old and new employers and the employee.

**26.4.5.3
Transfer of occupational pension scheme rights**

At the time of writing (early 2001) the provisions of occupational pension schemes relating to old age, invalidity and survivors' benefits were not automatically transferred, but this was likely to change. Accrued pension rights up to the time of the transfer must be protected. *reg.7*

Where the transferor employer operates an occupational pension scheme, the transferee employer is not obliged to set up a scheme for the transferred employees. *Adams & others v Lancashire County Council and BET Catering Services Ltd [1997] IRLR 436 CA*

The Government Actuaries Department has issued guidance that businesses and organisations tendering for local authority contracts should provide a pensions package 'broadly comparable' with the local government scheme. Provision for potential costs should thus be included in all such tenders, because it may turn out that local authority occupational pension rights do transfer even if other occupational pension rights do not. If the employer wishes it can apply to become an associate member of the Local Government Pension Scheme; if accepted the transferred employees will be able to remain in the scheme.

Only occupational pension schemes are excluded from TUPE. Other pension rights—for example, an employer's contractual obligation to contribute to stakeholder or personal pension schemes—are transferred.

**26.4.5.4
Fair and unfair dismissal**

A dismissal by either the old or new employer takes effect as a dismissal, but is automatically unfair unless the employer can show it is for a fair reason [see **30.8**]. If the employer can establish that it is dismissing the transferred employee as part of changes in the workforce arising from economic, technical or organisational factors which are not connected with the transfer, it will have a defence against a claim of unfair dismissal. If the defence fails and the dismissal was by the transferor, the employee will generally have the right to claim against the transferee. *TUPE reg.8(2);
Litster v Forth Dry Dock and Engineering Co Ltd [1990] 1 AC 546*

In selecting employees to be made redundant, the transferred employees should be treated in the same way as the existing employees of the transferee employer.

**26.4.6
Trade union rights**

Any relevant collective agreements between the transferor employer and a trade union or unions are automatically transferred to the new employer. This means, for example, that transferred staff continue to be entitled to pay rises negotiated under such an agreement before the transfer, or arising after the transfer as a result of national agreements. *TUPE reg.6*

If the transferred undertaking retains a separate identity, any recognition of an independent trade union by the transferor is transferred to the new employer. But if the transferred undertaking is merged into the transferee's business and loses its identity, union recognition is not transferred. *TUPE reg.9*

26.4.7 Consultation

The transferor and transferee employers must consult either the recognised trade union(s) or elected employees' representatives before effecting a transfer [see **30.2.3** for the rules for such consultation].

Collective Redundancies and Transfer of Undertakings (Protection of Employment) (Amendment) Regulations 1999 [SI 1999/1925]

The union(s) or elected representatives must be informed of when the transfer is to take place; the reasons; the legal, social and economic implications for affected employees; and whether the employer intends to take measures in relation to affected employees, which in practice means whether the new employer intends to make any material changes in existing working practices or conditions. *TUPE reg.10*

The information has to be given 'long enough before a relevant transfer to enable consultations to take place', and consultation must begin 'in good time'. The regulations contain an exception for special circumstances. *reg.10(7)*

If an employer fails in its duties the union or employees may take an action in the employment tribunal for breach of duty. The maximum compensation awarded is generally four weeks' pay. *reg.11(11)*

26.4.8 Transfers between associated employers

For the purposes of employment legislation two employers are treated as **associated** if one is a company which is directly or indirectly controlled by the other employer, or if both employers are companies which are controlled by the same third party [see **9.6** for more about company groups and control]. *Employment Rights Act 1996 s.231*

In common usage **associated employers** also refers to other similar relationships, for example where an organisation which is not a company is controlled by another organisation.

Transfers between associated employers are treated in the same way as other transfers between employers.

FOR FURTHER INFORMATION

Asylum & Immigration Act. Immigration & Nationality Department: 020-8649 7878; www.ind.homeoffice.gov.uk

Criminal record checks. Criminal Records Bureau: 0870-9090 811; www.crb.gov.uk

Equal opportunities in recruitment. See organisations at end of chapter 25

Work permits. Work Permits (UK): 0870-5210224; www.workpermits.gov.uk

Transfer of undertakings. ACAS: www.acas.org.uk; see telephone directory for local office

Work with children and vulnerable adults. Department of Health: www.doh.gov.uk

Home Office: www.homeoffice.gov.uk

Social services and education departments

Chapter 27
PAY AND PENSIONS

Topics covered in this chapter

This chapter provides an overview of matters relating to wages, PAYE, statutory sick pay, statutory maternity pay and pensions. It covers:

For sources of further information see end of chapter.

Double-underlined section headings indicate additions or significant changes since the first edition.

**27.1
PAYMENT OF
SALARIES
AND WAGES**

Traditionally **wages** are paid on an hourly, daily, piecework or similar rate, and a **salary** is a fixed weekly, monthly or annual rate regardless of the amount of work. **Remuneration** refers to any payment for work. These terms are used interchangeably, and under employment law **wages** or **pay** mean 'any sums payable to the worker in connection with his employment'.   *Employment Rights Act 1996 s.27(1)*

27.1.1
What counts as pay

For most employment law and tax purposes, pay includes:

- any fee, bonus, commission or other payment in connection with the worker's employment, regardless of whether it is covered by the contract of employment;
- holiday pay, statutory sick pay, statutory maternity pay and guarantee payments [see **27.1.9**];
- pay for time off as allowed under statute for public duties [see **24.30**] or trade union duties [see **32.5**];
- pay while suspended on maternity or medical grounds [see **27.1.10**];
- pay in lieu of notice, where paid under a contractual provision [see **27.4.11**];
- luncheon vouchers, gift vouchers and other vouchers with a fixed monetary value which can be exchanged for goods or services;
- reimbursement for expenses not incurred solely for work;
- some benefits such as accommodation, use of a company car etc [see **27.4.3**]. *Employment Rights Act 1996 s.27(1),(5)*

The following are not classed as wages for employment law purposes, but may be subject to tax:

- pensions;
- redundancy payments [see **27.4.11** and **31.6.4**];
- a lump sum payment on retirement;
- compensation for loss of office;
- payment in kind other than vouchers or tokens with a fixed monetary value;
- tips or gratuities paid directly to the worker by a third party [see **27.4.9**]. *s.27(2)*

The following are not classed as wages for the purposes of employment law, and in general are not taxable:

- reimbursement for genuine out-of-pocket expenses incurred solely for work purposes;
- a loan or advance on wages from the employer [see below]. *s.27(2)*

Specific rules apply to what is classed as pay for the purposes of minimum wage [see **27.2**].

27.1.1.1
Loans to employees and advances on wages

If a loan from an employer to an employee is in the form of an advance on wages, the full amount of pay before deduction of the advance is taxable when the employer recovers the advance.

An employer cannot make a deduction from wages to recover a loan or advance unless the right to make this type of deduction is explicit in the contract of employment, or the employee has given consent to the deduction before receiving the loan or advance [see **27.1.4**]. Any loan by a charity should be reasonable and for a good reason, such as enabling the employee to buy a season ticket.

27.1.2
Rate of pay

Subject to the obligation to pay at least the national minimum wage [see **27.2**], the employer is free to choose how much to offer for any job (except where salaries are set by statutory arrangements or an employer has negotiated pay levels with a trade union). However once the rate of pay and any arrangements for increments have been set, they can generally be changed only with the consent of the employee [see **23.7**].

Men and women, and in most cases part-timers and full-timers, must be paid the same for like work or work of equal value [see **25.4** and **25.12**].

There is no statutory obligation to give cost of living increases, annual increments or any other pay rises. Before making a contractual commitment to regular pay rises—especially if they will be linked to an external scale or an indicator such as the retail price index over which the organisation has no control—the organisation should be very confident it will have adequate funds to meet its commitments.

If increments are linked to satisfactory appraisals, great care must be taken to ensure appraisals are fairly done in ways which are not discriminatory on the basis of sex, racial group or disability.

27.1.3
Itemised pay
statements

All employees and workers [see **27.2.1** for definition of worker in this context] must be given an itemised pay statement at or before the time of payment showing:

- gross amount of wages (full amount before any deductions);
- amounts deducted for tax and national insurance;
- for deductions of a fixed amount, the details and amount of each deduction *or*, if a separate standing statement of deductions has been made, the total figure for fixed deductions;
- for variable deductions, the amount and purpose of each;
- the net amount payable (after all deductions);
- where different parts of the net payment are paid in different ways, the amount and method of each part payment.

Employment Rights Act 1996 s.8

If a statement of fixed deductions is given, it must be given to the worker in writing at or before the time of the payment when the deductions are made. It must include, for each deduction, the amount, the intervals at which it is made and the purpose. A new statement of fixed deductions must be issued at least once every 12 months. If any detail is changed, the employer must give written notice of the change, or must issue a new statement of fixed deductions which then remains valid for 12 months. *s.9*

If an itemised pay statement or statement of fixed deductions is not given at or before the time of payment, or is given but does not include all required information, the employee can bring a claim in the employment tribunal, and can be awarded the amount of all unnotified deductions in the 13 weeks before the claim was brought. *ss.11-12*

27.1.4
Deductions
from pay

An employer may not make any deduction from wages paid to an employee or worker [see **27.2.1** for definition of worker in this context, and **27.1.1** for a definition of what is classed as wages] unless:

- it is required or authorised by virtue of a statutory provision (for example income tax, national insurance, repayment of student loan, or court order);
- the worker has been overpaid wages or expenses (but there are exceptions to this; see below);
- the worker has taken part in a strike or other industrial action;
- the deduction is authorised by the worker's contract [see **24.17**];
- the worker agreed to the deduction in writing before the act which gave rise to the deduction;
- a court or tribunal has ordered the worker to pay the employer, and the worker has given his or her prior written agreement to the amount being deducted; *or*
- the contract authorises the employer to make a deduction and pay it over to a third party, or the worker has authorised this in writing (for example trade union subscriptions). *ss.13-16*

27.1.4.1
Overpayments

If the employer overpays wages or expenses because of an error of fact, it may claim the overpayment back from the worker or deduct it from a future payment. Errors of fact include, for example, adding up sums incorrectly, making a payment to the wrong person, or paying for hours which an hourly-paid worker did not work.

If the employer overpays because of an *error in interpreting the law*—for example, failing to operate PAYE properly—the overpayment can be deducted or claimed back only if the worker agrees.

Even where deduction for overpayment is allowed, the courts may prevent recovery. Legal advice should therefore generally be sought before any deduction is made.

Sunderland Polytechnic v Evans [1993] IRLR 1996;
Avon County Council v Howlett [1983] 1 All ER 1073 CA

27.1.4.2
Contractual and prior consent

Unless a deduction is authorised by statute or is to recover an overpayment, it may be made only if it is explicitly authorised by the written contract or a written agreement. The agreement must have been made prior both to the deduction and to the circumstances which gave rise to the deduction. Thus if a worker receives a loan from the employer or causes the employer a loss and then signs an agreement for the loan or loss to be recovered by deductions from salary, the agreement is not valid. The employer can recover the amount only by taking legal action against the worker, or by the worker making the payment voluntarily.

27.1.4.3
Disciplinary penalties

A deduction can be made for disciplinary matters only if the disciplinary proceeding is being held by virtue of a statutory provision (for example for a group such as the police whose disciplinary processes are governed by statute), or if the right to make the deduction is explicit in the contract. *Employment Rights Act 1996 s.14(2)*

This means that unless the contract allows [see **24.18**], an employer cannot make a deduction:

* for unauthorised absence (but workers paid wages only for hours worked do not have to be paid if they do not work);
* because a worker did not do his or her work properly;
* to cover damage to the employer's property;
* because the worker took money from the employer, or because her or his till was 'short';
* for any other reason, unless it is related to disciplinary proceedings held by virtue of a statutory provision.

Even during a disciplinary investigation, a worker can be suspended without pay or on reduced pay only if the contract allows [see **24.39**] or the suspension is linked to a disciplinary proceeding held by virtue of a statutory provision.

For workers in retail employment, even if deductions are allowed they cannot generally be more than 10% of the gross wages payable to the worker for the day when the shortage occurred. *ss.17-22*

27.1.4.4
Trade union subscriptions

Deductions for trade union subscriptions can be made only if the employee has authorised the deduction in writing within the last three years, and has not withdrawn the authorisation. A deduction for a subscription can be increased only if the employer notifies the employee at least one month before any increase in the deduction (unless the reason for the increased subscription is an increase in wages), and at the same time informs the employee that he or she has the right to withdraw authorisation at any time.

Trade Union and Labour Relations (Consolidation) Act 1992 s.68

27.1.5
'Weekly pay' and 'normal hours'

When the amount of a statutory payment or benefit depends on the level of weekly pay:

* if pay does not vary according to the amount of work done, **weekly pay** is the amount due under the contract of employment;
* if pay varies according to the amount of work done, number of hours worked or commission earned, **weekly pay** is the average for the previous 12 weeks. *Employment Rights Act 1996 ss.221-228*

If hours vary from week to week, weeks in which the employee earned nothing from the employer do not count in the calculation. Instead, previous weeks in which there were earnings are included, to bring the total number of weeks in the calculation up to 12.

Different rules apply when calculating normal hours and weekly pay for the purpose of minimum wage [see **27.2**] and working time rights [see **28.2**], and there is a statutory definition of weekly pay for the purpose of redundancy payments [see **31.6.1**].

27.1.6
Performance-related pay

Performance-related pay is additional pay if the employee's work reaches agreed standards or targets. Charities and other organisations can give a contractual or discretionary right to performance-related pay. Great care must be taken to ensure performance assessment is fair and does not discriminate because of sex, racial group or disability.

Performance-related pay is subject to tax and national insurance in the usual way.

27.1.7
Profit-related pay

Profit-related pay was a scheme under which employees could be paid a specified amount each year free of tax. It ended on 31 December 2000.

27.1.8
Cash in hand

Cash in hand refers to the practice of paying cash to workers without deducting tax and/or national insurance, sometimes without keeping proper records of the workers' name, address and national insurance number, and sometimes without declaring the payments as required to the Inland Revenue.

Unless the worker is genuinely self-employed in relation to this work [see **34.1.3**], it is the employer's obligation to operate PAYE, deduct tax and national insurance as required and account for it to the Inland Revenue. If this is not done the employer could be required to pay to the Inland Revenue the tax and NI which should have been deducted, and will be able to recover this from the worker only if he or she agrees [see **27.1.4.1**]. There may also be penalties for late payment.

If the worker's income is under the NI threshold *and* he or she has no other taxable income, tax and NI do not need to be deducted. The only valid way the employer can confirm that the worker has no other taxable income is by getting the worker to sign form P46 [see **27.4.1**].

Even where the worker is earning less than the NI threshold and has signed a P46 to say he or she has no other taxable income, the employer must keep proper records of payments made to the worker. If the worker is paid more than £100 total during the tax year, this must be notified to the Inland Revenue at the end of the year.

27.1.8.1
Cash in hand and tax evasion

From 1 January 2001 tax evasion is a statutory offence, and anyone with untaxed income is liable to up to seven years imprisonment and an unlimited fine. Organisations which pay cash in hand should be aware of the risk to the organisation for failure to operate PAYE, and the risk to the worker for tax evasion and possibly also for benefits fraud if the worker is receiving state benefits. *Finance Act 2000 s.144*

27.1.9
Guarantee payments

Employees who have worked more than one month and who are on wages rather than a fixed salary are entitled to **guarantee payments** for days when they are contractually obliged to work, but the employer provides no work because there is not enough work or for any other reason affecting the normal working of the employer's business.
Employment Rights Act 1996 ss.28-29

Guarantee payments are payable:

- at a statutory daily rate (£16.70 as at 1/4/01) or at the employee's usual daily rate, whichever is lower;

- in any three month period, only for the number of days the employee normally works per week. *s.31*

If an employer reduces hours or pay to less than 50% for at least four consecutive weeks, or for six or more weeks within a period of 13 weeks, an employee who has worked more than two years may be able to claim redundancy pay [see **31.6**]. *Employment Rights Act 1996 ss.147-148*

An employee on a fixed-term contract of three months or less, or on a contract for a specific task which is not expected to last more than three months, does not become eligible for a guarantee payment until he or she has been continuously employed for at least three months.

27.1.10
Pay during medical and maternity suspension

After one month's employment most employees, except those on a fixed-term contract of three months or less or a contract for completion of a task which is expected to last for three months or less, are entitled to be paid their normal wages or salary for up to 26 weeks when suspended on medical grounds as required by a statute or a code of practice issued under the **Health and Safety at Work Act 1974**. *ss.64-65*

This entitlement applies only to suspension for reasons covered by the **Control of Lead at Work Regulations 1980** *[SI 1980/1248]*, **Ionising Radiations Regulations 1985** *[SI 1985/1333]* and **Control of Substances Hazardous to Health Regulations 1988** *[SI 1988/1657]*.

A woman is entitled to full pay if health and safety regulations prohibit her from doing her normal work because of pregnancy, childbirth or breastfeeding, and no suitable alternative work is available [see **28.7.7**]. *Employment Rights Act 1996 ss.66-68*

27.1.11
Pay during notice period

During the notice period, regardless of whether the employer or employee has given notice of termination, the employee is entitled to full pay. This applies even if there is no contractual entitlement, for example an employee on sick leave who has used all his or her sick pay entitlement.

27.1.12
Discretionary payments

Many voluntary sector employers offer staff more generous arrangements than their contract provides for, such as bonuses, additional paid sick leave, paid sabbaticals or paid compassionate leave. Even where the organisation makes clear that these extra benefits are non-contractual and are entirely up to the employer's discretion, a court may still find the employer in breach of contract if the discretion is exercised in a way which is unreasonable. *Clark v Nomura International plc [2000] IRLR 766*

27.2
MINIMUM WAGE

Virtually all employees and workers are entitled to national minimum wage, which is (as at 1/4/01):

- £3.70 per hour for workers aged over 21, to be increased to £4.10 on 1 October 2001 with a proposed increase to £4.20 from October 2002;
- £3.20 per hour for workers aged 18 to 21, to be increased to £3.50 on 1 October 2001 and £3.60 from October 2002;
- at the young workers' rate for workers aged over 21 who are undergoing accredited training during their first six months working for a new employer.

The minimum wage is reviewed annually so up-to-date information should always be obtained when setting pay rates for low paid jobs, and appropriate provision should be made in budgets and grant applications.

Information about minimum wage is available on the internet and from the minimum wage helpline [see end of chapter].

27.2.1
Entitlement

A 'worker' is anyone who works under:

- a contract of employment, i.e. in an employment relationship; *or*
- under any other contract where they have to do the work personally (cannot sub-contract it), except where the work is being done for someone who is a client or customer of the person's own profession or business undertaking. *National Minimum Wage Act 1998 s.54*

The contract does not have to be in writing. In practice this means that virtually everyone who receives pay or consideration (something else of material value—see **23.2.3**) is entitled to minimum wage, unless they are genuinely self-employed and are carrying out the work as part of their self-employment. Minimum wage must be paid to agency workers, homeworkers, pieceworkers and commission workers, to foreign workers who are working in the UK, and to workers who usually work in the UK but are temporarily working outside the UK.

The reduced rate for workers aged 22 and over who are undergoing accredited training can be paid only if there is a written agreement between the employer and worker, stating that the worker will take part in a course of accredited training on at least 26 days during the first six months of employment. A copy of the agreement must be kept for at least three years.

National Minimum Wage Regulations 1999 [SI 1999/584], reg.13(2)-(6)

The following are not entitled to minimum wage:

- workers under the age of 18;

- trainees on the national traineeship, modern apprenticeship, foundation modern apprenticeship, advanced modern apprenticeship and similar government schemes, who are 18 years old, or are at least 19 and under 26 and in their first year of training;

- workers participating in specified government-funded schemes (such as New Deal) or European Social Fund-funded schemes designed to provide training, work experience or temporary work or to assist the person in seeking or obtaining work;

- during the first three weeks when a worker who has been participating in such a scheme is employed, under government-sponsored arrangements, for a work trial period;

- students on higher education courses, who are on up to a year's work experience required for the course;

- some people who have been homeless or living in a hostel for homeless people, and are now working in a scheme for homeless people and are receiving accommodation and other benefits, which may include money, from the scheme;

National Minimum Wage Regulations 1999 [SI 1999/584] reg.12;
NMW Regulations 1999 (Amendment) Regulations 2000 [SI 2000/1989]

- workers who live in a household as part of a family which is not their family and share the household work, such as au pairs, companions and nannies; *NMW Regulations 1999 reg.2(2)*

- residential members of religious communities;

Employment Relations Act 1999 s.22

- jobs done under informal arrangements between friends or neighbours;

- some volunteers and voluntary workers [see **35.3.3**];

- a person who is genuinely self-employed.

27.2.2
What counts as pay

'Pay' is defined differently for the purposes of minimum wage than for other employment law purposes [see **27.1.1**] or for tax [see **27.3.2**]. When calculating minimum wage, the following count as pay:

- gross pay, before deduction of tax, national insurance and most other authorised deductions [see **27.1.4**];

- repayments made by the worker to the employer, for example where a worker pays back the employer for a season ticket loan, rather than the employer deducting the repayment from the worker's pay;

- special allowances, for example for working in dangerous conditions, working unsocial hours, working in a particular area (such as London weighting), being on call—but only if these special allowances are consolidated into standard pay;

- payments made as part of an incentive, merit or performance-related pay scheme;
- bonuses;
- tips, gratuities and service charges that are collected by the employer and then paid to the worker, or are pooled before being distributed to the worker.

27.2.2.1
Accommodation offset

The value of accommodation provided by the employer counts as pay, but only (as at 1/4/01) to a maximum which is the lower of:

- 50p for every hour worked in the pay reference period [see **27.2.2.3**], reduced proportionately for each day in the pay period that accommodation is not provided;
- £2.85 for every day accommodation was provided in the pay reference period; *or*
- £19.95 per week. *NMW Regulations regs.36-37*

In determining the value of accommodation the hourly rate calculation generally applies for workers who do less than 40 hours per week, and the daily rate for workers who do more than 40 hours per week.

27.2.2.2
What does not count

The following do not count towards minimum wage pay:

- a loan or advance on wages (but it counts when it is repaid to the employer, either directly by the worker or by deduction from wages);
- the employer's contribution to pension schemes;
- redundancy payment or lump sum on retirement;
- rewards under a staff suggestions scheme;
- a premium (additional payment) above the worker's basic rate pay, for working overtime, or at particular times (such as bank holidays), or on particular duties (such as shift working);
- a premium above the employer's normal hourly rate for such work, for working nights or at weekends;
- special allowances [see **27.2.2**] that are not consolidated into standard pay;
- reimbursements or allowances for clothing, travel, subsistence and similar costs necessary for the work;
- reimbursement for other expenditure incurred for work;
- payments made by the worker for expenditure necessary for work (for example, travel costs) but not reimbursed by the employer;
- payments by the worker for tools, equipment, uniforms and other items necessary for the work and purchased from the employer;
- the value of accommodation above the offset [see **27.2.2.1**];
- the value of benefits in kind, such as meals, luncheon vouchers, fuel, a car or use of a car, assistance with removals, medical insurance, etc.

regs.9, 31-36

Although the above do not count towards pay for the purposes of minimum wage, some of them do count towards the definition of pay for employment law and/or tax purposes [see **27.1.1** and **27.3.2**].

27.2.2.3
Pay reference period

The **pay reference period** is the worker's actual pay period, to a maximum of one calendar month. For daily paid workers the pay reference period is one day, for weekly paid workers one week, for monthly paid workers one month, and for workers paid less frequently it is one month. Specific rules apply where money earned in one reference period is not paid to the worker until the next period, or where the worker receives an annual bonus. *reg.10*

27.2.3
Hours of work

The hours for which minimum wage must be paid depend on how the worker is paid. For this purpose there are four types of work: time work, salaried hours work, output work, and unmeasured work.

**27.2.3.1
Time work**

Time work is where a worker is paid according to the number of hours worked. The hours may be fixed or variable, and include:

- time when the person is required to be at work (either as basic work hours or overtime) and is at work;
- time spent on training at or away from the place of work during normal working hours;
- time when the worker is at work but cannot work, for example because equipment has broken down;
- time on standby or on call at or near the place of work (but not time on standby or on call at home);
- time travelling in connection with work during normal working hours or the normal range of hours, including lunch and tea breaks on board the train, bus, plane etc (but not travel between home and work);
- time waiting for a train, or changing trains or other form of transport (but not lunch or tea breaks while waiting for transport).

National Minimum Wage Regulations 1999 [SI 1999/584] regs.3, 7, 15, 20

Minimum wage must be paid for all time work hours.

Lunch and other rest breaks, periods when the worker is absent from work or is on holiday, sick leave and maternity leave, or absence while engaged in industrial action do not count as 'hours' for minimum wage purposes—even if, for example, the person works during their lunch break. Any pay received for these periods is not counted as minimum wage pay.

Where a worker is provided with suitable facilities for sleeping at or near the place of work, time when he or she is permitted to sleep and is not working does not count as work time for this purpose.

**27.2.3.2
Salaried hours work**

Salaried hours work is where a worker is entitled under his or her contract to an annual salary, is required to work a basic minimum number of hours in a year (which may be expressed in weekly terms, for example 35 hours per week), and is paid in equal instalments (usually 12 monthly or 52 weekly instalments, but it could be 26 fortnightly or six bi-monthly instalments, or whatever). *regs.4, 16, 21-23*

Work is considered to be salaried if the basic payment is the same each time, apart from variations resulting from a performance bonus, a pay increase, pay for working overtime, or the worker leaving part-way through the pay period.

Salaried hours workers include those who work only part of the year, such as school staff, but receive equal payments through the whole year.

The hours for which minimum wage is payable are calculated in the same way as for time workers [see above], except that hours of absence, such as rest breaks, lunch breaks, holidays, sickness absence and maternity leave are payable if they form part of the worker's basic minimum hours under the contract. So if a person is required to work 35 hours per week including lunch breaks, time at lunch is counted as work hours. If the person is required to work 35 hours excluding lunch breaks, the lunch break does not count as work hours and minimum wage is not payable for it, even if the person works through the lunch period (unless the employer counts this as overtime and makes an additional payment for it).

The following do not count as hours for minimum wage purposes:

- time when the worker is on reduced pay or no pay due to sick leave, maternity leave or other long-term leave;
- time when the worker is engaged in industrial action.

27.2.3.3
Output work

Output work is paid according to the quantity of items produced or made, or the number of sales or deals made by the worker. It is usually called piecework or commission work. The employer will either need to pay at least minimum wage for the number of hours actually worked, or will need to agree a 'fair estimate' of the hours to be worked.

NMW Regulations regs.5, 17, 24-26

The fair estimate must be in writing, comply with statutory requirements, and be supported by a contract between the worker and employer which sets the agreed piece rate. One agreement can cover a number of pay reference periods if the worker must do the same amount of work in each of them.

27.2.3.4
Unmeasured work

Unmeasured work is work which is not time work, salaried hours work or output work. It includes work where certain tasks must be done but there are no specified hours or times when they must be done. The employer requires the worker to work when needed or when work is available. The employer can pay minimum wage for every hour worked, or come to a 'daily average' number of hours.

regs.6, 18, 27-29

Unmeasured work for minimum wage is different from **unmeasured time** for the purposes of the working time regulations [see **28.2.1**].

27.2.4
Records

Employers must keep adequate records to show that workers are being paid at least minimum wage. For workers clearly paid over minimum wage there is no need to keep extra records. Where a worker is paid at or not much above minimum wage, detailed records of hours worked, overtime and time off should be kept, adequate for the employer to show that minimum wage has in fact been paid.

Where there is a training agreement [see **27.2.1**], fair estimate agreement [see **27.2.3.3**] or daily average agreement [see **27.2.3.4**], a copy must be kept. Records must be kept for at least three years after the end of the pay reference periods following the pay period that the records cover. However it is advisable to keep records for at least six years.

27.2.5
Enforcement

A worker who believes he or she is not being paid the minimum wage has a right to see the employer's minimum wage records. The request must be in writing, and the employer must produce the records within 14 days of the request, or within such time as is agreed with the worker. The worker has a right to be accompanied by another person when inspecting the records, and has a right to make a copy of the records.

National Minimum Wage Act 1998 s.10

A worker who is denied access to records or is not being paid the minimum wage can bring a claim in the employment tribunal or court. The worker can be awarded an amount to bring payments up to minimum wage (backdated to 1 April 1999), or where access to records is denied, can be awarded up to 80 times the minimum wage.

ss.11, 17

Rather than going to a tribunal or court, the worker can inform the enforcement agency, the Inland Revenue. The Inland Revenue can issue an enforcement notice, requiring the employer to pay minimum wage for each named worker (backdated to 1 April 1999). If the employer does not do this, there is a penalty of twice the amount of minimum wage (i.e. £7.40 as at 1/4/01) for each day from the time the enforcement notice was issued, and for each worker named in the enforcement notice who has not been paid the money due.

ss.19-22

In addition there are six criminal offences, each punishable by a fine of up to £5,000: refusal or wilful neglect to pay the minimum wage, failing to keep national minimum wage records, keeping false records, producing false records or information, intentionally obstructing an enforcement officer, and refusing or neglecting to give information to an enforcement officer.

ss.31-33

A worker who is dismissed or victimised because of seeking to enforce his or her right to minimum wage, or is dismissed because he or she is becoming eligible for minimum wage (or for a higher rate), can bring a claim of unfair dismissal or victimisation. There is no qualifying period to claim unfair dismissal in these situations.

National Minimum Wage Act 1998 ss.23-25

27.3
PAYE

Every employer, even if it has only one part-time employee, must register with the Inland Revenue and operate the **pay as you earn** (PAYE) scheme in respect of all workers to whom it applies. Operating PAYE incorrectly can have serious implications, and it is sensible to undertake a regular review of PAYE arrangements with the organisation's auditor or other financial advisor.

This book does not cover PAYE, income tax and national insurance in detail. The Inland Revenue and Contributions Office have a helpline and provide detailed information [see end of chapter].

The Scottish parliament has powers to charge different rates of income tax, so organisations with staff based or working in Scotland may need to take advice on the tax position.

27.3.1
People covered by PAYE

PAYE applies to every individual paid by an organisation in return for work, even one who might not normally be thought of as an employee, unless the individual:

- is recognised by the Inland Revenue as self-employed in relation to the work [see **34.1**]; *or*

- earns less than the weekly tax threshold [see **27.4**], and has no other taxable earnings.

Tax does not need to be deducted from wages of full-time students who work only during the holidays, provided the student signs **form P38(S)**. National insurance contributions may be payable.

27.3.2
What counts as pay

PAYE covers not only wages or salary, but also commissions and bonuses, one-off or lump sum payments, sick pay, maternity pay, holiday pay, tips collected by the employer and distributed to employees [see **27.4.9**], some payments on termination of employment [see **27.4.11**], and other money payments. PAYE may also cover the provision of 'perks' and other non-money benefits, such as accommodation or personal use of a company car [see **27.4.3-27.4.7**] and LETS [see **27.4.10**].

Special rules apply to people who work abroad.

27.3.3
Employer's duties

The employer has a duty to register for PAYE, operate it and keep all legally required PAYE records. If this is not done the employer could be held liable for all tax and national insurance contributions (NICs) which should have been deducted and paid to the Inland Revenue, plus interest, plus penalties for late payment.

The employer must send tax and national insurance payments monthly to the collector of taxes. If the average monthly payments of tax and NICs are less than a specified amount (£1,500 in tax year 2001-02), payments can be sent quarterly instead of monthly.

At the end of each tax year an annual return (**P35**) must be completed and sent to the inspector of taxes by 19 May. Each person employed as of 5 April must be given, by 31 May, **form P60** showing their total taxable income during the tax year, how much tax and national insurance was deducted and their tax code.

The value of benefits provided to employees and expenses paid to them must be itemised by the employer on form **P11D** or **P9D** [see **27.4.8**] and submitted to the Inland Revenue by 6 July unless the employer has a dispensation from having to file them [see **27.4.8.1**] or has entered into a PAYE settlement agreement [see **27.4.8.2**]. The same information must be provided to the employee by 6 July.

When workers for whom PAYE has been operated leave work they must be given **form P45** showing taxable income during the tax year, tax deducted and the tax code.

27.4 INCOME TAX

The rate at which income tax is paid depends on the amount of **taxable income** (income from all sources which is subject to tax, minus tax allowances and tax reliefs). For 2001-02, tax rates are:

- 10% (starting rate) on taxable income up to £1,520;
- 22% (basic rate) on taxable income from £1,521 to £28,400;
- 40% (higher rate) on taxable income over £28,400.

For 2001-02 the **threshold** above which PAYE must be operated is £87 per week (£378 per month) from all employments.

27.4.1 Tax allowances and codes

Everyone who receives taxable income is entitled to receive a certain amount free of tax. These **tax allowances** change each year. Tax allowances for earnings are divided by 52 to give the amount of tax-free pay which can be earned in a week, or by 12 to give the monthly tax-free amount. A **tax code** represents an employee's total allowances and enables the employer to work out tax on earnings above the allowances.

When a person first does paid work for an organisation:

- the employee must give the employer a **form P45** showing taxable income and tax paid so far in the tax year and the tax code, which will enable the employer to know how much tax to deduct; *or*
- the employer must give the employee **form P46**, on which the employee must indicate whether he or she has any other paid work, and if so which is the main work. This form enables the employer to know how to operate a temporary code until the tax office advises what the person's tax code should be.

If the employee has only one source of earned income, the employer does not have to deduct tax unless the employee earns more than their personal allowance. But if the employee has other employments as well, the allowance will be given at only one place of employment, or will be divided by the tax office between them. An employer might have to deduct tax even from earnings of as little as £1 per week, if the employee's allowance is all being used elsewhere.

The same applies if the person has taxable income from a source other than employment, and all or part of the personal allowance is set against that income. This particularly applies to pensioners, whose personal allowance is set against their taxable pension income.

It is the employee's obligation to notify the tax office of any changes which might affect the tax code, or to notify the employer and the employer notifies the tax office. Even if an employer knows an employee is entitled to additional allowances, the tax code must not be changed until the employee or employer notifies the tax office of the change and the inspector of taxes issues a new tax code.

27.4.2 Tax reliefs and credits

Individuals may also be entitled to tax reliefs and/or tax credits. With **tax reliefs**, tax does not have to be paid on the income used for certain outgoings, or tax which has been paid is rebated in some way.

27.4.2.1 No tax deducted by employer

Some tax reliefs are dealt with by the employer deducting the amount from the employee's earnings before working out how much tax is payable on earnings. Tax reliefs handled like this include payments to occupational pension schemes [see **27.9.3**], and payments to charities under a payroll giving scheme [see **46.3**].

**27.4.2.2
Tax relief at source**

Tax relief is available on some life insurance policy premiums and premiums for some types of medical insurance for people over 60, and pension contributions up to a specified limit. These tax reliefs are dealt with automatically by the insurance or pension company.

**27.4.2.3
Tax relief claimed
by taxpayer**

Some reliefs are obtained only if the employee claims them through self-assessment. These include tax relief on some loans, maintenance payments, some work-related expenses [see **27.4.3.2**], some vocational training, and additional tax relief for higher rate taxpayers on pension contributions and on donations made to charities under gift aid [see **46.2**]. Relief is usually given by an adjustment to the person's tax code.

**27.4.2.4
Children's tax credit**

From 6 April 2001 **children's tax credit** replaces the married couple's allowance and additional personal allowance for single parents or couples with a child aged up to 16 at the beginning of the tax year. It allows a parent or other person with a child up to 16 years old to earn a specified amount without paying tax on that income. Eligibility is reflected in the employee's PAYE code.

**27.4.2.5
Working families' and
disabled person's
tax credits**

Working families' tax credit and **disabled person's tax credit** [see **27.4.2.5**] are different. These are state benefits, paid by the employer then recovered by the employer through the PAYE process.

Working families' tax credit is available to one- or two-parent families with children, where at least one parent works a minimum of 16 hours per week. It consists of a basic tax credit, an additional credit if one earner works more than 30 hours per week, and a tax credit for each child. It may also include childcare credit, which covers 70% of eligible childcare costs to a weekly maximum (as at 6/6/01) of £135 for one child or £200 for more than one. WFTC replaced family credit.

Disabled person's tax credit works in the same way as WFTC and is available for certain people with an illness or disability, who work for at least 16 hours per week. DPTC replaced disability working allowance.

Women who are receiving statutory maternity pay or maternity allowance and previously worked 16 hours per week are treated as meeting the work requirements.

When an employee is entitled to WFTC or DPTC, the employer is sent a notification to start paying tax credits (**form TC01**) and a certificate of payments (**form TC02**). The employer must then pay tax credit at the daily rate for the period shown on the TC01, unless the employer does not expect to make three consecutive payments to the employee within the dates tax credits are payable, or the employee left employment before the start date for tax credits.

Tax credits are paid for seven days per week, with a week starting on Tuesday. They are paid with wages, and must cover the same pay period as the wages paid on that day. The tax credit paid to an employee is entered on the P11. There is no tax or national insurance on tax credits.

The total tax credits paid to employees are then deducted from the tax, national insurance and student loan repayments due to the Inland Revenue. If the amount paid out in tax credits is more than the amount owed to the Inland Revenue, the employer can apply to the Inland Revenue on **form TC11** for funding to cover the tax credits.

If the employer stops paying tax credits before the date on the TC01 for any reason other than receiving a stop notice, the employer must complete form TC02, and give parts 2 and 3 to the employee.

**27.4.2.6
Other tax credits**

At the time of writing (early 2001) the government had announced plans to introduce, in 2003, **employment tax credit** for people in low paid work who do not have children, and an **integrated child credit** bringing together existing forms of child support.

27.4.3
Out-of-pocket expenses

If an employee pays for work-related expenses, the tax treatment depends on whether the employer reimburses the employee or the employee remains out of pocket. The rules are complex and advice should be sought from a PAYE enquiry office or an accountant. The tax rules for employees' expenses are different from the rules for expenses incurred by volunteers [see **35.2**] and self-employed workers.

27.4.3.1
Reimbursement by employer

An employer's reimbursement of an employee's out-of-pocket expenditure is not classed as wages or remuneration and is not subject to tax or national insurance provided that:

* the expenditure was genuine (was actually incurred);
* the expenditure was necessary for the work; *and*
* the Inland Revenue and/or the Contributions Office allow reimbursement for this type of expenditure to be paid free of tax and/or national insurance.

Any other reimbursement is subject to tax and NI. An exception is small incidental personal expenses such as newspapers and laundry while an employee is on a business trip or attending work-related training involving an overnight stay. An employer can pay up to £5 per night for stays in the UK and £10 for stays abroad free of tax (tax year 2001-02).

Reimbursement for travel between home and the usual place of work is subject to tax and NI.

Virtually all reimbursements to employees, even those which are allowed by the Inland Revenue, must be notified to the Inland Revenue and the employee on form P11D or P9D unless the organisation has a dispensation from filing these forms [see **27.4.8**].

27.4.3.2
Expenses not reimbursed by employer

If the employer does not reimburse for some or all expenses, the employee may be entitled to tax relief on some expenditure. This might be in the form of a **flat rate deduction** agreed between the Inland Revenue and the relevant trade union. If a flat rate deduction has not been agreed, the employee can recover the amount spent only by claiming relief on a self-assessment tax return. Tax relief is available for:

* buying and maintaining tools which are not provided by the employer and are used only for work;
* buying and maintaining special working clothes which are not provided by the employer and are used only for work;
* travel expenses necessary to do the job (but not travel to and from the usual place of work);
* other necessary expenses incurred wholly and exclusively in doing the work;
* wear and tear on a car provided at the employee's own expense to do the job;
* some fees which have to be paid by an employee in order to carry on a profession;
* subscriptions to some professional bodies and societies.

27.4.4
Relocation expenses

Payment for **relocation expenses** of up to £8,000 (tax year 2001-02) is not subject to tax or national insurance provided:

* the move is necessary to enable the employee to take up a new job (for the same employer or a different employer) or to carry on the same job at a new location;
* the employee's current home is not within reasonable travelling distance of the new workplace; *and*
* the payment covers costs which are covered by this exemption [see Inland Revenue leaflet IR134 *Income Tax and Relocation Packages*].

27.4.5
Cars and driving

Reimbursing employees for use of their own cars, or allowing them to use a work vehicle for private use, has tax and national insurance implications which must be considered by the employee and employer. Details are in IR125 *Using Your Own Car for Work*, IR161 *Tax Reliefs for Employees' Business Travel*, IR172 *Income Tax and Company Cars*, and booklet 490 *Employee Travel: A tax and NICs guide for employers*

27.4.5.1
Use of private vehicles for 'business' use

Employees' use of their private cars to carry out an organisation's work is called **business use**, even if the organisation is not a business. The Inland Revenue's **authorised mileage rates** set the maximum which can be reimbursed tax-free for business use of cars. The rate depends on the number of miles reimbursed and the size of the car, and is the same for petrol and diesel engines. Tax-free rates for 2001-02 are:

	Up to 1500cc	1501-2000cc	Over 2000cc
Up to 4000 miles	40p	45p	63p
Over 4000 miles	25p	25p	36p

An employer who reimburses employees for business use of their cars can choose, from 6 April 2002, to pay an additional 5p per mile for each employee who travels as a passenger in the car on a business journey. This additional amount is paid to the employee and is free of tax and national insurance.

The authorised reimbursement rate for bicycle use for work purposes is 12p per mile, and for motorcycle use 24p per mile (2001-02 rates).

An employer can pay less than the authorised amounts, or nothing at all. In these situations the employee may then be able to claim tax relief on the amount which has not been reimbursed [see **27.4.3.2**].

The Inland Revenue rates are lower than National Joint Council for Local Authorities (NJC) rates. If an employee receives more than the Inland Revenue amounts, the excess is subject to tax and NI. Reimbursement for travel between home and the usual place of work, even at or below the Inland Revenue rate, is also subject to tax and NI.

If employees use private cars for work purposes they must notify their insurer [see **20.8**].

27.4.5.2
Use of company cars for private motoring

If the employer provides an employee or a member or his or her family or household with a car which can also be used for private motoring, the employee is assumed to receive **car benefit**. Tax and employer's **class 1A national insurance**, but not employee's national insurance, are payable on the car benefit, at a **scale charge** (also called **car benefit charge**). This is 35% of the new list price of the car at the time it was registered (including VAT, delivery charges, and accessories).

Accessories added after the car was registered increase the car's value, and therefore the car benefit, in the year they are added and each additional year. But accessories added solely for use by people with a disability do not increase the car benefit.

Before tax and NI are assessed, the scale charge is reduced:
- by one-third, if the car was used for 2,500 to 17,999 business miles during the year, or by two-thirds if it was used for 18,000 or more business miles;
- by a further one-third, if the car is four or more years old at the end of the tax year;
- pound for pound, for the employee's own contributions for private use of the car and for the employee's contributions of up to £5,000 towards the cost of the car and/or accessories.

A company car which is an employee's second car is assessed in the same way, except that the reduction for business mileage is only one-third and is given only if it is used for 18,000 or more business miles.

Information about company cars must be provided to the Inland Revenue on **form P46(Car)**.

27.4.5.3
Tax and car emissions

From April 2002 car benefit charge is reduced to 15% of the car's price, for cars emitting carbon dioxide at or below a qualifying level, and will increase to 35% depending on the emission level. Cars without an approved figure of CO_2 emissions or registered before 1 January 1998 will be taxed according to engine size.

27.4.5.4
Transport for disabled workers

Where a disabled person is provided with a vehicle for travelling to and from work or receives some or all of the costs of these journeys, income tax and national insurance are not charged on the amount received or the value of the vehicle.

27.4.5.5
Cash in lieu of car

A cash alternative to a car is subject to tax and national insurance in the same way as any payment to an employee.

27.4.5.6
Fuel

The value of fuel provided free of charge by an employer for an employee's private use is also subject to tax and employer's class 1A national insurance, based on the car's engine type and size. If the organisation is VAT registered it must account for VAT on the fuel.

27.4.6
Childcare

The tax situation for childcare costs depends on what is provided:
- if the employer provides a free or subsidised workplace nursery or playscheme on its own or jointly with others, there is no tax or national insurance on the value of the childcare or subsidy;
- if the employer provides childcare vouchers, the employee must pay tax and national insurance on the value if she or he earns more than £8,500 per year (including the value of the vouchers) or is a company director of the employer organisation, but the employer does not have to pay employer's NICs;
- if the employer directly engages and directly pays the fees for a nursery, playscheme, childminder or nanny, the rules are the same as for childcare vouchers;
- if the employer provides the employee with financial help towards the cost of childcare, the amount is subject to tax and employee's and employer's NICs.

Working parents who receive working families' tax credit or disabled person's tax credit may be entitled to a tax credit for up to 70% of childcare costs [see **27.4.2.5**].

27.4.7
Other benefits

Other taxable 'perks' and benefits include accommodation, meals, season tickets and other fares, luncheon vouchers worth more than 15p per day, medical insurance or medical care, flat-rate expense allowances, Christmas gifts or meals if the value is high, gifts from clients and virtually everything else which has a monetary value.

Some benefits and perks which have been exempted from tax include:
- limited private use by an employee of items provided by the employer for the employee's work, such as computers and fax machines, where these remain the employer's property and the total annual value of the equipment does not exceed £500 (the annual value of the employer's equipment is generally 20% of its value);
- mobile phones, and line rental for mobile phones (but vouchers or cash towards the cost of mobile phones or calls are taxable);
- general welfare counselling provided by the employer;
- contributions to employees' individual learning accounts;
- tea, coffee and similar light refreshments provided by the employer;
- accommodation services and supplies used in the performance of duties away from the employer's premises—but cars, buildings, boats or aircraft are not exempt.

Inland Revenue booklets P7 *Employer's Further Guide to Pay As You Earn* and 480 *Expenses and Benefits: A tax guide* contain detailed guidance on taxation of employee benefits. In many cases the rules are complex, so unless the tax and national insurance situation is absolutely clear, prior clearance should be sought from the organisation's PAYE office.

27.4.8
Form P11D and P9D

Unless it has a dispensation [see **27.4.8.1**], the employer must notify the Inland Revenue annually by 6 July on **form P11D** of all reimbursements for expenses and other benefits to:

- employees who earn £8,500 or more per year, including the expenses and the value of the benefits;
- all company directors, including employees who are also company directors;
- all members of the employer's governing body, if the employer is an organisation which is not registered as a company [see **chapter 14** for more about payments to governing body members].

Notification must be made on form P11D even if the reimbursements or benefits are not subject to tax or national insurance.

Form P9D is used for taxable reimbursements or benefits totalling more than £25 reimbursed to employees who earn less than £8,500 per year and are not company directors or governing body members. Non-taxable reimbursements and benefits do not have to be included.

The information on the P11D or P9D must also be provided to the employee by 6 July, and the employee must notify it to the Inland Revenue on a self-assessment tax return. It is the employee's obligation to ask for a tax return if one is not provided by the Inland Revenue.

If the benefits or reimbursements listed on the P11D or P9D are taxable, the Inland Revenue will issue a revised tax code so tax can be deducted from future payments to the individual. If the reimbursements are not taxable (because they meet the criteria set out in **27.4.3**), the employee should indicate this on his or her tax return.

27.4.8.1
Dispensation

If the only entries on the P11D would be reimbursement of expenses genuinely incurred wholly in the course of the business, the employer can obtain dispensation from having to submit the forms by writing to the inspector of taxes or using form P11DX in leaflet IR69. There is no need for a dispensation from form P9D, because this does not have to be filled in if the only reimbursements or benefits are free of tax.

Although an employer with a dispensation does not have to send details of expenses payments to the Inland Revenue, it must provide the information to the employee by 6 July. It should be made clear to the employee that these payments are covered by the employer's dispensation and do not have to be disclosed on the employee's tax return.

27.4.8.2
PAYE settlement
agreement

To avoid the employer having to fill in form P11D and P9D and notify the employee of small-scale or occasional taxable expenses payments and benefits, and the employee then having to declare them on a self-assessment tax return and pay tax on them, the employer can make a **PAYE settlement agreement** with the Inland Revenue. This is a formal contract between the employer and the Inland Revenue under which the employer—not the employee—pays the tax and national insurance on taxable expenses payments and benefits.

27.4.9
Tips

Tips and gratuities are subject to tax and national insurance. If the employer collects a service charge and pays some or all of it to staff, this must be itemised on the pay slip [see **27.1.3**] and the employer deducts tax and NI in the usual way. The same applies to tips added to the restaurant bill and paid by cheque or credit card. If the staff collect and keep their own tips, or if they pool the tips and share them among themselves, each worker is responsible for paying his or her own tax and NI on them through self-assessment.

**27.4.10
LETS**

Organisations which are part of a local exchange trading scheme (LETS) may pay wholly or partly in LETS credits. LETS credits are in general treated by the Inland Revenue as income, and the person who earns them may have to pay tax and national insurance on their value. Receiving LETS credits could also affect eligibility for welfare benefits. Any organisation considering using LETS or other non-money schemes as a form of payment should seek advice from their PAYE office and Letslink UK [see end of chapter].

**27.4.11
Pay on termination
of employment**

Contractual pay in lieu of notice is subject to tax and national insurance in the usual way. Non-contractual pay in lieu of notice is generally treated as damages rather than pay so can usually be paid without deduction of tax and NI [see **30.6.6**].

Statutory redundancy pay is not subject to tax or NI. Contractual redundancy pay is subject to tax and NI, but the Inland Revenue may agree to exempt payments up to £30,000 [see **31.6.4**]. There is no tax of NI on a discretionary payment (one which there is no contractual obligation to make) of money and/or non-cash benefits, such as a car, of up to £30,000 total. Payments which appear to be non-contractual but are given as a matter of course may in fact be contractual, and advice should be sought before making them.

Other payments on termination, for example on retirement, are generally treated in the same was as redundancy payments but advice should be sought from the Inland Revenue.

**27.4.12
Building contracts**

An organisation which spends more than £1 million per year, averaged over three years, on construction work is called a **contractor** and must comply with special tax provisions. Construction work includes the development of new buildings, and the repair and maintenance of existing buildings.   *Income and Corporation Taxes Act 1988 ss.559-567*

A contractor must deduct tax and national insurance from all payments to construction workers, unless the worker holds a valid CIS5 or CIS6 sub-contractor's tax certificate. A contractor can apply to its local tax office to allow local managers to make payments without deducting tax, provided the contracts are for minor repairs or maintenance work and do not exceed £1,000. Inland Revenue IR 14/15 *Construction Industry Tax Deduction Schemes* provides more details.

An organisation with a substantial construction programme under the £1 million annual average threshold may undertake other building work, for example redecorating its existing premises, without realising that it has moved into the 'contractor' category. Failure to deduct tax from payments makes the organisation liable.

**27.5
NATIONAL
INSURANCE**

Employers are required to deduct employees' **class 1 national insurance contributions** (NICs) and pay them to the Inland Revenue, along with an employer's contribution towards each employee's NI. NICs are forwarded to the Contributions Office, which is now part of the Inland Revenue. NI applies to employees aged between 16 and state pension age (currently 60 for women and 65 for men, but to be equalised upwards to 65 for women from 2010 to 2020).

A specified number of NI contributions are needed to entitle employees to certain state benefits. Further information about this is available from any local benefits office or at www.dwp.gov.uk.

Different national insurance rules apply to lecturers and examiners. Self-employed people pay **class 2 and 4 national insurance**.

Although national insurance and income tax are both collected under PAYE, they are covered by different legislation. This has given rise to contradictory rulings and inconsistencies in what is subject to tax and what is subject to NI. Tax and NI are now being brought into line with each other, and over time the anomalies should disappear.

27.5.1
Limits and
thresholds

The **lower earnings limit** (LEL) for national insurance is £72 per week (£312 per month, £3,744 per year) in tax year 2001-02. Statutory sick pay, statutory maternity pay and redundancy pay are available only to employees who earn at least the NI lower earnings limit.

The **earnings threshold** at which NI contributions (NICs) become payable is £87 per week (£377 per month, £4,525 per year) in 2001-02. From April 2001 the tax and national insurance thresholds are, for the first time, aligned at £87 p.w.

The **upper earnings limit** (UEL) is £575 per week (£2,491 per month, £29,900 per year) for each employment in 2001-02. The UEL is the point at which employee's NICs stop. There is no upper limit for employer's NICs.

If an employee has more than one employment with earnings above the earnings threshold, NI is payable in each. But an employee who is already paying the full employee's NICs (up to the upper earnings limit) in another job can apply to the Contributions Office for form CA2700. The Inland Revenue will then advise the employer if employee's NICs do not need to be deducted. Form CA2700 only lasts for one tax year so the employee must apply for it each year.

27.5.2
Employee's NI
(primary)
contributions

Employee's class 1 NICs are also called **primary NICs**. The rate for the employee's NICs depends on whether the employee is a member of an occupational pension scheme which is contracted out of SERPS, the state earnings-related pension scheme (to be renamed state second pension or S2P from April 2002) [see **27.9.3.2**].

For employees with weekly earnings above the earnings threshold, employee's NICs in 2001-02 are 10% on earnings from the threshold to the upper earnings limit if the employment is not contracted out, or 8.4% if the employee is a member of a contracted-out pension scheme.

Married women and widows used to be able to pay **reduced liability** class 1 contributions. This is no longer possible, but a woman who had reduced liability on 5 April 1978 is entitled to keep it unless her circumstances change. The rate is 3.85% on earnings between the earnings threshold and the upper earnings limit.

People over state pension age (currently 60 for women and 65 for men) do not pay employee's NICs, but must give the employer a CA4140, CF384, CF381 or some other definite proof of age.

27.5.3
Employer's NI
(secondary)
contributions

Employers are required to make an additional contribution towards each employee's national insurance. **Employer's class 1 NICs** are also called **secondary NICs**. They are sent to the Inland Revenue with the employee's tax and NICs. For employees who are not contracted out of SERPS, the employer's NICs in 2001-02 are 11.9% on earnings above the earnings threshold. There is no upper limit.

For employees in a contracted-out occupational pension scheme the rate is reduced for earnings up to and including the upper earnings limit, but is at full rate for earnings over the UEL.

Although people over pension age do not have to pay employee's NICs [see above], the employer's contribution must be paid in the usual way.

27.5.3.1
Class 1A and 1B
contributions

Where the employer must pay NICs on company car use or other expenses payments or benefits that are subject to national insurance, these are **class 1A NICs**. Where employer's NICs are paid on expenses payments or benefits that are the subject of a PAYE settlement agreement [see **27.4.8.2**, these are **class 1B NICs**.

27.6
SICK PAY

Most employees are entitled to 28 weeks of **statutory sick pay** (SSP) from their employer in each **period of incapacity for work** due to illness or injury. The SSP rate in tax year 2001-02 is £62.20 per week. This cannot generally be recovered from the Contributions Office, but in some cases the employer may be able to recover it [see **27.6.1**]. Employees who are not entitled to SSP may be entitled to **incapacity benefit**, which is paid through the local benefits office.

Tax and national insurance are payable on SSP. Detailed information about SSP is in CA30 *Statutory Sick Pay Manual for Employers*, free from the Inland Revenue.

Most voluntary sector employers also give **contractual sick pay**. SSP and incapacity benefit are assumed to count towards contractual entitlement, but some organisations specify that contractual entitlement is in addition to state benefits. For example a contractual entitlement to half pay would be made up of SSP plus additional pay to bring the total to half pay. This is different from an entitlement to 'SSP or incapacity benefit plus half pay'. The statement of employment particulars or written contract [see **23.5.3** and **24.22**] must specify sick pay entitlement.

27.6.1
Recovering SSP

Under the **percentage threshold scheme**, statutory sick pay can be recovered from the Contributions Office if an employer's total SSP costs in any month are more than 13% of the total national insurance class 1 contributions (employees' and employer's combined) for the month. NI class 1A and 1B contributions [see **27.5.3.1**] are not included in this calculation. The amount recoverable is worked out by subtracting the 13% figure from the total SSP paid in the month.

27.6.2
Sickness records

Because statutory sick pay can generally not be recovered, there is little incentive to deal with the paperwork, and many employers are lax about sickness records. However such records are essential:

- if the employer has high SSP payments and is entitled to recover some from the Contributions Office [see above];
- if an employee is ill for more than 28 weeks and becomes eligible for incapacity benefit from the Benefits Agency;
- to ensure the employer has adequate absence and medical records for personnel purposes and to help the employer determine whether the employee may be legally disabled and entitled to the protection of the Disability Discrimination Act [see **25.5**].

Employers must keep SSP records for at least three years. **Form SSP2**, available from the Contributions Office, may be used for absence records but does not have to be.

The SSP regulations do not specify what proof of incapacity to work must be kept. But the employer needs to be able to prove to the Contributions Office or Benefits Agency, if required, that every person to whom SSP was paid was genuinely unable to work. It is sensible, but is not legally required, to require employees to provide an employee's statement of sickness (**form SC2**) for any absence lasting four to seven days, and a medical certificate for an absence of more than a week.

Sickness records constitute **sensitive personal data** and must comply with the relevant provisions of the Data Protection Act [see **38.3.4**].

27.6.3
Entitlement to SSP

27.6.3.1
Qualifying days

An employer who operates statutory sick pay only has to pay SSP for absence on **qualifying days**. These are the days (at least one per week) when the employee normally works, and should be agreed between the employer and employee. They may be included in the written contract of employment [see **24.22**] but do not have to be. Special arrangements apply if the employer and employee agree that there are no days on which the employee is normally required to work, or cannot agree the normal working days.

27.6.3.2
Period of incapacity for work

A **period of incapacity for work** (PIW) exists when an employee is too ill to work for at least four days, even if these are not normal working days. Each PIW starts a new period of entitlement unless it occurs within eight weeks of a previous PIW. In this case the two are linked to form one **linked PIW** and there is no new period of entitlement.

27.6.3.3
Period of entitlement

A **period of entitlement** starts on the first day of the PIW. The first three qualifying days in a period of entitlement are **waiting days**. No SSP is payable for waiting days.

A period of entitlement ends when:
- the employee is fit to return to work;
- the employee ceases to send in doctor's certificates;
- the employee's maternity pay period starts;
- the employee ceases to be employed by the employer;
- the employee reaches maximum SSP entitlement of 28 weeks payment in the PIW;
- a linked PIW lasts for three years; *or*
- the employee is detained in legal custody.

If an employee is dismissed and the main or only reason for the dismissal was to avoid paying SSP, the employer will have to continue paying SSP until the entitlement would have ended for another reason. If an employee leaves and SSP was paid in at least one of the eight weeks prior to the end of the contract, the employer should provide **form SSP1(L)** if the employee requests it.

In each PIW the maximum entitlement is 28 weekly payments. After this the employee receives incapacity benefit from the Benefits Agency.

27.6.3.4
Entitlement during pregnancy and after childbirth

A pregnant woman who is unfit for work is entitled to SSP until her entitlement to statutory maternity pay begins [see **27.7.2**]. During the 18-week period of entitlement to SMP she cannot receive SSP even if her illness is completely unrelated to the pregnancy or childbirth.

27.6.3.5
Eligibility

An employee is **excluded** from SSP if, on the first day of the period of incapacity for work [see **27.6.3.2**], he or she:
- had average weekly earnings for the past eight weeks of less than the national insurance lower earnings limit (£72 in 2001-02);
- was aged under 16 or over 65;
- had received a national insurance sickness, invalidity or maternity benefit within the previous eight weeks;
- had reached maximum entitlement for SSP;
- had provided a **leaver's statement**, form SSP1(L), showing that 28 weeks SSP had already been paid by a previous employer, and there were less than eight weeks since the last date of SSP shown on the statement; *or*
- was in custody.

If an employee is not entitled to SSP the employer must provide **form SSP1**, available from a local benefits office, which will enable the employee to claim incapacity benefit. The exclusion lasts throughout the period of incapacity and subsequent linked periods.

A woman is disqualified from receiving SSP if on the first day of the PIW she is within the 18 weeks when she is entitled to statutory maternity pay [see **27.7.2**]. This applies even if she has returned to work during the 18-week period, or if the sickness is completely unrelated to pregnancy or childbirth. She reverts to receiving SMP or maternity allowance, and can then be reconsidered for SSP entitlement if she is still ill when the 18-week SMP period ends.

An employee on a fixed-term contract of three months or less who has not been employed for longer than 13 weeks is excluded from SSP. Separate contracts with eight weeks or less between them are counted together for this purpose.

A new employee who has done no work for this employer is excluded unless he or she had a contract with this employer during the previous eight weeks.

SSP is not payable during a stoppage due to a trade dispute, unless the employee can show that he or she was not directly involved in it.

27.7
MATERNITY PAY

Most pregnant women who are employed are entitled to **statutory maternity pay**. Those who are not are normally entitled to **maternity allowance**, which is paid through the Benefits Agency rather than through the employer. Information is in CA29 *Statutory Maternity Pay Manual for Employers*, available from the Inland Revenue.

If an employer has a **contractual** obligation to pay more than SMP, SMP makes up part of this payment. Only the SMP part of the payment can be recovered from the Contributions Office [see **27.7.4**].

27.7.1
Eligibility for SMP

The **qualifying week** for SMP is the 15th week before the **expected week of childbirth** (EWC, also called **expected week of confinement**). A week runs from Sunday to Saturday. To be eligible for SMP, a pregnant woman must:

* have continuous employment [see **23.4.6**] of at least 26 weeks continuing into the qualifying week;
* have average weekly earnings of not less than the national insurance lower earnings limit (£72 in 2001-02) for the eight weeks up to and including the qualifying week;
* still be pregnant at the 11th week before the EWC, or have had the baby by then;
* notify the employer of the date her maternity pay period is due to start at least 21 days beforehand or, if that is not reasonably practicable, as soon as possible;
* not be working for the employer [see below]; *and*
* give the employer medical evidence of her pregnancy (**form Mat B1**) at least 21 days before maternity leave and maternity pay begin.

'Must not be working for the employer' means that the woman must:

* be on leave, even if the leave is for sickness or another reason unconnected with the pregnancy;
* have resigned after the beginning of the qualifying week for a reason wholly or partly connected with her pregnancy; *or*
* have been dismissed by the employer or had her employment terminated without her consent, for example by redundancy, after the beginning of the qualifying week.   *Statutory Maternity Pay (General) (Modification and Amendment) Regulations 2000 [SI 2000/2883]*

Provided she meets all the necessary requirements, the woman is entitled to statutory maternity pay from the employer even if she gives notice that she does not intend to return to work. If she is not entitled to SMP she should be given **form SMP1** so she can claim maternity allowance from the Benefits Agency.

27.7.2
Maternity pay period

SMP cannot start until the beginning of the 11th week before the EWC unless the baby is born before then. If the woman wants to continue working, SMP can be postponed for any period until the birth.

SMP is payable only for weeks when the woman does no work at all for the employer. If the woman works for another employer before the birth, the first employer remains liable for her SMP. If she works for another employer after the birth, the first employer's liability for SMP ends. If she returns to work before the end of the SMP period, she no longer receives SMP.

SMP remains payable even if the child is stillborn or dies after birth.

**27.7.3
SMP rates**

SMP is payable for a total of 18 weeks. It is paid at the **higher rate** for the first six weeks, then **lower rate** for the remaining 12 weeks. The higher rate is 90% of the woman's normal weekly earnings during the eight weeks up to and including the last payday before the end of the qualifying week. The lower rate is £62.20 in 2001-02.

At the time of writing (early 2001) the government had announced that maternity pay would be extended to 26 weeks from April 2003, and would go up to £75 from April 2002 and £100 from April 2003.

If a backdated pay increase is awarded which increases the employee's normal weekly earnings during the relevant period, her normal weekly earnings must be recalculated and any SMP arrears must be paid to her.

SMP is subject to tax and national insurance in the usual way. There is nothing to stop it being paid in a lump sum, but this could create problems if the woman subsequently becomes ineligible for SMP, for example because of working for another employer after the birth.

**27.7.4
Recovering SMP**

Unlike SSP, the employer can recover SMP from the Contributions Office by deducting the relevant amount from its PAYE payments.

The amount which can be recovered is generally 92% of the gross (pre-tax and NI) SMP paid to the woman (tax year 2001-02). However an employer can claim 105% of the SMP if it qualifies for **small employer's relief** (SER). SER is available if the employer paid, or was liable to pay, £20,000 or less gross class 1 national insurance contributions in the previous tax year (to be increased to £40,000 from April 2002). Class 1A and 1B contributions [see **27.5.3.1**] do not count towards this total. The 105% allows small employers to recover not only all of SMP, but also some of the employer's class 1 national insurance on the payment.

**27.7.5
Contractual
maternity pay**

An employer may provide contractual maternity pay higher than statutory maternity pay and/or for a longer period, but cannot recover the additional amounts from the Contributions Office.

If the employee does not return to work after maternity leave, the employer cannot require her to return any SMP. The employee can, however, be required to return some or all contractual maternity pay, provided this is explicit in the contract of employment. An employer might, for example, require her to return all or some contractual maternity pay if she does not return to work, or does not return for a minimum period. Any such minimum period must be reasonable.

Boyle and others v Equal Opportunities Commission [1999] 83 EOR 39 ECJ

**27.7.6
Pension
contributions during
maternity leave**

All rights, including pension rights, continue during ordinary maternity leave [see **28.7.4**]. Pension rights during additional or contractual maternity leave depend on whether the woman has an occupational pension or another type of pension, and on her specific contractual and pension arrangements [see **28.7.5**].

**27.7.7
Paternity and
adoption pay**

At the time of writing (early 2001) the government had proposed two weeks of paid leave for fathers from 2003, at the same rate as statutory maternity pay. It had also proposed that one adoptive parent should be entitled to the same entitlement as for SMP, with the other entitled to statutory paternity pay.

27.8
STUDENT LOAN
REPAYMENTS

Where an ex-student started higher education after August 1998 and is earning over £10,000, student loan repayments are made by deduction from pay. Repayments are calculated at 9% of earnings over £10,000. The employer must not start making deductions until receiving a notice to start student loan deductions (**form SL1**), or receiving from the employee a P45 with a Y in the student loans box. Deductions must be entered on the P11, and are paid to the Inland Revenue along with tax and national insurance.

When an employee for whom student loan deductions are being made leaves, the employer must enter Y in the student loans box on the P45, unless a **stop notification** has been received for the employee.

27.9
PENSIONS

27.9.1
State pensions

People of state pension age are entitled to a **basic state pension** if they (or for married women, their husband) have paid national insurance contributions for the required number of years. The state pension is fixed annually and is not based on the amount earned.

State pension age is 60 for women and 65 for men, but is being equalised between 2010 and 2020. Women born before 6 April 1950 are eligible for their state pension at age 60; those born between 6 April 1950 and 5 April 1955 will become eligible at between 60 and 65; and those born after 5 April 1955 become eligible at 65.

Employees who have paid full rate national insurance contributions for some or all of the period since April 1978 are also entitled to a **state earnings related pension** (SERPS, also called **additional pension**). This is being reduced, and by 2010 will be 20% of average yearly earnings over the 40 years before retirement (adjusted for inflation).

Increasingly, employees need to make alternative arrangements for a retirement pension or look to their employer to do so. But there is no obligation for employees to take out pensions, nor are employers under any statutory obligation to contribute to a pension scheme.

27.9.1.1
State second pension

From 6 April 2002 SERPS will be renamed **state second pension** (S2P). The main change is that the following people will be treated for S2P purposes as if they had earned £9,500 per year:

* people earning more than the national insurance lower earnings limit (£3,744 per year in 2001-02) but less than £9,500;
* carers who throughout the year receive child benefit for a child under six, are entitled to invalid care allowance, or are given home responsibilities protection because they are caring for a sick or disabled person, and who have no earnings or earn less than the lower earnings limit;
* people receiving long-term incapacity benefit or severe disablement allowance who have no earnings or earn less than the lower earnings limit. *Child Support, Pensions and Social Security Act 2000 s.30*

The £9,500 amount is called **deemed earnings**.

For people who have contracted out of SERPS, there will be national insurance rebates and S2P top-ups to ensure they are no worse off than they would have been if they had stayed in SERPS. *ss.31-32*

After stakeholder pensions have become established, the intention is to make S2P pensions flat rate. The objective is to provide an incentive for moderate earners to opt out of the state scheme.

27.9.2
Pension options

Possible pension arrangements are:

* the employee relies solely on SERPS/state second pension;
* the employee stays in SERPS/S2P, but tops up with a **personal pension** [see **27.9.5**] or **stakeholder pension** [see **27.9.6**];

- the employee contracts out of SERPS/S2P and takes out an **appropriate personal pension** (sometimes called a **rebate only pension**) or **stakeholder pension**, under which the Contributions Office rebates to the pension plan part of the employee's and employer's national insurance contributions [see **27.9.5.2**];

- the employer organises a **group pension plan**, comprising a number of individual personal pensions and/or appropriate personal pensions all taken out with the same pension provider [see **27.9.4**];

- the employer provides an **occupational pension scheme**, which the employer decides is either additional to SERPS/S2P or contracted out of SERPS/S2P [see **27.9.3**].

An employee cannot be required to join a pension arrangement.

Information about pensions is provided by the Inland Revenue, the Financial Services Authority, the Occupational Pensions Regulatory Authority and the Pensions Advisory Service [see end of chapter]. It is also provided by solicitors, accountants and a very wide range of financial advisors, some of whom are tied to particular companies or products and cannot provide independent advice.

27.9.3
Occupational pension schemes

Occupational pension schemes, sometimes called **employer's** or **company pension schemes**, are offered by employers. They are regulated by the Occupational Pensions Regulatory Authority.

Employees who are trustees of a scheme have a statutory right to paid time off for pension scheme business.

Employment Rights Act 1996 ss.58-60

27.9.3.1
Final salary or money purchase

An occupational pension scheme may be:

- **final salary** (also called **defined benefit** or **salary related**), giving a pension based on the employee's salary at or near retirement and how long he or she was a member of the scheme; or

- **money purchase** (also called **defined contribution**), where the contributions paid into the scheme are invested and on retirement are used to buy a pension, so the amount depends on the value of the investment and the cost of purchasing an annuity (to provide a regular pension) at the time of retirement.

To ensure adequate funds for a salary related scheme, the employer may be obliged to make very large contributions to the scheme well into the future. This commitment should be taken on only after taking detailed legal and financial advice. Organisations with such schemes will also need to take detailed advice about how their potential liability is shown on their balance sheet.

27.9.3.2
Contracted in or out

With a **contracted-in** scheme the employee remains within SERPS/S2P [see **27.9.1**] and pays full national insurance, while taking out a separate pension through the occupational scheme. The employer might or might not contribute to this.

With a **contracted-out** occupational scheme, the employee gives up the right to SERPS/S2P and the employer and employee pay reduced national insurance contributions. Special rules apply to the amount the employer contributes to the occupational scheme.

27.9.3.3
Contributory or non-contributory

For occupational schemes the employer sets the contribution, if any, to be made by the employee. If the employee is required to contribute, it is a **contributory** occupational pension scheme. If the employee does not have to contribute, the scheme is **non-contributory**.

27.9.3.4
Additional voluntary contributions

An employee who wants to contribute more than the specified amount to an occupational pension scheme may pay **additional voluntary contributions** (AVC) linked to the occupational pension scheme, take out a **free-standing additional voluntary contributions** (FSAVC) plan with any insurance company, or (subject to rules about maximum levels) contribute to a **stakeholder pension** [see **27.9.6**].

**27.9.3.5
Tax relief on pension contributions**

Employees get tax relief [see **27.4.2.1**] on contributions to occupational pension schemes, up to a limit based on the percentage of the employee's salary represented by employee's and employer's contributions to the pension. The maximum contribution to an occupational pension scheme (including additional voluntary contributions and free-standing additional voluntary contributions) on which tax relief can be claimed is 15% of salary, with a maximum salary of £95,400 (in 2001-02).

From 6 April 2001 pension contributions are made net of tax (after tax has been deducted) and the pension provider reclaims the tax from the Inland Revenue.

**27.9.3.6
National insurance contribution**

If the occupational pension scheme is not contracted out of SERPS/S2P, there is no reduction in national insurance contributions for the employer or employee.

If the scheme is contracted out, the employee and employer pay national insurance contributions at the contracted-out rate [see **27.5.3**]. The employer must generally contribute to the scheme an amount no less than the difference between the full and contracted-out NI rates.

**27.9.3.7
Occupational pensions and sex equality**

Occupational pension schemes with different pension ages for men and women contravene the requirement for men and women to receive equal pay for work of equal value, so men and women must be allowed to take their pension at the same age.

Barber v Guardian Royal Exchange Assurance Group [1990] 2 All ER 660

**27.9.3.8
Occupational pensions and part-time workers**

Part-time workers were traditionally excluded from many occupational pension schemes, but the European Court of Justice held that this constituted indirect sex discrimination [see **25.2.4**].

*Bilka-Kaufhaus GmbH v Weber von Hartz [1986] IRLR 317 ECJ;
Vroege v NCIV Instituut voor Volkshuisvesting BV, C-57/93 [1994] IRLR 651 ECJ*

Further ECJ and House of Lords rulings on the period of eligibility held that part-timers are eligible for occupational pension rights back to 8 April 1976, when the first relevant ruling was made under the Equal Treatment Directive. *Shirley Preston & others v Wolverhampton Healthcare NHS Trust & others (ECJ 16/5/2000) C-78/98; [2001] 96 EOR 44 HL*

Part-time workers are therefore entitled to access to the employer's occupational pension scheme back to 1976 (or to whenever their employment with the employer started, if later), provided they are still employed by the employer, or made a tribunal claim for membership of the occupational scheme within six months of leaving the employer. If the pension scheme is or was contributory, the employer may require the worker to make contributions for the relevant period.

From 1 July 2000, employers who operate occupational pension schemes or make any other pension provision must provide it to part-time workers on the same basis as full-timers who are engaged in broadly similar work under the same type of contract (open-ended, fixed-term etc), unless there is an objective reason for not doing so.

Part-time Workers (Prevention of Less Favourable Treatment) Regulations 2000 [SI 2000/1551]

**27.9.3.9
Problems of occupational schemes**

An occupational pension scheme may be expensive to administer, so a scheme for an individual employer is likely to be suitable only if at least 100 employees join. This problem can be overcome by joining an industry-wide scheme [see **27.9.3.10**].

For employees, a problem with an occupational scheme is that when they move to another employer, they cannot continue contributing to the scheme. Depending on the scheme, the options will be:

- to leave contributions in the scheme;
- to get a refund of their contributions to the scheme, less administrative costs and tax, if they leave within two years of joining the scheme; *and/or*
- to transfer contributions to the new employer's occupational scheme or to a personal pension plan [see **27.9.5**].

Where members of the Local Government Pension Scheme are transferred to the private sector as a result of privatisation or contracting out of public sector services, the new employer may apply to LGPS for **admitted body** status. If the employer is admitted, relevant employees are able to remain in LGPS.

**27.9.3.10
Industry-wide schemes**

Some voluntary organisations may have access for their staff to an occupational pension scheme run by a local authority, an umbrella voluntary sector body such as the National Housing Federation, or a similar body. Other schemes such as those run by the Pensions Trust (020-7636 1841; www.thepensionstrust.org.uk) and London Pension Funds Authority (020-7369 6000; www.lpfa.org.uk) are available solely for voluntary and charity sector employees.

If an employee moves to a new employer who is also a member of the scheme, the employee can stay within the scheme.

**27.9.3.11
Socially responsible
investment**

From 3 July 2000, trustees of occupational pension schemes must state their ethical and environmental policies in their annual statement of investment. They are not required to operate a socially responsible investment policy, but the availability of information about their policies may make it easier for organisations to choose a pension provider, or to influence their provider.

**27.9.4
Group personal
pension plans**

A group personal pension plan is not an occupational pension scheme, but is a personal pension plan [see below] arranged by the employer for a group of employees. Because a number of staff join the same personal pension plan, administrative costs are reduced and more of the contribution can be invested towards the pension. The employer may be able to negotiate a return of some or all of the commission, which can also be used to enhance benefits.

**27.9.5
Personal pension
plans**

Any employee can take out a personal pension with an insurer or other provider. All personal pension plans are **money purchase**, providing benefits based on the amount of money in the fund at retirement and the cost of buying an annuity at the time of retirement.

Some employers contribute a fixed percentage of the employee's salary to a personal pension, or a fixed percentage up to a maximum amount. Part-time workers must be offered contributions on the same basis as a comparable full-time worker, unless there is an objective reason for not doing so [see **25.12**].

Personal pension plans are not linked to a particular employment, and can be maintained regardless of changes during the person's working life. But a future employer which has its own occupational pension scheme or group personal pension plan might not be willing to contribute to an individual personal pension plan.

**27.9.5.1
Tax relief on pension
contributions**

Contributions are made to personal pension plans net of tax (after tax has been deducted). The insurer recovers from the Inland Revenue the basic rate tax which the employee has paid on her or his contribution, and applies the money to the employee's pension fund. A taxpayer who pays higher rate tax [see **27.4**] can recover the additional tax through self-assessment.

The maximum contribution on which the Inland Revenue will allow tax relief is on a sliding scale based on the person's age, ranging from 17.5%

of earnings at age 35 or less to 40% of earnings at age 61 and over. Tax rules vary depending on the start date of the employee's most recent employment, but for most employees the maximum earnings which can be taken into account are £95,400 (tax year 2001-02).

Booklet IR78 *Personal Pensions: A guide for tax* from the Inland Revenue explains tax on personal pensions.

27.9.5.2
National insurance and contributions

With an **appropriate personal pension plan** (an approved contracted-out plan, sometimes called a **rebate only** plan), the employee gives up the right to SERPS/state second pension from the date of contracting out. Unlike contracted-out occupational pension schemes, the employee and employer continue to pay full national insurance contributions. The Contributions Office then contributes the difference between the reduced and full rates (the **NI rebate**) to the employee's pension plan.

27.9.6
Stakeholder pensions

A **stakeholder pension** is a form of personal pension intended primarily for employees earning between £10,000 and £20,000, but also available to others. The rules are set out in the **Welfare Reform and Pensions Act 1999** and the **Stakeholder Pension Schemes Regulations 2000** *[SI 2000/1403]*. Comprehensive and comprehensible information is available from the Occupational Pensions Regulatory Authority [see end of chapter].

Stakeholder pensions are intended to be low cost, good value, portable and accessible. The government's intention is to encourage people who might not ordinarily take out a pension to do so, in order to reduce dependence on SERPS/state second pension.

From 8 October 2001 all employers who are not exempt must offer access to a stakeholder pension scheme for all relevant employees. Even where the employer does not have to offer a scheme, or does not have to offer it to certain employees, it may do so voluntarily.

There is no obligation for the employer to make a contribution to the scheme, although it may choose to do so. It is likely that in the longer term, the government will make employer contributions obligatory.

27.9.6.1
Exempt employers

An employer is exempt from having to provide access to a stakeholder pension scheme if:

- the employer has fewer than five employees;
- all employees earn below the national insurance lower earnings limit (£72 per week in 2001-02);
- the employer offers an occupational pension scheme [see **27.9.3**] which all employees, except those aged under 18 or within five years of retirement, are eligible to join within a year of starting work; *or*
- the employee offers all employees, as a contractual right, personal pension arrangements that meet certain criteria.

The personal pension criteria that must be met are:

- the employer agrees to contribute at least 3% of basic pay (pay calculated before tax, national insurance etc, but excluding commission, overtime and bonuses) into a personal pension on the employee's behalf;
- the employer offers a payroll deduction facility to members of the scheme; *and*
- the scheme imposes no penalties on employees who transfer out of the scheme or stop making contributions.

The employer can make its personal pension contributions conditional on the employee contributing the same amount, up to 3% of basic earnings. The employer can contribute more than 3% but cannot require the employee to do this. For arrangements in place before 8 October 2001, matching may be allowed at any rate that has been agreed between the employee and employer.

27.9.6.2
Relevant employees

Unless the employer is exempt, access to a stakeholder pension must be offered to every employee who:

- is not eligible to join an existing occupational pension scheme [see **27.9.3**] within 12 months of starting work with the employer (unless the reason for ineligibility is that the employee is under 18 or is within five years of the normal pensionable age for the scheme);

- has been continuously employed for more than three months; *and*

- has had earnings at or above the national insurance lower earnings limit [see **27.5.1**] for three consecutive months.

The only exception is an employee who is not eligible to make contributions because of a restriction imposed by the Inland Revenue.

Apart from some government employees, stakeholder pension contributors must be resident in the UK.

27.9.6.3
Identifying a scheme

By 8 October 2001 all employers, except those who are exempt or who did not have five or more employees in the three months up to that date, must consult relevant employees and designate a registered stakeholder pension scheme. The consultation process is not set down in the legislation, so employers can consult relevant employees in any appropriate way, or may consult all employees.

Where the number of employees increases to five in the three months before 8 October 2001, the employer must designate a scheme within three months from the date the number of employees reached five. After 8 October 2001, an employer who ceases to be exempt has three months to comply. There are penalties of up to £50,000 for failure to provide or operate a stakeholder pension scheme.

Registered schemes are listed on the Occupational Pensions Regulatory Authority's website [see end of chapter], but the organisation should seek independent financial advice before choosing one. Some scheme providers can set up payroll deduction facilities as part of their service, which may be helpful for small organisations. The employer can, if it wishes, designate more than one scheme.

The employer must then:

- provide employees and organisations representing them with basic information about the scheme;

- offer payroll deductions from employees' earnings;

- pay the deductions to the stakeholder pension scheme provider within 19 days from the end of the month in which the deductions are made;

- maintain records of employee deductions and payments to the scheme;

- check from time to time that the scheme is still registered with OPRA.

The employee can choose whether to opt in or out of SERPS/state second pension. For opted-out contributors, national insurance rebates operate in the same way as for appropriate personal pensions [see **27.9.5.2.**].

An employee can change the amount of his or her contribution once in any six-month period, by giving notice to the employer. The employer may, if it wishes, agree to accept more frequent changes.

Employees can choose to join a different scheme, in which case they will have to make their own payment arrangements unless the employer agrees to make deductions for that scheme. Employees can also choose not to join any scheme, and can change their mind at any time.

27.9.6.4
<u>Tax treatment</u>
<u>and concurrency</u>

Contributions to stakeholder pensions are made net of tax, and the pension provider reclaims basic rate tax from the Inland Revenue. The maximum that can be paid into a stakeholder pension is £3,600 per year, including tax (tax year 2001-02).

Concurrency means being able to contribute to a stakeholder pension scheme even if the person is already contributing to another type of pension scheme. The tax relief rules [see **27.9.3.5** and **27.9.5.1**] apply to the total contributions.

The only people who cannot contribute to a stakeholder pension as well as another scheme are:

- 'controlling' company directors who are members of their company's final salary occupational pension scheme [see **27.9.3.1**];
- employees who are members of their employer's occupational pension scheme and have earned more than £30,000 in each of the last five years.

FOR FURTHER INFORMATION

Income tax and national insurance. Local Inland Revenue PAYE office

Inland Revenue/Contributions Office helpline: 0845-7143 143;
www.inlandrevenue.gov.uk

A Practical Guide to PAYE for Charities, by Kate Sayer (Directory of Social Change, 020-7209 5151; www.dsc.org.uk)

Maternity pay. Maternity Alliance: 020-7588 8582; www.maternityalliance.org.uk

Minimum wage. Department of Trade and Industry helpline: 0845-6000 678;
www.dti.gov.uk/er/nmw and www.tiger.gov.uk

Lets. Letslink UK: 020-7607 7852; www.letslink.org

New employers. Inland Revenue helpline: 0845-60 70 143

Pensions (including stakeholder pensions). Financial Services Authority: 0845-606 1234; www.fsa.gov.uk

Occupational Pensions Regulatory Authority (OPRA): 01276-627600; www.opra.gov.uk
and www.stakeholder,opra,gov.uk

Pensions Advisory Service (OPAS): 020-7233 8080; www.opas.org.uk

State pensions. Department for Work and Pensions information line: 020-7712 2171;
www.dwp.gov.uk

Tax credits. Disabled person's: 0845-60 55 858; www.inlandrevenue.gov.uk

Working families: 0845-60 95 000; www.inlandrevenue.gov.uk

Chapter 28
WORKING TIME AND LEAVE

For sources of further information see end of chapter.

Double-underlined section headings indicate additions or significant changes since the first edition.

28.1 WORKING TIME RIGHTS

Rights related to working time are granted in the **Working Time Regulations 1998** and other legislation. The main provisions of the Working Time Regulations, which are intended to protect the health and safety of employees and other workers, are:

- a limit of 48 hours on average weekly working time [see **28.2**], although employees can choose to work longer;

- a limit of eight hours average normal daily working time, with some exceptions, for night workers [see **28.2.4**];

- compulsory health assessments for all night workers [see **36.3.1**];

- minimum daily rest breaks [see **28.3.1**];

- minimum daily and weekly rest periods [see **28.3.2**];

- four weeks paid annual leave [see **28.4.1**];

- record-keeping obligations;

- possible fines and imprisonment for failure to comply with the regulations.   *Working Time Regulations 1998 [SI 1998/1833]*

Some of the rights include **flexibilities**, under which the rights can be changed or even excluded (not implemented). Other rights are absolute and there is no flexibility, even if the worker agrees.

Basic information about working time rights is available from Workright and the DTI website. The Health and Safety Executive information line or local authority environmental health department can deal with questions relating to the weekly and night working time limits and health assessments, and ACAS provides advice on time off, rest breaks and paid annual leave [see end of chapter for contact details].

28.1.1
Who is covered

Working time rights apply to all workers [see **22.1.2**]. This includes all employees, whether full-time, part-time, sessional, temporary or fixed-term, as well as most others who are paid or receive consideration (something of value) for their work. Unpaid trainees are also entitled to working time rights. For agency workers the obligations generally fall on the party which actually pays the worker.

Working Time Regulations 1998 [SI 1998/1833] regs.42, 36

The rights do not apply to people who are genuinely self-employed and doing work for customers or clients of their own business, or to volunteers who are not working under a contract [see **35.3**].

Some working time rights apply differently to **adolescent workers**, who for working time purposes are defined as workers who are above the minimum school leaving age but under 18 [see **28.5**]. The hours of school-age workers are subject to separate legislation.

At the time of writing (early 2001), working time rights did not apply to doctors in training or to workers, except for young workers, where the employer is engaged in the business of transport. Under European directives, rights must be extended to transport workers by 1 August 2003. Junior doctors must have all working time rights other than the 48-hour week by 1 August 2004; the 48-hour week must be implemented by 1 August 2009 or in some cases by 1 August 2012.

28.1.2
Collective and workforce agreements

Some working time rights can be adapted through agreements with individual workers, a **collective agreement** between an independent trade union or unions and the employer, or a **workforce agreement**. A workforce agreement is used where there is no collective agreement or mechanism for setting terms and conditions by collective agreement.

reg.23

A workforce agreement can apply to all the relevant members of the workforce, or only a particular group. **Relevant members** of the workforce are employees and other workers employed by the employer, whose terms and conditions of employment are not covered, wholly or in part, in a collective agreement. A **particular group** is a group of relevant members who undertake a particular function, share a workplace or belong to a department or unit within the employer's business.

sch.1

The workforce agreement may be agreed by the relevant workers or by workers' representatives. Where it is to be agreed by representatives:

- the employer determines the number of representatives;
- the candidates for election must be members of the relevant workforce or particular group;
- a worker who is eligible to be a candidate cannot be unreasonably excluded from standing;
- all the members of the relevant workforce or particular group, as applicable, are eligible to vote for their representatives;
- everyone entitled to vote can vote for as many candidates as there are representatives to be elected;
- reasonable steps are taken to ensure that voting is done in secret and the votes are fairly and accurately counted.

The agreement must be in writing, and for a specified period of not more than five years.

When the agreement has been negotiated, the employer must provide copies to all the workers to whom it is intended to apply, along with information and guidance to help them understand it fully.

The agreement must then be signed by the workforce or group representatives. A representative who is not a member of the relevant workforce or group on the date the agreement first becomes available for signing cannot sign it. If the employer has 20 or fewer workers on the date the agreement first becomes available for signing, it may be signed either by the representatives or by the majority of workers employed by the employer.

28.1.3
Enforcement

The regulations relating to weekly and night working limits and health assessments are enforced by the Health and Safety Executive. The regulations relating to time off, rest breaks and annual leave are enforced through employment tribunals.

All workers are protected against dismissal or other detriment for:

* refusing to exceed a 48-hour week, or refusing to 'agree' to work more than 48 hours if they do not want to;
* refusing to work during rest periods or to give up annual leave;
* refusing to sign a workforce agreement which varies any of the protections in the legislation, or which says they do not apply;
* carrying out activities as a workforce representative;
* making an allegation that the employer is not complying with the regulations.

Any dismissal connected with asserting these rights is automatically unfair, with no qualifying period.

28.2
HOURS OF WORK

Employers must take all reasonable steps to ensure that workers are not required to work more than an average of 48 hours for each seven-day period, unless they have signed an opt-out.

Working Time Regulations 1998 [SI 1998/1833] reg.4

28.2.1
Working time

Working time is time when a person is working, at the employer's disposal and carrying out the worker's activities or duties.   *reg.2*

This includes, for example:

* business lunches;
* travel time where travel is required as part of the work (but not routine travel between home and work);
* time worked at home, where the employer has agreed beforehand that the work can or must be done at home;
* training directly related to the worker's job;
* time spent working abroad, if the worker works for an employer who is based in the UK.

Where there is doubt about what counts as working time, workers (or their representatives) and the employer can agree what counts as working time.

Working time does not include:

* rest breaks when no work is done;
* time spent travelling outside normal working time;
* day release courses;
* training that is not job-related.

A preliminary European Court of Justice opinion in 2000 suggested that in order to be classed as working time, only one of the three elements has to be present: working, *or* being at the employer's disposal, *or* carrying out the worker's activities and duties. If this is upheld the definition of working time will change significantly.

28.2.1.1
On call time

The government's original guidance was that **on call time** was not working time unless the person was actually working. However, guidance issued by the DTI in early 2001 states that time when a worker is restricted to their workplace ('at the employer's disposal') is working time, even if they are not actually carrying out their duties. Time when they are on call but are away from the workplace, and thus free to pursue leisure activities, is not working time. Where the status of on call time is an issue, it may be necessary to seek specialist advice.

28.2.1.2
Unmeasured time

The 48-hour limit does not apply to **unmeasured time**, where a worker's time is not measured or predetermined, or where it can be determined by the worker. So where the number of hours is not set by the employer or in the contract, and is not monitored by the employer, there is no limit. This applies only to managing executives and others with autonomous decision-making powers, family workers, and workers officiating at religious ceremonies.

Working Time Regulations 1998 [SI 1998/1833] reg.20

28.2.1.3
Voluntary overtime

Another aspect of unmeasured time is where a salaried (rather than hourly paid) worker is required or expected to work a stated number of hours or is required to complete a stated amount of work, but voluntarily works additional hours.

In this case all the hours required by the employer—either explicitly, or implicitly where there would be a likely detriment if the worker did not do the extra hours —count towards working time. Hours worked on a genuinely voluntary basis are not counted.

Working Time Regulations 1999 [SI 1999/3372]

To ensure everyone is clear about which hours do and do not count towards working time, it is good practice for the employer to state explicitly that additional hours are not required and are worked voluntarily. The employer then has a duty to ensure that the work it requires can be done within the obligatory hours. A worker cannot be required to work 'voluntary' hours, and cannot be dismissed or subjected to a detriment if he or she refuses.

Alternatively the worker and employer can agree that the worker will opt out of the 48 hour limit [see **28.2.3**]. In this situation it does not matter whether working time is measured or unmeasured.

28.2.2
Average weekly
hours

The **reference period** for computing average weekly working time is generally 17 weeks. Exceptions are:

- where the worker has worked less than 17 weeks, in which case the reference period is the number of weeks they have worked;

- where a different reference period of up to 52 weeks has been agreed in a collective or workforce agreement [see **28.1.2**]; *or*

- where the regulations specify that the reference period can be extended to 26 weeks. This includes situations where the work is done at a significant distance from the worker's home so it is advantageous to work longer hours for a short period, to get it done more quickly; where the work is carried out 24 hours a day, as in residential institutions; where there is a foreseeable surge in activity, such as seasonal work; or where the work is affected by an unusual and unforeseeable event.

Working Time Regulations 1998 [SI 1998/1833] regs.4, 21

Average working time is calculated by adding up the number of hours worked in the reference period, and dividing by the number of weeks in the reference period. If the worker has taken paid annual leave up to the four weeks allowed in the regulations [see **28.4.1**], maternity leave or sick leave during the reference period, those days are not included as part of the reference period. Instead, the days when the person works immediately after the reference period are counted as part of the reference period, up to the total number of days taken off during the reference period. (So if a person took off five days sick leave during the reference period, the first five days they work after the reference period count as part of that reference period.)

Where a person has worked more than 48 hours average during part of a reference period, they are entitled to reduce their hours to bring the total for the period down to 48 hours.

Barber & others v RJB Mining (UK) Ltd [1999] IRLR 285

28.2.2.1
Record keeping

The employer must keep adequate records to show that workers are not working more than 48 hours per week on average. Where the person's weekly hours are well under 48 and they have no other work, there may be no need to keep detailed records. But if they have not signed an opt-out agreement [see **28.2.3**] and their hours are close to 48, or if they have other work which counts towards the 48 hours, the employer may need to keep detailed records and monitor working time quite closely.

28.2.2.2
Workers with more than one job

The 48-hour limit applies to the total number of hours worked, so a person who averages 24 hours in one job and 25 in another is exceeding the limit. *Each* employer has a duty to ensure that workers do not exceed the 48-hour total. This may involve requiring workers to inform the employer if they are doing other work and the average number of hours in that work [see **24.40**]. Alternatively each employer can protect itself by asking the worker to sign an opt-out agreement [see below], under which the worker agrees that they may work more than 48 hours.

28.2.3
Opt-out agreements

An individual worker may agree at any time to opt out of the 48-hour limit, but cannot be forced to do so. The agreement must be in the contract of employment or in another written form. The worker can cancel the agreement at any time by giving at least seven days notice, or such longer notice period—which can be up to three months—as has been specified in the written agreement.

Working Time Regulations 1998 [SI 1998/1833] reg.5

The notice is a simple signed and dated statement saying:

> I [name] agree that I may work for more than an average of 48 hours a week. If I change my mind, I will give my employer _____ days/months notice in writing to end this agreement.

The employer must keep records of who has opted out, but does not need to keep detailed records of the hours worked. An opt-out agreement covers only the 48-hour limit. It does not cover other working time rights.

Working Time Regulations 1999 [SI 1999/3372]

28.2.4
Night work limits

Employers must take all reasonable steps to ensure that the normal hours of work for night workers are not more than eight hours in each 24-hour period, averaged over a 17 week reference period. The reference period can be extended in some situations.

Working Time Regulations 1998 [SI 1998/1833] reg.6

Night time means 11 p.m. to 6 a.m., or such other period as agreed in a collective or workforce agreement [see **28.1.2**] or in a legally binding agreement between the employer and an individual worker or workers. The agreed period must be at least seven hours and must include the period from midnight to 5 a.m.

Night workers are any workers whose daily working time includes at least three hours of night time on most of the days they work, or on a proportion of days as agreed in a collective or workforce agreement, or sufficiently often that working such hours is 'normal' for them.

To calculate average night work:

- add up the normal hours of night work over the reference period;

- calculate the total number of days in the reference period, and subtract from this the number of days of weekly rest [see **28.3.2**] the worker is entitled to over the period (this will be two days per week for workers aged 16 and 17, and one day for workers aged over 17);

- divide the first number by the second number.

Overtime is not included as hours worked unless the worker's contract requires them to work a fixed amount of overtime.

The eight-hour average is not an eight-hour limit. For example, a worker aged over 17 is allowed to work six days in a week. If their normal night hours are four shifts of 12 hours, they normally have 48 hours of night work per week. 48 divided by six is eight, so they are still within the eight-hour average despite working 12 hours on each shift.

All night workers must be offered a free health assessment before they start working nights and on a regular basis, usually annually, while they are working nights [see **36.3.1**]. In some situations night workers may have the right to be transferred to work which is not at night.

28.2.4.1
Special hazards

There is an absolute (not average) limit of eight hours per 24 where night work involves special hazards or heavy physical or mental strain. Such work must be identified in a collective or workforce agreement [see **28.1.2**] or through a health and safety risk assessment [see **36.3.1**].

Working Time Regulations 1998 [SI 1998/1833] reg.6(7)

28.2.4.2
Exceptions and compensatory rest

The night work limits do not apply where:

- the worker's time is unmeasured [see **28.2.1.2**];

- the worker has to work at a significant distance from home, and chooses to work longer hours over fewer days to complete the work more quickly;

- the worker constantly has to work in different places, making it difficult to work to a set pattern;

- the work involves security or surveillance to protect property or individuals;

- the work requires 24-hour staffing, such as hospitals, residential institutions and media;

- there are busy peak periods, for example over the summer or the holiday period; *or*

- there is an emergency or other unforeseeable situation. *regs.20, 21*

In these situations—apart from where the worker's time is unmeasured—the worker is entitled to **compensatory rest** equal to the rest time the worker has missed. Workers over the age of 17 years must be given 90 hours of rest per week [see **28.3.1** and **28.3.2**], and 16- and 17-year-old workers are entitled to more [see **28.5.2**]. *reg.24*

28.2.5
Flexible hours

At the time of writing (early 2001) the government was considering giving parents of young children a legal right to ask to work flexible hours, and requiring employers to consider such requests seriously.

28.2.6
Sunday working

Apart from those who are employed to work only on Sundays, shop workers cannot be required to work on Sundays, and have the right not to be dismissed, selected for redundancy or subject to any detriment for refusing to work on Sundays. The rights are enforced through the employment tribunal. *Employment Relations Act 1996 ss.36-43*

Where the contract does not require Sunday working but the employer asks the shop worker to do this work and the worker agrees, the worker must sign an **opt-in** agreement. Where the contract requires Sunday working the shop worker may give the employer a signed and dated

opt-out notice. The opt-out does not come into effect until three months after its date. During the notice period the worker must work Sundays if required to do so, and cannot be dismissed or subject to any detriment because of having given an opt-out notice.

28.3
REST

28.3.1
Rest breaks

Workers aged 18 and over are entitled to an uninterrupted 20-minute break when the actual (not average) working day is more than six hours. This has to be during the working day, not at the beginning or end, and should be away from the workstation if the worker has one. The break may be paid or unpaid. The entitlement to a rest break may be modified or excluded (removed) by a collective or workforce agreement [see **28.1.2**].   *Working Time Regulations 1998 [SI 1998/1833] reg.12*

The employer has to ensure workers can take the break, but does not have to make them take it.

Additional breaks may be necessary for health and safety reasons, for example where a worker is engaged in monotonous tasks or computer work [see **36.4.7**]. The employer may make these breaks obligatory.

The same exceptions and compensatory rest rules apply to rest breaks as to night work [see **28.2.4.2**].

Workers under age 18 are entitled to longer breaks [see **28.5.2**].

28.3.2
Rest periods

Workers aged 18 and over are entitled to:

- a daily rest period of 11 consecutive hours between each working day; *and*
- a weekly rest period of 24 consecutive hours in each seven-day period, or two 24-hour periods in each 14-day period.   *regs.10, 11*

The weekly rest period is additional to statutory annual leave entitlement [see **28.4.1**].

The rules relating to daily and/or weekly rest periods may be changed or excluded by a workforce or collective agreement. The same exceptions and rules relating to compensatory rest apply as for night work [see **28.2.4.2**].

Workers under age 18 are entitled to longer rest periods [see **28.5.2**].

28.3.2.1
Shift workers

The 11-hour daily rest does not apply where:

- a worker changes shifts and it is not possible to take the full 11 hours before the new shift pattern starts; *or*
- a worker's hours are split up over the day and it is not possible to have a break of 11 consecutive hours, for example a cleaner who works mornings and evenings.   *reg.22*

Such workers are entitled to compensatory rest [see **28.2.4.2**].

28.4
ANNUAL LEAVE

28.4.1
Entitlement

All workers are entitled to four weeks paid annual leave per year. At the time of writing (early 2001) there was a 13-week qualifying period before a worker became entitled to annual leave, but the government had announced its intention to remove the 13-week requirement and to issue rules about how to calculate entitlement.   *reg.13*

Where a worker is entitled to paid time off for bank or public holidays, these count towards the four weeks statutory entitlement [see **28.4.4**].

Entitlement to additional annual leave is a contractual rather than statutory right. Employers may need to review contracts of employment and contracts with other eligible workers [see **28.1.1**] to ensure contractual provision complies with the statutory requirements.

Special rules apply to school-age workers [see **28.5.3**].

28.4.1.1
Record keeping

There is no statutory obligation for the employer to keep records of annual leave taken, but such records should be kept for management and personnel purposes.

28.4.1.2
Annual leave during sick leave

An employment tribunal decision in March 2000 found that a worker is entitled to paid annual leave even when off work on long-term sick leave and receiving only statutory sick pay or no pay. However there is no obligation on the employer to notify the worker of this right. At the time of writing (early 2001) this decision did not set a precedent, so up-to-date advice should be taken.

Brown v Kigass Aero Components Ltd [2000] 11 Emp LJ 9

28.4.1.3
Compulsory leave

The employer can require a worker to take all or part of their leave entitlement at specified times, for example on bank holidays or during a Christmas or summer shutdown. The employer must give notice in advance, either by specifying the leave date(s) or period(s) in the contract of employment, or by giving notice of at least twice the period of leave to be taken. For example if the employer is requiring the worker to take one day off, two days notice must be given. The notice period can be extended through collective or workplace agreements or contractual arrangements.   *Working Time Regulations 1998 [SI 1998/1833] reg. 15(2)*

28.4.1.4
Pay in lieu of leave

Statutory annual leave cannot generally be replaced by pay or extra pay in lieu of leave, except where a worker leaves or is dismissed during the leave year and has not taken the full leave entitlement [see **28.4.2.2**]. However the employment tribunal has accepted that a person working irregular and temporary hours may agree a specific increase in the hourly rate of pay, to cover paid leave during periods away from work.

Johnson v Northbrook College 25/20/1999 Cas 3 102727/99

28.4.2
Leave year

The leave year is usually specified in the contract of employment or a collective or workplace agreement, or may be agreed between workers and the employer. In the absence of agreement, each leave year starts:

- on 1 October if the worker started work with the employer on or before 1 October 1998;
- on the date the worker started work with the employer, if this is after 1 October 1998.   *WTR 1998 reg. 13(3)*

28.4.2.1
Carry over

Statutory annual leave is available only for the leave year to which it applies. There is no entitlement for untaken statutory leave to be carried over into the next leave year, nor is the employee entitled to payment in lieu of untaken leave. Where the employer allows statutory leave to be carried over it will not be statutory leave for the next year, but enhanced contractual leave.

Contractual leave can be carried over or be replaced by pay if the contract allows or the employer and employee agree.

28.4.2.2
Starting or leaving during the leave year

Where a worker starts or leaves during through a leave year, entitlement is proportionate. A worker who leaves during the year is entitled to pay in lieu for leave not taken, even if dismissed for gross misconduct.

reg. 14

Where a worker leaves during the leave year and has already taken more leave than he or she is entitled to for that portion of the year, a collective or workforce agreement [see **28.1.2**] or the contract of employment may require the worker to 'pay back' the additional time. The agreement or contract may specify that this will be done by working for the relevant amount of time, and/or repaying the employer the value of the additional time taken.   *reg. 14(4)*

A collective or workforce agreement [see **28.1.2**] may allow the employer to make a deduction from pay to recover payment for leave taken in excess of entitlement only if the contract explicitly allows for such a deduction [see **27.1.4**].

28.4.3
A week's leave and weekly pay

Where the normal working week is a specified number of days per week, the statutory annual leave entitlement is four times that number of days. For part-time workers or where the normal working week is a specified number of hours, it may be easier to specify the annual leave entitlement as four times the number of weekly hours.

Weekly pay for the purposes of annual leave pay is determined in the same way as for other employment law purposes [see **27.1.5**]:

- for a worker with regular hours, their pay is the number of hours specified in the contract of employment (excluding overtime, unless the contract requires a minimum amount of overtime to be worked);

- for a worker with variable hours, the average hourly rate of pay multiplied by the average of their normal weekly working hours over the previous 12 weeks;

- for a worker who does not have normal working hours, the average pay received over the previous 12 weeks, excluding weeks with no pay.

28.4.4
Public holidays

There is no statutory entitlement to bank and public holidays, although most voluntary sector employers give contractual entitlement to them. Where there is contractual entitlement, the contract should make clear:

- whether the leave is paid or unpaid;

- if paid, whether bank and public holidays count towards the entitlement specified in the contract, or are additional;

- any requirement or right to work on bank and public holidays, and if so any arrangements for time off in lieu [see **24.19**].

Part-time workers must be given the same rights as comparable full-time workers [see **25.12**, and **24.19** for a sample contract clause].

28.4.5
Notice of leave

Unless specified otherwise in contracts of employment or a collective or workplace agreement, the worker can choose when to take leave but must give the employer notice of at least twice the amount of leave to be taken—so one day's leave requires two days' notice, three weeks' leave requires six weeks' notice etc. The employer can agree to leave with shorter notice.   *Working Time Regulations 1998 [SI 1998/1833] reg.15*

The employer can refuse to allow a worker to take the leave requested. Such refusal is called a **counter-notice** and must be given within a period equivalent to the period of leave. So if the worker requests one day's leave, a refusal must be given within one day of the worker giving notice; if the worker requests three weeks' leave, a refusal must be given within three weeks of the request.

Alternatively an employer can exclude the worker's right to specify holiday dates. This is normally done in the contract of employment, but can be done in a collective or workplace agreement or other legally binding agreement with the worker. In this situation the worker does not have a right to specify dates, so the employer can simply refuse without having to comply with the counter-notice requirements.

28.5
YOUNG WORKERS

Under the Working Time Regulations, **adolescent workers** from school leaving age to their 18th birthday have some special protections.

The rights of **school-age workers**, from 13 to compulsory school leaving age, are set out in the **Children and Young Persons Acts 1933** and **1963**, and various **Children (Protection at Work) Regulations**. Detailed information is available from the local authority education department.

The rules on adolescent and school-age workers do not apply to young volunteers unless they are working under a contract [see **35.3**]. Good practice is generally to apply the rules to all young volunteers.

Specific health and safety rules apply to workers under the age of 18 [see **36.4.2**], and for school-age workers there are rules about the type of work they can do.

28.5.1
Hours of work

The 48-hour weekly limit [see **28.2**] applies to 16- and 17-year-olds in the same way as to over-17s. However at the time of writing (early 2001) the government was consulting on placing limits of eight hours per day and 40 hours per week on their working time, prohibiting young workers from working between 12 midnight and 4 a.m., or prohibiting work between either 10 p.m. and 6 a.m. or 11 p.m. and 7 a.m.

In relation to school-age workers, 13- and 14-year olds cannot work more than five hours on Saturday and weekdays when they are not required to attend school, and those from 15 to school leaving age cannot work more than eight hours. On Sundays the maximum is two hours for all workers from 13 to school leaving age.

Children (Protection at Work) Regulations 1998 [SI 1998/276] reg.2

School-age workers cannot work before 7 a.m. or after 7 p.m. on any day. On a day when they are required to attend school, they cannot work during school hours (9.30 a.m.-4.30 p.m., including the lunch break), and cannot work for more than one hour before school starts, or for more than two hours total.

School-age workers cannot work more than a total of 12 hours during a week when they are required to attend school. During school holidays, the maximum 13- and 14-year-olds can work is 25 hours per week. For 15- and 16-year-olds the maximum is 35 hours.

28.5.2
Rest

A young person under school leaving age who works more than four hours in any day must have a one-hour rest break.

Workers aged 16 and 17 are entitled to a 30-minute rest break when daily working time is more than 4½ hours. If the worker is employed by more than one employer, their total working time is considered when determining whether they are entitled to a rest break.

Working Time Regulations 1998 [1998/1833] reg.12(4),(5)

The exceptions that apply for adult workers [see **28.3.1**] do not apply to young workers. A young worker's right to a rest break can be changed or excluded only if:

- there are unusual or unforeseeable circumstances which are beyond the employer's control;
- the work to be done by the young worker is temporary and must be done immediately; *and*
- there is no adult worker available to do the work instead of the young worker. *reg.27*

Workers aged 16 and 17 are entitled to a 12-hour rest break in each 24-hour period they work. The 12 hours do not have to be consecutive if periods of work are split up over the day or are short. *reg.10(2),(3)*

They are entitled to 48 hours weekly rest in each seven-day period. This cannot be averaged over a fortnight. In some situations a young worker's weekly rest entitlement can be reduced to 36 hours. *reg.11*

A young worker's right to a weekly rest break can be changed or excluded only in unusual and unforeseeable situations [see above], and equivalent time off must be given in the following three weeks. *reg.27*

28.5.3
Annual leave

Workers aged 16 and 17 are entitled to the same annual leave as over-17s [see **28.4.1**]. Workers between 13 and school leaving age must have each year at least two consecutive weeks leave during school holidays.

28.5.4
Study leave

Employees aged 16-17 who are not in full-time secondary or further education and left school with few or no qualifications must be given reasonable paid time off for study or training. Paid time off must also be given to 18-year-olds who want to complete study or training they began at 16 or 17. Further information is available from the Department for Education and Skills [see end of chapter].

Right to Time Off for Study or Training Regulations 1999 [SI 1999/986]

Employers must cover the cost of wages, but government funding is available to help cover the cost of the study or training, and for support costs such as books, equipment, travel or childcare expenses. The local learning and skills council can provide details.

28.6
SICK LEAVE

There is no statutory entitlement to **sick leave**, so an employer can decide how much sick leave to offer, either in the contract of employment or on a discretionary basis. During sick leave employees are likely to be entitled to **statutory sick pay** [see **27.6**], and the employer may offer additional **contractual sick pay**.

If the sickness is legally a disability [see **25.5.1**] and the organisation has 15 or more employees or others working under a contract, the organisation is legally obliged to take all reasonable steps to enable the worker to continue working [see **25.5.4**]. This could include, for example, making changes to job responsibilities, hours of work or place of work, adapting premises or equipment, or providing assistance.

Ultimately, it is up to the employer to decide whether it is necessary to dismiss a worker on the basis of being unable to carry out the work as required, with no other suitable work available [see **30.8.3**]. But it is unfair dismissal to dismiss an employee solely or mainly because he or she is receiving statutory sick pay, and if the sickness is legally a disability it could be unfair dismissal and unlawful disability discrimination to dismiss a worker unless the dismissal is justifiable [see **25.5**].

The fact the an employee is entitled to up to 28 weeks statutory sick pay or a period of contractual sick pay does not prevent the employer from fairly dismissing the employee during that period. But fair dismissal is harder to demonstrate during periods of entitlement to sick pay. Where the organisation has taken out permanent health insurance for the employee and dismissal will deprive the worker of the benefit of the insurance, the courts have said there must be very substantial grounds for such dismissal [see **20.4.3** for more about this].

Workers on long-term sick leave may be entitled to four weeks fully paid annual leave even though they are not at work and are not being paid, or are being paid only SSP [see **28.4.1.2**].

28.7
MATERNITY
ENTITLEMENTS

Information on statutory maternity entitlements is available from the Maternity Alliance [see end of chapter]. These do not need to be set out in the contract of employment, and if they are included advice should be taken to ensure they are summarised accurately.

Many voluntary sector employers have contractual provisions which are different from the statutory provision. Where contractual and statutory provisions differ, the woman may take advantage of whichever is more favourable to her.

It is important to ensure there is no discrimination on the basis of pregnancy or childbirth [see **25.2.6**], and that general contractual provisions are not discriminatory. If an employee is entitled, for example, to training or development opportunities, or to performance appraisal linked to pay rises, she must not be deprived of these simply because she has been on maternity leave. *Caisse Nationale d'Assurance Vieillesse des Travailleurs Salaries v Thibault [1998] IRLR 399 ECJ*

**28.7.1
Time off for
ante-natal
appointments**

All pregnant women are entitled to paid time off for ante-natal care provided by a doctor, midwife or health visitor. This includes medical appointments, relaxation classes, parentcraft classes and other recognised care. *Employment Rights Act 1996 ss.55-56*

Except in the case of the first medical appointment, an employer who requests it must be shown a certificate from a registered medical practitioner, midwife or health visitor confirming the pregnancy, and/or an appointment card or other evidence of the appointment.

**28.7.2
Eligibility**

Only employees are entitled to statutory maternity pay and maternity leave [see **22.1.1** for definition of employee in this context]. This includes part-time, fixed-term, temporary and sessional workers, provided they meet the legal definition of employee, but does not included others who are legally defined as 'workers' [see **22.1.2**].

Statutory maternity provisions involve a number of different dates. These may be based on the length of time the woman has worked for the employer, the expected week of childbirth, the actual week of childbirth, the date maternity leave started, or the date the woman intends to return to work.

28.7.2.1
Dates based on EWC

Eligibility dates are based on the **expected week of childbirth** (EWC—also called **expected week of confinement**). For these purposes a week always starts at midnight between Saturday and Sunday. The main dates, in order, are:

- 16th week before EWC (24th week of pregnancy): a stillbirth after the end of this week gives the woman full maternity entitlement (a live birth gives full entitlement at any time);

- 15th week before EWC (25th week of pregnancy): qualifying week for entitlement to statutory maternity pay [see **27.7**];

- 11th week before EWC (29th week of pregnancy): qualifying week for entitlement to additional maternity leave [see **28.7.5**], and the beginning of this week is the earliest that the woman can start ordinary maternity leave and statutory maternity pay unless the baby is born earlier;

- sixth week before EWC (34th week of pregnancy): maternity leave automatically starts if the woman is absent (even for one day) for a pregnancy-related reason after the beginning of this week.

28.7.2.2
Dates based on
the date of birth

The **compulsory maternity leave period**—the period during which the woman is not allowed to return to work—is two weeks after the actual date of birth.
Maternity and Parental Leave etc Regulations 1999 [SI 1999/3312] reg.8

28.7.2.3
Dates based on actual
week of birth

The week of the birth starts with the Sunday of the week when the birth actually took place. The beginning of the 29th week after the week of the birth is the latest date to return to work for women on additional maternity leave, unless she follows it with another leave to which she is entitled [see **28.7.5**].

28.7.2.4
Dates based on start of
maternity leave

The latest date that a woman can return from ordinary maternity leave [see **28.7.4**] is the first day after 18 weeks of leave, unless the baby was born less than two weeks before.

28.7.2.5
Qualifying period

Another set of dates, based on length of continuous employment [see **23.3.4** for definition] determines entitlement for leave and pay:

- **from the first day** the contract is entered into: entitlement to 18 weeks ordinary maternity leave [see **28.7.4**] and the right to return to the same job;

- **26 weeks** of continuous employment up to and including the 15th week before the expected week of childbirth: entitlement to statutory maternity pay, provided the employee earns at least the national insurance lower earnings limit [see **27.5.1**];

- **one year** of continuous employment ending with the beginning of the 11th week before the EWC: entitlement to additional maternity leave [see **28.7.5**], and in most cases the right to return to the same or another suitable job.

28.7.2.6
Duration of benefits

Ordinary maternity leave is 18 weeks, or until two weeks after the birth if this is later. Statutory maternity pay runs for 18 weeks.

Additional maternity leave runs for 29 weeks from the beginning of the actual week of the birth, and thus overlaps with ordinary maternity leave.

At the time of writing (early 2001) the government had announced that from April 2003:

- ordinary maternity leave (and statutory maternity pay) will be extended from 18 to 26 weeks;
- the qualifying period for additional maternity leave will be reduced from one year to 26 weeks, and additional maternity leave will run for 26 weeks after the end of ordinary maternity leave.

28.7.3
Notice of pregnancy and leave

At least 21 days before she intends to start maternity leave the woman must notify the employer that she is pregnant and the expected week of childbirth. This does not have to be in writing. She must also give notice, in writing if the employer requires, of when she intends to start her maternity leave. The woman does not at this point have to give notice of whether or when she intends to return to work.

Maternity and Parental Leave etc Regulations 1999 [SI 1999/3312] reg.4

If it is not practicable to give 21 days notice, she must give it as soon as reasonably practicable.

If required to do so by the employer, the woman must provide a **Mat B1** certificate from a registered medical practitioner or registered midwife indicating the expected week of childbirth. The woman will receive this when she is approximately 26 weeks pregnant. The right to return to work is forfeited if the employer requires a copy and the woman does not provide it.

28.7.4
Ordinary maternity leave

There are two types of maternity entitlement: **ordinary maternity leave** and **additional maternity leave**. These have different eligibility requirements, last for different periods, have different contractual entitlements during leave and give different rights to return to work. Maternity leave entitlements apply to live births at any time, and to stillbirths after 24 weeks of pregnancy.

Ordinary maternity leave is 18 weeks, or until two weeks after the childbirth if this is later than the 18 weeks. *regs.7-8*

28.7.4.1
Start of leave

Ordinary maternity leave cannot start earlier than the beginning of the 11th week before the expected week of childbirth, unless childbirth occurs before this. In this case the maternity leave period starts on the date of childbirth. If the woman continues working after the sixth week before the EWC, the maternity leave period starts as soon as she is absent from work for one day wholly or partly because of the pregnancy. *reg.6*

28.7.4.2
Rights during ordinary leave

All statutory and contractual rights—including, for example, the right to paid annual leave, a contractual right to a company car, a contractual right to pension contributions by the employer or any other benefits—continue during ordinary maternity leave. The only right that does not continue is the right to receive normal pay (but the woman may be entitled to maternity pay). *Employment Rights Act 1996 s.71*

28.7.4.3
Notice of return

During ordinary maternity leave the woman does not have to give any notice if she intends to return 18 weeks after the date her maternity leave started. But if she intends to return sooner than that, she must give at least 21 days notice. This notice does not have to be in writing.

Maternity and Parental Leave etc Regulations 1999 [SI 1999/3312] reg.11

If the employee does not give 21 days notice and returns to work before the end of the 18-week leave, the employer can require her to remain away from work for 21 days or until the end of the 18 weeks, whichever is sooner. If the woman insists on returning to work, the employer does not have to pay her until the notice or leave period would have ended.

The woman does not physically have to return at the end of ordinary maternity leave if she has notified the employer that she will be taking another leave to which she is entitled, such as sick leave or annual leave, immediately after ordinary maternity leave.

If she decides not to return, she must give notice of resignation in the usual way [see **30.6**]. The contract of employment may require her to return some or all contractual (but not statutory) maternity pay if she does not return, or does not stay for a specified period [see **27.7.5**].

28.7.4.4
Rights on return

After ordinary maternity leave the woman returns to the same job on the same pay and conditions as when she left. If she would have become entitled to an automatic pay increment or any other new rights during the time she was away, she is entitled to them as if she had never been on leave.

Employment Rights Act 1996 s.71

28.7.5
Additional
maternity leave

An employee who has at least one year's continuous employment [see **23.4.6**] up to the beginning of the 11th week before the EWC is entitled to **additional maternity leave**. This lasts for 29 weeks from the beginning of the actual week of birth. Notice must be given in the same way as for ordinary maternity leave [see **28.7.3**].

Maternity and Parental Leave etc Regulations 1999 [SI 1999/3312] regs.5-7

The rather complicated overlap between ordinary and additional leave means that the first 18 weeks of leave are ordinary leave, and any further weeks, up to 29 weeks after the beginning of the actual week of the birth, are additional leave.

28.7.5.1
Rights during
additional leave

For the first 18 weeks of leave, the woman has all contractual rights other than the right to her normal pay [see **ordinary maternity leave**, above]. For the additional period of leave, the only conditions which automatically continue to apply are:

- notice periods for termination of employment;
- the right to redundancy pay;
- disciplinary and grievance procedures;
- any conditions relating to the disclosure of confidential information or the acceptance of gifts or other benefits;
- any condition which says she cannot work for another employer.

reg.17

This means that after the first 18 weeks of leave she does not have a right to a company mobile phone or car, accrual of annual leave entitlement above the statutory four-week minimum, and other contractual rights unless the contract explicitly says that these rights continue during the entire additional maternity leave period.

28.7.5.2
Pension rights during
additional leave

In relation to pensions:

- if she is a member of an occupational pension scheme, the employer must continue to make contributions if she is receiving statutory and/or contractual maternity pay [see **27.7.5**];

Social Security Act 1985 sch.5

- the contract of employment or other pension arrangement may state that the employer will make contributions during additional maternity leave even if she is not receiving maternity pay;

- if she is a member of a personal (including stakeholder) pension to which the employer makes contributions, the employer must continue to make these contributions if the contract of employment or other pension arrangement states that they will be made during additional maternity leave.

28.7.5.3
Notice of return

At any time after 15 weeks from the start of maternity leave, the employer can write to the woman asking for the date the baby was born, and whether she intends to return to work at the end of the additional maternity leave period. The employer must provide information to help the woman calculate when additional maternity leave will end. The woman must reply in writing to the employer's letter within 21 days, giving the date of birth and indicating when she intends to return. Even if she says at this point that she intends to return, she can change her mind later and give notice of resignation in the usual way [see **30.6**].

Maternity and Parental Leave etc Regulations 1999 [SI 1999/3312] reg.12

The woman does not need to give any further notice to the employer if she intends to return 29 weeks after the beginning of the week when the baby was born. If she wants to return earlier she must give the employer 21 days notice of the return date. These and other rules relating to notice are the same as for ordinary maternity leave [see **28.7.4.3**].

reg.11

28.7.5.4
Failure to give notice of return

If the employee fails to reply to the employer's letter asking whether and when she intends to return, the employer may discipline the employee. If the disciplinary hearing reasonably and fairly results in dismissal, the dismissal will not be automatically unfair.

28.7.5.5
Rights on return

After additional maternity leave the woman is entitled to return to the same job or, if that is not reasonably practicable, a job which is suitable and appropriate for her.

Her terms and conditions relating to remuneration must be no less favourable than they would have been if she had not taken ordinary and additional maternity leave.

Other terms and conditions, including those relating to seniority, pay rises dependent on length of service, holiday entitlement above the statutory four weeks annual leave, pension and similar rights, must be no less favourable than they would have been if she had not taken additional maternity leave. In other words those rights continue to accrue during ordinary maternity leave, but not during additional leave (unless the contract or occupational pension scheme arrangements explicitly state that they do continue to accrue).

reg.18

28.7.5.6
Small employers

If the employer and all associated employers [see **26.4.8** for definition] combined have less than six employees immediately before the woman's additional maternity leave ends:

- the right to return to work does not apply if it is not reasonably practicable for the employer to offer the woman her previous job or suitable alternative work;

- the right to return on the same conditions of employment does not apply if it is not reasonably practicable for the employer to offer the same conditions or conditions which are no less favourable than the original conditions. *Employment Rights Act 1996 s.96*

28.7.5.7
Extending leave

Additional maternity leave can be extended only if the contract of employment gives a longer period of leave, or a longer period is agreed with the employer. A woman who wants to take further time off may be able to do so by taking parental leave [see **28.8.1**] or annual leave. A woman who takes parental leave immediately after additional maternity leave has the same rights on return as if she had returned immediately after the 29 weeks.

Maternity and Parental Leave etc Regulations 1999 [SI 1999/3312] reg. 18

If the woman is unable to return because of sickness the employer's usual sick leave rules apply, but legal advice should be sought before dismissing for sickness in these circumstances.

Employment Rights Act 1996 s.82(2)

28.7.6
Part-time working on return

At the time of writing (early 2001) the government was considering giving women the right to return to work part-time or on flexible hours after taking maternity leave, and was also considering proposals to give women the right to work part-time until the child is 16. In the meantime there is no statutory right to work part-time. But if an employer refuses, without objective justification, to allow a woman to reduce her hours, the woman may be able to bring a claim of pregnancy discrimination or sex discrimination.

28.7.7
Maternity suspension

A woman is entitled to **maternity suspension** if she is engaged in work which poses a health risk to her or her baby while she is pregnant, after she has given birth or while she is breastfeeding.

Suspension of Work (on Maternity Grounds) Order 1994 [SI 1994/2930]

She is entitled to full pay and continuation of all her employment rights if she is suspended because of these or other health and safety regulations relating specifically to pregnancy and childbirth, and no suitable alternative work is available.   *Employment Rights Act 1996 ss.66-70*

If she turns down an offer of suitable alternative work she remains employed and keeps her employment rights, but is not entitled to be paid during the period of maternity suspension.

28.7.8
Dismissal during pregnancy or maternity leave

Dismissal solely or mainly because of pregnancy is nearly always automatically unfair [see **30.9.1**]. A significant exception applies to the right to return after additional maternity leave if her employer has five or less employees [see **28.7.5.6**].

Dismissal is also likely to be fair if it is not reasonably practicable for her to return to her old job for a reason other than redundancy, and she has been offered another suitable job and refused it. This applies regardless of how many employees the employer has.   *s.96*

'Suitable' means that the work is suitable for the employee, appropriate for her to do in the circumstances, and on terms and conditions not substantially less favourable to her.

A woman can be dismissed during pregnancy or maternity leave or after childbirth if the reason is, and can be shown to be, totally unconnected with her pregnancy. Similarly, she can be made redundant if it can be shown that the redundancy was unconnected with the pregnancy and there was no suitable alternative work on terms and conditions that were not substantially less favourable to her.

A woman who is dismissed for any reason or made redundant while pregnant or on maternity leave must be given a written notice of the reasons for dismissal.   *s.92(4)*

28.7.9
Dismissal after pregnancy

Even if a dismissal takes place several months after the pregnancy or maternity leave ended, it can be unfair if the reason is related to the pregnancy, for example dismissal because of absence or incapability arising from post-natal depression. Legal advice should be taken before dismissing, or undertaking disciplinary action which could lead to dismissal, in this situation.

28.8
PARENTAL LEAVE

28.8.1
Entitlement

Mothers, fathers who are named on the birth certificate, adoptive parents and others with parental responsibility under the Children Act 1989 are entitled to 13 weeks unpaid **parental leave**. Others who want to take parental leave will need to make a consent order under the Children Act or apply to the courts for a parental responsibility order. An employer can use a workforce agreement [see **28.1.2**] to ease this requirement and allow co-habitees, same-sex parents etc to take parental leave even without a consent or parental responsibility order.

Maternity and Parental Leave etc Regulations 1999 [SI 1999/3312] regs. 13-14

Entitlement to parental leave does not start until the employee has one year's continuous employment [see **23.4.6**].

At the time of writing (early 2001) the leave was available only for children born or adopted on or after 15 December 1999, but the government had announced that it would be extended, on a backdated basis, to cover children who were under five on that date.

The leave is available for each parent and each child, so if a couple has twins and another child, the mother and father are each entitled to 39 weeks leave (3 x 13 weeks). Where the child is disabled (has been awarded disability living allowance), the government had announced its intention to extend parental leave from 13 weeks to 18 weeks.

The leave must be taken before the child's fifth birthday (or 18th if the child is disabled), or within five years of the child being placed with the family for adoption (or until the adopted child's 18th birthday, if this is earlier). *reg. 15*

At the time of writing (early 2001) the government was considering proposals to make some or all of the leave paid.

Requests for parental leave do not have to be in writing, but to avoid confusion it is sensible for the employer to require requests to be written. Parental leave is a right to take time off to look after a child; if it is used for any other purpose the employer may be able to discipline the employee.

It is unlawful to dismiss an employee or subject her or him to a detriment for reasons related to parental leave. *regs. 19-20*

28.8.1.1
Records

There is no obligation to keep parental leave records. But the leave is cumulative and transfers between employments, so if an employee changes jobs the employer is likely to be asked for details of leave taken. After changing employers, the employee must build up one year's continuity before becoming entitled to the remaining leave.

28.8.2
A week's leave

Where the amount of time an employee is contractually required to work does not vary from week to week, a week's leave is that amount of time. Where the amount of time varies or the employee does not work every week, a week's leave is the weekly average the employee is required to work over a 52-week period. *reg. 14*

28.8.3
Default provisions

Employers and employees can agree through workforce [see **28.1.2**] or collective agreements how the 13 weeks parental leave should be taken. But in the absence of such agreement, **default provisions** apply.

sch. 2

If a provision in a collective or workforce agreement is less favourable to employees than the relevant default provision, the default provision applies. *reg. 21*

All organisations should review contracts of employment to ensure parental leave provisions are no less favourable than the statutory requirements and the default provisions. Where the employer wants to make arrangements which are more advantageous that the default provisions, it should negotiate a collective or workforce agreement [see **28.1.2**].

28.8.3.1
Evidence of entitlement

Under the default provisions, the employer can require the worker to provide evidence of parental responsibility, the child's date of birth and/or placement for adoption, and if applicable the child's entitlement to disability living allowance.

28.8.3.2
Duration of leave

Under the default provisions, leave must be taken in blocks of one week, up to a maximum of four weeks leave in a year for each child. If the leave is to care for a disabled child it can be taken in one-day blocks, or multiples of one day, again up to maximum of four weeks per year.

A 'year' generally starts on the date the parent first became entitled to take leave for that child.

28.8.3.3
Notice and postponement

Under the default provisions, notice of intention to take leave must specify the start and finish dates and must be given at least 21 days before the start date. A father taking time off for the birth for the child must specify the expected week of childbirth and the amount of leave to be taken, and the notice must be given at least 21 days before the start of that week. Similarly an adoptive parent must specify the expected week of placement and the amount of leave to be taken, and must give notice at least 21 days before the start of the placement week.

A request for leave may be postponed by the employer for up to six months where the business cannot cope without the employee. No more than seven days after the request is given to the employer, the employer must give notice in writing of the reason for the postponement and the start and finish dates when leave will be permitted.

Leave cannot be postponed where a father is taking it at the time of or immediately after the child's birth, or if an adoptive parent is taking it at the time of the child's placement for adoption.

Where the employer postpones leave under the default provisions and as a result the child passes its 5th (or 18th, where applicable) birthday, the employee remains entitled to the parental leave.

Maternity and Parental Leave etc Regulations 1999 [SI 1999/3312] reg.15(d)

28.8.4
Rights during leave and on return

Parental leave rights are subject to anti-detriment and anti-dismissal protection.

The employee remains employed during parental leave, but has only the reduced rights that a woman has during and on return from additional maternity leave [see **28.7.5.1** and **28.7.5.5**]. Occupational pension rights are an exception. Unless the contract or pension scheme specifies otherwise, occupational pension rights accrue only if the leave is paid.

regs.17-18

An employee who takes parental leave for a period of four weeks or less, other than immediately after taking additional maternity leave [see below], is entitled to return to the same job.

An employee who takes parental leave at any time for more than four weeks is entitled to return to the same job or, if that is not reasonably practicable, to another job which is suitable and appropriate.

28.8.4.1
Parental leave after additional maternity leave

A woman who takes parental leave for a period of four weeks or less immediately after additional maternity leave is entitled to return to the same job unless it would not have been reasonably practicable for her to return to that job if she had returned at the end of her additional maternity leave, and it is not reasonably practicable for her to return to that job at the end of her parental leave. In that case she is entitled to return to another job which is similar. The exemptions for small employers [see **28.7.5.6**] apply.

**28.8.5
Paternity and
adoption leave**

At the time of writing (early 2001) the government had announced its intention to introduce, from 2003:

- two weeks paternity leave for fathers, paid at the statutory maternity pay rate;

- adoption leave for adoptive parents under which one parent can have the same pay and entitlements as maternity leave, and the other parent can have the same pay and entitlements as paternity leave.

**28.9
TIME OFF FOR
DEPENDANTS**

All employees, regardless of length of service, are entitled to reasonable time off to deal with unexpected or sudden emergencies relating to dependants, or to make long-term arrangements for dealing with the situation. 'Reasonable' is not defined but DTI guidance is that it will generally be a day or two.   *Employment Relations Act 1999 sch.4 pt.2;*
Employment Rights Act 1996 s.57A

There is no right to pay during this leave. For salaried workers the time will generally be paid. For daily or hourly paid employees the contract of employment may state that the leave is paid, or the employer may decide to pay on a case-by-case basis.

A dependant is a spouse, parent, son or daughter; or anyone (other than a tenant, lodger, boarder or live-in employee) who lives with the employee. It could also be someone else, such as a more distant relative or neighbour, who 'reasonably relies' on the employee, for example a neighbour who has no one else to help make arrangements for them if they are ill or injured.

Examples of situations where time off could be taken include:

- if a dependant gives birth, falls ill or has been injured or assaulted;

- arranging longer term care for a dependant who is ill or injured;

- dealing with the death of a dependant;

- dealing with an unexpected disruption or breakdown of care arrangements for a dependant;

- dealing with an unexpected incident involving the employee's child during school hours.

The right is intended to cover only unexpected situations. So if, for example, a child falls ill, this right would give the worker a day or two to take the child to the doctor and arrange childcare. But it would not give the worker the right to two weeks off to look after the child.

There is no need for prior notice, but the employee must tell the employer, in writing or verbally, the reason for the absence as soon as reasonably practical. The employee must also indicate the length of absence, unless this is impossible until the return to work.

An employee can bring a claim in the employment tribunal if the employer unreasonably refuses to allow time off under these arrangements, or has subjected the employee to detriment because of taking or seeking to take leave. A dismissal because the person has taken, or sought to take, justifiable time off is automatically unfair.

All organisations should review contracts of employment to ensure provision for compassionate, childcare and similar leaves are no less favourable than the statutory entitlement. Legal advice may be needed to ensure the various leave arrangements are consistent and clear.

**28.10
TIME OFF FOR
PUBLIC DUTIES**

Employees have a statutory right to time off, which may be either paid or unpaid, for public duties. This right covers duties as a justice of the peace, or as a member of a local authority, relevant health body, relevant education body (including school governing bodies), statutory tribunal, board of visitors to prisons or prison visiting committee, a water and sewerage authority, or the Environment Agency.

Employment Rights Act 1996 s.50

The employer must give reasonable time off to attend meetings of the body and its committees, or to perform duties approved by the body.

The time off must be 'reasonable' for the duties involved and the employer's needs. Disputes are settled by the employment tribunal.

The employer may give a contractual right to pay for such time off [see **24.30**], or pay on a discretionary case-by-case basis, or require the time off to be unpaid. If the employer gives paid time off it may want to limit the number of paid days. The employer and employee should be clear what happens to attendance allowances and other payments received by the employee from the outside body.

Time off is also available for trade union duties [see **32.5**].

FOR FURTHER INFORMATION

Working time rights. Workright: 0845-6000 925

DTI: www.dti.gov.uk/er/work_time_regs/index.htm

HSE infoline (weekly and night working limits, health assessments): 0541-545500

ACAS (time off, rest breaks, paid annual leave): see telephone directory for local office; www.acas.org.uk

Maternity rights. Maternity Alliance, 020-7588 8582; www.maternityalliance.org.uk

DTI: www.dti.gov.uk/er/maternity.htm

Parental leave. DTI: www.dti.gov.uk/er/parental_leave.htm

ACAS [see above]

Study leave for young workers. Training Information Service: 0345-665588; www.dfee.gov.uk/tfst.htm or www.dwp.gov.uk

Time off for dependants. DTI: www.dti.gov.uk/er/time_off_deps.htm

ACAS [see above]

Chapter 29
DISCIPLINARY MATTERS, GRIEVANCES AND WHISTLEBLOWING

Topics covered in this chapter

This chapter explains what has to be in disciplinary and grievance procedures, and provides models. It includes:

For sources of further information see end of chapter.

Double-underlined section headings indicate additions or significant changes since the first edition.

29.1
THE TERMINOLOGY

A **disciplinary matter** is one which involves an employer being dissatisfied with some aspect of an employee's performance or conduct. A **grievance** relates to an employee's dissatisfaction with the employer, the work or another employee or employees.

Whistleblowing refers to raising an issue where an employee believes the employer or fellow employees are acting in a way which is unlawful, falls below proper standards, or is contrary to the organisation's purpose or policies.

29.1.1
Disciplinary

Not surprisingly, given what it is called, disciplinary rules and procedures often seen as being purely about fault and punishment. In reality they should be just as much or more about setting boundaries and guiding staff towards better performance. As such they should not be a last resort, but an integral part of good management practice.

A **disciplinary procedure** or **disciplinary policy** sets out the steps to deal with a disciplinary matter [see **29.4** and **29.6**]. Matters relating to work performance are sometimes set out in a parallel **capability procedure**, which is phrased differently to make clear it is about competence rather than 'discipline'.

The procedure(s) should be accessible, generally in writing, and should be explained to staff with a clear indication of the consequences of breach. The procedure(s) might properly cover, for example:

- matters relating to work performance: quantity of work, quality of work, failure to do work or to meet targets or deadlines;

- matters relating to conduct: lateness, rudeness, unauthorised personal use of the organisation's facilities, offensive behaviour;

- breach of the organisation's policies, procedures and rules;

- matters relating to health and safety.

Disciplinary and capability procedures are management tools, and should not be seen or treated as a judicial procedure. The intention should always be to identify what is going wrong and why it is happening, decide how to put it right, get it put right, and enable the employee and organisation to get on with their work. In addition, good procedures properly followed are a vital part of protecting the organisation from claims of discrimination or unfair dismissal [see **30.8.2**].

29.1.2
Grievance and whistleblowing

Grievance and **whistleblowing procedures** [see **29.7** and **29.8**] set out the steps employees should take to raise matters which concern them, and the steps to be taken by the employer.

29.2
PROCEDURES AND THE CONTRACT

29.2.1
Procedures and statement of particulars

The written statement of employment particulars which must be given to virtually all employees [see **23.5**] or the written contract must indicate who the employee should go to if seeking redress for a grievance relating to her or his employment. If the employer has 20 or more employees on the date the employee's employment begins, the statement or contract must also:

- include disciplinary rules applicable to the employee, or make reference to a document which sets out these rules;

- indicate who the employee should go to if dissatisfied with any disciplinary decision relating to him or her;

- include the steps in making a grievance complaint or disciplinary appeal, or make reference to a document which contains these steps.
Employment Rights Act 1996 s.3

It is good practice even for employers with fewer than 20 employees to give this information. [For sample contract clauses see **24.37-24.39**.]

Any document referred to must be one which the employee has reasonable opportunities to read in the course of employment, or which is reasonably accessible in some other way.

The procedures contained or referred to in the statement of particulars do not need to cover health and safety matters, since these are governed by statute [see **36.2**] and/or must be covered separately in the employer's health and safety policy [see **36.2.6**]. *s.3(2)*

There is no statutory obligation to have a whistleblowing procedure, since the basic rules are covered in the legislation [see **29.8**].

29.2.2
Part of the contract or not?

Employees must be informed about how disciplinary and grievance matters are dealt with, but there is no requirement for the procedure to form part of the contract of employment.

From the employer's point of view, there are considerable advantages in making clear that the procedures are not contractual [see, for example, **24.37** and **24.38**]. As an organisation grows or its management structure changes, it may well need to amend its procedures. If the procedures are part of the contract, any change needs the employee's consent [see **23.7**]. If they are not part of the contract, reasonable changes can be made without consent, although the employer should consult trade unions or employees' representatives before doing so.

More significantly, any dismissal always carries with it the risk of a claim for unfair dismissal [see **30.9**]. With a contractual disciplinary procedure, the employer exposes itself to additional risks of a claim for breach of contract or **wrongful dismissal** [see **30.7**] if it does not follow its procedure exactly as stated.

29.2.3
Conflict between disciplinary and grievance procedures

Procedural difficulties sometimes arise if an employer starts disciplinary proceedings against the employee, and the employee simultaneously raises a grievance against the employer or a fellow employee.

If the matters raised are about separate issues they should be dealt with in logical order, or it may be possible to deal with them simultaneously but in separate proceedings.

If the issues raised in the grievance and disciplinary proceedings are the same or overlapping, it may be sensible to hold a combined session to deal with both matters. However the situation becomes complicated if the disciplinary and grievance procedures operate differently or have different sequences of appeals or compositions of hearing bodies.

If the organisation finds itself in a complex web of disciplinary action, appeals against disciplinary decisions, grievances and/or appeals against grievance decisions it may be necessary to take legal advice to ensure that matters are dealt with properly and fairly.

29.3
GUIDELINES FOR GOOD PRACTICE
29.3.1
The ACAS code and guidelines

The Advisory, Conciliation and Arbitration Service (ACAS) *Code of Practice on Disciplinary and Grievance Procedures* does not have the force of law but must be taken into consideration by any employment tribunal where its provisions are relevant. ACAS can give advice on disciplinary and grievance procedures and issues [see end of chapter].

The ACAS code makes clear that a disciplinary procedure should emphasise and encourage improvements in individual conduct, rather than being seen primarily as a means of imposing sanctions. It does not specify a procedure, because this depends on each employer. It does give guidelines, which are that disciplinary procedures should:

- be in writing;
- specify to whom they apply;
- provide for matters to be dealt with quickly;
- indicate the disciplinary actions which may be taken;
- specify which levels of management have authority to take various forms of disciplinary action, ensuring where possible that immediate superiors do not normally have the power to dismiss without reference to senior management;
- ensure that employees are informed of the details of the complaint against them, and where possible are given all relevant evidence against them prior to the disciplinary hearing;
- ensure employees are given an opportunity to state their case directly to those deciding the matter before decisions are reached;
- be non-discriminatory;
- give individuals the right to be accompanied by a trade union representative or fellow employee of their choice [see **29.3.4**];
- provide that any suspension is normally with pay [see **29.4.3**];
- ensure that disciplinary action is not taken until a full investigation has been undertaken, the employee's explanation has been heard and the investigation shows on the balance of probability that the employee committed the disciplinary offence;
- ensure that any penalty imposed on an employee is explained;
- ensure that except for gross misconduct [see **29.4.12**], employees are not dismissed for a first breach of discipline;

- provide a right of appeal and specify the procedure [see **29.4.14**];
- provide for appropriate confidentiality.

ACAS Code of Practice on Disciplinary and Grievance Procedures s.9

**29.3.2
Suggested
procedure**

The suggested procedure (but this is only suggested, not required) for an offence or problem other than gross misconduct is:

- for a minor offence or problem with work, a verbal warning, or for a more serious matter a written warning, setting out the nature of the offence and the likely consequences of non-improvement and clearly indicating that it is the first stage of the disciplinary procedure;

- a final written warning stating that a further offence or non-improvement may lead to suspension, dismissal or other penalty;

- suspension or notice of dismissal. *ACAS s.12*

The procedure should avoid a fixed requirement that all matters, however serious, must be dealt with initially by a verbal warning. The procedure should be flexible, allowing a written warning or even, for very serious matters, a final written warning as the first warning.

In developing a procedure, a careful balance has to be drawn between the need to be fair, the resources of the organisation, and the demands which might be made on senior managers' or governing body members' time. It is not uncommon for voluntary organisations to develop procedures which are so detailed that they take a disproportionate amount of time. Equally, it is not uncommon for organisations to have procedures which are so vague that vast time and effort (and argument) are put into working out what the procedure actually is.

Models for disciplinary and grievance procedures based on the ACAS recommendations are at the end of this chapter.

**29.3.2.1
Review**

Disciplinary rules and procedures should be reviewed periodically. Amendments should be introduced on reasonable notice, and after consultation with staff representatives. Where procedures form part of the contract, changes will generally require consent [see **23.7.2**].

**29.3.3
Proceedings against
senior staff member**

Even where procedures are clear and workable, they are often unclear about the procedure to be followed when disciplinary action has to be taken against the chief executive or other senior staff member. Attention should be given to this when drawing up the procedure.

**29.3.4
Right to be
accompanied**

Employees and others working under a contract [see **22.1**], including casuals, agency workers, home workers, and freelances who are not genuinely self-employed, have the right to be **accompanied** by a single trade union official or fellow worker of their choice where the matters involved are of a potentially serious nature. In relation to disciplinary matters, 'serious' means they could result in a formal warning or some other disciplinary penalty [see **29.4.7**]. For grievance matters there is a right to be accompanied where the grievance relates to the performance of a contractual or statutory duty by the employer.

Employment Relations Act 1999 ss.10-14

Where the companion is unable to attend, the worker has a right to request that the hearing or interview be postponed for not more than five working days [see **29.4.4.1**]. If the companion is a fellow worker, the employer must allow her or him time off to accompany the worker. There is no obligation on a fellow worker to act as a companion.

The companion has a right to address the interview or hearing, ask questions and confer with the worker, but does not have a right to answer questions on behalf of the worker.

Refusing to allow a companion, or subjecting the employee or companion to any detriment, could lead to an award by the employment tribunal of up to two weeks' pay.

29.3.4.1
Further rights

Some organisations' procedures go further than the statutory requirements. The procedures may, for example, allow workers to be:

- **represented** rather than simply accompanied, so the companion can answer questions on behalf of the worker;
- accompanied or represented by any person, not only a trade union official or fellow worker;
- accompanied or represented by any person who is not a lawyer.

The 'not a lawyer' restriction seeks to avoid the proceedings being dominated by lawyers and becoming too legalistic and costly. However if the organisation has legal representation at a disciplinary interview or hearing this could be seen as depriving the worker of a fair hearing. If the employer is to be legally represented in a particular case, it may wish to allow the worker such representation.

Where the organisation is a **public authority** for the purposes of the **Human Rights Act 1998** [see **60.3.2**], failure to allow the employee an equal right of access to a lawyer may be attacked as a failure to allow **equality of arms** (equality of access to support and information in hearings, tribunals and trials).

European Convention on Human Rights art.6

29.3.5
Non-existent or inadequate procedure

Employers with fewer than 20 employees do not have to have a written disciplinary procedure [see **29.2.1**], and it is not uncommon for larger employers not to have one. Even where there is a written procedure it is often unworkable, generally because the management structure has changed or because the procedure is too vague or cumbersome.

Where there is no written procedure the employer must act fairly and reasonably. Legal advice may be necessary to help ensure that actions are indeed fair and reasonable, especially if the matter is particularly controversial or sensitive or may give rise to dismissal.

Where there is a written procedure but it is unworkable, it may be possible to change the procedure if it is not part of the contract [see **29.2.2** and **23.7**]. Advice should be taken before making any changes if disciplinary action has already started or is about to start.

Where a procedure is part of the contract, changes cannot generally be made without the employees' consent—even if the procedure is outdated or unworkable. It is essential to take advice in this situation. Any disciplinary action which does not follow the contract could give rise to a claim for breach of contract, and a dismissal which does not strictly follow the procedure could give rise to a claim for wrongful dismissal [see **30.7**]. But following the procedure, if it is no longer fair and reasonable, could give rise to a claim for unfair dismissal [see **29.4.10**].

29.4
DEALING WITH DISCIPLINARY MATTERS

The key elements when dealing with disciplinary matters are:

- a thorough investigation;
- an interview or hearing giving the employee a chance to hear the complaint and put her or his side of the matter;
- making a fair and reasonable decision.

Dealing with disciplinary matters is never easy, but it is much easier if the organisation has clear rules, standards and procedures.

29.4.1
Informal warnings

Where an informal warning is given prior to disciplinary action, it should not be a vague 'get your act together' comment. Even informal warnings, like formal ones [see **29.4.8**], should identify the problem, the change required, and the consequences of failure to improve.

It is not necessary to keep a written record of informal warnings but it is sensible to do so.

**29.4.2
Assessing the
situation**

Typically disciplinary action starts when an employee's line manager feels that informal discussions or normal management and supervision procedures are not having the desired effect, or when a breach cannot be dealt with informally.

At this stage the manager should be thinking through the issues, and if appropriate discussing them with his or her manager, the chief executive, the head of the personnel committee and/or the governing body chairperson. The purpose is to clarify what is known about the situation, and to consider the possible implications of starting disciplinary action. Attention should be given to:

- the nature of the problem and why it might be occurring;

- whether it could be occurring for reasons under the employer's control, for example the employee having been given inadequate or conflicting information about rules or work expectations;

- whether it is gross or very serious misconduct requiring very urgent action;

- the steps necessary to investigate the matter fully;

- whether the matter can be fully investigated without the need to suspend the employee;

- the employee's length of service, overall record and any previous disciplinary action;

- whether there are any special factors, for example if the situation is or could be perceived as being linked to taking time off because of a disability or to look after children, the employee's involvement in trade union activities, or anything else which could possibly constitute unlawful discrimination or detriment by the employer;

- whether there is a recognised trade union, and requirements of any procedural agreement or other agreement with the union which needs to be considered and steps taken to comply with it;

- whether dismissal is a possible outcome;

- the likelihood of a tribunal or court claim being brought;

- whether the organisation has insurance to cover employment claims [see **20.4.2**], and if so whether advice must be taken from the insurer before starting any disciplinary action or issuing a warning.

The statutory right to be accompanied [see **29.3.4**] does not extend to discussions which are investigatory. It applies only to hearings at which a warning or other disciplinary penalty could be issued.

**29.4.2.1
Legal advice**

Unless the matter is very straightforward and is likely to be quickly and easily resolved, it is sensible to talk through with the organisation's legal advisors the issues and the procedure to be followed. Advice obtained at this stage can prevent mistakes which could lead to very large costs later.

It is also useful to get feedback from a solicitor or other unbiased third party on the relative seriousness of the issue. It is not always easy to maintain a sense of perspective, and treating an issue hastily or inappropriately could lead to claims for unfair and/or wrongful dismissal.

**29.4.2.2
Investigation**

If necessary the line manager should investigate the matter by interviewing people, taking statements and gathering documentation. Legal advice may be necessary on how to undertake the investigation in the most effective way, and in ways which do not pre-judge the outcome.

**29.4.3
Suspension during
investigation**

In some situations (such as alleged harassment or theft), the employer may consider it inappropriate for the employee to continue working during an investigation. But it is an implied term of a contract of employment that the employer will provide work [see **23.3.4**], so an employee may be suspended only if there is provision for this in the contract of employment [see, for example, **24.39**]. Any suspension must be on full pay unless the contract allows for it to be on reduced pay or no pay. Suspension during an investigation is qualitatively different from suspension as a disciplinary penalty [see **29.4.7**], and it should be made clear that the suspension is not a disciplinary action.

Provision for suspension in the disciplinary procedure does not, in itself, allow the employer to suspend unless the disciplinary procedure is part of the contract of employment [see **29.2.2**]. Suspension where there is no contractual provision for it or for an unreasonable period could entitle the employee to bring an action for breach of contract or constructive dismissal [see **30.4.8**]. In practice such a claim is unusual where suspension is used in a reasonable way and full pay is given.

29.4.4
Notification of interview

If appropriate the line manager should meet with the chief executive or chairperson to clarify the exact nature of the disciplinary complaint. This should then be set it out in a letter to the employee which states the date, time and place of the disciplinary interview or hearing, reminds the employee of his or her right to be accompanied and/or represented at the interview and gives an indication of the possible outcome if the disciplinary interview results in a finding that work or conduct is unsatisfactory. The letter might indicate that a verbal warning, written warning or final written warning might be given.

In stating the disciplinary matter, the letter should where possible give enough detail to enable the employee to prepare for the interview. All evidence, including copies of important documents such as records of attendance, statements from other people or records of performance should be provided to the employee in good time before the interview. If the employee asks for additional documents, these should be provided if they are relevant.

Ideally the person who is to hear the matter should avoid being too closely involved, or involved at all, in the preparation of the case, but this may not be possible in a small organisation.

29.4.4.1
Postponement

Where an employee or worker has a statutory right to be accompanied [see **29.3.4**] and the chosen companion is not available, the worker can propose another date within five working days beginning with the first working day after the date set for the interview. Provided the requested date is reasonable, the employer must reschedule the interview.

Employment Relations Act 1999 s.10(5)

'Working day' excludes Saturdays, Sundays, Good Friday, Christmas and bank holidays.

In addition to this statutory right to postponement, the employer may allow an employee to seek a postponement to prepare his or her case. In considering the request for postponement the person dealing with the disciplinary matter needs to bear in mind the urgency and seriousness of the matter, and the need to deal with disciplinary matters quickly. This will normally result in agreeing to postpone, but seeking to keep the delay as short as reasonably possible.

29.4.5
The interview

A disciplinary interview or hearing should, insofar as possible, follow the principles of natural justice. Key elements of this are that the person being judged (in this case interviewed) should have the right:

- to hear evidence against him or her;
- to state his or her case;
- to have the decision made by a non-biased person.

Employers should also bear in mind that employment tribunals may consider article 6 of the **European Convention on Human Rights** [see **60.3.1**], guaranteeing a fair, independent and impartial hearing, when determining whether a dismissal procedure has been fair.

29.4.5.1
Impartiality

In small organisations all management staff might be directly involved in the problem that has given rise to disciplinary action, and even members of the governing body may be closely involved. The courts and tribunals accept that in small organisations it may be impossible to find anyone who is unbiased. In this situation the people doing the interview, and hearing any subsequent appeal, must be aware of their bias and make every effort to act as impartially as they can.

It is very important to be clear, right from the beginning, who will hear any appeal, and if possible to exclude them from the early stages.

29.4.5.2
Conduct of the interview

The degree of formality of the interview should be appropriate to the organisation and the situation. The ACAS guide refers to a need to interview the employee, not judge him or her, before deciding whether a disciplinary penalty is necessary and what it should be. The interview should be treated as a formal interview, not as a trial.

At the interview the employee should be told what has been alleged. The employee should already know this in considerable detail, because it would have been set out in the letter giving notice of the interview and in the accompanying documents.

The employer may simply tell the employee what the allegations are, call people to give evidence, or rely on written statements. If the employer asks people to make a statement at the interview, the employee should be given the opportunity to question each of them.

In considering what is fair, the courts and tribunals have not gone so far as to require employers to conduct a sort of judicial enquiry, with every witness called to give evidence and to be subject to the employee's cross-examination. However in most situations it will be fair to allow the employee such an opportunity. There will be very few occasions indeed where it is fair to use anonymous evidence.

If a new fact which is part of the allegation emerges in the interview, the employee may request an adjournment to obtain a witness or some other material in repudiation of it, or simply to consider his or her position. The employer should consider this request seriously.

After the employer has set out all its information, the employee must be allowed to state his or her case. Only in very exceptional circumstances (such as the employee refusing to attend the interview) would it be fair to give a disciplinary penalty without hearing the employee's response.

Having heard the response, the employer must come to a conclusion about what the facts were and what it believes actually happened. If further investigation is needed before a decision can be made, the interview should be adjourned so that this can be looked into.

29.4.5.3
Non-attendance

If the employee does not attend the disciplinary interview but has an excuse acceptable to the employer, the employer should postpone the interview. If the employee does not give a reason for non-attendance, gives an unacceptable reason or persistently misses rescheduled interviews, the employer may be justified in making a decision about a disciplinary penalty without hearing the employee's side.

A decision to proceed without hearing the employee should be made only if this is justifiable and reasonable. If the disciplinary procedure forms part of the contract of employment [see **29.2.2**], a decision to proceed without hearing the employee may generally be made only if the disciplinary procedure allows for this.

29.4.6
Making a decision

The employer merely has to come to a **reasonable decision**. The matter does not have to be proved beyond reasonable doubt; indeed, this may be impossible.

The decision does not need to be made at the conclusion of the interview. ACAS states that it is generally good practice to adjourn before making a decision.

The interviewer(s) may decide that the case against the employee is not proved, that it is proved but no further action needs to be taken, or that it is proved and a disciplinary penalty is appropriate.

29.4.7
Deciding the
disciplinary penalty

A **disciplinary penalty** or **sanction** is the action taken by the employer if its investigation shows that the employee's conduct or work was indeed unsatisfactory. The usual penalties are disciplinary warnings or, ultimately, dismissal. Penalties might also include loss of some privileges (such as loss of pay, loss of the right to use the organisation's facilities for personal use or loss of the right to work paid overtime), or suspension on reduced or no pay. Penalties involving loss of anything to which there is a contractual right (including pay) can be imposed only if this is provided for in the contract [see **27.1.4**].

Factors in deciding the penalty should include:

- full background circumstances relating to the employee, in particular length of service, position and general behaviour;
- previous disciplinary proceedings, especially those of a similar nature, and any warnings which are still outstanding;
- how the employer has dealt with similar disciplinary issues in the past (because the employer should behave consistently);
- whether the contract or any other document prescribes a defined penalty for this misconduct;
- any relevant reason, excuse or background circumstance.

The employer must believe (and believe that an employment tribunal would also believe) that the penalty is reasonable, taking all the factors into account.

29.4.8
Warnings

A **disciplinary warning** is a notice that the employee's conduct or work is unsatisfactory. Whether verbal or written, a warning must always be identified as such and should include:

- the type of misconduct or inadequate performance;
- the facts found;
- any disciplinary penalty in addition to the warning;
- if appropriate, what changes or improvement are expected;
- any time period for such change or improvement, and if appropriate when and how it will be reviewed;
- the consequences of further misconduct or lack of improvement;
- any right of appeal and the timetable for the appeal [see **29.4.14**];
- the date after which the warning will be disregarded if work or performance improves and there is no further disciplinary problem, or the fact that it will stay permanently on record.

For a first penalty, a verbal warning may be appropriate if the offence is minor, but for more serious matters or for a repeat offence the first penalty may be a written warning or even, for very serious matters, a final written warning. Repeated verbal or written warnings are unlikely to be effective, and may well become counter-productive.

For a verbal warning the employer should keep a written record of what has been said. It is good practice to give a copy to the employee.

A **final written warning** must cover the same issues and must state clearly that if conduct or work remains unsatisfactory, the next step will or may be dismissal.

29.4.8.1
Disregarded warnings

Most warnings should be given a date after which, if there is no further problem, they will be disregarded in any future disciplinary matter. The period might range from a year for a minor offence or problem, to five years or more for a serious or repeated offence. For some serious matters, especially those which have ended in a final written warning, the disciplinary warning might never be disregarded.

The date on which a warning will become disregarded needs to be decided on the basis of the particular disciplinary matter and other background circumstances. The disciplinary procedure should not specify a standard period after which all disciplinary warnings, or all warnings of a certain type, are disregarded.

29.4.9
Other disciplinary penalties

If there is explicit provision for it in the contract (and this is unusual for voluntary organisations), there may be other disciplinary **penalties short of dismissal**, such as suspension on reduced or no pay, a fine, disciplinary transfer or demotion. None of these may be used unless the contract of employment explicitly allows it.

Even if such penalties are contractually allowed, the employee is likely to be able to claim constructive dismissal [see **30.4.8**] if they are imposed inappropriately.

29.4.10
Dismissal

Dismissal is the ultimate disciplinary penalty and gives rise to vast numbers of employment tribunal and court claims. To reduce the risk of this, the employer should be aware that:

- a dismissal which does not comply with the contract of employment, for example does not give the necessary period of notice, may give rise to a claim for wrongful dismissal [see **30.7**];

- if the disciplinary procedure is part of the contract [see **29.2.2**], a dismissal which has not strictly followed the procedure is likely to be wrongful;

- if the employer dismisses on short notice and this deprives the employee of the chance to qualify to claim unfair dismissal, this may give rise to a right to claim damages;

- special care is needed when dealing with dismissals which could be seen as linked to racial group, sex, disability, working part-time, trade union activity, or asserting a health and safety right or another statutory right, because the employer may have to show that the dismissal was not in fact for any of these reasons, and was therefore not automatically unfair;

- if the employer does not use a reasonable procedure, for example does not give the employee an opportunity to put her or his side of the story, the dismissal may be unfair [see **30.8.2**];

- if the employer does not give at least one warning that dismissal may occur (except for summary dismissal), the employer is likely to be held to have acted unreasonably and therefore unfairly;

- if the reason for the dismissal is not justifiable and fair, the dismissal may be unfair.

The employee does not have to have worked any minimum period in order to claim wrongful dismissal, or unfair dismissal for one of the automatically unfair reasons such as race, sex or disability discrimination or the assertion of a statutory right. To claim unfair dismissal for other reasons the employee has to have worked for a one year qualifying period [see **23.4.6**].

If at any stage in the disciplinary proceeding it appears that dismissal may be an outcome, legal advice should be sought.

29.4.10.1
Dismissal with notice

Even if the employee has been warned that his or her actions could result in dismissal, notice must be given in the usual way [see **30.6**]. Pay in lieu of notice can be given if the contract allows for this.

29.4.10.2
Summary dismissal

Summary dismissal [see **30.4.7**] is dismissal without notice or pay in lieu of notice. It should be used only in cases of gross misconduct [see **29.4.12**], only after an investigation to substantiate the case against the employee, and generally only where the employee has been given a clear indication that action of that type may result in such dismissal.

29.4.10.3
Dismissal during probationary period

It is not uncommon, particularly where the disciplinary procedure is contractual, to include a clause in the contract stating that the procedure does not have to be followed during a probationary period [see **24.31**]. Unless this is explicit, dismissal during the probationary period should follow the same procedure as for any other dismissal.

29.4.11
Settlement

Frequently at some stage of a disciplinary action where dismissal is a possibility, the question of an agreed **settlement** arises. Settlement protects the employer from contractual claims which can be brought in the court, but in order to protect against claims in employment tribunals the settlement must follow strict guidelines [see **33.2.2**].

29.4.12
Gross misconduct

The tribunals and courts have refused to define what constitutes **gross misconduct**. It is essentially an action so serious that it destroys the employer/employee relationship of trust and confidence [see **23.3.3**] and justifies immediate (summary) dismissal without warning and without notice.   *Neary v Dean of Westminster [1999] IRLR 288*

Disciplinary procedures frequently list the key areas which an employer considers gross misconduct [see **29.6.4** for example]. The procedure should state clearly that the list is not exhaustive, and that other types of action can also be treated as gross misconduct.

The ACAS guidance and employment tribunal rulings make clear that in most circumstances it is unfair to dismiss an employee without first giving a warning. Gross misconduct is an exception to this general rule, allowing the employer to dismiss without giving a warning or notice [see **30.4.7** for more about summary dismissal].

Even in cases of gross misconduct the employer must act fairly. An investigation should be carried out, and the employee should be allowed to provide his or her response before as impartial as possible an interviewer or panel. If this is not done the dismissal could give rise to a claim for wrongful and/or unfair dismissal.

The fact that the contract of employment, disciplinary procedure or other document lists particular behaviour as gross misconduct does not automatically mean that summary dismissal for such behaviour is fair. If the employee challenges the dismissal, the tribunal will look at whether the basic rule was fair, and whether it was fairly and reasonably applied in the particular circumstances.

29.4.13
Criminal offences

If an employee is charged with a criminal offence committed in the course of employment, the employer should deal with the matter giving rise to the charge through the normal disciplinary procedure or through the procedure for gross misconduct [see above].

If the employee is charged with a criminal offence committed outside employment, the action to be taken should be based on his or her suitability for work.

There is no need to wait for the outcome of criminal proceedings, and doing so may involve the employer in inordinate delay.

Conviction in the criminal court—whether for an action within or outside work—does not normally justify dismissal or other penalty by the employer unless the disciplinary procedure has also been followed.

29.4.14
Appeals

ACAS guidelines say that an appeal procedure should exist and an employee should be able to appeal against dismissal. It is good practice to allow appeals at earlier stages of the procedure, although it may not be a good use of time to allow them at verbal warning stage. An example of an appeal procedure is in the model disciplinary procedure [see **29.6**].

Key principles in operating an appeals procedure are:

* matters should be dealt with as quickly as possible;
* if possible the appeal should be heard by a different person or persons at a more senior level, although the courts and tribunals recognise that for small employers this may not be possible.

The nature of the appeal should be made clear. Some appeals do not review the finding of facts, only the penalty imposed after the finding of facts. Much more commonly, the appeal is a re-hearing so that all issues are again explored. This can provide an opportunity to correct procedural defects made at an earlier stage.

There generally should be time limits after which an appeal cannot be lodged, so that appeals do not arise many months after the initial disciplinary action. Five working days is generally appropriate.

The procedure or notice should make clear whether an employee dismissed at the hearing remains an employee until the appeal is heard, and if so on what terms, or ceases to be an employee and is reinstated if the appeal is successful.

Even where an employee is being dismissed, there is no obligation on her or him to appeal. An employee who believes he or she has a valid claim for wrongful and/or unfair dismissal may simply accept the dismissal and claim compensation.

29.5 GRIEVANCES

A grievance procedure should follow the same basic principles as a disciplinary procedure, allowing employees to present their concerns and have them heard and dealt with in a fair, impartial manner. The usual procedure is to encourage employees initially to discuss the matter informally, if possible, with the person who is the cause of the grievance. If this is not possible or the outcome is unsatisfactory, the employee can take up the matter in writing with his or her manager (or a specified person above, if the grievance concerns the manager). There may then be a procedure for referral to a higher body, and an appeal procedure. For a model grievance procedure see **29.7**.

Records of grievances raised and the employer's response or action and reasons should be retained. Such records should be kept confidential, subject to data protection rules [see **36.2**]. Copies of minutes or notes from grievance meetings should be given to the individuals concerned.

Employees and others working under a contract have the right to be accompanied at interviews where grievances are being heard concerning the employer's breach of a contractual or statutory duty [see **29.3.4**]. In other situations the employer's procedure may allow a companion to attend.

In some organisations the grievance procedure may be the only formal way that a worker can raise concerns. Other organisations may also have a **whistleblowing policy**, to deal with issues arising under the **Public Interest Disclosure Act 1998** [see **29.8**], and/or a **harassment** or similar policy under which concerns about any form of discrimination or oppressive behaviour may be raised.

29.6
MODEL DISCIPLINARY PROCEDURE

COMMENTARY

Set out below is [Organisation's] current disciplinary procedure. This does not form part of your contract of employment, but represents [Organisation's] current practice which it may vary from time to time.

The second sentence should be included if the disciplinary procedure is not intended to form part of the contract [see **29.2.2**]. If the procedure is part of the contract, which is inadvisable, this should be stated.

Double-underlined headings indicate significant changes since the first edition of *Voluntary Sector Legal Handbook.*

1. **Purpose and scope**

    Disciplinary matters cover non-performance or inadequate performance of duties, breaches of contract or the employer's rules, and other misconduct affecting your work or the organisation. The procedure is intended and designed to improve performance and resolve difficulties, rather than to punish infringements.

2. **Principles**

2.1 The procedure is designed to establish the facts quickly and to deal consistently with disciplinary issues.

2.2 No disciplinary action will be taken until the matter has been fully investigated.

2.3 At every stage you will have the opportunity to state your case at a disciplinary interview and to be accompanied, if you wish, by a trade union representative, a fellow worker or a non-lawyer friend. You have a right to a request postponement of the interview for up to five working days if your chosen companion is not available.

The suggested clause goes beyond the statutory requirement [see **29.3.4**], allowing the worker to be accompanied by anyone, other than a lawyer, rather than only a trade union official or fellow worker.

2.4 Prior to a disciplinary interview you will be told the nature of the alleged offence or problem, the nature of the evidence and the range of possible outcomes, and you will be reminded of your right to be accompanied.

2.5 If at any stage a warning is given it will include the reason for the warning, any required improvement, and when the situation will be reviewed. It will indicate that if there is inadequate improvement or a repeat of the offence, a further warning or a final written warning may be given or, if applicable, that you may be dismissed.

    You will be told whether the warning will be kept permanently in your personnel file, or will be removed after a specified period. Unless the warning is permanent, it will not be used in disciplinary matters after the specified period provided your progress is satisfactory and you are not involved in any further disciplinary matter within the specified period.

2.5 You have the right to appeal against any disciplinary warning other than a verbal warning. The appeal procedure is set out in section 6 below.

Because verbal warnings are given only for first offences or minor problems, it may not be worth the time for appeals against them.

3. **The procedure**

3.1 Verbal warning

    If, after investigation and an interview with you, your conduct or performance is found to be unsatisfactory, your manager *[or whoever]* or, in his/her absence his/her deputy, may give you a formal verbal warning. A written record will be kept of the discussion, agreed actions and when the situation will be reviewed. You will be given a copy of this.

3.2 Written warning

If an investigation and interview with you about a disciplinary matter indicates that it is too serious to be dealt with through a verbal warning, you may receive a written warning as your first warning.

You may also receive a written warning if a review after a verbal warning or a previous written warning shows that there has been inadequate improvement in your conduct or work, or if an incident of unsatisfactory work or conduct occurs after a verbal warning or a previous written warning.

Many disciplinary procedures state or imply that whatever the nature of the offence, short of gross misconduct it must be dealt with first by a verbal warning (or sometimes two or three), then by a written warning (or two or three), and then by a final warning. A verbal warning may be appropriate for a minor matter, but the first occurrence of a more serious matter may require a written or even a final written warning.

3.3 Final written warning

A final written warning may be given if an initial offence is very serious, if conduct or performance remains unsatisfactory when reviewed after a verbal or written warning, or if an incident of unsatisfactory work or conduct occurs after a verbal or written warning. This will make clear that any recurrence of the offence, other misconduct or continued inadequate performance will or may result in dismissal.

3.4 Dismissal

If conduct or performance does not improve satisfactorily or if further misconduct occurs, you may be dismissed.

Dismissal will not occur unless it is authorised by the board of trustees or by an individual or committee explicitly authorised by them to make a dismissal decision.

Where notice of dismissal would expire before the outcome of any appeal is known, you will be treated as suspended without pay until the outcome is known.

Except in situations of gross misconduct [see below] an employee should be given at least one warning that dismissal might occur.

Note that even for dismissal after a disciplinary procedure, the employer must give notice as specified by statute or in the contract of employment, whichever is longer [see **30.6**]. Pay can be given in lieu of notice if the contract provides for this.

4. **Gross misconduct**

Gross misconduct includes any action which threatens the organisation, its work or reputation, people connected with the organisation or members of the public, or which destroys the employer's necessary relationship of trust with you. Examples include theft, damage to the organisation's property, fraud, incapacity for work due to being under the influence of alcohol or illegal drugs, physical assault, threatening behaviour, gross insubordination, conduct endangering any person, gross negligence, harassment, discriminatory behaviour, or serious breach of professional ethics, breach of standards of good conduct, or misuse of computer, email or internet access. This list is not exhaustive and other actions may also constitute gross misconduct.

If, after investigation, it is found that you have committed an act or acts of gross misconduct, the normal consequence will be dismissal without notice and without pay in lieu of notice.

The organisation may want to list other examples of particular importance to it. Any list must clearly state that it is by way of example only, and is not exhaustive.

The fact that a behaviour is listed as gross misconduct does not mean that it is always, in the particular circumstances, reasonable to treat it as such.

5. Suspension

While any alleged misconduct other than gross misconduct is being investigated or pending hearing of an appeal against dismissal, you may be suspended and will be paid your usual salary. In case of alleged gross misconduct, you may be suspended at your usual pay, or at reduced pay or without pay during the investigation, disciplinary action or any appeal against dismissal.

The employer is entitled to suspend only if the contract of employment explicitly makes provision for this [see **24.39**]. Suspension must be on full pay unless the contract allows for reduced or no pay. Allowing suspension only in the disciplinary procedure is not enough, unless the disciplinary procedure forms part of the contract.

6. Appeal

You are entitled to appeal against any written disciplinary warning or other disciplinary decision. To do so you must notify the chair of the board of trustees *[or whoever]* or her/his authorised deputy in writing within five working days of receiving the written warning or other written notification of the penalty. The chair *[or whoever]* or her/his deputy may, at her/his discretion, extend this period. Your notice must specify the issues you wish to appeal or contest.

The chair *[or whoever]* or her/his deputy will appoint an appeal panel made up of three members of the board of trustees. If possible, these will be people who have not been directly involved in the disciplinary procedure at any previous stage. If the chair or deputy wishes, one board member may be replaced by an independent external person.

A meeting of the panel will be convened as quickly as is reasonably practicable. You will be given at least two working days notice of the meeting. You are entitled to be accompanied at the appeal meeting by a trade union representative, fellow employee or non-lawyer friend.

You will be given the decision of the meeting in writing. The decision is final.

Delete 'written' from the first sentence if appeal against verbal warnings is also allowed.

Including a time limit for the appeal avoids the possibility of an appeal being lodged many months later.

Either the disciplinary procedure or the notice given to the employee should make clear what happens during an appeal against dismissal [see **29.4.14**].

29.7
MODEL GRIEVANCE PROCEDURE

COMMENTARY

Set out below is [Organisation's] current grievance procedure. This does not form part of your contract of employment but represents [Organisation's] current practice, which it may vary from time to time.

The second sentence should be included if the grievance procedure is not intended to form part of the contract of employment [see **29.2.2**]. If the procedure is intended to form part of the contract, which is inadvisable, this should be stated.

This procedure should be used to settle all disputes and grievances which you wish to raise concerning other employees, your work, the organisation or other matters relating to your employment. The purpose is to settle any grievance fairly, simply and quickly.

Where the organisation also has harassment and/or whistleblowing policies, this section should be expanded and be cross-referenced to them.

1. If your grievance concerns another employee, you should if possible first discuss and try to resolve it with that person.

2. If this does not resolve the matter, or if the matter involves your employment rather than another employee, you should refer it to your manager *[or the director, the chair of the board, or whoever]* or, in their absence, to his/her authorised deputy. If the matter concerns your manager you should refer it to his/her manager, or if s/he has none, to the chair of the board of trustees *[or whoever]*.

Use the title of the post, not the name of the current post holder. At this stage it should not go to the highest level (in most organisations, the whole governing body) because this would not keep anyone available for the appeal stage.

3. Unless there is a good reason for not doing so, a grievance matter should generally be raised within one month of the incident to which it refers.

If a time limit is included it should not be fixed, but should be defined in terms of 'should generally'.

4. You will be given an initial reply in writing within a reasonable period, which will generally be within two weeks of your raising the matter. If it is not possible to give a complete reply at this stage, you will be given a further written reply as soon as reasonably practicable.

Many procedures include very rigid timetables. If the grievance procedure is part of the contract, this could easily give rise to a claim for breach of contract if the relevant person does not reply within the specified time. Even where the procedure is not part of the contract, it is preferable to make this clause flexible.

5. If the matter remains unresolved, the person dealing with it will refer it to a meeting of the senior management team *[or the board's personnel committee, or a panel appointed by the board, or whoever]* or to a committee of some of them. The meeting will be held as quickly as is reasonably practicable.

The second stage should still allow for a different person or persons to be involved at appeal stage.

Avoid saying that the meeting must be held within a specified time.

6. You are entitled to attend this meeting and if you wish, to be accompanied by a trade union representative, a fellow employee or a non-lawyer friend. You and/or the person accompanying you are entitled to address the meeting. Where your grievance concerns the employer's failure to comply with a contractual or statutory duty, you have a right to a request postponement of the interview for up to five working days if your chosen companion is not available.

There is a statutory right to be accompanied if the grievance relates to the employer's failure to comply with a contractual or statutory duty, or if the grievance relates to a disciplinary matter which could result in a disciplinary warning or other penalty [see **29.3.4**]. The suggested clause goes beyond the statutory requirement, allowing the worker to be accompanied by anyone, other than a lawyer, rather than only a trade union official or fellow worker.

7. The decision of the panel will be given to you in writing as soon as is reasonably practicable after the meeting.

Appeal

8. If a matter which you think should be referred to a panel is not referred, a meeting is not held within a reasonable period or you are dissatisfied with the decision of the panel, you should write to the chair of the board of trustees *[or whoever]* specifying the issues you wish to appeal or contest.

In a large(ish) organisation grievances are likely to stop at chief executive level, rather than being referred on to the governing body, unless they involve very senior staff. In a smaller organisation, they may go on to the governing body.

9. The chair of the board of trustees *[or whoever]* will ensure that the matter is considered at the next meeting of the board or a committee appointed by it *[or senior management team or whatever]* (unless there are less than five working days between receipt of your request and the date of the meeting, in which case the chairperson may hold it over until the following meeting).

   You are entitled to attend this meeting to present your case, and if you wish, to be accompanied by a trade union representative, a fellow employee or a non-lawyer friend. You and/or the person accompanying you are entitled to address the meeting.

10. The decision of the board of trustees or committee *[or whatever]* will be given to you in writing as soon as is reasonably practicable after the meeting. Their decision is final and there is no further right of appeal.

11. You should ensure that there is no unreasonable delay in the implementation of this procedure.

    This gives the employee the right to put pressure on management if they are delaying dealing with the matter.

29.8 WHISTLEBLOWING

In general it is a serious disciplinary matter for an employee to breach confidentiality by revealing information about the employer's activities. But where disclosure would reveal or prevent malpractice or an unlawful act, there may be a **just cause** defence in disclosing the information. This is often referred to as **whistleblowing**.

In these situations the **Public Interest Disclosure Act 1998** protects employees and workers from victimisation or dismissal, provided they comply with the statutory procedures. There is no limit on the compensation that can be awarded to an employee who is unfairly dismissed or subject to detriment because of whistleblowing.

For the purposes of this Act, a 'worker' is a person who works under a contract of employment or other contract where he or she has to provide services personally [see **22.1**], agency workers, home workers whose work is controlled by the employer, medical practitioners in the National Health Service, and some trainees on work experience.

Employment Rights Act 1996 s.43K

The Public Interest Disclosure Act amends the Employment Rights Act 1996. Its complex provisions provide protection only if a disclosure falls into one of six categories and is made through one of six routes. If the subject matter is not in one of the categories or a non-protected route is used, the employee or worker is not protected from victimisation or dismissal.

Organisations should develop a whistleblowing or disclosure procedure which encourages disclosure within the organisation as soon as staff become aware of potential problem areas. The organisation may specify that this disclosure should be through the usual grievance procedure, or through a different route. A clear procedure enables corrective action to be taken and reduces the risk of staff feeling the need to disclose information externally. For a model policy see *Establishing a Whistleblowing Policy*, £5 from the Institute of Chartered Secretaries and Administrators [see end of chapter].

Information and advice on whistleblowing is available from Public Concern at Work and the Campaign for Freedom of Information [see end of chapter].

**29.8.1
What can be
disclosed**

For a disclosure to be protected, the employee or worker must reasonably believe that the disclosure tends to show that one or more of the following has happened anywhere in the world or is likely to happen:

- a criminal offence;
- failure to comply with any legal obligation;
- miscarriage of justice;
- danger to an individual's health or safety;
- damage to the environment;
- deliberate concealment of information tending to show any of the above. *Employment Rights Act 1996 s.43B(1)*

Even if the disclosure shows one or more of the above, the disclosure is not protected if the worker commits an offence by making the disclosure (for example, contravenes the Official Secrets Act), or if legal professional privilege applies. *s.43B(3),(4)*

**29.8.2
Who it can be
disclosed to**

The legislation encourages disclosure to the employer. A disclosure is protected if it is made to:

- the employer;
- someone to whom the employer, under its disclosure policy, authorises disclosure to be made;
- a person other than the employer whom the employee or worker believes in good faith has a legal responsibility for the matter;
- a legal advisor; *or*
- a minister of the Crown, where the employee or worker works for a government department or agency.
Employment Rights Act 1996 ss.43C-43E

**29.8.2.1
Prescribed person**

A disclosure is protected if it is made to a **prescribed person** [see below], provided the employee or worker:

- makes the disclosure in good faith;
- reasonably believes the information disclosed is substantially true; *and*
- reasonably believes the prescribed person is authorised to deal with such matters. *s.43F*

Prescribed persons include the Charity Commissioners, the Commissioners of the Inland Revenue, the Health and Safety Executive and similar regulatory bodies, but not the police.
Public Interest Disclosure (Prescribed Persons) Order 1999 [SI 1999/1549]

**29.8.2.2
Disclosure to others**

A disclosure to others, for example an MP, the police or media, is protected only if the employee or worker:

- makes the disclosure in good faith;
- reasonably believes the information disclosed is substantially true;
- does not make the disclosure for personal gain;
- is acting reasonably, in all the circumstances of the case, in making the disclosure; *and*
- reasonably believes he or she will be subject to detriment by the employer if disclosure is made to the employer or a prescribed person, *or* believes it is likely that evidence relating to the matter will be concealed or destroyed if disclosure is made to the employer, *or* the employee or worker has already disclosed the information to the employer or a prescribed person, and appropriate action has not been taken. *Employment Rights Act 1996 s.43G*

In deciding whether a disclosure to a person other than the employer or a prescribed person is protected, the following issues are considered:

- the identity of the person to whom the disclosure is made;

- the seriousness of the matter;

- whether the matter is likely to continue or recur;

- whether the disclosure is made in breach of the employer's duty of confidentiality to another person;

- any action the employer or person to whom the disclosure has been made has taken or should have taken as a result of a previous disclosure;

- whether in making the disclosure the employee or worker complied with the employer's procedure for disclosure.

Employment Rights Act 1996 s.43G

29.8.3
Exceptionally serious breaches

For very serious breaches, disclosure can be made without the normal attempt to resolve the matter internally or through a prescribed person. For a disclosure of this type to be protected, the employee or worker must show that:

- the disclosure was made in good faith;

- he or she reasonably believes the disclosure is substantially true;

- the disclosure is not made for personal gain;

- the matter disclosed was of an exceptionally serious nature; *and*

- in all circumstances it is reasonable to make the disclosure.

s.43H

FOR FURTHER INFORMATION

Disciplinary and grievance procedures. ACAS: see telephone directory for local office; www.acas.org.uk

Whistleblowing. Campaign for Freedom of Information: 020-7831 7477; www.cfoi.org.uk

Institute of Chartered Secretaries and Administrators: 020-7580 4741; www.icsa.org.uk/icsa

Public Concern at Work: 020-7404 6609; www.pcaw.co.uk

Chapter 30
TERMINATION OF EMPLOYMENT

For sources of further information see end of chapter.

Double-underlined section headings indicate additions or significant changes since the first edition.

30.1
GETTING IT WRONG

In most cases termination of the contract of employment is straightforward, with the employee giving notice. Occasionally a problem may arise from an employee not giving proper notice, but far more frequent are problems arising from the employer dismissing an employee without giving proper notice, or without following proper procedures or having a justifiable reason. The resultant wrongful and unfair dismissal cases can be very damaging and expensive, with potentially large financial awards. Uninsured legal costs and a large award could cause the insolvency of an incorporated organisation or personal bankruptcy for members of the governing body of an unincorporated organisation.

As well as the financial costs, a hasty badly planned dismissal can also have long-lasting negative effects on the organisation. If a claim of wrongful and/or unfair dismissal is brought, large amounts of staff and governing body time are likely to be consumed in preparing the case and attending the tribunal or court, and staff and volunteers may well be divided and demoralised. An organisation's good name may be damaged and funders may reconsider continued funding.

To reduce the risk of this happening it is essential to take early legal advice when an employee is being dismissed, to ensure that the employer deals properly with every aspect of the dismissal.

30.2 STATEMENT OF REASONS FOR TERMINATION

An employee who has at least one year's continuous employment [see **23.4.6** for definition], whose contract is terminated for any reason, is entitled to a written statement of the reason(s) for the termination if they ask for it. The employer must give this within 14 days of the request. *Employment Rights Act 1996 s.92(1)-(3)*

All female employees, regardless of length of service, must be given written notice of the reason for dismissal, without having to ask for it, if they are dismissed while they are pregnant or if their maternity leave period would be ended by the dismissal. *s.92(4)*

If the statement is not provided or is untrue or inadequate the employee may refer the matter to the employment tribunal [see **33.2**]. The tribunal may make a finding as to the reasons for the dismissal and award two weeks' pay. *s.93(1),(2)*

30.3 REFERENCES AND REPORTING

30.3.1 References

Unless the contract of employment explicitly states that the employer will give a reference, or such an obligation is implied because of special circumstances, there is generally no legal obligation on an employer to provide one. However failure to provide a reference to a worker who has claimed, or threatened to claim, sex discrimination could in itself constitute sex discrimination, and the same may apply in relation to other forms of discrimination [see **25.1**].

An employer who does provide a reference has a duty of care to the employee to ensure it is accurate and fair and does not give a misleading impression [see **26.3.1**]. An employee who is unable to obtain a future job because of an inaccurate or malicious reference might be able to make a claim against the employer. This would not apply if the job was lost because of an accurate reference.

Spring v Guardian Assurance plc and others [1994] 3 All ER 129; IRLR 460

A subsequent employer relying on an inaccurate reference provided by the original employer might also have a claim against that employer.

30.3.2 Dismissal of childcare and care workers

Where an employer, employment agency or employment bureau dismisses or ceases to use a worker, whether paid or unpaid, on grounds of misconduct which harmed or placed at risk a child or vulnerable adult, there is in many cases a duty to refer that worker to the secretary of state for health [see **36.8.2**]. Even where an organisation working with children or vulnerable adults is not under a duty to report the worker, it may choose to do so. Guidance on what does and does not have to be referred is available from the local social services department or from the Department of Health [see end of **chapter 26**].

Protection of Children Act 1999 s.2; Care Standards Act 2000 ss.80-84

The same reporting rules apply where the organisation:

- would have dismissed or considered dismissing a worker because of misconduct in relation to a child or vulnerable adult, but the worker resigns, retires or is made redundant before dismissal;
- suspends the worker because of such misconduct; *or*
- transfers the worker to a position in the organisation which is not a care or childcare position, because of such misconduct .

Organisations may also be required or choose to refer an individual who has been dismissed or transferred for other reasons or who has resigned or retired, where:

- information which was not available at the time becomes available; *and*

- the organisation forms the opinion that if the information had been available, it would have dismissed or considered dismissing the person on the grounds of misconduct which harmed or put at risk a child or vulnerable adult.

After referral and investigation, the worker may be placed on the Department of Health's **Protection of Children Act (PoCA) list** and/or its **Protection of Vulnerable Adults (PoVA) list** [see **26.3.4**]. It is an offence for a person on these lists to apply for or offer to work with children or vulnerable adults (depending on which list they are on), or to take or continue in such work.

30.4 TERMINATION WITHOUT NOTICE

Contracts of employment, like any other contract, can be terminated in a number of ways [see **18.11**]. Some, but not all, require notice of termination.

The most common forms of termination without notice are:

- termination by **frustration** [see **30.4.1**];

- termination by **agreement**, including expiry of a fixed-term contract [see **30.4.3** and **30.4.4**];

- **retirement** required under the contract of employment [see **30.4.5**].

Termination without notice may also occur when the contract is **repudiated** (seriously breached) by the employer or employee, leading to **summary** or **constructive dismissal** [see **30.4.7** and **30.4.8**].

30.4.1 Frustration

A contract is terminated by frustration if something happens which makes it impossible for the contract to be carried out, for example:

- the activity carried out under the contract becomes illegal;

- the employee dies;

- the employee is conscripted;

- the employee is imprisoned for an extended period;

- the employee becomes permanently disabled in a way which makes it impossible to do the job, it is not reasonable to make adaptations to enable her or him to continue working, and alternative work is not available [see **25.5**];

- the employee is ill for an extended period [see **30.8.3.1**];

- the employer (if an individual) dies;

- an unincorporated association or trust is dissolved [see **21.7- 21.8**];

- a corporate body (company or industrial and provident society) is wound up and therefore ceases to exist [see **21.3-21.6**].

A frustrated contract is terminated by action of law, rather than by a party to the contract. Generally there is no dismissal, and therefore no right to claim unfair dismissal, wrongful dismissal or a redundancy payment. The exceptions are frustration due to death of the employer (if an individual) or where the organisation is dissolved or wound up. Termination for these reasons entitles employees to redundancy pay if they have worked for the necessary qualifying period [see **31.6.1**]. However if the organisation is dissolved or wound up and its work is transferred to another employer, the contract is transferred as part of the transfer of undertakings [see **26.4**] and is not frustrated.

In some cases, such as conscription or an employee's death, it is clear that frustration has taken place. In other situations the question of frustration may become the subject of complex legal debate.

30.4.1.1
Long-term sickness

If an employee has a long-term illness, it may in some cases be possible to show that the contract has been frustrated. Factors taken into account include the terms of the contract, especially in relation to sick pay, how long employment was likely to last if there had not been sickness, the nature of the employment, the nature of the sickness, how long the sickness has continued, the prospects of recovery, and the duration of past employment.

The longer the worker has been employed by this employer, the less likely it is that the contract will be considered to be frustrated by sickness. But the sickness may be a valid reason for dismissal [see **30.8.3.1**].

Marshall v Harland & Wolff Ltd [1972] 1 WLR 899; 2 All ER 715

If the employer has 15 or more employees or others working under a contract it is essential, before making any decision to treat long-term sickness as frustrating the contract, to consider whether the sickness is legally a disability [see **25.5.1**] and the worker therefore has protection under the **Disability Discrimination Act 1995**. At the time of writing (early 2001) the government had announced that the 15-worker exception would be removed by October 2004.

30.4.1.2
Imprisonment

Imprisonment for a relatively short period does not necessarily frustrate a contract. Legal advice should be taken before claiming frustration or dismissing an employee on the basis of imprisonment, especially if the imprisonment is for a short time and is for a reason which does not affect the employee's suitability for the job [see also **30.8.4.1**].

30.4.2
Unsatisfactory references, medical checks etc

If employment is explicitly made conditional on receipt of satisfactory references, medical check, criminal record check, confirmation of qualifications etc, it may be terminated if these are not received or are unsatisfactory [see **26.3**]. It is the employer's decision whether they are satisfactory. An employee who has worked for at least one month is entitled to a statutory period of notice [see **30.6.1**].

30.4.3
Termination by agreement

The employer and employee may simply agree that employment will cease. This termination by **mutual consent** does not constitute dismissal. The employee is not entitled to claim redundancy pay, wrongful dismissal or unfair dismissal, and entitlement to jobseeker's allowance and other welfare benefits may be affected.

Because the employer may in effect have given the employee no choice but to agree, the courts or tribunal will look closely at an alleged termination by agreement if it is later disputed [see **30.10.3.1**].

30.4.4
Expiry of fixed-term contract

A contract for a fixed period of time [see **22.3.2**] ends at the expiry of the defined period. But non-renewal constitutes dismissal for the purposes of the unfair dismissal and redundancy legislation. An employee who has the necessary period of continuous employment [see **31.6.1** and **23.4.5**] is entitled to claim a redundancy payment or unfair dismissal if a contract for a specified period is not renewed when it expires.

Employment Rights Act 1996 ss.95(1), 136

30.4.4.1
Waiver of right to claim redundancy pay

The main difference between fixed-term and open-ended contracts is that an employee with a contract for a fixed term of two years or more can be asked or required to waive the right to claim redundancy pay when the contract ends [see **24.5** for a sample waiver clause]. The waiver cannot be used for temporary contracts [see **22.3.1**] which do not have a fixed ending date. Nor can it be used with contracts to complete a task [see **22.3.3**], because ending such a contract is not a dismissal, so no right to claim redundancy pay arises. *s.197(1),(3)*

The waiver, if included, covers only the right to redundancy pay. It does not remove the employer's duty to undertake a fair dismissal or redundancy procedure, nor does it waive other redundancy rights.

The waiver of the right to redundancy pay does not have to be included in the original contract. It can be agreed in writing at any time before the fixed-term contract expires, but an employer cannot *require* the employee to waive the right except when the contract is originally agreed. *Employment Rights Act 1996 s.197(4)*

A waiver agreed after the original contract has been agreed may not be valid unless it is signed as a deed [see **18.3**], or the employee has received a payment or other consideration in return for giving up his or her statutory rights [see **18.10.2**]. This is a technical matter, and the employer should seek legal advice before asking an employee already on a fixed-term contract to agree to a waiver.

30.4.4.2
Continuation after
expiry

If a contract with a waiver is subsequently extended or renewed on substantially the same terms, the waiver may continue to apply. But at the time of writing (early 2001) the law on this was extremely uncertain. Up-to-date advice should be taken, and the waiver should explicitly be included in any extension. *Employment Rights Act 1996 s.197(5);*
British Broadcasting Corporation v Linda Kelly-Phillips [1998] 5 PLC 62

Where an employee simply continues working after the original ending date, without agreeing and signing a new waiver, the waiver will not carry over. If the contract is subsequently terminated because of redundancy, the employee will be entitled to redundancy pay.

Re-engagement (rather than extension) occurs when the new work or conditions are substantially different from the previous contract, or where there has been a gap of more than one week between the old and new fixed-term contracts. In the case of re-engagement, a waiver will be possible only if the new contract is for at least two years.

If there have been several periods of fixed-term employment, a tribunal will look at the terms of the final contract.

The **EU Directive on Fixed-Term Contracts**, which was due to be implemented in the UK in mid-2001, may change the rules on fixed-term contracts.

30.4.4.3
Termination before
expiry

A fixed-term contract should generally contain provisions allowing for termination before its expiry, in which case notice as required in the contract must be given. The usual rules relating to fair dismissal and termination by notice apply [see **30.6**]. A waiver of the right to claim redundancy pay applies only to non-renewal at the time of expiry, so the employee may be able to claim redundancy pay if the reason for the pre-expiry termination is redundancy.

If the fixed-term contract does not include provision for termination before expiry, termination by either side is a breach of contract. If the employee resigns or the employer dismisses the employee before expiry, the aggrieved party may generally bring a claim for damages [see **18.12.2**]. The court will not require the employee to remain in the job and is unlikely to require the employer to reinstate the employee.

30.4.4.4
Fixed-term contracts
and unfair dismissal

Prior to 25 October 1999 it was possible to include in some fixed-term contracts a waiver of the right to claim unfair dismissal. This right was removed by the **Employment Relations Act 1999**, so an employer's failure to extend or renew a fixed-term contract could be unfair dismissal if there is not a fair reason (usually redundancy) for the contract's termination, and/or if the employer has not gone through a fair dismissal or redundancy procedure.

30.4.5
Retirement

Many employers have a **normal retirement age**, either set out in the contract of employment or ascertainable by custom and practice. Retirement age may be 65 or any age above or below this, but must be the same for women and men. If the employer does not have its own normal retirement age, it is 65. *Employment Rights Act 1996 s.108*

Setting a normal or compulsory retirement age is unlikely to be unlawful age discrimination when new age discrimination legislation is enacted [see **25.9.1**]. At the time of writing (early 2001) dismissal of an employee at or after the normal retirement age did not constitute unfair dismissal, but this had been challenged as unfair sex discrimination and legal advice should be sought [see **25.9.1**]. Similarly an employee made redundant on or after becoming 65, or after reaching the employer's normal retirement age if this is younger, is not entitled to redundancy pay [see **31.6.1**], but this may also change.

30.4.6
Early retirement

Early retirement is a form of termination by agreement, with an early retirement settlement which is usually the same as, or more advantageous than, the redundancy pay the employee would be entitled to. Unless it is absolutely clear that the employee is resigning, he or she may still have the right to claim unfair and/or wrongful dismissal, so the protection of a settlement agreement [see **33.2**] should be sought.

30.4.7
Repudiation by employee and summary dismissal

Repudiation occurs when one party gives a clear indication that they no longer intend to be bound by a contract, usually by doing something fundamentally contrary to the contract. Repudiation by an employee may occur if, for example, the employee commits an act which is:

- in clear breach of an agreed term of the contract;
- **gross misconduct** [see **29.4.12**] fundamentally undermining the employer/employee relationship; *or*
- defined in the contract as one which justifies summary dismissal.

The employee who steals from the till is an obvious example, but others are less clear. In one case, repudiation was held to have occurred when an employee borrowed only a small amount of money from the till and left an IOU—because he knew the employer would not have granted permission for such a loan.   *Sinclair v Neighbour [1967] 2 QB 279*

Disobedience on one occasion is generally not sufficient to show repudiation unless it is a crucial matter or is coupled with considerable rudeness and insolence. Each matter is judged on its own merits.

Where the employee has repudiated the employer may be justified in dismissing without notice (**summary dismissal**) [see **30.4.7**].

30.4.7.1
Summary dismissal without repudiation by employee

Unless repudiation has occurred, dismissal without notice constitutes wrongful dismissal [see **30.7**] and may also be unfair on the basis that the employer did not act reasonably [see **30.8.2**].

Where the tribunal or court does not accept that the employee repudiated the contract, the situation becomes reversed. Now it is the employer who has repudiated the contract, by acting in a way which was in fundamental breach by dismissing without proper notice [see **30.4.8**].

30.4.7.2
Not treating action as repudiation

Even where the act would undoubtedly be seen as repudiation, the employer or employee do not have to treat the contract as repudiated. The employer in the Sinclair case [see above], for example, could have allowed the employee to continue working, thus acknowledging a continuing contract, and the contract would not be repudiated.

30.4.8
Repudiation by employer and constructive dismissal

An employer may repudiate a contract by committing a serious breach of its obligations to its employees, for example:

- dismissing without giving the required notice, unless summary dismissal is justified [see **30.4.7**];
- reducing pay or requiring the employee to move to new offices many miles away, without consultation, notice or a provision in the contract allowing this;
- requiring an employee to work in an unhealthy or unsafe situation;

- sexual, racial, disability or other harassment, or failing to take reasonable steps to protect the employee from such harassment;
- violence, abuse or bullying, or failure to take reasonable steps to protect the employee from this;
- demoting the employee without reason;
- varying the contract in a way which is detrimental to the employee, without the employee's agreement [see **23.7.3**];
- any other action which seriously undermines the employer/employee relationship.

If an employee leaves because of an action like this, the employee may allege **constructive dismissal**. The dismissal is 'constructed' out of the employer's behaviour towards the employee, indicating an intention not to be bound by the contract. In a situation of constructive dismissal the employee does not have to give notice of resignation, and may be entitled to claim wrongful and/or unfair dismissal.

30.4.8.1
Acts by rogue trustees

The action of an individual member of the governing body, even if unauthorised, could give rise to a claim for constructive dismissal if it provokes an employee into resigning. To reduce this risk:

- members of the governing body, personnel committee or similar bodies should be aware that they are not authorised to criticise employees' work except within the framework of the organisation's supervision, disciplinary and other procedures;
- an employee at the receiving end of such comments should be told clearly that the comments are not authorised by the employer;
- it should be made clear to all relevant employees that the criticisms are not supported or endorsed by the employer (or where the comments may to some extent be supported, it should be made clear that the rogue trustee's *actions* are not supported);
- the organisation's grievance procedure should allow for employees to take action in this type of situation;
- governing body members who are aware of such comments should do what they can to prevent them or protect the employee from them;
- the organisation should do, and be seen to do, everything in its power to control the behaviour of the governing body member.

In some situations it may be appropriate to suspend or remove the person from the governing body [see **11.5.4** and **11.5.6**].

30.4.8.2
Employee not treating action as repudiation

The employee does not have to treat the contract as repudiated. He or she may continue working despite the employer's action, waiting to see if the employer will rectify the act. If the employer does not do so, the employee may resign and sue for damages later [see **33.6.2**].

This course of action is not possible where the employer summarily dismisses without justification. The employee might well want to ignore the employer's repudiation and continue working, but his or her only remedies are to seek damages for wrongful dismissal, and/or compensation or reinstatement for unfair dismissal.

30.5
TERMINATION
WITH NOTICE

For termination with notice, notice as required by statute or under the contract must be given [see **30.6**]. An employer's failure to give the required notice constitutes wrongful dismissal.

30.5.1
Resignation

An employee may resign at any time by giving the notice required by her or his contract of employment or by statute [see **30.6.1**], whichever is longer. Leaving without giving the required notice could constitute **wrongful termination** [see **30.7.3**], but except for very senior or valuable employees an employer is unlikely to do anything about it.

30.5.2
Unsatisfactory
probationary period

Many contracts specify a probationary period [see **24.31**] during or at the end of which the employer or employee can terminate employment without giving the full notice required in the contract of employment. The shorter notice allowed during the probationary period should be specified in the contract. If the probationary period is more than one month the notice required should not be less than one week, as this is the statutory minimum [see **30.6.1**].

For dismissal during or at the end of a probationary period, the employer may specify in the contract that the disciplinary procedure does not have to be followed. Even with this provision, it is good practice to ensure the employee is given at least one warning that dismissal may occur. If the contract does not exclude the disciplinary procedure during the probationary period, it applies in the same way as usual [see **29.4**].

30.5.2.1
Contract conditional on
satisfactory
probationary period

Some employees are hired on the basis that their contract of employment will not be confirmed until they have satisfactorily completed the probationary period. Regardless of this, for the purposes of employment rights their contract is created when the offer of work is made and accepted; their period of continuous employment [see **23.4.6**] begins when the contract specifies or (if earlier) when they actually start work; and the employer must give a written statement of employment particulars within two months of their starting [see **23.5**].

If the probationary period ends successfully the employer does not confirm that the contract will start, but in effect confirms that the contract which is already in existence will not be terminated and will continue. If the probationary period is not successful, the employee is dismissed according to the terms of the contract.

30.5.3
Express dismissal

Dismissal, including redundancy, occurs when the employer gives notice to the employee. Proper notice according to the contract or statute, whichever is longer, must be given, unless misconduct is so serious that it justifies summary dismissal without notice [see **30.4.7**]. Dismissal without proper notice, or which in any other way contravenes the contract, constitutes **wrongful dismissal** [see **30.7**].

Notice of dismissal must be given or sent individually to an employee, and must clearly indicate that it is a notice of dismissal. If notice is given verbally, it is sensible to confirm it in writing.

A dismissed employee may be able to bring a claim for **unfair dismissal** if the dismissal is for an unfair reason [see **30.9**], is for a reason which is not a fair reason [see **30.8**], or is carried out in a way which is not fair and reasonable [see **30.8.2**].

30.5.3.1
Pre-employment
termination

When an offer of employment is unconditionally made and accepted, a contract of employment comes into existence. If the employer terminates the contract, even before the person has started working, it could give rise to a claim for wrongful dismissal unless the required notice (with pay) is given. If the reason is connected with pregnancy, childbirth, trade union activities or anything else where dismissal is automatically unfair, the employee will be entitled to claim unfair dismissal.

Sarker v South Tees Acute Hospital NHS Trust [1997] IRLR 328

30.6
NOTICE

Unless employment is being terminated for a reason which does not require notice [see **30.4**], the employer or employee must give the notice required under the contract or statute. If there is a difference between statute and the contract, or between statute and what is implied, the longer period always applies. *Employment Rights Act 1996 s.86(3)*

30.6.1
Statutory period
of notice

The statutory minimum applies to virtually all employees who have worked more than one month. In the first month of employment there is no statutory right for an employee to be given notice. Thereafter the minimum which must be given by the employer is:

- during the first two years of continuous employment [see **23.4.6**], one week's notice;

- then one week's additional notice for every full year of continuous employment, to a maximum of 12 weeks' notice.

Employment Rights Act 1996 s.86(1)

After the first month of employment the statutory minimum which the employee must give to the employer is only one week, regardless of how long he or she has been employed. *s.86(2)*

30.6.1.1
Employer giving short notice

If an employer tries to deprive the employee of employment rights—such as the right to claim unfair dismissal—by giving inadequate notice so that the termination date falls before the expiry of the necessary qualifying period, the effective date of termination [see **30.10.1**] is postponed to the date on which notice would have expired if the employer had given notice as required by statute [see **30.6.1**]. The employee will then have the necessary qualifying period to claim unfair dismissal. This provision does not apply to a proper dismissal with no notice for gross misconduct. *ss.92(7), 97(2)*

In some situations where the employer gives short notice, the employee's statutory notice entitlement may not be enough to take her or him into the qualifying period. But if there is an entitlement to longer contractual notice [see below] that would go into the qualifying period, the employee may be able to sue not only for the usual damages for dismissal without notice, but also for the loss of the potential right to claim unfair dismissal which would have arisen if sufficient notice had been given. *Robert Cort & Son Ltd v Charman [1981] IRLR 437*

30.6.2
Contractual period of notice

Where the contract of employment specifies a notice period different from the statutory period, the longer period applies. Many voluntary sector contracts say that the employer will give one month's notice. This is invalid for anyone who has worked five or more years, who under statute is entitled to five or more weeks' notice.

30.6.3
Implied period of notice

Even if the written contract does not explicitly specify the period of notice to be given by each party, a period longer than the statutory minimum may be implied [see **23.3.4**] by the court. For example it is generally implied that monthly paid employees are entitled to at least one month, even if their statutory entitlement is less than this.

The longer an employee has been in employment and the more senior he or she is, the more likely it is that an extended period of notice will be implied. In the absence of an agreed notice period in the contract, the courts have found that periods of six and even 12 months are appropriate for very senior members of staff.

Custom and practice in an industry or the accepted practice within an individual organisation may also be implied into the contract.

30.6.4
Waiving right to notice

The employer or employee can at any time waive their right to notice. For example an employer can agree to accept only four weeks' notice from an employee who is contractually obliged to give eight weeks' notice, or an employee may agree to accept pay in lieu of notice.

Employment Rights Act 1996 s.86(3)

30.6.5
Pay during notice period

During the notice period employees are entitled to full pay even if they would not otherwise be receiving pay, for example because they are on sick leave and have used all their sick pay entitlement [see **27.1.11**].

30.6.6
Pay in lieu of notice

Pay in lieu of notice means dismissing an employee and giving payment for the notice period, without allowing him or her to work through the period. Pay in lieu of notice is sometimes referred to as PILON.

30.6.6.1
No contractual provision

Technically an employer may lawfully terminate a contract by giving pay in lieu of notice only if the contract explicitly provides for it or the employee agrees. However, if there is no contractual provision and the employer breaches the contract by giving pay in lieu, there is little point in the employee bringing a claim against the employer. The remedy for dismissal without proper notice is payment of damages [see **33.5.3**] calculated by reference to the employee's loss, generally the amount of salary the employee would have received in the notice period—so all that the employee would get by bringing a claim against the employer would be an amount equal to the payment in lieu of notice.

An employer who gives pay in lieu of notice where there is no contractual provision has broken the contract. This has the effect of releasing the employee from his or her contractual obligations, such as a non-competition clause [see **24.41**].

Because pay in lieu of notice without a contractual entitlement is legally damages for breach of contract, it is unlikely to be subject to tax and national insurance if it is under £30,000.

30.6.6.2
Discretionary provision

Where the contract says the employee *may* be entitled to pay in lieu of notice or the employer *may* make such payment, this is a discretionary provision.

30.6.6.3
Non-payment of
pay in lieu

Where there is discretionary provision or no contractual provision for pay in lieu, an employer who dismisses without notice generally makes a payment covering the full notice period. But if the employer dismisses without making the payment and is subsequently sued by the employee, the employer may be able to argue that the employee had a duty to mitigate his or her losses [see **18.12.2**] by seeking paid work during the notice period. The court or tribunal, in awarding the pay in lieu to the employee, may reduce the amount if the employee had other earnings during the notice period or did not take steps to mitigate loss by seeking other employment.   *Cerberus Software Ltd v Rowley [2001] ICR 376 CA*

30.6.6.4
Contractual provision

Where there is a contractual entitlement to pay in lieu, the employee is entitled to the full amount even if she or he goes immediately into a new and better-paying job. Contractual provisions such as non-competition clauses [see **24.41**] continue to apply through the notice period (and beyond, if this is part of the contract). The pay in lieu of notice is subject to tax and national insurance in the usual way.

30.7
WRONGFUL
DISMISSAL

The principles on which **wrongful dismissal** are based arise out of the ordinary law of contract [see **18.6-18.12**]. Like any contract, a contract of employment can be terminated only in accordance with the terms of that contract. If those terms are broken by the act or manner of dismissal, the employee has been wrongfully dismissed.

A claim for wrongful dismissal may be brought in either the court or the employment tribunal [see **61.4** for the court process and **33.3** for the tribunal process]. The award is generally damages for the amount of the employee's loss between the date of termination and the date the employer could lawfully have terminated [see **33.6.1**].

Where wrongful dismissal has occurred, the employer and employee may seek to settle between themselves. A condition of such settlement is often that the employee will not bring a claim against the employer. A settlement preventing the employee from bringing a claim in the employment tribunal is enforceable only if it complies with strict rules [see **33.2.2**]. A settlement under which the employee agrees not to bring a claim in court does not have to comply with any formalities, but to protect the employer it should be in writing. Legal advice should be taken before entering into any such agreement.

30.7.1
When wrongful dismissal occurs

Wrongful dismissal is not about the *reasons* for the dismissal and whether they were justified; it is solely about *procedure*. So a dismissal, for example for persistent lateness, could be justified and 'fair' but could still be wrongful if the employer did not follow the appropriate steps or give the required notice.

The most common forms of wrongful dismissal are:

- prematurely ending a fixed-term contract when the employee has not committed a breach which justifies this, or when the contract does not allow for termination before its expiry;
- dismissing without notice or with too short notice where there is no repudiation or contractual entitlement to dismiss summarily;
- dismissal without following the disciplinary procedure, where the disciplinary procedure is part of the contract.

Dietmann v LB Brent [1988] ICR 842, IRLR 299 CA

Common problem areas giving rise to claims are fixed-term contracts with inadequate termination provisions, unduly long consultation periods before redundancy notices can be issued, and contractual disciplinary procedures which are unworkable.

An employer can reduce the risk of claims for wrongful dismissal by:

- ensuring that the contract of employment has sensible provisions, particularly for termination of employment;
- being aware of each employee's contractual entitlements, and ensuring these are complied with at all times;
- having a disciplinary procedure which is explicitly not part of the contract [see **29.2.2**], following the procedure rigorously if it is part of the contract, and ensuring that all aspects of dismissal comply strictly with statutory and contractual requirements.

30.7.2
Wrongful v unfair dismissal claims

From an employee's point of view, a claim of wrongful dismissal may in some situations be more appropriate than a claim of unfair dismissal because:

- there is no qualifying period of continuous employment, as there is for most unfair dismissal claims, so any employee can claim wrongful dismissal from the day the contract is created;
- the time limit for bringing a wrongful dismissal claim in the courts is six years, but in most cases only three months for unfair dismissal (or for a wrongful dismissal claim in the tribunal);
- grounds for exclusion from the right to unfair dismissal, for example being over retirement age, do not apply to wrongful dismissal cases;
- if the employee is highly paid and has a long period of notice or a fixed-term contract, a wrongful dismissal claim can be more financially advantageous than a claim for unfair dismissal, because there is no upper limit to the amount which can be recovered as damages;
- compensatory damages for unfair dismissal may be substantially reduced because of an employee's contributory conduct [see **33.4.2**], but there is no such reduction rule for damages for wrongful dismissal;
- at the time of writing (early 2001) financial assistance from the Community Legal Service Fund (formerly legal aid) is not available for unfair dismissal claims, but is available for wrongful dismissal claims if they are brought in the court rather than in the employment tribunal. However financial assistance has been available for employment tribunals in Scotland since January 2001, and may become available for tribunals in England and Wales [see **61.5**].

30.7.3
Wrongful termination by employee

While most cases in law deal with the employer's wrongful termination of the contract, it is just as possible for an employee to terminate wrongfully, usually by not giving the required notice. In this situation

457

the employer has a right to make a claim against the employee for damages, although in practice it may not be worth the effort of suing.

Many contracts contain provisions that if an employee leaves without giving the required notice or refuses to work out the notice period, the employer is entitled to deduct from the final salary payment an amount equivalent to the number of days that the notice is short. This is based on the principle that the employee's breach of contract causes a financial loss to the employer. However such a clause may not be enforceable, because it is more of a penalty than a genuine pre-estimate of the employer's loss. In order to deduct lawfully there would have to be a contractual clause allowing such deduction, *and* the employer would have to be able to show that it actually suffered a loss equivalent to the deduction.
Giraud UK v Smith [2000] 9 PLC 64 EAT

30.8
FAIR AND UNFAIR DISMISSAL

The principles of fair and unfair dismissal arise not from contract law, but from statutory employment protection legislation and the many cases which have arisen under it. In most (but not all) cases the employee must have worked at least one year for the employer or an associated employer in order to bring an unfair dismissal claim [see **23.4.5**].

Before taking any action which could conceivably give rise to a claim of unfair dismissal, an employer should seek legal advice.

30.8.1
Fair reasons

To be fair, a dismissal must arise from a **fair reason**. These are:
- the capability or qualification of the employee [see **30.8.3**];
- the employee's conduct [see **30.8.4**];
- redundancy [see **30.8.5** and **31.1.1**];
- statutory requirements [see **30.8.6**]; *or*
- some other substantial reason of a kind to justify the dismissal from that position [see **30.8.7**].   *Employment Rights Act 1996 s.98(1),(2)*

There must be a fair reason at the time of the dismissal. If the employer dismisses without good cause but subsequently discovers a good reason for the dismissal, the **after-discovered reason** cannot be used to justify the dismissal. But if the employee has been re-engaged after winning an unfair dismissal case, the after-discovered reason may become a legitimate reason to dismiss again.

W Devis & Sons Ltd v Atkins [1977] AC 931, 3 All ER 40

30.8.2
Fair procedure

As well as being able to show that the dismissal is for a fair reason, the employer must also be able to show that, considering all the circumstances, including its size and administrative resources:
- the employer acted reasonably in treating it as a sufficient reason for dismissal; *and*
- the dismissal is fair, based on equity (the principles of fairness) and the merits of the case.   *Employment Rights Act 1996 s.98(4)*

30.8.2.1
Reasonable responses

To be fair, dismissal must be a **reasonable response** in the circumstances. In assessing what is reasonable the tribunal does not substitute its own assessment for that of the employer, provided the employer can show that its decision to dismiss was within 'a band of reasonable responses', it acted reasonably, and the procedure for the dismissal was fair and reasonable.   *Midland Bank v Madden [2000] IRLR 208*

30.8.2.2
Procedural fairness

Even if a dismissal is for a fair reason and is a reasonable response, it may be unfair if the employer does not achieve a reasonable standard of procedural fairness. The tribunal will look at matters such as the nature of warnings given, whether a proper investigation took place before dismissal, whether the employee was fully informed of the issues and evidence, and whether there was a genuine opportunity for the employee to put his or her case.

This underlines the importance of properly conducting disciplinary proceedings and giving, except in cases where summary dismissal is justified, at least one warning that dismissal might occur [see **28.4**].

30.8.3
Capability or qualifications

Capability means skill, aptitude, health or other physical or mental quality necessary to do the job, and **qualifications** means any relevant degree, diploma, or other academic, technical or professional qualification.

Employment Rights Act 1996 s.98(3)

30.8.3.1
Ill health

One of the most frequent issues around capability involves illness or injury. To dismiss fairly because of persistent periods of short absence caused by sickness, it is generally necessary for the employer to issue a disciplinary warning [see **29.4**] and to give an opportunity for the employee's health to improve. Thought should be given to the possibility of alternative employment with the employer.

If the condition constitutes a disability under the **Disability Discrimination Act 1995** [see **25.5.1**], employers with 15 or more employees must adapt the job or offer suitable alternative employment if this is reasonably practicable. Failure to do so may constitute unfair dismissal and unlawful discrimination.

Before dismissing, the employer must take reasonable steps to find out the true medical position, generally by obtaining a medical report, so a reasonable decision can be made. In most situations the employee should be given the opportunity to comment.

It is not necessary to wait until all statutory or contractual sick leave entitlement [see **28.6**] is used before dismissing. However dismissal on the basis of sickness during the sick leave period, where it appears that the employee is likely to be able to return before the sick leave period expires, is likely to be unfair. The length of sick leave and the impact of the absence on the employer are factors affecting whether it is reasonable to dismiss. *Coulson v Felixstowe Dock & Railway Co [1995] IRLR 11*

An employer who provides health insurance [see **20.4.3**] for employees should seek specialist advice before dismissing an employee covered by the insurance. These policies often provide that after an initial period of absence during which the employee receives sick pay from the organisation, the insurance starts to pay a sum as replacement of lost salary. Normally the policy provides that this payment will continue for as long as the person suffers illness or disability. In a number of cases, the court has said that the existence of such insurance creates an implied term in the contract, that the employee will not be dismissed except for gross misconduct while receiving payments under the insurance.

Aspden v Webbs Poultry and Meat Group (Holdings) Ltd [1996] IRLR 521

In light of the above cases, it is possible that dismissal during a period of contractual sick pay, even if it is fair, could be seen as a breach of contract. An employer considering dismissal in this situation should seek legal advice.

In some cases the contract may be frustrated by long-term illness [see **30.4.1.1**].

30.8.3.2
Other reasons

Other reasons for dismissal under the 'capability' heading may be a lack of skill or ability, for example an inability to organise others or to provide the required quantity or quality of work. Capability is assessed in relation to the employer's needs, which may change over time. Lack of aptitude may be shown as a failure to achieve a level of skill in a test or required on the job, or as a general failure to achieve the desired results. If this failure stems from carelessness or negligence, it should be dealt with under the heading of conduct.

30.8.4
Conduct

A huge variety of conduct-related reasons have been found to be fair, including poor timekeeping, absenteeism, failure to cooperate, breach of rules or guidelines, failure to obey an instruction, and violence or harassment inside the workplace or outside in relation to fellow employees. It is up to the employer to define what is or is not acceptable conduct, but the definitions must be reasonable in the circumstances.

30.8.4.1 Criminal acts

Just as some criminal charges or convictions may not justify disciplinary action [see **29.4.13**], they may not justify dismissal. It is not enough for the employer simply to know that the police are taking action. The employer must make its own enquiries and come to its own conclusion that the offence was committed and that it has implications for the employment. The employer does not need to prove to itself that the employee is guilty before dismissing, merely to have reasonable grounds for believing that the employee is guilty. There is no need to wait for the outcome of any criminal prosecution.

If the offence occurs outside the workplace there must be some effect on the work for it to be a proper reason for dismissal. This includes the impact that the offence or alleged offence is likely to have on relationships with other employees, clients or service users.

Imprisonment may in some cases frustrate the contract [see **30.4.1.2**].

30.8.5 Redundancy

A redundancy exists when the employer intends to stop carrying on the activity for which the employee was employed either totally or at the place where the employee was employed, or when the need to carry out the work has ceased or diminished [see **chapter 31** for more about redundancy]. The dispute in redundancy situations is not generally about the reasonableness of the decision to create a redundancy situation, but whether the procedures used to select the individual were fair.

A tribunal has no right to examine, for example, the decision to close a department. The tribunal is however allowed to question whether it is a genuine redundancy, so it is important for an employer to have evidence about its financial situation, grant cuts or other reasons for closure or loss of the job.

Even in a redundancy situation, dismissal may be unfair:

- automatically because the person was selected for a reason which is automatically unfair [see **30.9.1**];
- because it is unreasonable, for example where an employer is making a number of people redundant on the basis of 'last in first out' and increases the number of redundancies in order to be able to dismiss a particular employee;
- because the employer failed to consider the possibility of alternative work [see **31.5**] or failed to consult as required [see **31.2**]; *or*
- where the employer failed to use reasonable criteria for selecting those to be made redundant, or the pool of employees from whom those to be made redundant would be chosen. The employer can use any criteria it chooses, but they must be fair and reasonable.

In addition to behaving reasonably, the employer must comply with statutory rules regarding consultation and notification in some circumstances [see **31.2**]. Employees have particular rights during the period after notice of redundancy [see **31.4**].

30.8.6 Statutory requirements

This category of fair reasons for dismissal covers situations where the law prohibits an employee from continuing in the job. Such situations include, for example, a driver who has been disqualified from driving, or a care worker or childcare worker who has been disqualified or banned from working with children or vulnerable adults [see **26.3.4**] and is thus not allowed to continue working in care or childcare.

30.8.7 Some other substantial reason

Some other substantial reason is a very wide category covering, for example:

- the changing needs of the employer;
- a reorganisation in the interests of organisational efficiency which does not fit the criteria for redundancy;
- an employee's refusal to agree changes in the contract for which the employer can show that there is a substantial reason (even if these changes are quite significant such as an increase in hours);
- an employee causing disharmony between other employees.

Employment Rights Act 1996 s.106

30.9 UNFAIR REASONS FOR DISMISSAL

If the reason for a dismissal is not fair [see above] or if the procedure is not reasonable, the dismissal is unfair. A dismissal is also unfair if it occurs for a reason defined in statute as unfair.

30.9.1 Automatically unfair

If the reason for a dismissal is automatically unfair, there is no qualifying period to be able to make a claim of unfair dismissal for it. All employees have this right, from day one of their employment.

30.9.1.1 Race, sex and disability

A dismissal is automatically unfair if it is solely or mainly because of the employee's:

- race, colour, ethnic group, national origin or nationality;
- sex, gender reassignment (transsexuality), or married status;
- disability—but an employee cannot claim unfair dismissal due to disability if the employer has fewer than 15 employees or others working under a contract, or if the dismissal is justified.

The legislation on race, sex and disability is covered in **chapter 25**. An employee can bring a claim not only for unfair dismissal but also for unlawful discrimination. In unlawful discrimination claims there is no ceiling on the damages which may be awarded.

At the time of writing (early 2001) discrimination, including dismissal, on the basis of **sexual orientation**, will be made unlawful by 2 December 2003 [see **25.7**]. Some **religions** are covered under the **Race Relations Act 1976**, and discrimination on the basis of religion and belief will be made unlawful by 2 December 2003 [see **25.8**]. Dismissal on the basis of **age** is likely to be made unlawful by 2 December 2006, but this may not apply to compulsory retirement age [see **25.9**].

30.9.1.2 Maternity and parental rights

A dismissal for virtually any reason connected with pregnancy, childbirth or maternity leave is automatically unfair and is unlawful sex discrimination. There is an exception for an employer with less than six employees where it is not reasonably practicable to allow the woman to return to work after additional maternity leave [see **28.7.5**].

Employment Rights Act 1996 s.96(2)-(5)

Dismissal is automatically unfair if the only or main reason is that the employee took, or sought to take, statutory parental leave or leave to deal with dependant emergencies [see **28.8** and **28.9**].

30.9.1.3 Health and safety

A dismissal is automatically unfair [see **36.3.3**] if the only or main reason for it is that the employee:

- was authorised by the employer or employees to deal with health and safety matters and was dismissed because of taking steps to do so; *or*
- took steps to bring a health or safety danger to the employer's attention, or refused to work in an unsafe situation, or took steps to protect him/herself or other people from danger. *s.100*

30.9.1.4 Sunday working

Shop employees cannot be compelled to work on Sundays, and it is automatically unfair to dismiss an employee working in a shop who refuses to work, or proposes to refuse to work, on Sundays or on a particular Sunday [see **28.2.5**]. *s.101*

30.9.1.5
Trade union
membership or activity

A dismissal is automatically unfair if the only or main reason for it is that the employee:

- is, or proposes to become, a member of an independent trade union;

- is taking or has taken steps in relation to trade union recognition [see **32.3.3**], or has voted or proposes to vote in a ballot in connection with recognition;

- has taken part in trade union activities either in work time if permitted by the employer or outside work time, or proposes to take part in such activities;

- is taking or took part in **protected industrial action** [see **32.8.1**];

- is not a member of a trade union or refuses to join a union.
  Trade Union and Labour Relations (Consolidation) Act 1992 ss.152, 156-161

30.9.1.6
Assertion of
statutory right

A dismissal is automatically unfair if the only or main reason is that the employee:

- claimed that the employer had infringed a statutory employment right; *or*

- brought proceedings against the employer to enforce a statutory employment right.　　　*Employment Rights Act 1996 s.104*

This covers dismissal for any reason connected with claiming a statutory employment right [see **23.4** for a list of these rights].

In most cases, only employees have the right to claim unfair dismissal on the basis of asserting a statutory right. But others who are working under a contract also have the right to claim unfair dismissal in relation to rights such as minimum wage, working time rights and whistleblowing [see **22.1.2**].

30.9.2
Dismissal on
transfer of
undertaking

Dismissal before or after a transfer where the Transfer of Undertakings Regulations (TUPE) apply is unfair if it is for any reason connected with the transfer [see **26.4**]. Although such dismissal is automatically unfair, an employee can bring a claim of unfair dismissal only if he or she has a one-year period of continuous employment with the employer or an associated employer [see **23.4.6**].

Dismissal may be fair if the employer can show that it is necessary for an economic, technical or organisational reason requiring changes in the workforce of either the original or new employer before or after the transfer.　　　*Transfer of Undertakings (Protection of Employment) Regulations 1981 [SI 1981/1794] reg.8*

30.9.3
Dismissal during
industrial action

Dismissal while taking part in **protected industrial action** [see **32.8.1**] is automatically unfair.

Dismissal while an employee is taking part in an unofficial strike or other industrial action [see **32.8.2**] is not fair, but the employee loses the right to bring a claim of unfair dismissal. However, a claim can be brought if other employees who took part were not dismissed, or if another employee who was dismissed at the same time has been offered re-engagement within three months of dismissal. In this case the time limit for bringing a claim is six months rather than three.
Trade Union and Labour Relations (Consolidation) Act 1992 ss.237, 238; Employment Relations Act 1999 sch.5

30.10
ENTITLEMENT TO
CLAIM UNFAIR
DISMISSAL

An employee dismissed for a reason which is automatically unfair [see above] has a right to bring a claim of unfair dismissal, with no qualifying period (apart from a TUPE dismissal). To bring a claim for a TUPE dismissal or other types of unfair dismissal, the employee must have at least one year continuous employment [see **23.4.6**] with the employer or an associated employer.

Application must generally be made to the employment tribunal within three months of the effective date of termination [see **30.10.1**, and see **33.3** for tribunal procedure]. In exceptional circumstances, the three-month deadline can be extended. If the tribunal finds that the dismissal is not fair, the tribunal may award compensation [see **33.4.2**] or in very rare cases require reinstatement or re-engagement [see **33.4.1**].

Employment Rights Act 1996 ss.94-134

Rather than go to tribunal, the employer and employee may agree a settlement. Often a condition of settlement is that the employee gives up the right to take the case to tribunal. This condition is binding only if the settlement follows strict rules [see **33.2.2**]. In any situation where the employer is settling by making a payment in addition to whatever is due to the employee, it is sensible to make the payment dependent on the employee signing a formal settlement which complies with the rules.

30.10.1
Effective date of termination

The qualifying period and the time limit for bringing a claim are based on the **effective date of termination**. [For redundancy purposes this is called the **relevant date**, see **31.6.1**]. Complex rules govern determination of the date. In general:

- if proper notice [see **30.6**] of dismissal or resignation is given, the date of termination is the date on which the notice expires;

- if the employee is dismissed on notice but is not required to work out the notice period, the date of termination is the date when the notice period expires;

- if the employee is dismissed without proper notice but is given payment in lieu of notice [see **30.6.6**], the date of termination is the date when the dismissal actually takes effect;

- if the employee is not entitled to notice (for example, in cases of summary dismissal, see **30.4.7**), the date of termination is the date on which the dismissal takes effect;

- the date of termination of a fixed-term contract is the date on which it expires. *ss.95, 97*

When a dismissal without notice is communicated to the employee by post, the dismissal takes effect from when the employee receives the letter—even if the letter states that dismissal is from the date the letter is written. *McMaster v Manchester Airport plc [1998] IRLR 112 EAT*

If the employer gives notice, and then the employee gives a shorter notice which takes effect earlier, the effective date is the date on which the employer's notice would have taken effect.

Employment Rights Act 1996 s.95(2)

30.10.2
<u>Qualifying employees</u>

In general only employees and apprentices have the right to claim unfair dismissal. Trainees, self-employed people, agents, non-employee 'workers' [see **22.1.2**] and others who are not employees generally cannot bring a claim. However in some situations 'workers' working under a contract, such as casuals or agency workers, may be able to bring a claim in relation to an automatically unfair reason for dismissal [see **30.9.1.6**].

Some employees have the right to bring a claim for an automatically unfair reason for dismissal, but do not have the right to bring a claim for unfair dismissal for any other reason. They include:

- employees over the contractual or normal retiring age for that employer, or 65 or over if the employer does not have a normal retirement age (but this may change; see **25.9.1**);

- employees who are employed under illegal contracts, for example where the employer and employee have conspired to avoid tax or otherwise breach the law, although in some circumstances a degree of illegality might not prevent a claim for unfair dismissal;

- employees on contracts which end on completion of a specified task.

In the past, employees of a UK-based employer who worked outside the UK were not able to claim unfair dismissal, but they now have this right.

30.10.3
Qualifying dismissal

To make a claim of unfair dismissal, the employee must have been dismissed. Dismissal normally occurs in three circumstances:

- the employer terminates the employee's contract of employment, usually by giving notice although in some situations dismissal can be inferred from the circumstances;

- a fixed-term contract is not renewed; *or*

- the employee is entitled to terminate the contract because of the employer's conduct, and does so [see **30.4.8**].

For the purposes of unfair dismissal the employee is not considered to be dismissed if he or she is re-engaged before the dismissal takes effect or the employer offers to renew the contract of employment within four weeks of the dismissal.   *EBAC Ltd v Wymer [1996] 537 IRLB 3 EAT*

30.10.3.1
Termination by agreement

If a contract is terminated by agreement [see **30.4.3**], the courts are reluctant to find that such agreements deprive employees of their statutory right to claim unfair dismissal. Unless it meets certain statutory requirements, any agreement between an employer and employee is invalid if it seeks to prevent the employee from exercising his or her right to make an application to the employment tribunal for any reason. An agreement, therefore, where an employer agrees to make a final payment to an employee, give a reference to an employee, or take other action on condition that the employee does not make a claim of unfair dismissal is invalid unless it is in the prescribed form [see **33.2.2** for the requirements].   *Employment Rights Act 1996 s.203*

30.10.4
Non-qualifying termination

A contract can come to an end without there being a dismissal which would give rise to a possible claim for unfair dismissal. This is the case, for example, when an employee resigns or reaches contractual retirement age, or when the contract is frustrated [see **30.4.1**].

If a contract is terminated by completion of the job (for example, if a person is employed to write a manual), the employee cannot claim unfair dismissal, even if the job has lasted longer than the qualifying period. In one case a man was employed for 31 different ship repair jobs over a five-year period, but when the last came to an end there was no dismissal nor any right to redundancy payments, because each job had been on a separate contract and no continuity of employment had built up. This is different from a fixed-term contract for a specified period or a series of fixed-term contracts for specified periods, where a person who has the necessary continuity is entitled to claim unfair dismissal.

Ryan v Shipboard Maintenance Limited [1980] IRLR 16

FOR FURTHER INFORMATION

ACAS: see telephone directory for local office; www.acas.org.uk

---

Chapter 31
REDUNDANCY

Topics covered in this chapter

This chapter explains the procedure for redundancy and redundancy payments. It covers:

For sources of further information see end of chapter.
Double-underlined section headings indicate additions or significant changes since the first edition.

31.1 DEFINING REDUNDANCY

31.1.1 Definition for dismissal and redundancy pay

There are two statutory definitions of redundancy: one for the purposes of fair dismissal and redundancy pay, and a much wider definition [see **31.2.2**] for the purposes of consultation.

For the purposes of determining whether a dismissal is fair and entitlement to redundancy pay, redundancy is defined as a dismissal attributable wholly or mainly to the fact that:

- the employer has ceased or intends to cease to carry on the business for the purposes for which the employee was employed;

- the employer has ceased or intends to cease to carry on the business in the place where the employee was employed; *or*

- the requirement of that business for employees to carry out work of a particular kind, or for employees to carry out work of a particular kind in the place where the employee was employed, has ceased or diminished or is expected to cease or diminish.

Employment Rights Act 1996 s.139(3)

In deciding whether an employee is redundant the employment tribunal applies a three-part test:

- was the employee dismissed?

- had the requirement of the employer's business for employees to do work of a particular kind ceased or diminished, or was it expected to?

- if so, was the dismissal caused wholly or in part by the cessation or diminution of work? *Safeway Stores plc v Burrell [1997] IRLR 200 EAT*

'Business' means any type of activity for which a person is employed, even if carried out by a charity or other voluntary organisation. The reduced need for the work may arise through lack of demand, lack of funding, or a decision by the organisation.

465

'Work of a particular kind' is 'work which is distinguished from other work of the same general kind by requiring special aptitudes, special skills or knowledge'.　　　*Amos v Max-Arc Ltd [1973] ICR 46; IRLR 285*

If the so-called redundancy does not meet the tests for redundancy:

- the dismissal is not fair on the basis of redundancy, and an employee with the necessary continuity of employment [see **30.10.1**] may be able to make a claim of unfair dismissal (unless the dismissal is fair on some other basis); *and*

- the employee is not entitled to a redundancy payment, even if he or she has the necessary continuity of employment.

Even if the redundancy is genuine the dismissal may be unfair if it is not carried out reasonably, for example if reasonable and fair criteria are not used to select the people to be made redundant or to select the pool from whom those to be made redundant are chosen [see **30.8.2**].

31.1.2
Specific situations

It is not always clear whether a redundancy exists. In this situation advice should be taken at an early stage, to ensure the organisation consults, gives time off to look for work, offers alternative work if available, and fulfils the other obligations specific to redundancy.

31.1.2.1
Voluntary redundancy

The term **voluntary redundancy** is sometimes used where employees are invited to apply for redundancy. Provided a genuine redundancy situation exists, a candidate for voluntary redundancy is treated in the same way as a person chosen for redundancy by the employer.

Using 'voluntary redundancy' as a way of dismissing an employee who is not genuinely redundant is a misuse of redundancy [see **31.7**].

31.1.2.2
Offer of suitable alternative work

The employer has a duty to offer suitable alternative work if any is available [see **31.5**]. If suitable work is offered and the employee accepts it, there is no redundancy if the new contract starts as soon as the old contract ends or within four weeks of the termination. If suitable work is offered and the employee unreasonably refuses it, he or she loses the right to redundancy payment.　　*Employment Rights Act 1996 s.141(2),(3)*

31.1.2.3
'Bumping'

If Worker A who is redundant is transferred to another post as alternative employment, thus leading to the dismissal of Worker B who holds that post, Worker A is not redundant but Worker B is. This is called 'bumping'. However this approach has been challenged, and should not be relied on without legal advice.　　*W Gimber & Sons Ltd v Spurrett [1967] 2 ITR 308; Church v West Lancashire NHS Trust [1998] IRLR 4*

31.1.2.4
Restructuring

If an organisational restructuring leads to a loss of jobs, it is a redundancy situation if there is no longer a need for particular work or for so many employees to do the work. If the restructuring does not lead to loss of jobs but some work is dropped, the employees who have been doing that work may be redundant but may be able to be offered alternative work from among the new jobs.

Where existing employees are invited to apply for new jobs a redundancy situation is created, but those who are appointed to the new posts have accepted alternative work and are therefore not redundant.

If there are fewer new posts than applicants, those who are not appointed are redundant. If there are the same number of new posts as applicants (or more posts than applicants), failure to appoint a suitably qualified employee would give the employee a claim for unfair dismissal.

31.1.2.5
Work at other locations

If the employee's contract of employment has a **mobility clause**, the employer can require the employee to move to another location (but note that such clauses may constitute unlawful sex discrimination; see **25.2.4**). If one workplace closes or has insufficient work, the employee is redundant there—but if there is suitable alternative work at another site and the employee can be required to move there under the terms of their contract, is the employee genuinely redundant? In this situation the tribunal looks at the factual situation. In one case, where an employee had worked in only one location, the court of appeal said there was a redundancy even though work was available on another site and there was a mobility clause in the contract.

High Table v Horst [1997] IRLR 513 CA

Regardless of whether the contract contains a mobility clause, the offer of work at another location may be suitable alternative employment [see **31.5**]. If there is no suitable work at other locations, or if the locations are so far away as to be unsuitable, the employee is redundant.

31.1.2.6
Transfer of undertaking

Where an undertaking is transferred to a new employer [see **26.4**] and the employee continues working, there is no redundancy. If the employee is dismissed before or after transfer for an economic, technical or organisational reason which requires a change in the workforce [see **26.4.5**], the dismissal might constitute redundancy.

31.2
CONSULTATION
AND NOTIFICATION

An employer who proposes to make an employee or employees redundant must in most cases consult the individuals who may be made redundant, with a view to finding alternatives to redundancy. In some situations collective consultation may also be necessary.

Fair consultation involves:

* consultations when proposals are at a formative stage;
* adequate information on which to respond [see **31.2.3.3**];
* adequate time for response; *and*
* genuine consideration of the response.

One aim of consultation is to explore alternatives to redundancy and whether alternative work is available. Voluntary sector employers often ask the employees, under the guise of 'consultation', to decide who should be made redundant. This is an improper use of the consultation process, and an abrogation of management responsibility.

Boulton & Paul Ltd v Arnold [1994] IRLR 532 EAT

Failure to consult a worker who is on maternity leave or absent for a pregnancy-related reason may be unlawful sex discrimination.

McGuigan v T G Baines & Sons 11/4/1997; 24/11/1998 EAT

31.2.1
Individual
consultation

Although there is no specific statutory obligation for an employer to consult individual employees prior to making them redundant, case law has established that individual consultation is an essential part of a fair procedure and an employer's reasonable conduct. Failure to consult would entitle the worker to claim unfair dismissal, unless the tribunal concludes that consultation would have been utterly futile [see **30.8.2**].

Mugford v Midland Bank plc [1997] IRLR 208; IRLB 13 EAT

Consultation may be with each individual separately, with them jointly in meetings, or a combination.

If the employer undertakes collective consultation [see below] the trade union or employee representatives may consult the individuals, but individual consultation by the employer may still be advisable.

31.2.2
Definition of
redundancy for
collective
consultation

For the purposes of the requirement to consult with recognised trade unions or elected employee representatives [see below], redundancy is defined very widely. For consultation purposes, redundancy is any dismissal 'not related to the individual concerned or for a number of reasons all of which are not so related'. This covers any dismissal not directly related to an individual employee's competence or conduct. This could include, for example, new working arrangements.

Trade Union and Labour Relations (Consolidation) Act 1992 s.195

31.2.3
Collective consultation

When the employer proposes to make 20 or more employees redundant within a 90-day period—using the wider definition of redundancy—the employer has a duty to consult any independent trade union(s) recognised by the employer [see **32.3.3**] or, where there is no recognised union, elected representatives of the employees likely to be affected by the redundancies. If some but not all employees are represented by a recognised union, the employer must consult both the union(s) and representatives elected by the other employees.

Collective Redundancies and Transfer of Undertakings (Protection of Employment) (Amendment) Regulations 1999 [SI 1999/1925]

Consultation must be with representatives of all workers who may be affected, not only those under threat of redundancy. The consultation must include discussion about ways of avoiding dismissals, reducing the numbers of employees to be dismissed and easing the consequences of dismissals, and the method of selection for redundancy. Consultation must be undertaken by the employer 'with a view to reaching agreement' with the representatives.

Trade Union and Labour Relations (Consolidation) Act 1992 s.188(6)

Where there is no recognised trade union, the regulations specify how representatives are to be elected. The representatives must be employees, must be chosen by the employees rather than the employer, and have the right to reasonable paid time off for training. It is unlawful for an employer to dismiss or subject to detriment any employee for a reason connected with participating in an election for employee representatives or serving as an employee or trade union representative.

Collective Redundancies and TUPE (Amendment) Regulations regs.12-13; Employment Rights Act 1996 ss.47, 103

31.2.3.1
Counting the numbers

When determining whether 20 or more employees are to be made redundant, all employees likely to be made redundant are included in the numbers, even if they are not entitled to redundancy pay or are volunteering for redundancy. The only employees who are not counted are those on fixed-term or task-completion contracts of 12 weeks or less.

For the purposes of counting, the employees to be made redundant must be 'at one establishment'. This clearly means all working in the same place, but can also mean working in different locations if all the locations are administered from one place. *Barratt Developments (Bradford) Ltd v Union of Construction Allied Trades & Technicians [1978] ICR 319*

31.2.3.2
Period of consultation

The consultation must begin 'in good time'. The minimum prescribed periods are:

- 30 days before the first redundancy takes effect if between 20 and 99 employees are to be dismissed within a period of 30 days or less;

- 90 days if 100 or more are being made redundant within a period of 90 days or less.

Trade Union and Labour Relations (Consolidation) Act 1992 s.188(2)

If special circumstances make it impracticable to carry out the consultation as required, the employer must take all reasonable steps to comply as much as possible. *s.188(7)*

Individual notices of dismissal should not normally be issued until there has been a sufficient period of meaningful consultation.

31.2.3.3
Provision of information

The employer must provide the union or employees' representatives in writing with:

- reason for the proposals;

- number and description of workers proposed for redundancy;

- total number of employees employed at the location;

- proposed method of selecting employees to be dismissed;

- proposed method of carrying out the dismissals;
- proposed method of calculating any redundancy payments in addition to those required by statute.

Trade Union and Labour Relations (Consolidation) Act 1992 s.188(4)

If it is not reasonably practicable, the full requirements do not have to be met. However, this is interpreted fairly strictly.   *s.188(7)*

If employees do not elect representatives within a reasonable time the employer must give the specified information to each affected employee.

31.2.3.4
Protective awards

If the employer fails to comply with the duty to consult collectively and provide information, the union or employees' representatives may make a complaint to the tribunal. This can be made before the dismissals or not later than three months after they have taken effect.   *ss.189-192*

Failure to consult does not prevent an employer from being able to make the redundancies. However the tribunal may make a **protective award** requiring the employer to pay each affected employee a week's pay for each week specified in the protective award. The length of the period of the protective award must not exceed that specified for the period of consultation [see **31.2.3.2**]. Where collective consultation is required but there is no specified period, the period of the protective award may be up to 13 weeks.   *s.189(4)*

31.2.3.5
Official notification

An employer must notify the secretary of state for employment if 20 or more employees are being made redundant in a 90-day period.

31.2.4
Other obligations
to consult

The contract of employment, contractual policies or a collective agreement with the union(s) may include specific requirements, for example to consult the recognised union(s) even if there are fewer than 20 redundancies. All provisions must be strictly followed. Failure to comply with contractual obligations could lead to claims for unfair and/or wrongful dismissal. The obligations under collective agreements may or may not be legally binding, but even if they are not binding, failure to comply with them could lead to a claim for unfair dismissal.

31.3
PERIOD OF NOTICE

An employee who is being made redundant is entitled to notice in the usual way [see **30.6**]. Individual notice must be given to each employee. A general announcement that the organisation or unit will close is not adequate. If the employee is required to stop work before the end of the period of notice (for example, if the employer closes) the employee is entitled to pay in lieu of notice for that period.

31.3.1
Precautionary notice

An organisation approaching the end of a funding cycle without knowing whether a grant or contract will be renewed may need to give employees notice of redundancy, stating that they will be redundant if the funds are not forthcoming. This is often called a **precautionary** (or sometimes **protective**) **notice of redundancy**.

If the grant or contract is then received, the notice of redundancy is usually said to be withdrawn. Technically a notice of redundancy cannot be withdrawn—so in legal terms the employer is offering the job with its new funding as suitable alternative employment [see **31.5**].

31.4
RIGHT TO TIME OFF

An employee who has been given notice of dismissal because of redundancy and has the necessary qualifying period for redundancy pay [see **31.6.1**] is entitled to reasonable time off with pay during working hours to look for another job or to make arrangements for training for future employment. There is no statutory requirement as to the amount of time an employee is entitled to take off, and the employer can decide what is reasonable in any situation.

Employment Rights Act 1996 ss.52, 53

If the employer does not allow paid time off the employee is entitled to be paid the amount he or she would have been entitled to if time off had been allowed, up to 40% of one week's pay.

Employment Rights Act 1996 ss.53(4),(5), 54(4)

If the employer neither allows paid time off nor pays for the time not allowed, the employee may bring a complaint in the employment tribunal and may be awarded up to 40% of one week's pay.

31.5 ALTERNATIVE EMPLOYMENT

The employer is under a duty to offer alternative employment for the employee if any is available, to start as soon as the previous contract terminates or within four weeks of the termination.

31.5.1 Suitable alternative employment

If the work offered is virtually the same as the old employment in terms of the capacity of the worker, the location of the work and the contract conditions, and if the work starts as soon as the previous work terminates or within four weeks of the termination, it is considered to be **suitable alternative employment**. There is generally no dismissal for redundancy and no break in continuity of employment [see **23.4.6**].

s.138(1)

However the employer and employee may, if they wish, agree a trial period of up to four weeks from the end of the previous contract. If the employer dismisses the employee during this period, the employee is treated as having been made redundant from the end of the earlier contract. But an employee who unreasonably terminates the new contract loses the right to a redundancy payment, because he or she is deemed to have refused an offer of suitable alternative work.

31.5.2 Other alternative employment

If the alternative employment differs in any significant way from the previous contract, the employee has a statutory right to a **trial period** of four weeks from the end of the previous contract. *s.138(2)*

The trial period can be extended by agreement, provided the agreement to extend is made before the employee starts the new work and is in writing. It must specify the date on which the extended period ends and the conditions which will apply after the period. *s.138(6)*

If the employee successfully completes the trial period there is no redundancy and no break in continuity of employment. An employee who resigns or is dismissed during or at the end of the trial period (whether standard or extended) is treated as having been made redundant under the previous contract. No further reason for resignation or dismissal needs to be given, and the right to redundancy pay remains.

There is no entitlement to redundancy pay if the employee leaves after the end of the trial period.

31.6 REDUNDANCY PAYMENTS

In addition to statutory entitlement to redundancy pay, many voluntary sector employers provide for **enhanced redundancy pay**. This may top up the statutory entitlement, and/or give redundancy pay to employees who do not yet have the qualifying period for statutory entitlement. Enhanced redundancy pay may be **contractual** [see **31.6.2**] or **discretionary** (non-contractual) [see **31.6.3**].

Regardless of whether they are entitled to statutory and/or enhanced redundancy pay, employees made redundant are entitled to:

- payment of all wages owed up to the relevant date;
- holiday entitlement for untaken holiday leave (with the daily rate calculated as 1/7th of weekly pay or 1/365th of annual pay); *and*
- pay in lieu of notice if the employee has not been given the full notice required by statute or contract [see **30.6**].

Special provisions apply if the employer is insolvent [see **21.9.5**].

A redundant employee who gets a job with a new employer remains entitled to statutory redundancy. Entitlement to enhanced redundancy pay depends on the contract of employment or the employer's policy.

31.6.1
Statutory
redundancy pay

To qualify for statutory redundancy pay, the employee must have two years of continuous employment [see **23.4.6** for how this is calculated]. Periods of employment before the employee's 18th birthday and from age 65 (or earlier, if the employer's normal retiring age is less than 65) do not count. *Employment Rights Act 1996 s.211*

31.6.1.1
Relevant date

Statutory redundancy pay and the qualifying period are calculated up to the **relevant date**, and the six-month time limit for bringing a claim in the employment tribunal is calculated from this date. The relevant date is the date on which the notice of dismissal due to redundancy takes effect. *ss.145, 153*

31.6.1.2
Qualifying employees

Virtually all employees with the necessary continuous employment are entitled to statutory redundancy pay. This includes:

- part-time or low-paid employees, even those who work very few hours or earn very little, provided they earn at least the national insurance lower earnings limit (£72 per week in 2001-02);
- temporary employees [see **22.3.1**];
- employees on fixed-term contracts for two years or more who have not waived their right to redundancy pay [see **30.4.4**].

31.6.1.3
Non-qualifying
employees

Among those who do not qualify for statutory redundancy pay are:

- employees who do not have two years' continuous employment with the employer or an associated employer;
- people who are not employees of the employer [see **22.6**] such as self-employed workers and staff supplied by employment agencies;
- employees who have reached age 65 or, if it is lower, the normal retirement age for the employer;
- employees on fixed-term contracts for two years or more who have waived their right to redundancy pay [see **30.4.4**];
- employees on contracts which end on completion of a specified task [see **22.3.3**].

31.6.1.4
Lay-offs and short time

Employees who have worked the necessary qualifying period and are laid off or put on short-time working may be entitled to statutory redundancy pay. **Lay-off** means no work was provided and the employee had no remuneration from the employer during a week; **short time** means the employee received less than half a week's pay. To qualify for redundancy pay there must have been four consecutive weeks of lay-off or short-time working or a series of six or more weeks within a 13-week period. *ss.147-152, 154*

31.6.1.5
Dismissal after
redundancy notice

An employee in a redundancy situation who is dismissed for misconduct which would qualify for summary dismissal [see **29.4.12**] loses entitlement to statutory redundancy pay. This applies regardless of whether the employer dismisses summarily (without notice) or with notice. An employment tribunal may, if it considers it just and equitable, reinstate some or all of the redundancy pay entitlement. *s.140(1),(3),(4)*

If the employee has already received notice of redundancy and is dismissed because of taking part in a **unprotected industrial action** [see **32.8.2**], he or she does not lose the right to statutory redundancy pay. However, the employer has the right to require the employee to make up the days lost by the industrial action, and if the employee refuses, the right to redundancy pay is lost. *s.140(2),(5)*

An employee dismissed for any other reason after receiving notice of redundancy remains entitled to statutory redundancy pay.

**31.6.1.6
Resignation after
redundancy notice**

If an employee who has received notice of redundancy then gives notice that he or she is resigning before the redundancy notice expires, the employer can require the employee to withdraw the resignation and work until the end of the redundancy notice. This notification must be in writing and must state that if the employee does not comply, the employer will contest the liability to make a statutory redundancy payment. An employee who then does not work out the notice is not entitled to redundancy pay unless the case is taken to employment tribunal and the tribunal orders payment.

Employment Rights Act 1996 ss.136(4), 142

The employer may choose instead to accept the resignation and allow the employee to leave before the end of the redundancy notice, with redundancy pay.

**31.6.1.7
Calculation of
redundancy pay**

Statutory redundancy payment is calculated on the basis of:

- the employee's age at the relevant date [see **31.6.1.1**];
- the number of years continuous employment, to a maximum of 20;
- the amount of gross weekly pay, to a maximum set each year by the government.

To calculate statutory redundancy entitlement:

- work out how many years of continuous employment [see **23.4.6**] the employee has;
- if 20 years or less, work out how many years are at age 18-21, how many at age 22-40, and how many at age 41-65 (or up to the employer's normal retirement age, if it is less than 65);
- if the employee has more than 20 years of continuous employment, take the 20 most recent years and work out how many are in each of the three age brackets;
- take the employee's current gross weekly pay or the statutory maximum (£240 as at 1/4/01), whichever is less;
- multiply the weekly pay by 1.5 for each year of service between age 41 and 65, by 1.0 for each year of service between age 22 and 40, and by 0.5 for each year of service between age 18 and 21;
- if the employee is over 64 but not yet 65 the award is reduced by one-twelfth for each completed month between the 64th birthday and the dismissal date.

Booklet PL808 *Redundancy Payments*, available from the DTI or on its website [see end of chapter] contains a ready reckoner for working out entitlement.

For employees with variable earnings, 'weekly pay' is the average pay in the 12 weeks before the relevant date [see **31.6.1.1**].

Complex rules govern what is and is not included as pay. Professional advice may be necessary if the employee earns less than the statutory maximum and it is therefore necessary to work out exactly what the weekly pay is.   *ss.221-229, 234*

If the employer has contributed to a pension scheme [see **27.10**], a lump sum or pension payable under the scheme may be offset against redundancy pay. Details of this are set out in DTI booklet RPL1 *Offsetting Pensions against Redundancy Payments*.

The employer must provide a written calculation of the entitlement. Failure to do so can result in a fine.   *s.165*

**31.6.2
Contractual
redundancy pay**

Many voluntary sector contracts of employment offer more than the statutory entitlement to redundancy pay. Very generous contractual provision—for example one month's pay for every completed year of service, with no maximum number of years—places a potentially heavy financial burden on the organisation if it has to make long-serving staff redundant. The governing body, especially in an unincorporated organisation, must ensure that the organisation has adequate assets to meet its contractual redundancy obligations.

Some charities believe that they are not permitted to make redundancy payments above the statutory minimum. This is not the case, and a charity may make any reasonable contractual arrangements which the trustees consider appropriate. Only unreasonably generous provision might be considered by the Charity Commission or the courts to be a misuse of charitable funds.

31.6.3
Discretionary payment

Where there is no contractual obligation to pay more than statutory redundancy pay, the employer may make a discretionary payment to thank the employee for her or his years of service.

31.6.3.1
Payment by charity

A charity can make a non-contractual payment only if it is reasonable in the circumstances and is in the interests of the charity, for example is seen as encouraging staff to view the charity as a good employer.

If the payment is primarily driven by consideration of the redundant employee's private interest rather than the charity's interest, it can be made only if the governing body has actual or implied power to make such a payment [see **5.4.3**], and:

- the Charity Commission gives consent;   *Charities Act 1993 s.27*

- in a charitable company, the payment can be justified by the directors' duty to have regard to the interests of the company's employees; *or*   *Companies Act 1985 s.309*

- in a charitable company that is ceasing or transferring all or part of the company's business, if the payment is authorised by an ordinary resolution [see **17.4.7**] of the company's members or in accordance with the articles of association.   *s.719*

31.6.3.2
Payment by non-charity

A non-charitable unincorporated association can make a non-contractual payment only if it is authorised by the governing document or by all the members. The rules for non-charitable companies are the same as for charitable companies [see above].

31.6.3.3
Discretionary payments becoming contractual

A 'discretionary' payment may become contractual by custom and practice [see **23.3.4**]. This has implications for tax and national insurance, because non-contractual payments up to £30,000 are not subject to tax and NI [see below}, while contractual payments are (although the employer can apply to the Inland Revenue for exemption).

An additional implication is that an employee who is not given a discretionary redundancy payment could claim breach of contract if other employees in a similar situation were given payments. If the employer does not want this to happen, the redundancy policy should make clear that enhanced payment is purely discretionary, and any payment should be accompanied by a statement that the employer is not to be regarded as being committed to making similar payments in future.

31.6.4
Tax and NI on redundancy pay

There is no tax or national insurance on **statutory** redundancy payments.

If the employer has a **contractual** obligation to make a redundancy payment above the statutory minimum, or if the employer regularly makes such payments even though there is no contractual obligation to do so, the payment should be subject to tax and NI. However the Inland Revenue may agree to exempt an amount up to £30,000 from tax and NI if the redundancy is genuine [see **31.1.1**], the employee has at least two years of continuous employment [see **23.4.6** for definition], and the amount is reasonable in relation to the length of service and rate of pay.

Inland Revenue Statement of Practice SP 1/94

A genuine **non-contractual** payment—one not provided for in the employee's contract and not paid in accordance with the employer's usual policy or practice—is free of tax of tax and NI if it is up to £30,000.

Written authorisation should be obtained from the organisation's PAYE office before making any enhanced redundancy payment, whether contractual or non-contractual, without deducting tax and NI.

The portion of any redundancy payment over £30,000 is subject to tax and NI.

A statutory redundancy payment does not affect jobseeker's allowance. Enhanced redundancy pay may affect entitlement to welfare benefits, and employees are advised to seek advice about this.

31.6.5
Non-payment of redundancy pay

31.6.5.1
Statutory redundancy pay

If the employer fails to make a statutory redundancy payment, the affected employee can apply to the Redundancy Payments Office. Addresses are available from the redundancy helpline [see below]. The RPO makes the payment from the National Insurance Fund and collects the amount from the employer.

If the employer is insolvent the employee can claim redundancy pay and certain other amounts from the National Insurance Fund [see **21.9.5**].

31.6.5.2
Contractual redundancy pay

These remedies do not apply to non-payment of **contractual redundancy pay**. If the employer is a company or industrial and provident society and is solvent, an employee who wants to recover contractual redundancy pay sues the organisation. If the organisation is insolvent the employee is treated as an unsecured creditor [see **21.9.3**].

If the employer is a trust or association, the employee could sue some or all members of the governing body. If the claim is successful and the organisation has enough funds, it indemnifies the individuals who have been successfully sued. If it does not have enough assets to indemnify the individuals, they could then sue the other governing body members for a contribution towards the payments [see **19.1.3**].

31.7
MISUSE OF REDUNDANCY

An employer wishing to dismiss an employee without facing the real issue—usually inadequate performance or unacceptable conduct—may call the dismissal redundancy even though it does not meet the criteria for a genuine redundancy. This approach leaves open the possibility of the employee bringing a claim for unfair dismissal, with the organisation unable to show that the dismissal met one of the criteria for fair dismissal [see **30.8.1**]. To prevent this, the employee should be required to enter into a formal settlement giving up the right to bring a claim against the employer [see **33.2.2**].

Calling a dismissal a redundancy preserves the employee's right to jobseeker's allowance, but could involve the organisation in making a fraudulent statement if it is asked by the Benefits Agency about reasons for the dismissal.

FOR FURTHER INFORMATION

Redundancy entitlements and pay. Redundancy payments helpline: 0500-848489; www.dti.gov.uk/er/redundancy.htm

Chapter 32
EMPLOYER-EMPLOYEE RELATIONS

Topics covered in this chapter

This chapter covers the rights of workers in relation to workplace participation and trade union membership, and provides a brief overview of the law on industrial action. It covers:

32.1 Employee involvement	**32.5 Rights of trade union members**
32.1.1 General duties	32.5.1 Check-off
32.1.2 Duties of companies	32.5.2 Paid time off for union duties
	32.5.3 Time off for union activities
32.2 Employee representatives	32.5.4 Objection to political fund
32.3 Trade unions	**32.6 Rights of trade unions**
32.3.1 Staff associations or 'house unions'	32.6.1 Collective bargaining
	32.6.2 Information and consultation
32.3.2 Independent trade unions	
32.3.3 Recognised trade unions	**32.7 Trade disputes**
32.3.4 Collective agreements	**32.8 Industrial action**
32.3.5 Management and unions	32.8.1 Protected industrial action
	32.8.2 Unofficial action
32.4 Trade union rights: All workers	32.8.3 Peaceful picketing
32.4.1 Selection for employment	32.8.4 Dismissal during industrial action
32.4.2 Detriment	32.8.5 Collective agreements not to take
32.4.3 Dismissal on union grounds	industrial action

For sources of further information see end of chapter.

Double-underlined section headings indicate additions or significant changes since the first edition.

32.1 EMPLOYEE INVOLVEMENT

32.1.1 General duties

European Union law places a heavy emphasis on encouraging or requiring employers to inform and consult employees about the organisation and its work, generally through **works councils** (usually called **joint consultative committees** in the UK) in addition to or instead of through trade unions. This has led to significant changes in UK legislation, which now provides for consultation on specified matters with elected employee representatives where there is no recognised union, or in some cases in addition to consultation with recognised unions. Legislation also encourages new forms of partnership and joint working between employers and unions. *Employment Relations Act 1999 s.30*

The EU **Directive on Informing and Consulting Employees** will require employers to inform or consult employee representatives on all crucial employment and organisational decisions, including potential job losses, and developments that could lead to substantial changes in work or in contracts of employment. This is expected to apply from 2004 to employers with 150 or more employees, from 2006 to employers with 100 or more employees, and from 2008 to employers with 20 or more employees in a single workplace or 50 or more in different workplaces.
EU Directive on Informing and Consulting Employees [2001/501 PC 0296]

A UK employer with more than 1,000 employees in the EU must have arrangements in place for providing transnational information and consultation arrangements when employees ask for this. This is usually through a European works council (EWC). *Transnational Information and Consultation of Employees Regulations 1999 [SI 1999/3323]*

32.1.2
Duties of companies

The directors of a company have a statutory obligation to 'have regard to the interests of the company's employees in general'. This duty cannot be enforced by employees, because it is owed to the company rather than to the employees. *Companies Act 1985 s.309(1)*

A company with more than a weekly average of 250 employees in the UK must include in its annual report a statement of what has been done during the last year to maintain or develop arrangements to:

- give employees regular information about matters concerning them;
- consult employees or their representatives on a regular basis;
- encourage involvement of employees in the company's performance;
- make employees aware of the financial and economic factors affecting the company's performance. *sch.7 pt.V*

32.2
EMPLOYEE
REPRESENTATIVES

For the purposes of consultation on redundancy [see **31.2.3**] and transfer of undertakings [see **26.4.7**] the employer must consult with representatives of any recognised trade union or unions [see **32.3.3**] or, if there is no recognised union, with elected employee representatives. The procedures for electing employee representatives are set out in regulations [see **31.2.3**]. For health and safety consultation [see **36.2.7**], employers may consult with individual employees, trade union representatives or elected employee representatives.

Employee representatives have a statutory right to paid time off for duties during consultation on redundancy, transfer of undertakings or health and safety.

32.3
TRADE UNIONS

Trade unions remain a primary channel for resolution of employer/employee matters, whether collective or individual. Legally a trade union is a temporary or permanent organisation which consists wholly or mainly of workers, and whose principal purposes include the regulation of relations between those types of workers and employers or employers' associations.

Trade Union and Labour Relations (Consolidation) Act 1992 s.1

An organisation is also a trade union if its members are trade unions as defined above, or representatives of such trade unions.

This definition refers not to employees, but to **workers**. This includes:

- people who work under a contract of service (employees and apprentices); *and*
- people who work under a contract for services (casuals, home workers, freelances etc), but not if the contractual relationship is one of professional and client. *ss.295, 296*

The certification officer, a government official, keeps a list of registered unions and if appropriate, certifies them as independent.

32.3.1
Staff associations
or 'house unions'

A **staff association** or **employees' association** is one in which all the members work for one employer or a group of associated employers. A staff association can register as a trade union, but may not be able to be certified as an independent trade union [see below]. These non-independent bodies are sometimes called **house unions**.

32.3.2
Independent trade
unions

A trade union may be certified as **independent** only if:

- it is not dominated or controlled by an employer, group of employers or employers' association; *and*
- it is not subject to interference by an employer, group of employers or employers' association, for example by an employer providing financial or material support. *ss.5-6*

Most statutory trade union rights are available only to independent trade unions. An employer may make an informal or contractual agreement to give such rights to a house union.

32.3.3
Recognised trade unions

If an employer agrees to negotiate with a trade union 'to any extent' for the purposes of collective bargaining, that union is considered to be **recognised** by the employer. Although recognition is often a matter of agreement between the employer and the union, a union has the right to require recognition in some situations [see below].

32.3.3.1
Voluntary recognition

Recognition may be negotiated between the employer and union(s), or may be implied from custom and practice. It does not have to be set out in an agreement, although it often is. An employer should seek advice before signing a recognition agreement. ACAS [see end of chapter] can work with employers and unions to achieve a voluntary recognition agreement.

Trade Union and Labour Relations (Consolidation) Act 1992 s.178(3)

Recognition of this type is not permanent, and may be withdrawn by the employer at any time.

An employer might say that it has recognised a union by according it courtesies and facilities such as a notice board or use of meeting rooms, allowing a union representative the right to speak on behalf of union members in disciplinary or grievance procedures, or consulting the union on various matters. This is not 'recognition', but simply acknowledgement. It does not confer the statutory rights which unions get when they are recognised by the employer as having the right to negotiate and strike a bargain with the employer.

32.3.3.2
Recognition through statutory procedure

Where voluntary recognition cannot be achieved, a union may require an employer with 21 or more workers to enter into a legally binding agreement to recognise a union. The number includes workers for associated employers, defined as where the other organisation is controlled by the first or they are both controlled by a third.

Employment Relations Act 1999 ss.1, 5, 6, 25, sch.1

The complex recognition procedures are explained in the *Code of Practice on Access to Workers during Recognition and Derecognition Ballots*, and are overseen by the Central Arbitration Committee. Recognition is awarded by the CAC in relation to a **bargaining unit** if it is supported by a majority of bargaining unit workers voting in the ballot, and by at least 40% of the workers entitled to vote. The CAC may award recognition without a ballot if more than 50% of workers in the bargaining unit are members of the union(s) applying for recognition. Union recognition through the statutory procedure is legally binding and covers bargaining about pay, hours and holidays.

An organisation which is approached for recognition should take early legal advice.

32.3.3.3
Recognition and transfer of undertaking

When an undertaking is transferred and retains a separate identity [see **26.4**], the new employer must continue to recognise any union(s) recognised by the original employer. Having recognised the union, the new employer may then be free to change or withdraw from the recognition agreement, unless recognition was achieved under the statutory procedure.

Transfer of Undertakings (Protection of Employment) Regulations 1981 [SI 1981/1794] reg.9

32.3.4
Collective agreements

Collective agreements are negotiated between one or more independent union(s) and an employer or group of employers.

Trade Union and Labour Relations (Consolidation) Act 1992 s.178

They may be concerned primarily with the relationship between the union and the employer, or with the rights of individual employees. Either explicitly or by custom and practice some or all the terms of the collective agreement may be incorporated [see **23.3.5**] into individuals' contracts of employment. Different rules apply to collective agreements whereby employees agree not to take industrial action [see **32.8.5**].

A collective agreement may codify certain rules under legislation, for example the employer's rules on parental leave where these differ from the statutory default procedures [see **28.8.3**].

A collective agreement is not legally binding on the parties unless it is in writing and indicates clearly that it is intended to be legally enforceable. If only part of the agreement is intended to be legally binding, this must be clearly stated.

Trade Union and Labour Relations (Consolidation) Act 1992 s.179

If an undertaking is transferred, the collective agreements of the original employer are transferred to the new employer.

Transfer of Undertakings (Protection of Employment) Regulations 1981
[SI 1981/1794] reg.6

32.3.4.1
Individualised contracts

Some employers offer workers better pay or other terms if they give up other rights provided through a collective agreement. This is referred to as **individualised contracts**. At the time of writing (early 2001) the government has power to create regulations:

- protecting workers from dismissal or detriment if they do not agree to enter into such a contract;

- allowing employers to offer individualised contracts with better terms—even though such contracts are detrimental to workers who do not sign them—provided the individualised terms are not linked to not joining a union. *Employment Relations Act 1999 s.17*

32.3.5
Management and unions

Confusion can arise during negotiations if senior staff are members of the same union as other staff but are perceived by staff as being part of 'management', or if some or all members of the governing body are members of the same union as their employees. Another problem is the imbalance which can arise if the employees receive technical back-up from their union in a dispute, while a governing body made up largely of service users or local people has little access to technical expertise.

In these situations everyone needs to be very clear about their role in any negotiations, and it is important to develop a cooperative rather than confrontational approach to resolving problems.

32.4
TRADE UNION RIGHTS: ALL WORKERS

All workers have a right to belong or not belong to a union, and to take part in union activities at appropriate times. Except for dismissal because of participation in unprotected industrial action [see **32.8.2**], dismissal on union grounds is automatically unfair [see **30.9.1**],. Trade union rights are buttressed by the **Human Rights Act 1998** which implements article 11 of the European Convention on Human Rights, protecting freedom of assembly and in particular the right to form trade unions.

32.4.1
Selection for employment

An applicant for a job may not be refused work on the basis of:

- being, or not being, a member of a trade union;

- being unwilling to accept a requirement to join, leave or remain in a union;

- being unwilling to accept a requirement to have union subscriptions deducted from wages.

Trade Union and Labour Relations (Consolidation) Act 1992 s.137;
Employment Relations Act 1999 sch.2

An employer cannot run a **closed shop** where all employees must be members of a particular union or unions. However, an employer may ask or encourage job applicants to join the union. If they all agree this has the effect of perpetuating the closed shop, but no one can be refused a job because they do not agree to join the union, nor can an employee be dismissed because he or she leaves the union.

32.4.2
Detriment

An employer cannot take any action, or deliberately refrain from taking any action, in order to:

- prevent the employee from joining a union or remaining in a union;
- compel the employee to join a union;
- penalise the employee or subject the employee to any detriment because he or she is a union member;
- prevent the employee from taking part in union activities at an appropriate time (outside the employee's working hours or at a time within working hours which has been agreed with the employer);
- penalise the employee for taking part in union activities.

Trade Union and Labour Relations (Consolidation) Act 1992 s.146

32.4.3
Dismissal on union grounds

An employee dismissed or made redundant on 'union grounds' is automatically unfairly dismissed [see **30.9.1**] unless the dismissal is because of participation in unprotected industrial action [see **32.8.2**]. There is no qualifying period, nor is there an upper age limit. In addition to the usual remedy for unfair dismissal, the tribunal may require the employment to be continued, and may make an additional special award on top of the normal compensatory awards [see **33.4.2**]. *ss.152-166*

'Union grounds' means being, or not being, a union member; joining, or refusing to join, a union; or taking part or planning to take part in activities of an independent union at an appropriate time. *s.152*

32.5
RIGHTS OF TRADE UNION MEMBERS

Members of a trade union which is recognised by the employer either through a voluntary agreement or through the statutory procedure [see **32.3.3**] have statutory rights. Members of unions which are not recognised by the employer have these rights only if the employer agrees to them informally or as part of the contract of employment.

32.5.1
Check-off

An employer is not obliged to deduct trade union subscriptions from union members' pay. But if an employer does operate **check-off**, the following rules apply:

- the employee must give written consent at least every three years;
- the consent form must be signed and dated, and automatically expires three years from its date;
- the employee may withdraw consent at any time by notifying the employer in writing;
- the employer may increase the amount of the deduction only after giving the employee one month's notice in writing, and reminding the employee of the right to withdraw at any time;
- the employer may stop deducting at any time, or require the employee to re-confirm consent to continue deducting even within the three-year period;
- if the union has a political fund [see **32.5.4**], the employer must not deduct the political fund contribution if the employee notifies the employer in writing that he or she is exempt from the obligation to contribute to the fund or has notified the union that he or she objects to contributing to the fund;
- an employee may make a complaint to the employment tribunal if union subscriptions are deducted without authorisation or if the deduction is increased without proper notification, and may complain to the county court if unauthorised political fund contributions are deducted. *ss.68, 68A, 86-88*

32.5.2
Paid time off for union duties

Officials of a recognised trade union have the right to paid time off to carry out duties connected with collective bargaining and other matters agreed by the employer, and to attend industrial relations training. The amount of time allowed must be 'reasonable in all the circumstances'. The ACAS code of practice on time off for union duties describes what is 'reasonable'.

Trade Union and Labour Relations (Consolidation) Act 1992 ss.168, 169

32.5.3
Time off for union activities

Members of a recognised trade union have a right to reasonable time off, which may be paid or unpaid, to take part in union activities. This right does not extend to taking part in industrial action, whether protected [see **32.8.1**] or not.

s.170

32.5.4
Objection to political fund

A trade union may use its funds for political purposes only if the funds are collected specifically for this and are kept in a separate **political fund**. A ballot on retention of the fund must be held every 10 years. A member has the right to object to making the contribution, and the union cannot then require the member to pay the contribution or subject the member to any discipline or detriment as a result of not paying.

ss.71-85

32.6
RIGHTS OF TRADE UNIONS

Recognised trade unions have certain statutory rights. An employer may extend these rights to other unions or to a joint consultative committee or other representative body.

32.6.1
Collective bargaining

An employer is required to provide information to representatives of a recognised trade union if the union requests it for the purposes of **collective bargaining**. There is a general duty to provide all available information if its lack would impede the union's ability to negotiate, but there are a number of exceptions to this general duty, such as information obtained in confidence, information relating to specific individuals (unless the individual has authorised disclosure), or information which would cause 'substantial injury' to the employer.

ss.181, 182

The information which should be disclosed includes:

- pay and benefits, including structure of the payment system, earnings analysed by work group, and details of fringe benefits;
- conditions of service, including policies on recruitment, redeployment, redundancy, equal opportunities etc;
- numbers of employees overall and analysed by age and sex, turnover, absenteeism;
- productivity and efficiency information;
- financial data, including assets, liabilities and loans.

ACAS Code of Practice on Information Disclosure, para.11

32.6.2
Information and consultation

Trade unions recognised by the employer have a statutory right to be informed and consulted in relation to health and safety [see **36.2.7**] and occupational pension schemes [see **27.9.3**]. If employees are to be transferred to another employer or more than 20 employees are to be made redundant within a 90-day period, the employer must consult the recognised union(s) or elected employee representatives [see **32.2**].

Trade unions recognised under the statutory procedure [see **32.3.3.2**] have a right to information and consultation on training of staff in the bargaining unit covered by the recognition agreement.

Employment Relations Act 1999 s.5

32.7
TRADE DISPUTES

A **trade dispute** is a dispute between employers and workers [see **32.3** for definition of worker in this context] or between workers and other workers, relating to one or more of the following:

- terms and conditions of employment;

- physical conditions in which workers are required to work;

- engagement, non-engagement, termination or suspension of one or more workers;

- termination or suspension of the duties of one or more workers;

- allocation of work;

- disciplinary matters;

- a worker's membership or non-membership of a union;

- facilities for trade union officials;

- consultation and negotiation procedures;

- recognition of a union.

Trade Union and Labour Relations (Consolidation) Act 1992 s.218

In a trade dispute or a dispute over union recognition ACAS [see end of chapter] may be approached by anyone to undertake **conciliation**, to enable the parties to reach a settlement, and/or **arbitration**, in which arbitrator(s) or the Central Arbitration Committee devise a settlement which is binding on the parties. *ss.210-212; sch.1A para.10(5)*

32.8
INDUSTRIAL ACTION

32.8.1
Protected
industrial action

Industrial action includes strikes, withdrawal of cooperation, refusing to undertake certain activities and working to rule. It is lawful for a union or its officials or representatives to encourage people to take part in a strike or other industrial action only if the union has carried out a **ballot** complying with the relevant legislation among its relevant members, and the action has been agreed by the members. The employer must be notified of the ballot. Industrial action, if approved, must start within four weeks of the ballot, but this can be extended for a further four weeks if the employer and union(s) agree, to allow more time for negotiation. *s.238A*

Industrial action approved through a proper ballot is **protected industrial action**. Dismissal primarily for a reason connected with participation in protected industrial action is automatically unfair [see **32.8.4**], and the employee cannot be sued, for example for breach of contract or inducing breach of contract. *s.219*

Any member of the union has the right to require the union to conduct a ballot before it undertakes or continues industrial action. *s.62*

Unless industrial action is protected, participation in it may constitute breach of contract or inducement to breach of contract by the employees involved. To safeguard employees, industrial action should never be undertaken without getting proper advice from a trade union. Similarly, an employer or individual should take legal advice before taking any steps to stop industrial action. The DTI [see end of chapter] publishes a guide for employers and employees on industrial action.

32.8.2
Unofficial action

If the industrial action has not been approved by ballot or is subsequently repudiated by the union, it is an **unofficial** or **unprotected** action. The trade union is legally liable for unofficial action carried out by its members unless it formally repudiates the action. *s.238A*

Participation in unofficial industrial action is generally a breach of contract by the employee, and there is generally no right to claim unfair dismissal for dismissal while taking part in an unofficial action [see **32.8.4**]. *s.237A*

Any individual can apply to the High Court to stop unauthorised or unlawful industrial action, if the individual can show that the industrial action would prevent or delay the supply of goods or services to him or her, or that the quality of the goods or services would be adversely affected. *ss.235A, 235B, 235C*

32.8.3
Peaceful picketing

Peaceful picketing is lawful provided:

- it is at or near the place of work of the worker who is picketing and the worker's employer is a party to the dispute, or in the case of a trade union official taking part in a picket, it is at or near the place of work of a trade union member whom the official is representing or accompanying in a dispute with the worker's employer; *and*

- the purpose is to obtain or communicate information or persuade a person to work or not to work.

Trade Union and Labour Relations (Consolidation) Act 1992 ss.220, 224

Picketing and other actions are unlawful if they try to make a person do or not do something unwillingly. *s.241*

A code of practice issued by the government in 1981 sets a limit of six on the number of pickets at any entrance to a workplace. This restriction does not have statutory force, but it has been used as the basis for injunctions against mass pickets.

32.8.4
Dismissal during industrial action

Dismissal while taking part in **unofficial industrial action**, which has not been authorised through a proper ballot, is not unfair (i.e., it is a dismissal for a fair reason) unless it can be shown that the principal reason for the dismissal was for maternity reasons or taking parental or other family leave, or because the employee took action on a matter related to health and safety or working time, serving as an employee representative or a protected disclosure (whistleblowing). *s.237*

Where action was official but is repudiated by the union, employees have one day's grace to return to work. *s.238*

Dismissal is automatically unfair [see **30.9.1**] if the principal reason is that the employee took part in **protected industrial action**, provided that the dismissal occurs:

- within eight weeks of the day the employee started industrial action;

- after the end of the eight-week period, where the employee had ceased to take part before the end of the period; *or*

- after the end of the period, where the employer had not taken reasonable procedural steps to resolve the dispute. *s.238A*

There is a six-month time limit for bringing an unfair dismissal claim. There is no qualifying period or upper age limit. *s.238*

32.8.5
Collective agreements not to take industrial action

Some employers and trade unions have negotiated national collective agreements restricting employees' rights to strike or take industrial action. Most collective agreements between employers and trade unions are automatically incorporated into employees' contracts of employment [see **23.3.5**]. But agreements limiting the right to strike or take industrial action are incorporated into individual contracts only if the trade union is independent [see **32.3.2**], the agreement is in writing and states that it is incorporated into individual contracts, the agreement is reasonably accessible and available, and individual contracts explicitly or impliedly incorporate the terms. *s.180*

FOR FURTHER INFORMATION

Trade union recognition and rights: DTI: www.dti.gov.uk/er/union.htm

ACAS: see telephone directory for local office; www.acas.org.uk

Voluntary sector trade unions. MSF: 020-7505 3054; www.msf.org.uk

Transport and General Workers' Union: 020-7611 2500; www.tgwu.org.uk

Unison: 020-7388 2366; www.unison.org.uk

Chapter 33
EMPLOYMENT CLAIMS AND SETTLEMENT

For sources of further information see end of chapter.
Double-underlined section headings indicate additions or significant changes since the first edition.

33.1 ENFORCING EMPLOYMENT RIGHTS

Most **statutory employment rights**, including rights relating to pay, unfair dismissal and discrimination, are enforced through employment tribunals. The main exceptions are health and safety claims; statutory sick pay and statutory maternity pay claims, which are enforced by the Contributions Office; and minimum wage, which is enforced by either employment tribunals or the Inland Revenue [see **27.2.5**].

In the past, most **contractual employment rights** were enforced only through the courts. But since 1994 breach of contract cases have been able to be brought in the employment tribunal as well.

Tribunal procedures are outlined here, and further information is available from the Employment Tribunals Service [see end of chapter]. Court procedures are outlined in **61.4**. Tribunal and court proceedings may be complex and give rise to large awards, so experienced legal advice and representation are generally advisable at an early stage.

33.1.1 Advice for employers and employees

The Department of Trade and Industry [see end of chapter] produces free information on all aspects of employment rights.

Advice on employment matters is available to employers and employees from solicitors, ACAS [see below], citizens' advice bureaux and some independent advice centres, and to employees from trade unions and law centres. Organisations can insure against the cost of legal advice and employment-related awards against them [see **20.9.3** and **20.4.2**].

33.1.1.1
Financial assistance

Employees on a low income may qualify for advice from solicitors under the Community Legal Service Fund (formerly legal aid). At the time of writing (early 2001) financial assistance is not available for representation at employment tribunal proceedings in England and Wales. However it became available for some tribunal cases in Scotland in January 2001, and may become available for some cases in England and Wales.

33.1.2
ACAS

The Advisory, Conciliation and Arbitration Service (**ACAS**), an independent body, produces codes of practice on many aspects of employment. It provides information and advice on employment matters, undertakes enquiries into disputes or areas of employment, and helps achieve settlement in collective disputes and individual cases.

If either the employee or employee requests it, ACAS can help the parties reach a conciliated settlement prior to a tribunal claim. If either party makes a complaint to the tribunal, ACAS has a statutory obligation to seek a conciliated settlement [see **33.3.3**] if the conciliation officer considers that there is a reasonable prospect of resolving the matter without its having to go to tribunal. In unfair dismissal cases, ACAS can provide arbitration as an alternative to the tribunal [see **33.2.3**].

33.2
SETTLEMENT

Given the costs and other problems raised by tribunal and court cases, the employer and employee should always consider attempting to reach a settlement by themselves or with the assistance of ACAS. This can be done before or after application has been made to the tribunal or court.

33.2.1
Breach of contract

The employer and employee can settle a claim for breach of contract, including wrongful dismissal, by the employer agreeing to make a payment or take other action such as re-engaging the employee, and the employee agreeing not to pursue the claim in the court or tribunal. There are no special formalities, but it is advisable for each side to take legal advice and for the agreement to be in writing.

33.2.2
Claims under
employment
legislation

Very strict rules apply to **compromise agreements** or **settlement agreements**, under which an employee agrees not to pursue a claim arising from the employer's breach of anti-discrimination or employment legislation, including unfair dismissal. Such settlements also frequently deal with related issues such as confidentiality and references.

33.2.2.1
Settlement
through ACAS

For a settlement agreement arranged by ACAS, either the employer or employee can contact ACAS [see **33.1.2**], with a view to reaching a settlement for discrimination or breach of employment legislation. A settlement arranged through ACAS binds both parties. The employee cannot take the case to tribunal or court, unless he or she was induced to enter into the settlement by a material and false statement by the employer.

33.2.2.2
Settlement
without ACAS

An agreement not arranged through ACAS is valid only if it is in writing and:

- it relates to a particular complaint or complaints (not all possible complaints);
- the employee has received independent advice from a qualified lawyer, certified trade union official or certified advice worker on the agreement and its effect on his or her rights;
- the employee's advisor is covered by professional negligence insurance against claims by the employee;
- the agreement identifies the advisor; *and*
- the agreement states that the conditions regulating compromise agreements under the Act are satisfied.

Employment Rights Act 1996 s.203

33.2.2.3
Non-binding agreement

If the employer signs an agreement or pays an employee to give up the right to claim in the employment tribunal, without complying with the compromise agreement requirements, the agreement cannot be enforced by the employer. The employee retains the right to make or continue with a claim, but any payment received from the employer may be taken into account in calculating entitlement to compensation [see **33.4.2**].

33.2.3
Arbitration
through ACAS

From May 2001 ACAS provides an arbitration scheme for straightforward unfair dismissal claims, as an alternative to employment tribunal hearings. Both the employer and employee must agree to arbitration. It is likely to be less expensive and less formal than tribunals, and unlike tribunal hearings is confidential.

33.3
TRIBUNAL
PROCEEDINGS

Employment (formerly industrial) tribunal proceedings are governed by complex rules which can only be summarised here. The rules are set out in the **Industrial Tribunals Act 1996**, as amended by the **Employment Rights (Dispute Resolution) Act 1998** and various regulations. The **Employment Tribunals Service** [see end of chapter] provides detailed information.

33.3.1
Time limits

The time limit for submitting an application to the employment tribunal is generally within three months of the action which gave rise to the claim. For cases involving unfair selection of employees for re-engagement after industrial action, disputes over redundancy payments and disputes over equal pay, the time limit is six months.

The time limit is usually strictly applied. There is a power to extend the time limit where it was not reasonably practical to present an application within the specified period, but this is rarely exercised. For race, sex and disability discrimination and some other cases, the circumstances in which the limit may be extended are slightly wider.

33.3.2
Application

The employee normally makes the application on **form ET1**, but there is no obligation to use this form. The form or other application is sent to the Employment Tribunals Service, which sends a copy to the employer and invites a response on **form ET3** within 14 days. If asked to do so before the end of the 14 days, the tribunal generally extends the period to enable the employer to take advice or prepare a full response.

Before or after submitting a response, the employer may ask the employee to clarify aspects of the complaint. If the employee fails to do so the tribunal may order the employee to provide **further and better particulars**. Similarly the employee can seek further and better particulars of the employer's response.

33.3.3
Conciliation

Following the issue of proceedings an ACAS conciliation officer is notified and contacts the parties with a view to effecting a binding settlement. If the intervention of an ACAS officer results in a settlement, the details are recorded on **form COT3**. Alternatively, a binding settlement may be reached independently by the parties [see **33.2.2.2**].

33.3.4
Preparation

If settlement is not reached, either party may ask the other to provide more details of the claim or response, to clarify matters. The parties should prior to the hearing agree a **bundle** of documents for use before the tribunal. This includes all relevant documents, including witness statements. If one party believes the other has important relevant documents which have not been disclosed, that party may apply to the tribunal for an order for **disclosure**. This requires the documents to be revealed (sent to the party who has requested them).

At least six bundles of documents should be prepared: for the party preparing the bundle and the other side, three for the tribunal, and one for the witnesses. The documents must be paginated.

Normally witnesses attend tribunal proceedings voluntarily, but if a witness considered important by either party refuses to come, the party can ask the tribunal to order their presence.

33.3.5
Pre-hearing review

The tribunal may hold a **pre-hearing review**, a short hearing which generally makes a decision on any preliminary issues, for example whether there is an entitlement to bring a claim before the tribunal or whether the employee has served a sufficient continuous period of employment to qualify to proceed with the hearing. The review may deal with other procedural issues such as ordering one party to produce documents or provide further details of the claim.

The review also looks at the prospect of success. If the case looks hopeless, the tribunal may require the party bringing the case to pay a deposit of up to £500 as a condition of being allowed to proceed. Or the tribunal can strike out, at any stage in the proceedings, an application or response (notice of appearance) on the grounds that the case has no real prospect of success. *Employment Tribunals (Constitution and Rules of Procedure) Regulations 2001 [SI 2001/1171]*

33.3.6
Hearing

The tribunal gives notice of the **hearing**. It may agree to a postponement in order that any criminal case be dealt with first, or for some other reason such as the unavailability of important witnesses.

The parties may be unrepresented, or represented by solicitors, barristers, trade union or employers' body officials, or any other person.

Apart from a few exceptional situations, the hearing is in public. At the hearing the procedure is generally first to establish any preliminary questions, for example whether the employee was actually dismissed. If that is to be dealt with first, the employee begins. If that is accepted, the employer usually begins.

Most cases are heard on the basis of oral evidence.

Each side presents its evidence, with the other side allowed to cross-examine. Representations may be made in writing, but this is likely to be much less effective. The tribunal asks any questions that it wishes.

After the hearing the tribunal makes its decision and sends it in writing to both parties.

33.3.7
Appeal

An appeal against an employment tribunal decision must be made to the employment appeal tribunal (EAT) within 42 days. An EAT can hear an appeal only if it is based on a point of law. After the EAT a case may be appealed to the Court of Appeal and ultimately, if leave to appeal is given, to the House of Lords or the European Court of Justice.

33.4
REMEDIES FOR
UNFAIR DISMISSAL

In cases of unfair dismissal there are two remedies: reinstatement or re-engagement, and the payment of compensation. In rare cases, costs may be awarded [see **33.5.4**].

33.4.1
Reinstatement and
re-engagement

A **reinstatement order** requires the employer to treat the applicant as if he or she had not been dismissed. This is rarely made.

A **re-engagement order** requires the employer, a successor of the employer or an associated employer to offer the employee employment comparable to that from which he or she was dismissed. A reinstatement order re-creates the status quo, but a re-engagement creates a new contract between the parties.

Reinstatement and re-engagement orders are made only if the employee wants to return to work, and if it is practicable for the employer to take the employee back. If the employer refuses to comply without good reason, the tribunal may award compensation. The ceiling on the compensatory award [see **33.4.2.2**] may be removed, and the tribunal may also make an **additional award** of between 13 and 26 weeks pay. In calculating awards based on pay, the maximum weekly pay which is considered is £240 (as at 1/4/01).

33.4.2
Compensation

In most unfair dismissal cases the tribunal orders the employer to pay **compensation** in the form of a basic award and a compensatory award.

33.4.2.1
Basic award

The **basic award** is based on the employee's age, length of continuous employment [see **23.4.6**], and gross weekly pay (to a maximum of £240 per week, as at 1/4/01). It is calculated in the same way as a redundancy payment [see **31.6.1**], except that service before age 18 is included.

This basic award may be reduced if the tribunal thinks it is just and equitable, for example if the employee is near retirement or refuses unreasonably to take an offer of reinstatement, or if the employee's conduct before dismissal caused or contributed to the dismissal. Any statutory, contractual or discretionary redundancy payment [see **31.6.2** and **31.6.3**] already made is deducted from the basic award. Sickness benefit paid by the Benefits Agency is also deducted unless the contract allows for it to be paid in addition to normal salary during sickness [see **27.6**].

Employment Rights Act 1996 s.122

If the employee has received jobseeker's allowance or income support, this does not lead to a reduction in the award against the employer. However the Benefits Agency recovers the amount of the benefits from part of the award made by the employer.

33.4.2.2
Compensatory award

In addition to the basic award, the tribunal makes an award it considers just and equitable to compensate the employee for financial loss. The limit to the award is £51,700 (as at 1/4/01). The limit rises annually on an index-linked basis.

The compensatory award is assessed by looking at a number of headings, based on case law guidance. These are:

- **Immediate loss of wages**, calculated by looking at the loss the employee has suffered at the date of the hearing. This is generally the difference between the pay and other benefits the employee was receiving, including any increases that would have occurred, and any pay earned during the period up to the hearing. If the employee immediately obtained a new job at higher pay than the old job, there is no order under this head.

- **Manner of dismissal**. A sum is rarely awarded under this head unless the way in which the employee was dismissed made it harder for her or him to find future employment.

- **Future loss of wages**. If the employee is unlikely to get replacement employment immediately, or is likely only to obtain employment at lower pay, the tribunal estimates the likely future loss before the employee gets a job or receives pay at the old level. The award under this head is likely to be higher if the employee can show that jobs are difficult to get, either because of general economic circumstances or because of personal circumstances such as age, state of health or injuries.

- **Loss of protection**. When the employee finds new employment, he or she will not be entitled to protection from unfair dismissal or be able to claim redundancy pay until the necessary period of continuous employment has been accumulated [see **30.10.1** and **31.6.1**]. A nominal sum, generally somewhat over £100, is awarded under this head to compensate for this lack of protection.

- **Loss of pension rights**. The government's actuarial department has produced guidelines to help tribunals assess this complex area.

- **Loss of fringe benefits**. The value of benefits such as car allowances, accommodation etc will be taken into account.

- **Expenses** incurred in trying to mitigate loss [see below], such as journal subscriptions, fares to attend job interviews, or start-up costs for self-employment.

33.4.2.3
Supplementary award

An additional award of up to two weeks' pay can be made if the employer prevented the employee from using an internal appeal procedure.

Employment Rights Act 1996 s.127A

33.4.2.4
Reduction of compensation

The tribunal has to assess whether the employee has taken reasonable steps to try to **mitigate** (reduce the level of) his or her loss by seeking replacement employment. If there is a failure or a partial failure to do this, the compensation may be reduced. *s.123*

Compensation may also be reduced where the conduct of the employee makes it reasonable and equitable to take this into account when assessing the employee's losses, or where the employee refused to use the employer's appeal procedure.

33.4.2.5
Special award

Compensation is calculated differently if the employee was unfairly dismissed for trade union reasons [see **32.4.3**]. The minimum basic award is higher, the compensatory award is calculated in the usual way, and there is a **special award** based on 104 weeks' pay. If the employer has been ordered to reinstate or re-engage the employee and has refused, the special award is based on 156 weeks' pay.

33.5
OTHER TRIBUNAL REMEDIES

In addition to dealing with claims for unfair dismissal [see above] and wrongful dismissal [see **33.6**], employment tribunals deal with a wide range of other claims on employment-related matters.

33.5.1
Redundancy

Unfair selection for redundancy is dealt with as an unfair dismissal claim.

If the employer does not pay statutory redundancy pay [see **31.6.1**], the tribunal will order the payment to be made.

If an employer fails to consult the recognised trade union(s) or employee representatives as required [see **31.2.3**], the tribunal makes a **protective redundancy award** requiring the employer to pay the redundant employees an amount equivalent to their earnings during the required consultation period (to a maximum of £240 per week, as at 1/4/01).

If an employee who is under notice of redundancy is not given reasonable time off to look to work or to arrange training [see **31.4**], the tribunal will make an award of up to 40% of one week's pay.

33.5.2
Discrimination

An employer may be ordered by the tribunal to pay a compensatory award [see **33.4.2.2**] if it is shown that the employer discriminated on the basis of the employee's race, colour, ethnic or national origin, nationality, sex, gender reassignment, married status, disability, part-time status, or trade union membership or lack of it, or if dismissal was on any of these grounds. *There is no ceiling to most of these awards*, and they can take into account not only actual or potential money losses, but also **injury to feelings**. Additional **aggravated damages** [see **61.4.7**] may be added if the employer was malicious or heavy-handed.

33.5.3
Other claims

For other employment-related claims the employer may be ordered:

- to pay arrears of minimum wage [see **27.2**];
- to provide an itemised pay statement [see **27.1.3**];
- to reimburse a worker for unlawful deductions from pay [see **27.1.4**];
- to pay guarantee payments [see **27.1.9**];
- to pay wages while the employee is on medical or maternity suspension [see **27.1.10**];

- to recompense the employee for time off to which he or she was statutorily entitled, but not allowed to take [see **23.4.1**];
- to provide a written statement of employment particulars [see **23.5**];
- to take steps in relation to a disabled worker [see **25.5.4**];
- to take other action or make other payments as necessary to ensure the employer meets its statutory obligations to the employee.

33.5.4
Costs

In the past, costs awards in the tribunal were rare. They are now likely to become more frequent, because from July 2001 employment tribunals have a duty to consider awarding costs where the case had no reasonable prospect of success or where one of the parties or its representative has acted vexatiously, abusively, disruptively or unreasonably. The costs limit in this situation is increased, from July 2001, from £500 to £10,000. *Employment Tribunals (Constitution and Rules of Procedure) Regulations 2001 [SI 2001/1171]*

If an applicant persists with a claim after being ordered to pay a deposit at a pre-hearing review [see **33.3.5**] and then loses, the deposit may be awarded as costs to the other party.

33.6
BREACH OF
CONTRACT CLAIMS

Claims for breach of the contract of employment, including wrongful dismissal, can be brought in either the court or tribunal for sums due under the contract, damages for breach of contract, and counterclaims by employers against employees who bring breach of contract claims. There is no qualifying period of employment for breach of contract claims in either the tribunal or court.

Only claims which arise or are outstanding at the termination of the employment—such as arrears of pay, accrued holiday pay or damages for wrongful dismissal—can be brought in the tribunal. A breach of contract claim to the tribunal by an employee must be made within three months of the date on which the breach occurred or the contract giving rise to the claim came to an end. Any counterclaim by the employer must be made within six weeks of the employee's claim.

Some contract claims are excluded from the tribunal and must be brought in the court [see **61.4** for procedure]. These include claims where the employment has not terminated, and claims relating to living accommodation, intellectual property [see **39.2.3** and **39.6.1**], restrictive covenants [see **24.40** and **24.41**], obligations of confidentiality [see **38.1.4** and **38.1.6**], and personal injuries. A claim to the courts must be made within six years of the date of the act which gave rise to the claim.

The maximum award in the tribunal is £25,000. In the courts there is no limit to awards, and the winner is generally awarded his or her legal costs. *Industrial Tribunal Extension of Jurisdiction (England and Wales) Order 1994 [SI 1994/1623]*

33.6.1
Damages for
wrongful dismissal

An employee who has been wrongfully dismissed is generally entitled to damages covering financial loss between the date the employer actually terminated and the date the employer could lawfully have terminated. Thus if the employer could have terminated on three months' notice, damages are three months' wages plus other benefits such as bonuses. If the contract was for a fixed term of 18 months with no provision for termination before expiry and it was terminated wrongfully after eight months, damages would be 10 months' salary. In the tribunal (but not the court) the award is limited to £25,000.

33.6.2
Suing on the
contract

If an employer acts in a way which entitles an employee to treat himself or herself as being wrongfully dismissed [see **30.4.8**], the employee may instead continue working and sue the employer for damages any time within the next six years. In some situations the employee may be better off by following this course of action.

An example is where the employer wrongfully changes the employee's contract of employment, typically by reducing or removing entitlement to enhanced redundancy pay [see **31.6.2**]. In this situation, if the employee resigns and claims wrongful dismissal, the damages would be limited to the period of notice he or she would have been entitled to, normally not more than 12 weeks. An employee who carries on working and later sues may be entitled to the difference between the old redundancy pay and the new lower level.

33.6.3
Injunctions

Although the courts generally do not enforce contracts of employment by injunctions [see **18.12.7**], they have shown some willingness to force employers to go through a disciplinary or grievance procedure where the employee has a contractual right to do so, or to force employees to honour post-termination obligations such as confidentiality and not competing. An injunction is however a complex and expensive remedy, granted only in very limited circumstances. It is available only through the courts, not the tribunal.

Dietmann v LB Brent [1988] ICR 842 CA; IRLR 299

33.6.4
Other breach of contract cases

A claim for breach of the contract of employment, other than those arising or outstanding at termination and dealt with in the employment tribunal, is dealt with in the courts in the same way as any other breach of contract case [see **61.4** for procedure, and **18.12** for remedies].

In calculating the amount of damages there will be deducted:

- usually, tax and national insurance;
- any other money received by the employee, such as payment in lieu of notice, compensation for unfair dismissal, non-contractual payments, and social security benefits covering the time which would have been the period of notice (but statutory and contractual redundancy payments are not deducted);
- if it was a fixed-term contract or there was a very long period of notice, a deduction to reflect **accelerated receipt**—the fact that the employee is receiving a lump payment immediately, rather than having to wait for payment.

33.6.4.1
Mitigation of loss

The employee has a duty to take reasonable steps to mitigate the loss, normally by seeking another job or perhaps becoming self-employed. If another job is found, the salary from that job will be deducted in calculating the damages. If the employee takes no steps to find another job, the earnings which might have been earned had those steps been taken will be estimated and deducted.

Where the claim is for the employer's failure to make a payment in lieu of notice specified in the contract, no deduction is made for other earnings or the employee's failure to mitigate. Where the claim is for the employer's failure to make a discretionary payment in lieu of notice, deduction may be made for failure to mitigate [see **30.6.6**].

FOR FURTHER INFORMATION

Employment rights. Department of Trade & Industry: www.dti.gov.uk/er/regs.htm

Conciliation & settlement. ACAS: see phone directory for local office; www.acas.org.uk

Employment tribunals. Employment Tribunals Service: 0845-795 9775; www.dti.gov.uk/er/individual/et.htm

Chapter 34
SELF-EMPLOYED WORKERS AND OTHER CONTRACTORS

34.1 CONTRACTS FOR SERVICE

Commercial firms, organisations and self-employed individuals who carry out work for others are **contractors**. If they in turn engage a business, organisation or self-employed person to do some or all of the work, that individual or body is a **sub-contractor**.

Contractors have a **contract for services** [see **22.1.3**], which may or may not be in writing. The relationship between an organisation and its contractors is governed by contract law [see **18.6-18.12**], regardless of whether the contractor is a self-employed individual or a huge firm, and whether the contract is for a small piece of work or a major project.

34.1.1 Self-employed individuals

People who are self-employed are generally not entitled to the same rights as employees, and are not taxed under PAYE. But:

- a person who calls himself or herself self-employed and is treated as such by the organisation could in fact legally be an employee, and thus be entitled to the full range of employment rights;

- a person who does work on a self-employed basis but not in the course of his or her profession or business may be a 'worker' [see **22.1.2**], and entitled to workers' rights but not employees' rights;

- people who are legally employees and 'workers' nearly always have to be taxed under PAYE, even if they call themselves self-employed;

- different criteria are used to define self-employment for tax purposes and for the purposes of employment law, so in some situations a person could be legally self-employed for the purposes of tax but an employee or worker for the purposes of employment or workers' rights, or *vice versa*.

34.1.1.1 Employment rights

Individuals who meet the tests for self-employment [see **34.1.3**] are not entitled to rights available only to employees [see **22.1.1**], and are not entitled to most rights available to the wider group of people legally defined as 'workers' [see below]. However if they are obliged to provide their services personally, rather than being able to sub-contract them, they are covered under the employment provisions of the race, sex and disability discrimination legislation [see **25.1.2** and **25.5**].

34.1.1.2
<u>Workers' rights</u>

Certain statutory rights, such as minimum wage [see **27.2**], working time rights [see **28.1**] and certain other rights, are not available if the person is carrying out his or her profession or business, and the organisation is his or her client or customer.

In other situations where the person is carrying out work on what may appear to be a self-employed basis, he or she is entitled to these rights. This is because these rights are available not only to people who are legally employees, but to a wider category of **workers**. A worker is any person, employee or otherwise, who is working under a contract [see **22.1**] and has to provide their services personally, but not where it is a client relationship.

National Minimum Wage Act 1998 s.54;
Working Time Regulations 1998 [SI 1998/1833] reg.2

So for the purposes of minimum wage, working time rights, part-time workers' rights and the right to be accompanied at disciplinary and grievance hearings, there is a distinction between **self-employed** individuals who run their own business and are not entitled to the rights, and other **workers** who may undertake work on a **freelance** basis and are entitled to the rights.

The secretary of state for employment has power to extend other employment rights to 'workers'. *Employment Relations Act 1999 s.23*

34.1.1.3
Tax status

As well as differences in employment rights, there are significant differences in the tax treatment of employees and self-employed people. Tax law uses different criteria than are used for employment law, and distinguishes between:

- people who meet the Inland Revenue tests for self-employment [see **34.1.3.10**], are registered with the Inland Revenue as self-employed for tax purposes, and pay tax through self-assessment;

- the vast majority of other workers, who are treated as employees for tax purposes and must be taxed under PAYE;

- individuals who do not meet the criteria for self-employment, but have earnings or other income which does not have to be taxed under PAYE and is therefore taxed under self-assessment.

Before treating a person as self-employed, it is essential to confirm that he or she will be self-employed in relation to the work. A number of 'tests' are used for this [see **34.1.3.10**]. A person can be self-employed in one capacity but employed in another, so the fact that the person is registered with the Inland Revenue as self-employed does not necessarily mean that he or she can be treated as self-employed for this work.

If the individual is not genuinely self-employed for this work, the organisation must treat the individual for tax purposes as an employee [see **27.3**]. It is the employer's responsibility to ensure that PAYE is operated if it should be [see **34.1.4**].

34.1.2
Businesses and
organisations

As well as self-employed individuals, an organisation might appoint a firm—a partnership, cooperative or company—or a voluntary or not-for-profit organisation to undertake work on its behalf. The deduction of tax and NI is not generally an issue, because the organisation rather than an individual is being hired. However the deduction of tax and NI may be an issue with some building contracts [see **27.4.12**], and for an individual who sets up a personal service company and undertakes work through the company [see **34.1.5**].

34.1.3
Tests for
self-employment

In some cases it may be clear that an individual is self-employed in relation to the work, but in many cases it is less clear. In looking at the relationship, there are two separate issues:

- whether an employment tribunal or court would treat the person as self-employed for this work for the purposes of workers' and employment rights; *and*

- whether the Inland Revenue and Contributions Office would treat the person as self-employed for this work for the purposes of tax and national insurance.

The relevant bodies reach their conclusion on the basis of various **tests for self-employment**. These are difficult to apply, and different tests may yield different results. Thus in some cases the Inland Revenue may accept that a person is self-employed for tax purposes, but an employment tribunal may regard the person as an employee for the purposes of a claim of unfair dismissal and redundancy—or *vice versa*.

Massey v Crown Life Insurance Co [1978] 1 WLR 676, ICR 590

The tests for self-employment are outlined here, but an organisation should apply them with caution. If in any doubt about whether an individual should be treated as an employee or as self-employed, the organisation should check with a solicitor, accountant or PAYE office. The individual's assurances that he or she is self-employed, or the organisation's opinion of how the tests apply, are not enough.

The situation will be clearer where the organisation has received written confirmation from its PAYE office that individuals in similar situations carrying out similar work for the organisation may be treated as self-employed, where the Inland Revenue has carried out an audit of the organisation's tax matters and accepted similar workers as self-employed (provided full facts were disclosed), or where the Inland Revenue and Contributions Office have explicitly accepted that the individual is self-employed for that work.

34.1.3.1
Non-tests

Working part-time—even very part-time—or as a job sharer has no bearing on whether a person is employed or self-employed, nor does being employed on a temporary, fixed-term or casual basis [see **22.3**]. A person who has many jobs or pieces of work, or works at home or at their own office is not necessarily self-employed.

A person who calls herself or himself or is called 'self-employed', 'freelance' or 'consultant' is not necessarily self-employed.

The fact that a person is self-employed in one situation does not mean that he or she is self-employed in all situations. An actor, for example, might be self-employed as an actor while being employed by a restaurant as a waiter and by a youth project as a drama leader.

Even the fact that a person is registered as self-employed with the Inland Revenue, can prove that he or she has previously paid tax as a self-employed person or is registered with Customs and Excise and has a VAT number, does not provide a guarantee that the person can safely be treated as self-employed. The person might be legitimately self-employed in other contexts, but not in this particular relationship.

34.1.3.2
The test of
personal service

An employee must be personally involved in providing a service to the employer, but a self-employed person does not necessarily have to undertake the work personally. So a very strong indication of self-employment is that the person can appoint or sub-contract someone else to do it. But this test is not conclusive the other way, because in many cases genuinely self-employed individuals are required to undertake the work themselves and do not have the right to sub-contract it.

34.1.3.3
The control test

Employment implies that the employer has the right to 'command' the employee, while self-employed people generally have more choice about what they do, how they do it and when they do it. However, employees may exercise considerable control over their own work, while others may agree to follow detailed instructions and still be considered self-employed. So the **control test** is not conclusive.

34.1.3.4
Integration test

Sometimes called the **organisation test**, the **integration test** looks at whether the person's work is integrated into the core of what the organisation does or is an 'add-on' or 'accessory'. If the work is not integral, the person may be self-employed. But this test creates all sorts of difficulties in defining what is and is not 'integral'.

34.1.3.5
Mutuality of obligation

In employment, the employer is obliged to provide work if it is available [**23.3.3**] and the employee has to do it. If the organisation has no obligation to provide work, and the person is free to take it or leave it when it is offered, self-employment is indicated.

In a leading case, waiters at a hotel were treated as self-employed but were given preference over other casual staff. It looked very much like a contract of employment, but the Court of Appeal agreed that they were not employed because the workers had a right to decide whether to accept the work and were free to obtain work elsewhere, and the employer was not obliged to provide work although it regularly did so.
O'Kelly v Trusthouse Forte plc [1983] ICR 728 CA, IRLR 369 CA

34.1.3.6
Documentation

Any written agreement for the work will be closely examined, to see whether it contains terms typical of employment such as references to salary (rather than fee), arrangements for pay during holidays or sickness (which self-employed workers do not generally receive), or dismissal (rather than termination of the contract).

34.1.3.7
Registration

If an individual providing a service is registered for VAT, this generally indicates that he or she is not an employee. But the rules used by the VAT authorities are different from those used by the Inland Revenue or the employment tribunal, so VAT registration is not, in itself, conclusive proof of self-employment.

If a person sets up a limited company or partnership, that body enters into a contract and the person does the work on behalf of the body, the person is not self-employed in relation to that work. He or she will be doing the work as a director or employee of the company, or as a partner in the partnership [see **34.1.5**].

34.1.3.8
The independent business test

The **independent business test** looks at whether the individual is genuinely in business on his or her own account, or whether he or she is in fact part of the organisation to which the service is being provided. At present this is often used as the fundamental test.

Individuals are likely to be considered independent if they:
- provide their own equipment and other resources;
- are, in effect, selling their services and expertise;
- invest their own capital in the business;
- run financial risks and stand to gain or lose financially from the business.
Lee v Chung and Shun Shing Construction and Engineering Company [1990] IRLR 236

A person who works for many different bodies and whose income is irregular is more likely to be considered independent than one who works most of the time for one body and is paid on a regular basis.

34.1.3.9
Intentions of the parties

If the results of the other tests are inconclusive, the intentions of the parties may be an important factor in clarifying whether the relationship between them is one of employment or of self-employment.

34.1.3.10
Inland Revenue criteria

The criteria used by the Inland Revenue and Contributions Office for the purposes of determining tax and national insurance liability are similar to the above tests and are set out in booklet IR56 *Employed or Self-employed*. This looks at whether the individual:
- takes risks with his or her own money in carrying out the work;

- is able to engage others to do the work;
- can decide when, where and how the work is done;
- has to put right unsatisfactory work in his or her own time and at his or her own expense; *and*
- provides his or her own equipment.

34.1.4
The importance of the distinction

Many rights and obligations apply to an employer's relationship with employees, but not with self-employed workers and other contractors [for the main differences, see **22.1.3**].

Because of the complexity and inconsistency of the various tests for self-employment, it is possible mistakenly to treat a person as self-employed when he or she is legally an employee. But sometimes employers do this deliberately in order to avoid having to operate PAYE, pay employer's national insurance and provide statutory employment rights. This may be done with the collusion of the individual, who as a self-employed person can claim more expenses against earnings than an employee can claim, and who might prefer to be paid gross rather than with tax and national insurance deducted by the employer.

34.1.4.1
Employment rights

An employer who wrongly treats a person as self-employed, regardless of whether this is deliberate or by mistake, could have claims brought against it by the individual for not providing workers' or employment rights such as maternity pay and paid holidays, and could face a claim for unfair dismissal if the contract is not renewed when it ends.

34.1.4.2
PAYE

If the organisation does not operate PAYE for the individual and the Inland Revenue finds that it should have, the organisation could be ordered to pay up to six years' income tax and national insurance contributions on payments to the individual, plus interest and possibly penalties for late payment. In some situations special rules apply to construction workers [see **27.4.12**].

Organisations which have perhaps wrongly treated workers as self-employed should take advice from a solicitor or accountant with tax expertise. Drawing the matter to the attention of the Inland Revenue may mean that it assesses the organisation for past failure to deduct, but if the matter is ignored and the Revenue discovers it in future, it may then assess for an even more substantial past failure.

The Inland Revenue seeks to bring as many people as possible within the PAYE net, and is likely to challenge any 'self-employment' which it considers actually to be employment. The Revenue has the skills, knowledge and resources to fight the case, while the organisation is likely to have to bring in expensive tax specialists. Because of this, the costs of a challenge to a Revenue ruling may be out of all proportion to the amount of money the organisation will save if it wins.

34.1.4.3
Registration as self-employed

The distinction between self-employed and employee is significant not only for the organisation, but also for the individual. From 31 January 2001 individuals must register with the Inland Revenue within three months from the end of the month in which they start self-employment. A person who fails to register may incur a £100 penalty.

34.1.5
Personal service companies (IR35)

Where an individual sets up a limited company or partnership and carries out work through that body, he or she does that work as a director or employee of the company or as a partner in the partnership, rather than on a self-employed basis.

A company or partnership controlled by an individual who personally carries out work for clients is referred to as a **personal service company**. Under rules referred to as **IR35**, such a company or partnership has to operate PAYE for the individual where:

- the company enters into a contract with a client under which the individual has to do the work personally, or can appoint a substitute only with the consent of the client; *and*

- the individual undertakes so much work for the client that the relationship is, in effect, an employment relationship.

IR35 does not affect organisations which enter into contracts with service companies or partnerships, because the organisation's relationship is with the company or partnership, rather than the individual.

IR35 also does not affect individuals who work on a self-employed basis rather than through a company or partnership controlled by them.

34.2 PROTECTING THE ORGANISATION

34.2.1 Entering into the contract

Before hiring anyone on a self-employed basis, the organisation should:

- consider whether the nature of the work, or the relationship between the organisation and worker, is such that an employment tribunal would say that the person is actually an employee or 'worker' and/or the Inland Revenue would say that PAYE should be operated;

- ask for confirmation, in writing, that the person is registered with the Inland Revenue as self-employed for this type of work;

- ask for the person's tax office and reference number, and if in doubt, check with the tax office about whether it is permissible to treat the person as self-employed for the work they are doing for the organisation.

If in doubt it is generally safer to treat the person as an employee. This will have cost implications for employer's national insurance, statutory sick pay, holiday pay, and other statutory and contractual entitlements.

If the person is to be treated as self-employed:

- ensure that an appropriate written contract [see **34.3**] is signed by both parties; *and*

- review the health and safety, negligence and other risks arising from the relationship and ensure the individual and organisation have appropriate insurance cover.

34.2.2 Terminating the contract

Before terminating a contract with a person who has been treated as self-employed, the organisation should carefully consider whether there is any risk of the person asserting that he or she is in fact an employee and therefore has the right to claim unfair dismissal. If there is any possibility of this, legal advice should be sought.

34.3 THE CONTRACT

As soon as one party offers to pay another in exchange for a service and the offer is accepted, a contract exists [see **18.6**]. There is no obligation to put anything in writing, but it is very good practice to have a written contract with all self-employed individuals and other contractors. An organisation which regularly uses contractors should consider developing a suitable model [see **18.8**]. If it is asked to sign a contract prepared by a contractor it should carefully consider the terms and if necessary take legal advice before signing.

34.3.1 What a contract includes

There are no rules about what must be included or how long a contract should be. A good contract should include, as appropriate:

- the names of the parties;

- the nature of the work, either in general or in detail, perhaps with reference to another more detailed document which is attached;

Dates and deadlines

- the start date and if appropriate the finish date or deadline, and any deadlines between start and finish;

- if there is no finish date, how the contract will be ended and the notice which needs to be given by whichever side is ending it;

Fee	<ul><li>the agreed fee and the basis on which it is made (for example per hour, per session or as a fixed fee for the job as a whole);</li><li>whether the fee includes VAT, is exclusive of VAT or is not subject to VAT;</li><li>if paid on an hourly or other open-ended basis, whether there is a maximum to the amount of time or money payable;</li><li>any penalties or compensation if deadlines are not met;</li><li>the circumstances, if any, when additional fees will be due (for example on publication of a second edition, or if rights to a publication are sold to another organisation);</li><li>agreed expenses, how additional expenses are agreed, and the receipts or other documentation the contractor needs to provide;</li></ul>
Payment	<ul><li>when payment will be made (for example monthly, on completion of the job, or one-third in advance with one-third midway through and one-third on completion);</li><li>the requirement to invoice the organisation, and the organisation's agreement to pay within 14 (or whatever) days of the invoice date;</li><li>any interest on late payment [for information about the statutory right to charge interest on late payments, see **18.7.3**];</li><li>if the contractor is an individual, the fact that he or she is responsible for all tax and national insurance on payments made to him or her and will indemnify the organisation for any liability in respect of tax and NI on those payments (the organisation still has to confirm that the person is indeed self-employed, but this clause allows the organisation to recover tax and NI from the individual if necessary);</li></ul>
Nature of the work	<ul><li>where and how the work will be done;</li><li>warranties that the contractor has the necessary skill and will take all reasonable care;</li><li>the organisation's agreement to provide information, access to premises etc reasonably requested;</li><li>issues around data protection and confidentiality of information;</li><li>support or facilities to be provided by the organisation (for example typing, photocopying, telephone, access to library etc);</li><li>obligation to indemnify if damage or loss is caused (for example injury, libel or financial loss);</li><li>what insurance, if any, the contractor is required to have and whether proof of insurance must be provided [see **34.3.2**];</li><li>agreement to comply with the organisation's policies on equal opportunities, health and safety etc;</li></ul>
Monitoring	<ul><li>to whom the contractor reports, how often and in what form;</li><li>if appropriate how and when the work will be reviewed, what happens if the brief has to be changed, what happens if the work is unsatisfactory, and how disputes about the work are to be handled;</li><li>whether interim reports, drafts etc are required, and deadlines for these;</li><li>procedure for terminating the work if there is a breach of contract and the matter cannot be resolved;</li></ul>
Rights	<ul><li>whether the contractor will hold copyright, patent, design or other rights to any work produced, or whether the right(s) will be assigned to the organisation or will be held jointly [see **chapter 39**];</li><li>how the work will be assessed or evaluated on completion, and what happens if the organisation is dissatisfied with it;</li><li>what rights, if any, the contractor has to use research data or written materials for other purposes;</li><li>any restrictions, for example not to do similar work for a competitor;</li></ul>

- if relevant who has the right to change the material for future use, what payments are made to the contractor for future use etc;

Completion and follow-up

- for consultancy type work, how and to whom recommendations will be submitted before a report is produced, and to whom the report is to be given;

- whether any follow-up is built into this contract, or whether follow-up, if any, is to be agreed later as a separate contract.

34.3.2
Liability and insurance

It may be appropriate for the organisation to require the contractor to be insured for risks arising from its activities. This might include public liability insurance [see **20.5.1**], professional indemnity insurance [see **20.5.3**], insurance against breach of copyright [see **20.5.6**], defamation [see **20.5.5**] or breach of confidentiality [see **20.5.7**], or whatever is appropriate for the work.

The organisation should check that all necessary insurance actually exists and adequately covers the possible risks. Where the contract extends over a long period, the organisation may wish to require proof of renewal.

The organisation is not normally liable for damage or loss caused by a contractor, but could be held liable where:

- the organisation authorised the action which caused the loss or damage;

- the organisation has a duty with strict liability [see **19.5.1** and **36.2.5**]; *or*

- the organisation has not taken care to select a competent contractor.

Pinn v Rew [1916] 32 TLR 451

It may be appropriate to include in the contract provision for indemnification if the organisation suffers any loss as a result of the contractor's activities. Where the risks are substantial, the organisation should require the contractor to take out insurance indemnifying it.

The organisation must ensure that its own insurance covers risks arising from the work, and that its insurance is not invalidated by, for example, the presence of a contractor or the fact that the work is being done by a contractor rather than an employee.

34.4
DISPUTES

The risk of dispute can be reduced by putting as much as possible in writing beforehand, building in procedures for regularly monitoring work, and dealing with difficulties or differences as they arise. If a dispute does arise, it is generally dealt with by the parties. They may call in an independent third party, but there is no obligation to do this unless it is required under the terms of their contract [see **61.2** for more about dispute resolution].

If one party is in breach of contract—for example if the contractor does not do the work as agreed or the organisation does not pay on time—the aggrieved party may take the other to court [see **61.4** and **61.6**].

FOR FURTHER INFORMATION

Tax and national insurance. 08457-143 143; www.inlandrevenue.gov.uk

Chapter 35
VOLUNTEERS

35.1
THE LEGAL POSITION OF VOLUNTEERS

There is no legal definition of a **volunteer**, although the **National Minimum Wage Act 1998** does refer to **voluntary workers** [see **35.3.3.1**]. In common usage volunteers are often defined as people who give their time of their own free will, without being legally obliged to do so, and without pay or other reward. However some people referred to by their organisations or themselves as volunteers do receive pay or other reward, and/or are under a contractual or other commitment to carry out the work.

35.1.1
Obligations of volunteers

All volunteers, with or without pay, must comply with the law relating to the organisation's activities and services. This includes, for example, the law relating to health and safety [see **chapter 36**], driving [**35.9.5**], work with children and vulnerable adults [**36.8**], equal opportunities in service delivery [**chapter 37**], confidentiality and data protection [**chapter 38**], public activities and events [**chapter 42**], provision of food and drink [**chapter 43**], and fundraising [**chapters 44-45**].

When carrying out their work they have a **duty of care** [see **19.5.1**] to the organisation, other workers, clients or service users, and members of the public with whom they come in contact.

Failure to comply with relevant law could lead to claims or even criminal charges being brought against the volunteer and/or the organisations for which he or she is volunteering.

Volunteers must also comply with the organisation's internal policies, rules and guidelines. Failure to do so could lead to the volunteer being asked to stop volunteering for the organisation.

35.1.2
Rights of volunteers and duties of organisations

The legal rights of volunteers, and the corresponding duties of organisations, are often unclear, for several reasons:

- in the past, the people who framed legislation rarely thought about the implications for volunteers;

- even now, with these implications more likely to be considered, legislation may be framed unclearly or without taking into account the full range of volunteering relationships;

- the term 'volunteer' is used to describe a very wide range of people, some of whom may in fact be employees for the purposes of tax and national insurance and sometimes also for employment rights;

- both the EU and the UK are increasingly extending employment rights, including minimum wage and working time rights, to a wider group of **workers** [see **22.1.2**], which could include some volunteers.

These issues are particularly important where the volunteer is paid anything other than allowed reimbursement of expenses [see **35.2.2**], receives anything else of value [**35.2.4**], or has a relationship with the organisation which is or could be seen as contractual [**35.3**]. In these situations a so-called volunteer could be entitled to workers' rights or the full range of employment rights. In addition, their pay or the value of other benefits could be subject to tax, and depending on the circumstances the organisation would have to operate PAYE or the individual would have to declare it through self-assessment.

Even where volunteers do not have workers' or employment rights:

- the organisation has a **duty of care** to them [see **19.5.1**];

- if the organisation has any employees it must comply with health and safety legislation [see **chapter 36**], and good practice is to do so even if there are no employees;

- volunteers have the same protection as anyone else in relation to data protection [see **38.3**];

- volunteers who are not legally employees own the copyright or other intellectual property rights to work they create for the organisation, unless the rights have been assigned to the organisation [see **39.2.3**].

Unless the volunteer is legally an employee, there is no statutory obligation to take out insurance to cover situations where the volunteer becomes ill or injured as a result of the organisation's negligence. But it is good practice to ensure they are covered under the organisation's employer's liability or public liability insurance [see **35.8**].

Volunteers are not protected under the employment provisions of the equal opportunities legislation unless they are legally working under a contract [see **35.3**], but may be protected under the service delivery provisions [see **35.6.1**].

The National Centre for Volunteering or Wales Council for Voluntary Action [see end of chapter] can provide basic information on legal aspects of volunteering. For complex matters it may be necessary to seek detailed advice from a solicitor or other advisor with specialist expertise in relation to volunteers.

35.2 PAYMENTS AND PERKS TO VOLUNTEERS

Organisations have no obligation to make any reimbursements or other payments, or provide any benefits, to volunteers. But in looking at many rights and obligations in relation to volunteers, key issues are the nature of any payments made or benefits provided to the volunteer, whether the organisation has created a relationship in which it is obliged to provide certain types of payment or benefits, and whether the individual is obliged to provide work in exchange for those payments or benefits.

In looking at the nature of payments and benefits, a distinction must be made between:

- allowed **reimbursement** of expenses [see below];
- **additional payments** which may be called reimbursement but are not in fact linked to genuine out-of-pocket expenditure;
- **remuneration**, which is payment (or something else of value) given in return for the work done by the volunteer;
- a **one-off payment** or gift given as a token of thanks to the volunteer;
- provision of **benefits** which are part of or necessary for the work, such as training or in some cases accommodation;
- provision of additional benefits or **perks**, such as reduced price admission to events, discounts on goods in the charity's shop, or training unrelated to the volunteer's work.

35.2.1 Reimbursement of expenses

Reimbursement of expenses repays a person for expenditure which:

- was genuinely incurred (the money was actually spent);
- was authorised by the organisation;
- was wholly for the organisation's work;
- was necessary for the work; *and*
- is properly documented [see **35.2.1.4**].

Reimbursement which meets these criteria and is allowed by the Inland Revenue [see **35.2.1.1**]:

- is not subject to tax or national insurance;
- should not affect volunteers on state benefits, although some benefits offices erroneously count travel expenses and reimbursement for meals towards the earnings disregard [see **35.10.2.3**];
- is unlikely to be treated by the employment tribunal or court as consideration creating a contract [see **35.3**] and entitling the volunteer to workers' or employment rights;
- can be made to governing body members of charitable trusts and associations without contravening charity law, unless the governing document explicitly prohibits such payment;
- can be made to governing body members of companies (whether charitable or non-charitable) or non-charitable associations provided the governing document allows reimbursement or it is authorised by the members of the organisation [see **14.2.3**].

Even where reimbursement meets these criteria it may not be allowed for asylum seekers who are volunteering [see **35.5.2**].

35.2.1.1 Reimbursements allowed by the Inland Revenue

The reimbursements allowed by the Inland Revenue depend on whether the volunteer is **unpaid** (receives only reimbursement for allowed expenses) or **paid** (receives additional payment or other remuneration).

All volunteers, regardless of whether they are paid or unpaid, may be reimbursed tax-free and without other implications for:

- travel expenses or mileage to do the work (but not necessarily travel between home and the usual place of volunteering—see below);
- actual expenditure incurred in the purchase of materials or services required to do the work (postage, photocopying etc);

501

- actual cost of specialist or protective clothing necessary for the work;
- actual cost of training, conferences, supervision etc necessary for the work, and directly related costs such as travel costs and accommodation or meals while attending such events.

Unpaid (but not paid) volunteers may be reimbursed tax-free for:

- travel expenses or mileage between home and the place of volunteering:
- actual costs of meals taken while volunteering;
- actual cost of creche, childminding fees or other dependant care costs incurred in order to be available for voluntary work.

It is good practice for the organisation to have limits on what it will reimburse for meals, childminding and similar expenses.

35.2.1.2
Mileage

Reimbursement for mileage is tax-free if it is reimbursed at or below the Inland Revenue **authorised mileage rate**. Volunteers must keep proper records showing journey details, mileage and purpose. The reimbursement rates allowed by Inland Revenue for car journeys are based on the car engine size and on the total number of reimbursed miles for the vehicle during the tax year. The rates are (tax year 2001-02):

	Up to 1500cc	1501-2000cc	Over 2000cc
Up to 4000 miles	40p	45p	63p
Over 4000 miles	25p	25p	36p

If the volunteer can show that mileage costs were genuinely above these rates, the Inland Revenue will allow the additional amount to be paid free of tax and NI.

Bicycle use can be reimbursed tax free at 12p per mile, and motorcycle use at 24p per mile (2001-02 rates).

If the organisation reimburses at higher than the Inland Revenue rates, the excess is taxable and may have significant implications [see **35.2.2**].

If the organisation does not reimburse, or reimburses at less than the authorised mileage rates, volunteers may be able to set the expenditure against their taxable income. They should seek advice on this from their tax office.

For more information see **27.4.5** and leaflet IR122 *Volunteer Drivers*, available from the Inland Revenue [see end of chapter].

35.2.1.3
Flat-rate expenses

Organisations with large numbers of volunteers, where the paperwork involved in reimbursing actual expenditure would be disproportionately time-consuming, may apply to the local Inland Revenue inspector of taxes for permission to make flat-rate expenses payments. Such consent is not granted very often.

Even where consent for flat-rate payments is granted, it covers only the tax status of the payment. Any element of the payment which is not reimbursement of genuine expenditure will be an unlawful payment if made to a charity governing body member, may affect state benefits, and may entitle the person to workers' or employment rights.

35.2.1.4
Documentation

Unless the Inland Revenue has authorised flat-rate payments, volunteers should wherever reasonable provide receipts or other documentation to verify their expenditure. The organisation decides what it requires, but there should be enough information to show that the expenditure was actually incurred, was wholly for the organisation's work and was necessary for the work.

It is good practice to devise a claim form setting out the volunteers' name, date of expenditure, nature of expenditure and reason for it, and amount. It should also have a space for a signature authorising the reimbursement, and the cheque date and number (if paid by cheque) or signature of recipient (if reimbursed by cash). The relevant documentation should be attached to the claim form. Where receipts are not available, for example telephone calls made from home, the volunteer should provide appropriate records or an explanation of how the amount was estimated, or a note should be made on the expenditure record indicating why there is no documentation.

35.2.2
Remuneration and other taxable income

Unless the person is on a training or return-to-work scheme which specifically allows payment tax-free, all payments apart from reimbursement of genuine expenses [see **35.2.1.1**] are subject to tax and national insurance. Taxable income thus includes:

- regular payments for work;
- a one-off payment, if the person has been told they will receive it or it is regularly given for this type of work;
- sessional fees;
- 'pocket money';
- anything called an 'expenses payment' or 'reimbursement' unless it complies with the rules for allowed payments [see **35.2.1.1**];
- lump sums 'to cover expenses', unless the Inland Revenue has agreed flat-rate payments [see **35.2.1.3**].

Where the payment is clearly for the work, it is classed as remuneration. Where it is called an expenses payment or something similar it may be classed either as remuneration or other taxable income, depending on the situation. The amount is irrelevant, and even a token payment is taxable.

As well as being taxable, the payment may also affect state benefits, may be unlawful if made to a member of the organisation's governing body [see **14.1.1**], and may be treated as consideration creating a contract and thus entitling the volunteer to workers' or employment rights [see **35.3**].

35.2.2.1
Tax

Volunteers who receive payments which are not proper reimbursement are generally treated for tax purposes in the same way as employees. They must fill in form P46, and the organisation is likely to have to operate PAYE for any volunteer who:

- receives more than the national insurance earnings threshold (£87 per week in 2001-02) from the organisation; *or*
- pays tax on earnings from other sources or pension, and receives more than £1 per week from the organisation.

Where volunteers receive 'enhanced expenses', such as mileage at more than the Inland Revenue rate, the Inland Revenue may allow this to be declared by the volunteer and taxed under self-assessment, rather than through PAYE.

For more about income tax and national insurance see **27.3-27.5**. If the organisation is not registered for PAYE it should contact the Inland Revenue's new employer helpline [see end of chapter]. If it is already registered it should generally treat paid volunteers in the same way as new employees.

At the end of the tax year the organisation must give all paid volunteers a record of what they have received as remuneration during the year, and may also need to provide a record of expenses payments [see **27.3.3** and **27.4.8**]. This organisation must also provide this information to the Inland Revenue.

35.2.2.2
National insurance

A paid volunteer who is paid more than the national insurance earnings threshold (£87 per week in tax year 2001-02) must pay employee's (class 1) NI contributions, and the organisation must pay employer's NICs [see **27.5**].

35.2.3
Honoraria and thank-you payments

An **honorarium** is a payment which there is no contractual obligation to make. If a person is told that he or she will receive a payment, or if the payment is always made so the person can realistically expect to receive it, it is not an honorarium. It is a one-off payment and should be treated the same as other payments [see **35.2.2**].

Provided that a one-off payment is given as a genuine thank you and is not given regularly, it may not be subject to tax. The organisation should take advice from its PAYE office or accountant before making such a payment. Even if a payment is not subject to tax it may affect state benefits, and may be unlawful if paid to a member of the governing body. In addition, the organisation may be restricted in its power to make such payments [see **49.2.7**].

35.2.4
Benefits, perks and non-money gifts

Meals provided during unpaid volunteering are not subject to tax, are not unlawful if provided to governing body members, and in general will not affect state benefits. However some benefits offices erroneously set them against the earnings disregard [see **35.10.2.3**]. The value of meals provided to paid volunteers is subject to tax.

Benefits with a financial value, such as protective clothing, training, or supervision, can be provided with no problem provided they are necessary for the work.

Small perks which are not necessary for the work, such as reduced-price entry to the organisation's events or small discounts at the charity's shop, small gifts such as flowers or chocolate, and occasional small-scale social events are not likely to be taxable, and should not affect state benefits. If made to a governing body member it could be an unlawful use of the organisation's funds [see **14.1.1**], but in practice neither the Charity Commission nor the organisation's members would be likely to take action against the organisation. The provision or promise of such benefits could possibly be seen as consideration creating a contract [see **35.3**], and thus have implications for workers' or employment rights.

Benefits or perks which are not necessary for the work and have a financial value, such as additional training, could be subject to tax, could affect state benefits, could create an entitlement to workers' or employment rights, and if made to a member of a governing body could be an unlawful use of the organisation's funds. The organisation should take specialist advice before providing such benefits.

The provision of accommodation is complex and advice should be taken. If the volunteer must live there in order to carry out his or her duties, all or some the value of the accommodation may not be subject to tax. It will, however, affect some state benefits.

35.2.4.1
Employment rights

If a volunteer claims workers' or employment rights, a tribunal or court could say that there is a contract giving entitlement to those rights [see below] if:

- it has been made clear that benefits or perks which are not necessary for the work will be given in return for the work (for example 'as a volunteer you will get training that will help you in your career'); *or*

- the volunteer is obliged to provide work in return for a benefit ('we will provide training to enable you to work for us, and you must then work for us for at least six months').

35.3
IS THERE A CONTRACT?

Entitlement to workers' and employment rights depends on whether there is a **contract** between the individual and the organisation, and if so the nature of the contract. Contract here does not refer to a document, but to the **relationship** between the parties [see **18.6**]. A contract may be written, verbal or implied (assumed from the nature of the relationship).

At its simplest, a **contract** in this context is a relationship which involves:

- **consideration** (payment or something else of material value) being provided in return for work; *and*
- the **intention** to create a legally binding relationship between the parties [see **18.6.1** for more about what a contract involves]. The courts and employment tribunals generally assume that if one party agrees to pay another for work, they intend the relationship to be legally binding. The parties do not have to state this explicitly.

Proper reimbursement for expenses allowed by the Inland Revenue [see **35.2.1.1**] is not likely to be classed as consideration.

If there is a contract it may be:

- a **contract of employment** [see **22.1.1**], entitling the person to the full range of employment rights;
- another type of **contract**, for example for casual work, where the person is not entitled to all employment rights but is entitled to the more limited rights available to **workers**, such as equal opportunities, minimum wage and working time rights [see **22.1.2**]; *or*
- a contract with a **self-employed** person, who in most cases is not entitled to statutory employment rights other than equal opportunities protection [see **22.1.3**].

35.3.1
The range of
relationships

The most likely relationships with so-called volunteers are:

- Remuneration and/or benefits (including training) not necessary for the work

  + an obligation to do the work, or a situation where the person does the work on a regular basis

  = **contract of employment**, with entitlement to the same rights as any employee (see for example the Migrant Advisory Service case, **35.3.2.1**).

- Remuneration and/or benefits not necessary for the work

  + one-off, occasional or non-regular work

  = **contract**, with entitlement to workers' rights such as minimum wage and working time rights (see the Welcare case, **35.3.2.1**).

- Benefits *necessary* for the work (such as training)

  + a clear obligation to do the work in return for the benefit

  = contract or contract of employment, depending on the nature of the obligation, with entitlement to workers' or employment rights (see the Relate case, **35.3.2.1**).

- Any of the above

  + an explicit statement that the parties do not intend the relationship to be contractual [see **35.3.4**]

  = *possibly* a non-contractual arrangement not entitling the person to workers' or employment rights, but this should not be relied on.

- Only genuine reimbursement, and/or training or other benefits necessary for the work

  + the person free to stop volunteering whenever they want (i.e. no explicit commitment 'to volunteer for at least six months')

  = no contract, therefore no entitlement to workers' or employment rights.

It must be emphasised that the above outline is intended only to illustrate the range of relationships, and does not mean that any particular relationship would or would not be defined by a court or tribunal as contractual. The tribunal cases described below illustrate the issues.

35.3.2
Tribunal decisions

Any court or tribunal case involving a volunteer is likely to mean trying to interpret the law in unusual ways. This can give rise to confusing and sometimes contradictory decisions. Any organisation faced with a claim or potential claim for employment rights by a volunteer should take advice from a specialist solicitor.

The fact that a tribunal or court finds that a contract has or has not been created does not affect, one way or the other, liability for tax and national insurance, because the Inland Revenue and Contributions Office use different criteria [see **35.2.2.1** and **35.2.2.2**].

35.3.2.1
Volunteers held to have a contract of employment

A 'volunteer' office worker who received £25 per week (subsequently increased to £40) 'to cover expenses' was held to have a contract because she did not incur any costs for travel, meals or other expenditure, and received the payment even when she was on holiday. The payment was clearly for the work, rather than reimbursement. Because she worked regular hours each week in the organisation's office, the contract was held to be a contract of employment. As the chair of the appeal tribunal remarked, in upholding this finding, 'This is a very simple case and it is perhaps, in a way, like the elephant—you know one when you see one'. The worker subsequently received £11,000 for unfair dismissal.

Migrant Advisory Service v Mrs K Chaudri [1998] EAT 1400/97

A contract does not have to involve payment. In one of the best-known cases, a counsellor who after training applied for a position as a volunteer was held to have a contract of employment, even though she did not receive any money payment, because:

- she was obliged to provide 600 hours of counselling after receiving training, or to repay the organisation if she left without good reason before providing the counselling;

- there was an expectation that after she had done a certain amount of counselling, she might be paid for future work;

- there was a long and formal written agreement, with detailed obligations on both parties;

- the agreement referred to the organisation as 'the employer'.

Maria DeLourdes Armitage v Relate & others [1994] COIT 43538/94

In a less clear-cut case involving a disability discrimination claim against a citizens advice bureau, it was held that a contract of employment was created by the obligations on both sides, which included:

- the organisation's agreement to provide training and travel expenses;

- the individual's obligation to complete the training within a specified period, to work specified hours, and to give reasonable notice of leaving;

- the individual being subject to disciplinary and grievance procedures.

Murray v Newham Citizens Advice Bureau [2000] EAT 1069/99

This case illustrates the importance of looking at the entire relationship between the organisation and its volunteers. The phrasing and scope of internal procedures could be critical in showing an intention to create a binding relationship, especially where the organisation requires the person to work at specific times or for a specified period. Volunteer agreements and procedures should be reviewed with this in mind.

35.3.2.2
Volunteers held to have a contract

In one case a 'volunteer' was not required or expected to work on a regular basis, but helped out occasionally in a project to pack up food and toiletries for refugees. Whenever she attended she received a payment of between £5 and £15, depending on the number of hours she worked. The tribunal held that she was working under a contract, but that it was not a contract of employment.   *Ailsa Elshami v Welcare*

Community Projects and Geta Leema [1998] COIT 6001977/1998

35.3.2.3
Volunteers held not to have a contract

In one case in 1944, auxiliary coastguards who were paid for their work were held not to have a contract of employment, because the coast guard was a voluntary public service and there was no intention to create legally enforceable obligations on either side. If this case were heard today it is likely that even if no employment relationship were created, there would be a worker relationship.

More recently, a St John Ambulance volunteer claimed she was working under a contract because a condition of membership was that she do 30 hours of duties each year. The tribunal held that this obligation was a condition of membership, not a contract to provide services.

Mrs Y B Uttley v St John Ambulance & another [1998] EAT 635/98

Where an organisation offers to pay for the work done by a volunteer but the volunteer does not take up the offer, this does not create a contract with the volunteer. *Mrs D Alexander v Romania at Heart Trading Co Ltd [1997] COIT 3102006/97*

A requirement that volunteers comply with an organisation's policies and rules is not comparable to a requirement that they provide work. The latter may create a contract; the former does not.

Gradwell v Council for Voluntary Service, Blackpool, Wyre & Fylde [1997] COIT 2404314/97

35.3.3
Volunteers working under a contract

'Volunteers' who are working under a contract of employment are entitled to the full range of statutory employment rights [see **23.4** for a list of these rights]. Volunteers who are not legally employees but are working under a contract which entitles them to **workers' rights** do not have the full range of employment rights, but are entitled to:

- protection under the employment provisions of the race, sex and disability legislation [see **35.6.1**];

- national minimum wage [see below and **27.2**];

- working time rights such as rest breaks and paid annual leave [see **28.1**];

- the right to an itemised pay slip and not to have unauthorised deductions made from payments from the employer;

- if working part-time, the same rights *pro rata* as comparable full-time workers on the same type of contract [see **25.12**];

- the right to be accompanied at disciplinary and grievance hearings [see **29.3.4**].

At the time of writing (early 2001) the secretary of state for employment has the right to extend a wider range of employment rights to people classed as workers rather than employees.

35.3.3.1
Minimum wage

The **National Minimum Wage Act 1998** refers specifically to **voluntary workers**, who are working for a charity, voluntary organisation, associated fundraising body or a statutory body. Such voluntary workers are not entitled to minimum wage if, under the terms of their work, they are entitled to and actually receive:

- no money payments at all; *or*

- no money payments except reimbursement of expenses actually incurred in carrying out their duties, or reasonably estimated to be or have been so incurred; *and/or*

- no money payments other than payment for subsistence (meals and living expenses, but not accommodation), provided that the work is done for a charity, voluntary organisation, associated fundraising body, or statutory body *and* the volunteer has been placed with that body as a result of arrangements made by a charity acting in furtherance of its charitable objects (such as a CSV type placement);

and they are entitled to and actually receive:

- no benefits in kind at all; *or*
- no benefits in kind other than training provided with the sole or main purpose of improving the volunteers' performance of the work they have agreed to do; *and/or*
- no benefits in kind other than some or all subsistence (meals etc) and accommodation, as reasonable in relation to the work.

National Minimum Wage Act 1998 s.44

This rule has the effect of entitling volunteers to minimum wage if they are working under a contract, whether written, verbal or implied, and receive, for example, training beyond what is necessary for their work, or if live-in volunteers receive 'pocket money' on a placement which is not a CSV-type placement.

National minimum wage does not apply to residential members of charitable religious communities who are paid for work by that community. It does apply where the charitable religious community is an independent school or provides further or higher education.

National Minimum Wage Act 1998 s.44A,
amended by Employment Relations Act 1999 s.22

35.3.4
Exclusion of contractual intention

If a person is obliged to work and receives remuneration or something else of value for the work, but the individual and organisation have explicitly stated that they see their relationship as voluntary and do not intend it to be legally binding, an employment tribunal or court *might* agree that a contract has not been created, and the person is therefore not entitled to workers' and/or employment rights.

The tribunal or court would look at the nature of the relationship, and whether it was reasonable for the parties to say that the relationship did not create a contract. Even if it is explicitly stated that the parties do not intend the relationship to be legally binding, the tribunal might find that in fact the 'volunteer' has a contract and is therefore entitled to workers' or employment rights.

An organisation which wishes to pay its volunteers or provide benefits without creating a contract should make clear in all relevant discussions, correspondence and the volunteer agreement, if there is one, that this is a voluntary relationship and is not intended to be legally binding [see **35.4**]. These statements will be taken into account if a volunteer subsequently claims employment rights, but will not be conclusive.

Where the relationship involves payment or provision of benefits in return for work, legal advice should be taken before making a statement that the relationship is not intended to be legally binding. Such a statement could be seen as an attempt to deprive workers or employees of their statutory rights, and is likely to be ineffective. At the very least, workers would still be entitled to minimum wage.

35.3.5
Unpaid volunteers

If a volunteer is not remunerated in any way for the work done for the organisation and does not receive any benefits from the organisation, there can be no contract, because the creation of a contract requires an exchange of consideration [see **35.3**]. Any agreement between the organisation and individual is unlikely to be legally binding on either party. There may be a moral obligation to comply with the terms of the agreement, but the obligation cannot be enforced in the courts and the person would not have workers' or employment rights.

However because of the possibility that something provided by the organisation, such as training or a discount at the charity's shop, could be seen as consideration, any correspondence or agreement should make clear that this is a voluntary arrangement and is not intended to be legally binding [see above].

It is very important to be aware that even a volunteer who receives no payment could be held to have a contract if the volunteer receives something else of benefit from the organisation, as in the Relate and New-ham CAB cases [see **35.3.2.1**]. The minimum wage implications, in particular, could be very significant.

**35.4
VOLUNTEER
AGREEMENTS**

There is no obligation to provide a volunteer agreement. It may be helpful, especially for long-term volunteers or those taking on a major task, to clarify the expectations for both parties, but for other volunteers such agreements may be seen as unduly formal or restrictive.

Where volunteers are given a letter or written agreement, it should:

- start with a statement that it sets out expectations and intentions, not binding obligations to offer work or to do it, and that the terms of the agreement are binding in honour only;
- state that neither party intends a contractual or employment relationship to be created, either now or in future;
- phrase time commitments in terms of hopes ('we hope you will stay with us for at least six months' rather than 'you must');
- make clear that payment will be made only for reimbursement of genuine, documented expenses;
- make clear that training, protective clothing etc will be provided to enable the person to carry out their voluntary duties, but the agreement should not offer benefits that are not necessary for the work;
- where benefits such as use of facilities are offered, make clear that these are discretionary and the organisation is not obliged to provide them;
- make clear that obligations to comply with the organisation's policies, such as equal opportunities, health and safety and confidentiality, are required for compliance with legal duties and for the proper performance of the organisation's work, rather than being obligations creating a contractual situation;
- avoid employment-related terms such as contract, sick leave, annual leave, disciplinary procedure, promotion and dismissal.

Depending on the nature of the voluntary work, the agreement might then include any or all of the following:

- nature and purpose of the voluntary work;
- hours and days when the volunteer is willing to work;
- name and position of the person who will supervise the volunteer or to whom the volunteer is responsible;
- positions supervised by the volunteer;
- what the volunteer hopes for from the organisation;
- what the organisation hopes for from the volunteer;
- the volunteer's agreement to abide by the organisation's objects and its equal opportunities, health and safety, confidentiality, data protection and other policies;
- meetings or events the volunteer is entitled to attend;
- training to be provided to enable the volunteer to do the work;
- level and type of supervision and support to be provided;
- arrangements for reviewing work and dealing with problems;
- whom the volunteer should notify if he or she is ill;
- how much notice the volunteer is asked to give when not available for volunteering (for example during holidays), and whom to notify;
- reimbursable expenses, and how to claim them [see **35.2.1.1**];
- arrangements and requirements for use of the volunteer's car [see **35.2.1.2** and **35.9.5**];
- arrangements for use of the organisation's vehicles;
- relevant insurances provided by the organisation [see **35.8**];

- insurance cover required for the volunteer to provide;
- notice the volunteer is asked to give when stopping volunteering;
- what will happen if the volunteer's work is unsatisfactory;
- what the volunteer should do if dissatisfied in any way.

The last two points are in effect disciplinary and grievance procedures. If there is any possibility that the volunteer could legally be a **worker** [see **22.1.2**], these provisions must include the right to be accompanied [see **29.3.4**].

35.5
VOLUNTEERS FROM ABROAD

There is no restriction on nationals of European Economic Area countries (European Union plus Iceland, Liechtenstein and Norway) serving as volunteers in the UK. For nationals of other countries, advice is available from the National Centre for Volunteering, Wales Council for Voluntary Action or the Immigration and Nationality Department [see end of chapter].

35.5.1
Non-EU nationals

Most nationals of non-EEA countries need a work permit to take up 'employment paid or unpaid' in the UK [see **26.2.9**]. A person with a work permit, and their spouse, can volunteer. Individuals who do not need a work permit for paid work do not need one to volunteer. Au pairs from outside the EEA are not allowed to undertake voluntary work.

35.5.1.1
Charity volunteering

A person coming to the UK from outside the EEA to take up voluntary work will be able to do so without getting a work permit provided:

- the work is for a registered charity;
- the work relates directly to the charity's objects, and is not purely clerical, administrative or maintenance; *and*
- the volunteer may receive accommodation, board, and pocket money of no more than £35 per week, but no additional remuneration.

There may be minimum wage implications in providing accommodation and pocket money [see **35.3.3.1**], and advice should be taken from a specialist solicitor.

If a visa is required to enter the UK, this will be a **volunteer visa** and must be obtained beforehand in the usual way. The maximum stay is 12 months, and the volunteer may not take paid work while in the UK.

Volunteers who do not need a visa and have arranged their voluntary work beforehand may apply to the British embassy or high commission in their country for entry clearance. This does not guarantee entry to the UK but may make it easier. Volunteers who do not need a visa and are already in the UK may apply for a change in immigration status to allow them to do the volunteering.

35.5.1.2
Overseas students

Overseas **students** may undertake paid or voluntary work, and do not need consent for part-time or holiday work. Voluntary work is treated in the same way as employment [see **26.2.9**], including the limit of 20 hours per week in term time unless the college agrees to more hours.

35.5.1.3
Working holidaymakers

Working holidaymakers are treated the same way for volunteering as for paid work [see **26.2.9**].

35.5.2
Refugees and asylum seekers

There are no restrictions on volunteering, paid or unpaid, for **refugees** and people given **exceptional leave to remain**.

Asylum seekers may volunteer if the volunteering is 'for a particular cause', rather than general administrative work. They can be provided with meals (or reimbursement for meals) while volunteering, and can be reimbursed for actual travel costs. All reimbursements must be properly documented. Advice should be taken before providing any other reimbursements or benefits, as these could jeopardise the asylum seeker's application for refugee status, and could also create a situation in which the organisation has unlawfully employed a person who is not entitled to work in the UK [see **26.2.9**]. The Refugee Council [see end of chapter] can provide advice.

35.6 EQUAL OPPORTUNITIES

35.6.1 Race and sex discrimination

The employment provisions of the **Race Relations Act 1976** and **Sex Discrimination Act 1975** make it illegal to discriminate on the basis of race, colour, ethnic group, national origin, nationality, sex, gender re-assignment (transsexuality) or married status against an employee or most other people working under a contract. They therefore apply only if a volunteer has a contract with the organisation [see **35.3**], but good practice is for organisations to comply with the Acts in relation to all volunteers. The Commission for Racial Equality and Equal Opportunities Commission put forward proposals in 1998 for including volunteers under the employment provisions of the race and sex legislation.

In any case it is unlawful to discriminate in provision of services, and providing opportunities for volunteering could in some situations be seen as providing a service. [For the employment provisions of the Race Relations and Sex Discrimination Acts see **25.2** and **25.3**; for the requirements on provision of goods and services see **37.2** and **37.3**.]

If volunteers are paid for their work or receive payment in kind, men and women should receive the same payments or benefits for work of equal value [see **25.4**].

35.6.2 Disability discrimination

The employment provisions of the **Disability Discrimination Act 1995** [see **25.5**] apply to employees and others working under a contract personally to provide a service, but only where the employer has 15 or more employees or workers under a contract. Volunteers who are not working under a contract [see **35.3**] are not covered by the employment provisions and are not calculated in counting the 15. The 15-worker minimum will be removed by October 2004.

Regardless of the law, good practice to not to discriminate against volunteers on the basis of disability unless such action is legally justifiable [see **25.5.3**]. Good practice also involves taking reasonable steps to attract disabled volunteers, and making reasonable adjustments to enable them to volunteer [see **25.5.4**].

All organisations, regardless of number of employees, must take reasonable steps to make premises, goods, services and facilities accessible or available to people with disabilities, and must not discriminate unjustifiably in service delivery against a person with a disability [see **37.4**].

35.6.3 Part-time workers

If volunteers working under a contract [see **35.3**] are paid for their work or receive other benefits, those working part-time should receive *pro rata* the same as a full-time comparator [see **25.12**].

35.6.4 Rehabilitation of offenders

Volunteering is treated in the same way as employment for the purposes of the **Rehabilitation of Offenders Act 1974** [see **25.10**].

35.7 HEALTH AND SAFETY

The employment-related provisions of health and safety legislation may not apply to volunteers in exactly the same way as to employees [see **36.2.1**], but it would be very poor practice indeed to treat volunteers differently from employees in this respect [see **chapter 36** for health and safety obligations]. In any case:

- employers must provide a safe place of work for employees, which could be jeopardised if different standards of health and safety are applied to volunteers;
- there is a statutory obligation for employers to protect the health and safety of the public, which in this context includes volunteers;

- health and safety risk assessments [see **36.3.1**] must take into account risks not only to employees, but to others affected by the organisation's activities;

- all organisations, even those which are not employers, have a duty of care [see **36.1.2**]. This includes duties to all volunteers, and in particular to younger or older volunteers, volunteers with special needs, or volunteers who are vulnerable.

All volunteers should know their rights and responsibilities in relation to health and safety, including their responsibility to carry out work carefully and not put themselves or others at risk.

If a volunteer is injured due to the organisation's negligence, the volunteer may sue the organisation. If a client or member of the public is injured or suffers loss as a result of the organisation's or a volunteer's negligence, the organisation and/or volunteer may be sued. If the volunteer or organisation is in breach of health and safety duties, the organisation or individual(s) involved could be fined.

35.8
INSURANCE

Organisations should consider the same insurance issues in relation to volunteers as for employees. Insurances are covered in **chapter 20**.

35.8.1
Claims by volunteers

An organisation must take out employer's liability insurance to cover claims from employees if they become ill or are injured as a result of the employer's negligence or beach of a statutory duty [see **20.4.1**]. There is no obligation to take out such insurance for volunteers, but it is good practice to do so. Some insurers include this as part of the employer's liability insurance, while others include it within an organisation's public liability insurance [see **20.5.1**]. The insurance policy should explicitly mention volunteers, otherwise they might not be covered.

The organisation might also want to provide **personal accident insurance** [see **20.4.3**], to cover accident or death arising from volunteering but not due to the organisation's negligence.

35.8.2
Claims against volunteers

Employers have **vicarious liability** for the negligent acts of their employees, and a claim for damage or loss caused by an employee is generally brought against the employer rather than the employee [see **19.5.3**]. The legal position with regard to vicarious liability for acts of volunteers is unclear, and a claim could possibly be brought by a client or member of the public against a volunteer who is uninsured.

To avoid this possibility, the organisation should ensure that its **public liability insurance** [see **20.5.1**], **professional indemnity insurance** [see **20.5.3**], **product liability insurance** [see **20.5.4**] or other relevant insurance covers volunteers' legal expenses and indemnifies (repays) them if any claim is successfully brought against them.

35.8.3
Age restrictions

Some insurers do not provide cover for volunteers over or under a specified age. It may be possible to negotiate extended cover, or the organisation may wish to consider changing its insurer. The National Centre for Volunteering can provide information about insurers who cover older and younger volunteers.

35.9
SPECIAL SITUATIONS

Information about the law as it relates to specific volunteering situations is available from the National Centre for Volunteering or Wales Council for Voluntary Action [see end of chapter]. Some of the more common situations are outlined here.

35.9.1
Criminal record checks

Volunteers are treated in the same way as employees for criminal record checks [see **26.3.3**]. At the time of writing (early 2001) most voluntary organisations did not have access to such checks unless the local police or the local authority's social services department ran the checks for them. From autumn 2001 all organisations working with children and vulnerable adults may obtain standard or enhanced disclosures through the **Criminal Records Bureau**, and from mid-2002 all employers will have access at least to basic disclosures. The fee for all checks is £12, but the charge is waived for standard and enhanced checks on volunteers. For more about criminal record checks, see **26.3.3**.

35.9.2
Work with children and vulnerable adults

Volunteers are often in close contact with children, young people and vulnerable adults. The organisation should take sensible steps to ensure volunteers are properly recruited, trained, monitored and supported, and should have proper procedures for receiving complaints or concerns from clients or other staff, and acting on these [see **26.3.3** for good practice guidelines].

Rules under the **Protection of Children Act 1999, Criminal Justice and Court Services Act 2000** and **Care Standards Act 2000** apply to volunteers in the same way as employees. These rules are explained in detail at **26.3.4**. They:

- allow for certain people to be banned or disqualified from working with children and/or vulnerable adults (elderly, ill, disabled);

- make it a criminal offence for a person subject to such a ban or disqualification to work in a **regulated position**, which includes the vast majority of positions involving direct contact with children or vulnerable adults;

- make it a criminal offence for an individual to offer work in a regulated position to a person whom they know is banned or disqualified from such work, or to allow such person to continue working;

- require certain organisations, and allow others, to undertake a criminal record check before offering work in a regulated position;

- require certain organisations, and allow others, to refer to the secretary of state for health people considered unsuitable to work with children or vulnerable adults [see **36.8.2**].

35.9.3
Young people as volunteers

In general there are no restrictions on children and young people volunteering, but points to be aware of are:

- it is sensible to comply with the restrictions on paid employment for children and young people of school age [see **25.9.2**];

- because of their immaturity and relative lack of experience, the organisation has a special duty of care to children and young people;

- as good practice, the organisation should comply with health and safety requirements relating to young people at work [see **36.4.2**];

- the organisation's insurance for volunteers [see **35.8**] may need to be extended to cover volunteers who are under 18, and some insurers may not be willing to cover volunteers below 15 or 16;

- children under 16 cannot take part in house-to-house fundraising collections without an adult [see **45.2.1**].

35.9.4
Fundraising

A volunteer fundraiser who is paid, even as little as £5 per day, and is not an employee of the organisation or its trading subsidiary must comply with the rules on professional fundraisers [see **44.5.3**].

35.9.5
Volunteer drivers

Information for volunteer drivers is available from the National Centre for Volunteering, Wales Council for Voluntary Action and Community Transport Association [see end of chapter].

35.9.5.1
Use of own vehicles

It is not generally necessary to notify the insurer if a volunteer uses his or her own car or someone else's car only for journeys between home and the usual place of volunteering. But the insurer must be notified in writing if the car is used for the volunteering itself [see **20.8** for more about vehicle insurance]. Failure to inform the insurer may render the policy invalid, because of the duty to provide all relevant information.

Driving as a volunteer is normally covered under the usual 'social, domestic and pleasure' policy, but some insurers class such journeys as business use and require the policy to be extended to cover such use. Regardless of whether the journeys are classed as business or as social, domestic and pleasure, some insurers require an additional premium for volunteer drivers, especially if there is substantial driving or it involves additional risk. The volunteer may be able to challenge the extra premium, or may wish to look for another insurer who does not charge extra for volunteer driving.

Although the organisation cannot generally insure the vehicle (that is the responsibility of the vehicle's owner, keeper or driver), the organisation can provide a policy to protect volunteer drivers' no-claims discount or to pay any excess if they have an accident while driving for the organisation.

To comply with its duty of care, the organisation should ask to see a valid driving licence and proof that the vehicle is insured for journeys made for voluntary work, is taxed and has an MoT certificate if required. Copies should be kept. It is good practice to ask to see these documents annually. In addition the volunteer should be asked in writing about past and pending driving offences.

If mileage is to be reimbursed the driver must keep a record of journeys [see **35.2.1.2**]. The organisation may want to ask volunteers to sign a statement on the mileage claim form along the lines of 'I confirm that my vehicle remains insured for these journeys, is taxed and has a valid MoT if required, and that there have been no changes to my driving licence. I further confirm that I have declared all past driving offences, and that if I am charged with any driving offence I will immediately notify you of the charge and the outcome.'

35.9.5.2
The organisation's vehicles

If the organisation has its own vehicles, proper records must be kept of who is using the vehicles and for what purposes. All relevant requirements in relation to the vehicle, drivers and insurance must be complied with [see **36.11**].

35.10
VOLUNTEERS AND STATE BENEFITS

Different benefits have different rules, and these change frequently and often significantly. As a result there may be problems of misinterpretation in relation to volunteers on state benefits, or different benefits offices may interpret the rules differently.

The basic rules are in the Benefits Agency's WK4 *Financial help if you are working or doing voluntary work*, and updated information can be obtained from the relevant benefits office. Further information specifically about how the rules relate to volunteers is available from the National Centre for Volunteering and Wales Council for Voluntary Action [see end of chapter].

'Payment' here does not include proper reimbursement [see **35.2.1.1**], but does include all other payments or benefits in kind, including luncheon vouchers. The situation is particularly complex where accommodation is provided to volunteers, and advice should be taken.

35.10.1
Notification

Before starting voluntary work the volunteer should inform the job centre, if receiving unemployment-related benefits, or the benefits office, if receiving other social security benefits. If the volunteer receives any pay (other than allowed reimbursement) and is in receipt of housing benefit or council tax benefit, the local authority must be notified.

It is good practice for the organisation to provide copies of WK4, or to remind volunteers that they are responsible for notifying the relevant agencies.

35.10.2
Jobseeker's allowance

For an unpaid volunteer receiving **jobseeker's allowance** (JSA) there is no restriction on volunteering provided he or she:

- notifies the job centre of all voluntary work;
- is actively seeking work, as required by the job centre;
- is, or can be, available to work 40 hours per week; *and*
- is available immediately to attend an interview or start work (but see below).

35.10.2.1
Immediate availability

JSA rules allow 48 hours notice of availability to attend interview or start a job if the person is doing voluntary work, and also allow the claimant to be unavailable:

- for one period of up to 14 days (excluding Sundays) in a calendar year while attending a workcamp in Great Britain run by a charity or local authority, provided the job centre has been notified beforehand;
- while working as a lifeboat rescuer or firefighter;
- while working as a member of an organised group helping in an emergency where there is serious risk to people's lives or health or to property of substantial value.

In early 2001 the government announced its intention to extend the 48-hours to one week, initially for a one-year trial period.

35.10.2.2
Notification

It may be helpful for the organisation to provide a standard letter for volunteers to provide to the job centre, saying that the volunteer will receive no remuneration, only the reimbursement of genuine and reasonable out-of-pocket expenses; that the volunteer can be contacted care of the organisation while volunteering if a job opportunity arises; and that the volunteer can be available on 48 hours notice to attend a job interview or take up a job.

35.10.2.3
Payment and notional earnings

JSA is reduced if the claimant is paid more than the **earnings disregard** of £5 per week, or £20 per week if he or she is entitled to the **higher earnings disregard**. Proper reimbursement [see **35.2.1**] does not count towards this but flat-rate reimbursements do, even if authorised by the Inland Revenue for tax purposes.

Even where claimants are not paid, the benefits office might treat them as having **notional earnings** if they are doing their usual work or it would be reasonable for them to be paid. Notional earnings are not generally assumed for voluntary work done for or organised through a charity, local authority or health authority.

35.10.3
Income support

People on **income support** due to unemployment must comply with the same rules as for jobseeker's allowance [see **35.10.2**].

For others on income support, the benefit is not affected by unpaid voluntary work, although notional earnings could be assumed [see above]. Income support recipients who are entitled to the higher **earnings disregard** have their benefit reduced if they are paid more than £20 in a week. For others on income support the earnings disregard is £5. The benefits office must be notified of all voluntary work.

35.10.4
Incapacity, disability and carer's benefits

A person receiving **incapacity benefit, severe disablement allowance** or income support based on incapacity is allowed to volunteer provided the benefits office is notified beforehand, the volunteering is unpaid (apart from proper reimbursement, see **35.2.1**) and it is not for a close relative. There is no statutory limit to the number of hours for unpaid volunteering, but some benefits medical officers have questioned whether a person who consistently volunteers for more than 16 hours per week is actually unable to work.

The 'voluntary' work can be paid provided the doctor says the work is therapeutic. The payment cannot be more than the therapeutic earnings limit (£60.50 per week as at 9/4/01), and the person cannot work for more than an average of 16 hours per week. From April 2002 there will be no need for confirmation that the work is therapeutic, but there will be a one-year limit on work paid at this level.

Also from April 2002 new provisions will allow an earnings disregard of £20 per week for everyone on incapacity benefit, severe disablement allowance or income support based on incapacity. This will allow claimants to earn up to £20 per week, with no time limit and no hours limit. As with a therapeutic earnings payment, such payment has implications for minimum wage, employment rights etc [see **35.2.2**].

Industrial injuries disablement benefit is not affected by paid or unpaid voluntary work, but the volunteering must be notified to the benefits office.

Industrial injuries reduced earnings allowance is not affected by unpaid voluntary work, but the person should check with the benefits office before taking on paid voluntary work.

Invalid care allowance is not affected by unpaid voluntary work, unless it stops the volunteer caring for the disabled person for at least 35 hours per week. The benefits office must be notified of the voluntary work. Paid voluntary work is acceptable provided the amount received is less than £50 per week. Above this amount the allowance stops.

Statutory sick pay (from an employer) and **sickness benefit** (from the benefits office) are not affected by volunteering, but the employer and/or benefits office may well question entitlement if the person is known to be working.

35.10.5
Other benefits

Unpaid voluntary work does not affect eligibility for, or the amount of, **housing benefit** or **council tax benefit**. Paid voluntary work must be notified to the local authority and might affect the amount.

Long-term volunteers living away from home can receive housing benefit, council tax benefits and income support for housing costs in relation to that home for only 13 weeks.

Statutory maternity pay is not affected by volunteering. **Maternity allowance** is not affected by unpaid voluntary work, but is not payable for any day on which paid work is done.

35.10.6
Pensions and widow's benefits

State retirement pension, **war disablement pension**, **war widow's pension** and **widow's benefits** are not affected by paid or unpaid voluntary work, and the benefits office does not have to be notified.

FOR FURTHER INFORMATION

National Centre for Volunteering: 020-7520 8900; www.volunteering.org.uk

Wales Council for Voluntary Action: 029-2043 1700; www.wcva.org.uk

Asylum seekers and refugees. Refugee Council: 020-7820 3085; www.refugeecouncil.org.uk

Drivers. Community Transport Association: 0161-367 8780; www.communitytransport.com

State benefits. Local benefits office; www.dss.gov.uk or www.dfwp.gov.uk

Tax and national insurance. Inland Revenue: 08457-143 143; www.inlandrevenue.gov.uk

New employer's helpline: 0845-60 70 143

Volunteers from overseas. Home Office Immigration & Nationality Directorate: 020-8649 7878; www.ind.homeoffice.gov.uk

PART V
SERVICES AND ACTIVITIES

Part V covers the law as it affects services and activities which are common to most organisations, such as health and safety, equal opportunities, publications and campaigning. The law relating to services provided by specific types of organisation, such as community care, education or overseas aid, is beyond the scope of this book.

Chapter 36
HEALTH, SAFETY AND SECURITY

Topics covered in this chapter

This chapter outlines the requirements for health and safety at work and the protection of service users and the public, including consumer safety. It covers:

For sources of further information see end of chapter.

Double-underlined section headings indicate additions or significant changes since the first edition.

36.1
HEALTH, SAFETY AND THE LAW

Each year over 400 people are killed and one million people suffer injury at work, with a further two million suffering work-related ill health. Millions more are injured as visitors to premises, users of services or purchasers of faulty goods. These figures illustrate the impact of inadequate health and safety practices.

Health, safety and consumer protection are areas of law where very different legal duties overlap and where multiple liabilities may arise. If, for example, an employee is injured by faulty equipment:

- the employer may claim, both in breach of contract and in breach of strict liability statutory obligations, against the supplier for supplying faulty equipment;
- the Health and Safety Executive or local environmental health department may prosecute the employer for a breach of the **Health and Safety at Work etc Act** or related regulations, and may issue a prohibition or improvement notice [see **36.2.8**];
- the employee may claim against the employer for breach of contract, for negligence and for breach of statutory duty.

Claims are frequently brought for both breach of statutory duty and negligence. While a claim of negligence involves showing that the employer did not take reasonable care, a breach of statutory duty may give rise to a **strict liability** [see **36.2.5**] where the employer is liable even if negligence cannot be proved.

36.1.1
The statutory framework

The cornerstone of health and safety legislation is the **Health and Safety at Work etc Act 1974** and its detailed **regulations**, in particular the **Management of Health and Safety at Work Regulations 1999** *[SI 1999/3242]*.

Approved codes of practice (ACoP) provide guidance on implementation. A breach of a code cannot itself be prosecuted, but may form evidence of failure to achieve proper standards. An employer who is prosecuted for a breach of health and safety law and has not followed the ACoP will have to show that it has complied with the law in some other way. As well as codes of practice, the Health and Safety Executive issues more detailed **guidance** on practical steps for implementation.

The **Factories Act 1961** covers any place, including out of doors, where people make goods or parts of goods, wash or fill bottles, sort or pack goods, or undertake printing or bookbinding. The Act does not apply if the goods are not to be sold.

Persons with responsibility for premises have a statutory duty under the **Occupier's Liability Act 1957** to take reasonable care to ensure that anyone who is authorised or permitted to come onto the premises is safe while they are there, and the **Occupier's Liability Act 1984** imposes a duty of care even to trespassers [see **59.5**].

Organisations are affected by **consumer safety** legislation both as purchasers and users of goods and services and as providers. A wide variety of legislation covers quality of goods and services, general product safety, and safety of specific goods and services [see **36.10**].

In early 2000 the government announced plans for a new offence of **corporate killing** under which an organisation could be charged where management failure is a cause of death. Governing body members could also be charged if directly implicated in a death.

36.1.1.1
The impact of Europe

European Union member states must seek to harmonise their provision for health and safety at work. Harmonisation is implemented through **directives**, which member states have a duty to adopt into their national law.

The overlap of EU directives and UK legislation can create confusion. Where one imposes a higher duty than the other, the higher duty prevails and the courts interpret UK law in a way which reflects the intention of EU law.

36.1.2
Common law duties

In addition to their statutory obligations, employers have a common law **duty of care** to protect the health and safety of employees. This is an implied part of the contract of employment [see **23.3.4**]. There is also a common law duty for occupiers of land or premises to avoid risk of injury or death for anyone who is on the premises [see **59.5**].

If an employer or person with responsibility for premises is in breach of this duty, a person who is injured or becomes ill (or the estate of a person who has died) has a right to make a claim for **negligence**. It is a legal obligation for all employers to have **employers' liability insurance** to cover claims by employees [see **20.4.1**], and any organisation which has responsibility for premises used by non-employees or which provides services or activities for the public should also have **public liability insurance** [see **20.5.1**].

36.1.3
Registration

Every place where people are employed must be registered with the local authority or, in some cases, the Health and Safety Executive. Organisations which are not registered should contact the local authority environmental health department for advice. Late registration of offices and similar premises is not penalised unless the non-registration was deliberate.

36.2
HEALTH AND
SAFETY AT WORK

The **Health and Safety at Work etc Act 1974** applies primarily to employers' obligations to employees. Some parts, but not all, cover:

- employers' obligations to workers who are not classed as employees;
- employers' obligations to visitors, including volunteers, contractors, clients or users of the organisation and members of the public;
- the obligations of self-employed people to themselves and to persons other than their employees;
- obligations of persons who are not employers, but who have responsibility for non-domestic premises used by visitors.

The emphasis is on taking 'reasonably practicable' steps to create safe workplaces and safe behaviour. In deciding what is reasonable and practical, the cost as well as the actual physical difficulties of providing safety arrangements can be taken into account. Ultimately the employment tribunal or court decides what is or is not reasonably practicable in any particular situation.

The standard of care required under health and safety law is the same for all organisations, regardless of their nature or size, and prosecutions can be brought against individual members of the governing body or others considered responsible for the breach.

36.2.1
Duties of employers

Employers have a duty to ensure, as far as is reasonably practicable, the health, safety, and welfare at work of their employees. This includes carrying out risk assessments [see **36.3.1**] and taking all reasonable steps to:

- provide and maintain a working environment which is safe and without risks to health, and which has adequate facilities and arrangements for welfare at work;
- provide and maintain equipment and work systems which are safe and are not harmful to health;
- ensure safe use, handling, storage and transport of materials;
- provide appropriate information, training and supervision;
- keep the workplace, and the means of access and exit, safe and free of risk to health.   *Health and Safety at Work etc Act 1974 s.2*

Employers have specific duties in relation to workers under the age of 18 [see **36.3.1.2** and **36.4.2**], women who are pregnant or have recently given birth [see **36.3.1.1**], and people who work at night [see **36.3.1.4**].

The obligations are the same even if the employees are part-time, temporary, on a fixed-term contract, casual or sessional [see **chapter 22** for definitions].

520

Workplace means any place where employees carry out work, which might include outdoors, clients' homes, employees' homes etc. Although employers have no control over those environments, they have an obligation to ensure safe systems and procedures.

Employers must make employees aware of general health and safety duties by displaying an approved poster or giving all employees an approved leaflet. These are available from HSE Books [see end of chapter].

Most employers must prepare a written health and safety policy and ensure employees are aware of it [see **36.2.6**], produce written risk assessments [see **36.3.1**], and consult safety representatives [see **36.2.7**].

If a contractor or self-employed person is working at a workplace, the employer must ensure they are safe, and must take reasonable steps to ensure they do not endanger the employer's employees. If appropriate, the employer must provide its own staff with training about how to maintain safety where there are workers who are not employees and may not be fully aware of the risks at work or the procedures for dealing with the risks.   *R v Swan Hunter Shipbuilders [1981] IRLR 403 CA*

36.2.1.1
Duties to workers who are not employees and to the public

Employers must take all reasonable steps to ensure that people who are not employees but who might be affected by their activities are not exposed to risks to their health or safety, and must provide information about health or safety risks. This includes trainees, people on work experience, volunteers [see below], and self-employed people and other contractors undertaking work for the employer [see **36.2.1.3**].
Health and Safety at Work etc Act 1974 s.3

All goods supplied by one employer to another for use at work must, insofar as reasonably practicable, be safe for use in the workplace, and if appropriate, information about health or safety risks and instructions about safe use must be supplied.   *ss.5, 6*

36.2.1.2
Duties to volunteers

The **Health and Safety at Work etc Act** does not apply where the organisation has no employees. This may mean that it does not apply where an organisation is purely volunteer. But organisations in this situation should comply with the Act nonetheless, because:

- the legislation sets out the basic standards of good practice;
- the organisation has a duty of care [see **36.1.2**] to everyone, and one way to comply with this is to comply with legislative requirements;
- where volunteers receive pay or something else of value in return for their work they may in fact legally be employees [see **35.3**], and the organisation may thus have to comply with health and safety law.

36.2.1.3
Duties to self-employed workers and other contractors

An organisation has the same responsibilities to self-employed workers or other contractors as it does to any member of the public [see **36.2.1.1**]. The organisation should ensure that the contract makes clear the contractor's responsibility for their own health and safety and for that of the employer's employees, clients and members of the public with whom the contractor will be in contact, and others at the employer's premises. The insurance and indemnification position should be carefully considered [see **34.2.2**].

A two-way flow of information should be established, with the contractor and employer informing each other of risks arising from their activities. The employer must also establish procedures to ensure that safety rules are maintained, and must take action if they are breached.

In some cases, a person is self-employed but is working under the control of an employer may be treated by the health and safety authorities as an employee for the purposes of health and safety legislation.

36.2.2
Duties of employees

Individual employees must take reasonable care for their own health and safety while at work, and for the health and safety of others who might be affected by their acts. Employees must inform their employer of any dangerous situation or gap in the safety procedures, and must not interfere with anything provided for health, safety or welfare purposes or use it inappropriately. *Health and Safety at Work etc Act 1974 ss.7, 8*

36.2.3
Duties of non-employees and the public

Everyone is prohibited from intentionally or recklessly interfering with anything provided in the interest of health, safety or welfare or using it inappropriately. This covers, for example, damaging a fire extinguisher or blocking a fire escape. *s.8*

36.2.4
Responsibility for premises

Anyone—even if not an employer—who is responsible for non-domestic premises where people who are not their employees work, visit or use the premises must take all reasonable steps to ensure that the premises, the means of access or exit, equipment and materials are safe and free of risk to health or safety. Persons considered responsible for premises include anyone who is the owner or tenant of the premises, has responsibility for repairs, or has responsibility under a licence or tenancy for the health and safety of persons using the premises. *s.4*

36.2.5
Level of care

Liability for breach of health and safety falls into three broad categories:

- **absolute liability**: where it must simply be shown that the event or act occurred;

- **strict liability**: where it must be shown that the event or act occurred and was wrongful (contravened the Act or regulations);

- **normal liability**: where it must be shown that the event or act occurred and was wrongful, and that the employer or other person intended it to occur, was negligent, or was reckless as to whether it occurred.

Offences of absolute liability are very rare and there is no defence. An example is charging employees for required safety equipment. Even if reasonable steps were taken to prevent the breach, the simple fact that it occurred constitutes an offence.

Most health and safety duties are strict liability. Normally the only defence is that it was not reasonably practical to achieve a specific safety standard. *s.40*

The employer or other person does not have to show that they did everything possible to prevent the problem or injury, but that they took reasonable steps to prevent foreseeable problems. A step may not be reasonable where there is a gross disproportion between the actual likelihood of risk and the cost in time, money and trouble in averting the risk. For example, a building society showed to the High Court's satisfaction that the cost of putting protective screens in all its premises was disproportionately large compared to the risk to its employees.

West Bromwich Building Society v Townsend [1983] ICR 257

36.2.5.1
Liability of governing body members

At the time of writing (early 2001) the Health and Safety Commission was consulting on new guidance for company directors, clarifying and confirming their personal liabilities and responsibilities. Governing bodies of all organisations, not only companies, should comply with the guidance and bring it to the attention of governing body members.

36.2.5.2
Liability of funders

Where a body provides a grant or other funding and exercises some control over the recipient's activities, the funder could be held liable for a breach of health and safety by the recipient.

36.2.6
Health and safety policies

All employers must have a health and safety policy, which must be in writing if five or more people are employed. It must include:

- a general statement of policy, expressing a commitment to safety;

- organisational information, such as who is responsible for particular areas of health and safety;

- arrangements for dealing with particular hazards. *HSWA s.2(3)*

A typical policy contains a general statement and details of the person(s) or postholder(s) responsible for overall implementation of the policy. This must be signed and dated by the responsible person(s).

The arrangements for dealing with particular hazards might include:

- first aid materials, and any trained first aiders [see **36.6**];
- the reporting of accidents [see **36.7.1**];
- fire safety arrangements [see **36.5**];
- where further advice and help can be obtained (typically the local HSE office, and any safety consultant or medical practitioner involved with the organisation);
- arrangements for health and safety training;
- special rules for contractors and visitors;
- particular hazards, including guidance for use, general safety rules, safety checks, maintenance checks and cleanliness;
- detailed arrangements for dealing with dangerous substances, body fluids, materials under pressure etc;
- arrangements for dealing with major hazards of any sort.

The HSE produces guidance on policies and a sample policy statement.

36.2.6.1
The link between the policy and risk assessments

The details of hazards and measures to deal with them should be based on the **risk assessments** required under the **Management of Health and Safety at Work Regulations** [see **36.3.1**].

The policy should generally be approved by the governing body. Risk assessments are more detailed and do not necessarily need governing body approval, although governing body members must be aware of the steps being taken to protect health and safety. It is advisable to review the policy annually, or whenever the organisation's activities change or it uses new premises. Risk assessments should be reviewed more often.

36.2.7
Consultation with employees

Where there is a recognised trade union [see **32.3.3**] at the workplace, a **safety representative** or representatives must be appointed and in some cases a safety committee established. Their duties are covered by the **Safety Representatives and Safety Committees Regulations 1977** *[SI 1977/500]*, an approved code of practice, and guidance notes issued by HSE. *Health and Safety at Work etc Act 1974 s.2(6)*

Where there is no recognised trade union, the employer must provide certain information about health and safety and consult employees about health and safety matters. This may be done directly, or through elected employee representatives. *Health and Safety (Consultation with Employees) Regulations 1996 [SI 1996/1513]*

36.2.7.1
Trade union safety representatives

A recognised trade union has the right to appoint an employee to:

- investigate accidents and hazards;
- look into complaints;
- investigate reportable accidents;
- inspect the workplace;
- inspect relevant documentation, except for information relating to identifiable individuals or covered by the Data Protection Act (unless the individual has consented), and information which could cause 'substantial injury' to the employer's business;
- attend meetings of the safety committee, if there is one;
- make recommendations for changes;
- make representations to the employer on behalf of groups and individual employees.

Safety representatives have a right to paid time off to perform their functions and undergo training. Like all employees, they are protected if an employer seeks to victimise them because of their health and safety activities [see **36.3.3.1**].

**36.2.7.2
Safety committees**

If at least two safety representatives request it, the employer must convene a **safety committee** within three months of the request. Before doing so the employer must consult the trade union, but the employer can determine how often the committee meets, its composition and how the meetings are to be run. *Safety Representatives and Safety Committees Regulations 1977 [SI 1977/500] reg.9*

**36.2.7.3
Elected representatives**

If employees are not represented by safety representatives appointed by a recognised trade union, the employer must consult each employee, or one or more employees elected **representatives of employees' safety** (ROES). The regulations do not specify how the election should be held. *Health and Safety (Consultation with Employees) Regulations 1996 [SI 1996/1513]*

Employers must consult in good time on any new work, procedures or equipment that could substantially affect employees' health and safety, and must consider points raised in the consultation.

ROES have similar rights to those of trade union safety representatives, but do not have the same rights to inspect the workplace or investigate accidents. The employer must provide reasonable facilities and training to enable ROES to carry out their duties, and ROES must be given paid time off in working time to stand as a candidate in an election and to perform their functions if elected.

ROES and individual employees are protected against victimisation or dismissal on the ground that they took part or intended to take part in consultation with their employer or in the election of a representative.

At the time of writing (early 2001) the Health and Safety Commission was consulting on harmonising the rights of union safety representatives and ROES, and providing better support and training for them.

**36.2.8
Implementation and enforcement**

The **Health and Safety Commission** has responsibility for the 1974 Act and relevant statutory provision. It carries out research, provides training and information, and submits proposals for regulations.

The **Health and Safety Executive** (HSE) is responsible for enforcing the Act through a system of inspectors. The HSE also supports the Commission by carrying out research and providing information.

The HSE shares its enforcement duties with **local authorities** and various government departments. Local authorities, through their environmental health departments, are generally responsible for enforcement in lower risk areas, including offices, warehouses, shops and leisure premises. The environmental health department will advise if they are not the appropriate enforcement agency.

Any agency or individual responsible for enforcing the Act has a right of access to premises, and when on the premises can question people, take copies of documents, demand facilities and assistance and take any steps necessary to investigate thoroughly.

If an inspector believes there is a contravention of health and safety legislation, or that there has been a contravention and a further one is likely, an **improvement notice** may be served. A **prohibition notice** is served if the inspector believes that an activity is likely to involve the risk of serious personal injury. Appeals are to the employment tribunal.

**36.2.8.1
Criminal prosecution**

Breach of many provisions of the Act or its regulations may give rise to a criminal prosecution in the magistrates' courts, or in the crown court for a more serious matter. Not only the person breaking the particular section or regulation is liable, but also any other person whose act or default contributed to the breach. So if a breach occurs:

- the employee who broke the regulation may be prosecuted;

- if the employer is a corporate body (a company or industrial and provident society), it may be prosecuted; *and*

- the members of the governing body and/or senior staff may be prosecuted. If the employer is a corporate body, the directors are personally liable.   *Health and Safety at Work etc Act 1974 ss.27, 37*

Facts giving rise to criminal prosecution for a breach of health and safety legislation can form the basis for a claim for negligence [see **19.5.1**] or for breach of a statutory duty if a person is injured or killed.

36.3
RISK ASSESSMENTS

The Health and Safety at Work etc Act is buttressed by the **Management of Health and Safety at Work Regulations 1999** *[SI 1999/ 3242]*, which provide the framework for risk assessments and related duties.

36.3.1
Carrying out risk assessments

All employers and self-employed people are under a duty to identify and assess hazards to employees and others arising from the work.
Management of Health and Safety at Work Regulations 1999 reg.3

The assessment must consider not only all relevant health and safety legislation, but also the **Fire Prevention (Workplace) Regulations 1997** [see **36.5**].

The steps in a risk assessment are:

- identify the hazards (dangers), which generally involves asking people involved in the organisation to identify hazards they perceive as affecting their activities, and taking into account information from the HSE, suppliers and general publications.;

- identify what could go wrong (risks);

- consider how likely the risks are to occur;

- look at how many people might be affected (including visitors, contractors and others coming to the premises), the type of injuries or illness which might occur, and how serious they might be;

- evaluate the risks, and decide whether existing precautions are adequate or whether more should be done;

- record the significant findings (only obligatory if five or more people are employed, but good practice for all employers);

- set a date to review the assessment and revise it if necessary.

The report on the risk assessment must cover:

- the hazards identified;

- the risks identified (what can happen, how likely it is to happen and how serious it is if it does happen);

- the people at risk, including any special risks for new or expectant mothers, where there are women of child-bearing age;

- protective and preventative measures in place and to be taken;

- fire safety;

- procedures to deal with 'serious and imminent danger' (fire, attacks, etc), and the person(s) who would deal with them;

- any information received from other employers who share the premises, regarding risks arising from their activities.

A risk assessment is not a one-off activity, but must be reviewed at regular intervals, or as activities or hazards change, or if there is reason to believe the original assessment is no longer valid.

36.3.1.1
Pregnant women and new mothers

Where the workforce includes women of child-bearing age and the work could involve risk to the health and safety of a pregnant woman, new mother or her baby, the risk assessment must take account of this risk.
Management of Health and Safety at Work Regulations 1999 reg.16

If risk cannot be avoided by other means, the employer must make changes to the working conditions or hours of a new or expectant mother or offer suitable alternative work. If this is not possible, she must be suspended on full pay for as long as necessary to protect her health and safety or that of her child.   *Employment Rights Act 1996 s.67*

If she normally works at night and her doctor or midwife provides a certificate saying she should not continue to do so, the employer must offer alternative work which is not at night. If this is not possible she must be suspended on full pay for the period covered by the certificate.

36.3.1.2
Young workers

Where an employee, potential employee, trainee or person on a work experience or similar programme is under the age of 18, the risk assessment must take account of the inexperience, lack of awareness of risks and immaturity of young people; the nature of the work, the workplace, equipment, substances and processes used in the work; and the training provided or to be provided to young workers. The risk assessment must be carried out *before* they start work and they must be told of the risks and the safety measures in place. Where the potential worker is still of compulsory school age, the results of the risk assessment must be communicated to their parents or person with parental responsibility.
Management of Health and Safety at Work Regulations 1999 regs.3(5), 10, 19

Such risk assessments should also be carried out for young volunteers.

There are restrictions on the amount of work that can be undertaken by children and young people of compulsory school age [see **28.5.1**], and at the time of writing (early 2001) the government was consulting on placing limits on working hours and night working for 16- and 17-year-olds. There are also restrictions on the type of work that can be undertaken by school-age workers [see **36.4.2**].

36.3.1.3
Young night workers

Alongside the obligations to all young workers, is a further duty to offer workers aged 16 and 17 a health and capacities assessment before they undertake any work between 10 p.m. and 6 a.m., and at regular intervals while the night work continues. This is similar to a health assessment for adult night workers [see below] but must also consider the worker's physique, maturity and experience, and must take into account the worker's competence to do the night work.
Working Time Regulations 1998 [SI 1998/1833] reg.7(2)

The obligation to offer a health and capacities assessment does not apply if the work if of an exceptional nature [see **28.5.2**].

36.3.1.4
Health assessments
for night workers

All night workers [see **28.2.4**] must be offered a free health assessment before they start working nights. This must be offered on a regular basis, generally annually, while they continue to work nights. The worker is not obliged to take up the offer of the health assessment.
reg.7

The assessment can be made up of a straightforward screening questionnaire, and a medical examination if the employer has concerns about the worker's fitness for night work. The assessment should take into account statutory restrictions on working time [see **28.2**] and the type of work that will be done. It must be linked to the risk assessment, which should cover specific risks relating to night work.

The questionnaire should be drawn up and assessed by a doctor, nurse or other suitably qualified health professional who understands how night working might affect health.

The employer can require a medical examination even if the worker has not completed a questionnaire or has not indicated a health condition on the questionnaire. The person who carries out the examination may produce a simple fitness for work statement which will be given to the employer, or clinical information which is confidential and can only be released to the employer with the worker's written consent.

If a qualified health professional advises that the worker has health problems which are caused or made worse by night work, the employer should if possible transfer the worker to work that is not night work.

36.3.1.5
Work off the premises or at home

Risk assessments must be carried out for work done at other premises, out of doors, in service users' homes, or in workers' own homes. Where it is not possible to carry out assessments in relation to specific premises—for example where staff visit many clients' homes—the assessment should identify the range of risks.

The Health and Safety Executive has published guidance (INDG226) on home working.

36.3.2
Principles of prevention

When deciding how to deal with risks, the regulations set out **general principles of prevention**. These include:

- try to avoid the risk altogether;

- evaluate risks which cannot be avoided;

- try to deal with the hazard itself (for example replace dangerous equipment, rather than put up a warning sign);

- adapt work procedures, equipment and workstations to the individual, paying particular attention to alleviating monotonous work;

- as technological changes make it possible for work to be done more safely, implement those changes;

- where something is dangerous, replace it with something non-dangerous or less dangerous;

- develop a coherent overall prevention policy which covers technology, organisation of work, working conditions, social relationships and the influence of factors relating to the working environment;

- where possible, make changes that affect employees as a group rather than making individual changes;

- provide appropriate information and training to employees.

Management of Health and Safety at Work Regulations 1999, sch.4

36.3.2.1
Health surveillance

If a specific health risk has been identified, **health surveillance** may need to be maintained to see whether the risk is having an adverse effect on any staff member's health. *reg.6*

HSE guidance is that surveillance should be implemented if there is an identifiable disease or health condition relating to the work, it is possible to detect the disease or condition, it is reasonably likely that the disease or condition may arise in the work conditions, and surveillance could help reduce the risks for the employee.

36.3.2.2
Emergencies

Specific procedures must be in place to deal with risks such as fires and bomb threats which would pose a **serious imminent danger**. These procedures must be notified to all employees, and if there are five or more employees must be in writing [see **36.5** for more about fire safety]. *reg.8*

36.3.2.3
Particular individuals

The employer must not only set up safe procedures, but must also take into account the particular capabilities of those undertaking them, adjust the procedures to ensure they are effective, and provide training if particular skills need to be acquired. This could involve, for example, providing translations of safety procedures. *reg.13*

The Management of Health and Safety at Work Regulations also cover duties to external workers, such as self-employed people or contractors, who come onto the premises. Regardless of whether they come regularly or only very occasionally, such as the annual visit of the auditor, they must be informed of hazards at the workplace and the protective and preventative measures in force. *reg.12*

**36.3.2.4
Temporary workers**

People on fixed-term contracts, agency staff and other temporary workers must be given information about the qualifications and skills they need to carry out the work safely, and any health surveillance being provided. For example, a locum providing cover in an advice agency should be told before commencing the employment, verbally and in writing, about the risks arising from advising potentially aggressive clients, the safety procedures in place, and arrangements for safety training.

Management of Health and Safety at Work Regulations 1999 reg.15

**36.3.2.5
Shared premises**

Where two or more employers share premises they have a duty to cooperate, exchange information and coordinate their protective measures.

reg.11

**36.3.3
Employees' duties**

Employees have an obligation to inform the employer of serious dangers or shortcomings in the health and safety arrangements, and to operate equipment in accordance with proper instructions received.   *reg.14*

Employers who do not take appropriate action, including disciplinary action, if an employee operates equipment unsafely or works in an unsafe manner, will not be able to show that they have properly monitored and enforced their safety procedures.

**36.3.3.1
Protection from
victimisation**

Employers must not victimise employees who complain or take reasonable action about health and safety. An employee, regardless of length of service, may bring a claim in an employment tribunal if he or she is dismissed, selected for redundancy or subjected to any other detriment because he or she:

- carries out, or proposes to carry out, any activities which the employer has designated the employee to carry out in relation to health and safety at work;

- performs, or proposes to perform, any functions as official or employer-acknowledged health and safety representative or safety committee member [see **36.2.7**];

- brings to the employer's attention, by reasonable means and in the absence of a representative or committee with whom it would have been reasonably practicable to raise the matter, a concern about circumstances at work which the employee reasonably believes are harmful to health or safety;

- in the event of danger which the employee reasonably believes to be serious and imminent and which he or she could not be expected to avert, leaves or proposes to leave the workplace or any dangerous part of it, or refuses to return while the danger persists; *or*

- in circumstances of danger which the employee reasonably believes to be serious and imminent, takes or proposes to take appropriate steps to protect themselves or other persons from the danger.

Employment Rights Act 1996 s.100

**36.3.4
Competent persons**

Employers must appoint one or more **competent persons** to implement action required as a result of the risk assessment.

Management of Health and Safety at Work Regulations 1999 reg.7

'Competent' is not defined in detail, but means having an appropriate balance of skills, knowledge and experience about the organisation's work, health and safety duties in general, and duties specific to the organisation. In small, relatively unhazardous environments, a person could probably be described as competent after reading relevant publications and attending a training course. For larger premises or where there are significant risks, considerable training may be necessary or the organisation may employ an outside specialist to carry out some of the functions required by the regulations.

36.4
SPECIFIC HEALTH AND SAFETY DUTIES

Many detailed duties apply to the physical work environment. The matters covered below are not comprehensive, and organisations are advised to contact the local environmental health department, HSE information line or the local HSE office [see end of chapter for details] for information specific to their activities, services and premises.

36.4.1
Workplace health, safety and welfare

All workplaces except domestic premises, means of transport, building sites and exploration and mineral extraction sites are covered by the **workplace regulations**. In general, **health** means protection from long-term injury or illness, **safety** means protection from immediate danger, and **welfare** means facilities for personal comfort at work.

Workplace (Health, Safety and Welfare) Regulations 1992 [SI 1992/3004]

36.4.1.1
Health

To minimise the risks to health:

- there must be adequate **ventilation**;
- the **temperature** must be reasonable (there is no specified minimum or maximum, although the approved code of practice recommends a minimum of 16°C (60.8°F) unless the work involves strenuous physical effort or food is being kept cold);
- there must be room thermometers in enough rooms to be able to measure the temperature throughout the workplace;
- **lighting** must be adequate and suitable, and should be natural whenever possible;
- floors, walls, ceilings, windows, furniture and fittings must be kept **clean**;
- **workstations** (the furniture or machinery where an individual works) must be appropriate for the individual and for the work, with equipment and materials within easy reach without requiring undue stretching or bending;
- if the work involves sitting, a suitable seat and, if necessary, footrest must be provided;
- there must be adequate **space** for each worker.

Workers must each have a minimum of 3.7m² (40ft²) of floor space and 11m³ (about 400ft³) of air space. In calculating floor space, the space taken by the worker's desk and chair may be included, but space taken by filing cabinets, photocopiers etc should not be included. In calculating air space, the room height above 3m (10ft) is not included.

36.4.1.2
Safety

To ensure the safety of employees and others using the premises:

- **premises** must be in a good state of repair, with any defects put right or action taken to prevent injury;
- **machinery** and other equipment must be kept in good working order and must not be used if it poses a threat to health or safety;
- there must be enough **space** for workers to move about easily and safely;
- **emergency lighting** must be provided if any person would be in danger were the normal lighting to fail;
- **floors** must not be slippery or dangerous and must have drainage if necessary, and flooring must be suitable for its purpose;
- all **staircases** should have handrails and guards unless they would obstruct a traffic route;
- any area where there is a risk of a person **falling** or being injured by a falling object must be indicated and if appropriate fenced;
- **storage units** must be appropriate for the items being stored, and must not be overfilled;
- stored items must be securely stacked, and not stacked too high;

- **doors** and gates should be safe, with guards to stop sliding doors from becoming derailed and upward opening doors from falling; powered doors must have a manual override in case of power failure; and it should be possible to see through doors which open both ways;

- **transparent surfaces** should be marked so people are aware of them;

- all **glass** that might present a risk of breakage and injury—primarily glass in doors and up to 80cm (33in) from the floor—must be safety glass or must be covered in safety film;

- **windows**, skylights and ventilators should be able to be opened, closed and cleaned without danger;

- windows should have guards to prevent anyone falling out;

- pedestrians must not be endangered by **vehicles** on the premises.

36.4.1.3
Welfare

For the welfare of employees:

- there must be separate **toilets** for men and women unless each toilet is in a separate cubicle with a door lockable from the inside;

- if workers need to change for work, there must be facilities for **changing** and for drying and storing clothing;

- suitable **washing** facilities, with hot and cold water or warm water, soap and towels, must be provided near toilets and changing areas, and in other areas if they are necessary for health reasons or because of the nature of the work;

- the washing and changing facilities should be separate for women and men unless the facility is intended to be used by only one person at a time and has a locking door;

- toilets, washing and changing facilities must be properly ventilated and lit, and must be kept clean and tidy;

- **drinking water** must be available and accessible, with cups provided unless the water comes in a jet;

- there should be suitable facilities for **rest** and **eating** (for people who work at desks, the desk is sufficient);

- if there are restrooms, there must be suitable arrangements to protect non-smokers from **smoke**;

- rest facilities must be available for pregnant and nursing women.

The number of toilets and basins depends on the number of employees on the premises at any time (so if, for example, an employer has 50 employees but only 25 are on duty at any time, there only need to be facilities for 25). For one to five employees there must be at least one toilet and one basin; for six to 25 employees there must be two toilets and basins; for each additional 25 employees or part of 25, there must be an additional toilet and basin.

If separate facilities are provided for women and men, they must be counted separately (so if, for example, there are eight men and 27 women, there would have to be two toilets for men and three for women, even though there are only 35 employees in total). Slightly different provisions apply where urinals are provided for men.

36.4.2
Young workers

Young people of compulsory school age cannot be employed for any job which requires them to lift, carry or move heavy items which would be likely to cause injury. They cannot work in a kitchen, cinema or disco, and there are limitations on their employment in street trading, performances, sport, advertising and modelling. The local authority's education welfare department or the Children's Legal Advice Centre [see end of chapter] can provide advice.

Children's and Young Persons Acts 1933 and 1963;
Children (Protection at Work) Regulations 1998 [SI 1998/276];
2000 [SI 2000/1333]; and 2000 (No.2) [SI 2000/2548]

There are restrictions on the hours that school-age young people can work [see **28.5.1**], and at the time of writing (early 2001) there were also plans to impose restrictions on 16- and 17-year-olds.

Special risk assessments must be carried before a person under 18 is employed [see **36.3.1.2**].

Employer's liability insurance [see **20.4.1**] should be checked to ensure it covers all young employees and volunteers.

36.4.3 Smoking

The risks involved in **passive smoking** are now well established, and employers may face liability in future if they fail to take this risk into account and do not comply with the HSE approved code of practice on smoking. In certain circumstances, illness arising from passive smoking may constitute an industrial illness.   *Clay v DSS, The Times 30/8/1990*

Where rest areas are provided for employees, employers must make provision to protect non-smoking employees from discomfort caused by tobacco smoke [see **36.4.1.3**]. Even where there are no rest areas, provision should be made to protect non-smokers from smoke. In particular, if an employer knows that an employee suffers an adverse physical reaction to cigarette smoke, the employer has a duty to take all reasonable and practical steps to reduce the risk of illness. In one case, an employee successfully claimed constructive dismissal [see **30.4.8**] when she resigned because she had to work in a smoke-filled office.

Holmes v St Andrews [1998] 6 PLC 66;
Waltons and Morse v Dorrington [1997] IRLR 488

The duty to non-smokers may go even further. In early 2000 a Dutch court ruled that employers must guarantee non-smokers a totally smoke-free working environment, and in Italy, where an asthmatic woman died after her employer refused to allow her to move to a less smoky environment, the employer and the woman's work colleagues were facing possible manslaughter charges.

HSE Books and Action on Smoking and Health [see end of chapter], can provide information on smoking policies. Smokers do not have a right to smoke at work, and employers may ban smoking by employees. However any smoking policy should be introduced only after proper consultation with all employees or their safety representatives. The policy, contract or employment and/or disciplinary policy should specify whether breach of a no smoking policy will be treated as a disciplinary matter, or even as gross misconduct.

Organisations may ban smoking by clients, visitors and others on its premises. If a ban is ignored, the employer can ask the person to leave.

36.4.4 Violence

The HSE definition of **violence** is 'any incident in which an employee is abused, threatened or assaulted by a member of the public in circumstances arising out of his or her employment'. An employer might define violence more broadly, to include bullying or harassment [see **36.4.5**], nuisance phone calls or attacks on property. A workplace definition of violence is also likely to include acts by fellow workers, management and members of the governing body [see **30.4.8**], as well as acts by service users, customers and members of the public.

If violence poses a threat to the safety of workers or members of the public the employer must do a risk assessment, take appropriate action to reduce the risks, and provide appropriate information and training to people who may be affected by the violence. Depending on the situation, procedures might be developed to cover:

- what individual workers are expected or allowed to do;
- specific responsibility for handling and defusing difficult situations;
- available back-up and advice;
- available equipment, such as personal alarms or 'panic buttons', and how and when they should be used;

531

- records of people entering or leaving areas of risk;
- when police or other assistance can or must be summoned;
- records of violent or potentially violent incidents;
- how incidents are investigated and, if necessary, witnesses interviewed;
- circumstances under which police or other authorities can or must be notified of the event (if they are not summoned to it);
- support for the person who has been threatened or attacked;
- learning from the incident and applying the lessons.

HSE Books, the Suzy Lamplugh Trust and the TUC [see end of chapter for details] can provide information and advice.

36.4.4.1
Physical restraint

Where employees or volunteers may have to deal with service users, customers or members of the public who may become violent, the organisation should have a clear policy on whether and under what circumstances physical restraint may be used, the type of restraint, and alternative methods of dealing with actual or threatened violence. People who may need to use physical restraint must understand the implications of engaging in action which could legally be assault.

Appropriate training must be provided, and detailed records should be kept whenever restraint is used. Incidents should be fully investigated, appropriate support should be offered to all those affected, and procedures should be amended to reflect lessons learned from the incident.

36.4.5
Bullying, harassment and victimisation

Bullying has been defined as 'offensive, intimidating, malicious, insulting or humiliating behaviour, abuse of power or authority, which attempts to undermine an individual or group of employees, and which may cause them to suffer stress'. Harassment involves causing alarm or distress, by verbal or other means, on more than one occasion or, in the case of sexual harassment, causing distress by unwanted behaviour based on sex or sexuality. Employers have an obligation to ensure employees' health is not jeopardised by bullying or harassment in the course of work, and to take steps to prevent such action when they know or should know that it is happening and could cause physical or mental harm to the employee.

Managers must have the right to comment on and criticise people's work and their behaviour at work. But criticism becomes bullying or harassment when it focuses on the individual rather than on their work or behaviour, is destructive rather than constructive, and results in a person feeling threatened or compromised. This can include constant criticism, constantly giving staff trivial tasks or tasks which are beyond their capacity (without providing appropriate training or support), constantly 'changing the goalposts' so staff are unclear what they are meant to do or how to do it, shouting, using threatening or abusive language, persistently picking on or attacking people in front of others or in private, ignoring people, deliberately excluding people from work activities, blocking promotion, and treating people in other ways that demean and degrade them.

Organisational policies on bullying and harassment should state that bullying or harassment, whether isolated or systematic, will be treated as a disciplinary offence. Failure to deal with such actions may lead to claims of breach of health and safety, sexual harassment, race discrimination, disability discrimination, unfair dismissal, breach of contract, and/or offences under the **Protection from Harassment Act 1997**.

36.4.6
Stress

The employer's duty to provide a safe system of work includes monitoring and minimising factors which may cause or exacerbate stress-related psychiatric illness. The factors may be physical, such as excessive noise or overcrowding, or psychological such as overwork, bullying or fear of violence.

Failure to develop practices which acknowledge and seek to reduce foreseeable illness caused by workplace stress may lead to legal action. A local authority, for example, was found to be in breach of its duty of care after an employee who had suffered a mental breakdown returned to work and repeatedly asked, unsuccessfully, for his workload to be reduced. Another local authority accepted liability for personal injury caused by workplace stress after a worker was transferred to a new job, was not given the training and support she needed in order to do the job, and suffered serious psychiatric illness as a result.

Walker v Northumberland County Council [1995] IRLR 35
Lancaster v Birmingham City Council, The Guardian 7/6/1999

But in another case where the worker had suffered a breakdown, the court refused to award damages because there was no mental illness or medically recognised complaint.

Rorrison v West Lothian Regional Council [1999] IDS Brief 655

36.4.7
Computers and display screens

Special provisions apply to display screen **users** (staff who use computers or microfiche as a significant part of their normal work) and **operators** (self-employed people carrying out work for an employer involving substantial time at a display screen).

Health and Safety
(Display Screen Equipment) Regulations 1992 [SI 1992/2792]

Laptop computers are covered if they are in prolonged use by a user. In addition, employers should be aware of manual handling risks arising from workers carrying a computer, printer and heavy papers, and risks arising from poor posture when using a laptop on trains or in hotels.

The display screen regulations set minimum requirements for:

- the **display screen** (clearly defined characters, no flicker, adjustable brightness and contrast, able to swivel and tilt, no reflections or glare), the **keyboard** (tiltable, separate from the screen, space to support the user's arms and hands), and the **software** (easy to use, appropriate for the person);

- the **workstation** desk (non-reflective, large enough), document holder if there is one, and the chair (stable, adjustable for height, back adjustable for height and tilt, with a footrest if requested);

- the workstation **environment**, including space, lighting, glare, noise, heat, radiation and humidity.

Employers must plan the activities of users so there are regular breaks from the screen. Display screen users (but not self-employed operators) are entitled to eye tests at the employer's expense if they request it when starting display screen work, at regular intervals thereafter, or when experiencing visual difficulties. The employer must supply any corrective equipment required by a display screen user.

Employers must provide training about display screen safety to users, and information about health and safety to users and operators.

The employer must carry out an assessment of every workstation used by a user or operator, covering risks such as upper limb disorders (repetitive strain injury/RSI), stress and visual difficulties. HSE guidance acknowledges that it is still difficult to predict the likelihood of RSI and related injuries, and advises employers to encourage early reporting by users of any symptoms which may be related to display screen work. The risks of RSI can be reduced by arranging work so the worker does not have to sit in the same position for long periods, can take regular breaks, and can adjust the equipment and chair.

The regulations do not acknowledge a link between computer work and reproductive or pregnancy problems, so there is no statutory obligation for an employer to provide alternative work for pregnant women. There is however an duty to undertake a risk assessment and make appropriate changes to the job [see **36.3.1.1**]. Given the possibility of risk, it would be good practice to offer alternative work if it is available.

36.4.8
Work equipment and lifting equipment

Work equipment must be suitable for its use and must be used only for purposes for which it is intended. It must be kept in good repair, and where there is a health or safety risk must be used only by trained people. Instructions and information about the equipment must be easily available, and must be known not only to the people who use the equipment but also to managers and supervisors.

Provision and Use of Work Equipment Regulations 1998 [SI 1998/2306]

Lifting equipment and hoists, in particular, must be strong and stable enough for each load, and must be marked to indicate safe load limits. Equipment intended to lift persons must be designed to prevent a person being crushed, trapped or struck or falling from the carrier.

Lifting Operations and Lifting Equipment Regulations 1998 [1998/2307]

36.4.9
Personal protective equipment

Adequate and readily available protective clothing and equipment must be provided. The suitability of the equipment for its purpose and for the staff using it must be assessed, suitable training and information must be provided, and equipment and clothing must be properly stored and must be replaced as necessary.

Personal Protective Equipment at Work Regulations 1992 [SI 1992/2966]

The regulations apply only to clothing or equipment used for health and safety reasons, such as raincoats, high visibility jackets, helmets, aprons and chef's hats. They do not cover uniforms or items which do not have a protective function.

The employer must take all reasonable steps to ensure protective equipment and clothing is used. Employees have a duty to use the equipment or clothing and to report any defect or loss to the employer.

The employer cannot charge employees for equipment or clothing required under these regulations.

Health and Safety at Work etc Act 1974 s.9

36.4.10
Manual handling

Where large loads or people are being manually handled, employers and staff are generally aware of potential problems and good practice. But the manual handling rules apply just as much to office and catering situations where smaller loads might be involved, and other workplaces where items are carried, lifted, pushed or pulled, or where the work involves twisting or stretching. Potential hazards must be identified and avoided where possible, steps must be taken to reduce the risk of injury to the lowest reasonably practicable level, and information must be provided about the risks and safe handling.

Manual Handling Operations Regulations 1992 [SI 1992/2793]

36.4.11
Hazardous substances

Harmful substances, including photocopier and laser printer toner and solvent-based products such as glues and oil paints, are covered by regulations known as **COSHH**. The risk must be assessed (the manufacturer's hazard data sheet does not constitute a COSHH assessment), exposure to the substances must be prevented or limited, protective equipment must if appropriate be issued, appropriate information and training must be provided to employees, health surveillance [see **36.3.2.1**] and/or monitoring of exposure must be implemented if appropriate, and the safety procedures must be regularly monitored and updated. For some substances there is a maximum exposure level (MEL) which it is an offence to exceed; for others there is an occupational exposure standard (OES) which sets maximum recommended level. Guidance on specific substances and COSHH monitoring is available from HSE.

Control of Substances Hazardous to Health Regulations 1999 [SI 1999/437]

36.4.12
Electrical equipment

All electrical systems must be constructed, maintained and used in ways which prevent the risk of danger, and portable appliances such as kettles and computers may need to be tested annually by a competent person. Employers, employees and self-employed people have an absolute obligation [see **36.2.5**] to comply with the electricity regulations in all matters under their control. Guidance is available from HSE.

Electricity at Work Regulations 1989 [SI 1989/635]

36.4.13
Gas

Persons responsible for premises must ensure that gas fittings and pipework are maintained in good condition. Every appliance must be checked for safety at not more than annual intervals, and defects must be put right. Inspection records must be maintained.

Gas Safety Management Regulations 1996 [SI 1996/551]

36.4.14
Building construction

Where building construction work, including design work or demolition, involves more than five people on site at any one time, lasts more than 30 days or will involve more than 500 person days of work, it is the responsibility of the organisation paying for the work to ensure that only competent people are employed as planning supervisor and principal contractor. The organisation must also provide relevant health and safety information to the planning supervisor, and ensure that resources are sufficient to enable the project to be carried out safely.

Construction (Design and Management) Regulations 1994 [SI 1994/3140]

36.4.15
Lifts

Occupiers of premises must ensure that all lifts are safe, properly maintained and inspected every six months, and that proper records are kept of maintenance and inspections. *Offices, Shops and Railway Premises (Hoists and Lifts) Regulations 1969 [SI 1968/849]*

36.5
FIRE SAFETY

Employers, landlords and others in charge of premises have primary responsibility for fire safety in the workplace. They must carry out risk assessments [see **36.3.1**] with specific regard to fire safety, provide measures to deal with any fire risks on their premises, appoint employees to implement fire safety measures, and liaise as appropriate with external emergency services, particularly in relation to rescue work and fire-fighting. There are criminal sanctions in the case of serious fire risks. Information about all aspects of fire safety and compliance with the regulations is available from the fire authority and in *Fire Safety: An employer's guide*, from HSE Books [see end of chapter for details].

Fire Precautions (Workplace) Regulations 1997 [SI 1997/1840];
Fire Precautions (Workplace) (Amendment) Regulations 1999 [1999/1877]

36.5.1
Information and training

All staff must receive fire safety training covering the action to be taken on discovering a fire or hearing the alarm, the location and use of fire fighting equipment, escape routes, the importance of keeping fire doors closed at all times, the importance of closing all doors and windows during a fire, how to evacuate the building (including how to deal with members of the public and people with different types of disability), assembly points, and the importance of not entering the building until the all-clear is given. Fire procedures must not require anyone to attempt to tackle a fire.

Notices must be prominently displayed where visitors can see them.

Fire drills should be held at least annually, or more often if the risk of fire is high or escape might be particularly difficult. A record of evacuation times and any problems should be kept, and action must be taken to put right any deficiencies.

36.5.2
Fire certificates

A fire certificate is required for work premises where 20 or more people are employed, or where 10 or more people are employed anywhere other than the ground floor. This applies even if the people are employed by different employers. Certificates are also required for non-domestic premises where sleeping accommodation is provided. Certificates are usually issued by the fire authority, and must be displayed as required in the certificate. *Fire Precautions Act 1971*

Provided there are no changes to the premises, a fire certificate is valid for the lifetime of the premises. If there are changes, the occupier or owner must notify the fire authority.

Premises which do not need a fire certificate must comply with regulations for non-certificated premises. The fire authority can provide guidance.
Fire Precautions (Workplace) Regulations 1997 [SI 1997/1840]

36.5.3
Warning systems

Fire alarms and smoke detectors as specified in the fire certificate must be provided in all premises requiring a certificate. For premises which do not require a certificate, the fire authority, commercial suppliers and health and safety advice centres can advise on appropriate alarm systems and smoke detectors.

36.5.4
Escape

Adequate escape routes must be provided from all buildings, enabling people to turn away from the fire, wherever it may be in the building, and reach a protected staircase or exit. Fire exits must be clearly marked with signs complying with the **Health and Safety (Safety Signs and Signals) Regulations 1996** *[SI 1996/341].*

All staircases and fire exits must be kept accessible and free from obstructions, and if locked or fastened they must be able to be easily and immediately opened. Special provision may be required for people with mobility difficulties or for premises used for public entertainment. If a fire exit is temporarily unusable, for example because of building works, all signs pointing to that exit should be removed.

36.5.5
Fire-fighting
equipment

Fire extinguishers should be placed in positions where a person would not have to move more than 30m (slightly under 100ft) to reach them. They must be clearly marked with the type of extinguisher, the method of operation and the types of fire they can be used on.

Fire extinguishers should be checked every month, and should be inspected annually by a trained person.

Fire blankets can be used for small fires, including fires involving electrical equipment, oil or cooking fat. They can also be wrapped around a person whose clothing has caught fire.

36.5.6
Access

Designated fire access areas, dry riser mains and sprinklers must be kept clear. For buildings over 18m (59ft) in height, special access provisions are required.

36.6
FIRST AID

All workplaces should have adequate facilities and equipment for staff who become ill at work. There is no statutory obligation to provide first aid to anyone other than staff, but duty of care [see **36.1.2**] means that facilities should also be available for others on the premises. Records must be kept whenever first aid is administered [see **36.7.2**].
Health & Safety (First-Aid) Regulations 1981 [SI 1981/917]

36.6.1
First aiders

It is recommended, but not required, that all work places should have at least one **suitable person** on duty as a first aider, and **appointed persons** to cover when the suitable person is temporarily unavailable. If the risks are low, one suitable person may deal with up to 50 employees. In riskier situations, there should be more than one.

'Suitable persons' must hold a certificate from a first aid course approved by HSE. Certificates are valid for three years, and update courses must be started while the certificate is still valid. Suitable persons must be able to leave their work in order to render help, and must have the physical capability to give that help.

If the work is high risk and there are large number of employees, a first aid room should be provided.

36.6.2
First aid boxes

Clearly visible first aid boxes, marked with a white cross on a green background, must be maintained. The size and number of boxes depends on the number of staff. First aid boxes must contain only the allowed materials, and nothing else. Employees who spend considerable time on the road or in isolated locations should be given portable kits.

36.7
INJURY AND ILLNESS
36.7.1
RIDDOR

Employers, self-employed people and anyone who controls work premises must report to the **Incident Contact Centre** [see end of chapter] serious injuries, near-misses and illnesses caused by or at work to staff, service users, contractors, visitors or members of the public.

Reporting of Injuries, Diseases and Dangerous Occurrences Regulations 1995 [SI 1995/3163]

Reportable events include:

* fatal incidents and death occurring within one year as a result of a reportable incident (even if the incident was not reported);
* accidents or incidents causing major injury;
* potentially dangerous occurrences which did not cause injury;
* **over-three-day injuries** causing more than three days incapacity for work, even if the person is actually at work or if the days are weekend or other non-work days;
* some work-related diseases.

The reporting requirements are explained in HSE31 *Everyone's Guide to RIDDOR 95*. In the case of death, a major injury or condition or a dangerous occurrence, a report must be made immediately by the quickest means, usually telephone, with a written report on **form F2508** within 10 days of the incident. Over-three-day injuries must be reported on form F2508 within 10 days of the incident. Diseases are reported on **form F2508A**. Additional reporting requirements apply if staff who are in contact with food have certain diseases.

A copy of the form must be sent to insurers, and another copy kept indefinitely by the organisation.

At the time of writing (early 2001) the Health and Safety Commission was consulting on proposals to require employers to investigate (not just report) reportable incidents and act on the findings.

36.7.2
Accident book

A record must be kept for at least three years of all accidents, dangerous occurrences and diseases, and incidents where first aid was administered. This record, called the **accident book**, must include the date and time of the occurrence, the full name and occupation of the injured person, the nature of the injury, where it happened, and the circumstances. For a reportable disease, the record must show the occupation of the person affected, the date of diagnosis and the name or nature of the disease. Where first aid is given, the record must also include the address of the person treated; the signature, name and address of the person making the entry; and the date of the entry.

It is good practice also to record, in the accident book or a separate incident book, minor accidents or incidents which were, or could have been, a danger to health or safety, such as an aggressive outburst.

36.7.3
Internal reporting

The organisation should establish procedures to ensure that notification is promptly given to the person's family or next of kin, the organisation's insurers, the safety representative(s) or safety committee, senior staff, head office and/or the relevant member of the governing body, and the person responsible for keeping personnel records.

36.7.4
Medical and maternity suspension

For certain work-related illnesses caused by exposure to lead, ionising radiation and some other substances, employees must be suspended from the activity involving the exposure [see **27.1.10**]. Women who are pregnant, have recently given birth or are breastfeeding must be suspended with full pay if they undertake certain types of work and suitable alternative work is not available [see **28.7.7**].

36.8
WORK WITH CHILDREN AND VULNERABLE ADULTS

It is an offence for paid or unpaid work with children knowingly to be offered to a person who has been disqualified by the court from working with children or who is on the **Protection of Children Act** (PoCA) list maintained by the Department of Health, for such a person knowingly to be allowed to continue working with children, or for a banned person to apply for, offer to do, accept or continue in work with children. This prohibition is very wide, and includes trustees of children's charities. There provisions are explained at **26.3.4**.

Criminal Justice and Court Services Act 2000 s.35

Similar provisions apply to **care workers** in care homes, hospitals and clinics, and people who provide domiciliary personal care for people who because of illness, infirmity or disability are unable to provide such care for themselves without assistance. For these positions care work cannot be offered or continued if the person is on the **Protection of Vulnerable Adults** (PoVA) list maintained by the Department of Health, and it is an offence for a person on the list to apply for, offer to do, accept or continue in care work. *Care Standards Act 2000 ss.80, 89*

A **child** is a person under the age of 18. A **vulnerable adult** is a person aged 18 or over to whom:

- accommodation and nursing or personal care are provided in a care home;

- personal care is provided in their own home under arrangements made by a domiciliary care agency; *or*

- prescribed services are provided by an independent hospital, clinic or medical agency or an NHS body. *s.80(6)*

36.8.1
Duty to check

Organisations defined as childcare organisations [see **26.3.4**], and all organisations employing care workers [see **26.3.4**], must check the PoCA and/or PoVA lists before offering paid or unpaid childcare or care work. Employment agencies or employment businesses supplying care workers or workers for childcare posts must check the lists before supplying workers for such posts, and organisations recruiting through such agencies must receive documentary evidence that such a check was carried out in the previous 12 months. The lists are checked as part of criminal record checks [see **26.3.3**] for relevant positions.

There is no statutory obligation for organisations which work with children but are not legally defined as childcare organisations to carry out checks, but funders may require it and it is good practice to do so.

36.8.2
Duty to refer

Care homes, clinics, domiciliary care agencies and other bodies regulated by the **Care Standards Act 2000**, and organisations legally defined as childcare organisations [see **26.3.4**] have a statutory duty to refer to the secretary of state for health details of persons considered unsuitable to work with children or vulnerable adults. Other organisations may refer, but do not have to.

The criteria for referral are that:

- the organisation has dismissed the individual on the grounds of misconduct (whether or not in the course of his or her employment) which harmed or placed at risk of harm a child or vulnerable adult;

- the individual has resigned or retired in circumstances such that the organisation would have dismissed him or her, or would have considered dismissal, on such grounds if the individual had not resigned or retired;

- the organisation has, on such grounds, transferred the individual to a position which is not a childcare or care position;

- the individual has, on such grounds, suspended the individual or provisionally transferred him or her to a position which is not a childcare or care position, but has not yet decided whether to dismiss the person or confirm the transfer; *or*

- the individual is no longer in a childcare or care position (because of dismissal, resignation, retirement or transfer to another position), and the organisation has become aware of new information that, had it been available while the person was in such a position, would have led the organisation to dismiss or consider dismissing on the grounds of misconduct which harmed or placed at risk of harm a child or vulnerable adult. *Protection of Children Act 1999 s.2; Care Standards Act 2000 s.82*

After referral the case is investigated and if appropriate the person is added to the PoCA and/or PoVA list. There are provisions for the individual to appeal, and to apply after a specified period for removal from the lists.

36.9 PUBLIC HEALTH

Public health regulations, enforced by the local authority's environmental health department, cover air quality, ventilation and pollution; drainage; waste and rubbish disposal; pests and vermin; food hygiene [see **43.2**]; public entertainment [see **chapter 42**]; and residential accommodation provided by the organisation for its staff, tenants, residents or visitors. Information is available from the local authority.

36.10 CONSUMER SAFETY

It is an offence to sell or in some cases provide goods which do not comply with the relevant safety requirements. The regulations generally apply to new goods, and to the sale of second-hand goods 'in the course of business' or 'in the course of trade'.

If in any doubt at all about whether something complies with the regulations, the organisation should check with the local authority's trading standards or consumer safety department—or not sell the item.

36.10.1 Sale of second-hand and donated goods

Although the sale of donated goods is not classed as trading for charity law and tax purposes [see **52.3.2**], the fact that goods are donated is irrelevant for consumer safety purposes. Goods sold in charity shops are covered by consumer safety legislation, as well as goods sold at jumble sales or similar events which are held regularly and could be seen as constituting a business or trade.

Even if one-off jumble sales, Christmas fairs and similar sales are not regular enough to constitute a 'business', it is not sensible to sell or allow others to sell anything which could pose a risk to health or safety.

At a car boot sale, table top sale or similar sale the person hiring the pitch is selling the goods and is responsible for ensuring the goods comply with the relevant legislation. The organisation hiring out the space might want to make it a condition that no second-hand electrical or gas appliances or dangerous toys are sold.

At the time of writing (early 2001) some aspects of consumer safety applied differently to new and second-hand goods, but they were expected to be standardised from early 2002.

36.10.2 Clothing and personal goods

Items which must not be sold 'in the course of business' include:

- children's anoraks and similar garments with hood cords;

- nightdresses, pyjamas, dressing gowns, bathrobes and similar garments without fire hazard information on a permanent label;

- crash and cycle helmets and riding hats, unless the organisation can guarantee that they comply with the relevant safety standards when they are sold.

36.10.3
Furniture and household goods

Many household goods may be sold only if they comply with safety requirements. In some cases, special labelling is required. If the organisation cannot guarantee that items comply with the requirements, they should not be sold. Examples include:

- new upholstered furniture and furnishings, including scatter cushions;

- second-hand upholstered furniture and furnishings if it was made since 1 January 1950 and is being sold in the course of trade;

- nursery furniture which contains any upholstery (but changing mats, play mats, baby bouncers suspended from doorways, cot bumpers, bedclothes, and baby carriers and slings designed to be worn outdoors can be sold);

- baby car seats;

- new and second-hand electrical goods (but even if it does not comply with the regulations it can be supplied as scrap or to a business which repairs and reconditions electrical equipment);

- gas appliances, and oil heaters and lamps.

36.10.4
Toys

All new toys, including those which are handmade, must satisfy the applicable safety requirements, have a CE marking (to be replaced by EN/European norm marking), and provide information about the manufacturer or importer. This requirement does not apply to second-hand toys, unless the toys were brought into the EU from a non-EU country and are subsequently being sold in the course of a business.

Handmade toys must be certified by the maker as complying with the relevant toy safety standard and must be labelled with the name and address of the individual, business or organisation who made it. Some toys must contain a warning or indication of precautions to be taken. Advice on the regulations and labelling is available from the local authority trading standards or consumer protection department.

36.11
TRANSPORT

Information and advice about all aspects of driver, vehicle and operator licensing, legislation, training and operations is available from the Community Transport Association [see end of chapter].

36.11.1
Vehicle licensing and safety

An organisation which operates cars, vans, minibuses (nine to 16 passengers), buses/coaches (more than 16 passengers) or other vehicles must ensure they meet all legal requirements and are roadworthy, and drivers are trained in their use and operation. Drivers must ensure that their vehicle complies with the full requirements of the **Road Vehicles (Construction and Use) Regulations 1986** *[SI 1986/1078]* and **Road Vehicles Lighting Regulations 1989** *[SI 1989/1796]*, as amended. The organisation must ensure that maintenance systems are in place to ensure the roadworthiness of vehicles, including regular checks, defect reporting, safety inspections, servicing and MoTs.

All minibuses and coaches carrying three or more children on an organised trip must provide a forward-facing seat with, as a minimum, a lap belt (lap and diagonal is preferable) for each child aged between three and 16. Seatbelts must be worn when fitted to a vehicle with an unladen weight of 2,540kg or less.

36.11.2
Driver licensing and safety

Ordinary driving licences (category B) cover vehicles with up to eight passenger seats. Drivers who passed their driving test before 1 January 1997 have a restricted D1 entitlement, which allows them to drive a minibus (nine to 16 passengers excluding the driver) provided they are 21 or over and the minibus is not being used for 'hire and reward' (unless operating under a permit). When their licence expires, normally at age 70, a medical test must be passed to retain the D1 entitlement.

Drivers passing their driving test on or after 1 January 1997 receive a licence covering vehicles with up to eight passenger seats. In order to drive a minibus, drivers need to take a second test to gain a full D1 (PCV) entitlement unless all the following conditions are met:

- the vehicle is used for social purposes by a non-commercial body, and is not used for hire and reward (unless operating under a permit);

- the maximum weight of the vehicle is no more than 4.25 tonnes, or no more than 3.5 tonnes excluding any weight attributable to specialised equipment for carrying disabled passengers;

- the driver is 21 or over, has held a car (category B) licence for at least two years, and is doing the driving on a voluntary basis; *and*

- if the driver is aged 70 or over, he or she meets the health standards for driving a D1 vehicle.

At the time of writing (early 2001) a government-appointed task force had proposed a special licence, requiring additional training, for people who drive at work; limits on work-related driving time; and making employers liable for accidents caused by employees' dangerous driving.

FOR FURTHER INFORMATION

Health and safety law and good practice. Health and Safety Executive: infoline 0541-545500, www.hse.gov.uk; more comprehensive subscription service at www.hsedirect.com

Health and Safety Books: 01787-881165, www.hsebooks.co.uk. Free publications from www.hse.gov.uk/hsehome.htm

Local H&S advice centres: details from Manchester Hazards Centre, 0161-953 4037

TUC Rightsline: 0870-600 4882, www.tuc.org.uk/rights/health.htm

British Safety Council: 020-8741 1231, www.britishsafetycouncil.co.uk

CHAT: 0151-227 5559; www.safety-training-lohp.co.uk

London Hazards Centre: 020-7794 5999, www.lhc.org.uk

Royal Society for the Prevention of Accidents (RoSPA): 0121-248 2000, www.rospa.co.uk

Bullying. Andrea Adams Trust: 01273-704900; www.successunlimited.co.uk/bully/AAT.htm

Children and young people as workers. Children's Legal Advice Centre: 01206-873820

Local authority education department

Consumer safety. Local authority trading standards/consumer safety department

Department of Trade and Industry Consumer Safety Unit: 020-7215 0361, www.dti.gov.uk/capc/ca

Fire. Local fire authority

Fire Protection Association: 020-7902 5300; www.thefpa.co.uk

Personal safety. Police crime prevention unit

Suzy Lamplugh Trust: 020-8392 1839, www.suzylamplugh.org

Joint website on workplace violence: www.workplaceviolence.co.uk

RIDDOR: Incident Contact Centre: 0845-300 99 23; www.riddor.gov.uk

Smoking. Action on Smoking and Health: 020-7935 0592, www.ash.org.uk

Transport. Community Transport Association: 0161-367 8780, www.communitytransport.com

Work with children and vulnerable adults. Department of Health: www.doh.gov.uk

Local authority social services department

Signs and other H&S items are available from various suppliers, including the British Safety Council and RoSPA.

H&S training is provided by British Safety Council, RoSPA and local H&S advice centres; training specifically for voluntary organisations by local hazards centres and CHAT; **fire prevention training** by the Fire Prevention Association; **approved first aid training** by local branches of the British Red Cross (details 020-7235 3454, www.redcross.org.uk) and St John Ambulance (020-7235 5231, www.sja.org.uk).

Chapter 37
EQUAL OPPORTUNITIES IN
PROVISION OF GOODS AND SERVICES

37.1
THE LAW AND
GOOD PRACTICE

When considering equal opportunities it is important to distinguish between:

- statutory requirements, which must be complied with;

- codes of practice and guidance issued by the Commission for Racial Equality, Equal Opportunities Commission, Disability Rights Commission or similar bodies, where failure to comply may be taken into account if a discrimination case is brought against the organisation;

- requirements imposed by the organisation's governing document, which must be complied with unless legislation overrides them;

- requirements imposed by the organisation's equal opportunities or other policies, which can be changed by the governing body;

- requirements imposed by third parties such as funders or donors.

An organisation cannot be required, either by its governing document or policies or by third parties, to do anything which is unlawful.

Much equal opportunities legislation concentrates on employment [see **chapter 25**]. This chapter looks at equal opportunities in relation to the goods, services, activities, facilities, premises and other benefits provided by the organisation. For ease of reference, the term 'services' is used throughout to refer to anything provided by the organisation to its members, beneficiaries or members of the public.

37.1.1
Equal opportunities
and human rights

The **European Convention on Human Rights**, implemented by the **Human Rights Act 1998**, includes a number of rights relevant to service delivery, including the right to private and family life (art.8), freedom of thought, conscience and religion (art.9), freedom of expression (art.10), and freedom of assembly (art.11) [see **60.3.1**]. Article 14 prohibits these or any other Convention right from being interfered with by discrimination. The definition of discrimination is extremely broad, and includes religion, property, birth or other status.

The Convention right not be discriminated against exists only in relation to other Convention rights. A claim for breach can be brought only against a public authority or body carrying out a public function [see **60.3.2**]. This includes some but not all voluntary organisations.

37.2
RACIAL GROUP

Under the **Race Relations Act 1976** discrimination on the basis of **racial group** (race, colour, ethnic origin, national origin or nationality) is generally unlawful. This means that no member of the public can be deliberately excluded from access to services simply because of their race, nationality etc. An organisation cannot refuse to provide services on the basis of a person's racial group, nor can it deliberately 'forget' to provide them, or provide different or inferior services. This applies regardless of whether the services are free or a charge is made.

Race Relations Act 1976 s.20

Organisations which are legally public authorities or carry out public functions [see **60.3.2**] must 'have due regard for the need to eliminate unlawful discrimination and promote equality of opportunity and good race relations'. This means they must consider the racial equality implications of all relevant activities. Other organisations do not have this explicit duty, but many voluntary organisations consider it essential to ensure that their services are widely publicised and accessible to all sectors of the community. *Race Relations (Amendment) Act 2000 s.2*

The **EU Directive on Combatting Discrimination on the Grounds of Racial and Ethnic Origin** *[2000/43/EC]* must be implemented in the UK by 19 July 2003, and may lead to some changes affecting service delivery.

37.2.1
Access to membership

Associations and clubs (organisations with members) generally cannot discriminate on the basis of racial group in choosing members or in providing services to their members.

37.2.1.1
Small clubs and associations

Clubs and associations with fewer than 25 members are allowed to use racial group as a factor in selecting members. This exception does not apply to trade unions and professional organisations [see **37.2.1.3**].

Race Relations Act 1976 s.25

37.2.1.2
Cultural associations

Clubs and associations are allowed to limit their membership and services to people of a specific racial group (not defined by reference to colour) if the main object of the organisation is to enable the benefits of membership to be enjoyed by people of that group. This covers, for example, a cultural association open only to members of a particular racial group and providing its services primarily to its members. But the racial group cannot be defined as 'black' or 'white'. *s.26*

Other clubs and associations cannot discriminate on the basis of racial group in providing services unless they can show that the racial group has a special need for the service [see **37.2.2.2**].

37.2.1.3
Trade unions and professional associations

Trade unions and other organisations of workers, organisations of employees, or organisations whose members carry on a particular profession or trade for the purpose of which the organisation exists, cannot discriminate on the basis of racial group in access to membership or to any of the benefits of membership. *s.11*

Such organisations are allowed to take **positive action** to ensure that people from all racial groups are fully represented at various levels in the organisation. They are allowed to:

- encourage people of a particular racial group to join, if at any time in the previous 12 months there were no persons of that racial group as members, or the proportion of members of that racial group was small in relation to the number of people of that racial group who were eligible for membership;

- encourage people of a particular racial group to take advantage of opportunities to hold posts in the organisation or provide preferential access to training to help prepare them for such posts, if there are no people from that racial group or only a small proportion holding posts.   *Race Relations Act 1976 s.38(3)-(5)*

Racial group cannot, however, be used as a factor in selecting people for membership or for posts in the organisation.

There is no provision for other organisations to take these forms of positive action.

37.2.2
Access to services

Although discrimination on the basis of racial group is generally unlawful, there are some situations where voluntary organisations may use racial group as a factor in providing access to services.

37.2.2.1
Charities

Charities can limit their services to a particular racial group if their governing document explicitly allows this, provided the group is not defined by reference to colour. If a charity's governing document refers to colour, that reference must be disregarded and the charity's services become available regardless of colour.   *s.34*

Other charities cannot limit a service or services to a specific racial group unless the group has a special need for the service [see below].

37.2.2.2
Special need

In some situations access to some services may be restricted or allocated first to members of a specific racial group. This applies only if:

- it can be shown that members of the group have a need which is different in kind from, or is the same as but proportionately greater than, the other population of the area covered by the organisation;

- the need is attributable to and distinguished by a characteristic specific to the racial group; *and*

- the special need relates to education, training, welfare or ancillary benefits.   *s.35*

The special need cannot be based simply on people's preference to be with people of their own racial group.

Unless the organisation is confident that it could, if challenged, justify the provision of separate services or preferential access to services, it should take advice from the Commission for Racial Equality [see end of **chapter 25** for details] before designating services in this way.

37.2.2.3
Fostering and boarding out

Racial group can be used as a factor when making fostering or boarding out arrangements by which a person takes children, elderly people or people in need of a special degree of care and attention into his or her own home and treats them as if they were members of the family.
                    s.23(2)

37.2.2.4
Training bodies

Providers of training may limit access to vocational training to people of a particular racial group, or encourage members of that racial group to take advantage of opportunities to do a particular type of work, if:

- at any time in the previous 12 months there were no persons of that racial group engaged in that type of work in Great Britain or in the area covered by the training provider; *or*

- the proportion of persons of that racial group involved in that type of work was small, compared to the proportion of people of that racial group in the population of Great Britain as a whole or the population of the area covered by the training provider.   *s.37(1)*

37.2.2.5
Education and training for people not resident in Great Britain

Racial group can be used as a factor in providing access to education, training and ancillary benefits for people who are not ordinarily resident in Great Britain. The provider of the education or training must reasonably believe that the person does not intend to remain in Great Britain after the course.   *s.36*

37.2.2.6
Sport and games

Discrimination on the basis of nationality, place of birth, or length of residence in any area or place is allowed when selecting a person or team to represent a country, place or area, or any related association, in any sport or game; or when pursuing the rules of any competition relating to eligibility to compete in the sport or game in question.

Race Relations Act 1976 s.39

37.2.3
Publicity

It is generally unlawful to publicise an organisation or its services in a way which indicates that the organisation discriminates, or would discriminate, on the basis of racial group. However such advertisements are allowed when the discrimination is permitted under the Act. *s.29*

37.3
SEX

The **Sex Discrimination Act 1975** uses concepts and terminology similar to the Race Relations Act 1976, so the section above on racial discrimination should be read before reading this section.

In general no one can be denied access to goods, services, activities, facilities or premises (all referred to here as services) on the basis of sex, regardless of whether the services are provided for payment or free of charge. *Sex Discrimination Act 1975 s.29*

Amendments to the Act make it unlawful to treat a person less favourably in relation to vocational training, on the basis that the person intends to undergo, is undergoing or has undergone gender reassignment (transsexuality). The amendments do not refer to transsexuality discrimination in relation to other goods, services or facilities.

Sex Discrimination (Gender Reassignment) Regulations 1999 [SI 1999/1102]

37.3.1
Exceptions

Although discrimination on the basis of sex is generally unlawful, there are some situations in which it is permissible to use sex as a factor in allowing access to membership or services.

37.3.1.1
Single-sex organisations

The governing document of a voluntary organisation may restrict its membership, and the services it provides to members, to one sex. If the main object of the organisation is to provide services for one sex, the organisation can do anything necessary to achieve this object.

Sex Discrimination Act 1975 ss.34, 43

37.3.1.2
Special care

Facilities provided at, or as part of, an establishment for people requiring special care, supervision or attention can be limited to one sex. This includes, for example, hospitals. *s.35(1)(a)*

37.3.1.3
Propriety and privacy

Services can be limited to one sex where:

- people are likely to be undressed;
- the service involves physical contact between the provider and service user and the service provider might reasonably object if the user were of the other sex; *or*
- the presence of men is likely to cause serious embarrassment to women users of the service, or *vice versa*. *s.35(1)(c)*

37.3.1.4
Communal accommodation

Residential accommodation may be limited to one sex if:

- it includes dormitories or shared sleeping accommodation which, for reasons of decency or privacy, should be used by one sex only; *or*
- it should be used by one sex only because of the nature of the sanitary facilities serving the accommodation. *s.46*

In providing access to residential accommodation, men and women must be treated as fairly and equitably as circumstances permit.

Where services are provided only to people using single-sex accommodation, it is not unlawful to provide them as single-sex services.

37.3.1.5
Education

Services may be limited to one sex in single-sex educational establishments, boarding accommodation, and further and higher education courses in physical education. *Sex Discrimination Act 1975 ss.26-28*

37.3.1.6
Training

Access to training for a particular type of work can be limited to one sex where it appears to the training provider that:

- at any time in the previous 12 months there were no members of that sex, or a disproportionately small number, doing that work in Great Britain or in an area of Great Britain; *or*

- persons of one sex have special need of training because they have been carrying out domestic or family duties rather than being in full-time employment. *s.47*

37.3.1.7
Sport and games

Participation in sporting events where strength, stamina or physique are important may lawfully be limited to men or women. *s.44*

37.3.1.8
Religious premises

Where religious doctrine requires facilities to be restricted to one sex or where a significant number of the followers of a religion would be offended if separate facilities were not provided, it is lawful to restrict facilities or services to one sex at places used for the purposes of an organised religion. *s.35(1)(b)*

37.3.1.9
Trade unions and professional organisations

Trade unions, other organisations of employees, employers' organisations and professional or trade associations may undertake **positive action** if they have no or disproportionately few members of one sex, or if posts in the organisation are held by no or disproportionately few persons of one sex. The allowed positive action is:

- encouraging persons of the under-represented sex to become members of the organisation;

- encouraging persons of the under-represented sex to take advantage of opportunities to hold posts in the organisation;

- providing access to training for persons of one sex to enable them to take up posts in the organisation. *s.48(2),(3)*

Sex cannot, however, be used as a factor in actually selecting people for membership or for posts in the organisation.

There is no provision in the Act for this sort of positive action to be taken by other types of organisation.

37.3.2
Publicity

It is unlawful to advertise an organisation or its services in a way which indicates that they are available only to women or to men, unless such limitation is lawful. *s.38*

37.4
DISABILITY

The **Disability Discrimination Act 1995** not only makes it unlawful to discriminate unjustifiably against people with disabilities, but also requires providers of goods, services, facilities and premises (collectively referred to as services) to take reasonable steps to adapt their services and premises. The non-discrimination provisions have been in effect since 2 December 1996. The provisions requiring adaptation of services came into effect on 1 October 1999, and the provisions requiring adaptation of premises will come into effect on 1 October 2004.

The provisions apply to all providers of services, regardless of number of employees and regardless of whether services are provided for a charge or free. The definition of disability is the same as for the employment provisions of the Act [see **25.5.1**].

Information about all DDA requirements is available from the Disability Rights Commission [see end of **chapter 25**], at www.disability.gov.uk, and from many disability organisations. The Disability Conciliation Service, contactable through the Disability Rights Commission, can work with disabled people and service providers to help resolve problems. The Centre for Accessible Environments (020-7357 8182, www.cae.org.uk) and some major disability organisations carry out access audits.

37.4.1
Exceptions

The provisions of the DDA do not directly apply to managing or disposing of premises *[ss.22-24]*, provision of public transport *[ss.32-49]*, and education in schools and further and higher education institutions *[ss.29-31]*, but these are or will be covered under separate regulations. Education is quite broadly defined and includes youth services; social, cultural and recreational activities; physical education activities to promote personal development; and assessment and research facilities.

Even where an organisation's own services are within an exemption, the use of its facilities or premises for other, non-exempt, purposes is not exempt from DDA provisions.

Also excluded are services which are not available to the public, such as those of a private club. This could apply to some non-charitable clubs and associations. It is unlikely to apply to charitable bodies, whose facilities must be available to the public [see **4.3.8**], even if that 'public' is restricted in various ways and may be relatively small.

37.4.2
Non-discrimination

It is generally unlawful:

- to refuse to provide, or deliberately not to provide, a service to a disabled person which is provided or would be provided to other members of the public;
- to provide a service of a lower standard to a disabled person than would be provided to a non-disabled person;
- to make a service available to a disabled person on different terms than it would be provided to a non-disabled person.

Disability Discrimination Act 1995 s.19(1)-(3)

In general it is not unlawful to refuse to provide an able-bodied person with a service which is provided to a disabled person, or to provide a service of a lower standard to an able-bodied person. However such discrimination is unlawful if the able-bodied person has brought or threatened to bring action against the provider of services because the provider discriminated against a disabled person. *ss.19(4), 55*

37.4.2.1
Exceptions

The non-discrimination provisions do not apply if the provider of services can show that providing a different service to a disabled person or refusing to provide a service is justified:

- for reasons of health or safety;
- because the disabled person is not capable of understanding or entering into a contract [see **18.6.2**] or giving informed consent;
- because providing the service, or the same standard of service, to a disabled person or people would mean that the service could not be provided to other people; *and/or*
- because the costs of providing the service to a disabled person are higher, and therefore it is justified to charge a higher rate than is charged to non-disabled people. However, the costs of providing the service cannot take into account any costs incurred because of obligations under s.21 of the Act [see **37.4.3**]. *s.20(4)*

37.4.2.2
Services for people with a specific disability

Charities set up specifically for people defined by reference to a physical or mental capacity may provide services only for those people, even though this discriminates against people with other disabilities. Organisations which provide supported employment may provide it for a specific group or groups of disabled people. *s.10*

37.4.3
Adaptations to services

Providers of goods, services and facilities must take reasonable steps to make their services available to disabled people. This includes, where it is reasonable:

- changing policies, procedures or practices which make it impossible or unreasonably difficult for disabled people to make use of a service;

- providing a service by an alterative method, where physical barriers make it impossible or unreasonably difficult for disabled people to use the service;

- providing auxiliary aids and services to enable disabled people to use a service, such as information on audio tape or a sign language interpreter. *Disability Discrimination Act 1995 s.21*

The duty to make reasonable adjustments is a duty to disabled people *in general*—so the service provider must anticipate the needs of disabled people, and take reasonable steps to meet those needs.

Under these provisions, service providers do not need to make any adaptations to physical features. So there is no obligation, under the provisions in force from October 1999, to make adaptations to the building itself, to the means of access to or exit from the building, or to fixtures, fittings, furnishing, furniture, equipment or materials in or on the premises—but these will have to have been made by 1 October 2004 [see **37.4.4**]. *Disability Discrimination (Services and Premises) Regulations 1999 [SI 1999/1191]*

37.4.3.1
Reasonable adjustments

'Reasonable' is not defined in the Act, and varies according to the type of services being provided, the nature of the service provider and its size and resources. In considering what is reasonable, factors which may be taken into account include:

- whether the steps to be taken would be effective in making it easier for disabled people to access services;

- how practicable it is for the service provider to take the steps;

- financial and other costs of taking the steps;

- disruption caused by taking the steps;

- the service provider's financial and other resources;

- amount already spent on making adjustments;

- availability of financial or other assistance.

37.4.4
Adaptations to premises

The final provisions of the Act come into force on 1 October 2004. Changes must be in place by the implementation date, not starting from that date. Under these provisions service providers must take reasonable steps to remove, alter or provide reasonable means of avoiding physical features that make it impossible or unreasonably difficult for disabled people to use a service, unless the service is provided by a reasonable alternative method. *DDA s.21*

Factors to take into account when considering whether adjustments are reasonable are the same as for adjustments to services [see above].

In many cases, compliance with the Act will require substantial physical alteration of buildings or grounds. This will involve substantial planning by organisations to meet the 2004 deadline, as well as making significant budgetary provision and ensuring that the need for adaptations is considered when taking on new premises.

Where a lease requires the landlord's consent for such alterations, such consent must not be unreasonably withheld. Landlords have only 21 days to reply, after which they are deemed to be withholding their consent unreasonably and the matter may be referred to the county court. The landlord may make the consent subject to one or more reasonable conditions. *s.27, sch.4 pt.II*

If a landlord unreasonably withholds consent and an organisation goes ahead and makes changes to comply with s.21 anyway, the landlord can require reinstatement only if it would have been legally justified in refusing consent in the first place.

37.5
OTHER EQUAL
OPPORTUNITIES
ISSUES

Public authorities and bodies undertaking public functions as defined under the **Human Rights Act 1998** [see **60.3.2**] cannot discriminate in relation to the rights guaranteed under the **European Convention on Human Rights** [see **60.3.1**]. Apart from this, there is currently no legislation in England and Wales covering discrimination on the basis of age, religion, sexual orientation and other grounds in provision of goods, services, facilities or premises.

37.5.1
Religion

Discrimination in service delivery on the basis of religion is not in itself unlawful, except in relation to Convention rights. Where goods or services are available elsewhere, it seems unlikely that refusal to provide them on religious grounds will be a breach of the Human Rights Act.

Discrimination on the basis of religion could be unlawful if the religious group is defined by the courts as an ethnic group as well as a religious group [see **25.8**] so is covered under the Race Relations Act, or if discriminating against or in favour of a particular religious group has the indirect effect of discriminating against or in favour of a racial group. This does not apply to services directly related to worship, or provided by a religious group only or primarily to members of that religious group.

37.5.2
Age

There are often very good reasons for providing services for specific age groups, and this is not unlawful provided it does not breach a Convention right. To avoid possible sex discrimination, any age criteria should be the same for men and women.

37.5.3
Sexual orientation

Discrimination on the basis of sexuality could constitute indirect sex discrimination [see **25.7**] or discrimination in relation to a Convention right. For example services can be provided specifically for gay men *and* lesbians, but any service only for gay men or only for lesbians would have to be within an exception allowed under the Sex Discrimination Act [see **37.3.1**].

It is good practice to ensure that services are welcoming and suitable to gay men and lesbians as well as heterosexuals, and to ensure that assumptions are not made that all service users are heterosexual.

Services funded by local authorities cannot 'promote homosexuality' but they can provide services to gay men and lesbians [see **40.2.5**].

37.5.4
Political and
personal beliefs

It is not unlawful in itself to discriminate against (or in favour of) someone on the basis of their political or personal beliefs. However the European Convention on Human Rights guarantees the right to undertake political activity and the right of freedom of association [see **60.3.1**], and discrimination in service delivery could breach these rights or the right not to be discriminated against in relation to other Convention rights. Implementation of the Human Rights Act is likely to lead to many cases balancing rights of freedom of conscience and expression with rights of privacy and protection from harassment.

Within organisations, the issue of how to deal with members or service users with racist, sexist or other unacceptable beliefs can be very divisive. Many organisations say they do not discriminate on the basis of political beliefs, but this can become problematic if the organisation's members or service users espouse extremist causes. Organisations may seek to clarify their position in a variety of ways, including making it a requirement of membership that all members accept the organisation's commitment to equality of opportunity, and making clear that the organisation's services are available to everyone regardless of their views, but will not be available to anyone who acts in ways which are racist, sexist or otherwise abusive while they are on the organisation's premises or taking part in the organisation's activities.

Chapter 38
CONFIDENTIALITY, PRIVACY, DATA PROTECTION AND FREEDOM OF INFORMATION

Topics covered in this chapter

This chapter explains the Data Protection Act and other issues around confidentiality, privacy, freedom of information and disclosure of information. It covers:

For sources of further information see end of chapter.
Double-underlined section headings indicate additions or significant changes since the first edition.

38.1
CONFIDENTIALITY, PRIVACY AND DISCLOSURE

In considering the information to which an organisation has access, it is important to differentiate between information which:

- there is a legal duty to disclose to the relevant authorities;
- there is a legal obligation to treat as confidential, private and/or protected [see below], and therefore able to be disclosed to third parties in limited circumstances;
- there is a legal duty to disclose to the person to whom it refers; *or*
- as a matter of policy the organisation treats as confidential and limits disclosure.

Especially in organisations where information is particularly sensitive it is sensible to treat risks to information as seriously as risks to health and safety, and to undertake risk assessments and implement protective and preventative measures in a similar way [see **36.3**].

38.1.1
Legal obligations

Legal obligations to maintain confidentiality may arise:

38.1.1.1
Duty to maintain confidentiality

- under statute, including the **Data Protection Act 1998** [see **38.3**] **Human Rights Act 1998** [see **38.1.1.2**], **Freedom of Information Act 2000** [see **38.2**], **Regulation of Investigatory Powers Act 2000** [see **38.1.5**], and **Official Secrets Act 1989**;

- explicitly under a contract, where one or both parties agree not to disclose certain information or use it for other purposes;

- implicitly under a contract, for example in contracts of employment where it is implied [see **23.3.3**] that the employee and employer will keep certain information confidential [see **38.1.6.1**];

- through professional duties or other special relationships, as in the relationship between counsellors and their clients.

Breach of a duty of confidentiality may give rise to a claim for damages, including damages caused by injured feelings, and orders preventing disclosure.

In some circumstances a contractual duty to maintain confidentiality may be overridden by the obligation or right to disclose information [see **29.8** and **38.1.1.3**].

38.1.1.2
Respect for private and family life

Where an organisation is a public authority as defined by the **Human Rights Act 1998** s.6(3) [see **60.3.2**], it is obliged to respect individuals' private and family life, home and correspondence in its decisions and actions. In addition, all UK legislation must now be interpreted in ways which uphold these rights.

Many voluntary and community organisations do not meet the definition of public authority so cannot have a claim under the Human Rights Act brought against them. But such personal information, correspondence, photographs etc may well be protected under the **Data Protection Act 1998** [see **38.3.2**] or by explicit agreement.

38.1.1.3
Duty to disclose information

As well as the duty to maintain confidentiality, there can also be a duty to disclose information. This may arise from:

- a common law duty of care (particularly in relation to children);

- a contractual obligation, for example, where a local authority purchases services from an organisation and requires the organisation to provide certain information—but an organisation must be careful not to enter into funding agreements requiring it to disclose information that it does not have the right to disclose;

- statute, for example the obligation to report drug sales or use [see **38.1.1.8**] or persons who harm or put at risk of harm children or vulnerable adults [see **36.8.2**], and the duty on some organisations to disclose under the **Freedom of Information Act 2000** [see **38.2**].

38.1.1.4
Issues around disclosure

Where there is a duty of confidentiality *and* a legal duty of disclosure (for example, a client disclosing to a counsellor that he or she is abusing a child), the person to whom the duty of confidentiality is owed should generally be informed of the duty of disclosure.

Where there is a duty of confidentiality without a legal duty of disclosure, disclosure without the consent of the person to whom the duty of confidentiality is owed could be a breach of confidentiality. Consent to disclose should be obtained, for example, a counselling client agreeing that the counsellor can discuss him or her in supervision sessions.

Where the organisation has informed clients, service users or others that it has a policy of not disclosing information without the knowledge or consent of the individual, that policy will generally be binding.

Confidentiality should not be promised—or should be promised only with clear exceptions—if legal obligations or the organisation's policy require, or might require, disclosure within the organisation or to an outside body.

Insurance is available to cover claims for inadvertent breach of confidentiality [see **20.5.7**].

38.1.1.5
Disclosure to parents or carers

For organisations which work with children there is no legal obligation to disclose any information to parents, unless such obligation is included as part of the agreement under which the organisation is doing the work. An exception is schools, where specific regulations give parents rights to information about their children. Where an organisation feels it is in the best interests of the child to pass on information to a parent but is uncertain about the confidentiality implications, it should seek advice from the social services child protection team.

For organisations working with adults, there is no legal obligation to pass information to the family or other carers.

38.1.1.6
Disclosure of abuse

In relation to child abuse carried out by persons other than the organisation's staff, the duty of care to the child would generally override any duty of confidentiality to the abuser, and cases of actual or suspected abuse should be reported to the local social services department's child protection team.

Abuse of adults, even if they are vulnerable, by persons other that the organisation's staff is not subject to a legal duty to disclose. If information is obtained subject to confidentiality, disclosure without the consent of the client could be a breach of confidentiality and breach of the Data Protection Act unless the client or another person is at risk of serious imminent harm.

38.1.1.7
Disclosure of abuse by staff

Under the **Protection of Children Act 1999**, **Care Standards Act 2000** and **Criminal Justice and Court Services Act 2000**, some organisations working with children and/or vulnerable adults are required to report to the secretary of state for health any action by a staff member, inside or outside work, which harms or puts at risk a child or vulnerable adult [see **36.8.2**]. Organisations which are not obliged to report have the right to do so, and may be required to do so by funders or by their own policies. This rule applies to all relevant staff, whether paid or unpaid, full- or part-time, permanent or temporary, and staff supplied by employment agencies or employment businesses.

38.1.1.8
Disclosure to police

Unless the police have a witness or search order, there is no general legal obligation to disclose information or allow access to the police, nor is there in general any obligation to pass on knowledge of a crime. However it is a criminal offence:

- deliberately to mislead the police;

- to receive a reward of any kind in return for not notifying the police about a criminal act; *Criminal Law Act 1967*

- not to notify the police about an act which could be construed as an act of terrorism [see **41.6**]; *Terrorism Act 2000 s.19*

- not to notify the police about an act which could be construed as drug trafficking. *Criminal Justice Act 1993 s.16*

Failure to reveal information to the police about the sale, distribution, production or use of illegal drugs may be seen as evidence of a lack of willingness to take reasonable steps to prevent drug misuse [see **59.5.3**].

Police with a search warrant can search for 'relevant evidence' to help in detection of crime. An organisation faced with police requests for legally confidential information should seek legal advice.

Where a crime is committed against an organisation or the organisation becomes aware of a crime, factors to consider include:

- insurance policies require notification to police before they will pay out on theft, burglary or similar claims;

- charity trustees' responsibility to safeguard the charity's assets [see **13.3.5**] should be considered before making any decision not to report a theft or similar act to the police;

- funders or supporters may react negatively if they discover that a criminal act known to the organisation has not been reported.

Complex internal debates can arise if, for example, an organisation is obliged for insurance purposes to notify the police about a theft which involves service users.

For disciplinary issues arising from criminal acts by employees see **29.4.13**, and for issues around dismissal see **30.4.7** and **30.8.4**.

38.1.1.9
Disclosure to court

The courts have power to require disclosure of confidential information in some situations, but some information is **privileged** and may not have to be revealed. Legal advice is necessary in this situation.

38.1.2
Confidentiality policies

In addition to ensuring compliance with its legal duties, organisations generally want to protect a wide range of information from disclosure. A **confidentiality policy** can make clear to everyone involved:

- what information is held by the organisation, why it is held, how long it is held and how it is used;

- what information is protected as **personal data** under the Data Protection Act [see **38.3.2**], what has further protection as **sensitive data** [see **38.3.4.2**], and what may not be covered under the Act but is considered confidential because the organisation and/or individuals involved believe it should be;

- who within the organisation has access to various types of information, and whether such access is automatic or needs to be authorised in each instance;

- the circumstances, if any, under which information is disclosed to parties outside the organisation, and the procedure to authorise such disclosure;

- procedures for compliance with the **Data Protection Act 1998** [see **38.3**] and, if applicable, the **Human Rights Act 1998** [see **38.1.1.2**] and **Freedom of Information Act 2000** [see **38.2**];

- links between the organisation's confidentiality policy and its whistleblowing policy [see **29.8**];

- penalties for breach of confidentiality.

A confidentiality policy, contract, or other agreement with a worker cannot prevent, or seek to prevent, the worker from making a disclosure which is protected under the **Public Interest Disclosure Act 1998**.

Employment Rights Act 1996 s.43J

38.1.3
Confidential information about individuals

Virtually all organisations which keep information about recognisable individuals, whether on computer or paper, must comply with the data protection principles [see **38.3.4**], and some may have to notify (register) under the Data Protection Act [see **38.3.8**].

Regardless of whether information about individuals is kept on computer or paper, issues may arise around:

- whether to allow the person to limit the purposes for which his or her personal information is used;

- whether to obtain information from third parties, and if so whether and how to check it with the individual concerned;

- under what circumstances personal information can be passed on to third parties, how the person concerned is informed, and how his or her consent is obtained;

- who within the organisation has the right to know sensitive information about individuals;

- whether to keep a record in the person's file of everyone to whom sensitive information has been passed on.

38.1.4
Confidential information about employees

Employers have an implied duty to maintain the employee's trust and confidence [see **23.3.3**], which includes not disclosing information about them. The duties of employers are clarified in a data protection code of practice on the use of personal data (not only confidential information) in employer/employee relationships, which at the time of writing was expected to be published by the information commissioner (the renamed data protection commissioner) in late 2001. The code may, in particular, require changes in the use of information collected as part of the staff recruitment process.

The duty of confidentiality to employees does not extend to withholding information which there is a statutory obligation to disclose to the police or other authorities [see **38.1.1.8** and **38.1.1.7**].

38.1.5
Monitoring staff communications

In general it is an offence to intercept telephone calls, email or other telecommunications. However employers have wide powers to monitor such communications to or from staff, without the consent of either the staff member or the other party, where it is done to:

- collect facts or evidence;

- ensure compliance with internal or external rules or regulations;

- monitor standards;

- ensure the effective operation of the employer's systems, for example to prevent computer viruses;

- prevent or detect crime;

- investigate or detect unauthorised use of the organisation's computer or telephone systems. *Telecommunications (Lawful Business Practice) (Interception of Communications) Regulations 2000 [SI 2000/2699]*

Although the employer does not need to obtain explicit consent for such monitoring, it must make all reasonable efforts to inform employees, volunteers and other potential users of the system that such monitoring may be undertaken. This may be done by, for example, having a recorded message that calls may be monitored, including a message in emails saying that emails may be monitored, and including a clause in contracts of employment and volunteer agreements stating that calls, email and other telecommunications may be monitored [see **24.46**].

In other situations it is an offence for the organisation to monitor telecommunications unless:

- both the sender and recipient have given explicit consent, or the organisation has reasonable grounds to believe they have given consent; *or*

- the communication is made on a secure internal system within the organisation, such as a secure office intranet or a purely internal telephone system. *Regulation of Investigatory Powers Act 2000 ss.1, 2*

Any monitoring, whether of telecommunications or other communications, must not breach rights protected by the **Human Rights Act 1998** [see **60.3.1**], and organisations should take legal advice before undertaking monitoring.

All information obtained through monitoring must comply with duties relating to confidential information [see **38.1.3** and **38.1.4**]. If it is subsequently stored or used, the processing must comply with data protection rules [see **38.3**].

38.1.5.1
Policy on staff communications

It is good practice for organisations to draw up policies or codes of practice on staff use of telephones, email and the internet. These should encourage responsible behaviour and good management practice and should safeguard staff privacy, while enabling employers to protect their legitimate interests. The policy should make clear that:

- office and mobile telephones, fax, email, internet and computer systems must be used only for the organisation's purposes, or may be used for personal use to the extent authorised by the organisation;

- telephone calls, emails and other communications may be monitored by the employer as permitted by the **Telecommunications (Lawful Business Practice) Regulations** [see above];

- permitted confidential and personal telephone calls or emails, such as between trade union representatives and members, will not be monitored or read by managers;

- emails containing libellous, racist, sexually explicit or other inappropriate material must not be sent or forwarded;

- emails must not be sent anonymously, and must not be sent in a way that makes them appear to come from another sender;

- email must not be regarded as secure, and information about clients, employees, contract tenders, legal matters, financial and similar confidential or sensitive information should not be sent by email except in specific situations where it is authorised;

- the organisation's credit card numbers, PIN numbers, internet or other passwords and similar information must never be disclosed in emails or used on the internet unless such use is authorised;

- staff should be aware of the risk of creating or varying contracts by email;

- all email communications belong to the employer;

- all incoming and outgoing emails must be printed out and kept, and/or must be retained on the computer for a specified period;

- use of the internet may be monitored;

- copyright material, including software, must not be downloaded from the internet unless such downloading is allowed, and where material is downloaded it must be used only as allowed;

- unauthorised or unreasonable use of systems is or may be a disciplinary matter, and use for any obscene, racist, unlawful or similar purpose may constitute gross misconduct justifying summary dismissal [see **29.4.12**];

- virus protection systems must be operational at all times;

- emails, computer files etc may be checked by others, for example if a worker is unexpectedly absent or has gone on leave without leaving forwarding arrangements.

Where telephone calls are monitored, it is good practice for the organisation to provide separate lines (which may be payphones) for private use by staff.

To avoid disputes about whether employees and volunteers have been notified that communications will be monitored, it is good practice to have them sign the policy, or for a clause stating that communications will or may be monitored to be included in the contract of employment or volunteer agreement. The policy itself should not be contractual, as the employer is likely to need to change it over time.

38.1.6
The employer's information and know-how

Employees' disclosure or use of information gained during their employment is a complex area, and legal advice should be sought before taking action in any specific situation. A court can grant an injunction restraining the employee, and anyone the employee has disclosed the information to, from making use of the information, and can grant damages to the employer for breach of contract.

An employer's right to take action to prevent an employee or former employee disclosing or using information depends on:

- the employee's job and the type of information involved;

- express (explicit) terms of the employee's contract of employment;

- whether it was made clear that the information was confidential;

- whether the relevant information can be easily isolated from other information which the employee is free to use or disclose;

- whether the person involved is a current or former employee;

- whether the information was available from other sources.

38.1.6.1
Current employees

During employment, employees are bound by any express clauses in their contract imposing duties to keep information confidential, as well as the implied duties:

- of confidentiality, which usually covers general information about the employer's business and **know-how** (the employer's processes and procedures) as well as trade secrets;

- to act in good faith and to act honestly;

- not to compete with the employer [see **23.3.3**].

An employer therefore has quite extensive rights to prevent current employees disclosing or misusing information acquired from their employment.

Some judges define **trade secrets** narrowly to include only secret formulae and processes, but others define them as any information used by an organisation which, if disclosed, would be liable to cause real or significant damage to the organisation. This could include, for example, the names of customers or the contents of the next catalogue. Voluntary organisations' most valuable information may be about sources of funding, donors, successful campaigns and ongoing research. It is impossible to say generally whether this type of information could amount to a trade secret, and legal advice should be sought if a problem arises or is likely to arise.

38.1.6.2
Former employees

The restrictions after employment are generally less far-reaching. The employer may seek to include express clauses in the contract which restrict use after the contract has terminated of information acquired during the term of the contract, or restrict the employee's right to compete. Generally only clauses which restrict use of genuinely confidential information and trade secrets are enforceable [see **24.41**].

Ex-employees are also generally bound by:

- a more limited implied duty of confidentiality;

- the fact that all work done by employees during the course of their employment belongs to the employer [see **39.2.3** and **39.6.1**];

- the fact that employees are likely to infringe copyright if they take reports, databases, computer programs or other material [see **39.2**].

Apart from this, employees are largely free to use information they carry away in their head. Therefore one of the key issues in any case is what constitutes a trade secret of the employer, which may be defined narrowly or quite widely [see **38.1.6.1**].

38.1.6.3
Protecting information

Sensible steps to protect sensitive or confidential information include:

- having a clear and comprehensive confidentiality policy, and ensuring all employees, volunteers, agency staff, self-employed workers and others understand how it applies to their work;

- marking documents and envelopes as confidential;

- being aware of when information is at risk of exposure, for example when it is being photocopied or is in view on a desk or screen;

- restricting circulation of confidential material;

- having safe storage for paper and computerised confidential information, and shredding documents before disposal;

- disclosing confidential information to third parties only if they have signed confidentiality undertakings;

- including express confidentiality clauses in employee contracts [see **24.45** for sample clause] and in contracts with self-employed people and other contractors;

- requiring employees who work on a particularly sensitive project to sign specific confidentiality agreements which extend after their contract of employment terminates [see **24.41**].

38.1.7
Unlawful acts

38.1.7.1
By the employer or employees

In general an employee cannot breach confidentiality by revealing information about the employer's activities, or activities carried out by employees on behalf of the employer. But where disclosure would disclose or prevent malpractice or an unlawful act, the **Public Interest Disclosure Act 1998** protects employees and workers from victimisation or dismissal if they reveal such information [see **29.8**].

38.1.7.2
By service users or others

Even where there may not be a statutory duty to disclose unlawful acts to the police [see **38.1.1.8**], voluntary organisations and their staff should not ignore or condone lawbreaking. In particular, it is an offence knowingly to permit or allow premises to be used for the sale or distribution of illegal drugs, or the preparation or smoking of opium or cannabis [see **59.5.3**]. To protect itself the organisation should have clear policies setting out:

- what is not allowed on the premises or while taking part in the organisation's activities, especially in relation to violence, harassment, drugs, alcohol, weapons and items which could be used as weapons;

- procedures for ensuring good supervision of all areas used for the organisation's activities;

- what staff, including volunteers and self-employed workers, and service users or members of the organisation or governing body should do if they become aware of unlawful acts or acts which contravene the organisation's policies;

- who is authorised to deal with the wrongdoing;

- sanctions for wrongdoing, which may range from warnings to a ban;

- situations in which the police must be notified or may be notified;

- who is authorised to contact the police or other authorities;

- clear and detailed record-keeping procedures, including records of action taken;

- implications for staff and service users of not complying with the organisation's policies and procedures.

38.2
FREEDOM OF INFORMATION

The **Freedom of Information Act 2000** will be implemented gradually, starting with central government in mid-2002, and will be fully implemented by 30 November 2005. When implemented it will provide a general right of access, although with significant exceptions, to information held by **public authorities** in the course of carrying out their **public functions**. At the time of writing (early 2001), regulations were expected to be passed defining charities and other voluntary organisations as public authorities if they appear to carry out public functions, or if they provide contractual services to a public authority where the provision of that service is one of the functions of the authority.

Freedom of Information Act 2000 s.5(1)

38.2.1
Right of access

Any person or body, even if not a UK resident or national, will be able to apply to any public authority for information. A fee may be payable. In most cases the applicant must be told, within a specified period ranging from 20 to 60 days, whether the information requested is held by that authority (the duty to confirm or deny whether it holds information) and, if the information is held, to have it communicated to him or her. Where the authority does not reply or does not provide the information the applicant may apply to the **information tribunal**.

ss.1, 8-10

38.2.2
Publication schemes

Public authorities must publish and comply with schemes relating to the publication of information. These may be off-the-shelf schemes approved by the information commissioner (the renamed data protection commissioner) or others, or may be drawn up by individual authorities and approved by the commissioner. Schemes must specify the classes of information the authority publishes or intends to publish, the manner of publication, and whether the information is available to the public free of charge or on payment. Material made available in accordance with a publication scheme is exempt from the right of access, so the authority does not have to respond to requests for it on an individual basis. *Freedom of Information Act 2000 ss.19-20*

38.2.3 Exemptions

There are many exemptions to the right of access, where the authority does not have to confirm or deny whether it holds information or communicate the information. Exemptions apply, for example, to:

- information available to the public in other ways, for example under a publication scheme [see above];

- information which could be prejudicial to national security, defence, international relations, or law enforcement;

- information defined as personal data under the Data Protection Act [see **38.3.2**];

- information held by a government department that relates to the formulation or development of government policy, or other information held by public bodies 'if, in the reasonable opinion of a qualified person, its disclosure would prejudice the effective conduct of public affairs'. *ss.21-44*

Information about the Act and its application to voluntary organisations is available from the Campaign for Freedom of Information and the Freedom of Information Unit in the Lord Chancellor's Department [see end of chapter].

38.3 DATA PROTECTION

The **Data Protection Act 1998** applies to **personal data**. This is information about identifiable living individuals (**data subjects**) held on computer (including websites) or other electronic equipment with automatic retrieval, and information held in paper-based record-keeping systems or other records (such as microfiche) where information about a specific individual can be readily located. Under the **Freedom of Information Act** [see above], personal data held by a public authority which does not fall within this definition will also be covered.

Organisations or individuals which hold personal data are **data controllers**. Many data controllers which hold personal data on computer must **notify** (register) under the Act [see **38.3.8**]. All data controllers, even if they do not have to notify, must comply with the **data protection principles** [see **38.3.4**] and other provisions of the Act.

The 1998 Act replaced the **Data Protection Act 1984**, and includes transitional periods during which systems in place on 23 October 1998 can comply with either the old Act or the new. Unless indicated otherwise, the information below relates to the 1998 Act.

The wide-ranging obligations under the Act, and particularly the rights of access, mean that organisations need to review the information they hold, whether they really need to keep it, how it is stored, who has access to it, how it is used, how long it is kept, and how it is destroyed.

Information about data protection is available from the Office of the Information Commissioner [see end of chapter for details] and in *Data Protection for Voluntary Organisations* (Directory of Social Change). The Data Protection Act is complex, and at the time of writing it was unclear how some of the provisions would be interpreted. Specialist advice should be sought if there is any doubt about how the Act applies, especially in relation to sensitive personal data [see **38.3.4.2**] or people's right to see and amend information held about them [see **38.3.6**].

38.3.1 Transitional provisions

The 1998 Act includes two transitional periods until its provisions are fully implemented. The first ends on 23 October 2001, the second on 23

October 2007. These transitional arrangements apply only to systems in place on 23 October 1998. Where the transitional provisions apply, organisations can start to operate under the 1998 Act at any time prior to the end of the relevant transitional period.

38.3.1.1
Until 23 October 2001

During the first transitional period the rules were relaxed in relation to manual (paper) data, data held on computer solely for the purposes of operating a payroll or keeping accounts, straightforward membership information held on computer by unincorporated membership organisations, and the right to object to the use of data for direct marketing. These relaxations end on 23 October 2001.

Data Protection Act 1998 sch.8 pt.II

38.3.1.2
Until 23 October 2007

Manual (paper) data that was held by the organisation on 23 October 1998 does not have to comply with most of the data protection principles [see **38.3.4**] until October 2007. Information added to the filing systems between 24 October 1998 and 23 October 2001 must comply with all the principles by 24 October 2001. Information added after 23 October 2001 must comply with all the principles as soon as it is added.   *sch.8 pt.III*

38.3.2
Personal data

The Data Protection Act applies only to **personal data**. This is any information from which a living individual can be identified, either directly or from other information held by or likely to be held by the data controller. If, for example, information is identified by code numbers but the organisation has a list linking each number with a name, the coded information is personal data. Data can be personal even if the organisation does not keep any name; for example a street number and postcode can be enough, combined with the electoral register, to identify an individual.   *s.1(1)*

Personal data does not have to be written. It includes visual, photographic, audio, biometric and other non-text data.

38.3.2.1
Retrieval and
filing systems

All information from which living individuals can be identified is personal data if it is used on, kept on or intended to go onto a computer or other electronic retrieval system.

If it is kept on paper, it is personal data only if it is in, or is intended to go into, a **relevant filing system**. This is a system containing a set of data, structured by name of individual or by other criteria which make information relating to a specific individual readily accessible.   *s.1(1)*

Other manual data may not be covered. This could include, for example, information kept in date order, where there is no cross-referencing system linking individuals to the date files.

The Office of the Information Commissioner provides guidance for determining whether manual data is or is not covered by the Act. However this guidance states that a key factor in deciding whether to treat data as within the Act is the extent of possible damage or prejudice to an individual if data protection principles are not observed. Using this criterion, *all* personal files, however 'unstructured', should be treated as falling within the Act.

For bodies defined under the **Freedom of Information Act 2000** as public authorities [see **38.2**], all information about individuals, even in unstructured systems, is covered by the Data Protection Act.

Freedom of Information Act 2000 ss.68-72

38.3.3
Data controllers and
data processors

Processing includes obtaining, recording, holding or carrying out any operation on information. Operations include organising, changing, retrieving, consulting, using, disclosing, erasing or destroying data.

A data **controller** is an organisation or individual which decides, either on its own or with others, how data is to be processed and the purposes for which it is to be used.

An organisation or individual which handles information on behalf of a data controller, but has no say in how the information is collected or used, is a **data processor**. Examples of data processors are payroll services, external fundraisers, or mailing houses.

The data controller must be satisfied that the data processor has adequate security [see **38.3.4**], and must have a written contract requiring the data processor to comply with these security obligations.

Data Protection Act 1998 sch.1 pt.II para.11

38.3.3.1
Employees and volunteers

Employees who handle information on behalf of their employer are not data processors. Although the Act does not explicitly mention volunteers, the information commissioner has said that they are not data processors in relation to the organisation for which they volunteer.

38.3.3.2
Joint activities

Where organisations undertake joint activities with other bodies, it is essential to establish who is or are the data controller(s) and who, if anyone, is a data processor, and how their relationship is regulated.

38.3.4
Data protection principles

All data controllers must comply with the eight **data protection principles**. The principles say that personal data must:

- be processed lawfully and fairly [see **38.3.4.1**];
- be obtained only for one or more specified and lawful purposes, and not be further processed in any manner incompatible with that purpose or those purposes;
- be adequate, relevant and not excessive in relation to the purpose(s) for which it is held;
- be accurate and, where necessary, be kept up to date;
- be held no longer than is necessary for the specified purpose(s);
- be processed in accordance with the rights of data subjects [see **38.3.6**];
- be held securely, with appropriate technical and organisational measures taken to prevent unauthorised or unlawful processing of personal data, and to prevent accidental loss or destruction of, or damage to, personal data;
- not be transferred to a country or territory outside the European Economic Area, unless that country or territory ensures an adequate level of protection for data subjects in relation to the processing of personal data.   *sch.1*

38.3.4.1
Conditions for fair processing

In order for data to be fairly processed (obtained, stored, used and/or destroyed), the data subject must know who is collecting it, why they are collecting it, what they intend to do with it, and to whom it might be disclosed. The data controller may specify the purpose(s) by notification to the information commissioner [see **38.3.8**], or directly to the data subject. Even where the purpose has been notified to the information commissioner, it is good practice to inform the data subject unless it is obvious from the context in which the data is collected.

The processing must comply with the data protection principles [see **38.3.4**], and must also meet at least one of the conditions set out in schedule 2 of the Act. If it does not meet one of the following conditions, the processing is automatically unfair.

- The data subject has given consent to the processing. This consent may be explicit, or may be implicit where the purpose is obvious, for example, a trainee at a training project giving information about his or her previous education and work experience.

- The processing is necessary to carry out a contract to which the data subject is a party—for example to buy goods or services from, or provide goods or services under contract to, the data subject—or for taking steps at the request of the data subject with a view to entering into a contract.

- The data controller needs to process the data in order to comply with a legal obligation, other than a contractual obligation.

- The processing is necessary to protect the vital interests of the data subject.

- The processing is necessary for the administration of justice or for government or other functions of a public nature.

- The processing is necessary for the legitimate interests of the data controller or of a third party to whom the information is disclosed. This condition is not valid where the processing or disclosure could prejudice the rights or interests of the data subject.

Data Protection Act 1998 sch.2

38.3.4.2
Sensitive personal data

Further requirements apply to the processing of **sensitive personal data**, consisting of information relating to:

- the data subject's racial or ethnic origin;

- the data subject's political opinions;

- religious beliefs or other beliefs of a similar nature;

- trade union membership;

- physical or mental health or condition;

- sexual life;

- commission or alleged commission by the data subject of any offence;

- any proceedings for any offence committed or allegedly committed by the data subject, the disposal of such proceedings or the court's sentence in any such proceedings.   *s.2*

Before a data controller can process sensitive data, one of the conditions relating to all personal data [see above] must be met. In addition, at least one of the following criteria must be met.

- The data subject has given *explicit* consent. Explicit is not defined, but is likely to mean the data subject has given written consent to the specific purposes for which the data is held, or has given verbal consent which is confirmed in writing by the data controller.

- The data controller must process the information in order to comply with a legal requirement relating to employment.

- The processing is necessary to protect the vital interests of the data subject or another person where consent cannot be given by or on behalf of the data subject, or the data controller cannot reasonably be expected to obtain the data subject's consent.

- The processing is necessary in order to protect the vital interests of another person, but consent by or on behalf of the data subject has been unreasonably withheld.

- The processing is carried out by a non-profit political, religious or philosophical body or a trade union, relates only to members of the organisation or others who have regular contact with it, does not involve disclosure of the personal data to a third party without the data subject's consent, and is carried out with appropriate safeguards for the data subjects' rights and freedoms. This condition does not apply to other voluntary, non-profit or charitable organisations.

- The data subject has deliberately made public the sensitive data, for example where a person stands as a candidate for a political party, and thus makes public his or her political affiliation.

- The processing is necessary in connection with legal proceedings, or to obtain legal advice, or to establish, exercise or defend legal rights.

- The processing is necessary for the administration of justice or to carry out government functions.

- The processing is necessary for medical purposes and is carried out by a health professional or a person who is under an equivalent duty of confidentiality.

• Information relating to racial or ethnic origin is collected and used only for equal opportunities monitoring.

Data Protection Act 1998 sch.3

Further conditions which may be met include:

• Information relating to physical or mental health or condition, or to religious or similar belief, is collected and used only for the purposes of monitoring and promoting or maintaining equality of opportunity. The data controller must comply with any written request from a data subject not to process this information about him or her.

• Sensitive personal data is processed solely for the purposes of research. It must not be used in making decisions or taking action in relation to any data subject unless the data subject gives explicit consent.

• The processing is in the substantial public interest; is necessary in order to provide confidential counselling, advice, support or any other service; and is carried out without the explicit consent of the data subject because the data subject cannot give consent, or it is not reasonable to expect the data controller to obtain the explicit consent of the data subject, or seeking such consent would jeopardise the provisions of the service.

• The information is necessary for specific purposes connected with establishing, administering, or determining eligibility for benefits under an occupational pension scheme.

• The processing is in the substantial public interest, is necessary in order to prevent or detect an unlawful act, and seeking the explicit consent of the data subject would prejudice that purpose.

• The processing is in the substantial public interest, is necessary in order to protect the public from dishonesty, malpractice, incompetence or seriously improper conduct by an individual or organisation, or to protect the public from mismanagement or failures in service provided by any organisation, and seeking the explicit consent of the data subject would prejudice that purpose.

• The information meets the above criterion and is processed by a journalist, with a view towards publication which the data controller reasonably believes is in the public interest.

Data Protection (Processing of Sensitive Personal Data) Order 2000
[SI 2000/417]

38.3.5
Disclosure

A data controller may disclose information about individuals to third parties only if the disclosure is fair, is compatible with the purpose for which the data is held, falls within one of the conditions for fair processing [see **38.3.4.1**], and in the case of sensitive personal data falls within one of the conditions for fair processing of sensitive personal data [see **38.3.4.2**]. A disclosure may not be fair if the data subject was not aware that disclosure of that type might take place, and almost certainly is not fair if consent was sought but was withheld.

38.3.5.1
Non-disclosure
exemptions

The data controller may (but in most cases does not have to) disclose data, even if such disclosure is unfair or incompatible with the purpose, in order to assist the prevention or detection of crime, apprehension or prosecution of offenders, or assessment or collection of tax or duty. Such disclosure must not breach schedules 2 or 3.

Data Protection Act 1998 ss.27(3),(4), 29(3)

A statutory duty to disclose to the police or other authorities [see **38.1.1.8** and **38.1.1.7**] overrides data protection obligations.

38.3.6
Subject access

Individuals have a **subject access right** to information about themselves, and a right to have the data corrected or deleted. A request must be made in writing by the data subject to the data controller. The data controller may charge up to £10. The request must be answered within

40 days of receiving the fee (if any) and all the information the data controller is entitled to. *Data Protection Act 1998 s.7*

Where answering the request would involve the disclosure of information relating to another individual (including identifying a person as the source of the information), the data controller does not have to comply with the request unless the other individual has consented to the disclosure, or it is reasonable in all the circumstances to comply with the request without the consent of the other individual. Even if it is not possible to provide all the requested information to the data subject, the data controller must still provide as much of the information as it can without disclosing the identity of the other person—for example by leaving out names or other identifying details. *s. 7(4),(5)*

With references, for example, the data subject is very likely to be able to identify the writer, so will have a right to see the reference only if the writer agrees. If another individual, such as a manager, can be identified from the reference, that person will also have to give consent.

The criteria used in determining whether it is reasonable to comply with a request for subject access without the consent of the other individual are:

- any duty of confidentiality owed to the other individual;
- any steps taken by the data controller to seek the consent of the other individual;
- whether the other individual is capable of giving consent; *and*
- any explicit refusal of consent by the other individual. *s. 7(6)*

An individual may seek compensation from the data controller if he or she suffers damage because information is inaccurate, has been lost, or has been destroyed or disclosed without this being authorised by the data controller.

38.3.6.1
Exceptions

Data subjects do not have access to data about themselves held only for the purposes of preparing statistics or carrying out research, where individuals cannot be identified in the final statistics or research.

s.33(4)

Access to personal data about the physical or mental health of a data subject held or recorded by a health professional may be withheld if the disclosure would be likely to cause serious harm to the physical or mental health of the data subject, or would be likely to lead the data subject to identify another person who has not consented to the disclosure of his or her identity. *Data Protection (Subject Access Modification) (Health) Order 2000 [SI 2000/413]*

Similarly some social work agencies, specified in regulations, have the right not to allow access to a data subject where the disclosure would be likely to cause serious harm to the physical or mental health or emotional condition of the data subject or any other person, or would be likely to lead to identification of another individual who has not consented to the disclosure of his or her identity. *Data Protection (Subject Access Modification) (Social Work) Order 2000 [SI 2000/415]*

Disclosure of information in adoption records and reports and statements and records of the special educational needs of children is prohibited or restricted. *Data Protection (Miscellaneous Subject Access Exemptions) Order 2000 [SI 2000/419] and (Amendment) Order 2000 [SI 2000/1865]*

38.3.7
Right to prevent use of data

Individuals may prevent a data controller from using information about them in certain ways:

- where the data controller requires the data subject to give consent for data processing under schedule 2 [see **38.3.4.1**] or explicit consent under schedule 3 [see **38.3.4.2**], the individual can refuse to give this consent;

- there is an absolute right to prevent the use of personal data for direct marketing [see **38.4.1**];

- individuals cannot be sent unsolicited direct marketing faxes [see **38.4.3**], and have the right to opt out of unsolicited direct marketing telephone calls [see **38.4.2**].

In addition, an individual can at any time prevent a data controller from using his or her personal data, where the use of that information would cause substantial and unwarranted damage or distress to him or herself or to another person. The request must be in writing, and the data controller must reply within 21 days stating whether it intends to stop the data processing, and if not why not.   *Data Protection Act 1998 s.10*

Where significant decisions about an individual are made solely on the basis of automated processes, the individual can require the data controller not to make decisions about himself or herself solely on this basis. This includes, for example, automated employment selection processes and creditworthiness scoring.   *s.12*

38.3.8
Notification

Unless all information kept on computer is exempt [see below], the organisation must **notify** the information commissioner, and must renew its registration every year. The fee is £35 (as at 1/4/01). It is an offence not to notify if required to do so.

The initial application for notification is made by telephone (01625-545740) or over the internet (www.dpr.gov.uk), and a partially completed application form is then provided. To complete the application, the data controller must choose the purpose(s) for which the data will be used, the data subjects for each purpose, data classes, and potential recipients of data. Options are provided, but if these do not fit, the data controller can make up its own entry.

Notification does not constitute any guarantee that data is being processed properly.

38.3.8.1
Exemptions from notification

An organisation does not have to notify (register) under the Data Protection Act if it keeps its information about individuals only on paper. Even if it keeps personal data on computer, it does not have to notify if all of its information is within the following categories:

- it keeps data about prospective, current or past employees, workers [see **22.1.2** for definition] or volunteers, and uses it only for appointment, dismissal, pay, discipline, superannuation, work management and other personnel purposes;   *Data Protection (Notification and Notification Fees) Regulations 2000 [SI 2000/188] sch. para.2*

- it keeps data about past, current or prospective customers or suppliers, and uses the data only to keep accounts or keep records of sales and purchases in order to ensure that the appropriate payments or deliveries are made, and/or uses the data to advertise or market the organisation's business, activities, goods or services or to promote public relations in connection with the organisation's activities, goods or services; *and/or*   *sch. para.3, 4*

- the organisation is a non-profit body and the data is used only to establish or maintain membership of or support for the organisation, or to provide or administer activities for individuals who are members or have regular contact with the organisation.   *sch. para.5*

In addition to the organisation meeting one or more of the above criteria for all personal data held on computer:

- the organisation must not disclose the information to any third party unless it is for the relevant exempt purpose or the data subject has given consent to the disclosure; *and*

- after the organisation's relationship with the individual has ended, the data must not be kept any longer than is necessary to carry out the relevant exempt purposes.

If the organisation keeps any other personal data on computer, or uses it for any other purposes, it is not exempt from notification.

Under the 1984 Act, organisations exempt from registering did not have to comply with the data protection principles or other requirements of the Act. This is not the case under the 1998 Act. Organisations exempt from notifying must comply with all aspects of the Act, apart from the obligation to notify.

38.3.9
The register

The **register of data controllers** is compiled from the application form and is at www.dpr.gov.uk. A certified copy of an entry may be obtained from the commissioner. The fee is £2 (as at 1/4/01).

38.3.10
Redress

Anyone can ask the information commissioner to carry out an **assessment** as to whether a data controller is carrying out the processing of personal data in compliance with the Act. If a data controller is contravening the Act, a data subject may complain to the information commissioner. The commissioner has powers to obtain warrants to enter and search premises, serve **information notices** requiring information to be provided, and serve **enforcement notices** requiring action.

A data subject may subsequently appeal to the information tribunal and, on questions of law, may make a further appeal to the High Court.

38.4
DIRECT MARKETING AND TELEMARKETING

The **Data Protection Act 1998**, telecommunications regulations [see **38.4.2**], and distance selling regulations [see **18.7.3**] introduced significant new protections for individuals and organisations in relation to direct marketing. The converse of these protections is a significant restriction on some forms of fundraising, marketing and possibly some forms of volunteer recruitment.

38.4.1
Direct marketing

Direct marketing is defined as 'the communication (by whatever means) of any advertising or marketing material which is directed to particular individuals'. This includes fundraising and soliciting support, as well as more obvious direct marketing of goods and services, and may also include direct approaches to individuals to recruit them as volunteers. It covers approaches made by post, fax, telephone, email or any other method directed to a named individual.

Personal data cannot be used for direct marketing unless this purpose has been specified when the information was collected [see **38.3.4.1**]. Even where this purpose was specified, an individual may at any time require the data controller to stop using, or not start using, his or her personal data for the purposes of direct marketing. As this is an absolute right, people should be given the right to opt out of receiving direct marketing materials, for example by putting a tick box on order forms or donation forms. Failure to offer this option may constitute unfair data processing [see **38.3.4.1**].   *Data Protection Act 1998 s.11*

As well as opting out of direct mail from specific organisations, individuals may opt out completely from some or all types of direct mail through the **Mailing Preference Service** [see end of chapter].

38.4.2
Direct marketing telephone calls

An individual, partnership or unincorporated organisation may opt out of receiving unsolicited direct marketing telephone calls by registering with the **Telephone Preference Service** [see end of chapter]. There is no charge for registration. Incorporated bodies cannot opt out of unsolicited telephone calls.

An organisation intending to make direct marketing telephone calls must check all the numbers it intends to ring against the numbers in the TPS register, or obtain software to suppress calls to registered numbers. This includes numbers from the organisation's own database, from other lists, or from public sources such as the telephone directory. The only numbers that do not have to be checked are those where the individual, partnership or unincorporated organisation has given explicit consent to receive direct marketing calls from the caller, or where the call is made to an incorporated body. Information about how to suppress calls to registered numbers and how to obtain the TPS register on disk or other electronic media is on the TPS website.

Telecommunications (Data Protection and Privacy) Regulations 1999 [SI 1999/2093], pt.V

It is an offence, punishable by a fine of up to £5,000, for an organisation to make an unsolicited direct marketing call to anyone who has opted out through TPS, unless the person being called has explicitly given consent for the organisation to make such calls to them.

38.4.3
Direct marketing faxes

It is an offence to send an unsolicited direct marketing fax to any individual, partnership or unincorporated organisation. There is no need for them to have opted out. Incorporated bodies may opt of receiving unsolicited faxes by registering with the **Fax Preference Service** [see box below]. Persons sending direct marketing faxes must check the numbers in the same way as for telemarketing calls [see above].   *pt.V*

38.4.4
Direct marketing email

The telecommunications regulations do not apply to the use of telephone lines for sending unsolicited direct marketing emails (often called 'spam'). However an individual can require a specific data controller to stop sending direct marketing emails [see **38.4.1**], and can register with the non-statutory **E-mail Preference Service** [see box below].

Email addresses are personal data under the Data Protection Act, so cannot be used or passed on to third parties unless these purposes have been specified to the data subject.

As well as contravening data protection legislation, use of the internet to send spam could be a breach of the sender's contract with their internet service provider (ISP).

38.4.5
Sale or provision of lists

The sale or provision of lists, including lists of email addresses, for direct marketing or any other purpose, or the compilation of personal data into directories, is unlawful unless the person has been informed that the data will be used in this way. The sale of lists also constitutes trading, and there may be implications for tax [see **52.4.1**] and VAT [see **53.5**].

FOR FURTHER INFORMATION

Data protection. Office of the Information Commissioner: 01625-545745; www.dataprotection.gov.uk

Direct marketing. Direct Marketing Association, 020-7321 2525; www.dma.org.uk

E-mail Preference Service: www.e-mps.org

Fax Preference Service: 0845-070 0702; www.fpsonline,org.uk

Mailing Preference Service: 020-7766 4410

Telephone Preference Service: 0845-070 0707; www.tpsonline.org.uk

Freedom of information. Lord Chancellor's Department: 020-7210 8500; www.lcd.gov.uk

Campaign for Freedom of Information: 020-7831 7477; www.cfoi.org.uk

Chapter 39
INTELLECTUAL PROPERTY

39.1 INTELLECTUAL PROPERTY RIGHTS

Intellectual property (IP) refers to non-tangible assets such as names, goodwill and rights arising from the creation and invention of new products and creative works. Most intellectual property is protected by various legal rights, some of which arise automatically and some of which are effective only if registered.

Rights which exist without registration are:

- copyright [see **39.2**];
- database right [see **39.2.7**];
- moral rights arising from copyright [see **39.3**];
- the right to prevent others exploiting a reputation and goodwill [see **39.5**];
- design right [see **39.7**];
- rights relating to confidential information [see **39.8**].

Rights established through registration are:

- registered trade marks [see **39.4**];
- registered designs [see **39.7**];
- patents [see **39.6**].

Basic information about IP rights is available from the Patent Office and on the UK Intellectual Property website [see end of chapter].

39.2
COPYRIGHT

Copyright is a property right which gives the copyright owner the right to use or exploit the work, decide how it may be used or exploited by others, and prevent unauthorised persons from using it. It protects:

- original literary, dramatic, musical and artistic works;
- sound recordings, films (including videos), broadcasts, and cable programmes;
- the typographical arrangement of published editions (what a book or other publication looks like); *and*
- database design and in most cases content.

Copyright, Design and Patents Act 1988 s.1

This covers most original written and artistic work, including articles, reports and books whether published or not, leaflets, fundraising materials, drawings, paintings, photographs, correspondence, music, dance, plays and theatrical productions, email and website design and content, and computer programs. It covers electronic information, on computers, floppy disks, CD-ROM etc, in the same way as material on paper, film, videotape, audiotape, CD or other media.

Copyright does not generally protect the name of an organisation, but can protect the particular way the name is written or designed, provided it is sufficiently stylised [see **39.9** for how to protect the name itself].

Copyright does not protect ideas or information [see **39.8**]. Once they are written down, that version of the ideas or information becomes protected by copyright, but other people generally have the right to use those ideas or that information. (As authors and copyright owners of this book we can stop you from using the words as we have put them together on this page, but we cannot stop you from using the information on this page to write your own factsheet on copyright.)

The person or persons who create a copyright work are referred to as its **author** or **creator**, regardless of the nature of the work or how many persons there are. The person who owns the actual work—for example a painting or a manuscript—is the **owner** of the work. The person who owns the copyright is the **copyright owner** [see **39.2.3**], who may or may not be the author or owner of the work.

The Patent Office [see end of chapter] provides information on all aspects of copyright, including EU and international copyright.

39.2.1
Creation

In the UK, copyright arises automatically as soon as a work is created and 'fixed' in some way, with no need for registration of any sort. An article, for example, is protected as soon as it is written on paper or computer, a drawing is protected as soon as it is drawn, a tune is protected as soon as it is recorded on a cassette or CD, and images on a website are protected as soon as they are created. If the copyright material is published, the particular form and appearance of the published edition or version may also be protected.

It is sensible for an organisation to keep a record of the author and date of creation of any work produced for or by it and regarded by it as a copyright work. Traditionally, authors have recorded the creation of a piece of work by posting a copy of the work to themselves by registered post and leaving the envelope unopened, thus showing that the work was in existence at the date it was posted. This is not necessary and it is usually enough to note on every draft of a work the date and author.

39.2.2
Duration

The duration of copyright protection varies depending on the type of work and the date the work was first created. For literary, artistic, musical and dramatic works, copyright lasts until 70 years from the end of the calendar year in which the author dies. If the work is created by two or more people, it remains protected until the end of the calendar year 70 years after the death of the last surviving author.

The copyright in the published edition of the work lasts for 25 years. Even where the content of a work is out of copyright, a particular presentation of it may be protected. The duration for films is 70 years, and 50 years for sound recordings, broadcasts and cable programmes. The start date for the copyright period varies for each of these. *Duration of Copyright and Rights in Performances Regulations 1995 [SI 1995/3297]*

Works protected by copyright in the UK are also protected in countries which are members of the Berne Convention and the Universal Copyright Convention, but they should include the © symbol [see **39.2.4**].

**39.2.3
Ownership**

The person who first creates a copyright work (the author) usually owns the copyright. If more than one person is involved each may own copyright in part, or they may jointly own copyright in the whole work.

There are two important exceptions to the rule that the original author of the work owns copyright:

- where the work is produced by an employee; *or*
- where the author **assigns** copyright to someone else [see **39.2.3.4**].

Regardless of who owns copyright, the duration of copyright for a literary, artistic, musical or dramatic work always depends on the date of death of the original author(s) of the work.

Ownership of copyright must be distinguished from ownership of the work itself. A person who owns a manuscript or work of art owns the work, but copyright remains with the author, his or her estate, or the person or company to whom the author has assigned copyright.

Ownership of copyright must also be distinguished from moral rights [see **39.3**]. Authors may retain moral rights even if they no longer own the copyright.

**39.2.3.1
Works produced by employees**

Copyright in any work created by employees in the course of their employment belongs to the employer unless there is an agreement to the contrary. *Copyright, Design and Patents Act 1988 s.11(2)*

The key points are whether the work was done 'in the course of employment' and whether there was an agreement to the contrary. To avoid uncertainty it is a good idea, but not essential, to include a clause in every contract of employment stating that copyright in everything done by the employee during the course of his or her employment belongs to the employer [see **24.44** for sample clause].

An employee who is working on a special project which could arguably be outside the course of his or her employment should be asked to assign copyright to the employer [see **39.2.3.4**].

**39.2.3.2
Works produced by volunteers**

Volunteers who produce copyright work should be asked to assign copyright to the organisation [see **39.2.3.4**], or should agree a licence setting out the purposes for which the organisation can use it [see **39.11**].

**39.2.3.3
Works produced by outside persons and agencies**

Copyright in work done by self-employed persons [see **34.1**] and others who are not employees belongs to them, not to the organisation which commissions them and pays for the work. If the purchasing organisation wants to own the copyright or share ownership with the author(s), this must be explicit in the letter commissioning the work, a contract or a separate assignment of copyright. If copyright will remain with the author, a licence should be agreed setting out the purposes for which the organisation can use the work and arrangements for agreeing further use in future [see **39.11**].

**39.2.3.4
Assignment of copyright**

For an assignment of copyright to be legally binding the author must either receive consideration (payment or something else of value) for the work which is being assigned—even if it is only a token amount—or the agreement must be in the form of a deed [see **18.3**].

Provided there is some payment, assignment can be verbal if it is agreed before the work is created, but to ensure the situation is clear to both parties it is sensible to put it in writing. Assignment after a work has been created must be in writing.

If an organisation does not secure ownership of copyright for a work:

- it will not be able to use the work for its own purposes—for example, publishing a research report or using a photograph in an annual report—without the agreement of the author(s) of the work;

- it will not be able to stop the author(s) of the work from using the work for other purposes; *and*

- it will not be able to bring an action for copyright infringement if anyone else uses the work, because only the copyright owner can bring such action.

These problems become particularly acute if the author cannot be traced or refuses to assign the copyright.

In some situations the organisation may agree that the author(s) of the work will retain copyright, with the organisation granted a licence [see **39.11**] to use the work for specified purposes and/or for a specific period. Under the terms of the licence the author might agree not to use the work or allow it to be used for any other purposes for a specified time.

39.2.4
Use of the © symbol

There is no legal requirement to use the © symbol to show a claim of copyright in the UK. If international protection is required, use of the symbol is obligatory for Universal Copyright Convention protection outside the UK.

Use of the symbol does not, in itself, prove ownership of copyright. However, the symbol followed by the name of the copyright owner and the year of copyright makes clear that copyright in the work is claimed, and should make it less likely that others will copy the work.

It also increases the likelihood that the copyright owner would be able to obtain damages from infringers, because it would be difficult for them to argue innocence if the work is marked with the symbol.

39.2.5
Use of copyright material

Copying, publishing or performing someone else's copyright material without permission is generally an infringement of their copyright. The copyright owner's legal remedies include an injunction against use of the material, an award of damages, or an account (award) of the profits made from the infringement. Infringement may also be a criminal offence if it involves commercial exploitation of copyright material.

Copyright, Design and Patents Act 1988 ss.16-27, 107-110

Permission to copy, publish or perform someone else's copyright material is generally referred to as a **licence** [see **39.2.5.4** and **39.11**]. A licence does not have to be in writing, but especially where the copying is substantial or is being done for the purposes of financial gain it is wise to put it in writing.

39.2.5.1
Educational use

Exceptions where it is not necessary to get the copyright owner's permission to copy literary works include:

- making a single copy of a short extract of a published work for research or private study;

- use of some copyright works for educational purposes, such as copying text to prepare for teaching or for inclusion in an examination paper, or for performing a dramatic or musical work;

- single copies of short extracts made by librarians, provided they have the appropriate signed declarations from the person requesting the copying. *ss.28-50*

The legislation does not specify how much of a published work may be copied before the copying infringes copyright.

39.2.5.2
Review and criticism

The Society of Authors and the Publishers Association have agreed that for the purposes of criticism or review, permission is not needed to quote a single extract of less than 400 words from a prose work, or a series of extracts each less than 300 words and totalling no more than 800 words, provided the total quoted is not more than 25% of the work. Similar limits have been set for quotations from poetry.

39.2.5.3
Newspaper cuttings

Anyone can clip articles from a newspaper, but if the articles are photo-copied, scanned or faxed, even for internal management purposes, consent is required. A licence is available from the **Newspaper Licensing Agency** [see end of chapter] which covers cuttings from most national newspapers based in England. The licence may be issued free of charge to registered charities provided they meet relatively strict criteria, including that the largest single source of the charity's income is donations from the public. At the time of writing (early 2001) these criteria were under review. Organisations which copy articles without a licence may face charges backdated to 1996, when the NLA was set up.

Even under the licence, copies may be made only for internal management purposes. Copying for other purposes—for example, reproduction in a newsletter—must be licensed by the publisher of the newspaper.

39.2.5.4
Copyright licence

Organisations which regularly copy from books, periodicals and journals may obtain a **copyright licence** from the **Copyright Licensing Agency** [see end of chapter]. This eliminates the need to obtain consent each time material is copied or scanned. There is no provision for free licences for charities. Licences for use of visual art and photographs are available from **Design and Artists Copyright Society.** For licenses for performing live or recorded musical works, see **42.3**.

39.2.6
Computers and electronic media

Copyright law in relation to electronic information, especially on the internet, is developing rapidly. Specialist advice may be needed, especially in relation to websites and computer programs.

39.2.6.1
Computer programs

Computer programs are regarded as 'literary works' and are protected by copyright. Running a program usually involves copying it, and converting a program into or between languages constitutes copying. To avoid breach of copyright, an organisation should have a licence from the manufacturer for each commercial computer program it uses.

Where anyone other than an employee designs programs or software for an organisation, the organisation should take legal advice to ensure copyright is assigned to it or a comprehensive licence is drawn up allowing it to use and adapt the program.

39.2.6.2
Electronic information

Documents, designs and other creative work on computer, disk, CD-ROM or other electronic media are protected in the same way as any other work. The text of a document is copyright to the writer, and the way the document is designed is copyright to the person who designed it. (If the work is created in the course of employment, the whole product is copyright to the employer.) Copying computer documents without permission of the author(s) is a breach of copyright unless it falls within a limited number of exceptions, such as compiling a back-up copy. *Copyright (Computer Programs) Regulations 1992 [SI 1992/3233]*

39.2.6.3
Domain names

As a name, a domain name cannot be protected by copyright, but the organisation's name, initials and/or domain name may be registerable as trade marks [see **39.4**]. Even without registration, it is possible to take legal action to assert the right to a domain name which has been registered in bad faith by a person who has no right to the name.

39.2.6.4
Websites

The internet is not a copyright-free zone; indeed, its international nature means it may be subject to the laws of several countries. Websites

571

are likely to be protected by copyright and unauthorised copying is likely to be infringement, although it may be unclear which country's laws would apply. Making an unauthorised link to another person's website may also be breach of their copyright.

To reduce the risk of others using its copyright material, an organisation should make clear that its website as a whole and every page is copyright, material may be downloaded and printed out for personal use but may not be reproduced or used in any other way without consent, and other websites may not create links to the site without consent.

To reduce the risk of breaching copyright, an organisation should:

- ensure the designer of the website, if not an employee, has assigned copyright in the design to the organisation;

- ensure the organisation owns the copyright of all material included on the website, or has permission to reproduce it on the website;

- not create links to any other websites without their written consent;

- where links are created, make clear that the material on those sites belongs to those sites;

- have a policy on internet use by employees, volunteers and others, making clear that copyright materials from the internet may not be downloaded or used without appropriate consent.

Personal data obtained over the internet, for example through membership forms or internet fundraising, must comply with data protection rules [see **38.3**], and internet fundraising must comply with fundraising rules [see **chapters 44-46**]. For registered charities, companies or industrial and provident societies, and organisations registered for VAT, the website should contain the same information as must be included on business stationery [see **16.1**].

39.2.6.5
Email

The copyright on emails generally belongs to the author, but if they are created as part of employment it belongs to the employer. If emails are created during work time but not as part of employment, copyright could belong to either the employer or employee. There are many other issues in relation to email, such as unauthorised use of email facilities and the employer's right to monitor email and internet use [see **38.1.5**].

39.2.7
Databases

A database is a collection of independent works, data or other materials, arranged in a systematic or methodical way and individually accessible by electronic or other means. This includes directories, membership and similar lists, encyclopaedias, and other lists or collections of information, whether on paper, disk, CD, or any other medium.

Database programs on computer are protected under copyright law [see **39.2.6.1**]. Database content, whether on electronic media or paper, is protected under copyright law if the structure, selection and arrangement involve sufficient skill and labour and are original enough to be 'an intellectual creation of the author'.

If database content does not meet the 'intellectual creation' test, but involves a substantial investment of financial, human or technical resources in obtaining or checking the data, it may have the lesser protection of **database right.** This prevents the unauthorised extraction (copying or other form of transfer) or re-utilisation (distribution) of all or a substantial part of the data, or repeated use of even a small part of the data. As with copyright, ownership rests with the person(s) who created the data, unless they are employees, in which case database right belongs to the employer. Protection is initially for a period of 15 years from 1 January in the year after the database is first created or (if later) marketed. If the contents are updated in a way which amounts to a substantial new investment, a further 15 years of protection begins.

Copyright and Rights in Databases Regulations 1997 [SI 1997/3032]

39.3
MORAL RIGHTS

In addition to protection of copyright works, the copyright legislation also protects the **moral rights** of authors. These are the right:

- of **paternity**, which gives the author of a work the right to be identified as the author, but only if he or she specifically asserts this right [see the copyright page of this book for an example];

- not to be falsely described as the author of a work;

- of authors and film directors to object to certain deletions or adaptations being made to their works if the effect is derogatory;

- to object to the publication of photographs or films commissioned by an individual.   *Copyright, Design and Patents Act 1988 ss.77-95*

There are a number of exceptions, for example that employees who produce works in the course of their employment do not have rights of paternity or the right to object to derogatory treatment of their work.

Moral rights are not transferred when copyright is assigned, but persons who hold these rights may assign, waive, or give up their rights.

39.4
REGISTERED
TRADE MARKS

Trade mark registration is a relatively cheap and simple but under-used procedure, which can provide a useful deterrent against unauthorised use of the organisation's name, logo or slogans, and can also help with disputes where someone else uses the same or a confusingly similar mark as an internet domain name.

Any word, sign or symbol—referred to as a **mark**—can be registered if:

- it can be represented graphically (in words or illustration); *and*

- it is capable of distinguishing the applicant's goods or services from someone else's.   *Trade Marks Act 1994 s.1(1)*

Trade marks may consist of words, designs, letters, numerals, or the shape of goods or their packaging. They cover slogans, jingles and colours, and may even be granted for smells, sounds and gestures. To do this, the smell or sound would be described in words, and the gesture would be described in words or pictures.

There are some restrictions on what can be registered, including a restriction on purely descriptive words in common usage (such as 'The Cancer Helpline' for a telephone helpline for people with cancer) unless the applicant can show that, through usage, it has built up a distinctive reputation linked to that name.

The marks most commonly registered by voluntary organisations are their name or names, abbreviations or initials, slogans, logos, domain names, names of events, and marks which are a combination of one or more of these. Information on trade mark registration is available from the Patent Office [see end of chapter].

39.4.1
Registration of
domain names

Domain names can be registered as trade marks. In deciding whether a domain name is distinctive enough to be eligible for registration as a trade mark, suffixes such as .com and .co.uk are generally disregarded. A name prefixed with e– is treated as if it started with 'electronic', and a name prefixed with m– is treated as if the m– were 'mobile'.

39.4.2
Registration classes

The **Trade Marks Register** is divided into 34 classes of goods and eight classes of services. The number of service classes is likely to be increased. The term **trade mark** is used to refer both to trade marks (for goods) and **service marks** (for services). Registration gives the owner the exclusive right to use the registered **mark**, but only in the registered class of goods or services.

The most likely classes for voluntary organisations are:

- class 16: printed materials, including publications, training materials, photographs, brochures;

- class 35, which was extended in late 2000 to include retail shops, including charity shops, and mail order services;

- class 36: charitable fundraising, charitable collections, managing and monitoring of charitable funds;

- class 41: educational services, training, entertainment, sporting and cultural activities, publication of books, reports and magazines;

- class 42: provision of food and drink, temporary accommodation, medical care, legal services, computer programming, services which cannot be placed in other classes.

A trade mark cannot be registered if it is already registered for the same class. To check the register, the applicant may conduct a search on the Patent Office website [see end of chapter] or at its offices in London or Cardiff, or use its search and advisory service (fee £82.25 as at 1/4/01).

39.4.3
Registration

The Patent Office provides official guidance on applications, or a solicitor, patent agent or trade marks agent can file applications on behalf of an organisation. Filing generally costs £500 to £1,200, which covers preparation and the application fee (£200 for a single class and £50 for each additional class, as at 1/4/01). There may be further fees if the application is opposed or the Patent Office objects to the registration.

Trade mark registration is permanent, but lapses if a renewal fee (£200 for a single class and £50 for each additional class, as at 1/4/01) is not paid every 10 years. If a trade mark is not used in a five year period, it may be struck off the register.

39.4.3.1
Organisations with trading subsidiaries

The applicant should usually be the organisation which uses the mark. If the organisation has a separate trading subsidiary which uses the organisation's name in connection with the sale of certain goods, the application may be filed in the organisation's name with the trading subsidiary then licensed to use the mark [see **39.11**], or the application could be filed in the name of the trading subsidiary.

If there is any risk of the subsidiary becoming insolvent, it is advisable for the parent organisation to retain the rights and license the subsidiary, so there is no risk of the rights being lost in the insolvency.

39.4.4
Use of the ® and ™ symbols

The ® symbol does not have to be used. If it is used, it may be used only for the class(es) for which the mark is registered. It is an offence to give the impression that something is registered when it is not, for example by using the symbol improperly. Anyone who prepares publications or is involved in trading should be made aware of the importance of proper use of the symbol, and should be clear which aspects of the organisation's work are and are not registered in relation to the trade mark.

The ™ symbol has no legal significance in the UK, but puts people on notice that the user of the mark regards it as their trade mark. The symbol may be used for marks which are not registered.

39.4.5
Use of trade marks

Registration of a trade mark stops others from registering the same mark in the same class, and from using the mark on goods or services in the class for which it is registered without the consent of the trade mark holder. Permission to use a mark should be recorded in writing in a licence [see **39.11**].

Registration may also stop another party registering or using the mark in other classes, if the trade mark holder can prove confusion or bad faith. However, registration is often sufficient to prevent others from registering or using the same or a confusingly similar name.

An exception to the prohibition on using the mark in the same class is **comparative advertising**. Use of a trade mark for this purpose is not infringement, provided the use is 'honest practice', and does not take unfair advantage of the trade mark or act detrimentally to the distinctive character or reputation of the mark [see **40.2.2**].

39.4.6
International trade mark protection

A trade mark can be registered through the Office for Harmonisation in the Internal Market [see end of chapter], based in Alicante, to cover all member states of the European Union.

Under the **Madrid Protocol**, a UK national who has applied for or registered a trade mark in the UK can apply to the World Intellectual Property Organisation in Geneva [see end of chapter] to make simultaneous applications in any or all of the other countries which have ratified the Protocol (48, at the time of writing).

39.5
PASSING OFF

Passing off is using a name, domain name, logo, slogan, packaging etc which is the same as, or very similar to, someone else's in a way which deliberately or unintentionally causes loss of goodwill or financial loss to them. An action for passing off can be brought by the organisation which has suffered the loss even if the name, slogan or whatever which is being misused is not registered in any way, and even if the organisation is a charity or not-for-profit body rather than a business.

The British Diabetic Association v The Diabetic Society [1996] FSR 1-72

Generally a court grants protection against passing off only if:

- the organisation can show it has an established reputation or goodwill in the name, slogan, logo, packaging, catalogue or whatever the other party is using to make its misrepresentation;
- the other party has deceived members of the public or trade in some way by means of the misrepresentation, or is likely to do so or enable someone else to do so; *and*
- the organisation has suffered or is likely to suffer damage or injury to its business, reputation or goodwill.

The key test is whether the organisation has established such a strong reputation in what it is seeking to protect that the other party's use of something similar would deceive or confuse members of the public.

An action for passing off is generally very expensive, because of the need to prepare detailed evidence proving the organisation's reputation and showing why the other party's actions are causing or are likely to cause damage or confusion. This is very different from an action for infringement of trade mark rights, where no damage or potential damage needs to be shown.

In particularly urgent cases, a court will sometimes grant an immediate (interlocutory) injunction to restrain the other party until the trial.

The remedies are an injunction, damages, and the defendant's profits from the passing off. Even when the action is successful, the organisation is unlikely to get all its costs paid by the other party.

39.6
PATENTS

Patents protect inventions by giving the owner the monopoly right to use the invention and the right to prevent others using it. Patents generally protect scientific and industrial discoveries, such as manufacturing processes or chemical or biological products. Information about patents is available from the Patent Office [see end of chapter].

To be patentable, the invention must never have been made public in any way, anywhere in the world, before the date the patent application is filed. It is therefore essential that details of potential inventions are not disclosed to anyone, even by word of mouth, unless it is under conditions of strict confidence, buttressed by a written confidentiality agreement.

Charities have a duty to safeguard the results of their research [see **39.10**], so it is particularly important for them not to jeopardise their right to patent discoveries or inventions.

39.6.1
Ownership of patents

The person entitled to apply for a patent is the inventor or inventors. However there is a presumption that an employer owns the rights to any invention made by employees in the course of their normal duties or in the course of a project specifically assigned to the employee.

Patents Act 1977 ss.39-43

If the invention is of outstanding benefit to the employer, the employee may be entitled to some personal benefit and can apply to the court or the Patent Office for compensation for his or her part in the invention.

For inventions by volunteers, self-employed persons and others who are not employees, the rights of ownership rest with the inventor unless they have been assigned to the organisation [see **39.2.3.4**].

39.6.2
Registration

Copies of patents and patent applications should be searched before any application for a patent is submitted. Information is available from the Patent Office [see end of chapter] on how to do this.

It usually costs at least £500 to register a patent, and much more if a patent agent is hired to handle the application. An application must be submitted to the Patent Office, or to the European Patent Office in Munich for a patent covering all EU countries. During the fairly lengthy procedure the Patent Office examines whether the invention described is patentable, and third parties can object to the application. If the application is approved, a further fee is payable.

39.6.3
Duration

A UK patent lasts for a maximum of 20 years from when the application was filed. The initial registration fee covers the first four years and after that an annual fee, which can be substantial, is payable. During the last five years a court has power in some circumstances to compel the patent owner to grant a licence to third parties.

39.6.4
Use of patented inventions

The patent owner may license any person to exploit a patent [see **39.11**]. If an unlicensed third party is using a registered patent, the patent owner may bring court proceedings to obtain an injunction, and may also obtain damages or an account (award) of their profits.

39.7
DESIGN RIGHTS

Design rights protect the appearance of an object—its shape or surface pattern. For designs of a functional nature, **unregistered design right** protection arises automatically. It lasts for 15 years from the first recording of the design or 10 years from the first marketing of the item, whichever is shorter.   *Copyright, Design and Patents Act 1988 ss.213-264*

For designs of manufactured items which have some element of 'eye appeal', protection arises only if **design registration** is obtained from the Patent Office. It lasts initially five years, then is renewable on five-year terms to a maximum of 25 years.   *Registered Designs Act 1949*

39.8
IDEAS AND INFORMATION

Ideas are intellectual property but cannot be protected while they are still in a person's head. They are also not protected if they are communicated verbally, unless they are disclosed under a confidentiality agreement. Once they are on paper or computer or in some other tangible form they are protected by copyright [see **39.2**], but others cannot be stopped from developing the ideas or using them in different ways.

As with ideas, there is no general law which protects rights in information and know-how (processes and procedures). Once the information is written it is protected by copyright, and the way it is stored may be protected by copyright or under database right [see **39.2.7**]. But the law will not stop someone from *using* the information unless:

- the information is by its nature confidential; *and*

- the information has been disclosed only in circumstances which imposed an obligation on the recipient to respect the confidentiality of the information, for example within the employment relationship [see **38.1.6**] or where there is a contractual obligation to use information only for the purposes of the contract.

In this case, unauthorised use is likely to be a breach of contract or a breach of the duty of confidentiality [see **38.1.1** and **38.1.6**].

39.9 PROTECTING NAMES AND LOGOS

An organisation's name, logo and reputation are valuable assets which it should consider protecting. In terms of intellectual property rights, there are at least three aspects to this:

- preventing other organisations from using the same or a confusingly similar name or logo;
- preventing individuals or organisations from using the name, for example for fundraising, without authorisation;
- ensuring that when an organisation authorises use of its name or logo for commercial purposes, it is properly recompensed.

39.9.1 Stopping others from using the name or logo

A charity may be required by the Charity Commission, within a year of registration, to change its name if it is the same as, or too similar to, another charity's registered name [see **8.8.2**], and a company may be required by Companies House to change its name within a year of registration if it is the same as or too similar to another company's registered name [see **8.8.1**].

Registration as a charity thus provides some protection against another registered charity using the name, and registration as a company provides some protection against another company using an identical name.

These registrations do not protect against any other type of organisation using the registered name, nor do they cover operating or trading names [see **8.5**], logos etc, or protect against use of a name which is similar but not 'too similar'. This protection can be obtained only by:

- registering the name, logo or other mark as a trade mark for the relevant class(es) of services or goods [see **39.4**];
- bringing a passing off action if the name or other mark is used in a way which damages the organisation [see **39.5**]; *or*
- claiming copyright [see **39.2**] not for the name itself (which cannot be copyright) but for the particular design of the name, for example the distinctive way 'Age Concern' is written, or for the logo.

As an alternative it may be appropriate for the organisation to start using a new logo, use a different operating name [see **8.5**] rather than the name which is being used by the other party, or even change its name [see **8.7** for procedure]. This may seem like 'giving in', but may be preferable to ongoing confusion or an expensive and perhaps ultimately futile action for passing off.

Use of a name or logo by 'branches' which purport to be part of an organisation but are in fact not linked to it can be particularly problematic [see **9.2**].

Use of an organisation's name as a domain name could be trade mark infringement if the name has been registered as a trade mark, or could be grounds for a passing off action [see **39.5**]. There are a number of dispute resolution procedures under which domain name registries will force the transfer of the name which has been registered in bad faith.

39.9.2 Unauthorised use for fundraising

Often an organisation's name or logo is used not by another organisation, but by its own supporters—individuals, branches, other organisations or commercial bodies—who use the name to fundraise. This can become a problem if the persons undertaking the activity bring the organisation's name into disrepute, or undertake activities which the organisation does not approve of. Charitable institutions (charities and other 'good cause' organisations) can in this situation seek an injunction to stop the fundraising [see **44.6.1**].

39.9.3
Commercial use

The Charity Commission advises charities to be wary of entering into arrangements where the charity's name is to be used by a commercial company in return for money, and advises trustees to have clear policies on companies it is prepared to work with.

Any such arrangements, including arrangements with a charity's own trading company [see **47.6.1**] must be carefully considered by the trustees, be kept under review, and be in the interests of the charity and on terms which are advantageous to the charity. The arrangements should be set out in a proper licence arrangement [see **39.11**].

Unless the arrangements are with a trading company owned by the charity or other organisation whose name is being used, they must comply with Charities Act rules for commercial participators [see **44.5.5**].

Advice must be taken about the tax and VAT implications of licensing a charity's name or logo [see **52.7.9** and **53.5.3**], and should be taken about the organisation's potential liability for faulty goods [see **18.7.3**] where a product is branded with the organisation's trademarked logo.

39.10
EXPLOITATION OF RESEARCH

Charities involved in research, whether as their main purpose or as incidental to their work, should comply with the Charity Commission's guidance on carrying out, funding and commissioning research. Such charities must consider how best to protect their intellectual property rights arising from the research, and take appropriate steps to ensure the charity benefits from any use of these rights.

Trustees have to *consider* these issues, but do not necessarily have to register or otherwise protect intellectual property rights. In some cases the trustees may feel that the charity's objects can be best achieved by making research results freely available, even though this could result in a loss of income to the charity. This is acceptable, provided it can be justified within the trustees' obligation to act always in the best interests of the charity and to safeguard its assets, including its intangible assets such as IP rights.

Where a charity funds someone to undertake research, it should retain the intellectual property rights for itself, or ensure that if the researcher or other owner of the rights exploits the rights commercially, the charity gets a proportionate share of the proceeds. This is likely to involve a complex licence or assignment of rights, and legal advice should be sought at an early stage in commissioning or funding the research.

39.11
LICENCES

The granting of a right to use someone else's intellectual property—regardless of whether the property is protected by copyright, by registration or in some other way—is called a **licence**. A licence may range from a short agreement allowing another body to use an organisation's name or logo for a specific one-off purpose or to reproduce a copyright illustration or article, to a hugely complex contract for exploitation of a valuable patent or software or to replicate an organisation's work through a franchise arrangement. To protect both parties, even simple licences should usually be in writing.

Unlike assignment, where the right itself is transferred, a licence gives only the right to use the work for a specified purpose and/or period. Ownership of the copyright or other right is not transferred.

39.11.1
What to include

All licences contain certain basic information, but for anything more than the simplest licence legal advice should be sought to ensure the organisation's interests are protected (regardless of whether it owns the rights to the work, or is entering into an agreement to use work where the rights are owned by others). This is particularly important in relation to patented discoveries and inventions, software, and work which has involved or will involve substantial time and/or money.

At the very least, a licence should cover:

- who is granting the licence, and who is being given it;
- what intellectual property right(s) the licence covers;
- whether the licence is being granted on an exclusive or non-exclusive basis (whether the licensor is granting the licence only to the licensee, or may grant it to others as well);
- what payment, if any, the licensee must make, and whether it is in the form of a one-off fixed fee, an annual fixed fee, a royalty or some other form of payment;
- the term (duration) of the licence;
- whether the licence can be terminated before the end of the term;
- which party is to deal with third party infringers;
- any requirements for confidentiality between the parties;
- any indemnities between the parties.

It is common for trade mark licences to allow the licensor to exercise quality control over the licensee's products or services, and for licences for the use of a name or logo to include provision for withdrawal of the right if the name or logo is used inappropriately.

Licences for trade marks and patents may be, but do not have to be, recorded at the Patent Office. There are advantages for the licensee if the licence is registered within six months of its being granted.

39.11.2 Payments for intellectual property rights

Income received for intellectual property rights may be taxable, even for charities [see **52.5.4**], and may be subject to VAT [see **53.5.3**]. The tax and VAT treatment of payments for IP rights is quite complex for both charities and non-charitable organisations, and expert advice should be sought from a solicitor or accountant before entering into a licence.

39.11.3 Franchises

A franchise [see **9.4.4**] is a complex licence where typically the franchisee receives the right to use the franchisor's name, advertising, goodwill, know-how, products, services, methods of operating etc. Legal advice should be taken before entering into any franchise agreement.

FOR FURTHER INFORMATION

Copyright, trade marks, patents, design rights. Patent Office: 0845-950 0505; www.patent.gov.uk

UK Intellectual Property: www.intellectual-property.gov.uk

Office for Harmonisation in the Internal Market: oami.eu.net [no www.]

World Intellectual Property Organisation: www.wipo.org

Licence to copy newspaper articles. Newspaper Licensing Agency: 01892-525273; www.nla.co.uk

Licence to copy books, journals, periodicals. Copyright Licensing Agency: 020-7631 5555; www.cla.co.uk

Licence to copy visual art and photographs. Design and Artists Copyright Society: 020-7336 8811; www.dacs.co.uk

Research by charities. Charity Commission: 0870-333 0123; www.charity-commission.gov.uk

Chapter 40
PUBLICATIONS AND PUBLICITY

40.1
PUBLICATIONS

When producing any publication, from a leaflet to a huge tome, or when setting up a website or producing film, audio or video productions or advertising of any type, the following issues must be considered:

- who will own the copyright of the work [see **39.2.3**];

- whether consent needs to be obtained from third parties for the use of copyright material or trade marks [see **39.2.5** and **39.4.5**];

- for publications, whether an international standard book number or serial number should be obtained [see below];

- whether anything in the publication or other production is or could be construed as being libellous [see **40.3**];

- the risk of defamation arising from websites, especially where the site includes dynamic content such as chat rooms or bulletin boards;

- whether other liabilities could be created, for example through providing information or advice that could lead to a negligence claim if a person suffers loss as a result of relying on it [see **19.5.1**];

- whether the publication or part of it could be, or come to be, treated as setting out terms of a contract [see **40.2.3.2**];

- if the organisation receives local authority funding, whether the publication or production complies with the requirements for local authority-funded publicity [see **40.2.5**];

- if the publication or production is an advertisement, whether it complies with the relevant aspects of the British Codes of Advertising and Sales Promotion [see **40.2.1**].

Organisations should be clear about who needs to give final approval to publications and other productions before they are produced.

40.1.1
ISBN and ISSN

International standard book numbers (ISBN), **international standard serial numbers** (ISSN) and bar codes are used by publishers, distributors and booksellers to make the book trade more efficient, and have nothing to do with copyright. They are available free [see end of chapter]. There is no obligation to obtain an ISBN, ISSN or bar code for any publication, but it is a good idea to do so if the publication is likely to be sold through the book trade.

ISBNs are assigned to books and other publications. They are not available for serials published more often than once a year or works which are updated more than once a year. ISSNs are available for publications published annually or more frequently. An annual publication may have either an ISBN or ISSN, or both.

Bar codes are based on the ISBN or ISSN and are used by bookshops and newsagents for their computerised systems. Information about bar codes for books is provided when an ISBN is obtained. Information about bar codes for periodicals is available from the Periodical Publishers Association [see end of chapter].

40.1.2 Periodical registration

A newspaper or magazine which contains public news or commentary on the news must be registered with Companies House [see end of chapter] if:

- it is published at intervals of 26 days or less;
- a charge is made for the periodical, or it is a free publication containing only or mostly advertisements; *and*
- the publisher is not a company incorporated under the Companies Acts. *Newspaper Libel and Registration Act 1881*

Registration is on form NLR1 with a registration fee of 50p (as at 1/4/01) with an annual return and filing fee of 25p each July.

40.1.3 Legal deposit libraries

Anyone who issues or distributes publications, including items such as pamphlets, newsletters, and posters, to the public must send a copy to the legal deposit office at the British Library within one month of publication [see end of chapter]. The deposited publications form the **national printed archive**. Depositing a publication with a legal deposit library does not confer copyright [see **39.2** for how copyright arises].

Copyright Act 1911 s.15

The legal deposit libraries in Oxford, Cambridge, Edinburgh, Dublin and Aberystwyth are entitled to receive every publication, but do not have enough space. Organisations wishing to send publications to them should contact the Copyright Libraries Agency [see end of chapter].

40.2 PUBLICITY AND ADVERTISING

Publicity, advertising and sales promotions should comply with the British Codes of Advertising and Sales Promotion. They may also be subject to rules on political publicity and advertising [see **41.4**], publicity by organisations funded by local authorities [see **40.2.5**], and commercial participation in fundraising and promotions [see **44.5**].

An advertisement or other written or printed notice encouraging members of the public to donate to or pay a registered charity must state that the organisation is a registered charity [see **7.3.1**].

40.2.1 The Advertising and Sales Promotion Codes

The **British Codes of Advertising and Sales Promotion**, developed by the Committee of Advertising Practice and administered by the Advertising Standards Association, apply to charitable and voluntary organisations as well as to commercial businesses.

The basic principles are that advertisements, sales promotions and the promotional element of sponsorship arrangements should:

- be legal, decent, honest and truthful;
- be prepared with a sense of responsibility to both consumers and society; *and*
- respect the principles of fair competition generally accepted in business.

The codes are available free from the Advertising Standards Authority [see end of chapter]. At the time of writing (early 2001) they were being reviewed and streamlined.

The Committee of Advertising Practice copy advice team, based at the ASA, provides free and confidential pre-publication advice on the content of advertisements. Organisations in doubt about whether an advertisement or sales promotion complies with the codes should seek their advice.

Organisations which use an agency to prepare their advertisements should make it a condition in their contract that the agency complies with the relevant codes and if appropriate seeks advice from the ASA.

40.2.1.1
What is covered

The codes cover:

- advertisements in UK newspapers, magazines, brochures, leaflets, circulars, mailings, fax transmissions, catalogues, follow-up literature, websites and other electronic and printed material;
- marketing databases containing consumers' personal information;
- advertising posters and other promotional media in public places, cinema and video commercials, and advertisements in non-broadcast electronic media;
- sales promotions and advertisement promotions.

The codes do not cover broadcast commercials [see **40.2.4**], press releases and other public relations material, or advertisements in foreign media. They do not apply to publicity on t-shirts, carrier bags, mugs etc, which is covered by trading standards legislation. Packages, wrappers, labels and tickets are not covered unless they advertise a sales promotion or are visible in an advertisement.

Specific rules apply to environmental claims, advertisements portraying children, advertisements or promotions directed at children, distance selling (where the buyer and seller do not meet face to face), and practices relating to lists and databases.

It does not matter whether the publicity is about the organisation itself, issues dealt with by the organisation, or something sold, provided free of charge or organised by the organisation. Nor does it matter whether the organisation pays for the publicity, receives it free of charge, or receives it as part of a sponsorship or other arrangement.

40.2.1.2
Complaints

Complaints to the ASA are investigated and if upheld, the advertisement must be withdrawn. The codes do not have the force of law but if an advertiser refuses to comply with an ASA decision the ASA may refer the matter to the director general of fair trading, who can then seek an injunction from the court.

The ASA's decisions are widely publicised, and an organisation which has a case found against it often receives considerable adverse publicity.

40.2.2
Advertisements

Detailed rules in the **Advertising Code** set out specific procedures to help ensure advertisements comply with the basic principles.

40.2.2.1
Truthfulness

Before submitting an advertisement for publication or putting it on a website, advertisers must hold evidence to prove all direct or implied claims which can be objectively substantiated. Advertisements should not be misleading, which means that:

- where evidence is unclear or there are differing interpretations of the evidence, this should be made clear;
- opinions should not be presented as fact;
- composite case studies should be truthful in the general impression they create, and it should not be implied that a composite is an individual person's experience;

- if a model is used in a photograph this should be made clear if it is a relevant factor;
- claims to be 'environmentally friendly' should not be made without qualification unless advertisers can provide convincing evidence to support them.

Obvious untruths or exaggerations which are unlikely to mislead are allowed.

40.2.2.2
<u>Comparative advertising</u>

Advertisers should not unfairly attack or discredit other businesses or their products. Explicit or implicit comparisons with other businesses or products are allowed, provided the comparison is not misleading, is objective, does not create confusion between the advertiser and its competitor, and does not discredit or denigrate the competitor or its products. [See **39.4.5** for using other organisations' trade marks in comparative advertising, and **40.4** for comments made maliciously.]

40.2.2.3
<u>Decency</u>

Advertisements should not contain anything which would be likely to cause serious or widespread offence, and should not cause fear or distress unless there is a good reason for doing so. If fear or distress is likely to be aroused—for example, in an advertisement for smoke detectors—it should not be disproportionate to the risk.

Unsafe practices should not be shown unless they are promoting safety, and nothing should condone or be likely to promote violence or anti-social behaviour. The rules are more strict for advertisements addressed to or featuring children, which should contain nothing which is likely to result in their physical, mental or moral harm.

40.2.2.4
<u>Privacy</u>

Written consent should be obtained before portraying any person or a person's possessions or property in an advertisement, unless the portrayal is a general crowd scene, property in a general outdoor location, or a person who is the subject of a book or film being advertised.

Advertisers who do not have consent to portray entertainers, politicians and others who have a high public profile should not portray them in an offensive or adverse way, and should not claim or imply an endorsement where none exists. Portrayal of members of the royal family is generally not permitted.

40.2.3
Sales promotions

The **Sales Promotion Code** follows the same basic principles and general rules as for advertising. The code is intended primarily to protect the public, but also applies to:

- trade promotions and incentive schemes, where goods or services are offered on promotional terms to wholesalers and others who will sell or distribute them on;
- the promotional elements of sponsorships, for example where a commercial business or its products are promoted or advertised as part of a sponsorship arrangement with a voluntary organisation.

Promotions involving adventurous activities should be made as safe as possible by the promoters. Promotions intended for or involving children under 16 should indicate whether an adult's consent is needed.

40.2.3.1
Promotions linked to charities and good causes

Special rules apply to promotions claiming that participation will benefit registered charities or other good causes, augmenting those required under the Charities Act 1992 for **commercial participation** [see **44.5.6**].

40.2.3.2
<u>Sales terms</u>

Claims or representations in any publication could be treated by the court as forming part of representations that induced a person to enter into a contract [see **18.7.6**]. Some publications, such as an advertisement or leaflet publicising goods or a service, could be treated by the court as part of the contract.

**40.2.4
Broadcast
commercials**

Broadcast advertisements on independent media are covered by:

- the **Radio Authority Code of Advertising Standards and Practice**, for licensed radio;

- the **Independent Television Commission Code of Advertising Standards and Practice**, for terrestrial, satellite and cable independent television.

Advertisements may be used to solicit donations (a **broadcast appeal**), to publicise an organisation and its work, to sell goods or to publicise services, activities, events or facilities.

Only charitable organisations which are wholly or mainly funded by donations from the public are allowed to use radio or television advertising to solicit donations or publicise their objects or needs. Non-charitable companies may promote the needs and objectives of charities provided they have the permission of the charity concerned, state whether any charity will benefit financially from the sale of goods, and state how any money donated to charity will be calculated.

Broadcast appeals by charities must:

- deal with the topic carefully and with discretion, respecting the dignity of people on whose behalf an appeal is made and not exaggerating the scale or nature of any social problem;

- not be misleading in any way about a charity's activities or how donations raised through a broadcast appeal will be used;

- not include comparisons with other charities;

- not address any fundraising message specifically to children.

Advertising by 'political' organisations or about 'political' issues is not allowed [see **41.4**].

Special rules apply when broadcast appeals are made by professional fundraisers or commercial participators [see **44.5.6** and **44.5.7**].

**40.2.5
Organisations
funded by local
authorities**

The **Local Government Act 1986** covers publicity issued by local authorities. This also applies to publicity issued by local authority-funded voluntary organisations, unless the organisation can prove that it raised the money for the publicity from a completely separate source, and shows the income and expenditure separately in its accounts.

The definition of publicity is wide, and includes printed materials and advertisements, badges, banners, t-shirts, carrier bags and similar items. It could also include campaigns, exhibitions, plays, conferences and any other kind of public communication.

The restrictions apply to publicity intended for the public or a section of the public. They do not apply to internal communication within an organisation, or publicity provided only to a closed group such as MPs or an organisation's members.

Detailed information about the restrictions and the government's code of practice on local authority publicity is available from the Local Government Information Unit [see end of chapter].

**40.2.5.1
Promotion of
homosexuality**

Local authorities and, by extension, organisations funded by them cannot intentionally promote homosexuality, publish material with the intention of promoting homosexuality, or promote the teaching in any maintained school that homosexuality is acceptable as a family relationship.   *Local Government Act 1986 s.2 as amended by
LGA 1988 s.28 [still generally referred to as 'Section 28']*

This ban does not prevent local authorities and voluntary organisations funded by them from supporting lesbian and gay organisations and activities, providing information and services to lesbians and gay men, and discouraging discrimination against lesbians and gay men. It does mean that care needs to be taken in the wording of publicity materials which refer to homosexuality, especially if the materials are intended for use in schools.

40.2.5.2
Party politics

Local authorities and, by extension, organisations funded by them cannot publish any material which wholly or partly appears to be designed to affect public support for a political party.

Local Government Act 1986 s.2

Charities cannot in any case engage in such publicity [see **40.3.6**], so this rule is unlikely to affect them. Local authority-funded non-charities which are involved in activities which could be construed as party political should be particularly careful:

- before a local or general election;
- when using simplified publicity, such as a slogan;
- when referring to politicians or political parties;
- when commenting on controversial matters or making comments which are part of a wider campaign.

See **41.4** for more about political publicity.

40.2.6
Email and the web

The rules that govern all publications apply just as strongly to emails and materials on the internet. Organisations need to ensure that the speed and rapid distributive powers of the medium are matched by policies to prevent misuse, defamation, breach of copyright and other potential problems [see **38.1.5**].

40.3
DEFAMATION

For the purpose of defamation law, 'publication' refers to anything made public by disclosure to one or more third parties. This wide definition means that an organisation could find itself liable even if a defamatory comment is made only in a 'private' conversation, letter or email.

Defamation may be either:

- **slander** [see **40.3.2**], which covers a transitory occurrence such as a statement made verbally or a gesture; *or*
- **libel**, if the comment is written or is recorded in any other permanent form such as video or on a website, or if it is broadcast or is made in the public performance of a play.

Defamatory comments made in a speech are slanderous; if the speech is recorded in a transcript, tape or video the comments become libellous.

Defamation claims must be brought within one year. Proof of actual damage is not required to make libel actionable. To bring a claim for slander a person must generally be able to prove he or she has suffered actual damage.

Defamation Act 1996 s.5

Defamation insurance is available [see **20.5.5**].

The **European Convention on Human Rights**, in particular article 10 on freedom of expression [see **60.3.1**], may affect UK libel law.

40.3.1
Defamatory comment

To be defamatory a comment must:

- refer to an identifiable living person or corporate body, either by name or in a way by which people who know the person or company would think that the comment referred to him, her or it;
- be published, which means it must be made, or be made available, to a third party (so a negative comment about a person made only to that person is not defamatory); *and*
- 'tend to lower the plaintiff [the person about whom the comment is made] in the estimation of right-thinking members of society generally, and in particular to cause him to be regarded with feelings of hatred, contempt, ridicule, fear and disesteem'.

Sim v Stretch [1936] 2 All ER 1237

If A makes a defamatory comment about B to C, B can bring a claim against A. If C repeats the comment, B can bring a claim against both A and C.

If A makes a defamatory comment about B directly to B, and B then repeats it to C and C repeats it to D, this does not make either A or C liable for defamation—because B is considered to have consented to making the statement public.

A statement may be defamatory even if it does not directly defame a person or company, but contains **defamatory innuendo**.

40.3.1.1
The internet and defamation

The internet poses potentially major risks of liability, because a defamatory comment can reach so many people so quickly. All organisations should have policies making clear that emails containing defamatory material must not be sent, even within the organisation, and must never be forwarded [see **38.1.5**].

Organisations which allow other people to post information to their websites should take steps to control the potential risks. These include terms and conditions of use, regular monitoring of content, insurance, and possibly running the website through a separate company, to isolate the risk.

40.3.2
Slander

For a statement to be slanderous, the person about whom it is made must generally be able to show that he or she has suffered damage which can be calculated in financial terms.

This requirement does not apply if a slanderous statement alleges or implies that the person committed an imprisonable offence, has a 'socially undesirable' disease or is unfit to carry on his or her occupation or profession, or if it implies that a woman has committed adultery or acted in an 'unchaste' way. In these situations, as in libel cases, there is no need for the person who is slandered to show that he or she has suffered damage as result of the slander.

40.3.3
Defences

Even if a comment has a defamatory effect, it is not unlawful if the person who made the comment can prove a defence.

40.3.3.1
Justification

Under the defence of **justification**, a defamatory comment is not unlawful if the person making the comment proves that it is true.

40.3.3.2
Privileged comment

Privileged comment means that a statement is not unlawful, even if it is defamatory, because it is justified on the basis of freedom of speech or protection of the public interest.

Privilege may be **absolute** which means it always applies, or may be **qualified** which means it applies only if the statement is made without malice.

Absolute privilege applies to:

- statements made in the House of Commons or House of Lords, parliamentary papers of an official nature, and statements made by officers of state to one another as part of their official duties;

- statements relating to judicial proceedings made by judges, advocates, witnesses or jurors in the course of the proceedings;

- fair, accurate and contemporaneous reports, including reports in radio and television broadcasts, of public judicial proceedings in the UK, the European Courts of Justice and Human Rights, and United Nations criminal tribunals;   *Defamation Act 1996 s.14*

- communications between lawyers and their clients.

Qualified privilege applies to:

- fair and accurate reports, including broadcast, of public proceedings of a legislature, court, public inquiry, international organisation or international conference anywhere in the world; extracts from reports and papers published by a government, international organisation or international conference anywhere in the world; and extracts from any register or other document required by law to be open to public inspection;   *Defamation Act 1996 s.15; sch.1*

- statements made in pursuance of a legal, moral or social duty, where 'the great mass of right-thinking people' would consider it their duty under the circumstances to make the statement (for example reporting a suspected crime to the police or suspected child or elder abuse to social services);   *Stuart v Bell [1891] 2 QB 341*

- statements made to protect the public interest or the interests or reputation of the person making the statement.

40.3.3.3
Fair comment

Opinions may be expressed, even if they have the effect of being defamatory, on matters of public interest and concern. This includes comments on public figures and on public works such as literary works and plays.

This defence of **fair comment** does not apply where:

- the opinion is expressed maliciously; *and/or*

- the opinion is not based on any fact, or the facts on which the opinion is based are incorrect.

40.3.3.4
Offer to make amends

A formal offer to make amends by apology, correction and payment of compensation and costs, is a complete defence unless the plaintiff can show that the defendant knew that the publication was false and defamatory, and referred to the plaintiff. If the offer to make amends is accepted, the court fixes the level of compensation.

Defamation Act 1996 ss.2-4

40.3.3.5
Responsibility for publication

Organisations are generally vicariously liable for the acts of employees [see **19.5.3**], so libels in emails, websites or other publications produced by staff will generally create liability for the organisation.

A newsagent, library, website operator or similar body which distributes a libellous publication may be able to show it did not commit a defamatory act if it can show:

- it did not know, and had no reason to believe, that what it did caused or contributed to the publication of a defamatory statement;

- it took reasonable care in relation to the publication; *and*

- it was not the author, editor or publisher of the statement.   *s.1*

40.3.4
Remedies for defamation

Defamation is a civil wrong—a tort—but unlike most torts, defamation cases are sometimes heard by juries. The remedies are injunctions to prevent repetition of the defamatory comment, and damages.

Newspapers and periodicals may be able to minimise damages by:

- proving they were not malicious or grossly negligent in making the statement;

- proving they published a full apology at the earliest opportunity, or if the periodical appears less often than weekly, offered to publish it in another periodical chosen by the plaintiff; *and*

- paying a sum of money into the court [see **61.4.8**].

Libel Act 1843 s.2

40.3.5
Criminal libel and harassment

As well as being a tort, libel (but not slander) may also be a crime. In a criminal libel case the defamed person does not have to be alive, as he or she does for civil libel, and the defamatory statement does not have be made to a third party, as it does for civil libel.

In some situations, defamatory verbal or written attacks on an individual may constitute harassment [see **19.5.1** and **36.4.5**], and threatening letters, electronic communication or other articles may be **malicious communication**.   *Malicious Communications Act 1988*

40.4 MALICIOUS FALSEHOOD

Although legitimate comparisons with someone else's goods or services are acceptable [see **40.2.2.2**], negative comments cannot be made with malicious intent. If the person about whom the comment is made suffers loss as a result of a statement made maliciously, he or she can bring an action for **malicious** or **injurious falsehood**. Malicious falsehood is different from defamation in that:

- it applies only to comments about goods and/or services;

- the person about whom the comment was made must prove that it was made maliciously, and that actual loss was suffered as a result of the comment;

- the estate of a deceased person may be sued for malicious falsehood, but not for defamation;

- legal aid is available for cases of malicious falsehood, but not for defamation.

FOR FURTHER INFORMATION

Advertising & sales promotions. Advertising Standards Authority: 020-7580 5555; www.asa.org.uk

ISBN. UK ISBN Agency: 01252-742590; www.whitaker.co.uk

ISSN. ISSN UK Centre: 01937-546959; www.bl.uk/information/issn.html

Legal deposit libraries. British Library: 01937-546298; www.bl.uk

Copyright Libraries Agency: 020-7388 5061; www.llgc.org.uk/cla

Newspapers/periodicals. Companies House: 0870-333 36 36; www.companieshouse.gov.uk

Periodical Publishers Association: 020-7404 4166; www.ppa.co.uk

Organisations funded by local authority. Local Government Information Unit: 020-7554 2800; www.lgiu.gov.uk

---

Chapter 41
CAMPAIGNING AND POLITICAL ACTIVITIES

41.1
VOLUNTARY ORGANISATIONS AND CAMPAIGNING

Many people believe, erroneously, that voluntary organisations cannot involve themselves in political activities. In fact the voluntary sector has always been at the heart of political life in the UK, and even charities are allowed to undertake some political or campaigning activity.

41.1.1
Defining 'political'

'Political' may be defined in a variety of ways, for example:

- **party political**, intended to affect support for a party or candidates;
- seeking to influence decisions and actions of **government** and public sector bodies at any level, from local to international;
- seeking to influence decisions and actions of any body which operates in the **public arena**, for example campaigning for a company which makes military goods to convert to non-military production, or for a restaurant to ban smoking;
- seeking to influence any sort of **change**, even if it is purely individual, such as encouraging people to pick up their litter.

Different definitions of 'political' are used for different legal purposes. 'Political' advertising or publicity is defined differently, for example, in the Independent Television Commission's and Radio Authority's Codes of Advertising Standards and Practice [see **41.4**], the **Local Government Act 1986** [see **40.2.5**] and the **Representation of the People Act 1983** [see **41.5.1**]. The Charity Commission uses a different definition [see **41.3.1**]. In addition, a decision about whether an activity is 'political' may depend more on the views of the person describing it than on any legal definition of what is and is not political.

Even 'non-political' activities such as fundraising could in some situations be legally defined as terrorism [see **41.6**].

589

41.1.2
The law on campaigning

Voluntary organisations which undertake political activities are affected not only by the rules specifically relating to those activities, but also by a range of other legal issues:

- the proposed activity must fall within the organisation's constitutional objects [see **4.2**];

- the organisation must have the power to undertake the proposed activity, either explicitly within its governing document or by implication [see **5.4.3**];

- the decision to undertake the activity must be properly made, and must be recorded in minutes or some other appropriate way;

- funds raised specifically for the activity must be used only for it, and funds raised for other purposes cannot be used for this activity;

- the proposed activity must not be in breach of any grant, contract or lease conditions;

- political advertising and publicity must in general comply with the requirement to be legal, honest, decent and truthful [see **40.2**];

- there are restrictions on the use of local authority funding for political publicity [see **40.2.5**];

- in the run-up to an election, there are strict rules on political activities [see **41.5**];

- no one may act in a way which is likely to incite racial hatred, provoke violence or cause alarm [see **42.7**];

- demonstrations and other public activities must comply with the relevant laws, and some require police permission [see **42.4**];

- some demonstrations and other activities may be defined as terrorism under the **Terrorism Act 2000**, as is any support for an organisation proscribed under that Act [see **41.6**].

41.1.3
Human rights and campaigning

The **European Convention on Human Rights**, incorporated into UK law by the **Human Rights Act 1998**, guarantees the rights to freedom of expression and freedom of assembly and association. But such rights are subject to limitations 'necessary in a democratic society', including national security, public safety, and the protection of the reputation or rights and freedoms of others. The Human Rights Act is likely to be used to challenge restrictions on political and campaigning activities. *European Convention on Human Rights arts.10, 11;*
Human Rights Act 1998 sch.1

The Human Rights Act also provides a framework under which individuals and organisations can challenge public authorities [see **60.3.2**] which infringe rights, or under which organisations carrying out public functions may be challenged by their service users or others.

41.2
NON-CHARITABLE ORGANISATIONS

Non-charitable unincorporated associations [see **1.2**] and companies [see **2.3**] may be set up with explicitly political objects. Industrial and provident societies must be set up to carry on a trade, business or industry [see **2.4**]. This is interpreted widely, but an IPS with purely or primarily political objects might not be able to register.

Provided they remain within the law, within their objects and powers and within the requirements of funders and others, there are no external constraints on the political activities of non-charitable organisations. However, funds received from a charity—whether as a grant, donation or membership fee—cannot be used in any way which breaches the rules on charity campaigning [see **41.3.3**]. To prove they have not misused charitable funds, the non-charitable organisation may have to show these funds and what they have been spent on separately in their financial records and annual accounts.

41.3
CHARITABLE
ORGANISATIONS

A distinction must be made between organisations established with political **objects** (set up to achieve a particular political purpose) and those which have objects which are not explicitly political, but which undertake political **activity**. This distinction is crucial, especially for understanding what charities can and cannot do.

41.3.1
Political objects

It is a basic principle of charity law that a charity cannot be established for political purposes [see **4.3.8**]. Political objects or purposes include:

- promoting the interests of a political party;

- seeking to change, support or oppose changes to the law or government policy at home or abroad;

- seeking to educate the public in accordance with one particular set of political purposes.

Since a charity's objects must be exclusively charitable [see **4.3**], an organisation which has one or more political objects cannot be registered or recognised as a charity. However this aspect of charity law must now be considered in light of the right to freedom of association guaranteed by article 11 of the **European Convention on Human Rights**, and some organisations previously rejected for charity registration because of 'political' objects may find registration possible.

41.3.2
Political activities

Charities cannot have a political purpose, but can use political means to carry out or achieve their charitable objects. So charities can undertake some political activities, provided those activities are directly related to the achievement of their objects.   *McGovern and others v Attorney General (Amnesty International Trust) [1982] 1 Ch 321; [1981] 3 All ER 493*

The Charity Commission's guidelines on acceptable activities are set out in the free booklets CC9 *Political Activities and Campaigning by Charities* and CC9(a) *Political Activities and Campaigning by Local Community Charities*. Where there is doubt about whether an activity is permissible, advice should be sought from the charity's legal advisors or the Commission. If the charity cannot carry out the activity, it may be possible for it to be done by a non-charitable body associated with the charity [see **9.7.2**], but the charity will not be able to fund it.

41.3.3
What is permitted

Provided the activity or expenditure is directly related to the achievement of the charity's objects and is within its powers [see **5.4.3**], the following types of political activity can be undertaken:

- entering into dialogue with government at any level;

- promoting and commenting on proposed legislation or policy changes;

- supporting or opposing changes in the law or public policy, and making representations to government about such changes;

- providing MPs, local councillors etc with information, research material and reasoned views;

- informing the public about the charity's activities and the information it has presented to government, with the intention of obtaining public support for its views;

- conducting research and telling voters how MPs or political parties have treated an issue or voted on it, as a way of enabling discussion and well founded argument to take place with politicians (rather than merely as a way of applying pressure on them);

- providing well reasoned and well founded material for its supporters to send to MPs and other politicians;

- presenting petitions to the Houses of Parliament, national or local government, provided each page states the purpose of the petition;

- commenting on broader public issues which relate to the charity's purposes or the way it delivers its services;

- seeking the support of MPs or local councillors on matters relating to its grants or contracts.

A charity may allow its premises to be used as a polling station, and may hire out its premises, when they are not being used for the charity's charitable activities, for MPs' or local councillors' surgeries or for meetings of non-charitable organisations, including political and campaigning bodies. All such lettings must be on a proper commercial basis.

A charity cannot support a political party, or seek to persuade members of the public to vote for or against a particular candidate or party. It may advocate a particular position even though a political party advocates the same position, but it must be clear that the charity's views are independent of the political party.

A charity may employ staff such as parliamentary officers to liaise with MPs and government or local authority officials. Their work must be focused on promoting discussion, rather than merely applying pressure.

41.3.3.1
Elections

A charity may, in the run-up to an election, prepare material which assesses and comments on the manifestos and other proposals of the parties as they relate to the charity's work. This must be done in a way which is reasoned, balanced and well founded, and must not breach the restrictions imposed by electoral law [see **41.5**].

A charity may provide candidates with appropriate material in order to persuade them of the worthiness of its cause.

41.3.3.2
European and
international activities

Although the Charity Commission's guidelines refer to MPs and parliament, similar principles apply to political activities involving MEPs, the European Union, foreign governments or the United Nations.

41.3.3.3
Demonstrations and
direct action

Where a charity wishes to organise, promote or participate in a demonstration or direct action, the charity trustees must ensure the activity:

- complies with the general rules on political activities by charities;
- is properly planned, with liaison with the relevant authorities;
- is at all times under the control of the charity or other organisers;
- is peaceful;
- does not put the charity, its trustees, its members or those participating in the event at significant risk of having civil or criminal proceedings brought against them;
- does not bring the charity or charities in general into disrepute.

41.3.4
The amount of
political activity

Campaigning and political activities must be ancillary to the charity's objects. This means that they cannot dominate the activities of the charity, and must directly further the charitable objects.

In addition, the activity must be a reasonable use of resources. The governing body has to believe that the activity will further the charitable objects, and has to assess the effort or resources put into that activity against the likely benefit. This must be done not only when the activity is commenced but at regular intervals, to ensure the charity's resources are not being wasted in a fruitless campaign.

41.3.5
Affiliation to
other bodies

The fact that an alliance or campaigning body is not charitable, or is charitable but includes non-charities among its members, does not preclude a charity from joining. But affiliation to a campaigning body or alliance cannot be used as a way of undertaking activities—whether charitable or non-charitable—which the charity itself cannot undertake.

Before joining any such body or alliance the charity must ensure that it will advance the charity's purposes, and that the charity's funds will not be used for activities which the charity itself could not undertake.

If an alliance or campaign starts to undertake activities which the charity would not be able to do, the charity will have to disassociate itself from these activities, and ensure that its name and any funds it has contributed are not used to support those activities.

41.3.6
What is not permitted

All activities undertaken by a charity must further its objects, so campaigning is not permitted on issues unrelated to the charity's objects. A charitable students union, for example, whose objects were in connection with its membership could not spend money campaigning against the Gulf War, nor could a students union campaign against withdrawal of free milk for schoolchildren since its objects did not involve the welfare of schoolchildren. *Webb v O'Doherty and others, The Times 11/2/1991; Bawdry v Feintuck [1972] 2 All ER 81*

Charities must not base their campaigning on inadequate information or unreasoned argument. In particular, they must not:

- collect data in a distorted way, to support preconceived views;
- distort research or its results;
- publicise or promote research which is partial or faulty, or is based on incorrect data;
- publicise material which they know, or ought to know, is inaccurate;
- fail to investigate the evidence in support of their position before using it;
- use purely emotive or unreasoned appeals, unless the nature of the medium being used (such as a poster or short advertisement) prevents a full exposition of the charity's detailed position;
- urge supporters or the public to take action without providing information to justify the action requested (this particularly applies to persuading supporters or the public to write to MPs);
- provide propaganda which does not allow people to make up their own mind, rather than providing information which allows them to come to their own conclusion.

The nature of the activity must not be inappropriate to charities. In particular, charities must not:

- undertake research for a third party, where they know the third party will use it for party political or propaganda purposes;
- support a political party, even if this seems the best way of obtaining their ends;
- seek to persuade people to vote for or against particular political candidates or parties;
- take part in party political demonstrations.

41.3.7
Penalties

Involvement in political activities which contravene the Charity Commission guidelines could lead to a number of consequences for the charity and its trustees.

41.3.7.1
Tax consequences

Tax reliefs for charities under s.505 of the **Income and Corporation Taxes Act 1988** [see **52.5** and **52.6**] are available only insofar as profits made or income received are used for charitable purposes. If a charity's funds are used for non-charitable purposes, such as improper political activities, tax relief will be lost and tax may become payable.

Because the governing body of a charitable organisation is supposed to act in a prudent manner to preserve the funds of a charity [see **13.3.5**], the members of the governing body could be personally liable to replace the funds lost as a result of unnecessary taxation.

41.3.7.2
Charity Commission

The Charity Commission recognises that the borderline between appropriate and inappropriate charitable activity may be unclear. If it believes a charity has engaged in unacceptable political activity it will investigate and seek explanations before taking any action.

The Commission's response will be influenced by the nature of the activity, how substantial it was, and whether the charity had previously been warned about such activity. Responses could include:

- providing help and advice to prevent a recurrence of the problem;

- taking proceedings against the trustees for repayment of the funds used for the improper political activity;

- taking proceedings in respect of any income lost to the charity because of unnecessary taxation [see above];

- seeking an injunction from the courts to prevent further activities of this nature.

In some cases the Charity Commission may publish the results of its inquiry into a charity's political activities. This is useful in enabling other charities to ascertain the Commission's position, but it could have a substantial negative impact on the charity's funders and its public image. Even if the Commission finds that the activity was acceptable, the mere fact that a charity's name has been linked to an investigation may have a negative impact.

41.3.8
Avoiding problems

To avoid unnecessary difficulties around political activities, all governing body members, ordinary members, employees and volunteers should be aware of what is and is not permissible for their charity.

It is advisable for each charity to draw up its own guidance relating the Commission guidelines to its own objects, and setting out procedures to be followed to ensure compliance. This can help ensure that governing bodies and staff neither adopt self-censorship policies which are more restrictive than they need to be, nor recklessly leap into affiliations or campaigns which are not allowed.

In some cases it may be appropriate to set up a separate non-charitable campaigning arm [see **9.7.2**], or for the activities to be undertaken by a non-charitable members' support group or similar body. The charity will not be able to fund activities which it could not itself undertake, so funding will have to be found from alternative sources.

There is nothing to stop the people involved in the charity from undertaking any activity in their personal capacity.

41.4
POLITICAL
PUBLICITY

Radio and television advertisements cannot be placed by or on behalf of any organisation whose objects are wholly or mainly of a political nature, nor can advertisements be directed towards any political end. Both the Radio Authority and the Independent Television Commission have Codes of Advertising Standards and Practice which include guidance. The Radio Authority and ITC interpret 'political' broadly, and do not allow advertisements for campaigns intended to influence legislation or executive action by central or local government.

Broadcasting Act 1990 ss.8(2),92(2)

In 1994 Amnesty International (British Section) sought to broadcast an advertisement which was humanitarian rather than 'political'. The Radio Authority rejected the advertisement, on the basis that Amnesty's objects were wholly or mainly political. When Amnesty sought a judicial review, the court suggested that 'wholly or mainly political' should be interpreted to mean at least 75%, and that 'a very material proportion of the objects pursued by Amnesty International are non-political'. It invited Amnesty to make a fresh application to the Radio Authority, after which the Authority reversed its decision and allowed the advertisement to be broadcast.

R v Radio Authority ex parte Bull and another, CA 17/12/1996

At the time of writing (early 2001) the Radio Authority and ITC are reviewing their codes, particularly in light of article 10 of the **European Convention on Human Rights**. This guarantees freedom of expression, including the right to receive and impart information and ideas without interference by public authority.

Print and non-broadcast electronic advertising relating to political matters should comply with the British Codes of Advertising and Sales Promotion, which means the advertising must be legal, decent, truthful and honest [see **40.2.1** and **40.2.2**]. The identity and status of all political advertisers should be clear. If their address or other contact details are not generally available, they should be included in the advertisement.

Voluntary organisations cannot use funding provided by a local authority for any party political publicity [see **40.2.5**].

41.5 POLITICAL ACTIVITIES DURING ELECTIONS

Significant exceptions to the need to be 'truthful and honest' apply to advertisements whose principal function is to influence opinion for or against a political party or electoral candidate contesting a UK, European parliamentary or local government election, or any matter before the electorate in a referendum. These advertisements do not have to comply with the requirements:

- to be able to provide documentary evidence to prove all claims made by the advertiser or in testimonials used in advertisements;
- not to mislead by inaccuracy, ambiguity, exaggeration, omission or in other ways;
- to ensure comparisons are clear and fair;
- not to attack or discredit others unfairly.

British Codes of Advertising and Sales Promotion s.12

41.5.1 Authorisation of advertising and activities

While the rules on advertising content are eased during election campaigns, the rules of authorisation of advertising—and virtually all other campaigning related to the election—become much more strict. Non-charitable organisations which engage in party political campaigning need to be careful not to breach these rules. The rules come into effect as soon as an election is called, and may also apply in the weeks before this if it is clear that an election will be called.

41.5.1.1 Support for or against candidates

Expenditure may generally be incurred on presenting a candidate to the public, presenting information to the public about the candidate's views or backing for the candidate, or disparaging other candidates only if the expenditure is authorised in writing by the candidate's election agent.

Representation of the People Act 1983 s.75

This means that publications or advertisements about a candidate or candidates or their views may generally be issued only with the consent of the election agent(s), and public meetings and public displays about one or more candidates or their views may be organised only with such consent. In addition, every event must clearly identify the election agent, and every publication must include the name and address of the printer and publisher. New rules, not in force at the time of writing (early 2001), will require all publications to include the name and address of the printer, the promoter (the person who caused the material to be published), and the candidate or party on whose behalf the material is being published.

Political Parties, Elections and Referendums Act 2000 s.143

Allowed exceptions to the consent rules are:

- information about a candidate, his or her views and support for the candidate may be published in a newspaper or periodical or may be broadcast on radio or television without the agent's consent, provided it is not an advertisement;
- total expenditure of less than the permitted amount [see below] during the election period does not need consent, provided the expenditure is not incurred as part of a concerted plan of action involving one or more other persons.

The permitted amount is £500 in respect of a candidate in a parliamentary election. For local government elections it is £50 plus 0.5p for every entry in the register of local government electors.

Political Parties, Elections and Referendums Act 2000 s.131

41.5.1.2
Support for or against
a political party

Limits apply to expenditure for or against a particular party or group of candidates, or for or against a particular issue where the issue is closely identified with a party or group of candidates, in national elections. The limits are £10,000 in England or £5,000 in Scotland, Wales or Northern Ireland during the election period. The value of expenditure in kind (property, services or facilities provided free or charge or at less than 90% of their market value) is included. *ss.85-89*

41.5.2
What voluntary
organisations can do

During an election campaign, charities and other voluntary organisations may:

- publish information about the candidates or their views in their own newsletters or magazines, provided the periodical would have been published at that time as part of its normal cycle of publication, and provided that for charities, the information is reasoned and is not intended to affect support for or against a particular candidate or party;

- comment on aspects of the parties' manifestos and proposals which are relevant to their own objects, provided that if a charity does this the comment must be balanced and based on reasoned information;

- undertake political activities which are not related to the election of a particular candidate or party, provided these are within the organisation's objects and powers and they comply with the general rules on charity campaigning [see **41.3.3**];

- make their views on these issues known to candidates and the public, including through the media.

41.5.2.1
Public meetings

There are differing views as to whether voluntary organisations may organise public meetings during an election campaign. Following a House of Lords ruling in 1976, some advise that all election-related public meetings during an election period require consent of the relevant election agent(s). However in 1992 the Home Office advised that voluntary organisations could organise public meetings and the cost of such meetings would not constitute an election expense to candidates.

If a charity arranges a public meeting during the election period, either all candidates must be invited to attend and speak, or none.

41.6
NEW DEFINITION
OF TERRORISM

Under the **Terrorism Act 2000**, terrorism is defined as the use or threat of action where:

- the action or threat of action is designed to influence the government or to intimidate the public or a section of the public;

- the action or threat of action is made for the purpose of advancing a political, religious or ideological cause; *and*

- the action involves serious violence against a person or serious damage to property, endangers a person's life other than that of the person committing the action, creates a serious risk to the health or safety of the public or a section of the public, or is designed to interfere seriously with or cause serious disruption to an electronic system. *Terrorism Act 2000 s.1*

This definition is very wide and potentially defines as 'terrorist' any individual or organisation, in the UK or abroad, who advocates violence or damage to property for a political, religious or ideological cause. This could include individuals or organisations campaigning against oppressive regimes or environmentally damaging practices.

**41.6.1
Banned
organisations**

Some organisations, which may be based either in the UK or abroad, are proscribed by the Home Secretary. Any support for them—even wearing their emblem or helping to organise a meeting which will be addressed by one of their members—is an offence.

Terrorism Act 2000 ss.3, 11-13

**41.6.2
Fundraising**

Even where an organisation is not proscribed, it is an offence:

- to invite a person to provide money or property as a donation, loan or in any other way, where the fundraiser intends it to be used or has reasonable cause to believe it may be used for terrorist purposes;

- to provide money or property as a donation, loan or in any other way, where the person providing the money or property knows or has reasonable cause to suspect that it will or may be used for the purposes of terrorism. *ss.15-16*

This could include, for example, fundraising in the UK for an organisation overseas that supports—even if it does not actually use—violence or property damage as a way of challenging a repressive regime.

Information about the implications of these rules is available from Liberty [see below]

FOR FURTHER INFORMATION

Political activities by charities. Charity Commission: 0870-333 0123; www.charitycommission.gov.uk

Activities during election campaigns. Electoral Reform Society: 020-7928 1622; www.electoral-reform.org.uk

Advertising. Advertising Standards Authority: 020-7580 5555; www.asa.org.uk

Independent Television Commission: 020-7255 3000; www.itc.org.uk

Radio Authority: 020-7430 2724; www.radioauthority.org.uk

Proscribed organisations. Liberty: 020-7403 3888; www.liberty-human-rights.org.uk

---

Chapter 42
PUBLIC GATHERINGS
AND ENTERTAINMENT

42.1
THE LAW AND
PUBLIC EVENTS

Any event which is open to the public and/or is held out of doors is likely to have to comply with a multitude of legal requirements—regardless of whether it is or is not publicly advertised, a charge is or is not made, or it is open to all or only a section of the public. Legal issues include:

- whether the event directly furthers the organisation's objects [see **4.2**], and whether it is within the organisation's powers to organise such an event [see **5.4.3** and **47.1.2**];

- whether VAT is chargeable on charges made for the event, and whether it is recoverable on the costs [see **chapter 53**];

- tax implications [see **52.4** and **52.6**];

- whether to run the event through a trading company [see **47.2**];

- whether a licence is required for the event or premises [see **42.2**];

- use of copyright material [see **39.2** and **42.3**];

- rules for bingo, gaming machines, lotteries etc [see **45.6** and **45.7**];

- rules on the provision or sale of food and drink [see **chapter 43**];

- restrictions in leases, restrictive covenants in deeds [see **56.7.2**] and other restrictions in agreements relating to premises;

- fire regulations about the maximum number of people on premises;

- whether the police or other bodies need to be notified [see **42.4**];

- the general obligation not to create a public nuisance [see **19.5.1**] or too much noise [see **59.10.3**];

- insurance [see **20.5.1** and **20.9**].

For many events or premises, several different licences may be necessary [see below]. At the time of writing (early 2001), proposals had been published for a single integrated scheme for licensing premises which sell alcohol, provide public entertainment or provide refreshment at night. Up-to-date information is available from the Department for Culture, Media and Sport [see end of chapter].

42.1.1
Freedom of assembly and association

The **Human Rights Act 1998** guarantees the rights to freedom of assembly and association under article 11 of the European Convention on Human Rights [see **60.3.1**], but these rights may be limited if necessary to maintain public safety, prevent crime and disorder etc. At the time of writing (early 2001) it remained to be seen whether restrictions on public gatherings will be challenged under these rights.

42.2
PUBLIC ENTERTAINMENT

Premises generally need to be licensed by the local authority for public music, dance or sporting events, plays, and film or video shows. The licence is usually in the name of one or more members of the governing body. If this person changes during the period of the licence, the local authority should be notified. Annual entertainment, theatre and cinema licences require **certificates of safety** for the premises. These may or may not be required for occasional licences.

42.2.1
Music, dance and sport

A **public entertainment licence** is generally required for:

- public dancing or music, or any other public entertainment of a like kind if held indoors, or if held out of doors in London;
- public music events held out of doors on private land outside London, if the licensing authority requires registration.

Local Government (Miscellaneous Provisions) Act 1982 s.1, sch.1;
London Government Act 1963 s.52, sch.12

Entertainment of a like kind includes sporting events of a martial nature such as boxing, wrestling, judo or karate.

Outside London, any requirement for outdoor music events to be licensed does not apply if the music is incidental to a religious meeting or service, garden fête, bazaar, sale of work, sporting or athletic event, exhibition, display or other event of a similar character.

Outside London, a licence is not required for music performed in a church or other place of public religious worship or as part of a religious meeting or service. In London a licence is required.

A licence is not required for an entertainment or sporting event held in a pleasure fair, or music incidental to entertainment in a pleasure fair.

42.2.1.1
Sunday events

In the past, admission charges could not be made for public dances held on Sundays. This has now been changed and charges can be made.
Deregulation (Sunday Dancing) Order 2000 [SI 2000/3372]

42.2.1.2
Application and fee

Outside London at least 28 days notice must be given to the local authority, police and fire authority. The period may be reduced in particular cases. In London the notice period is 21 days for a licence for up to one year, and 14 days for an **occasional music licence**, with notice given to the local authority and the commissioner of police.

There is no licence fee if an entertainment is held at a church hall, chapel hall or similar building occupied in connection with a place of public religious worship, or a village hall, parish hall, community hall or similar building. All or part of the fee may be waived if the entertainment is educational or is being held for a charitable or similar purpose.

42.2.1.3
Copyright

A public entertainment licence gives the right to hold an event at which music may be played, but does not give any right to play or perform copyright music at the event. Further licences are required for this [see **42.3**]. If copyright works other than music are performed, consent of the copyright owner is required [see **39.11**].

**42.2.2
Plays**

A play is any dramatic presentation given in person by one or more people where a major part of what is done involves playing a role. A play may consist of speech, singing or action, and includes ballet, opera, musical shows and even nativity plays. *Theatres Act 1968 s.18(1)*

**42.2.2.1
Theatre licence**

Premises—including charitable, church and community premises and outdoors—may be used for the public performance of a play only if they have a **theatre licence**. To obtain a licence, at least 21 days notice must be given to the local authority and chief officer of police. *s.12(1)*

If the play is of an educational character or is being performed for a charitable purpose, the licence fee is waived. *sch.1*

Plays may not be performed between 2 a.m. and 2 p.m. on Sundays in premises which are licensed under the Theatres Act or to which the Act applies. *Sunday Theatre Act 1972 s.2(1)*

**42.2.2.2
Public entertainment
licence**

A public entertainment licence [see **42.2.1**] is not needed for music at places where plays are performed if the only music is played as an introduction to a play, during the interval, at the end of a play or between performances, and the total time taken by the music is less than 25% of the time taken by the performance(s) of the play on that day at those premises. *Theatres Act 1968 s.12(2)*

**42.2.2.3
Copyright**

If the work being performed is copyright, the consent of the copyright owner(s) is needed [see **39.11**]. If copyright music is being performed, either live or recorded, a variety of copyright licenses may be needed [see **42.3**] even if a public entertainment licence is not required.

**42.2.2.4
Alcohol licence**

An alcohol licence is not required for a bar at premises with a theatre licence, provided the bar is open only during and immediately before performances and these times are within normal licensing hours. The clerk to the licensing justices [see **43.3**] must be notified of the intention to sell alcohol. *Theatres Act 1968 s.12(2); Licensing Act 1964 s.199(c)*

**42.2.3
Film and video
shows**

**42.2.3.1
Cinema licences**

In general, films and videos cannot be shown to the public unless the premises are licensed. However a **cinema licence** is generally not needed for showing a film or video:

- at a private house if the public are not admitted, and the event is **non-commercial** (not promoted for private gain, or the main purpose of showing the film or video is to show a product, advertise goods or services, or provide information, education or instruction);

- where adults (16 and over) are admitted free of charge, and the main purpose is non-commercial;

- where children (under 16) are admitted free of charge, the main purpose is non-commercial, and the showing is held in a private house or as an activity of an educational or religious institution;

- if the organisation showing the film or video is a charitable or voluntary organisation and has obtained an exemption certificate from the Home Office, *and* does not use the premises to show films or videos for more than three days out of any seven days;

- if the premises are not used for film and video shows for more than six occasions in any calendar year, provided the occupier gives seven days notice in writing each time to the local authority, fire authority and police authority; *or*

- if it is being shown by a film or video society which is non-profit and is open only to members, and where all payments received are applied only for expenses. *Cinemas Act 1985 ss.5-7*

A cinema licence is required in other situations, with at least 28 days notice to the local authority, fire authority and chief officer of police. Special rules apply for films shown on Sundays. *ss.1, 9*

42.2.3.2
Public entertainment licence

A public entertainment licence [see **42.2.1**] is not needed to show a film or video which includes singing, dancing or music. It is also not needed if music is played before or after a film, during the interval or between two films, provided the total time taken by the music is less than 25% of the time taken by the films on that day in those premises.   *s.19*

42.2.3.3
Copyright

Regardless of whether a cinema licence is or is not needed, it is likely to be necessary to obtain the consent of the copyright owner before a film or video is shown [see **39.11**]. Most videos are hired or sold on the basis that they may be shown only for domestic purposes.

Even though a public entertainment licence is not required for music in the film or video or incidental to its showing, music copyright licences are likely to be required [see **42.3**].

42.2.4
Community premises licence

Local authorities can issue a **community premises licence** (CPL) for church and village halls, youth and community centres and similar buildings which normally cater for a maximum of 300 people. The CPL may also be available for larger premises which are used infrequently or are never used to their full capacity. Local authorities can set their own requirements, but government guidance recommends:

- there should be a single licence to cover two or more of public entertainment licence, theatre licence and cinema licence;
- renewal notices should be issued for annual licences, so the need for renewal is not overlooked by the organisation;
- local authorities should provide a named contact for enquiries;
- local authorities should impose only conditions which are strictly necessary for public safety and the avoidance of nuisance;
- the fee charged for a joint application for two or more licences should be less than the total due for the separate licences;
- where the premises are exempt from a fee, the fee should not have to be paid even if the premises are used for financial gain, provided their overall use remains for community purposes.

42.3
PERFORMANCE OF COPYRIGHT MUSIC

A number of consents are required for performance of copyright music, whether live or recorded. These licences are all separate, and having one does not remove the need to have the others.

The licences are required for public events, and also for other public situations such as background music in shops, pubs and workplaces, street performances, processions, festivals, fêtes, use of music in day centres or for dancing or keep-fit classes, jukeboxes, or any performance of live or recorded music which is not within a purely domestic setting.

For more about copyright in general, see **39.2**.

42.3.1
Performing right

A **performing right licence** applies to the copyright of the music (and words, if any) and is available from the Performing Right Society (PRS) [see end of chapter]. This licence provides royalties to composers and songwriters (or to whoever owns their copyright) and music publishers. Depending on the type of licence it may cover live performance of music; public playing of recorded music on records, tapes, CDs or karaoke; jukeboxes; broadcasting music on radio, television or cable; and/or the right to play radio and television broadcasts which contain music through a loudspeaker (for example in shops) or show them publicly, for example in pubs or at community centres or day centres.

A PRS licence is not required for the use of copyright music during worship in churches or other places of worship.

PRS does not licence live performance of all or part of musical shows, operas, ballets etc, the performance of specially written music for plays, or other dramatic or theatrical productions. These permissions must be obtained from the copyright owner, who is usually the publisher.

The fee depends on the extent of music usage, the type of premises being licensed and the capacity of the premises and/or average attendance at events. There are special fees for community premises run by voluntary organisations. The first year's fee is reduced by one-third if the licence is applied for before performances have started.

42.3.2
Recorded music
and videos

A different licence covers the copyright on the particular performance of the music which is recorded on a record, tape or CD, and is available from Phonographic Performance Limited (PPL) [see end of chapter for details]. For music on videos the licence is from Video Performance Limited (VPL) at the same address. A PPL or VPL licence provides royalties to the performers on the particular recording, or to whoever owns the copyright on their performance.

Charitable and other organisations concerned with the advancement of religion, education or social welfare do not have to obtain a PPL or VPL licence if there is no admission charge for the event at which the music is played, or if *all* the proceeds of any admission charge are applied for the purposes of the organisation. The same applies for events which are 'beneficial' to charitable and other similar organisations. PPL may interpret the 'all' strictly, and may not allow the exemption if any of the proceeds are used for any other purpose, such as room hire.

Community Matters [see end of chapter] has a joint licensing scheme with PPL for the use of sound recordings in community buildings run by charitable organisations.

42.3.3
Record company

Another licence covers the copyright held by the sound recording manufacturer. It is available from the recording company.

42.3.4
Recording
performances

The above licences give the right to play or perform music, but they do not give the right to record the performance. Licences to record copyright music are provided by the Mechanical Copyright Protection Society (MCPS) [see end of chapter].

42.4
PUBLIC
GATHERINGS

A gathering is **public** if it is held in a public place, or is held in a private place where the public or a section of the public are permitted, with or without payment, to attend.   *Public Order Act 1936 s.9*

A **private place** is one which the public have the right to enter only with the consent of the owner, occupier or lessee. It includes a public place hired for the occasion by the organiser of the gathering.

Depending on its nature and in some cases on its size, a public gathering may be:

*   a public meeting [see **42.4.2**];
*   an assembly, which may or may not also be a meeting [see **42.4.3**];
*   a festival [see **42.4.4**];
*   a procession or march, which may or may not also involve an assembly or public meeting [see **42.4.5**];
*   a picket line [see **42.4.7**].

The local authority may have by-laws requiring it or the police to be notified of gatherings in public places.

Information about public gatherings is available from Liberty [details at end of chapter]. Especially for large-scale events or events involving any risk to participants or the public, it is sensible to take legal advice beforehand, and before organising any sort of public event it is essential to consider all aspects of insurance [see **20.5.1** and **20.9**]

When a charity is involved in a public gathering of a political nature, it must comply with the rules on political activities by charities [see **41.3**]. All political events during the run-up to an election must comply with specific rules [see **41.5**].

42.4.1
Admission, exclusion and problems

Regardless of the nature of the gathering, it is sensible to be aware of the possibility of problems and to have procedures for dealing with troublesome individuals or groups (either within the gathering or as bystanders), police intervention and similar matters.

42.4.1.1
Public gatherings in a public place

The police may take action to prevent obstruction at a gathering in a public place. This may involve removing or arresting individuals or breaking up the gathering if a breach of the peace [see **42.6**] occurs or is reasonably expected to occur, or arresting individuals for public disorder offences [see **42.6**], breach of conditions imposed on a public event [see **42.4.3** and **42.4.5**], and certain other offences.

42.4.1.2
Public gatherings in a private place

The owners or managers of private premises do not have to make their premises available to anyone. The only exception is during election campaigns, when any candidate has the right to use a publicly owned hall for an election meeting, provided the meeting is open to the public and the intention is to discuss election issues.

The organisers of a public gathering in a private place may refuse admission to any person, provided this is not done unlawfully on the basis of race, sex or disability [see **chapter 37**].

People who attend a public gathering in a private place, including a public place hired for the occasion, without paying an admission charge are there because the organiser allows them to be, and may be asked to leave at any time with no reason. A person who refuses to leave becomes a trespasser and can be removed using reasonable force [see **59.5.2**].

Where people pay an admission charge, the payment creates a contract. Unless they have contravened the conditions of admission it is a breach of contract to ask them to leave, and a breach of contract and an assault to remove them physically. If they have acted in a disorderly way or contravened the admission conditions they may be asked to leave, and if they refuse they may be removed using reasonable force.

The police may enter a public gathering in a private place only if asked to do so by the occupiers of the premises or the organisers of the gathering, or if they have reason to believe that a breach of the peace [see **42.6**] is being or is likely to be committed. They may help remove trespassers if asked to do so by the occupiers or organisers, and may arrest individuals for breach of the peace.

The organisers of the gathering must comply with all conditions in the hire agreement, lease or any other agreement for use of the premises.

42.4.2
Public meetings

In legal terms a **public meeting** is a public gathering [see **42.4**] held 'for the purpose of the discussion of matters of public interest, or for the purpose of the expression of views on such matters'. A public meeting held out of doors with 20 or more people is a **public assembly** [see **42.4.3**]. *Public Order Act 1936 s.9*

For the responsibilities and rights of the person chairing a meeting, see **17.2.7**.

It is unlawful for any person to disrupt or deliberately interrupt a public meeting or stop it from transacting the business for which it was called, or to disrupt a political meeting held as part of an election campaign.
Public Meeting Act 1908 s.1; Representation of the People Act 1983 s.97

42.4.3
Public assemblies

A **public assembly** is a gathering of 20 or more people in the open air. It may be a public meeting [see **42.4.2**] or another type of gathering. The local authority may require notification of public assemblies.

The senior police officer in the area where the assembly is being held may impose conditions if there is evidence that public disorder or intimidation may occur. *Public Order Act 1986 s.14*

The police may not ban an assembly unless it involves trespass. A **trespassatory assembly** is one:

- which is to be held, or is being held, without the landowner's consent on land with no access or limited rights of access; *and*

- is likely to cause serious disruption to the life of the community, *or* is on a site of particular historical or archaeological interest. *Criminal Justice and Public Order Act 1994 s.70*

Special permission is needed for assemblies in Hyde Park (Royal Parks Agency, tel 020-7298 2000) and Trafalgar Square (Greater London Authority, tel 020-7983 4234).

**42.4.4
Festivals, street parties, fêtes etc**

An outdoor festival, street party, fête open to the public or similar event must comply with the requirements for assemblies [see above] as well as licensing and copyright requirements [see **42.2** and **42.3**], food hygiene requirements [see **43.2**], and all other relevant rules. There may be important tax and VAT implications for running festivals, fêtes and similar events as a way of raising funds [see **chapters 52** and **53**]. Advice may need to be taken from an accountant or solicitor who specialises in charity matters.

In some situations the police have power to stop people within five miles of an outdoor festival site and direct them to turn back, to seize vehicles and sound equipment at a festival, and to direct people to leave the festival. *ss.63-65*

**42.4.5
Processions**

The police must be given advance notice in writing of any proposal to hold a public **procession** or **march** intended to mark or commemorate an event, publicise a cause or campaign or demonstrate support for or opposition to the views or actions of a person or body of persons. *Public Order Act 1986 s.11*

At least six clear days before the proposed date, the notice must be sent by recorded delivery post or handed to a police station in the police area where the procession is intended to start. If there are exceptional circumstances it may be hand delivered with less than six days notice. The notice must state the proposed date, starting time and route, and must include the name and address of at least one organiser.

The purpose of the notice is to inform the police, not to seek their permission. The senior police officer may however impose conditions if there are good reasons for doing so, or in some cases may apply to the court for a prohibition order. *Public Order Act 1986 ss.12-13*

In exceptional circumstances the police may, with the consent of the Home Secretary in London or the local authority elsewhere, ban all or some marches in an area for up to three months. *s.13*

Information about processions and marches is available from Liberty [see end of chapter]. In London the police have a code of practice for marches. This is for guidance only, and is not legally binding.

**42.4.6
Events near Parliament**

While Parliament is in session it is not permitted to carry banners or placards, distribute leaflets, or hold an open air meeting, assembly or procession within one mile of Parliament on the north side of the Thames. *Metropolitan Police Act 1839*

**42.4.7
Picketing**

Apart from the legislation on peaceful picketing by workers [see **32.8.3**], picketing is not specifically allowed or prohibited. It could, however, constitute trespass, obstructing the highways, behaviour likely to cause a breach of the peace and/or public disorder.

42.5
LOUDSPEAKERS

Loudspeakers may be used only between 8 a.m. and 9 p.m. Notice as required under local by-laws must be given to the police, and other local by-laws must be complied with.   *Control of Pollution Act 1974 s.62*

42.6
PUBLIC DISORDER

Organisers of public events, especially large ones on contentious issues, should have contingency plans and should ensure stewards are trained to deal with situations which might arise. For some activities it may be appropriate to have independent legal observers present. Liberty [see below] can provide advice on this.

Breach of the peace is a common law offence which occurs when harm is actually done or is likely to be done to a person, or in the person's presence to his or property, or when a person is in fear of being harmed or having his or her property harmed through an assault, affray, riot or other disturbance.   *R v Howell [1981] 3 All ER 383*

Other types of disorder occur if a person of 'reasonable firmness' present at the scene would fear for his or her safety:

- **affray**, where one person (or more) uses or threatens unlawful violence towards another person;

- **violent disorder**, where three or more people are present, and they use or threaten unlawful violence;

- **riot**, where 12 or more people use or threaten unlawful violence for a common purpose.   *Public Order Act 1986 ss.1-3*

It is an offence to use threatening, abusive or insulting words or behaviour or to distribute or display threatening, abusive or insulting words or signs within the hearing or sight of a person likely to be caused harassment, alarm or distress, or if the words or signs are likely to stir up racial hatred, or with the intention to frighten someone, provoke violence or stir up racial hatred.   *ss.4-6, 18, 19*

Possession of racially inflammatory material, even without distributing it, is an offence.   *s.23*

Going onto land without the consent of the landowner and with the intention of disrupting or obstructing lawful activity or intimidating people to deter them from engaging in lawful activity is **aggravated trespass** and is an offence (unlike ordinary trespass which is a tort, see **19.5**).   *Criminal Justice and Public Order Act 1994 s.68*

FOR FURTHER INFORMATION

Local licensing. Local authority

Licensing of community premises. Community Matters: 020-7226 0189; www.communitymatters.org.uk

Licensing of village halls. ACRE: 01285-653477; www.acreciro.demon.co.uk

Licences for places of worship, church halls etc. Churches Main Committee, 020-7222 4984

Licensing law. Department for Culture, Media and Sport: 020-7211 6000; www.culture.gov.uk

Music licensing. Mechanical Copyright Protection Society (MCPS): 020-8664 4400; www.mcps.co.uk

Performing Right Society (PRS): 020-7580 5544; www.prs.co.uk

Phonographic Performance Ltd (PPL): 020-7534 1000; www.ppluk.com

Video Performance Ltd (VPL): 020-7534 1000

Demonstrations etc. Liberty: 020-7403 3888; www.liberty-human-rights.org.uk

Chapter 43
FOOD AND DRINK

43.1 FOOD SALES AND CHARITY TRADING

Charities and other voluntary organisations may provide or sell food and drink:

- as a direct part of achieving their objects, for example in a residential home or a café training project for a charity's beneficiaries;

- as an activity ancillary to their objects, for example running a snack bar for people attending a charitable training centre or a bar for people attending performances at a theatre which is a charity;

- purely or primarily as a way of raising money, for example by running food stalls at a fundraising festival, or a restaurant at a theatre which is open to the public rather than only to people attending performances.

The sale of food and drink constitutes a trade and is subject to the rules on trading by charities [see **47.1**]. Running alongside these rules are the rules on sale or provision of alcohol by charities [see **43.3.1**].

Selling food and drink as a *direct* part of achieving a charity's objects is straightforward. The sales are primary purpose trading [see **52.6**] or sales where the work is carried out by the charity's beneficiaries [see **52.6.4**], so the charity can carry out the trading itself.

The sale of food and drink may also be carried out by a charity where it is directly linked (ancillary) to the charity's charitable activities [see **52.6.2**], provided certain criteria are met [see **43.3.1**].

Where the sale is not part of a charitable activity or ancillary to it but is carried on to raise funds or as part of a fundraising event, it can be carried out by the charity provided it meets the requirements for the concessions for fundraising activities or events [see **52.7**].

In other situations the charity will not be able to carry out the sales itself, and will have to set up a separate trading company [see **47.3**] or a members' club [see **43.3.2.3**] to run the bar, café, kiosk or whatever. If this is done, the parent organisation grants a sub-lease or licence to the trading company or members' club, allowing it to trade or to sell alcohol on the organisation's premises. The arrangement must fulfil all the usual requirements for charities' relationships with trading subsidiaries [see **chapter 47**].

The sale of food or drink may have VAT implications [see **53.5.1**], and advice should be sought from the organisation's accountant or solicitor.

43.2
FOOD HYGIENE

An organisation involved in the production, supply or sale of food must comply with the **Food Safety Act 1990, Food Safety (General Food Hygiene) Regulations 1995** *[SI 1995/1763]* and other regulations for specific types of food. They cover not only food prepared on the organisation's premises or bought in, but also food prepared at home for sale or distribution elsewhere. Detailed information and guidance are available from the local authority's environmental health department.

The organisation must ensure food is supplied or sold in a hygienic way, identify food safety hazards, and ensure safety controls are in place and are maintained and reviewed.

Food premises should:

- be designed and constructed to permit good hygiene practices;
- be clean and maintained in good repair;
- have adequate drainage, an adequate supply of drinking water and adequate hand-washing facilities;
- provide clean lavatories which do not lead directly into food rooms;
- have adequate lighting and ventilation;
- have suitable controls in place to protect against pests.

Rooms where food is prepared, treated or processed should have walls, floors and equipment that are easy to clean and where necessary disinfect, and adequate facilities for washing food and equipment and for the storage and removal of food waste.

Anyone whose work involves handling food must:

- wear clean and, where appropriate, protective over-clothes;
- observe good personal hygiene;
- routinely wash their hands when handling food;
- never smoke in food handling areas;
- report any illness, such as infected wounds, skin infections, diarrhoea or vomiting, to their manager or supervisor immediately;
- protect food and ingredients against contamination;
- receive adequate supervision, instruction and/or training in food hygiene. *Food Safety (General Food Hygiene) Regulations 1995 [SI 1995/1763] sch.1*

Slightly different rules apply to movable and temporary premises such as marquees and market stalls.

Some foods must be kept either at or above 63ºC, or below 8ºC.
Food Safety (Temperature Control) Regulations 1995 [SI 1995/2200]

43.2.1
Registration

Premises where food is prepared, stored, supplied or sold on five or more days in any five-week period must register with the environmental health department. The five days do not need to be consecutive. The registration requirements also apply to food provision out of doors.
Food Premises (Registration) Regulations 1991 [SI 1991/2825]

There are exceptions for:

- premises where the only provision of food is retail sale from an automatic vending machine; *reg.3(1)*
- premises controlled by a voluntary organisation or charity and used only by voluntary organisations or charities, where no food is stored for sale other than dry ingredients for the preparation of beverages, sugar, biscuits, crisps and similar dry products; *reg.3(3)*
- domestic premises used for the preparation of food to be sold at a market stall run by WI Country Markets Ltd (Women's Institutes).
Food Premises (Registration) Amendment Regulations 1997 [SI 1997/723]

43.3
PROVISION OF
ALCOHOL

Many leases and some freehold titles contain covenants [see **56.7.2**] prohibiting or restricting the sale or provision of alcohol on the premises. These may have been included for religious or moral reasons, or to prevent the risk of disturbance often associated with alcohol sales.

Leaseholders in this situation who want to sell or provide alcohol must obtain consent from their landlord. Freeholders may either obtain consent from the owner of the land which has the benefit of the covenant, or may need to apply to a **land tribunal** to have the covenant removed [see **56.7.2**].

Some charity governing documents prohibit the provision or sale of alcohol. In this situation it may be possible to amend the governing document.

Organisations which want to provide or sell alcohol should consider whether this might be considered objectionable by funders or the local community, especially where the religion of community members prohibits or discourages consumption of alcohol.

43.3.1
Alcohol sales and charitable status

The sale of alcohol cannot in itself be a charitable purpose, so it could jeopardise charitable status. To avoid this the charity may:

- arrange on an occasional basis for alcohol to be sold by a publican or other licensed person on an **occasional licence** [see **43.3.2.2**];

- set up a separate members' club which obtains a **club registration certificate** [see **43.3.2.3**] and undertakes the sale of alcohol;

- set up a trading company [see **chapter 47**] which obtains an **on licence** [see **43.3.2.4**] or **restaurant licence** [see **43.3.2.5**] and undertakes the sale of alcohol; *or*

- obtain an on licence as a charity, but agree to **restrictions** in the licence which ensure that charitable status is not jeopardised. .

The Charity Commission regards sales of alcohol as 'ancillary' and therefore acceptable in terms of charitable status provided that:

- the provision or sale of alcohol is not expressly prohibited by the charity's governing document, lease or property deeds;

- the area occupied by the bar and additional storage facilities does not substantially detract from the charitable use of the premises;

- the bar is open only when the premises are in use for a charitable activity or purpose; *and*

- the bar is open only to people who are attending the charitable activity, either as participants or spectators.

Further information is in Charity Commission booklet CC27 *Providing Alcohol on Charity Premises*.

43.3.2
Alcohol licensing

The appropriate licence or club registration certificate must be obtained before alcohol is sold on any premises or out of doors, or is given to people who pay an admission fee or other indirect charge.

A licence is not required if:

- the alcohol is not sold, and is not included in any admission fee or indirect charge; *or*

- the alcohol is sold at premises with a theatre licence and the bar is open only immediately before and during performances [see **42.2.2**].

Licenses are granted by the **licensing justices** at the magistrates' court. The licence is granted to one or more named individuals, usually members of the organisation's governing body. They are personally responsible for ensuring the conditions of the licence are not breached.

A licence may be issued for alcoholic drinks of all types, wine only, cider only, beer and cider only, or beer, cider and wine only.

Once a licence—other than for an occasional event—is obtained, the conditions need to be taken into account if a new building is being built or alterations are being made to the existing premises. One of the requirements of any licence is that the licensing authority is satisfied with the layout of the premises, and changes may be necessary to meet its requirements.

Failure to lodge a licence renewal application at the appropriate time may lead to its loss, so renewal dates should be carefully diaried.

43.3.2.1
Occasional permission

Charitable and voluntary organisations may obtain an **occasional permission** to sell alcohol at up to 12 events in any 12-month period. The permission cannot last more than 24 hours each time. Application must be made to the clerk of the licensing justices at least three weeks before the function. The application may be made by an officer of the organisation, or by a member of the organisation with an officer's written consent.

Licensing (Occasional Permissions) Act 1983;
Deregulation (Occasional Permissions) Order 1997 [SI 1997/1133]

43.3.2.2
Occasional licence

An existing licensee of licensed premises may obtain an **occasional licence** to supply alcohol on other host premises. Under this arrangement the licensee, not the host organisation, remains responsible for the supply of alcohol and may wish to retain all or most of the profits.

43.3.2.3
Club registration certificate

With a **club registration certificate**, alcohol may be sold by a genuine members' club to the members of the club. Detailed restrictions are imposed, for example generally requiring a delay of two days between becoming a member and being able to buy alcohol.

The licensed organisation must be a private body with a minimum of 25 members, and must be clearly under the control of its members. Charities and non-charitable voluntary organisations whose governing document requires them to be for the public benefit cannot obtain a club registration certificate, but they can grant a sub-lease or licence to occupy premises to a members' club. This arrangement is appropriate, for example, for community associations which want to run a bar in their community centre.

In practice such arrangements need to be approached with considerable caution. Trading subsidiaries can be set up in a way which allows the parent charity or other body to appoint the governing body members [see **47.5.1**], but this is not possible when setting up a members' club. The parent body has no control over the club except through the contract, licence or agreement between the two bodies. The club will be controlled by its own members, who may develop priorities very different from those of the parent charity. The club may attract a substantial membership whose interests are promotion of their drinking and social activities, and this may come to overwhelm the charitable public benefit objects of the charity. Those members may also, if the charity is set up in a democratic way, form a substantial voting bloc and effectively come to control the charity.

43.3.2.4
Justices' on licence

A **justices' on licence** is the type of licence normally granted to a public house. When granted to a charitable or voluntary organisation, specific conditions are normally imposed to prevent the bar facilities being used by the general public. These might include, for example:

- sales being limited to people attending events or activities at the premises;
- restrictions on advertising; *and/or*
- sales being limited to people who have been a member of the organisation for at least two days.

If alcohol is to be sold on a regular basis to people who are not attending charitable activities, it will be necessary to set up a separate trading company which applies for the licence and runs the bar [see **chapter 47**]. This does not have the difficulties of control which can arise with members' clubs.

Notice for an on licence must be:

- given to the clerk of the licensing justices at least 21 days prior to the licensing session;
- given to the police authority, fire authority, local authority environmental health department and parish council (if there is one);
- displayed at the site; *and*
- advertised in the local newspaper.

The magistrates generally visit the site, and at the hearing will require evidence of the 'need' for an on licence in the area. They may ask for plans and local maps showing other licensed premises.

The process of obtaining an on licence is considerably more difficult and expensive than obtaining a club registration certificate, and third parties such as other licensees may object. Because of these difficulties, it is common for organisations which want an on licence to start by seeking a **provisional on licence**. *Licensing Act 1964 s.6*

43.3.2.5
Restaurant and accommodation licence

Premises structurally adapted and genuinely used for midday and evening meals, or providing accommodation and at least one main meal (not just breakfast) may be licensed. This form of licence is easier to obtain than an on licence, as no 'need' has to be proved. *ss.93-101*

An extension outside normal licensing hours may be obtained by applying for a **supper hours certificate**. *ss.68-69*

Application with the required information must be served on the clerk of the licensing justices not less than 21 days before the licensing session. Similar notice must also be given to the police, fire authority, local authority and parish council, and must be displayed at the site and advertised in the local paper.

43.3.2.6
Proposed changes

At the time of writing (early 2001) the government had proposed a major revision of licensing law, including:

- a single integrated scheme for licensing premises which sell alcohol, provide public entertainment or provide refreshment at night;
- personal licences allowing holders to sell or serve alcohol for consumption on or off any premises possessing a premises licence;
- new measures on under-age drinking, including a new duty for people selling alcohol to satisfy themselves about customers' ages;
- personal licences to be issued for 10 years to those aged 18 or over without a relevant criminal record, following a test of knowledge of licensing law and social responsibilities;
- personal and premises licences to be issued by local authorities.

Information is available from the licensing justices, the Department for Culture, Media and Sport or Community Matters [see below].

FOR FURTHER INFORMATION

Food hygiene. Local authority environmental health department

Food Standards Agency: 0845-757 3012; www.foodstandards.gov.uk

Department of Health: 020-7210 4850; www.doh.gov.uk

Licensing law. Department for Culture, Media and Sport: 020-7211 6000; www.culture.gov.uk

Community Matters: 020-7226 0189; www.communitymatters.org.uk

PART VI
FUNDING AND FUNDRAISING

Part VI covers the organisation's income from voluntary sources (donations, grants, fundraising and legacies) and from trading activities, including contracts and service agreements.

Chapter 44
FUNDING AND FUNDRAISING: GENERAL RULES

For sources of further information see end of chapter.

Double-underlined section headings indicate additions and significant changes since the first edition.

44.1 FUNDRAISING AND THE LAW

A voluntary organisation's efforts to bring in money are subject to a wide range of legal requirements:

- charities, and in some cases a broader class of 'charitable institutions' [see **44.5.1**], are subject to limits and controls on fundraising;

- funds raised for a specific purpose may be used only for that purpose [see **44.2**];

- many fundraising activities, such as public collections and lotteries, are regulated [see **chapter 45**];

- the organisation may have to pay tax on the income, or on any surplus or profit arising from the income [see **chapter 52**];

- if payment is received for goods or services, the organisation may have to charge VAT to the purchaser [see **chapter 53**];

- the sale of goods and services is affected by contract law [see **18.5-18.12**], consumer protection law [see **36.10**], and many other aspects of law;

- an organisation which sells goods or services through a trading subsidiary must ensure the relationship between the two bodies is properly handled [see **chapter 47**].

Charitable, benevolent and philanthropic institutions [see **44.5.1** for definition] are subject to specific controls if they pay even as little as £5 per day to a person who is not an employee to carry out fundraising [see **44.5.3**], or if they are involved in a commercial venture where a business benefits from use of the charity's name [see **44.5.4**].

Fundraising is not, in itself, a charitable activity. Charities which do not have a power to fundraise [see **5.4.4**] should take advice before using resources in this way.

This chapter covers general rules on fundraising. The term **funds** is used throughout to refer not only to money but to property of any sort given or donated to an organisation. This could include anything from jumble or newspapers for recycling through to buildings and land.

44.2
FUNDS RAISED FOR SPECIFIC PURPOSES

Funds given for a specific purpose must be used only for that purpose. Use of the funds for any other purpose may constitute fraud or deception. If the funds are covered by trust law [see below], any use for which they are not intended may also be a breach of trust.

44.2.1
Trusts and constructive trusts

Trust law covers funds:

- given to or raised by unincorporated bodies, whether charitable or non-charitable, for charitable purposes [see **4.3**];

- given to or raised by a non-charitable association 'for the benefit of the members' [see **18.4.5**];

- given to or raised by any third party, such as an individual or commercial body, if the funds are for charitable purposes or for the benefit of identifiable individuals such as victims of a disaster;

- in some situations, given to or raised by charitable companies for a specific purpose.

Funds covered by trust law are subject to a **trust** between the donor, the persons responsible for the funds (the trustees), and the persons intended to benefit from the funds (the beneficiaries) [see **1.3.1**].

Where funds are raised by a charitable trust or association, the members of the governing body are trustees for the funds. Where funds are raised by individuals or a non-charitable association, a **constructive trust** for those funds arises. A constructive trust is one which is not deliberately created [see **6.2**], but may arise by legal construction or by interpretation of the conduct of the fundraisers. A **constructive trustee**, like any other trustee, is obliged to use the funds only for the purposes for which they were raised, and is personally liable for their use.

44.2.1.1
Funds raised through charges for goods and services

The rules on breach of trust do not apply when goods or services are sold, charged for, or provided under a contract or most service agreements [see **48.1**]. These situations are covered by contract law, not trust law. So long as the goods or services are provided as required, there is no obligation to use all the money to provide them. Some local authorities and similar purchasers make it a contractual condition that any surplus is returned to them [see **48.3.5**]. If this is not required, any profit may be used for any purpose within the organisation's objects.

44.2.2
Non-charitable purposes

Apart from a few exceptions [see **1.3.4**], trust law does not cover funds raised for non-charitable purposes. If funds are misused, the persons responsible may be liable for fraud or deception—but not breach of trust as well.

44.2.3
Alternative uses for charitable funds

Sometimes funds raised for a charity or for charitable purposes cannot be used as originally intended, either because too much or too little was raised, or because the purpose for which the funds were raised is no longer necessary or realistic. Even where there is a valid reason to use the funds for another purpose, this cannot automatically be done.

Where insufficient funds have been raised, the charity must first try to locate identifiable donors, and ask if they want their money back or will allow it to be used for a different purpose. Where donors cannot be identified or where there are surplus funds, the Charity Commission is likely to have to make a *cy près* scheme [see **5.5.4**] to allow the funds to be used for another purpose. The new purpose will be as near as possible to the original, and the scheme will allow for donors to claim their portion of the money or property up to six months after the scheme is made.   *Charities Act 1993 s.14(5),(6)*

The need for these procedures may be avoided by wording the application, appeal or publicity in a way which allows for alternative use of the funds. Examples are: 'Proceeds from this festival will be used for our summer playscheme *and other activities for local children*', 'Please give generously to support our work in the Middle East *and other areas of conflict*' or, even more general, *'Funds from this appeal may be used for our general charitable purposes'*.

44.2.3.1
Known donors

If donors must be contacted and the charity or fundraiser has their names and addresses, they must be contacted in writing. The letter must include specified information and should be accompanied by a disclaimer form. The wording for the letter and disclaimer is available from the Charity Commission.   *Charities (Cy-près Advertisements, Inquiries and Disclaimer) Regulations 1993 reg.4; sch.3*

A donor who signs the disclaimer is giving consent for the money or property to be used for the purposes that will be specified in the Charity Commission scheme. If the donor asks for the money or property to be returned, the charity or fundraiser must do this.

44.2.3.2
Advertisement

If donors cannot be identified or their addresses are not known, the charity must advertise in a newspaper or other periodical which is sold or distributed throughout the area in which the appeal was made, and is in the same language as the advertisement. The advertisement wording is available from the Charity Commission.   *reg.2, sch.3*

Where the appeal was for the benefit of an area contained wholly or mainly within a local authority area, a copy of every advertisement must also be fixed to two public notice boards in the relevant area.   *sch.2*

If a donor asks for a disclaimer, a form must be sent [see above]. If donors do not come forward, any remaining money or property will be covered by the Charity Commission scheme.

44.2.3.3
Public collections
and events

Enquiries and advertisements are not required for the proceeds of cash collections made in collecting boxes or in similar ways, or for the proceeds of any lottery, competition, entertainment, sale or similar fundraising activity. These funds are conclusively presumed to belong to donors who cannot be identified, and will be covered by the Charity Commission scheme.   *s.14(3)*

44.2.3.4
Difficult
identification

Where it would be unreasonable to make enquiries or advertise for donors, either because the amounts likely to be returned are very small or because so much time has elapsed since the money was raised, the court may order that such property can be covered by the Charity Commission scheme. The Commission should be contacted about this procedure.   *Charities Act 1993 s.14(4)*

44.2.4
Alternative uses for
non-charitable funds

The Charities Act rules on advertising and *cy près* schemes apply to all funds raised by charities, or raised by individuals and non-charities for charitable organisations or purposes. They do not apply to money or property raised by individuals and non-charities for non-charitable organisations or purposes, but the donor may take legal action if the funds are not used as the donor intended.

44.2.5
Fundraising for the
public sector

Charities should not use their charitable resources to provide services that the state is obliged to provide, but can provide additional or top-up services. This includes fundraising to enable health service bodies, local authorities or other public sector bodies to provide additional services, purchase equipment, or build specialist premises.

Where funds are being raised for equipment or buildings, it is important to clarify with the recipient body in writing, before fundraising starts, any conditions on the long-term use of the gift. Otherwise there is nothing to prevent the recipient from selling the equipment, using the premises for unintended purposes, or selling or demolishing the premises.

44.3
GRANTS,
DONATIONS AND
GIFTS

A grant, donation or gift may be given by an individual, business, organisation or public sector body, and may be in the form of money, goods, other property, services, publicity or facilities. The key point is that the contribution is primarily a **gift**, the donor receives nothing more than an acknowledgement in return, and no contract [see **18.6**] is created. The distinction between a grant or donation and a contract is often unclear [see **48.1** for more about this], especially in relation to sponsorship [see **52.3.3**] and local or health authority service agreements [see **48.1.3**]. Legal advice may be needed to clarify the position.

44.3.1
Enforceability of
terms and
conditions

Except where there is a statutory obligation for a public sector body to provide a grant (for example to students), grants and donations are given at the discretion of the donor or funder and can generally be stopped at any time—even if the promise of the grant or donation is made in writing. There may be a moral obligation on a funder or donor to provide what they have promised, but unless the promise has been made under deed [see **18.3**] or under a will, or the arrangement is actually contractual rather than a grant, the recipient's right to the grant or donation cannot be enforced in the courts.

44.3.1.1
Grant cuts by
public bodies

When a local authority substantially reduced two organisations' grants with only a few days' notice, the organisations sought judicial review [see **60.5.2**]. The court found that the council had acted lawfully in making the cuts, but:

- the council should have given written prior notice before a final decision was made, and should have given organisations at risk of cuts reasonable opportunities to make representations to the council;

- after the cuts were made, the appeal against them should have been heard by persons who were not involved in the original decision.

R v Haringey London Borough Council [2000] All ER(D) 1583

44.3.1.2
Use for other purposes

Grants and donations may be given for purposes ranging from the very general ('to support the organisation's work') to the very specific. The purposes may be defined by the recipient organisation in its application or appeal, by the funder or donor, or by both parties.

Funds must be used only for the purpose for which they are given. If they are used in any other way, the donor can take legal action to recover the money. Members of the governing body could be held personally liable to repay funds which have been misused [see **19.3**].

44.3.1.3
Non-compliance with
conditions

In addition to the **terms** specifying how the grant or donation is to be used and when it will be paid, there may be **conditions** setting out related requirements. These may range from the non-existent or virtually non-existent ('to acknowledge receipt of this donation'), to many pages of small print. If the recipient does not comply with the conditions, the funder or donor may withdraw the funding, ask for its money to be returned, or in extreme cases take legal action against the organisation and the members of its governing body.

44.3.2
Refusing
donations

A decision not to accept a donation, grant or other support offered to the organisation should be made only by the governing body, and only after careful consideration. The members of a charity's governing body have an obligation always to act in the best interests of the charity and its beneficiaries, and difficult issues may arise if what seems ethically or morally right is not necessarily in the organisation's financial interest.

A decision to **disclaim** (refuse) a gift can probably be justified if:

- the aims or activities of the donor are contrary to the organisation's objects and work;

- acceptance could negatively affect support from other sources;

- conditions placed by the donor are unreasonable or contrary to the charity's objectives; *or*

- the donation is the product of illegal activity.

In other situations, the issues are similar to those on ethical investment [see **54.6.2**], and a refusal may be harder to justify as being in the best interests of the organisation and its beneficiaries. The guidance on un-solicited donations from the Institute of Charity Fundraising Managers [see end of chapter] may be helpful in weighing up such decisions, and advice and if necessary consent should be sought from the Charity Commission.

44.4
ALLOWING OTHERS TO USE A CHARITY'S NUMBER

44.4.1
Legal issues

Many funders and donors are able or willing to give funds only to charities, but may wish to support an organisation which has not yet completed the charity registration process or is not registered because of its size. In these situations the funder or donor may want to make the grant or donation to a registered charity (the **intermediary charity**), which in turn makes a grant to the **recipient organisation**.

This arrangement is convenient for everyone concerned: the donor fulfils its criterion of being able to give only to charities, the inter-mediary has provided a useful service and the recipient has had access to charitable funds. But such arrangements are lawful only if:

- the original donor, if an organisation, makes its donation only for purposes which are properly charitable and are within its own objects and powers (so, for example, a funder prohibited from making grants to non-charities cannot get around this restriction by making a grant to a charity which then passes it on to a non-charity);

- the intermediary charity receives the donation only for purposes which are charitable and within its objects and powers;

- the intermediary passes on the funds for purposes which comply with the donor's wishes *and* are within its own objects and powers; *and*

- the recipient uses the money only for charitable purposes which comply with the wishes of both the original donor and the intermediary *and* (if it is an organisation rather than an individual) are within its own objects and powers.

Any breach of these rules may make the donation subject to tax [see **52.5**] and could be a breach of trust [see **44.2**] or *ultra vires* [see **4.7**].

By receiving funds and passing them on, the intermediary charity becomes responsible for how those funds are used by the recipient. An intermediary charity which indiscriminately allows others to use its charity number and channels funds for other organisations or individuals without proper procedures could find itself liable for a recipient's misuse of the donor's funds.

44.4.2
Internal guidelines

The governing body of an intermediary charity should create clear writ-ten guidelines covering:

- when the organisation may be involved as an intermediary;

- the limits within which staff may authorise such arrangements without express authority from the governing body;
- what procedures must be followed;
- the need for all authorisations to be reported to the next meeting of the governing body and to be minuted;
- the need to monitor the recipient's use of funds.

44.4.3
Funding agreement

The intermediary's rules should be reflected in a **funding agreement**. Because of the potential tax and charity law implications, it is sensible to have the agreement reviewed by an experienced solicitor before issuing it to potential recipients. The agreement should be entered into prior to the recipient using the intermediary's name or charity number in any application for funding or publicity related to the funding.

The agreement should specify:

- that the intermediary's name and number can be used only in connection with the application or activity specified in the agreement;
- that all activities covered by the funding must be legally charitable and clearly fall within the intermediary's objects and powers;
- that the intermediary will be given copies of all applications and related documents either automatically or on request;
- that all grants or donations received under the arrangement must be initially paid to the intermediary;
- when the intermediary will pay the money on to the recipient, and that the intermediary has no obligation to make any payment if funds are not received from the original donor;
- who receives any interest earned during any period between the intermediary's receipt of funds and paying them on to the recipient;
- the intermediary's obligation to pay over to the recipient the tax recovered if the donor's payment is made under gift aid [see **46.2**];
- whether the intermediary makes any charge to the recipient for the use of its charity number (such a charge may have implications for tax, see **52.4**, and VAT, see **53.5.3**);
- what the recipient needs to do to trigger release of the funds;
- a warranty or promise by the recipient that the funds will be used only for charitable purposes, and only for purposes specified in its agreements with the original donor and with the intermediary;
- arrangements for the recipient to report back to the intermediary and the original donor;
- any arrangements for the intermediary to monitor the accounts and relevant activities of the recipient, or to have access to such information on request;
- the intermediary's right to retain funds or return them to the original donor if the recipient does not comply with the agreement.

44.4.4
Financial procedures

To ensure there is no confusion about whose money it is and how it is to be used, the intermediary must have clear procedures for handling funds received on behalf of other organisations, including:

- how receipt of the funds and transfer to the recipient is recorded in the intermediary's account books as a restricted fund [see **50.2.8**];
- whether the money should be placed in a separate bank account;
- if the money is not kept in a separate bank account, how interest is calculated and recorded;
- how receipt of the funds from the donor is reported to the intermediary's governing body and the recipient;
- how the release of funds is authorised;
- safeguards to ensure the intermediary does not use the funds for other purposes;

- whether fidelity insurance [see **21.6.3**] is needed to safeguard the funds.

The receipt and disbursement of the funds will be included as part of the intermediary charity's annual income and expenditure, and may put it into a higher income/expenditure category where more detailed annual accounts or a full audit are required [see **50.2.3**].

44.4.5 Fundraising by non-charities for a charity

In the situation described above, a registered charity allows its charitable status to be used to raise funds for an individual or an organisation which is not a registered charity. Similar procedures, adapted as appropriate, should be followed where a charity allows a non-charity to use its number to raise funds for the charity.

Where the non-charity is a commercial body, such arrangements must comply with the rules on commercial participation [see **44.5.4**] and the charity's obligation not to allow its name to be used commercially unless this is beneficial to the charity [see **39.9**].

44.5 PROFESSIONAL FUNDRAISERS AND COMMERCIAL PARTICIPATION

The **Charities Act 1992 part II** and related regulations cover charitable institutions' use of **professional fundraisers**, arrangements with **commercial participators**, and other matters relating to fundraising. Information and advice are available from the Charity Commission, the Institute of Charity Fundraising Managers [see end of chapter] and specialist solicitors.

44.5.1 Charitable institutions

For the purposes of the fundraising regulations, a **charitable institution** is any body established for charitable [see **4.3**], benevolent or philanthropic purposes.

Benevolent and **philanthropic** are not defined in statute, and case law is complex. In general the terms apply to bodies which are predominantly rather than exclusively charitable. The Community Fund (formerly National Lottery Charities Board), which is allowed to support only charities and 'institutions established for charitable, benevolent or philanthropic purposes', defines them as not charitable but 'for the good of mankind' (philanthropic) or 'specifically well intentioned' (benevolent).

The Community Fund further states that organisations must have the essential attributes of charity (a spirit of altruism and a dedication to purposes worthy of public support) and must 'be free of any characteristics which are essentially alien to charity' such as the possibility of self interest or private benefit, or political or doctrinaire purposes.

While this is not a statutory definition, similar criteria are used for the purposes of the Charities Act 1992 fundraising regulations.

44.5.2 Connected companies

A **connected company** is one where one or more charitable institutions can exercise, or control the exercise of, all the voting rights at a general meeting of the company.   *Charities Act 1992 s.58(5)*

Trading companies set up and controlled by charitable institutions are connected companies, but are not professional fundraisers [see **44.5.3**] or commercial participators [see **44.5.4**] when they are acting in relation to an organisation which controls them. Despite this, the Charity Commission recommends that connected trading companies follow the rules for professional fundraisers and commercial participators even when acting for their parent body.

44.5.3 Professional fundraisers

Under the Charities Act 1992, a **professional fundraiser** is:

- an individual, partnership or corporate body who carries on a business for gain which is wholly or primarily engaged in **soliciting** money or other property for charitable, benevolent or philanthropic purposes (a **fundraising business**); *or*

- an individual or company who is not working for a fundraising business as defined above, but who is being paid or rewarded for soliciting money or other property for a charitable institution and who is not explicitly excluded from the definition of professional fundraiser [see below].   *Charities Act 1992 s.58*

44.5.3.1
Who is not a
professional fundraiser

The following are not professional fundraisers:

- a charitable institution or its connected company [see **44.5.2**];

- a commercial participator [see **44.5.4**];

- an employee or member of the governing body of the charitable institution for which funds are being raised or its connected company, provided the individual is raising funds in that capacity rather than in any other capacity;

- a person making a solicitation for a charitable institution or connected company as part of a radio or television broadcast;

- a person paid no more than £5 per day or £500 per year (excluding legitimate expenses) for soliciting funds for a charitable institution;

- a person who is paid no more than £500 in connection with soliciting funds for a particular fundraising venture.

A **volunteer fundraiser** who is reimbursed for genuine out-of-pocket expenses [see **35.2.1**] is not remunerated and is not a professional fundraiser. But a volunteer who is paid lump sum expenses which are more than genuine expenditure, or who is given an honorarium or any other payment, is a professional fundraiser if the payment is more than £5 per day, £500 per year or £500 per event above actual expenses.

A **promoter of a public collection** [see **45.2.1**] is a professional fundraiser unless he or she is an employee or governing body member of the organisation for which the collection is being held, or is a volunteer for the organisation paid no more than £5 per day or £500 per year total for his or her fundraising work for the organisation.

A **fundraising consultant** who gives advice on fundraising, without actually soliciting funds, would generally not be classed as a professional fundraiser. However the boundaries between 'giving advice' and 'soliciting funds' are unclear, and advice should be sought from an experienced solicitor, the Charity Commission or the Institute of Charity Fundraising Managers [see end of chapter].

44.5.3.2
Grey areas

There are many grey areas where it is essential to take professional advice, or to err on the side of caution and comply with all the regulations even if it is not certain that the person is actually classed as a professional fundraiser.

44.5.3.3
Challenge events

A participant in a **challenge event** such as 'cycle through the Andes' [see **45.5**] may be a professional fundraiser if he or she is not an employee or governing body member of the organisation for which funds are being raised, and receives a tour worth more than £500. Where the participant is a member of the governing body, the implications of receiving the tour must be considered in light of the governing body member's obligation not to benefit from the charity [see **14.6**]. If there is any doubt about this, the participant should consult the Charity Commission for consent to participate.

44.5.3.4
Agents and
fulfilment houses

Soliciting money or property may mean not only asking for it, but also **receiving** it as a result of a solicitation or processing responses to a promotion. So if, for example, a charitable institution has an agreement to pay a commercial business to receive donations from an appeal, crediting the donations temporarily to the business's account before they are paid over the organisation, the commercial business could be a professional fundraiser. The same may apply if a business is paid to send out information packs or to process catalogue sales. A business which undertakes this sort of work is called a **fulfilment house** and may well be classed as a professional fundraiser.

A fundraising business which telephones potential donors is a professional fundraiser, but so might be individuals or companies who answer calls from potential donors, if they tell callers anything about the charitable institution or its work, or if the money received goes into the fundraiser's account rather than direct to the charitable institution.

44.5.4
Commercial participators

A commercial participator is an individual, partnership or corporate body which carries on for gain a business other than a fundraising business [see **44.5.3** for definition], and who in the course of that business engages in a **promotional venture** (often called **cause related marketing**) to raise money for one or more charitable institutions [see **44.5.1**].   *Charities Act 1992 s.58(1)*

The essence of commercial participation is that the commercial participator hopes customers will be more likely to choose a particular commercial product or service because they know some of the purchase price will be donated to a good cause.

Examples are donations to charities or other good causes of 5p for every tin of beans purchased, 50% of a restaurant's profits on World Aids Day, £1 for each new account opened in July, 10p for each pack of Christmas cards, or a business agreeing to give £5,000 to an organisation and publicising this as a way to attract more customers.

A commercial participator's indication that a proportion or amount of money raised from the promotional venture will be given to one or more charitable institutions or will be applied for their benefit is a **representation**.

44.5.4.1
Who is not a commercial participator

A body involved in raising money for a charitable institution is not a commercial participator if:

- it is not a commercial business;
- it is a commercial business but is controlled by the institution for which it is raising funds [see **44.5.2**];
- it is a commercial business but is not carrying on the promotion in the course of its normal business;
- it buys the goods from a charitable institution as a straightforward contractual transaction and then sells them on the same as any other goods, without representing that some of the profits will be donated to the charitable institution; *or*
- the benefit to the charitable institution is not publicised in any way.

A **connected company** [see **44.5.2**] is not a commercial participator when it is acting in relation to a charitable institution which controls it, but it may be a commercial participator when acting in relation to other charitable institutions.

44.5.4.2
Protecting the charity and its name

The Charity Commission has said that any commercial use of a charity's name must be 'expedient in the interests of the charity and on terms which are advantageous to the charity'. The terms must be defined in detail, and must be reviewed regularly [see **39.9**]. The Commission's guidance *Fundraising through Partnerships with Companies* outlines the issues which need to be considered before entering into a commercial participation arrangement.

The burden is on the charitable institution to ensure that a commercial participation agreement is favourable to the organisation and protects its reputation. This includes ensuring a sufficient price is obtained for the use of its name, being very specific about the purposes for which its name and logo can be used [see **39.11**], ensuring the arrangements enhance (or do not detract from) the organisation's reputation, and minimising risk to the organisation.

44.5.4.3
Tax and VAT

Licensing a commercial participator to use an organisation's name or logo is a trading transaction. If the charity provides any promotion, advertising or other services, the income may be subject to income or corporation tax [see **52.7.9**] and/or VAT [see **53.5.3**].

Specialist advice on the legal, tax and VAT implications should be sought before entering into any commercial participation arrangement, to ensure it is structured in a way which avoids tax liability or is carried out through the charity's trading company.

44.5.5
Written agreements

A professional fundraiser or commercial participator must have a written agreement with the institution(s) for which it is raising funds. In many cases, the agreement will also involve the institution's trading subsidiary.   *Charities Act 1992 s.59(1),(2)*

The agreement must be signed by both (or all) parties. For the voluntary organisation, the signatory must be a member of the governing body or a person properly authorised by the governing body.

If there is no written agreement, or the agreement does not comply with the requirements, the professional fundraiser or commercial participator cannot enforce the agreement against the charitable institution without first getting a court order.

44.5.5.1
Professional fundraisers

An agreement between a charitable institution and a professional fundraiser must as a minimum contain:

- the name and address of each party to the agreement;
- the date on which the agreement was signed by each party;
- the period covered by the agreement;
- any arrangements for terminating the agreement before the end of the period covered;
- any arrangements for altering the agreement during the period;
- a statement of the principal objectives for the fundraising and the methods to be used to achieve those objectives;
- if more than one charitable institution is party to the agreement, how the decision will be made about the proportion of money or property each will receive; *and*
- provision for payment of remuneration and expenses to the fundraiser, and if it is not a fixed amount, how the amount is to be determined.   *Charitable Institutions (Fund-Raising) Regulations 1994*
                                        [SI 1994/3024] reg.2

44.5.5.2
Commercial participators

An agreement between a charitable institution and a commercial participator must include the information required for agreements with professional fundraisers [see above], and in addition:

- the proportion of the payment received by the commercial participator for goods or services, or the proportion of the proceeds of any other promotional venture, which will be given to or applied for the benefit of the charitable institution; *or*
- the donations which will be given by the commercial participator in connection with the sale of any goods or services.   *reg.3*

44.5.6
Statements to donors

Professional fundraisers and commercial participators raising money or soliciting property for one or more specific charitable institutions must make a statement at the time, making clear their relationship with the organisation(s) for which they are fundraising [see below for wordings].
                                        Charities Act 1992 s.60(1),(2)

If the professional fundraiser or commercial participator approaches a potential donor or purchaser, the statement must accompany the solicitation or representation. Commercial participators selling goods may not need to put the statement on each item; a notice prominently displayed at the cash till may be adequate. If a public collection is organised by a professional fundraiser, the collectors must display the statement. If an individual or company is paid to organise a fundraising event, any publicity which asks for donations or indicates that a charitable institution will benefit must include the statement.

Additional information must be included if the statement is made as part of a radio or television broadcast with an announcement that payment can be made by credit or debit card [see **44.5.7**], or if the solicitation or representation is made by telephone [see **45.3.2**].

If funds are being raised for a registered charity which has total income of more than £10,000 per year, every written or printed notice encouraging people to give to the charity must state that the organisation is a registered charity [see **16.1.4**].

44.5.6.1
Professional fundraisers

A professional fundraiser soliciting money or property for one or more specific organisations must include, as part of the solicitation, a statement clearly indicating

- the name(s) of the charitable institution(s), and if there is more than one, the proportion in which each is to benefit;

- in general terms, the method by which the fundraiser's remuneration in connection with the appeal is to be determined.

Charities Act 1992 s.60(1)

If a professional fundraiser is soliciting funds for charitable, benevolent or philanthropic *purposes* ('for cancer research') rather than for a specific institution or institutions, the statement must indicate:

- the fact that money or property is being solicited for those purposes rather than for a specific institution;

- how the decision will be made about how the proceeds will be divided among charitable institutions;

- in general terms, how the fundraiser's remuneration is to be determined. *s.60(2)*

44.5.6.2
Commercial participators

A commercial participator raising money for a charitable institution must include as part of any representation a statement indicating:

- the name(s) of the institution(s) concerned;

- if applicable, the proportion to be given to each institution;

- in general terms, the proportion of the payment for goods or services to be given to or applied for the benefit of the institutions, or the donations to be made by the commercial participator. *s.60(3)*

The net amount which will be given to the organisation, after deduction of expenses and costs, should be stated. Examples are '3% of the purchase price goes to Worthy Society, a registered charity' or '25p per item sold goes to Worthy Society'. If it is not possible to state a precise amount or percentage, the statement should say something like 'A minimum of 3%...' or 'It is estimated that 3%...'

44.5.6.3
Commercial promotions for charitable purposes

Separate regulations apply to individuals, partnerships or corporate bodies which carry on a business for gain other than a fundraising business, and which raise money for charitable, benevolent or philanthropic *purposes* (rather than for a specific organisation or organisations, which would make them commercial participators).

These businesses are required to make a statement indicating:

- the fact that the contributions raised are to be used for those purposes and not for a specific charitable institution;

- in general terms, the method by which it will be determined what proportion of the payment for goods or services will be used for those purposes or what donations will be made for those purposes;

- how a decision will be made about which charitable institutions will receive the contributions. *Charitable Institutions (Fund-Raising) Regulations 1994 [SI 1994/3024] reg. 7*

**44.5.6.4
The advertising and
sales promotion codes**

As well as complying with charity law requirements, promotions claiming that participation will benefit registered charities or good causes should comply with the **British Codes of Advertising and Sales Promotion** [see **40.2**].

These state that the promotion should:

- name each charity or good cause which will benefit, and be able if required to show that they consent to the advertising or promotion;
- define the nature and objectives of the organisation which will benefit, if it is not a registered charity;
- specify exactly what will be gained by the named charity or cause, and state the basis on which the contribution will be calculated;
- indicate if the promoters have imposed any limitations on the contribution they will make out of their own pocket;
- not limit purchasers' or supporters' contributions, and ensure any extra money collected is given to the named charity or cause;
- not exaggerate the benefit to the charity or cause derived from individual purchases of the promoted product;
- if asked, provide to anyone a current or final total of contributions;
- take particular care when appealing to children.

**44.5.7
Credit card
fundraising**

If a professional fundraiser makes a solicitation or a commercial participator makes a representation as part of a radio or television programme and there is an announcement that payment can be made by credit or debit card, donors who pay more than £50 are entitled to give written notice within seven days of the broadcast saying they want their money refunded. An announcement to this effect must be made as part of the broadcast. *Charities Act 1992 s.61(1)*

This right to a refund does not apply if the television or radio broadcast is made by the charity itself or a person speaking on its behalf, rather than by a professional fundraiser or commercial participator.

Similar rules apply where donations are made as a result of telephone fundraising [see **45.3.2**].

**44.5.8
Transfer of funds**

Money raised by a professional fundraiser or commercial participator must be paid to the organisation's governing body, or into a bank or building society account in the name of the organisation or its governing body, as soon as reasonably practicable after its receipt or at any rate within 28 days or within the period agreed with the institution.
Charitable Institutions (Fund-Raising) Regulations 1994 SI 1994/3024] reg. 6(2)

Money raised by a professional fundraiser should be transferred gross, before deduction of any fees or expenses.

Donated property must be kept securely and must be dealt with in accordance with the instructions of the organisation. If the property is sold or otherwise disposed of, the proceeds must be dealt with in the same way as money donations. *reg.6(3)*

**44.5.9
Fundraising records**

A charitable institution which has an agreement with a professional fundraiser or commercial participator has a right to see all books, documents and other records relating to the agreement, on request and at all reasonable times. Records kept in non-legible form (for example, on computer) must be made available on paper. *reg.5*

**44.6
UNAUTHORISED
FUNDRAISING**

It is not uncommon for individuals or commercial businesses to raise funds for good causes without informing the organisations for which they are raising money. Most of the time this is fine, but problems may arise when the fundraiser uses dubious methods, uses an organisation's name inappropriately, or does not hand over funds raised for the organisation.

44.6.1 Professional fundraisers

A charitable institution may take out an injunction to stop a professional fundraiser or commercial participator from raising money or property on its behalf if there is no proper agreement with the institution, and if the court is satisfied that the contravention is likely to continue.

Charities Act 1992 s.59(3)

Where there is a contract and a commercial participator or professional fundraiser uses inappropriate fundraising methods, they are (presumably) not fulfilling their contract with the organisation and the matter can be dealt with as breach of contract [see **18.12**].

44.6.2 Unauthorised fundraising by others

A charitable institution may take steps to stop an individual or corporate body which is not a professional fundraiser or commercial participator from raising funds on its behalf if it objects to the methods being used for fundraising, feels that the individual or corporate body is not fit and proper to raise funds for it, or does not want to be associated with the particular promotional or fundraising venture.

s.62

The organisation must give notice that if the fundraising is not stopped immediately, an injunction will be sought under the **Charities Act 1992** s.62. The notice must specify the circumstances which gave rise to the serving of the notice, and the grounds on which the application for the injunction will be made. At least 28 days must elapse between giving the notice and applying for the injunction.

Charitable Institutions (Fund-Raising) Regulations 1994 [SI 1994/3024] reg.4

If the person stops the fundraising activity after receiving the notice, but starts the same or substantially the same activities within 12 months of the date of the notice, the organisation does not need to serve another notice or wait 28 days before seeking an injunction.

44.6.3 False statements about charitable status

It is an offence for a person soliciting money or other property to say that an organisation is a registered charity when in fact it is not. But it is a defence for the person to prove that he or she believed on reasonable grounds that the organisation was a registered charity.

Charities Act 1992 s.63

44.6.4 Non-payment of funds raised

Any person who raises funds for a particular organisation or purpose is a **constructive trustee** [see **44.2.1**] for those funds, and is obliged to give them only to the organisation for which they were raised or use them only for the purposes for which they were raised.

Failure to pay over funds raised as a constructive trustee constitutes theft, and taking a cut from a collection or appeal without telling donors that this would happen is a breach of trust.

R v Wain [1993] and Jones v Attorney General [1976]
Decisions of the Charity Commissioners vol.2, April 1994

FOR FURTHER INFORMATION

Charity Commission: 0870-333 0123; www.charity-commission.gov.uk

Institute of Charity Fundraising Managers: 020-7627 3436; www.icfm.org.uk

The Fundraiser's Guide to the Law by Bates, Wells and Braithwaite and the Centre for Voluntary Sector Development (Directory of Social Change)

Chapter 45
FUNDRAISING ACTIVITIES

45.1
LEGAL ISSUES

Voluntary organisations undertake a vast range of fundraising activities, often without fully appreciating the legal implications [see **44.1** for a summary of these]. In particular, the tax and VAT implications [see **chapters 52** and **53**] must be fully understood, and attention must be given to licensing requirements [see, for example, **42.2**, **42.3** and **43.3**].

This chapter covers requirements for some fundraising activities. General aspects of fundraising, including the rules on professional fundraisers and commercial participation, are covered in **chapter 44**. Other types of fundraising are covered at various points in this book:

- advertising and commercials **40.2**;
- affinity credit cards **52.3.2**;
- appeals **4.3.8**;
- running a bar **43.3**;
- fundraising events and entertainments **42.2**, **52.7.1** and **53.4.13**;
- contracts and service agreements **chapter 48**;
- gift aid **46.2**;
- legacies **46.5**;
- use of an organisation's name and logo **39.9**;
- sponsorship **52.3.3**;
- sale of donated goods **36.10** and **52.3.2**;

- trading activities and the sale of goods or services **18.7**, **18.9**, **36.10**, and **chapters 47** and **48**.

The Institute of Charity Fundraising Managers [see end of chapter] has codes of practice on many aspects of fundraising. These should be followed as a matter of good practice.

45.2 PUBLIC COLLECTIONS

At the time of writing (early 2001) there was still no implementation date for part III of the **Charities Act 1992** [see **3.4.1**]. When and if it is implemented it will replace existing legislation on public collections, but until then:

- the **House to House Collections Act 1939** and related regulations cover **house-to-house collections** [see **45.2.1**];
- the **Police, Factories etc (Miscellaneous Provisions) Act 1916** s.5 and related regulations cover **street collections** [see **45.2.2**].

The regulations on public collections apply not only to charities but to any collection for a charitable, benevolent or philanthropic purpose [see **44.5.1**]. In practice, it is safest to assume that all public collections by or for voluntary organisations are covered by the regulations.

The rules on professional fundraisers [see **44.5**, and especially **44.5.6**] are likely to apply if the organisation is paying a company, or individuals who are not employees or governing body members of the organisation or its trading company, to carry out the collection. The rules also apply if the collector is not being paid but is receiving other consideration (something of material value) for doing the work.

At the time of writing a **Public Fundraising Regulatory Association** was being set up by leading charities, as a self-regulatory body for high street and door-to-door fundraising. Information is available from the Institute of Charity Fundraising Managers [see end of chapter].

45.2.1 House-to-house collections: the 1939 Act

For the purpose of the **House to House Collections Act 1939** a **house** includes a place of business, so pub crawls and other fundraising activities involving going from one place to another are covered. The rules cover collection of money or other property. This includes collecting pledges such as gift aid declarations and direct debit forms, collecting goods such as for a jumble sale, and the door-to-door sale of goods or services where some or all of the proceeds will be used for a charitable, benevolent or philanthropic purpose.

45.2.1.1 Licensing

No later than the first of the month before the month when the collection will start, an application must be made for a licence, specifying the purpose of the collection and the area in which it will be taken. In the metropolitan police district the application is made to the commissioner of police; in the City of London, to the Common Council; and elsewhere, to the local authority.

The time requirement may be waived if there are good reasons for doing so. A licence may be granted for up to 12 months or in some cases for up to 18 months. If a licence is refused or revoked, any appeal must be lodged within 14 days.   *House to House Collections Act 1939 s.2(4)-(6)*

If the collection is being taken for local purposes and is likely to be completed within a short period of time, a certificate may be granted exempting that collection from the need for a licence.   *HTHC Act s.1(4);*
House to House Collections Regulations 1947 [SI 1947/2662] reg.3, sch.1

Some large national charities are exempt from having to register with each local authority. Applications for exemption should be made to the Home Office no later than the first of the month before the month when the collection will start. As a matter of courtesy, an exempt charity is expected to inform the relevant local licensing authorities about the dates of its collections.   *HTHC Act s.3*

45.2.1.2
The promoter

The **promoter** is the person to whom the licence is granted or who has been exempted from the need to obtain a licence. The promoter must ensure that the collection is carried out strictly in accordance with the licence or certificate and all legal requirements are met.

45.2.1.3
Collectors

Collectors must be over the age of 16 and be 'fit and proper persons'.
House to House Collections Regulations 1947 regs.5, 8

45.2.1.4
Certificates and badges

All collectors must carry a **certificate of authority** in the prescribed form and wear an official badge. Both must be signed by the collector. Certificates and badges are available from the Stationery Office [see end of chapter]. Charities registered with the Home Office produce their own certificates and badges. *regs.3, 4*

Where collectors are paid or will receive a portion of the collection, they are likely to be classed as **professional fundraisers** under the Charities Act 1992 part II and must comply with those rules [see **44.5.3**], including telling donors that they are being paid.

The promoter must keep the name and address of each collector to whom a certificate and badge have been given, along with the number of the collecting tin or receipt book given to them. *reg.6(2)*

Collectors must return the certificate and badge to the promoter when the collection is completed or whenever required by the promoter, and the promoter must destroy them after the collection. It is an offence for a collector to display or use a badge or certificate which does not apply to the collection being taken, or which is designed to deceive.
House to House Collections Act 1939 s.5, HTHC Regulations 1947 regs.7, 17

45.2.1.5
The collection

Money may only be collected:

- in a sealed tin or box which can be opened only by breaking the seal, and which is marked with a clear indication of the purpose of the collection and an identification number;
- if the Home Secretary has given authorisation, in envelopes sealed by the donor; *or*
- if money is collected in any other way, by handing a receipt to the donor from a duplicate or counterfoil receipt book. *regs.6(1), 13*

The receipt book must be marked with the purpose of the collection and an identification number. Every receipt (with its counterfoil or duplicate) must be consecutively numbered and must include the number of the receipt book.

45.2.1.6
Counting up

Unless the collecting tins are delivered unopened to a bank, the money must be counted in the presence of the promoter and another responsible person. The amount and identification number of the tin must be entered on a list, which is then certified by the person making the examination. For an envelope collection, each envelope is treated as a collecting tin. *regs.12(1)-(3), 13(2)*

Money accompanying a receipt book must be counted by the promoter and another responsible person, tallied with the receipt book, and entered on a list with the receipt book's identifying number. *reg.12(4)*

45.2.1.7
Returns

A return must be made to the licensing authority, listing all donations and expenditure incurred in connection with the collection, within one month of the expiry of the licence. Exempt national organisations must make an annual account to the Home Office. If the organisation has to provide accounts for street collections [see below], they can be combined if the licensing authority agrees. *reg.14*

The return must include the purpose of the collection, the names and addresses of collectors, the amount collected by each person, the total collected, costs of the collection, and how the profit was applied.

45.2.2
Street collections:
the 1916 Act

Street collections are held 'to collect money or sell articles for charitable purposes' on a public road, pavement or footpath. They are covered by the **Police, Factories etc (Miscellaneous Provisions) Act 1916** s.5.

The licensing authority is the same as for house-to-house collections [see **45.2.1.1**], but unlike house-to-house collections there is no obligation to license street collections, nor are there standard national regulations. The **Charitable Collections (Transitional Provisions) Order 1974** *[SI 1974/140]* contains a model for local licensing authorities which choose to license street collections, but it is not obligatory and there are many variations in the requirements in different licensing areas.

The model rules state that collectors should not be paid. This has implications where the organisation is paying its collectors, or is paying a fundraising business which pays collectors. If collectors are being paid it is important to ensure this does not contravene local licensing rules.

45.2.3
Public collections:
Charities Act 1992

When and if it is implemented, the **Charities Act 1992** part III will repeal the earlier legislation on street collections and house-to-house collections. If part III is implemented as it was enacted:

- house-to-house collections and street collections will be called **public charitable collections** and will all be covered by the same legislation;   *Charities Act 1992 s.65*

- collections on private land intended for use by the public (railway stations, airports, shopping centres etc) will also be covered;

- collections will be authorised by permit rather than licence;

- all permits will be issued by local authorities (a change for London boroughs, where licences have been issued by the police);   *s.66*

- the police will no longer be able to exempt small local house-to-house collections from the need for a permit [see **45.2.1.1**];   *s.66*

- an application for a permit will have to be made at least one month before the first date of the collection;   *s.67(3)*

- the Charity Commission will be able to make an **exemption order** for collections by charities (but not other organisations) which cover all or a substantial part of England and Wales;   *s.72*

- new regulations will apply to the conduct of collections, certificates of authority, badges, and minimum age of collectors.   *s.73*

Many provisions are likely to change significantly before implementation. Up-to-date information is available from the Charity Commission or the Institute of Charity Fundraising Managers [see end of chapter].

45.2.3.1
Collections covered

As defined in the Act, a **public charitable collection** is one which:

- is made by going from one house or place of business to another;

- is on any public road, pavement or footpath;

- is in a building to which the public have access, such as a railway or bus station, airport, shopping precinct or similar building;

- is in a place to which the public have access which is not within a building and is not excluded from the regulations [see below]; *or*

- meets any of the above criteria but rather than (or in addition to) being an appeal to the public, it involves an offer to sell goods or services with a representation that all or part of the proceeds will be used for charitable, benevolent or philanthropic purposes.

s.65(1),(7),(8)

45.2.3.2
Collections not covered

As defined in the Act, a collection will not be public if it is:

- at a public meeting [see **42.4.2** for definition];

- in a churchyard or on other land occupied by a place of public worship, provided the land is enclosed or substantially enclosed;

- in a static collecting box (one which is not in the possession or custody of a collector);

- inside a building (except for buildings intended for use by the public, such as railway stations and shopping precincts);

- at events which people have purchased tickets to attend;

- at places where the public are admitted only for the purpose of that appeal (for example, a private home which opens its gardens only for a fundraising event).   *Charities Act 1992 s.65(2),(9)*

Collections in privately owned places, including railway stations etc, will also require the consent of the owner or landlord.

45.2.3.3
Refusal of permits

Under the Act a local authority will be able to refuse to give a permit on any of the following grounds:

- the collection may cause undue inconvenience to the public;

- another public collection is taking place on the same day or on the day before or after;

- the amount likely to be collected would be inadequate;

- the applicant or anyone else is likely to be paid an excessive amount in connection with the collection;

- the applicant has been convicted of dishonesty or an offence relating to a public collection;

- the applicant is not properly authorised by the organisation on whose behalf the collection is being promoted; *or*

- the applicant showed insufficient care and control in carrying out a previous public collection.   *s.69*

If a permit is given the local authority will be able to attach conditions, vary the conditions or withdraw it.   *ss.68, 70*

An appeal against refusal, conditions, variation or withdrawal will be able to be made to the magistrates' court within 14 days.   *s.71*

45.3
DISTANCE FUNDRAISING AND MARKETING

Distance fundraising and marketing include any situation where the fundraiser or seller does not meet face-to-face with the potential donor or purchaser, including fundraising and marketing by direct mail, telephone, email and internet.

Organisations involved in distance fundraising must ensure they comply with relevant provisions of the **Data Protection Act 1998** [see **38.3**], telecommunications regulations [see **38.4**] and distance selling regulations [see **18.7.3**]. If relevant, they must also comply with **Charities Act 1992** rules on professional fundraisers and commercial participators [see **44.5**].

The Institute of Charity Fundraising Managers [see end of chapter] has codes of practice on various types of distance fundraising and marketing.

45.3.1
Data protection

Individuals' names, addresses, telephone numbers, email addresses and other details can be used for fundraising or direct marketing only if the individuals have been told the information will be used for these purposes. They have an absolute right to notify the organisation at any time that they do not want their details to be used for these purposes.

Unsolicited direct mail, including fundraising materials, cannot be sent to an individual who has notified the organisation or has registered with the **Mailing Preference Service** [see **38.4.1**]. Unsolicited direct marketing telephone calls cannot be made to an individual who has notified the organisation or has registered with the **Telephone Preference Service** [see **38.4.2**]. Unsolicited direct marketing faxes cannot be sent to any individual, or to an incorporated body which has registered with the **Fax Preference Service** [see **38.4.3**].

45.3.2
Telephone

Under the ICFM code of practice on telephone fundraising:

- there must be a clear contract between the organisation and any external agency involved in the telephone fundraising, as required under the **Charities Act 1992** [see **44.5**];

- the organisation and any external agency must comply with the data protection and related rules, and the rules of the Telephone Preference Service;

- the caller must give his or her name and the name of the charity or other organisation for which he or she is ringing, and must state that the purpose of the call is to request support;

- if asked, callers from external agencies should supply the name and address of the agency and the cost to the charity of each call;

- all callers should be pleasant and honest, and accept termination of the call without argument;

- calls should not be made after 9 p.m., or to anyone under the age of 16, or by using random digit dialling by computer;

- where possible a pre-call letter should be sent, and should include the option for the recipient to refuse a call.

For rules on gift aid declarations made by telephone, see **46.2.2**.

45.3.2.1
Professional fundraisers and commercial participators

All professional fundraisers and commercial participators [see **44.5.3** and **44.5.4**] must give certain information to all potential donors, including those contacted by telephone [see **44.5.6**]. In addition, further requirements apply when a solicitation or representation is made by telephone or by another method which is oral, but is not a radio or television broadcast or is not made in the presence of the potential donors.

If a donor or purchaser contacted by telephone makes a commitment to give or pay more than £50 to the fundraiser or commercial participator, the fundraiser or commercial participator must within seven days of the payment being made give the person a statement of their right to have the payment refunded. A payment is 'made' when the person gives authorisation for the payment on his or her debit or credit card, or when a payment made by post is posted, or when a payment made in person is actually made.   *Charities Act 1992 ss.60(5),(6), 61(2),(3)*

The fundraiser or commercial participator is entitled to deduct administrative expenses from the refund and to require the return of any goods already sent. There is no obligation to refund payment for services already provided at the time the notice was sent.   *s.61(4),(5)*

The Charities Act refund provisions do not apply when the telephone call is made by the charitable institution itself or by a person who is not a professional fundraiser or commercial participator. They also do not apply when the person is a professional fundraiser or commercial participator but the donation is made direct to the charitable institution. However, similar refund rules under the distance selling regulations apply to all bodies, including charitable institutions, where the telephone is being used for the sale of goods or services [see **18.7.3**].

45.3.3
Direct mail

For direct mail fundraising or marketing, the most important legal obligations are under the **Data Protection Act 1998** [see **38.4.1**] and, where goods or services are being sold, the distance selling regulations [see **18.7.3**]. Direct mailings should comply with the **British Codes of Advertising and Sales Promotion** [see **40.2**].

45.3.4
Email

Unsolicited emails ('spam') can be sent to individuals provided they have been told their details will be used in this way and have not opted out of receiving direct marketing from the organisation. The individual can at any time require the organisation to stop sending unsolicited email. Emails must include the same details as on letters [see **16.1**].

45.3.5
Internet

At the time of writing (early 2001) the law relating to e-commerce was developing. Organisations undertaking internet fundraising or sales should comply with the law on distance selling [see **18.7.3**] and good practice as it would apply to other forms of marketing and fundraising, and should obtain up-to-date legal advice.

A registered charity with annual income over £10,000 must include its registered name and the fact that it is registered on all fundraising and marketing communications, including web pages [see **16.1.4**]. Certain other information, such as VAT number, may also need to be included [see **16.1**].

For the rules on gift aid declarations made by internet, see **46.2.2**.

45.3.6
Chain letters

Funds are sometimes raised by sending a letter asking recipients to contribute to an appeal and send the letter on to others. The Charity Commission discourages the use of chain letters because they can be difficult to stop and can give rise, when the appeal target has been met, to claims that the charity is misleading the public. The Institute of Charity Fundraising Managers [see end of chapter] has guidance giving further reasons why chain letters should not be used.

If chain letters are used to raise money for a charity or other organisation the letter must clearly state the name of the organisation. If it is a registered charity with income over £10,000 per year, the fact that it is a registered charity must be on every copy of the letter [see **16.1.4**].

45.4
SALES

Sales of goods or services, whether through a shop or in other ways, must comply with rules on restrictions on trading [see **47.1.2**], tax and VAT [see **chapters 52** and **53**], professional fundraisers and commercial participation [see **44.5**], and where appropriate the rules on distance selling [see **18.7.3**]. Further issues arise where sales are carried out through a trading company [see **chapter 47**].

45.4.1
Auctions

Auctions can raise particularly complex issues:

- where the auction is carried out by a third party, that party will almost certainly be a professional fundraiser or commercial participator, and those rules will have to be followed [see **44.5**];

- if goods are donated to a charity but auctioned by a non-charity, there may be problems around the charity transferring the goods to the non-charity, and the non-charity will have to pay tax on any proceeds of the sale that are not donated to the charity under gift aid [see **52.3.2**];

- the sale is zero rated for VAT purposes only if the goods are donated to a charity and are sold by the charity or by an individual or organisation which donates *all* the profits from the sale to the charity under gift aid, otherwise the sale is standard rated [see **53.5.1**];

- even if the sale is zero rated it could, if carried out by the charity, take the charity over the threshold for VAT registration [see **53.6.1**];

- if some of the profit goes to the donor of the goods, the sale will not meet the requirements for VAT zero rating, and may not be exempt from tax if carried out by the charity [see **52.3.2**];

- if the organisation has paid for the goods and/ or has to pay the fundraiser or auctioneer, the auction may not raise enough to cover costs;

- the organisation will need to take legal advice about the conditions of sale and the conduct of sealed bids, if used;

- depending on what is being sold, the organisation may want to take advice about whether it is reasonable to exclude or restrict liability for the quality and fitness of the goods, since goods sold at auction are not consumer sales and are not covered by the **Sale of Goods Act 1979** [see **18.7.3**].

Legal advice will nearly always be needed when undertaking an auction. Similar issues may arise with sales of nearly new goods.

45.4.2
Car boot sales

An occasional car boot sale does not require a licence if all the proceeds from the sale will be used for charitable purposes, or the sale is on private property with the owner's consent. In other situations a local authority licence is required. Even where the proceeds are for charity, a licence may be required if sales are held regularly.

Local Government (Miscellaneous Provisions) Act 1982

Care must be taken to ensure that such events are not used for the sale of pirated material, in breach of copyright or trade mark rights [see **chapter 39**].

45.5
CHALLENGE AND OUTDOOR EVENTS

Challenge events take two main forms:

- a person pays to take part in an organised event such as a parachute jump or mountain trek, and then raises sponsorship for a charity or other organisation; *or*

- the person undertakes to raise a minimum amount in sponsorship, then is allowed to participate in the event.

The event may be organised by the charity or other good-cause organisation, its trading subsidiary, or a third party.

Such events may be intrinsically risky, and often take place overseas. They raise complex issues around risk, insurance and potential liability, as well as tax and VAT.

The Institute of Charity Fundraising Managers [see end of chapter] has a code of practice for such events. Their basic guidance is:

- the organisation should carefully analyse potential benefits and returns;

- tax and VAT implications must be assessed;

- a risk assessment must be carried out;

- equipment and staff skills should be thoroughly checked;

- participants should be fully briefed on what the challenge involves, and on the environmental implications;

- the emergency services should be notified;

- any damage should be reported to the landowner.

45.5.1
Risk and insurance

Before organising a challenge event it is essential to undertake a thorough risk assessment and get advice about reducing risk and taking out appropriate insurances. Particular risks that need to be considered include:

- the suitability and fitness of participants;

- participants becoming injured or ill, either because of the organiser's negligence or for other reasons;

- availability of medical treatment, especially for events in remote areas or overseas;

- problems arising from defective equipment or vehicles;

- problems related to accommodation and food;

- travel cancellations or delays;

- risks arising from political unrest, crime targeted at tourists, or extreme weather conditions;

- worst case scenarios: death, kidnap, serious accident involving all participants;

- the organisation's or other bodies' failure to comply with contracts;

- the possibility of having to return payments to participants and/or sponsorship to donors if the event is cancelled or curtailed;

- participants not paying sponsorship income to the organisation;
- the overlap between insurances taken out by the organisation, the tour operator, and participants—who covers what, and whether there are any gaps.

45.5.2
Transport and accommodation

Where participants receive travel and accommodation, the organiser in effect becomes a package tour provider and must comply with the **Package Travel, Package Holidays and Package Tours Regulations 1992** *[SI 1992/3288]*. This requires specified information to be given in the brochure, before travel, and in a contract. Information is available from the Department of Trade and Industry.

For VAT purposes, the organisation is likely to be treated as within the tour operators' margin scheme (TOMS) [see **53.5.3**].

If flights are provided the organiser must be protected by an air travel organiser's licence (ATOL bond) or must act as an agent for an ATOL holder. This protects travellers if the organiser becomes insolvent. The Civil Aviation Authority has guidance for charities about what is involved and what needs to be included in initial advertisements and in the promotional material for the event.

45.5.3
Charity law

Under the **Charities Act 1992** part II, a person is a professional fundraiser [see **44.5.3**] if he or she:

- receives more than £500 per event to raise funds for a charitable institution, *and*
- is not an employee or governing body member of the organisation or its trading company, or an employee of a fundraising business.

The payment does not have to be in money. A person who receives a trip or event worth more than £500, in return for raising funds for the organisation, may be a professional fundraiser and need to comply with those rules. This could also apply where the participant initially pays for the event, but then receives a payment back from the organisation if he or she reaches a minimum sponsorship amount.

The organisation would have to have a fundraising agreement with the individual, and the individual would have to disclose information to donors about how much of the money raised actually goes to the charity or other organisation.

An organiser who is not a professional fundraiser may be a commercial participator [see **44.5.4**] and have to comply with similar rules.

45.6
LOTTERIES

A **lottery** involves payment (in money or in some other way) for an opportunity to win a prize by chance. A lottery with non-cash prizes is often called a **raffle**, **draw** or **tombola**. The Institute of Charity Fundraising Managers has a code of practice for raffles and lotteries.

45.6.1
Lotteries and the law

A lottery is unlawful unless it is a **small lottery** incidental to an exempt entertainment [see **45.6.2**], a **private lottery** [see **45.6.3**], a **society lottery** [see **45.6.4**], a local authority lottery or a lottery which is part of the National Lottery. A lottery which does not fall into one of these categories is unlawful. A '100 club', for example, in which 100 people regularly pay a sum and draws are held, is legal only if it fits the very specific requirements for a private or society lottery.

In addition to the **Lotteries and Amusements Act 1976** which specifically regulates lotteries, a number of other laws are relevant.

45.6.1.1
Charity law

If the lottery is organised by a registered charity whose annual income is more than £10,000, tickets and all publicity material must indicate that the organisation is a registered charity [see **16.1.4**].

If a lottery is organised or promoted by a person who is paid to do so, that person may be a professional fundraiser or commercial participator [see **44.5**], and if so must comply with the relevant requirements.

45.6.1.2
Tax and VAT

Lottery tickets are not subject to VAT [see **53.4.14**]. The proceeds of a small or society lottery run by a charity, or a society lottery run by a charity's trading company where the charity is the registered society, are not subject to income or corporation tax [see **52.7.3**] if they are used solely for charitable purposes.

45.6.1.3
Alcohol prizes

The view of the Home Office, which regulated alcohol licensing until mid-2001, was that the sale of a ticket at an exempt entertainment, giving an opportunity to win alcoholic drink as a prize in a small lottery, does not constitute a sale for which a liquor licence is required. However some alcohol and police licensing authorities require licensing for society lotteries with alcohol prizes, and some may even require a licence for small lotteries. Failure to obtain a licence in this situation could result in a fine of up to £1,000 or six months in prison—even for a small lottery. Lottery organisers should therefore:

- not have alcoholic beverages as prizes;
- confirm with the local licensing authority [see **43.3.2**] that an alcohol licence is not required;
- run the lottery as part of an event which has a bar licence; *or*
- obtain an occasional permission [see **43.3.2**] for the event.

45.6.2
Small lotteries

A **small lottery** run as part of an **exempt entertainment** does not have to be registered. An exempt entertainment is a bazaar, sale of work, fete, dinner, dance, sporting or athletic event or entertainment of a similar character.   *Lotteries and Amusements Act 1976 s.3*

In a small lottery:

- the lottery or other opportunities for gaming cannot be the only or primary inducement for people to attend the event;
- no money prizes can be awarded (but gift vouchers can be);
- no more than £250 can be spent on buying prizes;
- unless the premises are licensed for the sale of alcohol, care should be taken about the provision of alcohol as prizes [see **45.6.1.3**];
- there is no limit on the price of tickets or on the number sold;
- there is no age limit for buyers or sellers of tickets;
- tickets can be sold only at and during the exempt entertainment;
- the winners must be announced during the entertainment;
- the proceeds of the entertainment (after deducting its costs) and the proceeds of the lottery (after deducting the cost of prizes and printing tickets) must be used for purposes other than private gain.

45.6.3
Private lotteries

A **private lottery** is limited to a specific group of participants and cannot be publicly advertised. It does not need to be registered, but if run by an organisation must be authorised in writing by the governing body. Private lotteries are limited to:

- members of one membership organisation which is not set up for gaming, betting or lotteries, and other persons on the organisation's premises;
- people who all work on the same premises; *or*
- people who all live on the same premises.   *s.4*

In a private lottery:

- there can be no written notice or advertisement of the lottery except on the tickets, and on the organisation's premises or where the persons for whom the lottery is promoted work or reside;
- cash prizes may be given;

- unless the premises are licensed for the sale of alcohol, care should be taken about the provision of alcohol as a prize [see **45.6.1.3**];
- the front of the tickets must include the names and addresses of the promoters, the price, a statement of the persons to whom the sale of tickets is restricted, and a statement that prizes will be delivered only to the person to whom the promoters sold the winning ticket;
- there is no restriction on the price of tickets, but the price of every ticket must be the same (so no '5 for the price of 4' deals);
- tickets cannot be given away or sold for less than their full price;
- there is no restriction on the number of tickets sold;
- tickets must not be sent through the post;
- refunds must not be given;
- if the lottery is organised by an organisation the entire proceeds, after deducting the cost of printing and stationery, must be used for prizes, the purposes of the organisation, or both;
- if the lottery is organised by people who live or work on the same premises the entire proceeds, after deducting the cost of tickets and stationery, must be used for prizes.

45.6.4
Society lotteries

A **society** is any club, institution, organisation or association. For lottery law purposes (but not for most other purposes, see **9.2.3**) each branch or section of an organisation is a separate society even if it is not autonomous.

A **society** (or **society's**) **lottery** is one promoted on behalf of a society which is established and conducted wholly or mainly for charitable purposes, participation in or support of athletic sports or games or cultural activities, or other purposes which are neither for private gain nor a commercial undertaking. *Lotteries and Amusements Act 1976 s.5*

45.6.4.1
Local authority registration

An organisation which wishes to run a society lottery must register with the local authority if:

- the total value of tickets to be put on sale is less than £20,000; *and*
- the total of the tickets for this lottery, plus the value of those already sold or put on sale in all earlier lotteries in the same calendar year, is less than £250,000. *sch.1*

The initial application to the local authority must specify the purpose for which the society is established. There will then be a further application, with a registration fee (£36 as at 1/4/01) and an annual fee every January (£18 as at 1/4/01). Tickets must not be put on sale before the organisation is registered.

45.6.4.2
Gaming Board registration

An organisation promoting a society lottery must be registered with the Gaming Board [see end of chapter] if:

- the total value of tickets or chances to be put on sale in any lottery is to exceed £20,000; *or*
- the total value of tickets or chances to be put on sale in any lottery, added to the value of those already sold or put on sale in all earlier lotteries in the same calendar year, is to exceed £250,000. *sch.1A*

The application must be accompanied by the organisation's governing document (constitution) and a letter from the governing body authorising the promoter, who must be a member of the organisation, to act in that capacity.

The initial registration fee is £3,840 (as at 1/4/01). Registration lasts indefinitely but a fee (£142 as at 1/4/01) is payable every three years. Any change to the lottery must be notified to the Board at least four weeks before tickets for the new scheme are put on sale. Tickets must not be offered for sale before the organisation is registered.

45.6.4.3
Lottery
managers

A lottery **manager** (not the same as a **promoter**, the person who takes legal responsibility) must be a member or employee of the organisation for which the organisation is being promoted, a company wholly owned by the organisation, or an **external lottery manager**. An external lottery manager must hold a certificate issued by the Gaming Board.

Lotteries and Amusements Act 1976 s.9A

The Gaming Board advises organisations to ensure that any arrangement they enter into with an external lottery manager meets the organisation's requirements and provides safeguards against the poor results of a lottery or the financial failure of the lottery manager.

45.6.4.4
Tickets

Tickets in a society lottery must not cost more than £1 each, and all tickets must be sold at the same price (so a '5 for the price of 4' deal cannot be offered). The total value of tickets sold in a single lottery must not be more than £1 million, and the total value of the tickets and chances sold in all lotteries held in any calendar year and promoted on behalf of the same organisation must not be more than £5 million.

s.11(2),(3),(6),(7)

Tickets must include specified information. The printing of lottery tickets is a specialist business, and advice should be sought from the local authority about locating a reputable printer.

LAA s.11(1)(b),(3); Lotteries Regulations 1993 [SI 1993/3223] reg.7

If an organisation runs two or more lotteries on the same day, the tickets for each must be clearly differentiated with a different serial number.

LR reg.9

A person cannot be required to make any payment beyond the ticket price as a condition for participating in the lottery, and cannot be required to buy more than one ticket as a condition for winning a particular prize.

LAA s.11(4A); LR reg.12

Money received for a ticket cannot be refunded to the participant.

LAA s.11(4)

45.6.4.5
Ticket sales

Tickets for a society lottery cannot be sold to or by anyone under 16 years of age.

LR reg.3

Tickets cannot be sold from machines, and must not be sold in the street, except for sales from kiosks or shops with no space for customers.

LR regs.4, 5; Betting, Gaming and Lotteries Act 1963 sch.4 para.1

Tickets may be sold door-to-door, but not by a person visiting a house in an official, professional or commercial capacity not connected with lotteries.

LR reg.6

Tickets sold in the street or door-to-door are likely to be subject to the requirements for street collections [see **45.2.2**], house-to-house collections [see **45.2.1**] or (when implemented) public charitable collections [see **45.2.3**].

45.6.4.6
Prizes

No more than 55% of the actual proceeds of a society lottery may be used to provide prizes.

LAA s.11(11)

Even if prizes are donated so are not counted in the 55%, no prize may have a value of more than £25,000 or 10% of the total value of tickets or chances sold, whichever is greater.

s.11(5)

Advice should be taken from the police and licensing justices if alcoholic beverages are being offered as prizes [see **45.6.1.3**].

45.6.4.7
Expenses

If the proceeds of a society lottery do not exceed £20,000, up to 35% of the proceeds may be used to meet expenses without referral to the Gaming Board. If the proceeds exceed £20,000, the permitted percentage is 15% but the Board can authorise up to 35% for a particular lottery.

s.11(13)

Contributions towards the expenses of a lottery from a genuine third party may be regarded as a donation and do not have to be included as part of the allowed percentage. But any expenses met by the organisation on whose behalf the lottery is promoted, or by the organisation or cause which will receive the proceeds of the lottery, must be treated as part of the costs of the lottery and must be included in the total expenses.   *Lotteries and Amusements Act 1976 s.11(14),(15)*

All the proceeds of a society lottery, after deducting the cost of prizes and expenses, must be used for the organisation's purposes. The cost of the prizes and expenses cannot be more than 80% of the total proceeds (so at least 20% of the proceeds must be donated to the organisation).

s.5(4)

45.6.4.8
Returns

After the completion of each society lottery promoted under its scheme, the organisation must submit a **return** to the local authority or Gaming Board. For organisations registered with the Gaming Board, a fee, ranging from £82 to £404 (as at 1/4/01), is chargeable for each lottery where the total value of tickets or chances sold is more than £2,000.

The Gaming Board's standard **beneficiary receipts** must be signed by representatives of any organisation receiving part or all of the net proceeds of the lottery. These must be sent in with the Gaming Board return. It is sensible to keep a photocopy of the beneficiary receipts.

An organisation which sells more than £100,000 worth of tickets or chances in all its lotteries held in any one year must submit, within 10 months from the end of the year, **consolidated accounts** covering all the lotteries, with a report on the accounts by a qualifying auditor.

45.6.4.9
Records

Finances, tickets and records of each lottery must be kept completely separate from those of other lotteries. Detailed records must be kept of:

- all tickets ordered and received from the printer;
- tickets issued to each point of sale;
- tickets sold, returned unsold and not returned (with a brief note of the reasons for unsold tickets not being returned);
- all income received from the sale of tickets;
- banking records;
- all expenses, with relevant invoices, distinguishing between expenses met directly from the proceeds, those met by the organisation or beneficiary, and those met by donations from third parties;
- all prizes, with relevant invoices;
- winners and winning tickets;
- how the proceeds were distributed, if the beneficiary was not the organisation which conducted the lottery;
- if agents were employed, their remuneration and the number of tickets they sold and returned.

Records must be kept for at least two years, but unsold tickets may be destroyed if the destruction is witnessed by two responsible officers of the organisation and precise records are kept of numbers of the destroyed tickets. Because winning tickets may be claimed for up to six years, adequate records should be kept beyond the two year period to deal with any late claims.

45.7
COMPETITIONS

Unlike a lottery, a **competition** involves skill. Prizes cannot be offered if success does not depend to a substantial degree on the exercise of skill. A so-called competition may be actually be a lottery, and therefore subject to controls, if the skill level is so low that virtually anyone can move on to the winning stage and the winners are then determined by means of a draw.   *s.14*

Competition prizes can also not be offered for predicting the result of a future event, or for predicting the result of an event which has already happened but where the result is not yet ascertained or not yet generally known.

Provided the competition is lawful, it is not subject to any specific legislation but should comply with the **British Codes of Advertising and Sales Promotion** [see **40.2**].

Ticket sales for competitions are subject to VAT [see **53.5.3**], and the proceeds are subject to corporation tax [see **52.7.3**].

45.8
GAMING

Gaming is playing any game of chance except for lotteries. Information about gaming and licensing is available from the Gaming Board [see end of chapter] and the local authority's licensing department.

Occasional gaming as a means of fundraising does not jeopardise charitable status, and the proceeds are not subject to tax if they fall within the concession for fundraising activities and events [see **52.4.7**]. For charities, gaming which does not fall within the concession should be carried out through a trading company [see **47.2**].

45.8.1
Bingo and other games of chance

Gaming occurs only if money or something else of value is staked on the outcome, or is received later in return for tokens. So there is no licensing requirement if bingo, cards or other games are played only for fun, with no money (or anything else which is **money's worth**) changing hands.

45.8.1.1
Entertainments not for private gain

Even where money changes hands, bingo and other games of equal chance do not have to be licensed if:

- each player makes only one payment of not more than £4, which includes entrance fee and stake or ticket money, and does not make any further payment for the game;
- the total value of all prizes is not more than £400 in one day;
- the proceeds, after deducting prizes and running costs, are not used for private gain.   *Gaming Act 1968 s.41*

Games may be advertised, and children and the public may take part.

Separate sessions at the premises on the same day and promoted by the same person are treated as one session. For a series of sessions on two days each session is treated separately, and the total prize for the final game in the series cannot be more than £700.

45.8.1.2
Club activity

Games such as bingo, whist or bridge do not need to be licensed if they are played as one of the activities of a genuine members' club which has more than 25 members, only members and signed-in guests take part, and the daily admission charge is no more than 60p per day for bingo or £15 for whist or bridge clubs. There is no limit on ticket or stake money but it must all be returned to the players as prize money, and cannot be accumulated for jackpot or 'snowball' prizes. The game cannot be advertised to members of the public.   *s.40*

45.8.1.3
Club premises

If all the 'club activity' provisions apply but the club wants to charge up to £2 per person per day for bingo or similar games of chance, the premises must be registered with the local authority.   *pt.II*

45.8.1.4
Occasional fundraising events

Occasional games of chance as part of an **exempt entertainment** [see **45.6.2** for definition] do not need to be licensed, provided that the game is not the only or main reason for people attending. There are no limits on admission charges, stake money or the value of prizes. All the proceeds after deduction of expenses and prizes must be used for purposes other than private gain.   *Lotteries and Amusements Act 1976 s.15*

45.8.1.5
Other situations

Information about registration requirements for bingo and games of chance in other circumstances is available from the Gaming Board.

45.8.2
Darts and snooker

Darts and snooker are considered to be games of skill, so a gaming licence is not generally required. However, a **billiard licence**, available from the local authority, is required if a table is used for the public playing of billiards, snooker or pool and the premises do not have a liquor licence.

45.8.3
Amusement machines

Permits are obtained from the local authority for amusement machines:

- which pay out up to £5 in cash and £8 in tokens for a maximum 30p stake, and can be situated in family arcades, cafes, leisure centres and other areas used by children and young people under 18 as well as adults;

- which pay out up to £15 in cash-only machines for a maximum 30p stake, and can be located only in adult-only environments.

Gaming Act 1968 s.34

For amusement machines in licensed liquor premises, permits are obtained from the licensing justices [see **43.3.2**].

FOR FURTHER INFORMATION

Charity Commission: 0870-333 0123; www.charity-commission.gov.uk

Institute of Charity Fundraising Managers: 0870-600 5522; www.icfm.org.uk

Collection badges & certificates. Stationery Office: 0870-6005522; www.thestationeryoffice.com

Lotteries & gaming. Gaming Board of Great Britain: 020-7306 6200; www.gbgb.org.uk

Chapter 46
TAX-EFFECTIVE GIVING

46.1 TAX EFFECTIVENESS

All donations to charities and other voluntary organisations are tax effective, in the sense that the organisation is unlikely to have to pay income or corporation tax on them [see **52.3.1**]. But donations to some organisations are even more tax effective, because the recipient body is able to recover the tax paid by the donor, or the donor is able to get tax relief on the income used for the donation. In general only charities can benefit from this type of tax-effective giving, but some arts bodies which are not charities are also eligible, and in early 2001 the government announced that it would consult on extending these provisions to non-profit sports clubs.

Tax-effective giving includes:

- gift aid [see **46.2**];
- payroll giving [see **46.3**];
- gifts of shares and other assets [see **46.4**];
- legacies [see **46.5**];
- some donations from businesses [see **46.7**].

The rules relating to tax-effective giving are generally not complex, but must be strictly followed.

Charity trustees have an obligation to maximise their charity's income [see **13.3.5**]. This includes recovering tax whenever possible, so all charitable organisations should take every opportunity to encourage donors to give through gift aid [see **46.2**], and should ensure that gift aid declarations are sent to all donors who make eligible donations.

A company which makes donations for charitable purposes, by whatever method, must list them in its annual report if the total value is more than £200 [see **50.3.3**].

46.2
GIFT AID

Gift aid enables charities to recover basic rate tax on donations received from UK taxpayers. Detailed information is available from Inland Revenue (Charities) or the Inland Revenue website [see end of chapter].

Finance Act 1990 s.25; Income and Corporation Taxes Act 1988 s.339

There is no minimum or maximum on the gift aid amount, nor any limit on the number of gift aid donations a donor can make in any year. For individual donors, the only requirements are that they have made a gift aid declaration covering the donation [see **46.2.2.1**], and will have paid UK income or capital gains tax during the tax year of at least as much as the charity will recover. For company donors, the only requirement is that the donation comes out of their UK pre-tax profits [see **46.2.4**].

A gift aid payment must be made from income which the Inland Revenue can confirm has had income tax or capital gains tax paid on it. Gift aid therefore cannot be used to pass on money collected from a number of unidentifiable individuals, for example in collecting tins. It also cannot be used for donations from one charity to another, or donations to a charity from a non-taxpayer (such as a local authority, or a person who does not pay UK tax).

Gift aid cannot be used to donate to a foreign charity, but may be used for all UK charities as well as some national institutions, and non-profit associations for scientific research or for the advancement of trade.

The writing off of a loan to a charity is not a payment of a sum of money, so cannot be classed as a gift aid payment. However if the charity repays the loan, the lender can then donate that amount to the charity under the gift aid scheme, and the charity can recover tax on it.

46.2.1
Gift aid as payment for benefits

A payment made under gift aid is a donation. The donor cannot receive goods, membership services, or other services or benefits (including, for example, discounts on goods or services) in return unless these comply with the **donor benefit rules**. The maximum value of the benefits that a donor, or a person connected with the donor, can receive in return for his or her donations is:

- benefits worth up to 25% of the total gift aid donations (net of tax) in the tax year, if the total donations are £100 or less;
- benefits worth up to £25, if total donations are from £101 to £1,000;
- benefits worth up to 2.5% of the total donations, if total donations are from £1,001 to £10,000;
- benefits worth up to £250, if total donations are over £10,000.

Finance Act 2000 s.39(5A)-(5D)

If the donor receives benefits worth more than the allowed amount, the entire gift aid payment is treated as an ordinary donation and the charity is not able to recover tax on it.

Even if a benefit is acceptable for gift aid purposes, there may be VAT implications [see **53.5.3**].

46.2.1.1
Conservation and heritage charities

The donor benefit rules do not apply where the right of free or reduced price admission is provided to the donor or members of the donor's family, so long as:

- the admission is to view property, and the preservation of that property is the charity's sole or main aim; or the admission is to view wildlife, and the conservation of that wildlife is the charity's sole or main aim; *and*
- admission is open to the general public on payment of a donation.

s.39(5E)-(5G)

This means that the value of the free or reduced price admission is not counted when determining whether a donation to these charities is eligible for gift aid tax recovery.

Free or reduced price admission provided to non-family guests of the donor, and the provision of anything other than admission, must comply with the donor benefit rules.

46.2.2
Donations from individuals

Individuals make gift aid donations net of tax, and the charity then recovers basic rate tax from the Inland Revenue. Tax can be recovered as soon as the charity receives the donation, provided the donor has:

- made a gift aid declaration [see **46.2.2.1**] in writing or via the internet, which covers the donation;
- made a gift aid declaration orally, and the charity has sent a written record of the oral declaration [see **46.2.2.2**];
- made the donation under a deed of covenant that was in existence on 5 April 2000 [see **46.2.3.2**]; *or*
- made the donation under a deed of covenant that was made on or after 6 April 2000 [see **46.2.3.1**], and has also made a gift aid declaration covering the donation.

46.2.2.1
Gift aid declarations

A gift aid declaration may be made in writing (including fax), electronically via email or the internet, or orally. The Inland Revenue can provide examples of gift aid declarations. All declarations must include:

- the donor's name (ideally full name) and full address including postcode;
- the charity's name or acronym;
- a description of the donations covered by the declaration [see below]; *and*
- a statement that the donations are to be treated as gift aid donations.

Donations to Charities by Individuals (Appropriate Declarations)
Regulations 2000 [SI 2000/2074]

Written and electronic declarations must also include a note explaining that the donor must pay income tax or capital gains tax equal to the tax the charity will reclaim on the donation(s). There is no need for a signature or date, although for practical reasons it is sensible for written and electronic declarations to be dated.

46.2.2.2
Record of oral declaration

Where a declaration is made orally, in person or by telephone, the charity must make a written record and send a copy to the donor. The written record must contain the same information as a written declaration, plus the date the donor made the oral declaration, the date the charity is sending the written record to the donor, and a statement that the declaration will not take effect if the donor cancels it within 30 days of the charity sending the written record. At the time of writing (early 2001) there was no specified period for sending it.

Donations to Charities by Individuals (Appropriate Declarations)
Regulations 2000 [SI 2000/2074]

The donor does not have to sign or return the written record. The charity cannot reclaim tax until it has sent out the written record, but it can reclaim as soon as it is sent, without waiting until the 30-day cancellation period has ended.

46.2.2.3
Donations covered by a declaration

A declaration may be made at the same time as the donation, or before or after. It can cover:

- any or all donations made from any date after 5 April 2000;
- all future donations, or all donations until a specified future date;
- a single donation; *and/or*
- any other definition of donation(s), for example 'the donations covered by the direct debit mandate below', 'the donations covered

by the direct debit mandate below and all other donations made by me since 6 April 2000', or 'the enclosed donation, all other donations made by me since 6 April 2000, and all donations made in future until this declaration is cancelled by me in writing'.

Gift aid donations may include:

- donations made by named donors in collecting envelopes, provided each envelope includes the gift aid declaration or the donor has previously made an open-ended declaration to the charity;
- sponsorship, such as sponsoring someone to run a race, provided the sponsorship form includes the declaration;
- regular donations made through standing orders or direct debit;
- any other donation which fulfils the gift aid criteria and is covered by a declaration.

A declaration which is not limited to a specific donation or time period continues indefinitely.

46.2.2.4
Donations not covered by a declaration

The charity must have internal records enabling it to identify which donations are and are not covered by a declaration. When a donation is received that is not covered by a declaration, the charity should have procedures to ensure a declaration form is sent and the donor is asked, if he or she is a UK taxpayer, to complete it for the donation, and ideally for future donations.

The internal records must also ensure that declaration forms are not sent out in relation to payments made with CAF cheques, CAF vouchers or similar vouchers on which the Charities Aid Foundation or another charity has already claimed the tax, and that tax is not recovered on such donations.

46.2.2.5
Gift aid records

The charity must keep proper accounting records showing the donations received, the link to a gift aid declaration (through a code number or some other method of linking the donation to the declaration), and tax recovered. A charity which does not keep adequate records can be required to pay back reclaimed tax, with interest, to the Inland Revenue, and can be liable to a penalty. Records should include the written declaration or written record of oral declaration, any correspondence or changes relating to the declaration, correspondence relating to gift aid donations, financial records relating to donations received, and any other records relating to the donations. Records do not have to be kept on paper.

A charitable association, company or industrial and provident society must keep gift aid records until six years after the end of the accounting period to which the tax reclaim relates.

A charitable trust must keep records until the later of:

- the 31 January which is 21 months after the end of the tax year to which the tax reclaim relates (so records for a claim relating to tax year 2001-02 must be kept until 31 January 2004);
- one year after the tax claim is made, rounded to the end of the quarter (so records for a claim made on 25 May 2002 must be kept until 30 June 2003); *or*
- Inland Revenue (Charities) completing any audit it has started.

It is good practice for charitable trusts to keep records for at least six years.

Gift aid declarations which extend beyond the period covered by the tax reclaim must be kept, so they are available for the later periods.

46.2.2.6
Tax recovery

The charity can claim the tax as soon as it receives the money and a written or electronic declaration, or receives the money and an oral declaration and sends out a written record of the oral declaration.

The forms for tax recovery depend on whether the donations were received on or before 5 April 2000 or after that date, and whether donations are made under a deed of covenant that was in existence on 5 April 2000. The necessary forms and full information about tax recovery are available from Inland Revenue (Charities) [see end of chapter].

The deadline for reclaiming tax is:

- for charitable associations and companies, within six years from the end of the accounting period to which the claim relates;

- for charitable trusts, within five years of 31 January in the year following the end of the tax year to which the claim relates.

46.2.2.7
How tax is worked out

An example of how tax on gift aid donations is calculated is:

- the charity receives donations totalling £1,500 that are covered by gift aid declarations;

- to have £1,500 available after basic rate tax, the donors would have received £1,923.08 as part of their taxable income and would have paid basic rate tax of £423.08 (at 22% basic rate);

- the charity works out the tax that has been paid on the donations (£423.08), and reclaims that amount from the Inland Revenue.

The amount of recoverable tax can be worked out by:

- dividing the current basic tax rate by 100 minus the basic tax rate;

- then multiplying this amount by the total amount of the gift aid donations.

For example:

- current tax rate 22, divided by (100 - 22) = 22/78;

- 22/78 multiplied by £1,500 = £423.08 tax which can be recovered.

If basic tax rate were reduced to 20%, the charity would only be able to recover £375 on £1,500 gift aid donations (20/80 x £1,500). If the tax rate went up to 25%, the charity would be able to recover £500 (25/75 x £1,.500).

46.2.2.8
<u>Lower rate taxpayers</u>

Individuals with very low taxable income may pay income tax only or mostly at the starting rate (10% in 2001-02) and therefore not pay enough *basic* rate income tax to cover the amount reclaimed by the charity. This is not a problem, provided the donor has paid enough income tax and/or capital gains tax, at whatever rate, to cover the amount reclaimed. A donor who does not pay at least this much should cancel the gift aid declaration [see **46.2.2.10**].

46.2.2.9
Higher rate taxpayers

If a donor pays higher rate income tax (40% in 2001-02) or capital gains tax, the charity recovers tax at the basic rate and the donor gets **higher rate relief** on the difference between the basic rate and the higher or capital gains rate. If a higher rate taxpayer makes a £1,500 gift aid donation, for example:

- the higher rate taxpayer receives £2,500 as part of taxable income;

- the individual pays higher rate tax (40% of £2,500 = £1,000) and donates the remaining £1,500 to a charity with a gift aid declaration;

- the charity recovers basic rate tax on this (£423.08);

- the individual notifies the Inland Revenue of the gift aid donation on his or her self assessment tax return;

- the higher rate relief is calculated by adding the net amount after tax (£1,500) and basic rate tax (£423.08) to give a **grossed up** amount (£1,923.08). The basic rate (22%) is subtracted from the higher rate (40%). The individual gets this higher rate relief (18%) on the grossed up amount (18% of £1,923.08 = £346.15). The Inland Revenue either gives credit against tax due from the individual, or adjusts the individual's PAYE code [see **27.4.1**] to allow for the credit to be set against the tax due on earned income.

46.2.2.10
Non-taxpayers

Donors who are not taxpayers, or do not pay enough income tax and/or capital gains tax to cover the tax recovered under the gift aid scheme, must not make a gift aid declaration. If they have a declaration in place and cease to pay enough tax, they must notify the charity to cancel the declaration. Failure to do so could mean that they have to pay the tax specially to the Inland Revenue in order to cover the amount reclaimed by the charity.

46.2.2.11
Cancellation

A donor may cancel a gift aid declaration at any time. The cancellation does not have to be in writing, but to avoid problems the charity may ask for it to be put in writing.

If the cancellation is during the 30-day period after an written record of oral declaration has been sent [see **46.2.2.2**], the cancellation is retrospective and nullifies the declaration. If the charity has already recovered tax on the donation, it must repay the recovered tax to the Inland Revenue.

Cancellation of a written (including electronic) declaration, or an oral declaration more than 30 days after the written record was sent, applies to donations received by the charity on or after the date it is notified of the cancellation, or such other later date as the donor specifies.

Donations to Charities by Individuals (Appropriate Declarations)
Regulations 2000 [SI 2000/2074]

46.2.3
Deeds of covenant

A **deed of covenant** is a promise in the form of a legally binding deed [see **18.3**] to donate a stated amount to a charity. Tax on deeds of covenant is now recovered under gift aid. But because a deed of covenant is legally binding on the donor, charities may want to continue to encourage donors to make them, along with their gift aid declaration. For charities with a large donor base, covenants can provide virtually guaranteed income for an extended period, and covenants may be able to be used as security if the charity has to borrow from a bank.

46.2.3.1
Covenants made after
5 April 2000

A deed of covenant entered into after 5 April 2000 does not, on its own, allow the charity to recover the basic rate tax paid by the covenantor. For tax recovery, the deed of covenant (or any agreement) must be accompanied by a gift aid declaration [see **46.2.2.1**].

There is no longer a prescribed form of words for deeds of covenant, and there is no minimum period. A deed of covenant can be worded as a simple agreement to make a donation of a certain amount for an indefinite period or for a set number of months or years. To be binding, it must say that it is a deed, be signed in the presence of one witness, and say that it is 'delivered' [see **18.3**]. An agreement which does not meet these requirements is not legally binding, and can be cancelled or ignored at any time by the donor.

Law of Property (Miscellaneous Provisions) Act 1989 s.1

46.2.3.2
Covenants in existence
on 5 April 2000

For deeds of covenant taken out before 6 April 2000, tax is now recovered under gift aid without any need for a gift aid declaration. The charity should ensure that a declaration is in place for other (non-covenanted) donations, and for any subsequent covenants.

For donations made under these covenants (but no other gift aid donations) the charity can, if it is more advantageous, recover tax at the basic rate in force when the covenanted payment falls due rather than when it is made. *Finance Act 2000 s.41*

For payments received before 6 April 2000, tax is recovered under the old deed of covenant procedures. Claims no longer need to be accompanied by the old form R185, and as with all covenant tax claims, can be backdated six years. This means that where a pre-April 2000 deed of covenant is in place but the donor did not complete a form R185, the charity may still be able to recover tax on earlier donations.

Covenants in taken out before 6 April 2000 continue until they expire. Only in exceptional circumstances should the charity release the donor from the covenant, and replace it with an equivalent gift aid declaration and standing order or direct debit. Releasing a donor, including a charity's trading company, from a covenant means giving up the security of a binding promise of continued payments, and this would contravene the trustees' duty to safeguard the charity's assets.

**46.2.3.3
Termination**

Because a deed of covenant is legally binding on the donor, it cannot be cancelled by the donor. Even if the donor ceases to pay tax and must cancel his or her gift aid declaration [see **46.2.2.10**], the promise to make the donation remains in place until it expires. However, a charity may release a donor from the covenant if the donor becomes unemployed or for another valid reason is unable to continue making payments. The release should be in writing and should be kept with the deed.

**46.2.4
Donations from
companies**

From 1 April 2000 companies, including companies owned by a charity, make gift aid donations gross. The company donates the full amount to the charity, including tax, and claims tax relief when calculating its profits for corporation tax [see **47.7.3** and **52.2.2**]. There is no need for a gift aid declaration, and the charity does not recover anything from the Inland Revenue.

Finance Act 2000 s.40

The same procedure applies to donations made under company deeds of covenant, regardless of when the covenant was made.

Where a charity's trading subsidiary wishes to donate all its profits to the charity, there can be a problem because the profits are generally not accurately known by the end of the financial year. If the company were to donate too little it would have to pay tax on the retained profits; if it were to donate too much it would not be able to recover the overpayment from the charity. To avoid these problems, charity trading subsidiaries have a nine-month period from the end of the financial year during which they can make the gift aid donation to the charity, but set it against their profits for the previous year.

**46.3
PAYROLL GIVING**

The **payroll giving scheme** enables employees to make charitable gifts by deduction from their salary. It is different from gift aid because the charity cannot recover the tax paid by the donor. Instead, the deduction is made from the donor's gross pay before tax has been deducted—so the donor does not pay income tax on the money used for the donation. National insurance, however, remains payable on the full salary.

*Income and Corporation Taxes Act 1988 ss.86A, 202;
Charitable Deductions (Approved Schemes) Regulations 1986 [SI 1986/2211]*

From 6 April 2000 there is no maximum on the donations which can be made through payroll giving. Donors under payroll giving cannot receive any benefits in return for their donation, and payroll giving cannot be used for payments covered by a deed of covenant or gift aid declaration.

An employer's payroll giving scheme must be approved by the Inland Revenue. At the employee's request the employer deducts the amount from the employee's pre-tax salary and sends it to an **approved agency**, which then sends it on, within 60 days, to the employee's choice of charity. The best known agency is **Give As You Earn** (GAYE), operated by the Charities Aid Foundation, but there are a number of other agencies run by individual charities or groups of charities. Details are available from Inland Revenue (Charities) [see end of chapter].

People receiving pensions through an occupational pension scheme can join the employer's payroll giving scheme if tax is deducted from the pension under PAYE.

46.3.1
Government
supplement

For all donations made through a payroll giving scheme from 6 April 2000 to 5 April 2003, the government is giving a 10% supplement. This is distributed to charities by payroll giving agencies along with payroll giving donations.   *Finance Act 2000 s.38*

Some agencies provide participating employees with vouchers which the employees can then give to charities of their choice. The agencies may add the supplement to the employee's payroll giving account, in which case the vouchers given to charities will already include the supplement.

46.4
GIFTS OF ASSETS

When an individual disposes of an asset which has increased in value, **capital gains tax** is payable on the gain (the increase in value). There is an annual exemption for individuals (£7,500 in 2001-02). Above this CGT is payable at the individual's income tax rate. [For tax on gains realised by organisations, see **52.2.4**.]

The obligation to pay CGT applies even if the asset is given away. The value is assessed at its current open market value—which could mean that the donor is liable for CGT even through he or she has not been paid for the asset and thus does not have funds to pay the tax.

46.4.1
Gifts to charities and
certain other bodies

When an asset is donated to a charity or is sold to a charity at below market value, its value is assumed to be an amount which does not give rise to either a gain or a loss, so there is no capital gain and therefore no need for the donor to pay CGT. This also applies to gifts and sales below value to certain institutions listed in the **Inheritance Tax Act 1984** [see **46.5.2**].   *Taxation of Chargeable Gains Act 1992 ss.257, 258*

If the sale of the asset would make a loss, it may be advantageous for the donor to sell the asset to a third party, set the loss against tax liability, and donate the sale proceeds to the charity under gift aid.

46.4.1.1
Gifts of shares
and securities

In addition to relief from capital gains tax, there is also relief from income tax (for individuals) and corporation tax (for companies) on gifts of shares and securities to charities. This is claimed by the donor, not the charity, and is in addition to the donor's relief from capital gains tax. To qualify, the shares or securities must be:

- listed on a recognised stock exchange in the UK or elsewhere;

- donated to the charity, or sold to the charity at less than their market value, on or after 6 April 2000 (for an individual) or 1 April 2000 (for a company); *and*

- donated or sold to the charity with 'no strings attached'.
                                                           Finance Act 2000 s.43

Gifts of shares and securities can have particularly complex tax implications for both the donor and charity. Advice should be sought on maximising the benefits to both parties.

46.4.2
Gifts to
non-charities

If an asset is given to a non-charity, the donor will have to pay capital gains tax. Specialist advice should be taken to ensure this is minimised.

46.5
LEGACIES AND
LIFETIME GIFTS

A **legacy** or **bequest** is money or other assets left under the terms of a will. A **lifetime gift** is a gift of money or other assets made during the person's lifetime.

Inheritance tax is chargeable on the value of a person's estate at the day of death, plus, on a sliding scale, the value of gifts made during the seven years prior to death. There is no inheritance tax on bequests and gifts to a spouse, charities and some other organisations [see below], and on the first £242,000 (in 2001-02) of the remainder of the estate. Inheritance tax (40% in 2001-02) is payable on everything above this.

46.5.1
Legacy fundraising

Legacies are an important source of income for both charities and non-charities, and many organisations undertake campaigns to encourage supporters to make wills and to leave a legacy to the organisation. Provided the organisation has adequate powers to undertake this sort of fundraising [see **5.4.4**] there is no problem with a legacy campaign, but difficult issues arise if the organisation becomes too involved in the process of drafting wills. Involvement in, or funding of, the preparation of a will under which the organisation ultimately benefits may, unless handled very carefully, lead to a legal challenge on the basis of undue influence. There is also the risk of the organisation being sued for negligence if its advice does not meet professional standards.

Before undertaking a legacy campaign, the organisation should consult the Charity Commission's guidance *Paying for Wills with Charity Funds* and the Institute of Charity Fundraising Managers' legacy fundraising code of practice [see end of chapter].

The promise of a legacy is not legally binding [see **44.3.1**], and an organisation has no recourse in law if a donor who has promised a legacy subsequently changes his or her will.

46.5.1.1
Legacies to companies

Where a charitable or other voluntary sector company is encouraging donors to leave a legacy, it may want to ask them to include a clause making clear that if the company becomes insolvent, the bequest cannot be used to meet the company's obligations to its creditors. This follows a ruling that until an insolvent company is dissolved, bequests and donations to the company can be passed on to creditors.

Re ARMS (Multiple Sclerosis Research) Ltd:
Alleyne v Attorney General & another [1997] 2 All ER 679

46.5.2
Gifts to charities and certain other bodies

Gifts by an individual during his or her lifetime, on death or through a close company controlled by an individual are exempt from inheritance tax provided that they are to:

- organisations established for charitable purposes;
- specified institutions such as universities, museums, art galleries, the National Trust etc established for national purposes or public benefit (at the time of writing, consultation was taking place about whether this should also be extended to community sports clubs);
- local authorities, government departments or health service bodies;
- political parties; *and/or*
- registered social landlords (gifts of land only).

Inheritance Tax Act 1984 ss.23-26, sch.3

In order to qualify for this relief, the following conditions must be met:
- the gift must be irrevocable;
- no one else may have an interest in the asset;
- there must be no limit on how long the asset can be held by the donor, or other limits on the donor's right to transfer the asset;
- any conditions required by the donor must be met within 12 months of the date of the transfer;
- if the asset is land or a building, the gift must not have conditions requiring the donor, the donor's spouse or a person connected with the donor to use the property rent free or at a rent below the market rate;
- the gift must be used only for charitable purposes; *and*
- if the will creates a new trust, the purposes must be wholly and exclusively charitable [see **4.3**].

Bequests to existing charities and other organisations which qualify for relief from inheritance tax are made direct to the organisation, without deduction of any tax. Straightforward money gifts are not likely to be

CHAPTER 46: TAX-EFFECTIVE GIVING

complex, but charities should use a solicitor to deal with any other bequests. For example, if a charity is entitled to the residue of an estate and the executor sells the property, shares or other assets which make up the estate before passing the proceeds to the charity, the gains could be subject to capital gains tax [see **46.4**]. But if the executor is instructed to sell them on behalf of the charity, rather than on behalf of the estate, capital gains tax would not be payable.

46.5.3
Gifts to other bodies

Bequests to organisations which do not qualify for inheritance tax exemption are subject to inheritance tax. The detailed terms of the will determine whether the estate of the deceased bears the tax and the organisation receives the full specified sum, or whether the tax is deducted from the sum before it is paid over to the organisation.

If an organisation which is not exempt from inheritance tax receives a gift from a living person who then dies within seven years, the value of the gift is added back into the donor's estate when calculating the estate's liability for inheritance tax. The value added back is reduced on a sliding scale for each year the donor survived following the gift.

46.5.4
Changes and challenges

Some or all of the beneficiaries may, within two years after the person's death, agree a **deed of variation** altering the way the estate is distributed. This may be done to maximise inheritance tax relief, or for other reasons. A charity can be party to a variation only if it can show that the variation is in the best interests of the charity.

46.5.4.1
Contested probate

Gifts in wills may be challenged by anyone, but this is most commonly done by relatives who feel they have not been provided for under the **Inheritance (Provision for Family and Dependants) Act 1973**, or by a charity or other party who believes the will is invalid or has not been properly administered. This gives rise to **contested probate**.

46.5.4.2
Ex gratia payments

A charity occasionally feels that it has received a bequest which the donor may not actually have intended or which is unfair to the donor's dependants, and that it has a moral obligation to make an *ex gratia* payment to the donor's relatives or others, even if this is not in the charity's best interest. This may be done only with the consent of the Charity Commission [see **49.2.7**].

46.5.4.3
Disclaiming legacies

In some situations a charity may not want to accept a legacy, but it can refuse to accept only if this is in the best interests of the charity [see **44.3.2**] or the Charity Commission gives consent. An exception is Alcoholics Anonymous, which wished to have the right to disclaim legacies so that it could remain a self-help organisation and did not want to have more assets than it needed for its day-to-day work. It succeeded in getting a private Bill through Parliament allowing it to disclaim legacies. *Alcoholics Anonymous (Dispositions) Act 1986*

The Institute of Charity Fundraising Managers [see end of chapter] has a guidance note on the acceptance and refusal of donations.

46.6
PERSONAL CHARITABLE TRUSTS

Individuals who want to make substantial donations to charities may find it appropriate to set up a personal charitable trust, with objects to support charitable work in general or to support particular types of charitable activity.

In addition to the capital gains and inheritance tax advantages [see above] the trust can be made the beneficiary of a gift aid payment. The trust recovers the tax and the trustees, who generally include the donor, can make a series of smaller donations from the trust's income. The whole of the income should generally be utilised in each year, unless it is being retained for a specific purpose [see **54.8** for more about retention of reserves].

Some trusts have as their main capital asset a large number of shares in the founder's company or a property asset. This arrangement may allow the donor to avoid capital gains tax or inheritance tax, while still being effectively able to control the company or asset which has been given. An example is a majority shareholder in a private company, who sets up a trust for charitable purposes with his or her shares. The donor and two other connected people—perhaps members of the donor's family—are named as trustees. The donor and other trustees control the charitable trust and also, through their control of the trust, the company. On the donor's death no inheritance tax is payable (because the shares have been donated to the charitable trust) but the donor's family retains control of the trust and company. Such arrangements are complex and require specialist legal advice.

46.7
GIFTS BY COMPANIES

When a gift aid donation is made by a business registered as a company (rather than operating as a sole trader or partnership), it is doubly tax effective: the charity receives the tax the company would have had to pay, and the company can set the full amount (donation plus tax) against its pre-tax profits. Gifts by a charity's trading company may be set against the previous year's profits if made within nine months from the end of the trading company's financial year [see **46.2.4**].

Most other donations and gifts by a company or other business cannot be set against its income or profits, but there are a few exceptions.

46.7.1
Benevolent gifts by traders

Businesses can get tax relief by setting payments to voluntary organisations against their income or profits, but only if the payment:

- is wholly and exclusively for the purposes of the business;

- is made for the benefit of an organisation established for educational, cultural, religious, recreational or benevolent purposes;

- is made to an organisation which is local in relation to the donor's business activities, and which is not restricted to persons connected with the donor;

- is not of a capital nature; *and*

- is reasonably small in relation to the scale of the donor's business.

Inland Revenue Extra-statutory Concession B7

These payments are called **benevolent gifts by traders**. Typical examples are:

- small annual subscriptions to charities relating to the business's trade or professional vocation, such as a benevolent fund;

- small donations to local charities which benefit the business's employees;

- payments to sponsor a charitable activity, if the payment is made to advertise or publicise the business and is reasonable compared with the publicity involved (but note that sponsorship which explicitly benefits the donor may be subject to VAT, see **53.5.3**);

- expenditure on scientific research related to the business where the research is conducted by a charity (but note that this could have VAT implications, see **53.5.3**).

A business should not set any gifts against taxable profits without taking advice to ensure they comply with the requirements.

46.7.2
Gifts of assets

The gift of an asset from a company to a charity or certain other institutions is treated for capital gains tax purposes in the same way as a gift by an individual [see **46.4**]. The company does not have to pay tax on the disposal, but in general cannot set any loss relating to the asset against tax. Where the company gives shares or securities to a charity or sells them to a charity at less than market value, the value can be set against profits and thus reduce corporation tax [see **46.4.1.1**].

46.7.3
Gifts of equipment

A gift of machinery and plant to charities or to many schools, further education colleges and universities attracts tax relief for the donor, if:

- the gift is an article manufactured or sold by the donor or used in the donor's business;
- the donor receives no benefit from the charity or educational establishment;
- the article was eligible for capital allowances; *and*
- the claim is made within two years of the date of the gift.

Income and Corporation Taxes Act 1988 ss.83A, 84; Finance Act 1999 s.55

This provision applies to the gift of computers, office furniture, scientific equipment and similar items.

46.7.4
Secondment of employees

A **secondment** is a temporary 'loan' of an employee to another organisation [see **22.5.3**]. If the employee is seconded to a charity by a business (whether a company, sole trader or partnership), the cost to the business is allowed as a deduction in calculating the profits of the business. 'Cost to the business' is the employee's salary and related costs.
Income and Corporation Taxes Act 1988 s.86

The cost cannot be deducted if the secondment is to a non-charitable organisation.

46.7.5
Political donations by companies

A company must receive authorisation from its shareholders before it makes a donation of more than £5,000 to a political party or political organisation. This applies to donations to organisations which seek to influence support for a political party or influence voters in a referendum. It does not apply to donations to charities or to organisations simply seeking to promote public debate.
Political Parties, Elections and Referendums Act 2000 s.139, sch.19

46.8
LANDFILL TAX

Landfill tax is a tax paid by landfill site operators, based on the amount of waste which goes into their site. Under the **environmental bodies credit scheme**, site operators are encouraged to make voluntary contributions, of up to 20% of their landfill tax bill, to approved environmental bodies. The site operator then receives 90% tax credit on the voluntary contribution. *Landfill Tax Regulations 1996 [SI 1996/152]*

Charities and other organisations which meet certain criteria are eligible to receive contributions under this scheme if they are involved in land reclamation or restoration; anti-pollution, waste management, environmental protection and conservation activities; research and education on recycling, and development and promotion of products made from wastes; or development of markets for recycled waste.
Landfill Tax (Amendment) Regulations 1999 [SI 1999/3270]

Organisations must be registered with Entrust, a private regulator set up by the government to oversee landfill tax credits. At the time of writing (early 2001) the government was reviewing these arrangements.

FOR FURTHER INFORMATION

Charity Commission: 0870-333 0123; www.charity-commission.gov.uk

Institute of Charity Fundraising Managers: 020-7627 3436; www.icfm.org.uk

Gift aid & covenants. Inland Revenue (Charities): 0151-472 6038; www.inlandrevenue.gov.uk

Landfill tax. HM Customs & Excise: 08459-128484; www.hmce.gov.uk

Entrust: 0161-972 0044; www.entrust.org.uk

Chapter 47
TRADING COMPANIES

47.1 VOLUNTARY ORGANISATIONS AND TRADING

Trading raises some of the most complex legal issues voluntary organisations will face. These involve the interaction of:

- **constitutional** issues, around whether the trading is within the organisation's objects and powers;

- **charity law**, which puts some restrictions on trading (although not as many as some people think), and requires charities not to pay unnecessary tax on trading activities;

- **direct taxation** law, which provides charities and some other voluntary organisations with tax privileges which may be threatened by trading activities;

- **VAT** law, which defines a very wide range of activities as 'business supplies' and therefore potentially subject to VAT;

- **liability** issues, around the risks involved in trading and, in unincorporated associations and trusts, the potential personal liability of the members of the governing body;

- **practical and management issues**, which need to be carefully considered before starting trading and while trading.

Each issue is complex, and mistakes can be damaging. The time, financial investment, risks and liabilities involved in trading are frequently underestimated, and can lead to significant losses.

47.1.1
The meaning of
trading

In terms of corporation tax or income tax, an organisation is likely to be **trading** where it receives payment from anyone—service user, member of the organisation, member of the public, statutory body, commercial business or anyone else—in return for providing goods, services, facilities, publicity or any other benefit. Even if the organisation does not have to pay corporation or income tax on the profit or income, the activity is nonetheless trading.

Where the person making the payment receives nothing in return (or nothing other than a simple acknowledgement) the relationship is likely to be one of donor and recipient [see **44.3**], rather than a trading relationship. But the boundary between a donation or grant and a payment for goods or a service is often unclear, especially in relation to sponsorship arrangements [see **52.3.3**] and service agreements and contracts for services [see **48.1**].

The definition of trading for **tax** purposes, and the tax exemptions available for charities and in some cases for other voluntary organisations, are covered in **52.4-52.6**.

In **charity** terms, a distinction is made between **primary purpose trading** (trading in direct furtherance of the charity's objects, see **52.6**), and other activities which are referred to simply as 'trading'. But primary purpose trading is trading as well.

VAT law does not refer to trading, but to **business supplies** [see **53.3.2**]. Business supplies may be exempt or taxable, and if taxable may be subject to VAT at zero rate, reduced rate or standard rate.

47.1.1.1
The inter-relationship

The relationship between these aspects of 'trading' is complex:

- primary purpose trading by charities is exempt from corporation or income tax (provided the profits are used for charitable purposes), but it is a business supply for the purposes of VAT and depending on the nature of the activity will be either exempt from VAT or taxable;

- some trading activities by charities, even if they are not primary purpose, are exempt from corporation and income tax, but subject to VAT;

- some trading activities by charities are exempt from VAT, but subject to corporation or income tax;

- even if an activity is exempt from corporation or income tax when carried out by a charity, it is nearly always subject to tax when carried out by a body which is not charitable;

- some activities are exempt from VAT when carried out by a charity, but subject to VAT when carried out by a non-charitable body;

- some activities which are zero rated for VAT when carried out by a charity are standard rated when done by a non-charitable body.

Generalisations such as 'we are a charity so we don't have to pay tax' or 'that activity is exempt from tax so it must be exempt from VAT as well' are *never* wise.

47.1.2
Restrictions on
trading

There are no statutory restrictions on charities or other voluntary organisations carrying out any kind of lawful trading. However:

- a voluntary organisation may only carry out activities within its constitutional objects and powers or allowed by law [see **4.7**];

- charitable status may be jeopardised if a charity undertakes too much trading which is not primary purpose trading [see **52.6**];

- even where the trading is carried out by a charity, the profits will be subject to tax unless the trading is explicitly exempt from corporation and income tax and the profits are used exclusively for charitable purposes [see **52.5**];

- a charity which pays tax on its income or profits cannot recover the tax from the Inland Revenue—but if a non-charity donates some or all of its profits to a charity under gift aid, the charity receives the tax that the non-charity would pay on those profits;

- if a charity trades in a way which means it has to pay tax, the trustees will generally be in breach of their duty to avoid loss of the charity's funds [see **47.2.3**].

To bypass the constitutional limitations on trading, avoid jeopardising charitable status, be able to recover tax and/or sometimes to take advantage of favourable VAT treatment, organisations often set up a separate **trading company** or **trading subsidiary** [see **47.2**].

47.1.2.1
Restrictions in governing documents

Governing documents of charities and some non-charities may say that the organisation cannot undertake 'any permanent trading activities' or 'any substantial permanent trading activities' [see **5.4.4**]. Permanent in this context means not only 'ongoing and long-term', but also regular or frequent. Even with such a restriction, a charity can:

- undertake permanent trading which is directly related to the charity's primary purpose or where the work is carried out primarily by the charity's beneficiaries [see **52.6.1** and **52.6.2**];

- undertake trading ancillary to its primary purpose [see **52.6.3** and **52.6.4**];

- organise fundraising events which fall within Inland Revenue extra-statutory concession C4 [see **52.7.1**];

- undertake fundraising or trading activities which are not within ESC C4, but fall within the exemption for small-scale trading [see **52.7.2**];

- provide services defined in its governing document to its members.

If the governing document says that a charity cannot undertake 'any permanent trading activities *in furtherance of its objects*' or something similar, this may mean that it cannot undertake even primary purpose trading. Advice should be sought from an experienced solicitor or the Charity Commission before entering into any regular or substantial trading arrangements, even for primary purpose trading.

47.2
TRADING COMPANIES

Voluntary organisations may set up **trading companies** (also called **trading subsidiaries**):

- to carry out activities outside their objects and powers;

- to keep the risk of liability separate from the main organisation;

- because particular VAT advantages can be gained;

- because they want to separate certain activities from the main work of the organisation; *and/or*

- where the organisation is charitable, to protect its charitable status and/or enable it to recover the tax paid on trading profits.

Complex issues are involved in deciding whether to set up a trading company and actually setting it up. These need proper professional advice, information which members of the governing body can understand, and adequate time for discussion and decision making. Many organisations, especially charities, set up trading companies when they do not need to and there is no advantage in doing so, while others do not set up trading companies when they must or when it would be advantageous to do so.

47.2.1
When a trading company is not necessary

There are many situations where it is not necessary for a voluntary organisation to set up a trading company, even if it is carrying out trading. However, the organisation may choose to set one up anyway in order to keep certain activities separate from the main organisation.

47.2.1.1
<u>Charities</u>

A trading company is not necessary if a charity is acting within its powers [see **47.1.2.1**] and receives its income only from:

- genuine donations, grants and sponsorship which do not give any benefit to the donor other than simple acknowledgement [see **52.3**];
- membership subscriptions entitling the member only to the right to attend general meetings, receive annual reports etc [see **52.3.5**];
- the sale of donated goods [see **52.3.2**].

Provided the charity has the necessary power to trade and all the trading income is used for the charity's charitable purposes, a trading company is also not necessary for:

- trading activities directly related to its primary objects (primary purpose trading), ancillary to primary purpose trading, or carried out mainly by the charity's beneficiaries [see **52.6.1-52.6.3**];
- small-scale commercial activities carried out as an integral part of primary purpose or ancillary trading [see **52.6.4**];
- membership subscriptions covering only activities within the charity's primary purpose and/or internal membership benefits such as an internal newsletter [see **52.3.5**];
- fundraising events covered by the Inland Revenue's extra-statutory concession C4 [see **52.7.1**];
- small-scale fundraising and trading activities where the profit does not exceed £5,000 [see **52.7.2**];
- small-scale fundraising and trading activities where the profit exceeds £5,000, but does not exceed the lesser of 25% of the charity's income or £50,000 [see **52.7.2**].
- lotteries and raffles [see **52.7.3**];
- rents [see **52.7.4**];
- dividends, bank interest or other investment income [see **52.7.6**];
- gains on the sale of assets [see **52.7.11**].

Even though the charity will not have to pay tax on any of these types of income, it may need to charge VAT on some of the activities.

Where the charity is making use of the exemptions for fundraising and trading activities and/or fundraising events it is still vital to check that it has power to carry out this type of trade [see **47.1.2.1**]. If there is any doubt, legal advice should be sought.

47.2.1.2
Non-charities

For non-charities, there are generally no particular tax advantages in setting up a trading company. Indeed, a non-charitable voluntary organisation may want to do the opposite: to set up a charity to undertake its properly charitable activities, so that the charity can take advantage of tax exemptions [see **9.7.2** for more about this].

The profit from the activities carried out by a non-charitable voluntary organisation or its trading company will be subject to tax unless:

- its income is in the form of donations, grants, sponsorship giving nothing other than simple acknowledgement to the sponsor, and/or membership subscriptions [see **52.3**];
- it is selling donated goods [see **52.3.2**];
- the profit arises from members in a membership organisation or club paying for goods or services in their capacity as members [see **52.8.1**]; *and/or*
- it is running a fundraising event which meets the criteria for Inland Revenue extra-statutory concession C4 [see **52.7.1**].

47.2.2
Warning bells

Even if a trading company is not required at a particular point in time, the situation needs to be regularly monitored. The YMCA restaurant case illustrates the risks. The restaurant, which was initially opened to provide meals to the hostel residents who were the charity's beneficiaries, needed further income. It opened its doors to the public and was soon much more profitable. But in becoming profitable it had moved from existing primarily to carry out the charity's purpose, to a mix of uses in which providing services to unconnected third parties predominated. The profits therefore became liable to tax, and the trading should have been carried out by a trading company.

Grove v Young Men's Christian Association [1903] 4 TC 613

Existing activities should be regularly reviewed to ensure they can still be carried out within the charity. For all new developments or projects, consideration should be given to whether it is a legal requirement to set up a trading company, or there is a practical advantage in doing so. Trading which starts out exempt from tax but becomes non-exempt may lead to the charity being assessed for up to six years' previous trading.

47.2.3
When a trading company is necessary

If the trading activity is outside the organisation's objects and powers as set out in the governing document, the organisation must set up a separate entity to carry out the activity. This is especially important for charities, whose trustees will be acting in breach of trust if they act outside the charity's objects and powers [see **13.3.2**].

For a charitable organisation, the ability to shelter trading income from tax by using a trading company is an overwhelming advantage. If taxable activities are carried out within the charity, it will have to pay tax which cannot be recovered. This would be a breach of the trustees' duty to act prudently, maximise the charity's income and not pay unnecessary tax, and they could be made personally liable to pay the tax or indemnify the charity for the tax it has paid. It is therefore advisable for a charity to set up a trading company when it is carrying out activities which are subject to tax.

47.2.4
When there is a choice

If an organisation has a choice about whether to set up a trading company, it will have to consider its current and future activities, and weigh up the advantages of having a separate body to carry out particular activities against the disadvantages and financial costs of operating two organisations.

47.3
SETTING UP A TRADING COMPANY

It is possible to buy an off-the-shelf company or get a new company registered within 24 hours [see **6.3.1**], but it makes more sense to give careful thought beforehand to the trading company and to set it up properly right from the beginning. For general issues around setting up a subsidiary, see **9.6** and **9.7**.

47.3.1
Business planning

No trading company should be set up until there has been a proper and prudent consideration of its chances of success and the risk of failure. This generally involves the preparation of a full business plan setting out the company's commercial objectives and its financial projections. It should be prepared with, or at least commented on by, people with appropriate knowledge and professional expertise.

The preparation and consideration of a business plan should not be a once-only exercise, but should be repeated on a regular basis. For the charity or other voluntary organisation which is the owner of the trading company, the business plan is a vital tool in ensuring that the company achieves the aims set for it. It is also part of the process by which the governing body of the parent organisation can demonstrate that it has acted in an appropriate and responsible way in deciding to set up and fund the company.

47.3.2
Legal structure

It is generally important for trading companies to have limited liability [see **2.1.1**], so they are most commonly set up as a company limited by shares, or less frequently as a company limited by guarantee or industrial or provident society. These structures are explained in **chapter 2**.

The parent organisation usually owns all the shares in a company limited by shares or IPS, or controls all the votes in a company limited by guarantee [see **47.5.1**]. Other models are where a charity does not control a trading company but receives its profits, or where the trading company is the parent, with a subsidiary charity whose trustees are all or mostly appointed by the company [see **9.7.2**].

47.3.2.1
Industrial and
provident society

An **industrial and provident society** [see **2.4**] must have at least three members (unlike a company, which needs only one) and is expensive to set up, so this structure is rarely chosen for trading companies.

47.3.2.2
Company limited by
guarantee

The structure of **company limited by guarantee** [see **2.3**] is occasionally chosen. The main advantage is that the structure can be more or less identical to the parent organisation, but with different objects and no restrictions on distributing surplus. The main disadvantage is that the trading company cannot raise money by issuing shares.

47.3.2.3
Company limited by
shares

By far the most common choice is a **company limited by shares** [see **2.3.6**]. A company can be formed with only one member so the parent organisation can be the sole member, holding one share.

The memorandum of association is likely to contain general trading objects allowing the company to carry on any trade or business, and a general power to do anything incidental or conducive to this. It may also include as an object the procurement of profits or gains for the purpose of paying them to the charity. The articles of association generally follow the format of Table A in the **Companies Act 1985** but should be adapted as appropriate, especially in relation to the board of directors.

47.3.2.4
Partnership or
sole trader

Very occasionally, short-term trading activity may be carried out by an individual operating as a **sole trader**, or by a two or more individuals or corporate bodies who are authorised to trade to make a profit for the organisation. They are in effect undertaking the trading as agents for the parent organisation [see **44.2.1**].

Whenever two or more individuals or corporate bodies enter into a joint business enterprise [see **9.5**], a **partnership** is created in law. Even if there is no formal agreement or document, a partnership is created and the partners are jointly and separately liable.

It is rarely advisable to trade through a partnership or sole trader, because of the lack of direct ownership by the parent organisation, potential tax complexities for the sole trader or partners, and the potential unlimited liability of the sole trader or partners.

47.3.3
Joint ventures

Some trading activities are joint ventures between groups of voluntary organisations, or between a voluntary organisation and a commercial business, statutory body or individual. This may be registered as a separate company or industrial and provident society. If it is not, it is legally a partnership [see above].

A joint venture requires a specially prepared memorandum and articles of association (or other governing document), usually supplemented by a **shareholders' agreement** or **joint venture agreement** [see **9.5.4**]. This agreement sets out in more detail the terms of the intended joint venture, how control is to be exercised, how decisions are to be taken and, very importantly, how financial risk is apportioned and how the parties can withdraw. The agreement should be drawn up by a solicitor.

47.3.4
Accounting

Most charities and companies must consolidate their accounts with those of their subsidiaries [see **50.2.7** and **50.3.2**]. It is essential to consult the parent organisation's accountants and solicitors before making any decisions about the preparation and presentation of the accounts of the parent organisation or trading company.

47.4 FUNDING THE TRADING COMPANY

The first really difficult decision is usually where the money will come from to finance the trading company. This is by no means straightforward, even if the parent organisation is wealthy.

47.4.1 Charitable status of parent body

The ability of the parent organisation to finance the trading company depends not only on how much money it has, but also on the powers given to it in its governing document and on legal limitations on the organisation's power to make loans and investments.

47.4.1.1 Non-charitable organisations

Non-charitable organisations can set up and fund a trading company provided they have power to do so under their governing document. If they do not have such power, the members may be able to approve the activity and expenditure anyway [see **4.7**], or they may be able to amend the governing document [see **5.5**].

If a members' club or association is considering financing the trading company from funds accumulated from members' subscriptions rather than from other income, it should take advice as to whether this threatens the tax-exempt status of the subscription income [see **52.3.5**].

47.4.1.2 Charities

Charitable trusts and associations may invest in a trading company, provided the investment meets the requirements of the **Trustee Act 2000** [see **54.1.2**] and provided their governing document does not give them narrower investment powers. The Charity Commission's view is that charities seeking to set up a trading company should normally obtain the funds from commercial sources rather than using the charity's funds, but this recommendation is not widely followed.

Report of the Charity Commissioners 1980, para.11

47.4.2 Loans from commercial sources

The small percentage of organisations funding trading companies from commercial sources reflects the high costs of such borrowing, and the considerable difficulty in obtaining it.

Another problem is that commercial lenders often require guarantees by the parent organisation. But if a guarantee is given by a parent charity for a loan to the trading company, funds given to the charity for its charitable purposes may be subject to tax and are potentially at risk, and the governing body which authorises such a guarantee is likely to be in breach of its duty to safeguard the charity's funds. Similar considerations apply to non-charitable organisations unless there is clear authority in the governing document for such a guarantee.

However, without such a guarantee it is likely to be very difficult, especially when the company is starting, to borrow significant sums from outside sources. Or the lender may require guarantees from individuals, which puts them at risk [see **55.5.3**].

47.4.3 Donations

Charity Commission guidance indicates that trustees (acting as individuals rather than as trustees) or other benefactors of a charity may wish to acquire the initial share capital of the trading company and then donate it to the charity. However, this is unlikely to raise the money needed to establish the trading company properly.

It may be possible to persuade outside bodies to make a grant or gift to the trading company to cover its start-up costs, but such funds are not readily come by.

47.4.4 Share capital

A common method of funding a trading company is by the parent organisation acquiring sufficient shares to provide the trading company with adequate capital, thus investing in the company in the same way as the parent organisation would in any other company. A number of difficult and somewhat contradictory issues arise when considering whether to use this **equity funding** approach.

47.4.4.1
Prudence and risk

A charity's trustees must consider whether they have the power to make such an investment [see **54.1**]. Even where they have the legal power to make such an investment, they must take proper advice and make a proper decision about whether it is prudent to invest in a potentially risky trading venture [see **54.3.1**].

If the trading company fails, shareholders are lowest in the list of priorities for payment. For this reason, the Charity Commission generally does not favour equity investment by a charity in a trading company, other than the minimal number of shares needed to form the company.

47.4.4.2
Tax exemption

Even if a charity has power to invest in a trading company, and even if such investment can be shown to be prudent and not to put the charity's funds at risk, a further difficulty arises from potential loss of tax exemption on funds used for the investment.

Only **qualifying investments** are eligible for tax relief [see **52.5.4**]. Investment in unquoted companies (those which are not listed on a recognised stock exchange) is not specifically authorised, although such investment may qualify under the **Income and Corporation Taxes Act 1988** schedule 20 para.9(1).

Income and Corporation Taxes Act 1988 ss.505, 506; sch.20

Trading companies set up by a charity are unlikely to be listed on a stock exchange, but it is generally possible to obtain informal advice from the Inland Revenue that they will allow tax exemption on income used for investment in a charity's trading company. Before doing this they must be satisfied that the investment is made for the benefit of the charity, and not merely for the avoidance of tax. There is no provision for the Inland Revenue to give formal approval for such investment.

Before giving even informal advice, the Inland Revenue will wish to see evidence of the arm's length nature of the transaction and the benefit expected to arise for the charity. This further emphasises the importance of appropriate business plans and professional advice prior to committing a charity's funds to a trading company.

47.4.5
Loans by a charity

The restrictions on equity investments by charities [see above] also apply to loans by charities: to qualify for tax exemption a loan must be **qualifying** [see **52.5.4**]. It is possible to obtain informal advice from the Revenue about whether exemption will be allowed.

Loans must be very carefully structured in order to meet Charity Commission requirements. In particular:

- the usual issues of prudence apply [see **54.1**];
- where possible the loan should be secured on assets owned by the trading company, or by a third party guarantee or other security;
- the loan should be on full commercial terms, at a rate of interest appropriate to the nature of the loan and the risks involved;
- it should be properly documented, with clear repayment provisions.

47.4.5.1
Loans v equity finance

As if the whole area of financing for trading companies is not complicated enough, it is made even more complex by a difference in view between the Inland Revenue and the Charity Commission. If a company is liquidated, lenders are slighter higher up the list of creditors than shareholders [see **21.9.3**]. So the Charity Commission generally prefers charities to lend to trading companies rather than invest in them. The Inland Revenue, viewing loans as an inappropriate source of long-term financing, is more likely to approve the equity investment route.

47.4.5.2
Tax on loan interest

Generally a company, when paying interest to anyone except a bank, must deduct tax at the basic rate from the payment and account to the Inland Revenue on **form CT61**. However, if more than half of a company's share capital is owned by a charitable company, the trading company may make an election to the Inland Revenue for interest payments to the charitable company to be made gross. This can be done only if both bodies are incorporated and constitute a group [see **9.6.1**] for company purposes.   *Income and Corporation Taxes Act 1988 s.247*

If the parent charity is an unincorporated association or trust, it must deduct tax which the charity can then reclaim.

To be eligible for tax exemption, loan interest must be paid to the parent charity annually [see **52.7.7**].

47.4.6
Retaining profit

The difficulties in obtaining start-up finance also apply to **working capital**. For charities' trading companies, maximum tax efficiency is achieved by donating 100% of profits to the parent charity under gift aid [see **47.7.3**]. But this may leave the trading company with inadequate working capital, and unable easily to obtain funds from other sources.

In many cases this problem is eased by the trading company paying over only part of its profits within its financial year, and retaining the remainder as temporary working capital. As new funds come in, the previous year's profits may be donated to the charity under gift aid at any time in the nine months after the end of the financial year.

If the trading company still would not have enough funds, options are:

- the charity may allow the company to retain some profits to cover operating costs and finance future growth, even though the company must then pay tax on the retained profits; *or*

- provided it has power to do so and the rules on loans are followed [see **47.4.5**], the charity may lend the company sufficient funds to cover operating costs.

47.5
MANAGING THE
TRADING COMPANY

What starts out as a clear relationship between the parent organisation and its trading company may become unclear and potentially fraught a few years down the line. Procedures should be put in place from the beginning to minimise the risk of this.

47.5.1
Ownership and
control

Typically the trading company is a company limited by shares, **wholly owned** by the parent. This means that all of its issued shares are held by the parent organisation if the parent is incorporated, or holding trustees or nominees [see **18.4.4**] appointed by the parent if it is unincorporated.

If shares in the subsidiary are held by nominees or holding trustees rather than by the parent organisation itself, a clear agreement must be drawn up to ensure the parent organisation retains control.

If the trading company is a company limited by guarantee rather than by shares, it is **wholly controlled** by the parent organisation if:

- the parent organisation or individuals appointed by it are the only members of the trading company; *or*

- the parent organisation has the right to appoint and remove all the members of the trading company's governing body.

Where the trading company is wholly owned or wholly controlled, the parent body legally has final control. If the parent does not approve of decisions made by its representatives on the trading company's governing body it can appoint new representatives, or can use company law procedures to remove them from office [see **11.5.6**].

It is unusual for a trading body set up by a voluntary organisation to be unincorporated and therefore to be a partnership or sole trader, although it can happen [see **47.3.2.4** and **47.3.3**]. Appropriate agreements should be drawn up to ensure that the parent body ultimately chooses and can remove the people who run the trading business, or to ensure appropriate control in a joint venture.

47.5.1.1
Who can be a director?

The parent organisation can appoint anyone, including members of its staff, as members of the governing body of its trading company. It should be clear what happens to the appointment of staff when they stop working for the parent, and procedures should be in place to ensure that the company always has the minimum number of directors required under its governing document. There is nothing to stop staff of the parent organisation from being paid an additional amount for their service as directors of the trading company.

The parent organisation can also appoint members of its own governing body as members of the trading company's governing body. If the parent organisation is a charity, its trustees can be paid for serving as directors of the trading company only if the charity's governing document or the Charity Commission permits this.

In general it is advisable to have some people on the governing body of the trading company who are not directly linked to the parent organisation, and *vice versa* [see below].

47.5.2
Maintaining the boundaries

Particularly where members of the governing body or staff of the parent organisation are also governing body members or staff of the trading company, dangerous confusions and conflicts of interest may arise. For example if a trading company is having financial difficulties, it may be in its best interests to get a loan from the parent—but is it in the parent's best interest to make the loan? The case of the Royal British Legion, where £900,000 of charitable funds were lost after being lent to a non-charitable subsidiary, illustrates the risks where these issues are not separately weighed up by the two bodies and where the over-riding obligation to safeguard charity funds may not be fully appreciated.

Charity Commissioners, Royal British
Legion Leasehold Housing Association: Final Report of Inquiry, May 1992;
Decisions of the Charity Commissioners vol.1, August 1993, pp.24-25

While these sorts of dilemmas can never be easily resolved, it can be easier if:

- the trading company has a proper business plan;
- the objectives and targets set in the business plan are closely monitored and regularly reviewed, and any problems are identified and dealt with before they become serious;
- there are appropriate job descriptions for governing body members and staff of the trading company;
- agendas, meetings, minutes, financial records, correspondence and decision making of the two bodies are kept completely separate;
- the governing body of the trading company includes some members, perhaps with business, financial or legal expertise, who are not on the parent organisation's governing body, or better still, have no direct association with the parent. This not only enhances recognition that the company is a legally separate organisation with potential conflicts of interest with the parent, but also brings in a wider range of commercial and other experience.

47.5.3
Staffing issues

If the parent's staff will or may be asked to work for the trading company, a suitable clause should be included in the contract of employment [see **24.1**]. If there is no such clause, they should be consulted and their consent obtained for any changes in their terms of employment. Varying employees' contracts without their consent could be a breach of contract [see **23.7.3**] or, if an employee resigns, could be treated as constructive dismissal giving rise to a claim for unfair dismissal [see **30.4.8**]. If employees do not agree to work for the trading company, the organisation should take legal advice before proceeding.

If a charity's staff work for the trading company, the charity will need to charge the company for their time and related costs [see **47.6.3**].

There may be pressure to pay higher salaries or provide other rewards to trading company staff, especially if they are recruited from the commercial sector. This may cause friction with the parent body.

It may be appropriate to include additional clauses in employment contracts for staff working with the trading company covering, for example, preservation of commercial secrets [see **38.1.5**], disclosure of personal interests [see **24.42**], or non-competition during the period of employment and possibly for a reasonable period thereafter [see **24.41**]. In some situations it may be advantageous for the parent and trading company to hire staff jointly [see **47.6.3.1**].

47.5.4 Working relationships

Legally and financially the parent body and trading company must be clearly separated, but it is important to maintain close working links and good communication. In particular the activities of the two organisations should not be incompatible, and the trading company should not do anything which undermines the parent's objects or good name.

47.5.5 Management charges

In addition to recovering the costs of providing premises, staff and other resources [see **47.6**], many parent organisations make a general charge to cover supervision and management of the trading company. Recovery of the actual costs (based on a proper estimate) is acceptable for tax purposes, but a management charge which includes any element of profit is likely to be taxable. Even if there is no profit element it could be subject to VAT [see **47.6.4**].

An inflated management charge is sometimes made as a way of transferring the profits of the trading company to the charity. This is not a tax-effective way to transfer profits and could jeopardise the parent charity's tax exemptions [see **47.7.2**].

47.5.6 Insurance

Because the trading company is legally a completely separate body, it is not covered by any of the parent organisation's insurances [see **chapter 20**] unless this has been specifically agreed with the insurers.

47.5.7 Fundraising arrangements

The rules for professional fundraisers and commercial participators [see **44.5**] do not apply to the relationship between charitable institutions and their wholly owned trading companies, or where such companies are jointly owned by two or more charitable institutions.

47.5.8 Separation of accounts and administration

Bank accounts and financial records must be kept completely separate. Any money received by the trading company for the parent organisation (for example, donations sent in with orders for mail order goods) should be paid over immediately.

All paperwork and records, especially minutes, contracts and other legal documentation, must make absolutely clear which organisation is involved with each transaction. At a practical level, many organisations find it useful to have distinctly different cheques and headed paper, and to use different coloured paper for agendas and minutes for each organisation.

It would be a serious breach of its responsibilities if a parent organisation's governing body allowed itself to become liable for the debts of its trading company by making a decision at the wrong meeting, using the wrong headed paper or creating confusion in any other way.

47.5.9 Insolvency of trading company

Part of the reason for carrying on trading through a trading company is to protect the parent organisation if the trading activities fail. This protection can be badly undermined if clear separation is not maintained between the activities of the parent and trading company.

The arrangements between the organisations should always reflect the possibility of the trading company's insolvency [see **chapter 21**], and make provision where possible to give the parent a preferred position This may be done by, for example, securing loans by debentures or mortgages [see **55.5**], or ensuring that assets revert to the parent if the trading company becomes insolvent.

Whatever the parent organisation's feelings about its moral obligations, it should meet the debts of an insolvent trading company only after receiving definitive legal advice that this is appropriate and lawful.

47.6 PAYMENT FOR SHARED RESOURCES

The parent organisation must take care—especially if it is charitable—not to allow its funds or resources to be used for activities of the trading company which are outside the objects or powers of the parent.

All transactions between the two bodies should be on an arm's length basis and should be clearly documented. Even though the trading company's profits will be donated to the parent, the parent must make full charges to the company and the company must pay for them. There may be VAT implications in making these charges [see **47.6.4**].

Apart from anything else, commercial good sense requires that costs are properly apportioned. Otherwise it may not become apparent that the trading company is showing a profit only because the parent organisation is providing free staff time, premises and running costs. Furthermore, if a trading company becomes insolvent, a parent company which has proper records of the amounts it is owed may be able to recover those debts in the same way as other creditors.

47.6.1 Intellectual property

The parent body should carefully control the trading company's use of its intellectual property rights such as its name, logo, copyright, trade marks, patents, website and databases. A formal agreement should:

- ensure fair payment for use of the intellectual property, because it is not a proper use of a charity's resources to provide them free or at less than proper value to a trading company;
- control the manner in which the intellectual property is used;
- ensure that the right reverts to the parent if the trading company becomes insolvent or is wound up for any reason;
- contain provisions for reviewing the agreement;
- contain provisions for terminating the agreement;
- avoid tax liability for the parent on fees received for use of the rights.

See **39.11** for more about intellectual property licensing, **52.7.9** for tax on intellectual property, and **53.5.3** for VAT on intellectual property.

47.6.2 Premises

Subject to any constraints in the organisation's lease or other title documentation, mortgage or insurance restrictions, planning permissions, or other restrictions on use of the premises, a trading company may share premises with its parent organisation. The parent should recover at least the full costs of those premises and in most cases a full market rent.

Rate relief may not be available for the portion of the building used for non-charitable purposes [see **59.2.4**], so this will have to be recovered through the rent or borne by the trading company. The arrangement between the parent and trading company may be a lease or licence [see **56.4** and **56.5**], with careful thought given to whether it is prudent to grant a secure lease [see **56.4.7**].

47.6.3 Staff, equipment and overheads

The parent should create a legally binding agreement by which it can **recharge** the trading company at appropriate intervals for the costs of staff time, shared equipment, use of facilities and other overheads.

While it may be tempting to charge a mark-up on these services and make some profit for the parent, a parent which is a charity needs to think very carefully before doing this. The provision of such services is unlikely to be part of its primary purpose, and as non-primary purpose trading any profit would be subject to tax [see **52.4**].

The supply of staff, photocopying etc is subject to VAT, even if the parent body charges for them at cost with no mark-up [see **53.5.3**].

47.6.3.1
Jointly hired staff

One way to avoid substantial recharges for staff time is for relevant staff to be hired by both the parent and trading company. This can be done by having a joint contract which states that both organisations are jointly the employer [see **22.4**]. Simply putting into a job description or terms and conditions of employment that the staff member is supposed to work for both organisations does not create a joint contract.

For staff who are properly jointly hired, the two organisations can have an agency agreement whereby one handles payment of salaries, deduction of PAYE etc and then recovers these costs (and no more) from the other organisation. Provided this is a genuine agency arrangement it is not treated as a supply of staff for VAT purposes, and VAT does not have to be charged on the payments.

Joint contracts can raise all sorts of other issues, for example around what happens if one of the employers becomes insolvent, or if one employer but not the other wants to discipline or dismiss the worker, or ensuring time paid for by a charity is not used for non-charitable work. To ensure these issues are fully considered, legal advice should be taken before drawing up a joint contract of employment.

47.6.3.2
Separate contracts

Another way to avoid large recharges is for staff to have separate contracts with each organisation, with each employer paying the staff for its agreed hours and operating its own PAYE. This can help to clarify the separate roles and accountability of an employee who is working for both the parent and trading company, and can also make it easier to have a staff member on two separate salary scales if this is appropriate.

47.6.4
VAT

A variety of complex issues arise around VAT and the relationship between the parent body and trading company. VAT is explained in **chapter 53**, but specialist advice will be necessary.

47.6.4.1
Avoiding VAT registration

Especially when a trading company is being charged for a portion of running costs and staff wages with linked national insurance and pension costs, the parent body can quickly reach the threshold where it has to register for VAT (in 2001, £54,000 in any 12-month period).

VAT registration may be advantageous, because it enables the organisation to recover some or all of the VAT it pays out [see **53.1.1**]. But for parent organisations which do not want to register, it may be possible to avoid registration by reducing the amount which is charged by the parent to the trading company, for example by:

- having the trading company make as many of its purchases as it can direct from an outside supplier rather than through the parent;

- having the trading company pay its share of bills, for example for photocopying or telephone, direct to the supplier; *and/or*

- the parent and trading company hiring staff jointly [see **47.6.3.1**] or on separate contracts [see **47.6.3.2**].

47.6.4.2
Putting costs through trading company

Rather than putting all costs through the parent organisation and charging the trading company, it may be tempting to do the reverse: to put everything through the trading company, and have the company charge the parent for its use. This can be done, but:

- if the parent is a charity, the trading company will have to donate its profits back to the parent by gift aid, to ensure no tax is paid unnecessarily on the sums paid by the charity to the company;

- if the parent is a charity, it will be necessary to ensure that all amounts paid to the trading company can be properly regarded as being for charitable purposes only;

- the trading company is likely to have to register for VAT and then charge VAT to the parent, which the parent will not be able to recover unless it is VAT-registered, and perhaps not even then [see **53.6.8**];
- even if the trading company provides goods, services or staff free to the parent, it may have to charge VAT on the supply.

47.6.4.3
VAT group

If both the parent and trading company are registered for VAT, no VAT has to be charged on invoices between members of the same VAT group [see **53.6.7**]. An unincorporated charity cannot create a VAT group.

47.7
PROFIT SHEDDING

Profit shedding refers to the transfer of profits to another body for the purpose of reducing or eliminating the tax due on the profits.

47.7.1
Non-charitable parent

If the parent is not a charity, there is generally no tax advantage in transferring a trading company's profits to the parent. The best that the company can do is deduct from its taxable profits certain small donations to a parent organisation established for educational, cultural, religious, recreational or benevolent purposes, but only if these donations can be shown to benefit the business [see **46.7.1**].

47.7.2
Management charges

An inflated or spurious management charge [see **47.5.5**] should not be used as a way of transferring the trading company's profits to the parent. The Inland Revenue might not allow such a payment as a deduction from profits, so the trading company would have to pay tax on all or some of the amount—and in any case the charity will be liable for tax on any profit element in the charge, because it is not a form of exempt income [see **52.4**].

47.7.3
Gift aid

Gift aid [see **46.2**] enables a charity to receive from a trading company a donation from the company's profits, plus the tax the company would have had to pay on those profits. The company donates the full amount to the charity, including tax, and claims tax relief when calculating its profits for corporation tax [see **52.2.2**]. (This is different from the procedure for gift aid donations from individuals, where the donation is made net of tax and the charity recovers the tax from the Inland Revenue.) There is no need for the company to fill in any form for the charity, or make any commitment in advance to a fixed sum or fixed percentage of profits over a defined period.

47.7.3.1
The procedure

A gift aid donation must actually be transferred from the company to the charity; it cannot simply be shown in both sets of books. Most of the payment should generally be made in the year in which the profit arises. If there is any untransferred profit, it can be transferred up to nine months after the end of the financial year.

There are no provisions for the company to estimate final profits, pay over that amount and then recover any overpayment. The company should therefore be careful not to donate more than its final profits, as this might be a distribution contravening company law [see **47.7.7.4**].

47.7.3.2
Gift aid and sale of donated goods

If a trading company sells donated goods, these sales are eligible for zero rate VAT, but only if the company donates 100% of its profits from the sale of the donated goods to a charity. Such sales may raise complex issues around who the goods were donated to and who is selling them [see **52.3.2**].

47.7.4
Deeds of covenant

Where a trading company entered into a **deed of covenant** [see **46.2.3**] before 1 April 2000, the deed remains binding but the donation is made under gift aid [see above] and should be made gross (including tax) rather than net of tax.

The Charity Commission's view is that the parent charity should not cancel such covenants, because the deed of covenant is a legally binding obligation which technically safeguards the charity's interest. Instead, the charity should accept a gift aid payment in lieu of the payment due under the deed.

47.7.5
Dividends

Payment by dividends does not allow recovery of tax, but may be used when for some reason payments were not made by gift aid during the accounting year or the following nine months. Charity trustees have an obligation to maximise their tax recovery [see **13.3.5**], and should use dividends only if there is a specific reason for doing so and only after taking appropriate advice.

Where the parent organisation is non-charitable, dividends are the normal route for transferring funds to it.

47.7.6
Capital gains

Unlike a charity, the trading company is fully liable for tax on **capital gains** arising from the sale or disposal of assets [see **52.2.4**]. This can be avoided by:

• transferring the gain to the charity as a gift aid donation; *and/or*
• having assets such as freehold property which may give rise to a capital gain owned by the charity, rather than the trading company.

47.7.7
Issues in
profit shedding

In making a transfer of profits to the charity, a range of potential problem areas must be considered. These can be complex, and specialist advice is likely to be necessary.

47.7.7.1
<u>Loan backs from charity</u>
<u>to company</u>

To achieve the maximum tax saving, the trading company needs to donate all of its taxable profits to the parent charity under gift aid. But doing this can leave the trading company without operating capital [see **47.4.6**]. Companies may find that after making the transfer, there needs to be a hasty **loan back** of much of the transferred sum. This must meet all the requirements for loans by a charity to its trading company [see **47.4.5**]. In particular, great care must be taken to ensure that the overall liability of the trading company to the parent does not gradually grow to a level which breaches the charity trustees' duty of prudence.

The Inland Revenue is likely to look closely at situations where profit shedding payments are followed by loan backs, particularly if the pattern is repeated over a number of years. They may argue that profit shedding has not actually taken place, and consequently all the potential tax savings will be put at risk.

47.7.7.2
Profit retention

To ensure that the trading company has the necessary capital to operate effectively without having to enter into such loan arrangements, it may wish to retain a proportion of its profits—even though this will mean that the charity will not be able to recover the tax paid on them. Financial advice should be sought before making any decision about retaining or not retaining profits.

47.7.7.3
Taxable profit v
accounting profit

Sometimes the trading company's taxable profit is different from the profit shown in its accounts. This happens because some expenses, such as entertaining and depreciation of assets, are included in the trading company's accounts but are not allowed for tax purposes [see **52.2.2**]. This could mean that the profit for taxable purposes is higher than the profit for accounting purposes, and donating all the taxable profits could create an accounting loss and a lack of operating capital. The most likely cause of this discrepancy is depreciation in relation to fixed assets held by the trading company, and one solution may be for such assets to be bought and held by the charity. At the time of writing (early 2001) the government had proposed changes which would alleviate this problem, by aligning profits for tax and accounting purposes.

Chapter 48
CONTRACTS AND SERVICE AGREEMENTS

48.1
CLARIFYING THE DIFFERENCE

Public sector bodies are increasingly **contracting out** services which they formerly provided. In a separate but related development, many public sector bodies which formerly provided grants for voluntary organisations are changing those grants to service agreements or contracts.

There is a great deal of confusion about the distinction between grants, service (or service level) agreements and contracts, and the terms are used in a wide variety of ways. But what something *is* depends on the nature of the transaction, not on what it is called. Regardless of what an arrangement is called, if it meets the legal criteria for being a contract it is a contract, and if it does not meet the criteria it is not a contract.

To exacerbate the confusion, an arrangement has to be considered not only in terms of contract law, but also in relation to VAT [see **53.3**] and whether it is a trading activity for the purposes of tax and charity law [see **52.4.1** and **47.1.1**]. For example a purchase/funding arrangement could be a contract under contract law but not be treated as a business supply for the purposes of VAT law—or it might not legally be a contract, but still be a business supply for VAT purposes.

48.1.1
Grants

The essence of a **grant** is that it is a donation or gift to support an organisation, service or activity, with the funder having no right to receive anything in return other than perhaps a simple acknowledgement [see

44.3]. This is different from a contract [see below], where the organisation is paid to provide something *in exchange for* the payment.

A grant is given **in trust** [see **44.2**], and if it is not used for the purposes for which it is given the funder can ask for the money (or other property) back, or can take legal action for breach of trust. Provided the grant has been properly used for the purposes for which it was given, the funder is unlikely to be able to require repayment or take legal action if the recipient does not comply with administrative requirements such as providing statistics.

A grant is by its nature discretionary, and may be changed or withdrawn at any time by the donor. (This does not apply to grants which a public body has a statutory obligation to provide, such as grants for higher education.) A donor may withdraw a grant, reduce it or pay it late, for any reason or none. The recipient organisation is unlikely to have any recourse in law, unless:

- the grant or donation has been made as a **deed** [see **18.3**], in which case it is enforceable by the recipient in the same way as a contract would be [see **18.12**]; *or*

- in certain limited circumstances, a decision of a public body might be open to **judicial review** [see **44.3.1** and **60.6.2**].

48.1.2
Contracts

A **contract** is a legally enforceable agreement between two or more parties [see **18.6-18.12** for more about contracts in general]. An agreement is generally a contract if:

- it involves **consideration**, with one party paying the other (or providing something else of value) in exchange for goods, services or something else of value;

- each party has accepted the other's offer; *and*

- the parties intend the agreement to be legally binding.

An arrangement where one party pays for something is virtually always treated by the courts as contractual unless the parties explicitly state that they do not intend it to be legally binding [see **18.6.1**].

48.1.2.1
Legal enforceability

A contract can be enforced through the courts by either party [see **18.12**]. If the purchaser does not pay on time or fulfil its other obligations, the organisation can take action to require payment and can seek compensation for losses suffered. If the organisation does not do what has been agreed, the purchaser can take action to require it to be done, terminate the contract and/or seek compensation for its losses.

Legal action is, of course, the final step. The vast majority of contractual disputes are resolved by negotiation between the parties [see **18.12.1**].

48.1.2.2
Tax and VAT

Grant income is not subject to tax [see **52.3.4**] and is outside the scope of VAT [see **53.3.1**]. But an arrangement which involves payment received as **consideration** is likely to be classed by the Inland Revenue as trading [see **52.4.1**] and therefore potentially liable to tax, and is likely to be classed by Customs and Excise as a business supply [see **53.3.3**] and therefore potentially subject to VAT.

Different criteria are used for tax law, VAT law and contract law. A particular arrangement could be subject to tax and VAT but not be contractually binding, or could be contractually binding but not subject to tax or VAT because of the exemptions available for charities and some other voluntary organisations. It is essential to take specialist advice on these matters.

48.1.3
Service agreements

Terms such as **service agreement** and **service level agreement** have no meaning in law, and are used in dozens of different ways by different purchasers or funders of voluntary sector services. It is important to clarify what each person who uses the term means by it.

More importantly, all parties involved in a service agreement or SLA must be aware that the legal nature of an arrangement is not changed simply because of what it is called. The fact that 'service agreement' may sound less intimidating than 'contract' does not change the reality of what the arrangement is.

Some of the ways the terms 'service agreement' or 'service level agreement' are used are described below.

48.1.3.1
'Grant'

A service agreement or SLA may simply be a grant, perhaps with more detailed conditions of grant aid or a more detailed description of the service. It would be a matter for the Inland Revenue, Customs and Excise or the courts to decide in any particular case whether they perceive the agreement as a grant or as a payment for a service.

48.1.3.2
Non-binding agreement

A service agreement or SLA may clearly be an agreement to purchase services from the organisation, but with an explicit statement that the agreement is not intended to be legally binding. One of the key elements in creating a contract is the parties' intention to create a legally binding agreement [see **18.6.1**], so if both parties have agreed that the arrangement will not be legally binding, it cannot generally be enforced in the courts. But in exceptional cases a court might agree to hear a case involving an agreement which the parties had agreed would not be binding, and could find that the agreement was in fact binding.

Even if the arrangement is not legally binding, it is treated as trading for tax purposes and a business activity for VAT [see **48.1.2.2**].

48.1.3.3
Dependent on process

Some purchasers say that they award a contract after a formal process of competitive tendering [see **48.5**], and enter into a service agreement if there is no formal competitive process. But for legal, tax and VAT purposes, the process by which an agreement is reached is irrelevant.

48.1.3.4
Internal agreement

An agreement between departments or units *within* an organisation cannot be a contract, because there is only one party (the main organisation). Where organisations are structured so one budget-holding department or unit 'purchases' services from another, the agreements between departments are often called service agreements or SLAs.

48.1.4
Human rights
implications

In relation to the **Human Rights Act 1998** [see **60.3**], charities and other voluntary organisations are generally private organisations carrying out private functions, even when they are providing services to the public. As such they do not come directly within the scope of the Human Rights Act. But when a government agency, local authority or other public sector body contracts with a voluntary organisation to carry out a **public function** [see **60.3.2**]—or possibly even if the voluntary body receives a grant to carry out a public function—the organisation may come within the scope of the HRA in relation to that function.

In many cases the voluntary organisation will not be carrying out the public function, merely assisting the public body to carry out the function, so the HRA may not directly apply. However:

- the public body must ensure it operates within the framework of the HRA, so it is likely to require any organisation providing services on its behalf or with its funding to do so as well; *and*

- the courts must interpret all law, even relating to private bodies and private functions, in accordance with rights guaranteed under the HRA, so funders/purchasers are likely to require organisations to operate within the HRA framework even if it does not directly apply.

48.2
AGREEING THE
CONTRACT

Before the organisation enters into a contract or service agreement, the governing body must understand the terms and conditions, as well as the implications of it being (or not being) legally enforceable. The agreement should be approved by the governing body or by a sub-committee, officer or staff member explicitly authorised to do so by the governing body. Only an authorised person should sign a contract, and should indicate that they are signing on behalf of the organisation.

Legal advice will generally be necessary before entering into a service agreement or contract, at least until the organisation is accustomed to the process. Even where a contract or service agreement emanates from a previous grant funder with whom there is a relationship of trust, this should not lead to any less careful attention to detail. A checklist of key clauses and concerns can be very useful in reviewing contracts.

The Charity Commission's CC37 *Charities and Contracts* raises a range of issues for charities to consider before entering into a contract with a public body, including:

- ensuring all services provided under a contract (or any other funding arrangement) are within the charity's objects and powers;
- not using the charity's own resources to provide a service that a public body is legally required to provide at the public expense;
- the need to cost the service properly and set an appropriate price;
- appropriate ways to deal with potential conflicts of interest where a charity trustee has a connection with the purchasing body;
- issues when two or more charities jointly enter into a contract.

The guidance is suitable for non-charities as well as charities.

48.2.1
Power to contract

A contract may set out the powers under which the purchaser is acting, especially if it is a public sector body. If this is not included, the organisation should ensure the contract is within the purchaser's legal powers. Similarly the contact may set out the voluntary organisation's relevant constitutional objects and powers. Even if these are not specified, the organisation should enter only into agreements which are within its objects and powers [see **5.4.3**].

To make clear that the organisation is acting as an independent service provider, the contract might include a clause stating that neither the organisation nor its employees are an agent or partner of the purchaser. This ensures that the organisation will not be treated in law as an agent for the purchaser [see **18.5**] or be held to have entered into a partnership arrangement [see **9.5**].

48.2.2
Using model contracts

Model contracts for specific types of service are available from many umbrella or support organisations. It is always worth contacting a relevant organisation before entering into discussions about a contract or service agreement. Guidance, including model contract conditions, may also be available from the Improvement and Development Agency for Local Government [see end of chapter]. As with all model contracts, care should be taken to ensure they are appropriate to each situation.

48.2.3
Drafts

Most contracts go through several drafts before they are finally signed. It can be helpful to ensure that each draft is dated and marked 'Draft' or 'Subject to contract', so it is easy to see which is the most recent version but it cannot be taken as the final version. The most recent version should always be carefully scrutinised. Even an apparently minor change in wording or a typing mistake may have significant implications.

48.2.4
Annexes

Any document referred to in the contract and incorporated as part of it should generally be attached to the contract as an **appendix** or **annex**. Lists—for example of equipment, staff or clients—are usually referred to as **schedules** and should also be attached. A contract should not be agreed if the parties have not seen all the relevant annexes or other documents incorporated as part of the contract.

48.3
TERMS AND
CONDITIONS

There is no standard format for a contract, but set out below are some of the terms and conditions commonly included in contracts and service agreements between public sector bodies and voluntary organisations. For more about contract terms in general, see **18.7**.

48.3.1
Duration

The starting date and duration of the contract should be specified. The duration might be a specified period or ending date, or 'until terminated by either side in accordance with the terms of this agreement'.

A contract for a specified period which contains provision to be extended (rolled over) at agreed intervals is called a **rolling contract**. A three year contract, for example, might be rolled over for a further year after each satisfactory annual review. 'Rolling contract' also refers to a contract which continues (rolls on) until one party terminates it.

Public sector bodies are not allowed to enter into contracts which 'fetter their discretion' (prevent them making free choices). They must retain the right to find other providers, so they must not commit themselves contractually for a longer period than is reasonable.

48.3.2
Service specification

The service specification defines the service(s) to be provided and the required quantity and quality. It covers the nature of the service, who it is for, and quantity and quality criteria. The level of detail will depend on the nature of the service.

48.3.2.1
Service description

The service description should include:

- the aims of the purchaser and the providing organisation;
- the name or description of the scheme, project or activity purchased under the agreement, and its general nature;
- what the service is expected to achieve (service objectives);
- a description of the service.

The organisation should commit itself only to what it knows it can deliver—not what it aspires to. The service description should be detailed enough to make clear what is expected, but should generally avoid an over-rigid specification which does not allow for flexibility.

48.3.2.2
Users/clients

It may be appropriate to define the people for whom the service is intended. This may include, for example, eligibility criteria, referral and acceptance procedures, whether the organisation can refuse to accept potential clients referred by the purchaser, how users will be involved in decisions about services, how progress will be assessed, and procedures for discharge or onward referral to other services.

48.3.2.3
Quantity

Purchasers are increasingly unwilling to pay for a service without an indication of the quantity to be provided. These are sometimes called **output indicators**, and may be defined in terms of number of people, number of sessions or visits, opening hours or hours of availability. The providing organisation must be absolutely certain that it will be able to meet these obligations throughout the full period of the contract.

Where the quantity is given as a minimum, the contract should make clear what happens if more or less than the minimum is provided, and what happens if this is for reasons outside the provider's control.

Any contract requiring an open-ended service ('all clients referred by the purchaser' or 'all enquirers') needs careful scrutiny.

Particular attention should be given to terms such as 'every day' (does this mean 365/366 days a year, or only weekdays, or only weekdays which are not public holidays?) and 'during normal working hours' (whose normal working hours—the provider's or the purchaser's?).

If a new service is being started, adequate time and funding should be allowed for the start-up period.

**48.3.2.4
Quality**

Most contracts include **performance indicators** to assess the quality of service. While the organisation should aim for the highest standards, it should commit itself within the contract only to what it knows it can provide. Where quality or outcomes (results) are to be monitored, the organisation should ensure it knows how this will be done and that the monitoring processes are appropriate and transparent.

**48.3.2.5
Equality of opportunity**

The service specification may specify that the organisation must comply with equal opportunities legislation (which it has to do anyway) and/or with specific policies required by the purchaser. Care should be taken before committing the organisation to complying with the purchaser's (or anyone else's) equal opportunities policy, or any other policy which could be changed in future without the organisation's agreement.

**48.3.2.6
Management
responsibilities**

Depending on the nature of the service, it may be appropriate to specify:

- which decisions, if any, require consultation with the purchaser, and the procedures for such consultation and for resolving disputes;

- arrangements, if any, for a liaison group or other body to oversee or advise on services;

- whether the purchaser requires representation on the organisation's governing body or a committee overseeing the service, and a statement that such representative(s) shall not have voting rights, or shall not have voting rights on any matter relating to the contract;

- confidentiality of information and compliance with data protection rules, including provision for destruction or return of personal data at the end of the contract period [see **37.1** and **37.2**];

- the organisation's right to make all decisions, other than those covered in the agreement, about eligibility for services, method of provision and management of the service.

**48.3.2.7
Monitoring and
evaluation**

The contract should make clear whether the purchaser will monitor only the services provided under the contract or service agreement, or all the organisation's services. The contract might specify:

- how services will be assessed, how frequently and by whom;

- content and frequency of monitoring reports by the organisation;

- provision for inspections, surveys of users, meetings with users, and independent (external) assessment;

- the purchaser's right of access, if any, to the organisation's premises, services or information;

- procedures for negotiating changes in services due to changing needs or demand.

The purchaser has a right to require proof that services are being provided as required under the contract. Unless legislation or the contract specifies otherwise, it has no right to other information apart from charity and company annual reports [see **50.2.14** and **50.3.5**].

The organisation should consider whether monitoring imposes unnecessary costs, is unnecessarily intrusive, or requires disclosures which are not allowed under the Data Protection Act [see **38.3**]. Disclosure issues may be particularly relevant where the purchaser is a potential competitor to provide the service.

**48.3.3
Sub-contracting**

The contract may indicate whether the organisation is allowed to sub-contract some or all of the work. In some circumstances this might be a requirement, for example where a lead organisation is taking on a contract where some work will be undertaken by other organisations.

Where work is sub-contracted, the lead organisation remains responsible for the full contract, even for sub-contracted work, unless liability for sub-contracted work is explicitly excluded.

**48.3.4
Enforcement by
third parties**

A contract which provides a benefit to a third party—for example a contract between a voluntary organisation and a local authority under which the organisation provides services to a client—can be enforced by that third party [see **18.6.5**]. The contract should make clear whether it is intended for third parties to have this right, or whether—as will be generally be the case—the right is to be specifically excluded.

**48.3.5
Payment**

The section on financial conditions may include some or all of the following points.

**48.3.5.1
Price**

The stated price should specify the fee basis. This may be, for example:

- **fixed fee**: an agreed sum;
- **actual cost** basis: often with a fixed maximum sum, and perhaps with any unspent funds clawed back [see below];
- **block** or **volume** fee: an agreed sum for a minimum and/or maximum number of units (clients, hours, sessions etc);
- **unit** basis: an agreed sum for each unit (client, hour, session etc), often called **spot** basis when the unit is a person;
- **cost plus** or **block plus** basis: a fixed sum, plus an extra fee for each unit or for each unit above the agreed minimum or maximum.

Particular care should be taken with actual cost pricing, to ensure agreement about what is included in the cost. With a contract, the organisation is being paid to provide a service and so long as it is provided, it is no concern of the purchaser how much (or how little) it actually costs to provide it. **Clawback** should have no place in contract funding.

The contract should be clear about the period covered by the agreed fee, any provision for increases, and who meets extra costs arising because of legislative or regulatory change. The contract might specify whether a charge is to be made to users, and how the amount will be determined.

Where the purchaser is not paying the full costs of a service, the organisation should be certain it can cover the additional costs. The contract should indicate what happens if the organisation does not have adequate funds to provide the full service as required under the contract.

**48.3.5.2
VAT**

A quoted price is generally assumed to include any VAT which is payable, unless it explicitly says that VAT is not included [see **53.3.2** and **53.5.3** for VAT on services]. It is therefore essential to include a statement in all contracts and service agreements saying **all payments to be made under the agreement are exclusive of VAT**.

If the organisation is registered for VAT and has to charge VAT on the service, this enables it to charge VAT at whatever the current rate is, whereas if a VAT-inclusive fee is specified and the VAT rate then goes up, the organisation cannot increase the amount for VAT.

If the organisation is not yet registered for VAT but will or may have to register in future and charge VAT on the service, this statement enables it to charge VAT at the current rate when it registers.

Even if the service is exempt from VAT [see **53.4**], this clause allows the organisation to charge VAT if the service becomes subject to VAT.

Especially when changing from grant funding to service agreements or contracts, it is very important to obtain specialist advice about the potential VAT implications.

**48.3.5.3
Payment terms**

A contract should specify:

- the frequency of payment (monthly, quarterly etc), and whether it will be made in advance, midway through the period or in arrears;
- when payment is due (for example 15 days before the start of the quarter, 28 days after date of invoice);

- whether interest will be charged on late payments and if so whether this is on contractual terms or in accordance with the **Late Payment of Commercial Debts (Interest) Act 1998** [see **18.7.3**] (this Act entitles many organisations to charge interest even if this is not specified in the contract);

- whether payment is made automatically or only on submission of the provider's invoice;

- whether payment is contingent on the purchaser receiving monitoring or financial reports or other information from the organisation;

- what happens if the organisation has been underpaid or overpaid.

Particular attention should be given to cashflow, especially where payment is spread evenly across a period but the organisation will have substantial outlay at the start of the period or other peak times.

48.3.5.4
Financial monitoring
and review

Provision for financial monitoring may be included as part of a contract. The organisation may be required to provide financial reports or accounts to the purchaser, and procedures may be included for reviewing and varying unforeseen financial costs.

48.3.6
Staffing

The contract may specify matters such as staff numbers and/or ratios, qualifications, procedures for criminal record checks, and provision for staff training and development. It may have provisions relating to use of agency and temporary staff, use of volunteers within the contract, and/or cover during holiday, sickness, maternity and parental leave.

48.3.6.1
Transfer of
undertaking

An organisation taking over a service previously provided by a public sector body, another voluntary organisation or anyone else is likely to be affected by the **transfer of undertakings** regulations [see **26.4**]. This is a complex area and it is very important for the organisation to take independent advice (*not* from the local authority or other body from whom it is taking over the service) at a very early stage.

48.3.7
Premises, equipment
and other support

The contract should specify any support to be provided by the purchaser: training, use of vehicles or equipment, vehicle maintenance, premises etc. If the purchaser is providing accommodation, the contract might include provisions about this, but it is nearly always better to have premises matters in a separate lease or licence [see **58.2**].

If the contract provides for the purchaser to give premises, equipment or vehicles to the organisation or if the sum to be paid includes capital expenditure, the contract should clarify ownership of the items and any restrictions on their sale or disposal [see also **57.12**].

48.3.8
Indemnity and
insurance

The purchaser may require the organisation to indemnify it for any claims against it arising from the services provided by the organisation. The organisation must look carefully at the extent of the indemnity and whether it is possible to insure it, and must allow for the cost of such insurance.

A contract may specify that the organisation has to take out public liability insurance and other insurances, including insurance to indemnify the purchaser. It is not uncommon for a purchaser to require proof that the insurances are in place.

48.3.9
Information

The contract should contain a warranty that the purchaser has provided all the information it holds relevant to the delivery of the service, and will provide any further information as it becomes aware of it. This is especially important where the organisation is taking over a service previously provided by the purchaser.

48.3.10
Variation

Any contract may be varied (changed) if the parties agree, although in some situations further consideration (payment) may be necessary in order for the variation to be valid [see **18.10.2**]. The contract might include provision for regular reviews at which the need for variation is discussed, or may include the procedure for agreeing changes. There is no obligation on either party to agree changes proposed in future, and lack of agreement will generally leave the old terms in place.

48.3.11
Breach of contract

If either side does not fulfil its contractual obligations, this is a **breach of contract** [see **19.4**]. Ultimately the injured party can take the other to court [see **18.12**], but long before this happens the parties generally try to negotiate a settlement. The contract might include the procedure for such negotiation, and might also include provision for mediation or arbitration [see **61.2**].

Where the organisation is unincorporated and the members of the governing body are therefore potentially personally liable for the organisation's financial obligations, it is important to try to include a clause limiting liability to the extent of the organisation's assets or to the extent of the organisation's insurance [see **19.6.5**]. Legal advice should be sought about the wording of such a clause.

48.3.12
Termination

The contract is likely to include provision for either party to terminate the contract if the other is in serious breach, or a more general **break clause** allowing either party to terminate at any time or at specified times (for example after six months).

A break clause is often presented as advantageous to small organisations, on the basis that it allows them to withdraw from the contract if they are unable to provide the service as required. But it also allows the purchaser to withdraw. Serious consideration should be given to the implications of including any such clause, especially if the purchaser is not contractually required to give a specified period of notice.

Some local authorities seek to include a clause allowing them to terminate for any breach of contract, rather than only a serious breach. Such a clause may not be enforceable where the contract is long-running, the organisation has made a substantial investment or taken on substantial obligations (such as a lease), and the breach was neither a serious breach nor an accumulation of less serious breaches that taken together constituted a very serious breach.

Rice T/A Garden Guardian v Great Yarmouth Borough Council
[2000] TLR 26/7/2000

48.3.13
Renewal and
non-renewal

Unless the contract is for a time-limited service, it may include procedures and the timetable for negotiating an extension or renewal. It is important to ensure that if the contract is not to be renewed, the organisation has adequate notice of this and adequate funds to cover winddown or handover costs.

48.4
CONTRACTS WITH
INDIVIDUALS

As well as its contracts with public sector bodies and other purchasers, a voluntary organisation may have agreements with individual clients, users or residents. If the individual is paying for the service, a contract exists and the same issues should be considered as with any other contract [see above and **18.6-18.12**]. An individual who is not directly paying (or providing other consideration) for the service does not have a contract with the organisation. But if the organisation has a contract with a local authority or someone else to provide services to the individual, the individual will be able to enforce this contract unless the right to do so is explicitly excluded [see **18.6.5**].

Legally binding contracts of this sort are different from arrangements colloquially called contracts and made with clients, school pupils or other service users as a way to demonstrate commitment to a particular relationship or process. Although such arrangements may be called contracts, but are generally not legally binding.

48.5
ROUTES TO A CONTRACT

Competitive tendering takes place when a purchaser invites bids from a number of potential providers of goods or a service. Competitive tendering may be:

- compulsory, where legislation requires a public sector body to invite competitive bids [see **48.5.1**];

- required under a public sector body's standing orders [see **48.5.2**] or other rules; *or*

- voluntary, if the body is not required to invite competitive bids but decides to do so anyway.

For the tendering process, see **48.6**.

Contracts may also be issued non-competitively [see **48.5.2.2**], if the purchasing body's procedures allow this.

48.5.1
Public services contracts

Contracting authorities must invite competitive bids from across the EU for contracts for goods, services and works of more than a specified value. Social welfare and similar services are not covered by the rules.

Public Services Contracts Regulations 1993 [SI 1993/3228]; Public Contracts (Works, Services and Supply) (Amendment) Regulations 2000 [SI 2000/2009]

A contracting authority is:

- a government department, local authority, or other part of central or local government; *or*

- any organisation set up 'to meet needs in the general interest, not having an industrial or commercial nature', if the organisation is financed wholly or mainly by a contracting authority or if more than 50% of its governing body is appointed by a contracting authority.

This means that local authorities, health authorities, government agencies, learning and skills councils, NHS trusts and similar bodies must have competitive procedures, either open or select list [see **48.5.2.1**], for many large contracts. The same procedures could apply to voluntary organisations which fall into the definition of purchasing authority and enter into relevant contracts to purchase goods, services or works [see **18.8.3**].

Information about contracting authorities and public contracts is available from the Office of Government Commerce [see end of chapter].

48.5.2
Standing orders and other rules

Where the public contract rules do not apply, public sector bodies may be subject to other statutory rules, for example governing lettings or disposal of property. There may also be binding guidance, for example on the way funding issues are dealt with.

Even where there are no external rules, public sector bodies are likely to have to comply with their own standing orders. These are intended to ensure that contracts are awarded in a way which conforms to financial propriety and is in accordance with policy, and typically require competitive tendering for contracts of more than a specified value.

Many bodies put work out to tender even if they are not required to do so. In this situation the purchaser may have to comply with standing order procedures, or may be free to conduct the tender as it chooses.

48.5.2.1
Select list tendering

Where public contract regulations or standing orders do not require contracts to be advertised openly, the purchaser may invite bids from potential contractors on a **select list** or **approved list**. This allows for competition, without the cost of open advertising.

48.5.2.2
Contracts issued without competition

In some situations, local authorities and other public bodies can issue contracts without putting the work out to tender. This may give the provider considerable scope for negotiating the terms of the contract. Contracts issued non-competitively may become less common as local authorities and other purchasers operate increasingly within a best value framework [see below] which has competition as a basic principle.

48.5.3
The best value
framework

Best value, which replaced **compulsory competitive tendering**, requires local authorities and some other bodies to 'secure continuous improvement in the way in which its functions are exercised, having regard to a combination of economy, efficiency and effectiveness'.

Local Government Act 1999 pt.I

Best value authorities must draw up annual performance plans setting out services to be provided, current standards for those services, and projected improvements. All services and activities must be reviewed against these projections, on a five-yearly basis. Best value reviews are based on four principles:

* to challenge whether the service should be provided, and if so whether it is being provided in the most effective way;
* to consult the local community;
* to compare performance with the performance of other providers; *and*
* to compete, through market testing, tendering and other means, to determine who can best provide the desired quality and quantity of service.

Central government and the Audit Commission have wide powers to intervene, in order to monitor and if necessary take steps to ensure best value is achieved. Tendering is one of several ways by which authorities seek to achieve best value. Organisations involved in contracts, service agreements or grant funding from best value authorities must ensure they understand what the authority expects from them in terms of its annual plan, performance targets and reviews, and should consider how the need for competition may affect them in future.

48.6
THE TENDERING
PROCESS

Tendering processes vary greatly in formality and flexibility, depending on the size and nature of the contract and the applicable regulations. Successful tendering depends on a very clear understanding of the particular tender requirements and the competition.

In most tenders, the tender bid constitutes a legally binding offer which can be accepted or refused within a time limit. This one-sidedly exposes the bidding organisation to a potential obligation, while leaving the purchaser free to accept or refuse. This situation is exacerbated by the fact that the tender offer is generally on detailed contractual terms which are set by the purchaser and are heavily biased in its favour.

In some situations the service specification and/or contract terms may be open to negotiation before, and sometimes after, acceptance of a bid. A bidding organisation should do all it can to modify terms in its favour at an early stage, or if that is not possible, seek to agree that further negotiations can take place after the contract is awarded.

Some aspects of the tender process are explained here.

48.6.1
Specification

A tender specification describes the services, activities or goods which the purchaser wants to purchase. It is generally in two parts. The **service specification** sets out what is to be done or provided and similar matters relating directly to the service [see **48.3.2**]. The **terms and conditions** set out the terms under which the service or goods are to be provided.

Usually the purchaser draws up the tender specification, sometimes after consultation with potential providers or service users. But sometimes the purchaser might place the onus on the tendering bodies to specify the service and their terms. In this case the potential provider has to 'second-guess' what the purchaser wants and what other bidders will offer. It is important to obtain the maximum possible information from the potential purchaser and other sources before proceeding.

The preparation of a service specification generally requires considerable time and research. To avoid it being misused by potential competitors, distribution should be limited. It is also not unknown for purchasers to ask potential providers to draw up specifications, then not to offer the contract to any of them but to readvertise it using one of the provider's specifications as the purchasing body's own specification. Making clear that the specification is the copyright work of the bidding organisation [see **39.2.4**] may reduce the risk of this happening.

48.6.2
Costing and pricing

From the service and contract specifications, the service can be **costed**. Once the cost is known, a decision can be made about **pricing**—what to charge for the service.

If the purchaser has issued a detailed specification, the task is to find the most economical way of delivering the service, including the achievement of the quality criteria. The price should not be cut even if the costs turn out to be high, unless the organisation is certain it has adequate reserves or income to subsidise the service, and is certain that such subsidy is proper and appropriate. Tendering at a price below real costs without being able to 'top up' means that the service will not be able to be delivered (and the organisation will therefore be in breach of contract) or the organisation runs the risk of becoming insolvent.

There is more flexibility at the costing/pricing stage if the organisation has itself prepared the service specification and can adapt it to fit a particular pricing structure.

When setting a price for work, a reasonable figure should be included for contingencies. The need to build up reserves to develop the organisation and to meet costs at the end of the contract should also be considered.

48.6.3
Submitting the tender bid

Submitting the bid generally irrevocably commits the bidder, so it should be submitted only if all the implications have been fully considered and submission has been properly authorised. The tender specification may indicate the form in which the bid is to be submitted. If so, all instructions must be carefully followed. Deadlines are important and for competitive tendering cannot be stretched. Photocopies should be kept of everything.

If accepted a bid is usually taken as final but it may, if this is clearly agreed, be subject to further negotiation, especially if considerable time has elapsed since the bid was prepared or if circumstances have changed in some way. Changes should be agreed only after carefully reconsidering the implications for service delivery and cost.

FOR FURTHER INFORMATION

Guidance for charities. Charity Commission: 0870-333 0123; www.charity-commission.gov.uk

Model contracts. Improvement and Development Agency for Local Government: 020-7296 6600; www.idea.gov.uk

Public contracts. Office of Government Commerce: 020-7211 1300; www.ogc.gov.uk

Tax & VAT. See end of chapters 52 and 53

PART VII
FINANCE

Part VII provides an introduction to accounting, tax, VAT and other financial matters.

Chapter 49
FINANCIAL PROCEDURES AND RECORDS

49.1
RISK ASSESSMENT AND MANAGEMENT

In the same way that the organisation carries out ongoing health and safety risk assessments [see **36.3**], it should also undertake regular financial and security risk assessments. These look systematically at financial and related systems and procedures, identify key risks, assess adequacy of controls and gaps in the systems, and recommend changes to help reduce the risk of financial mismanagement or fraud.

The starting point should be 'What could go wrong if we had incompetent or dishonest staff, volunteers, fundraisers, finance director, chief executive, treasurer, board members, investment advisors? What procedures can we put in place now, to ensure we have proper safeguards when and if we do have someone incompetent or dishonest in post?'

Financial risk assessment is often carried out as part of the internal audit process [see **49.2.8**], but it should be undertaken even if the organisation does not have internal audit procedures in place.

Similar risk assessments should also look at:

- risks linked to information held by the organisation, including information about clients, donors and staff [see **chapter 38**];

- risks arising from use of computers and electronic communication;

- risks related to unpredictable income, such as appeals or events;

- risks to the organisation's reputation;

- any other risks faced by the organisation.

In charities, these risk assessments are necessary to comply with the trustees' duty to consider major risks to the charity and establish systems to mitigate them. Trustees of many charities must include in their annual report a statement of compliance with this duty [see **50.2.13**].

49.1.1
Carrying out a risk assessment

As with a health and safety risk assessment, a financial or other risk assessment looks at causes of risk, what can go wrong, how likely it is to happen, how serious it would be if it did happen, what is already

680

being done to reduce the likelihood of it happening or to minimise the negative impact if it does happen, what else could or should be done, and an action plan.

Any risk assessment, especially when undertaken for the first time, is likely to identify many areas of concern. Some can be dealt with immediately with little outlay of time or money. Others are more complex, and governing body members or managers may feel overwhelmed by all that needs doing. A simple technique for prioritising is to rate probability and impact for each area of risk, along the following lines:

- **Probability**: 1=very unlikely, 2=unlikely, 3=possible, 4=likely, 5=highly likely
- **Impact**: 1=insignificant, 2=fairly serious, 3=serious, 4=very serious, 5=major disaster

The ratings for probability and impact can be multiplied to give an indication of what should be prioritised.

49.1.2
Action plans

The risk assessments should lead to action programmes which include:

- deadlines and named responsibility for implementing changes;
- regular reports by senior management to the governing body on the action programme and new areas of risk;
- regular reports on internal controls, especially in relation to finance, and their adequacy.

Risk assessments should be repeated whenever there is a change in activities, services, premises or equipment, or at least annually.

49.2
FINANCIAL
PROCEDURES

When things go wrong—money goes missing, unauthorised expenditure is incurred, or the organisation finds itself unexpectedly in debt—it is too late to put proper financial procedures in place. The governing body and staff should have ensured this was done long before.

This is not only good practice; it is a legal obligation arising from the duty of charity trustees to protect their charity's assets [see **13.3.5**], the general duty of care of all governing body members [see **13.2.3** and **13.4**], and statutory requirements under the Charities, Companies, and Industrial and Provident Societies Acts.

All organisations need proper procedures to ensure:

- authority to authorise expenditure and payments is clearly delegated;
- all decisions about expenditure are made by people authorised to do so, and if appropriate are minuted or recorded in other ways;
- budgets and cashflows are prepared and monitored, and appropriate action is authorised and taken to increase income and/or reduce expenditure;
- the organisation receives money due to it, claims all tax and rate reliefs to which it is entitled, and recovers tax where it is able to;
- the organisation pays its bills on time;
- salaries are properly calculated and PAYE is properly operated;
- if required, the organisation registers for VAT and operates VAT;
- if tax is due, the organisation meets its tax liabilities;
- cash, cheques, stock, equipment and valuables are safeguarded;
- petty cash and bank accounts are operated properly;
- the organisation has policies on investments and reserves, complies with the policies, and reviews them regularly;
- all financial transactions are properly recorded, and the records are kept securely and safely;
- financial records are checked by at least one person who has not been involved in making the payment or writing up the records;

- the governing body, senior staff and others with responsibility for financial control receive regular financial reports;
- the financial records are checked or audited regularly—at least annually—by an appropriately qualified independent third party.

The Charity Commission's free CC8 *Internal Financial Controls for Charities* includes a basic checklist, and the *Charity Finance Internal Audit Checklist* (details 020-7819 1200) is more detailed.

49.2.1
Guarding against theft and fraud

A governing body which does not take proper precautions against loss, theft and fraud could be held to be negligent if money or assets go missing. The Auditing Practices Board has defined fraud as including:

- falsification or alteration of accounting records or other documents;
- suppression or omission of the effects of transactions from records or documents;
- recording of transactions without substance;
- intentional misapplication of accounting policies;
- wilful misrepresentation of transactions or of the organisation's state of affairs; *and/or*
- misappropriation of assets, or theft.

Fidelity insurance [see **20.6.3**] can protect the organisation against theft or fraud by staff, governing body members and others within the organisation. The insurer will require evidence that anti-theft and anti-fraud procedures are in place.

49.2.2
Segregation of duties

To minimise the risk of error or fraud, different stages of the financial process should be carried out by different people. Financial record keeping should be monitored and spot-checked by a line manager or the treasurer. If the treasurer is the only person handling money, keeping records and preparing financial reports, another member of the governing body should look through the records on a regular basis.

49.2.3
Authorisation of expenditure

Budgets should be approved by the governing body or an authorised sub-committee. It should be clear who can authorise expenditure within the budget; who (if anyone) can authorise expenditure outside budget; who monitors income and expenditure against the budget, to whom they have to report and how often; and who must take action if income is lower or expenditure higher than budgeted.

49.2.3.1
Expenses

Procedures for reimbursing mileage and other expenses to employees and volunteers [see **27.4.3** and **35.2.1**] should be clear. There are likely to be several procedural stages:

- authorising the expenditure at policy level, for example an agreement to reimburse volunteers for travel costs by public transport, or for car use/taxi if this is authorised by the volunteer's manager;
- authorisation of the expenditure itself, for example a supervisor authorising a journey for a specific purpose, or authorising a taxi;
- procedures to receive and check receipts or other documentation;
- authorising the reimbursement, for example the supervisor signing an expenses claim form or payment authorisation, confirming that the volunteer incurred the expenditure and can be reimbursed for it;
- making the reimbursement;
- if the reimbursement is made by cash, having the petty cash voucher signed by the person who made the payment and the person who received it.

It is sensible to devise an expenses claim form, and to require receipts, mileage records or other documentation. Reimbursements should always be authorised in writing by someone other than the person who is receiving the money.

49.2.4
Bank accounts

Decisions to open, change or close bank or building society accounts should be made by the governing body, in the form required by the bank or building society **mandate**.

British Bankers Association guidelines require banks and building societies to check with the Charity Commission and, if appropriate, the charity concerned before opening an account in a charity's name. For all organisations, even if not charities, banks and building societies will verify the identity of at least two signatories.

The organisation's money should not be kept in anyone else's account. If it has to be kept there temporarily—perhaps because it has been collected as cash at an event—careful records should be kept and it should be paid over to the organisation as quickly as possible.

Proper procedures should be in place to keep records of telephone and electronic transactions. Bank statements should be regularly reconciled with the cash books, chequebook counterfoils, paying-in slips and direct debit and standing order records, and any discrepancies should be sorted out. If money is transferred between accounts or between linked organisations, the transfers should be monitored and reconciled.

49.2.4.1
Signatories

Account signatories should be people currently involved in the organisation, so they are aware of authorisation procedures and the implications of the cheques or other documents they might sign.

As soon as a signatory leaves—or before if appropriate—the signatories should be changed. Banks often require the outgoing signatory to confirm the change, to stop people from falsely telling the bank that they are new signatories. If it is not possible or appropriate for the outgoing signatory to do this, the reason should be explained to the bank.

Cheques do not have to be signed by two people unless the governing document or internal procedures require it. But a governing body which allows cheques to be signed by only one person could be held to be negligent if that person misuses the cheques.

The governing document may specify the signatories [see **5.4.19**]. The Charity Commission's model governing documents state that signatories must be trustees, but this does not have to be included. Many organisations allow employees to sign cheques, but require cheques above a certain amount to be signed by at least one governing body member.

Procedures should be in place to ensure that non-cheque transactions, such as electronic or telephone instructions, standing orders and direct debits, are properly authorised by the required number of signatories. Particular care must be taken in relation to passwords for telephone or internet banking, and PIN numbers for bank card transactions.

If cheque signatories are not available to sign cheques, the cheque should be made out and sent to them for signature. It has been found to be negligent for a company director—and, by implication, anyone else—to sign a blank cheque. This means that if the cheque is misused, the signatory could be personally liable to make good the loss to the organisation. The same holds for partially completed cheques.

Dorchester Finance v Stebbings [1989] BCLC 498

49.2.5
Cash

The organisation should keep the minimum possible cash on the premises, ensure that it is covered under the organisation's contents insurance [see **20.6.2**], and consider fidelity insurance [see **20.6.3**].

If possible all counting of cash should be witnessed and both people should sign a document verifying the amount. Incoming cash should be paid into the bank as quickly as possible.

Especially in charity shops and other situations where a large amount of cash changes hands, precautions should be taken against theft and counterfeit notes. The police crime prevention unit can advise. Under health and safety law, appropriate precautions must be taken to protect staff who handle cash in situations where they could be at risk of attack or who must carry cash in public [see **36.4.4**].

49.2.6
Equipment and stock

An up-to-date inventory (**register of assets**) should be kept of all equipment and other assets. For companies and charities, this is a legal requirement. *Companies Act 1985 s.221; Charities Act 1993 s.41*

If the organisation sells goods, it should do a comprehensive stock check at least at the end of the financial year, and should keep other stock records or make other stock checks as appropriate. For companies this is a legal requirement. *Companies Act 1985 s.221(3)*

49.2.7
Ex gratia payments

An *ex gratia* payment is one which the organisation feels morally obliged to make, even though it has no power or contractual obligation to do so and the payment cannot be justified as being in the interest of the organisation. An *ex gratia* payment might be made, for example, when an organisation receives, through an oversight or technicality, a legacy intended for another beneficiary.

49.2.7.1
Charitable organisations

A charitable organisation may make an *ex gratia* payment only with an order [see **3.5.4**] from the Charity Commission, court or attorney general. The rules are explained in Charity Commission booklet CC7 *Ex Gratia Payments by Charities.*

A payment which there is no legal obligation or power to make but is considered by the trustees to be in the interests of the charity is not technically an *ex gratia* payment, but may be made only with a Charity Commission order. This could include, for example, a payment to show appreciation to a volunteer or employee for long service or for a particularly significant piece of work.

A payment made as a settlement to prevent a potential employment tribunal claim [see **33.2.2**] is not an *ex gratia* payment. Provided such a payment is within the charity's powers, Charity Commission consent is not required.

If trustees are not clear whether they have power to make a payment, they should consult a solicitor or the Commission.

49.2.7.2
Non-charitable companies and IPSs

An *ex gratia* payment may be made by a non-charitable company or industrial and provident society only if it is genuine, reasonably incidental to carrying out the organisation's business, and made for the benefit and prosperity of the organisation. Although donations to charities might not fall strictly within these criteria, company and IPS donations to charities are regarded as permissible on the basis that they preserve goodwill. *Parke v Daily News [1962] Ch 927*

In addition a non-charitable company (but not an IPS) may make an *ex gratia* payment to current or past employees, if the company is ceasing operation or being transferred to another company. The memorandum or articles of association may specify procedures for authorising this, or it must be approved by an ordinary resolution [see **17.4.7**].
Companies Act 1985 s.719

49.2.7.3
Non-charitable associations

There are no external restrictions on the right of a non-charitable association to make an *ex gratia* payment. A decision to make such a payment should be properly made by the members of the association.

49.2.7.4
Tax on ex gratia payments

Ex gratia payments to individuals, including a cash payment on retirement, are taxed as individual income. A non-cash gift with a value of up to £30,000 to a retiring employee is free of tax.

49.2.8
Internal audit

Internal audit is a process by which an authorised person or internal **audit committee** monitors, assesses and reports to the governing body on the effectiveness of the organisation's financial systems and controls.

The purpose is to look in detail at all procedures and ensure they are adequate to provide full and accurate financial information, keep money and other assets secure, and minimise the risk of fraud. The financial risk assessment identifies what can go wrong and what needs to happen to reduce the risk [see **49.1**], and the internal audit confirms that those safeguards are in place and are working, and makes further suggestions.

The internal auditor or **audit committee** should not be directly involved in the organisation's financial processes. It should not be the same individual or department which carries out the annual audit.

49.2.9
External audit

The purpose of an external (usually annual) audit is to inspect and verify the accounts [see **50.2.12** and **50.3.4**]. External audits are a vital part of good financial procedure and are advisable even where they are not a statutory or constitutional requirement. However, an external audit reports only on the past. It does not predict cashflow problems (for which proper budgets and cashflow analyses are needed), nor will it prevent fraud (for which proper internal procedures are needed).

49.3
FINANCIAL
RECORDS

All organisations must keep the financial records required by law, their governing document and funders. These records must:

- be clear and comprehensive enough to explain the organisation's financial transactions;
- provide adequate information for financial planning and control;
- give an accurate picture of the organisation's financial position at any given time; *and*
- enable the members of the governing body to ensure the organisation's annual accounts comply with all relevant legislation, the governing document and funders' requirements.

For companies and charities these are legal requirements. For industrial and provident societies the legislation is worded differently but the intention is similar.   *Companies Act 1985 s.221; Charities Act 1993 s.41;*
Friendly and Industrial and Provident Societies Act 1968 ss.1-2

49.3.1
What to keep

Financial records include:

- the **books of account**, also called **cash books**, which might be computerised or on paper;
- minutes and other authorisation of expenditure;
- documentation (letters, duplicate receipt books etc) to verify income;
- documentation (invoices, chequebooks etc) to verify expenditure;
- bank statements;
- records of the organisation's assets and liabilities;
- stock control records;
- investment records;
- records for specific purposes, such as PAYE, gift aid, VAT (if the organisation is registered for VAT), membership subscriptions.

Cross-referencing systems should enable easy correlation between the cash books, cheque counterfoils or petty cash vouchers, the relevant invoices or receipts and bank statements, and between bank statements and the organisation's authorisations for telephone and electronic transactions and for incoming and outgoing direct debits and standing orders. The intention should always be to maintain an **audit trail** enabling each item of income or expenditure to be traced. An expenditure item, for example, should be traceable from the budget to the authorisation, the order, the invoice, the cheque, the management accounts and eventually the annual accounts. The cash book entry for a gift aid donation must have a clear trail to the donor's gift aid declaration [see **46.2**] and the tax recovery claim.

The purchase of equipment, and in some cases stock, should be logged in the relevant inventory with a cross reference to the purchase authorisation and payment.

Where grants or donations are received for a specific purpose, the financial records must indicate this clearly and must make it possible to show that the money has been spent for this purpose [see **44.2**].

Books of account, whether on paper or computerised, should never have data erased or removed. If a correction is needed it should be added as a separate entry. If an entry is crossed through or altered in paper accounts, it must be initialled by the person making the amendment. Computerised information should not be able to be altered or erased.

The records should be guarded against loss. An up-to-date backup of computerised information should always be kept, away from the premises. The accounting books should be kept separate from the supporting documentation, so that if the books are stolen or destroyed they can be reconstructed from the documentation.

49.3.2
How long to
keep them

The minimum statutory periods for which financial records need to be kept after the end of the financial year to which they apply are:

- three years for PAYE records;
- three years for financial records and annual accounts of private limited companies (which voluntary sector companies are), or 20 years if the company was wound up by being struck off the register [see **21.4**];
- six years for financial records and annual accounts of registered charities (except charitable companies) and exempt and excepted charities [see **7.1.2** and **7.1.3** for definitions];
- six years for VAT records.

Despite these minimum periods, it is sensible to keep:

- at least one set of annual accounts forever;
- PAYE records for at least seven years, because the Inland Revenue can make adjustments going back six years;
- cash books and expenditure documentation for at least 13 years;
- documentation relating to the purchase or sale of major goods for at least 10 years, because claims under the **Consumer Protection Act 1987** can be made during that period.

If records are stored off the premises it is important to keep a record of where they are.

If a charity ceases to exist the final trustees must keep the records for the six-year period unless the Charity Commission agrees in writing that they can be disposed of. *Charities Act 1993 s.46*

FOR FURTHER INFORMATION

The organisation's auditor

Community accountancy projects

Charity Commission: 0870-333 0123; www.charity-commission.gov.uk

Chapter 50
ANNUAL ACCOUNTS, REPORTS AND RETURNS

For sources of further information see end of chapter.
Double-underlined section headings indicate additions or significant changes since the first edition.

50.1 REPORTING REQUIREMENTS

For companies, industrial and provident societies and/or charities, strict rules apply to annual accounts, the annual reports which explain and elaborate on the accounts, and annual returns. Additional requirements may be imposed by the organisation's governing document or funders.

Non-charitable unincorporated associations and non-charitable trusts do not generally have to comply with statutory requirements in the production of annual accounts and reports, but do have to comply with their governing document and the requirements of funders.

Specific requirements apply to registered social landlords and credit unions. These are not covered in this book.

50.2 CHARITIES

The rules on charity accounts are in the **Charities Act 1993** ss.41-49 and regulations made under the Act, and the Statement of Recommended Practice for Charities (**Charities SORP**). Free publications on all aspects of the charity accounting requirements are available from the Charity Commission, and books at various levels are available from publishers specialising in the voluntary sector and/or finance. For information and advice specific to their situation, charities should consult their accountant or auditor or the Charity Commission.

50.2.1
Financial year

In unincorporated charities (associations and trusts), the trustees set an **accounting reference date** (ARD). The first ARD must be between six and 18 months after the date of the charity's establishment, and the charity's **financial year** (FY) must then end within seven days before or after the ARD.

Charities (Accounts and Reports) Regulations 1995 [SI 1995/2724], reg.5(2)

Subsequent ARDs are then usually 12 months after the end of the previous FY, but if there is a good reason it may be any date six to 18 months after the end of the previous FY. The reason for choosing a date other than 12 months after the end of the previous FY must be disclosed in the accounts. A date other than 12 months after may not be chosen for two consecutive years.

Charitable companies and industrial and provident societies have other rules for determining their financial year [see **50.3.1** and **50.4**].

50.2.2
<u>Charities SORP</u>

Accounting and Reporting by Charities: The Statement of Recommended Practice for Charities (Charities SORP), published in 2000, applies to financial years starting on or after 1 January 2001. Its detailed recommendations for preparing annual accounts and reports apply to virtually all charitable organisations in England and Wales (even if not registered with the Charity Commission), Scotland and Northern Ireland. The only exceptions are charities such as registered social landlords which have their own SORP.

The full SORP applies only if gross income is over £100,000. Charities under this threshold which prepare accounts on a receipts and payments basis [see **50.2.9**] only have to comply with SORP paras.344-358.

Although the SORP is only recommended practice:

- some provisions are included in the Charities Act or in regulations produced under the Charities Act, and are therefore obligatory;

- even where a provision is not required, charities to which it applies are expected to comply with it unless doing so would present a distorted view of the charity's financial position. If SORP is not followed, this must be explained in the notes to the accounts.

50.2.3
Accounting
thresholds

Unlike SORP, most Charities Act rules on charity annual accounts, reports and audit apply only to unincorporated charities (trusts and associations) which are registered with the Charity Commission, and depend on the charity's **gross income** [see below] and **total expenditure** [see **50.2.3.3**]. Different rules apply to excepted charities which are not registered with the Commission [see **50.2.6.1**], exempt charities [see **50.2.6.3**], and charitable companies [see **50.3.2.1**].

50.2.3.1
Gross income

Gross income for the purpose of determining accounting thresholds is not the same as any traditional idea of 'income', nor is it the same as the **incoming resources** which must be included in accrual accounts [see **50.2.10.3**]. Gross income:

- includes income from all sources, whether received for specific or general purposes;

- includes the value of **non-cash** resources, such as land or equipment, and **intangible** resources such as free rent or photocopying;

- does not include the value of volunteers' time;

- does not include money or property received as **capital funds**, but this refers only to income received as permanent endowment or expendable endowment [see **50.2.3.2** for definitions];

- includes income received for what are colloquially called **capital** purposes, such as for the purchase of equipment, vehicles or buildings (unless income received for buildings is received in a form which makes it a capital fund as defined for Charities Act purposes);

- does not include proceeds or gains from the disposal of investments and assets;
- includes transfers from capital to income, and income from investments including property;
- does not include repayments for loans, or income received as a loan.

Charity Accounts and Reports: Core guide (Home Office), para.2.3.1

50.2.3.2
Capital funds

A **capital fund** may be:

- **permanent endowment**, where the terms of a money gift are that it cannot be spent, or the terms of a gift of assets are that they cannot be sold or disposed of, or if they are sold or disposed of the proceeds must be retained by the charity and not spent; *or*
- **expendable endowment**, under which the trustees cannot initially spend the money or dispose of the assets, but have discretion at some time in the future to spend the money, or to sell the assets and spend the proceeds.

Even if a capital fund is not given for a specific purpose, it is a **restricted fund** [see **50.2.8**] because it is not available to be spent.

Care must be taken not to confuse this meaning of 'capital' with the more common usage where **revenue funds** refers to income received for operating costs, and **capital funds** refers to income received for buildings, vehicles, computers or other major equipment.

50.2.3.3
Total expenditure

Total expenditure for the purposes of deciding the accounting thresholds is not the same as **resources expended** or **resources used** [see **50.2.10.3**]. Total expenditure includes revenue expenditure, as well as expenditure on fixed assets and investments, depreciation and provision for the downward revaluation of fixed assets and investments. It does not include losses on the disposal of fixed assets or investments.

50.2.4
Unincorporated charities

For unincorporated charities, different thresholds apply for the various requirements. Charities must monitor gross income and total expenditure carefully and ensure they follow the relevant rules.

50.2.4.1
Very small charities: income under £1,000

A **very small charity** has annual gross income under £1,000 and no permanent endowment [see **50.2.3.2**]. For a very small charity which is not registered with the Charity Commission, the rules are:

- **annual accounts**: receipts and payments account and statement of assets and liabilities [see **50.2.9**];   *Charities Act 1993 ss.41-42*
- **trustees' report**: not required;   *s.46(3)*
- **examination/audit**: only if required by governing document or funders;   *s.46(3)*
- **provide accounts to Charity Commission**: not required;   *s.46(3)*
- **to public**: within two months to anyone who requests it in writing. A reasonable fee may be charged.   *s.47(2)*

A very small charity which is voluntarily registered with the Commission must follow the requirements for a light touch charity [see below].

50.2.4.2
Light touch charities: income and expenditure up to £10,000

Light touch provisions apply to charitable unincorporated associations and trusts whose annual gross income *and* total expenditure are each £10,000 or less. The rules are:

- **annual accounts**: receipts and payments account and statement of assets and liabilities [see **50.2.9**], or accrual account and balance sheet [see **50.2.10**];   *s.42(1)-(3)*
- **trustees' report**: simplified form or full form [see **50.2.13**];   *s.45(1)*
- **examination/audit**: only if required by governing document, funders or the Charity Commission;   *s.43(3)*

- **to Charity Commission**: only if specifically requested;

  Charities Act 1993 s.45(3A)

- **to public**: within two months to anyone who requests it in writing. A reasonable fee may be charged. *s.47(2)*

50.2.4.3
Income or expenditure from £10,000 to £100,000

For charitable unincorporated associations or trusts with gross income *or* total expenditure over £10,000, and gross income not more than £100,000, the rules are:

- **annual accounts**: receipts and payments account and statement of assets and liabilities [see **50.2.9**], or accrual account and balance sheet [see **50.2.10**]; *s.42(1)-(3)*

- **trustees' report**: simplified format with receipts and payments account, or full format with accrual account [see **50.2.13**]; *s.45(1)*

- **examination/audit**: independent examination or full audit [see **50.2.12**]; *s.43(3)*

- **provide accounts to Charity Commission**: within 10 months from the end of the charity's financial year; *s.45(3),(4)*

- **to public**: within two months to anyone who requests it in writing. A reasonable fee may be charged. *s.47(2)*

50.2.4.4
Income and/or expenditure from £100,000 to £250,000

For charitable unincorporated associations or trusts whose gross income is more than £100,000, and whose gross income *and* total expenditure are each not more than £250,000 and have not been for the previous two years, the rules are:

- **annual accounts**: accrual account and balance sheet [see **50.2.10**]; *s.42(1),(2)*

- **trustees' report**: full format [see **50.2.13**]; *s.45(1)*

- **examination/audit**: independent examination or full audit [see **50.2.12**]; *s.43(3)*

- **provide accounts to Charity Commission**: within 10 months from the end of the charity's financial year; *s.45(3),(4)*

- **to public**: within two months to anyone who requests it in writing. A reasonable fee may be charged. *s.47(2)*

50.2.4.5
Income or expenditure over £250,000

For charitable unincorporated associations or trusts with income *or* expenditure over £250,000 in this financial year or either of the two previous years, the rules are:

- **annual accounts**: accrual account and balance sheet [see **50.2.10**]; *s.42(1),(2)*

- **trustees' report**: full format [see **50.2.13**]; *s.45(1)*

- **examination/audit**: full audit [see **50.2.12**]; *s.43(1),(2)*

- **provide accounts to Charity Commission**: within 10 months from the end of the charity's financial year; *s.45(3),(4)*

- **to public**: within two months to anyone who requests it in writing. A reasonable fee may be charged. *s.47(2)*

50.2.5
Charitable companies

For charities registered as companies, the rules are:

- **annual accounts**: in accordance with company law [see **50.3.2.1**] and with the Charities SORP [see **50.2.10**];

- **reports**: directors' annual report [see **50.3.3**] and full trustees' report [see **50.2.13**], which can be combined in one report provided it contains all necessary information; *s.45(1)*

- **compilation report/audit**: compilation report or full audit if required under company law [see **50.3.4**];

- **to Registrar of Companies and Charity Commission**: within 10 months from the end of the company's financial year; *s.45(3),(5)*

- **to public**: as required under company law [see **50.3.5.5**]; and within two months to anyone who asks for it in writing. A reasonable fee can be charged. *Charities Act 1993 s.47(2)*

50.2.6
Excepted and exempt charities

Charities excepted and exempt from registering with the Charity Commission [see **7.1.2** and **7.1.3**] are covered by some, but not all, of the accounting and reporting regulations.

50.2.6.1
Excepted charities not voluntarily registered with the Commission

For charities which are excepted for any reason other than being 'very small', and are not voluntarily registered with the Commission, the rules are:

- **annual accounts**: depending on its income and expenditure, as specified above; *s.42(1)-(3)*
- **trustees' report**: only if required by the Charity Commission; *s.46(4),(5)*
- **examination/audit**: depending on its income and expenditure, as specified above; *s.43(1)-(3)*
- **to Charity Commission**: only if specifically requested; *s.46(4),(5)*
- **to public**: within two months to anyone who requests it in writing. A reasonable fee may be charged. *s.47(2)*

For 'very small' charities, see **50.2.4.1**.

50.2.6.2
Voluntarily registered

Excepted charities voluntarily registered with the Charity Commission must comply with the rules for their level of income and expenditure.

50.2.6.3
Exempt charities

Charitable industrial and provident societies or other exempt charities must comply with the SORP provisions appropriate to their level of income. Further rules are:

- **annual accounts**: as required by any legislation which governs it; or, if there is no legislation, an income and expenditure account and balance sheet at least every 15 months; *Charities Act 1993 s.46(1)*
- **trustees' report**: not required under charity law, but a report is likely to be required under other legislation and/or SORP; *s.46(1)*
- **audit**: as required under the relevant legislation;
- **to Charity Commission**: no requirements; *s.46(1),(5)*
- **to public**: within two months to anyone who requests it in writing. A reasonable fee may be charged. *s.47(2)*

50.2.7
Branches, special trusts and subsidiaries

An unincorporated charity must include within its main accounts all the income and expenditure of branches, projects or groups which are not separately registered as charities [see **9.2.3**], and **special trusts** for which it holds funds. The main accounts should also include supporters' groups, fundraising groups etc which raise funds only for that charity [see **9.2.4**].

Income and expenditure of branches, supporters' groups etc must be included in the main accounts gross, rather than net with the expenditure deducted from the income. The groups' assets and liabilities must also be included.

Trading companies which the charity controls [see **9.6.2**] should be consolidated with the main accounts.

Charity branches which are separately registered with the Charity Commission and have their own charity numbers should not be included unless the Commission has defined them as **subsidiary charities**.

50.2.8
Unrestricted, restricted, designated and capital funds

In drawing up a charity's annual accounts, there must be separate columns or pages for:

- **unrestricted** or **general funds**, which the trustees have discretion to decide how to use;

691

- **restricted funds**, which have been given to or raised by the charity for a specific purpose and may be used only for that purpose [see **44.2** for more about funds raised for specific purposes];
- **capital** (or **endowed**) **funds** [see **50.2.3.2**], if applicable.

Restricted funds and capital funds are also called **special trusts**.

Designated funds are not the same as restricted funds. Designated funds are money or property received by the charity for general purposes, but which the trustees have decided will be used for a specific purpose. The decision to use them for that purpose is purely an internal matter rather than an agreement between the charity and donor(s), and the trustees can change their decision. With restricted funds, the trustees cannot decide to use them for another purpose. Designated funds should be set out in a note to the accounts.

50.2.8.1
Grants, donations and gifts

Grants, donations and gifts—whether money, assets or in kind—are unrestricted if they are generally for the charity's primary purposes. If they are for a specific purpose, client group or geographic area, they are restricted income.

50.2.8.2
Fees, sales, contracts and service agreements

Income from fees or other charges made for goods, services or facilities, including income from service agreements or contracts to provide services, should be treated as unrestricted income. However some agreements called contracts or service agreements may in fact be grants [see **48.1**] and may therefore be restricted income. If there is any doubt about the status of such arrangements, advice should be taken from the charity's accountant or auditor about how to show it in the accounts.

50.2.8.3
Interest and dividends

Interest earned on bank accounts and from investments is general income if it is earned on general funds, and forms part of the relevant restricted fund if it is earned on restricted funds.

50.2.8.4
Expenditure

Expenditure out of income received for a restricted or capital purpose must be shown in those columns, and expenditure from general funds must be shown in the 'general' column. Transfers between the columns must be shown.

50.2.9
Receipts and payments accounts

Charitable associations and trusts with income and expenditure of £100,000 or less may prepare accrual accounts [see below] or, if they wish, simplified annual accounts consisting of a **receipts and payments account** and a **statement of assets and liabilities**. The Charity Commission provides a form which may be used for these accounts. *Charities SORP 2000 paras.350-356*

Expenditure in a receipts and payments account can be shown either in natural or functional categories [see **50.2.10.6**].

50.2.9.1
Changing to accrual accounts

Where the charity changes from receipts and payments to accrual accounting or vice versa, the previous year's accounts must be restated in the new format. Charities likely to reach the £100,000 threshold at which accrual accounts become necessary may find it advantageous to prepare them in that format even though it is not yet required.

50.2.10
Accrual accounts and balance sheet

It is beyond the scope of this book to consider the detail of full accrual accounts, but this summary should help organisations know what information is likely to be required by the person who prepares the annual accounts, and should help trustees understand the accounts. Accrual accounts are sometimes called **income and expenditure accounts**.

50.2.10.1
Accrual basis

Instead of including all the income and expenditure actually received and spent in the period, an **accrual account** is adjusted to show only the income and expenditure which actually relates to the period. So if, for example, £50,000 is received as a grant but £8,000 is a late payment for the previous year and £12,000 is an advance payment for the next year, the accounts for the year in which the cash is actually received would be adjusted to show only £30,000 as grant income.

Accrual accounts must always be accompanied by a **balance sheet** [see **50.2.10.8**] which shows the organisation's assets and liabilities at the end of the financial period covered by the accounts. In the example above £8,000 would have been shown as an asset (money owing to the organisation) in the previous year's balance sheet, and £12,000 would be shown as a liability in this year's balance sheet (because the organisation could have to return it if it does not 'deliver' the £12,000 worth of services for which it has received advance payment).

50.2.10.2
Material items

The SORP refers throughout to **material** items. Information is material if its inclusion or exclusion would be likely to influence a reader in relation to the accounts and report as a whole, or in relation to that particular item. The trustees decide whether an item is material. If in doubt, it should be included. *Charities SORP 2000 app.1 para.21*

50.2.10.3
Statement of financial activities

Charities must prepare a **statement of financial activities** (SoFA) rather than using the usual format for accrual accounts. The SoFA is intended to make it easier for people to understand how a charity is using its money. The requirements are explained in the SORP.
paras.56-156

Instead of being divided into the usual headings of 'income' and 'expenditure', the SoFA's headings are **incoming resources** and **resources used**. Each has separate columns for unrestricted and restricted funds, capital funds if relevant, and designated funds if the trustees wish [see **50.2.8**].

The main distinctions between a SoFA and a conventional income and expenditure account are:

- a SoFA includes all **incoming resources** (money and the value of donated goods, services or facilities), whereas an income and expenditure account shows only money income;

- a SoFA includes all **resources expended**, including the value of donated goods sold or given away or services and facilities used, whereas an income and expenditure account shows only money expended;

- for larger charities, outgoing resources must be divided into **functional** rather than **natural** categories [see **50.2.10.6**];

- gains on revaluation of investments and buildings are included.

Special accounting provisions apply to transfers between funds, gifts in kind, cash collections, life subscriptions, trading activities, permanent endowment, investments, loans, branches, charities with subsidiaries or connected charities, and other specific situations. Many of these provisions were clarified or amended in the revised SORP in 2000.

Figures for the previous financial year should be shown alongside those for the year covered by the accounts. *para.23*

50.2.10.4
Incoming resources

Incoming resources should be shown as:

- donations, legacies and similar income;

- incoming resources from the operating activities of the charity, distinguishing between activities in furtherance of the charity's objects and other activities for generating funds;

- investment income;

- other incoming resources. *para.59*

50.2.10.5
Intangible resources

Intangible incoming resources such as free rent or savings on reduced-rate facilities should be included in the SoFA if they are quantifiable and material, and the charity would otherwise have had to pay for them. A corresponding 'resources used' entry must be made.

The value of **volunteers' time** should not be included as an incoming resource or a resource used, but their contribution should be included in the notes to the accounts or in the trustees' report.

50.2.10.6
<u>Charitable and other</u>
<u>expenditure</u>

Expenditure is usually shown in **natural** categories such as salaries, premises costs, office costs etc. Charities still need to keep their day-to-day accounts under these headings, but if gross income is over £250,000 the figures must be grouped in the SoFA into **functional categories** which relate to the charity's activities. The natural breakdowns are then shown in the notes to the accounts.

Charities with income of £250,000 or less may use natural rather than functional headings in their annual accounts, regardless of whether they prepare receipts and payments or accrual accounts.

The **functional** categories are **charitable expenditure** and the **cost of generating funds** (fundraising and publicity). Charitable expenditure is divided into:

- grants made by the charity;
- costs of activities furthering the charity's objects, including salaries, administration, management and related costs;
- support costs;
- management and administration: the costs of running the charity as an organisation (rather than the costs of running its charitable activities) including, for example, the costs of AGMs and governing body meetings, audit fees, charity registration etc.

For an organisation which carries out more than one charitable activity, the charitable expenditure section should be subdivided into the various activities, for example day care, advice, respite care.

Expenditure covering more than one category—for example, the salary of a manager who spends part of her time managing day care, part managing respite care, part fundraising and part dealing with trustee matters—should be allocated on a reasonable and consistent basis to the relevant cost categories. The basis for the allocation should be explained in the notes. *Charities SORP 2000 para.284*

50.2.10.7
Summary income and
expenditure account

A charity may have to prepare a **summary income and expenditure account** as well as a SoFA if it is a company limited by guarantee [see **50.3.2.1**], or its governing document or funder requires it. A summary account is different from the **summarised** (abridged) accounts that may be included in publicity materials [see **50.2.15**].

If the SoFA includes only revenue transactions, the one set of accounts may meet requirements for both a SoFA and a summary income and expenditure account.

The summary income and expenditure account does not have to distinguish between restricted and unrestricted funds. *paras.335-338*

50.2.10.8
Balance sheet

The **balance sheet** shows the charity's net worth on the last day of the financial year. It includes **fixed assets** held for the charity's use and for investment purposes, **current assets** realisable within one year, and **liabilities**. *paras.181-182*

The balance sheet must be signed by one or more trustees who have been authorised to sign, and must specify the date on which the accounts were approved by the trustees.

50.2.10.9
Cashflow statement

A **cashflow statement** should be included if in the present or previous financial year, the charity met at least two criteria of:

- gross income of more than £2.8 million;
- balance sheet total of more than £1.4 million;
- weekly average of more than 50 employees. *paras.272-276*

50.2.11
Disclosures

Where a SoFA is prepared, the Charities SORP requires certain information to be included in the SoFA or in the notes to the accounts. Charities must ensure this information is kept and is made known to the person preparing the annual accounts.

50.2.11.1
Transactions with trustees and connected persons

Notes to the SoFA should disclose payments to or transactions with **connected persons**. A connected person is an individual or corporate body who:

- is a trustee of the charity, or a holding trustee or custodian trustee for the charity [see **18.4**];

- has donated material assets to the charity;

- is a child (including illegitimate child), stepchild, parent, grandchild, grandparent, brother or sister of any person included above;

- is an officer, employee or agent [see **5.3.2**] of the charity;

- is the spouse or co-habitee of any person included above;

- is a firm or institution controlled by any person or persons included above, or in which any such person is a partner; *or*

- is a corporate body in which any person included above has a substantial interest (20% or more of the share capital or voting rights), or in which two or more persons included above together have a substantial interest.   *Charities SORP 2000 app.1 para.26*

The notes should include specified information about the transactions. In relation to trustees, the notes must show:

- transactions directly or indirectly involving trustees personally;

- the amount remunerated, directly or indirectly, to trustees by the charity or a company controlled by the charity [see **9.6.1** for definition], or the fact that the trustees have not been remunerated;

- how many trustees have been reimbursed for expenses during the year, the total amount reimbursed and the nature of the expenses, or the fact that none have been reimbursed.   *paras.157-170*

50.2.11.2
Grants

If the charity made grants to individuals, the number of grants and total value must be included in the SoFA, the notes or a separate publication such as its annual review. If it made grants to institutions totalling more than 5% of its total expenditure, the accounts, notes or a separate publication should include details of all or the 50 largest grants over £1,000, along with an analysis and explanation of the grants. Information about institutional grants does not have to be disclosed if there is a specific reason not to reveal it and the reason itself is disclosed.
                              paras.138-146

50.2.11.3
Other disclosures

Other disclosures which should be made, if applicable, in the notes to the accounts are:

- the fact that the charity has purchased trustee indemnity insurance [see **20.10**] or certain other insurances, and the cost;   *para.170*

- the total emoluments (salary or other remuneration, and benefits in kind as defined for taxation purposes) paid to the charity's employees during the year, and the average number of employees during the year;   *para.171-172*

- the number of employees whose emoluments for the year were £40,000 or more, in bands of £10,000;   *para.173-175*

- the total amount payable to the charity's auditor or independent examiner;   *para.176-177*

- *ex gratia* payments [see **49.2.7** for definition] or waiver of rights to property to which the charity is entitled [see **44.3.2**], with the nature and date of Charity Commission or other authority for each such payment or waiver if such authority is required.   *para.178-179*

50.2.12
Examination
and audit

If the gross income of a charitable trust or association is over £10,000, it must have its accounts independently examined or audited. If its gross income or total expenditure is over £250,000, or was over this in either of the previous two financial years, it must have a full audit. Requirements for appointing, changing or removing an examiner or auditor and their rights are covered in **chapter 51**.

If an audit is not required under charity law but is required by the governing document, it may be possible to amend the governing document to require 'such audit or examination (if any) as is required under the Charities Act 1993 or subsequent enactments' [see **5.5** for amendment procedures].

After examining or auditing the accounts, the examiner or auditor must make a statement in the required format stating that the accounts are satisfactory, or include a statement in the accounts if there is reason to believe that proper records were not kept, the accounts are not in accordance with the records, or there has been material expenditure or action outside the charity's objects or trusts.

Charities (Accounts and Reports) Regulations 1995 [SI 1995/2724] regs.6-7
and 2000 [SI 2000/2868] reg.4

If the examiner or auditor expresses no concerns about the organisation's accounts, accounting procedures or financial position, the report is **unqualified**. If concerns are expressed, the report is **qualified**.

Under the **whistleblowing** provision, an auditor or examiner must inform the Charity Commissioners in writing if he or she believes there are reasons for the Commission to institute an inquiry [see **3.5.9**] or act for the protection of the charity. *1995 reg.6(5)*

50.2.12.1
Independent
examination

An independent examiner is 'an independent person who is reasonably believed by the trustees to have the requisite ability and practical experience to carry out a competent examination of the accounts' [see **51.4.2**].

Charities Act 1993 s.43(3)(a)

The examiner must carry out defined procedures which are intended to provide a reasonable assurance that records have been properly kept and the accounts are in accordance with the records.

50.2.12.2
Full audit

If the charity's income or expenditure is over £250,000 or has been in either of the previous two financial years, it must have a full audit by an auditor authorised under the Charities Act [see **51.4.1**]. A full audit may also be required by funders or under the governing document.

The auditor must be satisfied that the accounts give a **true and fair view** of the organisation's financial transactions and position, and that the charity is a **going concern** which will continue in operational existence for the foreseeable future [see **21.2.1**].

Accounting Standards Board, Statement of Standard Accounting Practice No.2

50.2.13
Trustees' report

The report required to comply with charity law is sometimes known as the **statutory report**. This need not be the same as a more descriptive report or **annual review** produced for publicity purposes.

50.2.13.1
Simplified report

A simplified statutory report, rather than a full report, may be prepared by charities with income and expenditure of £100,000 or less who prepare receipts and payments accounts [see **50.2.9**]. It must contain:

- the charity's name as it appears in the register of charities, and any other name it uses;
- its charity registration number and, if it is a charitable company, its company registration number;
- its principal address and, if it is a charitable company, the address of its registered office;

- its objects, or the trusts on which its assets are held;
- names of everyone who was a trustee (member of the governing body), holding trustee or custodian trustee [see **18.4**] at any time during the financial year covered by the report;
- names of any person or body entitled to appoint a trustee;
- a description of the charity's organisational structure, such as its divisions, departments, branches or subsidiaries;
- a description of any assets held by the charity or its trustees on behalf of another charity, including the other charity's objects and any special arrangements relating to those assets (this includes where a charity acts as a custodian trustee or its trustees act as holding trustees for the assets of another charity);
- a brief summary of the main activities and achievements during the financial year.

    Charities (Accounts and Reports) Regulations 1995 [SI 1995/2724] reg.10

If the inclusion of a trustee's name could put her or him in personal danger, the Charity Commission can dispense with the need to include that person's name. This provision does not apply to the statutory reports of charitable companies, where under company law the names of all members of the governing body must be disclosed.

The trustees' report must be signed by one or more trustees who have been authorised to do so by the other trustees.

50.2.13.2
<u>Full report</u>

For charities whose gross income is over £100,000, or for those under this amount which prepare accrual accounts, the trustees' report on activities should include:

- everything required for a simplified report [see above];
- a full review of all activities in relation to the objects;
- how the charity or its trustees are constituted (unincorporated association, trust, limited company, incorporated trustee body, etc) and the type of governing document it has;
- any restrictions imposed by the governing document on how the organisation can operate;
- the names of the principal officers (in this context meaning employees);
- names and addresses of the organisation's bankers and if applicable its solicitors, auditor or independent examiner, investment advisors and other principal advisors;
- summary of specific investment powers, and whether these are granted by the governing document, the Charity Commission or in another way;
- investment policy (if applicable), and the performance of investments;
- policies (if applicable) on reserves and grant making;
- a statement that the trustees have reviewed major risks to the charity and implemented controls to mitigate risk [see **49.1**] ;
- confirmation that the accounts comply with current statutory requirements and the requirements of the charity's governing document.   *Charities SORP 2000 para.31*

It should also include significant transactions, developments, achievements and changes in activities during the year, important events since the end of the year and likely future developments.

50.2.14
Providing reports to the Charity Commission and public

All registered charities with income or expenditure above £10,000 must submit their annual report and accounts, examined or audited if required, to the Charity Commission within 10 months from the end of the financial year to which they apply. The Commission makes them available for public inspection.   *Charities Act 1993 s.49*

Charities with income and expenditure up to £10,000 do not have to submit accounts unless the Charity Commission requests them.

All charitable organisations, even if not registered, must provide a copy of their most recent annual accounts and report within two months to any member of the public who requests it in writing. A reasonable fee may be charged for this.   *Charities Act 1993 s.47*

50.2.15
Summarised accounts

Before a summary of a charity's examined or audited accounts is published or circulated in any way, including on a website, it must be checked by the examiner/auditor. The summary must give a fair and accurate summary of the full accounts and must include specified statements by the trustees and the examiner/auditor.

Charities SORP 2000 paras.292-297

50.2.16
Charity annual returns

A charity **annual return** is a form sent by the Charity Commission, which charities with gross income or total expenditure over £10,000 must fill in and return within 10 months from the end of its financial year. The return is accompanied by a **database update form**, whose purpose is to ensure the register of charities is up to date. Charities whose gross annual income and total expenditure are both £10,000 or less only need to submit the database update form.

Charities Act 1993 s.48

Between returns, the Commission must be notified of any changes in the charity's correspondent, address or other details on the register of charities. There is no need to notify change of trustees until the next return.   *s.3(7)(b)*

50.3
COMPANIES

This book can only briefly summarise company law as it relates to annual accounts and reports. Free booklets explaining the requirements are available from Companies House and the Charity Commission [see end of chapter]. Voluntary sector companies should consult their accountant or auditor for further information and advice.

50.3.1
Financial year

A company's **accounting reference date** (ARD) is the last day of the month in which the anniversary of incorporation occurs. A company's ARD can be altered at any time by giving notice to Companies House on **form 225**.   *Companies Act 1985 ss.224-225*

The directors can agree to end the company's **financial year** on any date within seven days before or after the ARD.   *s.223*

A subsidiary undertaking's financial year must be the same as its parent company's [see **9.6.1**], unless the directors of the parent company believe there are good reasons for it not to be.

50.3.2
Annual accounts

50.3.2.1
Individual accounts

Every company must produce annual **individual accounts**. The accounts must include a **balance sheet** [see **50.2.10.8**] and a **profit and loss account** (or, for a voluntary organisation, an **income and expenditure account**). Insofar as possible the accounts should comply with the Companies Act 1985 schedule 4, but the need to give a true and fair view of the company's financial position is the primary consideration.   *s.226*

50.3.2.2
Group accounts

If the company is a parent company [see **9.6.1** for definition], it may also have to prepare **group accounts** with a consolidated balance sheet and consolidated profit and loss (or income and expenditure) accounts for the parent and all its subsidiary undertakings.   *ss.227-230*

50.3.2.3
Small and medium companies and groups

The rules on the form and content of individual and group accounts are less onerous for small and medium-sized companies and groups.

For these purposes, a **small company** or group must meet at least two of the following criteria:

- weekly average number of employees not more than 50;
- turnover (total revenue income) not more than £2.8 million;
- balance sheet total not more than £1.4 million.

Companies Act 1985 ss.246-249

At the time of writing (early 2001) the government had proposed increasing the turnover threshold to £4.8 million and the balance sheet total to £2.4 million.

A **medium-sized company** or group must meet at least two of the following criteria:

- weekly average number of employees not more than 250;
- turnover not more than £11.2 million;
- balance sheet total not more than £5.6 million.

At the time of writing the government had proposed increasing the turnover threshold to £19.2 million and the balance sheet total to £9.6 million.

50.3.2.4
Charitable companies

A charitable company prepares its accounts under Companies Act requirements, rather than Charities Act requirements. Some Companies Act rules, in particular on audit exemption [see **50.3.4.1**], are different for charitable and non-charitable companies.

Charities Act 1993 ss.41(5), 42(7), 43(9)

Although a charitable company's accounts are prepared under company rules, they must comply with the Charities SORP [see **50.2.10**] or must explain why they do not. SORP requires a **statement of financial activities** [see **50.2.10.3**] which is different from the income and expenditure account format required under company law. If its SoFA includes non-revenue transactions, a charitable company may also need to prepare a summary income and expenditure account [see **50.2.10.7**] in order to comply with Companies Act requirements.

50.3.3
Report of the directors

The directors must prepare a report on the accounts which must be agreed by the board and signed on their behalf by a director or the company secretary. *Companies Act 1985 ss.234, 234A*

The directors' report may be a short report issued with the annual accounts. It is not necessarily the same as a descriptive annual report or **annual review** to publicise the organisation's activities. A descriptive report may be used to meet Companies Act requirements only if it contains all the information required under company legislation.

Charitable companies must produce annual reports complying with both company and charity requirements [see **50.2.13**]. The company and charity reports may be separate or combined.

50.3.3.1
Small companies

The report of the directors of a small company [see **50.3.2.3** for definition] must include:

- the names of everyone who, at any time during the financial year, was a director of the company;
- the main activities of the company during the year and any significant changes;
- interests held by directors or their immediate families in the shares or debentures of the company, its subsidiaries or parent company;
- each contribution of more than £200 to a political party or EU political organisation or for a purpose affecting public support for a political organisation (charitable companies will not have made any such contributions);
- each contribution of more than £200 for charitable purposes;
- a statement that the company has taken advantage of exemptions for small companies, if it does not include the additional information required for the reports of medium companies. *sch.7; sch.8 para.15*

50.3.3.2
Medium and large companies

The report of the directors of a medium [see **50.3.2.3**] or large company must include additional information, including liability insurance paid for by the company for its directors, senior managers or auditors [see **20.10**], and specified information about the health, safety and welfare of the company's employees. The company's accountant or auditor can provide advice on what needs to be included. *Companies Act 1985 sch.7*

If the company has a weekly average of more than 250 employees, the directors' report must also include information about the employment, training and advancement of people with disabilities within the company, and how the company is involving employees in decisions about the affairs, policies and performance of the company.

50.3.4
Audit

Many companies are exempt from having to have an audit [see below]. Other companies, unless dormant [see **50.3.7**], must have an audit each year by a qualified auditor. The nature of the audit and the type of report produced by the auditor depends on the size of the company.

If the articles of association require a full audit even though one is not required under company law, they can be amended by special resolution [see **17.4.7** for procedure] to require 'such audit or reports (if any) as are required under the Companies Act 1985, the Charities Act 1993 and subsequent enactments'.

The process of appointing, changing or removing an auditor is closely regulated by the Companies Acts [see **51.3**].

50.3.4.1
Exemption from audit

An individual company must have a full audit if it is:

- a charitable company with total turnover (revenue income) of £250,000 or more, or more than £1.4 million in assets; *or*

- a non-charitable company with total turnover more than £1 million (£350,000 for financial years ending on or before 31 July 2000), or more than £1.4 million in assets.

Below these levels the company is exempt from having a full audit, unless its articles of association or funders require an audit. A company which takes advantage of the exemption must state this on the balance sheet. *Companies Act 1985 ss.249A -249E;*
Companies Act 1985 (Audit Exemption) (Amendment) Regulations 2000
[SI 2000/1430]

Members holding 10% of the voting rights of the company can require the company to have a full audit by giving notice in writing at the company's registered office at least one month before the end of the financial year.

50.3.4.2
Audit exemption report

A individual charitable company with turnover between £90,000 and £250,000 and less than £1.4 million in assets does not need to have a full audit unless its articles of association or funders require it. Instead, it may have a simpler **compilation report** (sometimes called an **accountant's report**) prepared by a **reporting accountant**. The company must include an **audit exemption certificate** with its balance sheet.
Companies Act 1985 ss.249A -249E

As with companies exempt from audit [see above], members holding 10% of the company's voting rights can require a full audit.

At the time of writing (early 2001) audit requirements for charitable companies were being reviewed.

50.3.4.3
Groups

A group of non-charitable companies is exempt if it meets the threshold requirements for an individual non-charitable company [see **50.3.4.1**].

Any group which includes a charitable company must have an audit if the gross income exceeds £350,000, or £420,000 on a consolidated basis.
s.249B

50.3.4.4
Full audit

For a full audit, the auditors must make a report stating whether, in their opinion, the accounts have been properly prepared in accordance with the Companies Acts and give a true and fair view of the financial situation. If the auditors cannot for any reason state that the accounts have been properly prepared and give a true and fair view, they must give a **qualified report**.   *Companies Act 1985 ss.235, 237*

50.3.4.5
Approval

The accounts and report must be approved by the board. The balance sheet must be signed on their behalf by a company director, and the directors' report must be signed on their behalf by a director or the company secretary.   *ss.233(4), 234A(3)*

50.3.5
Filing, circulation and publication

Once the annual accounts and reports have been signed, every copy which is presented to a general meeting, circulated or published in any way, including on the internet, must be complete and must include the names of the persons who signed the balance sheet, the directors' report and the compilation or auditor's report.   *ss.233, 234A, 240*

50.3.5.1
Laying before general meeting

The annual accounts, directors' report and auditor's or compilation report (if there is one) must be presented to (**laid before**) a general meeting within 10 months from the end of the financial year to which they apply, unless the company has passed a resolution to dispense with this requirement [see below]. The general meeting at which the accounts are presented is usually the annual general meeting, but it does not have to be unless this is specified in the articles of association.   *s.241(1)*

The accounts and reports must be sent to every person who is entitled to receive notice of general meetings [see **17.4.4**] at least 21 clear days [see **17.2.3** for definition] before the meeting, unless company members have agreed that the accounts and reports can be communicated electronically [see **50.3.5.3**]. Where the accounts and reports are sent on paper, they may be sent out less than 21 days before the meeting if this is agreed by every member entitled to attend and vote at the meeting.   *s.238*

The accounts are often said to be **approved** at the annual or other general meeting, but this approval by the company members is not necessary unless it is required under the articles of association. Under company law the company members simply **receive** accounts which have already been approved by the directors. If company members do not like what the accounts show they can question the directors, express their concern, pass a resolution calling for the directors to act differently, or ultimately remove the directors [see **11.5.6** for procedure]. But they have no right to refuse to accept the accounts, unless the articles give them this right.   *s.241(1)*

50.3.5.2
Elective resolution not to lay accounts

A private company may pass an elective resolution [see **17.4.7** for procedure] to dispense with having to lay the annual accounts and reports before a general meeting.   *s.252*

The elective resolution applies to the financial year in which it is made and subsequent years. While it is in place the accounts and reports must be sent out at least 28 days before the end of the 10-month period after the financial year, to everyone entitled to receive notice of general meetings [see **17.4.4**]. They must be accompanied by a notice informing members of their right to require the accounts to be laid before a general meeting. The procedures for making such a request and calling the meeting are set out in the Act.   *s.253*

50.3.5.3
Electronic communication

A company may seek the agreement of its members to the distribution of annual reports, accounts and other information through electronic communications—for example by displaying information on a secure section of a website, and notifying members by email or fax that the information is there. Strict rules apply to electronic communications

with company members. These rules are expanded in guidance from the Institute of Chartered Secretaries and Administrators [see end of chapter]. *Companies Act 1985 (Electronic Communications) Order 2000*
[SI 2000/3373]

50.3.5.4
Submission to
Companies House

The annual accounts, directors' report and auditor's or compilation report must be filed with Companies House within 10 months from the end of the financial year. This means *exactly* 10 months, so if the company's financial year ends on 28 February, the accounts must be in by 28 December, not 31 December, but if the financial year ends on 31 January, they must be in by 30 November not 1 December.
Companies Act 1985 ss.242(1), 244(1)(a)

Small companies [see **50.3.2.3** for definition] may submit modified accounts consisting only of an abbreviated balance sheet, without a profit and loss/income and expenditure account. *sch.8 paras.17-18*

The accounts may be filed even if they have not yet been laid before a general meeting [see **50.3.5.1**].

The reports must have original (not photocopied) signatures as follows:

- balance sheet signed on behalf of the board by a director;

- directors' report signed on behalf of the board by a director or the company secretary;

- report of the auditor or reporting accountant signed by the auditor or reporting accountant.

The accounts and reports, like all documents submitted to Companies House, must have the company's registered number prominently on the first page, and must be in black on white A4 paper. They can be in Welsh if the company's memorandum of association says that its registered office must be in Wales. Otherwise if any part of the accounts or reports is not in English a translation certified to be accurate must be included. *ss.255E, 242(1)*

If the accounts are not in the proper form, for example if a signature is missing, they are treated as not having been submitted on time. Companies House recommends that accounts are submitted to Companies House at least three weeks before the due date, so there is time to put right any problems.

*Failure to submit properly produced and signed accounts and reports on time leads to many voluntary organisations being fined and struck off the register of companies [see **21.4.2**].*

There are **automatic penalties** for the company ranging from £100 if the accounts are between *one day* and three months late, to £1,000 if they are more than 12 months late. In addition the directors may be held personally liable and may have charges brought against them, and the company may be struck off the register. It is very important to avoid this, as reinstatement is very costly and involves a court hearing. Being struck off may have other damaging consequences, including exposing members of the governing body to personal liability, and giving grounds for the termination of leases and other agreements. *s.242A*

Extensions are granted only if there is a very good reason, and not if the accounts are already late. Application is made to the companies administration branch at Companies House.

50.3.5.5
Making reports available
to the public

Company reports are open to the public at Companies House, and copies may be requested by any member of the public. A company must make its audited accounts and reports available to company members and debenture holders, and the accounts of charitable companies must be made available within two months to any member of the public who requests them. *Companies Act 1985 s.239; Charities Act 1993 s.47(2)*

50.3.6
Summarised accounts

If **summarised** or **abridged company accounts** are published in any way, including on the internet, they must not include the auditors' report, and must include statements in a specified form. It is usually advisable to have summarised accounts prepared by the auditor or reporting accountant. *Companies Act 1985 s.240(3)*

50.3.7
Dormant companies

A company is **dormant** if there has been no significant accounting transaction during the financial year. A dormant company is exempt from the requirement to have its accounts audited. *s.249AA;*
Companies Act 1985 (Audit Exemption) (Amendment) Regulations 2000
[SI 2000/1430]

The exemption for a dormant company applies only to the audit requirement (since it has had no financial transactions, there is nothing to audit). It must prepare and submit annual accounts and a directors' report, and must comply with all other requirements such as submission of annual return and election of directors.

Since the introduction of rules removing the need for many companies to have any kind of audit [see **50.3.4.1**], there is less need to put a company into dormancy.

50.3.8
Company annual returns

Every company must submit an annual return each year. This is a straightforward procedure designed to keep the register of companies up to date, and is separate from the requirement to submit the annual accounts and reports. *Companies Act 1985 s.363(1),(2)*

Companies House sends **form 363A** (blank) or **363S** (a shuttle form, already filled in) to the company. The form must be filled in or updated, then signed by a director or the company secretary and returned with the filing fee (£15 as at 1/4/01). Failure to file on time carries penalties.

50.4
INDUSTRIAL AND PROVIDENT SOCIETIES

An industrial and provident society's financial year must end between 31 August and 31 January unless it has authorisation from the Registrar of Friendly Societies for it to end at another time.
Industrial and Provident Societies Act 1965 s.39(2),(3)

50.4.1
Annual accounts

IPSs must prepare an annual **revenue account** and **balance sheet**. The revenue account can cover the whole society, or there can be two or more revenue accounts dealing with specific aspects of the society's work. The balance sheet must cover the whole society.
Friendly and Industrial and Provident Societies Act 1968 s.3(2),(4)

A society which has one or more subsidiaries must produce group accounts, although it is possible to apply to the Registrar of Friendly Societies to exclude one or more subsidiaries if there are good reasons for doing so. *ss.13-15*

50.4.1.1
Audit or report

IPSs must in general have a full audit carried out by a qualified auditor. However the members may pass a resolution at a general meeting not to have a full audit if:

- the IPS's turnover for the year did not exceed £350,000 (£250,000 for charitable IPSs); *and*

- the total value of its assets at the end of the financial year did not exceed £1.4 million. *ss.4, 4A*

The resolution may be vetoed by 20% of the votes cast at a meeting or 10% of the members eligible to vote. If the resolution is passed and turnover was more than £90,000, the IPS must have a **reporting accountant** make a report on the accounts. This is similar to a company compilation report [see **50.3.4.2**]. *s.9A*

Housing associations, credit unions and IPSs with a subsidiary cannot be exempt from having a full audit. *s.4A(3)*

At the time of writing (early 2001) it appeared likely that IPS rules would be changed to reflect changes in company audits [see **50.3.4.1**].

50.4.1.2
Approval

The IPS's audited accounts must be approved by the committee and signed by the secretary and two directors acting on behalf of the committee.   *Friendly and Industrial and Provident Societies Act 1968 s.3A(1)*

50.4.1.3
Filing, circulation and publication

The accounts form part of the annual return [see **50.4.2**] and must be sent to the Registrar of Friendly Societies each year with (if required) the accountant's or auditor's report. The accounts and return must be submitted within seven months from the end of the IPS's financial year.
Industrial and Provident Societies Act 1965 s.39(1); FIPSA s.11(1),(2)

The revenue account and balance sheet must not be circulated or published unless they have been audited or reported on (if required) and signed, and are accompanied by the relevant report.   *FIPSA s.3A*

A copy of the most recent balance sheet and relevant report must be on public display at the society's registered office.   *IPSA s.40*

Unless the governing document requires it, there is no obligation to send accounts to all members, but if any member or person interested in the funds of the society requests the accounts they must be sent free of charge.   *IPSA s.39(5); FIPSA ss.11(5), 13(7)*

One of the few requirements of the Charities Act 1993 which applies to charitable IPSs is that they must make their most recent annual accounts and report available within two months to any member of the public who requests it. A reasonable fee may be charged to cover the cost.   *Charities Act 1993 s.47(2)*

50.4.2
Annual returns

An annual return must be submitted to the Registrar of Friendly Societies within seven months from the end of the financial year. There is no annual filing fee for IPS returns.   *IPSA s.39*

50.5
NON-CHARITABLE ASSOCIATIONS

There is no statutory obligation for a non-charitable unincorporated association to prepare accounts or have them audited, but this may be required by its governing document or funders. If the governing document does not require annual accounts, the governing body or the members at a general meeting may require the treasurer or any other person to prepare accounts (and it would be a good idea to amend the governing document to make this an annual requirement; see **5.5** for procedure). They may also require the accounts to be audited or to be examined by a suitable independent person [see for example **51.4.2**], and might want to amend the governing document to require this as well.

FOR FURTHER INFORMATION

Local community accountancy project.

Charity accounts and audit. Charity Commission: 0870-333 0123; www.charity-commission.gov.uk

Charity Finance Directors Group: 020-7793 1400; www.cfdg.org.uk

Company accounts and audit. Companies House: 0870-333 3636; www.companieshouse.gov.uk

Company electronic communication. Institute of Chartered Secretaries and Administrators: 020-7580 4741; www.icsa.org.uk

Industrial and provident societies. Financial Services Authority: 0845-606 1234; www.fsa.gov.uk

Chapter 51
AUDITORS

51.1
THE NEED FOR AN AUDITOR

Unless it is required by statute, the organisation's governing document, funders, or the organisation's members, there is no obligation for an organisation to have its accounts audited.

Many small and some medium-sized organisations are exempted from the need for any kind of statutory audit, or may opt for a simpler **independent examination** [see **50.2.12**] or **compilation report** [see **50.3.4** and **50.4.1**] rather than a full audit. If there is a conflict between the governing document and statute—if, for example, the governing document requires a full audit when statute allows a simpler scrutiny or none at all, or *vice versa*—the higher requirement prevails. It may be possible to amend the governing document [see **50.2.12** and **50.3.4**] to bring it into line with statutory requirements.

Where the requirement of funders is higher than the statutory requirement or what is required under the governing document, it may be possible to negotiate with funders to change their requirement.

51.1.1
Finding an auditor

Persons eligible to carry out statutory audits are defined in the legislation for each type of organisation and are explained in this chapter. The organisation's governing document or funders may impose a different requirement, for example requiring an audit by 'a qualified auditor' when under statute an independent examiner would be sufficient. As with the audit requirement [see above], the higher requirement prevails. It may be possible to amend the governing document or negotiate with funders to bring those requirements in line with statute.

The voluntary sector is a specialist area, with complex accounting and reporting provisions [see **chapter 50**]. Auditors with a real knowledge of the sector are relatively rare, but organisations should make every effort to find one already familiar with the sector and with the type of work carried out by the organisation. The advice on finding an accountant [see **60.10.3**] applies to auditors as well, although not all accountants are able to carry out all types of audit.

Particular care is needed when choosing someone to carry out a charity independent examination [see **51.4.2**]. Independent examiners do not need to be professionally qualified, but the governing body does need to be satisfied that they have the necessary ability and experience.

**51.1.2
Cost**

It is vital to obtain quotes prior to appointment, but this should not be the only basis for selection. Care should be taken to ensure quotes are for the same service, and to find out what further charges are made for additional services (for example, advice on VAT) and the basis for calculating them. Once an auditor is appointed, a new quote should be obtained for each year, or changes in the fees should be monitored.

**51.1.3
Expectations
and role**

The form and content of statutory audits are specified by law and in **statements of auditing standards** (SASs) and **practice notes** issued by the Accounting Practices Board. For non-statutory audits, the form and content may be specified in the governing document or may simply be arranged between the organisation and its auditor.

Qualified auditors generally provide a **terms of engagement** letter setting out the contract between the auditor and the organisation. This may seek to limit the role of the auditor, both to narrow the grounds on which the organisation could make a claim against the auditor for breach of contract or negligence [see **51.7**], and to make clear the limits of the service provided. If services outside those specified are subsequently required, additional fees may be charged. The terms of engagement must be carefully considered by the governing body, with particular attention given to the need for additional services.

Where the auditor is not professionally qualified, it is even more important that the governing body and the auditor understand exactly what is expected of the audit and the auditor. To protect both parties, this should be set out in writing.

**51.1.3.1
The auditor's role**

The core of the auditor's role is ensuring that the accounts give a **true and fair view** of the organisation's financial affairs (or, for charity examinations, that the accounts are consistent with the financial records). Professional auditors must point out weaknesses in financial systems, but there is no duty on the auditor to ensure those weaknesses are rectified. That responsibility rests with the governing body.

Under the **whistleblowing** provisions in the Charities Act 1993, charity auditors or independent examiners have to report **deliberate or reckless misconduct** in administering the charity to the Charity Commission [see **50.2.12**]. For other types of audit, auditors should report fraud to the governing body—but the responsibility for detecting and preventing fraud rests with the governing body, not the auditor. Unless the client organisation specifically requests it, the auditor will not be searching for fraud.

The provision of advice on tax and VAT matters does not generally fall within the scope of an audit, and an organisation which requires this service should make this clear.

The organisation should also clearly specify if it requires the auditor to carry out other tasks, such as filing the audited accounts with the Charity Commission and/or Companies House, or submitting the accounts to funders or other bodies. It is the responsibility of the governing body, not the auditor, to ensure this is done.

**51.2
RIGHTS OF
AUDITORS**

To ensure they obtain all relevant information and are able to present their views to the organisation's members, auditors for companies, industrial and provident societies and charities have statutory rights.

51.2.1
Companies and IPSs

Auditors and reporting accountants for companies and industrial and provident societies have a statutory right:

- to have access at all times to the organisation's books, accounts and all related documentation;
- to require relevant information and explanations from the organisation's directors, company/IPS secretary and employees (and it is an offence for them knowingly to make a misleading, false or deceptive statement to the auditor);
- if auditing a parent body, to require information and explanations from its subsidiary undertakings [see **9.6.1**] and their auditors;
- to receive the same notices of general meetings and other documentation as company or IPS members receive;
- to attend general meetings, and to speak (but not vote) on any topic which concerns them as auditor;
- in companies, to require a written resolution [see **17.4.12**] which concerns them as auditor to be considered at a general meeting rather than be dealt with without a meeting.

Companies Act 1985 ss.389A, 390;
Friendly and Industrial and Provident Societies Act 1968 ss.9(5)-(7), 9B

51.2.2
Charities

An auditor or independent examiner carrying out an unincorporated charity's statutory audit or examination has the right:

- to have access to any books, documents or other records which relate to the charity and which the auditor or examiner considers necessary to inspect;
- to require information and explanations from past or present charity trustees, holding or custodian trustees [see **18.4**], officers [see **5.3.2**] or employees.

Charities (Accounts and Reports) Regulations 1995 [SI 1995/2724] reg.8

There is no statutory right to receive notice of a charitable association's general meetings or a charitable trust's trustee meetings, but it is good practice for the organisation to provide this.

51.3
COMPANY AUDITORS

The basic rules on company audits, including exemption from the need to have a full audit or from the need to have any audit, are set out in **50.3.4**.

51.3.1
Eligibility

To carry out a full audit for a company, the auditor must be a member of a recognised supervisory body and be registered as a company auditor under the rules of that body. To make a compilation report, the accountant must be eligible to carry out full audits, or must be a member of a recognised supervisory body, be engaged in public practice and not be ineligible for appointment as a reporting accountant under the rules of the supervisory body.

Companies Act 1985 s.249D; Companies Act 1989 s.25

The recognised bodies and the initials used by their members are:

- Institute of Chartered Accountants in England and Wales (ACA, FCA);
- Institute of Chartered Accountants of Scotland (CA);
- Institute of Chartered Accountants in Ireland (ACA, FCA);
- Association of Chartered Certified Accountants (ACCA, FCCA).

Members of the recognised bodies in Scotland and Ireland can carry out company audits in England and Wales.

An auditor may be an individual, corporate body or partnership. A person or firm appointed as a company auditor or reporting accountant must not have any connection with the company, or with an officer [see

5.3.2] or employee of the company, which would make him or her ineligible for appointment.   *Companies Act 1989 s.27*

51.3.2
Appointment

A company's first auditor or reporting accountant is appointed by the directors at any time before the first general meeting at which annual accounts are presented [see **50.3.5**], and holds office until the conclusion of that meeting. At each general meeting at which annual accounts are presented, the auditor must be reappointed or a new auditor appointed.
Companies Act 1985 ss. 384(1), 385

A casual vacancy in the post of auditor may be filled by the directors or by a general meeting. Special notice [see **17.4.7**] is needed for a general meeting resolution to fill a casual vacancy or to reappoint a retiring auditor who was appointed by the directors to fill a casual vacancy. The notice must also be sent to the person proposed to be appointed and, if the casual vacancy was caused by the resignation of an auditor, to the auditor who resigned. While the vacancy continues the former auditor, if any, may continue to act as auditor.   *s.388*

51.3.2.1
Resolution not to
appoint annually

For a private company which has elected to dispense with laying annual accounts before a general meeting [see **50.3.5**]:

- the first auditor is appointed by the directors;

- the auditor must be reappointed or a new auditor appointed at a general meeting within 28 days after the accounts have been sent to the members; *or*

- the company can pass an elective resolution [see **17.4.7** for procedure] to dispense with the obligation to appoint the auditor annually. The auditor is then deemed to be reappointed at the expiry of the 28-day period after the accounts have been sent to the members each year.   *s.385A*

Where the company has passed resolutions not to lay the accounts before a general meeting and not to appoint the auditor annually, the auditor continues to serve unless he or she is removed [see **51.3.5.5**] or the company makes itself dormant and thus does not need to be audited [see **50.3.7**].   *s.386*

51.3.3
Remuneration

If the auditor or reporting accountant is appointed or reappointed by a general meeting, the general meeting must also agree the remuneration (the amount to be paid to the auditor) or must state how the remuneration is to be decided. Often the general meeting delegates to the directors the right to set the remuneration. If the directors appoint the auditor, the directors decide the remuneration.   *s.390A(1),(2)*

The amount of remuneration, including expenses and benefits in kind, must be stated in a note to the annual accounts. If the auditor or an associate is paid for other services during the year, this must also be disclosed.   *ss.390A(3)-(5), 390B*

51.3.4
Resignation

An auditor or reporting accountant has the right to resign at any time, regardless of any agreement with the company. To do this, the auditor must deposit at the company's registered office a notice of resignation, and a **statement of circumstances** [see **51.3.5.3**] connected with his or her ceasing to hold office.   *s.392*

Within 14 days the company must:

- send a copy of the notice of resignation to Companies House with **companies form 391**; *and*

- if the statement contains circumstances which the auditor thinks should be brought to the attention of members or creditors, it must be dealt with in the same way as a statement of circumstances when an auditor is being removed [see **51.3.5.3**].   *ss.392(3), 394*

The auditor has the right to require the directors to convene an extraordinary general meeting to receive and consider an explanation of the circumstances connected with the resignation.

Companies Act 1985 s.392A

The provisions on attendance at general meetings and notification to Companies House are the same as for removal of an auditor.

51.3.5
Removal

A company may remove its auditor or reporting accountant at any time by ordinary resolution [see **17.4.7** for procedure] at a general meeting, regardless of any agreement between them. However there are safeguards to ensure that a whistleblowing auditor is not being removed as a way of concealing the company's bad practice.

51.3.5.1
Notice of removal

Special notice [see **17.4.7**] is needed to remove an auditor before the end of his or her term of office or to appoint any auditor other than the retiring auditor. This is not necessary if the auditor is being proposed for removal at the general meeting at which his or her term would have ended anyway [see **51.3.2**] and no one is being proposed as a replacement.

ss.391, 391A

As soon as it receives notice of a resolution to remove or replace an auditor, the company must send it to the auditor who is proposed for removal and to any person being put forward as a replacement. It must also be sent within 14 days to Companies House.

If an auditor is removed and/or appointed, Companies House must be informed within 14 days on **companies form 391**.

51.3.5.2
Representations

An auditor proposed for removal has the right to make **representations** to the company, which the company must circulate to everyone to whom notice of the general meeting is sent (or has been sent). If the representations are received too late to be sent out, the auditor can require them to be read out at the meeting.

s.391A

51.3.5.3
Statement of circumstances

An auditor proposed for removal must deposit at the company's registered office a **statement of circumstances** which includes:

- any circumstances connected with ceasing to be auditor which he or she thinks should be brought to the attention of the company's members or its creditors (the people to whom it owes money); *or*
- a statement that there are no such circumstances. *s.394*

If the statement includes such circumstances, the company must send it within 14 days to every person entitled to be sent copies of the accounts [see **17.4.4**]. Alternatively the company may apply to the court not to do this if it thinks the statement is being used 'to secure needless publicity for defamatory matter'. The company must inform the auditor that it has made this application.

51.3.5.4
Attendance at general meetings

The auditor has the right to attend the general meeting at which his or her removal is proposed, and to speak on any matter which concerns him or her as auditor.

Even after an auditor has been removed, he or she has the right to receive notice of a general meeting and all documents sent to company members for the meeting, and to attend and speak at the meeting on matters of concern to him or her as former auditor, if the meeting is:

- the one at which his or her term of office as auditor would have expired, had he or she not resigned or been removed; *or*
- the one at which an auditor will be appointed to replace him or her.

ss.391(4), 392A(8)

51.3.5.5
Removal of auditors not appointed annually

If the company has elected not to appoint auditors annually [see **51.3.2.1**], any member of the company can propose that the appointment is terminated.

s.393

A member cannot deposit more than one such notice during any financial year. The directors must notify Companies House of the resolution within 14 days, and must convene a general meeting to be held within 28 days of the date of notice of the meeting. They must put an ordinary resolution [see **17.4.7** for procedure] to the meeting as to whether the appointment of the auditor should be terminated. The notification procedures for removal of the auditor [see above] must be followed.

If it is agreed to end the appointment, the auditor is not considered to be reappointed when he or she next would have been. Companies House must be notified of the removal of the auditor on **form 391** within 14 days of the general meeting.

51.4 CHARITABLE TRUSTS AND ASSOCIATIONS

For the rules on independent examination and audit for charitable unincorporated associations and trusts, see **50.2.12**. Many funders require full audits even where these are not required by statute.

There are no specific statutory procedures or regulations for the appointment, resignation or removal of a charity's auditor or examiner, or how their remuneration is determined. If the governing document sets out procedures for appointing or removing the auditor or examiner and determining remuneration, these must be followed.

It is good practice to invite the auditor or examiner to the general meetings of a charitable association or meetings of the trustees of a charitable trust, but there is no statutory requirement to do so.

51.4.1 Full audit

A full audit of a charitable trust or association may be carried out only by a person registered to do company audits [see **51.3.1**]

Charities Act 1993 s.43(2)

51.4.2 Independent examination

An independent examiner does not have to be professionally qualified, but the trustees must be satisfied that the examiner has the 'requisite ability' and relevant practical experience to understand the charity's accounts and financial position. The Charity Commission strongly recommends that only qualified accountants should carry out examinations if the charity's income is more than £100,000 or it has assets worth more than £1 million.

An independent examiner should have no connection with the charity which might inhibit the impartial conduct of the examination. This means, at the very least, that the examination should not be carried out by anyone closely involved in the charity's administration, a major donor, a major beneficiary, or a close relative, business partner or employee of such a person.

Anyone appointed as an independent examiner should contact the Charity Commission or consult its website for the necessary information and instructions.

51.5 INDUSTRIAL AND PROVIDENT SOCIETIES

For audit requirements for industrial and provident societies see **50.4.1**. An audit may be carried out by a person eligible to audit companies [see **51.3.1**], or who was approved as an IPS auditor prior to the Friendly and Industrial and Provident Societies Act 1968 and has continued to act for the IPS every year since then.

Friendly and Industrial and Provident Societies Act 1968 s.7

An IPS's rules must specify whether the auditor is appointed by the members at a general meeting or by the governing body.

A qualified auditor who has been appointed is automatically reappointed unless he or she is removed by a resolution at a general meeting, resigns in writing, or becomes incapable or ineligible because of a connection with the IPS or ceasing to be a qualified auditor.

s.5

A resolution to not reappoint a qualified auditor or to appoint someone other than the existing auditor must:

- be given to the IPS at least 28 days before the general meeting at which it will be considered;

- be sent immediately to the auditor concerned; *and*

- be sent to the members with the notice of the meeting or at least 14 days before the meeting, or be publicised in a newspaper or in some other way.

Friendly and Industrial and Provident Societies Act 1968 s.6(1)-(3)

If the auditor proposed as a replacement is not eligible to serve or states in writing that he or she does not want to be appointed, the meeting may reappoint the retiring auditor or appoint another person even though proper notice of this has not been given.   *s.6(4)*

A retiring auditor always has the right to make written representations which the society must make available to members, to attend and speak at the general meeting, and to insist that the written representations are read out at the general meeting.   *s.6(6),(7)*

51.6
NON-CHARITABLE
ASSOCIATIONS

Non-charitable associations are bound only by the terms of their governing document, and by funders' requirements.

If the governing document does not require an audit or the equivalent of a charity independent examination, the members may pass a resolution requiring it, or may be able to amend the governing document [see **5.5** for procedure] to make it a requirement.

51.7
LIABILITY OF
AUDITORS

Auditors may be liable if they are in breach of their contract (terms of engagement) with the organisation [see **51.1.3**].

If an auditor is negligent (in breach of their duty of care), the organisation may be able to sue for loss. In certain circumstances, third parties who have relied to their detriment on inaccurate or misleading audit reports may have a claim against the auditor.

Auditors who audit limited companies cannot limit or exclude liability for negligence. If there is a statement in a company's articles of association or in a contract between the company and its auditor stating that the auditor is exempt from liability for negligence, or stating that the company will indemnify the auditor against liability, the statement is void.   *Companies Act 1985 s.310*

Chapter 52
CORPORATION TAX, INCOME TAX
AND CAPITAL GAINS TAX

Topics covered in this chapter

This chapter introduces the range of taxes which voluntary organisations might have to pay, in particular corporation tax, income tax and capital gains tax, and exemptions.

For sources of further information see end of chapter.
Double-underlined section headings indicate additions or significant changes since the first edition.

52.1
VOLUNTARY
ORGANISATIONS
AND TAX

Voluntary organisations, including charities, are subject to the same taxes, VAT and rates as anyone else—but may be eligible for a wide range of **exemptions** and **reliefs**. Tax matters are extremely complex, and eligibility may be jeopardised simply because the necessary forms are completed incorrectly. **Proper advice is essential**.

52.1.1
The range of taxes

A voluntary organisation may have to deal with:

- corporation tax or income tax on its profits or surplus [see **52.2**];

- corporation tax or capital gains tax on the increased value of its assets, when it sells or disposes of them [see **52.2.4**];
- employer's national insurance contributions (NIC) [see **27.5.3**];
- income tax and employee's NIC deducted from employees' pay and paid to Inland Revenue on behalf of the employees [see **27.3**];
- value added tax (VAT) or excise duty on goods or services it purchases [see **53.1**];
- VAT it charges on goods or services it provides [see **53.1**];
- duty on imported goods;
- business rates or council tax on property owned, occupied or used by the organisation [see **59.2** and **59.3**];
- stamp duty on some property transactions, transfers by deed and transactions in shares [see **57.10.1**].

52.1.1.1
Exemptions and extra-statutory concessions

Charities are generally exempt from all or part of these taxes, except VAT, import duty, and tax and national insurance on wages. For some exemptions, certain criteria may have to be met.

In addition to the exemptions set out in legislation, the Inland Revenue has published a range of **extra-statutory concessions**. The Revenue does not have to apply these, but does so. There is no appeal against the Revenue's decision in cases involving extra-statutory concessions, so activities where tax relief is granted by concession must precisely follow the rules [see for example **52.7.1.1**].

52.1.1.2
Tax recovery

As well as exemptions from income or corporation tax on most of their income, charities are able to recover tax paid by individual donors on donations made under gift aid [see **46.2**].

Under the gift aid scheme, organisations or businesses which owe corporation tax on their profits can donate some or all of the profit and the tax due on it to a charity. The charity is given the full amount, including tax, and does not have to recover the tax from the Inland Revenue.

52.1.2
Who is liable?

The liability for an organisation's tax payments depends on the organisation's legal structure and on how it is treated under tax law.

52.1.2.1
Incorporated organisations

A corporate body (company or industrial and provident society) is liable for its own tax. Individual members of the governing body or organisation are unlikely to be held personally liable for taxes unless they have been involved in tax evasion or fraud, or are negligent in dealing with the organisation's tax affairs.

52.1.2.2
Trusts

In a body set up as a trust [see **1.3**], the trustees are liable for the trust's taxes. They could be held personally liable if the trust does not or cannot pay.

52.1.2.3
Unincorporated associations

Unincorporated associations [see **1.2**] are treated in the same way as companies for most tax purposes. Tax assessments are issued in the name of the organisation and in the first instance the association, rather than the individuals involved, is liable for its taxes.

Income and Corporation Taxes Act 1988 s.832(1)

But unlike a company or IPS, the members of the association do not have limited liability. Unpaid tax may be recovered from the treasurer or another officer or member of the governing body, who then has a right to be indemnified (repaid) by the association [see **19.6.7**] if the association has adequate assets.   *Taxes Management Act 1970 s.108*

52.1.2.4
Branches

Whether a branch or the parent organisation is liable to pay tax depends on the nature of the relationship. If the branch is legally separate [see **9.2.2**] it is liable for tax. If it is legally part of the parent body, the parent is ultimately liable for the branch's tax obligations.

52.1.2.5
Charities

A charity is unlikely to have to pay income or corporation tax on income or profits, or capital gains tax on the sale of assets. If it does owe these or other taxes, liability depends on its legal structure [see above].

The members of a charity's governing body are under an obligation to recover all taxes due to the charity, and not to pay tax unnecessarily [see **13.3.5**]. If they fail to fulfil these obligations they could be personally required by the Charity Commission or court to indemnify (repay) the charity for its loss. This is unlikely if the trustees have acted honestly, reasonably and with reasonable care. Trustee indemnity insurance [see **20.10**] may possibly provide cover in the rare situations where a trustee is made liable.

52.2
INCOME AND
CORPORATION TAX

The principal direct taxes are:

- **income tax** on the income of individuals and trusts, covered by the **Income and Corporation Taxes Act 1988**;

- **capital gains tax** on the capital gains of individuals and trusts, covered by the **Taxation of Chargeable Gains Act 1992** [see **52.2.4**];

- **corporation tax** on the profits and capital gains of companies, industrial and provident societies and unincorporated associations, covered by the **Income and Corporation Taxes Act 1988**.

Charitable organisations are generally exempt from these taxes.

52.2.1
Tax rates and
schedules

The rates for income tax, capital gains tax and corporation tax are subject to alteration in each year's Finance Act. Current rates are available from the Inland Revenue or on its website.

For corporation and income tax, profits or income are worked out differently depending on their source. Each source is defined in the legislation as a **schedule**, with some schedules subdivided into **cases**. Profits or gains from a trade or profession, for example, are assessed under Schedule D cases I and II, rents are assessed under schedule A or schedule D case VI, and income from securities is assessed under schedule C, schedule D case IV or schedule F.

52.2.1.1
Companies, IPSs
and associations

There are five rates of **corporation tax** (2001-02) for companies, industrial and provident societies and associations:

- starting rate (10%) on the first £10,000 of taxable profit;

- a marginal rate of 22.5% on profits between £10,000 and £50,000;

- small company rate (20%) on profits from £50,001 to £300,000;

- a marginal rate of 32.5% on profits between £301,000 and £1.5 million;

- main rate (30%) on profits over £1.5 million.

For groups of companies or organisations where one controls the other or both are under common control [see **9.6**], the figures of £300,000 and £1.5 million are divided between the organisations in the group, so the higher tax rates become payable sooner.

52.2.2
Calculating taxable
income or profits

Charitable organisations are unlikely to have to pay income tax or corporation tax, but non-charities which receive income from sources other than donations and grants may well have to, and trading companies will have to pay corporation tax on any taxable profits which are not donated to a charity under gift aid.

Income for the purpose of calculating taxable profit is not the same as income for accounting purposes. Non-taxable income [see **52.3**], such as grants and donations, is included in the ordinary annual accounts, but is excluded from tax accounts. The situation is even more confusing because charities which prepare accrual accounts [see **50.2.10**] must show all **incoming resources**, including gifts in kind and intangible income, in annual accounts, but these are not shown in tax accounts.

Similarly, some **expenditure** may not be able to be set against taxable income. This expenditure is not shown in the tax accounts, but must be shown in the ordinary accounts.

Complex rules govern what is or is not a proper deduction or expenditure for tax purpose, and advice should be sought before drawing up tax accounts. At the time of writing (early 2001) the rules on drawing up accounts for tax purposes and for accounting purposes were being simplified and brought into line with each other.

**52.2.3
Losses**

If a trade makes a loss, the loss may be set against profits in any area of operation in that accounting period. Any balance may be carried back against profits in accounting periods within the previous three years. If there is still a balance or no claim is made, the loss may be set against later profits in the same area of trade.

Income and Corporation Taxes Act 1988 ss.393, 393A, 396

**52.2.4
Capital gains**

A **capital** (or **chargeable**) **gain** arises when an asset which has increased in value is given away, sold, exchanged or disposed of in any way, other than in the course of a trade. (In a trade, the sale gives rise to profit rather than capital gain.) Tax is charged on the increase in value, with an allowance for gain due to inflation.

Companies, industrial and provident societies and unincorporated associations pay tax on capital gains as part of corporation tax. Bodies set up as trusts pay capital gains tax. Charitable organisations are generally exempt from tax on capital gains [see **52.7.11**].

**52.2.5
Submitting returns**

Under **corporation tax self-assessment**, an organisation with taxable profits or chargeable gains estimates and pays its tax not later than nine months after the end of its accounting period and files a statutory return within 12 months from the end of the period. Automatic penalties apply for late returns. The accounting period usually ends on the organisation's **accounting reference date** [see **50.2.1** and **50.3.1**].

If the estimate is too low, the organisation has to pay the unpaid tax plus interest. If the estimate is too high, the Inland Revenue makes a repayment with interest. A return must be filed even if the organisation does not actually have to pay tax on its profits because it has donated all of them to a charity under the gift aid scheme.

Trusts which have taxable income file income tax returns for each tax year (6 April to 5 April).

Charities with no taxable profits or chargeable gains do not need to submit a tax return unless they are sent one by the Inland Revenue.

**52.3
NON-TAXABLE
INCOME**

Certain income—donations, grants, some membership subscriptions—is not subject to tax regardless of whether the recipient organisation is charitable or non-charitable. Specialist advice may be necessary to ensure the organisation is clear about what is and is not taxable.

**52.3.1
Donations**

Money, property, goods, services, facilities, publicity or anything else received as a **donation** is not subject to corporation or income tax—provided the donor receives nothing more than a simple acknowledgement. If the donor receives a benefit of any kind or if for any reason the donation is not 'pure profit' for the organisation, the donation may be subject to corporation or income tax (and possibly also VAT; see **53.3.1**).

The status of 'donation' is not jeopardised if the recipient organisation provides a sticker or small 'flag' to acknowledge the donation, a small acknowledgement in an annual report or other publications, or a small plaque which is clearly an acknowledgement of a gift rather than publicity for the donor. Beyond this, the boundaries become unclear. Specialist advice about the tax and VAT implications should be sought if a donor requires anything more than a simple acknowledgement, or before seeking 'donations' which give some sort of benefit to the donors.

Charities can maximise the value of money donations by encouraging the use of gift aid [see **46.2**].

52.3.2
Sale of donated goods

The sale of donated goods is exempt from corporation and income tax in the same way as direct cash donations. In addition the sale of donated goods is generally, but not always, zero rated for VAT [see **53.5.1**]. This is not the same as being exempt from VAT.

Profits from the sale of bought-in goods are subject to corporation or income tax [see **52.4.1**], but may fall within the exemption for small-scale trading [see **52.7.2**]. Sales of bought-in goods may also be subject to VAT [see **53.5.3**]. Organisations which sell both donated and bought-in goods must have adequate systems to keep the income separate.

52.3.2.1
Goods donated to charity and sold by non-charity

A potential complication arises when goods donated to a charity are sold by its non-charitable trading company [see **chapter 47**]. Because of the trustees' duty to safeguard a charity's assets [see **13.3.5**], the charity cannot give away an asset—the donated goods—to a non-charity, even where the charity owns the non-charity and will eventually get all or most of its profits. Options include:

- goods can be donated to and sold by the charity;

- goods can be donated to and sold by the trading company;

- goods donated to the charity can be sold by the trading company as agent for the charity.

Where goods are donated to the trading company, it should be made clear on signs or other notices that all goods are donated to the trading company which donates all (or some) of its profits to the charity.

If the agency arrangement is used, advice should be taken about the VAT implications.

52.3.2.2
Some profit to donor

The sale of 'donated' goods where some of the income is paid to the donor and the voluntary organisation keeps the remainder (for example some auctions and nearly new shops) does not generally qualify for the reliefs available for donated goods, but may in some cases. A voluntary organisation should not enter into such arrangements without taking advice from its solicitor, its accountant or Inland Revenue (Charities).

52.3.3
Sponsorship

The term **sponsorship** is used in many ways. Sponsoring someone to do something such as running the marathon is a donation. Sponsorship by a business or individual where the sponsor receives only a simple acknowledgement, such as a small logo on an annual report, is also a donation, and is not subject to corporation or income tax. But if the sponsor receives significant publicity or any other benefit as a result of its sponsorship—for example the organisation using the sponsor's logo or corporate colours in a significant way or mentioning the sponsor's products or services, or by the sponsor getting use of the organisation's logo—the sponsorship income may be classed as taxable trading income [see **52.4.1**]. It may also be subject to VAT [see **53.3.1**].

To reduce liability for tax and VAT it may be possible to arrange for the sponsor to divide the payment, making a straightforward commercial payment to cover the value of the benefits and a donation to cover the non-business element of the sponsorship.

Allowing a product to be branded with the organisation's trademarked logo not only has tax and VAT implications; it may also involve the organisation in liability for faults in the product under product liability legislation [see **18.7.3**]. Agreements for product sponsorship therefore need very careful drafting.

**52.3.4
Grants**

Grants received by voluntary organisations are not subject to corporation/income tax, unless they are to subsidise a non-charitable trading activity [see **52.4.1**] such as a charity shop or fundraising event.

A 'grant' which is actually a payment in exchange for a service could be considered by the Inland Revenue to be trading income [see **48.1** for problems in distinguishing between grants and payments for services]. Unless the service falls within the primary purpose of the charity carrying it out [see **52.6.1**], the 'grant' could be subject to corporation or income tax. Even if it is primary purpose and is not subject to tax, it could be subject to VAT [see **53.5.3**].

**52.3.5
Membership
subscriptions**

Membership subscriptions paid to voluntary organisations, whether charitable or non-charitable, are exempt from corporation or income tax provided they are basically a donation to the organisation, entitling the member only to rights under the constitution such as the right to attend and vote at general meetings [see **10.1.4**].

If the subscription entitles the member to any benefits, it is a trading activity [see **52.4.1**]. Any profit is potentially taxable, but there are a number of exemptions for both charities and non-charities. If some of the benefits are exempt and some not, the portion of the subscription that covers the non-exempt benefits is taxable.

Special rules apply to subscriptions to housing associations, trade associations, professional associations and some other bodies.

Even subscriptions which are exempt from corporation and income tax may in some situations be subject to VAT [see **53.4.11**].

**52.3.5.1
Charities**

If a membership subscription is paid to a charity, any profit is exempt from tax provided the benefits are directly related to the charity's **primary purpose** [see **52.6.1**], for example being able to attend arts workshops run by an arts charity, and the profits are used for the charity's charitable purposes.

Membership subscriptions to a charity can be paid with a gift aid donation provided the value of any benefits is not more than the allowed proportion of the donation [see **46.2**].

**52.3.5.2
Non-charities**

If a membership subscription is paid to a non-charity where the members have a constitutional right to share in the profits of the organisation, the membership subscription may be exempt from tax as **mutual trading** [see **52.8.1**]. Otherwise any profit on the subscription is subject to tax. Non-charities in this situation may want to structure their subscription rates in a way that ensures no taxable profit arises.

**52.4
TAXABLE INCOME**

Apart from genuine donations, grants and the 'donation' element of membership subscriptions, virtually all income received by voluntary organisations, including charities, is potentially subject to corporation, income and/or capital gains tax. This includes income from trading [see below], property [see **52.7.4**], bank interest and investment income [see **52.7.6**], sale of assets [see **52.2.4**] and other sources.

However there are substantial exemptions from tax for charities, and in some cases for other organisations [see **52.5**]. These exemptions generally apply only if the income or profits are used for charitable purposes [see **52.5.2**].

**52.4.1
Trading**

In tax terms, **trading** is defined as 'every trade, manufacture, adventure or concern in the nature of trade'.

Income and Corporation Taxes Act 1988 s.832(1)

This far-from-helpful definition is an old one, and has been subject to much litigation about what is or is not truly a trade. Whatever its imperfections, this definition is likely to cover most situations in which a voluntary organisation charges for goods, services, facilities, publicity, use of its name or logo, admission to events or other benefits, or is paid to provide these.

Many activities which are not typically thought of as trading are in fact trading activities, for example making a charge for photocopying or training courses, charging day centre users for meals or activities, or making a management charge for helping an organisation or project. For more about what is and is not trading, see **47.1.1**.

Most trading carried out by charities, and some carried out by non-charitable voluntary organisations, is covered by an exemption or extra-statutory concession [see **52.5**]. But where there is no exemption or ESC, all profit arising from the trading is subject to tax. This applies regardless of whether:

- the trading is intended primarily to meet a community need, primarily to raise money for the voluntary organisation, or both;
- the organisation making the profit is charitable or non-charitable;
- the price or fee is set with the intention of breaking even, making a small profit or making a substantial profit; *or*
- payment is made by the end user or by a third party.

52.4.1.1
Reducing tax liability

Where its trading falls outside the exemptions and extra-statutory concessions [see **52.5**], a charity should generally set up a non-charitable **trading company**, which donates some or all of its profits and the tax due on those profits to the charity under gift aid [see **47.7**].

Similarly, a non-charitable voluntary organisation might be able to set up a charity to undertake the properly charitable aspects of its work [see **9.6.2**]. The non-charity could then donate some of its profits to the charity under gift aid, and thus avoid tax on those profits.

52.4.1.2
Volunteer time and gifts in kind

If an organisation has taxable income, it may be able to set against it the value of volunteer time, rent-free accommodation, free services etc which it has received and would otherwise have had to pay for in order to carry out the taxable activities. Advice should be taken from the auditor or local tax office before making any such deduction.

52.4.1.3
Voluntary donations

Where trading is not eligible for an exemption or extra-statutory concession, tax can be reduced by charging only a small amount for the goods, service or event (thus minimising taxable profits), and asking for a supplementary voluntary donation. To be non-taxable the donation element must genuinely be voluntary, so cannot be obligatory or entitle the donor to additional benefits. Specific rules apply where a voluntary donation is suggested for a fundraising event [see **52.7.1.2**].

52.5
ELIGIBILITY FOR CHARITY EXEMPTIONS

Apart from donations, grants etc [see **52.3**], a charity's income or profit is taxable unless:

- a tax exemption or extra-statutory concession applies to that type of income or profit; *and*
- the income or profit which would otherwise be taxable is used only for the charity's charitable purposes.

Trading or other activities which are not exempt from tax should be carried out through a trading company [see **47.2**].

52.5.1
Charities and charitable purposes

For tax purposes, a charity is defined as 'any body of persons or trust established for charitable purposes only'.

Income and Corporation Taxes Act 1988 s.506(1)

A body registered with the Charity Commission is automatically treated by the Inland Revenue as a charity. *Charities Act 1993 s.4(1)*

A charity registered with the Commission which has taxable income or will recover tax through gift aid should apply to Inland Revenue (Charities) [see end of chapter] for an **Inland Revenue charity registration number**. This is different from the charity registration number given by the Commission.

Charitable organisations which are exempt or excepted from the need to register with the Charity Commission [see **7.1.2** and **7.1.3**] apply to Inland Revenue (Charities) for recognition of their charitable status and an Inland Revenue charity registration number.

52.5.2
Exemptions and extra-statutory concessions

The tax exemptions for charities are set out in the **Income and Corporation Taxes Act 1988** s.505 and in various **extra-statutory concessions** [see **52.6**]. These cover most potential sources of income for charities and charitable purposes. But the exemptions are specific and carefully defined, and do not cover all sources of income.

The organisation's solicitor or accountant or the Inland Revenue (Charities) [see end of chapter] should be consulted if there is any doubt at all about whether income is eligible for exemption.

52.5.3
Qualifying expenditure

To qualify for exemption, the taxable income or profit must be used only for the charity's charitable purposes. This is called **qualifying expenditure**.   *Income and Corporation Taxes Act 1988 s.506*

Qualifying expenditure includes:
- costs of the charity's charitable activities;
- the purchase of assets to be used to further its charitable activities;
- grants from the charity to another charity to fulfil the charitable purposes of the donor charity;
- reasonable administrative, management and fundraising costs;
- interest or other finance costs on the above;
- qualifying investments and qualifying loans [see below].

Payments to bodies outside the UK are qualifying expenditure only if the charity has taken reasonable steps to ensure that the payment will be used for charitable purposes [see **52.10.3**].   *s.506(3)*

Income or profit used for **non-qualifying expenditure** is subject to tax. There are detailed procedures for determining tax liability if some income is used for qualifying and some for non-qualifying purposes.

52.5.3.1
Endangering tax relief

Tax relief may be endangered if:
- the Inland Revenue considers the level of administrative, management or fundraising expenses is unreasonable;
- the income is used to raise further money in a way which is not itself charitable or eligible for tax relief, for example by subsidising fundraising events or funding a trading subsidiary [see **47.4**]; *or*
- the income is simply accumulated because no immediate use can be found for it (rather than being accumulated for a clearly defined objective within the charitable purposes).

52.5.4
Qualifying investments and loans

To be eligible for tax relief, surplus income must be invested in specified investments or loans. These **qualifying investments** are:
- bank deposit accounts and building society accounts;
- local authority and government bonds;
- shares and securities of companies quoted on a recognised stock exchange;
- unit trusts;
- interests in land (excluding mortgages);
- common investment funds and common deposit funds established for charities;

- investments made for the benefit of the charity and not for the avoidance of tax, and approved by the Board of the Inland Revenue.

Qualifying loans include loans to another UK charity to be used for charitable purposes, loans to beneficiaries of the charity which are made in furtherance of the charity's purposes, and other loans approved by the Inland Revenue.

All investments made by a charity must be within its investment powers [see **54.1**].

**52.5.4.1
Non-qualifying
investments and loans**

If a surplus is used in any way other than a qualifying investment or loan, tax relief on the income used for those purposes may be denied or restricted. The most common non-qualifying investments or loans are those to an unlisted company, typically the charity's own trading subsidiary [see **47.4.4** and **47.4.5**].

Income and Corporation Taxes Act 1988 sch.20

**52.5.4.2
De minimis exception**

A *de minimis* ('too small to bother about') exception applies to charities whose total income and gains are less than £10,000 in the accounting period. They are eligible for tax exemption even if they invest in non-qualifying investments or loans.   *s.505(3)*

**52.6
PRIMARY PURPOSE
TRADING**

The exemptions and extra-statutory concessions are very specific and apply only if all the relevant rules are met, and only if the relevant income is used for charitable purposes [see **52.5.3**].

**52.6.1
Primary purpose**

Profits from trading by a charity are exempt from corporation/income tax if the trade is actually carrying out a **primary purpose** of the charity.   *s.505(1)(e)(i)*

Primary purpose is defined by reference to the charity's objects as set out in its governing document [see **5.4.2**]. Primary purpose trading must *directly* achieve these objects, so the wording of the objects clause is crucial. The exemption applies, for example, to:

- charging beneficiaries or service users for charitable services or for goods directly related to the charity's purposes (such as selling mobility aids to people with mobility disabilities);
- contracting with a local authority to provide services to clients;
- a council for voluntary service whose objects are to improve the efficiency of other charities charging consultancy fees for services provided to those charities;
- an arts education charity selling art publications;
- a heritage charity charging admission to its properties.

'Means to an end' trading ('the profits from this activity will allow us to carry out our primary purpose') is not covered under this exemption, but might be covered under extra-statutory concession C4 for fundraising events [see **52.7.1.1**], or under the exemption for small-scale trading [see **52.7.2**].

Even if it is exempt from corporation and income tax, primary purpose trading may be subject to VAT [see **53.4.1**].

**52.6.2
Work carried out by
beneficiaries**

Another form of exempt trading is where the work in connection with the trade is carried out mainly by the charity's beneficiaries, and the profits are applied solely to the charity's purposes.   *s.505(1)(e)(ii)*

This exemption covers the sale of goods produced mainly by beneficiaries, or charges for services provided mainly by beneficiaries. 'Mainly' means 'probably...more than half'. The 'probably' means that advice should be sought if there is any doubt.

Fawcett Properties Ltd v Buckingham County Council [1960] 3 All ER 503

Examples are a café run by a charity set up to work with people with learning difficulties and staffed primarily by people with learning difficulties, or the sale by a refugee support charity of goods made by unemployed refugees.

The provisions on trading ancillary to the primary purpose and the *de minimis* provisions for non-primary purpose trading [see below] apply.

Even if the trading activity is exempt from corporation and income tax, it may be subject to VAT [see **53.3.2**].

52.6.3
Ancillary trading

The primary purpose exemption applies as well to trading activities which are not in themselves primary purpose, but which are undertaken as an integral part of carrying out the primary purpose or work by beneficiaries. This is called trading **ancillary** to the carrying out of a primary purpose. Examples are a bar or café open only to people attending the charity's charitable activities or using its charitable services, or renting accommodation to students attending a college.

52.6.4
De minimis
exception

Some trading activities are partly primary purpose, carried out by beneficiaries or ancillary to this, and partly non-primary purpose (perhaps because the activity is not within the charity's primary purpose or ancillary to it, or because the activity is primary purpose but the users are not the charity's proper beneficiaries). The non-primary purpose element is not eligible for tax exemption, but in practice a small amount of such trading is ignored by the Inland Revenue.

The Revenue's guidance on this *de minimis* ('too small to bother about') provision is that the income:

- must arise from trading which is not clearly separable from the primary purpose trading;

- the annual turnover (pre-tax income) on the non-primary purpose trading must be less than £50,000; *and*

- the annual turnover on the non-primary purpose trading must not be more than 10% of the total turnover from primary and non-primary purpose trading combined. This total does not include income from donations, grants and other non-trading income.

If the concession is not available, the non-primary purpose trading should be carried out through a trading company [see **47.2**]. If this is not done, the charity will be liable for tax on the profit from *all* the trading, not only the non-primary purpose portion.

52.6.5
Mixed trading

The boundary between primary purpose trading, ancillary trading and other trading depends entirely on the wording of the charity's objects and the nature of the trading. For example, for a charitable theatre:

- charging admission to its plays is primary purpose trading;

- the sale of pre-theatre drinks, programmes and ice cream to theatre-goers is ancillary to the primary purpose;

- selling drinks to non-theatre-goers before the play is non-primary purpose but is likely to be covered by the *de minimis* provisions;

- opening the bar all day or when there are no performances is non-primary purpose trading, but may be covered by the exemption for small-scale trading [see **52.7.2**]. If it does not fall within the exemption, it should be carried out through a trading company.

Inland Revenue (Charities) [see end of chapter] can advise.

52.7
OTHER
EXEMPTIONS FOR
CHARITABLE
PURPOSES

As with primary purpose trading [see above], other tax exemptions for charities apply only if the requirements are strictly met and the income is used solely for charitable purposes [see **52.5.3**]. These exemptions cover fundraising events, small-scale trading, lotteries, and income from property and investments.

52.7.1
Fundraising events

Fundraising events are a form of trading even if the money is being raised for charitable purposes, but the profits may be exempt from tax under extra-statutory concession C4 [see below] or the exemption for small-scale trading [see **52.7.2**]. Where the profits from a fundraising event are taxable it may be possible to reduce tax by asking for part of the fee or admission charge as a voluntary donation [see **52.7.1.2**].

An event which is exempt from tax under ESC C4 is also exempt from VAT [see **53.4.13**]. Other fundraising events may be subject to VAT, even if they are exempt from corporation and income tax [see **53.3.2**].

52.7.1.1
Extra-statutory concession C4

Extra-statutory concession (ESC) C4 is based on exemption criteria under VAT law. Under these rules, profits **of fundraising events** such as carnivals, concerts, discos, dinner dances, film shows, exhibitions, sports events, dinners, auctions of bought-in goods, bazaars, jumble sales and car boot sales are not taxed provided:

- no more than 15 similar events are held in one location in the organisation's financial year; *or*
- if more than 15 similar events are held in the same location, the gross income for each is below £1,000 per week.

Value Added Tax Act 1994 sch.9 gp.12

ESC C4 applies to events organised not only by charities, but also by other voluntary organisations. Detailed information is available from the Inland Revenue (Charities) and Customs and Excise [see end of chapter]. Decisions about eligibility for this concession are made by Customs and Excise rather than by the Inland Revenue.

Specific premises such as theatres or sports arenas are separate locations. If events are held in general purpose premises such as community centres or village halls, the events are in separate locations if the venues are in different villages or boroughs. For events on the internet, the charity's entire website is treated as one 'location'.

Each type of event is considered separately, so it would be acceptable to have 15 fetes, 15 concerts and 15 firework displays in a year, repeating this across the country or even across a county if the locations were sufficiently widely dispersed. And if each type of event did not bring in gross takings of more than £1,000, more than 15 of that type of event could be held in the same location.

A two- or three-day event with a single admission ticket is only one event. But a series of events on separate dates count as separate events, even if a season ticket can be purchased. If the same event, such as a concert or theatre performance, is repeated on several days, each one counts towards the 15.

The concession applies not only to profits from the event itself but also from advertising, programmes, souvenirs, raffle tickets, refreshments and other incidental activities, provided the source of income is genuinely incidental to the event and is not a separate profit-making activity. In considering this, Customs and Excise looks at the amount of income from that activity relative to income from the main event.

Even if the event meets all the above criteria, it might not be eligible for the concession if it is commercially organised, very large and likely to make large profits. An organisation arranging this sort of event, or any other where it is not clear that ESC C4 applies, should consult a Customs and Excise VAT office.

52.7.1.2
Voluntary donations

Where trading income is too high to qualify for tax exemption under ESC4, it may be possible to reduce it by charging a limited amount for the event, and suggesting that people make a voluntary donation (which would not count towards trading income). Such donation must genuinely be voluntary, so:

- it must be clearly stated on all publicity material, including tickets, that anyone paying the minimum amount will be admitted to the event or will receive the stated goods or service even if they do not pay the donation element;
- the additional payment must not give the person any particular benefit (such as a better seat at a concert);
- donors must be free to choose how much additional to give, even if the organisation has indicated a desired amount;
- for film or theatre performances, concerts, sporting fixtures and similar events, the minimum charge must not be less than the usual price for a commercial event of the same type; *and*
- for dances, dinners and similar events, the sum of the basic minimum charges made must not be less than the total costs incurred in arranging the event.

52.7.2
Small-scale trading

Trading activities which are not events are exempt from corporation and income tax provided:

- they are carried out by a charity which uses the profits solely for its charitable purposes; *and*
- the total turnover from all the activities does not exceed the annual turnover limit, or if the total turnover exceeds the limit, the charity had a reasonable expectation that it would not do so.

Finance Act 2000 s.46

The annual turnover limit is the larger of:

- £5,000; *or*
- 25% of the charity's annual incoming resources, subject to a maximum limit of £50,000.

Incoming resources means the total receipts of the charity from all sources [see **50.2.10**].

If trading income exceeds the turnover limit it may still be exempt from tax if the charity can show that at the start of the tax year, it expected the turnover to be lower than it turned out to be, or it expected the charity's incoming resources to be higher than they turned out to be. The Inland Revenue will look at budgets, relevant figure for previous years, minutes of relevant meetings and similar documentation.

52.7.3
Lotteries and competitions

Proceeds from charity lotteries (including raffles, tombolas, draws etc) are exempt from corporation and income tax provided:

- the lottery complies with the **Lotteries and Amusements Act 1976** as a small lottery or society lottery [see **45.6**]; *and*
- the income is used solely for charitable purposes.

Finance Act 1995 s.138

The exemption applies to lotteries run by a charity, and society lotteries run by a charity's trading subsidiary where the charity is registered as the society under the Lotteries Act.

Lottery ticket sales are exempt from VAT [see **53.4.14**].

Proceeds from a competition, where participants win on the basis of merit or skill, are subject to corporation or income tax and may also be subject to VAT [see **53.5.3**].

52.7.4
Income from property

Tax is normally payable on rent and other profits arising from land and buildings. But rents or profits from land or buildings vested [see **18.4**] in trustees for charitable purposes are exempt from corporation and income tax provided the income is used for charitable purposes only.

Income and Corporation Taxes Act 1988 s.505(1)(a)

Strictly speaking this exemption does not apply to land owned by charitable companies, because such land is not 'vested in trustees for charitable purposes'. But in practice the relief can be claimed by all charities.

This exemption does not apply to capital sums received from selling or developing land [see **52.2.4** and **52.7.5**].

Even if a charity is exempt from corporation or income tax on rents or other income from its property, the provision of other services, such as room bookings or conference facilities, may be subject to tax as a trading activity unless it falls within an exemption [see **52.7.2**].

Rents and other property income may be subject to VAT [see **53.4.16**].

52.7.5
Development of land

Profits from the development of land may be subject to tax, even for charities. Some exemption may be obtained by transferring the land to a company wholly owned by the charity or making other arrangements under the **Income and Corporation Taxes Act 1988** s.776. This is a highly specialist area requiring legal and financial advice.

52.7.6
Investment income

Interest on **deposits** at UK banks and building societies is subject to tax, which is generally deducted before the organisation receives the interest. Interest on **government bonds** and similar securities is also generally paid net of tax. **Dividends** from UK companies are paid net of tax [see **52.7.6.2**].

52.7.6.1
Exemptions for charities

Provided the income arises from a **qualifying investment** [see **52.5.4**] and is used for charitable purposes only, charities are eligible for exemption from corporation and income tax on interest, annuities, and dividends on shares assessed under tax schedule C [see **52.2.1** for explanation of schedules], yearly interest and other annual payments assessed under schedule D, and any distribution assessed under schedule F.

Income and Corporation Taxes Act 1988 s.505(1)(c)

The exemption also covers bank interest even if not yearly, interest and dividends payable gross by building societies, and profits from discounting transactions (where the investor receives a discount rather than interest) assessed under schedule D. *Finance Act 1996 s.146*

Under these exemptions a charity may ask a bank or building society to pay interest gross, without deduction of tax, and may ask the Bank of England to pay interest gross on government bonds.

If tax is deducted at source before the charity receives the income, the charity must recover the tax from the Inland Revenue.

52.7.6.2
<u>Tax on dividends</u>

When UK companies pay dividends and other distributions, they pay **advance corporation tax**. In the past, recipients of the distribution received a **tax credit** to show the tax had been paid, and non-taxpayers such as charities could recover all or some of the tax.

Tax recovery for most recipients ended in 1997, and for charities in 1999. But charities are eligible for special compensation payments, representing a decreasing proportion of the distributions they receive, until tax year 2003-04. Information about this transitional relief is available from Inland Revenue (Charities).

52.7.6.3
Places of worship

There is exemption from tax under schedule C in respect of interest, annuities, or dividends on shares which are in the names of trustees and are intended to be used solely for the repairs of any building used solely for worship, provided the income is actually applied to those purposes.

Income and Corporation Taxes Act 1988 s.505(1)(d)

52.7.7
Annual payments

Annual payments are exempt from tax provided:

- the payment is annual (even, in some cases, if the money is paid at intervals of less than a year);

- it is pure income or profit in the hand of the recipient with no element of current cost needed to generate the income; *and*
- the money is used for charitable purposes.

Annual payments include interest, some royalties [see **52.7.9**], and a range of other payments. Information is available from solicitors, accountants and the Inland Revenue (Charities).

Income and Corporation Taxes Act 1988 s.505(1)(c)

52.7.8
Payments from one charity to another

If a charity receives from another charity a payment which is not for goods or services or does not cover the full cost of the goods or services paid for, and if the income is not exempt from tax under any of the other exemptions, it is treated as an annual payment and is exempt in that way. *s.505(2)*

52.7.9
Intellectual property

Income from a **licence** to exploit an organisation's intellectual property, for example the right to use its name, logo or copyright, may be subject to tax as a trading profit or may be classed as an annual payment [see **52.7.7**] and thus qualify for relief if paid to a charity. This is a difficult area and advice should be taken in each case.

Lawrence v Inland Revenue Commissioners [1940] 23 TC 333

Copyright royalties forming part of the income of a publishing trade are taxed as trading profits. Other copyright royalties, for example inherited copyright, are normally taxed as an annual payment and are eligible for relief if paid to a charity. Income from **royalties on patents** is not eligible for tax relief even when paid to a charity.

Even where they might be exempt from tax, royalties and other intellectual property income may be subject to VAT [see **53.5.3**].

52.7.10
Overseas income

Income paid to UK charities from abroad may be exempt as yearly interest and other annual payments [see **52.7.7**], or primary purpose trading [see **52.6.1** and **52.6.2**]. In practice the Inland Revenue also exempts other overseas income, particularly rents and bank interest.

A UK charity which receives income from which foreign taxes have been withheld may be able to recover the tax from the relevant tax authorities. Inland Revenue (Charities) [see end of chapter] can advise on this, and can provide standard repayment claim forms.

Income from investment in offshore funds is exempt from tax if used for charitable purposes. *Income and Corporation Taxes Act 1988 s.761(6)*

52.7.11
Capital gains

A capital or chargeable gain arises when an asset which has increased in value is disposed of [see **52.2.4**]. Capital gains by charities are exempt from tax provided the gain is used for charitable purposes. The exemption is available even if the remaining proceeds from the sale (those additional to the gain) are used for non-qualifying purposes [see **52.5.3**].

Taxation of Chargeable Gains Act 1992 s.256

Where the asset sold forms part of the charity's permanent endowment [see **13.3.5**] the terms of the endowment may prevent the charity from using the gain directly for charitable purposes, requiring it to be reinvested in similar assets. This does not negate exemption.

52.8
TAX EXEMPTIONS FOR NON-CHARITIES

Non-charitable organisations pay corporation tax under corporation tax self-assessment on virtually all their income or profits unless it arises from donations, grants, the sale of donated goods or the non-taxable element of membership subscriptions [see **52.3**]. Non-charities are also exempt from corporation tax on:

- mutual trading [see below];
- fundraising events covered by extra-statutory concession C4, provided the profits are all used for charitable purposes [see **52.7.1.1**];

- lotteries, where the non-charity is a charity's trading company [see **52.7.3**].

52.8.1
Mutual trading

In some non-charitable membership organisations the members are entitled, under the constitution, to a share of the organisation's profits. Where this applies and the members pay for goods or services from the organisation in their capacity as members, it is called **mutual trading**. Examples might be the sale of drinks and food to the members of a members' club, or a sport club's fees for members to use its facilities.

Even if the members do not actually take their share in the profits, the profits from mutual trading are not subject to corporation tax.

If non-members pay for goods or services, or if the members pay for goods or services which are not directly related to their involvement as members (for example hiring the facilities for a private party, or buying t-shirts or mugs), the profits are taxable. Sales to signed-in guests are sometimes allowed tax-free by concession, provided the organisation is only open to members and guests, and the guests are not allowed to buy alcohol.

Even if mutual trading is not subject to corporation tax, it may be subject to VAT [see **53.3.2**].

52.8.2
Further reliefs

A few exemptions and concessions are available to specific types of non-charitable voluntary organisation.

52.8.2.1
Industrial and provident societies

Under **extra-statutory concession C5,** industrial and provident societies which have made a trading loss in an earlier year can offset the loss against investment income arising in a later year.

52.8.2.2
Scientific research associations

Some non-charitable scientific research associations can claim most of the same tax reliefs as charities. The status of these bodies is determined by the Department of Trade and Industry.

Income and Corporation Taxes Act 1988 s.508

52.9
TAX AND OUTGOINGS

Tax is affected not only by the source of income and whether the organisation is or is not charitable, but also by the way income is used. Tax exemptions for charities are available only if the relevant income is used for **qualifying expenditure** [see **52.5.3**], and for all organisations complex rules govern which expenditures can be set against income. This section looks at some of the tax issues relating to an organisation's expenditure or other outgoings.

52.9.1
Running costs of membership organisations

The running costs of membership organisations are assumed to be covered by membership subscriptions. As this income is not subject to tax [see **52.3.5**], the costs of running the organisation cannot be claimed as a tax deduction.

If the organisation receives taxable income from trading activities, the costs of running these activities can be deducted from the trading income.

52.9.2
Grants to other organisations

Grants made by a charity to another voluntary organisation are generally outside the scope of tax [see **52.3.4**], provided the grant is within the donor charity's primary purpose. But if a grant is made for any other purpose or in order to avoid tax, it will not be eligible for the exemptions and the income used for the grant will subject to corporation or income tax.

52.9.3
Donations and grants to individuals

In considering donations or grants to individuals, attention must be given to the tax consequences both for the donating organisation and for the recipient.

52.9.3.1
One-off payments

One-off payments by charities to individuals—for example, a grant to purchase essential furniture—are normally treated as donations with no tax consequences for the donating organisation or the recipient.

52.9.3.2
Regular payments

Regular payments are normally treated as income in the hands of the recipients, and the recipients may have to pay income tax if the payments plus their other taxable income exceeds their personal allowance.

If the organisation making the regular payments is a charity and the payments are made for its charitable purposes, payments will have no tax consequences for the charity. If the organisation is not a charity but is a club, society, residents' association or similar body run for the benefit of its own members, regular payments have no tax consequences for the organisation if they are made out of the organisation's untaxed income (received from subscriptions, mutual trading, donations etc). If the payments are made out of taxable income (received, for example, from trading activities), they cannot be set against the income as a way of reducing corporation tax liability.

52.9.3.3
Payments to people receiving state benefits

Where a grant or other financial support is given to individuals receiving welfare benefits, careful thought needs to be given to the impact of such payments on their welfare benefit entitlement. In general people receiving income-related benefits can receive up to £20 per week (as at 1/4/01) as a charitable payment, without it affecting their benefit. Advice on this complex topic can be obtained from solicitors specialising in welfare benefits law and from organisations such as the Child Poverty Action Group and the National Council for One Parent Families.

52.9.3.4
Scholarships

Unlike most regular payments to individuals, scholarships are generally not taxed as income. *Income and Corporation Taxes Act 1988 s.331*

However, if a company sets up an educational trust to provide scholarships for children of employees, the award is assessed as a benefit to the parent and he or she will be taxed on it. *s.165*

52.9.3.5
Research grants and prizes

The tax treatment of research grants depends on the circumstances, including the terms of the grant, the residence and employment status of the researcher and the country where the research is carried out. A research fellowship or other award payable over a period would be taxable income in the hands of the recipient, but the recipient would be able to deduct sums properly spent on travel, research books and other necessary expenditure to carry out the research.

52.9.4
Payment of interest

Where an organisation pays interest on anything other than a loan made by a UK bank or a hire purchase agreement, it may be required to deduct basic rate income tax and pay the tax to the Inland Revenue on **form CT61** within 14 days of the end of the quarter in which the interest is paid. Advice should be sought from Inland Revenue before paying interest on any loan to which this might apply.

52.10
OVERSEAS TAX ISSUES

Some aspects of the taxation of income received from abroad are dealt with above [see **52.7.10**]. Many other complex tax issues, generally requiring specialist advice, arise for charities which operate overseas, receive income from abroad or make expenditure abroad.

52.10.1
Europe

Although VAT may be harmonised across Europe, the EU has at the time of writing (early 2001) accepted no directives on harmonisation of direct tax (income, corporation and capital gains tax). If such a directive is ever adopted, it could have very serious implications for voluntary organisations.

52.10.2
Fundraising

Generally a UK charity raising funds abroad needs to register a local charity or not-for-profit organisation if it wishes to take advantage of any tax exemption in that country.

52.10.3
Making payments abroad

If a UK charity makes charitable payments abroad it is subject to both the special requirements of the Charity Commission [see **4.3.8**] and the tax requirement that payments made to bodies outside the UK only count as qualifying expenditure [see **52.5.3**] if the charity has taken all reasonable steps to ensure that the payment will be applied for charitable purposes. *Income and Corporation Taxes Act 1988 s.506(3)*

To ensure that funds used for the payments are not subject to tax, the organisation should have a written agreement with the overseas recipient stating that the funds must be used for a purpose which is legally charitable under UK law, and should have appropriate reporting and monitoring procedures in place. In some situations it may be advisable to obtain Inland Revenue approval in advance.

52.10.4
Overseas charities operating in the UK

If a charity is not based in the UK but operates or fundraises here, it may suffer significant tax disadvantages:

- tax on UK income such as interest will be deducted at source, and it will not be able to recover the tax;

- it will not be able to use gift aid to recover tax paid by donors;

- it will not be eligible for the tax exemptions which are available only to charities.

Overseas charities suffer particular disadvantages if they are based in a country which does not have a double taxation agreement with other countries, for example an offshore tax haven such as the Cayman Islands. Because there are no reciprocal agreements, tax withheld on income is not recoverable.

These disadvantages can normally be overcome by setting up a UK registered charity. The overseas charity will need to ensure that the UK charity qualifies for registration here, especially if a significant number of its governing body members are based abroad [see **3.4.6**].

FOR FURTHER INFORMATION

Community accountancy projects

Charities Tax Reform Group: 020-7222 1265

Charity Finance Directors Group: 020-7793 1400, www.cfdg.org.uk

Charity Taxation: A definitive handbook by Adrian Randall and Stephen Williams (Jordan Publishing)

Corporation, income & capital gains tax. Inland Revenue local tax office, www.inlandrevenue.gov.uk

Charity tax reliefs & exemptions. Inland Revenue (Charities): 0151-472 6038; www.inlandrevenue.gov.uk

VAT. HM Customs and Excise: 0845-010 9000; www.hmce.gov.uk

Chapter 53
VALUE ADDED TAX

Topics covered in this chapter

This chapter explains how charities and other voluntary organisations are affected by VAT, when they can save on VAT and when they have to charge VAT to their purchasers, customers or clients. It covers:

For sources of further information see end of chapter.
Double-underlined section headings indicate additions or significant changes since the first edition.

53.1 VOLUNTARY ORGANISATIONS AND VAT

Organisations which ignore VAT do so at their peril:

- if an organisation (including a charity) does not register when it has to, it will face substantial penalties;

- if it does not register voluntarily when it would be advisable to do so, it may lose the opportunity to claim back some VAT it has paid;

- even if an organisation does not have to register, it may pay unnecessary VAT if it does not know about the reliefs available to charities and other voluntary organisations.

Every organisation should regularly review its VAT position. Many organisations assume their auditor will alert them to the need to register, but it is not generally within the scope of an auditor's terms of engagement [see **51.1.3**], and in any case the auditor may lack specialist expertise in this complex area.

With proper planning, voluntary organisations can often make substantial savings on VAT. This chapter provides an introduction, but cannot cover all the possibilities and is not a substitute for specialist advice. Further information is available in numerous free publications from the local VAT office or the Customs and Excise website [see end of chapter], *A Practical Guide to VAT for Charities* by Kate Sayer (Directory of Social Change), and more detailed technical guides. The Charities' Tax Reform Group [see end of chapter] campaigns for better tax treatment for charities, especially in relation to VAT.

53.1.1
How VAT works

VAT is calculated completely differently from corporation tax, income tax and capital gains tax [see **chapter 52**]. It is a tax not on profits, income or gains, but on the **supply** of goods or services. The **value** of the supply is taxed, so VAT may apply even if the goods or services are supplied free of charge or make no profit.

53.1.1.1
Inputs and outputs

Charities and other voluntary organisations generally pay VAT in the same way as everyone else. This is **input tax**, because it is a tax on **inputs**—goods and services coming into the organisation.

An organisation may have to register for VAT and charge VAT on some or all of the goods and services it provides. This is **output tax**—a tax on goods or services going out of the organisation.

53.1.1.2
Basic principles

The basic principles of VAT are:

- all goods, services, facilities and everything else provided, purchased or received by the organisation, including by mail order or via the internet, are **supplies**;

- a supply is **non-business** [see **53.3.1**] or **business** [see **53.3.2**];

- a business supply is **exempt** from VAT [see **53.4**] or **taxable** for VAT [see **53.5**];

- a taxable supply is subject to VAT at **zero rate** [see **53.5.1**], **reduced rate** [see **53.5.2.1**] or **standard rate** [see **53.5.3**];

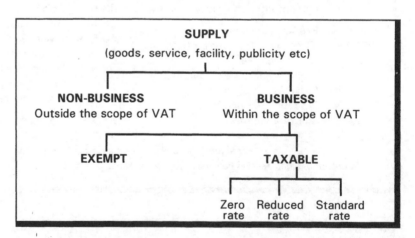

- when an organisation (or anyone else) purchases business supplies, it pays **input tax** on them unless the supplies are exempt or zero rated or are purchased from a supplier who is not registered for VAT;

- charities and some other voluntary organisations are eligible for a few zero ratings on goods or services they purchase which would normally be standard rated [see **53.2**]. It is important to be aware of these reliefs, as they are available even if the organisation is not registered for VAT;

- if the organisation provides taxable supplies whose total value in any 12-month period is more than the **registration threshold** (£54,000 in 2001), it must register for VAT [see **53.6.1**], charge **output tax** on its taxable supplies and pay the output tax it collects to Customs and Excise;

- if it makes taxable supplies whose value is below the threshold it can **register voluntarily** [see **53.6.9**];
- when it is registered it can recover **input tax** on some or in some cases all of the goods and services it purchases;
- if some of its supplies are taxable and some are non-business or exempt, it can usually only reclaim the portion of input tax which has been paid on goods or services which were used for the provision of taxable supplies [see **53.6.8**].

Other EU member states do not treat charities and voluntary organisations in the same way that they are treated for VAT purposes in the UK. If VAT is harmonised across the EU, it is likely to be disadvantageous for UK charities.

53.1.2
Assessing whether to register

Some charities and voluntary organisations must register for VAT [see **53.6.1**]. Others cannot register even if they want to [see **53.3.1.2**], while others may be able to register voluntarily [see **53.6.9**].

Assessing whether an organisation has to register for VAT is not a once-and-for-all matter, but something which must be constantly monitored. If it appears at any time that the organisation should be registered for VAT, advice should be taken immediately from its accountant or auditor. *Penalties for failing to register are severe*.

If the organisation does not have to register because all its income is **non-business** in VAT terms [see **53.3.1**] or **exempt** from VAT [see **53.4**], the people involved should be aware of the need to re-assess the situation if:

- the organisation starts receiving income for goods or services which are defined as **business** supplies [see **53.3.2**], for example if it starts providing services under a contract rather than under grant funding, or if it starts organising large-scale fundraising events or charging clients for services; *and/or*
- it starts providing goods or services which are not exempt, or in some cases if it uses the profits from the provision of exempt goods or services to subsidise other work.

If the organisation provides **taxable supplies** [see **53.5**]—goods or services which are neither non-business nor exempt—but does not have to register because their value is below the **registration threshold** [see **53.6.1**], it should consider whether to register voluntarily [see **53.6.9**]. If it does not register voluntarily, it should monitor the value of its taxable supplies on a monthly basis and be prepared to register as soon as the value for the preceding 12 months reaches the threshold, or is likely to exceed it in the next 30 days.

53.2
RELIEFS FOR CHARITIES AND SOME OTHER ORGANISATIONS

All charities, even if they are not registered for VAT, are entitled to a few reliefs. For VAT purposes a charity is any body registered with the Charity Commission, or exempt or excepted from having to register with the Commission [see **7.1.2** and **7.1.3**] but recognised as charitable by the Inland Revenue and/or Customs and Excise.

Some reliefs are also available for other voluntary organisations.

The relief takes the form of zero rating on goods or services purchased by the organisation which would normally be standard rated, so VAT is charged to the organisation at 0% rather than 17.5%. These reliefs are not available in other EU member states and are under threat from VAT harmonisation.

The organisation usually has to provide a declaration on its headed paper to the supplier at the time it orders or purchases the goods or services, confirming it is eligible for zero rating. The supplier then charges VAT at zero rate (i.e. no VAT) instead of standard rate. It is the purchaser's responsibility to provide the declaration. The supplier is not obliged to find out whether the purchaser is eligible for relief, or to make the declaration available to the purchaser.

The wordings for the declarations are in the relevant VAT notices, available free from any Customs and Excise VAT office or the Customs and Excise website [see end of chapter]. If in doubt about whether a zero rating applies, check with a specialist advisor and/or the local VAT office. There are penalties for making an incorrect declaration.

Some goods and services are always zero rated regardless of who is purchasing them [see **53.5.1**].

53.2.1
Advertising

From 1 April 2000 zero rating for charity advertising was significantly extended, and applies to:

- all advertisements (including job recruitment advertisements) placed by a charity in any media—print, radio, television, cinema, internet; *and*

- services connected with the design and production of the advertisement.   *Value Added Tax Act 1994 sch.8 gp.15 items 8, 8A-8C;*
VAT (Charities and Aids for the Handicapped) Order 2000 [SI 2000/805]

Zero rating applies only if the advertising is in someone else's publication, time or space, so does not apply to design and production of advertisements to be placed in the charity's own publications or of posters to be placed in the charity's windows.

It also does not apply to services connected with the charity's own website. Preparation of material to be placed on someone else's website is zero rated, but not design and production of materials to be placed on the charity's own website, or fees paid to an internet service provider to host the website.

Zero rating applies only if the services are supplied to the charity, so does not apply where design and production are done in-house—even if the advertisement will be placed externally.

Advertising targeted to specific individuals rather than to the public is not covered, so zero rating is not available under these rules for direct mailing, telephone fundraising, or emails. However under other rules zero rating is available for some fundraising materials [see **53.2.2**] and printing [see **53.5.1.5**].

If a qualifying advertisement is prepared but is subsequently not used, the design and production costs remain eligible for zero rating.

The declaration to claim this relief is in VAT notice 701/58 *Charity Advertising and Goods Connected with Collecting Donations*. If VAT has been paid on items which could have been zero rated, the charity can make a declaration asking the printer, publication, agency etc for a credit note. There are penalties for wrongly claiming zero rating.

53.2.2
Fundraising
materials

Stationery used specifically for fundraising appeals, collection boxes, and lapel stickers and similar tokens are eligible for zero rating under a Customs and Excise concession. The declaration to claim zero rating is in 701/58 [see above].

The only stationery eligible for zero rating under this concession is:
- collecting envelopes which ask for donations of money;
- similar envelopes used by religious organisations in their planned giving schemes;
- pre-printed letters appealing solely for money for the charity;
- envelopes used in conjunction with appeal letters and for forwarding donations, provided they are over-printed with an appeal request related to the appeal contained in the letter.

Collecting boxes and buckets may be made of any material, but to be eligible for zero rating must be tamper-proof and must include the name of the charity, either by indelible printing or embossing, or by having raised letters. Ordinary household buckets cannot be zero rated, but special tamper-proof lids used to seal such buckets are zero rated.

Lapel stickers, pins, badges, ribbons, artificial flowers (if they are the charity's symbol) and other small items designed to be worn on clothing are zero rated, provided they are of nominal value. 'Nominal value' means they are given free to donors or in return for a suggested donation of no more than £1, and cost the charity considerably less than £1. Only items designed to be worn on lapels (or similar) are zero rated. Other items are not, even if they are just a larger version of a lapel item.

Zero rating is not available for general stationery, raffle tickets, or other fundraising materials. If a charity buys its own materials to make stickers etc, the materials are not zero rated.

53.2.2.1
Other zero ratings

Some leaflets and other printed materials are always zero rated [see **53.5.1.5**]. If a printed item is eligible for both types of zero rating it may be better to use the zero rating specifically for charities, because this also allows for zero rating of the artwork, typesetting etc.

53.2.3
Disability-related goods

Charities and in some cases other voluntary organisations are entitled to zero rating on the purchase of some goods for use by people with disabilities, or for use in providing services to people with disabilities.

53.2.3.1
For blind and visually impaired people

Zero rating is available on:

* sound recording equipment, including parts and accessories but not including cassette tapes, supplied to charities caring for the blind or the severely visually impaired;

* sound recording equipment (but not tapes) supplied to voluntary bodies such as talking newspaper associations and used by them to make sound recordings on magnetic tape;

* radios and cassette recorders (but not tapes) supplied to charities for free loan to blind and severely visually impaired people.

Value Added Tax Act 1994 sch.8 gp.4

The declaration is in VAT notice 701/1 *Charities*. This equipment may also be imported free of VAT.

53.2.3.2
For chronically sick and disabled people

If a charity purchases specially designed equipment which it intends to make available to people who are chronically sick or disabled for their domestic or personal use, the purchase is zero rated. The zero rating applies regardless of whether the equipment is to be provided free or for a charge. It covers:

* some medical or surgical appliances;

* toilet aids and adjustable beds;

* wheelchair lifts;

* motor vehicles adapted for carriage of a person in a wheelchair or on a stretcher and no more than 11 other persons;

* boats adapted for use by people with disabilities;

* other equipment and appliances designed solely for use by a chronically sick or disabled person;

* construction of ramps, bathroom/toilet adaptations, alarm systems and some other building alterations.   *sch.8 gp.12; VAT (Vehicles Designed or Adapted for Handicapped Persons) Order 2001 [SI 2001/754]*

Zero rating applies when a charity provides, extends or adapts a bathroom or lavatory in residential accommodation for disabled people, or in a day centre where at least 20% of the centre's users are disabled.

VAT (Charities and Aids for the Handicapped) Order 2000 [SI 2000/805]

Further information and the declarations are in VAT leaflet 701/7 *VAT Reliefs for People with Disabilities*.

53.2.4
Vehicles, medical and scientific goods

Zero rating is available for some vehicles, medical and scientific equipment, medicinal products, and supplies of drugs and chemicals when they are purchased by charities and some other organisations.

53.2.4.1
Vehicles, medical and scientific equipment

Zero rating applies to the purchase of some equipment by or for charities which provide care or medical or surgical treatment for people who are chronically sick or disabled, non-profit research institutes, hospitals and health authorities. The equipment covered is:

- ambulances;
- motor vehicles with 51 or fewer seats designed or substantially and permanently adapted for the safe carriage of people in wheelchairs;
- motor vehicles with seven to 50 seats for use by an eligible body providing care for blind, deaf, learning disabled or terminally ill people mainly to transport these people;
- medical and scientific equipment;
- other relevant goods used in medical and veterinary research, training, diagnosis or treatment.

Value Added Tax Act 1994 sch.8 gp.15 note 3

To be eligible for zero rating, the item must be:

- purchased for its own use by a charitable institution providing domiciliary, residential or day care or medical or surgical treatment for people who are chronically sick or disabled;
- purchased for its own use by another eligible body, using funds provided by a charity or from voluntary contributions; *or*
- purchased by another body for donation to an eligible body, using funds provided by a charity or from voluntary contributions.

sch.8 gp.15 items 4-7

Under an extra-statutory concession, zero rating is also available to:

- charities whose sole object is the provision of care services to meet the personal needs of people with disabilities; *and*
- charities which provide transport services exclusively to people with disabilities.

Resuscitation training models are zero rated when purchased by charitable institutions which provide care, medical or surgical treatment for people with disabilities or provide rescue or first aid services, or not-for-profit research institutes using charitable funds to purchase the models.

Further information and the declarations are in VAT notice 701/6 *Charity Funded Equipment for Medical, Research, Veterinary etc Uses* and information sheet 8/98 *Charities: Supply, repair and maintenance of relevant goods.*

53.2.4.2
Medicinal products, drugs and chemicals

Medicinal products can be zero rated when supplied to a charity engaged in the treatment or care of people or animals, medical or veterinary research, or testing the efficiency of medicinal products. Drugs and chemicals used for medical research can be zero rated when supplied to a charity engaged in medical or veterinary research.

sch.8 gp.15 items 9-10

The declaration is in VAT leaflet 701/1 *Charities.*

53.2.5
Rescue and first aid equipment

For charities providing sea rescue or assistance, lifeboats and lifeboat equipment are zero rated. The declaration is in VAT leaflet 701/1 *Charities.* *sch.8 gp.8 item 3*

Equipment supplied solely for rescue or first aid services by a charitable institution providing such services is eligible for zero rating in the same way as medical and scientific equipment [see **53.2.4.1**], as is resuscitation training equipment. In some situations warning sirens may also be eligible for zero rating.

53.2.6
Building works

VAT on building works is particularly complex and requires specialist advice.

53.2.6.1
Relevant residential and charitable purposes

Relief from VAT in the form of zero rating is available if the building is to be used for a **relevant residential purpose** or a **relevant charitable purpose**.   *Value Added Tax Act 1994 sch.8 gp.5 notes 4, 5*

Relevant residential purposes are use as dwellings or accommodation, including short-term accommodation. Relevant charitable purposes are:

- for purposes defined as **non-business** in VAT terms [see **53.3.1**]; *or*

- as a **village hall** providing social or recreational facilities for a local community, or for other buildings such as community centres and sports pavilions, constructed and used similarly to a village hall.

'Similar to a village hall' means that the premises are used by the local community, and any economic activities are incidental to that use. Activities in which the local community participates directly, such as a jumble sale or plays performed by an amateur dramatic group, do not threaten zero rating, but other business activities, including lettings, could. For new buildings, a certain amount of commercial use is allowed, by concession [see below]. If in any doubt at all about whether zero rating applies, advice should be taken before claiming it.

If the building changes to a non-qualifying use or is disposed of within 10 years, the VAT saved may be payable. This can happen quite easily, for example if a service which has been grant funded starts to be purchased under a contract and therefore ceases to be non-business, or if the charity starts to charge fees to service users.   *sch.10 para.1*

Further information about zero rating on property and the declarations are in VAT leaflets 708 *Buildings and Construction* and 742 *Land and Property*. It is very important to take advice before making these declarations.

For charities which cannot zero rate their building works, substantial savings can be made by entering into **design and build schemes**. This should be done only with appropriate professional advice.

53.2.6.2
New buildings

Provided a new building will be used for a relevant charitable or residential purpose [see above], zero rating is available to charities for:

- services purchased in the course of constructing a new self-contained building (but not the separate services of architects, surveyors or persons acting as consultants or in a supervisory capacity);   *item 2*

- materials, hardware and other goods provided as part of the above zero-rated services;   *item 4*

- the sale by the person constructing a new building, of the freehold or the grant of a lease for a period exceeding 21 years.   *item 1*

Under an extra-statutory concession, zero rating is available for new buildings even if the building is partly used for business use, provided that:

- the building is used solely for non-business activity for 90% or more of the time it is available for use;

- 90% or more of the floor space is used solely for non-business activity; *or*

- 90% or more of the people using the building are engaged solely in non-business activity.

Organisations should consult their VAT advisor or Customs and Excise before relying on this concession to obtain zero rating.

53.2.6.3
Existing buildings

Zero rating is also available:

- for certain works to enable disabled access [see **53.2.3.2**];

- to charities, for services purchased in the course of constructing an annex or extension with internal access to an existing building, provided the annex has its own primary access and is capable of functioning independently of the existing building, and provided the building is used for a relevant charitable or residential purpose [see **53.2.6.1**];   *Value Added Tax Act 1994 sch.10 para.1 note 17*

- for sale or grant of a lease for more than 21 years by the person converting all or part of a non-residential building into a building intended solely for a relevant residential purpose;   *item 1*

- to registered social landlords registered with the Housing Corporation, for conversion services when a non-residential building is converted for a relevant residential purpose;   *item 3*

- to charities which convert a non-residential building for a relevant residential purpose, and which are prevented by legal constraints from selling converted property.   *by concession*

Refurbishment of an existing building can generally be considered a 'new' building only if no more than one perimeter wall is left standing. But Customs will sometimes class a refurbished building as 'new' even if more of the old building remains.

Zero rating is available for alterations to a listed building or scheduled monument, but not for repairs or maintenance. Special provisions apply to repairs of listed churches [see **53.5.3.8**].   *sch.8 gp.6*

53.2.7
Goods purchased in the EU

A VAT-registered organisation buying goods in another EU member state does not pay VAT when it imports the goods. Instead, it accounts for the VAT at the relevant UK rate when it fills in its next VAT return. A VAT-registered UK charity or other body eligible to purchase the goods listed above at zero rate can account for the goods at zero rate on its VAT return.

An organisation which is not registered for VAT pays VAT at the rate in the country where the goods are purchased. It cannot take advantage of UK zero ratings for the goods.

If an organisation spends more than the VAT threshold (£54,000 in 2001) on goods—but not services—purchased from other EU countries in any calendar year, it is required to register for VAT. This applies even if it would not otherwise be required to register.   *s.10*

53.3
SUPPLIES

All goods, services and facilities provided by an individual, business or organisation are **supplies**. Something is a supply even if it is funded completely by grants and donations or no charge is made for it. It is a supply even if it is produced or provided by volunteers or by a charity's beneficiaries. Everything an organisation provides to someone else is a supply.

Supplies are either **non-business** or **business**. For VAT purposes, the terms 'non-business' and 'business' have nothing to do with whether the supplier is a non-commercial body or a commercial business. The terms refer to whether something is outside the scope of VAT (a non-business supply), or within the VAT net (a business supply).

53.3.1
Non-business supplies

For VAT purposes, a supply is non-business *only* if it is defined as such in the VAT legislation or regulations. **Non-business supplies** are:

- the receipt of donations, legacies, grants and other voluntary contributions, provided no supply is made to the donor other than a simple acknowledgement such as a sticker or a mention in an annual report;

- simple acknowledgements provided by a charity or other voluntary organisation in return for sponsorship (but if the organisation provides anything more than this, the publicity or whatever else is provided becomes a business supply);

- the supply of advertisements in the organisation's programmes, brochures etc, provided at least 50% of the advertisements are from private individuals rather than commercial businesses (but these are likely to be zero rated anyway, see **53.5.1.5**);
- services provided in return for membership subscriptions to members of charities or organisations established for political, religious, philanthropic or patriotic purposes, so long as the subscription gives the members only the right to vote at general meetings and to receive reports on the organisation's activities and finances;
- services provided free of charge by voluntary organisations (but see **53.3.1.3** for special arrangements for national museums);
- welfare services and related goods supplied by charities **consistently below cost** to **distressed people** [see below] for the relief of their distress;
- provision of places of worship and religious services;
- the portion of income from affinity credit cards which is not classed by Customs and Excise as a business supply;
- dividends received on shares;
- the acquisition or disposal of shares or other securities.

53.3.1.1
Welfare services

Welfare services and related goods are **for the relief of distress** if they are for the relief of poverty, the support or relief of people over 65 years old, the treatment or care of people suffering from any disease or disability, the care of women before, during and after childbirth, or the prevention of disease or disability. **Consistently below cost** means that the recipients are consistently charged no more than 85% of the cost of providing the service, and the other 15% or more is subsidised from the charity's own funds.

53.3.1.2
If all supplies are non-business

Non-business supplies are **outside the scope of VAT** and are completely ignored for VAT purposes.

If all of a charity's or other organisation's supplies are non-business:

- it cannot register for VAT;
- it will not have to charge output VAT on any goods or services it provides;
- it will not be able to recover input VAT on its purchases;
- it may be eligible to make some purchases at 0% VAT [see **53.2**].

53.3.1.3
National museums and galleries

The activities of local authorities and the BBC are non-business, but under special rules they are allowed to recover VAT on their purchases. From 1 April 2001 these provisions are extended to some national museums and galleries. *Value Added Tax Act 1994 s.33; Finance Act 2001 s.98*

Where museums and similar bodies charge admission the charges are standard rated, but some cultural organisations can choose to make the charges exempt from VAT [see **53.4.8**].

53.3.1.4
If some supplies are non-business

Where some supplies are non-business and some are business, the organisation is making **mixed supplies** [see **53.6.8.2**]. Depending on the nature and value of its business supplies, it may have to register for VAT or be able to register voluntarily. If it registers, it will not be able to recover VAT on goods or services used for non-business supplies.

53.3.2
Business supplies

For VAT purposes, a business is any trade which is not explicitly defined as non-business—even if the goods or services are provided free, or without the intention of making a profit. *s.94(1)*

Business supplies include, for example:

- the receipt of funds where the donor or funder requires, is promised or expects to receive something in return;

- sponsorship where the sponsor receives advertising, publicity, or other benefits such as use of a charity's name or logo;

- the sale of donated goods;

- advertisements in programmes, brochures etc, if half or more of the advertisements are from commercial businesses;

- membership subscriptions which give members the right to benefits such as discounts, admission to events, advice, publications etc;

- admission charges for premises or events;

- rent or hiring out premises;

- photocopying, management charges or other services;

- welfare services and related goods supplied by charities to distressed people for the relief of their distress [see above], where the recipients are charged more than 85% of the cost of the service;

- all other goods and services provided by charities and other voluntary organisations for which a charge is made, even if the charge is only nominal and does not cover the full cost of the goods or services, and regardless of whether the charge is made to the end user, to a third party purchaser (such as a local authority), or both;

- interest received by non-charities (but not charities) on accounts at banks, building societies and other financial institutions;

- the portion of income from affinity credit cards which is treated by Customs as a payment to the charity for promoting the card.

A business has been defined in the courts as 'a serious undertaking earnestly pursued' so a one-off activity, on its own, might or might not constitute a business activity. *National Society for the Prevention of Cruelty to Children v Customs and Excise [1992] VAT Tr 417*

53.3.2.1
If some or all supplies are business supplies

If some or all of a charity's or other voluntary organisation's supplies are business supplies:

- it needs to consider whether the supplies are exempt [see **53.4**] or taxable [see **53.5**];

- if the supplies are taxable, it may have to register for VAT [see **53.6.1**] or may choose to register voluntarily [see **53.6.9**];

- regardless of whether it registers, it may be eligible for zero rating on some goods and services it purchases or receives [see **53.2**].

53.3.3
Services provided under contracts and service agreements

Where services are provided under a contract or service agreement, the transaction between the organisation and the purchaser may be a business supply [see **48.1**]. The situation is complex, and organisations should take specialist advice before entering into a contract or service agreement, or into a grant which could be construed as a payment for a service.

Customs and Excise may regard something called a contract or service agreement as a grant and therefore a non-business supply and outside the scope of VAT, or may regard something called a grant as a business supply and therefore within the scope of VAT. And to complicate matters further, something may be a business supply for VAT purposes but not be subject to corporation or income tax—and something which is neither a business supply nor subject to tax may still be a contract for the purposes of contract law.

And to make it even more complicated, VAT status can change even if the service remains the same. A day care service provided by a charity for elderly people may be, for example:

- **non-business** (and therefore completely outside VAT) if it is grant-funded and/or any charges to clients are consistently below cost;

- **business** but **exempt** from VAT [see **53.4**] if any profits are ploughed back into the day care service;

- **business** and **standard rated** if any profits are used to subsidise another service provided by the charity, or if the purchaser of the service is a local authority or similar body (under a contract or service agreement) rather the clients themselves.

Specialist advice about the VAT implications is essential when entering into a contract or service agreement. It is also important to ensure all contracts or service agreements include a clause enabling the organisation to charge VAT to the purchaser [see **48.3.5**], and to ensure the VAT situation is clear before the contract starts.

53.3.3.1
Services not provided to or for purchaser

Where a service is provided to the final users and not to the local authority, health authority or other purchaser, Customs and Excise has said in some cases that there is not a business supply to the purchaser. In the case of a citizens advice bureau, for example, the CAB makes supplies to the clients (which are free, and therefore non-business), and some VAT tribunals have ruled that there is no supply to the local authority which funds/purchases the service under a service agreement or contract. *Hillingdon Legal Resources Centre Ltd v Customs & Excise Commissioners [1991] VAT Tr 39; Wolverhampton CAB [2000] 16411*

However in many similar situations Customs has said that there is in fact a business supply to the purchaser/funder, even if services are provided direct to the final users—so advice is essential in each situation.

53.3.3.2
Services provided on behalf of purchaser

Where the local authority or similar body has a statutory duty to provide a service, it may pay an organisation to provide the service on its behalf. Where the service is provided under a contract, it is a business supply. Where it is provided under a grant or service agreement, Customs and Excise will look closely at the actual arrangement. It is likely that these arrangements, whatever they are called, will be considered a business supply between the organisation and the local authority, because the authority is receiving the benefit of the service—even though the service is actually being provided direct to the final users.

53.3.3.3
Services directly purchased by purchaser

Where a local authority or other body purchases a specified number of places (for example in a nursery, day care centre or training workshop) or pays for services to be provided to specified individuals, this is a business supply from the service provider to the purchaser.

53.4
EXEMPT SUPPLIES

All business supplies are either **exempt** from VAT or **taxable** for VAT. Some supplies are exempt only when provided by charities; some are exempt regardless of who provides them.

Exemption from VAT is completely separate from exemption from income or corporation tax [see **52.5**]. Even if the income or profit from an activity is exempt from income or corporation tax, the activity may nonetheless be a taxable supply for VAT purposes.

If everything an organisation provides is exempt, or is a combination of exempt plus non-business:

- it may be able to make some supplies taxable by providing them in a way which removes the exemption [see **53.4.1**], thus enabling it to register for VAT and recover VAT in relation to those supplies;
- if it cannot or does not want to do this, it will not be able to register;
- if it is not registered, it cannot reclaim VAT on its purchases;
- it may be eligible for zero rating on some goods or services it purchases or receives [see **53.2**].

Complex analysis may be necessary to determine whether a supply is exempt. For example, if a charity is contracted to manage a local authority children's home, is it providing services for children (which are exempt) or is it providing management services to the local authority (which are not exempt)?

Where supplies are partly exempt (or partly exempt plus non-business) and partly taxable, the organisation is providing **mixed supplies**. For the implications of this see **53.6.8**.

53.4.1
'Otherwise than for profit' basis

Some of the supplies listed below are exempt only if they are supplied on an **otherwise than for profit** basis. This does not mean that they are supplied at or below cost, or without intending to make a profit. It means that any surplus or profit made on the supply must be used **only for the same type of supply**. If the profit is used for any other purpose, the original supply is not exempt.

In many cases an organisation does not want to be exempt, because it wants to register for VAT and be able to reclaim at least some of the VAT it pays out. It may seek to make a profit, however small, on the activity and use the profit for another type of activity. This then makes the activity standard rated [see **53.5.3**]. Alternatively it may set up a profit-making trading subsidiary to run the activity [see **chapter 47**].

53.4.2
Health services

The following supplies are always exempt, regardless of whether provided by a charity, non-charitable body or commercial business:

- hospital and nursing services;
- care or medical treatment in registered nursing homes and care homes;
- all services by recognised medical practitioners and persons (including unqualified staff) working under their direct supervision.

Value Added Tax Act 1994 sch.9 gp.7

In mid-2001 a VAT tribunal ruled that care in care homes, but not nursing homes, should be standard rated rather than exempt. This decision was expected to be challenged.   *Kingscrest Residential Care Homes v Customs and Excise Commissioners, The Guardian 28/6/2001*

Provision of transport services for people who are sick or injured, in vehicles specifically designed for the purpose, is also exempt.

Further details are in VAT notice 701/31 *Health*.

53.4.3
Welfare and care services

Welfare services and related goods are exempt from VAT if they are made by a charity on an **otherwise than for profit** basis [see **53.4.1**].

A supply is eligible for this exemption if it involves 'the provision of care, treatment or instruction designed to promote the physical or mental well-being of elderly, sick, distressed or disabled people'.

sch.9 gp.7 item 9

Care means continuing personal contact in looking after, helping or supervising people, for example bathing, dressing or feeding them. Care also includes routine domestic tasks such as cooking, cleaning and shopping, where an assessment shows a risk to the person's physical or mental health or welfare, because the person cannot do the task safely or adequately or without significant pain or discomfort. The provision of emotional support to carers, or routine tasks on a carer's behalf in order to give them a break, are also covered under this exemption.

The provision of accommodation or catering is not included in this exemption unless it is **ancillary** to the provision of care, treatment or instruction [see **52.6.2** for explanation of ancillary].

Provision of welfare services on an **otherwise than for profit** basis is not the same as provision **consistently below cost**, which is a non-business activity [see **53.3.1.1**]

Further details are in VAT notice 701/1 *Charities* and information sheet 6/99 *Charities: Liability of routine domestic tasks*.

53.4.4
Services for children

Services provided by nurseries and playgroups registered under the **Children Act 1989**, or by homes for children registered under the Act (or, from April 2002, under the **Care Standards Act 2000**) or exempt from registering are exempt from VAT, regardless of who provides the services (but see **?** for a possible change in this rule).

Value Added Tax Act 1994 sch.9 gp.7 items 4, 9

Services for the protection of children and young people are exempt if provided by a charity on an otherwise than for profit basis [see **53.4.1**].

item 9

53.4.5
Probation services

Services provided in probation/bail hostels and bail hostels approved under the **Powers of Criminal Courts Act 1973** s.49 are always exempt, regardless of who provides the service.   *item 4*

53.4.6
Spiritual welfare

Board and lodging for a religious retreat, admission to a religious convention, and spiritual welfare provided by a religious community to its resident members in return for a subscription or other payment required as a condition of membership, are exempt if provided by a charity on an otherwise than for profit basis [see **53.4.1**].   *item 10*

53.4.7
Education and training

Eligible non-profit-distributing organisations (charities and other voluntary organisations, not-for-profit research institutes, schools, universities etc) are exempt from having to charge VAT on:

- education of a type provided in schools or universities;
- research provided to another eligible body;
- vocational training [see below];
- conference facilities, accommodation, catering etc when supplied to another eligible body for an exempt educational purpose (but usually not audio-visual equipment and other equipment provided for the organisers or instructors, rather than for the direct use of the students or trainees themselves).

VAT (Education) (No.2) Order 1994 [SI 1994/1124]

The services must be supplied on an otherwise than for profit basis [see **53.4.1**]. Further information is in VAT notice 701/30 *Education and Vocational Training*.

53.4.7.1
Vocational training

Vocational training includes training, retraining or providing work experience for:

- any trade, profession or employment;
- voluntary work connected with carrying out activities of a charitable nature; *or*
- voluntary work connected with education, health, safety or welfare.

Conferences, seminars and similar events intended to improve the participants' work performance as employees or as charity volunteers are included in this category.

Vocational training under a government-approved training scheme is always exempt, regardless of who provides it. This includes all training ultimately funded by a learning and skills council, local enterprise company, chamber of commerce, or the European Social Fund under a scheme approved by the Department for Education and Skills.

53.4.8
Cultural services

A cultural body which is managed and administered on a voluntary basis by people who have no direct or indirect financial interest in its activities may, if it wishes, exempt admission charges. This includes admission charges to museums, galleries, art exhibitions and zoos, and to theatrical, musical and dance performances of a cultural nature.

Value Added Tax Act 1994 sch.9 gp.13

The EU directive on which this exemption is based states that it should apply to bodies which are managed and administered on an *essentially* voluntary basis. It is thus unclear whether the exemption is available only to organisations where the governing body and staff are voluntary (as the UK legislation may imply), or to organisations which have voluntary governing bodies but paid staff (as the EU directive may imply). At the time of writing (early 2001) a case involving the Zoological Society of London had been referred to the European Court of Justice for clarification.

Information about the cultural services exemption is in VAT notice 701/47 *Culture*. The exemption is not the same as the special VAT arrangements to enable some national museums and galleries not to charge admission [see **53.3.1.3**].

53.4.9
Sport and physical education

Sporting and physical education services are exempt from VAT if they are supplied by non-profit-distributing bodies which are:

- membership bodies providing the services to members who are granted membership of at least three months; *or*
- non-membership bodies providing the services to any individuals.

Value Added Tax Act 1994 sch.9 gp.10

Exemption also applies to membership subscriptions to sports clubs, where under the terms of the governing document the subscriptions cannot be distributed to club members, and must be used for operating and improving facilities. Supplies by a membership body to non-members are standard rated.

To be eligible for exemption, any payments to staff must not be determined or varied with reference to the organisation's income or profits.

Further details are in notice 701/45 *Sport and Physical Education*.

53.4.10
Youth clubs

Recreational, educational, social and cultural activities provided to members of youth clubs in exchange for their subscription are exempt. Entertainment, food, drink and purely recreational holidays are taxable at the appropriate rate. Details are in VAT notice 701/35 *Youth Clubs*.

sch.9 gp.6 item 6

53.4.11
Membership subscriptions

Membership subscriptions to philanthropic, political, religious, philosophical or patriotic bodies, and to trade unions and similar organisations, professional associations, learned societies and some trade associations, are exempt, provided the subscription entitles the member only to:

- the right to participate in the organisation's management and receive reports on its activities; *and/or*
- benefits which relate to the aims of the organisation, are provided in return for the subscription, and do not include provision of any right of admission for which non-members have to pay.

Value Added Tax Act 1994 sch.9 gp.9 item 1;
Value Added Tax (Subscriptions to Trade Unions, Professional and Other Public Interest Bodies) Order 1999 [SI 1999/2384]

Membership benefits which do not meet these criteria—for example the right of free or reduced-price admission where non-members have to pay—are either exempt, zero rated or standard rated, depending on the nature of the benefit.

Organisations which have negotiated zero rating for the portion of subscription income covering magazines, newsletters and zero-rated publications can retain the zero rating.

Details are in VAT notice 701/33 *Trade Unions, Professional Bodies and Learned Societies*, information sheet 11/99 *Exemption of Subscriptions*, and notice 701/5 *Clubs and Associations*.

53.4.12
Food and drink

Sales of food and drink by charities from trolleys, canteens or shops are exempt from VAT if the sales are connected with the welfare of people in hospital, prisons etc. These sales are not exempt if they are not connected with such welfare, are made to staff, or are sales of excisable goods such as tobacco and alcoholic drinks.   *VATA sch.9 gp.7 item 9*

Tobacco and alcoholic drinks are always standard rated. Supplies of food and drink which are not exempt may be either zero rated [see **53.5.1**] or standard rated [see **53.5.3**].

The rules are in VAT notices 701/1 *Charities*, 701/14 *Food*, and 709/2 *Catering and Take-away Food*.

53.4.13
Fundraising events

In general, fundraising events are subject to VAT. But they are exempt from VAT and also from corporation or income tax [see **52.7.1**] if they meet a number of criteria, which are set out in VAT notice CWL4 *Fund-Raising Events*.

Value Added Tax Act 1994 sch.9 gp.12;
Value Added Tax (Fund-Raising Events by Charities and Other
Qualifying Bodies) Order 2000 [SI 2000/802]

Unlike the tax exemption for fundraising events [see **52.7.1**], the VAT exemption is not necessarily advantageous. Exemption means that organisations registered for VAT will not have to charge VAT on tickets, goods sold at the event and sponsorship for the event—but they cannot recover VAT on the expenses of the event. If it would be advantageous for an event not to be exempt from VAT, the organisation should try to arrange the event so that it does not qualify for the exemption. This will then have implications for tax—so such a decision is likely to require specialist advice.

53.4.13.1
Qualifying bodies

A fundraising event is exempt from VAT if it is a **qualifying event** [see below] and is held by:

- a charity or charities holding the event to raise money for charitable purposes;
- a corporate body wholly owned by a charity, which has agreed in writing to transfer all its profits to the charity [see **47.7**]; *or*
- a non-profit-making organisation which is a **qualifying body** holding the event to raise money exclusively for its own benefit. Qualifying bodies are those with political, religious, philanthropic, philosophical or patriotic objects; trade unions, professional associations, learned societies, pressure groups, and bodies established primarily to provide facilities for participating in sport and recreation.

Value Added Tax Act 1994 s.94(3); sch.9 gp.12 item 1

Advice should be taken before involving a charity's trading company in exempt events, particularly where the company is VAT-registered. Exempt income from the one-off event may reduce the company's ability to recover some input tax, unless the exempt income falls within the *de minimis* provision for partial exemption [see **53.6.8.2**]. Participation in exempt events also requires the trading company to transfer *all* its profits, from all sources, to the charity, which can leave the company without adequate operating capital.

53.4.13.2
Qualifying events

A wide range of events are covered by the exemption [see **52.7.1** for examples]. Events are exempt from VAT provided:

- no more than 15 events of a similar type are held in the same location during the organisation's financial year; *or*
- more than 15 events of a similar type are held in the same location, but the gross income from them is not more than £1,000 per week.

For more about the rules relating to events see **52.7.1**.

All income from the event is exempt, including admission charges, the sale of commemorative brochures and advertising in the brochures, sales of other goods by the charity or qualifying body at the event, and sponsorship directly connected with the event.

53.4.13.3
Joint events

If two or more qualifying bodies [see **53.4.13.1**] enter into an informal agreement to organise an event, each qualifies for the exemption. If the agreement is more formal and creates a separate legal partnership [see **9.5**], the new entity is exempt only if it is itself a qualifying body.

**53.4.13.4
Events organised by
others**

When a non-qualifying company or other non-qualifying body organises an event to raise money for a charity, the income donated to the charity is covered by the exemption. If the organising body retains any of the income to cover its own expenses, this is treated as payment for its agency services and is subject to VAT.

**53.4.13.5
Non-qualifying events**

An event which is not exempt is standard rated [see **53.5.3**]. If the organisation is VAT registered it will have to charge VAT on tickets, advertising, souvenirs etc. This increases the cost to customers, but enables the organisation to recover the VAT it has paid in organising the event, purchasing the souvenirs etc.

**53.4.13.6
Reducing VAT on
non-qualifying events**

A VAT-registered organisation which wants to reduce the amount of VAT it has to charge on admission tickets can set a low admission price, with a voluntary additional donation. The donation is non-business [see **53.3.1**] and there is no VAT on it provided it is genuinely optional. The criteria are the same as for voluntary donations for tax purposes [see **52.4.1**]. Customs officers can and do check that the conditions are met by the organiser.

**53.4.14
Lotteries**

Lottery tickets [see **45.6**] are an exempt supply. Where winning a prize is dependent on any element of skill, it becomes a competition and the entrance fee is standard rated [see **53.5.3**].

Value Added Tax Act 1994 sch.9 gp.4 item 2

**53.4.15
Premises bookings**

Hiring out premises is exempt from VAT, but if the charge covers services other than pure rent (for example caretaking or use of audio-visual equipment), VAT may be chargeable on that amount.

In some situations the organisation can choose to waive the exemption on premises hire charges [see **53.4.16.1**]. If it does this it will have to charge VAT to individuals and some groups, but will be able to recover the VAT it pays on goods or services related to the premises. It cannot charge VAT to a charity or charities which hire the premises for non-office non-business purposes [see **53.3.1**]—in other words, it *can* charge VAT to charities which hire premises for office or business purposes.

**53.4.16
<u>Property</u>**

Rent on residential dwellings and property used for a relevant residential or charitable purpose [see **53.2.6.1**] or the disposal of such property is exempt from VAT.

sch.10 para.2(2)(b)

Rental income from other premises is generally exempt, as are most disposals of premises other than the sale of newly constructed buildings. In order for rental income to be exempt, there must be a **licence to occupy land**. The criteria for determining whether a licence exists for VAT purposes is not the same as determining whether a licence exists in relation to property rights [see **56.5**].

Examples of licences in a VAT context include:

- rental of office space, farm land etc for the licensee's exclusive use, or where another person's right to enter does not impinge on the rights of the licensee;
- hire of a hall or meeting room (including use of shared kitchen);
- hire of advertising hoardings, display stands, space for kiosks and vending machines.

If other people have the right to use the same space at the same time, a licence may not exist and the rental income will be standard rated rather than exempt. An example is shared business premises where neither business has its own specified space.

Issues around property and option to tax [see below] are explained in VAT notice 742 *Land and Property*. VAT relating to property is very complex and it is essential to get professional advice.

53.4.16.1
Opting to tax

Where there is (or will be) a licence to occupy commercial premises, and the premises will be wholly or mainly used for standard-rated or zero-rated purposes, the landlord can choose to charge VAT. This is called **opting to tax**.

The decision to tax must be notified to Customs and Excise in writing within 30 days. After a three-month period during which the decision can be changed, it is irrevocable for 20 years and all supplies relating to those premises, including their construction or sale, are standard rated. It is essential to take professional advice before opting to tax if the organisation receives or is going to receive rents, and to consider the implications if the organisation's landlord can opt to tax [see **58.2.3**].

Opting to tax enables the landlord to recover VAT on the purchase of goods and services relating to the premises, but it makes rents higher. This does not affect VAT-registered tenants, which can recover the VAT they pay on the rent. But it will negatively affect tenants who are not VAT-registered or who can recover only part of their VAT.

In some situations the option to tax does not apply. In particular, it may not apply if at the time a landlord acquires a property, there is an intention or expectation that the property will be occupied or used by a person who funded the acquisition or development, or by a connected person. This includes not only obvious funders, but anyone who lends money for the acquisition or development, provides a guarantee, or directly pays for some construction costs. *Finance Act 1997 s.37*

53.5
TAXABLE SUPPLIES

If goods or services are not defined as non-business [see **53.3.1**] or exempt [see **53.4**], they are **taxable** for VAT. Taxable supplies are subject to VAT at **zero**, **reduced** or **standard rate**.

53.5.1
Zero rate

Some supplies are classed as taxable, but at **zero rate**. To a purchaser the effect is the same as if they were non-business or exempt: there is no VAT on them. But to the provider, there are significant differences:

- the value of zero-rated goods and services is included in the total when determining whether the organisation has reached the registration threshold [see **53.6.1**], but the value of non-business and exempt supplies is not included; *and*

- if the organisation is registered for VAT, it can recover the VAT paid on goods or services purchased for the purposes of making zero-rated supplies—but it cannot recover the VAT on goods or services purchased for the purpose of making non-business supplies, and in many cases cannot recover it for exempt supplies either.

Organisations whose supplies are all or mostly zero rated have the best of all worlds: they do not have to charge VAT to their clients or customers, *and* they can recover all or most of the VAT they pay out.

In most cases the goods and services listed in this section are zero rated both when the organisation supplies them, and also when the organisation purchases them.

53.5.1.1
Donated goods

The sale or hire of donated goods is zero rated when the goods are sold or hired out by a charity, or by an individual or organisation which has a written agreement to transfer to a charity all the profits from the sale or hire of the donated goods. The goods must be offered for sale or hire either to the general public, or exclusively to people with disabilities or people receiving means-tested benefits.
Value Added Tax Act 1994 sch.8 gp.15 items 1,1A

By concession, sales by a charity are also zero rated where the goods are of such poor quality or so unsafe that they cannot be offered to the public, and are therefore sold on as scrap or for use as rags. This concession covers only the sale of items that are unsuitable for sale—not items that were offered for sale but were not purchased.

Other sales or hire of donated goods are standard rated.

Where the donation is made by a VAT-registered donor, the donation is zero rated. This means the donor does not have to account for VAT on the donated goods. The goods may be donated for sale, hire, export or a combination. *Value Added Tax Act 1994 sch.8 gp.15 item 2*

**53.5.1.2
Supplies to charities**

Goods which are eligible for zero rating when purchased by charities or other eligible bodies [see **53.2**] are also zero rated when supplied by a charity or other eligible body, provided the body purchasing the goods makes the necessary declaration of eligibility.

**53.5.1.3
Supplies to sick and disabled people**

Specially adapted goods and equipment supplied to people who are chronically sick or disabled [see **53.2.3**] are zero rated if they are not exempt [see **53.4.3**]. Zero rating also applies to the provision of some building adaptations which are necessary or desirable because of the disability. *sch.8 gp.12 items 7-13;*
VAT (Charities and Aids for the Handicapped) Order 2000 [SI 2000/805]

**53.5.1.4
Exported goods**

Goods eligible for zero rating when supplied to charities or other eligible bodies in the UK may also be zero rated when supplied to a charity or eligible body in an EU member state. To satisfy the requirements for zero rating, the charity or eligible body which is purchasing or receiving the goods must not be registered for VAT in its own member state, and must provide evidence to show that all conditions of the appropriate relief are met.

Goods exported outside the EU are zero rated.

Goods given by charities to countries outside the EU (for example as relief or educational supplies) are normally classed as non-business but can be treated as zero rated. This enables the charity, if it is VAT registered, to reclaim the VAT paid out in purchasing the goods, or if it is not registered and the value of the donated goods is over the registration threshold, to register and reclaim VAT.

**53.5.1.5
Printed matter**

In producing or selling printed materials, zero rating applies to:

- books, booklets, brochures and pamphlets;

- leaflets, provided at least 50 are supplied and any portion intended to be completed, detached and returned takes up less than 25% of the whole leaflet;

- newspapers, journals and periodicals;

- children's picture books and painting books; printed, duplicated or manuscript music; and maps, charts and topographical plans.
Value Added Tax Act 1994 sch.8 gp.3

Zero rating applies to the production of the printed matter, regardless of whether the item is printed, instant-printed or photocopied, and also applies to its sale. It does not apply to preparation of the artwork, typesetting etc, which is standard rated.

The special zero rating for charity advertising and fundraising materials [see **53.2.1**] may be available for design and production of advertising artwork, leaflets which do not qualify for zero rating, and other standard-rated printed materials.

For more information see VAT notice 701/10 *Printed and Similar Matter.*

**53.5.1.6
Food**

The supply of much food and drink is zero rated, but prepared foods or foods supplied in catering are standard rated. Food and drink supplied by charities from hospital trolleys, shops and canteens is generally exempt [see **53.4.12**].

53.5.2
Reduced rate

53.5.2.1
Fuel and power

The VAT **reduced rate** of 5% applies to the supply of fuel and power to buildings:

- where at least 60% of the building is used for domestic or non-business [see **53.3.1**] charitable purposes; *or*
- regardless of the use of the premises, if only a small amount of fuel or power is supplied. *Finance Act 1994 s.42*

Other supplies of fuel or power are standard rated. An organisation which pays for gas and electricity direct to a landlord may be paying full VAT even though it is eligible for reduced rate. In this situation it may be advantageous to negotiate with the landlord to install meters and pay separately for fuel and power.

Organisations which pay standard rate VAT on fuel may also have to pay **climate change levy** on their fuel use.

53.5.2.2
Energy-saving materials

From 1 April 2000 the 5% reduced rate applies to installation (but not DIY installation) of specified energy-saving materials in all homes, including residential homes, and in non-business charity buildings. Eligible materials include building insulation, insulation for plumbing fittings, draught-stripping for windows and doors, central heating and hot water system controls, and solar panels.

Reduced rate also applies to:

- installation, maintenance and repair of central heating systems in the homes of qualifying pensioners, if funded under a government grant scheme;
- grant-funded installation of heating system measures in the homes of 'less well off' people;
- installation of security measures such as locks and smoke alarms in the homes of qualifying pensioners, when installed at the same time as energy-saving materials or central heating systems.

Further information is in VAT information sheet 1/00 *Reduced Rate for the Installation of Energy Saving Materials*.

53.5.2.3
Housing regeneration

Many building works are zero rated [see **53.2.6**]. From May 2001, reduced rate VAT is available for some other building works, including renovating dwellings that have been empty for at least three years, or converting property into housing, a dwelling into a care home, or a house into multiple occupancy. *Finance Act 2001 s.97*

53.5.3
Standard rate

All goods, services and other supplies, including those provided by charities, are **standard rated** unless they are defined in VAT legislation or regulations as non-business [see **53.3.1**], exempt from VAT [see **53.4**], zero rated [see **53.5.1**] or reduced rated [see above].

An organisation making standard-rated supplies may be obliged to register for VAT [see **53.6.1**], or may choose to register voluntarily [see **53.6.9**]. When it is registered it must charge VAT to clients, purchasers or customers who buy standard rated goods or services. It is also able to reclaim all or some of the VAT it pays when it buys goods or services.

Some standard-rated supplies are:

- provision of environmental, arts, consultancy or other non-exempt services [see **53.4**];
- provision of care or welfare services which are not specifically non-business or exempt [see **53.4.1**];
- provision of staff, services, or other benefits to another organisation, including a subsidiary [see **53.5.3.1**];
- in most cases, services provided under a contract with a local authority or similar body, and in some cases services provided under a service agreement or an arrangement called a grant [see **53.3.3**];

- fees, sponsorship or a 'donation' for use of an organisation's name, logo or copyright material;
- membership subscriptions that do not meet the criteria for exemption [see **53.4.11**], or the portion of the subscription that does not meet the criteria;
- sales of competition tickets (but not lottery or raffle tickets);
- fundraising events that are not exempt [see **53.4.13**];
- sale of calendars, t-shirts, mugs and similar items, unless they are being sold at an exempt fundraising event [see **53.4.13**];
- sale of donated goods by a non-charity which does not have a written agreement to donate to a charity all its profits from the sale of the donated goods [see **53.5.1.1**];
- sale of bought-in (non-donated) goods in charity shops;
- provision of publicity, tickets or other benefits in return for a so-called 'donation' or sponsorship.   *for example, Customs and Excise Commissioners v Tron Theatre Limited [1994] STC 177 C5*

53.5.3.1
Provision of staff

Where an organisation provides staff, the full charge to the receiving organisation is subject to standard rating. This includes not only the agency fee or commission, but also the staff member's salary, national insurance, pension and other related costs. However at the time of writing (early 2001) a concession was in place under which VAT was chargeable only on the agency fee, provided the receiving organisation paid the worker direct.

When VAT is extended to include salary and related costs there will be significant implications where, for example:

- a non-registered organisation uses agency staff;
- a non-registered organisation has an agency or another organisation operate its PAYE, and is billed for salary, employer's national insurance and perhaps an administration charge, all of which may have VAT added to them;
- a charity charges its associated trading company for use of the charity's staff, and thus makes taxable supplies high enough to have to register for VAT; *and/or*
- a trading company charges its non-registered charity, and the charity cannot recover the VAT it has to pay out.

Specialist advice should be sought from a solicitor or accountant about whether it is possible to reduce the VAT burden in such situations. It may be possible, for example, to have another organisation calculate PAYE but not actually pay the salaries (so it only has to charge its administration fee), for a charity and its trading company to employ staff under a joint contract of employment or similar arrangements [see **22.4**], or for a charitable company and its trading company to form a VAT group and not have to charge VAT to each other [see **53.6.7**].

53.5.3.2
Provision of
home care staff

Under an extra-statutory concession, there is no VAT on the salary and related costs element when an individual is charged for the provision of home care staff. To qualify for this exemption the work must be domestic or personal care carried out in the individual's own home, and the individual must be unable to carry out domestic or personal tasks safely or adequately, or without significant pain or discomfort. At the time of writing (early 2001) Customs and Excise was consulting on details of this provision.

53.5.3.3
Grant making and
grant assessment

The provision of grants is not, in itself, subject to VAT. However at the time of writing (early 2001) there is uncertainty as to the circumstances in which the provision of services to assess and distribute a third party's grants, or other money provided by a third party, is subject to VAT.

53.5.3.4
Postage and packing

Postage and packing or delivery charges are standard rated. However where they are included as an integral part of the purchase price, their VAT rating is the same as the goods. So if a book is priced at £20 'including p&p' the book element is zero rated [see **53.5.1.5**] and so is any p&p element, but if the price is £20 plus p&p the book is zero rated and the p&p is standard rated.

Standard rating applies even though postage stamps, when purchased from the post office, are exempt. This is because the book supplier is not providing the postage *per se*, but is providing the service of getting the book to the customer—and that service is standard rated.

At the time of writing (early 2001) a case in the House of Lords was looking at whether a delivery service can be exempt where the supplier makes a delivery charge *exactly* equivalent to the exempt delivery charge (in this case a Parcelforce charge).

53.5.3.5
Freelance/consultant
costs

The same principle applies when a consultant, freelance worker or other contractor who is VAT registered charges a client for photocopying, postage or fares. When the consultant paid for them the postage and fares were exempt, and the photocopying may have been zero rated. But the consultant charges the client for the overall service, including photocopying, fares etc, and the overall service is standard rated. This applies even if the elements are itemised separately on the invoice.

53.5.3.6
Tour operator's
margin scheme

Organisations which buy in travel for the direct benefit of the traveller—for example for overseas challenge events [see **45.5**]—may come within the tour operator's margin scheme (TOMS). Details are available in VAT notice 709/5.

53.5.3.7
VAT on property

Some building works are zero rated [see **53.2.6**] or reduced rate [see **53.5.2.3**]. Some rents and property disposals are always exempt [see **53.4.16**]; others are generally exempt but the landlord or seller can opt to charge VAT [see **53.4.16.1**]. Most other transactions related to property are standard rated. Difficult issues are raised by rent-free periods, reverse premiums and surrenders, and in the situation where someone builds property for itself or supplies land to itself. As with all matters relating to VAT on property, professional advice is essential.

53.5.3.8
VAT on repairs to
listed churches

Alterations to listed buildings are zero rated [see **53.2.6.3**], but repairs and maintenance are standard rated. The government proposed in late 2000 to implement reduced rate VAT for repairs to and restoration of listed churches, synagogues, mosques etc, but the European Commission was opposed to this. Instead, from April 2001 government grants, comparable to the amount that would have been saved if VAT had been reduced, are available for such repairs.

53.6
REGISTRATION

To determine whether an organisation has to register for VAT, the value of all taxable supplies—zero rated, reduced rated and standard rated—is totalled. The value of exempt [see **53.4**] and non-business [see **53.3.1**] supplies is not included, nor is income from the disposal of capital assets such as office furniture, computers, vehicles etc.

53.6.1
Compulsory
registration

An organisation must register within one month:

- if at the end of any month, the value of taxable supplies in the previous 12 months is above the threshold (£54,000 in 2001); *or*
- if at any time, there are reasonable grounds to believe that the value of taxable supplies in the next 30 days will exceed the threshold.

Value Added Tax Act 1994 sch.1 para.1

It registers by contacting the local Customs and Excise VAT office and completing **form VAT1**. It will have to provide recent financial accounts to show when it reached or expects to reach the threshold, and to show that it did not reach the threshold before this.

VAT registration is in the name of a **taxable person**. In this context 'person' means not only a human person or incorporated organisation [see **2.1.1**], but also an unincorporated association [see **1.2.1**]. Trusts [see **1.3.1**] register in their own name but Customs and Excise must be notified of the names of trustees and all subsequent changes.

VAT can usually be recovered on goods and services purchased in the six months prior to registration and on assets held at the time of registration, but only to the extent that the VAT relates to the supply of taxable goods or services. Advice should be sought about this.

53.6.2
VAT records and returns

After registration the organisation must:

- charge VAT at the appropriate rate on all its taxable supplies;
- issue **tax invoices** for all taxable (including zero-rated) goods and services supplied, including those sold via the internet, showing VAT registration number, date of supply, nature of supply, VAT rate and other required details;
- obtain proper VAT receipts for all expenditure on which it is eligible to recover VAT;
- keep financial records showing the VAT on goods or services provided or sold by the organisation (**output tax**) and the VAT on goods or services purchased by or provided to the organisation (**input tax**);
- fill in a monthly, quarterly or annual return, as appropriate;
- pay to Customs and Excise the VAT owing if the output tax (VAT collected) is more than the input tax (VAT paid);
- keep all VAT records for at least six years from the end of the year to which they apply.

At the time of writing (early 2001) the government had proposed a flat rate scheme under which organisations with taxable supplies up to £100,000 can calculate VAT as a percentage of their turnover, rather than keeping internal VAT records of all their purchases and sales. This provision is unlikely to be appropriate for organisations which make mixed zero-rated, exempt and/or non-business supplies.

53.6.3
Cash accounting

Usually VAT is accounted for on the date the goods or services are supplied, not the date payment is made or received. But if the value of all taxable supplies made by an organisation is expected to be less than £600,000 (in 2001) for the next 12 months, the organisation can choose to use the **cash accounting scheme**. With this, the organisation accounts for input VAT on the date it pays for goods and services, and output VAT on the date it actually receives the payment. This can make bookkeeping more straightforward. Cash accounting is explained in VAT leaflet 731 *Cash Accounting*.

53.6.4
Annual accounting

Usually VAT returns are made quarterly, but organisations eligible for cash accounting can opt for the **annual accounting scheme**. Details are in VAT notice 732 *Annual Accounting*.

53.6.5
Deregistration

An organisation may deregister, if it wishes to, if the value of taxable supplies in any 12-month period falls below the **deregistration threshold** (£52,000 in 2001). It will have to repay to Customs and Excise the VAT it has recovered on goods or assets it still holds, if this VAT is more than £1,000 in total.

53.6.6
Branches

Independent, autonomous branches or sections [see **9.2.2**] are generally treated separately for VAT purposes. If they are legally part of the main organisation, all their taxable income is added together to determine whether registration is necessary. If the main organisation registers, the branches will have to charge VAT on the taxable goods and services they provide, and will be able to recover the VAT they pay on goods or services they purchase to make their taxable supplies.

53.6.7
Group registration

Two or more bodies under common control as defined for company law purposes [see **9.6.1**]—such as a charitable company and its trading company—can register for VAT as a group. This is explained in VAT leaflet 700/2 *Group Treatment*. An unincorporated body which controls a company cannot register as a group.

Group registration means only one VAT return has to be submitted, and there is no need to charge VAT on intra-group supplies. This could be an advantage where one part of the group (for example, the charitable company) is not registered for VAT and is therefore unable to recover the VAT it has to pay to other parts of the group.

The disadvantage is that all members of a group are jointly and severally liable for the VAT. If one part of a group fails, the other part(s) of the group would have to meet its VAT liability.

The Charity Commission's view is that meeting such a liability is not a misapplication of charity funds, provided the charity had entered into the registration honestly and reasonably at a time when it appeared to be in the best interests of the charity. A charity setting up a VAT group should therefore ensure that it records the advice and discussions leading to the decision to create the group.

53.6.8
Mixed supplies and partial exemption

Many VAT-registered organisations provide **mixed supplies**—non-business [see **53.3.1**] and/or exempt [see **53.4**] supplies together with taxable supplies. In this situation VAT is only recoverable on purchases relating to taxable activities. This is called **partial exemption**.

The organisation should ensure that purchases of goods and services are allocated to the activities they are for. If a purchase relates to non-business or exempt activities as well as taxable activities (for example, telephone or photocopying costs), these costs will have to be apportioned to the different VAT categories. Various methods can be used for this, such as the percentage of income the organisation receives for each type of activity, the cost of providing each activity, the number of staff employed in each activity, or any other reasonable basis agreed with Customs and Excise.

At the time of writing (early 2001), a House of Lords decision had redefined the way mixed supplies should be treated. Customs and Excise was considering how to implement the changes and whether to make an extra-statutory concession continuing the old approach during a transitional period.

Because of the complexities of mixed supplies and partial exemption and the possibility of rule changes, advice should be sought from an accountant who specialises in charities and other voluntary organisations. It is essential to ensure that proper records are kept and criteria for allocation and apportionment are used which allow for maximum recovery of VAT.

53.6.8.1
Non-business supplies

VAT cannot be recovered on goods or services used to make non-business supplies. VAT therefore cannot be recovered on the portion of the purchase which is to be used for services funded solely by grants, donations etc, services provided free by charities, or other non-business activities.

53.6.8.2
De minimis rule

VAT on goods or services which are used to make exempt supplies cannot in general be recovered. However there is an exception if the amount of input tax relating to the exempt supplies is *de minimis* ('not worth bothering about').

An organisation within the *de minimis* limit is allowed to recover the VAT it has paid on goods or services used to make the exempt supplies.

The VAT can be recovered if input tax relating to exempt supplies is less than the *de minimis* limit (in 2001, an average of £625 per month), and is no greater than the amount of input tax relating to taxable supplies.

Although VAT can be recovered on exempt input tax, it cannot be recovered on goods or services used to make non-business supplies.

The *de minimis* rule is explained in VAT notice 706 *Partial Exemption*.

53.6.8.3
Working it out

If a VAT-registered organisation purchases something which will be used to make non-business, exempt and taxable supplies, it needs to apportion the cost (and the input VAT) to each type of supply. It then:

- can recover all the input VAT on the portion used to make taxable supplies;

- can recover the input VAT on the portion used to make exempt supplies if—and only if—the value of this input VAT is less than £625 per month on average, *and* is no more than half of the total input VAT used to make exempt and taxable supplies combined;

- cannot recover the input VAT on the portion used to make exempt supplies if it does not meet these *de minimis* criteria; *and*

- cannot recover any of the input VAT on the portion used to make non-business supplies.

53.6.9
Voluntary
registration

An organisation which makes taxable supplies whose value is below the registration threshold [see **53.6.1**] can choose to register voluntarily. It will then have to charge VAT on its taxable supplies, unless they are zero rated. It will be able to recover the VAT it has paid out on goods and services related to the provision of the taxable supplies, and may also be able to recover VAT on its exempt supplies if they meet the *de minimis* criteria [see above].

Before registering voluntarily, the organisation should take specialist advice to ensure the benefits will outweigh the additional administrative costs, and to ensure that VAT charges will not have negative effects on its members, clients or other purchasers of its goods or services.

An organisation which makes only non-business [see **53.3.1**] and/or exempt [see **53.4**] supplies cannot register voluntarily, unless the special zero rating relief for goods exported by a charity outside the European Union applies [see **53.5.1.4**].

53.7
APPEALS

Disagreements on VAT which cannot be settled with the local VAT office may go to the **VAT tribunal**. Appeals must be lodged with the tribunal (not the VAT office) within 30 days of the date of the VAT office's decision. If the organisation has already asked the VAT office to reconsider its decision and the decision is confirmed, the appeal must be lodged with the tribunal within 21 days of the confirmation. Information about appeals is in the VAT leaflet *Appeals and Applications to the Tribunals*.

FOR FURTHER INFORMATION

HM Customs and Excise: 0845-010 9000; www.hmce.gov.uk

Charities Tax Reform Group: 020-7222 1265

Chapter 54
INVESTMENT AND RESERVES

54.1 INVESTMENT DUTIES AND POWERS

Investments are money, land, stocks and shares, items of value and other assets held by an organisation in order to earn income or increase its overall worth. In this chapter, the term 'investments' is generally used to refer to stocks and shares, money, land, and any investment assets expected to produce income or a capital return.

Unless it is a common investment fund or common deposit fund [see **54.4.2**], a charity or other voluntary organisation is unlikely to have investment as an object. An organisation, therefore, may invest only to the extent that it has constitutional or statutory power to do so, and only if the investment is ancillary to achieving the organisation's objects and the organisation complies with any restrictions imposed by the governing document or statute.

The organisation's governing body may authorise investments or a particular investment policy provided it is not contrary to statute or the governing document. In some situations a third party, for example a donor, may specify how its funds are to be invested. But no one can require an investment which is prevented by law or by the organisation's governing document.

Investment is a particularly complex area, and appropriate advice should always be sought.

54.1.1 Who is a trustee?

In relation to much of the law relating to trustee duties when investing, a **trustee** is different from a charity trustee. Under charity law, a

charity trustee is a member of the governing body of *any* charity, whether unincorporated or incorporated [see **11.1.17**]. But in relation to duties when investing, a trustee is:

- a member of the governing body of a trust [see **1.3.1**], regardless of whether it is charitable or non-charitable;

- a member of the governing body of a charitable unincorporated association [see **1.2.1**] or a body established by royal charter [see **2.5**];

- a person who holds money, land or other property as a **holding trustee** [see **18.4.4.**] or **custodian trustee** [see **18.4.2**], on behalf of individuals, a trust or an unincorporated association, whether charitable or non-charitable.

Directors of companies and industrial and provident societies are not trustees in relation to their investment duties, even if they are charity trustees.

Duties when investing are explained below. For charities, the basic principles are set out in Charity Commission booklets CC14 *Investment of Charity Funds: Basic principles* and CC14a *Investing Charity Cash.*

54.1.2
Trusts and charitable associations

All trustees of associations and trusts have statutory and common law duties in relation to investments. Trustees include trustees of all trusts whether charitable or non-charitable, members of the governing body of charitable associations and bodies established by royal charter, and holding and custodian trustees [see **18.4.4** and **18.4.2**] who hold investments on behalf of charities or non-charities.

The trustees' investment duties and powers are governed primarily by their governing document and the **Trustee Act 2000**, with some residual duties and powers under the **Trustee Act 1925**, the **Settled Land Act 1925**, and the **Trustee Investments Act 1961**. Investing outside the powers granted by statute or the governing document, or failing to comply with investment duties, is a breach of trust and may also be a breach of statutory duty, for which the trustees can be held personally liable.

54.1.2.1
Statutory duty of care

All trustees have a general duty of care to their beneficiaries [see **54.1.2.2**]. In the case of investment and a wide range of activities associated with it, there is also a statutory duty of care under the **Trustee Act 2000** which must be exercised in relation to investment in stocks, shares and similar investments, and land. The statutory duty does not explicitly apply to investment in items of value such as works of art.

The statutory duty of care obliges trustees to exercise **such care and skill as is reasonable in the circumstances**, having regard in particular to any special knowledge or experience that the trustee has or holds himself or herself out as having. For a person acting as a trustee in the course of a business or profession, the duty of care requires particular regard to any special knowledge of experience that it is reasonable to expect of a person acting in the course of that kind of business or profession.

Trustee Act 2000 s.1

This duty of care applies when:

- investing;

- reviewing investments;

- acquiring land or exercising powers in relation to land;

- setting investment criteria;

- selecting investment advisors;

- choosing to do without advice;

- selecting agents, nominees and custodians [see **13.5.2**];

- determining the terms and statement of policy under which agents, nominees and custodians are to act, and reviewing such terms and policies.

sch.1

54.1.2.2
General duty of care

In addition to their statutory duty of care, charity trustees must invest in the best interests of the beneficiaries or the charity, to maximise the financial return on the investments and to minimise the risks to which the organisation is exposed [see **13.3.5**]. This duty overrides the trustees' personal views or priorities, and may have implications for organisations wishing to invest ethically [see **54.5.2**].

Cowan v Scargill [1985] Ch 270

The obligation to maximise the financial return means that charity trustees who do not invest surplus income, or who put it into an account where it does not earn proper interest, could be in breach of trust.

Inland Revenue Commissioners v Helen Slater Charitable Trust Ltd
[1981] 3 All ER 98

54.1.2.3
Delegation

Although trustees have a general duty to act personally and collectively [see **13.3.8** and **13.3.9**], they may in some situations delegate investment decisions [see **54.3.2**].

54.1.2.4
Investment in land

Subject to their duty of care and to any restrictions in their governing document, trustees have power to acquire freehold or leasehold land in the UK as an investment or for any other reasons, and to invest by lending on a mortgage of land in the UK. *Trustee Act 2000 ss.3, 8*

Sales or lettings of charity land must comply with the **Charities Act 1993** [see **56.11**].

54.1.2.5
Standard investment criteria

Trustees have a statutory duty to have regard to **standard investment criteria**. These are:

- the suitability of acquiring or retaining that type or class of investment;
- whether the particular investment is a suitable one within that asset class; *and*
- the need for diversification [see **54.3.3**], insofar as it is appropriate.

Before making any investment, they must generally obtain and consider professional investment advice [see **54.3.1**], unless they reasonably conclude that it is unnecessary or inappropriate. *ss.4-5*

The restrictions on investments contained in the **Trustee Investments Act 1961** were repealed by the **Trustee Act 2000**. Within their duty of care and other duties and within any requirements imposed by their governing document, trustees are free to invest as they choose.

54.1.2.6
Governing document

If the governing document of a trust or unincorporated association permits 'any investment for the time being authorised by law' or 'authorised by the Trustee Investments Act 1961' (or similar wording) the trustees may make any kind of investment, provided they act in accordance with the duties imposed by the **Trustee Act 2000**. But if the governing document contains restrictions on investment, those restrictions will apply.

A charitable association or trust whose governing document includes an amendment power may alter the governing document to modify powers of investment. Prior written consent must be obtained from the Charity Commission [see **5.5.1**]. *Re Jewish Orphanage*
Charity Endowment Trusts [1960] 1 WLR 344; Soldiers', Sailors' and
Airmen's Family Association v Attorney General [1968] 1 WLR 313

If a trust, whether charitable or non-charitable, or charitable association or trust does not have an amendment power, the Charity Commission or court may grant or vary powers of investment. The Commission can also give one-off consent for the acquisition of particular investments.

**54.1.3
Non-charitable
associations**

The investment powers of non-charitable associations are governed by their governing document and by any directions given by the association's members or by funders or donors. It may be possible to widen the powers by amendment [see **5.5.1** for procedure].

If a non-charitable association's investments are held by holding or custodian trustees [see **18.4.4** and **18.4.2**], investment powers are governed by the **Trustee Act 2000** unless the deed appointing the trustees specifies otherwise.

**54.1.4
<u>Companies</u>**

Directors of companies, whether charitable or non-charitable, are not subject to the duties and do not have the powers set out in the **Trustee Act 2000**. However they have a fiduciary duty and a duty of care [see **13.2** and **13.4**]. These duties are not quite as high as the duties of trustees under the **Trustee Act 2000**, but directors investing on behalf of a company should treat their duties equally seriously.

The memorandum or articles of association usually gives the widest investment powers. Where the powers are limited, they may be amended [see **5.5.2** for procedure]. Charitable companies should take advice about whether it is necessary to obtain the prior written consent of the Charity Commission before amending their powers of investment, or adding powers to use nominees or delegate investment decisions.

**54.1.5
Industrial and
provident societies**

Directors of industrial and provident societies are not subject to the **Trustee Act 2000**, but like company directors [see above] must exercise fiduciary duty and duty of care.

Unless its rules state otherwise, an industrial and provident society has statutory power to invest in a range of investments, including the shares of other industrial and provident societies. The IPS's rules may extend the statutory powers. *Industrial and Provident Societies Act 1965 s.31*

**54.2
<u>HOLDING
INVESTMENTS</u>**

The way investments are held will depend on the organisation's legal structure and the size and nature of its investment portfolio.

If the trustees of a charitable trust or association have incorporated the trustee body [see **1.4**], the trustee body generally holds the investments. Otherwise some or all of the charity trustees hold the investments as **holding trustees** [see **18.4.4**] or they appoint a **custodian trustee** [see **18.4.2**] to hold the investments for them if the portfolio is relatively small with infrequent changes. If the investment portfolio is large, the trustees may appoint a **nominee company** [see **18.4.4**] to hold them.

Subject to their duty of care [see **54.1.2.1**], trustees have a statutory power to appoint nominees (holding trustees or a custodian trustee) or custodians to hold their investments. If the trust or association is charitable and is not exempt from registering with the Charity Commission [see **7.1.2**], the trustees must follow the published Charity Commission guidance, available from the Commission or on its website, in selecting a nominee or custodian. The functions of such nominees or custodians must be regularly reviewed. *Trustee Act 2000 ss.19, 20, 22*

As incorporated bodies, companies and industrial and provident societies can hold investments in their own name [see **2.1.1**]. There is no need to appoint a nominee or custodian, although the company or IPS may do so if its governing document gives it this power.

**54.3
INVESTMENT
DECISIONS**

Trustees or members of the governing bodies of companies and industrial and provident societies may, provided it is not prohibited by the governing document and provided they exercise the appropriate duty of care [see **54.1.2.1** and **54.1.4**], undertake investment themselves without seeking outside advice, where they reasonably believe such advice is not needed. They may also employ a stockbroker, financial advisor, accountant, solicitor or bank to act in an **advisory capacity**, advising about investments but leaving the final decision to the organisation. In some situations they may delegate decision making [see **54.3.2**].

54.3.1
Advice

Governing bodies of charitable and non-charitable trusts and charitable associations must seek professional advice before investing and must consider the advice before making investment decisions, unless they consider it unnecessary or inappropriate to take such advice.

Trustee Act 2000 s.5

While taking advice may not be a strict legal requirement for companies, industrial and provident societies and non-charitable associations, they have a general duty of care so it is also essential for them to seek and consider such advice.

Investment advice should be impartial and be given by someone with sufficient experience of the type of organisation and investment. Evidence of appropriate care taken in the selection of advisors should be preserved, and the terms of appointment and any instructions to the advisors should be in writing and retained. All investment advice should be in writing.

54.3.2
Delegation

A governing body which wishes to delegate the right to make investment decisions or manage its investments may do so only if:

- it is a trust or a charitable association and the governing document does not prohibit such delegation; *or*

- it is a company or industrial and provident society and its governing document explicitly allows such delegation.

Provided delegation is allowed and the governing body exercises the appropriate duty of care, the governing body can hire a stockbroker, financial advisor or **institutional fund manager** as a **discretionary manager**, who will select investments within an overall policy set by the organisation, manage the investments, and monitor and report on performance. Such an arrangement takes a considerable administrative and management burden off the members of the governing body. In particular, a manager is likely to:

- act as a **nominee** [see **18.4.4**] and hold the investments in its name, or arrange for a bank or other third party to act as nominee;

- handle collection of dividends, response to rights issues [see **54.8.1**], and perhaps recovery of tax from the Inland Revenue [see **52.7.6**];

- take day-to-day decisions about investments.

54.3.2.1
Statutory power to
delegate

Trustees [see **54.1.1**] have a statutory power to delegate some investment management responsibilities to stockbrokers and similar professionals [see **13.5.2**]. Before delegating such powers, trustees have a legal duty to draw up a written policy statement to ensure the agent acts in the best interests of the organisation. This policy statement must be regularly reviewed, and revised if necessary. Trustees must also assess whether the agent has complied with the statement.   *ss.15, 22*

The statutory power to delegate does not override any restriction on delegation in the governing document. If such restrictions exist, the governing document can be amended [see **5.5**]. Registered charities require Charity Commission consent for such amendment.

54.3.2.2
Constitutional power

A charitable company whose memorandum or articles of association do not include power to delegate investment decisions may make an amendment in the usual way [see **5.5.2**]. Advice should be taken about whether prior Charity Commission consent is needed.

A non-charitable organisation without power to delegate investment decisions may amend its governing document in the usual way [see **5.5**].

The power to delegate should include safeguards allowing delegation only to qualified professionals, requiring them to act only in accordance with the organisation's agreed investment policy and requiring them to report back regularly to the governing body [see **54.3.4**].

54.3.2.3
Investment managers

Investment decisions should be delegated only to persons regulated under the **Financial Services Act 1986**. Publications such as *Charity Finance* provide information about the performance and charging policies of investment managers and common investment funds.

Investment managers may charge an annual fee, typically 0.5% to 1.5%, based on the capital value of the fund, or a commission on each share dealing. Commission arrangements run a risk of **churning**, where the manager makes an undue number of transactions in order to generate higher commissions.

54.3.3
Diversification

Whether investing directly or through an investment manager, trustees must have regard to the spread of investments and how well they meet the standard investment criteria [see **54.1.2.5**]. Even where the spread is achieved by investment in a common investment fund [see **54.4.2**] or unit trust, consideration should be given to the spread between fixed interest stock, which normally generates better income, and equities which generally give better protection against inflation.

Highly speculative investments should be avoided, because their potentially higher returns are likely to be linked to substantial risks.

Specialist investments such as futures options or foreign currency deposits are not suitable unless advised for a particular purpose. Charities concerned about particular investments recommended to them may seek the Charity Commission's prior approval for the investment.

54.3.4
Reviewing and assessing performance

Trustees must regularly review the performance of investments, agents and custodians, and should ensure their records show they have done this and the reasons for decisions. Such review will require looking again at the situation and aims of the organisation and its investment policy, all within the framework of the standard investment criteria [see **54.1.2.5**]. *Trustee Act 2000 s.4(2)*

Even where the organisation does not have to comply with the Trustee Act or has explicit investment powers so wide that it can invest in high risk ventures, the duty of prudence applies. Operating with less care than is required under the Trustee Act could be a breach of that duty of prudence. *Nestlé v National Westminster Bank [1994] 1 All ER 118; Bartlett v Barclays Trust Co [1980] Ch 515*

Part of the process of drawing up an investment policy [see **54.5**] is deciding how to assess the performance of the investments. Investments may be assessed against standard indices such as those produced by FTSE, or against specialist indices which measure the returns of charitable funds. No index should be chosen unless the governing body is satisfied that it provides an appropriate indicator for the organisation's investment objectives. Professional advice may be needed before selecting the index against which to monitor.

54.4
SPECIFIC INVESTMENTS

While many investments will be in bank deposits [see **54.4.1**] or stocks and shares, organisations may also invest in land [see **54.1.2.4**] or in special investment vehicles available only to charities [see **54.4.2**]. In some situations organisations may wish to purchase assets speculatively, with a view to selling them at a profit [see **54.4.3**].

54.4.1
Cash deposits

The deposit of small to medium sums requires prudence but is more a matter of practicalities, balancing accessibility, high rate of return, and the cost of transactions. Charity Commission booklet CC14a *Depositing Charity Cash* covers issues relevant to non-charities as well as charities.

A promise of unusually high rates of return needs to be treated with considerable care. In a worst case situation, deposits of up to £20,000 are protected against loss of up to 90%. Organisations should check that their deposits are covered by this scheme.

Credit Institution (Protection of Depositors) Regulations 1995 [SI 1995/1442]

Larger depositors will generally wish to spread the deposits and risk, and should take advice from professionals who are members of the Investment Managers Regulatory Association (IMRO).

54.4.2
Common investment funds and common deposit funds

Common investment funds (CIFs) are schemes established by the court or Charity Commission, and are similar to unit trusts [see **54.8.1**]. All charities have a statutory right to participate in CIFs unless this is prohibited by their governing document or they do not qualify as a participant under the CIF's rules. *Charities Act 1993 s.24*

CIFs allow an investment to be diversified over a much wider portfolio than would be economic for smaller charities. Some CIFs seek high income, while others seek to balance income and long-term growth.

Administrative and management advantages are:

- the purchase and sale of investments is simpler and cheaper than buying them individually;

- there is less paperwork than holding individual investments;

- the investor has access to advice from a large and skilled fund management organisation at a low cost;

- income is paid gross so it is not necessary to reclaim tax from the Inland Revenue.

For non-charities, unit trusts provide similar advantages.

Common deposit funds (CDFs) operate like bank accounts but enable the investor's funds to be placed in a range of bank and building society accounts. *s.25*

CIFs and CDFs are explained in Charity Commission leaflet CC15 *Common Investment Funds and Common Deposit Funds*, and CC15a lists current CIFs and CDFs.

Although CIFs and CDFs are likely to be a suitable home for investment by many smaller charities, they need to be reviewed regularly to ensure they remain appropriate.

54.4.3
Speculative purchase of assets

Because of the obligation for charity trustees and other trustees to avoid speculative investments, they generally should not purchase works of art, other commodities or foreign currency with a view to making a gain from their eventual sale. This does not apply to organisations which purchase assets as part of their primary purpose (for example museums) or which need foreign currency for their work, and which subsequently find they must sell some of these assets.

If a charity does purchase assets of this type with a view to making a gain from their eventual resale, the resale might be considered a trading activity rather than the realisation of an investment, and the profit from the sale may not be eligible for tax exemption [see **52.4**].

54.5
DEVELOPING AN INVESTMENT POLICY

To be able to show that they have invested prudently, the governing body must develop a coherent approach to investment. This starts from an analysis of the reasons for holding investments, which may be:

- provision for **short-term expenditure**, where the funds will be spent in the relatively near future on running costs, provision of services, grant making or capital expenditure;

- provision for **longer term expenditure**, where the funds are put aside for an expected but not immediate expenditure such as repairs or redecoration to premises, long-term expansion plans or a predicted cycle of future expenditure needs;

- creation of a **permanent** or **semi-permanent fund**, where the intention is to keep the capital intact but use the income from the fund to meet long-term expenditure;

- creation of a **permanent endowment**, a permanent investment fund where use of the capital is prohibited by the terms under which the funds are held; *and/or*

- where the organisation operates a **company pension scheme** [see **27.9.3**], creation of reserves to meet pension obligations to staff.

The purposes for which the assets are held will determine which types of investment are appropriate, and whether the investment income (interest or dividends) will be withdrawn or reinvested.

Charities are limited in their ability to accumulate funds for general purposes, without clear plans for how they will be used [see **54.7.2**].

54.5.1
Investment strategy

An analysis of the reasons for investment may reveal that different pools of funds need to be created, with different investment strategies. Key issues are likely to include:

- **liquidity**: whether the money needs to be readily accessible, or can be put into investments such as property or fixed-term stock where it is more difficult to get access to it;

- **frequency of access**: whether withdrawals are likely to be occasional and substantial, or frequent and smaller;

- **growth**: the desired level of growth, and over what period;

- **risk**: the level of acceptable risk, and in particular whether the risk of a reduction in the value of the invested funds is acceptable;

- **income**: whether the organisation needs a regular income from the investment and if so how often, or intends to reinvest any income.

Trustees whose investment powers were broadened by the **Trustee Act 2000** should review their investment strategies to take advantage of the wider range of investments now available to them.

The strategies should be written into one or more investment policies. Strategies and policies must be reviewed regularly to ensure they are being properly implemented, are fulfilling their objectives, and remain relevant. This may involve obtaining professional advice on appropriate measures for assessing success [see **54.3.4**].

54.5.2
Ethical investment

Non-charitable bodies are generally free to create their own guidelines for investment, either as part of the governing document or as policy decisions by the governing body or the organisation's members.

Charitable bodies have a general duty to invest in the best interests of the beneficiaries or the charity [see **54.1.2.2**] and must generally get the highest return possible, taking into account their need for liquidity and security of funds. Ethical or environmental considerations may be taken into account only in limited circumstances.

Issues arising from ethical investment are covered in a number of publications, and information is available about the ethical behaviour of specific companies [see end of chapter].

54.5.2.1
Guidelines for trustees

In a case brought against the Commissioners of the Church of England, the Bishop of Oxford argued that their policy of investing in arms companies and companies which perpetuated apartheid in South Africa was against the ethical principles of the church and was therefore in breach of trust and should cease.

The judgment in this case set out guidelines for ethical investment:

- if ethical criteria are to be used they must be based on the needs of the beneficiaries of the charity, not on the trustees' views;

- in most circumstances, the key criterion must be obtaining the best return on the investment with security;

- investments which directly impede the furtherance of the charity's objects may be excluded, for example a charity for alcohol abusers could exclude investment in breweries or companies owning pubs;

- where large numbers of investments are excluded and the financial risks for the charity are therefore greater, the arguments in favour of excluding those investments must be proportionately stronger;

- in justifying ethical exclusions the trustees cannot simply implement the directions of the membership, if those directions are contrary to their legal duties as trustees.

Harries v Church Commissioners for England [1993] 2 All ER 300

54.5.2.2
Ethical investment policies

Before drawing up an ethical investment policy which excludes any investments, the governing body must be absolutely clear what they mean by each restriction and must take advice from an investment advisor about the potential impact on investment returns.

If the impact is likely to be negative, the charity may have to take a less principled approach. For example, an absolute ban on investment in any company involved in the manufacture, supply or servicing of arms or other military equipment would exclude a high proportion of the larger UK companies. The impact of such a restriction might be reduced by specifying, for example, that companies are excluded only if a certain proportion of their turnover is linked to military supplies.

Thought should be given to what happens if a previously suitable investment becomes unsuitable. If its policy is very tightly defined, an organisation may need to disinvest very quickly if a company moves into prohibited work. Shares may have to be sold at a disadvantageous time, and the sale itself creates financial costs.

54.5.2.3
Positive policies

Instead of or in addition to excluding certain investments (a **negative policy**), some policies actively encourage investment in certain types of enterprise (a **positive policy**). The same underlying principle applies as in the Bishop of Oxford case: the primary concern must be to maximise the return to the charity. The fact that a company's or other enterprise's work or use of its profits meets ethical criteria can be only a secondary consideration.

54.5.2.4
Ethical unit trusts

Ethical unit trusts enable organisations to tailor their ethical investments without having to investigate dozens of companies. In deciding to invest in ethical unit trusts, the same principles apply as for other types of ethical investment.

54.6
PRACTICAL MATTERS

As well as ensuring that decisions about investments are properly made and regularly reviewed, the governing body must also ensure that practical matters relating to the investments are adequately dealt with.

54.6.1
Security and procedures

Regardless of who holds or manages the investments, appropriate procedures must be in place to ensure effective communication and security. Such procedures should cover:

- recording transactions;

- rapid collection of and accounting for income;

- allocation of income between particular funds;

- predicting income or capital receipts due, checking arrival, ensuring prompt banking and adequate record keeping;

- for charities, prompt recovery of any tax [see **52.7.6**];

- safeguarding the certificates, auditing the investments, and reconciling audits against the certificates actually held;

- careful control of any disposal, particularly ensuring that multiple signatories are required and if possible requiring separate signatories for the disposal of assets and the control of the certificate representing those assets.

54.6.2
Stamp duty

The transfer of stocks and shares is generally subject to **stamp duty** [see **57.10.1**] or in some cases **stamp duty reserve tax**. The rate for both taxes is 0.5%. Charities are exempt from these duties.

54.6.3
Tax

Investment income is subject to income tax or corporation tax [see **52.2**]. Most investment income received by charities is exempt from tax, provided the investment is a **qualifying investment** under the **Income and Corporation Taxes Act 1988** sch.20 [see **52.5.4**].

Tax is generally deducted at source, before the income is paid to the investor or reinvested, and charities must recover the tax from the Inland Revenue. Since 1999 charities have not been able to recover the full amount of tax deducted from dividends from UK companies, and after 2004 there will be no provision for recovery of this tax [see **52.7.6**].

Gains from the sale of investments are subject to tax on the gain [see **52.2.4**] but charities are exempt from tax if the gain is used for its charitable purposes [see **52.7.11**].

54.6.4
Accounting for
Investments

Investments, including land held for investment purposes rather than for the charity's own use, should generally be shown on a charity's balance sheet as a separate category within fixed assets [see **50.2.10**]. Land held for the charity's own use is not an investment, but a tangible fixed asset which should also be shown on the balance sheet under the overall heading of fixed assets.

Where the intention is to hold the asset for less than 12 months, this may be a short-term asset which should be shown on the balance sheet as a current asset.

Investments should be valued at market value as of the balance sheet date. For assets other than shares a 'reasonable approach' should be taken, which may be the trustees' best estimate of market value.

All organisations—not only charities—should take advice from their accountant or auditor about how to show the value of investments, and gains and losses from investments, in their annual accounts.

54.7
RESERVES

The term **reserves** may refer only to cash funds held by an organisation, or to the value of shares, stocks and bonds. Reserves are sometimes called **accumulated funds**. Reserves are divided into:

- **general** or **unrestricted reserves**, which can be used for any purpose at the discretion of the organisation;
- **designated reserves**, being held for a specific purpose decided by the organisation, but which could be used for another purpose;
- **restricted reserves** or **restricted funds**, being held for a specific purpose specified by the donor or by the terms of the appeal, and which can be used only for that purpose [see **44.2**];
- **permanent funds**, sometimes called a **capital fund** or **permanent endowment**, a form of restricted fund where the organisation is prohibited from spending the capital and can only spend the income from it;
- **expendable endowment**, a capital fund which the trustees have power to convert into income, and then spend.

Reserves held for general or designated purposes are sometimes called **administrative retention**, because the governing body makes a managerial or administrative decision to hold on to those reserves.

54.7.1
Income and capital growth

Unless the terms on which restricted or permanent funds are held specify otherwise, any income arising from a reserve fund (interest, dividends, gains from the sale of shares etc) becomes part of the same restricted fund. Similarly if there is a loss (for example, if shares are sold at a loss), the loss is borne by the restricted fund.

Some investments produce **capital growth** rather than income. Where the organisation holds a capital fund (permanent or expendable endowment) the capital growth is added to the capital fund, rather than being available to spend. With expendable endowment the trustees have power to use this capital growth as income, but with permanent endowment the trustees do not have this flexibility.

In mid-2001 the Charity Commission issued guidance relaxing the rules on permanent endowment. Under these provisions the Charity Commission may, in some circumstances, authorise trustees who hold permanent endowment to reallocate capital resources as income. This allows the trustees to invest on a **total return** basis for both capital growth and income.

54.7.2
Charities and reserves

Charity trustees are obliged to use a charity's funds for its charitable purposes. But this does not mean that charities are not allowed to build up any reserves. The governing document or the terms on which restricted funds are held may allow, or even require, the charity to build up reserves. Even if the governing document says nothing about reserves, there is an implied power to ensure the organisation has enough to meet its operating costs for a reasonable period, and to hold reserves for future general or specific (designated) charitable expenditure.

Examples of appropriate reasons for holding reserves include:

- future purchases of major equipment or premises;
- a major future development;
- safeguarding against anticipated and unanticipated fluctuations in income and expenditure;
- receiving an unexpectedly large legacy or other major donation and not wanting to spend it all at once.

In a consultation document in 1995, the Charity Commission suggested that operating reserves of three months' to two years' running costs were appropriate for most charities, but in guidance published two years later (CC19) this was not included. The Commission accepts that there is wide variation in the needs of charities. Its operational guidance suggests that reserves would be 'too high' if they were more than three years' gross expenditure, unless the charity could justify the higher amount.

If charity trustees allow excessive reserves to accumulate or do not have a reason for accumulating them, the Charity Commission may seek an explanation. In addition the Inland Revenue could require tax to be paid on the income held as reserves and/or the income from the reserves, because the income is not being used for charitable purposes [see **52.5.1**]. If there is a specific reason for wanting to accumulate reserves which might be considered excessive, the Charity Commission may make an order [see **3.5.4**] allowing this.

54.7.3
Reserves policy

An organisation's auditor should be able to advise on a realistic assessment of needs and appropriate levels of reserves to meet those needs. Based on this advice, the organisation should develop a **reserves policy** which should set out:

- why the organisation needs reserves;
- what level of reserves it seeks to hold for general purposes (often stated in terms of a specified number of months' operating costs);

- what designated reserves the governing body wishes to hold, and for what purposes;
- whether any restricted and permanent reserves need to be held, and for what purposes;
- how the reserves will be built up;
- the form in which the various funds should be held;
- how the income earned by reserves is to be used;
- how the policy and its application will be monitored and reviewed.

The reserves policy must be very closely linked to the investment policy [see **54.5**].

Many funders, especially public sector bodies, operate a short-sighted policy of not allowing organisations they fund to build up even small-scale reserves, reducing funding for organisations which have reserves, and/or operating **clawback** if the organisation builds up savings. This approach puts organisations—and therefore the services they provide—at risk. Sensible funders should recognise the need for the organisations they fund to maintain adequate reserves.

54.7.4 Accounting for reserves

Charities must show general funds, restricted funds and capital (permanent) funds separately in their accounts [see **50.2.8**]. Non-charitable organisations do not have to make this distinction in their accounts, but may choose to do so because it gives a more accurate picture of the organisation's financial position.

FOR FURTHER INFORMATION

Ethical investment. Ethical Investment Research Service: 020-7840 5700; www.eiris.org

Investment by charities. Charity Commission: 0870-333 0123; www.charity-commission.gov.uk

Regulatory bodies. Financial Services Authority: 0845-606 1234; www.fsa.gov.uk

---

Chapter 55
BORROWING

55.1 BORROWING POWERS

A voluntary organisation may borrow money only if it has power to do so. The nature of the power depends on its legal structure, whether it is charitable, and powers granted under its governing document.

A few organisations have a statutory power to borrow, but for most the power must be explicit in their governing document [see **5.4.4**]. The clause must be read carefully to ensure that any proposed borrowing is allowed. The clause may, for example, give the organisation the right 'to borrow money and charge all or any part of the property of the organisation with repayment of the money so borrowed'. This allows the organisation to use its assets as security for a loan, but does not allow it to guarantee a loan taken out by another organisation, such as its trading subsidiary [see **47.4.2**]. Unless the power to borrow is absolutely clear, it is essential to get legal and financial advice before borrowing.

55.1.1 Companies

A company's memorandum of association virtually always includes either a specific borrowing power, or a broad general power under which a power to borrow can be implied. If it does not, it should be amended in the usual way [see **5.5.2**] before undertaking any borrowing. If the company is charitable, the prior written consent of the Charity Commission may be needed for the amendment.

55.1.2 Industrial and provident societies

An industrial and provident society's rules must state whether it has power to borrow, and any limit on the borrowing and on how the loan can be secured.   *Industrial and Provident Societies Act 1965 sch.1 para.8*

IPS rules often contain limitations on the rate of interest to be paid on borrowing. If the specified rate of interest is unrealistically low, an application should be made to the Registrar of Friendly Societies to vary the restriction.

55.1.3 Unincorporated associations

Unincorporated associations defined by statute as literary or scientific institutions have a statutory right to borrow money on the security of their property in order to pay costs related to the property.
Literary and Scientific Institutions Act 1854 s.19

Apart from this, an unincorporated association can borrow money, commit its members to repaying a loan, or use the association's property as security for a loan (including a mortgage) only if the power to do so is explicit in the governing document.

The constitutions of many unincorporated associations do not contain borrowing powers. Before any small-scale borrowing, such as a temporary small overdraft, the governing body should obtain the explicit approval of the association's members. Before any substantial borrowing, the constitution must be amended [see **5.5.1** for procedure]. For a charitable association, the amendment may require the prior consent of the Charity Commission.

55.1.3.1
Personal liability

In an unincorporated association, the individual(s) who sign the borrowing agreement, the members of the governing body who authorise the borrowing and/or the members of the governing body at the time the debt is due to be repaid could be held personally liable if the organisation is unable to meet the terms of its borrowing.

It may be possible to create a borrowing arrangement in which the lender agrees to limit his or her right to repayment of principal and interest to the extent of the funds of the organisation [see **19.6.5**]. This means that if the organisation does not have enough funds, the lender does not get repaid. Commercial lenders, in particular, are unlikely to be willing to agree to this limitation on their right to be repaid.

55.1.4
Trusts

A trust may borrow only if the trust deed includes power to do so. A trust which does not have explicit power to borrow will need to amend its governing document [see **5.5.1** for procedure]. The consent of the Charity Commission may be required.

The issues of personal liability are the same as for an unincorporated association [see above].

55.1.5
Charitable organisations

In addition to the general requirements set out above, charity trustees have a duty to act prudently [see **13.3**], and must comply with Charities Act requirements prior to taking out a mortgage and other borrowing using a charity's land or buildings as security [see **57.11.1**].

55.2
OVERDRAFTS

An **overdraft** facility provided by a bank is a simple form of loan. An overdraft is not for any specific period, and the bank may withdraw the facility and require immediate repayment at any time. If the organisation expects to need the facility for a significant and predictable period, it may be advisable to enter into a loan agreement. This removes the risk of being required to pay the amount unexpectedly, and may also offer lower rates of interest.

Banks are unlikely to allow a significant overdraft or loan without seeking security in the form of a charge on the organisation's assets [see **55.5.2**] or a guarantee [see **55.5.3**].

55.3
UNSECURED LOANS

An **unsecured loan** does not give the lender any charge on (right to) the organisation's assets if the loan is unpaid. The loan may be given by a bank or other financial institution, or by an individual or organisation. A voluntary organisation which receives frequent loans from individuals or bodies which are not financial institutions should take advice to ensure it does not contravene the regulations on money lending and financial services.

55.3.1
Loan agreements

Especially where the borrowing is from a supporter of the organisation, there may be a temptation to 'keep it simple and informal', but all borrowings should be properly documented.

Key issues are the amount of the loan, repayment terms, provision for payment and calculation of interest, and any special provisions, such as higher interest if payment is late. The repayment arrangements are particularly important, and the organisation must be confident it will have adequate funds when repayment is due.

For substantial loans, legal advice should be sought before drawing up the agreement, to ensure the organisation's interests are protected and, in unincorporated organisations, to try to reduce the potential risk to individual members of the governing body [see **55.1.3.1**].

55.3.2
Interest-free loans

An organisation's supporters are often willing to provide interest-free loans, either short term or long term. As with any loans, these should be carefully documented.

Advice is particularly important for both the organisation and the lender when significant interest-free loans are being made to a charity. If the loan is intended for investment rather than immediate use, the Inland Revenue must be satisfied that the lender has not made the loan as a way of avoiding tax on the investment income. To comply with this requirement, the loan agreement should make clear that the lender has no right to specify how the loan is to be invested or how the income earned from the investment is to be used.

Income and Corporation Taxes Act 1988 s.660

55.3.3
Loans from governing body members

There are no restrictions on members of a governing body making interest-free loans to their organisation, but the lender and other governing body members need to be aware of potential conflicts of interest, especially if the organisation finds itself unable to repay the loan.

55.3.3.1
Charities

The prohibition on members of charity governing bodies gaining personal benefit from their charity [see **14.4.3**] means that they can charge interest to the charity only if:

- the charity's governing document explicitly allows members of the governing body to receive interest on loans to the charity; *or*
- the Charity Commission has authorised the payment of interest to the governing body member(s).

If the governing document allows payment of interest to trustees, it may set a maximum rate. This might be a specified percentage, or 'X% above the base rate at X bank'. If a percentage set in the governing document is no longer appropriate, it can be changed only with the prior written consent of the Charity Commission. If the governing document does not specify a maximum rate, the governing body decides. The person(s) making the loan must not take part in any discussion or decision about the loan terms and conditions.

Charities should not try to get around these rules by obtaining the loan from the spouse, other close relative or business partner of a governing body member, or from a company controlled by the governing body member or a person close to her or him. Interest payments in these circumstances could also constitute a personal benefit for the governing body member.

55.3.3.2
Non-charities

Non-charities with power to borrow may pay interest to members of their governing body who make loans to the organisation, unless the governing document prohibits such payment. The governing document may set a maximum interest rate for such loans.

55.4
CREDIT FINANCE

Especially when acquiring equipment, an organisation may obtain credit through **credit finance**. The major forms of this are hire purchase, finance leases and operating leases.

55.4.1
Types of finance

Hire purchase is a contract allowing the purchaser to use an asset while paying for it over time. The seller retains title until payment is complete. Only then does the purchaser acquire legal title.

With a **finance lease**, the asset is still owned by the finance house or other lessor at the end of the lease period, but the finance agreement may allow the organisation to acquire ownership of the asset for a reduced price or to hire it for a further indefinite period for a nominal sum. Finance leases are sometimes used for cars.

With an **operating lease**, the organisation obtains a limited right to use the asset through the hire period. At the end of the period the lease is renewed or the asset is returned to the owner.

55.4.2
Implications

Each form of finance has different financial and tax implications. These are beyond the scope of this book, and organisations are strongly advised to take advice before entering into any significant credit finance.

All agreements, regardless of the type of finance, are likely to be subject to comprehensive and sometimes onerous standard terms imposed by the hiring or leasing company. These must always be carefully considered before the document is signed. Although the terms are standard, they are in fact frequently negotiable [see **18.8.2**].

Few forms of credit finance can be terminated without substantial penalty, so all such agreements must be treated with considerable caution—regardless of the verbal assurances which might be given.

The legislation which protects consumers who use these forms of finance to purchase goods does not generally apply to organisations. However some protection may be obtained under the **Unfair Contract Terms Act 1977** and the **Unfair Terms in Consumer Contracts Regulations 1994** *[SI 1994/3159]*.

55.4.2.1
Authorisation

Many organisations and businesses have experienced very serious problems with credit finance, particularly with photocopier and equipment leases entered into without proper authorisation and without proper attention given to the small print [see **18.8.2**].

It is vital to establish a clear policy setting out who is authorised to make decisions about whether to enter into any form of credit finance, who can agree the terms, and who can sign the agreement. But any such policy is a purely internal matter within the organisation. If an unauthorised person enters into a contract, it is binding on the organisation provided the person acting on behalf of the organisation appears to the other party to be authorised [see **18.5.5**]. However if the organisation has a clear policy about who can and cannot enter into agreements, it may be able to claim compensation from the person who took the unauthorised action.

55.5
SECURED LOANS

Few lenders, except the organisation's wealthy supporters, are likely to make a substantial loan to an organisation without requiring security or **collateral**. This is likely to be in the form of a **charge** over the organisation's land and buildings (a **mortgage**), a charge over its other assets (**debentures**), a promise to cover the debt if the organisation defaults (**guarantee**) or **retention of title** to goods. A charge gives the lender the right to the asset if the borrower does not repay the loan.

Company mortgages, charges and some retentions of title must be registered within 21 days at Companies House on **form 395**, with a £10 fee. Records of mortgages and charges must be kept in the company's **register of charges** [see **16.3.9**], **register of holders of debentures** [see **16.3.11**] and, if appropriate, the **register of directors' interests in the company's shares and debentures** [see **16.3.12**]. When some or all of the mortgage or charge has been repaid, Companies House must be notified on **form 403a**, and the register of charges must be updated.

Charges on the assets of an industrial and provident society, and subsequent changes in the amount owing, must be notified to the Registrar of Friendly Societies [see **16.4.4**]. There is no obligation for an IPS to keep a register of charges, but it is good practice to do so.

55.5.1
Mortgages

For substantial loans, a mortgage is likely to be the lender's preferred form of security. Mortgages are dealt with in **57.11**.

55.5.2
Debentures

Companies and industrial and provident societies may enter into a form of charge over other assets such as equipment, stocks of publications or other items, money in bank accounts, money owed to the organisation, and intellectual property rights. This type of charge is called a **debenture** or **debt stock**.

Unlike shareholders, who buy a part of a company, holders of debentures simply lend money to the organisation for a fixed period at a fixed rate of interest, with their loan secured against the organisation's assets. A **fixed charge** is a charge on a specific asset or assets. A **floating charge** is a charge on the assets held from time to time, such as stock or money due to the organisation.

Most banks routinely secure overdrafts and loans to incorporated organisations with a standard form of debenture. This gives the bank the first rights to the organisation's assets if the organisation is unable to repay the loan, with power to appoint a **receiver** who will take possession of the organisation's assets and dispose of them. Only after the receiver appointed by the bank has secured payment out of these assets will any remainder pass back to the liquidator who will then wind up the company or IPS [see **21.5** and **21.6** for more about winding up companies and IPSs]. In mid-2001 the government announced proposals that would remove or reduce banks' rights in insolvency situations.

55.5.3
Guarantees

A bank or other lender may seek personal guarantees from individuals or other organisations if an organisation has few assets, or if it is an unincorporated association or trust and therefore finds it difficult to take out a loan secured against its assets. The organisation needs to think very carefully before asking anyone to provide a guarantee, since it imposes on the guarantor potentially onerous obligations, not only for the loan itself but also often for interest and legal costs.

Similarly, any individual or organisation asked to provide a guarantee should consider it carefully, and especially consider the worst case situation where the organisation defaults on the loan. It is advisable for any potential guarantor to obtain independent legal advice.

An organisation guaranteeing another organisation's loan is potentially liable for the borrowing, so can give a guarantee only if it would itself have the power to make that borrowing. In the case of a charity without such power, Charity Commission consent must be obtained.

55.5.4
Retention of title

Where goods are supplied by or to an organisation, some security can be obtained by including retention of title provisions in the supply agreement. These displace the normal rule that ownership of goods passes to the purchaser when they are delivered, even if they have not yet been paid for. The clause will provide that the goods remain in the ownership of the supplier until the full price is paid. If the clause has been properly drafted and the purchaser fails to pay, the supplier has the right to recover the goods.

PART VIII
PROPERTY

The decision to buy freehold land or take on a long lease involves the organisation in substantial expenditure and a long-term commitment which may be overlaid with ancient rights and covenants. Even a shorter lease or licence may involve the organisation in a myriad of obligations, some of which could extend long after the organisation leaves the property.

'Land' and 'property' means the land itself, as well as buildings and some objects on the land.

Part VIII covers some of the main issues relating to property.

Chapter 56
LAND OWNERSHIP AND TENURE

Topics covered in this chapter

This chapter explains freeholds, leases, tenancies, licences and sub-letting, and how land is registered. It covers:

Double-underlined section headings indicate additions or significant changes since the first edition.

56.1
VOLUNTARY ORGANISATIONS AND PROPERTY

Ownership or control of land has always been of vital importance. The law in this area is therefore very old and complex, with a huge body of statute and common law going back beyond the mediaeval period.

As well as the general law, land is often subject to specific rights and restrictions set out in the title documents or contract, and special rules apply to charity land. Even the simplest property transaction is likely to have potentially complex implications, and mistakes can be costly. Legal advice should always be sought before buying or selling land, or entering into a lease, tenancy or licence as either landlord or tenant.

Chapter 57 explains how freeholds and leases are acquired and disposed of, and **chapter 58** explains typical business leases.

56.1.1
The term 'property'

The terms **realty**, **land** and **property** are used interchangeably to refer to **real property** (freehold land) and **chattels real** (leasehold interests in land, and buildings and other immovable property on freehold or leasehold land).

'Property' is often used in a broader sense, to cover all of the organisation's assets. Those which are not realty are either **chattels personal** (movable property, such as furniture or vehicles) or **choses in action**

771

or **things in action** (intangible assets which the owner has a right to but does not have at present, such as money due on a debt).

In some contexts it may not be clear whether 'property' refers only to buildings and land, or to everything owned by the organisation.

56.1.2
Land ownership and tenure

The most important land rights are:

- freehold (ownership) [see **56.3**];
- lease (exclusive right of occupation) [see **56.4**]; *and*
- licence (right to use) [see **56.5**].

Only freeholds and leases are **legal estates** and give rights to the land. A **licence** is not legal estate; it is only a contract or permission.

Law of Property Act 1925

56.2
POWERS RELATING TO PROPERTY

An organisation may have statutory power to acquire and dispose of property, or may need to have such power in its governing document.

Registered social landlords are subject to special restrictions when dealing with property. These are not covered in this book.

56.2.1
Companies

Companies generally have in their memorandum of association the power:

- to buy, take on lease, mortgage and develop property for the use of the organisation or for investment purposes;
- to take property in exchange for other property;
- to alter, improve and maintain property and to build, maintain, equip, alter and demolish buildings;
- to sell property or dispose of it in other ways;
- to make regulations relating to any property.

These powers may be explicit, or may be implicit in a general power 'to do anything lawful to attain the organisation's objects'. Legal advice should be taken before entering into a property transaction if the memorandum does not contain either the relevant power or a general power. If property is being purchased to earn income from it rather than to use it for the organisation's activities, explicit power to invest may be necessary [see **54.1.4**].

Charitable companies are subject to charity law requirements on property [see **56.2.4**].

56.2.2
Industrial and provident societies

Unless its rules indicate otherwise, industrial and provident societies have all the powers relating to real property set out above. Charitable IPSs are not bound by most Charities Act rules on property, but do have to include the required statement in documents relating to mortgages and transfer of property [see **57.11.1** and **57.12.4**].

Industrial and Provident Societies Act 1965 s.30(1);
Charities Act 1993 ss.36(10)(a), 37(1)(b), 38(7)

56.2.3
Trusts and unincorporated associations

Unless their governing document specifies otherwise, trusts and charitable associations have a statutory power, subject to a duty of care [see **54.1.2**], to acquire freehold or leasehold land in the UK as an investment, for occupation by beneficiaries or for any other reason, and have the same rights in relation to the land as any other owner. This statutory power is in addition to any other powers specified in the governing document. If the organisation is charitable, it must comply with charity law requirements [see **56.2.4**]. *Trustee Act 2000 ss.1, 2, 8*

If a trust or charitable association will ever want to acquire land outside the UK, the governing document should include power to do so.

The power of a non-charitable unincorporated association to undertake property transactions is governed by its governing document.

56.2.4
Charities

Charities' powers depend on their legal structure [see above] and governing document. Powers relating to property will generally be implied (assumed to exist) if use of land is necessary to achieve the charity's objects.

Rosemary Simmons Memorial Housing Association
Limited v United Dominion Trust Limited [1987] 1 All ER 281

56.2.4.1
Duties of charity trustees

The normal duties of charity trustees apply to all land transactions by charities. This normally means obtaining and acting on appropriate professional advice, including, as appropriate:

- a structural survey;

- advice on the value of the property or level of rent;

- legal advice as to the suitability of the title for the purpose intended, planning permission, and any onerous covenants or restrictions [see **56.7**].

If proper advice is not taken and the charity suffers a loss on a property transaction, the trustees could be held by the Charity Commission or court to be in breach of trust, and could be personally required to make good the loss to the charity.

In addition to the general duty of prudence [see **13.3**] and the duty of care when investing [see **54.1.2**], special rules apply to mortgages [see **57.11.1**], selling or disposing of land or surrendering a lease [see **57.12**], and selling or disposing of permanent endowment [see **57.13**].

56.3
FREEHOLD

In legal terms a freehold is an **estate of fee simple absolute in possession** and gives rights to the land forever. These are the most fundamental and far-reaching rights over land, and do not in normal circumstances require any further payment to a third party for the perpetual occupation of the land. Even a freehold title, however, may be subject to a wide range of restrictions and obligations affecting the land or endowing it with additional rights [see **56.7**].

Although freehold is a permanent ownership, it can be lost if a third party occupies the land without permission for more than 12 years. Such occupation is called **adverse possession**, and is often referred to as **squatter's rights**.

56.4
LEASES AND TENANCIES

A **lease** is the right to occupy a freeholder's land for a defined period or a succession of periods, combining a contractual relationship with a property relationship. It is in effect a contract by which the freeholder or a leaseholder grants a legal estate to the lessee (often called a tenant) for a limited period. It gives the lessee or tenant the exclusive right, with some exceptions, to occupy the land and to exclude the landlord and others [see **56.4.4**].

In contrast to freehold which is a perpetual right, a lease must have a definite or potentially definite time limit, often called the **term**. The interest retained by the freeholder—the right to re-occupy the land when the lease has expired—is the **reversion**.

Most leases provide for the payment of some rent to the landlord. This may range from peppercorn or nominal to a full market rent which is increased at regular intervals, often referred to as **rack rent**.

The detailed terms of a typical business lease are dealt with in **58.2**. While the relationship of landlord and tenant is primarily governed by what the two parties agree, many statutory and other rules affect the relationship.

56.4.1
Liability

If the organisation entering into the lease is not incorporated with limited liability [see **2.1.1**], the signatories are personally liable for ensuring the terms of the lease are complied with, unless the lease specifically states otherwise. This includes payment of rent, any obligation to repair, and all other obligations. If the organisation defaults, the signatories or others defined under the lease are liable to make good the default. They then have a right to be indemnified (repaid) by the organisation [see **19.6.7**] if the organisation has funds to do so, and in some cases may be able to make a claim against other members of the governing body or members of the organisation [see **19.1.3**].

The landlord may be willing to agree that the liability of the signatories will not be greater than the organisation's ability to indemnify them [see **19.6.5**]. If this is not possible a person signing a lease, especially for a long term, on behalf of a trust or unincorporated association should take independent legal advice before doing so.

56.4.2
Leases

A **lease** is the contract by which the freeholder or a tenant of the land grants a tenant or sub-tenant the right to occupy the land. For fixed-term periods of more than three years, the lease must be signed as a deed [see **18.3**].   *Law of Property Act 1925 ss.53, 54*

If the person granting the lease (the **lessor**) is a tenant of the freeholder, the lessor grants an **underlease**. If the lessor has an underlease, the new lease is a **sub-underlease.**

Leases are often drawn up in duplicate with one part, the **lease**, signed by the landlord and the other part, the **counterpart**, signed by the tenant.

56.4.2.1
Premiums and rent

Tenants may pay the landlord for the lease in a variety of ways. There will be a rent which can vary from a small or nominal rent (a **ground rent**) ranging from a peppercorn to a few hundred pounds a year, to a full market rent with regular increases (a **rack rent**).

Where the rent is nominal the landlord will generally expect some other consideration, either an initial capital payment (a **fine** or **premium**) or another obligation such as constructing a building on the land.

Any combination of length of the lease (the **term**), size of premium and level of rent is possible. The most common are:

- for the sale of flats: long term (typically 99-125 years), large premium (full sale price) and very low rent (£50-£250 per year);

- for a building or development lease: medium to long term (20-99 years), a premium, relatively low rent reflecting the undeveloped site value, and the obligation to erect a new building on the site;

- for commercial property such as office, workshop or retail premises: short to medium term (up to 20 years), no premium, full market rent reviewed at three to five year intervals (**rack rent**).

For more about premiums in business leases see **58.2.3**.

56.4.3
Tenancies

A lease for a period of up to three years without a premium is often called a **tenancy agreement** (although in practice the term **tenancy** is used to refer to any type of lease). Unlike a longer lease or one with a premium, a tenancy agreement does not have to be in the form of a deed and may take the form of an informal written or verbal agreement.

In common usage the terms **tenant** and **lessee** refer to a person with a lease as well as one with a tenancy.

56.4.4
Exclusive possession

Lessees and tenants have **exclusive possession**, giving them the right to sole use of the property and the right to exclude everyone else, including the landlord. Exclusive possession is one of the features differentiating a lease or tenancy from a licence [see **56.5**], even though leases and tenancy agreements generally provide for many exceptions, such as a landlord's right of inspection and rights of access in an emergency or to do work on other land.

56.4.5
Changes in tenant
or freeholder

Once the freeholder lets the land the tenant may, unless prevented by the terms of the lease, **assign** the lease to another person [see **58.2.7**].

Alternatively the tenant may, unless prevented by the terms of the lease, retain the lease but **sub-let** all or part of the property. The new lease is then a **sub-lease** [see **56.9**].

Freeholders may sell their interest in the reversion [see **56.4**]. The right to possession of the land then reverts to the new freeholder when the original lease expires.

56.4.5.1
Leases granted before 1
January 1996

A lease granted before 1 January 1996 is a contract between the two original parties for the entire period of that contract. Thus the first freeholder and the original tenant are contractually bound to each other for the whole period of the lease, regardless of how many times the lease is assigned or the reversionary rights are sold.

Each new freeholder and each new tenant (**assignee**) is bound to observe the terms of the original lease during the period that they occupy the role of landlord or lessee. But if an assignee breaches the lease, the landlord can look to the original tenant for compensation.

The landlord must notify the original tenant of mounting arrears for which they may be liable. If this is not done within six months of when the arrears become due, the landlord loses the right to claim those arrears from the original tenant.

Landlord and Tenant (Covenants) Act 1995 s.17

An original tenant who pays the arrears of a defaulting assignee has a right to be granted an **overriding lease**. The original tenant becomes the assignee's landlord, and can enforce the collection of rent or evict the assignee. *ss.19-20*

56.4.5.2
Leases granted from
1 January 1996

For leases granted on or after 1 January 1996—unless they were granted as the result of an agreement, option or court order prior to that date—the obligations of the original freeholder and tenant after they assign their interest are substantially different. Pre-1996 forms of lease, guarantee and assignment document must therefore be fully reviewed before being used for any new leases.

For leases from 1 January 1996, the original tenant is released from its obligations after the lease has been assigned to a new tenant. However, leases nearly always include provisions giving the landlord the right to require the outgoing tenant to guarantee the new tenant's obligations through an **authorised guarantee agreement**. If this guarantee is in place, the outgoing tenant remains liable until the new tenant assigns to yet another new tenant. *ss.5, 11-16*

The landlord is not automatically released from its obligations if the lease is assigned to a new tenant, but may apply for release by serving a notice in the prescribed form within four weeks from the date of assignment. The tenant has the right to object to this. *s.6*

As with pre-1996 leases a former tenant has the right to be informed within six months of any liability for arrears of a later tenant, and has to right to be granted an overriding lease if it pays these arrears.

56.4.6
Registration of lease

When a lease for more than 21 years is granted or transferred, it must be registered at the Land Registry [see **56.6.2**]. The Registry issues a **land certificate** which with the lease forms the document of title.

56.4.7
Tenancies with
security

Charities and other voluntary organisations are covered by statutory provisions on business leases and tenancies, and may be entitled to a new tenancy as of right on expiry or termination of the original [see **58.7**]. In general all business tenancies, including weekly tenancies, are covered by these security provisions, provided that:

- there is a lease or tenancy, not a licence [see **56.5**] or tenancy at will [see **56.4.8.3**]; *and*

- the tenancy does not fall within specified exclusions [see **56.4.8**].

The security provisions apply only to property actually occupied by the tenant for the purposes of its business or not-for-profit activities, and where the business or activities are carried on by the tenant. Thus security of tenure is not available for parts of the premises sub-let to or used by other organisations, or even a subsidiary of the tenant.

An organisation taking on premises, either as a tenant or sub-tenant, or renting out premises needs to be fully aware of the implications of the security of tenure provisions before entering into any lease or tenancy agreement.

56.4.7.1
Term of years

A lease or tenancy for a **term of years** is granted for a fixed period, although it may contain provisions for early termination or surrender [see **58.8.2** and **58.8.3**]. If the provisions for security of tenure apply, the lease or tenancy continues on the same terms at the end of the period unless the landlord or tenant gives notice as required under the **Landlord and Tenant Act 1954** ss.24-28 [see **58.7**].

56.4.7.2
Periodic tenancy

A **periodic tenancy** is initially granted for a short period, from a week to as much as a year. The tenancy then continues for a succession of such periods until terminated by the landlord or tenant. If the security of tenure provisions apply, the tenancy continues until the landlord or tenant gives notice as required under the Act [see **58.7**].

56.4.7.3
Statutory tenancy

A **statutory tenancy** is created when a lease or tenancy for a term of years or a periodic tenancy is continued past its expiry or termination. It can be ended only by the procedures specified in the Act.

56.4.8
Tenancies without security

Certain types of business tenancy do not have statutory security of tenure. These include short-term tenancies, tenancies where the landlord and tenant agree to exclude security of tenure, tenancies at will, and tenancies at sufferance.

56.4.8.1
Short-term tenancy

Security of tenure is not created for business tenancies where:

- a fixed-term tenancy for six months or less is granted, without any provision for renewal beyond the six months; *or*

- the landlord renews such a fixed-term tenancy once only for a further six months or less.   *Landlord and Tenant Act 1954 s.43*

A further renewal brings the tenancy within the protection of the Act.

A short-term tenancy without security cannot be created if the tenant, or any predecessor of the tenant in the business or activity, has already been in occupation for more than 12 months.

56.4.8.2
<u>Court order</u>

If the tenant is likely to occupy the premises for more than one year but both the landlord and tenant agree to exclude security of tenure, they can apply to the county court for an order excluding security of tenure. There is a small court fee. Some courts are able to deal with the application and make the order within one week or less.

The application must be made prior to the grant of the tenancy. If it is necessary to allow the proposed tenant into the premises prior to the grant of the order, this should be done under a tenancy at will [see below] or short fixed-term agreement.

Rather than agreeing a series of short leases, the parties frequently agree to the grant of a longer lease of three to five years, which can then be terminated by either party by notice at any time. The advantage of this is that only one application to the court is necessary.

At the time of writing (early 2001) the government had announced proposals which, if implemented, will enable security of tenure to be excluded without obtaining prior court approval.

56.4.8.3
Tenancy at will

A **tenancy at will** can be ended immediately by either side, without having to give a period of notice. It may be used, for example, where tenants surrender their lease but cannot move out on the due date and the landlord allows them to remain, or where a tenancy does not have security of tenure and the lease expires while a new lease is still in the course of negotiation.

56.4.8.4
Tenancy at sufferance

A **tenancy at sufferance** arises when the tenancy has ended but the tenant remains without the assent or dissent of the landlord, and without a statutory tenancy. It is a state just short of unauthorised occupation [see **59.5.2**].

56.5
LICENCES

Unlike a freehold, lease or tenancy, a **licence** does not give the right to exclusive possession [see **56.4.4**]. It is not a legal estate, but merely a contract giving permission to use premises or land.

A licence may be for a very temporary occupation such as the right to erect a market stall for the day, or may be a long-term arrangement very similar to a lease or tenancy. Typically under a licence the landlord, rather than the occupant, is responsible for repairs, insurances and rates, and either side can terminate on short notice.

A genuine licence does not create any security of tenure [see **56.4.7**], and the licensor does not have the wide range of remedies open to a landlord under a tenancy [see **58.4**]. In particular, there is no right of distress for rent [see **58.4.3**].

56.5.1
Lease or licence?

Because long-term licences are often used to avoid creating security of tenure, there has been a great deal of litigation about what constitutes a licence. For a lay person it is risky to try to assess whether an agreement is a tenancy or a licence, and even lawyers may not agree.

If something called a licence is in fact a lease, the tenant may have security the landlord does not wish to grant. Or if something referred to as a lease is in fact a licence. the tenant will not have the security it thinks it has. For both parties, clarity is essential.

One of the key factors in determining whether an agreement is a lease or a licence is whether there is exclusive possession [see **56.4.4**]. But if the agreement says that the tenant must share occupation with the landlord or others and in reality no such sharing is intended, the court may well ignore the written words and look at the intended reality.

Another factor is whether rent is payable, but calling a payment a 'licence fee' rather than rent does not necessarily mean that the agreement is a licence rather than a lease.

The documentation will be looked at to see if it contains words such as 'tenancy' and 'rent' which would imply the intention to create a lease rather than a licence, and whether the general tenor of the obligations are more characteristic of a lease or a licence.

The basic function of the agreement is also important. When a charity has been granting a right in exercise of its charitable purposes, the courts have been more willing to define it as a licence than they have been in situations where the intention has clearly been for a commercial landlord to deprive an occupant of statutory rights. However no organisation should make assumptions about how its particular situation would be defined. Legal advice is essential.

56.6
LAND OWNERSHIP AND REGISTRATION

An incorporated organisation can own land, including leases, in the name of the organisation, but unincorporated bodies cannot. Legal advice should be taken before undertaking any actions involving land ownership or its registration.

56.6.1
How land is held

56.6.1.1
Incorporated organisations

If the organisation is a company limited by guarantee, company limited by shares or industrial and provident society, it is a legal person [see **2.1.1**] and can own a freehold or lease in its own name.

Because these organisations have **limited liability** and a landlord stands to lose out if the organisation becomes insolvent, a landlord may require individuals to act as **guarantors** for a lease [see **58.2.9**]. Any-one asked to guarantee a lease should take independent legal advice before agreeing to do so.

56.6.1.2
Incorporated trustee bodies

The trustees of an unincorporated charity may apply to the Charity Commission to incorporate the governing body (the charity trustees), without incorporating the charity as a whole [see **1.4**]. This enables the charity to hold land in the same way as a company [see above], but this type of incorporated body does not have limited liability.

56.6.1.3
Unincorporated trusts and associations

If the organisation is an unincorporated association or trust which has not incorporated its trustee body [see above], it is not a legal person and is unable to hold or rent property in its own name. The title to any free-hold or leasehold property owned by an unincorporated body or lease held by the body must be vested in individuals as holding trustees [see **18.4.4**], or in a corporate body as a holding trustee or custodian trustee [see **18.4.2**]. The Official Custodian for Charities [see **3.5.3**] can hold land for charities. Unless the governing document requires property to be held in a particular way, the governing body can decide. For a model deed for vesting property in holding trustees, see **18.4.5**.

The title documents or lease are in the name(s) of the individuals or corporate body holding the property, and should say that the property is held on behalf of the organisation. This makes clear that the individuals or corporate body hold the **legal title**, but the organisation is the **beneficial owner** with sole right to use and benefit from the property.

In addition the deed vesting the property in the holding trustees should say that the organisation will indemnify the holding trustees if they are held liable for any defaults of the organisation.

56.6.2
Title deeds

Freehold land was traditionally transferred by **conveyance**, a document recording the date of transfer from the previous owner to the new one. The new owner would be given copies of all the previous convey-ances and deeds, perhaps going back hundreds of years.

These conveyances and deeds form the **title deeds**, providing evidence that what has been bought was genuinely owned by the previous owner. The title deeds also record rights and restrictions affecting the land [see **56.7**]. If the land is held by a charity or on trust for it, this must be specified in the title deeds.

Where land is registered [see below] the title deeds are replaced by a **land certificate** issued by the Land Registry.

56.6.3
Land Registry

In most cases land ownership is recorded at the **Land Registry**. Records cover freehold properties, leases of more than 21 years, and charges and other matters affecting them. Failure to register ownership or rights over land within two months can lead to a loss of those rights.

Land Registration Acts 1925 and 1997

The Land Registry issues a **land certificate** which contains a copy of entries on the land register, and sometimes other documents referred to in the entries. Land is transferred by completion of **form TR1** which is lodged at the Land Registry with the land certificate. The central records and the land certificates are amended to show the change of ownership and any new restrictions of rights.

The land certificate will state whether the land is registered with **title absolute** (the most secure and absolute form of title), **good leasehold** (a lesser form of title for leases), or **possessory title** (the least secure form of title).

If the property is mortgaged another certificate, called a **charge certificate** is issued to the lender. The land certificate is then kept at the Land Registry until the mortgage is discharged.

The registration must indicate, in a specified format, if the land is held by or in trust for a charity. If land comes to be owned by a charity without a transfer taking place, or if an exempt charity becomes a non-exempt charity, the trustees must apply for an appropriately worded restriction to be inserted in the land title at the Land Registry.

Charities Act 1993 s.37(7),(8),(10)

56.6.4
Land charges register

Most land is registered [see above]. For the limited amount of land that is unregistered, the **land charges register** lists any charges affecting the land, including mortgages, contracts for sale (**estate contracts**, see **57.6.2**), restrictive covenants and easements [see **56.7**], and a variety of other claims.

If a charge which should have been registered was not registered, the charge would not generally bind the new owner when the land was sold or a lease was assigned.

56.7
PROPERTY RIGHTS AND RESTRICTIONS

Most property rights date back centuries and are enshrined in common law; others arise from statute law, the title deeds or lease provisions. Some of the most common rights and restrictions are explained here.

56.7.1
Easements

An **easement** is a right in favour of a third party landowner, generally the occupier of neighbouring land. A typical example is a right of way. This right attaches to the land, so even if the current owner was not party to the agreement to grant the right, free passage must be allowed in accordance with the right.

An easement may be created by deed but may also arise because of long use (**prescription**) or be implied in some special circumstances.

The land with the right is called the **dominant land**, and the land subject to the right is the **servient land**.

56.7.2
Restrictive covenants

Land is frequently the subject of **restrictive covenants**. These are restrictions which benefit neighbouring land, for example preventing the site being used for non-residential purposes. A restriction may be of almost any nature so long as it is capable of being for the benefit of the neighbouring or nearby land and is of a negative rather than positive nature. Restrictive covenants continue indefinitely.

If covenants no longer have any useful purpose, application to have them removed may be made to the **lands tribunal**. This is generally done only if the restriction is obsolete or prevents reasonable use, and if the person with the benefit of the covenant is not losing any practical advantage. Occasionally it is ended even where the person with the benefit is disadvantaged, if money is an adequate compensation.

56.7.3
Positive covenants

Land is sometimes subject to positive covenants—an obligation to do, rather than not do, something. Positive covenants can generally only be enforced between the parties who originally made the agreement.

56.7.4
Rights of light

After 20 years the windows of a building acquire a right to continue to receive light. This may later prevent an adjoining landowner putting up a building which cuts off that light, or may enable the person owning the right of light to be compensated by the person wishing to put up the building.

Prescription Act 1832 s.3

To prevent rights of light being acquired, the neighbouring owner may take steps under the **Rights of Light Act 1959** or obstruct the light in the 20 years after construction.

56.7.5
Rights of way

A right of way may be in the form of an **easement** [see **56.7.1**] benefiting one or more pieces of land. It will have been created by deed or by implication, as when a landowner sells a landlocked piece of land and the law implies a right of access over the vendor's retained land. On any sale, such rights pass to the new owners unless they are explicitly excluded.

Law of Property Act 1925 s.62

The other form of right of way is a **public right of way**. This may have been created by ancient usage, custom, implied grant, agreement under the **Highways Act 1980**, or dedication. Where a highway has been used by the public for 20 years it is presumed to be **dedicated** and becomes a permanent public highway. Generally only the surface of the way becomes public, and the landowner retains the subsoil.

56.7.6
Boundaries and party walls

The legal ownership and indeed the position of boundaries is often hard to ascertain. In normal circumstances there is no obligation on anyone to mark the boundary, put up any fence or maintain it.

If a boundary wall exists it may be a shared **party wall**, and any dealings with or work on it are subject to special rules. In particular, anyone intending to build on a boundary or to repair a party wall or fence must notify the adjoining owner. Anyone intending to carry out an excavation within three metres, or in some cases six metres, of a building or buildings must notify the owner(s), even if there is no party wall or there is land or a building between.

Party Wall Act 1996

Although a party wall is divided vertically, each side has a right of support.

Law of Property Act 1925 s.38

56.7.7
Access to adjoining land

When access to adjoining land is needed to carry out basic preservation works and there is no easement [see **56.7.1**] allowing access, it is possible to apply to the court for an access order. This does not include access to carry out rebuilding, alteration or improvement. An order might not be made if it would cause undue hardship or interference, and if made may be subject to conditions.

Access to Neighbouring Land Act 1992 s.1

56.7.8
Fixtures and fittings

An object on land may be:

- a **building** or other object considered to be part of the land itself;
- a **fixture** attached to the land or building; *or*
- a **chattel** attached to the land or building.

When land is purchased, it includes the fixtures but not the chattels. A great deal of dispute has occurred about what turns a chattel into a fixture. Key tests are the degree and permanence of attachment, and the purpose of their attachment. An object attached to facilitate enjoyment of the object, such as a picture screwed to the wall, is a chattel, but decorated wooden panels forming part of the design of the building would be fixtures.

Where a tenant has fixed an object to the building, the law is likely to agree that the tenant may remove it if this can be done without causing damage. These are referred to as **tenant's fixtures**. However if a tenant installs fixtures which cannot be removed without causing damage, such as a central heating system, these become **landlord's fixtures**. Removal of landlord's fixtures could constitute theft from the landlord.

56.8
MULTIPLE OWNERS

A freehold or lease may be owned solely by one person or organisation, or jointly by two or more. Multiple ownership of a freehold or lease may be a **joint tenancy** or **tenancy in common**. These are technically trusts of land, and are subject to statutory provisions.

Trusts of Land and Appointment of Trustees Act 1996

56.8.1
Joint tenancy

With a **joint tenancy**, all the owners of a freehold or lease own the whole, with none of the owners having rights to a distinct portion. Ownership must be in equal shares. If one owner dies the **right of survivorship** applies, and the property automatically becomes the property of the surviving owner or owners. Where the owner is a corporate body which is dissolved, the liquidator will dispose of the share or it will be *bona vacantia* and will be vested in the Crown [see **21.4.2**].

Law of Property Act 1925 s.36

56.8.2
Tenancy in common

A **tenancy in common** is much more frequently used for multiple ownership by organisations. If individuals or organisations own a property as tenants in common, each owns its individual share. The shares do not need to be equal, and each party is free to dispose of its share. The size of the differing shares will need to be set out in an agreement or deed between the tenants in common.

The death or dissolution of an owner does not lead to the other owners acquiring that share. The share passes under the deceased owner's will if the owner is an individual, or as part of the process of distributing its assets if it is an organisation which has been dissolved [see **21.1**].

s.34

56.8.3
Issues and problems

Where a freehold or lease is held jointly, complex statutory provisions apply under the **Trusts of Land and Appointment of Trustees Act 1996**. The owners or tenants should draw up, on the basis of legal advice, an agreement for their shared occupation. This covers, for example, share of ownership, mutual obligations, share of income, share of maintenance and other costs, input into decisions about usage or sub-letting, the right to force a sale of the property, and procedures to resolve disputes.

Without such an agreement, it will generally be assumed that the parties own as tenants in common in shares equal to their contribution to the purchase.

Most jointly held leases provide that the parties entering into the lease are jointly and severally liable [see **19.1.3**]. This means that each tenant is liable to the landlord for the whole of the obligations under the lease, for example to pay the whole rent. Each has a right to recover from the other tenant(s) if it pays more than its share, but this right means little if the other tenants are unable to pay.

A jointly held lease requires the agreement of both or all parties for any rent review or change in the lease, and also generally requires the consent of both or all organisations if the lease is to be surrendered [see **58.8.3**].

56.9
SUB-LETTING

The complexities of joint tenancies and tenancies in common mean that it is usually advisable to avoid jointly held leases, and to opt instead for one organisation to take the lease of the whole and to grant the others a sub-lease of part. A normal form of lease will set out very clearly their mutual rights and obligations, and avoids the complex agreements needed for jointly held leases.

In sub-letting the landlord must decide whether to grant a licence [see **56.5**], grant a tenancy but ensure that no security of tenure arises [see **56.4.8**], or grant a tenancy with security of tenure [see **56.4.7**].

A charity is under a legal duty to make the best use of its resources [see **13.3.5** and **57.12**]. It should be satisfied it is charging a fair market rent or fair licence fee, unless a convincing argument within the statutory criteria [see **57.12**] can be made that it is in the best interests of the charity and its beneficiaries not to do so. Examples are letting to a beneficiary, or to another charitable body to advance the letting organisation's charitable objectives.

Several other issues need to be considered before sharing or sub-letting premises:

- whether the proposed letting or licence is in breach of the terms of the organisations's own lease or any covenants in its title;
- whether there are planning permission considerations [see **59.9.1**], or the sub-letting will constitute a development [see **59.9.3**] for planning purposes;
- what notice period each side requires;
- whether the sub-let will affect exemption from rates [see **59.2**], or cause the premises to be re-rated as separate units with a possible increase in the total amount of rates payable;
- whether a service charge is to be made to cover repairs, insurance, heating, reception services, cleaning etc, and how these costs will be apportioned between the letting organisation and the tenant;
- tax implications [see **52.7.4**];
- VAT implications, and in particular whether to elect to charge VAT on lettings of the premises [see **53.4.16**];
- who will take responsibility for the arrangements and obtain appropriate legal advice on the documentation.

Charities Act requirements [see **57.12**] apply to all tenancies granted by charities, whether secure or without security. Technically they do not apply to licences, but it is good practice to follow these or similar procedures.

Sometimes an established organisation informally offers the use of its premises to new groups or projects 'to tide you over till you find your own place' or 'just for the duration of the campaign'. Even arrangements such as these should be put into writing, and legal advice taken to ensure security of tenure is not created if this is not the intention.

Chapter 57
ACQUIRING AND DISPOSING OF PROPERTY

For sources of further information see end of chapter.

Double-underlined section headings indicate additions or significant changes since the first edition.

**57.1
PROPERTY
TRANSACTIONS**

This chapter looks at steps that an organisation typically goes through in purchasing a freehold [see **56.3**], taking on a lease [see **56.4**], or disposing of a freehold or lease. For a short tenancy or a licence [see **56.5**] some of these steps may be omitted but care should be taken before doing so, because most steps are designed to protect the potential purchaser or tenant. Organisations should not in most circumstances attempt to undertake a property transaction without legal advice from an experienced solicitor. In addition charities should get information about charity law requirements from the Charity Commission.

57.1.1
Initial considerations

Prior to embarking on any purchase or lease, the governing body will need to ensure it has the necessary power to buy, sell or lease property [see **56.2**], and if it is an unincorporated association or trust will need to be clear about how the property is to be held [see **56.6.1**].

57.1.2
Typical stages

No property transaction is 'typical', but most go through most of the stages outlined below. It is theoretically possible to complete a property transaction in a matter of days, but this very rarely happens.

For taking a new lease for an office, typical stages would be:

- Day 1: the desired property is identified and negotiations begin.

- Day 14: the organisation's structural survey reveals problems, so the price is renegotiated. Heads of terms [see **57.4**] are agreed.

- Day 17-30: solicitors are instructed. The landlord's solicitor prepares a lease and possibly a contract [see **57.7**]. The organisation's solicitor undertakes a local authority search [see **57.5.3**], and raises enquiries before contract [see **57.5.2**] with the landlord's solicitor.

- Day 30-50: the organisation's solicitor explains the lease and contract to the organisation, then seeks to negotiate improvements in the lease and contract terms with the landlord's solicitor.

- Day 55: the lease and contract are agreed and contracts are exchanged.

- Day 56-66: the organisation's solicitor searches at the Land Registry and Companies House to ensure good title will be given on completion. The landlord's solicitor prepares a separate **engrossment** (clean copy) of the lease for execution by each party.

- Day 67: completion takes place. The solicitors exchange identical copies of the lease, and the initial rent and any premium are paid. The organisation can now move in.

- Day 68-98: the organisation's solicitor deals with post-completion matters, including the stamping and registration of the lease.

This scenario is subject to considerable complication and delay, and time should be allowed for this.

Careful thought must be given to issues arising from terminating an existing lease or licence. It may be risky to give notice before contracts are exchanged (Day 55 in the above outline), but leaving it this late may mean that the organisation must continue paying rent on the old lease for a considerable period.

57.2
SAFEGUARDS

Caveat emptor—the principle that it is up to the buyer to find any problem—generally applies to land transactions, but the purchaser or tenant is not entirely unprotected.

57.2.1
Misrepresentation or fraud

If an owner or landlord deliberately misrepresents matters, a purchaser or tenant may be able to bring a claim. However, many leases and contracts for sale of property provide that certain representations not actually written into the contract or lease do not give rise to a claim.

In general it is not an offence *not* to give full information about the property. There is no obligation to disclose matters such as lack of planning permission or physical defects, but if asked the vendor cannot give false or misleading information. Certain information, such as a defect in the title of the seller, does have to be disclosed.

A false or misleading claim by a property developer or estate agent may constitute a criminal offence. *Property Misdescription Act 1991*

57.2.2
Implied covenants

An **implied covenant** is a promise which the court will assume exists, even if it is not explicit.

57.2.2.1
Covenants for title

Covenants for title imply promises into the contract, transfer, lease or mortgage about the nature of the vendor's or landlord's ownership. The extent of the implied covenants depends on whether the transfer is expressed to be **with full title guarantee** or **with limited title guarantee**. If these phrases are omitted, covenants for title will not be implied. *Law of Property (Miscellaneous Provisions) Act 1994*

Full title guarantee implies that:

- the owner or landlord has a right to convey the property;
- the owner or landlord will do whatever is necessary to vest the land in (formally transfer it to) the purchaser or tenant;
- the property is free from any encumbrance or third party rights, except those that the owner or landlord does not know about and could not reasonably be expected to know about, and there is no liability on the owner or landlord for anything the tenant actually knows about;
- since the last sale the vendor has not created an encumbrance or charge or let anyone else do so, and is not aware of any such encumbrance or charge;
- where a lease is being assigned, the lease still continues and is not voidable because of any breach of the tenant's covenants [see **58.2.2**].

ss.2-4

Other terms are implied when mortgaging. *s.5*

With limited title guarantee means that the covenants are slightly more limited. In either case, the full list of covenants may be amended by particular provisions.

57.2.2.2
Implied by statute

Some implied covenants arise from statute. The **Landlord and Tenant Act 1985**, for example, imposes a duty on the landlord to repair in certain residential tenancies.

57.2.2.3
Derogation from grant

A covenant that a landlord must not **derogate** from the grant of the lease is always implied. This stops the landlord from doing anything which makes the premises substantially unfit for the purposes for which they are let, or which substantially deprives the tenant of its 'use and enjoyment' of its property. The emphasis is on an act by the landlord. If the premises are unusable at the beginning of the tenancy this is not a derogation from a grant, because it was up to the tenant to be aware of the unsuitability prior to signing the lease.

57.2.2.4
Implied by the courts

Covenants may be implied by the courts in certain very limited circumstances where the covenant is fair and obvious, does not contradict any agreed term, and is necessary to the business efficiency of the contract. The more detailed a lease or tenancy, the less willing a court will be to imply a term.

57.2.2.5
Quiet enjoyment

In the past, a covenant for **quiet enjoyment** was generally implied into a lease. This prevents the landlord from physically interfering with the property or harassing the tenant. This is no longer implied, and must generally be included in the lease as an **express covenant**. The right of quiet enjoyment can be limited, for example if the landlord makes clear that someone else has a right of way over the land.

57.3
INITIAL STEPS

A prospective purchaser or tenant first needs to ensure that the property is indeed as they think it is, and to determine whether the asking price or rent is reasonable. If the organisation is a charity it must also comply with charity rules on acquiring property, which are set out in Charity Commission booklet CC33 *Acquiring Property*.

57.3.1
Valuation

A price or rent should generally not be agreed without first obtaining professional valuation advice from a surveyor or a qualified and experienced estate agent. Purchase prices and rents offered are often highly speculative and open to considerable negotiation.

57.3.2
Inspection and survey

The potential purchaser or tenant should undertake a careful and methodical inspection of the property, noting any matters which may need further investigation. These might include, for example:

- evidence of recent building works which would have needed planning and building regulation approval;

- a path at the back over which others might have a right of way;

- evidence that anyone other than the vendor is occupying or using the premises and thus might have rights to the premises;

- the need for rights over other land, such as a fire escape over the roof or other shared facilities;

- access for people with disabilities [see **37.4.3**].

For virtually all freeholds and the majority of leases, the potential purchaser or tenant should have a **structural survey** of the building and land. Where undeveloped land is being developed or a new development is planned, an environmental survey should be undertaken.

Before doing a survey for a lease or tenancy the surveyor should have a full copy of the lease, because the terms set out in the lease will affect his or her report. The majority of leases are full repairing leases [see **58.2.4**], under which repair can extend to full replacement, for example of a roof. The words 'keep in good repair' in a lease mean put into good repair and then keep it in that condition. A surveyor can help ensure the potential tenant is fully aware of the condition of the premises and potential costs in repairing and maintaining them.

If defects are revealed by the survey, a potential tenant or purchaser may seek repairs or improvements, a rent-free period, reduction of rent, a **reverse premium** (the landlord or assigning tenant paying a capital sum to the incoming tenant) or a price reduction.

57.4
HEADS OF TERMS

At some stage the vendor and purchaser or landlord and tenant will strike a deal. The main terms may then be set down in a non-binding document called **heads of terms**. This is often drawn up by the agents selling or letting the property. It is very important to get professional advice on heads of terms before agreeing them, because subsequent variation can be difficult.

57.4.1
Freehold

The heads of terms for a freehold purchase are generally very short, consisting of the price, size of deposit and suggested completion date. The completion date may later be varied. Additional terms may be included such as fittings [see **56.7.8**], works to be undertaken prior to completion, or events on which completion is conditional [see **57.6.1.1**].

57.4.2
Lease or tenancy

Heads of terms for a lease or tenancy should be more detailed, with each issue thought about and carefully negotiated. Typical heads of terms are set out below. For the clauses in the lease itself, see **58.2**.

- Amount of rent, what it includes, and length of any rent-free period. If agreement cannot be reached, a compromise may be a low starting rent, stepping up during the period to the first rent review.

- Whether there is any restriction on the landlord's right to charge VAT on the rent [see **53.4.16**].

- Rent reviews, their timing, and any special methods of review [see **58.2.10**]. Typically rent reviews are upwards only. Tenants should press for reviews which can be either upwards or downwards.

- Length of the term of the lease.

- Any rights of surrender or early termination [see **58.8.2** and **58.8.3**]. These are better than rights of assignment or underletting, where there may be delays in finding a suitable new tenant and/or obtaining landlord's approval, and the organisation may be liable even after it has underlet or assigned the lease [see **56.4.5**].

- Whether the lease has security of tenure under the **Landlord and Tenant Act 1954** [see **56.4.7**]. If it is a business lease, the landlord may wish to exclude a tenant's normal right to renew the lease at the end of the term [see **56.4.8**]. If the tenant agrees to this, the tenant will have lost its right to a new lease and its right to have the court fix the rent for the further lease [see **58.7**]. This may enable the landlord to extract more than the market rent at a renewal, by taking advantage of the tenant's wish to avoid the expense and inconvenience of finding and moving to new premises.

- Uses of the property allowed by the landlord [see **58.2.5**].

- Any restrictions on the tenant's right to sub-let or assign the lease [see **58.2.7**].

- Additional rights such as car parking or use of common facilities.

- Whether any repairing obligation is full [see **58.2.4**], internal only, or limited, for example to keeping the property 'wind- and watertight' or 'in its current condition'.

- Service charge, any limitations on increases, and what it includes [see **58.2.3**]. The level of a previous service charge is no indication of what it may be in future. The survey may have highlighted potential major repairs, and if the service charge is to cover these it is essential to be aware of this. The total service charge may be capped so it does not increase by more than, say, the retail price index, or particular items of major repair may be excluded. Unless so specified, there is no limit on future increases.

- Who will insure the property [see **20.6.1**]. This is generally the landlord, who will then require the tenant to contribute a share of the insurance premium. This insurance generally covers the ground and building only, and not the tenant's contents or fittings.

- Deposit required, if any, and conditions for return of the deposit [see **58.2.3**].

- Who will pay legal and surveyor's costs, including costs of the superior landlords. Tenants are increasingly resisting attempts to make them pay the landlord's costs.

- Time limits for exchange of contracts or completion.

- Works of repair or fitting out to be carried out by either party before or after completion.

- Any precondition to completion, such as a grant of planning permission or consent of a superior landlord to change of use.

- References to be provided.

If the organisation does not have limited liability [see **2.1.1**], the people who sign the lease could be held personally liable for it. To protect them, a clause can be included, if the landlord agrees, saying that the signatories are liable only to the extent of the organisation's resources [see **56.4.1**]. If an organisation is considering taking on a substantial lease, this might be the time to consider incorporation [see **chapter 2**].

If the organisation has limited liability, the landlord may require a deposit, or a guarantor or guarantors [see **58.2.3**]. Anyone who guarantees a lease could become personally liable if the organisation becomes insolvent.

57.4.3
VAT

It is important to be clear about the VAT implications of any property transaction. The rules are complex (see, for example, **53.4.16**) and advice is essential. Typically the purchase price, premium and/or rent and service charge as specified in the contract are exclusive of any VAT payable. Therefore VAT at the current rate will be added to the stated price if the transaction is liable for VAT, or may be added to the rent during the course of the lease. Organisations which cannot recover the VAT must be absolutely clear whether VAT will or may be added.

57.5
INVESTIGATING
TITLE

One of the key steps which must be taken by a purchaser or tenant to protect itself is the professional examination, by the organisation's solicitor, of the title being proffered in the lease or sale. The solicitor also undertakes other enquiries relating to the property.

57.5.1
Title documents

Generally the title documents [see **56.6.2**] are looked at in detail where a freehold is being sold or a lease for more than 21 years is being granted. For shorter leases the tenant may have to assume that the landlord has a title which enables the grant of the lease.

The title documents will show:

- whether the vendor has unambiguous evidence of its ownership and right to dispose of the property;
- whether the extent of the property is shown correctly;
- any covenants, restrictions or burdensome obligations [see **56.7**];
- any mortgage on the land;
- any third party's consent needed for the transaction;
- any other important matters affecting the land.

57.5.2
Enquiries before contract

The organisation's solicitor raises a series of questions with the vendor or landlord. The solicitor should be briefed on any points which are important to the organisation.

Frequently the contract or lease excludes answers or representations unless they are made in correspondence between the purchaser's solicitor and the vendor or landlord. Issues which have already been discussed may thus need to be dealt with again in correspondence.

Replies from a vendor or landlord tend to be uninformative or evasive, and need to be read carefully. If information is inadequate, the organisation's solicitor should be asked to press for clearer answers.

57.5.3
Local search

A **local search** is a formal enquiry to the local authority where the land is located, to find out what has been registered on the **local land charges register**. This is not the same as the land charges register [see **56.6.4**] or land register [see **56.6.3**]. It contains a limited amount of information about the property, for example details of planning permission, or whether the local authority has a charge over the property for the recovery of an improvement grant.

The solicitor asks the local authority standard questions about matters such as responsibility for maintaining the road, charges for the use of drains and major redevelopments. The enquiries are by no means comprehensive, and in particular may show little about planning permissions granted for neighbouring property or major local redevelopment. As with replies from landlords, it is important to look carefully at the answers and where necessary to ask the solicitor to seek further information.

A visit to the planning office often reveals more information, so an organisation concerned about local development should also visit the planning office or ask the solicitor to do so.

57.5.4
Established use

The local search will reveal some or all **planning permissions** [see **59.9.1**] or any **established use certificate** [see **59.9.2**]. However, many buildings came into use prior to planning legislation, and the search may reveal little. For a small charge the local authority will generally confirm its view of the current use. If greater certainty is required, the authority may issue an **established use certificate**, which provides protection for continued use of the land for particular purposes.

The local authority may also provide a history of all planning applications in respect of the property. This usefully reveals what the authority has refused permission for as well as what it has granted.

57.5.5 Building and fire regulations

If the building was recently erected or there is any indication that it has been altered or extended, evidence of compliance with building regulations must be obtained. For matters involving building or fire regulations there is an overlap of responsibility between the surveyor and the solicitor, and the organisation should be clear who is supposed to resolve outstanding matters in these areas.

57.5.6 Plans

At some stage the solicitor will generally send the potential purchaser or tenant the plans to the property, although some leases do not include a plan. The organisation should check any plan against its own understanding of what is being sold or let. Plans are a very frequent source of error, partly because it is not standard practice for the solicitor investigating title to visit the site unless specifically requested to do so, and the solicitor may thus not have a full idea of what to look out for while investigating title.

57.5.7 Other enquiries

In some local areas, the solicitor may also make enquiries to ascertain whether there is any danger of subsidence or flooding, or may check whether any of the land involved is registered as a common.

57.5.8 Title insurance

Title insurance may be obtained where the investigation of title has revealed defects in the title, such as a long-ignored covenant preventing land being used for its current purpose. Such insurance may cover any loss in value of the property arising from such defects, and/or may cover the cost of defending legal proceedings.

57.6 CONTRACTS AND AGREEMENTS

Prior to exchange of the final contracts [see **57.7**] or transfer of the freehold or lease, the parties may enter into a variety of preliminary contracts or agreements.

57.6.1 Contracts

Instead of an immediate sale or grant of a lease, the parties may enter into a contract for this to happen later (an **estate contract**). Estate contracts are virtually always used in house or flat purchases as well as where, for example, a building has not been vacated by the previous tenant but the landlord and the new tenant wish to bind each other to go forward with their agreed transaction.

To be legally enforceable, an estate contract must be fully set out in writing and must be signed by both parties. *Law of Property Act 1925 s.40; Law of Property (Miscellaneous Provisions) Act 1989 s.2*

57.6.1.1 Conditional contracts

A contract may be **absolute**, with the parties bound to put it into effect on a particular date, or **conditional**, with the parties bound to proceed only if a specified event occurs. Such a condition might be outline or detailed planning permission being given for a change of use, or a satisfactory survey. Conditional contracts need very careful drafting so that it is absolutely clear whether the condition has been fulfilled.

57.6.2 Verbal contracts

In very limited circumstances, the court may enforce rights over land without a written contract. An example is where by agreement the future tenant has started to occupy the property, perhaps paying rent and making improvements, and it would be unfair to allow the landlord to say that the tenant had no rights because there was nothing in writing. Such a situation can create considerable legal difficulty and should be avoided.

57.6.3
Building agreements

A **building agreement** is a form of contract by which the purchaser or prospective tenant agrees with the owner or landlord that following the completion of building works on the site, the property will be sold or a lease granted. The agreement may provide that the owner, a third party, or the purchaser or incoming tenant actually undertakes the building works. It normally contains detailed provisions for the works.

The process of developing land can be undertaken without a building agreement by proceeding straight to the grant of a lease, often referred to as a **building lease**. Under such an arrangement the incoming tenant is normally obliged to construct, within a strict timetable, a building on the site.

57.6.4
Lockout agreements

Very occasionally a seller may agree with a purchaser not to offer the property to anyone else or hold negotiations for a period. Considerable litigation has occurred about such agreements, and neither party should enter into one without legal advice.

57.7
EXCHANGE OF CONTRACTS

Normally a contract provides for the lease to be granted or the sale to be completed at a later date (the **completion date**), but simultaneous exchange of contracts and completion is not uncommon.

Exchange of contracts generally refers to the date on which the contract binding the parties to enter into the sale or lease comes into force. Typically the contract is drawn up in duplicate, with one copy signed by the vendor or landlord and the other signed by the purchaser or tenant. The two copies are then exchanged and dated on the day on which it is agreed that the parties will be henceforth bound.

Prior to that date, to indicate that neither party wishes to be legally bound, all correspondence and documents passing between the parties and their lawyers or agents are headed **subject to contract**. This phrase is important because without it, a legally binding contract might be created without the parties intending it.

Since the contract will legally bind the parties, it should not be exchanged until:

- all searches, surveys and enquiries have been undertaken;
- necessary planning permissions have been obtained, unless the contract is conditional on this;
- any necessary funding or mortgage has been fully secured, unless the contract is conditional on this;
- if either the purchaser/tenant or vendor/landlord is a charity, the Charities Act requirements have been complied with [see **57.11-13**];
- property insurance is in place [see below].

Contracts normally use or incorporate standard terms, of which the most widely used are set out in the **standard conditions of sale**. These terms run to two very tightly typed pages, and cover in detail a very wide range of possibilities.

57.7.1
Insurance

Normal property insurance arrangements need to be put in place for damage or liability to third parties from the time of exchange of contracts until completion of the purchase or taking on the lease. It must be clear whether this is the responsibility of the vendor/landlord or the purchaser/prospective tenant.

57.7.2
Deposit

Where a purchase price or premium [see **56.4.2**] is to be paid, the contract usually provides for a deposit, typically 10%, to be paid when contracts are exchanged.

An estate agent may seek payment of a small deposit before exchange of contracts. Such payment should not usually be made. If it is made, there should be a clear agreement that it is returnable if the transaction does not go forward.

57.7.3
Late completion or non-completion

If the purchaser or tenant fails to complete as specified in the contract, the vendor normally becomes entitled to interest on the purchase price. The potential purchaser or tenant risks losing their deposit and may face a claim for damages.

A failure by the landlord or freeholder to complete may allow the tenant or purchaser to withdraw or to apply to the court for an order requiring the transaction to be completed (**specific performance**) and damages.

57.7.4
Auctions

In a sale by auction the contract is made when the auctioneer accepts the highest bid. The contract terms are set out in the auction particulars. All the purchaser's preliminary investigations [see **57.5**] will have had to be done prior to bidding.

57.7.5
Options and rights of first refusal

A deed, contract or provision in a lease may give a right or obligation which comes into effect at a later date, for example a right to a grant of a further lease at the end of the first lease, or the right to purchase the reversion [see **56.4**] if the landlord ever wishes to sell it. To be fully binding these rights must be registered with the Land Registry [see **56.6.3**], or be entered on the land charges register [see **56.6.4**] if the landlord has a lease of less than 21 years. If they are not registered, a third party may not be affected by them.

Options and rights of first refusal need careful drafting. A badly worded option could create a lease perpetually renewable for 2,000 years, which may be more than the governing body wants to commit itself to.

Law of Property Act 1925 s.145

57.8
BEFORE COMPLETION
57.8.1
Searches

If the transaction has to be registered with the Land Registry [see **56.6.3**], searches will be made there to ensure there has been no change in the position on the title since copies of the title documents were produced prior to exchange. If a property is an unregistered freehold or long lease, searches of the land charges register will be undertaken.

Searches may be made to ensure an individual vendor is not bankrupt, or to ensure an incorporated vendor has not charged the property, gone into liquidation or been struck off the register of companies.

The purchaser's solicitor will normally raise **requisitions on title**. These are further questions to the vendor's solicitor, and include a request for a **completion statement** setting out the amount the vendor or landlord believes is due for payment at completion.

57.8.2
Early occupation

Often the parties wish to allow the purchaser or tenant into occupation before completion. This can be done under the terms of the contract or under a separate agreement, normally a licence [see **56.5**], or a tenancy at will or short fixed-term lease [see **56.4.8**].

Access should not be given or taken unless all the terms have been agreed and in the case of a lease the full wording has been agreed. Resolving any outstanding matters can be extremely difficult once possession has been given.

Where a tenant is assigning or sub-letting, completion may be delayed by the lack of a superior landlord's consent. The current tenant may want to allow the new sub-tenant to move in while waiting for the consent, but if this is done it may be a breach of covenant entitling the landlord to forfeit (end) the current tenant's lease [see **58.4.2**].

57.9
COMPLETION

If a deed is required for the completion it will need to be properly executed [see **18.3**].

If the property is being purchased with the aid of a mortgage [see **57.11**], this will usually be completed simultaneously with completion of the sale or the grant of the lease.

**57.9.1
Payment**

Completion is normally arranged by telephone, with the monies being sent by post or electronic transfer. Any payment will normally be by banker's draft or an inter-bank transfer of funds. Only if the amount involved is small might an ordinary cheque be accepted.

At completion of a lease any premium is due, along with the rent and service charge, if any, for the first period, and any required contribution towards insurance. There may also be a contribution towards the landlord's legal costs, sometimes a contribution towards the landlord's surveyor's costs and perhaps also a contribution to one or more superior landlords' costs.

The organisation's solicitors will expect their fees and any stamp duty payable [see **57.10.1**]

**57.10
AFTER COMPLETION**

Further procedures must be carried out after the freehold has been transferred or the lease has been granted or transferred.

**57.10.1
Stamp duty**

After completion, the purchaser's or tenant's solicitor will arrange for any stamp duty to be paid to the Inland Revenue. This is a tax on a range of legal transactions, including commercial leases, agreements for leases, conveyances or transfers of any other kind (including stock transfers), and declarations of any use or trust.

**57.10.1.1
Stamp duty on sales
and premiums**

There is no duty (as at 1/4/01) if the purchase price is £60,000 or less, or the premium for a lease [see **56.4.2**] is £60,000 or less and annual rent is £600 or less. Above this, stamp duty (as at 1/4/01) is:

- 1% on a purchase price or premium of over £60,000 to £250,000, or on a premium of £60,000 or less where the annual rent is above £600;
- 3% on a purchase price or premium of over £250,000 to £500,000;
- 4% over £500,000.

**57.10.1.2
Stamp duty on leases**

The stamp duty based on a lease premium [above] is separate from, and in addition to, any duty based on rent.

There is no stamp duty based on rent where a rental lease or agreement for lease is for less than seven years or for an indefinite term, and rent is no more than £5,000 per year. Certain transfers within the same group of companies [see **9.6.1**] are exempt from stamp duty.

For other leases and agreements for leases, stamp duty is on a sliding scale from 1% to 24% of the average annual rent, depending on the period of the lease. Where the landlord can charge VAT, stamp duty is calculated on the rent plus VAT even if the landlord has not actually elected to charge VAT on the rent.

Where the lease is in the form of a lease and counterpart [see **56.4.2**], the landlord pays stamp duty of £5 on the counterpart.

There are financial penalties if documents are submitted more than 30 days after completion. If a document is not stamped it cannot be produced in any court action by the defaulting party and is therefore unenforceable.

**57.10.1.3
Charities and
stamp duty**

Charities are exempt from stamp duty on:

- conveyances, transfers of securities, and assignments of existing leases or grants of new leases to the charity (but not by the charity);
- common investment schemes and common deposit schemes for charities, and unit trust schemes set up specifically for charities;
- deeds of covenant.

Exempt transfers of land, leases or securities must be **adjudicated** by being stamped 'not liable' by the Stamp Office.

Where a charity is a landlord, it is not exempt from the £5 stamp duty on a counterpart lease.

57.10.1.4
Registered social landlords

Registered social landlords (housing associations etc) which are charitable are eligible for the same exemptions as other charities. In addition all RSLs, whether charitable or non-charitable, are exempt from stamp duty on:

- all transfers of land or buildings to resident-controlled RSLs;
- transfers between RSLs;
- transfers to RSLs from local authorities and housing action trusts;
- acquisitions by RSLs which are assisted by public subsidy.

Finance Act 2000 s.130

57.10.2
Land registration

Where the transaction involves registered land [see **56.6.3**] or the creation of a registerable interest in land (most frequently the grant of a lease for more than 21 years), the title will be submitted to the Land Registry for registration and the issue of a **land certificate**.

57.10.3
Notification to landlord

In some cases, typically where a sub-lease is being granted or a lease is being assigned, there may be an obligation to notify the superior landlord formally about the details of the transaction, and to pay a small fee.

57.10.4
Safe storage

Finally, the documents must be stored safely. Frequently the solicitor arranges this. The organisation should retain a complete set of copies for its records, and keep a note of where the originals are stored.

57.11
MORTGAGES AND CHARGES

A **mortgage** is an obligation secured against property. Using property as security for a loan creates a **charge** on the property [see **55.5**].

If the mortgagee defaults, the mortgagor can sue the mortgagee, take possession of and sell the mortgaged property, foreclose (transfer ownership of the property to the lender), or exercise a statutory power to sell the mortgaged property. Mortgagors often add other powers to the agreement, for example to appoint a receiver to take the income from the mortgaged property, or to grant leases after taking possession of the property.

Generally mortgages or charges must be registered on the land charges register for unregistered land [see **56.6.4**] or at the Land Registry for registered land [see **56.6.3**]. Unregistered charges are only effective in certain circumstances.

Companies and industrial and provident societies which mortgage or charge land must register the charge with, respectively, Companies House or the Registrar of Friendly Societies within 21 days [see **55.5**].

57.11.1
Charities and mortgages

Prior to using property as security for the repayment of a loan, a registered or excepted charity, but not an exempt charity [see **7.1** for definitions] must obtain and consider proper written advice about the charge.

Charities Act 1993 s.38

The advice must be in writing from a person who has no financial interest in the loan and who the trustees reasonably believe to be qualified by his or her ability and practical experience in financial matters. The advice must confirm that:

- the loan is necessary to enable the charity to carry out the particular course of action for which the loan is sought;
- the terms of the proposed loan are reasonable; *and*
- the charity has the ability to repay the loan on those terms.

Before mortgaging land under any other circumstances, for example to secure the return of a grant, the charity must obtain a Charity Commission or court order [see **3.5.4**].

Neither advice nor an order is necessary if the charity has special or general authority under statute to mortgage its property.

57.11.1.1
Statement on mortgage documents

For all charities, including exempt charities [see **7.1.2**], the loan document must state:

- that the land is held by or in trust for a charity;
- whether the charity is exempt from having to register with the Charity Commission;
- whether the charity has special or general authority to take out the loan;
- if the charity is not an exempt charity and does not have special or general authority, that it has obtained an order of the court or the Charity Commissioners or has taken and considered advice as required. *Charities Act 1993 s.39(1),(2)*

A loan to a charity which does not comply with these conditions may in some circumstances not be valid or enforceable. *s.39(4)*

57.12
DISPOSAL OF CHARITY LAND

Non-charities are governed only by their governing document in selling, leasing or disposing of land, but charities must comply with special rules. These are set out in Charity Commission booklet CC28 *Disposing of Charity Land*. Land includes ground, buildings or parts of buildings.

57.12.1
Connected persons

A court or Charity Commission order [see **3.5.4**] is required if a charity's land (including a lease) is to be sold, leased or otherwise disposed of to a **connected person**, or to a trustee for or a nominee of a connected person. A connected person is:

- a trustee of the charity, or a holding trustee or custodian trustee [see **18.4**] for the charity;
- anyone who has given any land to the charity;
- a child (including stepchild or illegitimate child), parent, grandchild, grandparent, brother or sister of any trustee or donor of land;
- an officer or agent [see **5.3.2**] or an employee of the charity;
- a spouse of any person listed above, including a co-habitee;
- an institution controlled by any person falling within any of the above ('control' means that the person can ensure that the organisation does what he or she wishes);
- an institution controlled by two or more persons listed above;
- a body corporate in which any connected person, or two or more corporate persons, hold one-fifth or more of the share capital or the voting rights. *s.36, sch.5*

The sale of charity land to a trustee of or for the charity is voidable (can be invalidated). This may apply even if the trustee retires from her or his post before the sale. If it is in the best interests of the charity to make such a sale, the Charity Commission may give consent.

57.12.2
Leases of seven years or less

If the charity is granting a lease of not more than seven years to a non-connected person [see above] and is not asking for a premium or fine [see **56.4.2**], it does not need to get an order provided that:

- prior to entering the lease or agreement for the lease, the governing body obtains and considers the advice of a person they reasonably believe to have the requisite ability and practical experience to provide them with competent advice on the proposed lease; *and*
- having considered the advice, they are satisfied that the terms of the lease are the best that can reasonably be obtained. *s.36(5)*

57.12.3
Leases of more than seven years and sales

A charity may make a grant or surrender of a lease for longer than seven years, sale or other disposition without an order only if the disposition is to a non-connected person [see **57.12.1**], and the trustees:

- have obtained and considered a surveyor's written report [see below];

- have advertised the property as advised by the surveyor; *and*

- are satisfied that the terms of the sale or lease are the best that can reasonably be obtained for the charity.   *Charities Act 1993 s.36(3)*

The surveyor must be a fellow or professional associate of the Royal Institute of Chartered Surveyors or the Incorporated Society of Valuers and Auctioneers. The trustees must reasonably believe the surveyor has ability and experience to undertake a valuation of this particular sort of land and the particular area in question.   *s.36(4)*

The surveyor must act exclusively for the charity and must prepare a written report complying with detailed regulations.
    Charities (Qualified Surveyors' Reports) Regulations 1992 [SI 1992/2980]

Unless the surveyor advises otherwise, the trustees must advertise the proposed sale or lease in the manner specified in the report.

If the trustees do not obtain a qualified surveyor's report, do not agree with it, do not advertise as specified in the report or do not feel they have got the best deal for the charity, they must obtain a Charity Commission or court order before selling or leasing the property. The Commission is unlikely to make an order without very good reason.

57.12.4
Statement and certificate

A contract, lease, conveyance, transfer or other disposition by a charity must state:

- that the land is held by or in trust for a charity;

- whether the charity is exempt from having to register with the Charity Commission;

- whether the charity has statutory special or general authority to dispose of the property; *and*

- if the charity is not an exempt charity and does not have special or general authority, whether the disposition needed a court or Charity Commission order.   *Charities Act 1993 s.37(1)*

If the charity is a company and does not have 'charity' or 'charitable' in its name, the document must state that it is a charity.   *s.68(1)*

The document must contain a certificate that the transaction has been sanctioned by an order of the Commission or court, or that the trustees have power to make the disposition and have complied with the provisions of the Charities Acts so far as they apply.   *s.37(2)*

57.12.5
Exceptional situations

An order need not be obtained before a sale in some specific situations:

- where a sale is made under any court order, Act of Parliament or specially established scheme;

- where a lease is granted at less than the best rent to a beneficiary of a charity, for the purposes of the charity (for example, a charity for elderly people providing low-rent housing for their beneficiaries); *or*

- where the disposition is made by one charity to another charity for less than the best price, and the disposition is **within the objects and powers** of the first charity (for example, an under-fives charity selling to another under-fives charity for less than market value).
    s.36(9)

These exceptions *do not* mean that a charity can automatically let or sell at below market value to any other person or charity. This can be done only if it is clear that such a transaction furthers the interests of the charity more than a sale at market value would.

57.12.6
Special trusts

If land is held on trusts which stipulate that it must be used for the purposes or a particular purpose of a charity, the trustees must generally place public notices before the land is disposed of. These notices must give the opportunity for representations to be made for at least one month. This requirement does not apply if the property being sold or leased will be replaced with other property which will be held on the same trusts, or the property is being let for not more than two years.

Charities Act 1993 s.36(6),(7)

57.12.7
Other requirements

Disposals by registered social landlords, parish or community councils, schools, churches and certain other organisations are covered by specific legislation, as are disposals of open spaces. Legislation includes the **Housing Act 1996** s.9, **Cathedrals Measure 1999**, **Pastoral Measure 1983**, and **Redundant Churches and other Religious Buildings Act 1969**.

57.13
DISPOSAL OF PERMANENT ENDOWMENT

Permanent endowment is land or other assets, such as paintings or an investment fund, which the charity receives on condition that it not be spent, disposed of or used for other purposes.

In general a permanent endowment of money or investments cannot be spent, land or buildings cannot be sold, mortgaged or otherwise disposed of, and other assets cannot be sold or disposed of. But in some situations the Charity Commission or court may authorise their disposal. These are explained in Charity Commission leaflet CC38 *Expenditure and Replacement of Permanent Endowment.*

FOR FURTHER INFORMATION

Acquiring & disposing of charity land. Charity Commission: 0870-333 0123; www.charity-commission.gov.uk

Stamp duty. Inland Revenue: 0870-603 0135; www.inlandrevenue.gov.uk

Chapter 58
BUSINESS LEASES

58.1
THE COST OF A LEASE

The majority of leases now granted for offices, shops and industrial premises are on **full repairing and insuring** terms (FRI). The tenants pay all the costs arising from the premises, either directly through their obligations to keep the building in repair, decorated and clean, or indirectly through service charges or other obligations to contribute towards costs incurred by the landlord. Before entering into a lease or tenancy agreement, organisations need to be fully aware of the potential costs over the duration of the lease.

Landlords prepare leases to protect themselves. But the terms are negotiable, and tenants should be wary of unsuitable or unfair terms. They should also ensure that any promise or assurance previously given by the landlord or its agent is explicitly incorporated into the lease.

Leases are technical legal documents, and advice should be sought before entering into one as either tenant or landlord.

58.2
A TYPICAL LEASE

There is no standard wording or layout for leases. The typical contents of a business lease are outlined here.

58.2.1
Introductory matters

58.2.1.1
Definitions

58.2.1.2
Interpretation

58.2.1.3
Term and extent of premises

58.2.1.4
Rights, exceptions and reservations

58.2.1.5
Rent

The first part of the lease includes the date and details of the landlord, tenant and any guarantor [see **58.2.3.5**]. If the landlord is not the freeholder, the lease may be called a sub-lease or underlease [see **56.4.5**].

The **definitions** section is very important, because words are sometimes defined in an unusual or far-reaching way which has important effects on the meaning of the clauses later in the lease. Defined words are likely to start with a capital letter in the lease, to show that they are being used in the specific way defined in this section.

Particularly important in the **interpretation** section is the typical provision that two or more tenants are **jointly and severally** (separately) **liable**. This means that each tenant is individually liable for the full amount of all the obligations, without any obligation on the landlord to pursue any of the other joint tenants [see **19.1.3**].

The **habendum** clause (Latin *habere*, to have) specifies the length of the lease, and is often combined with the formal words by which the landlord grants the lease or tenancy to the tenant and the **parcels clause** defining the property granted ('the Premises').

A more detailed description of the property may be included in a schedule attached to the lease, or the description may be by reference to an attached plan. The words used in the lease to refer to the plan indicate its degree of importance. If a plan is to take precedence over the written description, the phrase 'more particularly described in the plan attached' are used here. If the written description is definitive, the phrase will be 'outlined in red [or whatever colour] on the attached plan for the purpose of identification only'. Plans are a frequent source of error and should be carefully checked.

These sections will also generally specify the rights granted to the tenant, and that the grant is subject to certain exceptions and reservation of benefits for the landlord. The details are often set out in a schedule.

Rights typically granted to the tenant include a right of way, rights over escape routes, a right of support from adjoining buildings, use of common facilities such as toilets and lifts, use of parking or loading spaces, rights of running pipes and wiring, and right of access to undertake inspection or repair.

Common law implies that the tenant gets the benefit of any rights used by the premises at the time the lease is taken on. But most modern leases exclude this implication, so all necessary rights, however obvious they may seem, should be spelled out.

An **exceptions and reservations** clause prevents the tenant getting the benefit of rights which might otherwise be implied, and gives rights to the landlord.

Rights excepted from the tenant typically include mineral rights and the right of light [see **56.7.4**]. Excepting the right of light gives the landlord the right to develop adjoining premises.

Rights reserved to the landlord typically include right of passage, the right to run pipes and wiring through the premises, and right of access to inspect or do works.

The **reddendum** clause (Latin *redire*, to come back) defines what is **reserved** as rent. In addition to the normal rent, a modern lease is likely to reserve as rent all other sums due from the tenant to the landlord under the lease, for example the service charge or a contribution to insurance.

The reason is that when a tenant is in arrears, the landlord can use special methods such as distraint [see **58.4.3**] to recover unpaid rent, but not to recover non-rent sums. It is therefore in the landlord's interest to ensure that all monies are technically defined as rent, even if they would not conventionally be thought of in that way.

58.2.1.6
Premium or fine

Some leases require the tenant to pay a capital sum, known as a **fine** or **premium**, for the grant or assignment of the lease [see **56.4.2**]. This may happen where:

- the lease is being granted for a long period;
- there is a great demand for the particular premises, and the landlord seeks an immediate cash payment; *or*
- the lease has a rent below market rent, either intentionally where the landlord seeks only a nominal rent, or on assignment because upward movement of rents since the last rent review means rent is below the current market level.

If the premises are in poor condition or the rent is over the market level, the tenant may require a payment to move in—a **reverse premium**—as compensation, or may negotiate a rent-free period.

58.2.2
Tenant's covenants

The longest section in the lease is generally the **covenants** (promises) by the tenant. Typical covenants cover rent and other payments, maintenance and repair, use of the premises, and insurance. In these covenants the landlord may seek to ensure that every possible obligation, cost or liability which arises is the responsibility of the tenant.

In addition to the covenants listed here, there may be a host of other restrictions or requirements. Every lease, and every clause in it, needs careful consideration.

58.2.2.1
Limitation of liability

The tenant's liability is generally unlimited. A tenant which does not have limited liability [see **2.1.1**] may seek to limit liability to the assets of the organisation [see **19.6.5**], so that signatories to the lease or members of the organisation's governing body do not become personally liable. Landlords are likely to be reluctant to agree this, and may require a guarantor or a deposit [see **58.2.3.5**]. Organisations should resist pressure to provide personal guarantors, and anyone approached to be a guarantor should take independent legal advice before agreeing.

58.2.3
Rent and other payments

The first covenant is to pay rent. The landlord's right to charge VAT on the rent is generally not mentioned here, but is in a clause at the end of the tenant's covenants [see **58.2.3.4**].

Other clauses will detail other sums payable by the tenant, such as business and water rates, a share of insurance, service charge, taxes and other outgoings. These clauses are often very widely defined, and tenants may find themselves liable for large sums in addition to rent.

Special tax provisions may apply when rent is paid to a landlord based overseas. Information is available from the local Inland Revenue office.

58.2.3.1
Service charge

The service charge clause will deal with:

- what the service charge includes and how it is calculated;
- whether the tenant must make interim payments before the full cost is known;
- whether interest is charged if the landlord borrows money to finance works covered under the service charge;
- what accounts and evidence of the expenditure are to be provided to the tenant.

The tenant needs to understand that this is generally an open-ended liability, and the clause needs to be considered carefully to ensure it is reasonable. Tenants need to be aware of that major repairs or renovations, such as re-roofing and a new lift, can result in a huge service charge.

58.2.3.2
Sinking fund

Some leases provide for the landlord to set a service charge of more than is spent, and place the balance in a **sinking fund** to cover large occasional costs such as lift replacement or re-roofing. If this is not done, a tenant at the time of major repairs may have to bear its share of the full cost of a large repair, even though its lease is short or about to expire.

To protect themselves, tenants should have a full survey done so that potential major repairs are highlighted [see **57.3.2**], or seek limitation on the maximum service charge liability [see **57.4.2**]. They should also seek to ensure that this fund is held on trust, so that it cannot be used for any other purposes, and if the landlord goes into liquidation the funds are not available to meet the demands of the landlord's creditors.

58.2.3.3
Landlord's costs

The clause on landlord's costs typically obliges the tenant to pay, in a variety of situations, not only the landlord's solicitor's costs but also the costs of surveyors, experts, court fees, bailiffs and even the landlord's administrative costs. The tenant should seek to limit these obligations and at least try to agree to pay only 'reasonable and proper costs'.

58.2.3.4
VAT

Modern leases generally include an explicit clause that VAT is payable in addition to any other sums [see **57.4.2**]. Generally for non-residential accommodation the landlord will be free to elect to charge VAT at any time [see **53.4.16**], unless the tenant manages to agree a specific provision preventing this. If charged, VAT will be added to the rent.

58.2.3.5
Guarantors

Either within the lease or in a separate deed, the landlord may require a third party to guarantee the tenant's obligations if the tenant defaults.

A guarantor has been described as a fool with a pen, because the role is potentially extremely onerous and once taken on cannot normally be terminated. In most cases the guarantor has no control over potential liabilities, nor is there any obligation for the guarantor to be kept informed as they arise.

In addition to an obligation to meet the rent—which may rise substantially during the term—the guarantor will be obliged to honour the tenant's other obligations, including obligations for repairs and even a possible obligation to rebuild the entire premises [see **58.2.4**].

Guarantors should be separately advised from the tenant about the implications of the obligations they are taking on.

58.2.3.6
Deposits

An alternative to guarantors which may be more attractive from a tenant's point of view and has some advantages for a landlord is a deposit. This is often referred to as a **rent deposit** but the wording generally provides that the deposit is available to meet any claim by the landlord under the lease. Issues which need to be agreed are:

- the amount of the deposit;
- whether it is increased when rent is increased at rent review;
- whether there is a time limit on the deposit after which the tenant is entitled to its return.

On assignment of the lease the deposit is returnable.

Landlord and Tenant (Covenants) Act 1995

The tenant should seek to ensure that the deposit is held by the landlord on trust [see **58.2.3.2**].

58.2.4
Maintenance, repair and alteration

The repair clause needs to be read carefully, in conjunction with the definition of the premises [see **58.2.1.3**], to see exactly what falls within the tenant's obligation to repair. The clause may require the tenant simply 'to repair', or it may be a **full repairing** clause obliging the tenant 'to repair, renew, replace and rebuild'. This could require a tenant who rents a building in unsound condition to replace it completely if ordinary repairs are not possible.

The phrase 'to **keep in good repair**' is often misunderstood. It means putting the premises into good repair even if they were in poor repair when they were taken over.

A repairing clause may be moderated by excluding liability for **fair wear and tear** or **inherent defects**, such as faults in the original design.

If the tenant is only required to keep the building as it found it, a schedule describing the original state of disrepair should be included.

**58.2.4.1
Shared facilities**

The tenant is likely to be required to pay a share of the repair, rebuilding or replacement costs for any shared facility such as party walls, drains or access road.

**58.2.4.2
Fitting out**

The landlord may seek to oblige the tenant to fit out the premises for use or to make improvements. If improvements are made because of obligations included in a lease, future rents will generally be based on the value of the improved premises.

**58.2.4.3
Decoration**

The decoration clause requires the tenant to redecorate some or all of the premises, normally with differing timescales for the interior and exterior. The landlord's consent may be required to change the colour or to make other changes in decoration.

**58.2.4.4
Alterations**

The lease may totally prohibit alterations, or allow some degree of freedom, for example to install non-structural partitions. If the lease requires the landlord's consent, it is likely to require the tenant to pay all the costs associated with that consent. If surveyors or engineers are involved, these costs can be significant. It is therefore best to get any consent for the work written into the lease.

**58.2.4.5
Compliance with statute**

The lease generally requires the tenant to comply with a range of statutes such as the Health and Safety at Work Act, Disability Discrimination Act and any orders or notices delivered by statutory authorities. This could involve the tenant in very expensive works such as installing an external fire escape, upgrading fire alarms, or improving access for people with disabilities. The likelihood of such costs arising should be investigated before taking the lease.

**58.2.4.6
Planning permission**

Normally the tenant is allowed to apply for planning permission only with the landlord's consent. If such consent is likely to be needed immediately, it should be dealt with before the lease is granted. If it is likely to be needed in future, an exception should be added to the clause to allow such an application.

**58.2.4.7
Access**

The landlord will want rights of access to the premises for various purposes. The tenant needs to consider whether these are reasonable. If possible, the right should be restricted to circumstances where it is absolutely essential for the landlord to have access.

**58.2.5
Use of premises**

The **user clause** limits the ways in which the premises may be used. The tenant must consider its own use, the use of potential assignees or sub-tenants, and the effect on the rent review.

The uses permitted by the lease must be wide enough to include all the tenant's activities not only at the start of the tenancy, but at any time during its likely length including any renewal.

If the tenant may want to move before the end of the lease and cannot surrender the lease (return it to the landlord), it will have to try to find someone to take an assignment [see **58.2.7**]. If the permitted use is very narrow, it is likely to be difficult to find an assignee. Tenants who might be in this situation should seek to include a wide permitted use in the lease.

User clauses may allow additional uses with the landlord's consent. The law does not imply an obligation on the landlord to behave reasonably in giving or refusing such consent.

**58.2.5.1
Permitted use and
the rent review**

If the rent is to be reviewed by reference to market rents [see **58.2.10**], it is normally assumed that the use permitted is that allowed by the lease. If the use permitted is very narrow, the market rent will generally be lower; if it is wide, the market rent will be higher.

Some rent review clauses make the valuer assume that the premises are available for any use or a variety of uses specified in the rent review clause, rather than those specified in the tenant's covenant. In this case there is no advantage for the tenant in accepting a narrow user clause.

**58.2.5.2
Regulations**

For a building which has multiple occupants or for buildings forming part of an estate, a landlord frequently reserves the right to impose additional detailed rules for the good management of the estate. This may be reasonable if the rules are limited to good management and do not infringe the tenant's rights under the lease.

**58.2.6
Indemnity and
insurance**

An indemnity clause generally requires the tenant to pay costs or losses arising out of any claim within the premises, for example a claim arising from a person being injured on the stairs. To be able to meet its obligations, the tenant will have to take out appropriate insurance [see **chapter 20**]. The requirements may be very wide, and the tenant should ensure that its insurance covers all the liabilities.

**58.2.6.1
Buildings insurance**

The tenant may be prohibited from insuring the building. This is to protect the landlord against its own insurers refusing to pay on a claim on the grounds that the tenant's insurers should meet the claim.

However even where the landlord has taken on an obligation to insure, it may have insured against only a limited range of risks, perhaps fire and flood. A tenant who is obliged to put and keep the building in repair would then find itself liable if the building is damaged through an uninsured risk, such as a car crashing into it.

To avoid this happening, the lease should specify that the landlord is obliged to insure the building against all normal risks, or should not prevent the tenant from insuring the building. The tenant should insist on seeing the landlord's insurance [see **20.6.1**], and should consider what is covered and what remains uninsured. If some risks are uninsured, the tenant needs to consider insuring against these. The tenant should also seek to ensure that the lease obliges the landlord to inform the tenant of any change in the insurance provision.

The lease is likely to oblige the tenant to comply with the landlord's insurer's requirements. These may involve purchasing equipment or making modifications to the premises. The lease will forbid doing or allowing anyone to do anything which invalidates the insurance.

**58.2.6.2
Rent during rebuilding**

The tenant remains liable to pay rent even if the building is destroyed or uninhabitable, unless the lease contains a proviso suspending or waiving rent in these circumstances. The waiver period is generally limited to two or three years, and will be covered by insurance taken out by the landlord. If there is no waiver of rent, the tenant should take out insurance to cover the rent during any period of liability when the building is uninhabitable.

**58.2.6.3
Tenant's use**

The insurance covenant also generally requires the tenant to pay any additional premium arising from a particular use by the tenant.

**58.2.7
Assignment**

If there is no restriction in the lease, the tenant is free to assign, sub-let, underlet or mortgage the property without any consents [see **56.4.5**]. However, most leases impose some restrictions.

58.2.7.1
Assignment and sub-letting

The tenant may be prevented from sharing the premises, or from assigning or underletting part of them. Without this restriction, the landlord could end up with a multiplicity of tenants if the original tenant went into liquidation or did not renew the lease of the whole premises. Landlords are more likely to agree to sharing or sub-letting if the sub-tenant is not given security of tenure [see **56.4.8**] or if the sub-tenant is a branch or subsidiary of the tenant.

A tenant generally has a right to assign the whole and perhaps also to underlet the whole. Generally only in short leases or in special circumstances are these rights excluded. However the landlord's consent is generally required to such assignment or sub-let [see below].

The lease frequently includes detailed provisions designed to provide additional protection for the landlord following assignment, such as the right to require the new tenant to provide guarantors or a deposit and to enter into direct covenants with the landlord.

A landlord may seek to prevent assignment at a premium, or may try to require a premium to be shared with the landlord. These provisions are somewhat unusual and tenants often successfully resist them.

58.2.7.2
Landlord's consent

If a covenant requires the landlord's consent for assignment or sub-letting, the law implies that the consent should not be unreasonably withheld. *Landlord and Tenant Act 1927 s.19*

Case law on what is 'reasonable' generally turns on whether:

- the landlord's reversionary interest in the property [see **56.4**] will be affected;
- the landlord's neighbouring properties will be affected; *and*
- the proposed tenant is a responsible or respectable person or organisation capable of meeting the rents.

58.2.7.3
Authorised guarantee agreement

The lease may require the tenant to provide an **authorised guarantee agreement** [see **56.4.5**] if the tenant subsequently assigns the lease. If such an agreement is in place, the tenant is liable for defaults by its assignee.

58.2.7.4
Mortgage

If the premises are being let at less than market rent because a fine or premium has been paid [see **58.2.1.6**], or if inflation in market rents subsequently leaves the lease rent behind, the lease is a valuable asset which the tenant may wish to charge as security for borrowings.

But landlords may put restrictions on the property being mortgaged or charged, because if they decide to forfeit the lease [see **58.4.2**] they may face the prospect of the person holding the charge applying to the court to reverse the forfeiture in order to preserve their security. Whether this restriction is important depends on whether the lease has a value on the open market.

If the tenant is contemplating charging or mortgaging the property, the forfeiture provisions need to be examined carefully. These are often worded in a way which renders the lease worthless as security for a charge [see **58.4.2**].

58.2.8
Break clause

A **break clause** gives the tenant, the landlord or both of them the right to terminate the lease before expiry, on giving the specified period of notice. Organisations are often persuaded by property agents that if the tenant has a break option, the landlord should have one too. This may appear logical but can put the tenant at a significant disadvantage.

Whether it is fair for the tenant to have a break clause at all will depend on the surrounding circumstances, particularly lease terms such as the length of the term, the existence of rent review provisions and tenant's right to assign the lease or sub-let.

58.2.9
Landlord's covenants

In contrast to the tenant's covenants the landlord's covenants are often very brief, frequently no more than an obligation to allow the tenant peacefully to enjoy occupation of the premises [see **57.2.2**]. But they may include a variety of other obligations.

Where such obligations are included, the landlord may wish to qualify them. This might be done, for example:

- by making the obligations dependent on the tenant not only paying the rent but also observing the other terms of the lease;
- by expressing them not in the absolute terms normally imposed on tenants, but in terms such as 'use reasonable endeavours';
- by limiting the obligations to the period in which the landlord owns the reversion [see **56.4**], thus escaping liability if it assigns its reversionary interest;
- if the landlord is an unincorporated organisation, by limiting the personal liability of the lease signatories and members of the governing body to the amount of the organisation's assets [see **19.6.5**].

In a normal modern full repairing and insuring lease, the landlord will want to ensure that it is able to recover from the tenant all the costs of complying with its obligations, so that its income from rents is not eroded by the rising costs of compliance with its obligations.

58.2.9.1
Insurance

Leases generally provide for the landlord to insure the premises. The tenant should ensure that the landlord's obligation to insure is wide enough to cover all likely occurrences [see also **58.2.6.1**].

Where the tenant is liable for repairs [see **58.2.4**] it must be absolutely clear whose insurance covers repairs caused by damage to or destruction of the building. This clause should include a proviso that the tenant is not liable for rent or repair if the landlord receives a compensatory payment from the landlord's insurer.

One issue which may be covered is what happens if, following destruction of the premises, the landlord cannot or does not wish to reconstruct the premises. The landlord generally seeks to include a provision that it has a right to all the insurance money. The tenant needs to consider whether it should be entitled to a share, and if so should seek to include a provision for fair shares to be decided by an independent arbitrator. A right for the tenant to surrender the lease or for the landlord to terminate if the premises are destroyed may also be included.

Tenants negotiating leases should ensure that they have a right to copies of relevant insurance policies held by the landlord [see **20.6.1**].

58.2.9.2
Repairs

Unless the tenant has taken on all the obligations of repairing the building [see **58.2.4**], the tenant will be dependent on the landlord carrying out works to common parts, the main structure, roofs, accessories etc. It is very important for the landlord's obligations for such repairs to be spelled out in appropriate detail. If this obligation is not written in, the tenant may have no right to make a claim for losses caused by lack of repair.

58.2.9.3
Management and other services

Particularly in multiple occupancy buildings the tenant may be dependent on the landlord for a range of other services, including cleaning, lighting and heating common parts, reception, common kitchens, toilets and a variety of other facilities. A clear obligation on the landlord to provide these needs to be included.

58.2.10
Rent review

Many leases, particularly those for more than three to five years, contain provisions for the rent to be reviewed. The most common form of review is a **review to market rent** [see **58.3** for procedure].

Alternatively the lease may link the new rent to an indicator such as the retail price index or the turnover or profitability of the tenant, or simply provide for a fixed percentage increase. The implications of any such indicator need careful consideration. The RPI, for example, has on occasion increased much faster than commercial rents.

For voluntary organisations, the tenant's funding may dictate the sort of reviews it can accept. It may be essential for it to negotiate for the right to surrender [see **58.7.3**] if the rent is reviewed to a level it can no longer afford. Landlords generally resist such rights if they can.

One of the key issues in a rent review clause is whether the review is **upwards only**, requiring the new rent to be the same as or higher than the current rent, or is **reviewable either way** and allows a lower rent to be set if market rents have dropped.

58.2.10.1
Assumptions for
the review

Where rent is to be reviewed to market rent, the review clause will set out the assumptions on which the review is to be based. Even quite small variations in wording may have significant impact [see **58.2.5.1**].

Improvements carried out by the tenant during the period of the current lease are generally excluded from the review, provided the tenant has received all necessary consents from the landlord and provided the improvements were not required under the lease. If this assumption is included, there may need to be explicit provision as to whether improvements by the tenant during an earlier lease or under a contract prior to the grant of the lease [see **57.6.1**] will be considered.

All the assumptions need to be looked at carefully to see if they are fair. An example of an unfair review clause is one which seeks to have the assessment made on the assumption that the landlord has carried out its obligations, even if this is not the case.

58.2.10.2
Time limits

Time limits are important in any property transaction, but may have particular bearing on rent reviews. For example, some review clauses contain a provision that if the landlord serves a notice on the tenant suggesting an increased rent and the tenant fails to serve a counter-notice rejecting it within a time limit, the new rent is whatever has been specified by the landlord even if it is well above market rent.

A key issue in negotiating time limits is whether the party affected loses its rights if the time limit is not met. If the time limit is to be strict, the clause generally states that 'time is of the essence'. Even if time is not of the essence, it may be possible for one party to make it of the essence by writing to the other setting a deadline specifying that time is of the essence in meeting that deadline.

Review clauses tend to allow the rent to be agreed a reasonable time prior to the rent review date, or in many cases at any date thereafter. This can have serious consequences for the tenant. If the landlord takes no steps to activate the rent review on the due date, the tenant may feel a certain sense of relief. Such relief is misplaced, because unless there is a limit on when the landlord can activate the review, it may be activated several years later. Modern review clauses generally provide that no matter how long the gap between the rent review date and the actual review, the new rent is backdated to the review date. In addition, many clauses provide that interest is payable on the backdated rent as if it was rent in arrears. A delayed rent review could therefore create a large payment for the tenant. To avoid the risk of a large retrospective claim, the tenant as well as the landlord should have the right to initiate the rent review.

58.2.11
Forfeiture

Leases contain a clause specifying circumstances which give rise to a landlord's right to **forfeit** (end the lease) [see **58.4.2**]. Generally the right to forfeit is given for:

• any breach of any of the tenant's covenants [see **58.2.2**];

- the rent being unpaid for a defined time after it is due, regardless of whether any demand has been made for the rent.

Forfeiture clauses frequently allow forfeiture if the tenant becomes insolvent or bankrupt, or suffers any of a wide range of events which indicate that it is about to become insolvent [see **21.2**]. Such provisions generally make it impossible to use the lease as security for any loan.

In recent years landlords have also started including provisions allowing them to forfeit the lease if a guarantor becomes bankrupt. Tenants should seek to resist such provisions.

58.2.12
Provisos

The main part of a lease normally ends with a series of miscellaneous provisions. These may cover, for example:

- the service of notices;
- interest payable on late payments;
- what happens to property left behind when the tenant leaves;
- exclusion from the lease of any representations made by the landlord prior to the grant of the lease;
- exclusion of the normal rule that acceptance of rent by the landlord waives any previous breach [see **58.4.2.1**];
- special provision for early surrender of the lease [see **58.7.3**];
- if the organisation is a charity, any clause required by the Charities Act [see **57.12.4**].

58.2.13
Execution

Unless it is for three years or less at a full market rent without any fine or premium, a lease must be executed as a deed [see **18.3**]. If there is a plan of the property it should be signed by the lease signatories, but the signatures do not have to be witnessed as they do for a deed.

58.3
RENT REVIEW
PROCEDURES

Rent reviews during a lease are subject to the exact wording of the lease [see **58.2.10**]. In a **review to market rent**, a typical procedure is for the landlord to serve a notice specifying the desired new rent. In a majority of cases the rent is then agreed by negotiation.

58.3.1
Arbitration or
review by expert

If the landlord and tenant cannot reach agreement, the parties agree a suitable arbitrator or expert to assess a new rent. A clause in the lease normally provides that if they cannot agree an arbitrator, one will be appointed by a neutral party such as the president of the Royal Institution of Chartered Surveyors. Alternatively the landlord and tenant may agree to a rent review by a professional acting as an expert, a less formal procedure than arbitration. The general principles underlying arbitration and expert reviews are outlined in **61.2.2** and **61.2.3**.

The arbitrator or expert assesses market rent on the basis of **comparables**. This is evidence of similar lettings within recent months, which gives an indication of the current market level. Normally both landlord and tenant employ solicitors or surveyors to gather information on comparables and make the arguments about rent level.

At an arbitrator's rent review hearing the parties may be represented by solicitors and are likely to call surveyors to give expert evidence on comparable rent levels. If evidence is being submitted about rent levels which the parties have not dealt with directly themselves or through their surveyors, proper evidence of the rent level together with a copy of the lease must be submitted to the arbitrator.

58.3.2
After the rent
review

After the rent is fixed, whether by agreement, arbitration or an expert, a **rent memorandum** setting out the new rent is normally signed by both parties, with a copy attached to the lease and to the counterpart held by the landlord.

58.4
LANDLORD'S
REMEDIES

Because of the ancient history of the landlord/tenant relationship and its special nature, a landlord has substantially more ways of enforcing its rights than under a simple contract.

58.4.1
Suing

The landlord may sue the tenant for rent or other sums due. For leases granted before 1 January 1996 the landlord may be able to sue not only the current tenant but also the original tenant, provided the landlord serves a **default notice** on the original tenant in a prescribed form within six months of the money becoming due [see **56.4.5**]. For leases granted on or after 1 January 1996 the original tenant is not automatically liable for the default of a subsequent tenant, but the landlord may in some situations be able to bring a claim.

58.4.2
Forfeiture

A landlord has a common law right to end (**forfeit**) a lease where the tenant is in breach of a covenant. To do this the landlord must take possession, re-let or obtain a possession order. There are a number of statutory restrictions on forfeiture, contained primarily in the **Law of Property Act 1925** s.146. Forfeiture clauses in modern leases considerably extend the landlord's rights.

58.4.2.1
Waiver

The landlord loses its right to forfeit if it does something amounting to a **waiver** of the tenant's breach which gave rise to that right. Waiver is an act which acknowledges a continuing tenancy.

Demanding or accepting rent is a common act of waiver, since rent can only be demanded or accepted if the tenancy is still in existence. Other actions which waive are distraining for rent [see **58.4.3**] or taking a court action for rent due after the right to forfeit arose.

If the landlord obtained the right to forfeit because the tenant breached a covenant of a continuing nature, then despite the waiver the landlord regains the right to forfeit if the breach continues. Examples of continuing breach include failure to repair, or using premises in breach of the user clause [see **58.2.5**]. If the tenant's breach was of a non-continuing nature, such as failure to pay a particular rent instalment, there must be a further breach of covenant before the landlord regains the right to forfeit.

58.4.2.2
Method of forfeiture

The landlord can exercise its right to forfeit by taking proceedings through the court, or by **peaceable re-entry** where the landlord simply changes the locks, goes back into possession of the premises and thereafter excludes the tenant.

In either case, the landlord must first generally serve on the tenant a notice under the **Law of Property Act 1925** s.146 specifying the breach, requiring its remedy if it is capable of remedy, and requiring the tenant to make compensation in money for the breach. Such a notice is not required if the only default is rent arrears. A **section 146 notice** may well look like yet another letter, and may contain no indication that the landlord intends to forfeit.

If the tenant fails to meet the requirements set out in any notice or the breach is not capable of being remedied, the landlord can go forward with the forfeiture. If the landlord takes court proceedings the court has discretion, having regard to all the circumstances, to prevent the forfeiture. If the landlord has already forfeited, the court may allow the tenant back into occupation. If this happens, the landlord will be entitled to recover its reasonable expenses properly incurred in connection with serving the section 146 notice.

58.4.2.3
Forfeiture for failure to repair

If a landlord seeks to forfeit because the tenant has not put or kept the property in repair, the section 146 notice must advise the tenant of its right to serve a counter-notice claiming the benefit of the **Leasehold Property (Repairs) Act 1938**. If the tenant serves such a counter-notice, the landlord must obtain the leave of the court before enforcing its right to re-enter. *Leasehold Property (Repairs) Act 1938 s.1*

58.4.2.4
Forfeiture for rent arrears

If forfeiture is sought for non-payment of rent, it is not always necessary for the landlord to serve a section 146 notice. The court has a right to give the tenant relief from forfeiture, and normally does so if the tenant applies to the court within six months and is able to pay the arrears.

Law of Property Act 1925 s.11

58.4.3
Distress

Distress (also called **distraint**) is an ancient remedy by which a landlord can, without a court order, ask bailiffs to go onto the premises and seize the tenant's goods. Normally this is done in two stages:

- by taking **walking possession**, by which the goods are seized but not removed from the premises;
- then, if the tenant does not pay within a short period, by taking away the goods and auctioning them.

If a tenant is insolvent, distress gives the landlord a major advantage over other creditors. By seizing and selling the goods prior to a liquidation, it in effect obtains preference for its debt [see **21.9.3**].

Very occasionally distress can be used to assist a tenant where a landlord distrains on all the tenant's goods by taking walking possession, leaving the tenant with custody of them. The goods then cannot be seized by any other party, for example the VAT authorities or the tenant's bank.

Distress is governed by complex rules and should only be undertaken through certificated bailiffs, and only after taking advice about the potential Human Rights Act implications in relation to right to respect for home and right to peaceful enjoyment of possessions [see **60.3.1**].

58.4.4
Schedule of dilapidations
58.4.4.1
During tenancy

The landlord may inspect the property at any time, serve a **schedule of dilapidations**—a list of alleged defects in repair or unauthorised alterations—and require the tenant to rectify them. Most leases allow the landlord to enter the premises and do the works itself if the tenant fails to take action. It may be possible for the tenant to dispute some or all of the items on the schedule of dilapidations.

58.4.4.2
At end of tenancy

At the end of a tenancy the landlord will often send its surveyor to prepare a list of alleged defects and the alleged cost of putting them right. It is not uncommon for the landlord or surveyor to ignore any limits on the tenant's repairing liability as set out in the lease [see **58.2.4**]. In addition the surveyor may overstate what is wrong or include trivial matters, or the pricing of the items may be open to argument.

There is in any event a statutory limitation on how much the landlord can recover by way of compensation. The maximum is the reduction of value in the landlord's interest in the premises. This can be less than the cost of putting the premises in tenantable repair.

If the landlord intends to refurbish or redevelop the premises at the end of a tenancy, the tenant may have no liability. An unscrupulous landlord may nonetheless try to obtain compensation, and the tenant may find it difficult to discover the landlord's intentions for the building.

In any event, the sums claimed are open to negotiation. In the case of a substantial claim, advice should be sought from a surveyor or solicitor.

58.4.5
Damages

Damages are compensation awarded by the court for the landlord's loss. They may be the cost of putting right the tenant's defaults, plus loss of rent if re-letting is delayed. Damages for lack of repair are limited to the damage to the value of the landlord's reversion [see **56.4**], and may not be available where the landlord is going to demolish or refurbish at the end of the term. *Landlord and Tenant Act 1927 s.18*

**58.4.6
Specific
performance**

The court may order the tenant to discharge its obligations under the lease, for example to carry out repairs. However, this is a remedy at the discretion of the court. The court may refuse an order which would require detailed supervision, and award damages instead.

**58.4.7
Injunction and
damages**

If the landlord wishes to stop particular behaviour by the tenant, it may apply to the court for an injunction ordering the behaviour to cease and may claim damages. This is in the court's discretion.

**58.4.8
Other consequences**

A tenant's breach may have other consequences. It may, for example, allow the landlord to withdraw money from the deposit, trigger an action against a guarantor, or cause the tenant to lose rights under the lease. An example is where the tenant has a right to surrender [see **58.7.3**], but the lease provides that this is conditional on the tenant having observed all the covenants and conditions in the lease.

**58.4.9
Action by landlord**

Most leases reserve a right for the landlord to enter and carry out works if the tenant fails to observe the terms of the lease. Generally this covers repairs, but it may cover other areas such as ending nuisances. If no right is reserved the landlord will not generally be able to come onto the premises, and doing so would constitute trespass.

**58.5
TENANT'S
REMEDIES**

The tenant is much less well provided for by the law, and has no rights equivalent to forfeiture or distress. A tenant has to rely therefore on court action or one of the few other available remedies.

**58.5.1
Court action**

If the landlord breaches an obligation in the lease or implied by the law [see **57.2.2**], the tenant may be able to get an injunction to restrain further breaches and compensation for any damage or loss caused. For example, if the landlord does not fulfil a covenant to repair and the tenant's goods are damaged as a result, the tenant will be able to require the landlord to repair and to provide compensation for the loss of goods and for any loss arising directly from the damage.

**58.5.2
Set off**

If the tenant has a clear and quantifiable claim against the landlord, the tenant may be able to **set off** the sums due to the tenant from the landlord against any claim by the landlord for rent or in proceedings. Many modern leases explicitly deprive the tenant of the right of set off, so advice should be taken before exercising the right.

**58.5.3
Self-help**

If a landlord is in breach of its obligations, a tenant might itself take the required action. For example, a tenant might undertake repairs which are the landlord's responsibility, and then set off the cost against future rent. This remedy should be used with considerable caution and only after advice. The tenant must particularly be careful not to trespass on land it has no legal right to enter.

**58.5.4
Receiver**

The High Court has power to appoint a receiver of the property. This is an unusual step but might be taken where the landlord cannot be located or has failed to comply with orders to carry out vital repairs.

**58.5.5
Repudiation**

It has been accepted by the courts that where the landlord is in breach of the terms of a lease, the lease may in some situations be **repudiated** (cancelled) by a tenant on normal contractual principles [see **18.11.6**]. This is despite the fact that a lease is an interest in land, which normally could not be terminated in this way. However because of the nature of the landlord/tenant relationship, repudiation may only be possible in the case of extremely serious breaches. Case law on repudiation is unclear, but the possibility of such action could be raised as a way of exerting pressure on a landlord to remedy a breach.

58.6
SECURITY OF
TENURE

A tenant of premises used for business purposes (including not-for-profit purposes) may be entitled to a new tenancy as of right on the expiry or termination of the original. This security of tenure applies not only to premises, but also to open ground if this is used for the purposes of the business.

To obtain the new tenancy, the original tenancy must meet defined criteria [see **56.4.7**] and certain procedural steps must be taken within fixed time limits. At the time of writing (early 2001) the government had proposed simplifying lease renewal procedures, and moving away from the strict time limits.   *Landlord and Tenant Act 1954 pt.II*

This security is in addition to the security inherent in most fixed-term leases or tenancies, which generally cannot be terminated by the landlord prior to their expiry if the tenant observes their terms.

A tenant who does not have statutory security of tenure, generally because the relevant provisions of the **Landlord and Tenant Act 1954** been excluded by court order [see **56.4.8**], will have to agree any renewal with the landlord.

58.6.1
Procedure at expiry
of a lease

If the landlord and tenant in a business tenancy to which the Act applies take no action when the original lease term expires, the tenant remains a tenant despite the expiry of the lease, **holding over** under the protection of the Act. The tenancy becomes a **statutory tenancy** on the same terms as the old tenancy, including the same rent. However the landlord has a right, if it feels the current rent is too low, to apply to the court to set a new **interim rent**.   *s.24A*

58.6.1.1
Section 25, 26 or 27
notice

If either party is not happy with a statutory tenancy, it can serve notice ending the arrangement. These notices are:

- a **section 25 notice** given by the landlord, indicating whether it is willing to grant a new tenancy and if not, why it opposes the grant of a new tenancy;

- a **section 26 notice**, in which the tenant requests a new tenancy;

- a landlord's counter-notice to a **section 26 notice**;

- a **section 27 notice**, by which a tenant with a fixed-term tenancy or lease who does not wish to stay gives three months notice expiring at the end of the lease or on a quarter day (25 March, 24 June, 29 September, 25 December) thereafter.   *ss.25-27*

A section 25 or section 26 notice must be in a specified form. A pre-printed form can be obtained from legal stationers. A section 26 notice must be given between six and 12 months before the new term will begin, so organisations wishing to proceed in this way should begin planning approximately 15 months before the current lease ends.

The whole procedure is complex and must be carried out within strict time limits, so it is very important to take advice at all stages. For example, the landlord for the purposes of the 1954 Act is not necessarily the person to whom the tenant is currently paying rent, but may be that person's landlord or the landlord superior to both of these.

58.6.1.2
Counter-notice

Once a section 25 or 26 notice has been served, the other party must respond within two months. A tenant who does not respond loses its right to require the grant of a new tenancy. A landlord who does not respond loses its right to oppose the grant of the tenancy. This fairly short time limit is frequently ignored, with disastrous consequences.

A landlord serving a section 25 notice will have indicated whether it is prepared to grant a fresh tenancy, and if not, the grounds on which the tenancy will be opposed. For its counter-notice the tenant merely has to notify the landlord that it is not willing to give up possession. A clear letter will suffice, although printed forms are available.

A landlord providing counter-notice to a tenant's section 26 notice and intending to oppose a new tenancy must state the grounds on which it will base its opposition. *Landlord and Tenant Act 1954 s.30*

58.6.1.3
Grounds for opposition

The only permissible grounds for a landlord's objection are:

- breach by the tenant of its repairing obligation [see **58.2.4**], persistent delay in paying the rent, or breach of another substantial lease obligation;

- the landlord has offered and is willing to provide alternative accommodation which is suitable;

- the tenancy was created by sub-letting part of a property and the landlord will be able to get more rent by letting as one unit;

- the landlord intends to demolish or substantially reconstruct the premises; *or*

- the landlord intends to occupy the premises itself. This ground can be used only if the landlord purchased the premises at least five years prior to the end of the tenancy, and at all times since the purchase the tenants have occupied under a tenancy or successive tenancies which fall within the Act. *s.30(1)*

58.6.1.4
Court application

Not less than two months nor more than four months after receipt of the section 25 notice or the making of the section 26 request, the tenant must make an application to the court for the new tenancy. These time limits are based on calendar months, so if the section 25 notice is served on 31 December the two months will expire on 28/29 February and the four months on 30 April.

Once the application is made, both parties frequently agree that proceedings should be stayed while discussion and negotiation take place.

The tenant can withdraw it if it becomes clear that the landlord has good grounds for resisting the application. A landlord can apply for an **interim rent** to be fixed if it feels that the current rent is too low.

58.6.2
The new lease

If the landlord does not oppose the grant of a new lease, its grounds for opposition are found to be invalid or it fails to comply with the procedural requirements, the court will grant the tenant a new lease for the premises occupied by the tenant for its business, for a term of up to 14 years. If it has sub-let it will not get a tenancy for that part.

Generally the new lease follows the old, but the court has wide discretion to vary this. The court also fixes the new market rent. *s.34*

58.6.3
Compensation

If the landlord opposes the grant of a new tenancy on grounds of wanting to let the property as one unit or planning to demolish, reconstruct or occupy the premises, and a new tenancy is not granted, the outgoing tenant may in some cases be entitled to compensation, based on the rateable value and how long the tenant has been in occupation. *s.37*

Tenants may also be entitled to a statutory right to compensation for improvements they have made to the property. To qualify the tenant must comply with strict time limits and procedural requirements both in serving a notice on the landlord prior to making the improvements, and at the end of the tenancy. Compensation is whichever is less: the net addition to the value of the property directly attributable to the improvement, or the cost of the improvement. There is provision for reference to the court if compensation cannot be agreed.

Landlord and Tenant Act 1927 ss.1-3, 9

58.7
ENDING A
TENANCY

The principal ways in which a tenancy comes to an end are:

- the original term granted has expired;

- the lease or tenancy agreement gives one or other party the right to end the lease;

- the landlord accepts a surrender from the tenant;

- the tenant purchases the freehold and the tenancy ends as it is merged with the larger freehold interest;

- the landlord forfeits the lease because the tenant is in breach of its obligations under the lease [see **58.4.2**];

- either the landlord or the tenant terminates a periodic tenancy by a notice to quit;

- a section 25 or section 26 statutory notice is served [see **58.6.1.1**];

- in certain cases where a demolition order, closing order or derelict land order has been made by the court;

- there is a total destruction of the premises and the site on which they rest, for example by sea erosion;

- the lease is disclaimed by a liquidator of a company or trustee in bankruptcy under the **Insolvency Act 1986** ss.178-182.

A tenant cannot end a fixed-term lease prior to its expiry if there is no specific provision allowing it, and the landlord does not wish to accept a surrender. When taking on a lease with no right of surrender, the tenant should consider carefully exactly how long the premises are needed for, and whether it will be possible to dispose of the premises before then by assignment or sub-letting.

58.7.1
Expiry

At the end of a tenancy with security [see **58.6**] the tenant may either continue in occupation under the Act, give notice to the landlord [see **58.6.1.1**], or vacate the premises ending the tenancy. Tenants without security are obliged to vacate unless the landlord and tenant agree a renewal.

58.7.2
Notice under lease

Where the lease or tenancy agreement allows, a party may have the right to end the term. This is often called a **break clause** [see **58.2.8**].

58.7.3
Surrender

A lease may be surrendered (given back to the landlord):

- by voluntary agreement between the parties;

- by operation of law, for example when a tenant takes a longer lease before the old lease expires, and the old lease is deemed to have been surrendered and replaced by the new lease;

- because the lease provides for surrender, for example that the tenant must offer to surrender before seeking to assign the lease;

- by being implied from unequivocal actions, for example if the tenant gives up possession and the landlord accepts the keys and takes over occupation.

Formal surrender must be in writing, and for a lease of more than three years must be by deed. *Law of Property Act 1925 ss.52, 53*

In an implied surrender the situation may be unclear, so it is preferable for the agreement to be set out in writing.

58.7.4
Notice to quit

A statutory [see **58.6.1**] or periodic [see **56.4.2**] tenancy may be terminated by a **notice to quit**. The amount of notice required and the date on which it must expire are governed by complex common law rules. The notice requirements of the **Landlord and Tenant Act 1954** ss.25 and 27 [see **58.6.1.1**] must be observed.

Chapter 59
PROPERTY MANAGEMENT AND THE ENVIRONMENT

59.1
PROPERTY RESPONSIBILITIES

In the pressure to deal with the organisation's services, activities, campaigns, finances, fundraising, employees and volunteers, inadequate attention is often given to matters relating to property. But an organisation can find itself in serious difficulties if it is not fully aware of the legal implications of occupying or managing premises.

Some of these issues, such as insurance and health and safety, must be considered as soon as the organisation starts operating, even if it is operating from someone's front room. Others become important when the organisation buys its own premises or takes on a lease, or when it rents out or takes bookings for its surplus space.

Responsibility for the various aspects of property management should be allocated to named individuals, especially being sure someone is at all times responsible for ensuring compliance with any lease or tenancy agreement. If this is not done, any activity of the organisation could breach the terms of the lease and lead to forfeiture by the landlord [see **58.4.2**], or vital time limits such as those for rent reviews [see **58.3**] or continuation of the lease [see **58.7.1**] could be missed.

The organisation needs to ensure that individuals with these responsibilities have appropriate experience and training, have access to professional advisors, and maintain a diary highlighting key dates.

As an organisation's property management becomes more complex, a decision needs to be made about whether to use its own staff, or use outside professionals. If the decision is to use in-house staff, the costs of hiring properly qualified persons or training unqualified staff should not be underestimated. Property management is a complex and highly technical business, and small mistakes can have large consequences. For example, if the organisation wishes to evict a highly unsatisfactory tenant, the simple act of sending the tenant a rent demand could negate the organisation's right to end the lease [see **58.4.2**].

But if an outside person is to be appointed to manage the organisation's property, the organisation must ensure it has power to appoint an agent. Trusts and charitable associations have power under the **Trustee Act 2000** to appoint agents [see **13.5.2**]; other organisations must have power to appoint agents under their governing document.

59.2 NON-DOMESTIC RATES

Non-domestic property is subject to **uniform business rates** (also called the **national non-domestic rate**). These are levied on any property which is not used solely for residential purposes. Refuges, hostels and other properties used solely for accommodation are subject to council tax [see **59.3**]. Where a property is used primarily for residential purposes but is also used as an office or for other non-domestic purposes, the valuation officer decides whether to charge a business rate for the non-domestic part of the premises.

59.2.1 Valuation of property

Business rates are based on the **net annual value** of the property. This is the annual rent the property could be let at on the open market, as assessed by the Inland Revenue's valuation officer. This method of valuation means that an historic building which is very expensive to maintain might have a very low or even zero rateable value.

Buildings in a poor state of repair are valued for rating purposes as if they were in a reasonable state of repair.   *Rating (Valuation) Act 1999*

When a building is first built or brought into a separate rating assessment, the valuation officer values it and sends the occupier and the rating authority a **proposal of assessment**. Non-domestic properties are revalued every five years.

An appeal can be made within six months of any change in valuation. Many firms of surveyors have rating departments, and may handle an appeal on a 'no reduction, no fee' basis. During the appeal period, rates must be paid based on the valuation officer's valuation.

59.2.2 The rate

The uniform business rate for a property is its rateable value times the **national multiplier**. The national multiplier is set each year by the government, except for the City of London which has a separate procedure and sets its own multiplier.

59.2.3 Empty property

If premises are unoccupied for six weeks or less, the owner is liable for rates in the usual way. If they are empty for more than six weeks but less than three months, no rates are payable for that period. After three months the owner is liable for 50% rates, except for warehouses and industrial premises which are exempt.

59.2.4 Rate relief

59.2.4.1 100% mandatory relief

Places of religious worship belonging to the Church of England or the Church of Wales or certified under the **Places of Worship Registration Act 1855** are fully exempt from rates, as are their administrative offices, church halls and similar buildings used in connection with a place of worship. The phrase 'or similar buildings' has been widely interpreted to include church-owned buildings used for youth clubs, recreation and accommodation.

Local Government Finance Act 1988 sch.5 para.11;
Glasgow City Corporation v Johnstone [1965] AC 609

Full rate relief is also available for premises used wholly for:

- training, day care etc for people who are or have been ill or are disabled;
- welfare services for disabled people;
- workshops and other employment-related facilities for disabled people, as specified in the **Disabled Persons (Employment) Act 1944** ss.3(1) and 15.   *Rating (Disabled Persons) Act 1978*

If only part (but at least half) of the premises is used for these purposes, the rate relief may be proportionately reduced.

59.2.4.2
80% mandatory relief

A property is entitled to 80% relief from rates if the ratepayer is a registered, excepted [see **7.1.3**] or exempt [see **7.1.2**] charity and the property is used wholly or mainly for charitable purposes. It may also receive discretionary relief [see below].

Local Government Finance Act 1988 ss.43(6), 45(5),(6)

59.2.4.3
Discretionary relief

The local authority may, at its discretion, allow relief to a charity on all or some of the remaining 20% of the rate.   *ss.47, 48*

Charity trustees are obliged to safeguard their charity's assets and not pay unnecessary taxes, so they must apply for mandatory and discretionary rate relief.

Rating authorities may also grant discretionary relief of up to 100% to:

- not-for-profit bodies using property for educational, social welfare, philanthropic, religious, literary, artistic or scientific purposes;
- not-for-profit clubs, societies or other organisations, such as sporting clubs, using property for recreational purposes.   *s.47(2)*

Criteria used in deciding eligibility for discretionary rate relief include whether the organisation:

- encourages young people, elderly people, people with disabilities and people from ethnic minorities to take part;
- makes its facilities widely available;
- provides education or training;
- is actively involved in local or national organisations.

Rating authorities are required to give notice to the ratepayer of changes in relief. In cases of hardship the rating authority has power to reduce or return non-domestic rates.

59.2.4.4
Mixed use

Rate relief for charities is available only for premises actually used for charitable purposes, and not for related purposes such as fundraising. Administration and management are classed as 'charitable' when they are directed to the achievement of charitable objects. Premises used partly for charitable purposes (including administration and management) and partly for other purposes are eligible for rate relief if more than half the use is charitable.

Fawcett Properties Ltd v Buckingham County Council [1960] 3 All ER 503

Where staff have accommodation on the premises, relief is available if the occupant is there for the better performance of his or her duties and these advance the charitable purposes of the organisation.

Royal Philanthropic Society v County [1985] 129 SJ 854

59.2.4.5
Charity shops

Shops run by charities are eligible for the same reliefs as charities, provided the proceeds minus expenses are paid to the charity. Donated goods must account for more than half the value of the shop's sales. Shops run by a charity's trading company [see **chapter 47**] are not eligible for mandatory rate relief but are generally granted discretionary relief if more than half their income is from the sale of donated goods.

Local Government Finance Act 1988 s.64(10)

59.3
COUNCIL TAX

Council tax is a tax on property used for residential purposes. Liability generally rests with the occupier of the dwelling but the owner, rather than the occupiers, is liable if the property is:

- a hostel, residential care or nursing home, or religious community;
- in multiple occupation;
- a student hall of residence or a dwelling occupied solely by students;
- the residence of a minister of religion; *or*
- occupied by staff who live there in order to carry out work for an owner who lives elsewhere.

Certain persons are disregarded for the purposes of council tax, and there is a discount for properties occupied by only one person (or by one person and a disregarded person or persons).

An organisation liable for council tax on its dwellings needs to be clear whether and if so how it will recover the tax from occupiers.

Empty dwellings are exempt from council tax for up to six months. Dwellings undergoing substantial structural alterations or repair works are exempt during the works and for six months after substantial completion of the works.

59.3.1
Dwellings for disabled people

A dwelling specially adapted for use by a physically disabled adult or child can be put in the next lowest valuation band if:

- it is not already in the lowest valuation band;
- it contains sufficient floor space to permit a wheelchair to be used, or has a specially adapted additional bathroom or kitchen, or has a room other than a bathroom, toilet or kitchen which is used primarily for meeting the needs of the disabled person; *and*
- the facility listed above is essential for the disabled person, or is of major importance to his or her wellbeing.

59.4
WATER CHARGES

Water and sewerage charges are payable by the occupier of the premises (whether residential or business) or by the owner of properties in multiple occupancy. These are generally based on a standing charge and a charge for volume of water used. Some sewerage companies use other charging criteria, such as the size of the site area. Charities and similar organisations may be entitled to discounts from some water companies.

59.5
LIABILITY TO AND FOR PEOPLE ON THE PROPERTY

Anyone who owns, controls or occupies land or buildings has a wide range of obligations to prevent **invitees** or **licensees**—people who come onto the premises with permission—from being injured. Many of these obligations also extend to **trespassers** who are on the premises without permission.

A landlord has a duty of care to put right any defects in premises which it has an obligation or right to remedy. The landlord is not liable to a tenant if the defect is the result of the tenant failing to comply with its obligations to repair [see **58.2.4**], but may be liable to third parties if the landlord has a legal obligation to put right the defect if the tenant defaults.

Defective Premises Act 1972

If a lease, tenancy or contract gives the tenant's invitees or licensees the right to use common parts of the premises still in the landlord's occupation, the landlord has a duty of care to see that such people are safe while using the premises for those purposes. Such a duty cannot be restricted or excluded.

Occupier's Liability Act 1957 s.1

For any organisation which has employees, duties in relation to premises also arise under health and safety legislation [see **chapter 36**].

The liabilities arising from these duties should be insured against by taking out public liability insurance [see **20.5.1**].

59.5.1
Liability under
contract or licence

If the organisation charges for the use of its land or premises, a contract or licence arises between the person using the land and the organisation. Examples of this include:

- charging for entry to a fête (licence to enter for the fête);
- hiring out land for a car boot sale (licences to bring cars onto the land and to attend the sale);
- charging a room hire fee for a training course on the organisation's premises (licences to the organisation which books the space, to the trainer who teaches the course, and to students who attend).

This type of contract does not have to be written; it is implied (implicit) whenever someone pays for the use of land or premises.

Thought needs to be given to the exact terms under which entry is allowed. These terms and conditions may be imposed by putting up a clear sign at the point of entry, printing them on an admission ticket, or asking the person to enter into a formal agreement embodying those terms [see **59.7**].

In any agreement, including one governing use of premises, liability for causing personal injury or death cannot be excluded [see **19.6.6**]. Public liability insurance should be taken out to cover such claims [see **20.5.1**]. This may be the responsibility of the licensee or the landlord.

Other claims which may arise from a licensee's occupation include loss or damage to property, or financial loss. These can be excluded in the contract, and the organisation needs to consider whether to do this or to take out insurance against such claims arising. The court may rule that certain unfair exclusions are invalid [see **19.6.6**]

In addition, the organisation may need to reserve a right to terminate the licence prematurely, for example reserving a right to exclude individuals because of unacceptable behaviour.

59.5.2
Trespassers and
squatters

A person on premises without permission is a **trespasser**. It is technically a trespass to enter anyone's land without permission even for a few minutes. Consent to enter is implied in many situations or may be explicit under a licence, but such consent may be withdrawn before or after the person has entered the land. For example:

- it is implied that an occupier grants consent to others to walk up the front path to ring the bell, but this implication is removed if a sign makes clear that such access is not permitted;
- an organisation implies by its 'open' sign a licence to enter, but a staff member may revoke the licence by asking a visitor to leave;
- invitees and licensees have no right to remain on the property, and are trespassers if they come onto property outside the terms of a licence agreement or refuse to leave when properly asked to do so.

The person with the right of occupation may use reasonable force to eject a trespasser who does not leave when asked to do so [see **42.4.1**], but it is usually better to call the police in these circumstances.

The **Criminal Justice and Public Order Act 1994** gives the police powers in connection with mass trespass [see **42.4.3**], makes it an offence to fail to leave following a possession order, and narrows provisions in the **Protection from Eviction Act 1977** preventing the use of violence to secure entry to premises.

Criminal Justice and Public Order Act 1994 ss.56, 58(1), 71

Squatting is a trespass. **Squatters** may be evicted through the civil courts using a speedy procedure (order 113 in the High Court or order 24 in the county courts).

59.5.3
Drug use on premises

A person with management responsibility for premises has a legal duty not to knowingly 'permit or suffer' the sale or distribution of illegal drugs, preparation of opium, smoking of cannabis or opium, or preparation of illegal drugs.   *Misuse of Drugs Act 1971 s.8*

In 1999 the director and manager of a day centre were sentenced to five and four years imprisonment for failure to take adequate steps to stop drug dealing on the centre grounds. The sentences were subsequently significantly reduced, but their appeal against conviction was unsuccessful.   *R v Wyner and Brock [2000] The Times 28/12/2000 CA*

This case raises significant issues for staff or governing body members who are aware that drugs or other illegal substances may be used on their premises or who are aware of other unlawful activities. It is not enough for the organisation to have a policy saying it does not allow the sale, distribution, preparation or use of illegal substances; it must take active steps to prevent the illegal activities. In addition, it was held in this case that it was unlawful for staff to comply with a confidentiality policy that prevented disclosure of names to the police [see **38.1.1**], even though it was a condition of their contract of employment that they comply with it.

Permitting possession of illegal drugs or other substances, or working with people who are under the influence of illegal substances, is not an offence.

59.5.4
Banning people from premises

A person who does not pay an admission or similar charge has a right to be on premises only if the owner or occupier of the premises allows, and can be asked to leave at any time for any reason. However, where an organisation is providing public services and users of those services have access to the premises, a person may in some situations have an implied right to be on the premises unless they have explicitly been warned that they will be banned.

Wandsworth London Borough Council v A [21/12/1999] CA

Where the person has paid for the right to be on the premises, it is advisable to clearly reserve the right to require the person to leave, for example by a clause on the ticket or by displaying a notice. Regardless of whether the person has paid or not, refusal to leave within a reasonable time when asked means the person becomes a trespasser [see **59.5.2**].

59.6
ACCESS, SAFETY AND SECURITY
59.6.1
Disability access

The **Disability Discrimination Act 1995** requires employers with 15 or more employees or others working under a contract to make reasonable adaptations to premises to enable a person with a disability to be appointed or to remain employed [see **25.5.4**]. At the time of writing (early 2001) the government had said that the exemption for small employers would be repealed by October 2004.

All providers of goods, services and facilities, regardless of number of employees, must by 1 October 2004 have taken reasonable steps to remove, alter or provide reasonable means of avoiding physical features that make it impossible or unreasonably difficult for disabled people to use a service, unless the service is provided by a reasonable alternative method [see **37.4.4**].

Detailed information about the requirements and good practice is available from the Disability Rights Commission and the Centre for Accessible Environments [see end of chapter for details].

59.6.2
Safety and security

Premises must be healthy and safe as required under the **Health and Safety at Work Act 1974** [see **chapter 36**].

Owners, tenants and occupiers of premises have obligations under the **Fire Precautions Act 1971** and various regulations [see **36.5**]. The local fire safety officer can advise on all aspects of fire safety.

Advice should be sought from the local police crime prevention officer about how to make premises secure. Failure to ensure that premises and contents are secure could invalidate some insurances [see **20.6**], and could breach the governing body's obligation to safeguard the organisation's assets [see **13.3.5** and **13.2.1**].

The noise made by alarm systems is controlled under the **Control of Noise (Code of Practice on Noise from Audible Intruder Alarms) Order 1981** *[SI 1981/1829]*.

A guard dog cannot be used unless warning notices are clearly displayed, and the dog is under the control of the handler or is secured and cannot freely roam the premises.   *Guard Dog Act 1975*

59.7
HIRING OUT
PREMISES

When an organisation becomes involved in hiring out rooms, halls, playing fields or any other facility, it is advisable to have a clear written agreement with the hirer prior to the commencement of any hiring. An example of an agreement for hire is set out below, but every agreement needs to be drafted to reflect the particular situation and activities involved.

Insurance is vital. It is sensible for the organisation to extend its own third party/public liability insurance [see **20.5.1**] to cover the hirer, and not to rely on the hirer's duty to indemnify the organisation.

If the hiring involves more than normal furnishings—for example if it includes the use of catering facilities or training equipment—it could constitute a trading activity and be subject to tax and VAT.

For licences granted for longer term occupation, see **56.5**.

59.7.1
Model hiring
agreement

Date of Agreement:

BETWEEN [hiring organisation] of [address] ('the Organisation') and [the hiring body] of [address] ('the Hirer')

1. The Hirer may use _____ Room together with the following equipment: _____

    on the _____ day of _____ 20__ from _____am/pm to _____ am/pm

    for the purpose only of _____.

2. The fee is £ _____ [+ VAT at the standard rate, if the organisation is registered for VAT and has elected to charge VAT, or if the booking is subject to VAT because it includes extra facilities].

3. The Hirer will pay:

    (a) a deposit of £_____ not later than ___ working days before the date of hire; and

    (b) the balance not later than _____.

4. ___% of the fee is due if a booking is cancelled with less than ____ days notice.

5. The Hirer agrees to abide by the Organisation's conditions of hire set out below/overleaf and any directions given to it by the Organisation.

Signed on behalf of the Organisation: _____

Signed on behalf of the Hirer: _____

Conditions of Use

1. The Hirer may use the premises only for the use set out above/ overleaf.

2. In particular, the organisation may not use the premises for any of the following: consumption of alcohol; support for a particular political party or election candidate; or any illegal, obscene, pornographic or disreputable purpose.

3. The Hirer must ensure that no more than ____ persons are in the room at any time.

4. The Hirer must ensure that neither it, its activity nor any person in the premises for its purposes or allowed into the premises by the Hirer causes any noise or other nuisance or annoyance to any other user of the premises and/or neighbouring properties.

5. The Hirer will not itself, or let any of its invitees, obstruct the adjoining highway or any routes to or from the hired room.

6. The Hirer is responsible for all matters relating to health, safety or security arising out of its activities. The Hirer will immediately notify the Organisation if it becomes aware of any risk to health, safety or security within the room or the building of which the room forms part, or on any access routes.

7. The Hirer must comply with all fire, safety, security and other regulations displayed by the Organisation, and with all directions given by the Organisation.

8. The Hirer is responsible for any damage to the Organisation's property or facilities arising out of its use of the room or the activities of any persons using the room during the hire period.

9. The Hirer may not sub-hire or allow any other person to use the premises.

10. The Hirer (if an individual), the person who signs this agreement on behalf of the Hirer (if the Hirer is an organisation), or a person authorised by that person in writing must be present at all times.

11. The Hirer will not undertake any activity requiring a licence or the consent of any third party without (a) informing the Organisation and obtaining the Organisation's consent; (b) obtaining any necessary licences or consents; and (c) providing a copy of any such licence or consent to the Organisation as soon as it is obtained.

12. The Hirer is responsible for leaving the premises clean and tidy, and returning all furniture and equipment to the position it was in at the start of the booking. If the room is not left in its original condition a charge of £_____ will be made for each hour or part-hour of caretaking/cleaning. This additional fee will be invoiced and will be due within two weeks of the invoice date.

13. The Hirer will indemnify the Organisation against any claim, cost, loss or damage arising out of the Hirer's use or the actions of any person in the premises for the Hirer's purposes or allowed into the premises by the Hirer, or arising from any breach of this agreement.

14. If the Hirer fails to pay any money due it must pay interest on the overdue amount at 2% per month or part of a month until the amount is paid in full.

15. The Organisation may cancel the hire at any time if it cannot make the room available for reasons beyond its control, or because of any reasonable concern about the Hirer or its use of the room.

16. The Organisation may at any time require any person to leave the premises if there is or may be a breach of these rules or if there is inappropriate behaviour.

17. The Organisation shall not be liable to the Hirer for any loss, damage or expenses (other than personal injury or death) caused by reason of any cancellation, breakdown of equipment, cessation or interruption of any service or supply, or interruption or curtailment of use of the room.

59.8
WORKING FROM HOME

Many voluntary organisations operate from the home of a governing body member, employee or volunteer, or an organisation may agree that staff or volunteers can undertake some or all of their duties from home. Even if the amount of work or the space it takes up is insignificant, a number of issues should be considered by anyone working at home.

59.8.1
Insurance

People working from home have a duty of disclosure [see **20.3.4**] to their insurer. They should ensure that their insurance policies, and those of their landlord if they are tenants, are not invalidated because of the work. They should also be aware that contents insurance may not cover equipment or goods used partly or solely for work purposes, and a special policy or an extension to a domestic policy may be necessary.

An employer should ensure that its employer's liability insurance or insurance covering volunteers [see **20.4.1**] covers activities based outside its main premises. If equipment or goods owned by the organisation are used at the worker's home, it should be absolutely clear who is responsible for insuring them in the worker's home and in transit.

59.8.2
Health and safety

The organisation has a duty of care and a range of statutory duties to ensure the place of work is safe and will not have negative effects on staff members' health or safety [see **36.2**]. These duties apply to staff wherever they are located, and work at home is no exception.

Where the work involves the use of equipment, for example computer screens, the regulations governing their use [see **36.4.6**] apply with the same force in the home environment, regardless of whether the equipment is supplied by the employer or the employee.

59.8.3
Breach of covenant

Most leases for residential premises contain covenants preventing the premises being used for other purposes. Many freehold residential properties also have restrictive covenants on the title limiting their use to residential. Use of the home for the purposes of an organisation might breach these covenants.

In the case of a lease or tenancy, the landlord might seek to forfeit (end) the lease [see **58.4.2**] or obtain an injunction to prevent work use of the flat or house. Provided the work ceases, the courts are unlikely to allow forfeiture if a long lease has been purchased for a premium. But for a monthly or weekly tenancy or a licence, the landlord is more likely to be successful in an application for a possession order.

59.8.4
Planning permission

Limited work activities undertaken at home may not be extensive enough to constitute development as defined in the Planning Acts [see **59.9.1**]. However, extensive use of a home for the activities of an organisation may well constitute development requiring planning consent.

If home-based activities involve large quantities of post, visits from the public or clients, or any nuisance to neighbours, complaints may be made to the planning authorities. The authorities may then seek to end the use by means of an enforcement or stop notice [see **59.9.6.3**].

59.8.5
Tax and rates

Extensive working from home, especially if part of the premises is used solely for work purposes, could have significant effects on tax and rates:

- part of the premises could be assessed for business rates;
- it could breach the mortgage terms and lead to withdrawal of the loan;
- when the dwelling is sold, capital gains tax could be payable on the part used for work purposes.

A person working at home should seek advice from an accountant before claiming a portion of rent or mortgage as a business expenditure for tax purposes.

59.9
PLANNING LAW

When buying or taking on premises, ascertaining the current planning use is one of the key tasks [see **59.9.1.1**]. However, the impact of the legislation is much broader than this.

59.9.1
Planning permission

Planning permission is needed for most development of property and some changes of use. It is obtained through the local authority's planning department. Advice for voluntary organisations is available from Planning Aid [see end of chapter].

59.9.1.1
Land use classes

There are 14 classes of land use divided into four broad categories. Classes most likely to apply to voluntary organisations are:

A1 shops;

A2 financial and professional services provided to visiting members of the public (which could include, for example, law centres);

A3 sale of food or drink for consumption on the premises or hot food for consumption off the premises;

B1 business use as offices (other than those covered in A2), for research and development, and for light industry which can be carried out in a residential area without detriment to amenities;

B2 general industrial;

B8 storage and distribution of products;

C1 hotels and hostels;

C2 residential institutions providing accommodation with care;

C3 dwellings for up to six people living together as a single household, including those where care is provided for residents;

D1 non-residential institutions, including nurseries, day centres, educational centres, arts centres etc.

Town and Country Planning (Use Classes) Order 1987 [SI 1987/764]

59.9.1.2
Definition of 'development'

Development is defined as carrying out building, engineering, mining or other operations on land or making any material change in the use of any building or land. *Town and Country Planning Act 1990 s.55(1)*

Anything which involves development needs planning permission unless it falls within an exception. The main exceptions are:

• maintenance, improvements or alterations which affect only the interior or have no material effect on the external appearance;

• use of a building or land within the grounds of a dwelling for any purpose incidental to its enjoyment;

• use of land for agriculture or forestry;

• change of use within a use class;

• listed buildings [see **59.10.1.1**], which are covered by separate rules.

Further exceptions include:

• developments within a dwelling house;

• minor operations such as fencing, access ways and exterior painting and decoration;

• certain changes of use, for example from a use in B2 (general industrial) or B8 (storage and distribution) to a use within B1 (business), subject to a maximum floor space restriction.

Town and Country Planning General Development Order 1988 [SI 1988/1813]

59.9.1.3
Restricted developments

All new buildings, other than extensions to dwellings, are developments requiring permission, and some demolition also falls within the definition of development. Building operations which require planning permission have been widely defined and include, for example, putting up a portacabin, erecting a translucent roof over a patio, and attaching a radio aerial to the exterior of a building.

An external sign generally needs planning permission only if it is illuminated or is a hanging sign. *Town and Country Planning (Control of Advertisements) Regulations 1992 [SI 1992/666]*

Material changes of use have been very widely defined. There has been much litigation about it, and guidance should generally be sought.

59.9.2
Established use

If a development has taken place without planning permission, the local authority may take enforcement proceedings [see **59.9.6.3**]. However, action cannot be taken if a change was a change of use to a dwelling or the development was the result of an operational development, and it occurred more than four years previously; or it was another type of change or development and occurred more than 10 years previously.
Planning and Compensation Act 1991 ss.191, 192

It is possible to apply for a certificate of the lawfulness of established use or development, or a certificate of lawfulness of a proposed use or development [see **57.5.4**].

59.9.3
Development plans

Local authorities have an obligation to draw up long-terms plans for their area. These must be referred to when making decisions about individual planning applications. *s.54A*

An organisation which intends to develop land it owns or occupies should become involved in the development planning process. Otherwise it may find that land it wants to use has been designated for different purposes under the plan.

59.9.4
Planning agreements and planning gains

Local planning authorities are allowed to control development either by imposing conditions within the planning permission or by entering into separate **section 106 agreements**. *s.106*

Such agreements may be permanent or temporary, and may restrict the use of land, require payments, or define activities to be undertaken. A typical example is where planning permission is granted to a supermarket chain, on condition that the chain build a community centre on the site and let it to a local organisation for a peppercorn rent. Voluntary organisations are frequently the beneficiaries of such **planning gain**, and should keep this in mind when developments are being planned.

An organisation may, if it is carrying out its own development, be asked to enter into a section 106 agreement. This needs careful consideration, because of the burdensome obligations which can be imposed.

A section 106 agreement can be modified only by agreement between the planning authority and the other party, or following an appeal to the secretary of state for the environment. Such an appeal cannot be made during the first five years of an agreement.

59.9.5
Objecting to planning applications

Developments may be announced by a notice on the site, or neighbours immediately adjacent or across the road might be directly notified. Major developments must be advertised in local newspapers. Local newspapers frequently carry lists of proposed applications.

Objection may be made by letter or petition, or objectors may be allowed to speak at planning meetings. Effective objections are based on a thorough understanding of relevant planning law, the local plan, environmental issues and issues of architectural merit. It is usually helpful to involve a solicitor and/or planning consultants at an early stage.

59.9.6
Enforcement

59.9.6.1
Planning contravention notices

Planning is enforced by the local authority. Enforcement frequently starts with the service of a **planning contravention notice**. This is served if it appears to the local authority that there has been a breach of planning control. *s.1*

The recipient must respond within 21 days, giving information about how the property is being used. The notice constitutes a halfway house between discussions with the planning authority about an alleged breach and enforcement of an actual breach, and gives the local authority more information on which to decide what action to take.

An organisation receiving such a notice should immediately take professional advice. Failure to respond within 21 days is punishable by a substantial fine, as is providing a misleading response.

59.9.6.2
Breach of condition
notice

A **breach of condition notice** is served when a condition attached to a planning permission has not been complied with. Failure to comply with a notice can give rise to an unlimited fine, unless the recipient took reasonable measures to comply with the conditions or is no longer in control of the land. There is no right of appeal.

Planning and Compensation Act 1991 s.2

59.9.6.3
Injunctions and
enforcement notices

Where it appears to a local authority that there has been a breach of planning control, the authority has a choice of possible remedies:

*   applying to the court for an injunction requiring action to be taken or activities to be stopped;

*   serving an **enforcement notice** on the owner or occupier, requiring the breach to be remedied within a specified time unless the notice is appealed against by public enquiry or via written representations;

*   serving a **stop notice**, which takes effect within three to 28 days and immediately blocks continued use. But if the local authority wrongly serves a stop notice, the person served may be entitled to compensation.   *ss.5, 9*

59.9.7
Other action

Development of land might also give rise to:

*   a landlord taking action for breach of the terms of the lease;

*   a claim under the **Public Health Acts**; **Control of Pollution Act 1974**, particularly ss.60 and 61; **Environmental Protection Act 1990** ss.79 and 82; or under the law of nuisance [see **19.5.1**];

*   public pressure on the organisation to cease a use.

59.10
PROTECTING THE
ENVIRONMENT

In addition to ordinary planning regulations, a variety of conservation measures may be used to protect buildings and the environment. Alterations to or development of listed buildings or conservation areas [see below] require a separate application for listed building and/or conservation area consent, in addition to an application for planning permission.

59.10.1
Conservation

59.10.1.1
Listed buildings

Buildings are **listed** if they are of special architectural or historic interest. This may include both their intrinsic worth and their association with important events. Grounds or specific items attached to the building may also be protected.   *Listed Buildings Act 1990*

It is an offence to demolish, alter or extend a listed building without consent from the local planning authority. Consent for alterations may have conditions attached. If these involve undertaking works in a particular way or using particular materials, the cost of maintenance or alterations may be hugely increased.

59.10.1.2
Conservation areas

Local authorities have a duty to consider whether any part of their area is of special or historic interest, and can designate that area as a **conservation area.** Within a conservation area demolition is more strictly controlled, and some rights to carry out development [see **59.9.1.2**] are restricted.   *s.69(1)*

59.10.1.3
Tree preservation

Except in limited circumstances, trees cannot be felled without a licence. If a particular tree is protected, it is an offence to cut or lop it without permission from the local authority.   *Forestry Act 1967 s.9*

59.10.2
Pollution

Pollution of the air, land or water is a **statutory nuisance**. Pollution here includes noise and heat. *Environmental Protection Act 1990*

Specialist advice should be sought by any organisation which is responsible for an industrial or unusual process which causes or could cause pollution. Attention should also be given where an organisation occupies or manages property on which there are potentially polluting substances. Even if the organisation takes care to ensure these substances do not cause pollution, they could be held liable if pollution occurs as the result of acts of vandals or other third parties.

59.10.2.1
Contaminated land

Local authorities were required to draw up, by mid-2001, registers listing contaminated land where there is some actual or potential hazard to health or the environment, and were to gain powers to require land owners to clean up contaminated sites. Where contamination is an issue it is possible to carry out specialist surveys, for example of the soil and subsoil.

59.10.2.2
Ozone depleters

Organisations which use refrigeration, air conditioning equipment or firefighting equipment should check with suppliers to find out whether they contain ozone depleter substances such as CFCs or halogens. Strict rules apply to the disposal of such items. Information is available from the Environment Agency.

59.10.3
Noise

The emission of noise prejudicial to health or which creates a nuisance is a statutory nuisance. Local authorities may impose conditions relating to noise on planning permission for new buildings, or may issue noise abatement notices. Where a noise abatement notice has not been complied with, the local authority may seize and remove any equipment which it believes is being or has been used in the emission of the noise in question. *Environmental Protection Act 1990 ss.79-80;*
Noise Act 1996 s.10(7)

59.10.4
Waste management and recycling

Waste management—the deposit, transport, treatment, disposal or recovery of waste—is strictly controlled under the **Environmental Protection Act 1990** and the **Waste Management Licensing Regulations 1994** *[SI 1994/1056]*, **Environment Act 1995**, and **Special Waste Regulations 1996** *[SI 1996/972]*. A waste management licence may be required. Information is available from the Environment Agency and WasteWatch [see below].

Businesses which produce more than 50 tons of packaging (including items sent as unsolicited direct mail) per year and have a turnover of more than £2 million must register with the Environment Agency or a recycling compliance scheme, and must recycle a specified proportion of packaging. This does not apply to charities, but could affect trading companies involved in large-scale mailings or the sale of packaged products. *Producer Responsibility Obligations (Packaging Waste)*
Regulations 1997 [SI 1997/648]

FOR FURTHER INFORMATION

Disability access. Centre for Accessible Environments: 020-7357 8182; www.cae.org.uk

Disability Rights Commission: 08457-622 633; www.drc-gb.org

Planning: Planning Aid: 0207-636 9107; www.rtpi.org.uk/planaid

Pollution, waste management & recycling. Environment Agency: 0845-933 3111; www.environment-agency.gov.uk

WasteWatch: 0870-243 0136; www.wastewatch.org.uk

To understand how the law affects voluntary organisations, it can be helpful to understand where the law comes from and how it operates. Part IX explains this, and provides advice on finding a solicitor or accountant and finding out more about legal and related matters.

Chapter 60
HOW THE LAW WORKS

**60.1
TYPES OF LAW**

The law is divided into public and private law. **Public law** governs the behaviour of the state and of people towards the state, while **private law** governs the rights and obligations of individuals and groups and their relationships with each other

**60.1.1
Public law**

The main categories of public law are:

- **constitutional law**: rights, duties and freedoms, the structure of national and local government and the structure of the courts;

- **administrative law**: appeals and complaints about how governmental and quasi-governmental bodies administer the law;

- **welfare law**: individuals' rights to benefits from the state;

- **criminal law**: punishment for breaches of the law [see **60.5**].

**60.1.2
Private law**

Within private law, legal action is brought by and against individuals or corporate bodies, not by or against the state, and courts award suitable **remedies** [see **60.6.2**]. Private law is often called **civil law**.

The main types of private law are:

- **contract law**: deals with agreements between two or more persons or organisations which are intended to be legally binding [see **18.6**];

- **property law**: deals with ownership, possession and succession rights [see **56.3** and **56.4**];
- **trust law**: a division of property law which deals with persons holding property on behalf of others [see **1.3**];
- **tort**: covers civil wrongs which are not breaches of contract or trust, such as negligence, libel and trespass [see **19.5**] (some torts are also criminal offences);
- **family law**: deals with marriage, divorce rights, children's rights and the rights and duties of parents.

60.2
SOURCES OF LAW

Many countries have written constitutions setting down the structure of the state and the rights of people within the state. In the UK there is no formal constitution (technically, power still resides with the monarch) and many rights arise from the common law [see below] or equity [see **60.2.2**] rather than from formally enacted statute law.

60.2.1
Common law

Before the Norman conquest of England in 1066, each region had its own systems of law and its own courts. The Normans set out to establish a legal system which applied to the entire population. This came to be known as the **common law**, because it was to be common to everybody regardless of where they lived.

60.2.1.1
Precedents

During the reign of Henry II (1154-1189) the common law took its present form. Various courts were established, each dealing with a particular aspect of the law, with judges who toured the country. Their decisions were recorded and came to be used as **precedents**. In time this became a formal system with the preceding cases creating a uniform body of the common law, and judges bound to follow a precedent if the facts were the same in the case before them.

Precedents still form the basis of common law, with lower courts generally bound to follow precedents set previously by higher courts in similar cases. Since 1971 the ranking of the main courts [see **60.5.1** and **60.6.1**] in English law has been:

- **county courts** and **magistrates' courts**, whose decisions do not set legal precedents;
- **crown courts** and the **High Court**;
- **Courts of Appeal**;
- **House of Lords**.

Well over half a million past cases are on record, dating back hundreds of years, although cases dating from before the introduction of formal legal reporting in 1866 are not necessarily accepted as precedents.

In cases involving European Union law, decisions of the **European Court of Justice** [see **60.2.5.4**] are binding on all other courts, including the House of Lords.

With the implementation of the Human Rights Act [see **60.3**], decisions made in foreign courts on related issues and decisions in the **European Court of Human Rights** [see **60.2.5.5**] may be taken into account.

60.2.1.2
Case reporting

Decisions are now recorded in a variety of journals and specialist publications known as **law reports**. When referring to cases there is a standard format for the case name, the year in which it was reported, an abbreviation of the law report in which the case was published, and the page number. For example *Trustees of the British Museum v Attorney General [1984] 1 WLR 418* is in the first volume of the *Weekly Law Reports* of 1984 on page 418.

A table of all cases cited in this book, with the abbreviations for the relevant law reports, is on **page 865**.

60.2.1.3
Civil law countries

Elsewhere in Europe, law is generally based not on common law but on legislated codes, of which the most famous is the Code Napoleon. Systems based on such codes are referred to as **civil law**. For a different use of the term civil law, see **60.1.2**.

60.2.2
Equity

Historically, common law remedies were based on payment of money **damages** to compensate the wronged party. But sometimes damages were not appropriate. To deal with these cases a separate system of courts, derived from the ecclesiastical courts, evolved alongside the common law courts. Parties unhappy with the decisions of the common law courts or in situations where damages would not have been an appropriate remedy could take their cases to this **Court of Chancery**.

The Chancery Court based its judgments on **equity** (from the Latin *aequitas*, fairness) and made orders requiring acts to be done (**specific performance**) or **injunctions** requiring them not to be done.

Since the **Judicature Acts 1873-75**, equity and the common law have been dealt with in the same courts.

60.2.3
Local customs

A **local** (and hence not 'common') **custom** may be law in its own area if it has existed since 'time immemorial' and applies only to that locality. Examples are rights of way and agricultural rights.

60.2.4
Statute law

Statutes are laws enacted by Parliament. English law is rooted in the doctrine of **Parliamentary sovereignty**—the supremacy of Parliament over all courts. This means that Acts of Parliament are superior to all other English sources of law, and that a statute cannot be challenged under English law as illegal or unconstitutional, but stands until repealed by Parliament.

Since the UK joined the European Community (now the European Union) in 1973, some EU law overrides English law, and the **European Court of Justice** has in some areas been able to overrule both Parliament and the courts [see **60.2.5**]. Contrary to popular belief, it rarely does.

Since implementation of the **Human Rights Act 1998**, parts of the **European Convention on Human Rights** have become part of UK law. If the UK courts fail to give a remedy for breach of a Convention right or Parliament fails to amend legislation incompatible with the Convention, a person or organisation whose rights have been breached can petition the **European Court of Human Rights** [see **60.2.5.5**].

60.2.4.1
Enactment

Proposed laws are put forward as **bills** by members of the House of Commons or House of Lords. The bill is debated by the House in which it is proposed, and is either rejected or goes forward to a committee. This committee, which may consist of the entire House, discusses the bill and makes amendments. The House then votes on whether to accept the bill, reject it or make further amendments. If accepted it goes to the other House, where it goes through the same process..

After being passed by both Houses of Parliament (except for finance bills, which do not need consent of the Lords), the bill must be given **royal assent**. The monarch may technically refuse to pass any law, but in practice she always gives assent. As soon as assent is given the bill becomes an Act of Parliament and becomes law, unless it contains a clause stating that it does not come into effect until a later date.

Bills are on the internet at www.parliament.the-stationery-office.co.uk and Acts are at www.legislation.hmso.gov.uk/acts.htm. The statutes cited in this book are listed in the table of statutes on **page 857**.

60.2.4.2
Interpretation

The courts must accept statute law, but since October 2000 must interpret all law compatibly with the **European Convention on Hu-**

man **Rights** [see **60.3**], and may declare legislation incompatible with the Convention. Parliament is not obliged to change the law to make it compatible, but if it wishes to do so there is a 'fast track' procedure. Until it is changed, the law remains in force even though it is incompatible with the rights granted under the Convention.

Ambiguities in the wording of statute law provide scope for interpretation. When there are disputes over meaning, the courts consider Parliament's intention in introducing the law, and may consult Hansard, the record of Parliamentary debates, for this purpose.

60.2.4.3
Statutory instruments

Many statutes now do not set out the detail of the law, leaving this to be done by supplementary **statutory instruments** (SIs) made under the Act. Statutory instruments are laid before Parliament but are not passed in the same way as Acts.

All statutory instruments cited in the book are listed in the table of statutes on **page 857**.

Draft and final statutory instruments are on the internet at www. legislation.hmso.gov.uk/stat.htm.

60.2.5
European law

Depending on their nature, laws of the European Union may apply to all or some member states, and may or may not need to be enacted by the individual states.

European **regulations** are laws of the European Union which apply immediately in all member states. They are binding without reference to national governments.

Decisions are binding only on a named state, individual, company or group, and are most often used to grant exemption from a piece of legislation. They sometimes need legislation by the state involved.

Directives are orders to the governments of all member states to enact a particular law within a prescribed time. If a member state does not do so, the European Court of Justice can enforce the law.

European law cited in this book is listed on **page 864**.

60.2.5.1
European Commission

The **European Commission** is made up of one representative (commissioner) from each small EU member state and two from each large member state. The commissioners are nominated by their national governments, but are independent of those governments and take an oath to work in the common European interest and not to support their own government against European policy. The Commission is the only European body which can initiate legislation.

60.2.5.2
Council of Ministers

The **Council of Ministers** is made up of one delegate, normally the foreign minister, from each member state. When the Council is debating a particular subject, the delegates are each country's minister for that subject (for example when the council is debating agriculture, it is composed of each member state's minister of agriculture). Delegates to the Council represent their own governments.

As the delegates are full-time ministers in their own countries and have little time for European work, the **Committee of Permanent Representatives**, made up of permanent delegates from each member state, considers Commission proposals on behalf of the Council.

Final decisions on whether to pass legislation rest with the Council. It votes by qualified majority voting, with each delegate's vote weighted according to the size of their state's population.

The Council's decision must be unanimous on budgetary matters and on issues of employment rights and the free movement of persons. If a member state feels that 'vital national interests' are at stake in any proposed legislation, that state may insist that the Council must be unanimous in passing that law. In effect, this gives every member state the right to veto any piece of legislation.

60.2.5.3
European Parliament

The **European Parliament** is made up of elected representatives (MEPs) from each member state. The number from each state is based on its population.

The European Parliament has very limited powers. It can amend or delay the budget and can dismiss the entire Commission (but not individual members), but otherwise it acts as an advisory body. In disputes it usually sides with the Commission's pro-European stance against the Council's pro-national government stance.

The Parliament's lack of power compared to the unelected Council and Commission has led to concern about a 'democratic deficit'. It is likely that the Parliament will eventually be given greater powers.

60.2.5.4
European Court
of Justice

The duty of the **European Court of Justice** is to ensure that member states uphold the laws of the European Union.

The European Court of Justice is composed of one judge from each member state, plus one additional judge. Judges must be 'independent beyond doubt', and do not represent national interests.

The parties to any case requiring an interpretation of European law which reaches a court from which there is no appeal (in the UK the House of Lords) may submit the case to the European Court of Justice. Decisions of the ECJ must be accepted by all member states.

60.2.5.5
European Court of
Human Rights

The **European Court of Human Rights** in Strasbourg is not part of the EU. Its role is to enforce the **European Convention on Human Rights** [see **60.3.2**].

60.2.6
Delegated law

The UK Parliament can give other bodies the power to make binding laws within a specific framework. An Act, for example, may give the relevant secretary of state power to make regulations (statutory instruments) relating to that Act. Local authorities have many delegated powers to make **by-laws** on local matters. Bodies such as the National Health Service, police, and independent or semi-independent bodies set up by statute to carry out a particular task, may be authorised to make by-laws on matters relevant to their work.

Parliament may at any time revoke these laws or take away the power to make law. If one of these bodies makes a law which covers a matter outside its powers, the courts may rule the law *ultra vires* ('outside the powers') and the law will not stand.

60.3
HUMAN RIGHTS

The implementation of the **Human Rights Act 1998** on 2 October 2000 introduced into UK law most of the substantive rights embodied in the **European Convention on Human Rights** (ECHR). The UK had been a signatory to the Convention for nearly 50 years, and cases could be taken from the UK to the European Court of Human Rights in Strasbourg. But since October 2000:

- all acts of public authorities [see **60.3.3**] must be compatible with Convention rights; *Human Rights Act 1998 s.6*

- individuals, associations and corporate bodies have the right to bring a claim in the UK courts against a public authority or a private body carrying out a public function [see **60.3.3.3**], for breach of a Convention right; *s.7*

- government ministers must declare that each new bill is compatible with the Convention, or must indicate that the government wishes to proceed with the bill even though a statement of compatibility cannot be made; *s.19*

- when hearing cases on any matter, courts and tribunals must inter- pret all legislation consistently with Convention rights, and must take into account judgments of the European Court of Human Rights and other relevant decisions;   *Human Rights Act 1998 ss.2-3*

- certain courts can declare that existing legislation is incompatible with the Convention, in which case it can be reviewed by Parliament on a fast track basis.   *ss.4, 10*

Information about the Human Rights Act and the Convention is avail- able from the Lord Chancellor's Department, Justice and the British Institute of Human Rights. The National Council for Voluntary Organi- sations is monitoring its impact on voluntary organisations through the Human Rights Policy Network [see end of chapter].

60.3.1.1
Horizontal effect

Claims under the Human Rights Act can be brought only against **public authorities** or private bodies carrying out public functions [see **60.3.3**]. But all legislation, even in relation to purely private relation- ships such as between a private landlord and tenant or between two individuals, must be interpreted consistently with the Convention, and this is having a significant effect on how all law is interpreted and ap- plied. This sideways—rather than direct—effect is often referred to as **horizontality**.

60.3.2
Convention rights

Rights under the **European Convention on Human Rights** are set out in **articles** and additional **protocols**. The rights granted by incor- poration into UK law are: *Human Rights Act 1998 sch.1*

Article 2: right to life

Article 3: prohibition of torture, inhuman and degrading treatment or punishment

Article 4: prohibition of slavery and forced or compulsory labour

Article 5: right to liberty and security of person

Article 6: right to a fair and public trial or hearing in the determination of a person's civil rights and obligations or criminal charges against a person

Article 7: no punishment without law (the right not to be found guilty for an action or inaction which was not a criminal offence at the time it happened)

Article 8: right to respect for private and family life, home and corre- spondence

Article 9: freedom of thought, conscience and religion, including free- dom to manifest religion or belief, in public or private, through worship, teaching, practice and observance

Article 10: freedom of expression, including freedom to hold opinions and to receive and impart information and ideas without interference by public authority and regardless of frontiers

Article 11: freedom of peaceable assembly and freedom of association

Article 12: right to marry and found a family

Article 14: prohibition of discrimination in the exercise of other Convention rights

Protocol 1

    Article 1: protection of property and peaceful enjoyment of posses- sions

    Article 2: right to education

    Article 3: right to free elections

Protocol 6: abolition of the death penalty except in time of war.

60.3.2.1
Absolute rights

The right to life, the prohibition of torture and of inhuman and degrading treatment or punishment, the prohibition of slavery, and no punishment without law are **absolute** rights, also called **unqualified** rights. The Convention does, however, set out exceptions. The right to life, for example, is not breached if it is absolutely necessary to use force in specified circumstances such as protecting a person from unlawful violence or lawfully arresting a person.

60.3.2.2
Limited rights

For some rights, the Convention sets out specific circumstances in which the right may be **limited**. These rights are the prohibition of forced or compulsory labour, the right to liberty and security, the right to a public trial (but not the right to a fair trial), the right to marry and found a family, and the right to education.

The allowed limitations are very specific, and may not be exceeded. The right to a public trial (article 6), for example, may be limited by the exclusion of press and the public from all or part of a trial if this is necessary to protect the interest of juveniles or the private life of the parties. The right to liberty (article 5) may be limited in specific situations, which include lawful arrest and detention, and detaining an illegal immigrant, a person of unsound mind, a person addicted to alcohol or drugs, or where detention is necessary to prevent the spread of infectious disease.

60.3.2.3
Qualified rights

The main **qualified** rights are the rights to respect for private and family life, home and correspondence; freedom of thought, conscience and religion; freedom of expression; and freedom of assembly and association. The government may pass laws to limit these rights, but only if such limitation or qualification is necessary in a democratic society and meets other criteria set out in the Convention.

For example laws may be passed allowing restriction to the right to freedom of expression (article 10), if this is necessary for national security, public safety, the prevention of disorder or crime, protecting the reputation or rights of others, or preventing the disclosure of information received in confidence. The right to respect for private and family life (article 8) can be qualified if this is necessary for national security, public safety, the economic wellbeing of the country, the prevention of disorder or crime, or the protection of the rights and freedoms of others.

60.3.3
Public authorities

Public authorities are prohibited from acting incompatibly with Convention rights, and it is only against a public authority that a person may bring a claim for breach of a Convention right.

Human Rights Act 1998 ss.6-8

A **public authority** is any body, organisation or individual 'certain of whose functions are **functions of a public nature**'. This was deliberately left undefined in the legislation, and at the time of writing (early 2001) it was unclear how it will be interpreted. *s.6(3)*

60.3.3.1
Pure public authorities

Bodies such as the courts, government departments, executive agencies, the police and local authorities, are clearly public authorities. They are sometimes called **pure public authorities**.

A claim under the Human Rights Act may be brought against a pure public authority in relation to all its functions, including employment.

60.3.3.2
Hybrid bodies

Many other bodies are quasi-public or private, but carry out some public functions. They are sometimes called **quasi-public authorities, functional public authorities** or **hybrid bodies**. They are public authorities in relation to their public functions, but private bodies in relation to other functions.

In determining whether something is a public function and therefore the body is a public authority in relation to that function, factors taken into account include:

- the degree of state control;

- whether the body has special powers beyond those normally available to a body of that type (such as the NSPCC, which is a private body but has certain statutory child protection functions);

- whether the body is responsible for providing a public service under control of a public authority (such as dentists, who are likely to be public authorities in relation to their work for the NHS, but private bodies in relation to work they do privately);

- whether the government would have to perform the function if the body did not do it, for example regulating a key profession as the Law Society does;

- possibly, in the specific case of voluntary organisations, the source of the organisation's funds.

A claim can be brought against a quasi-public or private body only in relation to its public functions. At the time of writing (early 2001) it was unclear whether the employment relationship in these hybrid bodies will be seen as a public function when the worker is carrying out a public function (and therefore be subject to claims under the Human Rights Act), or whether the employment relationship will always be treated as private, regardless of the nature of the employee's work.

The differentiation between public and private functions and the resultant definition of 'public authority' is very complex and will be much litigated. Organisations which are concerned about whether they could be carrying out public functions and therefore could be public authorities should take care to ensure they do not breach Convention rights. This is good practice even if the organisation is a purely private body and thus does not face the possibility of claims against it under the Human Rights Act.

60.3.3.3
Voluntary organisations as public authorities

The vast majority of voluntary organisations are private bodies. This is true even for charities which must by definition be set up for public benefit [see **4.3.8**]. However for the purposes of the Human Rights Act a voluntary organisation is likely to be carrying out a **public function** and therefore be a public authority in relation to:

- services or activities carried out under statutory powers, such as the RSPCA's or NSPCC's enforcement work;

- work that would normally be the responsibility of central government, a local or health authority or other pure public authority, such as a local Age Concern providing day care services that social services has a statutory obligation to provide;

- services or activities that are clearly being carried out for or on behalf of a public authority, for example under a contract.

At the time of writing (early 2001) it was unclear whether services or activities funded by a grant from a public authority are public functions. Even if they are not, the public authority will, in giving the grant, be exercising a public function, and will almost certainly have a duty to ensure the grant is used in ways that are consistent with the Convention. Grant conditions are thus likely to be extended to require grant recipients to act compatibly with the Convention. This is good practice even if it is not required by funders.

60.3.3.4
Private acts by voluntary organisations

A case under the Human Rights Act can be brought against a charity, voluntary organisation or other 'hybrid' body only in relation to its public functions—not in relation to its private acts. Private acts include:

- work which is clearly not being carried out for or on behalf of a public authority, and is not funded by a public authority;

• private relationships such as the employment relationship—although, as indicated above, it is possible that the employment relationship could be classed as a public function where the worker is carrying out the organisation's public functions.

60.3.3.5
Bringing a claim

Only a 'victim'—a person whose rights have been breached—can bring a claim under the Human Rights Act. This includes individuals, groups of individuals, unincorporated associations and corporate bodies.

60.3.4
Implications for voluntary organisations

Where a voluntary organisation is clearly carrying out a public function, clients, service users or others who believe that their Convention rights have been breached in relation to that function will be able to bring a claim against the organisation under the Human Rights Act.

Regardless of whether the organisation is carrying out a public function, all clients, service users and others have a right to bring ordinary claims under other legislation. The courts must interpret this legislation compatibly with Convention rights.

A simple example is an organisation which publishes, without consent, personal information about a client. In this case:

• the client may bring a claim under the Data Protection Act [see **38.3**], and the court will interpret data protection law compatibly with Convention rights, in particular article 8 of the Convention which gives the right to respect for private life;

• if the information was published as part of carrying out a public function—if, for example, it was included in a research report that was produced for and on behalf of a local authority—the client could also bring a claim against the organisation under the Human Rights Act, for breach of article 8;

• if the publication was part of the organisation's private function, for example its own research report, the client could not bring a claim against the organisation under the Human Rights Act.

60.3.4.1
Respecting human rights

All organisations, regardless of their work or funding, should act compatibly with the Convention. In particular:

• an organisation which is clearly carrying out public functions must ensure it acts compatibly with Convention rights in carrying out those functions, in order to reduce the risk of a claim against it under the Human Rights Act;

• an organisation which might be carrying out public functions should ensure it acts compatibly with Convention rights in carrying out those functions, to reduce the risk of an HRA claim;

• even if the organisation is not carrying out public functions, it should act compatibly with the Convention as a matter of good practice;

• even if the organisation is not itself carrying out a public function, the terms of grant funding from a public authority may require it to act compatibly with the Convention;

• if any legal case is brought against the organisation, for any reason, the court will take into account the human rights implications;

• if the organisation supports clients in their dealings with public authorities, it may be able to assist clients in bringing a claim against the authority for breach of human rights.

60.4
PERSONNEL OF THE LAW

Legal work is carried out not only by solicitors and barristers, but by a range of other personnel. An understanding of their role can be helpful in understanding and making the best use of the legal system.

60.4.1
Solicitors

Solicitors deal with most aspects of legal work. Some of their work is done in court, but much of it is legal paperwork and legal advice. Solicitors may appear in county courts and magistrates' courts, and may appear in crown courts when dealing with appeals or sentencing from cases in the inferior (county and magistrates') courts. A very small number of solicitors are permitted to appear in the higher courts.

There are about 66,000 solicitors in England and Wales, regulated by the **Law Society**. Solicitors may practise alone or in partnerships. In selecting a solicitor it is important to try to find one with appropriate experience and expertise [see **60.10.3** for how to find a solicitor].

60.4.2
Legal executives and paralegals

Legal executives work with solicitors' firms, and must have considerable practical and formal training before admission into the Institute of Legal Executives. They are able to give legal advice provided they are working under the authority of a solicitor.

The term **paralegal** is sometimes used synonymously with legal executives, but paralegal encompasses a wide variety of personnel who may or may not have any formal training or qualification.

60.4.3
Barristers

Barristers must act alone and not enter into partnerships, although they share offices known as chambers. They are regulated by the **Bar Council**. They usually specialise in a particular field of law, and may appear in any court. They are generally engaged by a client's solicitor rather than by the client, thus involving two sets of fees for the client.

After 10 years, a barrister can apply to become a QC or **Queen's Counsel** (when the monarch is a king, the title is King's Counsel). This is called **taking silk**, because of the silk robes QCs wear in court. A barrister who is not a QC is referred to as a **junior barrister**.

60.4.4
Justices, magistrates and judges

The majority of **judges** are still drawn from among barristers but increasingly, particularly in the lower courts, some are solicitors.

Magistrates' courts and youth courts are presided over either by lay people who undertake the role on an unpaid basis after very limited training (**justices of the peace** or **JPs**) or lawyers who are paid for the work (**stipendiary magistrates**). Lay justices are assisted by a legally qualified **clerk** who advises on the law.

60.4.5
Prosecution

Formerly the police decided whom to prosecute for most crimes. This function is now undertaken by a government department, the **Crown Prosecution Service**, which is staffed by lawyers.

The **director of public prosecutions** is appointed by the attorney general. The DPP is a civil servant who is responsible for starting criminal prosecutions.

60.4.6
Law officers and lord chancellor

The **attorney general** is usually an MP, and is appointed by the monarch on the advice of the prime minister. The post is political, so a change of government means a change of attorney general.

Where cases are of constitutional importance the attorney general represents the crown (the state) in civil cases and acts as prosecutor in criminal cases. The attorney general supervises the director of public prosecutions, advises the government on legal issues, answers questions in Parliament on legal issues, and acts as head of the English Bar. The attorney general has the power to call a halt to any criminal proceedings by means of the **royal prerogative**.

The **solicitor general** acts as the attorney general's deputy. Despite the title the solicitor general is generally a barrister, not a solicitor.

The **lord chancellor** has three main roles: speaker of the House of Lords, a Cabinet post; most senior judge in the House of Lords, which is the highest court; and head of the Lord Chancellor's Department, which controls the courts and appointment of judges, and deals with human rights, data protection and freedom of information.

60.5
ENFORCEMENT OF
CRIMINAL LAW

Crimes are considered to be offences not only against individuals, but also against the community and the state. Criminal law is enforced by the state through the criminal courts. The state or occasionally a private individual brings the action, and the court decides on guilt and administers sanctions, usually based on **punishment**, to offenders.

60.5.1
Criminal courts

60.5.1.1
Magistrates' courts

Magistrates' courts deal with the vast majority of criminal cases. Each geographical area has its own magistrates' court, dealing with crimes committed in its area. Magistrates' courts deal with:

- summary trials (not triable by a jury) for minor offences which carry a penalty of not more than six months' imprisonment or a fine;
- preliminary matters, such as bail, on more serious cases which are being sent to the crown court for trial by jury;
- a wide variety of other functions including liquor licensing, some family law matters and enforcement of many regulations.

Magistrates' courts are bound by precedents set in the higher courts, but their own decisions do not set any precedents.

Defendants may appeal to the crown court against their sentence, or to the divisional court of the Queen's Bench Division [see **60.6.1.2**] on points of law.

60.5.1.2
Youth courts

The **youth courts**, formerly called juvenile courts, deal with young offenders except in homicide cases.

60.5.1.3
Crown court

The **crown court** replaced a number of older criminal courts in 1971. It sits in a number of locations throughout England and Wales, and is able to try cases committed anywhere in England or Wales. The best known is the **central criminal court** or **Old Bailey**. The crown court deals with:

- appeals against convictions or sentencing from cases tried in the magistrates' courts;
- passing sentence on people found guilty by magistrates when the magistrates do not have jurisdiction to pass an appropriate sentence;
- hearing cases on indictment (offences triable by judge and jury);
- a few items of civil work.

Crown court cases are divided by seriousness into four classes. The class determines whether cases are heard by **High Court judges**, **circuit judges** (appointed to hear cases in a particular area) or **recorders** (part-time judges appointed on a temporary basis).

The crown court is bound by decisions of the Queen's Bench Division of the High Court [see **60.6.1.2**], the Court of Appeal (criminal division) and the House of Lords.

60.5.1.4
Court of Appeal
(criminal division)

The **Court of Appeal (criminal division)** hears appeals against decisions of the crown court. Appeals on points of law are always heard, but appeals against a sentence are only heard by leave of the court. An offender may ask the home secretary to order the court to hear the case, but the home secretary is under no obligation to do so. Victims of crime or those acting on their behalf can appeal for a light sentence to be extended.

The court can quash (overturn) the decision, make the sentence longer or shorter, or order a retrial.

The appeal court is not bound by its own precedents, but it is bound by decisions of the House of Lords.

60.5.1.5
House of Lords

The **House of Lords**, as the highest court, is not bound by precedent when making decisions. It hears appeals if the courts certify that a point of law of public importance is involved and leave to appeal is granted by the courts or by the Lords themselves. Although the Lords are the highest court, their decisions may be overturned by the European Court of Justice if the case involves European Union law [see **60.2.5.4**], or the European Court of Human Rights if the case involves the European Convention on Human Rights [see **60.2.5.5**].

60.5.2
Criminal sentencing

Sentences—usually punishments—are imposed when a person is found guilty of having committed a criminal offence. Sentencing in criminal cases follows guidelines laid down in the **Criminal Justice Act 1991**. Sentences include:

- **absolute discharge**: when an offence has been committed, but the court rules that the offender was not at fault so there is no punishment;

- **conditional discharge**: no sentence is given, but if the offender commits another offence within a period of between one and three years, he or she will also be sentenced for the original offence;

- **fine**: may be levied as the punishment for any crime other than one for which a fixed punishment is laid down by law, and may also be levied in addition to other sentences;

- **community service order**: requires the offender to work unpaid for a fixed time;

- **probation**: aims to rehabilitate by setting conditions about the offender's activities and requiring regular meetings with a probation officer, with possible imprisonment if the terms are not met;

- **combination order**: combines community service and probation;

- **imprisonment**: is supposed to be given, under the **Criminal Justice Act 1991**, only if it is the punishment fixed by law, if the offence is so serious that only imprisonment is justified, or if only imprisonment would protect the public from the offender;

- **suspended sentence**: means that the offender is sentenced to prison but is released, and may have to serve the sentence if another crime is committed within the period of the sentence;

- **compensation orders** and **costs**.

An offender who is sentenced to a term of less than 12 months is regarded as a **short-term prisoner** and is released unconditionally after serving half the sentence. An offender sentenced to more than one year but less than four years may be released after serving half the sentence, but will remain on **licence** until the three-quarters point of the sentence.

Offenders sentenced to more than four years may be released on **parole** after serving half the sentence or are automatically released on licence after serving two-thirds. For some sexual and violent offences the licence period can be extended even beyond the period of the sentence. Prisoners sentenced to life imprisonment can be released only by the home secretary.

60.6
ENFORCEMENT OF CIVIL LAW

The civil courts deal with matters arising from private law [see **60.1.2**]. Their purpose is not to punish, but to decide disputes and to right wrongs. For the process of civil litigation, see **61.4**.

60.6.1
Civil courts

County courts deal with civil matters involving:

60.6.1.1
County courts

- adoption, guardianship and legitimacy of children, undefended divorces and minor probate disputes;

- equity matters (trusts, mortgages etc) and possession of land;

- winding up companies and (in some, but not all areas) bankruptcy;

- extortionate credit agreements;

- patent matters;

- all claims arising from personal injury which seem likely to be less than £50,000;

- claims in contract [see **18.12**] or tort [see **19.5**] up to £15,000;

- a range of other civil matters.

Claims under £5,000 are dealt with under the **small claims procedure**, and for those between £5,000 and £15,000 there is a **fast track** procedure. The court may hear larger claims if both parties agree.

County courts are bound by the decisions of the High Court, the Court of Appeal (civil division) and the House of Lords. Their own decisions do not create precedents.

60.6.1.2
High Court

The High Court of Justice, usually called the **High Court**, deals with contract and tort claims worth more than £15,000 (£50,000 for personal injury claims) and certain specialised claims such as libel.

The High Court is divided into the Family Division, the Chancery Division and the Queen's Bench Division. Each division may hear any High Court action, but for convenience specialises in particular areas:

- **Family Division**: marriage, divorce and custody of children, guardianship and adoption of children, non-contentious probate;.

- **Chancery Division**: company law, property, trusts, mortgages, administration of the estates of the dead, taxation, contentious probate;

- **Queen's Bench Division**: all other civil matters, mainly contract and tort. It hears applications for *habeas corpus* and hears appeals from magistrates' courts on points of criminal law. Specialist courts exist within the Queen's Bench Division, such as the **commercial court**, dealing with banking and insurance matters, and the **admiralty court**, for admiralty matters.

The High Court is bound by its own past decisions (except for the divisional court of the Queen's Bench Division, which is not bound by its own past decisions on criminal matters), and by decisions of the Court of Appeal (civil division) and the House of Lords.

60.6.1.3
Court of Appeal
(civil division)

The Court of Appeal (civil division) hears appeals from the county courts and High Court on matters of fact or law. It also deals with questions on legal matters arising from tribunals [see **60.8**]. Unlike the criminal division, the civil division of the Court of Appeal is bound by its own precedents, but it is not bound by decisions of the criminal division. It is also bound by decisions of the House of Lords.

60.6.1.4
House of Lords

The House of Lords is, as with criminal matters, the highest court, and is not bound by its own precedents. It deals with appeals from the Court of Appeal and, if all parties agree, appeals disputing the interpretation of a point of law subject to a binding precedent directly from the High Court (bypassing the Court of Appeal). Appeals may be made only by leave of the Court of Appeal or the House of Lords. Where European law is involved, a further appeal may be made to the European Court of Justice or European Court of Human Rights.

60.6.2
Civil remedies

The most common remedies in civil cases are orders to do or stop doing something (**specific performance** or **injunctions**), or **damages** to provide financial compensation. Civil remedies are explained in **61.4.7**.

Orders may also be made in **judicial review**, where the court reviews quasi-judicial or administrative decisions of public bodies.

60.7
OTHER COURTS

Coroners' courts deal with inquests on unnatural deaths, and can commit suspected murderers for trial. They also deal with treasure trove cases, involving money and valuables deliberately hidden whose owner is unknown.

The **Privy Council Judicial Committee** is part of the Privy Council, a body appointed to advise the monarch. It is technically unable to make decisions, but advises the monarch on decisions. It is not part of the court system, so does not set precedents. It hears appeals from:

- ecclesiastical courts, on matters concerning the clergy or church buildings;
- courts in the Channel Islands, the Isle of Man and some Commonwealth countries;
- the admiralty court;
- doctors struck off the medical register.

60.8 TRIBUNALS

Tribunals are boards—not courts—to which Parliament grants a judicial function. There are large numbers of tribunals, such as employment tribunals [see **chapter 33**], lands tribunals [see **56.7.2**], the solicitors' disciplinary tribunal and the General Medical Council tribunal.

The composition of tribunals varies but typically consists of two lay persons and one person, often the chair, with a legal qualification.

Some organisations, such as professional bodies, have their own **internal tribunals** to deal with, for example, employment or membership issues.

60.9 JURY TRIAL

Trials in the crown court and some civil cases, mainly those involving fraud, defamation, malicious prosecution and false imprisonment, are tried by jury. The number of jurors varies: in county courts it is eight, 12 in the High Court and crown court, and between seven and 11 in coroners' courts.

Jurors are chosen randomly from names on the electoral register, and must serve unless they are ineligible or are in a group permitted excusal and ask to be excused. People are ineligible to serve on a jury if they have received certain criminal sentences, suffer from a mental disorder, are members of religious orders, or work in the administration of justice. Groups permitted excusal are members and officers of Parliament or the European Parliament, doctors, dentists, nurses, veterinary surgeons, pharmacists and members of the armed forces.

60.10 FINDING SPECIALIST HELP

A book such as this can highlight areas of concern and explain general points, but cannot replace a professional advisor. This is why we have emphasised, throughout the book, the importance of seeking advice.

Voluntary organisations are at the crossroads of an unusually complex set of rules and laws. The interaction of charity law, special tax and VAT rules, complexities of their own unusual internal structures and governing documents, and rapidly changing government policies mean that the voluntary sector has a very particular need for expert and up-to-date advice.

Unfortunately, probably less than 5% of the 66,000 practising solicitors in England and Wales have had any significant contact with the voluntary sector, and probably only one quarter of 1% could properly describe themselves as experts in voluntary sector and charitable law matters. The same sort of percentages apply to accountants. Despite the difficulties, organisations should make an effort to seek out advisors with voluntary sector experience.

60.10.1 Support organisations

For straightforward issues, advice may be available from voluntary sector support organisations. These include:

- **National Council for Voluntary Organisations**: 0800-7298 298; www.ncvo-vol.org.uk.
- **Wales Council for Voluntary Action**: 029-2043 1700; www.wcva. org.uk.
- **Scottish Council for Voluntary Organisations**: 0131-556 3882; www.scvo.org.uk and **Northern Ireland Council for Voluntary Action**: 028-9087 7777; www.nicva.org. Note that this book does not cover the law in Scotland and Northern Ireland.
- Local councils for voluntary service may be able to provide advice to local organisations. Details are available from the **National Association of Councils for Voluntary Service**: 0114-278 6636; www. nacvs.org.uk. Some CVSs have specialist advice services for accountancy and/or employment law.
- Information and advice for community associations, especially those running community centres and similar premises: **Community Matters**: 020-7226 0189; www.communitymatters.org.uk.
- Information and advice for organisations in rural areas: **Action with Communities in Rural England** (ACRE): 01285-653477; www. acre.org.uk.

Umbrella bodies and federations can often provide information on legal matters to their member organisations. Law centres and citizens advice bureaux may be able to advise on some matters, but many do not advise employers on employment matters, even where the employer is a management committee or board of trustees of a voluntary organisation. Some areas have community accountancy projects which can provide advice and practical help on financial matters.

60.10.2
Legal update services

Voluntary sector specialist solicitors or advisors may provide newsletters or internet-based update services. The authors of this book both have such services:

- James Sinclair Taylor, **Sinclair Taylor & Martin Solicitors**: 020-8969 3667; www.sinclairtaylor.co.uk.
- **Sandy Adirondack**: 020-7232 0726; www.sandy-a.co.uk.

60.10.3
Finding a solicitor or accountant

The Law Society (0870-606 6575; www.solicitors-online.com) can provide names of practising solicitors and law firms with charity expertise, and legal directories listing solicitors and law firms and their areas of expertise are available in reference libraries. Voluntary sector periodicals such as *Charity Finance* (020-7819 1200) and *Third Sector* (020-8709 9050; www.api.co.uk) carry advertisements for a range of professionals. Names can also be obtained from other organisations which have used solicitors or accountants for similar matters.

Even where a solicitor or accountant advertises in a reputable voluntary sector publication or is recommended by another organisation, it may be sensible to ask for and take up references.

60.10.4
Choosing a solicitor or accountant

Whether choosing from one of the voluntary sector guides or simply selecting from among local solicitors or accountants, a variety of factors need to be borne in mind.

60.10.4.1
Size

Larger accountancy and law firms tend to be more expensive than smaller ones, but this is not invariable. There is often greater breadth of expertise within a larger firm, but many smaller specialist practices have greater specialist knowledge than the larger firms.

A compromise may be to choose a smaller or less expensive firm for straightforward work, and to seek specialist advice—for example on VAT—from a larger or more specialist firm. The strategy of having several professional advisors has some advantages, such as allowing comparison in price and quality of service. But good professional advice is based on a thorough understanding of an organisation and what it is trying to achieve, and this understanding takes time to build up. Using several advisors in the same field may mean paying a greater price or risking decisions being made by a person who does not have a full understanding of the implications for the organisation.

Another factor is that a small piece of work for an occasional client may take a lower priority than work for a regular client. On the other hand the advisor may be more complacent about the regular client, and give higher priority to wooing the occasional client.

60.10.4.2
Personnel

When selecting a professional it is important to discuss whether the work will be done by a partner (which is likely to be more expensive) or will be delegated. Delegation does not imply inferior service, but it is important to be aware of how the work will actually be handled.

60.10.4.3
Cost

For some types of work, particularly those which do not involve conflict or a third party—such as audit, property purchase, updating a staff contract or drawing up a constitution—it should be possible to get a quote or pre-estimate. However for more complex areas such as conducting negotiations on a funding agreement, undertaking litigation or resolving an outstanding tax dispute, professionals would probably refuse to give more than a general estimate.

Professionals generally charge on the basis of an hourly rate. Particular points to query are whether the rate includes or is exclusive of VAT, and whether the rate may be reduced for straightforward work or increased for particularly urgent, large or complex work. Where costs are a particular concern, it is reasonable to set budgets and require the advisor not to exceed the budget without written agreement.

Pro bono (free or reduced-rate services provided by professionals) may be available but the organisation will have much less control over who does the work and when it is done.

60.10.5
Terms of
appointment

Accountants and increasingly solicitors provide detailed terms of appointment. These should be examined carefully to ensure that the service specified includes all the required work. A specification solely for an audit, for example, will not include general advice on how to improve the organisation's accounting systems [for more about terms of appointment for auditors, see **50.1.3.**]

The terms of appointment will also specify payment conditions. Most professionals are willing to organise payments in a way that does not put pressure on the client's cashflow if this is requested in advance.

60.10.6
Disputes

Dissatisfaction with service or the bill should be discussed thoroughly with the person who provided the service or delivered the bill. If this is unsatisfactory it should be raised at a higher level within the firm. Most firms will be prepared to offer a reduction or compensation if there is a genuine problem with the service they have provided.

60.10.6.1
Solicitors

For work which does not involve the courts, a client can require solicitors to obtain a **remuneration certificate** from the Law Society confirming that the bill is (or is not) reasonable. A deposit of 50% of the amount due must be made. Where the client is served with a notice drawing its attention to the right to require a remuneration certificate, the right is lost if action is not taken within 30 days.

Where the disputed bill involves court proceedings the client can apply to have a detailed assessment of costs by the court. At a formal hearing a court official examines the work done by the solicitor and approves or otherwise the bill. The client has a chance to make its comments at the hearing.

The Office for the Supervision of Solicitors (0845-608 6565; www.oss. lawsociety.org.uk) deals with complaints about poor service or improper behaviour. The OSS has limited power to order compensation. Complaints of negligence are made through the courts. Advice should be taken from a different solicitor before bringing legal action for negligence against a solicitor.

60.10.6.2
Accountants

The Institute of Chartered Accountants (020-7920 8100; www.icaew. co.uk) does not have a procedure for intervening if an accountant's bill is disputed, but can provide an advice pack for this situation. They can also provide advice in cases of unethical or other unacceptable behaviour.

60.10.7
Other professionals

For surveyors, architects, engineers and similar professionals, it is generally much less crucial that they have voluntary sector experience. As with other professionals, clear agreements are the key to a successful relationship.

FOR FURTHER INFORMATION

Human rights. Lord Chancellor's Department: 020-7210 8500; www.lcd.gov.uk

Justice: 020-7329 5100; www.justice.org.uk

British Institute of Human Rights: 020-7401 2712; www.bihr.org

Human Rights Policy Network (NCVO): 020-7520 2473; www.ncvo-vol.org.uk

---

Chapter 61
DISPUTE RESOLUTION
AND LITIGATION

61.1
DISPUTE
PROCEDURES

Most disagreements and disputes are resolved informally and relatively amicably, and require no further action. But some are so serious or intractable that they require formal procedures, intervention by an outside person, and/or legal action.

Disputes or problems within organisations, or between an organisation and an individual or other body, may be dealt with:

- through internal procedures such as disciplinary and grievance procedures [see **chapter 29**] and complaint procedures;
- through procedures, if any, set out in the governing document;
- by involving a regulatory body such as the Charity Commission [see **3.5.2** and **3.5.8**];
- by involving an outsider as a mediator or arbitrator [see below]; *or*
- by legal action through the courts.

A contract or agreement between the parties may set out a procedure to be followed prior to legal action, and may specify that an outside person is to be or may be called in to resolve or help resolve the matter. Before taking action through the courts, the governing body must consider whether it has a power to conduct or settle litigation [see **5.4.3**], and charities should consider specific issues relating to **charity proceedings** [see **61.8**].

61.1.1
Time limits

Many methods of resolving disputes, especially if the courts are involved, have time limits. Failure to observe these will generally cost that party its right to claim, and may involve liability to the other party. As soon as any dispute or claim arises, the organisation must take steps to ensure that any time limits are monitored and observed.

61.2 ALTERNATIVE DISPUTE RESOLUTION

Alternative dispute resolution (sometimes called **appropriate dispute resolution**) involves a range of techniques to try to resolve disputes without having to take legal action through the courts. While there has been scepticism about some types of ADR, it is now actively encouraged as an alternative to court proceedings.

In March 2001 the government announced that wherever possible it would use mediation or arbitration, rather than litigation, to resolve government legal disputes. It also said it would include ADR clauses in all standard procurement contracts. Voluntary organisations which carry out work under public sector contracts may be required in future to agree to ADR clauses in their contracts, and to use ADR where appropriate to resolve contract disputes.

61.2.1 Mediation

Mediation, sometimes called **conciliation**, is an informal but structured process where one or more independent **mediators** help the disputants reach an agreed resolution. A mediator does not take sides or impose solutions, but helps the parties work towards resolution.

A successful mediation ends with a solution which the parties to the dispute are willing to accept. It is usually put in writing and signed by the parties, and may include a procedure for reviewing it to be sure it is working. A mediated settlement is generally legally binding and can, if necessary, be enforced in the courts.

Mediation may be particularly appropriate where the parties need to preserve a working relationship and it is preferable to try to avoid the adversarial approach of litigation, and where the parties are committed to working together to try to find a solution, but need some outside help. If the parties cannot reach a mediated settlement, they retain the right to use arbitration or litigation.

61.2.1.1 Mediation clauses in contracts

If both parties agree, mediation clauses can be included in contracts to purchase or provide goods or services, leases and other contracts. Clauses can also be included in an organisation's internal procedures. The Centre for Dispute Resolution [see end of chapter] can advise on appropriate wordings.

61.2.1.2 The courts and mediation

Because the courts are trying to speed up and simplify the process of resolving disputes [see **61.4**], they are in some cases encouraging potential litigants to use alternative dispute resolution, particularly mediation. If a person unreasonably refuses to participate in ADR, the court can make a costs award against them—even if they subsequently win their case in court.

61.2.1.3 Mediation for voluntary organisations

Organisations providing mediation services for voluntary organisations include the National Council for Voluntary Organisations/Centre for Dispute Resolution (CEDR) scheme and some community mediation projects, which can be contacted via Mediation UK [see end of chapter].

61.2.1.4 ACAS

ACAS, which provides dispute resolution services between employers and employees [see **33.2.3**], makes a distinction between what it calls mediation, where its officers provide solutions, and the type of mediation described above, which it calls **conciliation**. For straightforward unfair dismissal cases, ACAS offers **arbitration** [see **33.2.3**].

61.2.2 Experts

In some situations a contract, lease or agreement under dispute may provide for resolution by an **expert**, or parties to a dispute may agree to use this method. This is more formal than mediation [see above], but less formal than arbitration [see below].

Experts are different from arbitrators in that:

- they give their own opinion, rather than deciding between the parties' cases;

- if they ask for or allow evidence to be submitted to them, there are no formal rules governing their procedures;

- in cases of a wrong decision a court can overturn an arbitrator's decision on the basis of misconduct or wrongly applying the law, but an independent expert can only be sued for negligence.

**61.2.3
Arbitration**

In **arbitration**, an **arbitrator** hears evidence from both parties and makes an award to one party or the other. Arbitration procedures are governed by the **Arbitration Act 1996**, and the arbitrator's decision is legally binding.

Arbitration is widely used in leases for fixing rents at rent review [see **58.3.1**]. Contracts may also allow for arbitration. A typical clause is:

> Any dispute arising out of or in connection with this contract shall be referred to and finally resolved by an arbitrator agreed by the parties or, failing agreement, by an arbitrator appointed, on the application of either party, by the President or a Vice President of the Chartered Institute of Arbitrators.

Where an agreement contains a binding arbitration clause, either party can require arbitration prior to any court proceeding.

Arbitration is similar to litigation but is more private, generally quicker and generally less intimidating. It is more formal and judicial than mediation, and tends to be more expensive. The arbitrator will normally give a **reasoned award**, which is like the judgment of a court, if asked to. The arbitrator is paid by the parties to the dispute and will generally not release the award until the costs of the arbitration have been paid.

A decision by an arbitrator can generally be challenged in the courts only if it is alleged that the arbitrator made a mistake in law, and only if the court believes the issue is likely to have a substantial effect on the rights of the parties.

An arbitrator does not have to be qualified, but it is advisable for an arbitrator who is not qualified to take advice about the conduct of the arbitration. Qualified arbitrators may be contacted via the Chartered Institute of Arbitrators [see end of chapter].

**61.2.4
Ombudsmen**

For some types of work there is an ombudsman to whom complaints can be made after complaints procedures have been followed or, where there are no complaints procedures, a reasonable effort has been made to resolve the dispute. Tenants of registered social landlords, for example, have a right to complain to an ombudsman appointed by the Housing Corporation. The decision of an ombudsman is final.

**61.2.5
Disputes within
industrial and
provident societies**

Some industrial and provident societies have provisions in their rules for disputes between members and the society or disputes arising from the rules to be referred to the Registrar of Friendly Societies. This procedure no longer exists, and all such disputes must be referred to the county court. This requirement does not apply to disputes with outside bodies or internal disputes on other matters.

Friendly Societies Act 1992 ss.83-84

**61.3
CONSIDERING
LITIGATION**

Litigation is the process of making a formal legal complaint about a civil matter [see **60.1.2**]. If the matter is not resolved between the parties, litigation ends in a court trial.

An organisation's decision to take legal action or to defend an action brought against itself should not be taken lightly. The process can be long, costly in time and money, and emotionally draining, although civil procedure reforms known as the **Woolf reforms** are intended to speed up the processes. On the other hand, the cost to the organisation may be even greater if such action is not taken.

A desire for justice may not be fulfilled by legal action. Technical considerations, the passage of time, the costs and the relative power of the parties can all conspire to produce results far short of 'justice'. Even where the claimant (the person bringing the action) obtains the judgment it seeks, it only has an order. The claimant, not the court, then has the task of enforcing the order, again through technical and sometimes frustrating procedures.

61.3.1
Before litigating

Before making a decision to proceed with litigation, some of the factors which should be carefully considered within the organisation and with its legal advisor are:

- whether there is a legal right that can be enforced, or simply a moral right;

- whether, if judgment is obtained, the court will have a power to provide an adequate remedy [see **61.4.7**];

- whether the defendant is worth suing;

- whether the organisation has the legal power to litigate [see **5.4.3**];

- the cost implications, including whether these are covered by insurance [see **20.9.3**];

- how long the process might take;

- issues where the case involves **charity proceedings** [see **61.8**];

- the implications of diverting the time and energy of staff and governing body members from the normal work of the organisation, not only during the trial itself but during all the preparations, meetings, briefings, research etc;

- the public relations implications, which may be negative (for example interfering with fundraising, or alienating supporters or funders) or positive (such as reducing the risk of similar losses or problems, or demonstrating a firmness of purpose).

A decision to enter—or not enter—into litigation should be made by the governing body or under clear and explicit delegated authority.

61.3.1.1
Choosing a legal advisor

Much litigation is routine and well within the capabilities of most competent general firms of solicitors. Solicitors can also supplement their expertise by choosing appropriately qualified specialist barristers. But litigation is a formal affair, and quickly exposes a lack of experience in a legal advisor. Organisations should not be afraid to ask whether the firm has a litigation specialist, and to ask whether they have experience in the relevant type of litigation. [See **60.10.3** for advice on finding a solicitor.]

Location may also play a role. If the proceedings are to be conducted in the High Court in London, solicitors outside London may feel the need to instruct local agents as well as London barristers.

61.3.1.2
Cost of professional advice

The hourly cost of solicitors varies widely, from £70 in a one-person rural solicitor's firm, to at least £100-£200 for larger firms in urban areas, and perhaps several hundred pounds per hour for complex matters involving substantial sums. Similarly a newly qualified barrister may receive £100 for a short and routine court appearance, but a senior barrister's daily fee may run into many thousands of pounds.

Despite the inclination to choose on the basis of lowest cost, this may be a false economy. An expensive but highly experienced solicitor may well end up costing less (and having a better chance of success) than a less expensive but less experienced solicitor.

For technical disputes where success or failure may depend on the weight of expert evidence, large fees may be required by engineers, doctors, architects and other professionals. If the litigation lasts for an extended period, such input may be regularly required.

As litigation is a contest, the amount of legal work will depend on the tactics adopted by each side and cannot be determined in advance. Any estimates given in advance will be very provisional indeed.

61.3.1.3
Award of costs
and damages

The losing party to a court action, unless he or she has a **certificate of public funding** (formerly legal aid), will have to meet his or her own **legal costs** [see **61.4.8**], and generally a portion of the other party's. This can range from a very limited amount in small claims cases, to up to 75% of the winner's costs in other cases, so can add considerably to the loser's costs. (Note that different cost rules apply in the employment and other tribunals.)

Even if the winning party is awarded costs, these will not be for the full amount. It is still likely to have to meet at least 25% of its legal costs, and possibly much more. So even winning can prove costly.

Where there are interim court hearings before the trial, it is usual for the party who loses the application to have to pay some or all of the other side's costs, usually within 14 days of the hearing.

Defendants must also think seriously about the **damages** they could be ordered to pay if they lose the case [see **61.4.7.1**]. The claimant could also become liable for damages if the defendant makes a counterclaim [see **61.4.2.3**]. There is no limit on damages in court cases, or in discrimination cases in the employment tribunal.

61.3.1.4
Indirect costs

There are also likely to be indirect costs such as locum staff to cover for staff involved in the case, and perhaps lost income if donors, funders, members or clients are antagonised by the proceedings.

61.3.1.5
Liability for costs

If the organisation is unincorporated, any legal action will be brought against some or all governing body members, rather than against the organisation itself [see **1.2.5**]. If the organisation is an unincorporated trust, the trustees should consider at the outset an application for a court order requiring the trust to indemnify its trustees for costs and liabilities. This is called a **Beddoes order**, but it is not much use if the trust does not have adequate funds to indemnify the trustees.

Very serious consideration must be given and legal advice should be taken if the organisation does not have insurance to cover the legal costs and any damages, and there is any possibility that the costs and damages could be more than the organisation's assets.

If this situation arises and the organisation is incorporated with limited liability [see **2.1.1**], the organisation would be insolvent and would have to be wound up.

If the organisation is not incorporated with limited liability, the members of the governing body could be held personally liable for any or all of the amount owing by the organisation.

See **chapter 19** for more about liability, and **chapter 20** for more about insurances.

61.3.1.6
Issues for charities

The governing body of a charity has a primary duty to safeguard the charity's funds [see **13.3.5**], and any decision to enter into litigation must be in the best interests of the charity.

Charities do not require the Charity Commission's consent to take or defend legal proceedings, but if the litigation is an unusual type, for example libel, or might involve substantial costs the charity's trustees should seek the Commission's advice before proceeding.

**61.3.2
Deciding not to
litigate**

All these factors, and in particular the costs, mean that the vast majority of disputes or claims never lead to litigation. They are resolved through negotiation between the parties or through an alternative dispute resolution process, or the matter is simply dropped.

A legally binding agreement not to take legal action in the courts, in return for an apology, cash settlement or other settlement, is referred to as a **compromise agreement**. Where a compromise agreement relates to a potential employment tribunal claim, it must follow specific rules [see **33.2.2**].

**61.4
THE LITIGATION
PROCESS**

No legal case is exactly like any other, and procedures and the course of the action vary greatly from case to case. In addition there are particular procedures for specialist sub-branches of litigation such as libel (one of the few types of civil case where jurors are involved), patent law and complex commercial matters.

The **Woolf reforms** have significantly changed the litigation process. New **civil procedure rules** (the CPR) apply in county courts and the High Court. The procedure is intended to be less adversarial than before, with emphasis on dealing with cases quickly and encouraging the parties to cooperate with each other.

Much of the language has also changed. The person who initiates the litigation was previously called the plaintiff but is now called a **claimant**, although the person against whom the case is brought is still known as the **defendant**, and both the claimant and defendant are **litigants**. (There may be multiple claimants or defendants.) Latin terms such as *in camera* and *ex parte* have been replaced by **in private** and **without notice**.

**61.4.1
Preliminary stages**

61.4.1.1
Consulting insurer

As soon as there is any possibility of litigation, the organisation should find out whether the matter falls within any of its insurance policies [see **chapter 20**]. Insurance may cover the act giving rise to the litigation, or only the legal costs. If there is any possibility that the act is covered by insurance, the insurer must be consulted immediately.

Failure to consult the insurer immediately, any admission of liability or taking certain steps without the insurer's consent may release the insurance company from any obligation to cover the loss or costs.

If the issue is covered by insurance, it is likely that the insurance company will deal with all negotiations with the other party and will conduct any legal action against the other party. If the insurer is dealing with the matter, the organisation itself must not get involved in any discussions with the other party.

Where the insurance simply covers legal costs, the organisation can generally select its own solicitor and conduct the action. It may however need to obtain the insurer's consent for various steps.

61.4.1.2
Taking legal advice

The organisation may want at this stage to consult a solicitor or other legal advisor, or may decide to proceed further on its own. It is generally advisable to take legal advice sooner rather than later.

61.4.1.3
Documents

The organisation also needs to consider carefully what it puts into writing about the situation, even for its own use. Unless such documents fall within certain limits and are therefore **privileged**, they may have to be disclosed to the other side. This may weaken the organisation's case—but inability to provide relevant documents may also weaken its case [see **61.4.3.2**]. For this reason, documents which may later be needed as evidence in a legal case should not be discarded, destroyed or altered.

61.4.1.4
Without prejudice communication

If there is a risk of litigation, nothing should be said or put in writing to the other party without legal advice or very careful thought.

Unless specified otherwise, any communication with the other party is **open**. The content of open discussions or correspondence can be disclosed in later court proceedings.

But by starting settlement offers—either verbal or written—with the words **without prejudice**, the parties are able to hold discussions about settlement on the basis that neither side will be allowed to disclose what was said in these discussions or letters in later court proceedings. For example, an organisation in dispute with a computer manufacturer might offer without prejudice to accept £5,000 and a new computer. If the manufacturer refuses the offer, the manufacturer cannot later at the trial say that the offer to accept £5,000 and a new computer is evidence of the level of loss suffered by the organisation.

In certain limited circumstances, without prejudice offers may later be disclosed to the court. For example, a computer manufacturer who makes a substantial settlement offer might indicate that if the organisation wins less than the offered amount as damages at the trial, the manufacturer will disclose the offer during arguments about who should bear the costs of the action. In this case, the manufacturer's offer would be made **without prejudice save as to costs**, and would be called an **offer to settle** or **part 36 offer**.

61.4.1.5
Agreeing an offer

If a without prejudice offer of settlement is unconditionally accepted, the correspondence or discussion then becomes open and a binding agreement will be reached. This will be disclosable to the court.

61.4.1.6
Letter before action

If its demands are not met, the claimant generally writes a final **letter before action** giving a deadline after which it will commence proceedings. If such a letter is not written and the claimant commences proceedings without warning, the court might not award costs to the successful claimant, on the basis that a letter before action might have secured settlement without the need for proceedings.

For some types of claims, including personal injury, libel and clinical negligence, **pre-action protocols** (procedures) set out the steps to be followed and the information that must be disclosed at this stage.

61.4.2
Starting the proceedings

61.4.2.1
Legal advice

Before starting or deciding to defend proceedings, the organisation will need to take advice from its solicitor, and may also seek a barrister's opinion. This may be expensive, but may be advisable because:

- the solicitor may not have specialist expertise or may not have recent experience of litigation in the particular field;
- the process of writing the case down in order to instruct the barrister may provide a salutary concentration of the mind;
- a barrister who is not involved in other ongoing relationships with the client, as a solicitor may be, may be more objective in his or her assessment of the likely outcome.

The solicitor may arrange a meeting with the barrister to clarify points or allow fuller discussion. This meeting is called a **conference**.

The barrister's opinion may be given in writing, as an **advice**. A barrister's opinion is just that—an opinion—and does not provide an authoritative prediction of the outcome.

61.4.2.2
Payment on account

A solicitor who instructs a barrister or expert becomes personally liable for ensuring they are paid. Most solicitors are therefore unwilling to incur liability for such costs unless the client has paid a sufficient sum into the **client account** held by the solicitor. Solicitors also generally ask for payment on account of **costs** to ensure their own fees are covered. Interest on these accounts belongs to the client.

61.4.2.3
Claim form

Proceedings are generally started when the claimant presents a **claim form** (formerly called a **writ** or summons) to the High Court or a county court and pays a fee to the court. The claim form is then issued and must be **served on** (delivered to) the defendant. The claim form may contain a detailed statement of the claimant's claim, or may simply state the general nature of the claim and include the details in a separate **particulars of claim** (or statement of claim) which is served later.

The claim form or separate particulars of claim must include a **statement of truth**, in which the claimant confirms that he or she believes the stated facts are true.

Generally with the claim form there will be an **acknowledgement of service** form on which the defendant can indicate whether it intends to defend the proceedings. A defendant who wishes to defend then files its **defence**, and if it believes it has a claim against the claimant, may make a **counterclaim**. A fee is payable to the court when making a counterclaim. The defendant may also wish to **join** (bring) other parties into the action if it feels that they also have some sort of responsibility.

The defence, and counterclaim if made, must contain a statement of truth and must be filed at court and served on the claimant.

The response to the claim form and necessary materials must be filed within strict time limits. Failure to act within the limit may result in judgment being entered against the defendant in default of its response.

61.4.3
Before trial

When a defence is filed, the court will issue **allocation questionnaires** for each party to complete and return to the court. This enables the court to allocate the case to the right track [see below], and to make directions about how the case will be conducted, for example:

- fixing a hearing to discuss directions;
- allowing one or both parties to ask the other to clarify their claim or defence (a **part 18 request**);
- allowing the parties to use expert evidence at trial, either in the form of a report or in person;
- ordering disclosure [see **61.4.3.2**].

Where the court allows expert evidence, it often orders the parties to appoint the expert jointly.

61.4.3.1
Allocation of case

Using the **allocation questionnaires**, the court decides the track on which the case will proceed. These are:

- **small claims**, for most disputes worth less than £5,000;
- **fast track**, for claims between £5,000 and £15,000 where the trial is likely to last for one day or less;
- **multi-track**, for claims over £15,000.

The High Court can hear only claims over £15,000 (£50,000 for personal injury claims). County courts can deal with all cases, and will hear all except very large claims.

61.4.3.2
Disclosure

Each party is likely to be required to serve on the other a full list of the relevant documents which it holds. After the list has been served the other party can inspect and take copies of those documents.

This process is referred to as **disclosure** (formerly called discovery). It is very important and both parties have a wide duty to preserve and disclose documents relevant to the case, even if the documents harm their position.

Documents which are **privileged** from disclosure do not need to be disclosed. Privilege generally arises because the documents were prepared as part of the claim or in expectation of making or defending it, for example letters to and from the parties' solicitors.

61.4.3.3
Interim orders

In addition to these more routine steps, a party may apply to the court for an **interim order** to protect its position. If, for example, an organisation feels that neighbouring building works are damaging its buildings, it may seek an interim injunction to restrain further works.

The application may be made on the same day as the original claim form, or at any time thereafter. Except in very urgent cases or where surprise is essential, prior notice of the application must be given to the other party.

Interim orders are powerful tools, even including a **search order** (formerly called an **Anton Piller order**), and orders forcing compliance with court rulings or earlier orders on pain of losing the case (an **unless order**: 'unless you do this, you will lose the case').

61.4.4
Settlement

Attempts to settle the matter may take place at any stage. This may happen if, for example, documents produced in disclosure or the sharing of experts' reports give extra force to one party's arguments for a settlement. Or a well resourced organisation may wear down the resolve of a smaller one whose legal arguments may be good, but which may be less able to sustain them in the face of complex and expensive proceedings.

As the date of trial approaches the pressures for settlement may intensify, in order to avoid the cost and stress of the trial itself.

A settlement reached before trial may be embodied in an **order of the court** consented to by both parties. This enables either party to take action if the other party fails to comply with what has been agreed.

61.4.4.1
Hoping it goes away

The progress of an action is largely in the hands of the claimant, although the courts increasingly seek to ensure that proceedings are not unduly delayed. A claimant may simply cease to take any further action, and unless the defendant has a significant counterclaim, the defendant is likely to let matters rest. Both sides may simply want to forget about the matter, or may hope it will go away if it is ignored.

This strategy is risky for the claimant or for a defendant with a counterclaim, because if it delays too long the other party may apply to have the case struck out for want of prosecution. If the case is struck out the claimant (or defendant on its counterclaim) will not be able to proceed, and is very likely to have costs awarded against it.

If the defendant ignores matters it may have an **unless order** brought against it [see **61.4.3.3**], threatening loss of the case if it does not act.

61.4.5
Right of audience

Solicitors, barristers and others who have a right to speak for a party in court or at a tribunal are said to have a **right of audience** in the court. Each court or tribunal has its own rules about who has this right.

Individuals can always represent themselves. Barristers generally have a right of audience, and solicitors have the right in the lower courts. Organisations are generally allowed to be represented by a staff member or other unqualified person, but this must be confirmed beforehand.

61.4.6
Trial

The trial usually opens with the claimant, either directly or through its solicitor, barrister or other **advocate** (person representing it), opening the proceedings and calling witnesses in support of its claim. After each witness has given evidence, the defendant is able to cross-examine. If the cross-examination reveals new issues, the claimant may be able to re-examine the witnesses on these new issues. The defendant similarly presents its evidence, then both parties sum up.

61.4.7
Judgment and remedies

After summarising the facts the judge gives a judgment and may make an order, referred to as the **remedy**, which will be set out in a written judgment of the court. The most common remedies are:

- orders requiring **payment of a debt**;

- orders authorising **possession of a property** (land or building);
- **injunctions**: orders requiring a party to perform an action or prohibiting a party from performing an action [see for example **18.12.7**];
- **specific performance**: orders requiring a party to carry out a contract [see **18.12.6**] or take some other specific action;
- **damages** [see below].

61.4.7.1
Damages

Damages are financial compensation for the wrongs suffered, with the object of placing the party in the same financial position as if the contract had been fulfilled, or the tort (wrong) or breach of statutory duty had not been committed.

If the court feels that the claimant was wronged but has not suffered any loss or has not suffered substantially, it may award only a token amount as **nominal damages**.

Aggravated damages are extra damages if the court feels that the injury was aggravated by the defendant's conduct or motives.

Very high **exemplary damages** may be awarded where the court considers that the defendant committed the wrong for self-serving reasons or to make a profit, and the profit will exceed the claimant's loss—for example where a landlord evicts a tenant in order to rent at a better price. Exemplary damages may also be awarded to punish oppressive, unconstitutional or arbitrary acts by government.

Rookes v Barnard [1964] AC 1129

It is unusual for the court to award aggravated or exemplary damages and they should not be claimed in ordinary contract or tort claims.

Where the full loss is not known—typically in medical or accident cases—a **provisional award** may be made before the final assessment of the full amount.

61.4.8
Assessment and award of costs

The court generally awards costs to the winner of the case, so in addition to any other remedy, the loser is ordered to pay the legal costs of the winner.

The costs do not cover the winner's full costs. The proportion to be paid by the loser is either agreed between the parties or is assessed by the court. It is now common for judges to make a **summary assessment** of the costs at the end of a short hearing, on the basis of the winner's written summary of costs. Alternatively a court official may undertake a **detailed assessment of costs** (formerly called **taxation**), which involves reviewing the winning party's legal bill and assessing an amount which the official feels is fair. In normal circumstances this is 50% to 75% of the actual cost paid by the winning party.

Costs covered by the losing party are referred to as **party and party costs**. The actual cost paid by the winner, in the form of a bill from its own solicitor, is called **solicitor and own client costs**.

Although costs are normally awarded against the loser, there are some exceptions, for example:

- costs are not generally awarded against losers who have a certificate of public funding (legal aid);
- if the loser offered to settle prior to judgment or paid a sum into the court at a figure at or above the final judgment, costs may be reduced or lowered;
- the loser may have won awards of costs in preliminary hearings, and so may receive costs from the winner in respect of these.

The award of costs is discretionary. In a case where there are many issues and each party wins on some of them, the judge may order each party to pay costs for the issues that they lost, or may simply say that each side must pay its own costs.

61.4.8.1
Security for costs

Where the court believes that a party might not be able to meet the damages or the other party's costs if it loses the case, the court might order a sum to be deposited with the court, or might halt the proceedings until security for those costs is given. This particularly applies to organisations with limited liability.

61.4.9
Enforcement

Obtaining judgment merely gives the person in whose favour it has been given an order of the court for the remedy. The court does not, except in very unusual circumstances, take any steps to enforce the order. It is up to the winning party to decide whether and how to do this.

61.4.9.1
Execution

If the party against whom judgment is given fails to obey the order of the court, for example does not make the payment within the specified time, the person in whose favour judgment has been given may apply for **execution**. Under this process **court bailiffs** (called **sheriffs** in the High Court) enter the premises of the person against whom judgment has been given. If the judgment is for money they seize goods on the premises sufficient to meet the money judgment, or if the order is for possession they take possession of the premises.

Execution cannot be levied against specified categories of goods, for example personal clothing and tools of the debtor's trade.

Bailiffs in the county court are court officials, and there can be considerable delay before it is possible to obtain an appointment for them to attend to execute. In the High Court the sheriffs are independent and generally available at much shorter notice.

Execution is effective against an organisation or individual who can be traced and who has significant saleable property. But problems can arise if the bailiffs have difficulty in gaining entry to the premises, or if there are suggestions that the property on the premises is owned by someone other than the person against whom judgment was given.

When the bailiffs first attend they generally take **walking possession** by seizing control of the goods but not actually removing them from the premises. The creditor is then given a short period of time before the goods are removed. The goods are then generally auctioned.

61.4.9.2
Garnishee order

If it is known that there is money in bank or other accounts, the court will make a **garnishee order** requiring the bank to pay the money over.

61.4.9.3
Charging order

If the debtor owns property or shares, the court may make a **charging order** to put a charge (similar to a mortgage) over them.

61.4.9.4
Attachment of earnings

If the person against whom judgment has been given is employed, the court may order the employer to deduct amounts from the person's salary and pay them to the court to satisfy the judgment.

61.4.9.5
Bankruptcy or winding up

If a judgment of £750 or more remains unmet, this provides grounds for an application to wind up an organisation [see **21.5.4**] or to bankrupt an individual. The winding up or bankruptcy creates a completely separate case and requires a new set of proceedings.

61.4.9.6
Contempt

Where an injunction or other direct order of the court is disobeyed, the court can impose a fine or imprisonment for **contempt of court**.

61.4.10
Appeals

In many cases it is possible to appeal, provided strict time limits are met. However, the further up the court system a matter progresses [see **60.5.1**], the more constraints are imposed requiring leave (permission) to be given before appeals are taken. This is done to prevent the courts becoming clogged with appeals with little chance of success.

61.5
COVERING THE
COSTS

61.5.1
Insurance

Legal expenses insurance [see **20.9.3**] covers the costs of litigation. An organisation with this insurance must generally contact the insurer before taking any steps towards settlement or litigation. Insurance policies are also available to cover damages arising from a very wide range of claims [see **chapter 20**].

After-the-event insurance may be obtained to finance a case where there is a high prospect of success. If the case is lost the insurer will pay the other side's costs and also, under some schemes, the loser's costs. The insurer will require sufficient information to enable it to assess the risk, and the premium may be substantial.

61.5.2
Conditional fees

Some solicitors now offer **conditional fees**, sometimes called no-win no-fee. These means that the client only pays fees if the case is won, although it may have to pay disbursements (the solicitor's expenses).

Conditional fees and after-the-event insurance are frequently used by claimants in personal injury litigation. Their use outside this context is recent, and they are generally unlikely to be suitable or available to voluntary organisations contemplating litigation.

61.5.3
Certificate of public
funding (legal aid)

The **Community Legal Service Fund** may meet the reasonable fees of solicitors and barristers acting for individuals who meet the criteria for a **certificate of public funding** (formerly legal aid). This involves rigorous means-tested financial criteria, and tests as to the merits of their case. Public funding is generally not available for organisations, or for individual members of a governing body who are being sued as a representative of an unincorporated organisation rather than in their individual capacity.

Public funding from the Community Legal Service Fund is not available for all types of action. In particular it does not cover libel, or cases where conditional fees may be available, such as most personal injury cases. It is not available for tribunals, but does cover advice and preparation for a tribunal hearing. At the time of writing (early 2001) the government had proposed making funding available for VAT, income tax and Protection of Children Act tribunals, and it is possible that it will become available for employees bringing claims in the employment tribunal [see **33.1.1**].

The courts do not, in normal circumstances, enforce costs awards against publicly funded litigants [see **61.4.8**]. So if an organisation brings an action against such an individual, the organisation will have to meet its own costs even if it wins the case. This may be a consideration in deciding whether to continue with an action.

61.6
DO-IT-YOURSELF
LITIGATION

In actions involving **small claims** of up to £5,000 in a county court, a less formal procedure is used, and generally solicitors' costs are not awarded to the winning party. This is to encourage individuals to undertake their own proceedings.

Organisations can undertake actions larger than this without a solicitor, but the potential difficulties should not be underestimated. Where an organisation routinely needs to make claims which are unlikely to be contested—for example, recovering rent arrears from property let out—it may well be sensible to train some staff members to conduct routine litigation. Qualified legal advice should be available to these staff, and procedures should be in place to transfer cases to solicitors if they become more complex.

61.7
TRIBUNAL
PROCEDURE

Procedures in tribunals are generally similar to court procedures, but are less formal. Tribunals were developed partly to reduce the need for expensive legal representation, so do not generally make costs awards in favour of the winner. But tribunal proceedings may be technical and complex, and it is usually sensible for the organisation to be legally represented. For procedures in employment tribunals, see **chapter 33**.

Tribunals rarely have direct powers of enforcement, so court action will be needed if an award is not complied with.

Appeals may initially be to a higher level of tribunal, but the final appeal is generally to the courts. The courts accept appeals from tribunals on only a narrow range of issues.

61.8 CHARITY PROCEEDINGS

Charity proceedings are a very limited type of legal action where the court is asked to exercise its jurisdiction over the way a charity operates. Charity proceedings cover:

- matters relating to charitable status, such as an appeal against the Charity Commission's refusal to register a charity [see **7.2.9**];
- a challenge to a Charity Commission order;
- an application by the trustees to have the court decide matters relating to its governing document;
- claims involving breach of trust by the trustees [see **19.3**];
- claims that the trustees have acted unconstitutionally.

Charity proceedings can be brought only by one or more of the charity's trustees, the charity itself if it is incorporated, two or more people living in the charity's area of benefit [see **4.1**] if it is a local charity, or a person 'interested in the charity'. *Charities Act 1993 s.33(1)*

There have been a number of cases about who is a 'person interested in the charity'. Ordinary members of the public would be unlikely to have a sufficient interest, and even a founder or substantial donor would probably not be considered an interested person, unless he or she was also a trustee. *Bradshaw v University College of Wales [1987] 3 All ER 200*

But parents of children attending a school run by a charity, and a local authority where the charity owned land have been found to be interested persons. *Gunning v Buckfast Abbey Trustees Registered, The Times 9/6/1994; Re Hampton Fuel Allotment: Richmond upon Thames London Borough Council v Rogers [1988] 2 All ER 761*

Registered and excepted charities [see **7.1.1** and **7.1.3**] must obtain the Charity Commission's permission before taking charity proceedings. If the Commission refuses, consent must be obtained from a Chancery Division judge of the High Court. *Charities Act 1993 s.33*

Charities themselves may be subject to proceedings brought by the attorney general or the Charity Commission. *s.32*

To protect themselves from personal liability in charity proceedings, trustees of charitable trusts may seek a **Beddoes order** [see **61.3.1.5**], and governing body members of any charity may seek **section 29 guidance** from the Charity Commission [see **3.5.2**].

FOR FURTHER INFORMATION

Alternative dispute resolution. ACAS: see local telephone directory; www.acas.org.uk

Centre for Dispute Resolution: 020-7600 0500; www.cedr.co.uk

Chartered Institute of Arbitrators: 020-7837 4483; www.arbitrators.org

Mediation UK: 0117-905 6661; www.mediationuk.org.uk

Legal aid. Community Legal Service Fund: www.justask.org.uk

TABLE OF STATUTES
AND STATUTORY INSTRUMENTS

Statutes and statutory instruments can be purchased from the Stationery Office (tel 0870-600 5522; www.thestationeryoffice.com), or can be downloaded free at www.legislation.hmso.gov.uk. Text of UK statutes and statutory instruments is © Crown Copyright.

EUROPEAN LEGISLATION

TABLE OF CASES

LAW REPORTS

AC	Appeal Cases	IRLR	Industrial Relations Law Reports
A&E	Adolphus & Ellis	ITR	Industrial Tribunal Reports
All ER	All England Reports	KB	King's Bench Reports
All ER(D)	All England Reports Direct	LJ Ch	Law Journal Chancery
BCLC	Butterworths Company Law Cases	LJ Ex	Law Journal Exchequer
Beav	Beavan	LJ KB	Law Journal King's Bench
CB	Common Bench Reports	LJ QB	Law Journal Queen's Bench
CBNS	Common Bench Reports, New Series	LSG	Law Society Gazette
Ch	Chancery	LT	Law Times New Series
Ch App	Chancery Appeal Cases	M&W	Meeson & Welsby
ChD	Chancery Division	NSWLR	New South Wales Law Reports
COIT	Central Office of Industrial Tribunals	QB	Queen's Bench
DLR	Dominion Law Reports	QBD	Queen's Bench Division
EG	Estates Gazette	RR	Revised Reports
EmpLJ	Employment Law Journal -	SJ	Solicitors' Journal & Reporter
EOR	Equal Opportunities Review	Stark	Starkie
Eq	Equity	STC	Simon's Tax Cases
Ex	Exchequer	TC	Tax Cases
FSR	Fleet Street Reports	TLR	Times Law Reports
Hare	Hare	VAT Tr	VAT Tribunal
HL; HL Cas	House of Lords Cases	WLR	Weekly Law Reports
ICR	Industrial Cases Reports	WN	Weekly Notes
IRLB	Industrial Relations Law Bulletin	WWR	Western Weekly Reporter

INDEX

879

If you have trouble finding what you are looking for in the index or find any errors, please contact Sandy Adirondack at sandy@sandy-a.co.uk or 020-7232 0726, so we can improve the entries next time.